D1601134

Weimar in Exile

Weimar in Exile

The Antifascist Emigration in Europe and America

———————————

JEAN-MICHEL PALMIER

Translated by David Fernbach

VERSO

London • New York

This work was published with the help of the French
Ministry of Culture – Centre National du Livre

This work is supported by the French Ministry for Foreign Affairs,
as part of the Burgess programme headed for the French Embassy
in London by the Institut Français du Royaume-Uni

Liberté • Égalité • Fraternité

RÉPUBLIQUE FRANÇAISE

First published as *Weimar en exil*
© Editions Payot 1987
This edition published by Verso 2006
Translation © David Fernbach 2006
All rights reserved

1 3 5 7 9 10 8 6 4 2

Verso
UK: 6 Meard Street, London W1F 0EG
USA: 180 Varick Street, New York, NY 10014-4606
www.versobooks.com

Verso is the imprint of New Left Books

ISBN-10: 1-84467-068-6
ISBN-13: 1-978-84467-068-0

British Library Cataloguing in Publication Data
A catalogue record for this book is available from the British Library

Library of Congress Cataloging-in-Publication Data
A catalog record for this book is available from the Library of Congress

Typeset in Times by Hewer Text UK Ltd, Edinburgh
Printed in the UK by Bell and Bain Ltd, Glasgow

To the memory of

Carl von Ossietzky, Erich Mühsam, Emil A. Reinhardt, Theodor Lessing, Albrecht Haushofer, Georg Hermann, Erich Knauf, Adam Kuckhoff, Fritz Reck-Malleczwesen, who died in concentration camp or were murdered by the Nazis;

Kurt Tucholsky, Walter Benjamin, Ernst Toller, Walter Hasenclever, Carl Einstein, Ernst Weiss, Stefan Zweig, Balder Olden, Alfred Wolfenstein, who took their own lives in exile;

and to all the German antifascists who never saw Germany again.

But no complaints in our mouths;
Winter will not last for ever.
One day, we shall shout with joy:
Oh, my home, I see you again.
Then the soldiers of Börgermoor
Will no longer march
With spade on shoulder
Through the bog.

'The Peat-Bog Soldiers'
written in the Bögermoor concentration camp

The key question, in fact, is this: how can we become *beasts*, beasts in such a sense that the fascists will fear for their domination? A beast is something strong, terrible, devastating; the word emits a barbarous sound. But who believes you can fight barbarism by playing at angels? That would mean trying to parry a sabre blow with the naked fist. We have to understand that goodness must also be able to injure – to injure savagery. [. . .] Understand me, I am not saying that we have to go and kill Hitler. That would be bestial, but not intelligent. But we must use murderous weapons, or else the plague will continue until the end of time, at least the end of our time. How can we writers achieve a writing that kills?

Bertolt Brecht, 'The Intellectual Beast Is Dangerous'

There are times in which, for a writer who wants to have some influence, it is not good to write. Times in which the tapping of the typewriter is not as useful as that of the machine-gun. But the latter simply obeys the former.

Kurt Tucholsky, 'Learning to Laugh Without Crying'

There is no document of culture that is not also a document of barbarism.

Walter Benjamin, 'Poetry and Revolution'

Contents

Introduction

I always found the name false which they gave us: Emigrants.
That means those who leave their country. But we
Did not leave, of our own free will
Choosing another land. Nor did we enter
Into a land, to stay there, if possible for ever.
Merely, we fled. We are driven out, banned.
Not a home, but an exile, shall the land be that took us in.

Bertolt Brecht, 'Concerning the Label Emigrant'

I

Already in 1933, the number of intellectuals, writers and poets who fled the Nazi dictatorship rose into the thousands. The Reichstag fire, and the ensuing wave of terror, arrests and acts of barbarism, gave the exodus signal for Germany's progressive intelligentsia. They found themselves abruptly thrown onto the paths of exile, while their books were burned outside the universities in medieval ceremonies and the SA ransacked their apartments, threw manuscripts and libraries into the street, and lynched their families and friends. Many among them were certainly Communists, Socialists, Jews, sincere republicans, pacifists, or convinced antifascists. But not all left Germany simply to save their own lives. Some deliberately chose exile as the air at home had begun to stink. They refused to become accomplices, if only by their own silence, and could no longer recognize their country in the laws that legalized terror and sadism. As Heinrich Mann asserted, they not only embodied the honour and dignity of Germany, but the 'better Germany', that of the mind and the heart.

The blood spilled in every German town went together with the bleeding of culture. It was not just the representatives of Weimar culture that the Nazis murdered, but everything profound and revolutionary that the Republic had created. From a people of poets and thinkers (*Dichter und Denker*), Germany had become, in words of Karl Kraus that were often repeated, a country of judges and executioners (*Richter und Henker*). The advent of National Socialism, even before signalling a kind of deep-freeze and regression from which German culture would emerge only with great difficulty, gave rise to a haemorrhage that nothing could staunch. Within just a few months, Germany was drained of its writers, poets and actors, its painters, architects, directors and professors. Never before had any country seen a comparable blood-letting of its cultural life. Few intellectuals, indeed, had seriously envisaged leaving Germany until they were forced precipitately to do so. The Nazi terror caught them unprepared. The majority fled illegally, at risk of their life, and often with neither valid passport nor money. Used as they were to repression of various kinds, even under the Weimar Republic, the Nazi dictatorship had surprised them by its violence, rapidity and effectiveness. Even the most pessimistic lacked imagination when it came to considering what this would mean in concrete terms. Those who fled at the start of 1933 were the most far-sighted, and even none of them foresaw that their exile would last more than ten years.

The preferred countries of refuge were France, Austria and Czechoslovakia, where the emigrants could live freely while remaining close to Germany – unable to believe in the new regime's durability. In his poem 'Thoughts on the Duration of Exile', Brecht sadly expressed the illusion that so many of his fellow émigrés shared at this time:

Don't knock any nails in the wall
Just throw your coat on the chair.
Why plan for four days?
Tomorrow you'll go back home.[1]

It is easy today to reproach the intellectuals of the Weimar era for their errors and illusions. At the time, however, who did not share these? Is it legitimate even to speak of 'resignation' or 'self-blinding', as certain historians do? No party of the left really believed, in 1933, that it would be possible for the Nazis to remain in power without any constructive programme. The illusions of the intellectuals, even the most political among them, were those of the parties as well. But if the intellectuals shared these mistakes and dogmatisms, they were often more clear-headed. It was among them, very early on and most forcibly, that the idea of a united front against National Socialism emerged. The warnings that they repeated throughout the exile period proved uncannily prophetic. How can we not recognize today that if practically none of the forecasts of the German Communist party in the 1920s were accurate, almost all those of Kurt Tucholsky sadly were so, even those that seemed at the time most extreme and pessimistic.

The Weimar Republic's writers paid very dearly for these errors and illusions, often with their lives. They were a strange generation, crushed and martyred by history, and compelling our admiration. Their political consciousness had often been forged in the mud of the trenches. Individuals as varied as Erwin Piscator, Ernst Toller, Carl von Ossietzky and Fritz von Unruh were all awakened to politics amid the battles of the Great War. Their aim on return from the front was to place their art at the service of the revolution, or at least to struggle for a more just society, believing that democracy could be born from the ruins of the Reich. Communists, Socialists, pacifists, republicans, liberals and non-partisan writers, these intellectuals embodied throughout the 1920s an aspiration towards liberty, a critical and moral conscience that was almost unique. This has constantly to be borne in mind, to understand the hatred the Nazis displayed towards them and the sadism with which they were to treat them.

To retrace their story would mean giving an account of the various waves of repression that struck them head-on: the First World War that decimated the expressionist generation, the crushing of the Spartacists and the Bavarian workers' councils with the ensuing murder of some and arrest of many others, and finally the repressive measures to which they fell victim under the Republic even before the Nazi terror. The Weimar Germany we have mythologized was extremely repressive towards its intellectuals, and the artistic upsurge which immortalized the period developed despite the state and often against its laws. A number of the Third Reich's repressive measures had their origin under Weimar. The struggle against 'left-wing art' and 'cultural Bolshevism' started well before Hitler, and the intellectual freedom that the Nazis suppressed for more than a decade had already been considerably restricted by the Republic. The treatment inflicted on writers between 1919 and 1933 already showed certain aspects of Hitler's cultural policy, if without its barbarity.

Whether they lived in Berlin or Munich, saw themselves as 'proletarian intellectuals', fellow-travellers of the KPD or simply liberals, this 'literary left', the orphans of a Republic that did not cease to betray them, was richly diverse ideologically as well as artistically. They were also perhaps the last generation of intellectuals to believe in the power of the word over history. Whether writers or political activists, their fates were often similar. After the Reichstag fire, the Nazis arrested not only four thousand Communist cadres and officials, but also journalists, writers, poets and actors. Alongside KPD deputies and workers of the Red Front could be found the pacifist Carl von Ossietzky, editor of *Die Weltbühne* and moral conscience of a whole generation, the poet Erich Mühsam and the actor Hans Otto, all of whom were later brutally murdered. What role had these intellectuals ultimately played in the Weimar Republic? What influence did they have in the face of political events? Did they have even the least power to act on their time? Their appeals and manifestos to put poetry, literary and theatre in the service of the revolution were certainly legion – from Fritz von Unruh to Ernst Toller, Friedrich Wolf to Erwin Piscator. But did they manage in any degree at all to inflect the course of history? 'I want to act on this time,' declared Käthe Kollwitz. But what effect did her engravings of famine and war have on the violence and hunger of her day?

On closer inspection, there could never have been a more striking contrast between the cultural richness of an era and the mediocrity of its political representation. This overestimation of the role of intellectuals under the Weimar Republic, an overestimation for which they were themselves partly responsible, as shown when their professions of faith are opposed to their capacity for effective action, was most striking of all in the year 1933. Rare indeed were the writers remaining in Germany who avoided any compromise with the new regime. Still more rare were those who can be labelled anti-Nazi rather than simply non-Nazi. While the 'internal émigrés', faced with the literary dictatorship organized by Goebbels and the general flattening of artistic life, could take refuge only in an exaltation of nature or the inner world, the real opponents of fascism remained without any decisive influence. If it was they who enabled the true face of National Socialism to be known abroad, and if thanks to them it was possible to maintain that an 'underground Germany' did exist, the desperate struggle that they waged never managed to put the regime in jeopardy. Europe remained oblivious to the Hitler danger, it drove the nightmares from its sleep and refused to wake up. As for the German masses, deprived of their political organizations, it was too late for any writings to act on them. Undoubtedly, as Brecht maintained, the truth is revolutionary, but it is not sufficient simply to make it known for it to become a mortal weapon, a truth that kills.

When the fate of the literary emigration is considered, the questions become still more complex. These thousands of writers, poets, artists and intellectuals who left Germany in 1933 – voluntarily or perforce – what could they do in exile that might obstruct the Nazi machine, given that Hitler's rise to power was already their supreme defeat? With its multiple faces, internal conflicts and prodigious diversity, the anti-Nazi emigration certainly produced some thousands of works – novels, poems, plays, manifestos – yet these had few echoes within Germany itself. Until 1935, Willi Bredel, Heinrich Mann, Bertolt Brecht and J. R. Becher seemed to believe in the possibility of an upsurge of collective awareness in Germany if only the truth could be introduced there. Yet no resistance movement managed to shake the regime. Exile saw the birth of some of the finest works of contemporary German literature: we need only note Thomas Mann's *Doctor Faustus*, Klaus Mann's *Mephisto* and *The Volcano*, Lion Feuchtwanger's *Exile*, *The Seventh Cross* by Anna Seghers or *The Death of Virgil* by Hermann Broch, the novels of Ernst Weiss and Heinrich Mann and the plays of Brecht. Without a doubt this emigration maintained the honour and dignity, even the very survival, of German culture. Yet it could do practically nothing against the dictatorship. On the literary as well as the political level, its representatives continued to debate in their magazines the questions that had divided them in the 1920s. Not even Nazism and the collective fate it imposed on them managed to reconcile them.

What could be more disheartening than this contrast between the émigrés' valiant efforts to make known the truth about the menace of Hitler and the stubborn refusal to listen to them? What more uncanny than the desperate efforts to revive publishing houses and magazines in exile and the little interest that they aroused? Leafing today in libraries and archives through the hundreds of books, pamphlets and tracts written by the exiles of 1933, one can only feel an immense sadness for the often complete ineffectiveness of their struggles. In another of his exile poems, 'To Those Born Later',[2] Brecht seems to have foreseen the questions that would one day be addressed to him and his generation:

You who will emerge from the flood
In which we have gone under
Remember
When you speak of our failings
The dark time too
Which you have escaped.

To be sure, the martyrdom of this generation forces our admiration. And yet it was only belatedly that the 'literature of exile' found its true place in modern literature and became a focus of interest. And this fact alone already merits discussion.

II

Both in Germany and in the lands to which these writers emigrated, it was only in the early 1970s that the antifascist emigration aroused in-depth investigation. During the four decades that followed the initial emigration, and the three that succeeded the collapse of the Nazi regime, their very existence seems to have been forgotten. Certainly there were works that mentioned them, and many written by the émigrés themselves that sought to draw a balance-sheet, however provisional, on their struggles and achievements, from as far back as 1935–38.[3] Yet these were most often just more or less autobiographical documents, analyses that were necessarily incomplete. It was not just that despite magazines and personal contacts the émigrés had little information on the various groups that they formed; they lacked also the necessary critical distance.

A certain political development was needed before interest turned towards them – especially in the Federal Republic. Not only did it have to be recognized that they belonged to German literature, but exile had no longer to be equated with desertion or treason. It had also to be recognized that none of the literary worthies of the Third Reich had left any work that resisted the passage of time. When the literary productions of the Nazi period are examined, all that is found is an immense cultural vacuum.[4] The initial studies on German literature in exile, despite their value, were lacking in information. No historian could hope to offer a global perspective on the emigration. Besides, these attempts also often bore only on limited periods. Walter A. Berendsohn, in the first part of his work, studied the emigration up to the War, while the second part remained only a manuscript. In reading these early works it is often hard to find one's way among all the questions that remain without response:[5] is the omission of some name or other an accident or not? Analysis of the ideological position of this or that group of émigrés is often made difficult by the fragmentary character of the presentation. What should one infer from the multiple denunciations and accusations with which they are burdened? None of these works, moreover, claimed to be at all exhaustive: their characteristic titles are 'Introduction' (W. A. Berendsohn) and 'Synopsis' (F. C. Weiskopf).

A number of anthologies also contributed to make known works written in exile, even if at first these were not widely distributed. That of Richard Drew and Alfred Kantorowicz, 60,000 copies of which were printed in 1947, bore witness to a genuine – if at that time very limited – interest in the émigrés that seemed to be developing in Germany. Some of these were lucky enough to find a new place in German culture on their return from exile, and in both East and West their books were published anew.[6] But exile itself was rarely the object of deeper study: most often it was ignored by historians in the Federal Republic in the 1950s and 60s.

Throughout the years marked by the climate of Cold War, the émigrés of 1933 were kept at a distance and often attacked. Many criticized them for having left Germany, abandoning their country and returning in the uniform of foreign armies. It was forgotten that if they had left Germany it was often to avoid an absurd martyrdom, that several of the greatest representatives of German culture committed suicide in exile, unable to bear this separation from their country, and that they all took the road of exile with iron in the soul. Yet they were still reproached for having contributed to the devastation of Germany, having lived 'on the terraces of emigration' in New York, Mexico City or Los Angeles while Hanover, Dresden and Berlin were being bombed. They were 'bad émigrés' and 'Communists', as opposed to the good 'internal émigrés' who never left their homeland.[7]

The award of the Büchner Prize to Anna Seghers seemed to mark a certain official recognition of exile literature. And yet resentment towards antifascists showed itself on many official occasions. With an almost unimaginable lack of awareness, certain people lambasted Willy Brandt during his 1961 election campaign with the words: 'What did you do in your twelve years abroad?' Elsewhere, even after the War, some historians still found it hard to get a perspective of any depth on an emigration that was extraordinarily diverse in both literary and political terms. The 'exile literature' included works by 'avant-garde' writers such as Hermann Broch, Robert Musil, Carl Einstein and Ernst Weiss, contemporary 'classics' (Thomas Mann), popular writers (Lion Feucht-wanger, Oskar Maria Graf), 'socialists' (Heinrich Mann, Alfred Döblin), 'proletarian writers' (Willi Bredel, Ernst Ottwalt, J. R. Becher, Friedrich Wolf), former expressionists (Ernst Toller, Georg Kaiser, Carl Sternheim, Alfred Wolfenstein, Albert Ehrenstein, René Schickele, Fritz von Unruh, Walter Hasenclever) and Dadists (George Grosz, John Heartfield, Wieland Herzfelde, Karl Schwitters). Besides Communist exiles there were various Social-Democratic groups of both right and left, orthodox and dissident, as well as pacifists, liberals, republicans, Christians, conservatives, aristocrats, national-revolutionaries, monarchists, turncoats from the Nazi movement itself, also former prominent figures from Weimar governments (Heinrich Brüning, Rudolf Breitscheid, Rudolf Hilferding, Joseph Wirth). What makes it all the harder to grasp the complexity of political divisions is that the ideas of their representatives continued to evolve in different directions. The subsequent division of former exiles between the GDR and the Federal Republic gave these conflicts a further twist.

In the aftermath of the Second World War, German literature had reached a kind of zero point. Continuity was broken; the majority of writers fêted in the

Nazi years had literally not survived the regime that honoured them. As well as those who rallied to Nazism there were those who had supported it momentarily (Gottfried Benn), the 'internal émigrés' (from Ernst Wiechert to Ernst Jünger), those who rejected emigration (Ernst Glaeser) and those who changed camp more than once (Arnolt Bronnen). The debates on the existence of an 'internal emigration', as well as the polemics around the return of Thomas Mann, well illustrate the extreme difficulty of rebuilding this shattered unity in the 1950s. The young writers of the postwar era felt on the whole very little concern for an 'exile literature' that they hardly knew.[8] Their explorations took other paths,[9] even if they sensed a certain vacuum.[10] As for the writers who returned from exile, they often found they had little in common with the new generation, whose efforts they judged as 'pessimistic' and 'formalist'. Even when a certain number of works by the exiles were republished, they seemed to many just items in an anthology, closed chapters of a history that was no longer relevant. René Schickele himself foresaw this fate when he wrote in his diary on 11 December 1933: 'If Goebbels manages to wipe our names from the German picture, we are dead. Phantoms of a diaspora in an arid land. Even the next generation will know nothing more of us.'[11]

In the Federal Republic most literary scholars took little interest in the literature of exile, especially since some of them[12] had championed Nazi authors under the Third Reich. Even when the émigré writers became an object of study, the emigration as such remained neglected. Matthias Wegner's book *Exil und Literatur. Deutsche Schriftsteller im Ausland 1933–1945*[13] was one of the first works of literary criticism to take émigré literature as a specific subject, and place it in its due social and historical context. Studies bearing on the literary emigration, moreover, dragged behind those devoted to political emigration. As early as 1952 Erich Matthias published a well-documented study on the Socialist emigration: *Sozialdemokratie und Nation. Ein Beitrag zur Ideengeschichte der sozialdemokratischen Emigration in der Prager Zeit der Parteivorstandes 1933–1938.*[14] A certain number of doctoral theses were subsequently devoted to the political émigrés, but those by literary scholars were rare.

The first German efforts on the history of antifascist emigration aimed above all to gather documents on the exiled writers. Thus the Deutsche Bibliothek at Frankfurt, officially transformed in 1968 into the Sammelstelle für Exilliteratur in den BRD, directed by Hanns W. Eppelsheimer then by Kurt Köster, collected some 13,000 magazines and volumes published during the emigration.[15] This still forms the most substantial centre of exile documents.[16] Others followed one at a time: the Sammlung Berendsohn (Frankfurt) holds some 1,800 letters from Walter A. Berendsohn in connection with *Die humanistische Front*; the archives of the Emergency Rescue Committee which saved so many émigrés are also held in Frankfurt. These archives, together with Eppelsheimer's index comprising names and biographical data for all the writers who chose exile, at first interested only a tiny number of specialists. In 1960, Manfred Schlösser published an anthology, *An den Wind geschrieben. Lyrik der Freiheit (1933–1945)*,[17] which collected poems written in exile and in concentration camp. Other documents concerning émigré life were collected in Matthias Wegner and

Egon Schwarz, *Verbannung. Aufzeichnung deutscher Schriftsteller im Exil*,[18] and
Hermann Kesten's *Deutsche Literatur im Exil. Briefe europäischer Autoren
(1933–1949)*.[19] The originality of these volumes was to insist on the material
conditions in which so many of the exiles' works were written. More significantly, the exhibition organized in 1965 by the Deutsche Bibliothek, 'Exilliteratur 1933–1945',[20] stimulated a lively interest in several countries. Between 1967
and 1969 various institutes initiated series of microfilms (today conserved at the
Institut für Zeitungforschung in Dortmund) of the principal periodicals of
emigration. At the same time, Liselotte Maas published a remarkable *Handbuch
der Exilpresse* which, without attaining the rigour and comprehensiveness of the
works of H. A. Walter, contained bibliographic details on the main exile
periodicals.

From the years 1969 to 1975 onwards, works on the literary emigration
gathered pace and reached out beyond a specialist readership. The Deutsche
Bibliothek, the Archiv des Deutschen Gewerkschaftsbundes, the Forschung-
Institut der Friedrich-Ebert-Stiftung, as well as the Akademie der Künste in
West Berlin, started to assemble large collections of documents on the emigration. A systematic repertory of these was drawn up, counting no less than 17,000
bibliographical references. Significant republications appeared, from the Schil-
ler-Nationalmuseum at Marbach as well as from the Deutsche Bibliothek. The
same period saw the creation at Hamburg University of an Institut für
Exilliteratur, directed by Professor H. Wolffheim, and a committee to coordinate these different explorations was organized by the Deutsche Forschung-
gemeinschaft. After 1970, signs of interest in the exile literature grew too
numerous to mention here. In 1973 there appeared Hans-Christof Wächter's
book *Theater im Exil. Sozialgeschichte des deutschen Exiltheaters 1933–1945*
and the volume of studies edited by Manfred Durzak, *Die deutsche Exilliteratur
1933–1945*. In the same year the city library of Worms organized an exhibition,
'Verbannt, Verboten, Verdrängt', devoted to writers exiled or persecuted by the
Nazis. The Akademie der Künste, under the leadership of Professor Walter
Huder, initiated a number of exhibitions on exile theatre. Doctoral theses were
now frequently devoted to writers expelled from Germany, and an impressive
number of articles appeared on the literary emigration. In 1976–77, *Stern*
magazine published an investigation by Jürgen Serke, *Die verbrannten Dichter*,[21] tracing the destiny of a number of authors whose books were burned or
proscribed.[22] In 1978 an event was presented in Berlin, in the context of the
Berliner Festwoche: 'Zwischen Anpassung und Widerstand, Kunst in Deutschland 1933–1945. Szenen, Lieder und Gedichte aus dem Exil'. The series of
volumes published by H. A. Walter, *Deutsche Exilliteratur, 1933–1950*,[23]
retracing the cultural policy of the Weimar Republic towards progressive
writers as well as their persecution under the Third Reich and the reception
they met with in the different countries of exile, not only marked the high point
of these studies on exile literature but provided future scholars with a still
unequalled resource.

It should also be noted that from 1970 onwards the 'exile literature' seemed to
become a research theme for a new generation.[24] In the space of a few years

Georg Heinz published no less than thirteen volumes devoted to these writers (*Deutsches Exil, 1933–1945*). The majority of works by émigrés started to be republished systematically. Special collections were created, such as Fischer Verlag's Bibliothek der Verbrannten Bücher, which published some of the most celebrated writings by German antifascists in exile.[25] A slow but undeniable process reintegrated these not only into literature but also into collective memory.

In the German Democratic Republic studies of the exile period developed much earlier. The anti-Nazi emigration, together with the socialist and progressive literature of the Weimar Republic, were reclaimed by the young GDR as its inheritance, right from its foundation. It was not necessary to overcome the same resistance,[26] especially as some of the most celebrated among the exiles had chosen to establish themselves here on their return to Germany. This was the case with Friedrich Wolf, Gustav von Wangenhem, J. R. Becher, Alexander Abusch, Arnold Zweig, Alfred Kurella, Wolfgang Langhoff, Anna Seghers, Willi Bredel and Bertolt Brecht. Many of the emigrants' works were republished from the early 1950s onward, and became regular classics even when they were still unobtainable in the Federal Republic. Indeed, it was often only necessary for an author to be distinguished by some kind of honour in the GDR to be immediately labelled a 'Communist' in West Germany: Lion Feuchtwanger and Arnold Zweig are cases in point. After the anthology by Alfred Kantorowicz and Richard Drews, *Verboten und Verbrannt*, which related the fate of 750 antifascist writers, Dietz Verlag published the study by F. C. Weiskopf, *Unter fremden Himmeln*. In 1962 Horst Ecker devoted a doctoral thesis to *Die Beiträge der deutschen emigrierten Schriftsteller in der neuen Weltbühne, 1934–1939*. Hans Baumagar studied the struggle of the émigrés against fascism (*Der Kampf der sozialistischen deutschen Schriftsteller gegen den Faschismus, 1933–1935*; diss. Berlin 1964). In 1966, finally, Klaus Jarmatz proposed a synthesis, *Literatur im Exil*. Essays and monographs were devoted to the majority of exiled writers, as well as bibliographic works such as Horst Halfmann's *Bibliographien und Verlage der deutschsprachigen Exil-Literatur*.[27] In parallel with these explorations, a certain number of émigré periodicals were reproduced in facsimile, for example *Das Wort*. More recently, a broad project devoted to the emigration, the result of a collective labour undertaken by the Akademie der Wissenschaften der DDR and the Zentralinstitut für Literaturgeschichte under the direction of Werner Mittenzwei, Ludwig Hoffman, Wolfgang Kiessling and Eike Middell, led to the publication of six volumes devoted to the various countries which hosted significant émigré colonies.[28]

Research on the exiles steadily spread beyond the German frontiers and was enriched by foreign works or in-depth monographs on one particular country or another. The emigration in Czechoslovakia was studied by Gertrud Albrechtova (*Zur Frage der deutschen antifaschistischen Emigrationsliteratur*, Prague 1964) and by Bohumil Cerny (*Schwarze Front u. Ceskoslovensku 1933–1938*, Prague 1966). The emigration in Switzerland has been the object of several studies, in particular Alfred A. Häsler (*Das Boot ist voll. Die Schweiz und ihre Flüchtlinge 1933–1945*, Zurich 1962) and Peter Stahlberger (*Die züricher Verleger Emil Oprecht und die deutsche politische Emigration*, Zurich 1970). The Swedish emigration has been magisterially studied by Helmut Mussener, a student of W. A. Berendsohn (*Exil in Schweden. Politische und kulturelle Emigration nach 1933*, Munich 1974). The Stifts-ochlandsbibliToteket at Västeras also organized an archival centre on the activities of German émigrés.[29]

In the United States, despite the large number of writers, actors, artists and film-makers who took refuge there (especially after 1939–40), interest in the émigrés was slow to take off.[30] On the initiative of John M. Spalek, Guy Stern and Joseph P. Strelka, a seminar was held in the late 1960s on the theme 'German Literature in Exile', in the context of the Modern Language Association. These first studies from the side of literary criticism were complemented by a certain number of sociological studies and personal testimonies. One of the most important documents remains the report of the Davie Committee on 'recent emigration of European origin': *Refugees in America* (New York 1947). The book by Laura Fermi, daughter of the émigré nuclear physicist from Italy (*Illustrious Immigrants. The Intellectual Migration from Europe 1930–1941*, Chicago 1968) insists on the contribution all these émigrés made to American culture, but fails to analyse their relationship to the antifascist struggle, their actual conditions of existence, and their destiny under McCarthyism. The study by Joachim Radkau, *Die deutsche Emigration in den USA. Ihr Einfluss auf die amerikanische Europapolitik* (Düsseldorf 1971) is focused above all on the ideological diversity of the antifascist emigration and on the influence, by no means certain, that it exerted on American intervention in the European war. A number of American Germanists (Manfred Durzak, Alexander Stephan, Reinhold Grimm, Johst Hermand) have subsequently specialized in German exile literature and in the 'internal emigration', while the fate of individual émigrés in relation to American culture has been the subject of steadily deeper research.[31] The *rencontre manquée* between American culture and so many émigrés, as well as the indisputable legacy of these émigrés to America, have become research themes with many dimensions.[32]

If we consider the case of other countries such as France, the attitude towards this antifascist emigration had an added complexity.[33] The little interest that the German exiles attracted for a long time contrasted with their qualitative importance. If France only took in a few dozen émigré writers, these included some of the most representative of the Weimar Republic: Heinrich Mann, Lion Feuchtwanger, Bertolt Brecht, Anna Seghers, Erich Maria Remarque, Alfred Döblin, as well as political figures such as Rudolf Hilferding, Robert Breitscheid, Willi Münzenberg, Franz Dahlem, Walter Ulbricht, and critics such as Berthold Jacob, Alfred Kerr, Leo Schwarzschild and Georg Bernhard. There can be no doubt that this refusal of interest in the German antifascist emigration is related to the denial of a page in our own history that gives no cause for celebration. The first important French work on the emigration was published under the direction of Gilbert Badia in 1979,[34] in the form of a collective volume. Alongside historical studies of the antifascist emigration in France, this contained very detailed analyses of the development of French policy towards the émigrés, and the repressive legislation that led to their internment in French concentration camps. Almost simultaneously with this there appeared *Vivre à Gurs. Souvenirs d'une émigrée allemande dans un camp d'internement français, 1940–41* by Hanna Schramm, describing her internment in the Gurs camp, accompanied by an essay by Barbara Vormeier on French policy and the establishment of these camps.[35] These volumes were subsequently complemented by a collection of interviews with German antifascist refugees in France,[36] and a new volume devoted to the reception of exiles between 1933 and 1938.[37] Several research teams have been working in France on the specific problems of these antifascist émigrés who took refuge in 1933 in Paris and southern France.

These few works are mentioned here simply by way of example, to show both the delay but also the scope of this rediscovery of German literature in exile. Today this is not just a subject for isolated scholars, but for officially recognized teams and university departments, both in Europe and in the United States. In Federal Germany, moreover, *Exilforschung* has become on occasion a site of theoretical and ideological conflict.[38] Historians and sociologists argue over methods of study and the precise delimitation of this new field of research. As well as studying the writers who left Germany in 1933, a question now debated is the significance of their rediscovery. While at the first international symposium on *Exilliteratur*, held in Stockholm in 1969, the lack of interest from West German literary scholars could be deplored, this reproach was no longer valid by 1975. Several international colloquia have been regularly organized in Europe as well as in the United States: in Luxemburg (1968), Copenhagen (1972), Vienna (1975), Alabama (1975) and California (1980), with the participation of both émigrés and children of émigrés, as well as of historians and political figures (Willy Brandt for example has often attended). Various exhibitions have often been organized around this theme, in many countries around the world.[39] While historians of the exile remain as divided as ever,[40] the majority of exile works are now available, as well as those that were burned or destroyed under the Third Reich.[41] One of the most pressing questions is perhaps to know whether their inheritance can still be reintegrated into German culture, and how this might be achieved.[42]

III

Despite the number and scope of these works, attempts to take the measure of the emigration of 1933 in terms of its output, its forms of struggle, and its fate remain both impassioned and discouraging. The countless problems that the investigator encounters bear as much on the nature of the subject as on the methods and sources by which it can be approached.

The first striking fact about the antifascist emigration is its extent and diversity. Historians do not fully agree on the number of those who left Germany in 1933: 59,000; 60,000; 65,000? League of Nations figures show more than 100,000 refugees from the Reich who left in successive waves between 1933 and 1935. Just taking the few thousand German-speaking intellectuals, writers and artists,[43] it is hard to find a way to summarize their collective destiny without individual biographical sketches. The majority of 1933 exiles had little in common apart from leaving their country because of National Socialism.[44] They included political activists as well as writers, poets, actors, painters, architects and film directors, not to mention workers. They represented virtually all the artistic and political tendencies of the Weimar Republic: ex-Chancellor Heinrich Brüning and Nazi dissident Otto Strasser were exiles as much as the Communist Franz Dahlem. Of course, their respective opposition to fascism does not have the same significance.

The reasons that drove them onto the road of exile were indeed quite different. Some feared for their lives, and risked arrest and concentration camp. Others could have remained in Germany without being disturbed; they went into exile out of disgust for the new regime, solidarity with others, and basic morality. The coordinates of the 1933 emigration were not those of 1938. In the first years of the Hitler regime, all who left Germany were its opponents, many of them Jewish but by no means all. After the promulgation of the Nuremberg laws, the rampant anti-Semitism and the occupation of a large part of Europe by Nazi armed forces, a large number of 'racial' émigrés left Germany who were not necessarily political opponents. In Italy, undoubtedly, they would not have fled from the fascist regime and their departure would not necessarily have been accompanied by any political stand. The diversity of this emigration and the reasons that drove so many men and women to quit their country make it hard to grasp this as a single phenomenon. Statistically, they were all émigrés, whether they were anti-Nazi writers, political activists, or representatives of the apolitical Jewish petty bourgeoisie. In the various countries where they took refuge, however, they formed separate worlds. And political émigrés of Jewish origin did not hide their disdain for their apolitical co-religionists, certain of whom no doubt would even have supported Hitler had he renounced his anti-Semitism.

The diversity of the countries in which the émigrés found refuge is also a complicating factor in studying their activities. If in 1933 they remained in those countries bordering on the Reich, or at least of Germanic culture, not believing in the durability of the new regime, the success of Hitler's armies and the fall of France drove them ever further away. By 1940, many were prepared to embark for any destination in order to escape the Gestapo, if the country would accept Jewish refugees without a visa, or simply if a ship was available. Thus there were émigrés not only in the majority of European countries (even Italy), but also in North America, the West Indies and New Zealand, in Palestine, India and Shanghai – a city that hosted several Yiddish theatres.

It is impossible moreover to consider this emigration as a static environment: it was triggered in successive waves tied to political events – the return of the Saarland to Germany, the annexation of Austria, the invasion of Czechoslovakia, then of the Netherlands, the fall of France. It always remained very fluid and was constantly in motion. Émigrés moved from one centre to another in search of work and opportunity, because political struggle was better organized, because magazines, publishing houses or friends were to be found. At the ideological level, this emigration was also in constant flux, exile acting as a historical accelerator. In the course of 'changing countries more often than shoes' (Brecht), they changed both personalities and ideas. Politicians who had played a leading role under the Weimar Republic were often inactive in exile. Apolitical writers became activists, many who would formerly have been described as 'bourgeois' became fellow-travellers of the Communist party, Socialists became instigators of a new conservatism, and enthusiastic Communists became fanatical anti-Communists. An ideological diagram of the emigration in 1945, moreover, would have little in common with that of 1933. Who would have imagined that Thomas Mann would become one of the leading lights of the emigration, first as a Czech citizen, then as an American, that Heinrich Mann would work with his old enemy J. R. Becher to create an antifascist Popular Front with the Communists, that a Jew like Alfred Döblin would convert to Catholicism along with his entire family, and Franz Werfel write a novel in homage to the Virgin Mary for having escaped the Gestapo?

The difficulty of combining all these parameters, of describing the common struggle waged by groups of exiles who were often isolated from one another, of exploring both their literary and dramatic creations and their political activities, makes any projected synthesis both necessary and problematic. And added to these inherent difficulties of the exile phenomenon are those of the sources of information. It was not just the émigrés themselves who were scattered across the globe, but also the evidence of their activities, the journals and documents that make it possible to retrace their history. Describing the itineraries of this exile needs recourse to multiple sources of information. It is important to follow the logic of events that led them to leave Germany, the conditions of reception that they encountered, and the impact of international events on their situation. It is necessary, for intellectuals and writers, to know their situation before 1933 in order to measure what exile meant for them, and in what way it would modify their creative activity. A full knowledge of their works is often as indispensable as a reading of their diaries, their correspondence, and their memoirs. To read all the representative works of Weimar literature could itself take a number of years.

The analysis of literary production in exile poses problems that are infinitely more complex. A considerable number of documents were either lost by the exiles themselves (manuscripts, memoirs, correspondence), were not preserved (reviews, books), or were destroyed by the Gestapo (for example, the celebrated 'Library of Free German Books' in Paris). In their flight from Hitler, they often had to abandon their libraries and their manuscripts.[45] It proved impossible to overcome these gaps and losses when material was slowly gathered together after the War. Despite efforts to regroup them, the archives of exile are scattered among a number of countries.[46] It is not always easy to consult them. As for the official files on the émigrés in the countries where they took refuge, they are still not always accessible, even in France. Much information is to be found in their autobiographies (Heinrich Mann, Leo Marcuse, Alfred Kantorowicz, Rudolf Leonhard, Arthur Koestler, Manès Sperber, Franz Dahlem, Gustav Regler, Carl Zuckmayer), but these often present gaps, whether deliberate or not.

Certain episodes of exile were not recorded, being deemed at the time without interest. And written sometimes twenty years after the events that they relate, these works inevitably contain errors and – more seriously – were drafted subsequent to a further political development. The climate of suspicion that reigned among the émigrés, and their divergent political evolution, explain the fact that certain passages in their memoirs served primarily as a settling of accounts with their past. This is particularly true, for example, of the memoirs of Arthur Koestler, *The Invisible Writing*, where his Communist commitment of the 1920s and 30s is described from the perspective of a virulent anti-Communism. It is necessary therefore to learn to separate the facts from the tendentious interpretation that is often given them, and to compare one account with another, as well as with documents and oral evidence.

It is unfortunate that research on the German exile only started to develop intensively in the 1970s. By this time, the majority of those who played a leading role in this antifascist emigration were dead; any survivors were only young people in 1933. With the disappearance of the great figures of exile, whole sections of their history have become inaccessible. While certain exiles returned to live in Germany, or in France, Austria or Switzerland, others remained in their countries of exile, especially the United States, and it is in New York or California that they had to be studied.[47] Taking also into account that a number of major names among the exiles had nothing more to say, that it is often impossible to establish rigorous biographical details on some of them, that in other cases their full output in exile is not known, that several used indecipherable pseudonyms,[48] and that by the time many of their number could be tracked down and contact made they had often died, this will give an idea of the travails that the majority of historians of the antifascist emigration experienced.

There is now an abundant literature on the German emigration: not a month passes without an article or book on the subject appearing either in Europe or the United States, not to mention the conferences periodically organized around the world on these themes. Added to the difficulty of following all these publications individually is the need to consider them all from a critical point of view, in so far as they bear on political issues. Finally, a further difficulty bears on the choice of a style of approach: the phenomenon of emigration is so complex that it is unclear how to get to grips with it. It is impossible to restrict oneself to just one of its aspects. The exile works from 1933 to 1945 cannot be studied without taking the antifascist struggle into account, which in itself requires a return to the literary and political life of the Weimar Republic. It is also necessary to take account of the conditions of life of the refugees in the different countries where they settled. Novels such as Heinrich Mann's *Henri IV*, Feuchtwanger's *The False Nero*, Klaus Mann's *The Volcano* or Anna Seghers's *The Seventh Cross* would be incomprehensible outside of this context. It is hard to isolate 'exile literature' from 'political literature': the same writers often wrote magazine articles and pamphlets. If Golo Mann could maintain that it is possible to read his father's *Joseph and His Brothers* without reference to his exile, one could hardly comprehend *Doctor Faustus* without reference to Thomas Mann's reflections on Germany between 1940 and 1945. Moreover, every work written in exile bears its weight of suffering, as Feuchtwanger so well showed, and it is impossible to understand the creation of the exiles without reference to the conditions in which this was born. The first inquiries on 'German literature in exile', therefore, gradually gave way to the investigation of exile as a global phenomenon.[49]

IV

The scope of the subject, and its complexity, suggest that it should either be tackled collectively or that its scope should be very closely delimited. Every aspect of this antifascist emigration can be used to provide material for dozens of studies, from Socialist emigration in Sweden to exile theatre in Czechoslovakia, the reception of refugees in France, the historical novel as a specific genre of exile literature, the relationship of Brecht and Weill in America, or the Yiddish theatre in Shanghai. The choice of approach undertaken here is explained by a number of reasons. This investigation of German exile seeks to grasp the fate of a culture, in the wake of certain number of studies already undertaken on German artistic life in the 1920s and early 30s.[50] It is impossible to analyse the richness of Weimar culture without raising the question of its destruction and survival after the advent of National Socialism. Among all the myths to which the Weimar Republic has given rise, that of the power of 'left-wing art' is one of the most durable. Yet while certain historians today reproach Kurt Tucholsky for having contributed to 'destabilizing' the Weimar Republic by his criticism, this author himself maintained that despite all his success, he never managed to get a single policeman dismissed. The majority of authors whose names remain associated with this culture were condemned to exile in the space of a few weeks. It needed only a number of months for the National Socialist regime to establish by terror a power that only the intervention of foreign armies could destroy. Many of the greatest representatives of this culture did not even escape with their lives, and it was as a prisoner in concentration camp that Carl von Ossietzky was awarded the Nobel Prize. Even this did not manage to free him.

It is astonishing that the extraordinary fate of this generation and its relationship to history has been so little examined. However different their itineraries, the most common feature of all these intellectuals was their origins in the liberal petty bourgeoisie. They were radicalized very quickly, attracted either by pacifism or Communism. If those who rallied to the Communist movement in the early 1920s often followed a relatively clear trajectory, no matter that they ended up feeling they had been cheated by history, those who remained outside the parties, the 'independent writers' of the Weimar Republic, were faced with the most tragic contradictions. Often condemned to inefficacy as a result of their idealism, they gathered around symbols such as Ossietzky's *Weltbühne*. If they were led to play a historical role, this was often despite themselves, because they were caught up in the maelstrom of events, because they believed in a certain morality and could not tolerate being unable to realize their ideas in practice. In general, they held themselves aloof from active politics, for which they often had scant esteem, and preferred ideological debate. This was one of the origins of both the grandeur and the weakness of Weimar culture. The First World War had radicalized their pacifism, and in the wake of this they never ceased hating war and militarism (Helmut von Gerlach, Kurt Tucholsky, Ernst Toller, Carl von Ossietzky). Revolting against the Wilhelmine Reich and its reactionary values, after the defeat of the Spartacists they dreamed of seeing a genuine democracy established in Germany. Without being Socialists, they were ready to serve the Republic; without being Communists, they shared a hatred for exploitation and injustice, for the cause of the working class. Their political commitment was quite often not premised on any doctrine, and the principles they maintained were often fairly vague, as with the pacifism of Gerlach and Ossietzky, the libertarianism of Kurt Hiller and Erich Mühsam, the 'ethical Bolshevism' of Piscator or the militant humanism of Heinrich Mann. For these people, political action was identified with a certain ethical – even messianic – radicalism, which finds such great expression in the early essays of Georg Lukács or Ernst Bloch. If they often forsook their literary careers to become polemicists and political journalists, it was because the revolt that Germany inspired in them now left them no peace.

These ideals of humanity and justice were defended in all their works. 'Revolutionaries of the spirit', experimenting to breaking point with the contradictions of '*Geist*' and '*Tat*' so well expressed by Heinrich Mann, they often believed in the power of a certain 'intellectual elite' to influence politics (Kurt Hiller, Franz Pfemfert), and if some of them abstained for a good while from discussing National Socialism, it was, as Tucholsky said, that 'it is impossible to look so low'. Often they were rejected by the parties. The Communists reproached them for their independence and refusal to join, the Socialists described them as 'soilers of their own nests'. As republicans, they felt constant disappointment with the Weimar Republic: the flag had undergone a slight change of colour, but the old institutions had remained in place. And when they sought to defend this Republic against itself, against the dangers that threatened it, it did not hesitate to imprison them for 'high treason'.

As idealists, they rarely raised the question of power. Culture was the sphere in which they reigned; this was where their glory, their honour and their kingdom were to be found. Their universe was often limited to Berlin, to its theatres, cafés, magazines and publishers. They thought that the Nazis, devoid of intelligence or culture, could do nothing against this world. What could their imbecility and barbarism achieve against the spirit? Often the break between their universe with its moral requirement and the political sphere was almost complete, hence the striking contrast between the artistic richness of the Weimar epoch and its relative political mediocrity. Dreaming of an ideal Republic, they were confronted by a Social-Democratic party which despised them, while their ethical and radical communism was hard to fit into any party structure. What often pushed many of them towards the KPD was less a reading of the Marxist classics than the novels of Tolstoy and Dostoyevsky, the films of Eisenstein, the end-point of the expressionist revolt against injustice with its aspiration for a 'new man'. This represented for them the only possibility of building a different and more humane world. As Brecht wrote in his poem 'Praise of Communism':

> It's quite straightforward, you'll understand it. It's not hard.
> Because you're not an exploiter, you'll quickly grasp it. [. . .]
> It isn't madness, but puts
> An end to all madness.
> It doesn't mean chaos
> It just means order.
> It's just the simple thing
> That's hard, so hard to do.[51]

Their idealism constantly came up against political realism, and the degradation of democracy in the Soviet Union; the anti-Communism of some of them later in life was often less the sign of a reconciliation with capitalism than the fury of having seen so many dreams collapse.

Those who turned towards Social-Democracy often experienced similar disillusion. The unloved Republic, threatened from every direction, required them to happily support a regime that was ill accepted; their refusal not to criticize was seen as a charge against them. Yet the same struggle is at work from the pedagogic style of Ossietzky to the satire of Tucholsky: to constrain the Republic to live up to its own ideals, to lead it to defend itself against everything that threatened it, to warn and warn again. What is striking in hindsight is that despite their idealism, they were able to recognize in time almost all the dangers.

In relation to their example, many discussions on 'commitment', the 'power of intellectuals' or the 'politicization of art' seem over-simple. The destiny of this intelligentsia, its behaviour, words, actions and writings in the years that saw the rise of fascism and in the course of exile, in the long series of struggles that it lost, are an extraordinary sociological example on which one may reflect, in the words of Gramsci, that it is 'possible to think the present, and a well-determined present, with a thought elaborated for the problems of a past that is very often distant and superseded'. Their rare victories are important to us, but their defeats still more. And none of their struggles can leave us indifferent. It is this trajectory in the history of an intellectual generation, its inscription and its traces, that we have set out to investigate across the collapse of the Weimar Republic, the rise of National Socialism and the course of exile. Turning Brecht's assertion that 'the intellectual beast is dangerous' into a question, we have sought to understand the ability of the writers, artists and intellectuals to act on their times. And it is precisely because the epoch of the Weimar Republic was one of the richest in culture that it strikes us as forming an almost unique example.

This study, therefore, does not claim to retrace the history of German literature in exile: a task to which several Germanists have devoted themselves. No more will it give an exhaustive survey of the activities of the antifascist émigrés, which will often be mentioned only by way of example. And neither will it disentangle the relations between different political factions in exile.

Important as these questions certainly are, their interest is above all a historic one. Not even the tragedy that exile represented for all those affected will form the essential part of our investigation. Why should this particular exile of 1933, just because it chased out of Germany some of the greatest writers of its time, be more worthy of study than any tragedy of contemporary exiles, who often experience a very similar situation, and who benefit today from far less interest and sympathy than those of 1933? Finally, there are no victories to celebrate: apart from the tribunal on the Reichstag fire, and the massive distribution of information on Nazi Germany between 1933 and 1938, the record is almost one of continuous defeat. The Saarland was returned to Germany, Carl von Ossietzky, Eric Mühsam, Edgar André and Ernst Thälmann were murdered in concentration camp. None of their warnings could prise Europe out of its lethargy or arrest the inevitable process that was leading to war.

Perhaps this concern to remember their story also displays the sense of a moral debt towards them. Golo Mann asserted in 1968, at a conference on the German exiles held in Luxemburg, that if the majority of whose who embodied that epoch were already old or buried, it was still possible

> to see some honour given to the memory of those whom no one esteemed during their lives, to whom no one lent an ear, whose failure to find an echo destroyed them, who [. . .] took their own lives for fear of falling into the hands of their own compatriots, their minds completely empty and exhausted – to see their memory honoured is indeed no more than simple justice. But this justice comes too late.

Those exiles that Goebbels described as 'corpses in waiting' and who now rest in cemeteries across the world, their works and names being sometimes almost forgotten, still witness, despite everything – *trotz alledem* – to the power of intelligence and morality. Erika Mann had engraved on the tomb of her brother Klaus: 'He who seeks to save his life will lose it.' The Communist Alfred Kantorowicz recalled the phrase that Pope Gregory IV had engraved on his own tomb: *Dilixi justiciam et odi iniquitatem – proptera morior in exilio* ('I loved justice and hated injustice – which is why I died in exile'). To these two epitaphs we can add a third, in homage to all those whose books were burned and whose names the Nazis sought to efface: the epitaph that Rosa Luxemburg chose as the testament of the revolution in the face of an order built on sand and blood: 'I was, I am, I shall be.'

The list of all those who helped me with the research required for this study is too long to be reproduced here. My acknowledgements go above all to those survivors of the emigration who agreed to reply to innumerable questions, whether in writing or interview. Some of them have died in the meantime. I would particularly mention Maria Ley Piscator, Lotte H. Eisner, Blandine Ebinger, Claire Goll, Nina Kandinsky, Ernst and Karola Bloch, Herbert Marcuse, Ernst Heidelberger, Curt Trepte, Vladimir Pozner and Clara Malraux. Besides the German historians of exile literature, in whose wake the present work largely follows, I am indebted to Gilbert Badia for having been able to take part in the research of his team at the University of Paris VIII-Vincennes on the reception of antifascist émigrés in France. His passion to communicate and his enthusiasm have been a source of encouragement. I would also like to acknowledge the other members of this team, in particular J. B. Joly, J.-P. Mathieu, J. Omnès and Hélène Roussel. A number of questions on the relationship of intellectuals to history are the outcome of discussions often of long date, with which the names of Henri Lefebvre, André Gisselbrecht, Jean Duvignaud, Kostas Axelos and Predrag Matvejevitch remain associated. I owe Bernard Theyssèdre and Olivier Revault d'Allones for having already started this research into Weimar culture in the context of the teaching of the UER d'Arts Plastiques of Paris I. Finally, Pierre Dommergues encouraged me to pursue this research in the context of a doctoral thesis at the university of Paris VIII-Vincennes.

The several investigations undertaken in Germany were made possible by a grant from the Alexander von Humboldt Foundation. The unique generosity of its reception and efficiency of its organization enabled me to stay in Berlin for a lengthy period. It is thanks to the Humboldt Foundation that I have been able to pursue my research at several German institutions. Professor Dr Walter Huder, director of the centre of archives of the Akademie der Künste in West Berlin, welcomed me as a researcher and put at my disposal his rich archives on exile theatre. I should like to thank him warmly here, as well as his colleagues and Alexander Eickelpasch. My study of a certain number of documents on the emigration in the United States was facilitated by a Fulbright grant which enabled me to stay in Hollywood.

This work could not have been published without the trust and friendship of Jean-Luc Pidoux-Payot, without whom none of the volumes that I have devoted to the cultural life of the Weimar Republic would have seen the light of day. More than a publisher, he has been for me a special partner, and my acknowledgements towards him are naturally without limit.

Part One
Exile in Europe 1933–40: From Reichstag Fire to Spanish War

Let us speak quietly, there is someone dying in the room. Dying German culture, it does not even have catacombs at its disposal inside Germany any more. Merely chambers of horror in which it is to be exposed to the derision of the mob; a concentration camp with visits from the public.

It is getting crazier and crazier. What is an honest, a talented person to do in this country. His simple existence is a danger to him, he must conceal it. Every kind of talent endangers the life of the person who possesses it, apart from that of cringing. Artists, who are such, are openly threatened with castration or prison; this is no joke, such mouths do not make jokes. People have learnt to take the ridiculous seriously.

Ernst Bloch, 'Jugglers' Fair beneath the Gallows', in *Heritage of Our Times*

Assassination of a Culture

This purification of our civilization must include almost every field. Theatre, art, literature, cinema, press, posters and displays must be cleansed of exhibitions of a world in the process of putrefication, and be put in the service of a moral idea, a principle of State and civilization.

Adolf Hitler, *Mein Kampf*

The first country that Hitler conquered was Germany; the first people he oppressed was the German people. It is wrong to say that all German literature went into exile. It would be better to say that the German people were exorcised [. . .]. There is hardly a literature that has been respected and honoured by the state to such a degree – in the form of total banishment – as the German literature of our time; when the fascists trample on it, this is their form of saluting it.

Bertolt Brecht, 'The Last Word' (1934)

It is significant that the only references to art and culture to be found in the programme of the NSDAP (adopted on 20 February 1920) relate to measures of repression. There is certainly the promise of free education for poor children and a reform of educational programmes (paragraph 20), but the most important paragraphs assert that only German citizens and not Jews can exercise an official function (paragraphs 4, 5, 6), envisage a reform of the press and measures against political slander (paragraph 23), and, more seriously still, threaten with prohibition writing that contradicts this programme. This was a constant of Nazism: in the years that preceded Hitler's conquest of power, cultural questions were raised only under the aspect of repression. Hitler, who never missed an opportunity to display his contempt for intellectuals – those 'knights of the inkwell' – or to mock their pretensions and inefficacy, proposed merely to 'rescue German culture from the refuse that encumbers it', i.e. from the pernicious influences that had perverted it. *Mein Kampf*, rather than any particular programme, is where the essence of National Socialism's 'cultural conceptions' should be sought.

At the same time as it destroyed the political structures of the Weimar

Republic, the Nazi regime raged against its culture and rooted out of intellectual
life everything that was hostile to its own values. By its new institutions it made
all creative liberty impossible. This policy was founded on some astonishingly
heteroclite conceptions, whose foolishness and platitude in no way predicted the
barbarism that was to come.

THE STRUGGLE AGAINST 'DEGENERATE ART'

If it reached a climax with the advent of the Nazis to power, the struggle against
'degenerate art' began under the Weimar Republic; the expression was already
used by von Papen. It was not the Nazis who invented the concept of
'degeneration' as applied to art: Max Nordau had popularized it in his essay
Entartung of 1898, which, blending the pseudo-medical theories of Lombroso
with his own crude positivism, undertook a systematic critique of modern art
from a psychiatric and moralizing standpoint. Denouncing the devastating
effects of modern art on the youth, Nordau even qualified certain artists,
representing both symbolism and the beginnings of expressionism, as 'higher
degenerates'.

Hitler seemed to take on board some of Nordau's prescriptions when he
asserted in Munich on 25 February 1920: 'We demand a law to struggle
against the orientation in literature and art that exerts a corrupting influence
on our national life, and the suppression of all publications and spectacles that
run counter to the demands that have just been presented', i.e. those of the
NSDAP. The connection made between modern art and pornography in *Mein
Kampf* announces the programme of a 'clean-up' of German cultural life.
Hitler intended to disembarrass this of 'cubist, futurist and expressionist
refuse'. The project of struggle against 'degenerate art' would lead not just
to the book burnings of May 1933, but also to the exhibitions of 'degenerate
art' organized later in Munich and to the almost total destruction of modern
art in Germany.

On 23 February 1929 the Combat League in Defence of German Culture held its
first event.[1] The occasion was a lecture by Professor Othmar Spann on 'The
Present Cultural Crisis', delivered at Munich University.[2] Though not officially
Nazi, this league founded by Alfred Rosenberg sought to make culture a site of
confrontation by uniting all reactionary forces hostile to 'left-wing art'.[3] The
league organized exhibitions and lectures in several German cities, taking on the
full range of plastic arts and indefatigably championing a 'return to the Nordic
ideal'.[4] Alexander von Senger even launched the idea of a 'national dictatorship
over artistic matters' and in 1930, under the chairmanship of Wilhelm Frick, a
public meeting was held in Weimar at which a motion was voted insisting on
'energetic measures against influences damaging to the people in the fields of
theatre, literature and the fine arts'. A bulletin distributed to members of the
league denounced the principal 'corrupters of German art', in which the names
of Erich Kästner, Kurt Tucholsky, Thomas Mann, George Grosz, Bertolt
Brecht and Wassili Kandinsky already appeared. Rosenberg's *Kampfbund*

managed to gain the support of nationalist circles and certain cultural groups, and soon claimed a quarter of a million members.[5] With a view to coordinating all the nationalist cultural associations, it published its own periodical, *Die Bildkunst*, which counted among its contributors various personages with future responsibility for cultural policy under the Third Reich (A. Rosenberg, Paul Schulze-Naumburg, Hans F. K. Günther). An artistic bulletin, *Deutsche Kunstkorrespondenz*, was even distributed for free. The success of this ultra-reactionary association was so great that it soon had to be partitioned into several groups, corresponding to music, theatre, the fine arts and literature.[6]

The first time that the Nazis managed to join a coalition government in 1929, in Thuringia, this cultural policy was immediately put into effect. The ministry for public instruction was handed to Wilhelm Frick, with Schulze-Naumburg as his advisor. A series of repressive measures was undertaken very rapidly to prohibit the distribution of left-wing works, hitting Erich Maria Remarque's novel *All Quiet on the Western Front* as well as the films of Eisenstein, Pudovkin and Pabst,[7] and examples of 'musical bolshevism' such as Hindemith and Stravinsky. At the same time, all modern works were removed from the museums. Though the protests provoked by these measures forced Frick to resign, they clearly prefigured the cultural policy that the Nazis would pursue when they came to power.[8]

Whereas Italian fascism could strike a sort of compromise with the country's avant-garde, futurism in particular, because of its overtly reactionary character,[9] the Nazis pursued with the same constant hatred everything that symbolized modern art. If Mussolini could find in futurism certain themes that melded with fascist ideology – the cult of modernity, the glorification of violence and war, an inflamed nationalism, contempt for women, the exaltation of the race and of militarism – there was no comparison in German art of the Weimar period, its overall content being progressive. Nothing that had been created here could serve the values of the new regime. Even those artists and writers who rallied to National Socialism did not escape the most virulent attacks if they had belonged to any avant-garde movements (Benn, Nolde).[10] The campaign against degenerate art intensified after 1933, especially following the Reichstag fire. It was no longer a matter of demonstrations by isolated groups, but a systematic policy of destruction and terror.

Whereas the majority of writers were condemned to exile, the most representative painters of the Weimar period and its different currents (expressionism, Dadaism, 'new objectivity') were expelled from the academies and could no longer exhibit (Otto Dix, Max Beckmann). In 1933, canvases by Schmidt-Rottluff and Pechstein could still be seen in Berlin. Until the following year, some expressionist painters sought to show that they were representatives of an 'authentically German' art, but soon after the majority were deprived of the right to exhibit, then even to paint, while their works were withdrawn from the galleries. Two hundred and sixty works by Otto Dix were seized from the museums and Dix himself was arrested in 1939 for having belonged to the Human Rights League prior to 1933. Several works by the sculptor Ernst Barlach were destroyed, and he was prevented from completing the monument to Theodor Däubler.[11] The painter Max Liebermann died in absolute solitude, and his wife committed suicide. The canvases of Karl Schmidt-Rottluff were also withdrawn from museums, likewise those of Kirchner, who similarly killed himself. These measures were taken in the name of the new 'Nordic' ideas of Rosenberg, which presented Nolde as 'negroid' and Barlach as 'semi-idiot'. Karl Hofer was expelled from the Akademie der Künste[12] as a 'Judeo-Marxist destructive element', and Paul Klee himself termed a 'murderer of German art'. Similar measures were taken against Kokoschka and Kandinsky, both the object of the Nazis' particular hate.[13] The man responsible for the measures taken in this area was the allegorical painter Adolph Ziegler, a specialist in academic nudes, which even in the Hitler era brought him the ambiguous soubriquet of 'painter of German pudenda'.

From 1935 on the first exhibitions of 'degenerate art' were organized. The Bavarian interior minister Adolph Wagner had twenty-six paintings suppressed from an exhibition organized at the Neue Pinakothek under the rubric 'Contemporary Berlin Art'. Among these undesirable works were those of Nolde, Beckmann, Heckel, Purrmann and Feininger. The chair of the New Secession was eventually arrested by the Gestapo and the group suppressed. In 1936 the campaign against expressionism became still more violent: all exhibitions of modern art were forbidden and its representatives no longer allowed to paint. The retrospective organized for Ernst Barlach and Käthe Kollwitz was also closed down. The canvases withdrawn from German museums – from impressionism and Van Gogh through the different currents of the Weimar period – were sold in Switzerland to the profit of party coffers or of Göring himself. Those that did not find buyers were burned at the firemen's barracks in Berlin. A large number of painters were condemned to emigration (Feininger, Beckmann, Kokoschka, Klee, Kandinsky), others 'to landscapes and still lifes' (Schmidt-Rottluff, Pechstein, Hofer, Heckel). As for the Bauhaus, it had been closed in 1933 as a 'Judeo-Bolshevik stronghold'. Officially charged with the purging of German cultural life, Frick was overtaken in zeal by Rosenberg's *Kampfbund*, which ceaselessly called for more radical measures.[14] The School of Fine Arts was occupied by the Nazis in February 1933 (with the support of Bernhard Rust, the Prussian minister for religion). Following violent confrontations between Nazis and students, it was decided to root out 'cultural bolshevism'. Several professors were examined, two of these immediately dismissed (G. Tappert, K. Lahs), and the school finally closed.

A similar struggle was waged to 'purify' music and theatre. The *Kampfbund* insisted that all Jewish composers, conductors and musicians be removed from musical life. Musical associations with Jewish members were immediately dissolved, while the struggle against 'decadent modern music' was intensified. Targets were the 'musical bolshevism' of Hindemith and the 'supreme decadent' Schoenberg, as well as the 'negroid and typically Jewish music' of Kurt Weill. At the same time, musical instruction was reformed under the direction of Hans Hinkel, president of the *Kampfbund* and secretary of state at the Prussian ministry of education, with a view to rooting out 'unhealthy elements'. While

Hitler's own taste was for Wagner, Goebbels, who was more attracted to Brahms, Schubert and Mozart, managed to get Richard Strauss named president of the Reich chamber of music, with Wilhelm Furtwängler as vice-president. Bernhard Rust obtained the dismissal of Schoenberg and Franz Schreker from the Prussian academy, which aroused the indignation of Furtwängler. On 11 April 1933, he drew Goebbels's attention to certain catastrophic aspects of National Socialist policy and requested that it should be 'clearly proclaimed that men such as Bruno Walter, Klemperer, Reinhardt, etc. should be able to continue to exercise their art in Germany'. In a public response in the *Berliner Lokalanzeiger*, Goebbels removed any shadow of doubt: 'It is your right to feel yourself an artist and see things from the artist's point of view. But that does not mean that you may adopt an apolitical attitude in the face of the development taking place in Germany. Politics is also an art, perhaps the most noble and complete one that there is.'

Goebbels thus refused to revise his decisions and keep as a norm only the 'distinction between good and bad', as Furtwängler had requested: 'Art, in the absolute sense, as liberal democracy understands it, cannot be accepted [. . .]. You can always continue to exercise your art in Germany. But to complain that men such as Walter, Klemperer, Reinhardt, etc. have had to abandon concerts here and there seems to me all the more out of place at this time as authentically German artists have often been condemned to silence during the last fourteen years.'

When Furtwängler presented Hindemith's opera *Mathis der Maler* in October 1934, the composer was violently attacked by the Nazi press and the *NS-Kulturgemeinschaft*, despite the protests of the conductor. Furtwängler had to resign from his official functions on 4 December 1934. Rosenberg and his followers likewise sought to prevent Richard Strauss from performing his opera *The Silent Woman*, the libretto having been written by 'the Jew Stefan Zweig'. Following the interception of his correspondence, Strauss also had to resign from his presidential post.[15]

The German theatres had their repertoires similarly purged. Hans Tietjen, responsible for the Berlin stage, was accused of having favoured Jewish actors[16] and replaced by Ludwig Ulrich, director of the Weimar Volksbühne.[17] Not only were progressive plays eliminated, but also those written by Jews, while at the same time several Socialist, Communist and Jewish actors were dismissed, arrested or murdered.[18] As for the overall artistic direction, this was from now on in the hands of Hanns Johst, a mediocre expressionist whose plays already prefigured the *Blut-und-Boden* jargon.[19] As the Berlin theatres were controlled by Göring, but those in the provinces by Goebbels, Rosenberg's demands were often contradicted. Though he had maintained on 8 May 1933 that he had no intention of 'putting a brake on artistic creation, as it is in art that the law of the personality is expressed', Goebbels soon reduced the theatre to a simple propaganda tool. The 'Day of the Stage' organized for 15 October 1933 was designed to give German theatre a new boost. In a number of cities open-air National Socialist stages were established like the Dietrich-Eckart-Bühne, created in 1936 for the occasion of the Berlin Olympics. These mediocre spectacles, saturated with propaganda, soon left the public cold. The majority of great actors were forced into exile, together with stage directors, although the number of theatres continued to rise under Hitler (299 in 1936 against 248 in 1934), and some major actors did remain in Germany.[20] German theatres were in fact paralysed both by censorship and by the poor quality of works now encouraged.

The whole of artistic life had to accept the new values or disappear. Nothing of what had made the greatness of Weimar culture was allowed to subsist. A few death throes still encouraged timid hopes among those who sought reasons not to emigrate. An exhibition of Italian 'futurist aeropainting' was held in Berlin in March 1934, sponsored by Goebbels, Rust, Göring, and Eugen Hönig (president of the Chamber of Fine Arts), and inaugurated by Marinetti himself along with Vittorio Cerriti, ambassador of fascist Italy. Nazi Germany was represented here by two former expressionists, Rudolph Blümmer and Gottfried Benn, vice-president of the Writers' Union. A few timid attempts were made to defend modern art against Rosenberg's attacks. Some young Nazi painters such as Otto Andreas Schreiber, and functionaries such as Hans Weidemann, sought in vain to save some expressionists near to Die Brücke or Der Blaue Reiter. The union of Nazi students also protested against the dogmas imposed on art. But the reaction was brutal: Otto Andreas-Schreiber was accused by Rosenberg of being an 'ultra-revolutionary of the Strasser type' and had to apologize publicly in the *Deutsche Allgemeine Zeitung* (14 July 1933).[21] An exhibition organized at the Ferdinand Moeller Gallery by Nazi students, 'Thirty German Artists', showing canvases by expressionist artists (all non-Jewish, including Barlach, Macke, Nolde, Pechstein, Rohlfs, Schmidt-Rottluft), was closed after three days by the interior minister, Wilhelm Frick. The nomination of Rosenberg at the head of the party's control commission for intellectual activities clearly marked the defeat of the opening attempted by Goebbels. Yet even after the failure of the Moeller exhibition, works by Nolde, Barlach and Feininger were still exhibited in January 1934, at the instigation of Schreiber and Weidemann, and no doubt with the support of Goebbels, despite attacks in the *Völkische Beobachter*. In April the same year, the Moeller gallery exhibited watercolours and lithographs by Nolde. Rosenberg then intervened directly with Goebbels, reproaching him with sabotaging the foundations of the National Socialist vision. The final point in these hesitations was marked by Hitler's speech in September 1934 when he reaffirmed the danger represented by these 'corrupters of German art'. Without being reconciled with Rosenberg, Goebbels ceased supporting the avant-garde artists and the *Kunst der Nation* magazine was banned in 1935.

From 1937 onwards, large exhibitions of 'degenerate art' were held in Munich. This phenomenon of the Weimar Republic was counterposed to 'authentically German art'. The choice of Munich, the city where Nazism was born, was a symbolic one. While the public were invited to admire canvases that conformed to the new regime's values – pallid imitations of naturalism, monotonous peasant scenes, Aryan and 'Nordic' nudes – works by Franz Marc,[22] George Grosz, Ernst Barlach, Paul Klee and Wassili Kandinsky were presented for mockery. So that the visitor should have no doubt on the appropriate judgement to make, alongside these works were displayed drawings by mental patients[23] and the prices at which the 'degenerate' works had been bought by museums. As these last referred to the period of inflation, people were led to believe that these artists had grown rich thanks to the ridiculous cultural policy of the Weimar Republic, during a period of general misery. The canvases were accompanied by posters of the kind 'Expression of the Jewish Racial Soul', 'The Invasion of Bolshevism in Art', 'Outrage to Heroes', 'German Peasants as Seen by Jews', 'Madness Elevated to a Method'. The fact that individuals as mediocre and challenged as the painter Adolph Ziegler and the photographer Heinrich Hoffman took part organizing these events should not give credence to the notion that Hitler and the supreme authorities of the NSDAP were not responsible for the birth of these exhibitions against 'degenerate art'; they were inaugurated by Goebbels, while Hitler himself was undoubtedly their instigator.

THE STRUGGLE AGAINST INSTITUTIONS

On 15 February 1932, in the *Deutsche Kulturwacht*, Hanns Johst had already demanded in the name of the Kampfbund für die Kultur, the magazine's sponsoring body, that the Prussian Academy of Arts should be disbanded. The pretext for this destruction was provided by a manifesto posted on Berlin walls,[24] bearing the signatures of two Academy members, Heinrich Mann and Käthe Kollwitz, and calling for a KPD/SPD united front against the Nazis in the elections of March 1933. The Nazis detested the literary section of the Academy[25] in particular because the writers whom they admired were poorly represented in relation to the republicans and liberals.[26] In August 1931, the Academy protested the censorship measures that now threatened literature, and the following year Heinrich Mann drew up a report proposing to condemn nationalist methods in literary criticism, in particular those of Paul Fechter.[27] Indeed, the very fact that the literary section had since 1930 been presided over by Heinrich Mann was sufficient to make it hateful to their eyes.

The Reichskommissar for science, art and education, Bernhard Rust, consequently demanded that the president of the Academy, Max von Schillings, a composer close to the National Socialists, should hold Heinrich Mann and Käthe Kollwitz responsible for the scandal aroused by this appeal and demand their resignation, in the absence of which the Academy would be dissolved. Schillings also opined that this appeal violated the statutes of the Academy, which was supposedly non-political,[28] and promised that a meeting would be held the same day to take a decision. Heinrich Mann, who was found at the cinema, was incited to attend his own trial as a matter of urgency.[29] Schillings begged him to renounce his office as president so as not to damage the Academy. Mann resigned, together with Käthe Kollwitz, 'in order to save the Academy from a difficult situation'. This withdrawal – presented as a voluntary decision – was in fact an exclusion, rendered official on 15 February 1933. The architect Martin Wagner resigned in solidarity, and Alfred Döblin informed von Schillings of the section's decision to meet in order to decide on this matter. Ludwig Fulda remarked that Heinrich Mann had only done his duty as a citizen, and the literary section published a text in which it expressed its solidarity with Mann, thanking him for having given the Academy the benefit of his prestige and reproaching von Schillings for taking an illegal decision. The Nazi press, for its part, railed against Mann, and Wilhelm Stapel's *Deutsches Volkstum* claimed, not without logic, that it was the entire section that had elected Mann to the presidency and should now all resign.

After the March elections, the majority of cultural organizations were similarly dismantled. Rather than attacking them head on, the Nazis preferred to provoke a crisis situation within them so that, by using their supporters, they could present their intervention as responding to the will of the majority. This process of fascisization of writers' organizations had started back in 1931. In that year an Arbeitgemeinschaft nationaler Schriftsteller, under the leadership of Walter Bloem, had already been founded within the SDS (Schutzverband deutscher Schriftsteller) presided over by Hans Richter. On 19 March 1933 a demand signed by Hanns Heinz Ewers was addressed to the leadership calling for the exclusion of Communist and pacifist members who were 'traitors to the fatherland'. The political ideas of members were soon passed in review, and those who were hostile to the 'new Germany' were excluded. Their names were published on 13 April in the *Neue Weltbühne*. They included Rudolf Olden, Theodor Plievier, Ludwig Renn, Anna Seghers, Ernst Toller and Arnold Zweig. The Berlin SDS group, which was very progressive, was immediately dissolved. In May 1933, Bloem was given an honorary position, and the real responsibility passed to the Nazi writer Götz Otto Stoffregen, cultural editor of the *Völkische Beobachter*.

A profession of faith[30] in favour of the new regime was required of each writer in October 1933. Authors of Jewish origin were given special numbers and forced to pay higher contributions. From now on, magazines and periodicals could not accept contributions from writers without knowing their numbers. As the numbers of 'undesirable' writers figured on special lists, it was easy to eliminate them. From 31 July 1933, the SDS[31] was transformed into the Reichsverband deutscher Schriftsteller (RDS), and the former organization officially dissolved in December. This new organization, supposedly non-political, was to decide which authors it was desirable to publish or to ban. In fact, only those members recognized as 'of German blood' (*deutschblutig*) could now publish freely, while others were forced into silence. As a preliminary repressive institution, the RDS conducted the indispensable work of purging that would lead to the Reichsschrifttumkammer.

After the leadership of the SDS had been led to resign, the same programme was applied to the literature section of the Prussian Academy of Arts, attacked once again. On 14 March 1933 Max von Schillings addressed a letter to thirty-one members of this section, making clear that in the new situation the section had to reorganize, and its members were asked to respond with a simple yes or no to the question, 'Are you prepared to put your person at the disposition of the Academy?' If yes, this involved a commitment not to engage in any political activity hostile to the government and to collaborate loyally in the cultural tasks that were now incumbent.

Of the twenty-seven members of the section who responded, eighteen replied in the affirmative, including Rudolf Binding, Walter von Molo, Stehr, Stucken, Gottfried Benn, Ludwig Fulda, Alfred Mombert,[32] Oskar Loerke, Gerhart Hauptmann, Mell, Franz Werfel, Theodor Däubler, Bernhard Kellermann, Fritz von Unruh and Georg Kaiser.[33] Rudolf Pannwitz refused to reply; Thomas Mann wrote from Switzerland on 17 March 1933 that he had no intention of acting against the government and he believed he had always served German culture, but he was in any case withdrawing from the Academy.[34] Alfons Paquet and Jacob Wassermann requested explanations; Paquet announced his decision to quit the Academy, and Wassermann asked if he was still eligible for membership, being Jewish: the response came on 18 April, confirming that he had effectively been excluded. Alfred Döblin wrote that he was not a 'politician', but as a Jew he did not see very well how to react to the '*völkisch*' movement. In a second letter (17 and 18 March) he announced his decision to quit the Academy, as likewise did René Schickele. Oskar Loerke, third secretary of the Academy, lost his post on 1 April. On 5 May 1933, Georg Kaiser, Bernhard Kellermann, Alfred Mombert, René Schickele, Fritz von Unruh and Franz Werfel received identical letters informing them of their exclusion. As there was now practically no one left, the Academy was 'renewed' and 'reorganized' for its meeting of 7 and 8 June.[35] If unanimity had not been reached on the new mission of the Academy, as witness the discussions between Blunck, E. G. Kolbenheyer and Schäfer, it was now around the new president Hanns Johst.[36] From now on the Academy was to lose all power. In the course of 1933 it sought in vain to come to the aid of a certain number of writers who had been sent to concentration camp 'by mistake', but its petitions remained without effect.[37] Wilhelm Schäfer still protested against the burning of books by Alfons Paquet, but other members of the Academy with reactionary ideas would also have their books banned (Grimm, Kolbenheyer). Discussion within the Academy, which had formerly been so lively, fell silent,[38] and thanks to the servility and mediocrity of its president Hanns Johst, its alignment with the new regime was soon complete. A new selection was made in October 1933, in favour of H. Claudius, F. Grenssen, Enrica von Handel-Mazzetti, Ricarda Huch, Ernst Jünger, H. Lersch, Schaffner, J. Schlaf and J. Wehner. Some of these, such as Jünger,[39] had the courage to refuse these compromising honours.

After the abolition of the SDS[40] and the literature section of the Prussian Academy of Arts,[41] the Nazis attacked in the same manner the German section of PEN, but with less success. The motive for the attack was an article by Carl Haensel published in the *Deutsche Allgemeine Zeitung*, which insisted that German literature should be represented within PEN by authors deeply rooted in the popular tradition. Following this, on 23 April, several new members were nominated, all National Socialist sympathizers: Stoffregen, von Schirach, Naso, Steguweit, Schauwecker, Weinbrenner and Bronnen. The plenary meeting subsequently accepted a second list of new members: Arenhövel, Hermann Bethge, Bley, Busch, Dietrich, Kohne, von Leers, Schlösse, Heyk and Schickedanz, all members or sympathizers of the NSDAP and very far from well-known. Anti-Nazi writers being now in a minority in the assembly, their opponents had no difficulty in occupying the leadership of German PEN. Here again, the illusion was maintained that the 'renovation' was not a political decision but an internal demand of the German section.

All that remained was to exclude members hostile to the regime. During the international congress of PEN held at Ragusa (now Dubrovnik) on 28 March 1933, it was announced that Ernst Toller and nine other members had been expelled for belonging to Communist organizations. But the Nazis had under-estimated Toller's cleverness and the magnitude of international reactions. The internal situation of German PEN, and the overall barbarism that characterized the cultural policy of the Third Reich, could not be a matter of indifference to foreign writers, especially given that the most eminent members of the German section (Thomas and Heinrich Mann, Erich Maria Remarque, Emil Ludwig, Stefan Zweig) had been replaced by authors better known for their anti-Semitic writings than for their literary qualities. Thus a certain number of foreign representatives decided to raise the question of the repression that was raging in Germany and the treatment inflicted on writers.

> Despite the reasons for this reversal being so readily apparent, it was impossible for the congress to involve itself in the internal modifications of the German section. But it could and should inform itself if the present members respect the three points that in some way form the charter of the Federation:
> 1. Literature, which is national in its origins, knows no frontier and must be able to circulate freely among the nations, irrespective of political or international accidents.
> 2. In all cases and especially in case of war, works of art, being the common heritage of humanity, must be protected from national or political passions.
> 3. The members of the PEN Club will use all their influence in support of mutual respect and understanding between nations.[42]

The American motion proposed by S. Camby recalled these three fundamental principles without insisting on the reasons for this warning. H. G. Wells, replacing John Galsworthy as president of PEN, wished at any price to avoid a break with the German section. The motion went on to maintain: 'It is needful to take precise measures to prevent PEN centres from being used as propaganda tools for the justification of persecutions inflicted in the name of chauvinism, racial prejudice and political bad faith.'

This did not rule out the possibility that the executive committee might be brought to take into consideration the state and activities of each section, and to 'initiate action against those that did not respect the aims of the federation'. Vague enough, yet still threatening, the Camby motion was applauded shame-lessly by the German delegates Elster and Busch. Sixteen other delegates insisted on their reports being heard: they demanded that the German delegates explain themselves on the subject of the Reich's cultural policy, the burning of books, the attacks on personal liberty, anti-Semitic persecution and the expulsion of intellectuals. The German representatives violently opposed any discussion that would raise accusations against the Nazi regime, finding support here from certain other delegations[43] and even threatening to leave. Benjamin Crémieux intervened to affirm: 'We are here without exception to prevent the temporal from seizing the spiritual and dominating it.' It was decided that the sixteen supporting delegations and five oppositional ones would meet to seek a means of reconciliation: 'In exchange for an unimportant modification which consisted in placing the three reproaches not in the conclusion but in the considerations of the text, the Germans accepted that they should be put to the vote. They simply demanded the right to abstain, so that any discussion took place only after the vote.'[44]

The president refused this and gave the floor to Ernst Toller, who spoke as a guest of the British PEN.[45] The Germans, Swiss and Austrians immediately left the hall. The Italians remained. After Toller came Schalom Asch, then again Toller who exposed the prevailing situation in Germany. The German delegation resigned only after its return to Berlin.

> A number of those who were unwilling for the Congress to tackle such a burning question have accused the Congress of playing politics. There is no one that merits that reproach except themselves. The PEN Club has the task of raising its voice each time that it notices facts that are contrary to its mission. It is neither a professional grouping nor a tourist association, nor, as has been very well said, an international of nationalisms. And if it had to keep silent, it would subsequently have to disappear.[46]

The Nazi press was unleashed against 'the Jew Toller' and 'the Jew Crémieux'. The German section of PEN was now replaced by a 'National Union of Writers' presided over by Hanns Johst. But it was re-established in exile by antifascist writers.[47]

NEW FORMS OF ORGANIZATION: THE REICH CHAMBERS OF CULTURE (*KULTURKAMMERN*)

A look at the new Nazi cultural organizations will enable us to understand how and why the destruction of Weimar culture could be so rapid and radical, and any literary opposition almost impossible.

German artistic life from now on was entirely in the grip of the propaganda ministry directed by Goebbels, who controlled literature and the plastic arts as well as the theatre and cinema. Every writer and poet, every painter and actor, had to belong to their respective organization on pain of being unable to practise their art and being reduced to silence and unemployment. Their role was that of a board of control, selection and repression. A decree explained that the task of the Reichskulturkammern[48] was to work together with the Reich minister of popular education and propaganda in order to promote German culture, settle material questions specific to these cultural professions and combine the efforts of different groups. Seven chambers of culture were established to this end (literature, theatre, music, cinema, plastic arts, press and radio). Only individuals affiliated to these chambers would be authorized to practise a cultural activity. No work could be exhibited, printed or broadcast without their agreement. The chambers controlled not just the creation of culture but also its material production and distribution. It was not only writers, poets, painters, actors and musicians who had to belong, but also publishers, journalists, booksellers, librarians, manufacturers of radio equipment or musical instruments, which enabled the establishment of an almost complete state monopoly. With their various ramifications, these instances were in a position to exclude, for racial or ideological reasons, any individual judged 'harmful' by the state. It was significant moreover that in 1938 the two vice-presidents of these chambers simultaneously occupied important positions in Goebbels's ministry, Walter Funck and Karl Hanke being secretaries of state. The submission of culture to propaganda was made all the more complete in that the presidents of each chamber and those responsible for the different sectors of cultural life were nominated by Goebbels himself. The presidents of the various chambers together formed the Reichskulturrat (Reich Cultural Council). A Reichskultursenat comprising individuals selected by the president was added to this. In this way, for example, the theatre *Kammer* was concerned not only with repertory, but also with actors, authors, dance associations, retirement homes for players, and the association of dramatic writers and composers. The 'literature chamber' for its part embraced journalists as well as writers, booksellers and publishers. The 'press chamber' also included journalists, as well as the managers of station kiosks, stenographers and paper merchants. Moreover, each chamber decided on relations between the different organizations that it supervised.

The president and his council exercised a continuous and absolute control over each individual 'cultural worker', who was naturally obliged to belong to their proper chamber. If the chamber rejected this membership or expelled the person concerned, this signified their elimination pure and simple from cultural life. If someone risked practising a profession falling within the sectors controlled by the chambers without their agreement, they were liable to a fine of up to 100,000 marks. Finally, in each district or *Gau*, a *Landeskulturverwalter* watched over the decrees of the chambers. If membership of these organisms guaranteed a certain material security, any creation outside of them was impossible both in theory and in practice, without resort to clandestinity.[49]

The Reich Literature Chamber
Directed by Hans Friedrich Blunck, later by Hanns Johst, this was one of the largest and comprised six sections.[50] From 1934 onward, it also had eight directors for professional associations (writers, librarians, directors of public libraries, bibliophiles, bookstores, book workers, etc.), as well as seven other corporate bodies which comprised such varied sectors as scholarships, literary prizes and book trades. No written material could escape it.[51]

Censorship was directly exercised by the minister of propaganda, but the chambers had the further task of drawing up blacklists of books to be banned. A decree of 25 April 1935 stipulated that the chamber of letters had to establish an index of all books and authors considered as 'un-German' (*undeutsch*) or hostile to the interests of the German nation. These lists contained new publications as well as translations and reprints of old works. Titles figuring on these lists had then to be confiscated by the Gestapo. This is how libraries and bookshops were purged of works by such authors as Thomas Mann, Stefan Zweig, Franz Werfel, Carl Zuckmayer and Franz Kafka. Finally, a selection was established from a strictly '*völkisch*' standpoint: the books retained were used for education and propaganda.[52]

The Reich Theatre Chamber

Presided over by Ludwig Körner and Eugen Klöpfer, actors who put themselves in the service of the regime, this chamber did not have to concern itself with censorship, which was exercised by the Reich office of dramaturgy (directed by Rainer Schlösser), following the decree of 15 May 1934. Its two first sections were responsible for legal organization, the third for opera and the selection of new German or foreign works. The fourth section concerned 'stage workers', governing salaries and conditions of work. The fifth was in charge of music halls, cabaret and circus, the sixth in charge of dance, the seventh of puppet shows, impresarios and so on.

The Reich Music Chamber

Directed from 1935 by Dr Peter Raabe, this supervised the distribution of musical works and the teaching of music. Its field of activities embraced popular music as well as the classics, and the elimination of 'un-German' and 'degenerate' music. After 1938 it had four sections: the first established the Aryan character of musicians, the second was concerned with the organization of music schools and teaching establishments, in close collaboration with the movement Kraft durch Freude and the Hitler Youth. This chamber also included a large number of professional associations, dealing with composers, with unpublished works by young musicians, with censorship, orchestral musicians, contracts and payments. The chamber also controlled the wages of some 60,000 musicians working in nightclubs and hotels. Manufacturers of musical instruments, publishers of scores and the like also came under this chamber. The third section's remit was with choirs and popular music, the fourth had charge of concert agents and impresarios. Censorship at the level of works was little developed, as the political aspect of musical works is hard to pin down, apart from musicians such as Paul Hindemith who were termed 'musical bolsheviks', or Jewish and Communist composers who as such were 'un-German' and hostile to the regime. The chamber also watched over the 'Aryan' character of musicians.

The Reich Cinema Chamber

Closely controlled by Goebbels, this was concerned with both the production of films and verifying their 'German' character, and was also responsible for economic and social problems of the cinema. It had ten sections (legal and financial aspects, cultural and political questions, press service, relations with German and foreign newspapers, artistic aspects, scenery, economic aspects of production, statistics, credits (the Filmkreditbank was established in 1933), producers and directors, cameramen, technicians, make-up artists, production and export of films, studios, distribution in Germany, theatre owners, measures to avoid needless competition, photography, relations between cinema and propaganda, documentaries, and so on.

The specificity of this chamber lay in its close links with the propaganda ministry. A large number of its members were directly at Goebbels's orders. As Nazi propaganda made incessant use of the cinema, a *Gaufilmleiter* had special charge of this problem. Finally, the effective control of the cinema was assured by the centralization of finance in a single bank whose director was the president of the cinema chamber.

The Reich Plastic Arts Chamber
This had five main groups and a large number of sub-groups. Its activities concerned sculpture, painting, architecture, garden decoration and graphic arts as well as the antique trade and art publishing. It not only controlled the works produced, but also their conditions of production, sale and exhibition, as well as art objects that were confiscated (especially from Jews). Artistic creation as a whole, the distribution of works and artistic trades were all subordinated to it. The most favoured were architects, whom Hitler saw as artisans of the Reich's greatness. A special post was created to supervise the manufacture of symbols of National Socialism, entrusted to Professor Hans Schweitze, better known under the pseudonym Mjölnir, who played an important role in the elaboration of Goebbels's propaganda in Berlin. This chamber paid out grants to artists independent of commissions. By the end of 1936, it counted 42,000 members, including 15,000 architects, 14,300 painters, 2,900 sculptors, 2,300 handicraft workers, 4,200 engravers, 1,260 designers and 2,600 art publishers. The absence of art critics here is notable, Goebbels believing that criticism was both pernicious and useless. A decree of 29 November 1936 stipulated that only direct accounts and reportage were authorized.

The Reich Press Chamber
This chamber was responsible for the political control of newspapers, periodicals, and all who were involved with them. If it did not itself see to repression and censorship, it nevertheless controlled all the professional organizations. Its president, Max Amman, made sure that it was a docile instrument, in full submission to the state power. As political journals were prohibited, just like opposition organs, the German press now contented itself with reproducing the information sent it each day by the propaganda ministry (which even stipulated the titles to articles and the space they should be given). By virtue of the decree of 1 November 1933, Amman was able to confiscate some 1,473 periodicals, with no compensation for the proprietors. At the start of 1933 there had been 4,703 periodicals in Germany; by 1944 there were only 977. In case of conflict, the party press was necessarily favoured. Just as important,

the Reichsverband der deutschen Presse, though subordinate to the Pressekammer, was in fact answerable directly to the propaganda ministry and controlled 15,000 journalists. Its chief was Wilhelm Weiss, director of the *Völkische Beobachter*. Schools of journalism were charged with training perfect zealots for the regime, deprived of any critical sense. It should be noted that pamphlets, reviews, children's books, religious and scientific publications were also controlled by special commissions. Even newspaper sellers had to belong to associations, which ensured an absolute control of the press.

The Reich Radio Chamber

From 1933 on, German radio became a centralized entity subordinate to the propaganda ministry. This meant that anyone practising a trade with any connection to radio was required to belong: sound engineers, technicians, journalists, announcers, even listeners, were dragooned into an organization. In 1932, Eugen Hadamovsky, future *Reichsleiter*, had the idea of bringing artists, engineers and listeners together in a vast corporation that would enable radio to be made into a gigantic means of propaganda. The organization was subsequently absorbed into the Reichsrundfunkkammer. Any possibility of independence was evidently excluded (it was forbidden to listen to foreign broadcasts), and information to be broadcast was naturally provided by the propaganda ministry.

This brief summary of the structure and ramifications of these 'chambers of culture' is sufficient to show that after their creation, any possibility of opposition in the field of art or literature was almost impossible. If no political resistance movement could establish itself without being immediately infiltrated and dismantled by the Gestapo, culture was still more closely surveyed. Outside of leaflets, clandestine or disguised writings brought in from abroad by the émigrés, no mode of cultural expression could escape the control of Goebbels and his ministry. The whole of Germany was thus rendered dumb. Those who did not want to serve the regime had to keep silent or take refuge in the celebration of inner awareness or rural values. Undoubtedly some antifascist works were produced under Hitler – paintings or poems – but secretly, at the risk of terrible danger, and with no real impact on the population. The majority of these were only known in fact after the collapse of the Third Reich. Any discussion on the attitude of artists and writers in the 1930s and 40s, those who remained in Germany, must take into account the existence of this complex spider's web of repressive instances. Everyone knew that if they broke the laws they risked martyrdom, and in the prevailing climate of fear their voice would likely remain without echo.

Yet if this intellectual annihilation reached its zenith with Goebbels's cultural dictatorship, the process of erosion of liberty had begun already under the Weimar Republic. It was one of the most absurd injustices of this regime that it so frequently and violently repressed those who sought to defend it.

ARREST, INTIMIDATION, ELIMINATION

In the immediate aftermath of the Reichstag fire, a large number of writers, intellectuals, journalists and actors, often not members of any party, were arrested by the SA on the basis of detailed lists prepared in advance, as Göring himself recognized at the Nuremberg trial. As few of these believed themselves in any real danger, they were often arrested during the night at their homes. Carl von Ossietzky was visiting friends when he heard the news of the fire. His friends urged him to leave Germany but he refused, contenting himself with removing his name from his door. He was arrested on 28 February, at the same time as the poet Erich Mühsam, who was trying to get to Prague. Ludwig Renn, freed on 28 January, was rearrested exactly a month later, and the SA immediately destroyed all his manuscripts. The same day they arrested Egon Erwin Kisch, Otto Lehmann-Russbüldt, Hermann Duncker, the lawyer Hans Litten, Harry Wilder, well-known for his interventions at Communist meetings, and the sexologist Max Hodann. All these arrests were carried out by sections of the SA, with the help of the police. The same fate would have struck Ernst Toller, Erwin Piscator and Theodor Plievier if they had been in their apartments. Unable to arrest them, the SA ransacked their libraries and manuscripts.[53] The same scenes were repeated in other German cities. The actor Wolfgang Langhoff was arrested in Düsseldorf, Willi Bredel in Hamburg, and a similar treatment was inflicted on Berta Lask, Anna Seghers, Alfred Apfel, Klaus Neukrantz, Manès Sperber, J. Sternfeld and Karl A. Wittfogel. Kurt Hiller still published an article in the 7 March issue of *Die Weltbühne*, 'Heroism and Pacifism'; his apartment was immediately devastated by the SA, who even tore up photos of his parents. He was arrested in Frankfurt on 23 March, freed five days later, arrested again on 2 April, released on 9 May and arrested once more on 14 July for having helped some young Communists to flee the country. Paul Zech was arrested while staying with a Jewish family, imprisoned in a cellar, then freed. In the meantime his library had been pillaged.

Certain writers managed to escape arrest, being well prepared. J. R. Becher had already fled,[54] Brecht was staying at a private clinic, Willi Münzenberg had taken the precaution of moving.[55] Ernst Toller and Erich Weinert were hunted throughout Germany, and it was mere chance that saved their lives. Some people were giving lectures abroad and learned in good time what was awaiting them. Friedrich Wolf, the Communist playwright, called at the police station in Stuttgart to protest against the banning of one of his plays. Overhearing a conversation with the chief of police, he realized there was an order out to arrest him, and took advantage of their momentary inattention to flee. Alfred Wolfenstein, Theodor Lessing and Walter Mehring managed to escape while the SA was ransacking their homes. Stefan Grossman, editor of the *Tage-Buch*, was questioned by the SA, but as he was seriously ill they did not take him away. The majority of writers were immediately taken to prison, concentration camp, or Gestapo dungeons, where they were savagely tortured.

The effectiveness of the SA shows that these arrests had been carefully prepared: the Nazis knew precisely the names of their adversaries and where to find them. Completely illegal, despite the police cover, these arrests were absurd as well as unjustifiable. None of the writers arrested could seriously be considered a real danger to the state; their writings and convictions were manifest, but not the least act of violence could be pinned on them. The heterogeneity of victims is also striking: they included Communists (Willi Bredel, Anna Seghers), radical democrats (Carl von Ossietzky, Otto Lehmann-Russbüldt), non-party people, left liberals (Stefan Grossman), antifascists (Walter Mehring), pacifists (Ernst Toller, Armin T. Wegner), socialists with no direct party connection (Theodor Lessing, Alfred Wolfenstein), anarchists (Erich Mühsam, Theodor Plievier) and libertarians (Kurt Hiller). In contrast to the sadism of the arrests, the lack of preparation of the victims has a tragic aspect.

This unleashing of violence struck publishers as well as writers. At the same time that these intellectuals were arrested, the premises and printing presses of left-wing journals were ransacked, especially those connected with the KPD or the activities of Willi Münzenberg.[56] In a few days these publishers lost more than four hundred thousand books, which for many heralded a mortal crisis.[57]

A number of arrested writers were able to leave Germany in the wake of international protests: Kurt Kläber and Otto Lehmann-Russbüldt (who would later emigrate to the Netherlands and England), Egon Erwin Kisch (on the intervention of Czechoslovakia, of which he was a citizen), Anna Seghers (who subsequently married Laszlo Radvanyi and acquired Hungarian citizenship, then emigrated to Switzerland, France and Mexico), Alfred Apfel, Manès Sperber (freed on the intervention of the Polish embassy, who then emigrated to Yugoslavia along with other Poles), Walter Zadek (freed on the intervention of professional organizations, who took refuge in the Netherlands), Justin Steinfeld (refuge in Czechoslovakia), Max Hodann (emigrated to Sweden), Eduard Claudius (emigrated to Switzerland), Berta Lask (emigrated to Czechoslovakia, then the Soviet Union).[58] Other writers were released in 1934, after being interned in concentration camp, such as Willi Bredel, Kurt Hiller and Wolfgang Langhoff.[59] The same year, Werner Hirsch, K. A. Wittfogel, J. Zerfass, Armin T. Wegner[60] and Ludwig Renn[61] were released. Some people were freed even later, such as Rudolf H. Ganz.[62] Several however were murdered in concentration camps or Gestapo prisons: this was the fate of Klaus Neukrantz,[63] Erich Baron, Erich Mühsam and Carl von Ossietzky. I shall relate here the martyrdom of these last two, which held a highly symbolic value for the whole generation for which they spoke.

Born on 3 October 1889 in Hamburg-Neustadt, Carl von Ossietzky[64] was only eighteen when he first attended a meeting addressed by August Bebel. This first contact with the workers' movement and the Social-Democratic Party was decisive for him. Close to such individuals as Theodor Barth, Hellmut von Gerlach, and Robert Breitscheid, who founded the Demokratische Vereinigung in Berlin, he became a member of its Hamburg section, and it was in its organ, *Das Freie Volk*, that his first theatre criticism appeared in February 1911. His articles denounced capitalism and the bourgeoisie, and urged on the struggle for freedom. He believed in socialism as an absolute ideal, and in a militant pacifism that he never stopped defending throughout the 1920s. In 1914 he was condemned to a fine for his anti-militarist articles, which did not prevent him from continuing to denounce the danger of a global war. When this broke out, he was sent to the front as a private soldier.

The experience of war marked him as deeply as it did Ernst Toller or Erwin Piscator. After 1917 he wrote many articles that affirmed his faith in pacifism and his support for the Spartacists. Though outside the Communist party, he followed its development sympathetically. From 1920 to 1922 he collaborated with the *Berliner Volkszeitung*, and took part in the foundation of the Friedensbund der Kriegteilnehmer which united former French and German soldiers in defence of peace. The pacifist rallies that he organized, sometimes together with Kurt Hiller, attracted up to a hundred thousand participants. A passionate democrat, Ossietzky was also a forceful defender of the Republic, while denouncing its inadequacies. He condemned the extremists who opposed it, and maintained that a genuine socialism in the Marxian legacy was not Communist. He simultaneously proposed a reform of the Reichswehr and its democratization. He insisted that it should not be used against the workers, and that paramilitary formations of the far right should be proscribed. He continued to believe in the Republic even when the murderers of pacifists were acquitted. In 1923 he took park in the foundation of the Republican party (RPD), though this failed to obtain a seat in the Reichstag. Disappointed, Ossietzky left this party and continued his work as a publicist, first of all in the *Tage-Buch*, founded by Leo Schwarzschild and Stefan Grossman,[65] constantly warning the Social-Democrats and denouncing everything that threatened the Republic. But the more he defended the Republic, the more it attacked him. In 1925 he was prosecuted by Stresemann, but his influence increased significantly when in January of the following year Siegfried Jacobsohn engaged him as a permanent contributor to the *Weltbühne*, of which he became editor after its founder's death (3 December 1926), also inviting Kurt Tucholsky to contribute regularly. Thanks to his courage and qualities, the journal won a new readership and steadily became the organ of the non-party intellectual left. In his articles Ossietzky constantly demonstrated what a genuine Republic would mean. He argued for a union of the forces of the left, even if, like Tucholsky, he always criticized the submission of the KPD to the Comintern. The magazine published documents on the reorganization of the Reichswehr and its clandestine activities, which led him to be prosecuted for treason. In December 1927 he was condemned to a month in prison. He took advantage of this to attack the administration of justice, launched a campaign against the death penalty, and took up the defence of pacifist journalists such as Berthold Jacob and Fritz Küster, accused of high treason in 1928. In February that year, he was accused once again of publishing censored texts by the Communist novelist Berta Lask.

It was only in 1930 that Ossietzky started to concern himself with the Nazi party, following the publication of a text by Willi Münzenberg, *Nationalsozialismus oder Kommunismus*. At this point he maintained that the NSDAP had no future. Hitler struck him as a puppet of heavy industry, and he doubted that this would finance indefinitely a party so ardently preoccupied with the renaissance of Teutonic divinities. He saw Nazism simply as a gathering of malcontents, and those marching behind its music, he claimed, did not know in what direction they were heading. If Hitler wanted to enter the government, he would have to become 'correct' and 'bourgeois'. Without ideas or principles, Nazism could not endure: no sympathizer of the NSDAP was even capable of explaining what made up the supposedly 'socialist' character of the party. Ossietzky did not believe that Hitler could possibly win a lasting victory; he trusted the intelligence of the voters. But as he took count of the headway being made by the Nazis among the German electorate, he called for a united front, published in the *Weltbühne* Trotsky's texts on fascism, and denounced the candidacy of Marshal Hindenburg. There were few, however, who listened.

In 1931, when the *Weltbühne* was tried for information published by Kreisler, Ossietzky and his contributor were sentenced to a year and a half in prison. Some people advised him to quit Germany, but he saw this as abandoning his ideas and refused.[66] He emerged from prison when the Weimar Republic was in its death throes.[67] Taking up once again the editorship of the *Weltbühne*,[68] he continued to attack the right wing and the Nazis, though he knew by now that 'the Republic had lost the battle'. On 7 March his journal ceased publication.

Ossietzky was one of the first intellectuals to be arrested after the Reichstag fire. Just as on his previous arrest, he had refused to flee. While terror already raged in the streets, he still believed in the force of moral ideas. Immediately after his arrest, he was taken to the Columbiahaus by the SA, together with Egon Erwin Kisch and Ludwig Renn. Transferred to Spandau, he was accused of having taken part in the Reichstag fire. On 6 April he was interned in the former prison of Sonnenburg–Neumark, transformed into a concentration camp, where he was tortured daily by the SA on account of his pacifist and anti-Nazi activities. He embodied everything that they despised: a certain conception of morality, courage, intelligence and generosity. Within less than a year he was reduced to the state of a mere skeleton covered with skin. Yet the Nazis could not gather the least 'proof' against him. Some foreign journalists, such as the American representative of Associated Press, H. G. Knickerbocker, the author of books of reportage on Germany, were permitted to see him in the camp. Ossietzky simply asked the reporter to send him books on the Middle Ages, an epoch which seemed to have returned once more. Yet despite this daily torture, the Nazis did not manage to destroy him. His martyrdom lasted for five years. He was offered his freedom if he publicly renounced his ideas, but did not even bother to respond. In February 1934 he was transferred to the camp of Papenburg–Esterwegen, in the middle of a marsh. His health, already dismal, deteriorated further, and he had to be excused from compulsory labour. Yet he continued organizing political discussions within the camp. Even after 30 June 1934, when the administration passed into the hands of the SS, Ossietzky continued to show his contempt, refusing to reply to them as he had been condemned to be silent. Those who met him at this time recall a man looking already aged, with hollow face, eyes deeply sunk in their orbit, and a waxy complexion. In 1935, following a KPD meeting in Brussels, committees for the release of Thälmann, Mierendorf and Ossietzky were established in Paris. His martyrdom became a symbol of Nazi barbarism, and even in New York committees were formed to defend him.

On 23 January 1936 the English journalist Wickham Steed wrote an open letter to the editor of *The Times*, demanding that, given the failure to obtain the release of Ossietzky, he should receive evidence of the admiration of antifascists across the world. These movements however failed even to obtain Ossietzky's transfer to a hospital. When a Red Cross representative requested to meet him in the course of a visit to Esterwegen, he was answered that there was no prisoner there of that name. When he insisted, two SS men finally carried in a man with a livid face, broken teeth, one eye closed and a broken leg, unable to utter his name. The Red Cross representative could only salute Carl von Ossietzky in the name of the civilized world. All he could murmur was: 'I only wanted peace.'[69]

The SS tried many times to murder him, and he owed his survival to the Communist prisoners in the camp. Thousands of signatures were gathered in his support. The Nazis then launched a campaign against the award of the Nobel Prize to a political opponent. Several personalities – the Nobel Prize winner Jane Addams, Baron von Weiszäcker, chancellors of English and American universities – multiplied their interventions at foreign ministries. Petitions in his favour circulated around the world and were addressed to Hitler. But the Nazis refused to release him, hoping that the candidacy of President Masaryk, put forward in opposition to Ossietzky, would finally prevail. While Thomas Mann intervened with the Nobel committee in Ossietzky's favour, the Norwegian writer Knut Hamsun, a convert to fascist ideas, sought with false documents provided by the Gestapo to prove that Ossietzky was a traitor to his country. The affair rapidly took an international dimension and the Nazis ended up supporting the candidacy of Baron de Coubertin, organizer of the Olympic Games. In order to save face, Göring had Ossietzky, by now almost in his death-throes, transferred to a Berlin hospital. To the surprise of the Nazis he was still alive and the world was interested in him, this man suffering with a heart ailment and tuberculosis, who in Germany was called a 'living corpse'.

Though he could scarcely speak, the Nazis still tried to wipe out his memory by making believe that he had abandoned his ideas and agreed to rally to the 'new Germany'. In Norway, demonstrations of workers, students and intellectuals continued to demand his release. Prisoner 562 at Esterwegen was awarded the Nobel Peace Prize on 23 November 1936. Hitler's response was to announce on 30 January 1937 that in future no German citizen would be allowed to accept the prize. Even so, the Gestapo would not release Ossietzky: he was under constant surveillance in the prison hospital where he was dying, and the prize money was confiscated. No intervention could now save him, and he died on 4 May 1938. A sculptor clandestinely executed his death mask. He was cremated in the Berlin suburb of Wedding, and no plaque was allowed to be placed on his tomb: even in death, this pacifist still inspired fear.[70]

No less tragic was the martyrdom of the Jewish poet Erich Mühsam. Born 6 April 1878 in Berlin, the son of a Lübeck pharmacist, he was already expelled from college for 'socialist intrigues'. In Berlin he joined the anarchist group of Gustav Landauer, then lived from 1908 to 1911 among the Munich *bohème*. A member of the Munich revolutionary council in 1918, he was condemned to fifteen years in a fortress (amnestied in 1924), whilst Landauer was trampled to death by the soldiery and Leviné shot. He soon won fame for his anarchist poems and his participation in revolutionary magazines (*Kain, Zeitschrift für Menschlichkeit*). Hating the state, capitalism and imperialism, he had already been arrested in 1910 for his propaganda activity among the unemployed. His works written in prison after the fall of the Bavarian *Räterepublik*, and his proletarian stage plays,[71] appeared in 1920 and won great acclaim. From 1926 he published the anarchist monthly *Fanal*. With his red beard and long hair, he was a figure of legend throughout Germany.

Mühsam was likewise arrested by the Gestapo in the wake of the Reichstag fire. Imprisoned at first in Berlin (April 1933), then in the KZ Sonnenburg,[72] he was aware that he would not get out alive. The SA broke his teeth. He became deaf and almost blind from their beatings. Each morning he was forced to dig his own grave and was placed it in as a sadistic joke. When his wife[73] visited him, she had to take away for washing his clothes covered with blood. Subsequently interned in the KZ Brandenburg, his health went into decline. Also suffering a heart condition, he was knocked about each day for having written proletarian plays and anarchist poems. So that he could not write any more, his hands were broken and even the Jewish prisoners were forced to beat and torture him. Soon he became so weak that he could no longer walk unaided.

In February 1934 he was sent to KZ Oranienburg. This old and infirm man was forced to clean out the camp latrines with his hands. When the SS took over the camp administration, Erich Mühsam knew that he now had not much longer to live. The SS regiment that arrived from Bavaria was well aware of Mühsam's activity in the Munich soviet. The camp commander effectively gave him twenty-four hours to hang himself. As he refused, wanting his death to at least create a scandal, he was hung in the latrines on 10 July 1934.[74]

These torments did not mean that the writers concerned were unaware of the outside world. They very often gave proof of an astonishing lucidity about the events they lived through or anticipated. The most rigorous and incisive analyses of the dangers that threatened democracy and the Republic were most frequently to be found from liberals, pacifists, and non-party writers such as Ossietzky, Toller, Mühsam, von Gerlach and Tucholsky, rather than in party pamphlets. In all the major battles that had to be waged – from the struggle against the right-wing squads, Hitler, censorship, the Reichswehr, to the united antifascist front – they unceasingly urged on the defenders of the Republic. But their courage and intelligence counted for practically nothing in the face of events.

After they had been already gagged under the Republic, the Nazis sought not only to eliminate them physically but to expel their works from the collective memory. Many could not even save their own lives.[75]

THE BOOK BURNINGS OF 10 MAY 1933:
BONFIRES OF THE INTELLIGENCE

Their most characteristic invention, and that which revealed them best, was the bonfire on which they burned books that they were incapable of writing: the sum, in fact, of an entire intellectual culture from which their own inadequacies had excluded them [. . .]. Germany, at this moment, brought forth its madmen and savages.

Heinrich Mann, *Hatred*

Following the decrees of 8 February 1933, all Marxist publications were proscribed. The Nazis had been resolved for a long while to eliminate all works that they viewed as hostile to their ideas or 'foreign to the German spirit'. If they sought to give a semblance of legality to the authoritarian reorganization of writers' associations, their attitude towards these works themselves, books in particular, reveals more than any other measure the style of the regime: they were simply burned.

Nazi propaganda sought to make believe that the autos-da-fé of 10 May 1933 were spontaneous actions expressing the will of the people – students in particular – and the enthusiasm elicited by the 'national revolution'. Though repeated by some historians of literature,[76] this thesis is quite erroneous. Everything indicates on the contrary that these book burnings were minutely prepared. The initiative supposedly came from the Nazi students, in particular the Deutsche Studentenschaft founded in 1919, and known for its anti-Semitic and reactionary ideas. January 1933 saw the organization of the Hauptamt für Presse und Propaganda der deutschen Studentenschaft, which took the first large-scale measures: works by Jewish authors were put on the fire. Each student had to 'purify' their own library, those of their friends and finally the public libraries. It was envisaged that bonfires of books would be kindled in front of the universities, and that all books thus confiscated would be thrown onto them. A ceremony followed by a torchlight retreat completed this 'purification of German culture'.[77] These measures were set in a general context marked by the boycott of Jewish or antifascist professors, the implementation of the ideas propounded by Hitler in *Mein Kampf* or in the Nazi students' *Zwölf Thesen wider den undeutschen Geist*, designed to abolish the distance between *Schrifttum* and *Volkstum*. The fifth of these theses, in particular, stated: 'The Jew can only think Jewish. If he writes in German, he lies. The German who writes German and thinks non-German is a traitor.' The seventh and tenth theses envisaged a struggle against the 'non-German spirit' and gave students the task of denouncing Jewish intellectualism and liberalism. This organization published in the journal *Nachtausgabe* (belonging to the Hugenberg company) on 26 April 1933 a list of works that deserved to be burned. Among others were to be found books by Schalom Asch, Henri Barbusse, Bertolt Brecht, Max Brod, Alfred Döblin, Ilya Ehrenburg, Albert Ehrenstein, Lion Feuchtwanger, Ivan Goll, Jaroslaw Hasek, Walter Hasenclever, Arthur Holitscher, Egon Erwin Kisch, Walter Lippmann, Klaus Mann, Roger Neumann, Ernst Ottwalt, Kurt Pinthus, Erich Maria Remarque, Ludwig Renn, Arthur Schnitzler,

Richard Beer-Hoffman, Ernst Toller, Kurt Tucholsky, Arnold and Stefan Zweig. These lists were drawn up in haste, to judge by misspelled names and wrong attributions. It seems that very few Nazis had read the works they were going to burn.

On 26 April a new series of actions took place: students, often accompanied by SA men in uniform, carried off '*undeutsch*' books from bookstores and libraries. On 10 May assemblies of students, professors and numerous spectators were held outside the universities. Books were brought in handcarts, wagons drawn by oxen, and lorries, preceded by Nazi fanfares. It was not only students who spoke in front of the bonfires, but also professors, rectors, and party functionaries. In Berlin, Alfred Bauemler, the Nazi publisher of Nietzsche, gave the inaugural speech; in Bonn it was Hans Naumann; in Cologne the Germanist Ernst Bertram, who had been a friend of Thomas Mann; in Nuremberg Karl Holz. Goebbels himself presided over the Berlin book burning. Volumes were thrown onto the flames accompanied by ritual imprecations designed to exorcise the anti-German demons concealed within: 'Against class struggle and materialism, for the popular racial community and the idealist attitude to life', 'Against decadence and moral corruption, to safeguard family and State', 'Against the falsification of our history and the deprecation of our great figures, for the honour of our past', 'Against the literary betrayal of soldiers of the Great War, for the education of the people and the spirit of truth . . .'

The 'herald' then adjured the crowd to burn the writings of Marx, Tucholsky, Ossietzky, Ernst Glaeser, Heinrich Mann, Alfred Kerr and Karl Kautsky.[78] Even today, it is impossible to see images of these book burnings or listen to the recordings made without a feeling of unease in the face of this medieval barbarism and perverse religiosity. Night and flames served to give this ceremony a still more disturbing mystical dimension, fire being at the same time the symbol of destruction and of resurrection.[79]

The idea was certainly not new. In October 1817 a famous book burning had already taken place in Germany: nationalist students in Fichte's time had gathered at the Wartburg castle where Luther had once taken refuge, to burn writings hostile to their political conceptions, just as Luther had burnt the papal bull exactly three hundred years before. The same ritual had already been established: a herald announced in loud voice the title of each work to be burned and the incantation was taken up by the crowd. Heinrich Heine had already prophesied that 'Where they start by burning books, they end up burning people.' Yet the auto-da-fé of anti-nationalist writings in 1817 was only a symbolic gesture: it was not even books that were burned but symbolic representations, papers with their authors and titles. In 1933, the burnings went together with waves of arrests, daily terror and the first concentration camps. And the works were attacked out of an inability to destroy the authors themselves. Alfred Döblin was hardly mistaken when he noted in his diary: 'The Jew who bears my name has been burned there.'

Reaction to these manifestations in Germany was timid, even if it is doubtful whether they were truly popular. Only some rare critics such as Bernhard

Diebold openly denounced the Nazi cultural policy. Few university rectors opposed the destruction of their libraries apart from Martin Heidegger, rector at Freiburg, who took under his protection the 'Jewish works' claimed by the Nazi students. Documents published by J. Wolf[80] show that the majority of German newspapers reported these 'ceremonies' sympathetically, describing them in detail without a trace of irony, even in the face of this astonishing symbolism: the proscribed works, from Marx to Tucholsky, carried in ox-carts preceded by the SA.[81] The foreign press, on the other hand, took umbrage at these burnings and reported them in terms scarcely favourable to the Reich. *Nouvelles Littéraires*, which immediately took on a number of antifascist refugees as contributors, gave an account which deserves to be quoted here:

> On the evening appointed for the sacrifice, the gloomy sky appeared unwilling to countenance a revival of this sad medieval custom. At ten o'clock a dense crowd had gathered outside the university on the Opernplatz, and a providential rain could still have saved the honour of German intellectual life, but all hope was lost when an hour later there arrived in the square a procession of students brandishing torches and surrounding heavy lorries loaded with books. Soon the bonfire took hold, on which the demonstrators started to throw their flaming torches; propelled by the wind, smoke and sparks fell upon the crowd, putting the film crew in an awkward position. But the spectacle would not be spoiled for such a trifle, and a great cry of joy arose when the students, forming a chain, started to throw books onto the flames: the burning pages flew up into the air and fell down upon the participants, who piously gathered the charred remains. Now a thundering voice through a loudspeaker proclaimed the anger of the German spirit [. . .]. Fuelled constantly, the brazier cast upward a steadily growing flame, which lit up those attending with a sinister light. A young girl beside me said quietly to herself: 'It's German intellectual life that's burning!' But others cried: 'See the black souls of the Jews fly away.'

The eyewitness concluded:

> One should perhaps laugh, but it is scarcely possible to avoid indignation. The foolishness of a ceremony of this kind has not escaped a large number of influential members of the National Socialist party, according to certain testimonies that I have received. It is probable, however, that the government does not have the power to oppose the students' enthusiasm.

Even if many foreign observers still failed to understand the symbolic importance of these acts, they perceived them as both macabre and disquieting. And it was not without reason that Thomas Mann claimed in a radio broadcast to German listeners of 26 June 1943 that of all the bloody acts that the Nazis had committed, the book burning of 10 May 1933 was the one that had most vividly struck the imagination of the whole world: 'The Hitler regime is the regime of book-burning and will remain so.' He added that this act continued to haunt

German émigrés abroad, whereas in Germany it was already a forgotten memory. On 10 May 1943, the New York Public Library and three hundred other major American libraries dipped their flags to half-mast in memory of the book burning.

The émigrés reacted to these events with a mixture of horror and impotent rage. Thomas Mann often recalled that he had been sent a charred copy of one of his books, and Stefan Zweig related in his autobiography that one of his friends had presented him with a book of his that a student had pierced with a nail.[82] Ernst Toller followed the appeal that opened his book *I Was a German*: 'Where were you, my German comrades?', with the note: 'Written on the day that my books were burned in Germany.' Heinrich Mann analysed at length the significance of the autos-da-fé in his essay *Hatred*, published in Paris in 1933. Alfred Döblin saw himself as symbolically burned as a Jew together with his books. Hanns Henny Jahn called the book burning the most important event of the century, in a letter of 20 June 1933.[83] It was also in reaction to this book burning that the Deutsche Freiheitsbibliothek was established by German refugees in Paris, with the view of collecting not only all the burned books but also works banned in Germany and the writings of antifascists.[84] Brecht evoked this episode in several of his poems, in particular the one dedicated to the Bavarian author Oskar Maria Graf, whose name had been forgotten on the proscription lists, which Graf considered a slanderous insult. He consequently wrote to Hitler to demand that this dishonour should be repaired:

> [. . .] a banished
> Writer, one of the best, scanning the list of the
> Burned, was shocked to find that his
> Books had been passed over. He rushed to his desk
> On wings of wrath, and wrote a letter to those in power
> Burn me! He wrote with flying pen, burn me! Haven't my books
> Always reported the truth? And here you are
> Treating me like a liar! I command you:
> Burn me![85]

Three days after the *Bücherverbrennung*, the Börsenverein für den deutschen Buchhandel published a list of works the distribution of which was 'not recommended'. These lists were established by the Prussian ministry for science, art and popular education. They denounced the enemies of the German people, who were called representatives of 'asphalt literature'.[86] The authors incriminated were Jews, Communists, Socialists, republicans and pacifists. The collection of works to be suppressed was divided into three groups: those which should be destroyed by fire (Erich Maria Remarque, for example), those which should be 'kept in the poison cupboard' (Lenin, Marx), and a third group of 'doubtful cases' which should be examined before being classed with the two previous. All these works however should be withdrawn from libraries,[87] with just one copy kept for the study of *Asphaltliteratur*. These 'blacklists' were conveyed to bookstores, together with 'white lists'[88] recommending works judged favourable to the new regime. Other lists, constantly updated, concerned fields as varied as history, politics and science.[89] The Deutsche Bücherei in Leipzig contained no less than five thousand titles published after 1933 that could not longer be read.

These measures naturally had major repercussions at the economic level: they reduced a large number of publishers to bankruptcy, and deprived a large number of German writers both of their readership and their livelihood.[90]

At the end of 1933, the periodical *Die Tat* could write:

> By a wave of the hand, the left intellectuals have been swept away. Their magazines and newspapers are banned. Other newspapers and major publishers have suddenly ceased to know them, even though a short while ago they were received with open arms and paid handsome royalties. The wheel has turned, and we quickly forget today the time when it seemed a matter of course in Germany that only the left knew how to write.

The Beginnings of Emigration

1. INTELLECTUALS' ATTITUDES TOWARDS NATIONAL SOCIALISM

We experienced something other than we were, wrote something other than we thought, thought something other than we expected, and what remains is again something other than we had in mind.

Gottfried Benn, *Double Life*

I can still see them met together in a Berlin building – ministers, parliamentarians, writers, all victims targeted by an uncontrolled violence that was already mounting, grasping for power and awaiting only the occasion to erupt. They had themselves aroused these coming excesses, precisely by their contempt as civilized people for such blind and barbarous forces. They grimaced at them in disgust, they felt waves of belated revolt, mad optimism, even curiosity. What was going to happen? They would soon know.

Heinrich Mann, *Hatred*

THE ANTI-INTELLECTUALISM OF NATIONAL SOCIALISM

Today's snobs and knights of the inkwell may well tell themselves that the great revolutions of this world have never been made under the sign of the pen [. . .]. All great movements are popular movements, volcanic eruptions of human passions and states of mind, aroused either by the cruel distress of poverty, or by the torches of the word cast among the masses – never by jets of lemonade from anaesthetizing literati and salon heroes.

Hitler, *Mein Kampf*

If fascism was essentially a violently anti-intellectual movement, it tempted nonetheless a certain number of writers hostile to both democracy and Communism.[1] A few major names rallied to fascism, believing in it for a longer or shorter time (such as Ezra Pound, Gottfried Benn, T. F. Marinetti, Knut

Hamsun, Martin Heidegger), but their adhesion was most often simply 'accidental' (Heidegger), or an aberration in their trajectory (Benn); the general mediocrity of the movement's votaries cannot be denied.[2] Nevertheless, in the 1920s a fairly sizeable number of intellectuals saw for a moment in fascism the possibility of arousing a crisis-struck Europe from its lethargy. Other names that could be mentioned include those of Gentile, Pirandello and Malaparte in Italy; Céline, Drieu la Rochelle, Robert Brasillach and L. Rebatet in France; H. S. Chamberlain, Rudyard Kipling, Edmund Blunden in the English-speaking world, as well as more temporarily T. S. Eliot, Williamson, G. B. Shaw, W. B. Yeats, Wyndham Lewis, Ezra Pound and R. Campbell; Arnolt Bronnen and Hanns Johst in Germany, or again Knut Hamsun and Panait Istrati. It is impossible to understand the commitment of these intellectuals to fascism[3] without taking into account the whole European situation between 1914 and 1930, the flare-up of nationalism that the War had aroused, the fear of revolutionary contagion, doubt in the face of democracy, the spectre of decline, and concern at the economic crisis which affected every country. Very few of these intellectuals could have imagined that their admiration for strong and anti-democratic regimes would lead in due course to Auschwitz. Often their connection was only with the idea and myth of fascism, and they held themselves aloof – except in France – from the fascist movements of their various countries.[4] It is often even hard to prove that a causal chain led from their philosophical or political visions to this direct commitment.[5] Certain authors whom one could justly consider as forerunners of these movements either kept their distance or even condemned them. Others, who would seem from all evidence ideological opponents, made their peace with fascism in power. In certain cases, indeed, their rallying to fascist doctrine defies all rational understanding. The logic that impelled a particular author to support or accept National Socialism can only be explained by taking into account the complexity and fluidity of the intelligentsia, as well as the doctrinal farrago of National Socialism which offered a number of different points of contact.

The 1920s and early 30s in Germany saw paradoxical developments on the part of many writers. Some of these, as more or less everywhere in Europe, seemed sometimes to rally to fascism out of pure provocation.[6] Absurd and repugnant as this intellectual fascism may seem to us, we must also recognize that it was not always the fruit of opportunism but often, as Ernst Bloch emphasized, of an aberrant and perverted idealism. It was sometimes the same conditions and aspirations that led some writers to believe in a proletarian revolution and others in a conservative revolution. Many of them had in common the experience of war, hatred for capitalism, a certain contempt for bourgeois culture, and the expectation of a new world. The same themes often peruade their works (G. Benn, J. R. Becher). They were equally enthusiasts for Nietzsche and Dostoyevsky, and the same quotations from *The Brothers Karamazov* can be found in Lukács, Bloch, Jünger and Moeller van den Bruck. On the left as on the right, they saw themselves as 'revolutionaries'.

It is easy today to divide these writers into hostile families: in actual fact the Weimar Republic, as far as its intelligentsia are concerned, was a regular ideological imbroglio.[7] There was not so much a clearly divided literary left and right, but rather certain fixed poles – the nationalist and anti-Semitic far right, the Communist party and its 'proletarian intellectuals' – between which a number of ideological bridges permitted a certain traffic. The boundaries between the groups were often vague, and it was not uncommon, among intellectuals and writers, to find phenomena of 'ideological contamination', exchange of terminology[8] or ideological reversals that were both surprising and spectacular, whether rapid or gradual. Often the ideologists themselves no longer seemed to know exactly where their troops were to be found. The polemic over Albert Leo Schlageter, the Freikorps fighter who was shot by the French for sabotage during their occupation of the Ruhr, is a good example: this future Nazi hero and martyr also awakened certain sympathies on the left.[9] What should one say of the attitudes of these various groups towards Soviet Russia? If for the Communists the Russian system embodied an actual ideal to construct in Germany, the right also experienced a certain admiration for it. National-bolshevism seemed even to dream of a union of the two regimes' respective virtues: a sort of alliance of Prussianism and bolshevism. Ernst Niekisch, one of the most interesting figures of this period, symbolized in his own person all the contradictions of these ideological currents. He had taken part in the Bavarian Soviet Republic, but remained apart from both Social-Democracy and Communism. A friend of Ernst Toller and Ernst Jünger, he steadily moved towards the ideas of a conservative revolution. The symbol of his movement was an eagle holding in its claws a sickle and a sword. Niekisch dreamt of a reconciliation between Germany and Russia, and mixed nationalist terminology with slogans taken from the left. He met Goebbels but never rallied to Nazism. A few months before Hitler seized power he published *Hitler, ein deutsches Verhängnis*. Until 1934 he continued his political activity around *Widerstand*, a magazine founded in 1926. He was arrested and questioned in March 1933, then released, but interned in concentration camp in 1939.[10]

Up until 1933 these antagonistic intellectual groups still continued to meet one another in Berlin. If Nazis and Communists clashed in the streets, it was not the same with writers. Ernst Jünger attended meetings at which Ernst Niekisch and Goebbels[11] were present along with actors such as Heinrich George and Valeriu Marcu (a friend of Béla Kun), as well as members of Strasser's Schwarze Front and friends of Röhm. Many of these right-wing groups were opposed to Hitler after 1933, and several participants at these meetings ended up in concentration camps. Jünger recalls the strange evenings organized by the publisher Ernst Rowohlt, who for his birthday celebrations invited authors as different as Bertolt Brecht, Ernst von Salomon, Thomas Wolf and Arnolt Bronnen. He acknowledged that it was only much later that he realized the macabre aspect of these gatherings. Surprising as they might seem, they are by no means incomprehensible: in Berlin in particular, writers, artists and actors formed a world both quite dense in its geographical concentration and marginal in relation to the rest of Germany and its political culture. They were united – both left and right – by a belief in culture and debate, even if they developed opposing ideological visions. And this belief, as

Klaus Mann recognized, sometimes constituted an effective screen that cut them off from reality.

A certain number of writers of the Weimar era underwent quite astonishing ideological developments. The conversion of Thomas Mann to democracy is a good example, even if it was not until he went into exile that he actually converged with the positions of his brother Heinrich and son Klaus. But an immense distance already separated *Reflections of a Nonpolitical Man* from his lectures of the 1920s in support of democracy and the republic. Ludwig Renn, who was arrested by the Nazis, went into exile and fought in the International Brigades, came from a right-wing background: his original name was Arnold Vieth von Glossenau. Kurt Hiller, as a libertarian, was notoriously anti-Communist before coming round to support an antifascist Popular Front. Some developments took place more slowly, others resembled regular conversions. The case of the army officer Scheringer, who passed from the right to Communism, is a well-known one.[12] The writer Peter Martin Lampel, an aviator from the First World War, member of the Black Reichswehr, and author of the celebrated play *Revolt in the House of Correction*, developed from the far right towards national-bolshevism and wrote anti-Nazi plays. Just as spectacular was the trajectory of J. R. Becher, an expressionist haunted by suicide and decline who developed into the most orthodox of Communists. Bodo Uhse, before being a Communist writer, was editor of a Nazi newspaper. Ernst Glaeser, a pacifist writer invited to the Congress of Soviet Writers, chose exile, then returned to Germany and was responsible for an aviation magazine. The anti-bourgeois expressionist dramaturge Arnolt Bronnen, a friend of Brecht, rallied to Goebbels before ending up a Communist. A naturalist writer as critical as Gerhardt Hauptmann compromised with the Nazi regime, while the reactionary poet Stefan George kept his distance. The actual logic that impelled certain writers in one direction or the other is not always clear, and often defies any sociological analysis. Ernst von Salomon, a 'nationalist hothead' and Freikorps member implicated in the murder of Walter Rathenau, had two brothers of whom one was active, like him, in the Schleswig-Holstein partisans, but as a member of the KPD, while the other joined the SA. Ernst von Salomon never hid his admiration for his Communist brother Bruno, and at one time even assisted him in editing a peasant newspaper whose ideology was sufficiently confused that articles could very well have been written by either.[13] As for Jünger, a representative of the revolutionary right, he not only kept up links with E. von Salomon, but also with Ernst Toller, Ernst Niekisch and Erich Mühsam, and attended the 'study group on planned economy' at which Niekisch debated with Georg Lukács.

The complexity of this ideological universe, however, played in Hitler's favour. With his demagogy, the extreme confusion of his slogans, his contradictory openings towards a mythical anti-capitalism and the support of the most reactionary right wing, he shamelessly borrowed terminology from all those intellectuals he despised, as long as it could serve his propaganda. While the majority of them saw in him nothing more than an ignorant and vulgar character – an insignificant loud-mouth, but useful in their struggle against the Republic – Hitler felt only a mixture of jealousy and hate for intellectuals, who did not act but lost themselves in incomprehensible political and philosophical discussions. Perhaps the only thing that genuinely united the conservative revolutionaries and the left was their certainty that Hitler was uncultured, and therefore not dangerous.

THE REACTIONARY CURRENTS OF THE WEIMAR REPUBLIC IN THE FACE OF NAZISM

I would not go so far as to say that such glimpses into the future were completely worthless. But they could only be vague [. . .]. I don't think I deceive myself in claiming that at that time the prospects of a new mass party were viewed with scepticism. Its feverish aspect was rather an argument against it.

Ernst Jünger, *Gärten und Strässer*

Rich and diverse as Germany's progressive culture in the 1920s was, it was never the genuine expression of the Weimar Republic but rather an ill-tolerated ghetto. It is too easy to forget that these years saw not only the work of Erwin Piscator, Heinrich Mann, Thomas Mann, Alfred Döblin, Ödön von Horvath, George Grosz, Fritz von Unruh, Kurt Tucholsky, Ernst Toller and Carl von Ossietzsky, but also of Ernst Jünger, Ernst von Salomon, Edgar Jung, Carl Schmitt, Otto Spengler, Stefan George and Moeller van den Bruck. Taken together, the ideological currents of the right certainly had a greater impact than the progressive culture, even if their role is less well-known.[14] The years after 1919 saw the growth of political irrationalism and mystical nationalism in the conservative periodicals, discussion clubs such as the Herrenklub, the Stahlhelme and their magazines, characters such as Moeller van den Bruck or the 'young conservatives' who developed rabidly anti-democratic ideas in the most varied journals,[15] giving lectures throughout the country.

If the majority of these periodicals had runs of only two to three thousand copies, *Die Tat* reached a print-run of 30,000 in 1932. The organ of the *Stahlhelme* sold 110,000 copies at a time when the organ of the liberal pacifist left, *Die Weltbühne*, sold no more than 13,000. It should be stressed that the zenith of these conservative magazines exactly corresponds to the three final years of the Republic. This anti-democratic and anti-liberal thought found its chief representatives in Moeller van den Bruck, Othmar Spann, Schmidt-Krannbal and Edgar Jung, and was developed around three main centres, the Deutsche Studentenschaft, the Deutscher Schutzbund, and the Juni Klub. Its periodicals display pell-mell the assertion of a mystical nationalism, a mélange of romanticism and idealism, appeals to the '*völkisch*' element in opposition to the 'republic of Jews and Marxists', a certain Spenglerian cultural pessimism, and the call for a social, political and spiritual renewal to be effected on the basis of an aristocratic conception of the world. Some, like the contributors to *Die Tat*, dreamt of regrouping the advocates of a national revolution in a way that would wipe out divisions between right and left. Undoubtedly the political readership for these reviews was restricted by the abstraction and frequent obscurity of their theories. But a number of themes developed by these authors were taken up by magazines of the far right and the '*völkisch*' vulgarizers.[16] If some were content to exalt a romantic passé-ism reminiscent of Novalis,[17] the most representative current was that of the 'conservative revolution' which sought to combine all energies against the decadent and hated Republic. Reflection on law and its philosophy played a large part in the elaboration of its conceptual arsenal (Schmitt, Smend). Irrationalism, often inherited from Klages, was intimately mingled with the experience of war in the development of this anti-democratic thought. Pacifist literature was very soon opposed by a 'war literature', Ernst Jünger being its leading figure with books such as *Storms of Steel, War as an Inner Event, Fire and Blood*. These works displayed both the aestheticizing of war dear to the futurists, and the glorification of a heroic life and ideal. It was from the Great War that Jünger, the most interesting individual in this group, drew his concept of 'total mobilization' (*die totale Mobilmachung*), later developed in *Der Arbeiter*,[18] a work which had its impact on a whole range of currents, from national-bolshevism to Heidegger. A further legacy of the Great War was the characteristic hatred of the left, the 'November traitors', 'the rear', responsible for the 'stab in the back'. The exaltation of national sentiment often acquired a *völkisch* tinge that heralded the mystique of the Nazi *Volksgemeinschaft*. Any work that condemned the War, wrote Friedrich Georg Jünger, was abject; he referred to the novel of Erich Maria Remarque, *All Quiet on the Western Front*, as a 'subhuman vision'. It was from the blood spilled by the soldiers that the popular racial community already claimed by the conservative revolution would upsurge. They opposed to Marxism a mystical nationalism, to the Republic the authoritarian state (*der totale Staat*), and to democracy the image of a charismatic Führer, 'tamer of the masses', a '*völkisch* Messiah', whose profile was already drawn in the writings of Hans Bechly,[19] W. Stapel[20] and Käthe Becker,[21] often associated with the image of a purified Reich, regenerated and elevated to the level of myth, an almost eschatological utopia (Stefan George, J. M. Wehner, Moeller van den Bruck).

It is easy to maintain today the innocence of these theories, on the pretext that they were not put into practice, and certain of their representatives even persecuted by the Nazis. It remains nonetheless that a large number of these themes can be found in debased form in Nazi language. Undoubtedly the conservative revolutionaries never reached more than a certain reading public. The abstract and ultra-philosophical character of their theories could not have engendered an actual mass movement. Ernst von Salomon maintains in *The Questionnaire*, with his customary irony, that the clearest proof of Ernst Jünger's intelligence is that he was able to understand the articles he wrote. If Hitler was hardly in a position to follow the reasonings of these champions of conservative revolution, he did not actually need to. But the theorists worked in his direction, even if this aristocratic and intellectual right seems far removed from the beginnings of the NSDAP. They struggled against the Republic, undermined faith in democracy, and provided ideas that could make Nazism acceptable and legitimize it. Moreover, not all champions of the conservative revolution were hostile to Hitler and his party. If they held him in low esteem, they recognized in him a kind of devilish ability, and viewed him as the only man able to 'get Germany out of the swamp', as Oswald Spengler put it. Ernst Jünger, who at this time saw Hitler as 'a kind of General Boulanger', wrote in his journal:

> The conservatives believed they had to 'infiltrate minds' and seize leadership in this way. The Communists were preparing to take over by civil war. One could learn from their theorists, Wittfogel for example, the stations by which they expected to reach their goal, following the recipes of the dialectic [. . .]. The general view was that there would be an enormous shock and that this would be beneficial [. . .]. These people [the Nazis], like the staff of a theatre, would raise the curtain, present all kinds of old-fashioned stuff and go away, after which the stage would be free. That is indeed what happened, but they occupied it longer than anyone foresaw around 1930.[22]

If a certain number of these intellectuals refused to rally to Nazism and formed a kind of aristocratic opposition or internal emigration, they still bear a historical responsibility that it would be vain to deny, Ernst Jünger in particular.

The philosophical ideas of the revolutionary or conservative right in the 1920s are not easy to analyse,[23] but part of their terminology can be found in a large number of writers. Though the term 'conservative revolution', which van den Bruck undoubtedly borrowed from Dostoyevsky, was also used by Thomas Mann, Mann himself underwent a genuine conversion to democracy. The Great War, which in many writers crystallized a veritable nationalist passion (Richard Dehmel, W. Schäfer, Arno Holz, Gerhart Hauptmann) did not leave him indifferent: he protested against the accusation of barbarism levelled against Germany, and when the Swiss painter Hodler denounced the bombardment of Reims cathedral, Mann did not hesitate to accuse the French of having used it for military purposes. While Romain Rolland published *Au-dessus de la mêlée*, Mann wrote his *Thoughts on the War*. Far from condemning the War, he saw it as an opportunity to purify and regenerate the world, and maintained that Germany should claim this war for its own, just like the writings of Luther or Kant. His essay 'Frederick and the Grand Coalition', published in December 1914, not only portrayed a legendary historical figure, but bore as its subtitle 'Contribution to the Requirements of the Day and the Hour'. The parallels between Prussia of 1756 and Germany of 1914 were many, and certain justifications for the actions of Frederick the Great could be applied equally to Wilhelm II (for instance the violation of Belgian neutrality). Mann presented the War as a solemn fate: Frederick had been chosen by the spirit of history 'in order that the destiny of a great people might be fulfilled'.[24]

These positions taken by Thomas Mann brought a response from Romain Rolland and from his own brother Heinrich.[25] The *Reflections of a Nonpolitical Man* (1918) almost amounted to self-justification. Democracy is denounced here as a danger to the artist, the authentic product of culture, to whom Mann opposes the 'intellectual', the creation of civilization. He celebrates irrationalism, the irresponsibility of art 'which absorbs matter and form', the 'retrench-ment that enables him to take shelter when the material situation is a bit chaotic'.[26] A republic represents anarchy, and Mann exalts the 'enthusiastic Germanity' of Houston Stewart Chamberlain against the admiration that his brother displayed for France and Zola. But from 1922 on Thomas Mann defended the Weimar Republic, immediately attracting the attacks of the reactionary press for his 'apostasy'. In numerous lectures, he affirmed his faith in democratic ideas before an often hostile audience, seeking to rally the student youth to his convictions while becoming a target for the Nazis. To those who maintained that the Republic was a creation of defeat and shame, he retorted that it was a creation of exaltation and honour. If he continued to defend Nietzsche and Schopenhauer, he polemicized against the theses of Otto Spengler, championed the 'unity of political and national life' and cried 'Long live the Republic!'[27]

Mann's positions continued to radicalize throughout the 1920s and 30s. He drew close to the proletariat and socialism, refused to read passages from his work but instead delivered political warnings, maintaining in his celebrated 'Appeal to Reason':

> And yet there are hours, there are moments of our common life, when art fails to justify itself in practice; when the inner urgency of the artist fails him; when the more immediate necessities of our existence choke back his own thought, when the general distress and crisis shake him too, in such a way that what we call art, the happy and impassioned preoccupation with eternally human values, comes to seem idle, ephemeral, a superfluous thing, a mental impossibility.[28]

Thomas Mann insisted on Germany's distress, and the difficulty of demanding healthy political thought from a people sick with despair. Whilst recalling his own class origin, his attachment to bourgeois culture and his independence from political parties, he waxed indignant at the results of the elections and the advances of the NSDAP. He denounced the intellectuals and academics who lent them their support, thus adding 'to the movement a zest of cultivated barbarism'. Nazism struck him as 'an immense wave of eccentric barbarism', 'a primitive fairground brutality of the democratic masses'. He noted bitterly:

> This fantastic state of mind, of a humanity that has outrun its ideas, is matched by a political scene in the grotesque style, with Salvation Army methods, hallelujahs and bell-ringing and dervish-like repetition of monotonous catchwords, until everybody foams at the mouth. Fanaticism turns into a means of salvation, enthusiasm into epileptic ecstasy, politics become an opiate for the masses, a proletarian eschatology; and reason veils her face.[29]

Like Ernst Bloch, Thomas Mann reproached the Nazis for confusing German culture with St Vitus's dance. Faced with the advance of National Socialism, he viewed it necessary to defend Marxism as the last bastion of democracy against barbarism. On 2 March 1931 he once more attacked the Nazis in 'The Rebirth of Decency', complaining of 'the triumphal penetration of forms of darkness, depressing and hostile to spirit and culture, of an unrestrained reaction that has in no way reached its culmination but is approaching this with an insolent rapidity; this reaction has been baptized by its pseudo-literary representatives and prophets with the name of revolution – the national revolution.'[30]

Mann recalled that all past revolutions were made for the people and not against them, that they sought to give life to words today considered laughable, such as liberty, truth and justice, whereas Nazism was the very triumph of non-spirituality, the cult of the primitive and irrational. Referring to the attacks directed against himself – the Nazis refused even to acknowledge him as a German writer – he repeated that to hold out a hand to Marxism was not to betray German culture or even bourgeois ideals, as these were indissolubly linked with a certain conception of liberty. It was in the last instance his attachment to humanism and the ideals of classical culture that led him to rise up in horror against both Hitler and Oswald Spengler's exaltation of Prussianism.[31]

Spengler's attitude, for its part, was equally symbolic of the multifarious ideological attitudes adopted towards Nazism by intellectuals who were hostile from the start to democracy and the Republic. Spengler was undoubtedly reactionary. In 1926 he linked himself with the industrial forces grouped around the Langmann association. Despite its lack of rigour, his vision of the *Decline of the West* managed to seduce a whole generation.

Chance had it that Spengler finished the first volume of *The Hour of Decision* at the moment that the Nazis were preparing to take power. In his preface, he reaffirmed his hatred for the 'sordid revolution of 1918', the 'betrayal by the inferior part of our people of that strong, live part which had risen up in 1914 in the belief that it could and would have a future'.[32] Spengler even saluted the 'national revolution of 1933' as a 'prodigious event', while deploring that it was 'noisily celebrated every day'. He expected 'a moral example' from the new government, not 'verbiage and violence'. Certain themes in his book drew close to Nazism, for instance a hatred of bolshevism, a glorification of the 'white nations' and an admiration for 'the strength of the Germanic race'. But despite the bellicose fever and Germanolatry that he shared with the Nazis, Spengler's vision of the world remained far removed from that of Hitler. The revolution he expected was to be made 'from above and not from below'. It had nothing to do with the plebs and the masses, who even if won to Nazi ideas inspired Spengler with a genuine horror. He despised anti-Semitism and distrusted racism; 'those who speak too much of breeding have too little of it,' he said against Nazi ideas. He dreamed of resurrecting the Second Reich and doing without a Third. As a defender of past privileges, Spengler championed a monarchist version of national dictatorship, and expected salvation from the Prussian spirit rather than from fascism. Still less did he believe in the possibility of a single party, or of isolating Germany from other nations, while the various European fascisms seemed to him only transitional stages: they bore within them too many weeds inherited from socialism. As for the Nazis, whom he often referred to simply by the term '*völkisch*', he reproached them for their clumsiness and irresponsibility. Like Jünger, he saw them as no more than executors, incapable of political action of any scope, good only for the task of burying the Republic. The real leaders should be representatives of an aristocratic elite, on a level with the leaders of industry, and it is symbolic that Spengler generally used the word *Führer* only in the plural. He distrusted the Nazis and despised them. If he had a certain respect for Mussolini, somewhat 'wiser' and less 'folkloric', he rarely mentioned Hitler by name and accused the Nazis of confusing politics with 'romanticism of feeling'. He opposed to them the virtues of the 'Prussian ideal', 'a very aristocratic spirit, directed against all kinds of majority, against the regime of the plebs and above all against herd qualities'. Spengler's convergence with the Nazis would thus be very short-lived.

Alfred Rosenberg, in *The Myth of the Twentieth Century*, reproached Spengler for his pessimism, but maintained in 1930 that he was 'three-quarters Nazi without knowing it'. Yet Spengler kept his distance from the new regime. He refused to be enlisted as an official thinker, rejecting identification with National Socialism or 'Prussian socialism', even if for a moment he seems to have dreamt of becoming Hitler's adviser, when he requested an interview in Bayreuth in the summer of 1933. The implicit critique of Nazism contained in *The Hour of Decision* did not escape the Nazi rulers. Spengler met with such hostility that he abandoned publication of the second volume.

The aristocrat Fritz P. Reck-Malleczwesen stated in his *Diary of a Desperate Man*[33] that the hatred Spengler bore for the Nazis 'pursued him even in his dreams'. His admiration for the Prussian spirit distanced him even from a regime that seemed to realize certain aspects of this. Reck-Malleczwesen himself embodied the attitude to be found among a certain number of 'aristocratic' opponents of the Nazis.[34] He saw Nazism as a grandiloquent, imbecile and criminal movement, and his *Diary* is full of contemptuous depictions of Hitler: 'We were in no way amused; we experienced the painful feeling that you might have when a fellow traveller whom you find yourself alone with in a train compartment reveals himself to be a lunatic,' he noted apropos a meeting with Hitler, at the home of his friend Clemens zu Franckenstein. He added that after Hitler's departure they opened the window to breathe the pure Bavarian air; 'it was not an unclean body that had occupied the room, but an unclean spirit.' Heinrich Mann would not have spoken any differently. Among the intellectual members of this aristocratic right, Reck-Malleczwesen has a particular talent in sketching a vitriolic portrait of Hitler:

> With his oily lock which fell down over his face when he was delivering his sermons, he resembled a scoundrel at a wedding who before getting down to business tells you how he's going to seduce the kitchen-maids [. . .]. I was increasingly surprised that between pork sausages and calf's feet this preacher Machiavelli, when I held out my hand to take leave of him, made the bow of a café waiter who has just received a good tip.[35]

In sum, Hitler for him was simply 'an abortion of refuse and slurry'. When he met him in 1932 in a Munich restaurant, together with his friend Friedrich von Mücke, they burst out laughing at his clumsy manners.[36] They were persuaded that a fellow like that could not be dangerous.

The same unawareness is shown by Ernst Jünger, who seemed to observe the rise of Nazism in the 1920s with an amused scepticism. He attended Nazi or Communist meetings with total indifference, not taking either of them seriously. His kingdom was one of ideas, and he felt only contempt for popular struggles. With his philosophical-political essays, however, he exercised an invidious fascination on a large number of writers and intellectuals of the right. Ernst von Salomon does not conceal, in his memoirs, the complete admiration he felt for him.[37] If he declared himself unable to debate with Jünger in theory, 'for want of the organs for magic and metaphysics',[38] he noted with still greater melancholy: 'At bottom, I always felt that he was far less interested in the value and direction of my efforts than in the scale of destruction I caused.'[39] Jünger had only contempt for the Nazis, and Hitler for him was just a 'dummy who supplanted the others because he offered more'.[40] But he had little sympathy for either the Communists or the Republic. When von Salomon questioned him on his political activities, he simply replied: 'I chose this observation post from where I can watch the bedbugs devouring each other.'[41] And he believed it better to have 'two extremist parties rather than one'.[42] In any case, he saw the Republic as doomed and the extremists simply as its gravediggers: they 'undermined a republic where there were liberals but hardly any republicans, aside from such isolated figures as Otto Braun, who demanded in vain a salutary blood-letting.'[43] If he was contemptuous of Hitler, he did not hide the fascination that Hitler exerted on him, even if he always kept his distance from the regime's demonstrations and honours and, like Benn, saw in the army 'the aristocratic form of emigration'. No sympathetic portrait of Hitler emerged from his pen: Jünger in the 1920s considered him a conjuror, a circus horse.

Ernst von Salomon, a member of the *Freikorps* and close to Major Erhardt, was more a writer-activist than a theoretician. His political autobiography remarkably reflects the ambiguous place that Hitler occupied in these right-wing intellectual milieus:

> From the fogs of conventional jargon we saw arise on almost all sides men whose language expressed a new community. The rigid divisions and idiocy of the closed camps of right and left, borrowed from the arrangement of seats in parliament, were suddenly outdated, and after an inflation of ideologies, one could once more undertake an objective discussion. This was a kind of intoxication. [. . .] But afterwards it appeared that in every discussion there was a silent guest who for most of the time did not show himself and yet dominated the discussion since he imposed its subjects and prescribed its method and orientation. This silent guest's name was Adolf Hitler.

He adds:

> Since he did not speak, his presence was disturbing. As these debates failed to take him into account, they turned round in empty air with their ideas and projects, their concerns and anxieties. [. . .] While the discussion proceeded with animation, fuelled by tea and whisky, and the fish and roast were awaited, the SA were marching outside with a 'firm and calm' step. Of all the plants that sprouted so rankly on all sides, none contained a remedy against the rise of National Socialism.[44]

No more than Jünger did von Salomon take the Nazis seriously. Their revolution for him was simply 'the harvest festival of an amateur gardening club'.[45] Brought up in the royal Prussian cadet corps, von Salomon inherited all its reactionary values and hated the Republic still more than did Jünger – even taking part in the murder of one of its ministers. As an activist he had a certain admiration for the SA and for Hitler's oratorical qualities. But like Erhardt, he saw him only as an 'idiot', a 'curious and repugnant being', understanding neither his character nor his doctrine.

Yet if they mocked Hitler as a petty-bourgeois parvenu, the majority of right-wing intellectuals envied his power and effectiveness. As Ernst von Salomon confesses: 'Not for a moment of my life could I have been a follower of his, but there was no moment either when the very existence of this man did not determine my behaviour, one way or another.'[46] Jünger for his part acknowledges in his *Journal* that his feelings towards Hitler were ambiguous. Though he compared him to 'a plant which thrives and grows tall at a high altitude, feeding on rotten soil and assimilating its strength',[47] he went to hear him and could not help himself admiring the fervour of this 'pale and enthusiastic' character, even if he found him demonic.[48] The theorists of the conservative revolution found readers, while Hitler fanaticized the masses. They knew that he alone was able to prevent Communism and destroy the Republic. They were often prepared to let him act, to use him, expecting that subsequently he would melt away and let them put their own ideas into practice. But Hitler despised them still more than they despised him, and as with the other parties of the right that supported him in this dupery, it was he who left the winner, thanks to the authority of a party with millions of members. Once in power, Hitler turned against these former supporters and the fragile community of this right-wing intelligentsia was broken: some like Ernst von Salomon kept a low profile, others like Jünger put into practice their aristocratic ethics in a war that they viewed as mere butchery. Declared adversaries had the choice either of exile (Otto Strasser) or going underground. Those who openly displayed their opposition found themselves in concentration camp (Ernst Niekisch).[49]

THE LITERARY LEFT AND THE
RISE OF NATIONAL SOCIALISM

It is precisely the vileness and fearsome character of this regime, and the mediocrity of its personnel, that prevented many of us from taking the measure of this evil in all its profundity and shattering significance. The seizure of power happened so suddenly, like a shock that could not be foreseen.

Bertolt Brecht, 'Notes on Heinrich Mann's *Courage*'

On the right there was little lucidity. But what about the left? In this Republic, prey to repression of all kinds, and with growing restriction on freedom, one might have expected that several writers would very soon become aware of the process leading to the triumph of Hitler and the enormity that a Nazi dictatorship would assume. The illusions nourished by the literary left were just as damaging, and faithfully reflected those of the workers' parties.

The progressive intelligentsia of the Weimar Republic comprised writers, poets, artists, liberal professionals, some academics, journalists and 'independent authors' who had little in common besides living in Berlin, writing for publication, and being hostile to the forces of the right. Several lived with difficulty from their writing, with articles which they placed in the capital's various newspapers and magazines. More interested in debating ideas than in politics as such, they were nonetheless led to radical positions. They often shared the illusion that an artistic avant-garde necessarily accompanied a political one as its spearhead. In general, they hardly loved the Republic, even if they defended it against the various threats to it. They held the Social-Democrats in low esteem and deplored the dogmatism of the KPD, while dreaming of reconciling the two. It was among them, accordingly, that the first champions of an antifascist Popular Front emerged. The Social-Democrats despised these over-critical intellectuals, who for their part had no desire to ally themselves with the murderers of Karl Liebknecht and Rosa Luxemburg. They thus formed a rather strange ghetto with variable borders and diverse ideologies, perpetually on the margin of the parties, enjoying a real intellectual audience but quite lacking any political power.

The Social-Democrats often hamstrung the intellectuals with repressive harassment, and almost considered them as enemies. As a general rule, their leaders, former workers,[50] had little interest in debating ideas, in marked contrast to the Communists. If the right saw them simply as 'traitors', the KPD violently attacked them for their refusal to join its organizations. This intellectual left had a number of different components. Alongside Communist writers and the 'intellectual proletarians' of the League of Proletarian Revolutionary Writers there was a sizeable number of fellow-travellers. Some intellectuals were sympathetic to socialism even if they did not identify with the Social-Democratic organizations. Many were non-party and saw themselves more as 'liberals', 'republicans' or 'pacifists'. They gathered around magazines and represented less an ideology than a certain political sensibility. They indefatigably denounced everything that seemed to run counter to their ideals, hoped for a rapprochement between Germany and France, a clean-up of the judiciary and army, and the establishment of a genuine democracy. When they saw their ideals thwarted, they often became profoundly pessimistic or developed a biting satire (Tucholsky) which attracted the hatred of both the right, as they were attacking Germany, and of the Republic, as they attacked its institutions.

These liberal intellectuals were scarcely loved by their Communist counterparts. Since Communism at that time embodied in the eyes of many intellectuals an absolute moral ideal, the KPD attracted a varied range of characters: Erwin Piscator, John Heartfield, Wieland Herzfelde, Willi Bredel, Ernst Ottwalt, Friedrich Wolf, Georg Lukács, J. R. Becher and Willi Münzenberg. Traumatized by the War, and inspired by the October Revolution, these intellectuals – fairly young for the most part – were seeking a utopia, rebelling against a society that they judged corrupt and murderous. As the Republic had killed off the Spartacist movement, their heart led them to join the cause of the proletariat, not without idealism. Often they identified above all with the party apparatus, and railed against non-Communist intellectuals in an unjust and sectarian fashion.[51] But one need only read the writings of Korsch, Lukács, Bloch, Brecht or Benjamin to measure the degree to which Communism in the 1920s served as a source of enthusiasm and confidence in the possibility of shifting history onto a new path.

One cannot deny the courage, idealism and faith that inspired this generation. Pacifists, liberals, republicans and Communists, they were passionately committed to a movement of revolt that often united them in the same combat even when their ideas divided them. The writings of Tucholsky, Ossietzky, Toller or von Gerlach show that in very many of the struggles waged to defend democracy and freedom in Germany they acted alone, hated all the more by the right in that many were of Jewish origin. They were often very lucid, more so than the parties. But vis-à-vis the Nazis, many displayed a veritable blindness; for a long while, they saw them as no more than one element among others, certainly an obstacle to democracy, but not one with any special significance.

A few writers undoubtedly showed genuine insight about Hitler, but they remained a minority in relation to those who, as H. A. Walter put it, viewed the rise of Nazism with 'a mixture of lucidity, illusion, pessimism and carelessness'. Even in the darkest hours, the intellectuals of the Weimar Republic displayed a surprising optimism. At the same time as they predicted an increasing repression, the success of Nazism and the dawn of a bloody dictatorship, they seemed still to believe in an upsurge of democracy, an action by the working class, or a collapse of the NSDAP following the erosion of its electoral base. They trusted in the laws of the Republic and the *Rechtstaat* as against the violence of the streets. The very fact that they predicted and announced the worst seemed at the same time to conjure it away and prevent it from being realized. Even up to 1933 nothing managed to change their minds: not the decrees and restriction of constitutional rights, nor the treason trials, nor the acts of terror committed by the Nazis.[52] Even the most clear-headed could not imagine that this terror would erect itself into a government. In his autobiography Ludwig Marcuse summed up this illusion as follows: 'For me and millions of others, there were just three years to run. We did not know this. We did not once foresee what was going to happen [. . .]. Even the most pessimistic could see the future only in terms of what was already familiar.'[53]

Was it even possible to predict at this point in time the contours of National Socialism in power? If the methods of the Nazis were already notorious, the perspective of a durable government seemed impossible simply by virtue of these methods. It is readily comprehensible here that the illusions of the writers, on the right as well as on the left, should follow those of the parties. Besides, the relationship of even the most progressive individuals to politics was often ambiguous. Alfred Döblin wrote very tellingly: 'They lived indeed like other German citizens in a state, but it was not their state. They certainly lived in Germany, but they were not in Germany.'[54] The rich cultural life that marked a city like Berlin sufficed to veil from their eyes the sinister political reality. Literary and aesthetic debates often seemed more interesting to them than unemployment statistics or election results. The steady deterioration of democracy did not prevent intellectuals from solemnly celebrating in 1931 the birthday of Heinrich Mann, or that of Gerhart Hauptmann the following year. Klaus Mann states in his autobiography[55] that writers felt it incumbent on them to take an interest in politics, but only as an onerous chore; the years 1928–30 were marked above all for them by cultural events. He himself knew very well that there were unemployed workers in Germany, but he trusted the government to remedy this. In the field of the arts all was well: theatres and cinemas were full of spectators, and artists were not impoverished. He noticed nothing of the 'crisis' that the newspapers were all so full of. He frequented cafés, nightclubs and theatres, aware that civil war was brewing between Nazis and Communists, but like the 'republicans' he kept faith with the institutions and trusted in Hindenburg. The release of *The Blue Angel* mattered more to him than the triumphs of Hitler or the prospects of a politics that he despised. Like Jünger he detected in Hitler an affinity with Charlie Chaplin, though far less funny. When he saw him in a Munich cake-shop, stuffing tarts into his mouth, he laughed out loud: 'Poor Schiklgrubber,' he thought, 'how can you hope to conquer Germany?' He saw in Hitler only a clumsy oaf, crude and childish, and wondered how anyone could find this unpleasant and hysterical individual at all magnetic. In a couple of years Hitler would be an unknown vagabond once again, and Klaus Mann could not prevent himself taking pity on him. Paying attention, he regarded him more closely and found that with his soft face he looked more like Fritz Haarmann, the child-murderer of Hanover, than Chaplin. Mann undoubtedly recognized that at that moment he felt a total foreigner in Germany. But he took no notice of the Nazi threat, and when his childhood friends became Nazis he just laughed at their lack of culture.

In his memoir, *Aller Tage Abend*,[56] the actor Fritz Kortner evokes the same heedlessness that prevailed among his profession. When the Nazi terror developed, with frequent attacks on left-wing performances, he himself, though a Jew and hated by the Nazis, did not think of his own safety. The life of the Berlin theatres concerned him more than Hitler's successes, an attitude that was broadly shared by his theatrical colleagues. Kortner recalls that the critic Alfred Kerr likewise never took the Hitlerite noise seriously, that what happened in the Prussian parliament passed him by, preoccupied as he was by two wars of his own to wage: a defensive one against the Austrian critic Karl Kraus,[57] and an offensive one against the critic Herbert Jhering, the friend of Brecht. Kortner also stresses that this war of literary reviews and newspapers did much to sidetrack the intellectual milieu from politics. While the Nazis were marching in the Berlin streets, he passed his evenings in discussion with Brecht, Ernst Deutsch, Hans Albers, Max Pallenberg, Erich Engel and Marlene Dietrich. When Nazi violence intensified, he learned to box.[58]

A further revealing witness of this unawareness is given by the celebrated diaries of Count Harry Kessler.[59] A friend of Valéry, Cocteau, Radiguet and Jouve, as well as of Piscator, Grosz, Toller, Reinhardt and Brecht, this republican aristocrat who frequented all the political, diplomatic and literary circles of the German capital, at ease with the likes of Rathenau, Noske and Severing as well as among actors and poets, was all the more hated by the right in that he came from a monarchist background.[60] If he had little regard for the Republic's official representatives, he took the Nazis for a gang of imbecile thugs and incessantly maintained that Germany was on the verge of civil war. This brilliant and cosmopolitan spirit had the occasion to discuss Hitler with the widest range of personalities.[61] Each day he noticed the deterioration in German conditions, and described it in his diaries, relating the literary or political views he had heard in the course of the evening. When his valet, more clear-headed than him, asked to resign, being afraid to fall victim of the hatred that the Nazis bore towards the count, he noted imperturbably: 'Today he came and said that he must leave my employ. His father [a Nazi] insists on this because there will shortly be "unpleasantness" in my household and he does not want his son to be involved.'[62]

While Kessler was visiting Paris soon after, the son of the former French ambassador, Roland de Margerie, urged him not to return to Berlin. But far from taking the Nazis seriously, Kessler still noted on 1 April 1933: 'It is difficult to say which feeling is stronger, loathing or pity, for these brainless, malevolent creatures.'[63] Forced into exile, he saw the Nazis seize Germany as if 'the sick soul of a sadistic murderer [had] suddenly awoken in Germany in millions of men.'[64] He impatiently awaited the collapse of the new regime.

The weak political awareness of these writers can be shown beyond doubt. But the same unawareness was often found among those close to the Communist party. As Manès Sperber wrote: 'We foresaw many things, if not all. We examined realistically the birth and unfolding of events, and we said to ourselves: yes, it may well start like this, and develop in this way, on condition that it encounters no obstacle. But we lived at that time as if nothing of the kind could ever happen.'[65]

Evoking the attacks that targeted Communist writers, Gustav Regler noted:

> They referred to us as Jews, which to us was no term of abuse, since we owed so much to the gifted minds of German Jews that Berlin without them was inconceivable [. . .]. At that time, almost everyone lowered their heads. Cincinnatus, seeing fires flare up on the horizon, abandoned his plough and went to restore order in Rome before returning to his peaceful countryside. No Berlin intellectual believed in this consular mission. The artists in my cell liked to spend their evenings arguing pleasantly in a cloud of pipe-smoke. They struggled like the devil to sell their paintings and place their subversive articles, and liked to sit around for hours on the imitation leather bar-stools of cafés, sleep with their wives or their mistresses, pursue a petty well-regulated life and be left in peace.[66]

In January 1933, a troupe of Communist actors were performing a political play titled *The Mousetrap* at the Kleines Theater on Unter den Linden. As no decree banning it had been issued, they imagined, wrote Regler, 'that the government, considering them the victors of tomorrow, would not take the trouble to stop them. They were confident that in a couple of weeks the play would be staged at the Nationales.' On 28 January, Regler spent the evening at the home of the actor Dewald, who amused himself by imitating Hitler and pulling his hair down over his forehead. His imitation was interrupted by a phone call from a friend, who told him that Hitler had just been named Chancellor. 'He hurriedly brushed the lock from his forehead. He gave us an apprehensive glance, as though he expected us to strike him dead.'[67]

And yet the subsequent memoirs of the émigrés, as H. A. Walter remarks, stress more their clairvoyance than the illusions of that time. The majority were far indeed from expecting the apocalypse, and if they sometimes did imagine the worst for a moment, they changed nothing in their daily round. Thomas Mann's publisher Gottfried Bermann Fischer, who claimed to have been aware of the Nazi danger early on, until 1933 still frequented the reviews at the Sportpalast and the tennis courts of the Grunewald. Theodor Wolff was an habitué of the racetrack and could be seen on the stand behind Chancellor von Papen.[68] Count Harry Kessler always attended literary evenings, Leonhard Frank the balls on the Kurfürstendamm. Even the greatest writers often seem to have shown little sensitivity to the Nazi phenomenon, as shown by the example of Stefan Zweig: 'So I am frankly unable to recall when I first heard the name of Adolf Hitler [. . .]. The name made no impression on me. I gave it no thought. There were so many, now long forgotten, names of agitators and *Putschists* in the confused Germany of that day which rose only to disappear.'[69] The Nazi magazines that he browsed seemed to him so badly written that he could scarcely take them seriously. When he saw the SA march by in Bavaria and attack the Social-Democrats, this disturbed him a bit, but Hitler's arrest after the failed putsch of 1923 reassured him. Besides, Hitler was too crude and vulgar to be dangerous:

> Even then we did not note the danger. The few among writers who had taken the trouble to read Hitler's book, ridiculed the bombast of his stilted prose instead of occupying themselves with his programme. The big democratic newspapers, instead of warning their readers, reassured them day by day that the movement, which in truth found difficulty in financing its enormous activities with no more than the contributions of big business and audacious borrowing, would inevitably collapse in no time.[70]

As a cultivated European, Zweig could not conceive how a man who had never been to university or even finished school, who had slept in night shelters and gained his living for years by shady means, could occupy the position held by Bismarck, Baron von Stein or Prince von Bülow. In September 1930, in the wake of the elections, Zweig still celebrated the 'understandable rebellion of youth' without being troubled by the goals this pursued. This brought him a response from Klaus Mann, 'Jugend und Radikalismus. Ein Antwort an S. Zweig',[71] which tempered his fine enthusiasm: young people were getting politicized, to be sure, but to the right. The same confusion could be found with Alfred Döblin, who in reply to a letter from the student G. R. Hocke, 'Wissen und Verändern', maintained that an intellectual should be above party and that his task was 'to separate socialism from the class struggle'. If some, like Ossietzky, championed early on the idea of an anti-Nazi united front, many, like Döblin, continued to believe in the intellectual's independence. For them, Nazism was just a buffoonery that would rapidly disappear. They experienced as much curiosity towards it as they did contempt. Some of them did not hesitate to attend NSDAP meetings as if they were circus performances.

Bermann Fischer tells[72] how in April 1932, during the presidential election campaign, he decided together with Carl Zuckmayer to attend a speech by Goebbels at the Berlin Sportpalast. They had been sent invitation cards by the actor Emil Jannings. 'If we had suspected what we were going to see,' Bermann Fischer writes, 'we would at least have left our wives at home.' In his zeal, Jannings had provided them with VIP cards. As soon as they arrived, SA men in uniform conducted them to special places, opposite the swastika flags and the official tribune. They sat in fascinated terror through the collective delirium that greeted the arrival of Hitler. Some Nazis soon recognized them and were astonished to see them in those seats. While Goebbels was speaking they slipped out, narrowly avoiding being lynched for not saluting. Even so, they had to rise when Göring made everyone sing the *Horst-Wessel-Lied*. 'If looks could kill, we would long have been dead under our chairs,' noted Bermann Fischer, claiming that he had never felt himself surrounded by such violent hatred. His only hope was to be mistaken for a foreigner. In was only after this experience that he took the Nazis seriously. As H. A. Walter remarks, these examples reveal very well the mixture of naivety, heedlessness and unawareness that characterized a large portion of the progressive intelligentsia, its belief in democracy and the power of intelligence in the face of stupidity and brutality.

Besides those who did not seem to see the danger that Hitler and his movement embodied, there were those writers who were more aware of what a Nazi triumph would signify but who continued to minimize its practical import. Lion Feuchtwanger estimated that a section of workers, frightened by Communism and disappointed by the Social-Democrats, could well be tempted by the idea of a 'national socialism' which, sustained by heavy industry, had a chance of coming to power. This correct deduction, however, did not prevent him, while awaiting the arrival of the dictatorship, from buying a house not far from Berlin.[73] It was only later in exile that he understood the incoherence of his attitude. Brecht for his part was well aware of what Hitler's arrival in power would mean, and early on envisaged – a very rare case – the necessity of exile, even confiding to Fritz Kortner that this might last forty years. Yet he too in August 1932, with the royalties from *The Threepenny Opera*, bought a house at Utling, on the Ammersee. In December 1931 Heinrich Mann likewise affirmed that darkness was falling on Germany, if it was not night already. In several essays he prophesied that the Nazi dictatorship would be one of the most bloody in history. Yet even he, who throughout the 1920s had lived in hotel rooms and guest houses, decided at that point to buy a property in Berlin . . . while awaiting this bloody dictatorship. Fritz Kortner displayed the same incoherence. A famous actor, Jewish and a convinced democrat, he was particularly hated by the Nazis. When the actress Käthe Dorsch, the girlfriend of Göring, warned him in 1932 of the risk he was running, and that he would most likely be arrested if the Nazis took power, he decided to leave Germany for Ascona. But when Chancellor Brüning banned the SA from wearing uniform, Kortner decided to return. While crossing Bavaria he stumbled on a Nazi rally and feared being recognized and lynched. All the same, he continued en route to Berlin.[74]

All these intellectuals, even when aware of the danger, sought to interpret the least setback to the NSDAP's progress as a definite averting of the peril. Georg Bernhard, a writer on the *Vossische Zeitung*, expected a Nazi defeat in April 1932. Klaus Mann saw Hindenburg's victory as an encouraging sign, which showed that Hitler would never come to power.[75] Harry Kessler noted in his diary on 4 July 1932 his joy at seeing many young people parade with the Iron Front: they were not *all* Nazis. The novelist Vicki Baum notes in her memoirs[76] that the publisher Ullstein, whose company was hated by the Nazis, still considered in 1932 that it was absolutely impossible that Germany should fall back into militarist madness, that Hitler was a ridiculous clown who could strike a response only in sick minds. When she told Ullstein of her intention to emigrate, he asked if she had lost her head. Leo Schwarzschild, an Ullstein editor and later a well-known émigré, also maintained in 1932 that if Hitler did take power, he would burn out very quickly, and that the federal structure of the *Länder* would resist any Nazification. Only Bavaria, in his opinion, might fall prey to Nazism. Arnold Zweig showed the same illusion: when the French ambassador, A. François-Poncet, told him of his fear that the Nazis would gain power, Zweig replied that Chancellor Severing 'would press the button and the security police would sweep Hitler out'.[77] The same attitude could be found in Fritz von Unruh and Hubertus Prinz zu Löwenstein.[78] As for Kessler, he noted in his *Diary* on 25 April 1932: 'On the whole, [Unruh] seemed to find the Republic's situation pretty desperate. On the other hand, he too says that if Hitler takes power, he would very soon be swept away, as he could not keep a single one of his promises, and that the Communists would then seize control. He seemed to view this development as inevitable.'[79]

These illusions are undoubtedly understandable: they were paralleled by those of the left, and fuelled by the Nazis' loss of two million electors in 1932. The irrational and riotous character of National Socialism, and Hitler's own incoherence, made a lasting victory seem scarcely credible. Even Thomas Mann wrote to Herman Hesse, on 22 December 1932, that 'the peak of lunacy' had been reached in Germany, and now the descent would begin. As for the poet Erich Mühsam, one of the earliest victims of Nazi terror, he wrote at the same time: 'They will never come to power.' This mixture of clear-headedness and illusion is found just as frequently in the pacifist milieus that the Nazis especially hated. Carl von Ossietzky lucidly analysed the deteriorating political situation in his articles for *Die Weltbühne*. On his release from prison, just before Christmas 1932, he even drew an astonishingly realistic picture of the German situation. And yet he never took heed for his own safety, imagining that moving house and not putting his name on the door would be enough to protect him from the SA. The issue of *Die Weltbühne* for 7 March 1933 announced to its readers the arrest of its editor-in-chief.

Kurt Hiller, Ossietzky's deputy on *Die Weltbühne*, analysed the political situation in similarly pertinent terms in two texts of 1932, 'Der Sprung ins Helle' and 'Selbstkritik links',[80] in which he proposed to the parties of the left a severe self-criticism, of both their ideas and their methods. He showed that the economic crisis was pushing voters towards the NSDAP rather than to the left. Between 'National Socialist mysticism' and 'Marxist empiricism', Hiller declared his choice for 'the critique of Kant'. With the advent of the Nazis to power, he predicted 'an era of mediocre brutality, of anti-intellectual sadism, in short of complete barbarism'. The only way to 'lance the National Socialist abscess', however, he saw in a 'purified pacifism'. In 1932, he invited the liberal intellectual left to organize itself around the candidacy of Heinrich Mann for president of the Republic. After the arrest of Ossietzky, Hiller once again analysed in the *Weltbühne* the irrationality of Nazi ideology. His lodgings were immediately ransacked by the SA. As there was no official arrest warrant against him, he made a complaint at the police station against persons unknown for house-breaking and theft. Taking temporary refuge in Frankfurt, he was arrested but then released, and arrested again on 14 July 1933.

Heinrich Mann, who had refused to run as candidate for the presidency and called on all opponents of Hitler to vote for Hindenburg – which brought a violent attack on him from J. R. Becher – had warned against 'bellicose nationalism' as early as 1923,[81] but two years later felt able to guarantee the stability of democracy. Mann maintained that a dictatorship would never be possible in Germany, as German militarism was dead. In 1931 he seemed more clear-headed. In an article 'We Go to the Polls', he denounced National Socialism and the 'blood-bath' that it was preparing: 'They will have to gas the masses,' he wrote, while still reaffirming his faith in the final defeat of Nazism. In 1930 he had described the Nazis as 'infantile and bloody puppets'. 'If they were capable of showing themselves energetic in other ways than boasting,' he wrote, 'they would have taken power long ago' ('The German Situation'). The following year he again announced that the Nazis 'are condemned to defeat', and in 1932 wrote that 'We have been spared the worst.'

If these are the illusions of liberal writers, there were then those of a third group, the Communists. Their positions are generally simpler to characterize, as they faithfully followed the line of the KPD. They saw in National Socialism a retrograde movement, which did not pose any real danger for the future. Often it was 'social-fascism' that they flagged as the main danger. Their optimism was disarming. Many believed that if Hitler did take power, he would immediately be swept away by the working class, and this fascist episode could only hasten the process of proletarian revolution, the Nazis having meanwhile drawn votes away from the Social-Democrats. Scarcely anyone at all among the Communist intellectuals believed in the danger of a prolonged dictatorship.[82] The Austrian Marxist Ernst Fischer visited Berlin at the invitation of Ernst Toller, and met there with Communist writers, in particular the ex-Dadaist publisher Wieland Herzfelde. Having attended a meeting addressed by Goebbels, Fischer shared with his Berlin friends his worry that the Nazis might seize power. His 'lack of political awareness' was ridiculed; as an Austrian he could not understand the German situation. When he evoked the possibility of a Hitler victory, he triggered general hilarity. John Heartfield and his brother Wieland Herzfelde treated him gently, reproaching him for his poor appreciation of the strength of the German proletariat and the determination of the KPD. Moreover, it was explained to him that at bottom Hitler even played a positive role, by taking votes from the Social-Democrats. Disappointed with the Nazis, electors would then turn to the Communist party. Ernst Fischer went on to ask whether it would not be prudent to block Hitler's rise in good time by an alliance of all workers' organizations, but he met with the response that this was impossible, as Social-Democracy was precisely 'the main social support of the bourgeoisie':

> An altercation broke out among the Communists. Soon everyone was speaking at once. Wieland Herzfelde sought to maintain some kind of order [. . .]. I kept silent and listened. Here there was hope. People were discussing. A new idea was being sought. They were moving towards a United Front. Suddenly a trenchant voice made itself heard, coming from the chest on which John Heartfield was seated: 'Comrades! I warn you to stop this discussion immediately. There is a social-fascist among us.' I looked around. Everyone's eyes rested on me. It was I who was the social-fascist. Shattered, I got up and took my leave.[83]

This mixture of dogmatism and optimism was to be found among both 'proletarian intellectuals' and fellow-travellers. Friedrich Wolf characterized the time, in one of the plays he wrote then, as that of 'victory over fascism'. Several declarations could be cited in which writers displayed the same illusions. What can be said of those who chose the wrong target and spent their time attacking liberals and pacifists, as if Tucholsky or Heinrich Mann were the danger to combat?

In contrast with the optimism of Communist intellectuals, certain figures gave proof of a radical pessimism and swayed between lucidity and resignation. Often they considered that the battle for democracy in Germany was already lost. The most typical example of this attitude is undoubtedly the sadness and despair that marked the final years of Kurt Tucholsky's life. Having already moved to France out of disgust for Germany, he still continued sending articles to the *Weltbühne*. The more the Republic's position deteriorated, the more ferocious his satire became. And with his increasing fame, he was hated all the more. At the same time, it was clear to him that his action had grown totally useless. Disappointed by the Republic, deploring the blindness of the political parties and the optimism of those writers who seemed genuinely to believe in the power of intelligence against barbarism, he repeatedly declared that he was tired of fighting for a lost cause, and that democracy could not be rescued. He realized that he had no desire to play the martyr and pay for the political aberrations of the left-wing parties who by tearing each other to pieces were letting Hitler come to power. All he would get from this would be an obituary, which as he wrote to his brother on 18 January 1931, he felt able to write quite unaided. In the face of Nazism he felt only an immense sense of nausea and despair.

Even those who did not share this radical despair sought less to abandon their illusions than to escape the situation. Klaus Mann acknowledges that in his circle there was talk of exile early on. He sunk himself ever more in his literary work so as not to see a political situation that was deteriorating by the day. But only a few intellectuals really envisaged the idea that this could get to the point of forcing them to emigrate. Arnold Zweig, persuaded by A. François-Poncet of the imminent Nazi danger, travelled to Palestine to prepare a future exile. But in May 1932 he returned to Germany. In a letter to Freud of 29 May 1932, he spoke of being 'deep in depression, which is connected with the rain, with Bavarian memories, with the grey sky, the terrible political situation in Berlin . . .'[84] Fritz Kortner describes in his autobiography the increasing consumption of drugs and alcohol among many intellectuals in the months preceding the Nazi seizure of power. Yet despite this despair, very few thought of leaving the country. Some had already established themselves abroad a while back: Emil Ludwig had lived in Switzerland since 1906, René Schickele (an Alsatian) and Joseph Breitbach lived in France; Wilhelm von Uhde and Carl Einstein had been in Paris since 1925, Rudolf Leonhard and Walter Hasenclever since 1927. Some preferred to remain abroad for fear of Nazi reprisals, though this did not prevent them from frequently visiting Berlin. Tucholsky lived likewise in France, Walden had been in the Soviet Union since 1930, along with Georg Lukács, Béla Balazs and Hans Günther. Alfred Kurella worked in Paris on the Communist publication *Monde*, he was secretary to Henri Barbusse and the International Committee Against War and Fascism. Arthur Koestler had worked abroad as a foreign correspondent since 1932, Lion Feuchtwanger was on an American lecture tour at the time that Hitler took power. Albert Ehrenstein and Erich Maria Remarque had lived in Switzerland since 1932 and 1931 respectively. A few, moreover, had chosen exile even before this was forced on them: the pacifist journalist Berthold Jacob moved to Strasbourg in 1932, and E. J. Gumbel, driven from his academic chair by Nazi students, had also settled in France. Returning to Berlin in 1932 after a lecture tour in the United States, Vicki Baum left Germany again soon after: the joy with which some of her friends welcomed the election of Hindenburg led her to foresee the worst. Many of them considered the battle for democracy as already lost.

It is easy today to wax ironic at the unawareness of the majority of German intellectuals in the face of the Nazi danger. But how should we explain the incoherence that marked the attitude of so many? If several were aware of the catastrophic situation in Germany, the greater part persisted in their belief in the strong organizations of the left, despite their division, in the combativeness of the working class, in respect for the constitution of which Hindenburg was the supposed guarantor. National Socialism, moreover, which had met with defeat in the 1932 elections, hardly seemed capable of forming a stable government. With the benefit of hindsight, it is easy to believe that it was already possible in 1930 to imagine what the Third Reich would be like. But for most observers of that time it was a mythical idea, equally absurd as the other themes of Nazi propaganda. No one could seriously imagine that Hitler, with his incoherent and demagogic programme, could stay in power, even in the worst of cases, for more than a few months. Many German writers, including some of the most progressive, may well have displayed a lack of imagination in conceiving the consequences of the Nazis' coming to power; but any subsequent survey of Hitlerism inevitably has little in common with those made before 1933. Ludwig Marcuse, in his autobiography, devotes a chapter, 'Before Sunset', to analysing his mistakes in appreciating the Hitlerite danger. He accuses himself, together with his generation as a whole, of having displayed a lack of imagination towards what he calls, in terms reminiscent of Bloch, the 'not-yet-happened' (*noch-nicht-da-gewesen*). Whether they were optimists or pessimists, he notes, the majority of writers painted the future in rose or in black, but in equally familiar colours. Nazism, however, and the regime that it engendered, was something scarcely imaginable and unknown, hardly more conceivable as a system, in Marcuse's expression, than a nuclear explosion would have been before Hiroshima.

ATTEMPTS AT REGROUPING AND ACTION (1932–33)

If this literary left cannot be accused of cowardice, however erroneous many of its appreciations and judgements, it has to be recognized that the means available to it in the face of Nazism were extremely limited: they consisted of warnings, exhortations, appeals and declarations published in journals and reviews which often were read only by the already convinced. If the most lucid writers – Ossietzky, Tucholsky, Toller and von Gerlach – were also marginal, this marginality, a condition of their freedom of judgement, was equally symbolic of their absence of power. Faced with the NSDAP's millions of electors and paramilitary formations, they continued the fight, their only weapon being their faith in intelligence and morality. The Republic that they so bitterly defended had often assaulted and gagged them, taking no heed at all of their warnings. Physically attacked by the Nazis, legally attacked by censorship, they were moreover divided into various groups with ideologies that were hard to reconcile, and their actions could only be realized by means of symbols, such as the proposed presidential candidacy of Heinrich Mann.

Astonishment at the despair and impotence that the majority felt in the final years before the Republic's collapse would thus be misplaced. A rearguard struggling to hold onto positions that were already lost, with no audience among parties, masses or Republic, they found themselves reduced to the state of unhappy Cassandras well before the years of exile. Even within the literary organizations they were a minority, these having been already infiltrated by Nazi sympathizers. Each time they sought to break the derisory 'non-political' facade they were expelled from these.

Yet it was among these intellectuals that the first champions of a Popular Front against fascism were to be found. John Heartfield, not exempt from dogmatism despite his prodigious talent, already thought in 1932 of developing an anti-Nazi propaganda common to all parties of the left. The idea of a Popular Front had been put forward already by Heinrich Mann in 1931, who proposed to Abegg, secretary of state at the Prussian interior ministry, a common action against the Nazis. Kurt Hiller, a libertarian who was little suspect of Communist sympathies, also proposed to create a union of left-wing anti-Nazi writers, and invited half a dozen groups to take part in a joint conference.[85] Despite a meeting that lasted four hours, nothing concrete emerged,[86] and his proposal for Heinrich Mann as candidate of the liberal left against Thälmann, Hindenburg and Hitler, symbolic as it was, was opposed by both Communists and Social-Democrats, the latter calling for a vote for Hindenburg.

It seems that the parties of the left ascribed little importance to these initiatives. The hostility between Communists and Socialists was too intense for such fragile gangways between the two parties to have the slightest chance of resisting their constant attacks.[87] The most striking example is that of the Iron Front established by the poet and playwright Fritz von Unruh, in opposition to the gathering of reactionary forces and to rekindle enthusiasm for the democratic ideal. At the start the SPD paid little attention to this organization, and sought to respond to its success by tying it to its own apparatus. But such examples of interest by a political party for an initiative taken by intellectuals were quite rare. More often, their efforts led only to the formation of small discussion groups, seminars such as the one on political and cultural questions that crystallized around Döblin (*Wissen und Verändern*), uniting writers, Socialist activists and students. Döblin did indeed publish accounts of these discussions that circulated among the intellectuals, but the audience remained extremely limited. The abstract character of these intellectual discussions on the margin of the parties generally prevented them from having the least impact on political reality.

In the final years of the Republic other anti-Nazi groups were established, sometimes financed by industrialists, such as one that Gottfried Bermann Fischer belonged to, but their interventions were complete fiascos, he himself admits, like when they tried to inject intellectual controversy into Nazi meetings. If some people were tempted, as Tucholsky was, to link up with the Communists in the face of the imminent danger of Hitler coming to power, they were often rejected as 'bourgeois intellectuals', or could not overcome their hostility towards tactics that they deemed dogmatic, bureaucratic, erroneous, and with no bearing on German reality. All the same, for many a rapprochement with the KPD, or even membership of it, provided the only possibility of concrete action, even if they did not approve all its ideas. Such were the trajectories of Friedrich Wolf, Erich Weinert, and Brecht himself. Thanks to the Communist party, they could at least reach a working-class audience. But the success of Weinert's songs or the plays of Wolf and Brecht should not lead us to misconstrue the almost total impotence of the intellectuals faced with the rise of fascism.

In the weeks between Hitler's appointment as Chancellor and the Reichstag fire, a certain number of intellectuals sought desperately to launch a rearguard action.[88] The Berlin group of the SDS sent an appeal to all its sections on 7 February, inviting them to mobilize against the censorship that was about to fall on the world of letters. The appeal declared: 'This is the final hour. Whoever remains silent today will not be able to open their mouth tomorrow.' A certain number of Communist writers took an active part in these propaganda actions. Gustav Regler related:

> We stuck posters on the walls in the Berlin suburbs. We organized protest-meetings of penniless workers evicted from their tenements, and fed as many as we could in our small apartments to give them the feeling, if only for an afternoon, that someone cared what happened to them. We filled backyards and back-alleys on Sundays with the sound of our singing and with our inflammatory speeches. We helped the Red Front youths who came within our jurisdiction to sell their newspapers and to deal with the Nazi patrols who tried to drive them off the streets.[89]

But he recognized that after Hitler had come to power, any further action seemed pointless: Regler thought of trying to shoot Hitler with his revolver, but was unsure if it was worth risking his life for a place in history.[90]

On 19 February the congress *Das Freie Wort* was held at the Kroll Opera. Alfred Kantorowicz launched an appeal in defence of intellectual freedom.[91] This organization hoped that by not raising political slogans it might escape prohibition. But its financial means were weak and the scope of possible action weaker still.[92] Expelled from the Prussian Academy for the appeal he had signed with Käthe Kollwitz, Heinrich Mann took part in a further meeting with Brecht, J. R. Becher, Ludwig Frank and Ernst Glaeser, to try and find some new means of struggle. Willi Münzenberg likewise sought to bring together a number of antifascist organizations. But these attempts had no more success than *Das Freie Wort*, that congress being dispersed by the police as soon as Rust, the Prussian minister of culture, was criticized.[93] The audience had to flee, singing the *Internationale*. This was perhaps the last free meeting held in Berlin.[94] Kantorowicz wrote in *Welt am Abend* that free speech had to be defended not just with words but with deeds. His home was immediately ransacked by the SA who came to arrest him. In the weeks that followed Hitler's appointment, groups of progressive intellectuals still met in Berlin to try and discover the last possibilities of resistance, but practically nothing was to be found. The only one that remained, exile, was something that the majority could not yet agree on. On 17 February Ossietzky still denounced the new regime's anti-Semitism, and Erich Mühsam took part in meetings of the SDS together with Rudolf Olden. Ten days later they were arrested by the Nazis and sent to concentration camps.

BETWEEN COLLABORATION AND ADHESION

Why [. . .] did we not stand in front of the synagogues with outstretched arms, to
protest and accuse? Because we knew that we wouldn't find an echo? It was not that, it
was something more serious. At bottom, we were already dead. We could no longer
live on our own resources.

                                                                    Ernst von Salomon

As far as I was concerned, and many others too, we had in any event to consider that
the new government had legitimately taken over the executive; there was no objection
to be made.

                                                                       Gottfried Benn

Still more difficult to depict is the problem of the collaboration of intellectuals,
writers and artists with the new regime and its institutions. If it is hard to write
the history of the attitude of German writers towards National Socialism *before*
1933, the history of the ideological and personal compromises made *after* 1933
is that much more so. The logic of these adhesions is not always evident.

Several German historians[95] use the categories 'Nazi', 'non-Nazi' and 'anti-
Nazi' to classify attitudes towards the Third Reich. This distinction is relatively
easy to make among those who went into exile – even if 'anti-Nazi' signifies
nothing very concrete politically, given the ideological diversity of the exiles.[96]
But it is far harder in relation to those who remained in Germany. The
discussion of the phenomenon of 'internal emigration' that took place after
1945 readily demonstrates this: many individuals who had compromised with
the Third Reich – writers in particular – and accepted official honours,
subsequently presented themselves not just as 'internal émigrés' and 'non-
Nazis', but even as disguised 'anti-Nazis', so well disguised indeed that no
one could have suspected. It is not always easy to understand what impelled one
writer to remain in Germany and another to leave. It was not necessarily those
authors 'furthest to the right' who supported the regime. Sometime the logic of a
certain adhesion is understandable even if somewhat surprising (Gottfried
Benn). That of Heidegger is less so. In such cases, it is necessary to introduce
multiple distinctions that take account of the point in time (adhesion at the start
of 1933 or later), the length of time (a few months, several years, the whole
duration of the regime), the official responsibilities accepted, positions taken
and writings. One cannot place on the same level the fanatical and constant
adhesion of Hanns Johst or Heinrich George, the passing support of Benn, and
the aberration of Heidegger in 1933. The reserved attitude of von Salomon
cannot be confused with that of Jünger, whose contempt for Nazism is again not
to be equated with the active resistance of Ernst Niekisch. What can one say of
the opportunism that so many writers, intellectuals and artists displayed – the
attitude of Gerhart Hauptmann, for instance?[97]

Undoubtedly the portrait Klaus Mann drew in his novel *Mephisto* was a
ferocious caricature of the lack of awareness shown by so many artists and
writers, transforming into a stereotype certain traits borrowed from the actor

Gustaf Gründgens[98] in order to depict the cowardice and opportunism that enabled them to make a career under the Third Reich. But such portraits, typical as they might be, could be duplicated for lawyers, academics, stage directors, dramatists or literary critics. And what about painters and architects? If those who sold their soul to the devil were legion, they did not all sell it in the same fashion. The gap between adhesion to fascism and struggle against it was not a matter of a simple geographical border. Certain exiles conducted no political activity in emigration and could scarcely be considered genuine adversaries of the regime, or else they defended the most reactionary political positions. And not all the artists who opted to stay in Germany had National Socialist sympathies. Besides those who rallied to the regime and made it a gift of their talent, many others lived in an uncomfortable position that is often hard to imagine. Actors such as Bernhard Minetti and Gustaf Gründgens belonged to this latter category. The attitudes of such people cannot be judged globally, but have to be carefully examined in detail.

When one considers the expressions of Nazism in the years up to 1933, the anti-intellectualism affirmed by Hitler, the platitude and mediocrity of the values claimed by the new regime and its barbarism, one might wonder how any intellectuals worth the name could rally to it. Yet it was paradoxically among students and academics that some of the movement's most fanatical zealots could be found. The 1920s saw a steady fascisization of the student milieu, which had traditionally been reactionary enough, and a systematic boycott of left-wing teachers. Individuals as famous as Max Weber were insulted, and well before the Nazi seizure of power, many teachers had been forced to abandon their posts as a result of hostile demonstrations by students (Theodor Lessing, E. J. Gumbel).[99] The Nazis found a good many converts among Germanists and philosophers, jurists and linguists. Some had supported Rosenberg from the early 1920s in his struggle against 'un-German culture'. A. Bartels, an anti-Semitic historian who purported to show that no Jew – even Heine – could write proper German, had been honoured in 1925 with a visit from Hitler. Professor Schulze-Naumburg had attacked the entire progressive art of the Weimar epoch on the same delirious racial criteria. Paul Fechter exalted '*völkisch*' literature. After 1933, the universities would not just capitulate before the Nazis, but support them with their erudition. In the majority of works and theses written under the Third Reich, the same racist clichés are to be found, the same spineless attempt to show that all the most fundamental tendencies of German culture find their culmination in National Socialism, that the classic authors – even Goethe and Schiller and Hölderlin – were its 'predecessors of genius'. At the same time as the idea of a racial university was celebrated, Hebel, Hölderlin, Schiller and Nietzsche were reread in the light of Hitler and Rosenberg. Literary history was falsified in order to eliminate Jewish or progressive authors. Jurists, who had done so much to undermine the democratic edifice of the Weimar Republic, came to serve as artisans of the new National Socialist legislation. They took their oath to Hitler and abandoned democratic law for the teaching of 'racial law'. Scientists bent themselves to denounce the influence of 'Jewish physics' and refute the theories of Einstein, to reform the teaching of biology on the basis of racist criteria, and to establish a 'racist and popular pedagogy' (Ernst Krieck, rector of Heidelberg University). They often attended or even organized book burnings at their universities, where books of their former colleagues were burned: Alfred Baumler, for example, the Berlin rector and friend of Goebbels, who sought to present Nazism as the philosophic pinnacle of the whole Western tradition. Hans Naumann, rector of Bonn University, defender of book burnings and specialist in Nordic mythologies, attempted in his delirious study of 1934, *Germanischer Schicksalglaube*, to translate Heidegger's *Sein und Zeit* into mythical 'Germanic' categories.[100] The most serious thing is that academics of worth fell into this trap, ending up defending positions that seemed the negation of everything they had previously believed in. Germanists were often the most exposed to this kind of ideological aberration, hijacked by the shoddy Germanism championed by National Socialism.[101] Two very different examples may serve to illustrate this attitude: the Germanist Ernst Bertram, and the philosopher Martin Heidegger.

A professor of German, Ernst Bertram (1884–1957) had written in 1918 a remarkable study on Nietzsche and the pictorial influences on his work, such as Dürer's engraving *The Knight, Death and the Devil*.[102] In 1909 he had begun a correspondence with Thomas Mann, and their friendship grew steadily stronger. They shared the same philosophical irrationalism and the same hostility to politics.[103] Mann viewed Bertram's essay on Nietzsche as the equivalent of his *Reflections of a Nonpolitical Man*.[104] Yet in 1933 Bertram took up a position of support for the new regime and became a Nazi, if trying to prevent the writings of his old friends Thomas Mann and Friedrich Gundolf from being burned or banned. While Mann had undergone a conversion to democracy, Bertram enclosed himself in a mythical Germanness that he purported to see realized in National Socialism, and it was in vain that Thomas Mann urged him to vigilance: 'Have you begun to see? No, for they are holding your eyes closed with bloody hands, and you accept the "protection" only too gladly. The German intellectuals [. . .] will in fact be the very last to begin to see, for they have too deeply, too shamefully collaborated and exposed themselves.'[105] Bertram, for his part, never ceased to disapprove of the position taken by Thomas Mann in favour of democracy. He urged him to the last not to declare himself an exile. Their relationship was interrupted when Mann took a public position in favour of emigration.

The case of Heidegger is still more surprising. Thought of as apolitical, and known essentially for his philosophical works, especially *Sein und Zeit*, his sympathy for National Socialism was unforeseeable. When he was proposed as rector of Freiburg University by his colleagues (a post he would hold from February 1933 to May 1934), he delivered a strange speech, 'The Self-Assertion of the German University', which was hard to reconcile with the surrounding world in its key ideas, as it used ambiguous terminology. At the end of the winter semester, Heidegger resigned his function in the wake of disagreement with the Nazi party, which sought to dismiss deans hostile to the regime whom Heidegger had appointed. Heidegger refused and did not attend the investiture of his successor Professor Koch, an authentic Nazi rector. Heidegger cannot be reproached for any *action*, quite the contrary. He was one of the rare academics to show genuine proof of courage, to oppose the book burnings, and refuse anti-Semitic demonstrations at his university – even to criticize National Socialism in his lectures. It remains the case, however, that by his authority he gave cover to various measures such as the withdrawal of Germany from the League of Nations, and encouraged his students to leave for 'labour service', while in his lectures, as well as in various proclamations that appeared in student journals, his ultra-personal philosophical language was confused with Nazi terminology. It is impossible to re-read his speech on the 'Freikorps hero' Albert Leo Schlageter without a certain malaise. In an interview published in *Der Spiegel* after his death, Heidegger tried to explain the reasons for his blindness in fairly ambiguous terms, and in a manner that was often hard to believe: 'At that time I did not see any alternative. Amid the general confusion of opinions and political tendencies represented by twenty-three different parties, what mattered was to find a national and especially a social position.'[106]

Heidegger's case is cited above many others, being all the more disturbing in that he was a major philosopher. However temporary, the aberration that led him to find in National Socialism a metaphysical dimension, the encounter between 'modern man and planetarily determined technique' as this is described in *The Worker* by Ernst Jünger, cannot be understood as an isolated phenomenon.[107] The attitude of so many German academics towards Nazism, and the small number of them who emigrated when they were not threatened for racial or political reasons, illustrate very well the capitulation of the university in the face of barbarism. This fortress of intelligence and spiritual independence, as its founder Humboldt had conceived it, had become in the course of the 1920s the graveyard of the democratic spirit.[108] It was not that these academics were convinced Nazis, quite the contrary. The majority had very little esteem for this vulgar and loud-mouthed movement. But they had no more esteem either for the Weimar Republic. If a number did support it, this was only pro forma, and without great enthusiasm. No declared Nazi could be found among the most eminent professors of this time, but neither were there any acknowledged Socialists and Communists. The foundation of the Institute for Social Research in Frankfurt was a response to this situation. The majority of teachers wanted to know nothing of Nazism. Those who took a position against Hitler in those years were rare in comparison with those who denounced the Republic. Chauvinistic, still believing in Germany's redemptive mission and the superiority of its culture, they had steadily drifted into more radical positions ever since 1914. Even those most critical of the imperial regime (Max Weber, Max Scheler, Georg Simmel) did not always escape the nationalist fever. The majority of their number used their positions to denounce liberalism, and railed against those colleagues who dared to take a left-wing standpoint. Brought up on Wilhelmine culture, they were foreign to the cultural life of their own time, which developed outside of the university. And if the savage enemies of democracy among them remained a minority, within this apolitical and bourgeois university it was they who exerted the strongest influence.

A second category who collaborated massively with the new regime was that of artists and actors. Only a few avant-garde painters, such as Emil Nolde, close to the expressionist group Die Brücke, joined the National Socialists early on, but many who had been eclipsed by this avant-garde saw in the Nazis' seizure of power the occasion to take their revenge. The mass of mediocre canvases painted under Hitler – those peasant allegories, imitations of classical works and academic nudes, this profusion of superannuated romantics – was not necessarily engendered by fanatical political convictions, but, as Arno Breker maintains, 'by honest German painters who wanted to work'.[109] Membership of Nazi organizations enabled these painters to live off their art for the first time. The condemnation of modern art, the exile of the greatest representatives of the art of the 1920s and the destruction of all progressive art, gave them the opportunity to be at last recognized, exhibited and admired. While others had to leave Germany or change their style, they could become 'official artists'. Yet the notion of 'Nazi art' is an illusion; the most one can speak of is an art encouraged by the Third Reich. A large number of works seen as characteristic of this epoch were often the imitation or continuation of earlier styles, a reprise of classical or neo-classical tradition, and could equally have been executed in other countries.[110] One need not even deny the talent of a certain number of painters and sculptors who became famous under the Third Reich. Some of these put their art at the service of the regime without themselves being Nazis. Others, like Albert Speer, the regime's official architect and minister for armaments, were seduced by Hitler early on.[111] The sculptor Arno Breker, whose neo-classical style was so highly praised in the 1940s, was never a member of the NSDAP and maintained that Hitler did not believe in artists being politically committed.[112] The ability to win official commissions was often the key element in these artists' adherence to the regime. Very few of them were genuinely won to National Socialist ideas.

It was the same reasons that often impelled film directors, theatrical producers and above all actors to remain in Germany. If it is scarcely astonishing that Leni Riefenstahl rallied to the new regime, who would have imagined that G. W. Pabst, nicknamed in the early 1930s 'Pabst the red', would refuse to leave? Under the Weimar Republic he had made films arguing for pacifism (*Four Footsoldiers*) and for Franco-German reconciliation (*The Mining Accident*), and the greater part of his works contain a very sharp edge of social criticism, from *Street Without Joy* to *Lulu* and *The Threepenny Opera*. This however did not prevent him from turning out more ambiguous films such as *Paraclese* and *Komödianten*.[113] And what about Veit Harlan, sadly famous as the director of *Jew Süss*? Known first of all as an actor – he played alongside Paul Wegener, Alexandre Moissi and Max Pallenberg, even working with Max Reinhardt – he was connected with a large number of progressive figures of the Weimar years, including the Communist actor Hans Otto.[114] While his friends emigrated or lost their jobs, like Leopold Jessner, Harlan commenced under the sponsorship of Göring, then of Goebbels, a directorial career that would lead him to the cinema. Agreeing to work within the 'chamber of culture', he carried out the regime's commissions, his main concern being that his wife should obtain leading roles. From one compromise to another he was caught up in the machine, and had to make, no doubt against his will, the most famous anti-Semitic film of this time, *Jew Süss*. It is true that he sought to play down its anti-Semitism and restrain Goebbels's madness, but he still put his talent at the service of the regime.

The case of actors is all the more tragic in that their attitude was often one of a genuine lack of awareness. While all who were of Jewish origin or known for their anti-Nazi ideas were forced to emigrate, others, including the most renowned, continued brilliant careers under the Third Reich, both in theatre and cinema. Doubtless there were some who really were won over to National Socialist ideas, such as Heinrich George, but the majority did no more than accept the regime's favours. Emil Jannings, 'Professor Unrat' in Sternberg's *Blue Angel*, met Hitler on several occasions and enacted a whole series of German heroes (Friedrich Wilhelm I, Alfred Krupp, Dr Koch) as well as playing in propaganda films such as *President Krüger* (1941). In that year he was proclaimed a 'state artist', after Goebbels had already awarded him the Goethe medal in 1938. Also appointed head of the governing committee of the Tobis, he was able to draw sumptuous benefits from the Third Reich.[115] The aristocrat F. P. Reck-Malleczwesen noted in his diary in August 1939:

> I paid a visit to Jannings, whose splendid residence on the Wolfgangsee had only one shadow over it: its proprietor's fear of war. He feared for his valuables and his collection of works of art, and for the selection of charcuterie that would garnish his table in the years to come. [. . .] He is a pot-bellied bourgeois who sees in the approaching world catastrophe an obstacle to his siesta by the lake.[116]

Jannings's attitude at the Nuremberg trial evidenced the same opportunism.[117]

A large number of actors who had become famous with their films of the 1920s, continued to play in propaganda films or in the various comedies that were so popular in the Nazi period. Werner Krauss, celebrated for his interpretation of Robert Wiene's *Caligari*, was to play the role of a doddering rabbi in *Jew Süss*, alongside Heinrich George, who was to be found in so many films of the Hitler era, including Hans Steinhof's *Hitler Youth Quex*. Otto Wernike, the police commissioner in Fritz Lang's *M*, played the lead in *S. A. Man Brandt*. Rudolf Forster, 'Mack the Knife' in *The Threepenny Opera*, also played in many films of the period,[118] the same as Gustaf Gründgens or Hans Albers. From reading their memoirs it would seem that the Third Reich had never existed. They sought to shine just as they had done with Reinhardt, Jessner or Piscator, without questioning their responsibility. Rare indeed were those who dared to refuse roles and interrupt their careers rather than serve the propaganda effort.[119] They were often astonished by the questions posed to them after the War: they were actors after all, their public was still there. They pretended to separate art and reality. Like Klaus Mann's Höfgens–Mephisto, they were ready to exclaim:

'What do men want from me? Why do they pursue me? Why are they so hard? All I am is a perfectly ordinary actor.'[120] If a few who were seriously compromised could not resume their career after the War without difficulty, or had to interrupt it for a while,[121] the greater part continued to act after 1945 as if National Socialism had been only a minor incident in their trajectory. It had in many cases enabled them to embark on a brilliant career in the place of certain exiles. Whether politicized or not, in accommodating themselves to the new masters they did not have to fear criticism: it no longer existed.

> The intelligentsia of this nation has been well and truly humiliated. But in its very humiliation, it still has the power to make the dictators admit the weak spots in their armour. They lack an audience, they lack people [. . .]. The regime has found its new literary recruits above all among the old and half-forgotten, the malcontents of mass-market publishing from days gone by. There are poor impotent figures with eyes yellow from spite, who despite trembling with envy, supported our proximity when they had to, desperately hoping that their hour would come. It is here. Let them hurry up and enjoy it, it won't last long.
>
> Heinrich Mann, *Hatred*

Klaus Mann maintains, not without reason, that German writers behaved better in relation to the Nazi regime than any other professional category. Though a few declared themselves in favour of the new regime, the number of these was far smaller in comparison with the philosophers, jurists, Germanists, historians, actors, painters, doctors or musicians who compromised themselves with the Nazis. The most significant writers of the Weimar Republic took their distance from the regime, kept silent or went into exile, even if Gottfried Benn rallied to National Socialism in 1933 and Gerhart Hauptmann showed an ambiguous attitude, while Ernst Wiechert and Ernst Jünger also remained in Germany.

The reasons for this massive exodus of writers after 1933 are clear enough: for an actor it was often possible to play the same roles in Berlin, Munich or Hamburg, before and after 1933, as long as they were neither a Jew nor a Communist. Gründgens played *Faust*'s Mephisto before Göring as he would have done before any political leader. A painter could continue to work if he did not belong to one of the 'decadent' currents. Without freedom, however, the writer could not exist. What he wrote or refused to write rendered him immediately responsible. And very few authors could accept this pseudo-liberty: many emigrated even if they were not directly threatened.[122]

Before discussing the composition of this emigration, it is interesting to explore the reasons that impelled certain authors to rally to the new regime. No more than the émigrés did these form a unity. It was not always those authors furthest to the right that collaborated with the regime. Conversely, others who seemed far removed from the Nazis defended it. The reasons for such adhesion are varied: study of Third Reich literature should not be limited to the official eulogists, but has to include also the fellow-travellers, all those prepared to lend their names to it, for whatever reason. Apart from anti-Semitic and ultra-nationalist literary critics, Hitler and his movement initially attracted only a very few writers. Authors of the right and far right were often more persuaded by Prussian ideas or those of the conservative revolution than by the kitsch and peasant myths dear to Alfred Rosenberg. Stefan George rejected the regime's honours to the point of being prepared to die in Switzerland, for fear of being given a state funeral.[123] Ernst Jünger, despite being admired by Hitler, refused the responsibilities that the new regime proposed to him.[124] Ernst von Salomon worked as a scriptwriter at UFA, and though his attitude was less rigorous than Jünger's, he also kept his distance from the regime.[125] Arnolt Bronnen, the expressionist playwright, had been led towards Nazism by his hatred for the bourgeoisie and his sincere admiration for Goebbels.[126] Throughout the 1920s, after having been friendly with Brecht and then Jünger, Bronnen gave vent to the most violent provocations on the Nazis' side, also devoting a novel to the Freikorps.[127] After 1932 he had little further contact with Goebbels and moved via anti-Nazism to Communism.

The attitude of Gottfried Benn was much stranger. A convinced nihilist, foreign to political reality and indeed reality of any kind, which he considered a 'capitalist category', the author of the expressionist masterwork *Pride and Other Poems*, he believed neither in progress, technique, money nor history. In his eyes an epoch justified itself only by the perfection of a few poems. A friend of Grosz, Becher, Klabund and Klaus Mann, he was certainly hostile to Marxism, deeply influenced by Nietzsche and a radical individualism. History for him had no meaning at all, the Weimar Republic was a collection of 'incompetent bureau-crats' and 'small shopkeepers'. Though a doctor specializing in venereal disease, he lived in relative poverty in Berlin, exalting the artist as asocial. It is true that the 'biological orientation' that was central in his work was for him a question of race and mythology, yet Benn was neither racist nor anti-Semitic. His entire aesthetic vision was dominated by a radical pessimism and by his belief in art as the 'final metaphysical revolt within nihilism'. His intransigence, his passion for solitude and his contempt for history distanced him from the Nazis. Yet in 1933 he refused to emigrate,[128] and despite maintaining that he had never attended a Nazi meeting or was even aware of the NSDAP programme – taking its anti-Semitism in particular as scarcely serious[129] – he decisively rallied to National Socialism.

When Klaus Mann went into exile in France on 9 May 1933, he wrote to Benn from Le Lavandou asking how he could keep up his membership of an Academy whose leading representatives had been expelled, or support a regime which had forced his friends into exile and evoked the horror of the whole world. Mann did not expect a reply,[130] but Benn responded with a trenchant speech on Berlin radio, 'A Response to the Literary Emigration',[131] reproaching the émigrés for sheltering in seaside resorts in the south of France instead of taking an active part in the construction of the New Germany, refusing to collaborate with a regime 'which would need the *Iliad* and the *Aeneid* to tell its history'. He accused them of betraying their country by combating Nazism from abroad, after learning German in school and owing everything to their nation. Benn ended his attack against the émigrés with a personal declaration of faith in the new regime, which he would later on try and minimize by attributing it to ignorance and naivety:[132]

> I declare myself personally in favour of the New State, because it is my own people who are beating a path in this way. Who am I to isolate myself from it? Do I know better than them? [. . .] My spiritual and material existence, my language, my life, my personal relations, the sum total of my mind, I owe first and foremost to this people. It is from them that our ancestors came, it is to them that our children will return, and as I was brought up in the country among the flocks, I know very well what a fatherland is.[133]

He maintained that it was his complete disinterest that justified his rallying to Nazism: 'It is the fanatical purity that you so flatteringly ascribe to me in your letter, precisely this purity of sentiment and of thought, that has led me to this position. [. . .] I have made my decision for the State, and I must accept on its behalf that you, from your side of the river, call out farewell.'[134] Benn's illusions, however, proved brief: by 1934, he maintains, he had lost faith in the regime and members of the Academy found it difficult to shake his hand. He was rapidly cold-shouldered and violently attacked as a 'cultural bolshevik'. After being designated to deliver the official speech on the death of Stefan George, he was banned in the event from appearing, and from the following year he no longer existed for official Germany.[135]

Benn rallied to National Socialism not out of opportunism but from sincere conviction. Yet it is impossible to believe in the total naivety that he claims to justify his aberration. Even without knowing in detail the NSDAP's programme, he had ample occasion in Berlin to acquaint himself with its style and expressions. Brecht wrote of Gottfried Benn: 'A doctor by profession, Benn published poems on the pains of women in labour and the paths of lancets through the human body. And now he has rallied decisively to the Third Reich.' But did Benn's poems and theoretical essays of the 1920s lead him fatally towards Nazism? Nothing is less certain. It is quite wrong to maintain – as Alfred Kurella did, for example, in the arguments of antifascist exiles about expressionism in 1938–39 in the review *Das Wort* – that his political development was determined by his aesthetic positions.

An especially interesting counter-example to this is provided by the greatest representative of German naturalism, Gerhart Hauptmann. An acerbic critic of Wilhelmine Germany, his work elicited both enthusiasm and scandal, and if the younger generation eventually turned away from him, this was simply because he was incapable of breaking a new path after 1914. Playing on his resemblance to the ageing Goethe, he enjoyed long years of triumph on the international stage, though the audience turned gradually more towards Wedekind or Hoffmannstahl. The scion of a family of Silesian weavers, the champion in Germany of Tolstoy, Ibsen and Zola, Hauptmann became known first of all for poems filled with social demands and above all for his drama *Before Sunrise*, staged by Otto Brahm in 1889. Despite cuts made by the censor, his works continued to enjoy great success, especially *The Skin of the Beaver*. His play *The*

Weavers was seen as a revolutionary work. Yet a writer who maintained under the reign of Wilhelm II that 'I hate this military dictatorship with its policy of provocation and drawn sabre' already displayed a disconcerting nationalism in 1914. Not only did he sign the 'manifesto of the ninety-three', but wrote poems exalting the War which brought violent criticism from both Franz Pfemfert, editor of the expressionist review *Die Aktion*, and Romain Rolland, who urged him to choose between Goethe and Attila. Surprised by this unforeseen support, the Kaiser awarded Hauptmann the 'Red Eagle of the Fourth Class', which the writer was pleased to accept. This did not prevent him in due course from being awarded the honours of the Republic in 1922 by President Ebert, and his seventieth birthday being celebrated in 1932 by all progressive writers.

Hauptmann assuredly embodied everything that the Nazis detested. Back in 1893, a play of his had already been described as a 'monstrous wretched piece of work', 'social-democratic-realistic, at the same time full of sickly, sentimental mysticism, nerve-racking, in general abominable.'[136] The *Deutsche Kulturwacht* attacked him in September 1933. But not only did Hauptmann not emigrate, he agreed to join the revived Academy and was decorated by Rudolf Binding in the name of the new regime.[137] On 1 May after the Nazis took power, Hauptmann hung a Nazi flag from his window and applauded Hitler's decision to leave the League of Nations.[138] Doubtless the Nazis were suspicious of him and never held him in high esteem.[139] All the same, he did not emigrate, and distanced himself from those that did.[140] This attitude had its rewards: his plays were newly staged in Germany in 1939, and his eightieth birthday was celebrated by Baldur von Schirach in Vienna.[141] Like other writers (E. Glaeser, H. Carossa), Hauptmann agreed to serve Nazi propaganda, and when Ferenc Körmendi asked him the reasons for his attitude, he could only reply: 'Because I am a coward, do you understand? I am a coward, you understand, a coward.'[142]

The full history of the compromises made by German intellectuals and artists remains to be written. The few examples mentioned here only give a selective idea. They show that the logic which led to such compromise was at all events far from clear. It was just as unpredictable that Gerhart Hauptmann would accept the regime's favours as that Stefan George would refuse them, that Max Hermann-Neisse would emigrate while Gottfried Benn attacked the émigrés so violently.[143] In most cases, neither their political ideas, which were often vague, nor the aesthetic currents to which they belonged, made it possible to foresee these attitudes. Exile was not only a political act but a moral one, which brought other considerations into play besides ideological ones.[144]

If one examines the writers who were representative of official Nazi literature, the eulogists of *Blut und Boden*, the reasons for their choice are more evident and a more rigorous classification is possible.[145] They included epigones of the Romantic tradition[146] such as Rudolf Binding, F. Barthel, Ina Seidel, Borries von Münchhausen, Hermann Stehr and E. von Scholz; opponents of rationalism such as H. F. Blunk (author of regional novels set in a prehistoric time), Hanns Heinz Ewers, Hanns Johst, Burte, W. Schäfer, E. E. Dwinger; Ernst Bertram and Hans Grimm. A certain number of writers who championed a 'higher order' also rallied to Nazism (Paul Ernst, Schumann, E. G. Kolben-heyer), together with those nostalgic for provincialism (Hermann Stehr, Emil Strauss, Friedrich Griese, H. Steguweit), partisans of the '*völkisch*' tradition (Hans Grimm, Hermann Claudius, H. Menzel, J. Weinheber, H. Lersch, H. Zöberlein), defenders of nationalism (K. Ziesel, R. G. Binding, H. Baumann, E. E. Dwinger, F. Schauwecker, B. Brehm, A. Bronnen) and adepts of the *furor Germanicus* (Blunck, Johst, G. Schumann, H. Anacker, Baldur von Schirach, L. F. Barthel, H. Böhme, Will Vesper, H. Zillich and W. von Scholz).

It is notable, from these various names mentioned, that one and the same author often illustrates several reactionary tendencies, future components of Nazi literature. These had often been marginal figures; few indeed had been considered major writers before 1933.[147] Virtually none of them survived the ephemeral glory that the Third Reich conferred on them. If some continued to rehearse the same reactionary values after 1945, a number of them sought to appear as 'internal émigrés'. Bards of war and nationalism, eulogists of their region and its peasant idylls, defenders of Aryan purity and Germanic values – if in some cases their rallying to Nazism was predictable, in many other cases it was not.[148]

The stance of a certain number of critics is also worthy of study. If the greatest of these, who wrote for the progressive press under the Weimar Republic and were longstanding opponents of National Socialism, did take the path of exile, others rallied to the 'new Germany'. Thus Paul Scheffer, a writer for the *Berliner Tagblatt* well-known for his progressive ideas – he had been the paper's correspondent in the Soviet Union, from where he wrote sympathetic reports – became a confidant of Goebbels and took over the paper's editorship. Just as strange was the case of the *Frankfurter Zeitung*'s Paris correspondent Friedrich Sieburg. When the writer Ernst Erich Noth took refuge in France, the editor-in-chief of the newspaper – which counted among its contributors some of the most famous writers in Weimar Germany – advised him to meet Sieburg,[149] but after a few minutes' conversation, Noth realized that he had entered the lion's den, as Sieburg had been won to the nationalist cause even while living in Paris.[150] Close for a while to General Schleicher, he subsequently joined the Nazis and gave lectures in Switzerland in support of the new regime, modestly terming himself an 'evangelist of the Third Reich'. He spoke in Paris on 22 March 1942 under the auspices of the group Collaboration. Doubtless he was more than a mere propagandist. Hans Daiber believed that 'he was not a wolf, he was a fox who sometimes howled with the wolves, but more tunefully.'[151] Sieburg had a real love for France, even if he sometimes adapted a stinging irony about this 'backward' country where nothing worked properly, and saw the French as a 'magnificent and unsupportable people'. His most famous book, *Is God French?* (Paris 1930), had a good reception. Despite his adherence to Nazism, several of his earlier books, such as *Is This Germany?* which criticized anti-Semitism and racism, and *The Red Arctic* that depicted the Soviet komsomols, were banned, and he was finally expelled from the chamber of literature. He was attacked by émigrés in a number of articles, and seen by them as a typical arriviste.[152] Sieburg maintained, however, that he had never been a member of the NSDAP, or even a genuine sympathizer, which is certainly false. His personality and celebrity undoubtedly give his case an exemplary value. But how many unknown Sieburgs were there as well?

2. THE DECISION TO EMIGRATE

The majority of those who left Germany did so out of fear or disgust at a regime whose highest representatives openly flaunted themselves as murderers.

Hermann Kesten

We left because we could not breathe the air in Nazi Germany.

Klaus Mann

THE REASONS FOR EMIGRATING

In 1933, over 53,000 emigrants left Germany, of whom 37,000 were Jews.[153] Not all left for the same reason. Some were forced to leave, others chose exile for moral or political reasons.[154] Sometimes their lives were not even in danger, but they no longer wanted to live in Germany. Without being directly persecuted, they were opponents of the regime. Many Jews who left Germany, on the other hand, were persecuted but not political opponents. The difficulty of analysing the overall phenomenon of emigration is due above all to the complexity and diversity of motives that impelled so many men and women to leave their homeland.

The most clear-cut reasons to discern are economic constraint and racial persecution. The climate of anti-Semitism, the expulsion of Jews from state employment and the liberal professions, the economic boycott and the Nuremberg laws signalled the collapse of their conditions of existence. Thrown out of their economic activities, they had to leave Germany, even those who cannot be considered as 'political émigrés' or even genuine opponents of the Nazis. They often emigrated not in 1933 but only towards 1938, hoping always for an improvement in their situation, or at least that no further anti-Semitic measures would be taken. Some even declared themselves ready to support Hitler if he abandoned anti-Semitism. Political émigrés of Jewish origin often judged very severely these 'racial exiles' devoid of any political consciousness.[155] The latter most often remained apart from the political emigration.

All declared opponents of National Socialism, all activists, were equally forced into exile. The withdrawal order issued officially by the Comintern to the German Communists came belatedly. If the most threatened adversaries of the regime sought already in January 1933 to escape abroad, many Communist and Socialist militants remained in Germany to try and create resistance networks. Several had to leave the country as the terror and repression intensified, but some of these subsequently returned – clandestinely so as not to meet a senseless martyrdom.

The case of writers was far more complex. They definitely formed a large part of the emigration of 1933, and were often among the first to quit Germany.

Some were directly threatened[156] and went into exile to escape arrest and concentration camp. Others left because they featured on the blacklists, because their books had been burned or they feared being the next victims of the repression.[157] Others again left for complex reasons without being directly threatened. In this third category it is practically impossible to distinguish a 'literary emigration' and a 'political emigration'. If they each included many Jews, it was not as Jews that they chose exile or were sent to concentration camp. Some of them were political writers, long-time adversaries of Nazism who went on to continue their struggle in emigration (Heinrich Mann), others did not believe in the possibility of such a struggle, despite being passionate opponents of Nazism (Kurt Tucholsky). Others again, who had not previously taken part in political struggle, became radicalized (Thomas Mann). Very soon all these exiles were considered by the Nazis as opponents by the sole fact of their having left Germany, even when, like Max Hermann-Neisse,[158] they were not involved in any political activity. But while writers transformed themselves into activists, former politicians virtually ceased to play any further role in the emigration.[159] The reasons that impelled so many writers to emigrate in 1933 are varied. Their exodus began already on 30 January and accelerated with the wave of arrests that followed the Reichstag fire (27–28 February) and the book burnings (10 May). The majority of authors threatened understood very well that the burning of their books was a symbolic way of burning them in person. One of the most clear-cut reasons that drove many intellectuals to leave Germany was simply the desire to save their lives.

On this point, it is impossible to stress too forcibly how wrong are certain assertions already made in 1933 that many writers left Germany 'too soon' or 'misguidedly'. Gottfried Benn for example claimed in his response to the émigrés of 24 May 1933 that 'nothing would have happened to them' had they stayed. The murders of Carl von Ossietzky and Erich Mühsam, the brutality suffered by the majority of artists, actors and writers arrested, showed what this 'nothing' really meant.[160] As Klaus Mann put it in *The Turning Point*, 'the only choice that remained was between an absurd martyrdom or opportunistic treason, concentration camp or falling in line'. The measures already taken by the Nazi government of Thuringia, the sadistic acts inflicted on writers after the Reichstag fire, the death threats, arrests, and the promise of the *Völkischer Beobachter* that many heads would roll, left little room for hope. Moreover, the laws passed 'for the protection of the German people', the establishment of the Kulturkammern, the concern to protect 'German blood and honour' and the fascisization or dissolution of all writers' organizations, were a threat to all. The effectiveness and scope of the dictatorship over culture left little possibility for any kind of 'literary opposition'.[161] The first measures taken by the Nazis against certain writers had exemplary value. Those who were not arrested and sent to concentration camp were watched daily and attacked by the SA. Count Harry Kessler noted in his diary:

> In the afternoon, as I was about to leave for Weimar for a day, I had a call from a young man who urgently requested to see me on behalf of Plievier. [. . .] The young

man, deathly pale, told me that at six o'clock this morning Storm Troopers arrived to fetch Plievier from the apartment he shares with him. They mistook another young man for their prey and beat him up terribly. On discovering their error, they smashed the apartment amid yells that they will yet avenge themselves on that swine Plievier, who is now hiding somewhere or other with not a penny in his pocket and unable to get away.[162]

Hermann Kesten, who left Berlin six weeks after the Nazis took power, wrote from Paris on 23 March 1933 to Ernst Toller:

> In Paris I feel I've been rescued. Do you already know that the SA came to look for you early this morning at your Berlin apartment? They also came to my house. There was a sudden knocking. It was the woman from the flat downstairs; her husband is an editor of some kind, I know him by sight. She trembled, and murmured: 'Police, SA, search.' They surely intended to come to our flat as well. We had to flee by the back stairs and get rid of some compromising papers. She then went back down to her flat. I was moved [. . .]. They took away the editor who has not been seen again. I often think of him, of our friends, and other victims.[163]

Even those who were not members of any party could be threatened by the laws for cultural 'purification' (*Säuberung*), whether or not their books had been burned on 10 May. This was the case with 'non-Aryan' writers, pacifists, left-wing sympathizers, and those who refused to join the new Nazi organizations. The list of persons arrested or sought by the Gestapo shows that this repression struck all progressive writers, whether close to the KPD or not. If Ossietzky, Ludwig Renn, Erich Mühsam, Willi Bredel, Kurt Hiller and E. E. Kisch had been arrested, Ernst Toller, Erwin Piscator, Kurt Tucholsky, Klaus Mann, Lion Feuchtwanger or Bertolt Brecht would have experienced the same fate had the Nazis been able to catch them.[164]

It took a number of weeks, however, for the majority of writers to realize how seriously they were threatened. Many still believed in the possibility of resistance, or in a rapid collapse of the regime. Ludwig Marcuse thought of emigrating as soon as Hitler took power, but only left on 28 March.[165] Leonhard Frank left Berlin for Munich thinking it would be safer there. A few months later he was forced to emigrate to Switzerland.[166] Even the most menaced, the Communist writers, still hesitated to leave the country. Gustav Regler watched the Reichstag burning but could not take the decision for exile.[167] Despite knowing that he was wanted by the police, he walked through Berlin to see if the brown virus had contaminated everything. Meeting the writer Erich Franzen, he learned that the police had already visited his apartment. Continuing to believe in a way out,[168] he wandered the streets, not knowing where to take refuge. A prostitute looked at him, hesitated and said: 'If you want a hide-out you can have my key.' It was only at that point that he realized how he resembled a hunted animal: 'Berlin contained hundreds of thousands of workers who yesterday had been my comrades. Now that the time had come there were only Korth and Franzen, two equally threatened writers, and a street-girl, to offer me help against being struck down.' He decided to take refuge in Worpswede at the home of his girlfriend, the daughter of the painter Heinrich Vögeler. Denounced by the Protestant pastor, he had to leave for Bremen, then Cologne, took refuge in the Saar and finally in Strasbourg.

The case of Alfred Döblin is just as characteristic. He heard the news of the Reichstag fire on the radio, without realizing what this would mean for him. His friends urged him to leave but he felt in no danger. When they managed to persuade him that he was under threat, he decided to leave Germany for a while, 'to let the storm pass'. On his way to the Anhalt station with a simple suitcase he noticed in front of the door of his building a man whose civilian coat poorly concealed a Nazi uniform, who eyed him suspiciously and followed after him. He had to run into the subway to escape him. Döblin travelled to Stuttgart and took refuge in a sanatorium in Kreuzlingen, but he already wondered if he hadn't been afraid for nothing. He wrote to his wife that he would come back in a day or two. She described to him the terror unleashed on Berlin and he understood that the time of exile had begun.

If any of these writers had remained in Germany their fate would have been very predictable: arrested and tortured in the Gestapo cellars by the SA or SS. The most fortunate would have got out disfigured and sick, with their teeth broken. Others ended in concentration camp. And yet the motive of saving their lives was not the only thing that drove them to quit Germany. These acts of sadism and terror struck the most political, those who had taken part in the antifascist struggles of the 1920s. Many others – perhaps the greatest number – emigrated without being threatened. They could often have remained in Germany without being disturbed, but refused out of solidarity with the persecuted, hatred for the regime, and concern for their own dignity. They knew that by remaining in Germany they would be as good as dead, as far as their existence as writers was concerned. Exile for them was not a material necessity, but a moral decision, an act of courage and clear-headedness.

Klaus Mann, in *The Turning Point*, explains that he himself was not directly threatened. He did not belong to those 'persecuted for racial reasons'. While he was not a 'pure Aryan', the Nuremberg laws would have counted him as an 'Aryan of second class'. Though scarcely loved by the Nazis – who particularly hated his sister Erika – he was not a political agitator. His conversion would doubtless have been accepted and made use of.[169] But he maintained that 'some people could no longer breathe the air of the Third Reich', and that 'Germany seemed to have been struck by a plague'. Since any opposition to the regime seemed impossible to him, and he had the soul neither of a martyr nor an opportunist, he saw no other solution but exile. 'Emigration wasn't good, but the Third Reich was worse.' Hermann Kesten likewise asserted[170] that for any writer there was a clear reason for emigration: they did not want to live under a dictatorship, and held to their dignity. Alfred Döblin recalled that freedom was the essence of artistic creation and that Hitler made this impossible.[171] Klaus Mann stressed the voluntary character of his own exile, even if 'nausea at anti-

Semitism may be as forceful a reason as its practical consequences'. A number of exiles of 1933 refused to be classified as 'racially persecuted' and lumped in with the massive emigration of German Jews, many of whom were not progressive. It is a fact that Bertolt Brecht, Heinrich Mann, Thomas Mann, René Schickele, Oskar Maria Graf, Georg Kaiser, Leonhard Frank, J. R. Becher, Fritz von Unruh, Ludwig Renn, Gustav Regler, H. H. Jahn, Bodo Uhse, F. and A. Busch were not Jewish. While certain of these – Heinrich Mann, Brecht, Becher, Remarque – were directly threatened by their expressed political convictions, it was not certain whether Irmgard Keun, Oskar Maria Graf, Max Hermann-Neisse, Ludwig Renn and Klaus Mann might not have been tolerated in Germany.

The example of Oskar Maria Graf, whose books the Nazis had forgotten to burn until he reminded them, is well-known. The same goes for Balder Olden, who until 1933 defined himself as 'a completely apolitical writer'. While his novel *Kilimandscharo* could be taken for a pacifist work, other books of his received a warm welcome in nationalist circles. A 'pure Aryan' and writer for conservative journals, he belonged to that category of writers who, in the eyes of those who remained in Germany, had gone into exile 'for nothing'. He, on the contrary, knew that he could not remain in the Reich without betraying himself: 'What would my task have been there? To close my eyes and ears, and write serene novels full of peaceful images of days gone by; to become a liar.'[172] What everyone had seen with their own eyes, he maintained, their mouths could not repeat and the writer could not write.

> I would have grown old in shame, to experience perhaps the dawn of a better world for which others had struggled. But under the cypresses my tomb would have become a dunghill. The only alternatives were suicide or – no, flight from Germany was not a flight from that! – The cries of the tortured echoed for those who wanted to hear them, resounding from thousands of voices across the frontiers of the Reich. It was impossible to think of anything else. How could we have managed to write about anything else?[173]

THE PROBLEMS OF EMIGRATING

Clear as the need to leave Germany was, the majority of writers only took this decision with iron in the soul, and most often in utter despair. The difficulties of tearing themselves from their homeland and their everyday existence were both material and psychological. The need to escape arrest, the SA, persecution and border controls was clear enough. But a reading of their diaries and correspondence shows that psychological obstacles were no less important than objective dangers. The émigré had often to leave his or her family, so as not to arouse suspicion.[174] They had to leave their apartment, abandon their library,[175] their manuscripts and their professional activities, confront innumerable material difficulties for which they were unprepared, as well as leaving their linguistic space, which writers could often not withstand.[176] By emigrating they fled their country, their source of inspiration, their language and their readers.

Many knew that they would no longer be published or read. Even someone as privileged as Thomas Mann, enjoying international fame, could write to Lavinia Mazzuchetti: 'I am much too good a German, far too closely linked with the cultural traditions and the language of my country, for the thought of an exile lasting years, if not a lifetime, not to have a grave, a fateful significance to me.'[177]

The same anguish is to be found in all émigré writers. Alfred Döblin wrote to Ferdinand Lion on 28 April 1933:[178] 'I cannot be a doctor abroad and write. Why? For whom?' Alfred Kerr, the most famous Berlin theatre critic, noted in his 'Voyage sentimental' published on 1 July 1933 in *Les Nouvelles Littéraires*:

> No one abandons their homeland for fun. We all love the countryside where we were children. We are attached to those places where we have paid tax. And then, to have to express yourself in a foreign language is very hard (do you detect this, readers?). On the other hand, to be held in a concentration camp for anti-Hitler declarations in verse or prose, to be the object not of humiliation but of attempted humiliation, even with the prospect of finding yourself dead (for accidents will happen) in these desolate places without the causes being known – there are people fatuous enough not to like that.

In Prague, Vienna, Zurich and Paris, Kerr continued to attend theatres, but with the desperate feeling that he was now simply a spectator: 'At the back of a box I was plunged into melancholy, for I brusquely recalled that I was no longer a drama critic in Berlin. I would not be able to utter my opinion there frankly. And I know, alas!, that there is no way back. Then I ask myself (one must confess the truth): "But how will German theatres manage without me?" ' With his immense pride, Kerr found it shattering to exclaim: 'Never again to write in German! It will be hard for me to take leave of this language to which I have given so much.'

Fritz Kortner, one of the most famous expressionist actors, similarly evokes in his memoirs the fearful sympathy he felt in the 1920s for the Russian émigrés in Berlin who waged 'a veritable battle with the language'. He maintained that one could doubtless learn a foreign grammar and vocabulary, 'but not that coloration of language in which a child is brought up'.[179] Even though threatened, he could not bring himself to leave Berlin and its theatres. When Leonhard Frank asked him on his return from a London tour why he had come back to Berlin, he could only reply: 'because they speak English, because there are no cafés, no bars like we have here, because I can't just meet you and the others, because my mouth has been formed to speak German and my head to read German books, because I have no friends there, and there is no night life like in Berlin.'[180] Even when the situation grew worse he could not resolve to leave his homeland. Amazed by his lack of awareness, Leonhard Frank urged Kortner to emigrate. 'If I were Jewish,' he claimed, 'I would leave tomorrow.' 'And you?' Kortner asked him. 'The day after,' Frank replied with a smile. He tried to prove to himself that the situation was not so desperate, and that 'Schleicher could well checkmate Hitler.' While waiting, he continued to play in Schiller's *Don Carlos*, despite the attacks of the Nazis who even made up a story of sexual assault to discredit him. The Marquis de Posa, who gave him his cue on stage, was played by a fanatical young Hitlerite, and Don Carlos by a young Jew aptly named Schiller. Basking in the audience's applause, Kortner felt that his place would always be in Germany. Even when his friend the actress Käte Dorsch, a familiar of Göring's, urged him likewise to emigrate, he still refused. When Hitler became Chancellor, however, Kortner left on a tour abroad, and did not return until 21 December 1947. He had to play in Denmark under police protection, as there were people there who wanted to lynch him. At Kovno, in Lithuania, the Jews called for a boycott of his company because of 'the Nazi actor Kortner'. Posters had to be printed to make clear that Kortner was Jewish and the company Austrian. But some actors really were won over to Nazism, and when they returned to Germany they proposed to Kortner to intervene in his favour even though the entire Nazi press was incessantly railing against him. His wife, more clear-headed, refused to return to Berlin. Kortner was finally warned that his safety could not be guaranteed, and he left for Vienna in utter despair.

Many writers, before they were able to leave Germany, had to remain underground for a while. Shelter in working-class districts patrolled by the police and infiltrated by Gestapo agents was far from safe, above all for KPD activists who were particularly wanted. A number of writers and activists had to stay for many weeks in hotels where identities were not checked. Their situation was all the more tragic in that very few, aside from Arnold Zweig, had envisaged before 1933 the possibility of leaving Germany in the event of a Nazi victory. In the space of a few days, therefore, a number of antifascists – Wilhelm Kasper, Ernst Schneller, Walter Strecher, Ernst Thälmann, Erich Birkenhauer, Werner Hirsch, Alfred Kattner – were rapidly apprehended. Many intellectuals did not even have a valid passport, or this had been withdrawn by the Republican authorities. They had no place of asylum to escape arrest, and sometimes lacked even the ready cash needed to board a train. The assistance they received was very limited: some took refuge with parents or relations, with friends, publishers or colleagues. Heinrich George, before he rallied to Nazism, lived for a while on assistance from other actors who had gone into exile. The less threatened helped the persecuted to flee. Edgar von Schmidt-Pauli, a member of the National party, enabled Theodor Plievier to quit Germany. Alfred Kantorowicz was also sheltered by a nationalist friend. Almost all, apart from Carl von Ossietzky, gave up the idea of returning to their apartments, for fear of being immediately arrested. John Heartfield remained clandestinely in Berlin until April 1933, Alexander Abusch in the Ruhr until June.

Before resolving to leave Germany, a number of them went to Bavaria, where the Nazi terror had not yet been unleashed. Some Social-Democrats (Robert Breitscheid, Rudolf Hilferding, Otto Wels) found a temporary refuge there, and so did a number of writers (Theodor Wolff, Hellmut von Gerlach, Leonhard Frank, Klaus Mann). Several still nourished the hope that Nazism would be limited to a bloody week in Berlin and that Bavaria, jealous of its independence, would resist, perhaps even restoring the Wittelsbach dynasty. In *The Turning Point* Klaus Mann portrayed Munich in January 1933 with its masked balls and

the applause that still greeted the anti-Nazi jokes of his sister Erika at the
Pfeffermühle cabaret. He described the 'grim and feverish merriment' of this
final week: 'The tangos and waltzes were punctuated by the grisly news and
rumours pouring in from Berlin. We danced at the Regina Palast Hotel when
the Reichstag burned [. . .].'[181] He learned of Thälmann's arrest while throwing
confetti. It was only with the arrival of the Nazi *Gauleiter* Ritter von Epp and
the arrest of Prime Minister Held that he decided to leave for Switzerland,
warned of the danger he ran by the family chauffeur – all the better informed in
that the man worked for the Nazis. The terror broke on Bavaria a week later.
Opponents were immediately expelled from government jobs, the archives of
the satirical magazine *Simplicissimus* were ransacked and many antifascists
arrested, including Oskar Maria Graf, W. Hallgarten, K. von Kauffungen, J.
Zerfass and W. Schaber.

In the course of these weeks that marked the beginning of the Hitler epoch,
traffic between Germany and its neighbouring countries still remained relatively
free. The most threatened individuals could take refuge abroad. But in the wake
of the economic crisis it had been forbidden since 1932 to take more than 200
marks per person out of the country. If a German citizen wanted to move
abroad and transfer their funds, there was a tax of 25 per cent. It happened that
a number of writers, for different reasons, found themselves out of Germany in
January 1933: Thomas Mann was on a lecture tour, Fritz Kortner travelling
with his theatre company, Hanns Eisler in Vienna, O. M. Graf in Austria,
Walter Hasenclever and Josef Roth in Paris. For those who remained in Berlin
departure was still fairly easy, on condition that they made the decision in good
time. Robert Neumann left Berlin as soon as Hitler was appointed Chancellor,
followed by Wilhelm Herzog who reached Paris on 14–15 February and Alfred
Kerr who left for Czechoslovakia on 18 February. Some still hesitated. Herzog
describes[182] how despite his advice, Heinrich Mann refused to leave for France,
as he was booked to give a lecture at the Academy on 4 April for the sixtieth
birthday of Jacob Wassermann. When Herzog told him that there was no way
he would be able to give his lecture, Heinrich Mann chided him as a 'bird of ill
omen'. Even after his expulsion from the Academy he could still not decide to
leave Berlin, despite the urgings of the French ambassador François-Poncet.
Walter Mehring left Germany a few hours before the Reichstag fire, while
Ossietzky and Hellmut von Gerlach still believed in the need to remain in the
country.[183]

After the Reichstag fire, controls became more rigorous. It was not just a
question now of intimidation and acts of vengeance, but of a systematic daily
surveillance. The Nazis checked bank accounts to see who was getting ready to
leave the country. Trains were also watched by the SA and SS. Anyone
travelling abroad was questioned, especially Jews, if they seemed to have a
lot of luggage. Special advice was given to the police to enable them to recognize
Jews.[184] Border controls were also reinforced. The object was not just to stop
Jews from taking 'German assets' out of the country, but above all to arrest
Communist militants or anyone suspected of being a danger to the Reich.[185]
Soon a visa was required in order to travel abroad.

The only remaining solution for those who wanted to emigrate was to disguise themselves as simple tourists, at the risk of being recognized, or to leave Germany illegally, sometimes at the risk of the lives. Some chose to cross the border over the Alps, others had recourse to foreign embassies.[186] From 1 January 1934 the visa requirement was suspended, but certain countries continued to insist on substantial payments for those wanting to cross to their territory.[187] The suspension of the visa did not indicate any degree of clemency on the part of the Nazi government: terror had already eliminated all opposition and this was simply no longer needed. The Jewish emigration from 1934–35 onwards was viewed in a different light: the Nazis even sought occasionally to make deals with the Zionist organizations to ensure a massive departure of Jews from Germany. The general refusal of European countries to accept them led to countless tragedies. Finally, even after 1934, the Gestapo tried to kidnap and return to Germany certain antifascist refugees already settled abroad, if they approached the German frontier.

Within less than two months the whole of German culture suffered a regular haemorrhage, with no precedent in history. The list of writers who left shows that this reached its peak between 15 and 30 March 1933.

Writers who left Berlin on:
28 February
J. R. Becher, B. Brecht, L. Lanis, J. Deutsch, A. Döblin, L. Marcuse, K. Grossmann, E. Jacobsohn, B. Frank, F. Wolfskehl

29 February
A. Kolbe

1 March
R. Olden, F. Pfemfert, B. Viertel, A. Polgar, A. Thomas

2 March
M. Hermann-Neisse, K. Wolff

3 March
F. Wolf

4 March
A. Wolfenstein, G. Tergit

8–12 March
H. Kessler, A. Kantorowicz

14 March
A. Zweig

15–20 March
W. Benjamin, E. Bloch, S. Kracauer, T. Balk, F. Erpenbeck, R. Fischer, B. Frei, A. Goldschmidt, J. Hay, F. Höllering, J. Hollos, B. Olden, H. Pol, H. Sahl, O. Strasser, H. Zinner, H. W. von Zwehl, G. Hermann, Leo L. Matthias, W. Speyer, M. Scheer, W. Sternfeld, G. von Wangenheim, P. Westheim, F. Bruckner, W. Herzfelde, F. Sternberg, J. Thoor, E. J. Aufricht, B. von Brentano, K. Otten, W. Türk, M. and F. Weiskopf and G. Bernhard.

The fall of the Bavarian government forced those who had taken refuge there to cross the frontier. L. Frank, L. Schwarzschild, J. Bornstein, K. Reinhold and R. Breitscheid left Munich on 10 March. R. Hilferding, E. Mann, K. Mann, H. Fischer, Ö. von Horvath,[188] H. von Gerlach, T. Wolff, A. Moritz Frey,[189] F. Schoenberger and T. Heine also left Germany before the end of March 1933. In April, still other opponents of the regime went into exile: Hans Jacob, Else Lasker-Schüler, E. Castonnier, S. Marck, H. zur Mühler, Hubertus Prinz zu Löwenstein, H. J. Rehfisch, K. Schnog and John Heartfield. These departures often took place in extremely dramatic conditions. Not only did the émigrés leave alone, without money, with just a few clothes, in fear of being stopped at the border, but they often had to escape police surveillance. John Heartfield, who managed to reach Prague on 20 April, had lived in hiding for six weeks, wanted by the SA, without daring to return to his apartment. He had to meet his wife in a public place so that she could give him all the money that she had: five marks! He tried to return home, but had to hide in a cupboard while the SA men who had followed him ransacked the apartment. He spent the night in this cupboard before being denounced in the morning by the concierge. He then fled to Berlin, hailing a taxi and explaining that the Nazis were after him. He was fortunate enough to come across a Communist activist who took him to some friends, the actors Heinrich Greif and Lotte Löbinger. He then took refuge in Schmiedeberg, before crossing the Czech frontier in the snow together with his brother Wieland Herzfelde. They then reached Prague by bus.

May 1933 saw the emigration of Anselm Rüst and N. Mühlen, and June that of Willi Hans. On 15 July, W. A. Berendsohn and E. Ottwalt. In summer 1933, Robert Musil, who had lived in Berlin since 1931, decided to return to Vienna. I. Heilbut and W. Hallgarten left Germany in August 1933. S. Friedländer, P. Zech, E. Ginsberg and A. Neumann emigrated in September and October.

These few examples, taken from lists drawn up by H. A. Walter, are doubtless insufficient to show the scope of the exodus from Germany then taking place, which drove over the border so many writers, poets, actors, producers, film directors and artists as well as political figures. We may just recall that besides the names already cited, Germany also lost in 1933: H. Budzislawski, W. Hegemann, H. H. Jahn, H. Marchwitza, A. Rosenberg, R. Breuer, H. Keisch, F. Burschell, W. Schoenstedt, M. Schroeder, A. Thalheimer, B. Uhse, H. Wendel, A. Durus, W. Bretholz, S. Heym, G. Kauder, K. Rosenfeld, A. Scharrer, M. Seydewitz, E. Weiss, K. Heiden, S. Thalheimer, E. Kuttner, A. Roda, C. Zuckmayer, G. Anders, E. Arendt, H. Arendt, U. Becher, A. Bessmertny, H. Bieber, F. Blei, E. Feder, H. Fleisch-Brunningen, E. Deutsch, R. Herrnstadt, F. Heymann, K. Hirschfeld, H. M. Hirschfeld, A. Holitscher, H.-A. Joachim, K. Korsch, W. Kreft, S. Lackner, F. Leschnitzer, V. Marcu, B. Menne, P. Merin, C. Misch, H. Natonek, F. Walter and O. Zarek.[190] This exodus, moreover, did not stop at the end of 1933. It continued, if with diminishing intensity, and ended only in 1940.[191]

We should note that the conditions of emigration steadily deteriorated between 1933 and 1940. Not only could later émigrés take only 40 marks instead of 1,200, but the total sum of assets that could be transferred abroad was reduced from 200,000 marks to 50,000. Often the intervention of a foreign government was required to enable certain individuals to emigrate, especially if they had already been arrested. Those who left Germany between 1934 and 1940 were generally writers who had not been involved in politics, and who opted for exile as a result of anti-Semitism and economic pressure. This belated exile steadily merged together with the massive exodus of German Jews after 1938. There are even some writers whose exile cannot be considered a political act. The material and psychological difficulties that accompanied exile were all the harder for individuals who were more or less unknown abroad, and did not benefit from any support, especially if they were already of advanced age. Some preferred to die in Germany in fear and humiliation rather than confront exile.[192]

THE POSSIBILITIES OF EMIGRATION

In 1933 Germany had common borders with ten countries.[193] It was relatively easy to cross one or other of these borders in the first few weeks of the Nazi regime, but the Gestapo surveillance grew steadily more intense. Directed first of all at the best-known opponents – writers or activists – this was rapidly extended to everyone else. While those equipped with a valid passport could still hope to reach France, Austria, the Netherlands or Czechoslovakia, lists of suspects were soon distributed to border posts in order to intercept them.[194]

The decision to emigrate was a function of motives that were political, moral, emotional and psychological, but also of a whole range of objective factors: the material and intellectual capacity to leave Germany and try to build a new life abroad. Statistics published by Gilbert Badia relating to emigration to France[195] show that these refugees were predominantly male (at least in the first period) and relatively young.[196] The number of refugees older than sixty was insignificant (0.6 per cent). Those who remained in Germany would be all the more persecuted if certain family members had taken refuge abroad, and thus they often provided opportunities of pressure and blackmail on the émigrés. Before leaving Germany, many had spent time underground. If political exiles often had access to support networks and connections abroad,[197] this transition to a clandestine existence was far harder for writers, many of whom had not even the first idea how to protect themselves. Though the Nazis initially allowed any German citizen possessing a passport to leave the country, foreign governments adopted a wide range of measures to deal with these refugees. Czechoslovakia accepted them all, with or without papers; the French attitude fluctuated, while Switzerland and Austria threatened to hand them back to the Gestapo. In every case, it was hard for refugees to get permission to work, and if they sought permanent exile, their goods were immediately confiscated by the Nazi government.

Despite all these difficulties, a large number of antifascists did manage to leave Germany. Some made use of clandestine crossing points to reach the Saar, Austria, Switzerland or France, crossing the border at night disguised as climbers or with local assistance. The German population had not yet been cowed by the Nazi terror and were ready to come to their assistance, while they also benefited from a very real current of sympathy abroad. But illegal crossing became increasingly difficult, once the borders were guarded by the SS and neighbouring countries sought to defend themselves from this influx of refugees. The only remaining option was to cross the frontier as a tourist, on condition that the police were not over-attentive to the traveller's identity. Ludwig Marcuse left Germany alone, while his wife remained to pack up his books. He took a first-class couchette on the train so as not to attract attention. The SA greeted him politely and let him continue his journey. He managed in this way to reach the Saar, and from there the south of France. Manès Sperber wrote:

> They all behaved as if, in order to pass unnoticed, it was sufficient to suppress their identity and resemble a traveller in his Sunday best going off to a family or professional gathering. [. . .] It was only when the conductor, having opened the door of our compartment, asked us with a marked cordiality to show him our tickets, that it became clear how, out of ten travellers, at least four were not ordinary passengers but refugees.[198]

The most common thing was for antifascists to reach the border by stages, approaching slowly so as not to arouse suspicion. Walter Mehring was warned by a government employee that he had to leave Germany within two weeks to avoid being arrested. He still wanted to deliver a lecture before his departure. When he arrived at the venue he noticed SA men who were evidently lying in wait. He was questioned, but managed to pass for someone else, maintaining he was just there for a cup of coffee. He then immediately took the train for Paris. Most frequently, exiles never spoke to anyone before reaching the frontier, for fear of being denounced.[199] Wieland Herzfelde made out he was taking his wife to the train, then jumped on when the train started moving. Alfred Kantorowicz left for Davos with a medical certificate attesting that he had a lung problem. Theodor Plievier reached Dresden, then lay low for a few days. On the point of being discovered, he took the bus to Prague while the police lay in wait for him on a train. Many émigré memoirs relate the astonishing devices they were forced to invent:

   Harry Wilder managed to leave Germany by passing for a commercial traveller: he had stolen some catalogues and samples as part of his disguise. Fritz Erpenbeck dressed himself up as a music-hall performer and reached Prague with a false contract for an engagement there signed by two directors: Dr Weiss and Freimann (in reality Bruno Frei and F. C. Weiskopf). His name figured on the wanted list, but he escaped the police thanks to a mistake in his first name as well as to the theatrical costumes he was carrying – quite unusual for a Communist editor. Friedrich Wolf took advantage of a stay in the Alps to cross the border on skis. The Social-Democrat leader Otto Wels, accompanied by Siegfried Crummenerl, also crossed the frontier in mountaineering guise. Franz Schoenberner, an editor with *Simplicissimus*, likewise left Germany across the mountains near Lake Constance (19 March 1933). Wilhelm Eildermann, a KPD member, crossed the mountains to Czechoslovakia in a snowstorm, fearing to find himself back in Germany.[200] Willi Münzenberg, actively pursued by the SA, could not think of leaving Germany by train since his photo had been sent out to all border posts. He waited until 28 February to reach the Saar, as that was the day of Carnival. Paying little attention, the police let him pass without noticing that he had handed them a passport borrowed from another comrade. He then took refuge in France.

The scenarios by which people managed to leave Germany became increasingly complex.[201] Émigrés had to take a larger number of stages so as to cover their tracks. At that time the Saar played a particular role in the émigrés' transit. Some people could benefit from unusual complicity. A number of writers, and even Communist activists, were helped by SA men to cross the border or escape arrest. There were often cases where personal relations overrode political opposition, or of former Communists who had joined the SA, which recruited its members in the same proletarian milieus.[202]

In this way the first émigré colonies came to be formed, in capitals of all countries adjacent to Germany, often less by genuine choice of a country of refuge than because this offered the possibility of leaving the Reich. Few indeed considered a remote exile. Their concern on the contrary was to return as soon as possible, after a defeat of the Nazi regime which they deemed imminent. France, Czechoslovakia, the Netherlands, Austria and the Scandinavian countries were the initial major countries of asylum, but the geography of exile gradually shifted as the Nazi grip extended. The majority initially kept within the German-language zone, often speaking not of exile but of a mere 'withdrawal'. Gustav Regler wrote to his son that he was simply 'on leave'.[203] Döblin saw in Nazism just a 'storm', Klaus Mann gave the Hitler regime a few weeks or months, Heinrich Mann expected to return 'tomorrow or the day after'. More pessimistically, Harry Kessler gave Hitler two years, ex-Chancellor Brüning 'a year and a half'. They all believed that the regime would rapidly run out of steam, lacking any solid economic programme or diplomatic support, and trigger a violent revolt against it. To the degree that the Hitler regime consolidated itself they put back the date, but the majority continued to believe in its rapid collapse. The exile publications display the same optimism. Commenting on the executions of 30 June 1934, *Die Rundschau* maintained that 'just as children cry in the dark when they feel more afraid, so Hitler's demonstrations are all the more noisy and grotesque as he senses his coming fall.' This optimism – Manès Sperber spoke later of the 'intoxication of hope' – lasted until the War broke out. Walter Landauer wrote to Hermann Kesten on 14 December 1939: 'I believe we'll shortly be finished with this *"Hitlerei"*'; he hoped to return to Germany in 1940. Even Brecht, in his poems 'Duration of the Third Reich' and 'Thoughts on the Duration of Exile', maintained that the Thousand-Year Reich would not last the winter.

When Lotte H. Eisner arrived in Paris on 31 March 1933, her brother-in-law greeted her with the words: 'Well, you've come to France for a holiday.' Almost half a century later, she had not forgotten the reply she made at that time: 'Yes, but I'm sure it will be a long one.' Few émigrés indeed imagined at that time that many of them would die before they could return to Germany.[204]

3. STRUCTURAL FEATURES OF THE
ANTI-NAZI EMIGRATION

AN EMIGRATION WITHOUT UNITY

The German emigration [. . .] is far too heterogeneous in its mentality, talents and
human value to be able to judge it en bloc. But its members are linked by one common
bond, that they are all victims of this regime, an honour of which maybe not everyone
is worthy.

Thomas Mann, letter to Eduard Korrodi, 29 November 1935

The German emigration after 1933 was an exile of elites.

Hermann Kesten

One of the specific traits of the emigration engendered by Hitler's seizure of
power was certainly its surprising and unmistakable diversity. The very term
'émigré' is ambiguous. There were those who rejected it, and Brecht's famous
poem, 'Concerning the Label Emigrant' is evidence of this. Whether they called
themselves *Emigranten*, *Exilanten*, *Verstossene*, *Vertriebene*, *Verbannte*, how
can one encompass, in a single notion, that some left Germany by choice, others
by force, and that the only thing uniting them was that they left Germany
because of National Socialism? The majority of definitions of this emigration
that are offered thus inevitably lack rigour. Helga Pross[205] defined exile as 'the
involuntary migration of isolated individuals or groups into a distant country'
as the result of political, social, religious or economic circumstances. But the
émigrés of 1933 were not all involuntary or proscribed. Some left Germany
voluntarily. And why just a 'distant country'? Was Brecht in Denmark any the
less in exile than Paul Zech in Argentina? Moreover, Pross's notion gives no
importance to either racial persecution or moral motivation. Werner Vordtriede[206] in his 'typology of an exile literature' proposed to consider as belonging
to this literature works written by authors animated by nostalgia, solitude,
sadness and suffering for their country. But this notion of quasi-metaphysical
exile could apply equally to Novalis or Hölderlin.[207] The antifascist émigré
might well be a stranger on the earth, but not just any kind of stranger.

Nazi jurisdiction distinguished in a fairly confused fashion two types of
émigrés: those who left Germany for 'racial' reasons – Jews for the most part,
who were excluded from economic and cultural life by the laws of 7 April 1933
and the later Nuremberg laws – and those who had expressed their opposition to
National Socialism either before or after 1933. In distinction to the 'racial
refugees', the Nazis termed the latter group 'political refugees' (*politische
Flüchtlinge*). This overly vague distinction hardly makes it possible to grasp
the emigration as a whole. Peter Stahlberger designates as 'political émigrés' all
those Germans who struggled against National Socialism in exile by way of
political or literary activity.[208] But the émigrés did not all have the same
relationship to politics. Some who had been apolitical in 1933 became politicized in exile. Others, politically active under the Weimar Republic, went into
exile but did not struggle against fascism. Stahlberger moreover restricts himself

to Germans, while it would be better to speak of a 'German-language emigration'. It was also because of National Socialism that Austrians such as Robert Musil, Hermann Broch, Stefan Zweig, Josef Roth and Alfred Polgar, Czechs such as Max Brod, Egon Erwin Kisch and Ernst Weiss, Hungarians such as A. Gabor, Julius Hay, Ödön von Horvath and Georg Lukács, Frenchmen such as René Schickele, Poles such as Manès Sperber, were found in the exile community. The occupation of Austria, then of Czechoslovakia, forced into exile opponents of Nazism and Jews who were not German nationals.[209]

The emigrants themselves never stopped stressing the heteroclite nature of their diaspora. Ludwig Marcuse maintained: 'I had the impression that there were dozens of left-wing political sects among the German exiles. If I try and list them today, I do not always succeed.'[210] And Golo Mann noted:

> The writers in exile had nothing to do with the German state as it now presented itself. They rejected it entirely, and this state likewise rejected them. This rejection, this independence and this freedom in relation to what had been decreed in the name of the German state was something they all had in common. Apart from this they actually showed very few common features, being a mixture of conservatives and revolutionaries, romantics and socialists, so that no common label was possible.[211]

Alfred Kantorowicz maintains in the same way that the émigrés 'did not form a unity. Every current (however sectarian), both intellectual and political, of Europe in the first half of the twentieth century was represented. [. . .] Apart from their hostility to Hitler, there was no common denominator that united the exiled German-speaking writers [. . .]. Those who left Germany represented every imaginable shade of the century's literature.'[212]

In the case of both writers and political activists, their diversity seemed to defy all classification. There certainly were particular 'currents' that displayed an effective unity: the Communists, for example. But between 1933 and 1945, a number of writers and militants would break with the party (Manès Sperber, Gustav Regler, Willi Münzenberg), some even becoming famous anti-Communists (Ruth Fischer, Arthur Koestler, Margaret Buber-Neumann). As for the Social-Democrats, if they did not display the same rigorous unity as the Communists in 1933, having already had the experience of internal dissidence, they developed into different groups that were often mutually hostile, each based in a particular place of exile: Prague, Amsterdam, Stockholm, Paris, New York. Divided into right and left, into currents that were reformist or revolutionary, accepting or rejecting a rapprochement with the Communists – in particular after the Front Populaire had been established in Paris – the range of their ideological shadings ran from those ready to ally with the Communists to those who preferred the Schwarze Front of Otto Strasser. Just to take the example of the refugee Social-Democrats in the United States during the Second World War, it is often hard to ascertain in what respect they were still Socialist. Exile did not manage to silence the fratricidal strife of the left-wing parties that had been so destructive under the Weimar Republic. On the contrary, this often intensified.[213] And there was no more unity among émigrés of the right or the Catholic centre – Strasser, Rauschning, Brüning, etc.

The literary emigration displayed the same heterogeneity. Divided on the political level between Communists, Socialists, republicans, pacifists, liberals, democrats, conservatives and apolitical, they were just as divided in the literary sphere. The émigré writers included expressionists, Dadaists, 'classics', proletarian novelists, popular novelists, avant-gardists, with nothing in common save that they wrote in German and rejected the Hitler regime. Klaus Mann indeed maintains that at least after 1933 the émigré writers shared the illusion of making up a community, but this is denied by many others. Thomas Mann and Lion Feuchtwanger, who had never met before 1933 despite living in the same town, may well have met regularly in exile, but Alfred Döblin claims that even in these years writers remained apart, 'each living for himself'. The material conditions of exile alone were enough to make any unity questionable. Hans Mayer rightly notes[214] that the inability of the majority of writers to give an adequate description of the exile experience was not because of any specific weakness of 'exile literature' but simply because the idea of exile as a collective fate is a 'fiction'. While all writers had in common a certain number of experiences – nostalgia for Germany, solitude, material difficulties, administrative harassment, linguistic conflicts – these problems inherent to any exile were experienced very differently as a function of their respective fame. In Switzerland, Hans Mayer recalls, the police expelled émigrés without resources, but 'a solid bank account well provided with solid Swiss francs guaranteed your safety as long as the money did not run out.'[215] Access to many countries depended on a number of factors – celebrity, usefulness to the host country, material resources. Money was lent to those likely to profit from it, while those who might be a burden on the country of asylum were systematically repulsed. For the émigré who lacked resources, the only recourse was disguised begging from aid committees, charitable organizations or more fortunate exiles. Thomas Mann would never have trouble finding a home or a country to settle in; many nations would consider it an honour to grant him citizenship. But this was clearly not the case with a Communist activist, an untranslated writer, or an unknown journalist. When Chancellor Brüning requested a visa, he was immediately received by the French consul in London. Many other émigrés had to wait months before they got a notice of refusal. And when what was at stake were the lives of antifascists in France threatened by the advance of the German army, obtaining an affidavit, the indispensable condition for reaching America, depended largely on the émigré's financial resources. Some fell into the hands of the Gestapo for want of money for a rail ticket to Barcelona or Lisbon. What was there in common even between two politicians such as Chancellor Brüning and Rudolf Hilferding, the one a professor at Harvard and guest of the highest political figures, the other abandoned in France without money and murdered by the Gestapo? The social differences among writers were still more acute. Some survived with difficulty in cheap hotels, trying to write novels that no one wanted to publish, eating in soup kitchens and scrounging a bit of money from magazines. Others, such as Mann or Feuchtwanger, never had to give up the luxury to which they had been accustomed before 1933. Heinrich Mann lived in a state close to poverty just a few kilometres from Lion Feuchtwanger, who dictated his bestsellers among his precious books and period furniture. Finally, the fact that such different reasons drove people into exile ruined in advance all émigré unity. It would be wrong to feel astonishment therefore at the contradictory character of the first classifications attempted by the émigrés themselves, as evidenced by essays of Alfred Döblin and Walter A. Berendsohn.

Döblin's brief work, *Die deutsche Literatur im Ausland seit 1933. Ein Dialog zwischen Politik und Kunst*, was published in Paris in 1938. He divided German literature into three currents:

1. A conservative current, oriented towards the past, comprising writers such as W. von Scholz, H. Stucken, R. G. Binding, W. von Molo, H. Carossa, H. Stehr, P. Ernst, J. Ponten, W. Schäfer, E. G. Kolbenheyer, as well as Ricarda Huch and Stefan George.
2. An intellectually revolutionary (*geistesrevolutionär*) current, represented by writers such as Georg Kaiser, Carl Sternheim, Fritz von Unruh, Bertolt Brecht, Ernst Toller, Else Lasker-Schüler, Alfred Wolfenstein, Franz Werfel, Franz Kafka, Ernst Weiss, Leonhard Frank, Hermann Kesten, Josef Roth, Anna Seghers, Gustav Regler, Ernst Jünger, Arnolt Bronnen and Ernst von Salomon.
3. A humanist current, comprising Heinrich Mann, Gerhart Hauptmann, Thomas Mann, Jacob Wasserman, Bruno Frank, Hugo von Hoffmannsthal and Arthur Schnitzler.

Döblin maintains that all three groups were affected by the *Gleichschaltung* of 1933, but in different ways. The conservatives were often tempted to accept it. The 'humanist' group, most seriously threatened by events, emigrated in large part, while the 'intellectually revolutionary' group split into a right and a left wing. Döblin's characterization is not completely wrong, but it is too vague to offer a precise analysis of the emigration. The '*geistesrevolutionär*' notion expresses this vagueness, as it is capable of covering expressionist writers, pacifists, monarchists, apolitical, Communist and far right.

The same ambiguity can be found in the essay by Walter A. Berendsohn, *Einführung in die deutsche Emigranten-Literatur*, the two sections of which were combined under the title *Die humanistische Front*. Alfred Kantorowicz remarks[216] that while this classification may be appropriate for Socialist, Communist, pacifist, liberal and republican writers, all those who left Germany for moral reasons or because of racial persecution, it is hard to include among the 'humanists' such right-wing figures as Chancellor Brüning, Hermann Rauschning, Otto Strasser (a deeply anti-Semitic Nazi dissident), or the SA émigrés in China. Yet Berendsohn also asserts the existence of a community among the emigrants and compares the emigration as a whole to 'an orchestra playing on a large number of instruments'.

The diversity of the emigration was a function of the broad ideological spectrum that it represented, but also of the heterogeneity of those whom the

Nazis forced into exile: Communists, Socialists, republicans, liberals, pacifists, monarchists, conservatives, Catholics and Protestants, as well as a mass of German and Austrian citizens of Jewish origin who had never been involved in any political activity. Despite this heterogeneity, however, it is possible to distinguish summarily at least three main components in the emigration engendered by National Socialism: the massive emigration of Jews in the wake of racial persecution, which reached its apogee after 1938; the political emigration made up of political activists and opponents of the regime; and the literary, artistic and intellectual emigration, which, without necessarily having taken part in antifascist struggle before 1933, rejected the new regime. These three categories, however, cannot be rigorously separated: the émigré Jews included genuine opponents of the Nazis, while many activists or anti-Nazi writers were of Jewish origin. It was not for the most part as Jews, however, that they emigrated in 1933, and it was not as Jews – with some notable exceptions – that they were sent to concentration camp. In the eyes of the Nazis, they were political opponents. Finally, the distinction between 'political émigrés' and 'literary émigrés' breaks down in a number of cases; activists and writers took part in common actions, wrote propaganda pamphlets, anti-Nazi leaflets and texts. Even those who had never been previously involved in politics felt 'forced into politics' as Thomas Mann put it. The exile of a poet who left Germany in 1933 was also a political act. The Nazis, for their part, rapidly came to consider all of them as oppositionists. Yet it is still hard to summarize the unity of these different components.

THE 'RACIAL' EMIGRATION

First the Jews had been deprived of their professions; they were forbidden the theatres, the movies, the museums, and scholars lost the use of the libraries; they had stayed because of loyalty or indolence, cowardice or pride. They preferred being humiliated at home to humiliating themselves as beggars abroad.

Stefan Zweig, *The World of Yesterday*

For my part, I would say: there are *also* decent Jews, a few, less than 10 per cent as the emigration figures show. I except them, I have the greatest esteem for them, for their silent suffering, but . . . But? The rest are worthless.

It is not true that the Germans had been Jewified. It was rather that the German Jews had been bochified.

Kurt Tucholsky, letter to Arnold Zweig

In 1933 the Jewish population in Germany was around half a million,[217] 76 per cent of whom had been born in the country, the remainder almost all in Eastern Europe. Some 80 per cent of the total were German citizens. Taken as a whole, this was one of the most assimilated Jewish communities in Europe. For several generations Jews had played a major role in Germany's political, economic and cultural life, and they often considered themselves more German than Jewish. Only the religious factor, which was generally quite weak,[218] made it possible to distinguish them. If the Jewish community was aware that its emancipation had been made possible by a certain climate of liberalism, the erosion of this ideal with the First World War and its aftermath was to deeply divide German Jews. Often assimilated into the bourgeoisie or petty bourgeoisie, they shared the reactionary and nationalist ideas of these classes. Ernst Bloch was profoundly shocked to see his professor Georg Simmel, who as a Jew could never reach the top of the academic hierarchy, in the uniform of a reserve officer.[219] A large section of the Jewish bourgeoisie were ready to support nationalist ideals and the expansionist policy of Wilhelm II. Often seeking to be still more nationalist and patriotic than non-Jewish Germans, they hoped thereby to escape any reproach from the right. And yet it was liberalism that best defined the aspirations of the majority of German Jews, as shown by their major role in literature and journalism.

This attitude was not shared by their children after 1914. Many of these questioned both assimilation – the 'Jewish–German symbiosis' – and liberalism. They were often tempted by Zionism, by a romantic return to Jewish tradition, or by commitment on the side of the workers' parties, Communism or a messianic socialism striking them as the best defence against a return of anti-Semitism.[220] It is this movement that explains works as close – and as distant – as those of Walter Benjamin, Gershom Scholem, Georg Lukács and Ernst Bloch.[221] The Jewish bourgeoisie remained outside these movements and generally disapproved of them. Attached to assimilation, they could not imagine that anyone could deny their membership of the national community.

On 1 April 1933, however, a general boycott of Jewish businesses was organized under the direction of Julius Streicher. A series of measures (7 April) excluded Jews from public offices. On 22 April, Jewish doctors were expelled from social security boards. This anti-Semitism, already of a scope that few had predicted, steadily increased until the promulgation of the Nuremberg laws that completely removed Jews from social, political and cultural life. The German Jewish community was tempted to see in the initial demonstrations no more than 'populist excesses' coming from uncontrolled elements. To protect themselves from reprisals, they were ready to give the lie to rumours from abroad that portrayed their situation in the gloomiest colours, though a reading of *Mein Kampf*, or the writings of Goebbels and Rosenberg, gave little room for ambiguity. A 'Union of German National Jews' was even formed, directed by Dr Max Naumann, which tried to reconcile Jewish interests with National Socialism. Leaving this extreme position aside, it is clear that the majority of German Jews did not seem to take Hitler's first measures seriously. A number of Jewish personalities publicly denounced the campaigns against Nazi anti-Semitism being organized abroad.[222] Feeling often more German than Jewish,[223] very few were prepared to emigrate. Not all even disapproved of the Nazi programme, even if they deplored its populist anti-Semitism. They too were champions of a national renaissance. As for the intellectuals, their relationship to the Jewish community was often highly tenuous. Kurt Tucholsky had broken with Judaism and saw himself as a Berliner.[224] Alfred Döblin had so little idea of Jews that he decided to visit Poland to see what they were like, and returned with an almost ethnological depiction.[225] Jacob Wassermann spoke of his trajectory 'as a German and Jew', while Fred Uhlmann evoked this assimilation very well in his novel *The Rediscovered Friend*.[226]

It was often Nazi anti-Semitism that gave back to German Jews an awareness of their identity. Yet the majority were sufficiently attached to Germany that they clung on to the least possibility of remaining, all the more so as there were very few countries prepared to accept them. The *Völkische Beobachter* waxed ironic, not altogether without reason, on the protestations of sympathy towards the mistreatment of Jews in Germany by foreign countries who sought to lock their gates in the face of Jewish emigration. Only 25,000 Jews left Germany during the first half of 1933, 50,000 between 1 July 1933 and 15 September 1935, and 100,000 in the two following years.[227] In leaving Germany, they had to abandon nine-tenths of their assets. Palestine was the only country ready to accept them, and this was the destination of 40 per cent in this period. For some, to be forced into exile was so insupportable that they preferred to take their lives rather than leave Germany, or later Austria. The boycott was sufficiently complete that the majority of Jews remaining in Germany could survive only with the help of Jewish charities.[228] After 1938 they were totally eliminated from economic life. Twenty thousand Jews were expelled from Germany even though they had lived there for many years. The '*Kristallnacht*' pogroms destroyed 7,500 Jewish shops and 191 synagogues, while 20,000 people were arrested and thirty-six murdered. Yet at the end of 1937, 350,000 Jews had continued to live in Berlin. The majority went into exile only when their conditions of existence, indeed of survival, were completely destroyed. Often it was then too late. And it was also for these Jewish émigrés that the separation from Germany seemed the most painful.[229]

Deeply attached to Germany, many of these Jewish émigrés had very little in common with political émigrés or oppositionists in exile.[230] They often avoided seeing them. The political exiles, for their part, displayed real annoyance when they heard *their* emigration, with its ideological motivation, equated with the 'racial' Jewish emigration. They were also affronted by the behaviour of these exiles, issuing from the Jewish bourgeoisie or petty bourgeoisie, who despite their exile had not acquired the least political awareness. Theodor Csokor describes[231] a Jewish businessman he met in Italy, who could not hide his admiration for Hitler and his regret at his stupid anti-Semitism.[232] Hans Jacob maintained that even in exile these émigrés remained Jewish Germans rather than German Jews.[233] Lion Feuchtwanger refused to be grouped together with 'those who would gladly have remained in Germany if they had not been deprived there of their means of existence'.[234] Klaus Mann often waxed ironic at those Jews who even in exile remained 'good citizens', 'good Germans', and refused to be seen as political oppositionists. On the boat taking him to the United States, Döblin could not conceal his anger in talking to some Jewish émigrés. One of them uttered views that were openly Nazi, even though he had himself been released from concentration camp. Döblin saw them dress for their evening and dance as if they were in Berlin or Frankfurt, and found them surprisingly strange.[235] It was for the same reasons that Heinrich Mann, in his essay 'In Defence of Culture',[236] regretted that the exile propaganda insisted so exclusively on anti-Semitic persecution. While he naturally recognized the need to denounce the suffering inflicted on the Jews in Germany, he believed that it was not just Jewish defence committees that should speak at meetings, as the emigration included opponents of the Nazis who were not threatened as Jews. He likewise emphasized in his autobiography: 'Even in the Academy of Fine Arts, convictions were proclaimed and members left it in the face of the new regime's anti-intellectual demonstrations. These included far more of so-called German race than Jews. It is even worth noting that the latter did not all leave when they could honorably do so. Several were expelled after having insidiously declared their support for the regime.'[237]

For the same reasons, Anna Seghers, a Communist novelist of Jewish origin, refused to be published in an anthology of Jewish writers banned in Germany that Hermann Kesten was preparing.[238] A number of émigrés, nonetheless, were continuously identified by their origins. Even Döblin, who ended up by converting to Catholicism together with his whole family, sent Kesten his 'best Jewish greetings'. Albert Ehrenstein projected in 1933 an essay on the Jewish question.[239] Sigmund Freud hesitated over publishing in London his essay on 'Moses and Monotheism' in which he claimed that Moses was an Egyptian. These emotional reactions to Nazi anti-Semitism were not made to smooth over differences between Jewish and non-Jewish émigrés. Franz Schonauer complained that the first number of Die Sammlung was almost entirely made up of contributions from Jewish writers,[240] believing it was very clumsy tactics to suggest that only Jews were enemies of the Nazi regime. Max Hermann-Neisse expressed himself in similar terms in a letter to Kesten of 17 January 1934. He recalled his completely 'Aryan' background and affirmed: 'The world should be shown that it is not just Jewish artists who have been driven out as Jews from this country that has gone mad, but also poets of "purely German" origin [. . .] who can or will no longer live in today's Germany.'[241] Their hostility towards certain apolitical Jewish exiles, whose only concern was the possibility of an early return to Germany, is all the more readily explained as the very reason these intellectuals had gone into exile was their refusal to accept anti-Semitism, the clearest expression of the regime's barbarity.

POLITICAL EMIGRATION

Political emigration formed the second component of the exile community. It was extremely diverse and reflected in this the great variety of ideological tendencies that Nazism intended to eradicate from German life. After the Reichstag fire, the workers' parties saw themselves deprived of any possibility of action, let alone opposition. Their only remaining choice was between underground work in the most perilous conditions, continuing their struggle in exile, or being sent to concentration camps. No party of the left was really prepared for illegal work. The wave of arrests that followed the Reichstag fire decimated the hierarchy of Communist cadres in a single night. Those functionaries who escaped arrest often had no further precise orders, while the party's centralized structure permitted only an organized form of struggle. The Social-Democratic party for its part did not long survive the Communists. Political activity was relaunched from exile in Prague, Moscow, Paris, London and Copenhagen, often on the basis of new divisions, even if a few clandestine Communist papers – *Das Ruhr-Echo, Die Hamburger Volkszeitung, Die Rote Fahne* – did make their appearance from March 1933 onwards. Until October 1935, the date of the KPD's 'Brussels conference', there was no real will for unity of the workers' parties against fascism at the official level. A self-criticism of Communist strategy was only undertaken with Dimitrov's speech at the Seventh Congress of the Communist International, which affirmed the idea of a single front against fascism. Divisions continued until 1945, and intensified to the degree that the Social-Democrats broke up into factions in the wake of European political events and the vicissitudes of exile.

Besides the two major workers' parties there were smaller political formations as well, dissenting Socialist factions as well as those issuing from the Catholic Centre, from conservative milieus, not to mention turncoats and dissidents from the NSDAP. As well as Communist, Socialists, liberals and republicans, the political refugees included conservatives, monarchists, and a few individuals who had played a major role in the Weimar years. The following attempt at classification is purely indicative, and makes no claim of comprehensiveness. It will however give a glimpse of the complex mosaic that the political emigration made up.

Aristocrat, monarchist, conservative and republican

If a large number of representatives of the Prussian aristocracy agreed to continue serving in the Hitlerite army, there were some who went over to the opposition. Some did so at the beginning of the Nazi era, forming a kind of 'internal emigration', others more belatedly, taking part in the plot against Hitler or rallying in the Soviet Union to the Freies Deutschland movement formed among POWs with a view to hastening the end of the War. Monarchist aristocrats who went into exile included Otto von Habsburg[242] and the former head of the Austrian defence force Ernst Rüdiger Fürst von Starhemberg.[243] The emigrants included a number of princes and counts: Max Karl Prinz zu Hohenlohe-Langenburg,[244] Hubertus Friedrich Prinz zu Löwenstein-Wertheim-Freudenberg,[245] Richard Graf Coudenhove-Kalergi[246] and Harry Graf Kessler, who had long been a republican.

Champions of the Austro-Hungarian monarchy

Otto von Habsburg was not the only monarchist in exile. After 1938 there was a significant Austrian legitimist emigration. The democratic parties, banned four years before the *Anschluss*, had been repressed by a clerical and fascisizing coalition which had to flee abroad in its turn after the Hitlerite invasion.[247] This monarchist opposition was one of the most disciplined, publishing a regular journal *Oesterreichische Post*. It rallied to its cause not only political figures such as Martin Fuchs, but also such writers as Franz Werfel, Alexander Roda-

Roda, S. Morgenstern and above all Joseph Roth, author of *The Radetsky March*, one of the most famous evocations of the old emperor Franz-Josef, a veritable hymn to the Austro-Hungarian monarchy that had been so liberal for the Jews.

Former political figures from the Weimar Republic

The majority of these did not play any major role in exile. If some, like Gustav Noske, remained in Germany, even profiting from a pension paid by the Nazis for having crushed the Spartacists, others chose a more or less discreet exile. Philipp Scheidemann, termed a 'November traitor' by the Nazis, left for Czechslovakia, then Denmark, where he died in 1939. Joseph Wirth, a left Catholic, emigrated to Switzerland and did not return to Germany until 1948; he had no influence at all throughout the exile years. Ex-Chancellor Brüning took no part in the exile struggle. The exiles included the former Prussian prime minister Otto Braun, who died in Switzerland in 1956, and some very important Social-Democratic figures such as Otto Wels (died in France), Robert Breitscheid and Rudolf Hilferding (handed by the French authorities to the Gestapo and murdered). There is generally a striking contrast between the high responsibilities that they exercised during the Weimar period and the little significance they had in exile. Heinrich Mann occupied a more important position in émigré politics than any parliamentarian of the Weimar Republic.

Conservatives

A certain number of conservative personalities also took the path of exile, even if the Nazis had not tried to arrest them. This was the case of the writer Balder Olden, a former officer of the imperial forces in Africa and author of the celebrated article 'Nothing in particular would have happened to me' (*Mir wäre nichts besonders passiert*). His novel on Africa had been hailed by the conservatives. He went on to play a major part in exile.

Catholics and Protestants

Though large sections of the German churches collaborated with the Nazi regime, a number of religious figures went into exile, the most well known being the theologian Paul Tillich. These were most often either theologians, churchmen, or figures who could endorse neither the suicide of the Catholic parties nor the collaboration of a section of the Protestant church with the Nazis. Prinz Hubertus zu Löwenstein, a member of the Reichsbanner, belonged to this left Catholic opposition, even fighting on the Republican side in Spain. Karl Spiecker published the review *Das Wahre Deutschland*.

Pacifists

This was one of the most substantial émigré families. If they tended to divide into various tendencies (some favouring an alliance with the Communists, others not), they counted in their ranks several former contributors to *Die Weltbühne*, friends of Carl von Ossietzky such as Alfred Falk, F. W. Foerster, Hellmut von Gerlach, Kurt Grossmann (secretary of the German Human

Rights League), Emil Gumbel (removed from his Heidelberg chair in 1933 for having denounced the crimes of the 'black Reichswehr'), Otto Lehmann-Russbüldt (member of the Human Rights League), Egon Erwin Kisch (well-known for his reportages, which he elevated to the rank of a literary genre), Berthold Salomon (aka Berthold Jacob), a contributor to *Die Weltbühne*, later kidnapped by the Nazis in Switzerland, released but ultimately murdered by the Gestapo, Ludwig Quidde (member of the Deutsche Friedengesellschaft) and Hermann Kantorowicz (one of twenty-five professors expelled from university in 1933 on Hitler's order for their pacifist ideas).

Alongside these pacifist figures can be ranked a certain number of writers with pacifist ideas, even if their ideologies were very varied: the libertarian Kurt Hiller, who had formed the group of 'revolutionary pacifists' in 1923, and Fritz von Unruh, an officer who had turned to pacifism after the Great War. A certain number of writers left Germany because of their pacifist ideas, such as Ernst Toller, Walter Hasenclever, Armin T. Wegner, Rudolf Leonhard, Leonhard Frank, René Schickele, etc.

National-bolsheviks and turncoats from National Socialism
The most significant among the latter category in exile was the Schwarze Front of Otto Strasser, who had left the NSDAP in July 1930 to form the opposition group Kampfgemeinschaft revolutionärer Nationalsozialisten, other members being Major Buchrucker, Herbert Blank and Eugen Mossakowsky. Strasser's group merged with the Tatkreis and the Bündische Jugend, a section of the Stahlhelme, the Werwölfe, the Order of Young Germans, and Claus Hein's Revolutionary Peasants to give rise to a heteroclite gathering under the name of the Schwarze Front: black, Strasser specified, 'for black suggests invisibility and intangibility to the German mind'.[248] Strasser went into exile in Austria and then Czechoslovakia, continuing his struggle against Hitler by publishing pamphlets and especially by establishing in Prague a 'black transmitter' broadcasting to Germany. His radio engineer, Rudolf Formis, was murdered in Prague by the SS on the Gestapo's orders, in particularly horrific circumstances. Strasser smuggled into Germany in the course of his exile a certain number of pamphlets and newspapers such as the *Huttenbriefe*.[249] Between 1933 and 1937 he used his magazine, *Deutsche Revolution*, to try and organize a 'third front' that rejected both collectivism and bourgeois individualism, as an alternative to the fascism/communism dichotomy. The confusion of his political ideas and his aspiration to a mystic and anti-Prussian socialism, not to mention his anti-Semitism, scarcely enabled him to play a major role in exile, even if the right-wing Social-Democrats and Brüning considered a rapprochement with him.

Hermann Rauschning was a further turncoat from National Socialism. Born 7 August 1887, he joined the Nazi party in 1931 and the next year represented the Danziger Landbund. In 1933, thanks to Nazi and Centre votes, he was chosen as president of the Danzig senate. After a conflict with Hitler he emigrated to Poland, subsequently to Switzerland, France, England and the United States. Known worldwide for two works, *The Revolution of Nihilism* and *Hitler Speaks*, he was the symbol in exile of the right-wing opposition to

Nazism, enjoyed a broad intellectual credit and exercised a certain influence through to the Cold War.

Fritz Thyssen had financed Ludendorff and Hitler in 1923, becoming a member of the NSDAP in 1931. But in 1939 he viewed the risk of a global conflict as the likely ruin of the German economy and broke with the Nazis. After the invasion of France he was arrested by the Gestapo, brought back to Germany and interned in a mental hospital at Babelsberg, then sent to concentration camp. Yet he still managed to emigrate, and died in Argentina in 1952.[250] The right-wing emigration also included a certain number of SA men who took refuge in Shanghai, several of whom never returned to Germany and in some cases settled in Taiwan.

Just as hard to classify are the exiles of a national-bolshevik stamp. A certain number of these remained in Germany and even formed for a while an open opposition, especially Ernst Niekisch and the Widerstand circle, but others emigrated. These included the playwright Peter Martin Lampel and the 'left people of the right':[251] Karl O. Paetel, close to Niekisch and Jünger, Hans Ebeling, Bodo Uhse, Ludwig Renn, Eduard Kobel. While some remained hostile to Communism, others drifted towards it, often mixing their attachment to 'revolutionary nationalism' with left-wing slogans, which makes their ideological positions hard to characterize.

Anti-Communists

Other groups of exiles formed around reviews and personalities were equally hostile to Nazism and to Communism. The most well-known example is that of the Deutsche Freiheitspartei (1936 to early 1937), which united in Paris and London elements that were heterogeneous and even mutually antagonistic. This included right-wing figures such as Hermann Rauschning, Social-Democrats such as Robert Breitscheid, and former members of the KPD such as Willi Münzenberg. The London group was led by August Weber and Hans Albert Kluthe, that in Paris by Otto Klepper and Karl Spiecker. They sought to establish contacts with opponents of the Nazis in Germany, especially in the army and universities. Their German colleagues were discovered by the Gestapo, and tried in Berlin in 1939. Their bulletins, the *Deutsche Freiheitsbriefe*, were distributed in Germany in the form of leaflets, and from January 1938 until November-December 1940 they published *Das Wahre Deutschland*. The Deutsche Freiheitspartei rejected any distinction between Communists and Nazis: 'A red dictatorship is as cruel as a brown one, and Stalin's crimes are no different from those of Hitler. We want nothing to do with people who defend this policy,' declared *Das Wahre Deutschland* in 1939.

Social-Democrats

Though the SPD had three times as many members as the KPD, this numerical superiority was not to be found in the exile milieu. A certain number of Social-Democrats remained in Germany and made their peace with the regime, others continued an underground struggle alongside the Communists, despite official instructions against this. The majority of Social-Democrats in exile were based in Prague, Paris and London.[252] They remained divided between different factions, which continued to evolve in the course of exile. The Prague leadership was first of all rejected by those who stayed in Germany, hoping in this way to salvage their party. They subsequently split over a number of questions (the respective responsibilities of the left parties in Hitler's victory, relations with the Communists, commitment to the Popular Front, relations with other exile groups, the future of Germany, etc.). Each group often published its own reviews and newspapers.

After the banning of the Social-Democratic Party on 23 June 1933, its leaders Otto Wels, Hans Vogel and Erich Ollenhauer left for exile, and the core of the party's activities shifted to Prague where the Parteivorstand der SoPaDe was formed around Wels. Vogel and Ollenhauer moved to London where they formed the Union deutscher sozialistischer Organisationen im Grossbritannien. The initial programme of the SPD in exile (July 1933) maintained the primacy of the struggle against Hitler.[253] The SoPaDe sought a leading place in the anti-Nazi fight. It proposed to gather and distribute information on the regime, and support the resistance. At the same time, the Socialists attacked the Communists and rejected any dictatorship of the proletariat (*Die historische Aufgabe der deutschen Sozialdemokratie*). In summer 1938 the Parteivorstand had to leave Prague for Paris, after the Czech government was constrained to give in to Hitler's demands and limit ever further the scope of exile action. After the dissolution of the Parteivorstand in 1940, Ollenhauer and Vogel moved to London as representatives of the Vorstand der sozial-demokratischen Partei Deutschlands. A number of German Socialist groups came together in London, united by a hostility to the Communists that was reinforced by the German–Soviet pact. In 1945 they published the *Politische Kundgebungen und programmatische Richtlinen der Union deutscher sozialisticher Organisationen in Grossbritannien*. Erich Ollenhauer had already defined on 6 December 1942 the *Möglichkeiten und Aufgaben einer geeinten sozialistischen Partei in Deutschland*, which still rejected any alliance with the Communists.

Other Socialist groups also played a significant part in exile activity. The Sozialistische Arbeiterpartei (SAP) had been formed in 1931 by Max Seydewitz and Kurt Rosenfeld as a splinter group from the SPD. Its founders decreed the dissolution of the party after 1933. But new SAP groups formed in exile, sometimes close to the Trotskyists, but separating from the latter when these condemned the idea of a Popular Front with the Communists. The SAP called itself 'Marxist-Leninist' but refused to submit to the Comintern. It published *Die Neue Front* which appeared in Germany until 1931, then in Paris from 1933 to 1939, with its main contributors being Peter Anders, H. Diesel, K. Frank, Paul Fröhlich, F. Sternberg, F. Thomas. There was also the *Marxistische Tribune. Discussionblätter für Arbeiterpolitik* with E. Bauer, Willi Brandt, John Ewars, Marta Koch, K. W. Neuendorf, K. Sachs and A. Schifrin. The SAP was especially active in the Scandinavian countries, Sweden in particular.

The diversity of Socialist émigrés in the United States makes it hard to analyse their theories. Some rejected any relationship to Marxism and claimed allegiance to Lassalle. They included Wilhelm Sollman (interior minister under

Stresemann), Max Sievers, Fritz Tegessy, and the Sudeten Social-Democrats Wenzel, Franzel, etc. They often displayed a very virulent anti-Communism, and their more right-wing elements considered a rapprochement with Otto Strasser's Schwarze Front. Several of them may be considered direct forerunners of McCarthyism. Certain dissident Socialist or oppositional groups were strong enough to bother the SPD leadership, others had no more than a few hundred supporters. Among the left oppositionists, the most well-known group was that formed in 1931 by Walter Löwenheim, with former Communists and opposition Social-Democrats from the party's left wing. When Löwenheim published in Prague in 1933 the pamphlet *Neu Beginnen! Faschismus oder Sozialismus. Als Diskussionsgrundlage der Sozialisten Deutschlands*, the name Neu Beginnen was taken over for the group. It included in particular Fritz Erler, Karl Frank, Waldemar von Koeringen, Richard Löwenthal, Erich Schmidt and Erwin Schoettle. Criticizing the SPD and the KPD for their failure to understand Nazism, this group tried to develop a new strategy, uniting between 300 and 1,000 followers under its slogans.

Very often, the exiled Socialist groups gathered around a figure or a journal, and it is impossible to analyse here the complexity of their ideological relations with the SoPaDe. Among those that need mention, however, are the *Zeitschrift für Sozialismus*, initially edited from Prague by Rudolf Hilferding, which set out to be an independent theoretical and critical journal; and *Der Kampf*, which appeared from May 1934 to 1938 under the direction of Otto Bauer. Founded by Austrian and German Social-Democrats (Otto Bauer, Karl Renner, Adolf Braun), this journal saw itself in the line of Friedrich Adler (who published a journal of the same title during the First World War) and proposed to unite Social-Democrats of the left. In 1938 it changed its name to *Der Sozialistische Kampf* and moved to Paris. It should be stressed that the majority of Socialist exiles remained divided over essential questions, the most important being that of the Popular Front and relations with the Communists. On top of the differences that originated in the political situation under the Weimar Republic and the fratricidal strife and distrust between the two workers' parties, new divergences opened up in exile. Right-wing Socialists such as Robert Breuer converged with the Communists, Robert Breitscheid defended the united front, while Friedrich Stampfer was always hostile to it and steadily moved more to the right. Some, like Erich Kuttner, would fight on their own initiative in the International Brigades, while others rejected this. In several cases, encounter with the American context often completed the distancing from any reference to socialism.

Communists

The Communists certainly displayed greater ideological unity than that of other groups, even if the same was not true of writers close to the KPD.[254] In 1932 the party had decided to set up an emergency network in case it was forced underground. That however did not prevent the massive arrest of its militants. Following the arrest of Ernst Thälmann, an exiled leadership in Paris was formed by Franz Dahlem, Wilhelm Florin and Wilhelm Pieck, the latter having senior responsibility. The other politburo members – John Schehr, Hermann

Schubert, Fritz Schulte and Walter Ulbricht – continued to represent the KPD leadership in Germany. Relations between the two leading groups were maintained by way of clandestine couriers. In autumn 1933 the Paris leadership prevailed on those members remaining in Germany to leave for Paris, for reasons of security. Only John Schehr remained in Germany after October 1933. Other Communists left for Prague or Moscow. On 16 January 1935 the politburo decided that the leadership would shift to Moscow, with Franz Dahlem and Walter Ulbricht responsible in Prague for illegal resistance. Though essential decisions on the work of the KPD in exile were shared between Moscow, Prague and Paris, Communist émigrés could be found in the majority of European countries, in North America and in Latin America.

The orthodoxy ultimately represented by the Soviet party was maintained throughout the exile years, but there were defectors from the unity that had existed in the KPD before 1933. A number of Communists who had been dogmatic enough during the 1920s, took their distance from the party and broke with it following crises that were more or less violent – the Spanish war, the anti-democratic developments in the Soviet Union, the Moscow trials and the German–Soviet pact, which so disoriented militants. If the certainty that only the USSR could successfully oppose fascism kept their criticism silent for a long while,[255] the German–Soviet pact and the new instructions given to activists, coming in the wake of the trials that condemned men whom they often knew to be innocent, had the result of causing many to break with the Comintern. Willi Münzenberg, Manès Sperber, Arthur Koestler, Gustav Regler, and later Wolfgang Leonhard and Alfred Kantorowicz, all experienced their separation from Communism as more or less painful, but some went on to become virulent anti-Communists. As for the Communist writers, whilst they formed a single front on the ideological level, that was not enough to remove the many enmities that continued to divide them in the climate of suspicion peculiar to exile.[256]

THE LITERARY EMIGRATION

Any emigration, in so far as it is active and pertinent to the country from which it originates, is a literary emigration.

Golo Mann

The third component of the antifascist emigration, the literary emigration proper, was just as divided as the political emigration from which it cannot easily be distinguished. As Hermann Kesten wrote:

The step into exile is a political step. The man who goes into exile wants to liberate his country or at least return home to a liberated country. [. . .] Almost always he leaves for exile because the situation in his homeland is illegal and inhuman, because freedom is limited or abolished and slavery elevated by dictatorship into a moral principle, because right and law are now worthless, human dignity is trampled underfoot, and political murder is the order of the day.[257]

It is symbolic that the first list published by the Nazis of opponents whom they were depriving of German citizenship consisted almost entirely of writers, even though many of these were non-party. Among these writers it is hard to apply any classification. W. A. Berendsohn distinguished in his 'humanist front' an individualist tendency bound up with the neo-Romantic tradition from before the Great War, and another tendency dominated by social preoccupations.[258] Such criteria however are not readily apparent. How for example would one class Alfred Döblin? Hildegard Brenner, in her 1967 study,[259] still seemed to follow Berendsohn's approach and group all writers around similarly vague categories such as 'humanist' or 'antifascist', despite the much broader material at her disposal. The same ambiguity is to be found in William K. Pfeiler,[260] who simply counts all the exiled writers as 'antifascist' and sees the unity of the literary emigration in the German language and a 'militant humanism'. As for Döblin's criteria, applied in *Die literarische Situation*,[261] which separated groups of writers into 'feudal', 'humanist' and 'progressive', they are scarcely more convincing than those used today by some scholars of an orthodox Marxist persuasion, who speak of 'bourgeois writers', 'progressive bourgeois', 'humanists', Marxists, Communist, Social-Democrats, etc. Was Heinrich Mann a 'Communist fellow-traveller', a revolutionary, a socialist or a 'progressive bourgeois'?

In point of fact, the literary emigration did not strictly present any unity. The ideological cleavages, as numerous – and still more vague – as those among activists in the political parties of the Weimar Republic, were combined with various literary and aesthetic tendencies. The emigration included Communist writers (Willi Bredel, J. R. Becher, Friedrich Wolf, Wieland Herzfelde), liberals (Stefan Zweig), 'progressives' (Heinrich and Thomas Mann), Marxists such as Brecht, monarchists (Joseph Roth), libertarian anti-Communists (Kurt Hiller), pacifists (Fritz von Unruh, René Schickele, Hellmut von Gerlach), conservatives (Balder Olden) and even former disciples of Stefan George.[262] Looked at from the standpoint of their literary allegiance, there are representatives of every tendency found in Germany in the 1920s and early 30s: expressionism (Hiller, Pfemfert, Schickele, Else Lasker-Schüler), Dadaism (Wieland Herzfelde), realism (Brecht), the proletarian currents (Ernst Ottwalt, Willi Bredel, etc.). Some were authors of avant-garde novels (Alfred Döblin, Carl Einstein), others of bestsellers (Lion Feuchtwanger, Vicki Baum, Erich Maria Remarque). Finally, if some could continue to write and publish in exile, many writers would be condemned to utter silence, and others found a publisher only with extreme difficulty. The literature of exile also had its stars and its pariahs.

The Movable Limits of Emigration: Herman Hesse, Thomas Mann and Ernst Glaeser

A reading of émigré correspondence shows how the separation between writers who went into exile and those who remained in Germany was not as total as one might imagine. At first contacts were maintained, despite rancour and incomprehension. There were personal ties that the separation could not simply abolish, but also appeals from émigrés to those who did not want to leave: appeals to vigilance, to courage, to probity. Undoubtedly the break with writers

who rallied to Nazism was a brutal one, such as that between Thomas Mann
and Ernst Bertram, or between Klaus Mann and Gottfried Benn. If the most
fanatical did not want to know anything about the émigrés, many writers who
remained in Germany sought to minimize the rupture. They continued to blind
themselves as to the nature of the regime and its cultural policy, and deemed the
exiles' accusations to be 'excessive'. It is hard to read today without a certain
discomfort certain passages in Gottfried Benn's reply to Klaus Mann. How
could he write about the exiles: 'Do you think that history is more active in
certain French spas?' In many cases, however, the break with the émigrés was
not so brusque. At the same time as exiled writers such as Ernst Toller and
Klaus Mann sought to open the eyes of those who remained in Germany,[263]
certain friendships – such as that of Alfred Döblin and Oskar Loerke – were
maintained across the barrier of exile.

   At the start, the dividing line that separated the exiles from the others was not
yet decisively drawn. In the months that followed the Nazis' coming to power,
some émigrés returned to the Reich illegally. Others who had left the country
hesitated to opt for a definitive exile.[264] A certain number of antifascist writers
who held foreign passports continued to live in Germany (Ödön von Horvath).
Finally, some German writers established themselves abroad without yet
acknowledging themselves as émigrés (Thomas Mann). Their distance from
the émigré journals could even be interpreted by the Nazis as a positive sign in
favour of the regime. Finally, some who had long since settled outside Germany
shared the same ambiguity to the extent that they had not taken a public
position on recent events.

   Herman Hesse is a good illustration of this attitude. He had already left the
poetry section of the Prussian Academy in November 1930, after being a
member since 1926. Living in Switzerland since the First World War, he could
not be considered an anti-Nazi émigré. Romain Rolland could thus write to
Madeleine Rolland on 18 September 1933:

> Apart from a few words at the beginning, on the inconveniences caused by events in
> Germany, he seemed to us to be quite undisturbed either materially or morally.
> Materially, no measures have been taken against him and he continues to be
> published there. Morally, his tranquillity, his pink complexion and rejuvenated air
> are evidence enough. From the height of his promontory on the Colline d'Or, he does
> not risk being submerged. He certainly expressed his utter contempt for the Führer,
> whom he deems unintelligent and used as an instrument tuned to the average German
> sensibility, but he confesses himself completely detached now from Germany and its
> fate. [. . .] He does not have a homeland. He is interested only in the universal and
> timeless values of the mind and is confident that these will remain intact under the
> passing torrents. [. . .] He saw Thomas Mann some time this year, who struck him as
> the one among the great émigrés who feels most seriously the ills of the time and his
> own duty.[265]

Yet if he maintained his detachment from Germany, Hesse could not remain
insensible to the fate of the émigrés. On 5 February 1936 he wrote to Romain

Rolland: 'My life at Montagnola is not quite as calm as you might think [. . .]. I find myself as ever between two hostile camps, and am attacked by both: now it is the Nazis in Germany, earlier on my colleagues there, and at the same time the German émigrés, whom I have constantly worked for in the last three years and for whom I have made great sacrifices.'[266]

Hesse was careful not to display his sympathies too openly: his books were still sold in Germany, and he could even visit there himself.[267] He was not officially part of the emigration,[268] even if in 1933 he received at his house Socialist émigrés and poets fleeing Germany (Heinrich Wiegand, Max Hermann-Neisse). The Nazis tolerated him, and he was proud of belonging neither to writers praised by the regime nor to the so-called *Asphaltliteratur*.[269] In exchange, he refrained from any political declaration against the regime, and did not sign any appeal in favour of the émigrés. One of his poems began with the symbolic verse:

Better to be killed by the fascists
than to be a fascist oneself.
Better to be killed by the Communists
Than to be a Communist oneself.

This prudence did not prevent Hesse from being attacked with increasing violence by National Socialist literary critics, who reproached him for his 'soulful solitude', his 'absence of deep links with the German people' and his relations with the émigrés. Yet he still maintained his distance from the emigration, even if Will Vesper accused him of having 'eaten Jewish bread'.

The case of Thomas Mann is still more complex. He became of course one of the great symbols of the antifascist emigration, and played a preponderant role both by his moral support and by the assistance he provided to the most destitute refugees. Yet the man who wrote: 'I am a man of balance. I instinctively lean to the left when the boat threatens to capsize on the right, and vice versa'[270] did not straight away view himself as an émigré. His rallying to the exile cause was the culmination of a complex development, both moral and political. If, in the face of the Hitlerite menace, he had not hesitated to ask his own class to make common cause with the Socialists, Thomas Mann could not consider without fear a rupture with Germany. For all his hatred for National Socialism, he felt too deeply attached to German culture and his mother tongue to decide on exile, all the more so as his fame in Germany and his assets there were both so considerable.[271] He was thus initially tempted to minimize the significance of the new regime. In a letter to Walter Opitz of 20 January 1933, he wrote: 'Yes, the situation in Germany is gloomy, but for once perhaps not as much as it seems.' Frequently attacked by the Nazis, Mann had escaped the unleashing of barbarism thanks to a lecture tour abroad. In March he was staying with his wife in Arosa, and intending to return to Germany at the beginning of April. The hostility of the Nazi press to his lectures on Wagner[272] should have incited him to prudence. Yet he remained deaf to the warnings of his friends, even his own son. Klaus Mann records[273] an astonishing phone conversation he had with him: Klaus tried to make him understand the risk he would run by returning to Germany, by saying that the weather was bad in Munich and it would better to remain a bit longer in Switzerland. Thomas Mann did not grasp the sense of the allusion, and replied that the weather was no better in Arosa. Klaus insisted, and asked for some time to get the Munich house into shape, but his father replied that he didn't mind the disorder and reaffirmed his intention to return. Throwing caution to the winds, Klaus urged him not to do so because of the Nazis.

Thomas Mann seems not yet to have believed in the reality of exile. He followed attentively the unfolding of political events, as his diary shows, listened to his children's reports and for a moment considered accepting Franz Werfel's invitation to stay with him in Venice. He decided not to return to Germany, but if political comments occupy a growing place in his Diary, he did not yet view himself as an émigré. On 13 March 1933 he wrote to Lavinia Mazzuchetti: 'It is only by sheer chance that I am outside Germany. On February 10 I set out with my wife for the Wagner celebration in Amsterdam, and from there according to schedule went on to Brussels and Paris. [. . .]. [O]ur stay here is being protracted by force of circumstance. [. . .] Whether we will or no, we have had to remain here.'

He did not yet believe that this terror could continue indefinitely:

> As long as individual acts of terrorism persist throughout the whole country, acts that the new holders of power have probably had to concede to their people within certain limits [. . .] it really would be foolish to return [. . .] I am on the list of those who have committed 'pacifist excesses' and 'intellectual high treason'. At any rate it is possible that within the near future some kind of law and order, a tolerably decent way of life, may be restored in Bavaria, so that I can return with my family.

The idea of a definitive exile he found insupportable:

> I am much too good a German, far too closely linked with the cultural traditions and the language of my country, for the thought of an exile lasting years, if not a lifetime, not to have a grave, a fateful significance for me. Nevertheless, we have had to begin looking around for a new base, if possible in the German-language area. At the age of fifty-seven *such* a loss of settled life and livelihood, to which I had become adjusted and in which I was already growing a bit stiff, is no small matter.[274]

The majority of letters Mann wrote at that time display the same anxiety. To Albert Einstein, he confided on 15 May 1933:

> I am much too good a German for the thought of permanent exile not to weigh heavily indeed, and the breach with my country, which is almost unavoidable, fills me with depression and dread [. . .]. For me to have been forced into this role, something thoroughly wrong and evil must surely have taken place. And it is my deepest conviction that this whole 'German Revolution' is indeed wrong and evil. [. . .] And to have warned as earnestly as possible against the elements which have brought about

this moral and spiritual misery will some day certainly accrue to the honour of all of us, although we may possibly be destroyed in the process.[275]

Yet despite his hostility to Nazism and his personal connection with a certain number of exiles,[276] Mann had still not taken a public position in favour of emigration, all the more so as various novels of his were due for publication in Germany.[277] His publisher Bermann Fischer constantly urged him to be prudent.[278] Mann still wanted his books to appear in Germany, and publicly refused therefore to support the magazine started by his son Klaus, *Die Sammlung*. But as Bermann Fischer notes,[279] he had already become, despite himself, not only the symbol of emigration, but of 'a better Germany, suffering and oppressed'. His books were not yet the object of official censorship, even if he was hardly loved by the Nazis. His break with the official organizations was not yet complete.[280] He certainly refused to reply to the questionnaire of the Prussian Academy of Arts, but he justified his refusal to Max von Schillings, maintaining that he had not the least intention of acting against the government, and that he believed he had always served German culture. He declared that he had left the Academy 'to concentrate on personal affairs'.[281] On 23 December 1933 he wrote to Julius Meier-Gräfe: 'After my letter to Blunck, I believed I would always be viewed as a German writer, and that other formalities were not required [. . .]. But yesterday, all the same, the sinister forms from the Reich Association reached me, with the demand to sign them without fail. I refused to do so, and if Bermann [Fischer], who is most affected by this, cannot find a way out, my exit from the Association will be sealed.' He added: 'At bottom, I am aware that my books were not written with a view to Prague or New York, but for the Germans [. . .]. On the other hand, what sense would it have to work in a country where people are ashamed of me and fear putting my name before the public.'[282]

Whereas his brother Heinrich considered emigration as a 'task' and set himself to gather together antifascist writers, Thomas Mann initially at least viewed the émigrés' activities in a negative light, especially their attempt to establish an exile press.[283] He held himself apart from their magazines and refused to give interviews.[284] Thus he wrote to Ernst Bertram on 9 January 1934:

My attitude, my verdict, are not determined or influenced by the spirit of exile. I stand for myself and have no contact at all with the German emigration scattered over the world. Moreover, this German emigration has no existence whatsoever as an intellectual and political entity. There is total individualistic splintering; and if the whole world has not yet reached a proper understanding of the grace and dignity of your Germany, the wholly uninfluential exiles are not to be blamed or credited for that. The widespread notion to the contrary among your fellow countrymen is totally benighted, and it would be a good thing if you opposed it.[285]

This distance towards the émigrés was still apparent in his refusal to participate in an international writers' congress to which Rudolf Olden had invited him. He declared himself opposed to the émigré propaganda, and indicated that his publisher did not want him to take part in such gatherings for the sake of his books. An awkward position, for if Mann upset the Nazis by his silence and insistence on remaining abroad, the émigrés reproached him for not taking a more overt position against the Reich. Thomas Mann was however preparing himself to abandon the publication of his books in Germany so as to write about politics. 'For a long time now, I've not worried about breaking with Germany, I desire this and would prefer my books also to be abroad.'[286] He describes the Reich as a 'veritable gaol'.[287] To the extent that his attitude towards Germany hardened, his sympathy for the émigrés steadily grew: he even regretted not being one of them.[288] On 14 October 1934 he wrote to Alfred Neumann: 'I believe in the honour of the emigration, and your work confirms for me that good things, the best and most important ones, arise now outside our frontiers, in an atmosphere of freedom, and not inside, in the barrack-room rottenness of the stupid military camp that still answers to the name of Germany.'[289] From 1934 onward, he seriously envisaged the possibility of having his books published outside Germany, and recognized ever more that the only worthwhile German literature was that produced in exile: 'My view is that the "émigré literature", on which a new Brandès may perhaps some day write a good chapter, is no bad thing. Neumann's *The New Caesar* and Frank's *Cervantes* are works of a *high level*, the new novel of my son Klaus (just stripped of his nationality) also marks a definite advance, and the best of all is René Schickele's great essay on Lawrence, an admirable work.'[290]

But for all that, Mann did not yet consider his exile an entirely voluntary act, even if he gradually ended up making it so. At the same time, he also sought to justify his public discretion, and his failure to take a stand in favour of emigration:

> I have tried to keep in touch with my German readership, which because of its nature and its intellectual formation is now in opposition and from which one day a movement against the regime currently in power may arise; and the contact would immediately be broken, i.e. my books which until now may be read would immediately be banned, if I pinned my colours to the mast more clearly than I have in any case done in some of my declarations of recent years.[291]

Mann's definitive and public rupture with Hitlerite Germany was provoked by an article of the Swiss critic Eduard Korrodi published on 25 January 1936 in the *Neue Zürcher Zeitung* under the heading 'Deutsche Literatur im Emigrantenspiegel' ('German Literature in the Émigré Mirror'). Korrodi took violent issue with an article by Leopold Schwarzschild that had appeared on 11 January in the *Neue Tage-Buch* published in Paris, which maintained that out of all German's cultural and material assets, only one had been completely saved: German literature, which was now completely outside the country.[292] Korrodi retorted to Schwarzschild that Thomas Mann's books were still being sold in Germany, that Mann had refrained from identifying himself with the émigrés and that in any case German literature could not be reduced to that of 'Jewish authors in exile'. Korrodi finally recalled that a number of major writers had remained in the Reich: Hans Carossa, Max Schröder, M. Mell, J. Schaffner, E. Strauss, Friedrich and Ernst Jünger, Ricarda Huch and Ernst Wiechert. His article, aggressive and unpleasant, was a violent attack on the émigrés and their publishers en bloc (in particular Querido Verlag and Allert de Lange in Amsterdam). It was accompanied by a letter from Herman Hesse, in response to an assertion by Georg Bernhard, explaining that he was not a 'German émigré' but a 'Swiss citizen'.

Thomas Mann could no longer avoid taking a more clear-cut position. On 3 February 1936 he sent a letter to the newspaper in which he acknowledged an element of truth in the Swiss critic's assertions: 'You are right; it was a distinct polemical error on the part of the editor of the *Neue Tagebuch* to assert that all or virtually all of contemporary literature has left Germany, or as he puts it, "has transferred abroad". [. . .] Leopold Schwarzschild [. . .] regards the current political struggle as far more important, honourable, and decisive than a whole world of poetry.' Mann also maintained that he was not certain that some writers who remained in Germany would not have preferred to be abroad, and that 'the boundary between exiled and non-exiled German literature is not so easy to draw; it does not coincide so precisely with the boundaries of the Reich.' While he refused to hurl anathema on the writers who had not emigrated, he also reproached Korrodi for confusing 'Jewish literature' with the entirety of antifascist emigration, recalling that many exiled writers were not Jews. While Korrodi saw the 'Europeanization of the German novel' as a Jewish influence, Mann claimed this merit for himself, maintaining that 'nothing good can possibly come of the present German regime, not for Germany and not for the world.' And he ended his letter with some lines from August von Platen that left no doubt on the fact that he too would now consider himself an émigré.[293]

The Nazis reacted immediately by depriving Mann of German citizenship, while the exile press and Schwarzschild himself thanked him for his courage in the name of all the émigrés. He immediately received many tokens of sympathy[294] and found himself rapidly transformed into a kind of intellectual leader of German literature in exile,[295] a position of which he was constantly proud. Thus he wrote to Herman Hesse on 9 February 1936: 'Sooner or later I had to declare myself in clear language, both for the sake of the world, in which a good many highly ambiguous, half-and-half notions of my relationship to the Third Reich prevail, and for my own sake as well. [. . .] After Korrodi's nasty trick of using my name to attack the exiles, I owed them some compensation, a profession of solidarity. The torrent of letters shows that I have warmed the hearts of many sufferers.'[296] In conclusion, 'I may well be expatriated and my books banned. But if that should happen, I can at least tell myself that either there will be war, or else within a few years the situation inside Germany will change so that my books may once again be distributed.'[297]

The letters Mann wrote in the following months all show that he did not regret his decision: he repeatedly attacked the Nazi regime, and with increasing violence. On 19 December 1936, the dean of the philosophy faculty at Bonn informed him of the university's decision to withdraw the doctoral title that he

had been awarded. Mann replied with a letter in which he noted the responsibility of the university for the present situation in Germany and the decision of
Harvard to award him a similar title, and stressed that a large number of ties
continued to attach him to Germany, where he would already be dead had he
remained there. Mann rejected all the more vehemently the right usurped by the
Nazis to identify themselves with German culture, when they had transformed
the country into an object of hatred and disgust for the entire world. From now
on therefore he would feel himself 'forced into politics', and play a growing role
in the emigration and the struggle against National Socialism – becoming,
according to Ludwig Marcuse, a kind of 'kaiser of all German émigrés'.

The case of Ernst Glaeser also illustrates the shifting borders of emigration, but
in an inverse sense. Whilst Thomas Mann had to overcome much apprehension
to accept the rift of exile, the inability to bear this same rift would lead Ernst
Glaeser to prefer the dishonour of a return to Germany, whatever the price to be
paid.
 For a number of reasons, Glaeser counted among the most remarkable
writers of the Weimar era. Issuing from the bourgeoisie, he broke with his class
and became a pacifist. His two novels, *Class 22* (1928) and *Peace* (1930), not
only met with great success but were hailed as progressive works in left-wing
milieus. He even seemed to be a kind of fellow-traveller of the Communists. But
for all that his books struck a somewhat ambiguous note: they describe the
experiences of a young German between 1914 and 1919, his political hesitations,
his encounter with the Great War and the Spartacist uprising, in a style akin to
that of the New Objectivity in painting. Glaeser left Germany more out of fear
than genuine political desire,[298] and settled first in Ticino, then in Zurich.
Several of his books were published in exile: *Der letzte Zivilist* (1935), *Das
Unvergänglich* (1936) and *Skizzen* (1937). Very rapidly, however, Glaeser found
this separation from Germany insupportable. Ernst Erich Noth, who was living
in Paris, was sent by *Nouvelles Littéraires* to interview Glaeser on the appearance of a French translation. He found him dead drunk:

> I could not understand at all what inadmissible things he was trying to drown in
> alcohol. I did not suspect his plans, and was unaware (though others such as Joseph
> Roth should have told me) that he had already crossed the German frontier, even
> before his official return to the Reich, to vote yes to Hitler in a plebiscite, and that in
> order to win the National Socialist regime's good graces he had informed the German
> consular authorities in Switzerland of the views and intentions of political refugees
> who had confided in him without suspicion.[299]

Glaeser complained of his isolation in exile, the lack of understanding he
encountered, the loss of his readership and the material difficulties he had to
confront. In his drunken state he made nationalist utterances to E. E. Noth and
criticized the weakness and uselessness of the émigrés. A few weeks later he
returned to Germany and called the émigrés 'traitors'. To gain pardon for
having left the Reich, he had to swear an oath of allegiance. Though he was

never a very honoured writer, for all that his return had a fairly spectacular character, he edited a Luftwaffe newspaper (*Adler im Süden*) published for the theatre of operations in North Africa and Italy. E. E. Noth comments: 'Positions of this importance were not entrusted by the Nazis to men in whom they did not have confidence. To win such a post, Glaeser must have given patent proof and convincing evidence of political and ideological submission.'[300]

Is this so certain? Was the editing of a small air-force paper really such an honour for a man who had been recognized and admired as one of the greatest writers of the 1920s? Though not a Communist, he had been invited in 1930 to the Second International Conference of Revolutionary Writers in Kharkov, and figured among the German delegates such as J. R. Becher, Ludwig Renn and Anna Seghers, being considered an objective ally of the working class. Even if his books were the subject of critical debate, his novels enjoyed such success – *Peace* in particular – that he was appointed to the new leadership of the League of Revolutionary Proletarian Writers (BPRS) and in 1934, during the First Congress of Soviet Writers, Willi Bredel praised him as the very representative of antifascist literature. Not only had his books attracted numerous attacks under the Weimar Republic (including a trial for blasphemy in Kassel in 1927), but they were solemnly burned by the Nazis on 10 May 1933 and withdrawn from public libraries. Glaeser's reversal thus seems all the more incomprehensible.[301]

Glaeser was severely judged by E. E. Noth who termed him a 'renegade' and 'traitor', and also by Brecht, who wrote in his *Journals*: 'types like GLÄSER must no doubt be treated as enemies of the people; he had been given the marxist line on the bourgeoisie; he went back, not, as he maintains, to participate in germany's defeat, but in the victory. the war he joined began as a crime not against the german people, but against other peoples.'[302] Other émigrés such as Alfred Kantorowicz seem however to have taken pity on Glaeser, or claimed not to understand him.[303] The reasons adduced by Glaeser to justify his return – 'homesickness' and his inability to bear exile – are likely enough. One might also remark, as did E. E. Noth, that his approach to fascism was always ambiguous. When he depicts it in his novel *Der letzte Zivilist* (*The Last Civilian*), he describes it as something that comes to disturb 'the peaceful calm and dignity of [his] region', and Noth maintains that 'if at that time one had probed Glaeser's book more deeply, and examined its real content instead of being content with superficial approval, one would have been struck by the absence of any deliberate and clearly expressed opposition to the Nazi regime.'[304]

It is true that Glaeser scarcely mentions Nazi atrocities and that his understanding of National Socialism was always superficial. But wasn't the same ideological vagueness present in all his novels? Arthur Koestler recalls in his memoirs a passage from Glaeser's novel *Class 22* that depicts the uncertainties of German youth. A young boy asks an old teacher what side he will take in the great uprising and what is his place. The teacher replies:

There is a collective destiny, and to revolt against it doesn't lead anywhere. History is not interested in the wishes of individuals. We are individuals. We are condemned to remain individuals. We can never get into the stream. [. . .] History has spat us out. We stand between the front lines. We are civilized but useless. If you remain honest, you will spend your life in depressing independence between the fronts. You will see everything and understand everything, you will survive new wars and new revolutions, but you will be alone, without friends, without a roof or a country, without echo and achievement . . .

The book ends with the boy's words: 'No, no, this will not be my destiny. I don't want to be a piece of phosphorescent driftwood left at the muddy bend. I want to be carried by the stream, in the stream, with the stream, part of the stream. I shall do everything to belong again. I shall go to Canossa. I shall deny myself as I have denied my parents. 'I shall write this very day a demand to be accepted again into the Collective.'[305]

Written in 1928, these words were strangely prophetic.

THE QUESTION OF INTERNAL EMIGRATION

So as not to lose his living
At a time when oppression was growing heavier
More than one person decided to stop speaking the truth
On the crimes of the regime, and the continuing exploitation
But at least not to spread the regime's lies:
Not to expose anything
But not to prettify things either. Those who behaved in this way
Seemed to confirm that they had resolved
At a time when oppression was growing heavier
Not to lose face: in reality
They were only resolved
Not to lost their living.

> Bertolt Brecht, 'To Those Who Have Been Brought into Line' (1935)

They are reminiscent of painters who cover the walls of a doomed ship with still lifes [. . .] They scribble their images without letting themselves be disturbed either by those in power or by their victims.

> Bertolt Brecht, 'Five Difficulties in Writing the Truth' (1939)

The notion of 'internal emigration' (*innere Emigration*) has elicited a good deal of discussion, theoretical as well as political. Neither the exiled writers themselves nor their subsequent exegetes have been able to agree on the scope of the concept, even on its validity. Whilst these polemics reached their apogee between 1945 and 1950, they continued to resurge in respect to particular writers who remained in Germany after 1933, and in works devoted to cultural life under the Third Reich.

The first major debate on internal emigration involved Thomas Mann, Frank

Thiess, Otto Flake and Wilhelm Hausenstein. It was provoked by an open letter from Walter von Molo to Thomas Mann that was published on 4 August 1945 in the *Hessische Post*. Von Molo invited Mann in urgent terms to return to Germany, and 'take back his place in the midst of this people for whom he has so long been an object of scandal, a people who remained silent in the face of the treatment that despots inflicted'. Thomas Mann mentioned this letter in fairly negative terms in *The Genesis of a Novel*.[306] On 18 August an article by Frank Thiess appeared[307] titled 'Die innere Emigration', which vexed Thomas Mann still more forcefully:

> . . . the O. W. [Office of War Information] sent to me a wrong-headed and provoking article by Frank Thiess from the *Münchner Zeitung*, in which a group called the Inner Emigration set itself up with a great deal of arrogance. Presumably those 'exiles within' were a community of intellectuals who had 'kept faith with Germany', not 'left her in the lurch of her misfortune', not looked upon her fate 'from comfortable box seats abroad', but honestly shared in it. They would have honestly shared it even if Hitler had won. Now the armchair had collapsed around the armchair lookers-on, and for this they took great credit for themselves, were lavish with insults towards those who had breathed the cold winds of exile and whose lot had been, for the most part, misery and death.[308]

Mann maintained that Frank Thiess lost face when an interview was published in Germany that he had given in 1933, and was clear evidence of his support for Hitler: 'And so the flock has lost its leader.' In his 1945 article, Thiess declared that an 'inner space' (*innere Raum*) had existed in Germany which the Nazis had failed to conquer. He valorized the fact of not having emigrated as a source of experience and enrichment, which the exiles had completely lacked. Maintaining that writers who had remained in Germany did not expect any reward for their fidelity, he attacked those who had left in 1933 – the 'emissaries of foreign embassies' – even while claiming not to want to damage them.[309]

In his response to Walter von Molo, 'Warum ich nicht zurückkehre' (*Augsburger Anzeiger*, 12 October 1945), Thomas Mann wrote that in his eyes, books published under the Third Reich lacked any value. They all gave off an odour of shame and blood. This response brought new reactions such as that of Otto Flake, who depicted Germany in its entirety as victim. Gottfried Benn, in his autobiography *Double Life*, likewise bent himself to justifying his attitude in moral terms: 'I maintain that many of those who remained in Germany and continued to occupy their posts did so because they hoped to keep free the places of those who left, and give them back when they returned. I say this not to defend myself or others – it is not the time for this – but I simply record a fact. That is how it was.'

He ended by claiming a certain commonality of fate: 'We have had our debates of conscience, we have had our hopes and doubts, we have had to pay in the coin of our internal and external defeats, exactly like those who departed from us. We have lived this in one way, they in another. [. . .] And I don't know why Döblin should now treat me as a scoundrel both in public and in private; that is his problem.'[310]

Bad faith and naivety? No doubt. But Benn rejected the accusation of opportunism and describes the years spent under Hitler as a daily torment. He maintained that there was nothing the émigrés could envy about his situation. The controversy continued with a still more aggressive article by Frank Thiess, 'Abschied von Thomas Mann', another piece by Wilhelm Hausenstein ('Bücher frei von Blut und Schande' in *Süddeutsche Zeitung*, 24 December 1945) and a reply by J. R. Becher to Thiess of 26 January 1948.

Besides the question of the return of the émigrés and their encounter with those who had lived through the Hitler era, this polemic on the internal emigration was set in a very particular historical context: it heralded the climate of anti-Communism and Cold War in which the 'good émigrés' were those who went into internal exile, while the 'bad émigrés', the antifascist exiles of 1933, were treated as 'traitors' and 'Communists'. The ideological function of the term 'internal emigration' was to establish the image of an 'other Germany' made up of anonymous oppositionists who all hated Nazism, support for which had been confined to a handful of fanatics and murderers foreign to the German people as a whole. These 'internal émigrés' would be the departure point for a new German culture, rejecting the 'totalitarian temptations' of fascism and Communism, and linking up with the classical humanist tradition that these authors had cultivated in their internal life, while refusing to abandon their homeland. Frank Thiess maintained in the same fashion that they did not have to resolve 'to leave our sick mother, Germany. It was natural for us to remain with her.' At the same time as new 'internal émigrés' were ceaselessly discovered and valorized, the exiles were correspondingly attacked and treated as 'partisans of Moscow': their works not republished, frequently reviled by the press, slandered at the highest level and banished from school textbooks. On the other hand, many literary lights of the Third Reich were magically 'de-Nazified' and presented themselves as disguised oppositionists. It is understandable in this context how so many émigrés who returned to Germany chose to leave again for a new exile: Alfred Döblin, Oskar Maria Graf, Armin T. Wegner.[311]

If we abstract from the subsequent context and seek to give an objective appraisal of this notion of internal emigration, a number of considerations present themselves:

1. The notion of internal emigration was not coined in 1945. As early as 1933, a certain number of writers who remained in Germany viewed themselves as émigrés.
2. The exiles themselves were very largely divided on the existence of this 'internal emigration'. The majority – even Thomas Mann at the start of his exile – seemed to grant it a certain credit.
3. One should not consider every writer who remained in Germany from 1933 to 1945 as equally tainted by National Socialism.

The term 'internal emigration' was used after 1933 by a number of writers who, whilst refusing for a whole range of reasons to go into exile, did not agree to join the Nazis' organizations. It appears in a good number of works that attest to an attitude of this kind.[312] Jochen Klepper[313] declared that he felt 'in spiritual exile'. Ernst Barlach described his 'life as an émigré in his own land'.[314] This attitude, moreover, was not peculiar to progressive authors. Gottfried Benn, in a letter to Ina Seidel of 12 December 1934, defined his joining the army as 'an aristocratic form of emigration'.[315] The same attitude can be found in the wartime diaries of Ernst Jünger and in his allegorical novel *Auf den Marmorklippen* (*On the Marble Cliffs*). It also corresponds to the life of Ernst Niekisch after 1933. While aware that he was hated by the Nazis, he continued to publish texts hostile to the regime until his circle was destroyed. Arrested by the Gestapo on a number of occasions, and threatened with death, he refused to go into exile and confides in his autobiography (*A Risky Life*) *Gewagtes Lebenn*, 'I did not want to be an emigrant'.[316]

Contacts moreover were maintained between émigré writers and those who, while remaining in Germany, refused to rally to Nazism. Alfred Döblin continued writing to Oskar Loerke, and Niekisch travelled abroad to meet various émigrés.[317] One of the most remarkable examples of 'internal émigrés' was undoubtedly that of the aristocrat Friedrich Perceval Reck-Malleczwesen, an ex-officer and columnist on the *Süddeutsche Zeitung*, who spelled out his hatred for the Nazis in his diary, eventually published in 1966 under the title *Tagebuch eines Verzweifelten* (*Diary of a Desperate Man*).[318] Though he buried the diary every day at a different place in the forest, to keep the Gestapo off his track, he was finally arrested in 1944 and died in Dachau the following year. A convinced monarchist, Malleczwesen felt only contempt and disgust for the Nazis, and silently addressed himself to the émigrés as follows:

> You who left Germany four years ago, do you have the slightest idea of our illegality and our life constantly threatened by a possible denunciation by the first hysteric to come along? It is a strange feeling to see you again in thought, to hear your voices sometimes on the radio, crossing the deep oceans to reach us from that world where we have so long now been forbidden to set foot, in places where just a few years ago we could chat together! I miss you even if, as was the case with most of you, you were opposed to my views and we were political opponents. [. . .] Can you manage to comprehend what it means to live year after year with hate in your heart, to go to bed with hate, to spend the night in dreams of hate and wake up again with hate in the morning? All this for years without the least legal safeguard, without the least compromise, without a single 'Heil Hitler!', without setting foot in the compulsory meetings, with the stigmata of illegality on your forehead. Do we still speak the same language after so many years?[319]

When asked about the reasons that had kept him from emigrating, Mallecz-wesen simply replied:

> I am German, and this country where I live has all my love. To uproot myself would be to perish . . . I tremble for each tree and each forest that disappears, for each quiet

valley that is profaned [. . .]. I know that this country is the beating heart of the world, I believe in its palpitations despite all this bloody mud. But I also know that what the one up there thunders and growls is the very negation of right, of honour, of all that makes life worth living . . . It is a caricature of Germany, scribbled by a mad ape that has broken its chain.[320]

Even if he remained in Germany, Reck-Malleczwesen never compromised with Nazism, and his whole diary is nothing but an immense cry of rage and impotent hatred against it. In what way did this hatred and pain divide him from the émigrés?[321]

The term 'internal emigration', moreover, is not found just in the private correspondence and diaries of some non-exiled writers, but was used by the émigrés themselves. Thomas Mann used it in 1934 in his essay 'Leiden an Deutschland', where he maintained that 'the internal émigrés in Germany and the external émigrés are united in the same absence of a homeland [*Heimat-losigkeit*].'[322] He repeated again in 'This Peace' (1938): 'German émigrés now have this frightful experience in common with those fellow countrymen still in Germany who shared their desires and hopes: the long-drawn-out torture of the growing realization, repudiated up to the last, that we Germans, inside our country and outside it, were not backed by Europe [. . .].'[323]

Mann makes clear that 'this "we" always denotes the German opposition both extra- and intra-muros'. The term 'internal emigration' appears again in a review of Hans Fallada's book *Wolf unter Wölfen* signed by Kurt Kesten in the magazine *Das Wort* (vol. 2, p. 135), and was used also by Heinrich Mann, Wilhelm Pieck, Paul Tillich and F. C. Weiskopf between 1934 and 1939. In his novel *The Volcano*, Klaus Mann likewise described 'those to whom their country has become foreign' as 'internal émigrés'. He maintained that 'the faces of whose who will return one day to Germany will bear the same stigmata as the faces of those who remained'. Klaus Mann's fictional Angel, the angel of those without a homeland, 'must gather the two facts of internal and external emigration'.[324] This assertion of a suffering shared by both exiles and certain writers hostile to Nazism who had remained in Germany, is found in authors as opposed to each other as Brecht and Thomas Mann.[325]

These links between writers in exile and writers within the Reich who were hostile to the regime were to some degree made official at the 1935 Congress for the Defence of Culture, when this was addressed by a writer from Germany who appeared wearing a mask (Jan Petersen). Alfred Kantorowicz maintained that for the émigrés, the two most important events of this congress were the appearance of Heinrich Mann at the tribune, representing the external emigra-tion, and that of Petersen, who brought the émigrés the greetings of a group of antifascist writers who continued to work inside the Reich, at the peril of their own lives. According to Kantorowicz, this was proof that an underground literature existed in Germany that had not been won over to Nazism, and when Petersen started his address, many émigrés began to cry.

The notion of internal emigration cannot thus be viewed as simply an invention of Frank Thiess, an ideological justification dreamed up after

1945. Rightly or wrongly, it corresponded to a certain hope for a revolt against Hitler, nourished by the émigrés up to the outbreak of the War, that was constantly disappointed, and went together with their overestimation of the opposition forces. The later refusal of Thomas Mann to admit the existence of this internal emigration went hand in hand with his deteriorating relationship to Germany, the almost complete loss of faith in the existence of a Germany not won to National Socialism that marked his essays of the 1940s written in the United States. Subsequent historians moreover show the same diversity of judgement.

Walter A. Berendsohn maintained, in a chapter of *The Other Germany. Illusion and Reality*,[326] that this 'internal emigration' was a contradiction in terms, since ' "internal emigration" only makes sense to describe people who withdraw from any activity, take no part in the life of their time and seek refuge in an inner world.' He acknowledged that a number of writers suffered under the Nazi regime, but did not accept that this was sufficient justification to describe them as 'internal émigrés'; keeping silent did not add up to opposition.[327] Franz Schonauer likewise claimed in his essay *Deutsche Literatur im Dritten Reich. Versuch einer Darstellung in polemisch-didaktischer Absicht*,[328] that 'internal emigration is a myth that needs destroying'. But this is an extreme position.

The opposing attitude is so as well. Historians of literature have often been tempted to consider the majority of writers who remained in Germany as internal émigrés, with the exception of a few particularly prominent Nazis. Thus Karl August Horst, in his study *Die deutsche Literatur der Gegenwart*,[329] classes even such official writers of the Third Reich (*Staatsschriftsteller*) as Blunck and Kolbenheyer among the opposition. The same goes for Wilhelm Kahle's presentation *Geschichte der deutschen Dichtung*,[330] which celebrates the literature of internal emigration as the genuine opposition to Nazism.

Apart from these entrenched positions, the majority of émigrés and historians of emigration allow a diversity of shadings. Alfred Kantorowicz rejected the radicalism of Walter A. Berendsohn and believed that some writers who remained in Germany were very close to the exiles in their material and intellectual positions. He cited the famous letter[331] that Ricarda Huch addressed to the president of the Academy of Arts, Max von Schillings, in which she announced her withdrawal from an institution from which Jews, pacifists, liberals and progressive elements had been expelled. She rejected the government's right to decide who was really 'German', declaring that its brutal and bloody methods repelled her, and that this 'Germanity' exalted by the Nazis was certainly not the character of her nation.[332] Kantorowicz also described the meeting of German writers held in the Soviet sector of Berlin in 1947, which brought together such different figures as Bernhard Kellermann, Peter Suhrkamp, Elisabeth Langgässer, Paul Wiegler, Axel Eggebrecht, Hans Henry Jahn, Karl Jaspers, H. Kasack, Walter von Molo, Ernst Niekisch, G. Wiesenborg, R. Pechel and Ernst Wiechert. He maintains that these writers who remained in Germany were no more united than the émigrés, that they were marked by the same ideological cleavages, but spoke the same language as the exiles. They had often had similar experiences. Karl Wolfskehl, who had emigrated to New Zealand, doubtless knew the same despair as Oskar Loerke, who remained in Berlin. A neo-Romantic exile such as Albrecht Schaeffer was undoubtedly closer to Wiechert, who remained in Germany, than to Brecht. Kantorowicz acknowledged that it was hard for all that to distinguish between 'genuine internal émigrés' and opportunists.[333] Klaus Mann likewise, in *The Turning Point*, recognized that among those who refused to go into exile there were some genuine oppositionists, but stressed that within the Reich the only choice was between compromise and martyrdom. Golo Mann paid homage to Ricarda Huch who continued her work in solitude and poverty, expressing her personal opposition despite being unable to have an effect on others,[334] also to Leopold Ziegler and Theodor Haecker, even suggesting that their books should be seen as part of émigré literature, since 'the Other Germany was not only in exile, it could also be found within the country'. The same attitude was taken by Alfred Polgar, who wrote in 1948:

> When the German people sold themselves to the devil, many opponents of the pact remained in the country: simply because it was impossible for them to leave. Others who could have left did not do so: perhaps because they felt unready for the adventure of emigration, because they believed that the devilry would not last long, or because away from the sky of their homeland, however dark this might be above their head, they would not have been able to breathe. It would be absurd to reproach them for remaining there.[335]

Polgar maintained nonetheless that he did not feel the slightest pity for them; he reserved his pity for those who died in the gas chambers.

It is clear then that the notion of 'internal emigration' was not just an invention of Frank Thiess. On the other hand, its existence cannot simply be taken for granted. Was Thiess the first to use the term?[336] And should he himself be counted among the internal émigrés? An examination of his work could serve as a touchstone for the concept. But if G. Weisenborn effectively did consider him an adversary of the Third Reich,[337] Thomas Mann mentioned a pro-Nazi interview of Thiess's, though this seems at present undiscoverable, just like the letter in which he supposedly expressed his disapproval of the regime. There remains his work.

The example usually given of Thiess's opposition to Nazism is his novel *Das Reich der Dämonen* (1941). Unfortunately, as R. Grimm has emphasized,[338] those passages that were effectively critical of the regime only figure in the 'improved' (*verbessert*) edition published after 1945. If the earlier printings are consulted (two impressions totalling 30,000 copies), they are completely absent. Thiess's other writings, moreover, show nothing specifically anti-Nazi; on the contrary.[339] On this point therefore Thomas Mann was right: the majority of Thiess's work contains elements favourable to the regime, his novel *Tsushima* was printed in a special edition for the army in 1936, and it is hard indeed to see him as an oppositionist, for all his affirmations.[340] The same doubts arise on an attentive reading of the works of most of these 'internal émigrés', as well as their declarations and professions of faith – Gottfried Benn, Ernst Jünger, Hans Blunck and even Ernst Wiechert.

The concept of 'internal émigré' should not be applied, then, without a detailed critique of both the works adduced and the texts that take up their defence. Sometimes even those authors with the best intentions did not escape the ideological context of the immediate postwar years. A sentiment of hostility towards the victorious foreign powers, the disarray caused by the fact that National Socialism had been overthrown by the intervention of enemy armies and not by internal resistance, and a certain guilt feeling at sharing this 'collective fate' led certain writers, even victims of the regime such as G. Weisenborn, to contribute to the construction of this legend of an 'underground Germany' foreign to Nazism, suffering in silence, these armies of intellectual resistance that were celebrated after the War.[341] A few writers such as Alfred Andersch, however, displayed their scepticism as to the reality of this literary opposition, and preferred to speak of a zero point (*Nullpunkt*) in German literature.[342]

It was not until nearly thirty years later that the first historical and critical studies on this internal emigration finally appeared. One of the most interesting remains that of Reinhold Grimm, 'Innere Emigration als Lebensform'.[343] Grimm believed that an internal emigration did indeed exist, even if there is no agreement on its limits, its representatives, or its influence. Basing himself on classifications applied to the resistance by Hans Rothfels,[344] he proposed to divide the literature of internal emigration into *innerdeutsche antifascistische Literatur* (oppositional literature) and *innerdeutsche nichtfascistische Literatur* (non-Nazi but non-oppositional). This is doubtless an interesting distinction, but unfortunately one difficult to apply, as where writers are concerned the boundary between 'anti-fascist' and 'non-fascist' is very vague. According to Grimm, the literature of literary emigration would be confined to the first category. Given the plethora of repressive bodies that weighed down on literature, the possibilities of expressing any kind of opposition in writing were extremely reduced. Grimm sought also to define internal emigration less by its concrete manifestations than as a 'form of existence', a concern that is methodologically valuable but extremely hard to apply: writings can readily be analysed, but 'existential attitudes' lend themselves to all sorts of interpretation. Gottfried Benn and Ernst Jünger, for example, both lived through the War years with a sense of sadness, solitude and hostility towards the regime. But was that enough to make them its opponents? Grimm cites as examples of this 'internal emigration as a form of existence' the case of Ricarda Huch, which everyone would certainly accept, likewise Werner Bergengruen, who publicly refused along with his family to hang a Nazi flag from his window or give the Hitler salute, also copying out leaflets of the White Rose group and the sermons of the bishop of Münster, Count Gallen. Grimm rightly emphasized how this attitude cut across political divisions, in a form of internal emigration shared by Christians and Communists, for instance Reinhold Schneider, Rudolf Alexander Schröder and Jan Petersen (Hans Schwalm), by liberals such as R. Pechel (editor of the *Deutsche Rundschau*), conservatives and aristocrats (F. P. Reck-

Malleczwesen), national-bolsheviks (Ernst Niekisch), right-wing figures such as Ernst Jünger and Gottfried Benn, and bourgeois progressives such as Adam Kuckhoff.[345] What united them all, according to Grimm, was a certain existential attitude and a common fate. Many of them met with arrest, persecution, concentration camp and death. Others were forced to hide their manuscripts, to circulate their texts clandestinely, deprived of any power but to cry their hatred of the regime, as did Ernst Wiechert or Albrecht Haushofer in his *Moabiter Sonette*. Some of them managed to reach a small number of readers (Reinhold Schneider) or publish abroad using pseudonyms (Bergengruen); others saw their manuscripts confiscated (Ernst Niekisch's *Das Reich der niederen Dämonen*). The rare works smuggled out of Germany had to take difficult routes. The famous novel of Jan Petersen, *Unsere Strasse* (1933–34) reached London hidden in a couple of cakes; some texts of Wiechert, such as *Der Dichter und die Jugend* (1933), then *Der Dichter und die Zeit* (1935) were taken down in shorthand and sent abroad before being published by Willi Bredel. Grimm recalls that Wiechert himself was sent to concentration camp, while many texts of his could not be published.

It is also impossible to deny that the attitude Grimm analysed was often subsequently invoked by writers such as Gottfried Benn for example in *Double Life*, or Ernst Jünger who never stopped claiming that even amid the worst devastations there was a haven of peace: this centre of the cyclone that he evokes in *On the Marble Cliffs*. The peaceful and simple nature hymned by Wiechert likewise links up with the image of refuge in an inner space so often exalted in German Romanticism. Grimm saw this as a consequence of Protestantism with its two kingdoms of earth and heaven, and the high value set on inwardness (*Innerlichkeit*) that Thomas Mann precisely questioned in 'Germany and the Germans': 'What constitutes this depth? Simply the musicality of the German soul, that which we call its inwardness, its subjectivity, the divorce of the speculative from the socio-political element of human energy, and the complete predominance of the former over the latter.'[346] The attitude of so many writers under the Third Reich, therefore, was understandable for Grimm only against the whole German philosophical and literary tradition.

Though the interest of Grimm's analysis and the information contained in it cannot be denied, it is hard to see this as sufficient. As Ralph Schell emphasizes,[347] the specificity of German writers' attitudes towards the Third Reich should not be confused with the whole history of German inwardness. Above all, a consideration of the 'internal emigration' as an existential attitude leads authors with hardly anything in common to be classified under the same heading; it leads to a fatal identification between genuine opponents of the regime, who sometimes paid with their lives for remaining in Germany, and conservatives who restricted themselves to a silent contempt. The same reproach could well be made to the East German historian Wolfgang Brekele, who in his study 'Die antifaschistische Literatur in Deutschland 1933–45'[348] sought to define a united antifascist front including the internal emigration: in his terms 'those who had not been influenced by Nazi ideology, had written humanist works and did not let themselves be mobilized by fascist politics'.[349] But this 'internal antifascist front' is an intellectual construct which never existed in fact, in contrast to the German antifascist front established in Paris, or the movement Freies Deutschland that united in the Soviet Union both German generals and Communists. Brekele had understandable difficulty in citing a single concrete manifestation of this 'internal antifascist front'. If the exiles were divided, those who remained in Germany were yet more so. While the emigration occasionally managed to bring together writers whose ideological positions were opposed (Heinrich Mann and J. R. Becher), the conditions of fascism in no way reconciled Communists such as Jan Petersen and Grünberg with religious opponents such as Bergengruen, Schneider and Wiechert. Brekele does indeed try to distinguish within this 'internal antifascist literature' a socialist camp and a bourgeois camp, the latter itself divided into 'left bourgeois' represented by Weisenborg, Kuckhoff and Krauss, 'Christians' (Wiechert, Schneider, Bergengruen) and 'reactionaries' (Jünger), but these classifications are too vague to enable any genuine understanding of their relationship to the Third Reich. Even if they did represent the survival of a few grains of freedom, their political attitude cannot be grasped with a single notion, given the very composition of this internal emigration, which included both adversaries of the regime who had not emigrated (Ricarda Huch), and others whose degree of opposition was very diverse – from Wiechert to Jünger. What finally should be said of those exiles who returned to Hitler's Germany, or of sympathizers with National Socialism who subsequently took their distance?

Furthermore, the Reichsschriftumkammer was in a position to ban any writing deemed subversive or hostile to the regime, and no publication could see the light without their authorization. Thus the very fact of publishing already meant a certain compromise in the form of collaborating with the system. Conversely, as there were several instances with the power to prohibit a book, the fact that a writer had been criticized by the regime did not necessarily mean that he or she was an opponent. Finally, a certain number of 'internal émigrés', whilst being opposed to the regime, nonetheless shared certain of its values (H. Carossa, E. Wiechert, E. Jünger).[350] Here again, the interpretation proposed by Brekele is questionable: does the fact of exalting nature, the simple life and inwardness in the face of the crimes of the regime constitute a 'humanist opposition' or simply an escape? If a writer cannot be reproached for not having emigrated,[351] the fact of continuing to publish was fraught with ambiguity. Non-Nazi works could appear, but was this true of works that were genuinely anti-Nazi?

The book burnings of 10 May 1933, the publication of 'blacklists', the purging of bookstores and libraries and the creation of the Reichskulturkammern signalled the alignment of all cultural life on the same ideological model. But however complete the repressive character of the system, some gaps and exceptions existed. Erich Kästner, whose works had been burned in 1933 and no longer was allowed to publish in Germany, still managed to have his books published abroad, and for the twenty-fifth anniversary of UFA even wrote the screenplay for *The Adventures of Baron Münchhausen*, the condition being that his name was not mentioned. Moreover, 'non-Nazi' works such as Wiechert's

Das einfache Leben (1939) and even more surprisingly Jünger's *Auf den Marmorklippen* (*On the Marble Cliffs*) of the same year, managed to appear, even though books by authors closer to the regime were sometimes banned.[352] On examining the attitude of representatives of the 'internal emigration' in their dual relationship to Nazi ideology and cultural organizations, one is led not only to reject the existence of a single front, but to distinguish attitudes that are both complex and diversified.

This in no way means that there were no 'literary opponents' under the Third Reich: simply that these were not a large number, and the majority paid for this opposition with their liberty or their life. The perfection of the system of oppression was enough to defeat those more credulous in the possibility of such opposition. Reduced to clandestinity, constantly pursued by the Gestapo, certain opponents managed nonetheless to circulate illegally texts that were in some cases essentially political. It was first of all the proletarian writers, members of the BPRS, who developed this underground activity. The Berlin section of the group continued to exist until 1935, managing even to publish its own journal, *Stich und Hieb*,[353] and to send to the *Neue Deutsche Blätter* in Prague documents on everyday life in Germany. This group consisted of writers and activists who were not well-known to the Nazis: Jan Petersen, Kurt Steffen, Berta Waterstradt, Walter Steller, Elfriede Brüning and Louis Kaufmann. Other writers not connected to the BPRS were also very active, such as Karl Grünberg who wrote unsigned articles in the Swedish press from 1933 to 1937. The activity of the BPRS came to an end when the group was dismantled by the Gestapo in 1935. Jan Petersen managed to emigrate, but other members were imprisoned. Similar groups existed in Hamburg, Magdeburg and Breslau. This literature consisted chiefly of leaflets, appeals and poems printed clandestinely in cellars, then posted on walls or dropped in letterboxes. It also included reportage and short stories. The authors of such texts often displayed great ingenuity in printing them, sometimes cutting the text into rubber blocks or linoleum. This technique had been used under the Weimar Republic with poems by J. R. Becher published in *Rote Fahne* and reprinted in book form in the USSR under the title *An die Wand zu kleben* ('To be Stuck on the Wall'). The same procedure was adopted towards the end of the War by the White Rose group.

Since clandestine printing presses were rare, this literature generally had to be printed abroad and smuggled into Germany in a number of different ways.[354] Besides these clandestine writings there were 'camouflaged writings' (*Tarnschriften*) produced by different anti-Nazi groups, especially those around Willi Münzenberg in Paris, consisting of political writings disguised as first-aid notes, tourist brochures, false German classics, etc.[355] We do not know the exact number of 'disguised' writings that circulated in Germany.[356] Doubtless their influence was extremely limited. They were incapable of effectively mobilizing opinion against Hitler, but their symbolic significance is undeniable. Besides, it was often opposition writers remaining in Germany that made possible the publication in the exile press of concrete information on conditions in the Reich, such as *Die Stimme aus Deutschland*, *Stimme der Illegalen*, and more generally testimonies published in *Deutsche Blätter*, *Internationale Literatur* or *AIZ*. A certain number of texts were written in concentration camps, many of which have not survived. Among the few that were subsequently published are the *Moabiten Sonette* of Albrecht Haushofer, killed by the SS on 23 April 1945, Bruno Apitz's novel *Esther*, written in Buchenwald, and the novel by Werner Krauss (a member of the Schulze-Boyssen resistance group) *Passionen der halkyonischen Seele*.

Finally, alongside writers who remained in Germany and sought to convey in their work a different vision from that of National Socialism, openly protesting against its values and embarking on clandestine action, we should also acknowledge that a minority who refused to exile themselves in 1933 cannot be considered subject to Nazi ideology. For the most part these were condemned to silence. The Dadaist Franz Jung, though very political in the 1920s, did not go into exile. Arrested by the Nazis in 1936, he was released on the intervention of Admiral Canaris, head of the Abwehr. He then took refuge in Prague, Vienna and Paris, and worked in a bank in Budapest, before being arrested by the Hungarian fascists. Managing to escape, he was captured by the Gestapo and taken to Vienna, but succeeded in reaching Italy and was interned in a labour camp until his liberation by the American army. Irmgard Keun, the lover of Josef Roth and author of many famous popular novels such as *Gilgi, eine von uns*, had several of her books destroyed by the Gestapo in 1934. Since this had not been ordered by any judgement, she complained. Harassed by the Gestapo despite being neither Jewish nor very political, she moved from Frankfurt to Amsterdam where her novel *Nach Mitternacht* was published by Querido Verlag in 1937. It was in Ostend that she got to know Roth, already weakened by alcohol and despair. A witness of the invasion of Holland, she was again arrested by the German police, but an officer provided her with a passport in the name of his cousin, which enabled her to return to Germany. She lived under a false identity until the end of the War.

What finally should one say of the companion of Brecht's youth, Marieluise Fleisser, who lived at Ingolstadt, her birthplace in Bavaria, without writing anything but loathing the Nazis? If the term internal emigration has any meaning, it is surely applicable to those writers who abstained from any literary compromise with the Third Reich, no matter that their number is extremely restricted.

The Stages of Exile in Europe

Scarcely had German authors established themselves in the Saar, in Alsace, in Holland, in Belgium, Austria, Czechoslovakia, Poland, the Balkans or Italy, but Hitler arrived and they were forced to flee or be brought back to concentration camps in Germany. Europe became for the exiles a hell with no escape. They ended up with no money, no passport, and no visa to go anywhere. They now simply had to submit to the ever harsher persecution of their old enemies, their compatriots, and their new enemies, the police of their countries of refuge. The pope, Italy, France, England and the Soviet Union all made agreements and pacts with Hitler. On the other hand, no agreement was made between the peoples on behalf of the persecuted. It was in no way surprising that so many of them fell into Hitler's hands, that so many exiles committed suicide, that so few have survived.

Hermann Kesten

It was a ghostly flock.

Stefan Zweig, *The World of Yesterday*

I will hunt them down to the ends of the earth until they perish.

Goebbels

There is practically no country in the world where German writers did not end up. From France to the Soviet Union, from Switzerland to China, from Finland to South Africa, from Brazil to Ireland, scattered over the globe they tried everywhere to spread their works and their ideas.

Wieland Herzfelde

Herzfelde's characterization of the anti-Nazi emigration is tragically true: there were at least forty-one countries in which German-language writers sought refuge between 1933 and 1945.[1] Not all these countries had the same importance in the history of emigration, and Manfred Durzak is right to distinguish 'countries of asylum' from 'countries of exile'. The former are those countries in which émigrés found refuge individually, the second those that enabled them to continue their literary and political activity.[2] The reasons prompting a large number of them to settle in countries that were both fairly remote and culturally distant are not always easy to grasp. It was often the possibility of reaching them without a visa, obtaining permission to stay or authorization to work that determined their choice of such a distant asylum.[3] This was why the writer Karl Wolfskehl emigrated to New Zealand, the expressionist poet Paul Zech to Argentina (he had a brother there, albeit a Nazi sympathizer), the Prague critic Willy Haas to India, and Yiddish theatre players to Shanghai. What about all those university professors who settled in Ankara? Or those who remained in the West Indies because a boat took them there and they could not go any further? For many of them, the final place of exile was not the object of choice: it was imposed on them as a fate, representing a possibility of survival, the only chance of escaping the Gestapo, prison, or concentration camp.

The countries of exile were themselves differentiated by a large number of factors: the number of émigrés they accepted, the conditions of existence encountered, the activities that could be practised. The high number of émigrés that settled in a country did not suffice to make it a particularly important stage in the history of emigration: there was a surprising disproportion between the richness and diversity of the antifascist emigration in the United States and the limited activity it could develop there. Capitals such as Paris, Prague, Amsterdam, Moscow, Mexico City or Santiago de Chile loom larger in the history of exile than New York or any other North American metropolis. Finally, the geography of this diaspora was far from static: it was made up of stages, way-stations, and temporary refuges. The émigré colonies constantly shifted, for internal reasons (the possibility of obtaining work, a residence permit or a visa; political regroupings) but especially for historical ones. In the first years that followed Hitler's coming to power, the anti-Nazi emigration remained encamped in Europe, in German-speaking countries or at least those contiguous to the Reich. With the reunion of the Saar to Nazi Germany, the occupation of Austria and Czechoslovakia, then Poland, the Low Countries and France, it rapidly dispersed ever further afield. A number of expressionist works had popularized the image of the 'way-station drama': now it was the entire German intelligentsia that had to experience this.

We shall limit ourselves first of all to sketching some basic aspects of this emigration in Europe and a few other countries, depicting the diverse conditions of reception that the émigrés met with, and what these different stages of exiles meant in the history of emigration.[4]

1. EXILE IN CZECHOSLOVAKIA

They are a fine people, the Czechs – imaginative, brave, and liberal. I am not only an admirer of Czechoslovakia but also a citizen of that country.

Klaus Mann, *The Turning Point*

The conditions of exile in Czechoslovakia, undoubtedly among the most favourable that the émigrés encountered, are explained by a number of factors.

First of all, the generosity of a people and its president, Masaryk, who had the courage to come to the aid of victims of Hitlerite persecution[5] despite the proximity of the Reich and its continual threats of reprisals. In 1933, the country had 700,000 unemployed.[6] Entry to its territory required no visa or special permit for German refugees, Jewish or otherwise. They were authorized to remain with or without a valid passport, on condition they did not seek work there. Several committees were rapidly created to come to their assistance, check the reasons that had driven them to exile, and gather information on the terror reigning in Germany. A Czechoslovak National Committee for Refugees from Germany had been founded in 1933, bringing together a number of organizations. When it was established that an émigré was a genuine refugee from Nazism, they would receive the famous *Evidenzbögen*, papers that without constituting an actual title to settle in the country, did offer legal protection. A number of measures taken in Prague in favour of the refugees in 1933 would be adopted in France at the time of the Popular Front government. These arrangements, supervised jointly by the police and the refugee committees, made it possible to legitimize their stay and avoid the infiltration of Gestapo agents or Nazi spies. If in theory émigrés were accepted only on a transitional basis, in practice they could until 1938 remain without problems. The Czech government certainly expressed certain preferences towards the émigrés: those who were apolitical or relatively so were preferred to Communist cadres. Yet it was in Prague that the Social-Democratic resistance was reconstituted, and the city was also a centre for many Communist intellectuals.[7] A number of Czech public figures (I. Zollschan, Max Brod, Dr Hubert Ripka) intervened with the government in their favour, circulating manifestos and appeals, especially in cases where their antifascist activities, far from contravening the asylum conditions, were perfectly legitimate. It seems that these petitions finally played a major part in the decisions taken by the Czechoslovak authorities towards the émigrés.[8]

This benign attitude aroused the hostility of the Reich, which protested on numerous occasions and threatened Czechoslovakia with reprisals if it allowed such activity to develop on its territory.[9] The Nazis also had at their disposal powerful organizations of supporters capable of upsetting the country's political balance. Though the NSDAP had been proscribed since 1933, many Nazi groups remained active under the rubric of 'gymnastic societies', such as the Sudeten-German Patriotic Front of Konrad Heinlein.[10] The activity of Hitler's agents in Czechoslovakia was particularly brutal: for example the murders of Professor Theodor Lessing and the radio engineer Rudolf Formis, a colleague of Otto Strasser. In two years the Gestapo attempted more than fourteen kidnappings,[11] and a Nazi agent, Viktor Wolf, tried to make out that the emigrants were forging counterfeit coins. A number of Gestapo agents raided émigré homes disguised as Czech police, with the complicity of Sudeten Germans who were fully bilingual. At the same time, many German firms were involved in distributing Nazi propaganda in Czechoslovakia, and informed the Gestapo on émigré activities. As for the Nazi students at the German University of Prague, they often demonstrated against professors hostile to National

Socialism.[12] A certain number of émigrés who had been deprived of German nationality[13] wished to acquire Czech citizenship, and the pro-Nazi elements opposed this with extreme violence.[14] The government was thus sometimes led to restrict émigré activity by calling the most active elements to order.[15] But on the whole, antifascists had great freedom of expression. Max Deri, Kurt Hiller, Ludwig Hardt, Anton Kuh, Heinrich and Thomas Mann all gave many lectures. Several were able to speak on the radio, and even to broadcast anti-Nazi programmes to Germany from transmitters that though illegal were tolerated, such as that of Otto Strasser's Schwarze Front.

Czech publishers such as Orbis Verlag produced the works of German émigrés, and until 1938 Prague was the exiled seat of the Social-Democratic leadership. Socialist, Communist and Trotskyist publishing houses all thrived, and if the Czech government intervened – as it did apropos the publication of *Simplicissimus* – so as not to envenom its relations with the Reich, it allowed the exile press to develop on condition that the responsible editor was Czech. This posed hardly any problem, given the close ties that united German writers with those of Prague. John Heartfield was able to exhibit his photomontages in spring 1934, which aroused a very lively response from Germany.[16] This attitude was sharpened in 1937, when the danger of German invasion increased and Goebbels offered to end a press campaign against Czechoslovakia if the country banned the émigré press.

Benès agreed to take certain measures, without really believing in the Reich-minister's sincerity. The *Neue Vorwärts*, organ of the SoPaDe, had to move to Paris, and from summer 1938 the *Neue Weltbühne* stopped publication. Yet on 25 June 1938 a *Volkskulturtag* could still be organized in Reichenberg, with the participation of Czech Communists and many German émigrés, including Heinrich Mann. As tension between Prague and Berlin continued to grow, however, émigré activities were increasingly restricted.

According to Kurt Grossmann, the number of émigrés settled in Czechoslovakia was quite considerable.[17] They included such leading political and literary figures as Brecht, Oskar Maria Graf, Rudolf Olden, F. Höllering, P. Kast, Kurt Hiller, Heinz Pol, Theodor Balk, L. Turek, M. Zimmering, Ernst Ottwalt, P. Nickl, W. Ilberg, Fritz Erpenbeck, Alfred Wolfenstein, Ernst Bloch and Heinrich Mann. The latter maintains in his autobiography[18] that the antifascist émigrés were not merely tolerated but received like family. This quite unique situation is explained by the liberal tradition of the Czech government, the existence of a German-language Czech literature, and above all by the close ties between Prague writers and those of Germany. The *Prager-deutsche Literatur* formed a particularly favorable milieu for the reception of the émigrés. Its multifarious tendencies included those symbolized by the names Rainer Maria Rilke, Franz Kafka, Franz Werfel, Egon Erwin Kisch, G. Meyrink, F. C. Weiskopf and Louis Fürnberg. Many of these writers had a readership that went well beyond their own country, and refused – Kisch for example – to see themselves as 'Sudeten Germans', preferring to call themselves 'German writers of Czechoslovakia'. Hostile to any nationalism, their hatred of Nazism was completely natural. These writers were all the more detested by the Nazis in that many were of Jewish origin and the others considered as 'traitors' to the cause of the Sudeten Germans and the 'greater Reich'.

The majority of émigrés in Czechoslovakia settled in Prague[19] where these German-language Czech writers already lived, though many had stayed for a while in Berlin. In 1925, F. C. Weiskopf had sought to establish a 'left front of progressive writers', uniting Socialists and Communists who were keen to establish their Czech identity. Having had to struggle for its own freedom, Czechoslovakia had a genuine understanding for the German antifascists. In his lecture 'Erfahrungen im Exil zu Prag', Wieland Herzfelde maintained: 'German-Czech: this may be a difficulty of language for us, but there is no opposition morally or ideologically.' It was in Prague that the *Neue Deutsche Blätter* was published, with 7,000 copies of its first issue (September 1933) containing the celebrated appeal by Wieland Herzfelde, 'Wir wollen deutsch reden', which proclaimed 'He who writes, acts. The *NDB* seeks to unite contributors and readers in common actions. We want to fight fascism with our literary and critical words. In Germany the Nazis are raging, we find ourselves in a state of war. There is no neutrality, not for anyone. Above all, not for writers.'[20]

The activities of antifascist émigrés were as rich in terms of literature and publishing as they were in politics.[21] After the banning of the SPD on 22 June 1933 and the annulment of its deputies' mandates, the members of its *Vorstand* took refuge in Prague and became the only official representatives of German Social-Democracy in exile. They sought to renew links with those who had remained in Germany, and smuggle clandestine writings and leaflets into the Reich. Besides the *Deutschland-Berichte der SoPaDe* published in Prague from June 1933, significant Socialist journals reappeared in Czechoslovakia such as *Neue Vorwärts* and *Sozialistische Aktion*. It was also in Prague that the famous 1934 manifesto 'Combat and Objective of Revolutionary Socialism: The Politics of the German Social-Democratic Party' was published.[22] The group *Neu Beginnen* – standing for a resistance action outside of the KPD and SPD – established itself there around W. Löwenheim, while the leaders of the two parties met in the city on 23 November 1935 to decide on united action.

The activity of the Communists was fairly substantial. With the mass arrest of KPD cadres, a number tried to flee Germany by clandestinely crossing the Czech frontier.[23] Many lived first of all in Strasnice, or organized clandestine work until the police expelled them in May 1937 following a press campaign against this 'nest of conspirators'.[24] They continued nonetheless to distribute illegal leaflets and journals, to struggle against the Nazi propaganda of the Sudeten Germans. Many German-language Communist journals reappeared in Prague, including *Der Funke*. Bruno Frei published a whole series of pamphlets, under the name Karl Franz, explaining the situation in Germany. In April 1933 Wieland Herzfelde's Malik Verlag published Rudolf Olden's *Hitler, der Oberer*. In March–April, F. C. Weiskopf, Wieland Herzfelde and Bruno Frei founded the journal *Gegen-Angriff*. Ties were established between the Communist exiles in Prague and Willi Münzenberg in Paris to coordinate their actions. *Gegen-*

Angriff, printed in Strasbourg, would appear as a daily during the Reichstag fire trial, and with its two editions – Paris and Prague – became one of the most important antifascist journals.[25] In March 1936 there appeared in place of *Gegen-Angriff* the *Deutsche Volkszeitung* directed by L. Breuer. Many émigrés of different tendencies assisted with these periodicals.[26]

At the Bertolt-Brecht-Klub, émigrés frequently gave lectures.[27] Ernst Bloch presented his theories on utopia. Texts were read by Erich Mühsam, Lion Feuchtwanger, Heinrich and Thomas Mann, J. R. Becher and Egon Erwin Kisch. Wieland Herzfelde even held a workshop for writers, while F. C. Weiskopf brought German exiles together with Czech writers. The cultural journal *Tvorba* published in 1935 an 'open letter to President Masaryk', requesting him to withdraw his candidacy for the Nobel Peace Prize in favour of Carl von Ossietzky. Committees of Czech and German writers staged works by émigrés such as Brecht's *Threepenny Opera* and plays by Friedrich Wolf. From 1934, frequent solidarity meetings were held to defend antifascists imprisoned in Germany, while the Czechoslovak *Schriftstellerverband* held an exhibition of books burned in Germany.

These activities were facilitated by the creation of a number of magazines and publishing houses. Malik Verlag, which had been established in Prague in April 1933, formed in Bruno Frei's words 'the first roof over the head of emigration literature'.[28] Besides *Der Gegen-Angriff*, the *AIZ* also appeared in Prague (later known as the *Volksillustrierte Zeitung*), as did *Neue Weltbühne* under the direction of William S. Schlamm, then Hermann Budzislawki, before moving to Paris in August 1939, as well as *Neue Deutsche Blätter* and *Simplicissimus* (subsequently *Simplicus*).[29] Prague was also the exiled seat of Strasser's Schwarze Front, which organized anti-Hitler broadcasts from its 'black transmitter', eventually silenced by the Gestapo.[30]

The constant attacks of the German press, and the Reich's direct interventions, forced Czechoslovakia to steadily restrict the activities of the émigrés. But the situation only began to deteriorate substantially in 1937. The government was then forced to limit émigré activity on its territory, so as not to inflame relations with Hitler's Germany. Between 1937 and 1938 the majority of antifascist journals had to emigrate to Paris. The situation worsened again on 21 May 1938 while German troops concentrated in Saxony. It became increasingly urgent for émigrés to flee Czechoslovakia, but where to? Max Brod wrote in his autobiography, *A Combative Life*: 'After the Munich agreement which left Czechoslovakia only an illusory sovereignty, I decided with a number of friends to emigrate to Palestine. [. . .] We did not think there was any great hurry. Hitler had publicly declared that now German Bohemia had been ceded to him [. . .] he had no intention of bringing a single Czech under his authority.'[31]

But the political climate of the Czech 'second republic' that followed the Munich agreement was increasingly suffocating for Czech writers as well as for the German émigrés,[32] even if still only a few realized the urgency of the danger. After the Munich agreement the British government had issued some 2,500 certificates permitting Sudeten Jews to leave for Palestine. But the administrative formalities were so complex that according to Max Brod, no more than a thousand of these were actually taken up. The Jews of Prague only received ten certificates, as the British did not consider them threatened.

Max Brod and his friends finally decided to leave for Palestine. Arriving at Cracow, they learned that their country no longer existed, that the Nazis had arrived in Prague and that theirs had been the last train out. The majority of Jews and antifascists who could not reach Britain, Palestine or the United States were massacred at Auschwitz, Theresienstadt, Mauthausen and Belzec. The expressionist playwright Paul Kornfeld, born in Prague in 1889, returned to his home town after the Nazis came to power. Refusing to emigrate, he was deported as a Jew in 1941, and died in the Lodz concentration camp.

2. EXILE IN AUSTRIA

The choice of Austria as a place of exile was easily explicable: a country of German language and familiar culture where émigrés did not even feel foreign. In 1932–33, moreover, no visa was needed between Germany and Austria. German citizens could live there as long as they liked, as long as they did not seek work. A number of Austrian figures had played an important part under the Weimar Republic. It was common for German journalists, especially Social-Democrats, to be regular contributors to Austrian newspapers, while Viennese writers were tied in many ways to those of Berlin.[33] Yet Austria was very parsimonious in its acceptance of German émigrés. It was generally only a stop on their itinerary, and many preferred to take refuge in Prague or Paris. Vienna hardly seemed safe to them.[34]

The Austrian government was not prepared to welcome to its territory any political émigrés who might strengthen the parties of the left. As early as autumn 1933 measures were taken to prevent the entry into Austria of a certain number of political refugees (including Will Schaber). The familiarity of Austrian culture was largely offset by an unfavourable political situation.[35] From 1932 onwards, Austria had entered a phase of systematic limitation of democracy and liberty. Chancellor Dollfuss did not conceal his sympathy for fascism, his successor Schuschnigg still less so, even if the irony of history was subsequently to present them both as martyrs and opponents of National Socialism.

Despite the favourable conditions that it might have offered, therefore, Austria ultimately attracted relatively few émigrés. Those who had fled National Socialism had no desire to fall into the hands of the 'Austro-fascists'. After 1936, moreover, anti-Semitic persecution became just as strong as in Germany, and equally cynical. If the majority of European countries saw the formation of committees to aid the refugees, practically none were established in Austria. Whilst the Austrian government declared itself anti-Nazi, and the NSDAP was actually banned on 19 June 1933, it did not tolerate antifascist activity on its territory. No significant anti-Nazi publication could be found in Vienna, and no publisher of exile literature apart from G. Bermann Fischer, whose position was often ambiguous. The *Neue Weltbühne* was published there for a while, until pressure from Chancellor Dollfuss forced it to leave for Prague. Otto Strasser recalled that the Viennese prefect of police, Steinhäusl, was a Gestapo spy.[36] He often sought to pin responsibility on émigrés for violent attacks that had actually been carried out by the Austrian fascists. At the time Hitler took power in Germany, workers' organizations and left-wing parties were being persecuted in Austria. If the Austrian government was bound to fear Hitler for the threat he represented towards its own country, its internal politics were already close to fascism, especially in its attitude towards the working class. On 8 March 1933, Dolfuss banned gatherings, public meetings and demonstrations, and considerably restricted press freedom, to such a degree that the monarchy seemed in hindsight to have been almost liberal. From 15 March 1933 the Austrian parliament ceased to play any role, and a genuine atmosphere of civil war prevailed in Vienna.

For a certain period, the Austrian government sought to violently repress the partisans of National Socialism, while restraining as far as it possibly could the power and activities of the workers' organizations.[37] Mediation between the government and the Socialists failed to get anywhere.[38] The Austrian Social-Democrats had only one real force at their disposal, the Republikanischer Schutzbund, but no more than the party itself did this want to launch a real struggle against Dollfuss. In February 1934, it finally fell victim to a provocation of Starhemberg's pro-Nazi movement and was defeated after several days of bloody confrontation. After July 1934, the pro-Nazi movements scaled up their activities. The Reich radio broadcast to Austria under the responsibility of Inspector Habitsch, in charge of Austrian questions. There were frequent acts of terrorism: occupation of the radio station, the murder of Chancellor Dollfuss, fighting in Carinthia and Styria. There was also an NSDAP group known as *Österreich* established in Munich. The participants in the 1934 putsch, who appeared to have been abandoned by Hitler, took refuge in Yugoslavia, but subsequently returned to Germany to establish an 'Austrian legion'. In August 1934, von Papen was nominated minister-plenipotentiary in Vienna, and took charge of reconstituting the pro-Nazi organizations, including the 'union of Reich Germans'. If some of these and too well known were forced to dissolve, new ones were formed in secret.[39]

The conflicts of 1934 claimed more than three hundred dead, and several members of the Schutzbund were murdered.[40] The Social-Democrat leaders – Otto Bauer, Julius Deutsch, Ernst Fischer[41] – emigrated to Prague, Moscow or Paris. A certain number of Austrian writers already decided at that point to go into exile (Klara Blum, Julius Hay, Friedrich Bruegel, Hedda Zinner, Stefan Zweig, Robert Neumann, Julius Braunthal). The measures that were subsequently taken against the opposition[42] only increased the parallels between the Austrian and Hitlerite regimes: the banning of the workers' parties, imprisonment, arbitrary arrest, etc. The majority of anti-Nazi émigrés felt immediately threatened, in the same way as Austrian progressive figures. It was not only the opposition leaders who had to leave Austria; writers such as Stefan Zweig were also forced to seek exile in England. Though scarcely political, Zweig suffered the humiliation of having his home in Salzburg raided, the police claiming to be looking for a Schutzbund arms depot.[43] Many émigrés left Austria in 1934 after the banning of the SPÖ (Oskar Maria Graf, Wilhelm Hoegner, Waldemar von Knoeringen, Fritz Sternberg). Among those who remained, several were arrested, such as the dramatist Julius Hay, accused of having published a clandestine journal during the street fighting.[44] It is not surprising, then, that those German émigrés who chose Austria after 1934 as their place of exile included relatively few who were very political. The majority of progressive Austrian authors did not want to have any further relations with the regime,[45] which appeared to them as a lesser evil only in comparison with Hitlerite barbarity. Those who remained in Austria, having failed to find another place of asylum, were condemned to clandestine work.[46] The majority of émigrés judged Schuschnigg's regime pretty severely. If Carl Zuckmayer speaks of it in his memoirs with a certain sympathy, most intellectuals, even the least politicized, denounced the repression that now reigned in Austria. F. T. Csokor and Robert Musil, though still living in Vienna, felt themselves exiles in their own country. Sigmund Freud did not dare publish his essay on *Moses and Monotheism*.[47] On 20 February 1934 he wrote to Ernst Freud: 'The future is uncertain; either Austrian fascism or the swastika. In the latter event we shall have to leave; native fascism we are willing to take in our stride up to a certain point; it can hardly treat us as badly as its German cousin.'[48]

While the émigrés could not trust a government that by 1937 no longer hesitated to return Communist or Social-Democratic refugees who had arrived illegally in Austria to the Gestapo, there were few Austrian intellectuals or writers prepared to offer them any support. Ernst Bloch and his wife, during their exile in Vienna, frequented the homes of the sculptor Fritz Wotruba, the composer Ernst Krenek, the publisher Zsolnay and Elias Canetti, as well as Franz Werfel and Alma Mahler.[49] But one could also encounter Chancellor Schuschnigg at the home of the latter couple. Karl Kraus, for his part, joked about the émigrés, not the Nazis, and when intellectuals left for exile, wrote: 'The rats are leaving the ship.' Already at the PEN Club congress of 1933, certain members of the Austrian section were forced to resign, including former president Felix Salten, for protesting about the book burnings in Germany.

One might well ask what impelled certain German émigrés to seek refuge in a country so heavy with threats. In general these were authors of Austrian or Hungarian origin[50] who had settled in Berlin around the mid 1920s and hoped to find support from Austrian friends (Franz Blei, Ferdinand Bruckner, Albert Ehrenstein, Julius Hay, Ödön von Horvath, Fritz Kortner, Peter de Mendelssohn, Robert Musil, Alfred Polgar, Hertha Pauli, Max Reinhardt, Alexander Roda-Roda, Paul Roubitzsek). Or else they were German authors for whom Austria was only the first step on their path of exile (Ulrich Becher, Mischa Boljansky, Bruno Frank, Paul Frischauer, Oskar Maria Graf, Wieland Herzfelde, Friedrich Wolf, Hedda Zinner, Carl Zuckmayer). Many left Austria before 1938,[51] and the number of antifascist émigrés steadily fell in the years after 1934. Moreover, after 11 July 1936 and the rapprochement between Germany and Austria that von Papen had mediated, it was foreseeable that the NSDAP would again be legalized and anti-Nazi propaganda forbidden. The climate of censorship and repression that prevailed in Austria also explains the limited character of émigré activity there. There was no major antifascist journal, even if G. Bermann Fischer managed to establish in Vienna, with the authorization of the Nazis, a division of his Fischer Verlag which produced works forbidden in Germany. He published there Peter Altenberg, Richard Beer-Hoffmann, Alice Beren, Alfred Döblin, Martin Gumpert, Moritz Hermann, Friedrich Heydenau, Hugo von Hoffmannsthal, Arthur Holitscher, Harry Graf Kessler, Annette Kolb, Thomas Mann, Arthur Schnitzler, Bernard Shaw, Jacob Wassermann and Carl Zuckmayer. After 1934, any real struggle against fascism in Austria became an illusion, with Social-Democrat activists reduced to clandestinity or arrested. Any émigré suspected of political activity risked immediate expulsion. When Hitler's armies invaded Austria on 15 March 1938, many Austrians gave them a triumphal welcome. The situation of émigrés then became completely desperate. In her memoir of Ödön von Horvath, Hertha Pauli[52] describes the anguish of refugees who witnessed in her apartment, with the blinds drawn, the entry of the Nazis into Vienna. Walter Mehring managed to cross the Swiss frontier, with the Gestapo already after him. Horvath took refuge in Czechoslovakia, Theodor Csokor in Poland. In a letter to Karl Kunschke,[53] Csokor described the wave of terror that gripped the Austrian capital, and even Alma Mahler recalls in her memoirs that it was not advisable to move around the city without a swastika on your car. A wave of fervent anti-Semitism took hold of the country. Oppositionists and Jews were forced to scratch off anti-Nazi posters with their fingernails. A large number were immediately arrested by the Gestapo, and many of them murdered.

A number of antifascist writers who did not manage to escape in time took their own lives. These included Hans Friedrich Enk, Alfred Grünwald and Egon Friedell, the celebrated art historian, who threw himself out of his window when he saw the Gestapo coming down the street. Hermann Broch, who lived in Alt-Aussee, was arrested by 'provincial Nazis'. He was both Jewish and known from his novels as an opponent of National Socialism. It was during his imprisonment, when he expected to be killed, that he had the idea for one of his finest works, *The Death of Virgil*. Thanks to the intervention of James Joyce and Stephen Hudson, he managed to leave Austria and find refuge in England, then the United States. Others were unable to escape: R. Auernheimer, F. Beda-Löhner, F. Bergammer, A. Golz, B. Herlig, A. Klahr, E. A. Reinhardt and J. Soyfer were arrested and sent to concentration camp. Some, however – Auernheimer, Bergammer, Elbogen, Engel and Klahr – eventually managed to reach exile in Britain or America.

The Austrian emigration then joined forces with the German anti-Nazi emigration in Prague, Paris, Zurich, London and Moscow. But in 1938, with the deteriorating international situation, the conditions of reception were worse than in 1933. Many Austrian exiles were sent back at the frontier, Jews above all, and most commonly they were refused any possibility of work. G. Bermann Fischer, Franz Werfel, H. Schnitzler, Albert Bassermann, F. Horch, Alfred

Polgar and Carl Zuckmayer first of all reached Switzerland, where they were forbidden activity of any kind. Even Czechoslovakia closed its borders after the *Anschluss*, to avoid too great an influx of refugees. In the *Prager Tagblatt* for 18 September 1938, Polgar reflected ironically on the situation of these refugees who tried to reach Switzerland or Czechoslovakia, comparing them to a drowning man: people see him from both banks, and would be ready to help him as long as he doesn't reach *their* side of the river.[54]

It was Britain that received the greatest number of Austrian refugees. In March 1938 a German PEN Club in exile was re-established in London under the chairmanship of Rudolf Olden, together with an Austrian PEN presided over by Franz Werfel and Robert Neumann. With the support of English figures such as Storm Jameson and Herman Ould, they sought to help the large number of threatened Austrian intellectuals with visas and material support. This is how Sigmund Freud, Elias Canetti, Hermann Brosch, Oskar Kokoschka, Theodor Kramer, Fritz Lampl, J. Lederer, C. Rössler and Hilde Spiel arrived in London. The majority were taken charge of by the Emergency Rescue Committee, and many emigrated to the United States with the aid of Hermann Kesten and Thomas Mann. A certain number still remained in Czechoslovakia, Switzerland or France (Vicki Baum, Oskar Baum, Richard Beer-Hofmann, Franz Blei, Ernst Deutsch, Hertha Pauli, Robert Pich, Alfred Polgar, Alexander Roda-Roda, Hans Sahl, Friedrich Torberg and Franz Werfel). A small number were allowed to remain in Switzerland (Rudolf Kassner, Robert Musil).[55] Others fell into the hands of the Gestapo in 1940 or committed suicide (Ernst Weiss). Some went into exile in Palestine (Martha Hofmann, Leo Perentz, Heinz Politzer), in South America (Egon Eis, Fred Heller, Paila Ludwig, Egon Erwin Kisch), in Italy (F. T. Csokor), in Yugoslavia (Alexander Sacher-Masoch, Hermann F. Manner), Sweden (G. Bermann Fischer, R. Braun) or China (Fritz Jensen, Susanne Wantoch). They were never able to form a single centre as Austrian authors, and remained dispersed.

3. EXILE IN THE NETHERLANDS

The Netherlands was relatively favourable to antifascist émigrés. The authorities did not require a visa for German, Austrian or Czechoslovak nationals, and accepted a large number of refugees without passports. The country's frontiers were also open to political exiles – provided they renounced political activity – and to Jewish refugees. Despite severe regulations governing work permits,[56] the Dutch authorities were fairly liberal in granting exiles permission to practise their profession if this was useful to the nation. The majority of witnesses – including Erika Mann, F. Landshoff, J. P. Kroonenburg and Walter Zadek[57] – agree that even after 1934, when the regulations became more severe, those who had found refuge in Holland while waiting to reach other countries were authorized to remain there. If the border controls could send back anyone unable to prove sufficient financial means, entry was allowed if their return to Germany would place their life in danger. This was very much more favourable than the measures in force in the majority of European countries. The ban on pursuing political activity is easily explicable: Holland was a neutral country, and the internal political situation had to be taken into account.[58] If National Socialism had few sympathizers in Holland, the same was true of Communism. Opposition to fascism often came from non-party groups: the Unity for Democracy founded in 1935, and the Vigilance Committee of Antifascist Intellectuals (1936). But if the Dutch government did not take any serious measure against the émigrés, neither did it do anything in their favour. The most effective help came from private sources: committees to aid Jewish refugees, Protestant and Catholic committees.[59] The Dutch population was more inclined to respond to humanitarian imperatives than economic ones. If political activities were officially forbidden, the émigrés often circumvented this ban and Holland became the preferred meeting-place between exiles and oppositionists who remained in Germany.[60] When such activity became too visible, the police were satisfied with expelling its agents to Belgium.[61] On 24 February 1934 a clandestine congress of Socialist youth was held at Laren, outside Amsterdam, with the view of forming a Fourth (Trotskyist) Youth International. Besides Dutch nationals, a number of foreign delegates took part in the conference, including eight Germans. The venue was discovered by the police and the delegates arrested. Most foreigners were expelled to Belgium, but the German Socialists (Franz Bobzien, Heinz Goldberg, Heinz Hose, Kurt Liebermann) were handed over to the Gestapo, together with a number of refugees.[62]

At least thirty thousand German émigrés took refuge in the Netherlands. Activists and writers as well as artists, they included actors and cabaret performers such as Rudi Nelson, Kurt Geron, Otto Walburg and Max Ehrlich. Holland was also a staging-post for other exiled writers. Max Hermann-Neisse, Joseph Roth, Klaus Mann, Walter Kolbenhoff, Irmgard Keun,[63] Ludwig Berger and Wolfgang Cordan stayed for a while in the country. In June 1938 alone, more than seven thousand political refugees were registered with the police. The real number was substantially higher, as those most at risk refrained from announcing their arrival, for fear of being handed to the Gestapo in the name of 'defence against elements dangerous to the state'. The majority of those who took refuge in Holland were progressive liberal writers. They found not only a readership – German literature, whether émigré or not, was widely reviewed in Holland – but also publishers. As the Dutch government did not consider this exile literature to be political activity, it was possible for Allert de Lange and Emmanuel Querido to set up significant publishing houses for German literature in exile. Some other publishers – van Kampen, de Gemeenschap, Contact, Sijthoff – disappeared from view, but those two rapidly became the most celebrated émigré publishers. Contact between Dutch and anti-Nazi publishers were established by Nico Rost,[64] who put Querido Verlag in touch with Fritz Landshoff, the former director of Kiepenheuer Verlag. In a similar way, links were established with Hermann Kesten and Walter Landauer, who contributed to Kiepenheuer and Allert de Lange Verlag.

The most remarkable figure among these exile publishers was Emmanuel Querido. Born in Amsterdam in 1871, into a family of Portuguese-Jewish origin, his brother Israel Querido was a well-known writer. In 1898 he founded a bookshop, then in 1915 a publishing house that had its first great success with the translation of Henri Barbusse's anti-war novels *L'Enfer* and *Le Feu*. He himself wrote an autobiographical novel under the pseudonym Joost Mendes, *The Race of Santeljanos*. Querido published socialist writings, and texts by Trotsky and Otto Bauer, while keeping his distance from any political party. Through Nico Rost as intermediary, he told Fritz Landshoff[65] of his decision to open his publishing house to German exile authors. He even undertook the direction of this project himself, which led to the formation of a German section of Querido Verlag. In 1934 this became independent from the parent company, and published novels by Alfred Döblin, Lion Feuchtwanger, Bruno and Leonhard Frank, Oskar Maria Graf, Irmgard Keun, Heinrich and Klaus Mann, Gustav Regler, Josef Roth, Anna Seghers, Ernst Weiss and Arnold Zweig, as well as political essays by Konrad Heiden, Emil Ludwig, Heinrich Mann, Rudolf Olden and Leopold Schwarzschild. Querido also published a number of works against Hitler's Germany such as the reportage by A. den Doolaards, *Swastika over Europe*, and J. de Kadts, *Fascism and the New Freedom*. The exiles' novels, published in editions of three thousand, enabled the payment of royalties to authors that often formed their only source of income. Arrested by the Gestapo in 1943, Emmanuel Querido perished in concentration camp along with his wife.

Allert de Lange had founded a publishing house in 1880 that was subsequently directed by Gerard de Lange.[66] Walter Landauer and Hermann Kesten, who worked there as readers, developed a practice quite close to that of Querido Verlag. Gerard de Lange had wanted initially to publish an anthology of German writers in exile. He was so touched by their fate that he decided to open a division of his publishing house for them. Other publishers made similar efforts. De Boeckenvrienden Solidariteit at Hilversum, founded by H. Kohn, published Dutch translations of works by German émigrés (E. E. Kisch, Ernst Toller, Bertolt Brecht, Theodor Plievier) as well as other antifascist authors. Der Arbeiderspers (Amsterdam) published the first testimonies on the concentration camps (Gerhard Seger, *Oranienburg*, 1934; Walter Hornung, *Dachau*, 1936), alongside novels by Ernst Glaeser and Lion Feuchtwanger.

It was also in Amsterdam, with Querido Verlag, that Klaus Mann established his magazine *Die Sammlung*, sponsored by André Gide, Aldous Huxley and Heinrich Mann, which counted among its contributors, during the first years of emigration, authors as varied as Günther Anders, J. R. Becher, Ernst Bloch, Bertolt Brecht, Bruno Frank, F. Hardenkopf, Max Hermann-Neisse, Else Lasker-Schüler, Rudolf Leonhard, Ernst Weiss and Arnold Zweig. The title of the review gives a fairly accurate idea of its intentions: to gather together exiled anti-Nazi writers despite their political differences. The Nazis immediately reacted by publishing in October 1933 a warning from the Reichsstelle zur Förderung Deutschen Schrifttums threatening to boycott all the writers who contributed to it and whose books were still on sale in Germany.[67]

The genuine success of émigré literature published in Holland was felt by the Nazis as a real competition with the literature of the Reich, capable of damaging the export of German books. *Die Neue Literatur* (published by Will Vesper) declared in 1934: 'The books of emigrants, all printed in Jewified Amsterdam by Dutchmen such as the Jewish publishers Querido, Allert de Lange and van Kampen almost completely dominate the market for German books here, and the genuinely literary books of New Germany are passed over in silence as they formerly were in Germany under the domination of the Jews.'

In response to this situation, the Gestapo flooded the Netherlands with Nazi pamphlets, and severe attacks from Goebbels forced the Dutch government to take measures against those émigrés who were too active (such as Heinz Liepmann) and forbid certain works that risked unleashing Nazi anger. The publishers of exile literature were also led to be rather more prudent.[68] Émigré political activity was nonetheless fairly significant in most areas of culture, a fact explicable by the quality of the refugee artists. These included conductors such as Bruno Walter, who in 1934 played in Amsterdam the works of composers hated by the Nazis such as Kurt Weill and Ernst Krenek, and a considerable number of actors and directors, many of whom were sent to concentration camps after 1940. German theatre companies played Schiller as well as Brecht, Ernst Toller and Friedrich Wolf. A certain number of these productions however were banned for fear of German reprisals, in particular Friedrich Wolf's *The Sailors of Cattaro* and Brecht's *The Mother*. In the same fashion, a certain number of broadcasts were censored, and the police interrupted a recital of Ernst Busch. Goebbels threatened the Dutch government with banning any performance of a German work in Holland if the country continued to tolerate this émigré theatrical activity. As it was hard to produce political plays, some directors limited themselves to progressive classical works: Leopold Jessner presented plays of Schiller exalting liberty in all the major Dutch cities.

The role of cabaret was also important. Erika Mann transported her Pfeffermühle to Holland, where it performed from 1934 to 1936. Another group, Ping-Pong (Dora Gerson, Erwin Parker, K. E. Wolff) interpreted antifascist songs or others banned in Germany. Rudi Nelson, one of the fathers of Berlin variety in the 1920s, also established the cabaret La Gaieté in Amsterdam and successfully mounted a number of reviews between 1934 and 1940. The Theater der Prominenten, grouping actors and cabaret artists who had formerly worked in Berlin, on screen as well as on stage (Willi Rosen, Siegfried Arno, Otto Wallburg), presented a number of reviews with sketches. A number of actors and directors managed to integrate into the Dutch cinema (Richard Oswald, Max Ophuls). Many representatives of the Bauhaus also settled in Holland (F. R. Wildenhain, Hajo Rose), as well as such well-known painters as Heinrich Campendounck, close to the Blaue Reiter, and Max Beckmann. Klaus Mann, Lion Feuchtwanger and Joseph Roth gave many lectures against fascism. An exhibition of émigré books was also organized by the bookshop Mensingh en Vissen in The Hague.

When the Nazis invaded Holland, a large section of refugees who had not managed to escape in good time were arrested, returned to Germany and interned in concentration camps. This did not stop Rudi Nelson and his friends from actually recreating their cabarets in concentration camp, such as the review *Total Verrückt*. Many émigrés were arrested and murdered in Auschwitz, including Emmanuel Querido, Max Sievers and Walter Landauer. R. Oering committed suicide in 1940. Some, like Irmgard Keun, owed their survival only to chance. Finally, among the emigrants to Holland were the parents of a little girl of four, born in Frankfurt in 1929, who managed to hide the diary that she subsequently kept, later known worldwide as *The Diary of Anne Frank*.

Holland's neighbouring countries Luxemburg and Belgium did not play a major role in the history of emigration. They were only staging-posts, places of temporary asylum. Annette Kolb and Karl Schnog stayed in Luxemburg, Max Sievers in Belgium, where the expressionist author Carl Sternheim also lived.[69] A certain number of exiles settled in Antwerp, as the mayor of the city, who was also chief of police, made clear his antifascist convictions by protecting German émigrés. The reports of the Reich consulate depict quite substantial émigré activities in the press (Social-Democratic and Communist). Three antifascist journals appeared in the city: *Unser Wort* (Trotskyist), *Deutschland Information des Zentral-komitees der KPD* (1938–39) and *Freies Deutschland* (published from early 1937 by Max Sievers). The curator of the Bibliothèque Nationale, Lode Baeckelmann, often came to the assistance of the émigrés and was supportive enough to archive their leaflets.

    Antwerp was also the site of major theatrical activity, as many actors or directors had taken refuge there.[70] And political refugees in Belgium included such varied figures as Salomon Dembitzer, Harry Domela (famous for having passed himself off for a long while as the eldest son of the Crown Prince), and Hans Bendgens-Henner, whose fate was especially tragic. He was expelled from Belgium to Holland (where he had initially settled) on the pretext of having crossed the frontier illegally on arrival from Amsterdam. After living clandestinely for a while, he was arrested and taken back to the border in November 1939. The Dutch police imprisoned him in Amsterdam for two months, before sending him to an internment camp for refugees. He requested in vain to be sent back to Belgium, where his family had settled without any resources. Even though he reminded the authorities that he had not applied for a work permit and that his politics were purely pacifist, his request went unanswered. His wife also intervened to no avail: she was denied the status of political refugee. Dutch friends managed to get him expelled again to Belgium, while Antwerp writers signed a petition in his favour. On 9 May 1940 he was interned again as a foreigner and deported to France, in a convoy of Jews, Nazis and Communists. Belgian soldiers handed them all over to the French army as 'fifth columnists'. His family was taken in by an Antwerp shopkeeper of Dutch origin. They moved back to Düsseldorf where he had himself been imprisoned. His son had to join the Hitler Youth so as not to die of hunger. Hans Bendgens-Henner was hanged on 15 November 1942.

    Émigré activities had little resonance in Belgium apart from radio broadcasts by Ernst Busch and Hanns Eisler, made possible thanks to a number of Socialists working for the Belgian radio. The émigré press was little read, and according to Heinz Kühn, hardly more than five copies of *Das Freie Deutschland* were sold at Brussels station. While the left showed a certain interest in the activities of German émigrés, the Flemish nationalists, attracted by the 'new Germany', were often used by the Nazis to spy on them. In April 1936, the Thirteenth Flemish Congress of Philology held in Gent was devoted to the new literary currents in Germany, but no criticism was made of the situation of German writers. From 1939, under the auspices of H. F. Blunck, the Reich sought a further rapprochement with the Flemish nationalists, a number of whom joined the SS. Flemish students were invited to study in Germany.[71]

4. EXILE IN BRITAIN

At many times in its history Britain had received a fairly sizeable number of refugees – after the revolutions of 1848, for example. In 1933, however, its attitude was very different. It is true that few anti-Nazi émigrés immediately thought of settling there. It was only with the annexation of Austria that it became a real land of asylum, especially for many Jews.[72] This situation is explained in large part by the economic crisis that Britain was suffering, and its high rate of unemployment. If German, Austrian and Czech citizens were in principle accepted without visa, the immigration authorities could always forbid access to refugees without financial resources[73] or suspected of Communist sympathies, even though this was in contradiction with the legislation on immigration that dated from 1905.

By 1937, more than 4,500 refugees had reached Britain, including major scientific and literary figures who benefited from the Notgemeinschaft Deutscher Wissenschaftler[74] or British aid organizations. After 1938, many refugees of Jewish origin were accepted, as well as Socialists from Vienna and Prague. A thousand scholarships were granted to exiled students, while British universities and colleges took on about fifteen hundred teachers. By virtue of its geographical situation, Britain did not have to fear an influx of clandestine émigrés, but it made efforts to keep Communists out of its territory.

These fairly unfavorable asylum conditions help to explain the very limited number of antifascists who sought to settle in Britain in 1933, doubting their ability to continue their literary or political activity there. Relations between Britain and Germany, at the cultural level, were relatively weak. Fred Uhlmann, who became in due course an English writer, acknowledges in his memoirs that he was almost totally ignorant of English culture.[75] Few German writers were translated. Unless they wrote in English, they had little chance of being published. Despite the geographical proximity, they felt totally isolated in London. This explains in part the negative judgements of the country made by a good number of émigrés. Those who took refuge there in 1933 were rarely political activists or committed writers. They were more likely to be scientists, academics, or representatives of the liberal bourgeoisie. Of those activists who did settle in England, the majority were liberal, Catholic, conservative or Social-Democrat. Outside of the universities, only the theatre and cinema were able to welcome representatives of Weimar culture. Fritz Kortner emigrated to England with his whole family, and sought to persuade Brecht and Leonhard Frank to follow. Among writers, there was no real ideological unity, at most a certain celebrity that went back before 1933. Thus René Fülop-Miller, Ferenc Körmendi, Richard Friedenthal, Otto Zarek, Stefan Zweig, Hermann Broch and Robert Neumann were already known from their books. These refugees also included a significant number of journalists: Stefan Lorant, editor-in-chief of the *Münchener Illustrierten* (who went on to found *Picture Post*), Arthur Koestler, correspondent for the *News Chronicle*, Sebastian Haffner, author of a famous and controversial study of Hitler,[76] Alfred Kerr, the great Berlin theatre critic, and Rudolf Olden, contributor to the *Berliner Tagblatt*. Finally, besides the Austrian writers already mentioned there were the poets Max Hermann-Neisse and Karl Otten, the latter an expressionist writer who went on to fight in the International Brigades. A few rare authors were able to see their works translated into English, particularly writers of historical and political essays. The only major activity of exiled German writers would be the organization of a PEN-Zentrum Deutschsprachiger Authoren im Ausland. It was C. A. Dawson-Scott, an English woman of letters, who had founded the PEN Club in 1921. Following the last conference of PEN at Ragusa (Dubrovnik), and the departure of the German section which rejected any questions on the situation of writers hostile to the Nazi regime, it was necessary to regroup the former anti-Nazi members. Other exiles such as Lion Feuchtwanger, Ernst Toller, Rudolf Olden and Max Hermann-Neisse envisaged the formation of a 'centre of free literature', a project that came to fruition during the Edinburgh conference of 1934, with Heinrich Mann as its president and Olden as secretary. Kurt Hiller, founder of the 'Neopathetic Cabaret', had also thought of establishing a 'literary club' in England, likewise Veit Valentin and Fritz Demuth, who organized the Luncheon Club together with K. Federn, Monty Jacobs, Max Hermann-Neisse and Karl Otten. But this activity remained very limited.

It was thanks to these émigrés, however, that important archival centres were established in England. In 1933, Alfred Wiener, secretary of the Centralverein Deutscher Staatsbürger Jüdischen Glaubens, had founded a centre of documentation on fascism and anti-Semitism with assistance from the University of Amsterdam, later known as the Wiener Library. This had more than 40,000 volumes when it was moved to London in 1939. Paul Hirsch had also established a library in Frankfurt for musical scores and works on musical history, which in 1936 was transferred to Cambridge University. In the same way, the collections of the Warburg Institute in Hamburg, devoted to the history of civilizations, were moved to England. More than 100,000 volumes reached English libraries in this way.

Yet ignorance of modern German literature and the absence of a German-speaking readership practically prevented the establishment of any publishing facilities in exile, of the kind that arose in Holland and Czechoslovakia. Few English publishers took the risk of publishing émigré authors, with the exception of the East and West Library and Imago Verlag, a publisher of psychoanalytic works established in 1938 after the exile of Freud. The reception reserved for émigrés in England, and their conditions of work, depended largely on how well known they were.

The entire British press fêted Freud on his arrival. He was begged for autographs. Besides Freud and Stefan Zweig, Hermann Broch was the major Austrian figure to find refuge in England, where certain of his novels had already been translated.[77] Elias Canetti also settled in London, as his work, unlike that of Broch, was already better known here than in Germany or Austria. A certain number of Socialist leaders also found exile in England, generally the least radical: for instance Stefan Pollatschek, contributor to the *Wiener Arbeiterzeitung*, Julius Braunthal, Bruno Heilig[78] and Hermynia zur Mühlem. A number of these remained in England and started to write in English.

A growing number of émigrés reached Britain after 1938, following a shift in British policy towards the refugees. The occupation of Austria and Czechoslovakia, and the intensification of anti-Semitic persecution, persuaded the British authorities to expand their assistance. A mutual aid group was formed around Lord Baldwin, and the Quakers – together with other religious figures – developed an intensive activity in favour of the refugees, with the result that by the end of 1938, some 11,000 refugees had reached England. Their number continued to rise with the Czechoslovak crisis, forcing the British parliament to approve a financial aid (the Czech Trust Fund) to cover the material necessities of refugees, chiefly housing. Besides those writers and artists who left Czechoslovakia for England – Ernst Sommer, Heinrich Fischer, Ludwig Winder, John Heartfield, Oskar Kokoschka – there were several detainees in concentration camp who obtained permission to emigrate. A reception camp for them was established at Richborough. At the same time, a number of writers reached London. Monty Jacobs, publisher of the *Vossische Zeitung*, and Richard Friedenthal, came directly from Germany, Moritz Goldstein from Italy, Fred Uhlmann from Paris.

The fairly harsh conditions of existence that the émigrés encountered scarcely left them the leisure to develop literary or political activity. In an economic situation that was highly unfavorable, it was often impossible for them to obtain a work permit. Their assimilation into English culture was difficult, and only a few mastered the language sufficiently to use it. The most favoured found employment at the BBC, at the Wiener Library or in the universities. Some contributed to the British press, but it proved impossible to establish a genuine exile press. It was not until 1941 that *Die Zeitung* appeared, a newspaper designed for distribution in the Reich. Its editorial team, largely British, published works by émigrés. Publishing activity, however, remained very limited, mainly the work of Socialist groups in exile. Very few works were published in German.[79] Before the start of the War, Fred Uhlmann established a German League for Culture, designed as a centre for émigrés. Its members included Stefan Zweig, Berthold Viertel, Max Hermann-Neisse, F. Reitzenstein, Walter Goehr and Franz Osborn. Many intellectuals believed that they benefited in general from public sympathy,[80] but the majority felt completely isolated. Christopher Isherwood, familiar with Berlin, described this attitude of a large part of the English intelligentsia towards refugees remarkably well in his novel *Prater Violet*,[81] depicting the travails of an Austrian director invited to make a sentimental film in London, whose worries for his country and his friends arouse only boredom and scepticism. Isherwood's narrator, though a friend of this émigré, declares:

> Perhaps I had travelled too much, left my heart in too many places, I knew what I was supposed to feel, what it was fashionable for my generation to feel. We cared about everything: fascism in Germany and Italy, the seizure of Manchuria, Indian nationalism, the Irish question, the Workers, the Negroes, the Jews. We had spread our feelings over the whole world; and I knew that mine were spread very thin. I cared – oh yes, I certainly cared – about the Austrian socialists. But did I care as much as I said I did, tried to imagine I did? No, not nearly as much.[82]

German émigrés managed for all that to liven up the London theatre, and establish a cabaret with Hugo Koenigsgarten, as well as the Freie Deutsche Kulturbund founded in 1939, which put on a number of exhibitions and concerts, remaining the most important émigré organization throughout the exile years. H. J. Rehfisch and H. Friedmann founded together with other exiles Club 43, where intellectuals could meet and discuss the most varied topics.[83] It was subsequently charged with intervening on behalf of German prisoners.

With Britain's declaration of war the situation of émigrés deteriorated, even if some now obtained work permits. Fearing a possible invasion, in May 1940 the government took severe measures against potential spies who might be hidden among the refugees. As in France, refugees were interned in special camps, and it was without irony that one of the commanders of these camps asserted: 'I would never have thought that so many Jews were Nazis.'[84] Even the most famous émigrés were not spared this fate, and Stefan Zweig's bitterness is readily understandable:

> Again I had dropped a rung lower, within an hour I was no longer merely a stranger in the land but an 'enemy alien', a hostile foreigner; this decree forcibly banned me to a situation to which my throbbing heart had no relation. For was a more absurd situation imaginable than for a man in a strange land to be compulsorily aligned – solely on the ground of a faded birth certificate – with a Germany that had long ago expelled him because his race and ideas branded him as anti-German and to which, as an Austrian, he had never belonged. By a stroke of a pen the meaning of a whole life had been transformed into a paradox; I wrote, I still thought in the German language, but my every thought and wish belonged to the countries which stood in arms for the freedom of the world.[85]

German and Austrian refugees were divided into three categories. Those in group A were immediately interned, those in group C were accepted as refugees on racial grounds or deemed genuinely antifascist. As for the refugees in group B, they were left in provisional freedom. This classification was not very rigorous, and Hans Eichner, an Austrian refugee, tells[86] how a rabbi suspected of being a disguised German spy was classed in group B. The classification into these different groups was carried out on the basis of questioning by a committee. In 1940, refugees between eighteen and sixty-five were interned as 'enemy aliens' after being asked to present themselves immediately to boards for their place of residence. They were then taken to the racecourse at Lingfield and put up in stables. After a few weeks they were transferred via Liverpool to the Isle of Man. Many were subsequently embarked on warships along with German prisoners, and transported to Australia.

To struggle against the despair that affected them, émigrés in these camps organized university classes and taught each other foreign languages. Fred Uhlmann writes quite truthfully:

> Our pride was our marvellous collection of more than thirty professors and lecturers, mainly from Oxford and Cambridge, some of them men of international reputation. I doubt if one could have found a greater variety of lecturers anywhere else – we had an *embarras de richesse*. What could one do if Professor William Cohn's talk on the Chinese Theatre coincided with Egon Wellesz' Introduction to Byzantine Music? Or Professor Jacobsthal's talk on Greek Literature with Professor Goldmann's on the Etruscan language? Perhaps one felt more inclined to hear Zunz on the *Odyssey* or Friedenthal on the Shakespearean stage?[87]

Divided on their arrival in Australia into two groups of a thousand each, they were now sent to camps at Hay in New South Wales, sheltered in twenty-eight-man barracks where tables had been constructed with old boards. Melbourne University offered them books, but as the censorship forbade any document to be sent out of the camp, they were forced to refuse. Nevertheless, they organized concerts thanks to a piano lent by the Quakers. According to Eichner, these camps were gradually transformed into an enormous German and Austrian university in exile, in which everyone was able to share their knowledge with their companions in misfortune. Many were subsequently sent from Hay to Tartura in Victoria. This exile continued until 1942, from which date they were gradually returned to Britain. Many then joined the Pioneer Corps or the Australian army. Some met with a particularly tragic fate: their ships were torpedoed en route to camps in Canada and Australia, with many drowned. After the War, a number of émigrés remained in England and played a far from negligible role in cultural life. These included F. Gottfurcht, E. Larsen, Martin Esslin, Robert Lucas, Alfred Lenger and Richard Friedenthal.

5. EXILE IN SWITZERLAND

Ziffel: Switzerland is a country famous for the freedom everyone enjoys. As long as they are tourists.
Kalle: I went there and didn't feel very free.

Bertolt Brecht, *Exile Dialogues*

For more than one reason, Switzerland embodied for a long while the very image of a country of asylum and exile. We need only recall the role that it played during the First World War. The Alsatian pacifist René Schickele, and Ivan Goll from Lorraine, found refuge, while Ernst Bloch worked out the arguments of his *Spirit of Utopia*, and both expressionism and the Dada movement developed there. In a letter to Hans Carossa of 7 May 1951, Thomas Mann described Switzerland as 'a country where German writers come to seek refuge and die'. Its political system, its proclaimed tolerance and neutrality, as well as its cultural and linguistic diversity and faith in humanitarian ideals, had attracted victims of religious and political persecution through the ages. From the eighteenth century on, it had welcomed such varied German exiles as Georg Büchner, Friedrich Freiligrath and Wilhelm Weitling, later August Bebel, Gustav Landauer, Willi Münzenberg and Erich Mühsam. And what should one say of the Russian emigration in Switzerland, which included Lenin himself? During the First World War, Zurich became the centre of all opponents of the war, the chosen land of pacifist magazines, of opponents of bellicose nationalism grouped around Romain Rolland, Marcel Martinet, René Schickele and P. J. Jouve. Expressionists, political activists and Dadaists met up in Zurich at the Cabaret Voltaire or on the editorial boards of avant-garde reviews, and it is hard to imagine the development of artistic life at the dawn of the 1920s without taking into account the centre of political and artistic agitation that was Zurich around 1914.

The stance that Switzerland adopted towards the refugees of 1933 rapidly shattered most of these illusions. Its policy towards the émigrés was selfish and severely restrictive,[88] and the harshness with which it treated refugees left a moral scar that nothing has yet been able to efface.

The laws governing Swiss conditions of asylum (1921, 1925, 1928) allowed individuals without citizenship or papers[89] to be admitted into the country, but clauses subsequently added between 1933 and 1938, under pressure of the economic crisis,[90] increasingly restricted the opportunity of benefiting from this right of asylum. All possibilities for foreigners to practise the least activity were gradually withdrawn.[91] It became possible to prohibit access to Swiss territory for a whole variety of reasons: saturation with foreigners,[92] undesirability,[93] or lack of means. After 1933, new laws not only enabled a constriction of the influx of refugees, but the rejection of those whose 'customs' were too different from the Swiss: Jews were expressly targeted by this restriction. It also became possible to refuse anyone who risked disturbing Switzerland's relations with neighbouring countries. Communists, and political activists in general, were considered damaging to good understanding with Hitler's Reich. Not only did political refugees have to present themselves to the police within forty-eight hours, but their residence was assigned and eventually they were interned in camps. Placed under police surveillance, these refugees were forbidden to practise any kind of activity, while they did not receive permanent residence permits and were always under threat of expulsion. All political refugees were questioned about their activities, the circumstances and reasons for their escape from Germany, and their means of existence. In certain cantons, including

Zurich, recognition as a political refugee was possible only if Swiss citizens could be found to guarantee the émigré financially. Permission to remain in the country was limited to three months, and it was possible to be refused even this, as an 'undesirable', someone 'unworthy of asylum', or a 'Communist without papers'. Political refugees were the target of all kinds of police harassment, searched, flushed out, and under constant surveillance. Moreover, the status of 'political refugee' was granted only to party leaders, writers, and functionaries who had played a public role under the Weimar Republic. It was stipulated that Jews, despite their persecution, could not take advantage of this. Only in 1944 (!) did they become eligible for this status.

The xenophobic character of these laws was admirably served by the anti-Semitism of the police chief for foreigners, Dr Heinrich Rothmund,[94] who applied them zealously. Swiss democrats, revolted by this situation, had to take into account the significant pro-Nazi movement in their country,[95] which forced the government to still stricter vigilance towards the refugees. A large percentage of the Swiss administration and bourgeoisie did not hide their sympathy for Hitler's Germany. Their anti-Communism was violently proclaimed, and many hardly bothered to conceal their anti-Semitism.[96] Some refugees – Communists and Jews in particular – were accordingly treated with extreme brutality. Any kind of activity – material, intellectual or artistic – was forbidden them,[97] and there is no example of another country where the conditions imposed on refugees were as severe. For fear of being deprived of German coal, Switzerland paralysed all antifascist activity on its territory. On this point, fascist Italy and Portugal often showed themselves more humanitarian towards German émigrés than liberal Switzerland, which did not hesitate to hand over illegal refugees to the Gestapo. This policy was all the more sorely felt in that the government showed nothing like the same severity towards the local Nazis. Even in its official publications, contempt for antifascists is visible: they were denoted in insulting language as '*diese Vögel*' ('these birds').

For the majority of émigrés, therefore, Switzerland would only be a short station in their exile. The country's policy and its standard of living both militated against definitive settlement there. By the outbreak of the War, Switzerland had accepted only 120 political refugees and eighteen 'famous exiles', whereas in 1950 it counted 1,213,000 immigrant workers. In both cases, indeed, this acceptance was only provisional. It is understandable why émigré correspondence should be so rich in recrimination against Swiss hospitality. Friedrich Wolf, who took refuge in the country in 1933, had to leave immediately, as did the expressionist publisher Kurt Wolff. Brecht, invited to Carona by Kurt Kläber, had to leave after a month, following harassment by the police for foreigners. Hans Marchwitza, who declared himself a 'revolutionary writer', was taken back to the border a few weeks later. The cases mentioned by H. A. Walter[98] need no commentary. One émigré who had published an article in a Socialist journal was denounced by an informer. He was immediately expelled for 'working without authorization'. Jewish lawyers who had defended Communist accused were refused the status of political refugee. Émigré actors playing at the Zurich theatre were classified as 'seasonal workers' and obtained permission to stay for just nine months. A few exceptions alone qualify this negative image of Switzerland: émigrés protected by important Swiss figures (as Wilhelm Hoegner was by Dr Hans Oprecht), or very famous émigrés such as Thomas Mann with his Nobel Prize, were treated with respect. Even antifascists recognized as political émigrés were constantly under police surveillance and threatened with expulsion on the slightest pretext.[99]

Nothing in principle escaped the prudence of Swiss legislation. When the Hungarian author Julius Hay notified the police of the birth of his son, it was stipulated on his passport that in no case would the baby be allowed to work in Switzerland. If a refugee undertook the least work he would be expelled. But if he stayed in the country without resources, he equally risked seeing the renewal of his authorization refused, and also being expelled. Moreover, if in the majority of countries labour legislation targeted those occupations that were most subject to competition, Switzerland legislated on intellectual work with the same intransigence.[100] Certain exiles were forbidden from writing, both for fear of German reprisals but also at the demand of Swiss writers who feared the talent of the new arrivals.[101] Theatrical directors such as Gustav Hartung were hard pressed to find work in Switzerland, even while Germans from the Reich were allowed to stage Nazi works.

Associations of writers and artists displayed the same chicanery.[102] As for publishers, with the exception of Emil Oprecht who was accused of damaging relations with Germany by publishing antifascist writings, they also refused to distribute the exiles' works. When G. Bermann Fischer thought of moving his Vienna publishing house to Switzerland, he came up against a virulent campaign by local publishers. After 1938, moreover, Swiss policy became even more severe: Jewish passports were stamped with a special sign at the request of the Swiss authorities, who threatened that they would require a visa for all German nationals if Jews were not expressly indicated. This anti-Semitic measure[103] enabled many refugees to be returned, and led to an ongoing collaboration between the Swiss and Nazi police. Between 1932 and 1939, seventy Communists were expelled from the country, and after 1939 a visa was required for all foreigners. Anyone who had entered Switzerland illegally – with the exception of women, children, the old and infirm – would now be returned to the frontier.[104] This sombre picture however does not take into account the support of the local population and of organizations such as the Communist and Socialist parties and the Red Cross. Literary and artistic figures as well as ordinary people devoted themselves to the refugee cause, out of humanitarianism as well as hostility to fascism. Official measures were often protested, and many people were saved thanks to this apolitical charity and anonymous generosity.

Switzerland thus did not play a major role in the history of antifascist emigration. Only a few émigrés managed to settle there, even among the most famous. Such celebrity, indeed, could make them still more suspect, in the case of authors known for their Marxist sympathies. The Communist poet Erich Weinert[105] was expelled, as well as Ernst Bloch who had been a refugee in Switzerland in the First World War. If the Swiss authorities showed somewhat more leniency towards Social-Democrats or conservatives, no one was free from the threat of expulsion: the antifascist journalist Walter Victor had his residence permit withdrawn in 1938 following his writings against Hitler. The illustrator Carl Meffert-Moreau, who managed to contribute to the Swiss press under a pseudonym, was also hunted out. Alfred Kerr had to leave the country for lack of means. Alfred Döblin stayed for a while in a hotel with his family, completely isolated. He wrote his novel *Babylonische Wanderung* in the reading room of the Zurich library. Erich Maria Remarque lived in Switzerland until 1939, without any connection with other émigrés. Emil Ludwig, known for his biographies of famous people, saw one of his novels banned (*Der Mord in Davos*). Brecht left Switzerland for lack of money, calling it 'a nation of hoteliers'. Georg Kaiser, who took refuge there in 1938, spoke of a genuine 'desert of the mind'. He died in poverty and almost forgotten. He too had been forbidden to write, after being one of the greatest expressionist playwrights. As for Tucholsky, in his letters from exile he broke out in insults about these 'eastern Swiss' whom he called 'worse than the *boches*'.

The majority of émigrés who wanted to continue their anti-Nazi activities did so illegally, as any political stand was forbidden, even if this had no connection with the Swiss situation. Activists worked under borrowed names, and had to move house constantly. Switzerland agreed to grant refugee status to a very limited number of exiles: Joseph Wirth, Wilhelm Hoegner, Otto Braun, Artur Crispien, Wilhelm Dittmann. Belonging to the Centre party or the Social-Democrats, these took no part in antifascist activity. Communists who had entered Switzerland illegally managed to re-establish cells in several Swiss cities,[106] but it was very hard to print underground journals and smuggle them into Germany.[107] A number of Swiss Socialists came to the assistance of the émigrés, and without their aid any political work would have been impossible. The émigrés also sought to inform *Reichsdeutsche* working in Switzerland of the crimes of Hitlerism. Certain newspapers, the *Süddeutsche Volksstimme* and *Süddeutsche Information* which were published legally, also gave out information on Hitler's Germany.[108]

In the artistic field, the émigrés' activities were very varied. Most of the exiles gathered in a small number of places, such as Fontana Martina close to Lago Maggiore. This abandoned village had been bought by the writer and publisher Fritz Jordi – a Swiss delegate to the Third Comintern congress in 1921 – who transformed it into an artists' colony.[109] From 1938, a number of German and Italian antifascists established themselves there. But it was the homes of Swiss citizens that formed the most important centres of emigration. Evening readings and discussions were organized around Wolfgang Langhoff, Anna Seghers and Bernhard von Brentano, as well as at the home of the writer R. J. Humm. The Rosenbaums welcomed the proletarian writer Hans Marchwitza, while the home of the publisher Emil Oprecht became a forum for exiles.

These émigré cultural activities were very largely dependent on the attitude of the Swiss organizations. After the Nazi seizure of power, the German book market was restricted for German-language Swiss authors. Goebbels tried unsuccessfully to draw them into Nazi organizations. Fearing the loss of German readers and the competition of the émigrés, the Swiss encouraged any kind of restriction bent on limiting the exiles' expression in the press, publishing and theatre. A certain number of literary figures however had an opposite attitude and helped the émigrés to pursue their activities. The Swiss critic Carl Seelig, not very political but a friend of Hermann Broch, Kurt Tucholsky, Brecht, Stefan Zweig and Robert Musil, came to the aid of many antifascist writers by organizing readings for them at his home or in churches. Still more important was the assistance of the publisher Emil Oprecht, who had previously published both Communist and anti-Communist works. A one-time member of the Swiss Communist party, he had begun his political career[110] in the Socialist youth movement of Willi Münzenberg. Hostile to nationalism of any kind, he dreamed of a United States of Europe. Oprecht detested fascism and published antifascist works whether their authors were Communist or conservative. In the Oprecht catalogue, the names of Ernst Bloch and Friedrich Wolf were to be found alongside that of Hermann Rauschning.[111] It was this opening for the émigrés, and his magazine *Information*, that permitted the establishment of a kind of discussion platform on fascism, something quite rare in Switzerland, which would play a significant role, at least until the outbreak of the Second World War.[112] After 1940 Oprecht confined himself to championing the idea of a United States of Europe, and published few further works by émigrés. Most of these had already fled Europe, and there was no way he could maintain his platform without coming up against the Swiss authorities. Despite his ideological hesitations, Oprecht played an essential role in the history of anti-Nazi emigration in Switzerland. Besides *Information*, he also re-established the famous Büchergilde Gutenberg, a collection of inexpensive progressive books which formed a genuine link between German émigrés and Swiss workers. Herman Hesse likewise came to the aid of the exiles, though avoiding any trenchant declaration against the Reich.[113]

While the publishing opportunities for exiles were very limited, a certain number of works played an important role in the struggle against fascism. *The Peat-Bog Soldiers* by Walter Langhoff, published by Spiegelverlag, had such success that Langhoff was asked to undertake a lecture tour, which attracted a large audience. The Swiss police banned him first from speaking in particular cantons, then in the whole of the country. We should recall that it was while Thomas Mann was staying in the country that the famous polemic with the Swiss critic Eduard Korrodi erupted, leading Mann to take a public position in favour of the emigrants. The review *Mass und Wert*, edited by Thomas Mann and Konrad Falke, which maintained in its founding programme, 'We aim to be artists and anti-barbarians', was founded in Zurich in 1937. Its decisive impulse was given by Golo Mann, and the review was to publish extracts from new works by Thomas Mann (*Lotte in Weimar*) and Robert Musil (*The Man Without Qualities*), as well as international authors such as Federico Garcia Lorca (*Blood Wedding*), Jean-Paul Sartre (*Les Murs*), Oskar Maria Graf, Walter Benjamin and Bertolt Brecht. The mutual hostility between Mann and Brecht should of course be remembered, as well as the mixture of conservative and progressive elements that *Mass und Wert* represented, keeping the most political contributors at a distance.

A certain development of antifascist theatre also took place in Switzerland, chiefly in Zurich thanks to the director of the Zürcher Schauspielhaus, Oskar Wälterlin, who had worked for a long while in Germany. Without being a political activist, he wanted to stage classic plays defending liberty and humanist values, and gathered round him a number of émigré actors and directors of high quality. Antifascist cabaret found its best illustration with Erika Mann's Pfeffermühle. Though violently attacked by the Nazis in 1931, at the meeting of the International Women's League for Peace and Freedom, she had founded her cabaret in January 1933 at the Theater Bonbonnière in Munich. More detested still than her father, it was impossible for her to continue the least activity in Germany. She decided to move to Zurich along with her whole company,[114] and the Pfeffermühle started up again there on 1 October 1933. A number of scripts were written for it by her brother Klaus, and one of the most notable participants was Therese Giehse, later known for her work with Brecht. The success of this cabaret was such that between 1933 and 1937 it gave performances in Czechoslovakia, Holland, Belgium and Luxemburg, despite the protests of the Gestapo and violent attacks by Nazi sympathizers, who in Switzerland in particular tried to interrupt the show with cries of '*Juda verrecke*', '*Hinaus mit der Juden!*' or '*Wir brauchen keine Juden in der Schweiz*' ('Death to the Jews', 'Out with the Jews', and 'We don't need any Jews in Switzerland'). Sometimes the performance needed police protection, and the famous cabaret was eventually banned. Between 1 January 1933 and its legal closure it gave more than a thousand performances.

Another important cabaret which formed a focus of cultural and political agitation in Switzerland was the Cornichon, directed by the playwright Walter Lesch. This had known far worse problems at its beginning. It likewise attacked both Hitler and Swiss policy towards the émigrés. With W. Lesch, Max Werner Lenz and Otto Weissert, it presented very political shows with émigré actors, including Dora Gerson (later murdered in concentration camp) and Katharina Renn. If it was extremely hard to organize antifascist theatre in Switzerland, a certain number of shows were indeed staged with political intentions: for instance Joe Mihaly's Agitprop choir, made up of Swiss workers and German exiles, whose montage shows recalled certain Berlin proletarian reviews of the Weimar period, especially the experiments of Erwin Piscator. In the same style, Hans Sahl (future secretary and collaborator of Piscator) established Jemand.

In the field of cinema, one should also mention the enterprise of Julius Marx, who, with the help of the theatre critic Bernhard Diebold – of Swiss origin, but who had worked for twenty-five years in Germany – tried to make films with the émigrés for the Thema company. Many émigrés were excited by the idea, but none of these projects came to fruition, as no company would finance antifascist films or any that touched on the racial policy of the Third Reich. Despite the efforts of Friedrich Wolf, Bernhard Diebold and J. Marx, their firm collapsed without a trace in 1939.

*   *   *

On 1 September 1939, Switzerland mobilized to defend its 'armed neutrality', and immediately took measures that considerably affected the life of those rare émigrés that it tolerated on its territory. While its policies towards them had never been exactly generous, they were about to worsen considerably. On 12 March 1940 the Bundesrat demanded the creation of internment camps for the émigrés. At the same time, their presence in certain public places – station platforms, cafés, etc. – was strictly forbidden. Ten work camps were immediately established.[115] Though Switzerland was well aware of the systematic massacre of Jews and oppositionists in the countries occupied by the Reich, its frontiers remained tightly bolted. These measures, according to a number of émigré witnesses, provoked genuine disgust among many citizens, who publicly attacked them. But the internal regulation of the camps (a ban on going out, discussion, etc.) was not alleviated until 1944, when there was no longer any doubt as to Germany's defeat.

Cut off from their international connections and deprived of any assistance, émigrés in Switzerland had to abandon antifascist struggle. They had to declare themselves immediately to the police on pain of being expelled. Once declared, a number of them were handed over to the criminal police. Many were treated extremely harshly and accused of the most absurd actions. Few new refugees managed to reach Switzerland until the end of the War. Those who had been interned remained in the camps, even when the Swiss Social-Democrats were in government.[116] And it was not without a certain unease that the latter had to read letters sent them by their German and Austrian comrades describing life in these camps. Only when hostilities came to an end were a certain number of voices raised against this regime – for example that of Karl Barth was denounced as a dark shadow on Swiss democracy, and questions were raised as to the motives of those responsible. The Swiss dramatist Ulrich Becher described the internment conditions of the refugees and became their spokesperson. A number of Swiss public figures started to ask themselves what these exiles, who had worn the uniform of common criminals, must have thought when they returned to play a political role in Germany after the War. What impressions did they take back of their Swiss exile? This question aroused lively apprehension among a number of Swiss politicians.

The activities of the internees were reduced to a minimum. In certain cases they were able to publish little newspapers such as *Die Lagerstimme*, but they were constantly accused of 'Communist intrigues'. Wilhelm Frank, Walter Fisch, Rudolf Singer and Karl Seliger were threatened with being handed over to the Gestapo. The law of 16 March 1942 forbade them any political or cultural expression. The celebrity of some internees gave them no protection at all: the singer Joseph Schmidt, well known for the film *A Song Goes Round the World*, died in one of these camps for want of urgent hospital treatment. Yet despite official prohibition, the internees organized clandestine discussion groups on politics, culture, economics and the future of Germany, to avoid being destroyed psychologically. They wrote poems and songs, staged theatre productions and agitprop sketches.

In 1941 an aid organization, the Kulturgemeinschaft der Emigranten, was set up for the benefit of the detainees and some of the constraints imposed on the émigrés were relaxed. Joe Mihaly and Carl Seelig, helped by members of the Zurich theatre, organized productions for them. Several were actually staged in the camps, in memory of victims of Nazism such as Ernst Toller, Erich Mühsam and Carl von Ossietzky. Plays by Lessing were also produced. On 25 May 1945, the Schutzverband Deutscher Schriftsteller was re-established. This belated improvement did not manage to wipe out the fact that for the majority of émigrés, Switzerland had been a veritable calvary.

6. EXILE IN SPAIN

Spain would not generally be counted as a country of asylum, for few opponents of Nazism thought of taking refuge there in 1933, apart from Karl Otten, Harry Kessler, Graf Keyseling, Herbert Schlüter and Werner Rings. Yet between 1936 and 1939 it became a key place of activity for all German antifascists.[117] Not only did exiles join the International Brigades to fight Franco and defend democracy, but writers, painters, actors, directors and poets pressed to put their talent at the service of the Spanish Republic, which is how Spain played such an important role in the history of emigration.

The reasons why Spain could not become a place of asylum are clear enough. The political situation had been especially disturbed since 1931: agrarian uprising, repressed workers' strikes,[118] intensified actions by the right, the aborted putsch of General Sanjurjoe in 1932. This struggle of the Spanish people to establish their rights might well have attracted antifascist refugees, but the obstacles to their settling in Spain were several: the cultural tradition was one they could not relate to, and there were few indeed who spoke the language. In Spain, moreover, unlike most European countries, there was practically no one who read German. At the political level, the progressive forces were very divided. Those who took refuge in Spain did so in isolation, to find better conditions of life, even though no committee to assist émigrés existed in Spain, nor could any publishing house be created. Those who managed to get published had to write for the Spanish press or have their articles translated.[119] Besides, the economic situation was extremely unfavorable.

Those German exiles who moved to Spain settled in the large towns (Barcelona, Valencia); they were often merchants of Jewish origin. It was practically impossible for an émigré to find an equivalent profession in Spain, and many had to practise manual trades. A certain number of refugees settled in the Balearic Islands where they pursued a diverse range of occupations; many had known Ibiza as a holiday centre before 1933, and hoped that poverty would be more bearable there in the sun. This was the case with Walter Benjamin, who settled in Ibiza and lived in diabolical economic conditions, as attested by Gershom Scholem and Theodor Adorno. He tried to write essays but was prevented from concentrating by the tourist commotion. He walked in the moonlight with the grandson of Gauguin, but finally returned to Paris in October 1933. There is something bitter and derisory in the fate of these first émigrés to Spain: Counts Kessler and Keyserling frequented the salons of local dignitaries, not their fellow émigrés. Dr Berger, a future member of the International Brigades' medical service, reared chickens on a farm; Erich Ardent and Else Perl opened a vegetarian restaurant. She soon committed suicide, unable to bear the conditions of exile, while he had to work as a servant for an anti-Nazi baron.[120] The majority of refugees felt foreign in this culture, which failed to offer them any platform. At most they could organize solidarity action amongst themselves. Besides, their antifascist activity immediately came up against a government ban, at least until 1935.

The situation changed dramatically after the elections of 1936, for which the democratic forces had regrouped in a Popular Front. The émigrés benefited from this élan, and at the end of 1935 a committee was established for the liberation of Ernst Thälmann. From 1936, Communist émigrés[121] publicly debated political and cultural questions. One of the first demonstrations of these émigrés was the organization of a People's Olympics in Barcelona, held from 22 to 26 July 1936. This was supported by the government, and attracted workers' sporting teams from a number of countries. When the generals' putsch broke out on 17–18 July, a number of German exiles formed the first internationalist fighters of the Spanish Republic.

With the menace of fascism gripping Spain, the life of the German émigrés was totally transformed: they found themselves caught up in a struggle that was remarkably similar to that which they wanted to wage in Germany. For many of them, fighting Franco and defending the Republic was a struggle against Nazism and Hitler. They could not remain indifferent to the intensifying struggle, and most often tried to join it. Those who found themselves in territory occupied by the fascist forces (such as Majorca) were arrested, and threatened with being handed to the Gestapo if they exercised the least political activity.[122] The pacifist Heinz Kraschutzki, publisher of *Das Andere Deutschland*, was imprisoned until the end of the Second World War, though many émigrés managed to reach other countries. Some German Jews, taking the Nazis at their word, agreed to return to the Reich, where they were immediately interned in camps if they could not pay a large sum of money for their release. Others straight away joined the Republican fighters.[123] These volunteers, who fought for the Republic from 1936 on, were not all exiles: a large number of them came to Spain not for refuge but to fight. They included antifascists from all over the world, including many from Germany.

Journalists, writers, exiles in Spain or voluntary fighters, shared the same fate regardless of nationality. The first groups, such as the Thälmann Group and the July 1936 Group, were formed spontaneously, while the Thälmann Centuria founded in Barcelona in August was the first sizeable body, with Hans Beimler and a group of Communist exiles from France playing an active part. The International Brigades, formed in mid October, sought to create a genuine people's army. 'Political soldiers', 'volunteers for liberty', they gave themselves the task of fighting alongside the Republic and the Popular Front.

If the role of émigrés in the battles waged to defend the Republic militarily is well known, the struggle on the cultural front was equally important. The fighters in the Brigades included writers, actors, poets, doctors and engineers, who used their various skills to aid the civilian population.[124] These social and cultural activities were both broad and hard. Half the Spanish population was illiterate, and from the beginning of the war more than ten thousand schools were established, as well as the cultural militia formed in January 1937 to teach soldiers on the battlefront. These were taught to read and write, as well as the foundations of socialism. As soldiers and cultural agitators, Willi Bredel and Hans Beimler were particular examples of this. A number of antifascist émigrés worked gratis in these campaigns, helping the peasants with the harvest so that the armies did not lack bread. A symbol of solidarity and internationalism, the Brigades were active in the cultural field as well as militarily. After losing an arm at the battle of Guadalajara, Ludwig Habermann was appointed head of a children's home built by the Brigades.

These cultural activities of the antifascists were still more important in the towns, especially Barcelona, which was not as immediately threatened as Madrid. Many émigrés took part in July 1936 in lively discussions on art and revolution, on political theatre, music or agitprop, and were tempted to develop in Spain the forms of cultural action that had already been realized in the Weimar period among the German proletariat. Erwin Piscator was invited to Barcelona in December 1936 by the Generalidad.[125] He declared that Spanish theatre should be at the level of the historical situation, and called for 'a total mobilization of art'. A number of 'red' and 'proletarian' reviews appeared, just as in Berlin. German and Spanish authors worked together on these shows. The aim was not just to use art against fascism, but to create a revolutionary culture able to respond to the needs of the time. Rereading the articles of Willi Bredel or Erich Weinert on cultural development in Catalonia gives a good sense of the role played by so many émigrés. These also became historians and chroniclers of the International Brigades.

A concert hall was established at the antifascist club in Barcelona, along with a classroom, a meeting room, a reading room and a library. Dance and song were involved as well as theatre and cinema. The German section gave lessons in Spanish, and wounded soldiers were welcomed there as well as activists. Ernst Busch interpreted revolutionary songs, Erich Weinert recited poems. In December 1937, a big event was organized for the anniversary of Hans Beimler's death. As announced in the first issue of Die Rote Sturmfahne – the organ of the Thälmann Centuria – 'our formation is a combat troop of the German Popular Front',[126] and it was in Spain that this Popular Front was put into practice.[127] Men of every nationality fought in the International Brigades, whether they were Communists, Socialists, or non-party. Cultural and military tasks were closely associated. The émigrés even organized antifascist radio broadcasts for transmission to Germany, and from January 1937 the German Communist party had a Deutscher Freiheitssender at its disposal, broadcasting also in Portuguese, Italian and Bulgarian. Besides information on the war in Spain, these transmitters in Madrid and Barcelona gave information on the German situation, and expressions of international solidarity. The success of their broadcasts[128] was relatively great, to judge from their echoes in the foreign press and the anger they provoked from the Nazis, who were unable to silence these voices from Spain. A large part of the material used in these broadcasts was brought from Paris: lectures on Hölderlin and freedom, Goethe and German youth, recordings of speeches of Heinrich Mann, testimonies of Hitlerite terror. Many émigré writers took part in the antifascist broadcasts from Barcelona. Besides texts of Heinrich Mann, later assembled in the collection *Courage*, writings by Feuchtwanger, Gustav Regler, Rudolf Leonhard and Alfred Kerr were transmitted, all appealing for unity. Cultural work was developed within the International Brigades in a similar fashion. The émigrés gave courses on the history of class struggle, and on social and cultural questions. As for the Spanish workers and peasants, they often learned to read and write from the Brigades.

The publication of newspapers was a particularly important activity. Ranging from simple typewritten leaflets giving information on battles, to newspapers (*Ataquemos, Hans Beimler, Todos Unidos*) and periodicals (*Pasaremos, A l'assaut, Adelante la 13e!, Le Soldat de la République, Notre Combat*), published in several languages in the midst of combat and in the worst situations, these formed a link between the fighters and a source of information on the antifascist struggle waged on the different fronts. There were battalion journals as well as brigade ones, and a central organ published reportage, photographs, and first-person accounts by fighters. Some of these journals were distributed in thousands of copies. Written by journalists, poets, officers and soldiers, these documents have an exceptional interest for the history of the Brigades. The political texts of Franz Dahlem are found alongside narratives by Willi Bredel and Ludwig Renn, poems by Erich Weinert and songs of Ernst Busch.

Even while fighting, the International Brigades felt that their struggle was a symbol, and that whether victorious or vanquished their story would serve as an example and a lesson. The fighters thus transformed themselves spontaneously into historians, gathering together a copious documentation on their life and their struggle. They wanted to ensure that the heroism of those who fought in Spain should never be lost. All the cultural and agitation material, newspapers and leaflets were sent to the historical section in Madrid, along with combatants' diaries.[129] The International Brigades also published books and pamphlets (Edicions del Comisariado de las Brigadas Internacionales): these included speeches, Comintern resolutions, photograph albums, even children's drawings, as well as novels, collections of songs and poems (Ernst Busch, Erich Weinert) and reportage (Egon Erwin Kisch). Hanns Eisler and Ernst Busch wrote and composed anthems for the Brigades.

Just as Piscator on his visit to Catalonia had encouraged a 'total mobilization of art' and the creation of revolutionary theatre, so a large number of theatre companies sprang up during the Spanish war with an audience both civilian and military. In 1938, an agitprop battalion gave performances inspired by the life of the soldiers, encouraging them to struggle and criticizing mistakes that had been made. As these pieces were directed at fighters of all nationalities, they chiefly employed shadowgraphs and mime. A number of these plays were written by exiles such as Ludwig Renn. Cinema likewise played an important role in the life of the Brigades. Erwin Piscator's film *The Revolt of the Fishermen of Santa Barbara* was screened, along with Eisenstein's *Que viva Mexico*, *Professor Mamlok* (from the play by Friedrich Wolf) and the Joris Ivens documentary *Spanish Earth* (1937, with the collaboration of Ernest Hemingway).

The importance of German émigrés in the Spanish conflict can also be seen in the organization of a major congress in Barcelona in July 1937 that continued, with less ceremony, the Congress for the Defence of Culture that had been held in Paris in 1935. The Spanish war was naturally an important subject of antifascist literature. At least twenty German writers took part in it as soldiers, officers, political commissars or artistic agitators, including Arthur Koestler, Ludwig Renn, Bodo Uhse, Willi Bredel, Gustav Regler, Hermann Kesten and Alfred Kantorowicz. The war left its mark on many works of world literature, including novels by Malraux and Hemingway. Even without taking part in the fighting, many German antifascists visited Spain, including Anna Seghers, Klaus Mann, Ernst Toller, Rudolf Leonhard and Prinz Hubertus zu Löwenstein. There were also a number among these antifascists and German émigrés who died in Spain: Hans Beimler, Franz Vehlow, Kurt von Appen, Georg Meyer, Paul Baumgarten, Philipp Mayer, Josef Graf, Richard Wagner, Willi Wille, Otto Volkmann, Paul Lose, Hans Schwindling, Karl Katz, Artur Becker, Wilhelm Pinnecke, Hans Erben and Wilhelm Glaser. Of the 450 fighters in the Ernst Thälmann Battalion, only eighty survived the war, and 3,000 of the 5,000 international volunteers who fought against Franco rest in Spanish soil.

After the defeat of the Republic, the antifascists of the International Brigades said their farewell to the people of Barcelona. Those who could not return to their own country without risk remained in demobilization camps. After the fall of Barcelona they covered the escape of refugees across the French frontier. The majority of them managed to cross the col du Perthus on 8 and 9 February 1939. They were disarmed and interned in French camps. After the armistice, a number who had not gone into hiding were handed to the Gestapo (Franz Dahlem, Heinrich Rau). Many were executed by the Nazis or perished in concentration camp.[130]

7. EXILE IN SCANDINAVIA

Denmark, Sweden and Norway remained at a certain remove from global political disturbances. Almost as hostile to fascism as to Communism, these countries aimed at remaining a haven of peace in a Europe where democracy was increasingly threatened. There were indeed in these countries both Communist parties and movements of the far right (e.g. the National Gathering in Norway), but the Social-Democrats gained the greatest share of the popular vote. Despite the liberal attitudes they adopted towards foreigners, and the large number of well-known German émigrés that they received (Walter A. Berendsohn, Bertolt Brecht), these countries did not play a major role in the history of emigration. Yet in the immediate aftermath of 1933, at least six thousand Germans found refuge there. This limited number contrasts with a well-developed network of aid committees. Subsequently, in particular after the occupation of Austria, many refugees who were directly threatened reached Scandinavia, often illegally. In 1938 something over a thousand individuals arrived in Denmark, four or five hundred in Norway, and 2,500 to 2,800 in Sweden.[131] These countries then took fairly severe measures to limit the number of emigrants, and like Switzerland, stamped the passports of Jewish refugees with the infamous 'J'. After 1940, many of these refugees had to flee once again to escape the Gestapo. But despite police surveillance of political refugees, the cultural activities and antifascist movement that they managed to establish were such as to give these countries a significant role in the story of the German and Austrian diaspora.

Denmark

Though Denmark required a visa for stateless emigrants, Germans, Austrians and Czechs could stay there for six months (three months after 1934) without this. They were nonetheless expected to provide for their needs, abstain from any political activity, and declare themselves to the police. The notion of 'political activity' was ill defined. Left-wing academics (Walter A. Berendsohn) were allowed to contribute to political journals, though Communists were not. Brecht himself had problems after staging his play *Round Heads and Pointed Heads*, attacking the racial policy of the Reich.

It was political émigrés in particular who settled initially in Denmark. The majority were Social-Democrats, often belonging to the party's right wing. Among the more famous, one should mention the trade unionist Fritz Tarnow who sought to unite the non-Communist left against the Nazis, and after 1940 played an important role in Sweden. Karl Raloff, former head of the Reichsbanner, published a number of antifascist works in Denmark. K. Rowold, a member of the SoPaDe, was also very active. As for Philipp Scheidemann, despite the important role he had played after 1918 in the Weimar Republic's infancy, he remained inactive in exile, until his death in 1939. Otto Buchwitz worked to set up a supposedly antifascist front that would unite everyone from the Communists to supporters of Strasser's Schwarze Front.

The Communist party was represented by a number of cadres and activists who chose Denmark to continue the struggle in Germany (Heinrich Wiatrek,[132] Herbert Warnke, Waldemar Verner). Many of these later worked in the wartime Freies Deutschland movement. Alongside these political émigrés from the two major workers' parties were a certain number of marginal figures such as Wilhelm Reich, who tried to combine psychoanalysis with Marxism and established in Copenhagen the Verlag für Sexualpolitik, and the writer Walter Hammer (arrested by the Gestapo in 1940). The émigrés' cultural and political life was concentrated in Copenhagen, at the Emigrantenhjem where they organized meetings, theatrical performances, conferences and exhibitions ('Der deutsche Kulturkampf', 1937). Several academics gave lectures, including Walter A. Berendsohn who taught literature there. A professor from Hamburg University, his major works appeared in exile and he became one of the earliest and most famous historians of exile literature. Berendsohn continued to write articles and give lectures, and managed to remain in Denmark until 1943, the Gestapo believing him already dead. Not only did Berendsohn play an active part in all these émigré activities, he also participated in the foundation of the Freies Deutschland Kulturbund (FDKB) and never returned to Germany. Other major figures of German emigration in Denmark included the Marxist philosopher Karl Korsch, the historian of religion Günther Zuntz, the jurist Fritz Bauer (subsequently author of a protocol for the prosecution of war criminals), and a number of writers: Wolf Harten, contributor to the Bücher-gilde Gutenberg in Switzerland, arrested by the German army in 1940 and doubtless murdered; Walter Kolbenhoff, author of *Untermenschen*, a novel on Nazism, later one of the founders of Gruppe 47; and the expressionist writer Hanns Henry Jahn.[133] Bertolt Brecht, after staying briefly in Switzerland and France, settled at Svendborg, encouraged by his friend Karin Michaelis. Despite expressing himself rather ironically about Denmark in his *Exile Dialogues*, the time he spent there was a very fertile period for him. It was in Denmark that Brecht wrote such varied works as *The Good Person of Szechwan*, *Señora Carrar's Rifles*, *Fear and Misery of the Third Reich*, *The Life of Galileo*, and the Svendborg poems. In August 1939 he took refuge in Sweden,[134] forced like other émigrés to flee the advance of the German army.[135]

Norway

Antifascist emigration to Norway was very limited. There were fewer émigrés here than in Denmark, let alone Sweden. Norway particularly welcomed left-wing Social-Democrats: one of the most famous was Willy Brandt,[136] who besides a very varied journalistic practice, also established contact with other groups of Socialist émigrés in France and Sweden. Brandt was one of the instigators of the campaign to obtain the Nobel Peace Prize for Carl von Ossietzky, imprisoned in a Nazi camp. After the invasion of Norway he moved to Sweden, where between 1933 and 1945 he published eight books. The SAP was also represented in Norway by O. F. Mayer, and other Socialist groups by Otto Friedländer, Max Seydewitz, and Willy Strzelewicz. A few German Communists also found their way to Norway, former combatants in the Spanish war (Hermann Matern, who after 1940 moved to Sweden, then the USSR), pacifists (Max Barth) and left-wing Socialists such as Joachim Joesten. Finally, among the writers and artists who settled in Norway one should mention the caricaturist T. T. Heine, and above all the Dadaist Kurt Schwitters, who subsequently emigrated to England.

Sweden

In contrast to Denmark and Norway, Sweden played a far more important role in the history of German emigration, managing – like Switzerland – to maintain its neutrality. This did not prevent the government building internment camps for antifascist refugees. The sizeable number of émigrés who moved there is explained by the relative ease of staying in the country without too much police harassment. The law of 1937, modifying one of 1928, stipulated in effect that in the case where a political refugee made himself liable to expulsion, he could not be sent back to a country where he would be in danger. Opportunities for work in Sweden were not plentiful (apart from manual work), even if no law actually forbade émigrés to practise a profession.[137] Though fairly industrialized from the beginning of the century, Sweden remained at a distance from most major European events. Its Social-Democrats developed a pragmatic policy, the Communist party ultimately split into several groups of left Socialists, and besides significant liberal parties, there were also conservative and nationalist movements that gave rise in 1933 to a youth movement that was overtly pro-Nazi.

In general, bourgeois milieus in Sweden viewed Germany with a certain sympathy and had a phobia about Communism or even left Socialism. The two National Socialist parties had little political significance,[138] but conservative circles approved of Hitler's anti-Communism even while disdaining the climate of terror that raged in Germany. Sweden remained neutral throughout the War, thankful for not having experienced invasion like Norway. The ruling coalition in 1939 included Socialists and Communists, and if the victims of fascism found popular sympathy, the government still allowed a German division to cross its territory, and avoided any confrontation with Hitler.

Until the end of the War, Sweden sheltered at least 5,594 antifascist refugees (figure for 1945). The laws regulating immigration (of 1927, 1932 and 1938) did however envisage certain measures to prevent an influx of refugees. Residence permits were limited to three months, and the provincial authorities were authorized to deport undesirables to the frontier. But in no case could émigrés be expelled to Germany. Support organizations, moreover, appeared very early on.[139] Alongside the Communist Red Aid, the Social-Democratic party and trade unions formed committees in aid of the refugees in May 1933, and an appeal in their favour was signed by two hundred prominent figures. Whilst conservative milieus wanted to see the policy towards the émigrés hardened, the Social-Democrats tried to alleviate it. After the annexation of Austria, however, a section of the population became alarmed at the large number of Jewish refugees who had found shelter in Sweden. Conservative circles brandished the spectre of unemployment and the 'Jewifying' of Sweden. From 1938, moreover, refugees had to prove that they would not be a burden on the Swedish state, or that they already had family living in Sweden. This measure basically applied to Jewish refugees, and was all the easier to apply as their passport was now stamped with a special 'J'.

The government's liberal policy had to take account of the right-wing movements and of students hostile to the arrival of overqualified academics.[140] In 1939 the government granted a further support of half a million krone to organizations working to assist the refugees, but on 16 February it also set up two new internment camps for Communist and Socialist refugees and combatants from the International Brigades. In 1941, measures were taken in favour of Jews, to facilitate their obtaining a residence permit in Sweden. Whilst it was liberal on the whole, Swedish policy was not without restrictions on permission to remain in the country. Like the majority of European countries, Sweden did not escape anti-Communism and even anti-Semitism: the section of Swedish police in charge of surveillance of immigrants collaborated closely with Gestapo agents.[141] The government of the time was subsequently criticized severely for the internment of antifascist refugees. This internment lasted up to three years, and those confined – Communists for the most part – were not accused of any specific offences and did not represent the slightest threat. The Swedish press and left-wing parties launched several campaigns in their favour, and they were eventually released in 1943.

Political refugees formed a large part of German emigration in Sweden. The most substantial component were Social-Democrats, divided despite their activism, of whom a hundred or so had settled in Sweden in 1933. On 11 February 1935 a SoPaDe group was founded in Stockholm (Lange, W. Homann, Paul Bromme), which by 1936 counted thirty-four members. This first group soon split into two fractions – right and left – divided both on the question of possible cooperation with the Communists and on the validity of the instructions given by the Prague leadership. The strategic questions – struggle against fascism, alliance with the Communists, Popular Front, future perspectives for Germany – were complicated by personality clashes, and right through to 1946 the different Social-Democrat groups published a number of analyses and programmes, enjoying a fairly wide freedom of activity.

The Communist emigration was also considerable: one to two hundred, according to H. Müssener. Not only were they very active in Sweden, they maintained connections with the resistance remaining in Germany. Despite some popular hostility, they managed to develop a number of activities: refugee aid, participation in the Freies Deutschland movement, publication of the weekly *Die Welt. Zeitschrift für Politik, Wirtschaft und Arbeiterbewegung* (with Karl Mewis, G. Hauser, F. Schwerder and F. Leopold). Several of these activists were arrested and interned in 1942. Alongside the two major parties of the left there were a number of other organizations, in particular the Sozialistischer Arbeiter Partei (SAP), very active in Sweden despite counting no more than about thirty members there. Champions of an antifascist front, they cooperated with Socialists and Communists in setting up aid committees, as well as maintaining contact with the SAP in Paris, the SoPaDe in Prague, Communists in other countries, and in a general way all the forces of the Popular Front.

These efforts to achieve unity of the left in exile gave rise also to other movements such as the Askaniakreis, which sought to unite Socialists and Communists and was active until 1939. Finally, the Austrian Socialist emigration was also represented in Sweden. The majority of these groups remained in contact with resisters in Germany, and established periodicals and information bulletins on the German situation. The political organizations were also supplemented with cultural groupings such as the Freies Deutschland Kulturbund (FDKB), whose activities were equally significant. Indifferent to the political allegiance of its members, this embraced conservatives (Dr Gallinger,

H. J. Schoeps) as well as Social-Democrats and Communists (the actor Curt Trepte). The events organized by this group included the staging of political plays, recitals from Goethe, performances of Mozart and Beethoven along with Hanns Eisler's 'Song of Solidarity' and 'The Peat-Bog Soldiers'. Several hundred German émigrés regularly took part in these activities.

The different groups of émigrés often worked on common actions. Besides the organization of a Popular Front, they united around cultural activities and commemoration ceremonies such as that held on 24 September 1944 for Wilhelm Leuschner, Ernst Thälmann and Robert Breitscheid. Stockholm was also the headquarters for various Austrian organizations (the KPÖ, *Die Österreichische Zeitung*, Freie Österreischische Bewegung), to the point that the émigrés in Sweden were sometimes referred to as the 'little International'. The work of the political emigration in Sweden was not restricted to the organiza- tion of meetings and discussion groups. Thanks to the support of Swedish sailors, Communist propaganda material, often originating in Leningrad, could be smuggled into Germany in double-bottomed suitcases.

The artistic and literary emigration in Sweden was also very significant. It included architects from the Bauhaus (Fred Forbat), sociologists (Fritz Croner) and philosophers (Ernst Cassirer, former rector of Hamburg University), along with linguists and historians of literature, whose work took on a new dimension through the process of exile. The best-known example is of course that of Walter A. Berendsohn, who reached Sweden from Denmark in 1943 and wrote several important works on Scandinavian literature. Exile theatre was represented by actors and directors such as Hermann Greid, Curt Trepte and Robert Peiper, and the plastic arts by Hans Tombrock, a friend of Brecht, as well as Heinz Buchholz, Walter Guber, Edgar Hannewald, Karl Helbig and Peter Weiss.[142] A substantial number of German writers also found refuge in Sweden. They produced such successful essays as Kurt Stechert's *Wie konnte es geschehen?* (*How Could It Happen?*, 1943), F. Rüch's *Frieden ohne Sicherheit* (*Peace without Security*, 1942), S. Neumann's *Der Koloss auf Stahlfüssen* (*The Colossus on Feet of Steel*), Otto Friedländer's *Deutschland nach Hitler* (*Germany after Hitler*, 1944) and *Der letzte Jude aus Polen* by S. Szende (*The Last Jew from Poland*, 1944). All these books played a significant part in the development of Swedish opinion towards Hitler's Germany. German literature was represented in Sweden by a number of leading figures: Kurt Tucholsky had settled there in 1929, though he stopped writing in 1933, as evidenced by his last letters, later published under the symbolic title *Letters of Silence*. He committed suicide in December 1935. Bertolt Brecht moved to Sweden in April 1939, invited by the Imperial Union of Amateur Theatres. He settled on the small island of Lindingö, at the home of the sculptor Ninan Santesson. *Mother Courage and Her Children* was written as the story of the Scandinavian camp-follower Lotte Svärd, drawn from the *Tales of Ensign Stahl* which the Swedish actress Naima Wifstrand had given him to read.[143] While in Sweden Brecht took part in several discussions with émigrés (Hermann Greid, members of the SAP) and even proposed writing a collective *Dictionary of Fascist Slogans*.[144] Hilde Rubenstein, the author of poems and plays, also found refuge in Sweden.[145]

If Peter Weiss was not yet a dramatic writer, it was nonetheless in Sweden that he started his literary career.[146] Finally, Nelly Sachs (Nobel Prize, 1966) reached Sweden in May 1940, obtaining Swedish nationality in 1952.[147]

Émigré publishing activity in Sweden was also substantial. After his departure from Vienna on 1 July 1938), G. Bermann Fischer settled in Stockholm and published more than 130 books between 1938 and 1948 (with Victor Zuckerkandl, Justinian Frisch and a 50 per cent holding from the publisher Bonnier). Collaboration with Querido Verlag in Amsterdam was maintained until 1940, but in Sweden Bermann Fischer published only works by authors who were already well known (Thomas Mann, Stefan Zweig, Franz Werfel, Carl Zuckmayer, Ernest Hemingway). In 1944, Max Tau also established the Neue Verlag, which published works by Lion Feuchtwanger and T. T. Heine.[148]

Theatre was another important field of activity for German émigrés in Sweden, often in association with the Freie Deutsche Kulturbund. The Freie Bühne – which included German, Austrian and Czech actors – gave performances in support of the émigrés from 1939 to 1942. Among the most important figures of this dramatic emigration were Curt Trepte, Verner Arpe, Peter Winner, Hermann Greid, Robert Peiper, Hans Verder and Harald Brixel. The Freie Bühne set out to stage works defending the democratic heritage of German culture. It focused on authors as different as Kleist, Schnitzler, Karl Kraus, Hasek, Nestroy, Stefan Zweig, Oskar Maria Graf, Bertolt Brecht, Arthur Koestler and Anna Seghers. Performances were often preceded by the recital of poems by Brecht, Hölderlin, Heine, Goethe, Schiller or Tucholsky. Brecht also wrote a propaganda piece for an amateur company in Riksförbund, *The Cost of Iron*. Like pieces he had written in Denmark, this was designed to warn Swedes against the dangers of their policy of neutrality. Finally, in the field of cinema, Paul Baudisch and Adolf Schütz wrote the screenplays for some sixty films.

Even though they felt isolated and were often viewed with disdain, the German émigrés in Scandinavia managed to develop a great variety of activities. This is explained by the fairly liberal character of the policy of these states towards them, and a genuine tradition of tolerance and democracy.

8. EXILE IN THE USSR

Study of antifascist emigration in the USSR raises a series of particular problems. As H. A. Walter has emphasized,[149] there are few reliable documents on this exile and the highly diverse activities of the German émigrés there. With few exceptions – such as Erwin Sinko – we possess little in the way of memoirs and testimonies written in the course of exile itself. The émigrés' activities, and the trajectories of their exile, often have to be reconstituted on the basis of their autobiographies, documents written in later years which can only be used with a certain caution. A number of them, Communists at the time of exile, later became radical anti-Communists – perhaps indeed because of their exile experience. It is also remarkable that the most influential literary figures, who would have been able to give the most detailed description of this emigration, wrote practically nothing on the subject or even avoided mentioning it at all (Lukács, Piscator). The massive liquidation of German antifascists who took refuge in the USSR, and the disappearance of their personal archives and manuscripts, only adds to these difficulties.

The same divergences are found also among historians. It is undeniable that with rare exceptions, the memoirs of German émigrés in the Soviet Union who survived the deportations and executions of the Stalin era give a very negative image (Erwin Sinko, Julius Hay, Wolfgang Leonhard, Margaret Buber-Neumann, Ruth von Mayenburg, Ernst Fischer, to give just some well-known names).[150] Krystina Kudlinska maintains on the contrary, in the chapter she devotes to this emigration,[151] that the émigrés in the USSR did not feel themselves foreigners, suffered no discrimination, could write and publish without problems, and take an active part in antifascist struggle. The few positive testimonies that she cites in support of this claim are not accompanied by any mention of the names of all those who were executed. David Pike's fairly comprehensive volume, *Deutsche Schriftsteller im sowjetischen Exil 1933–1945* (Frankfurt 1981), stresses the scale of repression and the large number of victims among the German antifascists. On the other hand, the work by Klaus Jarmatz, Simone Barck and Peter Diezel, *Exil in der UdSSR* (Leipzig 1979) emphasizes the scope of the émigrés' artistic, literary, dramatic and political activity, completely passing over the fact that many of them perished in labour camps. One might look in vain here for the least commentary on the death of Ernst Ottwalt, the Communist aesthetician and friend of Brecht, the arrest of Herwarth Walden, former director of the gallery *Der Sturm*, or the execution of Carola Neher, 'Polly Peachum' in Pabst's film of *Die Dreigroschenoper*. If it is impossible to tackle the history of German emigration in the USSR simply from the angle of its often tragic end, it is equally impossible to restrict it to a study of the émigrés' cultural activities, and say nothing of the political context in which these were located or what happened to the majority of these refugees after 1938.[152]

According to certain historians such as Klaus Jarmatz,[153] the USSR differed radically from other countries of asylum in the generosity of its welcome, the immediate application of proletarian internationalism in favour of the émigrés, and the readiness with which these were entrusted with tasks that were often important.[154] It was supposedly perceived less as a 'land of exile' than as a 'new homeland'. All this could theoretically have been true, and it was certainly the hope nourished by the majority of those who took refuge there. Even Arthur Koestler describes the emotion that gripped so many future exiles when they crossed the Soviet frontier.

According to its constitution of 1925 (article 22), the USSR granted the right of asylum to all who were forced to leave their country because of revolutionary activity. In actual practice, this right was granted to German émigrés only parsimoniously, and from 1936 on it was only those in danger of death who were allowed into the Soviet Union. Stalin seemed to have little desire to see a large number of German refugees arrive in the country, and after the murder of

Kirov in December 1934, a climate of distrust developed which severely affected all foreigners. In general, the Soviet government systematically granted asylum to functionaries of the KPD, and to a certain number of writers whose Communist convictions were well established. The acceptance of émigrés, however, was never as broad as the constitution envisaged.[155] The USSR invited and accepted individuals capable of filling particular posts.[156] Some Soviet writers even advised their German friends not to come.[157] The émigrés themselves were aware of the fact that the USSR was developing a practice of realpolitik towards them, taking care not to envenom its relations with the Reich.[158] In his paper *Gegen-Angriff*, Willi Münzenberg defended the USSR against the accusation of neglecting the émigrés made in the *Neue Weltbühne*. He retorted that such questions raised apropos the USSR's attitude towards the refugees were naive, as even if it had not organized a boycott of Hitler's Germany or any particular debates on the subject, its very existence was a blow against fascism, which it alone could effectively combat. Münzenberg's argument undoubtedly failed to convince: for many antifascists threatened with death, saving their life had also an incontestable strategic importance. H. A. Walter emphasizes that the USSR's policy towards the émigrés was not very realistic in any case, as the deployment of German Communist cadres in the Comintern organizations was by no means evident. Not suffering unemployment, unlike the majority of Western countries, the USSR could most likely have accepted a larger number of emigrants.[159] What prevented this was rather the climate of systematic distrust.

For those who were eventually authorized to settle in the USSR, the paths of exile were very diverse. Some were officially invited, including Theodor Plievier (by the Red Navy), Julius Hay (by the International Union of Revolutionary Theatre), and Erwin Piscator (to shoot a film). The majority of émigrés were subject to the same conditions: on their arrival in the USSR they were deprived of their passport, which was only returned to them on their departure. The length of their stay was established according to a complex calculation that was far from clear. Despite these difficulties, however, a sizeable number of Communist writers and functionaries chose the USSR as their country of exile, often less by necessity than by political conviction, such was their faith in Communism and the country that embodied this. It is symbolic that even Ernst Bloch thought of emigrating there. The fascination that the USSR exercised is readily explicable. The majority of German progressive intellectuals had hailed the October Revolution as the dawn of a new world. The new society being constructed embodied this in a number of ways.[160] They were passionate about its social achievements and artistic experiments, and wanted to see them at first hand. Throughout the 1920s, thanks to Lunacharsky's Narkompros, cultural ties steadily multiplied. Erich Baron published the magazine *Das Neue Russland* from 1924 to 1932. He had been secretary of the Friends of New Russia since 1922, and the organization's members included Holitscher, Goldschmidt, Kurella, Jung, Walden and Paquet. German newspapers and periodicals linked to the KPD, and the 'Münzenberg trust' above all, constantly put out enthusiastic images. Wieland Herzfelde, the former Dadaist, published Soviet writers such as S. Tretyakov in his Malik Verlag. All admired Gorky, whose plays were frequently performed in Berlin. Tretyakov's reportage style was mirrored by Willi Bredel and Ernst Ottwalt. The foundation of the League of Proletarian-Revolutionary Writers (BRPS) in 1928 marked the high point of German artists' admiration for the Soviet Union. Contacts between artists, both official and otherwise, were relatively numerous. Dadaists and constructivists met together. S. Dudov, who made the film *Kuhle Wampe* together with Brecht and Ottwalt, studied in the USSR before coming to Berlin. Walter Benjamin was asked to write the article on Goethe for the *Great Soviet Encyclopaedia*. In the fields of architecture and cinema, painting and theatre, Germans and Soviets seemed to be exploring the same paths.

It was in no way surprising, then, that a number of German artists had thought of settling in the USSR already in the Weimar period, especially when they were threatened with censorship (like Joseph Schneider, condemned to death in Germany). Several writers were invited to visit Moscow: Frida Rubiner in 1930, H. Damerius, Béla Balazs, H. Günther, Georg Lukács and Herwath Walden in 1932, then Berta Lask, Ernst Ottwalt and Erwin Piscator. After the Nazis came to power, certain writers, including some who were already refugees in other countries, also tried to reach the Soviet Union: Peter Kast, Franz Leschnitzer, M. Vallentin, Dora Wentscher, Erwin Hoernler, G. and I. von Wangenheim and Friedrich Wolf. In 1934, a further group already established in Prague emigrated to the USSR, with Willi Bredel, Anton Gabor, A. Durus-Kemeny, H. Weissbeck, A. Hotopp, G. Gog and Klara Blum. In 1935 they were joined by Fritz Erpenbeck and Hedda Zinner from Prague, Adam Scharrer from Paris, Alfred Kurella and J. R. Becher from Zurich, H. Greif and Erich Weinert from the Saar. After the annexation of Czechoslovakia, Ernst Fischer likewise emigrated to Moscow. At least thirty-five major German writers were now living there, joined by a number of painters (Heinrich Vogeler) and actors (Curt Trepte, Alexander Granach, Carola Neher), besides cadres and function-aries of the KPD. The incontestable reticence of the Soviet authorities to open their frontiers more broadly to émigrés did not rule out significant movements of solidarity towards them. The Soviet population, despite difficult conditions of life, displayed a genuine warmth towards the émigrés, despite not knowing the full story of the German proletariat's defeat or understanding the reasons for this exile.

In comparison with other countries, artists and writers in the USSR formed a relatively united community. The majority of German exiles were Communists (exceptions being Theodor Plievier, Herwarth Walden and Adam Scharrer). They often belonged to the BPRS, which did not rule out differences and rivalries among them that are often hard to analyse. Though Communists, they nonetheless formed distinct groups centred on particular individuals and periodicals. They often judged each other severely, and were themselves prey to the prevailing treason psychosis. Brecht did not hide his hostility towards the 'Moscow clique', which he wrongly attributed to Lukács's leadership. If these writers remained divided, the political émigrés were still more so, and the German emigration in the USSR cannot be depicted without taking account of their position in all these debates, whether they took an active part or not.

The majority of important members of the KPD lived in the Hotel Lux, the offices of the Comintern.[161] Wilhelm Pieck and Walter Ulbricht led a firmly structured leadership group, but there were also 'historic' members of the German Communist party who were now in disgrace, almost all of whom – like Heinz Neumann and his friends – fell victim to Stalin's repression. Neumann had been viewed as suspect ever since his arrival in Moscow.[162] In 1931–32 he was relieved of his functions on the KPD politburo for having 'deviated from the Comintern line on the question of the struggle against the National Socialists'. Despite this accusation he refused to make a self-criticism. Neumann emigrated to the USSR in 1935, after being imprisoned in Switzerland, while the Swiss government was considering the German demand for his extradition. He was housed by the Comintern and worked alongside his wife as a translator with a publishing house. Despite attacks launched against him, he refused to accept that he had conducted 'a work of splitting and opposition within the party'. The Comintern's international commission declared him guilty nonetheless of 'German fascism', according to his wife. At the end of 1936, Dimitrov, now general secretary of the Comintern, asked him on Stalin's behalf for a work on the Seventh International Congress of the Comintern, to include a critique of his political errors. Neumann refused and was arrested in 1937. His wife remained free for a while, before being imprisoned herself and deported to Karaganda. In 1940 Stalin handed her over to the Gestapo, along with other German refugees, at the bridge of Brest–Litovsk, and she was interned in Ravensbrück.

Though they often criticized the hierarchy that existed in the treatment of KPD functionaries, the majority of writers sought to keep their distance from narrowly political discussions, while frequently appealing for the protection of influential cadres. It is in fact hard to know what power even the highest cadres in the KPD still enjoyed in the USSR. As the majority of memoirs of former exiles attest, their activities generally took place in an atmosphere of general suspicion. While the majority of KPD functionaries were integrated into the Comintern apparatus, many writers and artists found work with a variety of cultural organizations, such as libraries, publishing houses, magazines and especially radio. On the material level, the majority enjoyed a security that many refugees in the Western countries often lacked. Their standard of living was often higher than that of their Soviet counterparts.[163] But this relative well-being clearly could not offset the ideological risks: was it better to fear dying of hunger, being expelled, or living in the permanent anxiety of being arrested for unpredictable reasons that defied all logic?

Almost all the émigrés – with the exception perhaps of a handful of cadres – suffered from the climate of generalized fear that marked Stalinist Russia. It is possible to cite certain texts by J. R. Becher or Friedrich Wolf declaring that they were considered as brothers, did not feel in exile, could take an active part in antifascist struggle, and so on. But the overall balance of German emigration to the USSR remains very negative: a considerable number of German antifascists – not to mention Poles – ended up in labour camps. And this unpleasant truth also forms part of the lived experience of the émigrés. It may well be true, as Erich Weinert maintains, that the exile in the Soviet Union did not have to fear his right of asylum being withdrawn, that he was welcomed by the whole country and his work highly appreciated, but this selective presentation is overly idyllic to the point of being scarcely credible.[164] Yet the richness and diversity of émigré activity cannot be denied, in culture as well as in politics. It was in the Soviet Union, at the Seventh Congress of the Communist International (25 July to 21 August 1935) that the change of strategy was decided that made it possible to construct the Popular Front. The KPD meeting held on 3 October 1935, outside Moscow for reasons of security, ended with Dimitrov's celebrated speech that called for unity of action between Communists and Socialists, marking the first serious self-criticism of the KPD in the struggle against fascism in Germany. Even if important centres of Communist emigration were also found in Prague and Paris, Moscow became from 1935 on the place where the strategy of the exiled KPD was elaborated. It was also in Moscow that the Freies Deutschland committee was created towards the end of the War, the story of which will be told below. On 3 April 1942 the KPD's central committee published a document on 'The New Steps Towards Realization of the Policy of Unity and Popular Front', in which a programme of 'salvation of people and country' was sketched out in five points, serving as a basis for the Freies Deutschland initiative. On 10 December 1941, in the prisoner-of-war camp 58, KPD representatives spent two days debating with German soldiers. This discussion led to the drafting of a manifesto to the German people signed by 158 prisoners. From April 1942 onwards, contact between German exiles and prisoners of war steadily developed. In June of that year, the manifesto was signed by more than 1,900 prisoners. At the end of June 1943, a new appeal led to the foundation of the Freies Deutschland committee, presided over by the poet Erich Weinert, with members including Wilhelm Pieck, Wilhelm Florin, Walter Ulbricht, Anton Ackermann, Willi Bredel, Friedrich Wolf, Gustav von Wangenheim and J. R. Becher. This manifesto called for an immediate end to a lost war, and laid the foundations for a state to succeed the Hitler regime. From 21 July 1943 to 3 November 1945, a special transmitter broadcast cultural and political programmes to Germany in support of the movement, and a newspaper developing the committee's directive was also widely distributed.

The cultural activities of émigrés in the USSR were equally important. The situation of writers was a priori very favorable. They were able to contribute to several German-language papers (there were twenty-one in the Soviet Union by 1939), readily publish their works and stage productions in workers' clubs and theatres. The majority of their works were published by the Publishing Co-operative of Foreign Workers in the USSR (later known as Das Internationale Buch), or by the Verlag für Nationale Minderheiten in Kiev. Often they were published in both Russian and German, in large print runs. At the same time, anthologies, and collections of letters and documents bearing on exile literature and theatre, were published from 1933 on.[165] The press was also very well developed. Besides the publications of the Communist International there were those of the German minorities in the Soviet Union, and several periodicals counting among the most important of the worldwide emigration. *Internationale Literatur* was published in Moscow from June 1931 to December 1945. Produced in Russian, German, English and French, this was the organ of the International Union of Revolutionary Writers until its dissolution in 1935.[166] Its first editor-in-chief was the Polish poet Bruno Jasienski, and its editorial board included both Soviet and foreign authors. Among the Germans were J. R. Becher, Ludwig Renn and Erich Weinert. After 1932, *Internationale Literatur* was directed by Dimanov, and Hans Günther was in charge of the German edition. From August 1933 J. R. Becher took over responsibility. Its editorial committee comprised such varied writers as Barta, Bredel, Gabor, Günther, Hupper, Lukács, Ottwalt, Tretyakov, Weinert and Wolf. Other names were subsequently added, under the impulse of the Popular Front policy. Alongside Soviet writers such as Gorky and Sholokov were the names of Henri Barbusse, Romain Roland, Heinrich Mann, Lion Feuchtwanger and Thomas Mann, Arnold Zweig and Oskar Maria Graf. Articles were also devoted to foreign literature and to questions of aesthetics. Among the most interesting columns, '*Wir rechnen ab*' – subsequently '*Glossen*' – published many articles on fascism and Hitlerite Germany, on the Popular Front, and on issues in aesthetic debates, such as the question of national culture and heritage, socialist realism, and the tasks of antifascist literature, written by Kurella, Gabor and Lukács.[167]

No less important, the review *Das Wort* also appeared in Moscow from July 1936 to March 1939. Its history, more complex than that of *Internationale Literatur*, coincides with the hope aroused by the Popular Front policy in the world of literature. Founded after the Congress for the Defence of Culture held in Paris in June 1935, this brought together writers from several countries, united by the same desire to oppose fascism and war. *Das Wort* symbolized the opening of the Popular Front, as against the strictly Communist allegiance of *Internationale Literatur*. Edited by Bertolt Brecht, Lion Feuchtwanger and Willi Bredel, and with Soviet finance, the review played a unifying role and was a place of publication for some of the most famous exile polemics, including the debates on expressionism provoked by Klaus Mann's letter to Gottfried Benn about his rallying to Nazism, and on the opposition between realism and formalism. We need only recall that these debates involved the most prominent figures in German aesthetics: Georg Lukács, Ernst Bloch, Anna Seghers, Herwarth Walden, Béla Balazs, Hanns Eisler, Bertolt Brecht, etc. The review disappeared with the German–Soviet pact and the collapse of the *Volksfront*. Seeking to be the organ of all writers who combated fascism, it welcomed liberals, Christians and non-party people as well as Marxists. A 'child of the Popular Front', as its editor Fritz Erpenbeck called it, *Das Wort* championed a revolutionary humanism able to unite both Stefan Zweig and Alfred Kurella. Alongside theoretical discussion, antifascist struggle, and the defence of liberty and democracy, *Das Wort* also shared with its readers poems by J. R. Becher, Brecht's *Fear and Misery of the Third Reich*, extracts from Willi Bredel's novel *Dein unbekannter Bruder* (*Your Unknown Brother*), reportages by Egon Erwin Kisch, texts by Lion Feuchtwanger, Oskar Maria Graf, Ernst Toller and Stefan Zweig.

Besides these periodicals, we should also mention the significant activity of German exiles on Soviet radio (Maxim Vallentin, Heinrich Greif, Ernst Fischer, Erich Weinert, Peter Kast, Hedda Zinner, Adam Scharrer, Berta Lask, Dora Wentscher, etc.). Few cinema projects reached fruition, however, apart from Erwin Piscator's film based on Anna Seghers's short story 'The Revolt of the Fisherman of Santa Barbara', Gustav von Wangenheim's *Kämpfer* (*Fighters*), on the Reichstag fire trial (1936), and *Professor Mamlok*, made in 1938 from the play by Friedrich Wolf. Lukács continued his works on aesthetics in collaboration with Lifschitz. Béla Balazs, his friend from youth, taught cinematic theory through to the end of the War. Herwarth Walden, Franz Leschnitzer, Blum, Wentscher and Rubiner also worked in institutes where German was taught. Some exiles took on important functions, such as J. R. Becher at *Internationale Literatur*, or Alfred Kurella who was in charge of the bibliographic section of the Moscow library for foreign literature. Alfred Durus-Kemenyi became secretary of the Moscow committee of the Union of Plastic Artists of the USSR.

Many émigrés also took an active part in the struggle against fascism. When Hitler's armies invaded the Soviet Union, several immediately asked to join the Red Army as ordinary soldiers. Many of them, including Friedrich Wolf and Willi Bredel, worked on writing leaflets and manifestos, and producing propaganda material encouraging German soldiers to desert. When the Freies Deutschland committee was founded, its first members included a number of exile poets (Weinert, Becher, Bredel, Wolf). The committee published not only leaflets and manifestos, but also a four-page newspaper, and from December 1943, an illustrated magazine *Freies Deutschland im Bild*, designed for German troops and prisoners. The programme of Freies Deutschland[168] was distributed in millions of copies among German soldiers. The Freies Deutschland movement subsequently spread to other countries, with H. Hauser in charge of the national committee for Western countries, and Ludwig Renn head of the movement in Mexico.

Among all these cultural activities, a fundamental place was held by theatre, and especially political theatre. The first regroupings of German actors in the USSR arose very early on, such as the Moscow Foreign Workers' Club to which a number of proletarian theatre troupes belonged. The famous Berlin company Kolonne Links, banned already by the von Papen government, had established itself in the Soviet Union in 1931. Gustav von Wangenheim, a central figure in Berlin agitprop, was invited to Moscow after he went into exile in Paris along with other Communist actors (Rober Trösch, Curt Trepte, Ingeborg Franke-Wangenheim), to establish a German theatre there. Performances took place in Moscow, Gorky, Ukraine and the Volga Republic. Many people had the idea of transforming this agitprop style into a genuine antifascist theatre in exile, capable of reaching an international audience. The Kolonne Links company, which on 25 February 1934 staged von Wangenheim's celebrated plays *Helden im Keller* (*Cellar Heros*) and *Agenten* (*Agents*) at the Foreign Workers' Club, gradually transformed itself into an antifascist exile theatre, with a repertoire that included proletarian works as well as Brecht and Weill's *Ballade vom Reichstagsbrand (Ballad of the Reichstag Fire)*. The system of sovkhozes and kolkhozes enabled these companies to undertake wide-ranging tours, stopping even in rural villages. This led also to the development of the Deutsche-Kollektivistentheater Odessa, which had opened a studio under the direction of Ilse Berend-Groas, formerly head of a proletarian agitation troupe in Kassel. Its very broad repertoire included Molière's *Malade imaginaire*, *Othello*, Schiller's *Intrigue and Love* and Brecht's *Señora Carrar's Rifles*, as well as proletarian pieces. The Deutsche-Kollektivistentheater Gebiets Dnepropetrowsk was likewise composed of émigrés and included actors from Max Reinhardt's company together with those from Proletkult and Maxime Vallentin. It staged a number of antifascist plays inspired by true stories: G. Hinze's testimony on the ten months he had spent in concentration camp in 1933, the sadism of the Gestapo, the murders of Hans Otto and Erich Mühsam, as well as spectacles composed around 'The Peat-Bog Soldiers' Song'. This collective gave more than 160 performances in a year, before over 45,000 spectators, in at least a hundred different venues. The shows were accompanied by political and cultural discussion.

The most interesting theatrical experiment among the antifascist exiles in the USSR, however, was that in the Volga German Republic, which in itself sums up the richness of the exile experience. This was a strange republic, which played a large part in the life and imagination of the émigré antifascists.[169] With its capital at Pokrovsi – subsequently called Engels – and its second city of Karl-Marx-Stadt, this was in the early 1930s a collection of villages and collective farms. The inhabitants had settled in the region as colonists in the time of Catherine II, their language being closer to that of Luther than to modern German. The majority knew no Russian. The republic had its own government and was very attached to its traditions.

In 1934 a number of cultural events took place in Engels, where there was already a German theatre. Several proletarian pieces were staged, and a number of agitprop troupes around Gustav von Wangenheim and Hermann Greid established themselves there. They were later joined by the theatre group inspired by Maxim Vallentin. This had been previously in exile in Prague, and it was on the invitation of Erwin Piscator, who in 1934 became president of the International Association of Theatre Workers (MORT), that it came to the USSR. The idea then developed of establishing at Engels, the Volga capital, a major antifascist theatre that would in itself be a symbol of Weimar in exile.

Despite the official consent of the Soviet government and that of the Volga Republic, the obstacles to the achievement of the project were enormous. First of all the language: the Volga Germans spoke a language scarcely comprehensible to the émigrés, and they knew nothing of fascism or Hitler, in whom they saw simply a new kaiser. To arouse them to politics and the actual situation in Germany by the use of theatre might have seemed impossible. And yet very soon the émigrés staged the first antifascist plays, as well as starting wall newspapers with information on the situation in Germany and later Spain. While itinerant theatre troupes travelled from one village to the next in carts, or in boats on the Volga, Erwin Piscator sought to establish this great antifascist theatre at Engels by attracting to the USSR a number of exiled actors and directors. His closest collaborators included Arthur Pieck (the son of Wilhelm Pieck) and Bernhard Reich, a director who had worked in the USSR since 1926. While seeking to transform the MORT into a means of international coordination, and the Engels theatre into a rallying place for all the exiles, Piscator wanted to set up a wide programme of dramatic presentations. The first plays he scheduled included works by Brecht, Wangenheim, Wolf, Zinner and Hay. He also envisaged shooting anti-Nazi films in several languages. Though none of these film projects came to fruition, on account of material difficulties and lack of coordination, the idea of an antifascist theatre immediately rallied a large number of actors and directors. Piscator had overall charge of the undertaking, with Bernhard Reich as his second-in-command. The pair spent two years working on the Engels project. Piscator tried to involve in his enterprise not only German actors and directors already established in the USSR (Alexander Granach, Carola Neher, Ernst Busch, Hermann Greid), but also those who were exiled in other countries. He claimed that in the Soviet Union there was work for all, whilst those who had settled elsewhere had built their house on sand, as they were not safe from a Hitlerite invasion. The only danger he brought to his correspondents' attention – for example E. Kalser who was living in Switzerland – was the risk of malaria in the Volga flood plain. To Otto Walburg he confided: 'If I had a son, I would not want him brought up anywhere but in the USSR, as here his future is assured. He can study and become what he wants. There will be work and progress for generations to come' (letter of 10 October 1936). The situation of émigrés was often so tragic that his enthusiasm was infectious: the news went round the world of the foundation at Engels of this enormous revolutionary theatre with tremendous resources and exceptional figures. L. Steckel even wrote from Zurich to Paul Zech in Argentina to advise him to keep in touch with this opportunity. Piscator proposed that Brecht should come and work in the USSR, though Brecht was far less sanguine on the prospects of the enterprise.[170]

Piscator also came up against growing difficulties in the realization of his plans. First of all, it seems that certain directors he had invited refused to come and work in the Engels theatre (von Wangenheim, Hans Rodenberg, Hermann Greid). On top of this came the unexpected dissolution of MORT, the very organization that was supposed to enable a number of foreign artists to come to the USSR. According to Bernard Reich, one of the reasons invoked for this dissolution was the typically Stalinist fear that it would permit the infiltration of spies. Piscator does not seem to have realized that in the long run this measure signalled the collapse of the Engels project. He travelled to Paris with Arthur Pieck, sent by the Comintern to examine the activities of the antifascist front. There he met the most active émigrés, in particular Willi Münzenberg, organizer of the counter-trial on the Reichstag fire and publisher of the *Brown Book*. He was getting ready to return to the USSR when he received a telegram from Reich (3 October 1936) enjoining him not to return, on the pretext that the renovation work had not yet been finished. There soon followed a letter from

Wilhelm Pieck, officially discharging him from his functions, and warning that he could not guarantee his safety if he returned. Piscator subsequently recognized that this warning might well have saved his life.

The Engels project and its failure is a good example of both the richness of the émigrés' activity in the Soviet Union and the extreme difficulties – very often political – that they encountered in the course of this. The Engels theatre, which managed to start operating amid dreadful administrative harassment, was eventually denounced as a bourgeois work of demoralization foreign to Soviet culture, and many of its collaborators were arrested. As for the Volga Republic, Stalin feared its inhabitants might be sympathetic to Hitler, and on 28 August 1941 had them deported to the Urals. The republic was officially dissolved on 7 September 1941, and not re-established until 29 August 1964.

The political climate prevailing under Stalin deeply marked the fate of those German émigrés who took refuge in the Soviet Union. As foreigners, intellectuals or professional activists displaying a wide ideological diversity, they were appropriate victims. Many were arrested without reason after the assassination of Kirov (doubtless perpetrated at Stalin's own behest) and either deported to Siberia or executed. These measures affected party cadres,[171] leaders and rank-and-file activists, as well as writers and poets. To describe their tragic fate, which has already been the object of detailed accounts as far as the writers are concerned, would go beyond the scope of this book. In the majority of cases, we still know nothing of the reasons for their arrest or what exactly happened to these émigrés, many of whom ended up in Siberian prison camps. Besides official arrests and executions, others simply disappeared or died in suspicious circumstances, such as Max Holz.

From 1936 onward, the Soviet press ceaselessly urged vigilance and the struggle against 'enemy infiltrators'. Even the *Deutsche Zentralzeitung* took up this appeal on 9 August 1936. The repression struck the émigrés in successive waves. KPD cadres were the first affected. On 27 April 1937, Heinz Neumann was arrested at the Hotel Lux. A search of his room revealed books not only 'of a Trotskyist character', but likewise 'Zinovievist, Kamenevist and Bukharinite'.[172] He disappeared into a Siberian camp, together with other Comintern cadres, whether German or not (Alichanov, Gorski). In September 1937 his wife was arrested, expelled from the KPD and condemned to five years in a labour camp as a 'socially dangerous element'. In the same fashion, Litten and Gresetski were sent to the Kolyma camp as 'Trotskyists' because they had received catalogues sent by émigré publishers. They were both executed as spies. The Polish Communists were especially affected,[173] and a large number of Germans were eliminated who had played an important part in the history of the KPD (August Kreuzburg, Klara Valter, Hermann Schubert, Hermann Remmele, Wally Adler and Betty Olberg, to mention just a few).[174] Writers were just as harshly affected as political cadres.[175] According to Julius Hay, the émigrés themselves were tempted to seek out traitors and fascist spies in their midst, thus giving credit to the most delirious accusations.[176]

It seems that it was the arrest of Ernst Ottwalt that marked the start of the persecution of émigré intellectuals. He was arrested in 1936, and died in a Siberian camp in 1943. Ottwalt was a Communist aesthetician and novelist, whose work was quite well known in the Weimar period. He was Georg Lukács's antagonist in a number of significant debates on the proletarian novel and the reportage novel in the *Linkskurve*, and worked with Brecht and Dudow on the screenplay of *Kuhle Wampe*. His novels include one that tells the story of an émigré who betrayed his comrades and worked for the Gestapo. The police suspected him of having written his own story, and he was arrested. (Paul Nizan in France met with a similar posthumous slander that had certain parallels with Ottwalt's case.) Nothing certain is known of his death.[177]

It is impossible to give the names of all the antifascist émigrés arrested after Ottwalt. One of the most significant was Herwarth Walden, founder of the art gallery and expressionist review *Der Sturm*. An admirer of Soviet Russia, he was already close to the Communists in the 1920s. He emigrated to Moscow in 1932, and worked quite regularly on *Das Wort* from 1937 to 1939 (under the pseudonym Walter Sturm). Walden was particularly involved in the great debate on expressionism of 1937–38. He worked for several years at the Foreign Languages Institute in Moscow, also publishing in *Internationale Literatur* articles on foreign literature, cultural life in the Third Reich, and music. He was arrested on 13 March 1941,[178] and deported to the camp at Saratov on the Volga where he died the same year. Hans Günther, born 8 September 1899, a contributor to *Rote Fahne* and *Linkskurve*, had been responsible for agitprop. He took part in several theoretical discussions in the USSR. Though one of the few émigrés with a good knowledge of Soviet literature, he was arrested as an 'enemy' and died at Vladivostok in 1938. The journalist Werner Hirsch, a close collaborator of Ernst Thälmann, was condemned to ten years in labour camp and died of hunger in Siberia. Albert Hotopp, in charge of KPD publications, was arrested in 1941 and died in a camp. Gregor Gog, who escaped from a Nazi concentration camp where he had been interned after the Reichstag fire, was sent to a Soviet camp in 1941 and died of tuberculosis in Tashkent in 1944. Like the Yugoslav Karlo Steiner, arrested in 1936 and not released until 1956, the Hungarian friend of Lukács, Joseph Lengyel, was condemned in 1938 to eight years of forced labour, then to a further ten years, and did not return to Hungary until 1955. The widow of the poet Erich Mühsam, Zensl Mühsam, accused of having abused Soviet hospitality, was condemned to twenty years' forced labour, though she had come to the USSR at the invitation of the Red Cross to speak of the martyrdom of her husband murdered by the Nazis. She returned to the GDR to die there in March 1962, at the age of eighty, after a campaign had been launched on her behalf by former émigrés.[179]

The same measures struck a number of actors. Though some of these were arrested but then released (Maxim Vallentin, Alexander Granach), one of the most tragic cases was that of Carola Neher. Famous from her work on stage and screen, the wife of the poet Klabund (who died before her exile), she remained the unforgettable Polly Peachum in the film version of *Die Dreigroschenoper* made by G. W. Pabst. She was rapidly put on the blacklist of actors as an anti-Nazi, and deprived of German nationality. She emigrated to the USSR after marrying the German-Romanian engineer A. Becker. In Prague she had met with Erich Wollenberg, a former KPD activist and political editor of *Rote Fahne*, who had broken with Communism in 1931. He had doubtless given her the addresses of friends in the USSR, and this would seem to have been the motive for her arrest. After the birth of her son, Georg Becker, she left her husband and started a relationship with Mikhail Koltsov, the editor of *Pravda*, in charge of Soviet publishing and a friend of Stalin (though he was nonetheless arrested in 1938 and executed). Not speaking Russian, Carola Neher had a great deal of difficulty in finding new engagements, though she did act in von Wangenheim's film *The Dimitrov Case*.

At the time of the Moscow trials, she was arrested with her husband as a 'Trotskyist spy' and imprisoned. Though she had attended lectures at the Arbeiterschule in the 1930s as a means of studying Marxism, she was never involved at all in politics and had certainly never read Trotsky. Margaret Buber-Neumann was doubtless one of the last people to have seen her alive in 1940: 'Carola Neher was in prison garb. Compared with our camp rags, it was almost elegant, and the elegant Carola wore it with an air. It consisted of a blue flannel blouse with red lapels, a dark blue skirt and a short jacket. As she had been doing a hard labour term, her lovely hair had been shaved off, but it was just long enough again to stay down.'[180] Condemned to ten years in prison for serving as a 'Trotskyist courier', she tried to commit suicide by cutting her veins in the Lubyanka prison. Her son, aged just one year, had been placed in an orphanage. Several witnesses agree that the NKVD tried to recruit her as a spy. After her refusal, she was sent back to camp. Her husband had been shot in 1937, and she herself was executed as a spy on 28 June 1942. After the War, as with other émigrés who had been killed, it was made out that she had preferred to remain in the USSR rather than return to Germany. Carola Neher's son was subsequently entrusted to an antifascist couple, Hermann and Ilse Tannenberg. Hermann was also executed and his wife deported to Siberia. (Only in 1972 did she receive permission to return to Germany, to die in an old people's home there.) The child was then brought up in ignorance of his true identity, and went on to teach music and composition in Odessa. He was only authorized to visit Germany in 1968, following efforts by Rudolf Lenk and several demands made to Leonid Brezhnev by German writers and artists, including Golo Mann, Günter Grass and Carl Zuckmayer. In March 1969 he wrote a letter to Rudolf Lenk that scarcely needs comment:

I lost my parents at the age of a year and a year and a half respectively, and I only learned their names last year, in 1968, at the age of thirty-four. For thirty years I tried to conjure up the presence of my mother by my side. As an infant, she took the form of a hope to see her appear, and in my maturer years, that of a persistent auto-suggestion of her spiritual presence. I have no doubt that her last thought before dying was of me.[181]

The birth of Carola Neher's son, as a Soviet citizen, had been reported in an issue of *AIZ* published in Prague.

It is clear that the German émigrés met with a tragic fate in almost all countries, that everywhere they had to face administrative and police harassment, incomprehension, hostility, hatred, poverty, despair and hunger. A number of them died in camps or in prison, committed suicide or were handed over to the Gestapo. The case of the anti-Nazi emigration in the Soviet Union was not exceptional in this respect. What made it most tragic, however, was that since the 1920s this country had represented for these men and women the hope of a new world, for which they were ready to give their lives. They had never imagined that they could be its victims. Thus of all the crimes of the Stalin era, this was undoubtedly one of the most absurd and revolting.

9. EXILE IN FRANCE

I loved a city whose inhabitants paraded their heart of gold in their songs and street cries, while at the same time they were astonishingly proud of their professed anti-Semitism.

Manès Sperber

THE RECEPTION OF ANTIFASCIST ÉMIGRÉS

A large number of German antifascists sought refuge in France after 1933.[182] They included some of the most illustrious figures of the Weimar Republic, in culture as well as in politics, and made up a total close to 30,000,[183] the largest component of the emigration that followed the Nazi victory. The reasons driving these émigrés to choose France included the country's reputation for hospitality,[184] its proximity to the Reich, and its less repressive legislation towards émigrés than that of many other European countries. It is harder to analyse the composition of this emigration. The majority were relatively young,[185] and mostly from the liberal professions. They included relatively few workers – even though the return of the Saar to the Reich in 1935 forced a number of these to take refuge in France. But the importance of the emigration in France was not simply a function of numbers, but rather the celebrity of some of the greatest writers from Germany (Heinrich Mann, Bertolt Brecht, Anna Seghers, Walter Benjamin, Carl Einstein, Ernst Toller, Alfred Döblin, Erich Maria Remarque, Lion Feuchtwanger) and Austria (Joseph Roth), along with figures who played an important role in the exile community such as Alfred Kantorowicz, Gustav Regler and Arthur Koestler, and politicians who had occupied key posts in the Weimar Republic, the Social-Democrats Rudolf Hilferding and Robert Breitscheid, the Communists Franz Dahlem, Walter Ulbricht and Willi Münzenberg. Their political role had been in some cases in government, in others as party functionaries or activists on behalf of their class. The exiles also included a good number of journalists, essayists and publicists (Georg Bernhard, Leopold Schwarzschild, Alfred Kerr), not to mention visual artists (Hans Hartung, Max Ernst), actors and directors (Peter Lorre, Erich von Stroheim, Max Reinhardt, Erwin Piscator).

These refugees arrived in a number of successive waves. In the wake of the Reichstag fire, it was chiefly militants from the left organizations and intellectuals who escaped to France, but in a fairly limited number. This rose from May 1933 onwards,[186] and the aid committees estimated that at least 7,300 refugees had already reached France by this date. German Jews also reached France in stages. Those who emigrated in 1933 did so for political reasons; they were opponents of the regime. Others did not leave Germany until the boycott of Jewish shops, the promulgation of the Nuremberg laws (1935) and above all the *Kristallnacht* of 1938. The return of the Saar to Germany following the plebiscite drove out a number of Saarlanders who did not want to be citizens of the Third Reich, as well as antifascists who had moved to the Saar in 1933. The annexation of Austria in 1938 also led to a number of Austrians seeking asylum in France,[187] while in 1938–39 a number of German exiles in Czechoslovakia also moved to Paris.

As Gilbert Badia has emphasized, these successive waves of migration, and the offsetting of arrivals in France by departures to North and South America as refugees felt endangered, make it hard to establish the exact number of émigrés. But the majority of writers (Kurt R. Grossmann, Gilbert Badia, Norman Bentwich) agree on a figure between 30,000 and 35,000. The political composition of the German emigration has also been estimated by several authors. One of the best documented accounts, that of Ursula Lankau-Alex,[188] counts some 10,000 political émigrés, who included 3,000 to 3,500 Social-Democrats, 4,000 to 5,000 Communists, a few refugees belonging to minor left-wing organizations, 500 to 600 pacifists and 250 to 300 Catholics.

France still enjoyed a positive reputation for its reception of refugees; many intellectuals admired its liberal tradition.[189] But the economic situation at the time of this influx aroused fears that the refugees would aggravate the crisis, even if this risk was altogether mythical given their limited number. The government also had to take into account the reactions of the right-wing press, and between 1933 and 1939 French policy developed from relative tolerance to a brutal rejection. In the first months of 1933, however, the refugees enjoyed a genuine sympathy. It is sufficient to read the press reports on German events, especially those of the literary press, to measure their impact on public opinion.[190] Anti-Germanism was of course widespread in France, above all among intellectuals of the right close to *Action Française*, from Charles Maurras to Léon Daudet. The anti-Semitism of this epoch, however, also had a violently anti-German dimension.[191] Efforts to elicit support for the victims of National Socialism thus developed chiefly in left-wing milieus, among the Communists, Socialists, and a certain number of progressive intellectuals. This aid was initially in the context of a movement of opposition to war and imperialism. In 1932, at the initiative of figures such as Henri Barbusse and Willi Münzenberg, a great anti-war congress had been organized in Amsterdam, followed by a rally against fascism at the Salle Pleyel in early 1933. The two movements joined forces on 20 April 1933 to create the Amsterdam-Pleyel committee, which saw aid to the victims of National Socialism as both a moral and a political task.[192]

The arrival of the first refugees gave rise to a number of interventions in the Chamber of Deputies to attract government intervention in their favour.[193] The Socialist deputy Jules Moch questioned interior minister Camille Chautemps on the reception given to émigrés at the French frontier: 'Is it the case, Monsieur le Ministre, that orders will be given to our border controls that those who have had to flee Nazi rifles or the submachine-guns of the Reichswehr will find in our country that fraternal welcome that has always been the glory and honour of France?'[194] Such instructions were indeed given on 20 April: French consulates were requested to deal with visa requests from German Jews in a liberal manner. It was even stipulated that refugees without passports should be admitted to French territory 'on the simple establishment of their status and armed with a safe-conduct permitting them to reach the address that they give. They will subsequently be allowed to obtain an identity card and the possibility of work.'[195]

This relative official understanding towards victims of National Socialism aroused the hostility of the right-wing press and Action Française, which railed against these '*métèques*' and the influx of German Jews. The attacks peaked in 1936 with a series of articles by Henri Béraud in *Gringoire*.[196] In papers of the right and far right, the German émigrés were viewed as disturbing elements, 'spies', 'beggars' or 'criminals'. They were accused – especially after 1938 – of poisoning relations with Germany and pushing for war. From 18 July 1933, therefore, the ministry of the interior[197] made clear that Jewish refugees accepted in France had to be bearers of a German passport, and on 2 August gave the instruction to return passport-less foreigners. Both consulates and the border police were requested to exercise due vigilance.[198] Those refugees permitted to work in France were mainly directed to the southwest for employment in agriculture.

Groups and committees in aid of the refugees were nonetheless formed very rapidly. Secours Ouvrier and Secours Rouge International concerned themselves chiefly with the Communists, while the Comité Matteoti helped Social-Democrats. Jewish émigrés were catered for by the Comité National de Secours aux Réfugiés Allemands Victimes de l'Antisémitisme, the American Joint Distribution Committee and the Quakers. Despite their valiant efforts, these committees had very restricted means. A number of official organizations, especially the military authorities, put unused premises at their disposal, to help shelter the growing number of refugees. Generally these were no more than abandoned barracks, often completely unheated, and with the swelling tide of refugees, the support of the committees proved increasingly insufficient.

But the situation of German refugees in France was to worsen considerably from 1934–35. The émigrés fell prey to a climate of growing xenophobia, stirred up by the far-right leagues. Successive governments increasingly gave way to pressure from the right, multiplying measures against the émigrés and foreigners in general.[199] It was the above-mentioned Henri Béraud who wrote on the Stavisky affair in *Pavés Rouges*: 'The foreigners in our midst, the debris of speculators, the vermin of hotel rats, the plague of spying, agitation, provocation, attacks and kidnappings and, capping it all, the permanent scandal of naturalizations in which politicians and officials seem to vie with each other for shamelessness – this is what the Stavisky affair has shown up.' It was in vain that the parties of the left – and Léon Blum – protested the injustice of these measures. They could not prevent expulsion orders from being carried out. The émigrés were often viewed as pariahs whose very right to live was rejected.

In January 1935, France received refugees from the Saar, those who had opposed reunification with Germany in the referendum. An Association d'Entraide pour la Sarre had been formed well in advance of the plebiscite. When the result was announced, 7,000 refugees from the territory arrived in France, both native Saarlanders and German antifascists who had taken refuge there. They were first of all sheltered in barracks, subsequently directed to the southwest with state support. But when it proved that the League of Nations would not meet the refugees' subsistence costs, the French government closed the shelters and cut off all assistance.[200] In the era of the Front Populaire, an office for refugees was set up under the Saarland Social-Democrat Max Braun. But after 1938 these no longer enjoyed any privileged status and were simply considered as 'German refugees'. The annexation of Austria and the new influx of refugees, many Jewish, did not lead France to any special measures in their favour. The only refugees accepted were those with visas supplied by the French consular authorities. Qualified as 'ex-Austrians', they simply joined the other refugees, as Rhinelanders had done after the remilitarization of the Rhineland.

The advent of the Front Populaire was however an important milestone in the life of the refugees. The new government immediately took measures to improve their condition, for instance cancelling the decree of 6 February 1935 that restricted the validity of identity cards issued to foreigners to the departments in which they had settled.[201] They were allowed to change their residence, and stateless persons were given legal status. Finally, a decree of 17 September 1936 created an identity certificate permitting refugees to visit any country that was a signatory to the Geneva convention. From this point on, the refugees did not have to fear expulsion. A 'consultative commission for German refugees' was established, to verify that identity certificates were issued only to genuine refugees. Its members included four Frenchmen and four émigré Germans (Albert Grzesinksi, Georg Bernhard, T. Tichauer and Willi Münzenberg).[202] The government now sought to regularize the situation of émigrés. At the same time, however, a circular of 14 August 1936 was addressed to departmental prefects, requesting that they 'no longer allow any German émigré to arrive in France, and proceed to return any foreigner, German subject or arrival from Germany who, entering after 5 August 1936, is not provided with the necessary identification documents'.[203] This improvement in the situation of refugees was very real: of 3,014 cases examined by the commission, 2,490 were recognized as 'genuine refugees'.[204] From 1938 to 1940, however, the situation of German émigrés turned into a real nightmare: the sympathy they had been shown during the Front Populaire era proved to be very short-lived.[205]

Reception Committees

What were the main bodies concerned with refugees in France? The first thing is to distinguish the reception of Jewish refugees from that of political refugees. The majority of Jewish refugees came under the remit of the Comité National de Secours aux Victimes de l'Antisémitisme en Allemagne',[206] which united the other aid organizations. This body enjoyed substantial funds, and was practically the government's only official contact on the refugee question.[207] It was financed by international Jewish organizations, and while it handled the reception of Jewish refugees in France, its main effort was to direct German Jews towards other countries, for fear that their presence in France would stoke up anti-Semitism.

The leading lights of this committee were either Jewish or sympathetic to the refugees – the chief rabbi Levy, Baron Edmond de Rothschild, former ministers André Honorat, Justin Godard and Paul Painlevé, and they requested Jewish communities in France to help in the reception of their co-religionists. By May 1933 the Comité National had already assisted more than 3,000 refugees. Other committees – the Fédération des Sociétés Juives, Secours Rouge, the Ligue Contre l'Antisémitisme – also came to their support. But the French Jewish community was divided on the attitude to adopt towards German refugees. While all Jewish representatives condemned the treatment inflicted on Jews in Germany, the more conservative were careful not to adopt a radical political position, and to avoid a blanket condemnation of the Hitler regime. In the course of a meeting called to coordinate efforts in support of German Jews, for example, Baron Robert de Rothschild, vice-president of the Consistoire Israélite in Paris, ruled out any political involvement.[208] Jacques Heilbronner summed up as follows the official position adopted by French Judaism at this meeting:

> France like other nations has its unemployed, and not all Jewish refugees from Germany are individuals who should remain here for the greater good of our country. There are between 100 and 150 major intellectuals that France has an interest in keeping, as scientists or chemists with secrets unfamiliar to our own [. . .]. These we shall keep, but out of the seven or eight thousand Jews, maybe ten thousand, who will arrive in France, is it in our interest to keep them?[209]

The committee saw its real powers of decision placed in the hands of individuals selected by Robert de Rothschild.[210] As a whole, the émigré German Jews were not received with genuine sympathy by Jews in France. Rather than genuine solidarity, these displayed a charity that was merely dutiful and restrained.[211] One cannot even say that the representatives of French Judaism nourished any great sympathy towards German refugees, Jews though they might be. The committee nonetheless accepted 15,000 refugees before its closure in July 1934, providing basic assistance in the form of identity papers, food, housing, and financial aid, with generosity but not without discrimination.[212] But as this assistance dwindled, the growing number of refugees soon overburdened the initial measures of support.[213] The Comité National only obtained from the military authorities permission to install refugees in three disused barracks (Porte d'Italie, Porte d'Orléans, Saint-Maur) and in a former hospital (Porte de la Villette), where they encountered truly wretched conditions.[214] It is true that the idea of the Comité National was to be only a sorting station for German emigration, and all those whose status as émigrés was in doubt were sent back to their countries of origin, until in 1937 the Gestapo threatened to arrest and imprison any Jews who sought to return to the Reich. Efforts were then generally made to send them to South America, South Africa, the French colonies or Palestine. From January 1934, these temporary shelters were returned to the military authorities, and on 1 August the Comité National closed its doors to all refugees, confining itself to simply giving advice.

Responsibility for political refugees was undertaken by a fairly large number of specialized committees, whose functioning has been the object of a recent study.[215] First place among the major organizations assisting German refugees was held by the Ligue des Droits de l'Homme (LDH) presided over by Victor Basch, which had 190,000 members and 1,500 branches spread across French territory. The Ligue came to the aid of those émigrés who received help neither from Jewish organizations nor from the Secours Rouge.[216] In April 1933, it established a 'German committee' to receive the refugees. The German pacifist Hellmut von Gerlach, former director of the Human Rights League in Germany, served as intermediary between the Ligue and the Comité National.[217] The German organization was re-established in Paris the same year, and worked closely together with the LDH in assisting the refugees. It had three sections, in Prague, Strasbourg and Paris.

The French Socialist party (SFIO) was involved in refugee aid through its 'immigration commission' established at the initiative of Jules Moch.[218] A Matteoti Foundation had already been formed in Zurich in 1926, to come to the aid of Italian refugees. The Socialist International established in August 1933 a Matteoti Committee to assist Social-Democratic émigrés.[219] Communist émigrés, for their part, were taken under the wing of International Red Aid, which displayed great effectiveness on their behalf.

All these organizations sought to assist refugees by pressing the French government to facilitate access to its territory for all individuals who were under threat. The Ligue des Droits de l'Homme often intervened when refugees were threatened with expulsion. Secours Rouge called public meetings, together with the LDH and the PCF, in defence of several of them.[220] Where German Communist refugees were concerned, International Red Aid was naturally most active.[221] Most of the initiatives taken by these committees linked up in a number of ways: of prime importance was to intervene on the political level so that frontiers were open, even to those refugees who were not in possession of valid papers. When reception was less generous than the exceptional regime established in April 1933 foresaw, the Ligue very often intervened in support of those affected. This type of intervention was still more necessary in 1935 towards the Saarland refugees. These organizations also offered legal aid to refugees who were threatened with expulsion, especially in the case of political activists who were continuing the antifascist struggle.[222] Finally, they also provided material aid to refugees by circulating subscription lists in their favour. International Red Aid called a 'week of solidarity with victims of German fascism' from 17 to 25 June 1933, to raise funds for both the clandestine German Rote Hilfe and the French Secours Rouge.[223] It also held dances, fêtes, and even a 'Big Red Christmas for German prisoners, political refugees and their children'. Secours Rouge organized sponsorship for political émigrés, the idea being that French workers' families would take partial responsibility for their support, though this did not prove very successful. Besides financial assistance, the organizations of the left worked to obtain the right to work for the émigrés, in the absence of which, as Secours Rouge put it, 'the mere right of asylum is turned into a right to die of hunger'.[224] The Ligue des Droits de l'Homme likewise sought to find families prepared to take in émigré children, and the Comité Matteoti developed similar forms of assistance. These organizations however often met with very serious obstacles.[225]

Reception of Intellectuals and Writers

The reception of intellectuals, writers and artists posed specific problems of its own, and it is interesting to describe briefly the relations they managed to establish with their French colleagues. While in the majority of cases their situation differed little from that of the refugees in general, they could at least hope to benefit from the support of their French counterparts, especially as they included some of the most famous cultural representatives of the Weimar era. Whereas the academic emigrants – though only relatively few of these settled in France – aroused early on the sympathy of a number of personalities who formed a Comité des Savants to come to their aid,[226] the reception of writers was more complex. It depended very largely on their celebrity, on their familiarity with the French language, on existing translations of their work, and on connections that they already had in France. They often benefited from the strong current of radicalism and political awareness that marked the French intelligentsia at this point in time.

What Herbert R. Lottmann described under the title 'Rive Gauche'[227] was not just a myth. There were few times when French writers felt as concerned by political events as in the early 1930s, when they were ready to make a commitment in the face of world events. They did so no doubt with naivety and idealism, but also with an undeniable generosity and great sincerity. Well before the popularization of the notion of *engagement* by Sartre, a group of writers – a certain elite – made its appearance on the international stage, leaving the domain of mere literature to take a position on international events, to contribute to the mobilization against fascist movements and in favour of their victims, to support the Front Populaire and the Spanish Republic and to defend the USSR.[228] Though Charles Maurras, Céline and Drieu la Rochelle attracted at the same time the youth of the right, the 'Rive Gauche' made its historical entrance with Gide, André Malraux, Henri Barbusse, Paul Nizan, Jean Guéhenno and a number of others, whose names were regularly to be found at the head of appeals, manifestos and petitions, and who seemed to have almost abandoned literary creation to take part in public meetings.

This intellectual left was a very complex phenomenon. It included veterans like Barbusse, established Communist writers (Paul Vaillant-Couturier and J. R. Bloch), young intellectuals who rallied to Communism (Paul Nizan), Radical-Socialists (André Chamson), writers who emerged from the bourgeoisie (Gide and Malraux), 'autodidacts' such as Jean Guéhenno, surrealists in revolt against the bourgeois world – Breton and Crevel – and 'humanists' like Jean Cassou. Several of them were to be found in 1932 in the Association des Écrivains et des Artistes Révolutionnaires (AEAR): Barbusse, Romain Rolland, Breton, Nizan, Aragon, Giono, Malraux, Gide, or in the Comité de Vigilance des Intellectuels Antifascistes founded by Rivet, Alain and Langevin. If the most spectacular of their initiatives was the visit by Gide and Malraux to Berlin to try and to Hitler and obtain the release of the accused in the Reichstag fire trial, their support for the German emigration took a number of forms. The refugees, by the information they carried on Hitlerite Germany, stoked up their revolt and their hatred of fascism. It is very likely that Malraux gathered from German émigrés the material for his book *Le Temps du mépris*. The celebrity and audience of French writers, the intellectual power that they wielded in newspapers, with publishers, with public opinion, in meetings and in reviews, enabled émigré antifascists to find spokespeople who amplified their words.

We should also note that some of the émigré German writers in Paris were French-speaking as well as Francophile, and in no way felt rootless in their new country. Many others came into contact with representatives of the French intelligentsia through encounters, recommendations and connections. The best introduction to the Parisian literary world was an invitation from one or other of the great writers. Between 1933 and 1935, this politicization of French writers reached a veritable paroxysm with their massive participation in the Congress for the Defence of Culture. But they were also to be found in many actions of the Thälmann committee, and public gatherings in support of the Popular Front. This development might supervene on the pacifism inherited from the First World War (Barbusse), or be triggered by contact with the Amsterdam-Pleyel committee or the claim of a 'militant humanism' (from Gide to Guéhenno), which explains both Gide's anti-colonialism, Malraux's antifascism, and an admiration for the USSR. Many at this time had a mythic image of the Soviet Union, which was slow to erode (from Gide to Nizan) and exerted an uncontestable fascination on French intellectuals.

The power these intellectuals ascribed to literature may well have been greatly exaggerated, and in their approach to many political problems they showed considerable naivety. Yet this intellectual movement has an indisputable importance, which makes its encounter with the German antifascist emigration all the more significant.

Many of the émigrés certainly had a strong desire to meet Gide or Malraux, and were often in a position to do so. As E. E. Noth wrote: 'In these early months of

1933, an émigré coming from Germany was something of a novelty, especially if they were Aryan.'[229] Contacts were often made by way of magazines and publishers. Noth enjoyed the support of Gabriel Marcel[230] who, as director of the Feux Croisés collection published by Plon, brought out Noth's novel *Die Mietkaserne* (*Tenements*) and put him in touch with Guéhenno (who edited the collection Les Écrits at Grasset). At Marcel's apartment on the rue de Tournon, Noth made the acquaintance of certain figures of the right, but also of poets and academics such as P. J. Jouve, Jean Wahl and Berdiaev. On the editorial board of the magazine *Europe*, Noth met Jean Guéhenno and got to know Eugene Dabit, author of *Hôtel du Nord*.[231] At the magazine *Vendredi*, where Guéhenno was also on the editorial board, he made contact with André Chamson and Jean Cassou. And it was on the advice of the literary critic Frédéric Lefebvre, at that time a contributor to *Nouvelles Littéraires*, that Noth decided to write in French.

The twin poles of attraction in Parisian literary life, at least for the German émigrés, were undoubtedly Gide and Malraux. Malraux's apartment on the rue du Bac became a regular meeting-place for German refugees. Clara Malraux acted as translator, and the visitors included Guéhenno, Gustav Regler, Gide, Manès Sperber, Paul Nizan and Léo Lagrange. Clara herself worked on antifascist propaganda material. Malraux was then at the peak of his fame with the publication of *La Condition humaine* (1933), and deeply concerned by events in Germany. As Gustav Regler wrote in his autobiography: 'The Malraux house had become for me what the court of Urbino had been for the émigré Leo X, or Venice for the banished Aretino [. . .]. Malraux was the ambassador of a hundred kingdoms, his house vibrating with the era, and though he sometimes kept a certain distance, not without nobility, for me he was a blessing.'[232]

It made perfect sense, then, for Clara Malraux to write in her memoirs: 'Within ourselves we had already created the Popular Front. It remained to create it outside.'[233] Manès Sperber describes the Malraux's apartment as one where 'antifascist émigrés, especially Italians but Germans as well, were constantly welcomed', and Malraux, for him, was 'the Saint-Just of antifascism'.[234]

But even this generosity had its limits. The French intellectuals might well be willing to sign petitions, and hear refugees' descriptions of Germany, but they rarely understood their distressful situation. Arthur Koestler noted: 'I was grateful for their help, but it depressed me that neither I nor any of my fellow refugees was ever invited to a French house.'[235] Even if they were invited, this was for discussion and not for dinner. When he met Gide for the first time, Manès Sperber was so stricken with cold – he lived at the time in an unheated room – that the glass of cognac Malraux offered him (without inviting him for dinner) sent him off to sleep while Gide was talking. 'This little incident, hardly noticed, was typical of the situation of an émigré intellectual.'[236]

What mattered most to the émigrés, however, was not so much material support as the impact that statements by these writers, with their audience among the French public, could have. If Malraux and Gide felt concerned for the émigrés, these for their part constantly opened the French writers' eyes to the danger that National Socialism represented also to France. Malraux's attitude was completely unambiguous. On 21 March 1933 he took part in the meeting organized by AEAR (which he had joined the previous year) to protest Hitler's seizure of power and the atrocities already committed in Germany. Using his status as recipient of the Prix Goncourt, Malraux missed no occasion to warn against the Nazi threat. Besides his visit to Berlin (4 January 1934) to try to rescue the Reichstag fire accused, he attended meetings of the Thälmann committee and antifascist gatherings, and he dedicated *Le Temps du mépris* to the 'German comrades'.

Gide himself set out to read *Capital*, and made a substantial financial contribution to assist German refugees. One need only read the texts assembled in his collection *Littérature engagée*[237] to measure the number and scope of his declarations against fascism. Though he never joined the AEAR, he agreed to preside at its meetings and his name figured on the committee in charge of the review *Commune*. He delivered the opening speech at the AEAR rally on 21 March 1933, under the rubric 'Fascisme', and asked: 'What can we do today for the oppressed side in Germany?' He was honorary president of the World Congress Against War and Fascism (a scion of the Amsterdam-Pleyel movement) held in Paris from 22 to 24 September 1933. On 4 January 1934, he travelled with Malraux to Berlin and co-signed the letter to Goebbels as 'delegate of the Dimitrov committee'. He again presided (at least in theory, as he was unable to attend) at the meeting in support of Dimitrov on 31 January 1934. Besides his participation in the Congress for the Defence of Culture, he took part in the meeting organized by the Thälmann committee on 23 December 1935, again at the Salle Wagram.

The reactions of the German émigrés towards these encounters with the most celebrated French writers were often complex. There was certainly an immense sense of gratitude towards them, even if the descriptions they give of Gide or Malraux are not always free from irony. These various literary salons certainly served as poles of attraction for many of the émigrés. As E. E. Noth wrote: 'Only colleagues who were really launched, or whose material security was somehow assured, could afford the luxury of refusing these invitations'. Noth himself frequented Charles du Bos, Daniel Halévy (who received guests on the quai de l'Horloge) and Drieu la Rochelle as well as Malraux, then Jean Cassou, Jean Guehénno and André Chamson, and again Julien Benda, Emmanuel Berl, François Mauriac, Gabriel Marcel and Abel Bonnard. Visiting Malraux's home and hearing him expound among his Oriental objets d'art, Noth listened in both fascination and astonishment.

In the eyes of the émigrés, these Paris salons and writers' homes were microcosms linked together by magazines, books, debates on ideas, and above all personalities.[238] It became unusual not to meet German émigrés at all these places. Koestler, Regler, Sperber, Willi Bredel and Willi Münzenberg all knew and visited Gide and Malraux, while the Communist Alfred Kurella lodged with surrealists in Montparnasse. Kurella was closely tied to André Thirion;[239] Manès Sperber also saw Bernard Groethuysen. And if Thomas Mann was right to deplore how Paul Valéry found the Nazi contempt for the intellect 'charming', there is no doubt that the whole intellectual left in France felt concerned by the events in Germany. On more than one count, its mobilization in the years 1933–35 was exemplary.

The power of these intellectuals was basically rooted in their established prestige, and their ability to make themselves heard both with the wider public and with political figures. A number of German émigrés also had links with French politicians. Besides the relationship between the KPD and PCF, Willi Münzenberg had contacts with such varied individuals as the Socialist Salomon Grumbach, the Radical-Socialist Pierre Commert (director of press services at the quai d'Orsay), Gaston Palewsky, Georges Mandel, Pierre Cot and Jean Giradoux (a significant contact in the eyes of the émigrés on account of his official position).

Some writers were also aided by academics in the German field studies, several of whom proclaimed their anti-Nazi convictions early on. E. E. Noth, who restarted his studies at the Sorbonne, profited from the protection of E. Tonnelat and Edmond Vermeil. Golo Mann taught at the École Normale Supérieure at Saint-Cloud, then at the University of Rennes. Alfred Döblin was helped by Robert Minder, whom he met in summer 1937. His book *Berlin Alexanderplatz* had been translated in 1933, and in the course of the winter semester of 1937–38, it figured in the programme of German studies.[240] On 18 December 1937 Döblin was invited by Henri Lichtenberger to deliver a lecture on Berlin, in the context of the Société des Études Germaniques. Finally, many scholars and scientists who were keen to assist the émigrés sought to facilitate their insertion in French academic life, or took part in campaigns of the Comité de Vigilance des Intellectuels Antifascistes or the Thälmann committee. The most famous of these included Jean Wahl, Lucien Lévy-Bruhl, Frédéric Joliot-Curie, Paul Langevin, Célestin Bouglé, André Mayer, Sylvain Lévi and Maurice Halbwachs.

The Settlement of Refugees

The mood of intellectual effervescence in Paris and the radicalization of a large number of French writers explains why so many émigrés sought to establish themselves in the capital, until poverty, lack of work and police harassment forced them to leave for the provinces.

If many refugees came to Paris expecting it would be easier there to find both work and help from the aid committees, the city attracted above all those intellectuals, writers and journalists who could not imagine recommencing their career anywhere else than in the French capital. There was also the mythology of Paris that had so fascinated progressive German writers of the Weimar era, even if not all of them nourished the same love for the city as did Walter Benjamin. Paris was familiar to them on more than one count. Some had already spent time there in the 1920s (Heinrich Mann, Walter Benjamin, Carl Einstein, Klaus Mann, Harry Kessler, Hermann von Keysserling). Tucholsky already lived there, happy to escape from Berlin. Manès Sperber had settled there in 1929. Philippe Soupault was an admirer of Heinrich Mann, who felt himself a disciple of Zola and brother to Anatole France. Klaus Mann was friendly with Jean Cocteau and especially with René Crevel. Thus despite the barrier of language, their German accent that so distressed the French, many of these intellectuals who arrived in Paris did not really feel in exile at all. With its cultural treasures, museums, bookshops, publishers, galleries and picture dealers, Paris was perhaps the only European city that could rival Berlin. They loved its atmosphere and its lightness, waxed lyrical over its street scenes and buildings, and constantly wandered around the Latin Quarter. Undeniably, some of the finest texts on Paris were precisely written by these German émigrés of 1933. Despite the precarious situation that they experienced in this 'capital of the nineteenth century', the city aroused their enthusiasm.

At the same time as they fell prey to bureaucratic harassment, deprivation, and often even hunger, these émigrés were ravished to discover Montmartre, rue Mouffetard and the balls of 14 July. Klaus Mann admirably described this émigré life in his novel *The Volcano*, with its meetings in cafés and little restaurants to exchange the latest news from Germany. Many were ready to love a city they had often dreamt of, but which with its blithe unawareness and egoism brought them each day a trail of chagrin and humiliation. Egon Erwin Kisch described the fate of German writers in Paris in an interview published by *Nouvelles Littéraires* on 5 August 1933:

> They try and contribute to newspapers, to get their books translated, to find any kind of work. All this almost without any success. Their poverty is extreme. In Prague, the Czech writers put on a few shows for the benefit of their German colleagues. Here nothing has been done, except the evenings organized by the AEAR. For the moment they can just about manage. But the winter will be terrible for the German refugee intellectuals. And despite this, they try and help those colleagues who have remained in Germany.[241]

This life can be glimpsed by reading Klaus Mann, Lion Feuchtwanger or the diary of Alfred Kantorowicz. Cooped up in the cheap hotels of the Latin Quarter or the 18th and 20th *arrondissements*, many lived in conditions bordering on destitution. Paris attracted them as one of the world's great cultural metropolises,[242] but at the same time the fear grew daily that they would be unable to hold out there. Within less than a year, a large section of the Berlin intelligentsia were trying to rebuild their lives in the French capital.

It is hard to imagine, for example, that a single hotel in the rue de Tournon housed at one time or other such guests as Joseph Roth, J. R. Becher, Alfred Döblin, Gustav Regler and Ludwig Marcuse. E. E. Kisch, for his part, lived for a while in Versailles, Arthur Koestler in Belleville, then Meudon, Manès Sperber in the Latin Quarter and then the Chevreuse valley, Döblin at Maison-Laffitte and Becher at the Porte d'Orléans. It was only too truly that Willi Münzenberg wrote to F. Brupbacher on 15 May 1933: 'Paris is becoming an immigrant city. Hundreds more arrive each day. You can meet everyone here. Up to now there are about 4,000.'[243]

At the same time as they loved the city and sought to settle there, many émigrés – and writers above all – were pained by a certain indifference towards them. As Manès Sperber noted: 'Everywhere, and in Paris above all, the German emigration was only one emigration among others, and neither the most unfortunate nor the most pathetic, not even the most disunited; but it was the most undesirable.'[244] And Koestler wrote in similar terms: '[T]here was something withdrawn, impersonal and chilling in their helpfulness.'[245] Thus despite the friendships that were made, many émigrés had the sense of being abandoned in their ghetto. Once again, it was Arthur Koestler who described those French people who 'grasp you in their arms' only to leave you alone again immediately after, 'shivering in the street, condemned to remain an eternal tourist or an eternal exile as the case may be.'

Sooner or later, as E. E. Noth wrote, 'the Paris sidewalk actually seemed to be above my means',[246] and many émigrés had to leave the capital for the provinces, hoping that life would be easier there and they might find work. Indeed, work permits were granted to those who agreed to move to a provincial department. Jobs were often available in agriculture, especially in the south-west. Noth, for his part, left for Provence. After Paris, the Midi formed the second major concentration of German émigrés, in some respects prefiguring southern California in the following decade. The symbol of this 'German colony' was Sanary-sur-Mer, where a large number of émigrés settled. Close to Toulon, Sanary was still at the time a little-frequented fishing village. Yet Ludwig Marcuse happily described it as the 'capital of German literature'; and indeed such eminences as Lion Feuchtwanger and Emil Ludwig were to be found on this 'byway of the *Weltgeist*' alongside Aldous Huxley and Marcuse himself.

Scattered among hotels and villas, the little colony held literary evenings and meetings to discuss both literature and the state of Germany. As well as the émigrés of Sanary, these were also attended by others who had settled in Provence. They included Hermann Kesten, Alfred Kantorowicz, Franz Werfel, Alma Mahler, Friedrich Wolf, Bruno Franck, Ernst Bloch, Bertolt Brecht, Ernst Toller, Alfred Kerr and Erwin Piscator, as well as Fritzl Massary (the daughter of Carl Sternheim), Wilhelm Herzog, Arthur Koestler, Rudolf Leonhard, Alfred Polgar and Balder Olden. Ludwig Marcuse could no longer remember which of the émigrés had first had the idea of moving to Sanary, but many thought they had found a new homeland in this village: 'The winter was short and scarcely severe – with roses, the first mimosas and carnations. For arrivals from the north like ourselves, it wasn't a winter at all. January was already springtime.'[247]

They would meet in the cafés around the port, happy to be paid so little attention. Ludwig Marcuse lived there for six years, in between visits to Paris. The village became a kind of large-scale literary café. And when Fritz Landshoff, former director of Kiepenheuer in Berlin, was hunting for authors for his new publishing house for exile literature, it was naturally to Sanary that he came, with a handful of contracts for Feuchtwanger, Toller, Arnold Zweig and Heinrich Mann. Thomas Mann called Sanary 'the happiest period of exile', and many émigrés really did feel that they had rediscovered a kind of community.

Heinrich Mann lived in Nice, not far from the Promenade des Anglais, and also in the town were Wilhelm Speyer, Theodor Wolff and Magnus Hirschfeld. E. E. Noth settled in Aix-en-Provence, Alfred Kantorowicz at Bormes-les-Mimosas, Balder Olden and E. A. Reinhardt at Le Lavandou. Provence also welcomed a number of exiled painters, while several German émigrés worked as gardeners.

Who today remembers the exiles of Sanary? In 1983, a German critic went to investigate the vestiges of emigration that could still be discovered there.[248] The owner of the hotel where so many émigrés stayed had long since burned the register with its illustrious names. He remembered his German customers from before the War, but didn't know what had happened to them. The hotel was later requisitioned by the Gestapo. Feuchtwanger's pleasant villa was still in place, as well as the windmill where Franz Werfel and Alma Mahler lived until their flight across the Pyrenees. Thomas Mann's house had been blown up by the Germans, who feared an Allied landing in the vicinity. But as the world situation worsened, the inhabitants of Sanary steadily grew more hostile towards these 'dirty *boches*'. In 1939, they had to report to the military authorities along with all other émigrés on the Côte d'Azur. The number was so great that the stadium at Antibes had to be turned into an internment camp. In his novel *Die Rechtlosen* (*Those Without Rights*), Walter Hasenclever described the strange life that they lived there. The municipal archives at Sanary still contain the death certificate of Franz Hessel, Walter Benjamin's friend who worked with him on a translation of Proust. In June 1941, the few émigrés who still remained in Sanary were imprisoned again in the brickworks at Les Milles, close to Aix-en-Provence. Lion Feuchtwanger described the wretchedness and desperation of those days in his book *The Devil in France*. The brickworks still exists today, and by insisting a little, one can visit the old building that the guards used as a refectory. Beneath a layer of dust, it is still possible to make out paintings done by the émigrés – maybe including Max Ernst – as well as the large rooms described by Feuchtwanger, the courtyard where useless shelters had to be dug, the narrow stairway, and the cubbyhole where Walter Hasenclever took his own life. Final traces.

THE POLITICAL ACTIVITIES OF
ANTIFASCIST ÉMIGRÉS IN FRANCE
The Forces in Play

Among the 10,000 political refugees in France were a good number of prominent figures – Socialist and Communist deputies, former ministers, senior officials of the Prussian government, party functionaries, and so on. The large number of German Communists who made for France is doubtless explained by the presence of a well-organized Communist party there.[249] The role they were to play was all the greater in that they displayed a theoretical and political unity, whereas the Social-Democrats were divided among themselves, and would remain so on all important questions, especially the strategy to adopt towards Nazism.[250] Along with the Social-Democrats, a certain number of independent left formations were also represented,[251] though these did not play any decisive role in the émigré community. The political formations of the Centre almost vanished after 1933, and if Catholics were represented by a few exiled political figures, they had no particular political expression. As for the pacifists, they were present in the majority of debates, in the form of a large number of writers, journalists and intellectuals who were members of the Human Rights League, contributors to *Die Weltbühne* and friends of Carl von Ossietzky; one need only mention the names of Hellmut von Gerlach, Kurt Grossmann, and Otto Lehmann-Russbüldt.

The differences marking the activities of the two big workers' parties are explicable first of all in terms of their respective structures. The KPD was hierarchical and its policy always displayed the same cohesion. The Social-Democrats, in contrast, were not only divided into several factions, each located in a different exile centre, but failed to agree on a coherent strategy after the Nazi seizure of power. The party leadership established in Prague (SoPaDe) was soon challenged by Social-Democrat groups located in Paris. If the Social-Democrats rejected with a greater or lesser degree of hostility, at least until 1935, any idea of cooperation with the Communists, some of them did champion a revision of party tactics, and a number of the younger elements wished to see the SoPaDe adopt a more 'revolutionary' strategy. Communist resistance, for its part, started already in 1933, while the Social-Democratic leadership looked askance at joint actions undertaken by Communist and Socialist workers in Germany against the Nazi regime. It was from fear of seeing some of its activists go over to the KPD that the Social-Democrats officially encouraged resistance.

From the beginning of exile, as Franz Dahlem recalls, collaboration was established between German Communists and the PCF. They organized common actions and appeals,[252] whereas relations between German Socialists and the SFIO were nothing like as close.[253] Though the SFIO approved the Popular Front policy, the SoPaDe in Prague remained hostile to it. Paris moreover sheltered a large section of the KPD's exiled leadership,[254] whereas no member of the SoPaDe settled in France until 1938.

The impressive number of committees, organizations, discussions and campaigns set up by the antifascist refugees in Paris certainly made the city the 'capital of the emigration', as Willi Münzenberg called it already in 1933. There were clandestine committees as well as legal ones, antifascist publishing houses and the INFA (Institute for the Study of Fascism), national and international bodies. This rich activity was due to a number of factors: the relative tolerance that the émigrés enjoyed, which was not the case in many other countries where all political activity was prohibited, and the large number of activists who settled there. A Comintern bureau for Western Europe had been formed in Paris in 1930, and the activities of the exiled KPD were facilitated by its existing relations with the PCF (even though the KPD lagged behind its French counterpart in its gradual abandonment of the struggle against 'social-fascism'). The organizations of International Workers' Aid, the contribution of Willi Münzenberg, and the Carrefour publishing house, were also important factors in the expansion of these activities. Actions undertaken by the Communists fell into several types. First of all, they took part in solidarity actions. Secours Rouge assisted antifascist political refugees whether they were Communist or not.[255] International Workers' Aid worked in close association with International Red Aid, and in March 1933 the Deutsche Hilfskomitee was formed with its headquarters in Amsterdam. This non-party committee later grew into the Welthilfskomitee für die Opfer des deutschen Faschismus (based in London) presided over by Lord Marley; Albert Einstein and Paul Langevin were honorary members, with Dorothy Woodman of the Labour party as secretary. The Deutsche Hilfskomitee included a large number of Willi Münzenberg's collaborators; its secretary was Alfred Kantorowicz.[256] Finally, committee supporters formed a Comité d'Aide aux Victimes du Fascisme Hitlérien in summer 1933, with its office at Francis Jourdain's address.

Relations with French Parties

The French police services watched political émigrés especially closely. But the thousands of German activists who were refugees in France sought an assistance from French organizations, both material and moral, that would symbolize the proletarian left. Attempts at regroupment and action were fragile, at least until 1935, since the French left was as divided as the German. In 1935, however, contacts between French left organizations and German political refugees multiplied. Here we shall just describe a few of these connections.[257]

The first type of connection between German political émigrés and the French left was that of solidarity actions designed to support both antifascist prisoners in Germany and émigrés who crossed the frontier and arrived in France. At the political level the object was to defend them and help them gain asylum. The various types of support presupposed the intervention of already existing organizations – political parties, trade unions, defence organizations, the Ligue des Droits de l'Homme, bodies linked to parties or to International Red Aid – as well as the formation of new support committees in which French and Germans would both be active. Some of these committees and bodies had an open character, others were clandestine or disguised. Many had links to French organizations, others had a broader remit, attached to the Comintern or the Socialist International.

Relations between the émigrés and the French left formations were directly political. They involved support for resistance within the Reich, various actions against fascism, the comparison of political analyses, debates and divergences between the parties over their understanding of events in Germany and perspectives for action (responsibility of the parties for the Nazis' coming to power, possibilities of organizing resistance, projects for unity between Socialists and Communists). These relationships were extremely complex and always shifting: they depended on European events, on the respective ideologies of the French and German parties, on developments in French politics (the Popular Front, Munich, etc.) and time lags in perspectives (adoption of the united front tactic by the PCF leadership in 1934, then the following year by the KPD, divergences between the SFIO and the Prague SoPaDe on unity with the Communists).

A final difficulty in analysing these relationships is posed by the very different relations that the underground leadership of the KPD had with the PCF, the Comintern functionaries[258] and the mass of Communist émigrés, whose activities are often hard to trace in full detail. What is necessary most of all, in the perspective of a study like the present one, is to gather evidence from as many different sources as possible, both personal memoirs and official accounts.[259]

Relations between the exiled KPD and the PCF were all the more indispensable in that a large section of its underground leadership had sought refuge in Paris. In May 1933, Franz Dahlem, Wilhelm Pieck and Wilhelm Florin arrived there to form the KPD's external leadership (*Auslandsleitung der KPD*), while John Schehr, Walter Ulbricht, Hermann Schubert and Fritz Schulte formed its internal leadership (*Inlandsleitung*). In autumn 1933, Walter Ulbricht also reached Paris. Franz Dahlem returned to Berlin in February 1934 to put the different underground groups in contact with the 'border leadership' or 'exile leadership'. The politburo itself was transferred to Moscow early in 1935, and following the arrest of the majority of members of the internal leadership who had remained in Germany, Dahlem and Ulbricht exercised this function from Prague, where an 'operational leadership abroad' was formed some time after 15 October 1935. This was transferred to Paris in October 1936, and remained there until 1939.

Apart from the period from January 1935 to September 1936, therefore, France was the seat of the most important organs of the exiled KPD. With the simultaneous presence of Willi Münzenberg and his publishing programme, and the formation in Paris of a German Popular Front, there can be no doubt that the French capital formed the centre of KPD activities after 1933. Yet according to the research of Jacques Omnès, the members of the PCF's political bureau seem to have been unaware at first of the presence of KPD leaders in France. It is not obvious, moreover, why Paris was chosen rather than Prague to establish this KPD leadership in exile.[260] According to Babette Gross, the companion of Willi Münzenberg, the possibility of shifting the leadership of the KPD's mass organizations to Paris had already been envisaged before 1933.

Franz Dahlem relates in his memoirs how liaison between the secretariat of the KPD's central committee and the leadership of the PCF was maintained by a liaison agent or by correspondence. Although both Maurice Thorez and Franz Dahlem lived at Ivry, direct contact was kept to a minimum for security reasons.[261] Two KPD cadre schools were held at Draveil, and the KPD's 'Berne conference' (30 January to 1 February 1939) was also held there. If relations between the KPD leadership and the PCF were broken in September–October 1939, following the repression against the Communists, they were renewed in 1940 in the context of the participation of both French and German Communists in the *Travail allemand*. Throughout their exile in France, the KPD leadership remained underground, generally abstaining even from meetings with other German émigrés. Alongside the connections between the underground emigration and the PCF, there were those that the 'legal' Communist emigration had with other organizations. The 'operational leadership abroad' was rigorously clandestine, but the 'emigration leadership' in France was an official organization with public activity directed by Siegfried Rädel.

If the rule for the Communist International was that Communist émigrés joined the parties of the countries in which they found themselves, this rule does not seem to have been followed very closely by the German Communists. They remained members of KPD cells, re-established in the majority of large towns where they stayed, which were themselves in contact with the PCF.

What makes it harder to study relations between the émigré German Socialists and their French comrades is that the leadership of the Social-Democratic party in Prague was challenged by various German Social-Democrat groups exiled in Paris. The Prague SoPaDe, however, viewed itself as the sole official representative of the directing committee of the SPD following its proscription in Germany.

The question of the responsibility of the SPD in Hitler's coming to power, like the questions of the organization of resistance and of united action with the Communists (rejected by the party leadership until 1935), triggered an ideological explosion of the Socialist emigration in its different centres. The German Social-Democrats in France certainly had contacts with the SFIO, but no common strategy was elaborated. The differences between the SoPaDe and the SFIO remained major, and reached their culmination in the era of the Popular Front, backed by the SFIO but rejected by the SoPaDe. In 1933 the SFIO had adopted Léon Blum's slogan: 'Neither say nor do anything that might fuel German nationalism and "revanchism".'[262] Blum himself claimed to be persuaded that 'Chancellor Hitler will respect international conventions.' Until 1934, Blum does not seem to have truly realized just what the advent of National Socialism meant for Germany. At the SFIO's congress in 1933 (14 to 17 July), only Salomon Grumbach and Georges Weill made reference to the Hitler regime and how this would sooner or later signify war.[263] Apart from this, the discussion was on 'socialist authenticity' and participation in the Radical government, not on events in Germany. The French Socialists were deeply pacifist. In no case did the new German government signal to them the need for any kind of turn in the party's policy on the question of disarmament.

At the same time, the Socialist party had to take a position on the reception of refugees. This was a question to which Blum was sensitive (the far right regularly attacked him as a rootless Jew), and Paul Viénot, under-secretary of state at the foreign ministry though not a party member, contributed to the formation of a 'consultative commission' for German refugees.[264] A number of Socialist figures intervened on their behalf. Jules Moch often took up their defence, as did Éduard Depreux and Raoul Evrard. Salomon Grumbach, a bilingual lawyer, represented several émigrés to the French government and the League of Nations, together with Paul Boncour. In 1933, the French Socialist Marcel Livian had contacts with exiled German Social-Democrats such as

Robert Breitscheid, Siegfried Crummenerl, Kreyssig and Paul Friedländer, later with Max Braun and Erich Ollenhauer.

The French Socialists were very active within the Ligue des Droits de l'Homme and the Matteoti Committee. The first solidarity body in this context was Défense Socialiste, intended to defend party members of foreign nationality. A 'commission to study questions bearing on immigration' had already been set up in 1930.[265] After its demise in 1936, the French party continued to support the German Socialists' official body,[266] and contacts with the Arbeiterwohlfahrt were expanded. Early in 1935 the SFIO formed a second association, Les Amis des Travailleurs Étrangers, while at the branch level, members were called on to aid refugees financially. Some money was paid to German Socialist leaders such as Robert Breitscheid.

The French Socialist press regularly attacked Hitler's policies. Jules Moch, then president of the immigration commission, was quick to raise the question of the reception of refugees in his interventions in the Chamber of Deputies. On 8 April 1933, Léon Blum gave a speech against Nazi racial policy, on the occasion of a meeting of the Ligue Internationale Contre l'Antisémitisme. The activities of exiled German Socialists also reached a certain audience. *La Vie du Parti* (a supplement to *Le Populaire*) published on 16 February 1934 the programme of the Prague SoPaDe, and informed its readers of resistance actions and perspectives of common struggle envisaged in France by the Socialists and Communists for the liberation of Thälmann and Seitz (the Socialist mayor of Vienna). The Socialists took several initiatives – parliamentary, material and legal – in support of the émigrés, trying to ease legislation towards them.[267] Blum questioned the government once again on the right of asylum when a hundred refugees without papers were threatened with being returned to the frontier after the Saar plebiscite.

Finally, when the Popular Front government was formed, a 'liaison centre for organizations of foreign workers' grouped together over a dozen bodies for immigrant workers and political refugees.[268] Marcel Livian makes clear that 'the refugee organizations did not immediately decide to form a liaison centre like that for workers'. Such a unification was however achieved with the Fédération des Émigrés d'Allemagne en France under the chair of the Social-Democrat Albert Grzesinsksi, former Prussian interior minister. The liaison centre for immigrants finally brought together the Association of Friends of Foreign Workers, the LICA and International Red Aid. It was at the initiative of the Fédération des Émigrés that a conference was held in Paris in June 1936, leading to the creation of an international bureau for the respect of the right of asylum. The Popular Front thus marked a period of unquestionable improvement in the situation of the émigrés.[269]

Though several meetings took place between the French Socialists and the German Communist and Socialist refugees, it does not seem that any collaboration or even an equivalent contact took place at the level of party leaderships. Max Braun, Robert Breitscheid and Rudolf Hilferding are the only German Socialist figures whose names appear in the memoirs of the French Socialist leaders. There were too many differences between the strategies of the

SoPaDe and the SFIO to allow for any political collaboration. After the *Anschluss*, more than 1,800 Austrian Socialists took refuge in Paris and set up an organization there. Otto Bauer made contact with Max Braun and founded a Socialist bimonthly, *La Lettre Socialiste*, as well as the *Arbeiterzeitung*. The French Socialists made frequent appeals in their favour until the interment of refugees began.[270] But if Léon Blum continued to receive letters from refugees requesting his assistance, Socialist interventions in the Chamber of Deputies were hardly in a position to influence government policy.

Antifascist Struggle

The combat waged by the émigrés against National Socialism from French soil was exceptionally intense and took a variety of forms. The richness of these activities is explained by the importance of the émigrés who took refuge in France (the leadership of the KPD, Willi Münzenberg), by the French ideological context, especially the intellectual mobilization against fascism that followed the riots of February 1934, and above all by the presence of a large number of émigrés – activists, writers, journalists – who helped to develop these forms of antifascist struggle. Their diversity was so great that it is hard to give an overall depiction, all the more so as it is impossible to dissociate it from the cultural, literary and artistic activities of the émigrés, in such cases as conferences, productions of antifascist plays, exhibitions and newspaper articles. A certain number of these activities will be analysed further on, from a theoretical standpoint. For the moment we shall mention them simply in their relationship to the specifically French context.

Pride of place must be given to information and propaganda activities. Most of the resistance centres established in Germany found it very hard to publish their own propaganda material, though the Communists managed to relaunch a certain number of underground papers. Very often, antifascist propaganda material was brought into Germany from neighbouring countries. Many anti-Nazi pamphlets were produced in France, especially in Paris, disguised as anodyne or classical texts (*Tarnschriften*) so as to put the censors off track, and smuggled into the Reich from Alsace, the Saar, Belgium or Holland. The importance of Paris as a centre of antifascist propaganda is explained by the presence of Willi Münzenberg, along with his team and his publications.

The task in hand was both to provide propaganda material to resisters who remained in Germany, giving them accurate information on the Reich against the press now in thrall to Goebbels's dictatorship, and to warn Europe what the advent of Hitler would mean. 'Border secretariats' were rapidly established, their role being to maintain contact with underground activists, to gather information on what was happening in Germany, and to transmit instructions. For this purpose, a large number of short publications were printed, with covers that disguised their content as writings banned in Germany, often by German émigrés. Printing these on bible paper made them easier to transport and camouflage, and they were smuggled into the Reich at the cost of severe hardship. Sometimes they were even disguised as Nazi publications.

The work of information and propaganda did not simply aim to introduce forbidden texts in Germany, but also to distribute all kinds of information that could discredit the Reich by revealing its true face. A significant exile press was thus developed on French territory, as well as antifascist book publishing, both feared by the Nazis. This was all the more effective in that the Paris émigrés included some of the best journalists and controversialists of the Weimar Republic, such as Leopold Schwarzschild and Georg Bernhard.[271] Willi Münzenberg, moreover, had been a specialist in KPD propaganda and continued to give proof of a prodigious talent.

In 1933 Kurt Rosenfeld and Sándor Rado founded Inpress, an international press agency against National Socialism. Maximilian Scheer was in charge of the German edition, Vladimir Pozner of the French. Inpress appeared until early in 1936. From early 1933 Scheer and Rudolf Leonhard published the newspaper *Die Aktion! L'Action*, 'the first voice of emigrants in Paris' and 'organ for the defence of German refugees and struggle against Hitlerite fascism'. From 1933 to 1936 there appeared the *Pariser Tageblatt* directed by Georg Bernhard, which continued as the *Pariser Tageszeitung* until May 1940.[272] Paris also saw the publication of a French edition of *Gegen-Angriff*, from 1933 to 1936, Communist in slant and directed in Prague by Bruno Frei. Under the title *Deutsche Volkszeitung* this became an important organ of debate in the Popular Front period. Leopold Schwarzschild's famous weekly *Das Neue Tagebuch* was also published in Paris from 1933 to 1940, and equally important was the *Neue Weltbühne*, which appeared first in Prague then in Paris until its proscription on 31 August 1939, directed by Hermann Budzislawski. In March 1936, Heinrich Mann, Robert Breitscheid, Max Braun and Bruno Frei founded the press agency *Deutsche Informationen*, which published three times a week a bulletin giving French newspapers information on Hitler's Germany.

The Social-Democratic exiles in Paris also developed their own press[273] – *Der Sozialistische Informationsbrief, Sozialistische Warte, Marxistische Tribüne, Neue Front, Neue Vorwärts, Deutschland-Bericht, Mitteilungen des Parteivorstandes, Informationsblätter* – reflecting the fragmentation of the SPD emigration. Other political groupings also had their journals, both the extreme left (*Der Funke, Der Internationale Klassenkampf, Die Internationale, Gegen den Strom, Unser Wort*) and KPD dissidents (Willi Münzenberg's *Die Zukunft*).

The impact of this exile press was backed by the accounts, stories and articles that appeared in the French press, to which a certain number of émigrés contributed. Egon Erwin Kisch and E. E. Noth both published several articles in *Nouvelles Littéraires*,[274] other émigrés in *Europe* or *Commune*, the journal of the AEAR.[275] One of the most famous French tribunes of the emigration was undoubtedly *La Dépêche de Toulouse*. Maurice Sarraut published in this newspaper many articles written by such prestigious émigrés as Heinrich Mann, Georg Bernhard, Theodor Lessing, Alfred Kerr, Thomas Mann, Theodor Wolff and Hermann Rauschning, regardless of the complaints that the German embassy made to his brother Albert Sarraut, minister of the interior. Between

1933 and 1940 the Toulouse paper published more than 170 articles by German émigrés,[276] including theoretical articles, commentaries on events, and dismal prophecies on the future of Europe: to read them today is to be struck less by their naivety and mistaken analyses than by the sinister truths that they sought to reveal.

Émigré publishing activity in France was significant in both Paris and Strasbourg. The most detailed study of this literature, by Hélène Roussel,[277] emphasizes that as well as those publishing enterprises directly tied to or financed by political parties, there was a very varied activity of non-party émigré publishing. Among the most famous achievements were the Phoenix-Bücher series, with fourteen titles of documents and essays, the Éditions du 10 Mai, and above all Willi Münzenberg's enterprises: Éditions du Carrefour, Éditions Sebastian Brant, Éditions Prométhée. To take just the example of Carrefour, between 1933 and 1937 it published some forty-five books and eleven pamphlets, particularly including works of documentation assembled by Münzenberg and his fellow workers, all highly important for understanding the political, economic, social and military developments of Hitlerite Germany.

The most striking example of these productions was undoubtedly the collection of documents on the Reichstag fire, published by Münzenberg as *The Brown Book*, which clearly established the innocence of the accused and the guilt of the Nazis. Together with the organization of a counter-trial in London, even before the opening of the trial in Leipzig, this remains the greatest – and perhaps the only – ideological success of the émigrés. From examining the series of titles published by Carrefour, it is clear that they provided an almost unique body of information on Hitler's Germany, its preparations for war, Gestapo activities abroad and the reigning barbarism at home. Following Münzenberg's break with the Comintern, Éditions Sebastian Brant continued this activity of information and propaganda into 1938 and 1939.[278]

The major achievements of the émigrés in France also included the establishment of the Institute for the Study of Fascism (INFA),[279] which operated in Paris from late 1933 to the first quarter of 1935. Its members included Arthur Koestler, Manès Sperber, and Oto Bihalji-Merin. Born from a joint initiative by Bihalji-Merin and Hans Meins (together with organizations depending on the Comintern), and with a board of sponsors comprising Paul Langevin, Lucien Lévy-Bruhl, Marcel Willard, Marcel Prenant, Henri Wallon and Francis Jourdain, the INFA had its offices first at 22 rue des Fossés-St-Bernard, later at 25 rue Buffon. It set out to 'struggle against the danger that fascism presents to civilization' by analysing fascist movements, gathering documentation on their activities, establishing archives and publishing information bulletins. Though the actual results of INFA activities remained fairly modest, this was a quite remarkable project. Among its achievements, besides conveying information to the French press, one should mention the antifascist exhibition organized in Paris in 1935,[280] supported by a number of organizations including the Comité de Vigilance des Intellectuels Antifascistes, the Ligue des Droits de l'Homme, the International Women's League for Peace, the World Committee against War and Fascism, and the International Association of Doctors Against War.

The exhibition opened on 9 March 1935 at the La Boétie Gallery (83 rue de la Boétie), and was accompanied by meetings and artistic events. INFA ceased to function late in 1934 for reasons that are not entirely clear.[281]

Another important émigré activity was the defence of imprisoned antifascists, activists and writers. The aim was to rally the maximum number of public figures to their cause, with a view to putting pressure on Germany. Though it was not an exile creation, the story of the Thälmann committee lies at the heart of this struggle.[282] Established in March 1933, at the initiative of International Red Aid, the committee's objective was the liberation of both Thälmann and the accused in the Reichstag fire trial. Other committees were created in April by Münzenberg and his colleagues, to support other prisoners and spread information on the reign of terror in Germany. Presided over by André Seigneur, a PCF staffer, the Thälmann committee brought together a number of famous intellectuals and achieved a genuine mobilization that went wider than the milieu of Communist sympathizers. Certain Socialists – Georges Monnet, Charles Morizet – took part in its activities, and from 1934 on public meetings were organized in which Communists worked together with members of the SFIO, which gave it official support. This committee was in fact made up of a French and an international section. In France, it was supported by such diverse individuals as Paul Langevin, André Gide, André Malraux and Henri Barbusse – names that figure on the committee's letterhead. Far from limiting itself to the defence of the KPD leader, it sought 'to enlighten French public opinion on the methods and aims of the National Socialist regime'.[283] While the delegation led by Gide and Malraux that it sent to Berlin on 4 January 1934 was its most famous initiative, the committee also sent several other delegations, often including workers, backed up by demonstrations in front of the German embassy. These sought to obtain news of the accused, and described to the French press the reception that they received. On a couple of occasions they were actually able to meet Thälmann,[284] and were many times received by senior officials, the Nazi government still being obliged to take account of international public opinion. Financed by the PCF, by Münzenberg and above all by collections, the committee continued and expanded its initiatives through to 1939. Its bulletin published campaign instructions, insisting on methods of mobilizing opinion. The movement for the liberation of Thälmann managed to achieve a mobilization of rare scope.

Besides these delegations, public actions such as the Thälmann week reached a large audience. A pamphlet published by Éditions Universelles, *Pour Thälmann*, which printed the addresses given at a public meeting organized by the committee at the Salle Wagram on 23 December 1935, shows how both Gide and Malraux again took an active part, making several interventions on behalf of the accused. These mobilizations reached quite a broad public, to judge by the statutory note at the end of the pamphlet, which reports some 3,200,629 signatures received by 4 January 1936 for the liberation of Thälmann. The committee went on to organize a conference on National Socialist legislation, as well as a 'people's tribunal' to inform public opinion on the atrocities committed in Germany, and on the situation of writers and oppositionists. Some demonstrations even amounted to popular festivals, with attractions and dances organized to raise funds for the committee. The Thälmann committee also tried in vain to obtain the release of the editor of *Die Weltbühne*, Carl von Ossietzky, providing the press with accounts of the conditions of his detention in the Sonnenburg concentration camp. It alerted writers' organizations throughout the world, and took an active part in the campaign to have Ossietzky awarded the Nobel Peace Prize, gathering thousands of signatures for this.[285] After the Nobel committee did indeed decide for Ossietzky, on 23 November 1936, a celebration was organized in Paris on 14 December, presided over by Aragon and with the participation of J. Perrin (Nobel Prize for physics), Julien Benda, J. R. Bloch and E. E. Kisch. Other actions were organized on Ossietzky's death.

These mobilizations were accompanied by the production of a large number of leaflets, appeals, petitions, papers, pamphlets and postcards, which it is hard today even to list. The Comintern weekly was quite right to note that the French committee's action had been 'exemplary'.[286] Though the Thälmann committee was a French organization, its activities were only possible thanks to the contribution of a number of émigrés who provided it with information on persecution in Germany. Many émigrés (Heinz Lohmar, Siegfried Rädel) also took part in the exhibitions organized by the committee. The absence of their names in public documents is naturally explained by the discretion forcibly imposed on foreigners.[287] Those émigrés most regularly found on the platform included the children, wives or widows of arrested antifascists (Frau Beimler, Martha André, etc.). It is likely that a good part of the documentation that enabled Malraux to write *Le Temps du mépris* and make his repeated interventions against fascism was furnished him by émigrés such as Gustav Regler and Rudolf Leonhard, who was for a while treasurer of the committee and president of the German Society of Men of Letters. Ernst Toller also attended the meeting of 17 April 1936,[288] and Friedrich Wolf that of 2 February 1939.

Not only did all these activities find a great resonance among the working class, but their audience was multiplied thanks to the large number of prominent intellectuals who gave the committee moral and material support. The presence of Gide, Malraux and Romain Rolland, and of Paul Langevin who agreed to preside at a number of meetings organized by the Thälmann committee, shows the extent to which they were aware of the danger that fascism presented to those values to which they were most attached. The fact that the majority of these figures were outside the Communist orbit was also very useful tactically, as Willi Münzenberg had shown throughout the 1920s.[289] Gilbert Badia is right to emphasize that the Thälmann committee was a major political symbol, not just by the strength of the mobilization it achieved, but as a contribution to the birth of a *Volksfront* for Germany. There can be no doubt that its activities contributed to a rapprochement of the two workers' parties. Whilst in 1933 these had organized separate demonstrations against Nazi persecution – the 'social-fascist' accusation was still brandished by the Comin-

tern – it was the Thälmann committee that around the turn of the year united
Socialist and Communist figures, for perhaps the first time, around the defence
of German antifascists. Finally, after the birth of the Front Populaire in France,
the committee again helped to bring together Socialist and Communist German
exiles.

This step towards the *Volksfront* was undoubtedly one of the high points of
German exile activity in France. Though Gilbert Badia rightly emphasizes[290]
that the formation of the Front Populaire was partly explained by the desire not
to repeat the mistakes that made Nazi victory possible in Germany, it is
symbolic that after the examples of France and Spain, it was Paris that saw
the birth of the German *Volksfront* that had not been possible under Weimar.
But while Socialists and Communists shared a common experience of emigration, and undertook together certain acts of resistance in the Reich, the
leadership of the SoPaDe still rejected any coordination at top level, and
polemics between the two parties continued. In July 1934, however, an agreement on a united front was concluded for the Saar plebiscite, and in June 1935,
at an International Workers' Aid demonstration in Montreuil, an appeal for the
unity of German émigrés was launched. The following month saw the formation
of a provisional committee to work for a *Volksfront*,[291] with the participation of
Communists, writers, and members of the small socialist groups, despite the
refusal of the SoPaDe. This provisional committee aimed at the formation of a
Popular Front that would bring all German émigrés under one flag. A first
public meeting was held in September, at the instigation of Willi Münzenberg,
with around sixty prominent figures being invited. Presided over by Heinrich
Mann, the conference took place at the Hôtel Lutétia. When the Popular Front
tactic was officially proclaimed at the 'Brussels conference' of October 1935, a
pact for united action between the parties was envisaged. The 'Lutétia committee' proposed to convene a conference of figures favourable to the idea of a
single front, to be held early in 1936. Throughout that year the committee
expanded its activities, publishing *Deutsche Informationen* (edited by the Communist Bruno Frei and the Socialist Max Braun). On 22 April, the Lutétia
committee elected a fifteen-strong executive and, despite the continuing opposition of the SoPaDe, circles of 'friends of the German Popular Front' were soon
created, which organized discussions and demonstrations, and launched several
joint appeals by Socialists and Communists. On 10 and 11 April 1937 a third
conference was held at the Hôtel Lutétia, attended by some three hundred
delegates. Though Willi Münzenberg had initiated many of these rapprochements, Heinrich Mann was their most passionate champion. Yet despite all
these efforts, the attempt at a *Volksfront* met with defeat, and in January 1938
the collaboration between Socialists and Communists ceased. The last attempt
at regroupment failed early in 1939.[292]

No less important in the history of émigré political activity in France was the
participation of a large number of exiled writers at the Congress for the Defence
of Culture in 1935, which opened on 25 June at the Mutualité. Over five days,
writers from across the world – including some of the greatest – discussed before
an audience of thousands the question of the defence of culture against the

fascist threat. In December 1934, on his return from Moscow, Henri Barbusse had drafted a manifesto calling for the formation of an international league of writers. Romain Rolland and Heinrich Mann initially refused to sign it, deeming it too political. A second text was then drawn up in February by Paul Nizan, André Malraux, J. R. Bloch and Ilya Ehrenburg. On 27 March, along with other writers including Barbusse himself, they reached agreement on the aims of the congress. Despite difficult material conditions, J. R. Bloch, Malraux, L. Gilloux, L. Moussinac and René Blech undertook the preparations for the meeting. Eight themes were selected – cultural heritage, humanism, nation and culture, the individual, the dignity of thought, the role of the writer in society, literary creation, and the writer and defence of culture – to be discussed from a variety of viewpoints. All the great names in French and exiled German letters were present for these debates, even if some of them, for instance Robert Musil, did not take the floor.[293]

It may have been naive to expect a congress of this kind to have an immediate political impact, but its first success was to enable writers from twenty-eight countries to debate ideas, and it amounted to one of the greatest intellectual mobilizations of the time. An International Association for the Defence of Culture was formed, with a bureau including Gide, Barbusse, Rolland, Heinrich and Thomas Mann, Gorki, E. M. Forster, Aldous Huxley, G. B. Shaw, Sinclair Lewis, S. Lagerlöf and Del Valle-Inclan. At a time when literature exercised a genuine power, the union of so many figures in a mobilization against fascism was a media event of great force. Beyond the divisions between Communists and Trotskyists, beyond the objections of Benda and Musil, beyond the pathos, idealism, enthusiasm and naivety that marked those years and that generation, there was a symbol here that still today demands admiration.

ÉMIGRE CULTURAL ACTIVITY
German Writers in France

Though the number of German refugees in France was not all that great, we have already explained how they included some of the greatest names in Weimar culture. Besides the famous writers already mentioned, there were also many of the publicists and journalists so numerous in Berlin in the twenties, as well as actors, stage directors and visual artists. The situation of the writers was very varied. It depended on their fame, but also on their knowledge of the French language and the connections that they had in Paris. While some were able to adapt to their new situation with relatively little difficulty – Feuchtwanger for example – this was certainly not the case with the majority. Only a minority of the émigrés could speak French, and it was rare exceptions such as E. E. Noth who were able to start writing immediately in the language of their host country. The possibilities of contributing to the French press were thus seriously limited. Almost all, however, took part in 'cultural work' (*Kulturarbeit*) against fascism. A number of French intellectuals, for their part, remained sceptical of the chances for these German writers to live and write in France. One article published on the front page of

Nouvelles Littéraires on 17 June 1933 was already titled 'Where then is Weimar?' and included the following paragraph:

> Where then are the representatives of that part of the German heritage, shunned and persecuted by Hitler, to settle, not only to live but to produce? These proscripts have the duty of illustrating by new works the traditions of thought of which they are the depositories. But where will be the geographic base of this wandering Germanism? Certainly exiled or misunderstood writers gravitate towards London or Paris by a natural movement, these now being the only two great capitals of freedom. But they risk perishing outside their linguistic milieu, constrained to a permanent mental translation. Russian writers have had bitter experience of this.

Paris and the south of France became for several years the new homeland of these German writers, and it was in France that some of the most representative works of German literature in exile were born. The majority of them felt the need to re-establish the organizations that united them before Hitler came to power. In May–June 1933 a number of them met in Paris with the aim of continuing their struggle in exile. Many contributed to Willi Münzenberg's *Brown Book*. The paper *Gegen-Angriff* which appeared on 1 May in both Prague and Paris also brought together writers and intellectuals, as did *Die Aktion* (Rudolf Leonhard, Maximilian Scheer). But the most important initiative was the re-establishment of the Schutzverband Deutscher Schriftsteller (SDS) in summer 1933, also the work of Leonhard. The members of this association henceforth met on Mondays, organizing meetings and reading their works. This was the first step in the regroupment of émigré intellectuals in their struggle against fascism. With the backing of French writers, the SDS organized actions in support of writers imprisoned in Germany, as well publishing its own journal, *Der Deutsche Schriftsteller*; it formed one of the chief platforms of German literature in exile, its members including such varied figures as Rudolf Leonhard, Ludwig Marcuse, J. R. Becher, E. E. Kisch, Anna Seghers and Alfred Kantorowicz.

The SDS soon undertook to gather all accessible documents on the Third Reich that might help to serve resistance to Hitler. While Münzenberg and his team were preparing the *Brown Book*, the SDS assembled an important documentation that was to form the Archive Antifasciste Internationale (IAA), conceived in April 1933 in the wake of a meeting of the support committee for victims of Hitlerism.[294] In February 1934 the IAA announced its intention of creating a Bibliothèque Libre Allemande in Paris. A founding committee was set up under the leadership of André Gide, Lion Feuchtwanger, Lucien Lévy-Bruhl, Heinrich Mann, Romain Rolland and H. G. Wells. This library[295] collected all the works banned, burned or censored by the Third Reich, together with writings that helped an understanding of fascism.[296] Inaugurated on 10 May 1934, exactly a year after the book burning in Berlin, the Deutsche Freiheitsbibliothek had its office in a painter's atelier on the boulevard Arago. It was directed by Heinrich Mann, Max Schroeder and L. Kralik, while Alfred Kantorowicz was its general secretary. The SDS and other émigré organizations met there, and exhibitions were also held on the premises. The library's archives and books were seized by the French police in 1939, and doubtless either destroyed or scattered.

Among the most famous émigré meeting-places in Paris – not counting the Café Mathieu and the Café Méphisto on the boulevard Saint-Germain – was the Deutscher Klub, already founded in 1925, which from 1933 became a regular centre for exiled writers. Heinrich Mann, Hermann Kesten, Bertolt Brecht, Josef Roth, Klaus Mann, Alfred Döblin, Lion Feuchtwanger and Walter Mehring took part in its events. Magazines such as *Das Neue Tage-Buch* and the *Pariser Tagblatt* also played a major role in the community of exiled writers. But their most symbolic political actions were undoubtedly their participation in the efforts to build a Popular Front, the Congress in Defence of Culture, and the *Brown Book*.

The situation with exiled academics was just as complex.[297] On 13 May 1933, with André Honorat (former minister of public instruction) in the chair, a meeting was held at the Sorbonne in the course of which a Comité des Savants was set up, with the task of deciding on the measures to be taken to assist their German colleagues expelled from their posts. This committee was basically concerned with scientists. Financed by the Universal Israelite Alliance, the American Joint Distribution Committee and the Rockefeller Foundation, this committee – thanks to the Indologist Sylvain Lévi – set up both documentation and finance for German refugee academics. In 1933, according to J. P. Mathieu, fifty-four German scholars received awards from the committee, enabling them to continue their work in French institutions.[298] Even if in the majority of cases France was only a staging-post in their exile – most frequently, they ended up either in Turkey or the United States – they included such eminent figures as the sociologist Gottfried Salomon, the statistician E. J. Gumbel, the educationist Erich Stern and the philosopher Erich Weil. Albert Einstein himself was offered a chair at the Collège de France.[299]

The Free German University
The Freie Deutsche Hochschule[300] was certainly one of the most interesting cultural institutions set up by the émigrés. In February and April 1934, the émigré press (*Pariser Tageblatt*) announced the formation of a 'school for German émigrés' (Deutsche Emigrantenschule), which seems not to have been realized.[301] In September of that year the reopening of MASCH (Marxistische Arbeiterschule) was announced, the Marxist school of the KPD that had been very famous in Germany. It was in the context of efforts to create a German Popular Front that the Free German University was founded, under the direction of Johann L. Schmidt. Opened on 19 November 1935, in the presence of Bodo Uhse, Manès Sperber, Georg Bernhard and Wolfgang Hallgarten, this brought together figures from very different political backgrounds. It combined elements from both MASCH and the Social-Democratic *Volkshochschulen*,[302] and sought to escape any kind of sectarianism. Even before opening its doors, it had been preceded by a People's University at which émigrés and French artists

gave tuition. The creation of these two universities was accompanied by the publishing of a free German university review, the *Zeitschrift für Freie Deutsche Forschung*. This was in large part the work of Johann Lorenz Schmidt, a pseudonym for Laszlo Radvanyi, Hungarian sociologist and economist, and the husband of Anna Seghers.[303] The People's University was presided over by the Social-Democratic journalist Robert Breuer.

These two universities gave lecture courses with reduced fees,[304] held in bookshops run by émigrés. Ties between the two universities and the exiles grew still closer in the period of the Popular Front. The People's University was more concerned with the teaching of émigrés, while the Free German University sought to channel the intellectual potential represented by the exiled academics. Far from wishing to restrict itself to an émigré audience, it sought to symbolize the German university free from National Socialist ideas, even if its non-émigré students remained few in number. It did however play a major role in the dynamic of the Popular Front. The teaching offered was very varied, even if it did not cover all fields of a regular university. Some French professors were invited to give lectures. The *Zeitschrift* for its part only saw three issues (July and November 1938, then 1939), but managed to bring together a number of strong contributors.[305] Moreover, contacts existed between contributors to the *Zeitschrift* and other scholarly initiatives undertaken by the émigrés. Thus Paul Honigsheim, who taught at the university in 1936, also directed the Paris branch of the Institut für Sozialforschung.

The Frankfurt School in Paris

Banned in 1933 for its 'hostility to the state', the Frankfurt Institut für Sozialforschung had already envisaged the likelihood of exile. Most of its library was confiscated.[306] On 13 April 1933, Max Horkheimer had been dismissed from the faculty, and Karl Wittfogel arrested (he was released in November). A bureau of twenty-one members was formed in Geneva in February 1933, as the administrative centre of the Institute, known from now on as the Société Internationale de Recherches Sociales, initially under the direction of Horkheimer and Friedrich Pollock. Outposts were subsequently opened in London and Paris. The Paris bureau was organized with the help of Célestin Bouglé (1870–1940), a sociologist who had studied under Durkheim, and director of the documentation centre of the École Normale Supérieure since 1920. He provided offices for the Institute within the complex on the rue d'Ulm.[307] The project was also supported by Maurice Halbwachs and Georges Scelle, both professors in Strasbourg, as well as by Bergson. It was also Bouglé who suggested to Horkheimer that the Institute's *Zeitschrift* could be published by the Librairie Félix Alcan.

Members and collaborators of the Institute active in Paris included Paul Honigsheim (director from 1933 to 1938), Hilde Weiss, R. Schröder, Walter Benjamin, H. Grossmann, O. Kirchheimer and G. Meyer. Among French contributors to the *Zeitschrift* were B. Groethuysen, M. Halbwachs, Alexandre Koyré, D. Lagache, Charles Le Cur, Henri Lefebvre and M. Leroy. Book reviews were also written by Raymond Aron, R. Polin and G. Friedmann.

Despite these contacts, however, it seems that very few French sociologists were really interested in the Institute's activities. Neither Aron nor G. Gurvitch, who later wrote histories of German sociology, make any reference to it, even though they were in a position to read these works, which was not the case with the majority of French sociologists. But the Durkheimian school that dominated French sociology was doubtless very hard to reconcile with the dialectical, Hegelian and Marxist inspiration of the Institute. Discovery of the Frankfurt School in France had to wait a further fifty years.

Theatre, Cabaret, Cinema

In 1933 a fairly large number of German actors, stage directors, film-makers and dramatists took refuge in France; some remained there until 1939, others soon left for Britain or America. There were also those who, after failing to establish themselves in Paris, decided to return to Germany. This was the case with such major figures as Gustaf Gründgens and G. W. Pabst. The large representation of the German stage and screen in Paris explains the diversity of émigré activity in these areas, which sought to make theatre and cabaret a means of agitation against National Socialism and to raise awareness of events happening in Germany.

One of the most symbolic achievements of these émigrés was the creation of the Franco-German cabaret Die Laterne, which offered antifascist shows from 1933 to 1939 and provided a number of émigrés with a livelihood. D. Luschnat and Anna Seghers founded a variety company in Paris, Der Ballon, several members of which had belonged to the most famous Berlin cabarets (Kabarett der Komiker, Tingel-Tangel, Katakombe, Truppe 31). This company soon disappeared, but a month later, Die Laterne presented shows twice weekly,[308] with songs, dance and sketches. The Laterne's actors included both German émigrés and native French.[309] It was thanks to this cabaret and its participants that Brecht's play Señor Carrar's Rifles was produced in Paris, as well as 99%, drawn from his Fear and Misery of the Third Reich.[310] The two most famous German émigré directors in Paris were Erwin Piscator and Max Reinhardt. Despite his efforts, however, Piscator was unable to find work in Paris, and his film project on Schweyk (with Noël-Noël or Fernandel) failed to get off the ground. He then left for New York, where Gilbert Miller attempted to stage his epic adaptation of War and Peace. As for Max Reinhardt, who enjoyed an international reputation, he received a triumphant welcome for his production of Johann Strauss's Die Fledermaus in November 1933; but this was the only show he was able to produce.

A certain number of antifascist works were also shown. Ferdinand Bruckner was already known before 1933; he emigrated to France where several of his plays were produced, some with a good deal of success.[311] Brecht arrived in Paris in 1933 to see The Seven Deadly Sins produced (for a very short season) at the Théâtre des Champs-Elysées, with music by Kurt Weill and choreography by George Balanchine. More important was the production of The Threepenny Opera in 1937, staged at the Théâtre de l'Étoile by E. J. Aufricht, who had produced it in Berlin in 1928 – as well as Mahagonny. These two productions, and his Jewish origin, had made him a target for Nazi hatred, and his last shows had been attacked by the SA.[312] After visiting Zurich and Prague, Aufricht – a great admirer of French theatre – decided to settle in Paris. He met up again there with Kurt Geron ('Tiger Brown' in *The Threepenny Opera*)[313] and Brecht himself, who was living at a small hotel near the Luxembourg. Unable to find work in Paris, Aufricht left for Normandy and turned to farming for a while.[314] On the advice of Kurt Weill and the son of Max Ophuls, he returned to Paris to recommence his career as producer and director.

It was the Exposition Mondiale of 1937 that gave Aufricht the occasion to consider a new production of *The Threepenny Opera* at the Théâtre de l'Étoile. The scenery was created by Eugène Berman (a Russian émigré); René Bergeron played Peachum, Yvette Guilbert took the part of Mrs Peachum,[315] Renée St-Cyr was Polly and Susy Solidor Jenny, while Raymond Cordy (an actor used by René Clair) played Tiger Brown. Raymond Rouleau, stage manager at the Théâtre de l'Œuvre, interpreted the role of Macheath and also took charge of the production, which had a great success. Following this, E. J. Aufricht tried an interesting theatrical experience at the Pigalle, which operated as a cinema until 11 p.m. He decided to have a 'Midnight Theatre' there,[316] along with a 'surrealist bar'. Despite its originality, however, this enterprise failed to meet with success.

Some works were also read by émigré actors, for example during SDS events – thus Friedrich Wolf's *Professor Mamlok*, in July 1933, by actors from Truppe 31, which went on to tour the USSR and Mexico. Others were created by companies that had only a limited existence, such as Maxim Blaustein's Neie Jydische Bühne, which in September 1933 staged Leonhard Frank's *Karl and Anna* at the 'Théâtre Pierre Levée'. The Arbeitergemeinschaft Emigrierter Deutscher Schauspieler likewise performed Arnold Zweig's *Semaels Sendung oder der Prozess von Tisza Eslar* (*Semael's Message, or The Trial of Tisza Eslar*) at the Théâtre Albert Premier. After the accidental death of Ödön von Horvath, his play *Glaube, Liebe, Hoffnung* (*Faith, Hope and Charity*) was staged by Alwin Kronacher,[317] by way of homage, at the Salle d'Iéna on 8 December 1938, and a company of Jewish actors performed a theatrical adaptation of Joseph Roth's novel *Hiob* (*Job*) at the Théâtre Pigalle in July 1939. The success of certain productions – for instance the extracts from *Fear and Misery of the Third Reich* – raised the hope for a moment of creating a German theatre in Paris, but the project failed for lack of resources.

Several film projects also deserve to be mentioned, even if they were not crowned with success. At least two antifascist films made in Moscow by German émigrés were shown in Paris: *Kämpfer* (*Fighters*) and *Professor Mamlok*. A number of German directors made films in France – R. Siodmak (*La Crise est finie*, 1934), Fritz Lang (*Liliom*, 1934), and Max Nossek (*Le Roi des Champs Élysées*, 1934). In 1936 G. W. Pabst filmed *Mlle Docteur (Salonique, nid d'espions)*, an insipid scenario saved by the presence of some wonderful actors: Pierre Fresnay, Louis Jouvet and Jean-Louis Barrault. *Jeunes filles en détresse* (with Micheline Presle), also made in France, was hardly one of his masterpieces. In 1939, Pabst returned to Hitlerite Austria. Max Ophuls made *La Tendre Ennemie* in France in 1935. He had also planned to shoot a film based on Schiller's *Intrigue and Love*. A significant number of UFA photographers, set designers and actors also sought with difficulty to find a place in the French cinema industry. Finally, it was in Paris that Gisèle Freund was to find fame as a photographer, and that the painter Wolf lived a semi-underground existence, turning subsequently to avant-garde photography.[318]

Visual Arts

The biological and racial criteria applied to art, and the pillorying of a large number of works representative of German painting in the Weimar era as 'degenerate art', led to a major exodus of all Jewish or 'avant-garde' artists.[319] A large number of them sought refuge in Paris,[320] even if they found many obstacles in the way of recommencing a career there. Some were already famous, others little known. If a large number of these artists were aware of the role that fell to them in the antifascist struggle, others – Kandinsky or Hans Arp – kept their distance from the émigré groups. The reasons that prompted so many artists to come to Paris are clear enough: in the same way as Berlin, Paris enjoyed the reputation of a European cultural capital, and the art market there was very developed.[321]

At least two hundred German artists reached France from 1933 onwards. Some of them had already stayed there periodically in the 1920s. The majority settled in Paris or in Provence. This exodus took place in successive waves, the Third Reich's policy in artistic matters being far from clearly established in 1933, as shown by the examples of Gottfried Benn and Ernst Nolde, the differences between Goebbels and Rosenberg over expressionism, and the attempt of certain academics to have this recognized as 'Nordic art' – not long before it was qualified as 'degenerate art'.[322] German artists in France in 1933 included Albert Flocon (Mentzel), Hermann Gowa, Kurt Lahs, Jean Leppien, Robert Liebknecht, Richard Lindner, Heinz Lohmar, Käthe Münzer-Neumann, Horst Strempel, Günther Strupp, Gert Wollheim, Fritz and Else Wolff and Ludwig Wronkow, as well as foreign artists who had been living in Germany (Cesar Domela, Jankel Adler, J. D. Kerzsenbaum and W. Kandinsky). Others who arrived later included Hanns Kralik, Leo Maillet (Mayer), Anton Räderscheidt, Francis Bott, Johnny Friedländer, Erwin Graumann, Hans Hartung, Eugen Spiro, Erwin Öhl, Max Beckmann, Arnold Fiedler, Heinz Kiwitz, Hans Bellmer, Gert Caden and Hermann Lismann, all of whom lived in France between 1933 and 1938. Though some of them had tried to continue their career, several had been sent to concentration camps or were directly threatened because of their Jewish origin. In 1938 came the turn of Austrian artists who reached France after the *Anschluss*. Finally, a number of German artists living in France since the 1920s became de facto émigrés in 1933 (Max Ernst, Otto Freundlich, Ferdinand Springer, Hans Reichel, Max Lingner). This sometimes delayed exile of visual artists confirms Klaus Mann's judgement: it was the writers who behaved best. While, with only some exceptions, few major authors agreed to collaborate with the Nazi government, a large number of artists remained in Germany after 1933 despite the official condemnation of their works (Ernst Barlach, Käthe Kollwitz, K. Schmidt-Rotluff, Karl Hofer, Karl Rössing, Otto Dix, W. Scholy). Some of these went into exile later, others preferred to stop painting or accepted that they were 'condemned to landscapes'. The number of artists who took part in underground resistance, however, was by no means negligible: Otto Nagel, Carl Lauterbach, Otto Pankok. Several of them (Alfred Frank, J. Levin, K. Schumacher, F. Schulze, H. Will) paid with their lives.[323]

The émigré artists in Paris generally experienced considerable material problems. Very few of them managed to organize individual shows, apart from Max Lingner and John Heartfield (Paris 1935).[324] Some were exhibited in various group exhibitions (Käthe Münzer, Eugénie Fuchs, Eugen Spiro, Victor Tischler, Fred Uhlmann).[325] It was often the inability to exhibit that led some of these to become designers or newspaper illustrators. A large number of artists were already politically active before 1933. Many subsequently took part in the big antifascist exhibitions such as that of 1938:[326] Heinz Lohmar, Alfred Hermann, Kralik, Kiwitz, Öhl and Hagen all designed posters for the Thälmann committee or scenery for antifascist plays. (Lohmar designed the sets for two Paris productions of Brecht.) More important still were the collective initiatives of émigré artists and their organizations. In 1933, under the patronage of the committee for the protection of persecuted Jewish intellectuals, a special room at the autumn Salon was devoted to Jewish painters expelled from Germany.[327] Many German painters also took part in different antifascist exhibitions, the most famous of which was that organized by the Thälmann committee in February 1938, 'Cinq ans de dictature hitlérienne'.[328]

One of the first major attempts to unite German artists exiled in France was the 'Collective of German Artists' founded early in 1936. The participants included Max Ernst, Otto Freundlich, Heinz Lohmar, H. Kralik, R. Liebknecht, E. Öhl, H. Stempel and Gert Wollheim.[329] The collective envisaged a number of meetings with debates – including a lecture by Max Ernst on 'surrealism and revolution'. A review edited by the collective, *Die Mappe*, does not seem to have survived the first issue. The collective's activities steadily declined and it seems to have died a death towards 1937.[330]

A far more structured organization was founded in autumn 1937, the Union des Artistes Allemands, successively known as the Union des Artistes Libres Allemands, Union des Artistes Allemandes Libres, and from spring 1938, Union des Artistes Libres. This new organization sought to be a broad assembly of exiled artists, and as Hélène Roussel makes clear,[331] its links were less with the spirit of the Weimar artistic far left than with the great tradition of German painting. A Union des Artistes Allemands, founded in 1903, had counted among its members such celebrated painters as Max Liebermann, L. Corinth, Slevogt, Kalckreuth and Hodler. Presided over by Eugen Spiro, who had belonged to the Artists' Union before 1933, when its school of painting was closed by the Nazis, and who was now president of the Ligue Internationale

Contre l'Antisémitisme (LICA), the new organization immediately planned a reply to the exhibition organized by the Nazis in Munich to stigmatize the art of the Weimar Republic. Max Lingner proposed a sponsoring committee bringing in French representatives of the art world and press, as well as the German and French Popular Fronts.[332] The émigrés were however divided over the direction to give the exhibition: a direct response to that of the Third Reich? A demonstration of the vitality of German art in exile? An exhibition of artists who were persecuted but remained in the Reich? Discussion was all the more lively in that other projects for a counter-exhibition – in Switzerland or England – were already under way. The art critic Paul Westheim found himself at the centre of most of these debates and played a major role. He had been since 1933 one of the most forceful adversaries of the cultural policy of the Third Reich.[333]

Though it had relatively significant resources at its disposal, the organizers of the exhibition envisaged in London could not win the support of émigré artists in Paris, as it rejected both Jews and émigrés on its sponsoring committee.[334] It explicitly maintained its abstention from a political standpoint. The London exhibition went ahead in July 1938 without any direct reference to the Munich spectacle. In the meantime, the founders of the Union des Artistes Allemands, along with the initiators of the collective of German artists, organized the Union des Artistes Libres chaired by E. Spiro,[335] with Kokoschka as honorary president. Far more structured, this organization set out to group together 'all German and Austrian artists, critics and art lovers scattered throughout the world'[336] who rejected National Socialism. It launched appeals to all artists to join the Union or its local branches, there being one for example in Prague.

Even if not all the exiled artists responded to this appeal, contacts were established with Max Beckmann, Paul Klee, F. Nussbaum, Theodor Balden, Bruno Taut, Walter Gropius, J. Albers and H. Vogeler – to name only the most famous. In France, this Union had some thirty members, but its activities involved a far larger number of individuals. The association was quite effective, to judge from the ties it managed to form. It became a genuinely representative organization of émigré artists, and it was doubtless to this end that the Union declared itself 'apolitical' and avoided taking a position on disputes among the exiles.[337] Neither did it support any particular artistic current.[338]

Its greatest achievement was the exhibition organized in Paris in November 1938 at the Maison de la Culture (rue d'Anjou) under the sponsorship of the SDS. The context for this was a week of German culture celebrating the thirtieth anniversary of the Schutzverband. This exhibition sought to show both 'degenerate works' and the works of émigrés, together with documents illustrating Hitlerite barbarism. Finally, the works of some seventy artists were displayed, including Spiro, Ernst, Klee, Grosz, Wollheim, Beckmann, Räderscheid and Krauskopf. Every current in German painting was represented, from expressionism to realism, at a time when expressionism was at the centre of debate in the review *Das Wort*.[339] Though French critics did not necessarily appreciate all the canvases on show – the gap between French and German artistic sensibility was quite large in the inter-war decades – the political impact of the exhibition, which focused attention on the fate of artists in Germany, was undeniable.

The Union des Artistes Libres also published a bulletin under the direction of Paul Westheim, *Freie Kunst und Literatur* (September 1938), which from October became the organ of the Cartel Cultural Allemand, founded in Paris, and uniting cultural organizations in the perspective of the Popular Front.[340] The models to be displayed in New York in 1939, in the context of the International Exhibition there, were also its work. Boycotted by Germany, this exhibition was to include a 'Free German pavilion', but the project was abandoned, doubtless from a combination of lack of funds and dissension among the émigrés, some of whom sought to present the project as a Communist initiative. The Union then opted for a less ambitious project: thirty models depicting the struggle of German people for freedom at different moments in their history. Even these models, however, do not seem to have been displayed, and this was the Union's last activity. Most of the refugee artists in France were interned in autumn 1939, though some continued painting in the camps. It is still possible to see at the camp of Les Milles, near Marseille, the famous frescos decorating the guards' refectory which Max Ernst helped to paint. A number of these artists managed to reach the United States or Mexico. Many lived in hiding during the Occupation, others were involved in the Resistance.

After the reprieve of the Popular Front government, the situation of the émigrés steadily worsened. They were deprived of the most basic liberties, their place of residence was assigned, and they fell prey to arbitrary police measures. The decree-law of 12 November 1938 established 'internment centres'. Violently attacked by the far right, when war broke out the émigrés were viewed as suspect and rounded up both in Paris and in the provinces. Many were arrested in August and September 1939, and from November they were sent off to internment or concentration camps from which they were only released in February or May 1940, often too late to escape the Gestapo.

The title Lion Feuchtwanger gave to the account of his internment in the Les Milles camp, *The Devil in France*, is readily understandable. Though it was in France that some of the most important works of German exile literature were produced – Klaus Mann's *The Volcano*, Heinrich Mann's *Henry of Navarre*, Friedrich Wolf's *Professor Mamlok*, Ferdinand Bruckner's *The Races*, Anna Seghers's *The Seventh Cross* and *Transit*, Lion Feuchtwanger's *Exile* – it was also in France that Ernst Weiss, Walter Hasenclever, Carl Einstein and Walter Benjamin took their own lives, while Rudolf Hilferding, Robert Breitscheid and Franz Dahlem were handed over to the Gestapo.

10. EXILE OUTSIDE EUROPE:
CHINA, TURKEY, PALESTINE

Whilst it seemed appropriate in this book to depict together the branches of German emigration on the American continent (United States, Mexico, Brazil, Argentina), and it is permissible to overlook the situation of émigrés in a few countries that did not really constitute lands of exile (Yugoslavia, Italy) or did not see particular activities develop (the West Indies),[341] the three examples of China, Turkey and Palestine are worth dwelling on, as they bear witness to the strange diversity of the road of emigration.

China

According to Gerhard G. Gerechter,[342] the number of Jews taking refuge in Shanghai from 1937 to 1940 was slightly over 17,000. At the end of the War they formed a Gemeinschaft der Demokratischen Deutschen, subsequently the Association of Refugees from Germany, and finally in New York the Gemeinschaft Ehemaliger Shanghaier. Strange as this emigration might be, it is explained by the fact that after European borders were shut tight, China was the only country still to accept émigrés with no visa, and the situation of Shanghai was especially favorable. Shanghai was accessible from Hamburg and Naples. The city had already welcomed White Russian refugees after the 1917 revolution and, even before that, Sephardic Jews from Baghdad. When the Gestapo agreed to release Jews interned in the Buchenwald or Dachau concentration camps, in 1938, this was on condition that they could immediately leave Germany, and Shanghai was the only possible destination. Most of them reached China via Siberia and Japan.

Not all of this emigration can be described as antifascist, as it had a very mixed character. Besides Communists, it included former SA men who had survived the 'night of long knives' and went on to become officers in Chang Kai-shek's army, as well as many Jews – artisans, merchants – expelled from Germany and a certain number of artists, especially actors. After 1939, it was increasingly hard to reach Shanghai[343] and the story of this emigration is far from well known.[344]

Among the thousands of Jews who found refuge in Shanghai were some two hundred actors who formed the European Jewish Artists Society[345] and staged several German classics such as Lessing's *Nathan the Wise*, also plays by Hoffmansthal, Brecht, Bruckner, Bruno Frank and Walter Hasenclever. As well as German theatre, an important centre of Yiddish culture developed in Shanghai, with its journal *Die Tribüne*.

If Shanghai received more than 18,000 German, Austrian, Czech and Romanian refugees, it was because one could stay there more or less indefinitely without papers. Since 1844, the city had enjoyed extra-territorial status. A town of contrasts with its wooden houses and modern architecture, its shopping streets and opium dens, prostitutes and European colonies, Shanghai underwent an immense expansion thanks to foreign capital. Despite political confrontations, and a certain climate of decadence that characterized the city, it managed to remain a kind of exceptional ghetto until shortly after the War.

The German emigrants reached Shanghai in three successive waves. First of all, in 1933, some academics and architects (Richard Paulick) arrived in the city without being in any way noticed. In 1935 their number rose and a support committee had to be formed. The second emigration period corresponded to the years 1938–39,[346] when a certain number of Jews interned in German camps were released and reached Shanghai as a result of international negotiations.[347] The third wave of émigrés followed the outbreak of war, when many refugees reached Shanghai by sea or by the Trans-Siberian railway. Many of these were Polish Jews fleeing the advance of Hitler's armies.

The overall character of the Shanghai emigration was petty-bourgeois. It included few well-known oppositionists, intellectuals or writers. Its political activities were very restricted, given the limited number of German or Austrian Communists who ended up there. According to Alfred Dreifuss, the majority of émigrés were not even resolutely antifascist, and impatiently awaited Hitler's disappearance to return to Germany, seeing Nazism as nothing more than a kind of natural calamity. They included doctors, members of the liberal professions, merchants and booksellers, who all strove to find some kind of activity in Shanghai. The ideological situation of these émigrés was further complicated by the fact that the city already had a German colony about 2,400 strong, a large portion of whom had no interest in events in their home country, while others did not hide their Nazi convictions. There was even a 'local branch' of the NSDAP and pro-Nazi newspapers, as well as a number of representatives for German firms who were notably sympathetic to the Hitler regime. The Gestapo worked together with the Japanese authorities, and after the Japanese occupation, these Shanghai Germans spied on and denounced anti-Nazi refugees. Anti-Communist Germans, moreover, were often supporters of Chang Kai-shek. It is symbolic that the representative of German heavy industry and armaments in Nanjing was in fact the brother of the celebrated actor Emil Jannings, 'Professor Unrat' in *The Blue Angel*. The most well-known former SA man among the refugees was Walther Stennes, an officer under Wilhelm II, who went on serve under Stresemann, Hitler and Chang Kai-shek. A member of the Freikorps, fanatical nationalist and participant in the 'black Reichswehr', he was mixed up in a whole series of scandals and crimes under the Weimar Republic. He went on to become SA leader in Prussia but came into conflict with Hitler in 1931, who accused him of fomenting a putsch and inciting opposition between the SA in Berlin and the Munich leadership. Arrested and interned, he was saved from execution by Göring who had him taken to the Dutch border. Stennes then travelled to China, became military adviser to Chang Kai-shek and tried to organize the Nationalist army and police along Prussian lines. He narrowly avoided arrest by the Japanese, and subsequently by the Americans, who accused him of refusing to denounce former Nazis in Shanghai who had collaborated with the Japanese army. Chang Kai-shek saved him once more by appointing him to the Chinese Military Commission.[348]

It goes without saying that there was no connection between left-wing émigrés and the SA. The Jewish émigrés, for their part, included a certain number of Zionists who published the *Shanghai Jewish Chronicle*.

In December 1941, the Japanese forcees, who until then had been stationed outside the city, invaded Shanghai and closed all British and American businesses and shops. US and British citizens were interned in camps, and the Japanese took over the city administration. Refugees from Germany and central Europe now faced a climate of misery, fear and famine. Émigré activity, which had never been very significant, was now greatly limited. A few Communists still managed to publish an information bulletin, *The Voice of China*, reporting on the political situation in China and the battles fought by the Communists.[349] A 'political salon' and a political training school were also established in Shanghai, likewise under Communist inspiration. These Communists – a few dozen in all – were condemned to illegality throughout the exile period, having to fear denunciation by spies, by Nazi supporters working for Chang Kai-shek and by the Japanese – and later American – authorities.

On 18 February 1943 a new period of uncertainty for the Shanghai refugees began. The Japanese government now decided to group 'stateless emigrants' in an actual ghetto. They had to sell their houses and shops at derisory prices and move to the district of Honju, while Chinese were invited to occupy the positions thus released. A. Dreifuss notes that no Chinese did so, out of opposition to the Japanese and pity for the refugees. A 'Stateless Refugee Office' was created by the Japanese, the military official in charge of it ironically calling himself the 'king of the Jews'. From now on, these émigrés could not leave their ghetto without a special passport. Besides, thanks to the Gestapo and its own spies, the Japanese army was perfectly aware of the names of Communist refugees and refused them passports. Many of these 'stateless' refugees died in the ghetto from either epidemics or bombardment. The more healthy were forcibly enrolled in a kind of Japanese home guard, the Pao-Chia.

On 1 November 1945, the Residents' Association of Democratic Germans in Shanghai was created, with a view to establishing contact with the Allies in order to prepare the return of refugees to Germany and to defend their rights. In fact, almost 99 per cent of the refugees had remained in Shanghai throughout the exile period, and were forced to practise the most varied trades. In most cases they had little opportunity for political or cultural activity. They were too few in number, lacked resources, and above all were too isolated from European culture. They did however manage to organize literary events and to set up a number of theatres in the most difficult conditions. With a very limited audience they staged plays by subscription, their repertoire including such famous and difficult works as Brecht's *Threepenny Opera* and plays by Hasenclever, Bruckner, Klabund, Lessing, Molnar, Schnitzler, Sophocles, Strindberg and Wolf, along with pieces by Shanghai authors, most often Austrian journalists or actors. These were often akin to operettas, and strongly marked by Jewish humour. No great innovations could be expected from this improvised theatre with some eighty performers (nineteen actresses, twenty-eight actors, nineteen male singers, fourteen female), but its very existence was a miracle. Its aim was not to combat fascism and promote Weimar culture, but simply to maintain a link between émigrés and European culture; and it succeeded in this to a surprising degree. This German and Austrian emigration to Shanghai, which continued to express its culture in the midst of hovels and opium dens, has a certain fascination.

Turkey

The presence of a significant German academic emigration in Turkey is no less surprising than the staging of the *Dreigroschenoper* by an amateur company in Shanghai or the development of a Yiddish repertory there. In spring 1933, Mustafa Kemal Pasha launched a wide-ranging programme of moderniza-tion,[350] which included developing the University of Istanbul. He accordingly decided to accept a number of refugee academics from Germany. The Not-gemeinschaft, an aid organization run by Philipp Schwartz and Albert Malche, the Swiss professor in charge of reorganizing the university, was authorized by the Turkish government to negotiate with such academics the possibility of positions for them. Thirty were immediately offered contracts to come and teach at the five colleges newly created in Istanbul. By November 1933 their number had grown to fifty. The majority were engaged for five years, and accepted the conditions that the government laid down: to learn Turkish and gradually begin to give lectures in that language. Philipp Schwartz himself taught for twenty years in Turkey as head of the Pathology Institute, before ending his career at the Warren State Hospital in Pennsylvaniaa. It was at his request that other scholars were invited to Turkey: the mathematician Richard Courant, the physicists James Frank and Max Born. Thanks to these émigrés, the Turkish university system was completely transformed by 1935. A large number of professors moved to Ankara, establishing new disciplines and institutes there. Though scientists were particularly numerous, these also included historians and linguists.[351]

The life of this community of exiled German academics was extremely strange.[352] Isolated both culturally and linguistically, they were forced back on their own resources. As they could no longer write in German or Austrian publications, British or American journals ceased arriving after the War broke out, and they could not read or write Turkish, they were led to publish their own journals in order to keep in touch with each other's works. The list of subjects covered ran from the Hittites[353] to Sanskrit, by way of surgery and dermatol-ogy. The language barrier was insurmountable for many academics. Even among those who studied Turkish seriously, only a few ever managed to use it for teaching purposes. Thus, in the first years of exile, they were forced to resort to interpreters who translated their lectures sentence by sentence.[354] The contrast between this specialized academic elite and the uneducated students was often dramatic. Facing these émigrés, specialists in the most varied scientific or literary fields, were the sons of peasants and soldiers, some of whom had never seen electric light before their arrival in Istanbul. Yet they set out to study biophysics with Dessauer, the history of the Hittites with Güterbock, or the most advanced medical techniques with Philipp Schwartz.[355] Unable to settle there, many of these academics struggled to reach the United States. Those who did not manage to do so were interned in camps for the duration of the War, along with Nazis who, according to L. Dieckmann, persecuted them more cruelly than their guards.[356]

Palestine

A large majority of those exiles who took refuge in Palestine were naturally of Jewish origin. Some of them saw this not so much as exile but as a return to their own land.[357] The Zionist idea that had become widespread since the beginning of the century aroused much debate in the German-Jewish community, even if Germany was the European country where Jews felt most assimilated. They had given so much to the German culture with which they identified. Some Jews had become highly nationalistic, and imbued with the ideals of the bourgeoisie, even if liberalism seemed to them a rampart against anti-Semitism. Almost all saw themselves as Germans rather than Jews, assimilation appearing to them completely natural. Kurt Tucholsky and Walter Benjamin were 'Berliners', and Alfred Döblin felt so unfamiliar with Jewish customs that he travelled to Poland to observe these.

After the First World War, Jewish youth often felt the contradictory temptation of a commitment to the parties of the left or a return to Jewish tradition. Some of them, according to Gershom Scholem, maintained that Jews had only been accepted in Germany to the extent that they renounced their identity. Intellectual Zionism in the first decades of the century strove to denounce this false Jewish–German symbiosis. The partisans of Zionism were certainly few in number in relation to the Jewish community as a whole. Scholem, a Zionist from an early age, estimated[358] that out of 600,000 German Jews, only 20,000 took part in the election of Zionist delegates. His personal trajectory is quite remarkable in this respect. He first became interested in the movement in 1921, after reading a lecture on Zionism. One of his brothers was '*deutsch-national*' (a right-wing nationalist), another apolitical, a third was a Communist deputy in the Reichstag (he died in Buchenwald). Zionism very soon appeared to Scholem and his friends as a way of breaking with the bourgeoisie and the cult of German-Jewish assimilation. While still a youth in Berlin, he developed a passion for Jewish mysticism, learned Hebrew, and left Germany for Palestine in 1923.

Such clear choices however were rare. Most Jewish intellectuals of this generation felt the pull of different poles of attraction. The example of Walter Benjamin is too well known to need detailed discussion here. At the time when Scholem was turning to Zionism, Benjamin was absorbed by philosophy and literary criticism. He subsequently adhered to Marxism and sought to reconcile the attachment to a religious tradition that profoundly marked his thought with a political commitment that was both enthusiastic and sincere. When Scholem urged him to learn Hebrew and join him in Jerusalem, Benjamin's response was to temporize, promise one thing and do another. In the end he was attracted by Moscow and Paris more than by Jerusalem, hesitated to leave Berlin and Europe, and was unable to choose between Brecht and Kafka, Marxism and Judaism. Benjamin's tragedy was also the profound manner in which he assumed all these contradictions.

Franz Kafka, who apart from short journeys to Berlin and Italy was unfamiliar with the world outside the Austro-Hungarian orbit, did take an interest in Zionism and tried to learn Hebrew, without however sharing the convictions of his friend Max Brod. The parallel between the Scholem/Benjamin and Brod/Kafka friendships is striking, and illustrates very well the contradictions experienced by so many Jewish intellectuals in the 1920s, both in Germany and in central Europe. But if Palestine exercised a certain fascination on many Jewish intellectuals, their relationship to it was primarily mythical and sentimental. In Berlin they dreamed of Jerusalem, but only a few tried to settle there. The beginning of anti-Semitic persecution, however, was to give Palestine a new reality. Hitler himself viewed Palestine as a 'Jewish territory', and in May 1933 the Reich authorities made contact with the Zionist leaders with a view to a possible massive Jewish migration.[359] The British government, which held a League of Nations mandate over Palestine, immediately took energetic measures to block this project, for fear of Arab reaction. Even so, an estimated 70,000 German-speaking Jews emigrated to Palestine between 1933 and 1939, in the wake of Hitler's persecution.

Though for some of these – intellectuals or not – Palestine represented a kind of dream, the encounter with reality brought a fairly brutal awakening. Jews they might be, but these émigrés felt deeply isolated culturally and linguistically, and constantly met with political antagonism.[360] Few indeed took the initiative to seek exile in Palestine before the rise of Hitler. The only German writer of Jewish origin to consider the possibility seriously was Arnold Zweig, who travelled there in 1932. His correspondence shows that his stay there was far from happy. Though he published with Querido Verlag in 1934 his *Bilanz der deutschen Judenheit. Ein Versuch* (*Balance-Sheet of German Jewry. An Investigation*), he confided to Freud in a letter of 21 January that year:

> I don't care any more about the 'land of my fathers'. I haven't got any more Zionist illusions either. I view the necessity of living here among the Jews without enthusiasm, without any false hopes and even without the desire to scoff. I am grateful for the stroke of fate which united us as young people with this remarkable phenomenon and which forced us to come here for the sake of our children and our young friends.[361]

Zweig's correspondence is an astonishing testimony to the malaise he experienced as a German writer in Palestine. He viewed cultural and political activity there as zero: 'People here demand their Hebrew, and I cannot give it to them. I am a German writer and a German European, and this fact has certain consequences.'[362] When his passport was due to expire, Zweig could not bring himself to demand a renewal from the Third Reich, but refused to break his link with the German people by requesting a Palestinian one. He declared himself a Jew, but with no relationship to 'Jewish nationality', dreamed of leaving Palestine but without knowing where to go.[363] The complaints uttered by Arnold Zweig – the sense of a loss of freedom, the rejection of nationalism and systematic opposition to the Arabs, fear of a 'cultural desert', rootedness in European culture, the impression of being rejected[364] – were echoed by many Jewish intellectuals who emigrated to Palestine but in no way felt at home there. Though there were some writers who managed to find a certain audience there, their case remains rather exceptional. Sammy Gronenmann, for example, had three of his dramas staged in Palestine, and Max Brod five, at the famous Habimah Theatre, where Brod became literary adviser.[365] Gershom Scholem, for his part, certainly managed the transition, and became a famous scholar at the University of Jerusalem. Max Brod, along with his Prague friend Felix Weltsch (librarian at the Hebrew University), seems to have found a new homeland in Palestine. Ludwig Strauss achieved a similar assimilation, and began to write in Hebrew. But other writers such as Jenny Aloni, Werner Bukofzer, Alice Schwarz, Georg Strauss, Manfred Sturmann and Max Zweig experienced more complex and conflicting destinies.

The example of Else Lasker-Schüler perhaps best symbolizes the contradictory feelings that Palestine aroused in so many German intellectual émigrés. The granddaughter of a rabbi, a strange and moving figure in the expressionist milieu of Berlin, close to the circle around *Der Sturm*, a friend of Herwarth Walden, Franz Marc, Karl Kraus, Georg Trakl and Gottfried Benn, she wrote from the early years of the century poems that were often very fine, drawing on biblical images and exalting Jerusalem – her 'Hebrew Ballads'. Detested by the bourgeoisie, whose values she offended, she became a favorite target of the SA, who called her a 'Jewish pornographer'. In spring 1933, after being attacked with iron bars by SA men, she took refuge in Switzerland. In Zurich, where she slept on street benches, she was arrested for vagabondage. At the age of forty-six, she had rarely had a fixed address. She lived in Switzerland by selling her drawings and reciting her poems. A production of her drama *Arthur Aronymus and His Fathers* was banned on 19 December 1936, as infringing Swiss neutrality.

Laske-Schüler visited Palestine for the first time in 1934, still haunted by Berlin. The mystic Jerusalem she had hymned in her poems had little relation to the real Jerusalem she discovered. Palestine struck her as 'a country torn apart and filled with social tensions'. Her book *The Land of the Hebrews*, published in Switzerland in 1937, is more than a travelogue, rather a series of mystic visions that continue those of the 1920s. But when an offer was made to translate them into Hebrew, she replied that in German they were already too Jewish. In 1937 she travelled again to Palestine but returned disappointed. Two years later she made a third journey and this time remained there. Unknown and almost forgotten, she died in poverty, depending on the generosity of some friends. Seeking to recreate in Jerusalem the atmosphere of Berlin, she founded a poetry club, Der Krall, where she read her poems by candlelight, accompanied by little bells and a hurdy-gurdy. Her political ideas were hardly taken seriously, and she was viewed as mad. Continuing to mourn the memory of Berlin, she wanted the pacifist expressionist Fritz von Unruh to become president of Palestine, and dreamt of a reconciliation between Jews and Arabs. Max Brod, who met her on several occasions, described her as a ghostly and pitiful apparition; he too saw her as suffering from mental illness. Her last collection of poems, *The Blue Piano*, appeared in 1943, and her drama *I and I* was never staged in her lifetime. Its characters included literary, biblical and political figures: Faust, Mephisto, Saul, David, Baal, Solomon, Max Reinhardt, Hitler, Göring, Goebbels, Hess, etc. Else Laske-Schüler died on 22 January 1945, and was buried at the foot of the Mount of Olives. At her request, the Kaddish was recited, and in German her poem 'I Know That I Soon Must Die'. Her tomb was destroyed by the Jordanians to build a road, and restored in 1968.

It was an evident fact that Palestine had no time for Berlin poets and writers. It was more sympathetic to manual workers and tended to view these intellectuals as useless mouths. The assimilation of Jews to German culture was so strong that it was scarcely possible to imagine transforming them into Zionists and persuading them to express themselves in Hebrew. Many Jewish antifascists found themselves completely isolated and even rejected. Their political commitment was often held against them; even in the 1920s, as Gershom Scholem recalled, young Jewish Communists and Zionists attacked each other as 'Jewish fascists' and 'red assimilationists'. It was all too clear that these Jews from Germany saw Berlin more than Jerusalem as their spiritual home. The newspaper *Orient*, run by German antifascists in Palestine, which took Ossietzky's *Weltbühne* as its model, was viewed by Palestinian Jews as 'too left'. Manfred Durzak[366] cites a letter from Wolfgang Yourgrau, who published this paper together with Arnold Zweig, to Walter A. Berendsohn, complaining of the boycott that the émigré Jewish antifascists suffered, treated as 'Communists', 'traitors to Zionism' or at best 'café intellectuals', insults reminiscent of the Nazi vocabulary. The offices of *Orient* were even bombed by right-wing Zionists in 1943, and despite the presence of several German-Jewish publishers in Palestine, it was impossible to publish works in German. At most, poetry collections were permissible in limited editions, such as those by Werner Kraft (1937), Else Lasker-Schüler, Heinz Politzer (1941) and Louis Fürnberg (1943).

Finally, strange as it might appear, there was a colony of German émigrés in India, even including such major figures of artistic life from the Weimar era as Willy Haas, publisher of the *Literarische Welt*, who hailed from Prague and had worked in both theatre and cinema. Haas requested a visa to emigrate after obtaining a contract with a Bombay film company. He found there a significant Jewish community, and it was possible for Jews to emigrate from Germany if an adequate number of people would guarantee their 'honesty'.[367] In his autobiography, Willy Haas gave a striking portrait of the India where he found refuge after escaping the Gestapo: he felt a complete foreigner there, even if the Parsees of Bombay reminded him of the old Jews of Prague. He spent his entire exile adapting Indian or European plays for the Bombay studios.[368] When war broke out, he joined the Indian army and was sent to Nepal and Tibet.

Exile as Everyday Tragedy

When Dante walked through Verona, people pointed their fingers at him and mur-
mured that he was in hell. Otherwise how would he have been able to describe all its
torments? He did not draw these from his imagination, he lived them, experienced them,
saw and felt them. He really was in hell, the city of the damned: he was in exile.

Heinrich Heine, 'On Ludwig Börne'

I do not know to what extent those who have never been forced to leave their country
can imagine life in exile, life without money, without family, without friends and
neighbours, without their familiar tongue, without a valid passport, often without an
identity card or work permit, without a country prepared to accept exiles. Who can
understand this situation: to be without any rights, rejected by their own country that
persecutes and slanders them, and sends murderers across its borders to kill them?
[. . .] They have no defence against the police, and the authorities expel them from one
frontier to another.

Hermann Kesten

When they left Germany in 1933, none of them imagined that their exile would
last twelve years. The majority of émigrés had not envisaged having to leave
Germany any more than they had thought they would have to protect
themselves from Nazi terror and the massive arrests that followed the Reichstag
fire. Brecht's poems 'Duration of the Third Reich' and 'Thoughts on the
Duration of Exile', just like the correspondence and diaries of so many émigrés,
show that they almost all thought they would be able to return to Berlin in a few
weeks, once the Nazi regime collapsed. Exile was not something unfamiliar to
them; they had read the poems of Heine and Dante, Ovid and Victor Hugo. But
it was only slowly that they became aware of the community of suffering that
marks the fate of exiles across nations and epochs.

It is almost impossible, moreover, to separate the works born in exile from the
weight of suffering and bitter experience that accompanied them. Emigration
has to be understood as a phenomenon *sui generis*, with multiple dimensions:
political, literary and theoretical as well as sociological and psychological. There

is an emigrant *Dasein* which determines the majority of exile creations. It may be that the novels Thomas Mann published after 1933 do not necessarily show the traces of his émigré existence, but this is certainly not the case with those of Lion Feuchtwanger or Anna Seghers, or even Thomas Mann's brother Heinrich and son Klaus. The political and literary debates among émigrés, moreover, are not always comprehensible outside of a certain context made up of fear and jealousy, obsession with betrayal, envy and poverty, which the émigrés themselves described as an 'emigrant psychosis'. The climate of suspicion, leading sometimes to denunciation, is a striking illustration of this. Doubtless the experiences that the émigrés of 1933 underwent were not always exceptional; they are the fate of all exiles.[1] But because they were undergone by distinguished writers and poets, and woven into the intimate fibre of their creations, these experiences still speak vividly to us today.[2]

The exile situation is an intimate tragedy that affects all aspects of existence: relationship to time – past, present and future, childhood memories – as well as space, language, ties to others and to oneself. To write on exile without being exiled oneself is almost impossible. One can only acknowledge the truth of the words repeated by so many émigrés: only those who have known exile can describe its heartbreak, others can only imagine it.

1. LEGAL PROBLEMS OF THE ÉMIGRÉ SITUATION
THE APPRENTICESHIP OF EXILE

They were no longer Germans, yet they still were. They lived, on sufferance, in countries that had received them but to which they did not belong.

Golo Mann

Merely, we fled. We are driven out, banned.
Not a home, but an exile, shall the land be that took us in.
Restlessly we wait thus, as near as we can to the frontier
Awaiting the day of return, every smallest alteration.

Bertolt Brecht, 'Concerning the Label Emigrant'

Exile was experienced all the more cruelly by the émigrés of 1933 in that it struck them so suddenly, without their being able to prepare for it either materially or morally. After leaving behind their town, country, family, friends and work, often also their library and manuscripts, the exiles found themselves in a country whose culture, language and customs might be completely foreign. Without friends, papers or visa, without permission to stay or permit to work, they had to relearn how to live. In a world that often seemed strange and hostile, they felt completely infantilized. Unable to earn a living, abandoned to bureaucratic chicanery, they had to plead their cause to support committees, where these existed, line up at counters to obtain subsidies, papers, information, advice, wait for hours or whole days at consulates, commissariats, prefectures of police, to try to sort out the legal imbroglio that their very existence presented.

Hated by their native country, ill received by their country of asylum, they were tempted to shut themselves up in their own isolation and seek only the company of other émigrés who shared the same bitter experiences. Scarcely did these émigré circles come into being, but they transformed themselves – often enough – into antagonistic microcosms in which everyone suspected each other,[3] amazingly subject to rumour, false news, and Gestapo spies. Whether they lived in Prague, Paris, Zurich or London, they found themselves in the same cafés and hotels (later in France in disused barracks), attentive to the least event in Germany that might foreshadow the coming collapse of the regime. Some of them went to the station every day to read the foreign papers. Scattered to the four corners of the world, they went on writing and expressing their complaints.[4]

Despite the common fate that united them, the exiles suffered deeply from economic differences and divergent treatment. Material worries inevitably supervened on the psychological torments of uprooting, separation from their native land and mother tongue. While the most famous of them could expect to find support, protection and money anywhere – what country would have refused to welcome Einstein or Thomas Mann, to offer them accommodation, nationality, a position? – the majority were condemned to live each day in growing solitude, anonymity and humiliation. When they went in search of a publisher, or a magazine that might accept an article, it was often less to defend their ideas than to buy a pair of shoes or settle a hotel bill. Once a famous author or actor, the exile steadily became just a 'refugee of German origin'.[5]

The Europe that notionally accepted them was a world disturbed and in crisis, ever ready to view them with contempt and hostility.[6] They often had nothing to offer but their ideas, their books, their courage and their hatred of Hitler. Each day they had to confront the egoism, blindness and pettiness of those who didn't want to know anything of their reasons for exile. As Golo Mann wrote:

> I would say that the exiled writer was an unwelcome guest. Europe in the late 1930s was poor and petty, anguished and inhospitable to foreigners. The Hitler regime was unloved, but those Germans who had rejected Hitler's domination and protested against it were not loved any more. Not to be en règle with the proper authorities, not to have a valid passport, was always something that aroused suspicion. The same questions: What exactly do you want here? How long are you going to stay? When are you leaving? – we've heard them so often, and not only from the mouths of bureaucrats. How much of our time has been wasted by this harassment, which we had to put up with in order to obtain anywhere a limited permission to stay, parsimoniously granted, how harshly did it act on our humiliated nerves [. . .]. Books have appeared on this subject [. . .] and they are really amusing to read. What was less amusing was to live it.

Hermann Kesten also noted: 'For thousands of years, the same prejudices and errors have accompanied émigrés across the countries in which they took refuge. They were defeated, so they were assumed to be in the wrong. They had been persecuted, so they were persecuted again even where they should have been protected. They were malcontents and unfortunates, so they were distrusted.'

Far from improving, their situation continued to deteriorate, despite international discussion of the refugee problem and the establishment of support committees. Each new wave of émigrés made the survival of the preceding wave more difficult. As the 1930s advanced, the conditions of reception became more draconian, and the reactions of public opinion to the refugees grew more hostile. After war was declared, they were interned, and when obtaining an American visa was the only way of escaping the Gestapo, it became that much harder to depart. It is in no way surprising that these years saw an increasing number of suicides. The majority of émigrés had no further hope.

This was the general context in which the exiles experienced their situation psychologically. In each individual story chance plays a considerable part, and there is no quite typical fate. Political activists, and intellectuals tied to political organizations, suffered less from solitude and despair than others who were more isolated. There are hardly any cases of Communist émigrés committing suicide. The exile was also less vulnerable if he shared the experience with his wife – how many émigrés owed their material and psychological survival to their partners, and at what price! The older he was, the less his prospects of social resettlement, his capacity for adaptation or restructuring of his personality. The fact of speaking the language of the country of exile, or learning it, knowing its culture and having connections there, counted for much. Even the feeling of exile varied from one émigré to another. There were those who could travel the whole world without feeling foreign. For others, the anguish of exile started with leaving Berlin, Munich or Frankfurt. Some émigrés managed to break any sentimental bond with Germany, and even stopped speaking German. Others listened in tears to reports of the Allied bombing of Dresden, Munich or Hamburg. While many refused to return to Germany after the War, what of those who returned to die there or take their own lives?

It was perhaps writers above all who felt most cruelly the trauma of separation from their native tongue, their childhood and their readership. This heartbreaking wrench was for a few of them a source of inspiration, but for many it meant annihilation. Even a writer like Kurt Tucholsky, after leaving for exile, felt that the act of writing had become an absurdity.[7] United as they were by a common fate, their situations still differed greatly as a function of their celebrity. Lion Feuchtwanger, Heinrich and Thomas Mann, Ernst Toller and Bertolt Brecht were all major writers who had been famous and admired under the Weimar Republic. But if Feuchtwanger or Thomas Mann could keep up the same easy lifestyle in exile, this was not the case with the great majority. Even writers such as Alfred Döblin and Heinrich Mann experienced a material situation quite close to poverty. Most of the exiled authors were unable to write in any other language but German. For want of publishers, some stopped writing and practised manual trades.

Separation from one's homeland meant for some a state of mourning. For a long time they dreamed of Germany, and not even Brecht or Becher escaped the nostalgia for native landscapes hymned by Max Hermann-Neisse. It was only slowly that the émigrés gained experience of their new situation,[8] though this did not make it any the less cruel. As it emerged that this exile would last a long time, they had to try and give their life a new material structure, even at the risk of never escaping from a state of semi-beggary. The long train of humiliations that accompanied exile was not the least negative aspect. Little by little, their relation to space and time,[9] to history, radically shifted. The beginnings of exile were often compared to unwanted holidays.[10] After the anguish of flight came a certain euphoria at having escaped Hitler. The exile did not yet think about the duration of his absence. He even refused to locate himself in relation to the present time. As Manès Sperber wrote:

> The exile is hostile to the *present*, the most ephemeral and yet the most important category of time. It is only in the past that he finds his justification and the reasons for hoping for a future that must make everything right, must overthrow the usurpers, as well as raising the exiles to front rank in the recovered homeland. This loss of the present, a loss desired and yet suffered day after day, prevents him from finding his feet in the land of asylum. He does not actually want this, being always en route; everything for him is provisional, each 'now' becomes a fleeting moment.[11]

The exiles were also assailed by a perpetual feeling of foreignness. The references to the novels of Kafka to be found in so many exile writings are not fortuitous. Solitary himself, the exile only encountered other solitudes. The indifference of others was his guarantee of a certain freedom, but also the source of his wretchedness. The first need of the émigré is to be able to ensure his survival. But how is he to work? Everywhere he comes up against selfish restrictions, and risks expulsion or a heavy fine. A prisoner of his own language, which he speaks now only with other émigrés, he finds himself unable to communicate with those who might become his friends, and is thrown back again on other exiles. In this way, little communities form around a hotel, a café or a village, each in its anguish creating its own ghetto. The exile gradually discovers that no one needs him, that he is redundant everywhere, and the little that he manages to gain is seen by others as theft or usurpation. Manès Sperber was certainly right in calling the anti-Nazi emigration 'the most undesirable of all'. When the exiles tried to warn, they were told to keep quiet. As a rule, no one listened to them. After arousing a mixture of interest and compassion, the émigré became a burden to be rejected, a problem to be handed over to an administrative department.

Now it was no longer just his connection to the material world that changed, but his relationship to others and to himself. Though sharing a collective fate, the exile is isolated and abandoned. As a loser, he feels himself to blame. Threatened, he accuses others. A wall of rancour and suspicion builds up around him.

It is an established fact that the exiles constantly accused one another of treason. Their collective misfortune did not succeed in uniting them; it often exacerbated opposition. Leopold Schwarzschild attacked Klaus Mann and

Lion Feuchtwanger as 'Soviet agents'. Brecht distrusted the 'Moscow clique'. Julius Hay feared both J. R. Becher and Walter Ulbricht. Gustav Regler was accused of denouncing his friends in exchange for release from the camp where he had been interned. He in turn complained of being denounced to the American authorities as a 'Nazi agent' by his former Communist friends. Émigrés in the USSR accused Hans Rödenberg of denouncing émigrés to the NKVD. But this generalized distrust was not restricted to political circles. It also cut across families, whom exile had dispersed or prevented from reuniting. Stefan Zweig had to leave his mother in Vienna. Alfred Döblin left Germany initially without his wife, and recounts in his *Schicksalreise* the vicissitudes through which he managed to find her again in 1940. For want of papers, Alfred Kantorowicz was unable to marry legally, and had to leave his father in Germany. Gustav Regler's son remained in Germany and fought in the Wehrmacht.[12] One of Döblin's sons, Klaus, after his demobilization in 1940 (he had fought in the French army), killed himself to escape the Gestapo; the other, Stefan, found himself in the '*zone libre*' but was interned in a labour camp after reaching Switzerland. As the end of the War approached, the émigrés felt a sense of anguish with news of the bombing of German cities; some, like Piscator, still had a brother in Germany. Nor did couples escape this psychosis of suspicion. Gustav Regler had married the daughter of the painter Heinrich Vogeler (who had emigrated to the Soviet Union and died in poverty and abandonment). When his wife declared that she wanted to see Germany again, he did not even dare to accompany her to the station, but declared that he was ready to give up politics if she returned safe and sound.[13] When she returned and he saw the swastika stamp on her passport, he wondered if she had not betrayed him and returned in order to spy on him: 'I looked at her neat, braided hair, her smooth white neck, the blouse of hand-woven material, everything about her that appeared flawless and unsullied [. . .]. Was she capable of betrayal? [. . .] I turned away my head, but the passport was still there, and she seemed to have become a stranger, herself stamped with the swastika.'[14]

If it is true, as a large number of émigrés maintain, that exile made them mature, it killed the weaker as much as it revealed the stronger. As a long trail of vexations and humiliations, traumas and psychological wounds, it was, as Alma Mahler asserts, 'a serious illness'.[15] Often it radically changed the personalities of the émigrés. Lion Feuchtwanger maintained that those who had been courageous sometimes became cowards, whilst the cowardly grew courageous, the modest greedy, the solitary asocial or servile: 'They are like fruit that has been plucked from the tree too soon, not ripe or even dry and bitter.'[16] And Manès Sperber wrote in similar vein: 'Many personal problems came to torment the fugitive extremely, and force him to seek immediate solutions, but as he found himself, through no fault of his own, in no state to even try and escape from these, he gradually got used to ending up leaving everything in suspense.'[17]

This shift in the émigré's personality as a result of the exile experience has been the object of interesting analysis on the part of the exiles themselves.[18] It played a major role not only in their creative work, but also in their respective political or religious development. It was hard to imagine that a writer like Ernst

Glaeser would abandon emigration and return to Germany, or that Thomas Mann would become an exile leader. How many counterparts did the protagonist of Ernst Ottwalt's novel, the émigré who became a Gestapo spy, have in real life?

While they changed countries, languages and cultures, the émigrés also saw their beliefs shift. Non-religious Jews became religious – even, like Döblin, converting to Catholicism – while believers became atheists. Former Jewish Communists became convinced Zionists. Orthodox Marxists finished up as reactionaries; some of the fiercest opponents of Communism in the 1950s had been equally fanatical Communists in the interwar years. Émigré correspondence and memoirs, therefore, cannot be read without a certain caution. Exile had its share of both generosity and egoism, fraternity and meanness, senseless hope and boundless despair. Its literary, philosophical and political expressions would be incomprehensible without the dramatic experience that fuelled and illuminated them.

REFUGEE STATUS

But very shortly he was awakened. A young man dressed like a townsman, with the face of an actor, his eyes narrow and his eyebrows strongly marked, was standing beside him along with the landlord. The peasants were still in the room, and a few had turned their chairs round so as to see and hear better. The young man apologized very courteously for having awakened K., [. . .] and then said: 'This village belongs to the Castle, and whoever lives here or passes the night here does so in a manner of speaking in the Castle itself. Nobody may do that without the Count's permission. But you have no such permit, or at least you have produced none.'

Franz Kafka, *The Castle*

The passport is the noblest part of a man. A passport, moreover, cannot be manufactured so easily. A man can be made any old how, the most dumb way in the world and without any rational motive, but a passport never can. The value of a good passport is always recognized, whilst the value of a man, however great it may be, is by no means necessarily acknowledged.

Bertolt Brecht, *Exile Dialogues*

Many émigré accounts that depict the quest for a residence permit, a passport or a visa, bear an undeniable affinity to the novels of Kafka. Like the Surveyor or Joseph K., the exile is confronted with powers that are both inflexible and anonymous – those of the Castle and its invisible masters – or more prosaically, the arbitrariness of an official, a prefect, an embassy attaché or a consul. Never a concrete individual, the refugee becomes a legal abstraction, a concept, an embarrassing problem for the offices and countries that shunt him from pillar to post. Klaus Mann sadly noted[19] how in a world of national states and nationalisms, a stateless man could only arouse distrust; for as Heinrich Mann put it, 'power only recognizes power'.[20] Whatever he does, the exile is always wrong. In his first weeks of exile in Paris, Klaus Mann was insulted by an

American woman in a restaurant for speaking German: a German could only be a Nazi. He was subsequently reproached for having left Germany: 'There was no reason for a decent and orderly citizen to run away from his country, no matter what kind of government happened to be in power.'[21] Discovery of what refugee status meant was experienced by the majority of émigrés of 1933 with a mixture of anguish and revulsion. Opposition is not loved anywhere, the poet Max Hermann-Neisse laconically noted.

A man, even a hungry man, is still a man, simply weaker. Without papers, however, the émigré is only a hybrid creature, whose physical reality may be undeniable but whose legal existence has become questionable. It is in no way surprising that the passport problem held such a place in the lives and works of the antifascist exiles.[22] After Hitler, it was often their main obsession.[23] Klaus Mann, in 1938, asked: 'What Frenchman, Englishman or American can imagine what it means not to have a passport? A man without a passport is a semi-man, unable to live. We, the emigrants, learned this, and we learn it again each day.'[24] He concluded, not without reason, that a valid passport was as necessary as a shadow, its loss as catastrophic as that obsessing Peter Schlemihl. When a German refugee's passport expired, he gradually lost his legal existence. Even Thomas Mann, as his correspondence and diaries show, was not free from this concern.[25] As for requesting the Reich authorities to renew a passport, this was either impossible or something an émigré could not bring himself to do. The situation was all the more catastrophic for the majority of refugees in that they did not even have a passport in the first place, or had not bothered about its validity. In any case, after 1938 almost all the émigrés found themselves with expired passports,[26] and few countries were ready to grant them new ones. This lack of a valid passport made movement increasingly difficult, even for well-known figures.[27] Their existence was in fact a real legal imbroglio; they were citizens of a neighbouring state, but their own country refused to regularize their situation, as if they were criminals or swindlers. They now found themselves abandoned to the arbitrariness of European regulations on immigration, and with police officials able to drive them from one frontier to another.[28] The need to prove one's identity, despite being deprived of documentation, constantly gave rise to tragic-comic situations such as even Kafka's black humour would not have dreamed up.[29] The climate of xenophobia that intensified in the years leading up to the War only aggravated the émigrés' situation.

The measures taken by the Reich, which stripped a large number of exiles of German nationality, added new elements to the legal complexity of their status. The German legal code only provided for deprivation of nationality in very limited cases.[30] The Hitler regime, however, arrogated itself the right to deprive anyone of German nationality if they failed to show loyalty to the state,[31] or refused to return to Germany when ordered to do so. These measures struck two categories of individual right away: Jews from the east to whom the Weimar Republic had granted German nationality, and anti-Nazi émigrés.

By 1936, the Nazis had published seven lists with the names of individuals who had been 'ausgebürgert' (deprived of nationality), about three hundred in total.[32] These were for the most part political opponents, artists, journalists and academics who were known for their antifascist ideas. By the end of 1938, five thousand others had been deprived of their nationality, followed by a further three thousand in 1939. The initial choice of names was fairly arbitrary, depending largely on texts that the émigrés had signed in exile. The first list of 23 April 1933 (*Liste I*) included Alfred Kerr, Heinrich Mann, Willi Münzenberg, Leopold Schwarzschild, Otto Wels, Phillip Scheidemann and Kurt Tucholsky.[33] Einstein was deprived of his nationality as a Jew and an opponent of the Nazi regime on the second list (24 March 1934). *Liste III* (1 November 1934) struck chiefly those who had called for a vote against the reattachment of the Saar to the Reich (Ludwig Renn), taken part in propaganda action against Nazism (John Heartfield), or written against Hitler (Konrad Heiden, Rudolf Olden). This third list also included the names of Hans Beimler, Max Brauer, Willi Bredel, Leonhard Frank, Carola Neher, Prinz Hubertus zu Löwenstein, Prinz Hohenlohe-Langenburg, Klaus Mann, Erwin Piscator, Gustav Regler, Otto Strasser, Bodo Uhse, Gustav von Wangenheim, Eric Weinert and Alfred Kantorowicz. Thomas Mann did not lose German nationality until 1936, both because of his international fame, and his delay in taking a clear stand against the regime and rallying publicly to the emigration.

The criteria governing the selection and order of victims were fairly contradictory.[34] This measure affected also the victims' families. A law of 2 November 1933 ordered the rectors of all universities to withdraw from antifascists the university honours they had previously been awarded. Besides the celebrated case of Thomas Mann, and his exchange of letters with the rector of Bonn University which had withdrawn his doctoral title, Freiburg University did the same in 1937 with Alfons Goldschmidt, withdrawing his doctorate in law. He was extremely surprised, as he had in fact never received this. Tübingen University did the same with Hermann Budzislawski. Finally, in September 1941, *Ausbürgerung* was applied to all Jews who had left Germany or were remaining abroad.

In a first phase, the émigrés generally did not take these measures to heart. They used them, in fact, for their attacks on the Reich, maintaining that by withdrawing their nationality the regime had conferred on them an honour of which they hoped to prove worthy. The measure seemed so absurd that it was hard to take it seriously. Alfred Falk, a member of the Human Rights League and the German Movement for Peace, who figured on the first list, even had it printed on his visiting card as an honorific title. Klaus Mann saw it as a way of combating the émigrés' protests: 'If we were no longer Germans, our denunciation would be a bit less scandalous', and deplored the stupidity of an administrative measure that pretended to separate people from the country in which they were born by a stroke of the pen.[35]

In fact, it did not take the émigrés long to perceive that this was not a mere aberration attesting only to the Nazis' impotent rage against them – comparable, as Leopold Schwarzschild put it, to the fable of the fox and the grapes. Even if European public opinion was well disposed towards those whom the Nazis had deprived of nationality, as far as the governments of the countries in which they had taken refuge were concerned they were now not simply German, however undesirable or burdensome, but 'stateless'. In certain countries, Switzerland for example, the loss of German nationality rendered any existing residence permit null and void, even if the émigré's passport was still valid. Moreover, it now became possible to refuse them a residence permit altogether. The majority of European countries were in no way minded to grant refugees a new nationality.[36] This could only be legally obtained if the émigré stayed between three and ten years in the country in question (as far as France and Belgium were concerned) and had adequate means of existence.[37] These conditions were supplemented by a range of additional clauses, such as knowledge of the language and culture, or performance of military service.[38] Some refugees therefore turned to Latin America, where it was possible to obtain nationality by procedures that were legally dubious, as well as costly.[39] A few fortunate exiles managed to obtain naturalization before 1939 in the country where they were resident, often only thanks to a good deal of support and recommendation. This is how Alfred Döblin became French in 1936, as well as Annette Kolb (with the assistance of Jean Giradoux, several of whose works she had translated into German). Bruno Walter and Friedrich W. Foerster likewise obtained French nationality in 1938,[40] as did Siegfried Trebitsch. Britain granted nationality to three prominent exiles: Erika Mann,[41] Stefan Zweig, and the former ambassador Baron Franckenstein. Austria offered Thomas Mann citizenship in 1936, if he would settle in Vienna, but the situation in Austria was so dangerous that he declined the offer. He finally took Czech nationality.[42] Carl Zuckmayer, a refugee in Austria since 1933, acquired Austrian nationality, and Franz Csokor became Polish in 1939; as a translator of Polish novels, he spoke the language perfectly. Other émigrés sometimes acquired Spanish nationality for serving as emissaries for the Spanish Republic (Gustav Regler, for example, on his mission to the United States). Alfred Wolfenstein also became a Czech citizen, as did Hans Habe (of Hungarian descent). But for every naturalization granted a writer, a hundred others were rejected. Many émigrés were forced to obtain papers illegally, while for women one of the simplest solutions was to contract a formal marriage with a citizen (Dutch or British) in order to obtain a passport. If a German citizen could become Portuguese for 10,000 Swiss francs, it only cost 2,000 or so for certain Latin American countries. This is how Valeriu Marcu travelled with a Honduran passport, Bruno Frank with one from Panama, and Leo Matthias with a Guatemalan one. These bogus passports were available only to the more moneyed émigrés, and did not always prove valid.[43]

THE QUEST FOR A VISA

Obtaining provisional refugee status did not give any kind of guarantee, as the émigré could not travel without a visa: a problem that in 1940 became so dramatic that it drove some people to suicide.

Ludwig Marcuse claims in his autobiography that he would gladly have given his soul for an American visa.[44] This is very easy to understand. In 1940, such a visa represented the only way of escaping arrest by the Gestapo and probable death. But even before 1940, the quest for a visa was already an established part of the émigré's calvary. If an exile wanted for example to visit other exiles in a neighbouring country, he needed not only a visa, but assurance that he would be authorized to return. For those who did not have a valid passport, obtaining a visa was often impossible, and the diversity of legal regulations in Europe transformed this hunt for a visa into a macabre farce. Stefan Zweig described this situation in *The World of Yesterday*, in terms so poignant as to need no further commentary:

> But I had to solicit the English certificate. It was a favour that I had to ask for, and what is more, a favour that could be withdrawn at any moment. Overnight I found myself one rung lower. Only yesterday, still a visitor from abroad and, so to speak, a gentleman who was spending his international income and paying his taxes, now I had become an immigrant, a 'refugee'. I had slipped down to a lesser, even if not dishonourable, category. Besides that, every foreign visa on this travel paper had thenceforth to be specially pleaded for, because all countries were suspicious of the 'sort' of people of which I had suddenly become one, of the outlaws, of the men without a country, whom one could not at a pinch pack off and deport to their own State as they could others if they became undesirable or stayed too long.

He also remembered the words of a Russian émigré: 'Formerly man had only a body and soul. Now he needs a passport as well, for without it he will not be treated as a human being.'[45] Zweig recalled nostalgically the period before the First World War, when an international border could be crossed as easily as a line of longitude. Whereas one's first steps in a new country used to lead to a museum, he remarks, they now lead to the police station or consulate:

> When those of us who had once conversed about Baudelaire's poetry and spiritedly discussed intellectual problems met together, we would catch ourselves talking about affidavits and permits and whether one should apply for an immigration visa or a tourist visa; acquaintance with a stenographer in a consulate who could cut down one's waiting-time was more significant to one's existence than friendship with a Toscanini or a Rolland. Human beings were made to feel that they were objects and not subjects, that nothing was their right but everything merely a favour by official grace. They were codified, registered, numbered, stamped and even today I, as a case-hardened creature of an age of freedom and a citizen of the world-republic of my dreams, count every impression of a rubber-stamp in my passport a stigma, every one of those hearings and searches a humiliation.[46]

Zweig also maintains that from the day on which he had to live with a foreign passport, something of his natural identity melted away. After 'training my heart' for nearly half a century to beat as a citizen of the world, he discovered that losing one's country means 'more than parting with a circumscribed area of soil'.[47] And yet few countries would have refused a visa to someone like Stefan Zweig. It was quite a different case for an author known for his radical political ideas, a Communist sympathizer, or a political activist. Hermann Kesten, who travelled to Amsterdam in 1938, was not allowed to return by train to France, Belgium refusing him entry on the pretext 'that he was not a Nazi', as he ironically put it. On 1 December 1938 he wrote to W. A. Berendsohn to obtain a Danish visa for Soma Morgenstern, the *Frankfurter Zeitung*'s correspondent in Vienna, whose Austrian passport had expired and who risked internment in Dachau. Very often, the exiles had the feeling that their fate hung on the arbitrary decision of some official, a secretary at a consulate or embassy. From 1940 on, the visa question became desperate: their only hope of leaving Europe was to obtain a US visa. Leonhard Frank had still not managed to obtain one by 1 October 1940.[48] He went every day to the Lisbon consul, and wrote to all his friends to come to his aid. Finally he obtained a Mexican visa, but this was no longer any use as his passport had expired. He then wrote to the Swiss publisher Emil Oprecht: 'If Thomas Mann learns that I've been given a Mexican visa, he will believe I've been saved, and won't do anything more to get me an American visa. Then I'm lost.'[49] Walter Victor also confided in a letter to Oprecht Verlag, on 13 July 1940, that 'the American consul in Marseille is the man on whom my fate depends'. Valeriu Marcu wrote ironically to Hermann Kesten on 27 September 1940: 'You cannot travel to Portugal without an American visa. Or at least possessing a valid passport – something that only the gods of Olympus possess.' Kesten's wife could only obtain a visa for Venezuela, Santo Domingo or Cuba. To get there, a US transit visa was needed, obtainable from the Marseille consul. To leave France, however, a transit visa for Spain and Portugal was also necessary. But France refused to give visas to antifascists, and without the French exit visa, it was impossible to obtain the Spanish and Portuguese visas.

As Alfred Polgar wrote: 'Hitler was quicker than the consuls, on whose good spirits the saving visas depended.'[50] Obtaining these required support, protection, and money, on all of which the majority of émigrés fell short.[51] This legal aspect of the émigrés' situation, therefore, was for each a source of daily suffering, before becoming a theme of exile literature or a chapter in a memoir.

2. THE ECONOMIC SURVIVAL OF THE ÉMIGRÉS

Every week and every month refugees arrived in growing numbers and each lot was poorer and in greater consternation than the one that came before. The first ones, those who had been prompt to leave Germany and Austria, had still managed to save their clothes, their baggage, their household goods; some even had a little money. But the longer one of them had placed trust in Germany, the greater his reluctance to wrench himself from his beloved home, the more severely he had been punished.

Stefan Zweig, *The World of Yesterday*

THE ÉMIGRÉS' MATERIAL SITUATION

And if I asked somewhere for something to live on,
They always said to me: what a cheek.

Bertolt Brecht, 'Poem V'

By leaving Germany the exiles had saved their lives, but often no more than that. They did not even know how they would survive the next few days. The majority of political activists had little money anyway and could not take it with them. The writers of the Weimar Republic, with a few exceptions, were not well-to-do. They found themselves cut off not only from their public, but also from their royalties. Their books had been burned or banned. Journalists could no longer hope to contribute to the German press. All knew that it would be hard to write in exile. If an author such as Thomas Mann or Lion Feuchtwanger was sure to be published and translated in most countries, this was not the case with others, either little known or reputedly difficult. As far as dramatists were concerned, they were well aware that few countries would agree to stage works officially condemned by the Reich. Even Horvath's old works were no longer performed in Vienna. In some countries, such as Switzerland, they were not even allowed to write. And if they tried, with iron in the soul, to follow another profession, they risked expulsion or withdrawal of their residence permit. The existence of exile publishing houses and a certain German-language readership until 1939 could keep some writers above the poverty line, but this linguistic and literary space steadily contracted as the grip of National Socialism spread. And even the royalties that some exile publishers generously paid were not enough to live on. The émigré reviews were poor and ephemeral, their print-runs were generally limited, and they were read by an equally impoverished public.

The example of writers, at least, suggests that social differences were further exacerbated in the exile situation. Thomas Mann was right to fear an SA attack on his house in Munich and the confiscation of his bank accounts, but he did not have to fear dying of hunger.[52] He might well recall that Old German had two words to denote an emigrant: *Recke* which meant someone banned, and *Elend* which meant someone without a country. But Mann always lived comfortably in exile, both in Europe and the United States, thanks to the proceeds that his books brought him from their international sales. In a tribute to Lion Feuchtwanger[53] he expressed his regret that Goebbels was never able to admire the splendid house where Feuchtwanger lived at Sanary, and the 'seaside castle' he owned in California. Few émigré writers knew such well-being. Most famous writers were impoverished by exile, and those less famous were completely ruined. The former had to curtail their lifestyle, the latter had to beg food from more fortunate colleagues or from committees.

Alfred Kantorowicz, for example, describes a typical day in the life of an exile, that of 27 September 1935. In his hotel room he discussed with three friends the possibility of founding a magazine, and met with a representative of the SDS. He worked for some time on his novel. As his wife had managed to get ten francs from the aid office, he was able to buy cigarettes, milk and bread.

Unfortunately he forgot to keep part of this money to pay for telephone calls, and the hotel refused to give him credit. A friend gave him one franc in exchange for some cigarettes and tea.[54] Arthur Koestler describes his emigration in France in fairly similar terms: 'During some weeks of extreme penury I was forced to sleep in a hayloft in a Paris suburb and to walk every day several miles on an empty stomach to the Party office where I worked without pay. I was lightheaded with hunger and my shoes were falling to pieces [. . .].'[55]

A few émigrés managed to transfer part of their assets, but these were only a small minority.[56] Not only was the export of capital forbidden, but anyone who left the Reich had to pay a tax (*Reichsfluchtsteuer*). The transfer of assets was also taxed at a very high rate if it was done legally.[57] The conditions of emigration continued to worsen from 1933 to 1938, this tax being replaced by the confiscation of assets. As a general rule, the émigrés saved little of what they possessed in Germany, not even their libraries or manuscripts.[58] The left organizations, for their part, often managed to preserve some of their assets. Willi Münzenberg avoided the confiscation of his publications by entrusting them to the Soviet embassy, and Max Horkheimer had already transferred abroad part of the finances of the Institut für Sozialforschung. It remains true despite this that the majority of exiles lost all their belongings on leaving Germany.[59]

POSSIBILITY OF WORK AND RE-ESTABLISHMENT

> There are places where I could earn a minimal income, and places where I could live on a minimal income, but not a single place where these two conditions coincide.
> Walter Benjamin, letter to Gershom Scholem, 28 February 1933

The difficulties that the émigrés met with in organizing their new existence are easy to imagine. Many activists lived off aid, or embarked on manual trades. As for those in the liberal professions, they had little prospect of re-establishing themselves, given the restrictive legislation of the countries in which they took refuge.[60] Only those academics who found places in foreign universities were more fortunate, though this depended on both their specialism and their celebrity.

The situation of writers was especially tragic. Very few still had the slightest possibility of getting their work published in Germany, though some did manage this by using pseudonyms or with the help of non-Nazi friends. Walter Benjamin continued publishing book reviews under a false identity until 1935, in the *Frankfurter Zeitung*. On 16 October 1935 he described his material situation to Max Horkheimer in the following terms:

> I am consequently now living as a boarder with some other émigrés. Beyond that, I have succeeded in obtaining permission to take my midday meal at a restaurant that has a special arrangement for French intellectuals. In the first place, however, this permission is only temporary and, in the second place, I can make use of it only on

those days I am not in the library, for the restaurant is very far from there. I will only mention in passing that I ought to renew my *carte d'identité* but do not have the 100 francs this requires. Since it involves a fee of 50 francs, I have also not yet been able to join the Presse Étrangère, which I was urged to do for administrative reasons.[61]

Ernst Erich Noth also managed to draw fictitious royalties for a novel already published and another that could no longer be published. The director of the *Frankfurter Zeitung*, Heinrich Simon, helped him until he was dismissed. In the same way, the *Berliner Tageblatt* assisted many of its former contributors. Some writers (Annette Kolb, Thomas Mann, René Schickele) remained in connection with Fischer Verlag until 1934. Those writers who had not taken a public position against the regime were still able to receive their royalties, but these were paid in Germany and it was increasingly hard to transfer them abroad. The book burnings of 10 May 1933, the promulgation of blacklists and the purging of publishing firms and bookshops, soon deprived most writers of any revenue.[62]

They had to try and publish their books abroad, or set up publishing houses in exile. In practice, only very well-known writers could hope to be translated into other languages. Others, and poets in particular, had no chance of interesting a publisher in an unknown work. For want of a readership, some authors stopped writing. As for the print-runs typical of these exile publishers (Emmanuel Querido, Allert de Lange, Emil Oprecht), they were often so limited that they could not be of great help to the writers concerned. There did indeed exist outside of Germany a potential readership for works in the German original (thirty to forty thousand, according to Wieland Herzfelde), but this was not enough to support émigré publishing. The market was saturated with books from the Reich, which reduced their sale price by 25 per cent for export, while it was often hard for bookshops to get hold of émigré works. Even the merger of Querido and Bermann Fischer in 1938 did not enable them to compete with Reich publications, and this collaboration did not endure. With the exception of publishers tied to political parties (as Graphia Verlaganstalt of Karlovy Vary was to the SPD, or Willi Münzenberg's Carrefour imprint to the KPD), few publishers were in a position to promote the works of exiles effectively. Apart from Querido Verlag, the German division of Allert de Lange, Bermann Fischer and Emil Oprecht, other exile imprints were ephemeral creations, and it was only in the USSR that exile works could achieve large print-runs. Others were often limited to a thousand copies or even less. Their publication was undertaken for ideological rather than commercial reasons, and the losses that arose from these works were compensated by the profit of others. Between 1933 and 1940 Querido Verlag published 110 titles by fifty-three authors, but only six of these authors were émigrés.[63] Bermann Fischer published seventy-five titles from 1936 to 1940 of which forty were by émigrés, Allert de Lange eighty-seven including fifteen by émigrés. As for the publishing firms set up by the exiles themselves, they published no more than some fifty titles altogether. Some publishers, out of solidarity, paid a kind of monthly stipend to a few exiled authors, in order to enable them to live and work. At least this stopped them from dying of hunger.[64]

*   *   *

Contributions to newspapers and magazines brought little financial return. The émigrés published more than 400 periodicals, but the majority of these had very small runs, soon disappeared, and were often bought only by other émigrés. Since these had little money, and the émigrés who sent in an essay, poem, review or article were many, they could only pay a derisory fee. Even as a regular contributor, no émigré managed to live from this. The payments were simply 'tips', as Max Brod called them.[65] Exiled authors often sought to contribute to a number of periodicals, and in the climate of poverty and humiliation that marked their lives it was not uncommon to see them quarrel or fall out over fees unpaid or too low. One of the most tragic examples of such misunderstandings was the break between Walter Benjamin and Klaus Mann.

Even when he lived in Berlin, Walter Benjamin was already burdened with financial worries. He lived as an 'independent writer', trying to place his articles in literary reviews or daily papers, often finding them rejected for their seeming obscurity or rarely paid for. On 28 February 1933 he wrote to Gershom Scholem:

> The little composure that people in my circles were able to muster in the face of the new regime was rapidly spent, and one realizes that the air is hardly fit to breathe anymore – a condition which of course loses significance as one is being strangled anyway. This above all economically: the opportunities the radio offered from time to time and which were my only serious prospects will probably vanish so completely that even 'Lichtenberg', though commissioned, is not sure to be produced. The disintegration of the *Frankfurter Zeitung* marches on. The editor of the feuilleton page has been relieved of his duties, even though he had demonstrated at least some commercial aptitude by his acquisition of my *Berliner Kindheit* at a ridiculously low price.[66]

Benjamin quickly realized that no newspaper in the Reich would accept any further work of his. As a refugee in Ibiza, he started to write without documentary support an article on the sociology of French literature for the *Zeitschrift für Sozialforschung*, 'since I can at least count on being paid by them'.[67] On 16 June 1933 he wrote to Scholem: 'Since leaving Berlin, I've averaged a monthly income of about 100 reichsmarks, and this under the most unfavorable conditions. I don't wish to imply that I might not manage to earn even less than this tiny sum.'[68] He sought to find new commissions for articles or to write under pseudonyms. He followed closely the development of new laws on the German press, to see if he would still be able to contribute to certain periodicals. Soon he asked Theodor Adorno, and especially his wife Gretl, to help him: 'If you were to put some noble logs on my hearth, you would be associated with my best hours, and the plume of my smoke above the house would blow over to you on the 15th.'[69]

From January 1934, Benjamin was completely dependent on the Frankfurt Institute, on Max Horkheimer,[70] and on the generosity of Brecht. As for the émigré periodicals, most of them did not pay their contributors at all. Thus, in a letter addressed to Brecht on 20 May 1935, Benjamin explained to him the pitiful incident that had led to his break with Klaus Mann, publisher of *Die Sammlung*, over his review of Brecht's *Threepenny Novel*:

> The long and short of it is that I viewed as an insult the proposed honorarium of 150 French francs for a twelve-page manuscript that had been commissioned by the editorial board – without having the slightest inclination to overestimate the market value of my production. In a short letter, I asked for 250 francs and refused to let him have the manuscript for less. Thereupon, even though it was already typeset, it was returned to me.[71]

In justified despair, Benjamin tried to get his article translated into Czech and published in Prague.

The émigré periodicals all paid derisory fees.[72] In the Weimar years these had been just something extra for intellectuals, but now they became one of their rare sources of literary income. The majority of émigrés, in their letters or memoirs, recount having waited for payment for an article in order to pay their hotel bill.[73] A further example of the distress of these writers in exile is given by the last years of Robert Musil. Well before the Nazis came to power he already lived in very precarious financial conditions. Only the support of a group of passionate admirers enabled him to continue his work.[74] He left Berlin in summer 1933 and returned to Vienna. While detesting the Nazis, Musil was fairly sceptical about politics in general. A new 'Musil society' was formed in Vienna by Bruno Fürst, with the support of a couple of dozen enthusiastic readers.[75] When the Nazis invaded Austria, he had to flee, and in December 1938 he settled in Zurich, protected by a Protestant pastor and the Committee for the Settlement of Refugee Intellectuals. There he spent the last years of his life in solitude and poverty. When the committee stopped supporting him, he could count only on the charity of private individuals. Swiss legislation prohibited him from publishing. He died on 22 April 1942, victim of a stroke, in the most complete destitution. According to his last wishes, his wife scattered his ashes in a forest. News of his death was announced in Germany with a brief sentence in the *Frankfurter Zeitung*. It was impossible to find a publisher for his posthumous works in Switzerland.

After the banning of their books in Germany, many émigrés tried hard to have them translated in the countries where they had taken refuge. Such translation, unfortunately, was possible only for the most famous authors, a privileged minority,[76] or for certain political essays that sometime achieved quite large print-runs,[77] which was rarely the case with novels. The fact of being translated into several languages was not however synonymous with commercial success,[78] and only a few authors managed to live off these translations (Thomas Mann, Lion Feuchtwanger, Vicki Baum, Erich Maria Remarque, Stefan Zweig, Emil Ludwig and to some extent Franz Werfel). As a general rule, translations did not bring in much money.[79]

Some writers carried out work related to their intellectual activities, especially translations, but these brought them neither money nor fame.[80] The translation of foreign works into German for émigré publishers was another meagre opportunity, but after 1938 it was no longer possible to work for publishers in Austria, Czechoslovakia or Switzerland. As for lectures and public addresses, these were possible only for the 'heroes' of the émigré world. In the majority of cases even they did not bring much in. Thomas Mann was alone in giving regular 'shows' in the United States, acclaimed often by a very motley audience who had come just to see 'the great European writer'. For many exiles lectures were just an opportunity for getting their work known. Frequent events of this kind were organized by the SDS in Paris, but generally they only attracted other émigrés. Besides, few authors apart from Thomas Mann were capable of expressing themselves in a foreign language. The general public only came out to see 'stars', whose glory was often passing: Emil Ludwig, author of historical biographies, could fill a hall, as could Hermann Rauschning, but Robert Musil drew an attendance of just fifteen. The organizers of the PEN Club only invited famous writers, for whom the earnings from these lectures were not a vital necessity. If some enjoyed these triumphal tours,[81] for others they were a forced labour that was necessary to keep body and soul together.[82] These lectures were also a way of struggling against Hitlerite propaganda,[83] but they were not enough for anyone to live on, and often had their humiliating side.[84]

Attempts to contribute to the foreign press could also prove very disappointing. As soon as they arrived in their country of exile, the émigrés tried to form links with progressive newspapers, both to draw attention to the situation in Germany and to try to write for them. Even if the fees paid were low, they were very much better than those paid by the exile press. Some émigrés did manage quite easily to contribute to German-language papers in Austria and especially Czechoslovakia. But this was not possible in Switzerland, where it was radically prohibited, or in France, as very few of the émigrés could express themselves correctly in a foreign language, with rare exceptions such as Heinrich Mann, Ernst Erich Noth or Alfred Kerr. Besides, many papers refused for political reasons to accept contributions from German refugees.[85] Far from increasing the papers' readership, their articles aroused the hate of all reactionary milieus, especially the far right. In certain cases, their contributions were officially banned after protests from the Reich authorities. And in any case, there were too many émigrés to hope for even the most modest regular employment in the foreign press.[86]

Each bulletin of a Hitler victory makes me lose my significance as a writer.
Bertolt Brecht, *Journals*, 25 February 1939

Dramatists might hope to draw a certain income from their work in countries where a German-language theatre existed. But these were little performed – even works by Toller, Brecht and Horvath – and theatres were generally reluctant to stage them, for fear of right-wing demonstrations against the émigrés. Apart from the few exile theatres, only one work of Brecht was performed in Sweden, and *The Threepenny Opera* had only four productions between 1933 and 1939, including one in Shanghai. Though plays by German émigrés attracted an intellectual audience, they failed to reach a wider public. Austrian theatres shunned the plays of von Horvath, and Walter Hasenclever tried unsuccessfully to interest British theatres in his work.[87] Though Friedrich Wolf's play *Professor Mamlok* had a certain success, this was only because Nazi harassment had caused a scandal on its production in Zurich. Political cabaret, more modest and less expensive, sometimes proved more effective as a means of propaganda.

A number of émigrés considered working for the cinema as a way of escaping their misfortune, especially after 1939 in Hollywood. A certain number of writers had already thought up film projects during their exile years in Europe.[88] But while many writers had worked for the German cinema before 1933, in exile they did so above all to earn a living.[89] For most émigrés the cinema proved a mirage, as witnessed by the number of aborted projects and screenplays never filmed.

Unable to continue their profession abroad, the majority of émigrés had to live from any expedient. The most well-to-do started by selling what they had been able to rescue from Germany, ending up with their books. Women sold their jewellery to pay for a hotel room, clothing or bread.[90] Some were helped by their families, who managed to send them funds clandestinely. Most frequently, it was thanks to the work of their wives that these émigré writers managed to escape destitution. If Ernst Bloch could write *The Principle of Hope* in his American exile, it was because Karola Bloch worked as a waitress and subsequently as an architect. In many European countries, legislation on women's work was less restrictive than on that of men. These wives were ready to undertake banal or humiliating work which their husbands would not. From being wives of literati and journalists, or working as actresses and teachers, they became cleaners, home helps, cooks and seamstresses. They experienced the anxiety of all refugees: without a work permit they could not practise a profession, and without resources they could not obtain a residence permit. They were generally prevented from exercising skills from which their host country would have profited.[91] If they worked without authorization they risked expulsion, and they risked the same if they were without resources.[92] They therefore undertook any kind of activity as soon as this was authorized.

There is a surrealist aspect to listing the jobs done by émigré writers between 1933 and 1945. Carl Zuckmayer, a dramatist, grew maize in Vermont; E. J. Aufricht, producer of *The Threepenny Opera*, reared cattle; the publisher Rolf Passer grew tobacco; Arthur Koestler was in turn monitor at a children's centre, cook, editor on piecework and home help. Elisabeth Castonnier sold papers in the Vienna streets, Max Zinnering washed dishes in a Paris restaurant, worked in a factory, became a builder's apprentice, a farmer in Palestine and proofreader for *Die Rote Fahne* in Switzerland. Franz Pfemfert, former editor-in-chief of the magazine *Die Aktion*, was a travelling photographer in the United States. To pay his passage to America, where he had obtained a teaching post, Leo Matthias had to start a cleaning business in Amsterdam, and save up for six months. Paul Zech (winner of the Kleist Prize in 1919) worked in Buenos Aires as a bar-room pianist and night watchman. Hans Natonek washed corpses in a morgue. A large number of intellectuals became secretaries, typists, book-keepers, hotel porters or errand boys. Many political activists became manual workers.[93] Poets such as Hanns Henry Jahn or Walter Hasenclever also worked as farmers. For the most part, the experience of exile meant a constant fear of destitution and appeal to the aid committees.

THE AID COMMITTEES

Whether international or private, underground or official, the various commit-tees formed to assist the German émigrés not only offered legal protection and moral support, but prevented them from drowning in poverty and despair. There were religious and political committees, set up by governments or by the major workers' parties, and they certainly helped alleviate the refugees' fate and did something to remedy their distress, in the face of the selfishness of most European governments. They represented a sincere effort of solidarity as well as an awareness of the need to assist in all possible ways those who had fought against fascism or been its first victims. There were many committees, though most émigrés claim to have been aware of just a small number, but their financial means were very limited, and went on shrinking as the number of émigrés grew and reaction towards them hardened. Their assistance was more-over only first aid, and limited to a strict minimum – legal defence, a little money, refectory tickets, a possible lodging in some kind of hostel. In no case could an émigré hope to live off this assistance for any length of time.

The support of these committees was supplemented by the efforts made by some literary or political figures and the most famous among the émigrés. For all the dissension among exiled writers, there is no doubt that Thomas and Heinrich Mann, Ernst Toller, Ludwig Marcuse, Franz Werfel and Stefan Zweig constantly used their prestige to rescue émigrés in distress, and their royalties to assist those most in need. It was thanks to them that a number of antifascists were able to obtain the necessary affidavits, 'emergency visas', financial guarantees or tickets that enabled them to leave for the United States in 1940. Many were ready to share their earnings with their poorest colleagues (Erich Maria Remarque, Stefan Zweig), and use these to establish bursaries for exiled writers or literary awards. A large number helped their colleagues materially at one point or another (Emil Ludwig, Ferdinand Bruckner, Ernst Toller, Lion Feuchtwanger, Carl Zuck-mayer). They organized collections to enable them to leave France. And many writers – including Joseph Roth – could only survive in exile thanks to the generosity of these others (in particular that of Stefan Zweig). Undoubtedly the daily life of the exile was somewhat eased by such actions, for all the rivalries, unavowed hatreds and old quarrels. Several managed to live from these little bits of help.[94] Derisory as these sums often were, they saved a large number of exiles from destitution or suicide, and it is impossible to stress too greatly the im-portance of such organizations as the Comité National des Réfugiés Allemands Victimes de l'Antisémitisme, which by November had already assisted 9,000 refugees, International Red Aid, the Matteoti Committee and the Ligue des

Droits de l'Homme. Even when financial aid was limited, legal assistance was often crucial in saving someone or other from expulsion or imprisonment. The émigré might be able to count on nothing more than a hot meal, a bed, some advice and a few francs, but this support was essential. In many countries it was accompanied by an upsurge of generosity on the part of a greater or lesser section of the population, and the protection and support provided by some prominent figures wishing to come to the aid of these refugees.[95]

There were hardly more than a dozen writers in a position to lead a more or less satisfactory existence in exile, in material terms. The others all experienced phases of relative equilibrium punctuated by poverty. Neither the aid from the committees nor the meagre opportunities of work which they found enabled them to live a normal life. Most were hurled down the social ladder, to a situation that few had previously known. Almost all underwent the same humiliations, even the most favoured, and what Alma Mahler says of Franz Werfel held for most of them: 'He was cherished by the gods from his childhood until his fortieth year. Nothing was lacking to make him happy: parents, sisters, family fortune, growing fame . . . and then, suddenly, the persecution against the Jews in Germany . . . His works were burned, he was no longer celebrated; in the eyes of the population, which now imposed its tastes, he was just a little Jew of mediocre talent.'[96]

3. PSYCHOLOGICAL EFFECTS

If, as Alma Mahler maintained, emigration was 'a serious illness', it was because it involved an upheaval in both material existence and the individual personality. Their relationship to such aspects of everyday life as space, culture, country and mother tongue kept shifting. These experiences were common to all the exiles, and if we pick out those of writers in particular, it is because they show this exile experience in striking relief through their novels, memoirs, diaries and correspondence.[97] Rooted deep as they were in German culture and language, they were perhaps the most sadly affected by this separation, which they never ceased to feel as a wound.

UPROOTING AND LONELINESS

It hurts to be uprooted.

Alexandre Granach, September 1935

He who is spared by hunger is prevented from sleeping by homesickness, like Heine.

Heinrich Mann

The feeling of uprooting and loneliness depended on personal as well as objective factors.[98] It varied greatly from one émigré to another. Walter A. Berendsohn, at home in Scandinavian languages and literature, doubtless felt less uprooted in Denmark than did Brecht. Heinrich Mann, Alfred Döblin,

René Schickele, Klaus Mann and Joseph Roth, who could express themselves in French, did not have confront a barrier that was so fearsome for other exiles. As Klaus Mann wrote: 'We lived in Amsterdam, Zurich or Paris without feeling in exile in these great cities. Paris had long been a kind of second home.' It is much harder to imagine the feelings of a German-Jewish actor in Shanghai, Paul Zech in Argentina or Willy Haas in Bombay. Some felt in exile as soon as they left Berlin, others when they crossed the German border, others again when the European coastline receded into the distance. Hans Natonek remarks that certain émigrés left Europe behind as one leaves a worn-out suit. He for his part kissed the American soil, afraid of being turned into a pillar of salt if he looked back.[99] Some writers managed to continue their work under foreign skies, in Paris or in Los Angeles, but others felt quite unable to write as soon as they were separated from German culture. Klaus Mann wrote his autobiography in English, but certain exiles lived with a fear of losing their mother tongue if they stopped speaking it, and were only able to express themselves in the dialect of their native region.

They had all left Germany in a state of sadness and panic, with the secret hope of returning very soon. Wolfgang Langhoff described his despair at leaving behind the last ramparts of the Black Forest, Rudolf H. Ganz his chagrin at leaving his city of Frankfurt. Fritz Kortner could not tear himself away from the Berlin theatres. Few indeed immediately realized what this separation from Germany would mean. The joy of having escaped the Gestapo or arrest by the SA was mixed with apprehension and curiosity about their new existence. Despite his sadness at fleeing Germany, Ludwig Marcuse could not prevent his ravished reaction to the countryside of Provence: 'Everything was sky blue, not just our morale.' For the first time in his life he saw fig trees, and the discovery of French wine and bread calmed the pangs of departure. Not only did they refuse to believe that their exile would last, but they trusted in a sympathetic welcome. Only slowly did they discover, in the words of Alfred Polgar, that not only had their country become foreign to them, but that the foreign land had not become their country.

Rejection by their homeland did not mean that they felt at home in their country of arrival. After the generosity with which some people received them, they experienced the pettiness and egoism of others. Their accent singled them out and disturbed those around them. Later on, they were often insulted for speaking German. The stigmata of the barbarism that had hunted them out of Germany were imposed upon them. A German, even a refugee, could not be a friend; the victim spoke the same language as his tormentor. It was at this point that they slowly began to feel the uprooting, the material and moral solitude, that led some of them to suicide. This often rapid degradation of the personality can be read on each page of some people's diaries and correspondence. Rejected by others, they withdrew into themselves and their little exile communities. These writers never wrote so much as they did in exile. They commented on their respective situations, explained their experiences, sadnesses and joys, exchanged manuscripts attentive to the advice of a friend or colleague who became both the editor and public that they were deprived of. Letters assumed a special importance in exile. It was these that bound the writers together, as well as to their country, their fate, their mother tongue and their common struggles, both political and in daily life. On 26 March 1939 Hermann Kesten wrote to Ernst Weiss, who committed suicide in Paris the following year: 'In recent weeks I've been living in utter despair and distraction. I want to write, but I scarcely have the strength to work. Yet I feel that only work can save us, at least morally: for can we be saved materially? I am so poor and disheartened.'

Living in cheap hotels or boarding-houses, the refugees gathered in small circles, often in cafés, to read their works, comment on the latest news from Germany – true or false – and share what little resources they had. In Paris or in Hollywood, a birthday was always an occasion to get together. Ernst Toller, one of the émigrés most terribly scarred by loneliness, threw a party for the fiftieth birthday of the poet Max Hermann-Neisse so that he would feel less abandoned. This old friend of George Grosz, exiled in London, was reduced to visiting the East End once a week to talk with a hotel porter who came from the same region as he did: as an uprooted poet, he cradled himself in the music of his native dialect. The genuine solidarity found among many writers is not an adequate symbol of this emigration. Jost Hermand asserted, not without reason,[100] that in the first years of exile there was never that 'humanist front' or 'antifascist front' that was so readily claimed after 1945. The prevailing mood among the émigrés was rather one of loneliness, despair, distrust and even hostility. As Wolf Frank wrote in 1935:[101] 'There were emigrants and emigrants. From start to finish it was not one single thing. [. . .] Businessmen were not concerned about political activists, nor were Social-Democrats for Communists [. . .]. The rich did not even want to hear of their poor companions in misfortune.'

These divisions were not absent even in the literary milieu, and added to the feeling of isolation. Literary styles, political options and living standards all divided them. Thomas Mann acknowledges that though living in Munich just as Lion Feuchtwanger did, he did not meet him until forty years later, in Sanary-sur-Mer in 1933. Mann refused to help the unfortunate Mynona (Salomo Friedländer) to reach the United States, as he didn't like him. Though his three cars were confiscated by the Munich SA, Mann never wanted for anything. In the Les Milles camp, Feuchtwanger was able to recruit 'domestic servants' among the poorer internees. But even Alfred Döblin, Heinrich Mann and Walter Benjamin often lived in a state close to destitution.

This was something that the countries that accepted refugees often did not want to know about, abandoning them to the charity of committees. Ludwig Marcuse, Arthur Koestler and Manès Sperber described in quite similar terms the discomfort they felt when their French friends mentioned the soirées they organized for one another, never imagining how much they would love to be invited. The psychological distress and black humour that mark the characters in Brecht's *Exile Dialogues*, who meet up in cafés or station waiting-rooms, are only too real. Declassed intellectuals, whose opinions on a novel or play are no longer of interest to anyone, they met just for the pleasure of escaping their loneliness and speaking German.

NOSTALGIA AND HATRED FOR GERMANY

The heart full of hatred and nostalgia! What an adventure to be an emigrant.

Klaus Mann, *The Turning Point*

Germany, pale mother . . .

Bertolt Brecht

I no longer have anything to do with the country, and speak its language as little as possible. I don't care if it collapses, or Russia invades – for me it's finished.

Kurt Tucholsky, letter to Arnold Zweig, 15 December 1935

'They were no longer Germans, yet they still were. They lived on sufferance in the countries that had taken them in, but to which they did not belong,' wrote Golo Mann. Of the many cruel experiences of exile, the ambivalence that they felt towards their own country was one of the most painful. From 1933 to 1945 this relationship continued to change, but all experienced that mixture of hatred and nostalgia so characteristic of émigré psychology. The hatred was reinforced with each new revelation of the atrocities committed by the Nazis and their growing success. The nostalgia was fuelled by time, and gradually transformed into a fear of dying without seeing Germany again. Though some émigrés managed to live in just one of these attitudes, the majority constantly swung between the two: they cursed the Third Reich while dreaming of their return to a Germany freed from National Socialism. They desired the defeat of the Nazis and an Allied victory, while weeping for the bombings that ravaged the cities they had so loved.[102]

Among the radically negative attitudes that some émigrés adopted towards Germany after 1933, that of Kurt Tucholsky is a particularly good example. Exiled in Sweden, he refused to see himself as part of the emigration, or believe in an exile literature, finding it ridiculous that the émigrés proclaimed themselves the 'genuine' and 'better' Germany when the country had become Nazi. He saw Germany only as a maleficent entity that he avoided speaking of. At one time Thomas Mann also seemed to adopt this position. After maintaining at the start of his exile that he could not imagine a prolonged separation from German culture, he later began to denounce Germany as dangerous and demonic. On 4 May 1935, he wrote to Karl Vossler: 'Melancholy? I know only horror.' Brecht took him severely to task for this impassioned attitude, which led him to identify the German people with National Socialism. But it is clear that after 1939 hatred triumphed over nostalgia for most of the émigrés. They often felt guilty in the eyes of others – the countries that had given them asylum – for being Germans, for belonging to the same nation and speaking the same tongue as those who had become an object of disgust and contempt for the whole world. Klaus Mann maintains that for a long time the only tie that bound him to Germany was that of a disconcerting foreignness, and that he felt nearly the same despair as Heine when he imagined his homeland in a dream.

Just reading a German paper, seeing a photograph of a party congress in

Nuremberg or a swastika flag was enough to give émigrés a feeling of nausea. Thomas Mann wrote: 'You can hardly imagine what we feel when faced with the present symbol of Germany, the swastika. We refuse to look at it, we turn away our eyes, we prefer to look at the ground or the sky [. . .]. When I was living in Zurich, I often had to pass the German legation flying this sinister flag, and I admit that each time I made a wide detour.' Klaus Mann wrote that 'the spectacle of a Germany transformed into a savage beast was not only anguishing but disgusting', and he recalled the words of his friend René Crevel before his suicide: '*Je suis dégoûté de tout.*'[103] In 1940, Alfred Kantorowicz noted in his diary[104] that he bore the fact of being German as a curse, and was ashamed of it. When he heard the Nazi radio rejoice in 1945 on the death of President Roosevelt, he wrote that there were hours when 'as a German, you wanted to hide your face from the Americans'.[105] At the same time, other émigrés, such as Paul Zech, wept bitterly on hearing the news of the bombing of German cities: the extracts from Stefan Zweig's letters already quoted are echoed by many émigrés in similar terms.

Faced with the grief that German developments caused them, many were tempted to deny their identity. Erich Maria Remarque replied in an interview: 'I am no longer German. I do not think German or feel German or talk German,'[106] and to an American journalist who asked him if he was sometimes nostalgic for Germany, he responded ironically: 'What makes you think that I'm Jewish?' But such clear-cut reactions were fairly uncommon. Ludwig Marcuse admits that even as a US citizen he still felt German: living in Beverly Hills he dreamed of Berlin, and walking in German streets.

Many exiles maintained, like Heine, that they had never dreamed so much of Germany as when in exile. Walter Hasenclever, who committed suicide in France, prayed for the German mountains and forests in a dream of spiritual transfiguration. The novelist Elisabeth Augustin, a refugee in the Netherlands, maintained that she had never felt nostalgia for Germany, but only for her childhood: 'What I lost,' she wrote, 'was a dream, a dream of Germany.' After leaving Vienna, Freud confided to Max Eitington: 'The feeling of triumph on being liberated is too strongly mixed with sorrow, for in spite of everything, I still greatly loved the prison from which I have been released.'[107] It was the same nostalgia for Germany that impelled Ernst Glaeser to break with his fellow émigrés and return there. Max Hermann-Neisse, a refugee in England, continued in his poems to proclaim his nostalgia for the German landscapes that he saw over and again in his dreams. Paul Zech wrote poems on the same theme in Argentina. The murder or kidnapping of some émigrés by the Gestapo also haunted many incessantly. Only rarely did they dare approach buildings where the swastika flag was flying. Most described the typical 'emigrant dream' they repeatedly had: finding themselves in a German town, surrounded by SA or SS, and waking up screaming. Some émigrés, like Armin T. Wegner, relived in their dreams for the rest of their lives their arrest by the SA.

The more they hated Nazi Germany, the more their notion of a homeland grew spiritual. Ex-Chancellor Brüning wrote in his diary:[108] 'I am steadily growing away from the usual characteristics that for most people form the notion of their country. For me, this is an idea.' Even after the War, they found themselves unable to rebuild the ties that exile had broken. Manès Sperber wrote: 'I did not go to Auschwitz. But it is there, just as in all the camps and ghettos, that my connection with everything that Germany had meant for me over the years had been turned into derision, broken, gassed and destroyed.'[109]

Some émigrés refused to return to Germany, others did return but felt strangers there. Then a new exile begun, sometimes more desperate than the original. And what should we say of those like Jean Amery, who returned to Germany only to take his own life; those who dreamed of returning to the village where they were born in order to die there; those who in their old age finally asked for their reinstatement as German citizens; or those who had a new desire to write poetry in German, after ceasing to speak it since 1933?

Often, after 1940, this nostalgia for Germany was transformed into a nostalgia for Europe as spiritual homeland. Even when they felt directly threatened, they left the continent only as a last extremity, with iron in the soul, and dreamed constantly of returning. 'If I had some money I would leave for Europe right away, to live perhaps in the south of France, and above all to breathe European air once again. Despite the fears of war, I would rather be there than in this beautiful and peaceful California.' So Christine Toller wrote to Hermann Kesten on 12 June 1939. There were many émigrés in America who expressed themselves in similar terms, each dreaming of the region, town or village that they most loved. 'I have a great nostalgia for Europe. How I would love to be able to take a walk in Ticino once again,' Brüning confided to Anna Herzog, and he wrote to Mona Anderson that 'the feeling of not seeing Europe again is like a stone on my chest.'[110]

As a language of pain, poetry itself seems inseparable from nostalgia. It was in exile that Max Hermann-Neisse and Paul Zech wrote some of their finest poems on Germany. Many, without this wrench, might never have been so sensitive to their country's landscapes. In his *Exile Dialogues*, Brecht accompanies their sad musings with evocations of the German countryside:

Woods of Bavaria, welcoming woods, cities on the edge of marshes [. . .]
And you too, Berlin, 'multiplied' town, living in the street and under ground
And you, Hanseatic ports
Teeming towns of Saxony
Cities of Silesia looking eastward
Always covered with smoke.

As if to excuse himself for slipping into this moment of emotion, Brecht suddenly exclaims: 'The meaning of the poem is: this country must be conquered, it's worth the trouble.'[111]

WRITING IN EXILE: THE MATERIAL SITUATION

A writer without a homeland is like a king in exile. The latter has no subjects, the writer has no readership. [. . .] Besides, the writer's language is bound to isolate him in the country where he is no more than a tolerated guest. His only instrument is his language, his only means of expression, a language that cannot be split apart from the things to express in it.

Golo Mann

Everything I've learned about writers since I've been an émigré, indeed everything I've learned about people in general, is that if you leave your country, you lose your influence and then you're nothing.

Alfred Döblin, 27 September 1935

Along with the feeling of being uprooted and proscribed, most writers had an obsession with destitution and social decay. If this was a feeling shared by other exiles as well, intellectuals were especially sensitive to it if they had enjoyed in Germany a certain material well-being and a very real prestige. The few exceptional cases of writers who managed to maintain their lifestyle in exile – Thomas Mann, Lion Feuchtwanger, Vicki Baum, Erich Maria Remarque, Stefan Zweig – should not make us forget the poverty of the others. Even Thomas Mann anxiously followed the negotiations about his property in Munich.[112] Though he managed to save some of his belongings, he did not escape the feeling of decay, of a 'déclassé existence' as he wrote in his diary in May 1933, which even brought him to tears.[113] As for Feuchtwanger, one of the most well-off of the exiled writers, it was during his internment at Les Milles, sleeping on damp straw, that he realized that he was a 'former German writer'. Alfred Döblin had to leave Zurich for want of money. Not having been rich in Berlin, he experienced severe poverty in exile, as did Heinrich Mann, former president of the poetry division of the Prussian academy, who depended on the help of others. Arnold Zweig's letters to Freud are full of tragicomic lamentations over the inadequate heating in the hotel where he lived, and his children who outgrew their clothes too quickly. Each further collapse of the material well-being they had formerly known then appeared as a new humiliation. They constantly recalled their past life: Stefan Zweig thought of the collection of manuscripts he had left in Vienna, Thomas Mann of his books and precious furniture, even Brecht in 1933 wrote a poem titled 'The Time When I Was Wealthy', remembering the seven weeks of 'real wealth' he had known thanks to the profits of the *Dreigroschenoper*.

When it was not their material distress that obsessed them, it was their past glory. Alfred Kerr realized in despair how when he now went to see plays, no one wanted to know his opinion of them. Fritz Kortner was astonished that another actor could play Richard III: this had always been his role. Ernst Toller felt like crying when he was asked in America what his profession was. Max Reinhardt, who had lived at Leopoldkron in a genuine castle, abandoned all his dreams in New York. Fritz Murnau depicted in his film *The Last of Men* the fate of a hotel porter whose personality collapsed when his smart uniform was taken away from him on the verge of his retirement. How can we imagine what it meant for a poet, an actor or a journalist to become a farm worker or a dishwasher in a restaurant? Very soon, the majority of exiles were confronted with the same situation: they had to leave the country that was dearest to them, move from one hotel to another, choose the poorest quarters or leave for the provinces. The least famous and the oldest were most cruelly affected. Salomo Friedländer, Kantian philosopher and satirist, left Germany for France at the age of sixty-two. In spring 1943 he was to be deported as a Jew, but given his age and weak condition, his non-Jewish wife was taken to Drancy instead of him. They survived at Ménilmontant to the end of the War. The old Mynona died utterly forgotten on 9 September 1946, and was buried in the Pantin cemetery. During the War years he was still writing *The Magic I*.

Exiled in Vienna in 1935, Ödön von Horvath didn't know if he would have anything to eat the next day. A. Berend was unable to seek medical attention as he couldn't pay for a doctor. Arthur Koestler admits having often suffered from hunger in Paris. E. E. Noth recalled that he turned over every coin in his pocket a dozen times before daring to buy a cup of coffee or visit the cinema. All feared illness as a catastrophe that could wipe out their meagre savings. It is also sad to read the occasional description of an exiled writer, formerly well-known, who now looked more like a drunkard or a tramp. It is unpleasant even to look at the last photographs taken of Joseph Roth, who committed suicide in Paris. Who would recognize in those bloated eyes and misty gaze the author of *The Radetzky March*?

As for writing, they continued as long as they were able. But reading these works of exile, one often forgets the tragic circumstances in which they were conceived. Both Lion Feuchtwanger and Alfred Kantorowicz have described writers dressed in rags, composing their novels or poems in unheated rooms. The poems of Ludwig Renn and the stories of Bodo Uhse were written amid the battles of the Spanish war. Willi Bredel wrote *Encounter on the Ebro* under the bombs falling on Madrid, while Friedrich Wolf's play *Beaumarchais* was written in the Vernet concentration camp, and Kurt Kerlow-Löwenstein wrote poems in similar circumstances. Rudolf Leonhard wrote *Germany Must Live* in the *maquis*, and Stefan Heym corrected the proofs of his novel *Peace with a Smile* as a soldier in the US Army.

Need we also mention that it took Max Hermann-Neisse three years to find a publisher for his collection *About Us Foreigners*, in a run of 500 copies, or that Paul Zech, one of the greatest expressionist poets, published only one single collection in his Buenos Aires exile – which sold eleven copies – and left fifty volumes of manuscript?

THE STRUGGLE WITH LANGUAGE

We are a sign devoid of sense
Far from our homeland
We have almost lost the power of speech.

Friedrich Hölderlin

What use thumbing through a foreign grammar?
The message that calls you home
Is written in a language you know.

Bertolt Brecht 'Thoughts on the Duration of Exile'

It is the German language that I feel to be my genuine homeland.

Lion Feuchtwanger

In a lecture given to the SDS in New York in 1939, on the theme 'destroyed language, destroyed culture', Ernst Bloch analysed the different attitudes that the émigrés adopted towards their own language. Some felt so rooted in it that they no longer managed to write in exile; others strove to stop using it from a hatred of what Germany had become.[114] In this way, Bloch argued, the German language was doubly threatened. *Intra muros*, it had become 'the devil's language', at the service of a bloody bestiality. *Extra muros*, it was scattered across the world.

Among the exiles' various torments, the struggle that most of them had to wage with language was one of the most debilitating. Apart from a few academics (Walter A. Berendsohn, for example), very few were able to continue their work in a foreign tongue. Some were at least able to express themselves in French or English, but very few could use either language fluently. We should remember that while the majority of antifascist émigrés who reached America had a solid classical education, they were generally unfamiliar with even basic English. For many of them, the language barrier aroused a feeling of unease, loneliness and fear. The émigré had daily experience of this in his relationships with the authorities or people he met in the street: his accent betrayed him as a foreigner. He was comical, disconcerting and triggered a reflex of distrust. When the War broke out, many antifascist exiles in France tried to pass as refugees from Alsace. Even at the start of their exile, émigrés tried to find spaces of German culture where they felt less out of place. 'Apart from Kalle, he knew no one in Helsinki who spoke German,' wrote Brecht in his *Exile Dialogues*.[115] As Günther Anders noted,[116] they were not only hunted from one country to another but from one language to another, which for some led to catastrophic difficulties in their ability to express themselves. In learning a new language they lost the use of German, and even writers did not always realize that their mother tongue was no longer intact.[117] G. Bermann Fischer, Thomas Mann's publisher, recalled[118] that the only language his children spoke fluently was Swedish. They went on to learn English in the United States, but continued to speak Swedish among themselves. Bermann Fischer and his wife, on the other hand, carried on speaking German, but addressed their children in Swedish to make themselves understood. Eventually the children replied in German to questions asked them in English. Oskar Maria Graf's son went to a German school in the United States, but like his father he would only express himself in Bavarian dialect; Graf indeed refused to speak anything else, even in New York. The exiles' correspondence is full of tragicomic laments about such language problems. Alfred Döblin was surprised that his accent aroused a mixture of amusement and discomfiture in France. Kurt Pinthus complained to Walter Hasenclever of his inability to learn English. Fritz Kortner took daily lessons with three English teachers. Leonhard Frank did likewise, but never managed to make himself understood in a London street. Hanns Eisler spoke a strange tongue and people found it hard to make out whether this was meant to be English or German. Walter Benjamin bravely set out to learn Spanish, by three different methods, but he feared the encounter with Danish.[119] And what about those academics who had to learn Turkish, Swedish or Hebrew? Max Brod became fluent in Hebrew, but Arnold Zweig, perhaps less motivated, never managed to learn the language. The calvary of Willi Haas, working in Hindi films without even speaking English, or that of the Yiddish actors in Shanghai, is scarcely imaginable.

If this situation was common to all the émigrés, those who worked with language – poets, writers and actors – experienced it most dramatically. Ludwig Marcuse maintained that few of their number over the age of thirty dared to express themselves in a foreign language.[120] Those writers who managed to do so were thin on the ground.[121] The situation of actors was just as desperate. As Marcuse put it, Albert Basserman spoke neither English, French, German nor American: 'he spoke Mannheim.' Elisabeth Bergner, for her part, spoke Bergner. On an American stage, their poor knowledge of English was comic, and what had made for the beauty and depth of their diction was now condemned to disappear. The impossibility of continuing to write in German was undoubtedly one of the many reasons for Tucholsky's suicide, defining himself as he did as 'a German writer who has ceased to write'. If Thomas Mann could not imagine distancing himself from German culture, Brecht was just as deeply rooted,[122] as indeed was Max Reinhardt.[123] And the reason that so many of the émigrés wrote poems was perhaps to rediscover a certain original relationship with their language.

THE TEMPTATION OF SUICIDE

We the banished. We the stateless. We the despised. What right do we still have to live?

Walter Hasenclever, shortly before his suicide

The artist has to keep his soul intact. A writer lost in morbid isolation, psychologically wounded, in prey to despair, what can he offer that might find favour with the public?

Golo Mann

When I saw him for the first time, I had the sense of seeing a man who would die in a matter of hours, simply from sadness.

Irgmard Keun, after meeting Josef Roth in Ostend in 1935

The road of exile was littered with the suicides of writers. What is astonishing, however, is not so much the high number of those who took their own lives, as the capacity of others to cling to life against all hope. For all of them, exile was a wound whose scar would never heal. If some chose voluntary death to escape torture by the Gestapo, or because they could no longer find the strength to hope, this ultimate act is often comprehensible only as following a slow and gradual destruction of their personality.[124]

For many writers, this despair started with being no longer able to write in the face of the triumph of what they had always combated. Condemned to silence, Tucholsky felt himself among the living dead. After his books were burned, Döblin asked what good it was to write, and for whom? Horvath, Sperber and Koestler felt the same anguish.[125] If a fairly large number of writers committed suicide, an even greater number admit having experienced this temptation. Carl Zuckmayer's fine text of 1942, *Appeal to Life*,[126] is perhaps one of the most poignant analyses of the distress of exile. He argued that each émigré life was a weapon, as the exile by his very existence bore witness against iniquity and barbarism. As long as they were alive, Hitler's triumph was not yet total. And Zuckmayer urged his comrades not to abandon their posts, even if they were 'bitter and cold', as 'none of us must die as long as Hitler lives': the last drop of blood beating in an émigré's heart was 'the symbol of the spirit and of freedom'.

But many did not hear this appeal. And the death that they chose, to put an end to a life that they saw as devoid of sense, or simply to escape the Gestapo, is often understandable only in the light of the experiences that they underwent and the general development of the personality. It would be vain to look to Brecht for a depiction of the brutal psychological development engendered by exile. But this is not the case with Franz Werfel, Walter Benjamin, Alfred Döblin and Stefan Zweig, all of whose correspondence betrays a gathering mental anguish. Even Thomas Mann, so discreet in his private life, could not stop himself depicting in his diary for 1933 and 1934 crises of depression, nervous collapse and floods of tears. It is true that the majority of suicides by exiled writers were bound up with particular political events (Franco's victory, fear of being handed to the Gestapo and taken back to Germany, certainty of not seeing Europe again). But it is often impossible to establish exactly what event, sometime a very small one on top of so many others, led a particular writer to take his own life. The majority of such suicides between 1933 and 1945 are explicable in terms of three phenomena: total lack of hope, as escape from immediate danger, or the gradual destruction of the exile's personality.

It goes without saying that these three kinds of cause were all involved in the majority of exile suicides. Walter Benjamin and Walter Hasenclever each poisoned himself both from despair and from fear of falling into the hands of the Gestapo. And a similar despair drove Stefan Zweig and Joseph Roth to death through alcoholism. As Klaus Mann wrote of the suicide of his friend René Crevel, in 1935: 'He took his own life because he was ill. He took his life because he feared madness. He took his life because the world had become mad. Why do people take their life? Because they don't want to live through the next half-hour, the next few minutes, because they *can't* do so. Suddenly, you get to the dead point, the point of death.'

If the majority of émigré suicides took place in 1939 and 1940, when Hitler seemed triumphant and they feared being arrested by the Gestapo, the daily life of exile still played an important part in this decision. 'Each morning I need the courage of a giant to keep living, simply to go on,' René Schickele wrote to Hermann Kesten on 15 December 1939. One fine day they simply didn't find that courage any more. It is certainly easy to ascribe these suicides to subjective considerations, to stress that Tucholsky was seriously ill, that Stefan Zweig could never stand being an émigré even though he scarcely suffered materially from his exile, that Ernst Toller had just left his wife, Walter Benjamin had attempted suicide before, and Klaus Mann, in his work as well as his life, was obsessed by the suicide of his friends. It remains true nonetheless that the death of all these antifascist authors has a historic significance.

Despite the violence of his satire with its corrosive humour, Kurt Tucholsky was astonishingly vulnerable. He had already settled in France in 1924, no longer able to bear life in Germany, and wrote for a number of Paris newspapers. On the death of Siegfried Jakobsohn, publisher of *Die Weltbühne*, he returned to Berlin to take over the direction of the magazine, which in 1927 he passed to his friend Carl von Ossietzky. Before going into exile in Sweden, he first lived in Paris and scarcely set foot again in Germany. Curiously enough, his last years were those of his greatest fame, a success however that had no effect: his satires were admired or hated, without really having the slightest influence. He thus had the feeling of writing in vain. Like other writers who believed in the Republic, he experienced the bitterness of seeing all his prophecies fulfilled one by one. On 10 May 1933 his books were burned at the order of Goebbels, who bore him an implacable hatred; he had already been deprived of German nationality on 25 April. Clear-headed as ever, he knew that his success as a satirical writer went together with complete political impotence. Problems of illness compounded the tragedy of history. Since 1931 he had suffered from a sinus inflammation, and despite several operations he lost the sense of smell and was in constant pain. The advent of Hitler meant the collapse of all his hopes, as well as the material basis of his existence. Exiled in a country whose language he could not understand, and faced with a lost cause, he could no longer find the least reason to write. He refused to link up with the émigré community, seeing in this belief in the power of spirit against force one of the most tragic illusions of the intellectuals of his generation. Since Hitler was in power, he himself felt defeated. He no longer meant anything, and constantly reiterated that the German children of tomorrow would be Nazis. The letters collected in the last volume of his correspondence, under the symbolic title *Letters of Silence*, show the depth of his despair. As he wrote already in 1933 to Walter Hasenclever: 'You can struggle for a majority that is oppressed by a tyrannical minority. But you cannot preach to a people the opposite of what the majority of them want. [. . .] If opposition doesn't come from within, we can never manage this, even if a few rags appear in Paris. I won't have any part in this.'

Tucholsky saw himself not just as a writer who had stopped writing, but as 'a German who has stopped being one'. He strove to stop thinking in German, even in his dreams. He kept his distance from other exiles, and from people in

general: 'I could never write in another language. [. . .] My need to communicate is zero.' Tired of life, disheartened by a Germany wallowing in barbarism,
he poisoned himself on 19 December 1935, leaving a note requesting that no
attempt be made to save him. The doctors overrode his wishes, but he died just
the same two days later.

Ernst Weiss, like Friedrich Wolf, Alfred Döblin, Gottfried Benn and R.
Sorge, was a doctor as well as a writer.[127] Born in 1882 in Brno, critics often
called him the German Dostoyevsky on account of the great torments of soul
experienced by his characters, suspended between dream and reality. The First
World War was a decisive test for him, as for all writers of his generation. From
1919 to 1933 he lived in Vienna, Prague, Munich and then Berlin, writing
strange 'detective stories of the soul' in which disease, death, destruction and
madness play a constant role. After the Nazi seizure of power he lived in poverty
in Prague, then in Paris, protected by Stefan Zweig and Thomas Mann, and
regularly seeing Joseph Roth, Walter Mehring and Hermann Kesten. His
material situation grew steadily worse: he carried on writing, in wretched hotel
rooms, some of the most important works of exile literature, such as his novel
Der Augenzeuge (The Eyewitness) in which he sought to understand the triumph
of Hitler in pathological terms. Weiss then fought for the Spanish Republic. His
morale broken by the triumph of Franco, he refused to leave Paris as German
troops approached, despite the urging of Walter Mehring. After writing more
than fifteen books, two plays, five volumes of stories, a book of essays and a
collection of poetry, he no longer believed either in literature or in his personal
salvation. As the German forces entered Paris, he took poison and cut his veins
in the bathroom, on 14 May 1940. In her fine novel Transit, Anna Seghers based
a character on him: a writer commits suicide, and a fellow exile looks for his
suitcase, abandoned at his hotel, in order to take over his identity.

When Ernst Toller was released from the fortress where he had been
imprisoned for his part in the Bavarian soviet republic, he maintained: 'I am
thirty years old, my hair is grey, but I am not tired.' He took an active part in all
the struggles to defend the Weimar Republic, without abandoning his pacifism
and his messianic socialism. Considered the greatest dramatist of the Weimar
years, his fame spread far beyond the German borders. As poet and dramatist, a
moral as well as a political figure, he was among the German authors most
admired across the world. In February 1933 Toller took refuge in Switzerland,
and on 23 April he was deprived of his nationality. He spent the following years
in London and Paris, giving numerous lectures, making appeals and interventions against National Socialism and in support of Republican Spain. He took
each ideological defeat as a personal one. After the fall of Barcelona, Franco's
victory and the defeat of the antifascist Popular Front, he sought refuge in the
United States. His personal disarray compounded the anguish he felt at the
course of history. Toller, the most frequently performed German dramatist of
the Weimar years, saw his plays disappear from theatres everywhere, and his
name fall into oblivion. Those who met him in New York describe a man
precociously aged, slowly succumbing to a deep despair. Even his play Pastor
Hall, the story of one man's struggle against Hitler, was a failure. His wife, the

actress Christiane Grantoff, who had followed him into exile, left him after three years of marriage.[128] His despair grew ever greater, and no one managed to console him.[129]

On 22 May 1939, Toller hanged himself in the bathroom of the Mayflower Hotel where he lived in New York. The only items on his desk were photos of Spanish children killed in the bombing. He had long depended for his subsistence on the support of friends. A man of the theatre, he ended up identifying himself with the hero of his play *Hopla wir leben!*, Karl Thomas, who hangs himself after coming to see the world as just an absurd machine. Long before his suicide, Toller had written prophetically: 'If you no longer have the strength to dream, you no longer have the strength to live.' At the age of forty-six, he could no longer manage to dream. His death passed almost unnoticed outside the émigré milieu. The Nazi press announced the news under the cynical headline: *Hopla, he's dead. Long live Germany*, adding the following commentary: 'Self-liquidation. According to American sources, the Jewish Communist émigré Toller hanged himself in a New York hotel. As is well known, Toller played a disruptive role in the Munich soviet republic.'

There is no point in seeking precise reasons for Toller's suicide. He was desperate, and could find no more reason to work or live.[130] His death was not just a consequence of the collapse of democracy in Europe. Nor is it explained by the loss of his wife. As Heinrich Mann rightly noted, thinking no doubt of Toller: 'In a case of suicide, one reason might be a woman, but not the only one.' And Toller did not kill himself just because his plays were no longer performed. All these things are indissociable. Just three people attended Toller's cremation. Even in death, his chagrin and sadness were insupportable, and the exiles discovered to their disgust that the American undertaker had dressed and made up the body as if he was going to a cocktail party. Walter Hasenclever and Joseph Roth criticized his suicide, but they were themselves to die of the same sickness, an absence of hope.[131]

Stefan Zweig was one of the rare émigrés able to maintain their former lifestyle in exile, despite experiencing its inevitable humiliations. Yet he too, a citizen of the world, on leaving his city and his homeland, steadily lost his 'belief in humanity', as he wrote on 24 January 1940 to Hermann Kesten. He had indeed left in Vienna his mother, too old to go into exile, as well as his belongings, the symbols of his refined existence, but he soon acquired British nationality and was able to lead the same bourgeois existence. Stefan Zweig did not feel the same 'compulsion to politics' as so many exiled writers, deeming this irreconcilable with the demands of his art. But the subtlety of his psychological plots now seemed to him derisory and displaced in view of the historical situation.[132] His break with Austria was not that traumatic: he had lived in Swiss exile during the First World War. But he felt this new exile all the more cruelly in that throughout his life he had kept his distance from any ideology and proclaimed a spirit of steady tolerance. The end of a certain humanist conception of the world, of the faith in liberalism that he saw as the very essence of the European spirit, meant the collapse of his world.

Settled in England, Zweig became obsessed by the loss of his readership and the fear that his novels no longer met their taste. He felt the annexation of Austria as a personal humiliation, and suffered a number of legal problems that typically vexed the emigrants, even if he was spared the most painful of these on account of his celebrity. As Europe gradually sank into barbarism, Zweig feared ever more for his own literary creation. He held himself aloof from other émigrés, and only rarely published in their periodicals. When the War broke out, he had no desire to leave Britain, even if it was, as he wrote to Hermann Kesten in January 1940, a 'lost outpost'.[133] The same year, however, he took ship for Brazil, where he successfully gave a series of lectures. Deciding to settle there, he wrote an enthusiastic book on his new homeland. He visited New York and Hollywood, meeting other émigrés there. Though he took no part in their struggle, he showed great generosity in helping them materially. His readership was still significant, but he felt increasingly alone. His world and his values had collapsed, and he could see no more meaning in life. When it seemed that the War would never finish, he took poison and died.

The majority of émigrés found Zweig's death completely senseless. If someone like him killed himself, who could summon the courage to keep on living? The letters between Thomas Mann and Zweig's first wife Friederike are eloquent on this point. When Friederike was surprised by Mann's silence, he could only reply that he disapproved of such a suicide and could not understand it. He wondered how Zweig had been able to forget the mission he was charged with as a writer, and consider his life a purely private matter (*reine Privatsache*). He felt both chagrin and indignation, equating this suicide with an act of desertion. Before committing suicide together with his wife Lotte, Stefan Zweig had left a declaration in which he said he was 'taking leave of life by a voluntary act and in full awareness', thanking 'Brazil, this wonderful country' that had been so hospitable to him. In a final message, he wished that his friends would finally see the dawn. For his part, he preferred to depart alone as he did not have the courage to await it.[134] Though Jewish, the *estrangeiro* was given a Catholic funeral, and thousands of Brazilians accompanied his body to the cemetery.

We could give many other examples of famous writers who chose suicide from despair and resignation. Franz Blei, writer and literary critic, and the editor of Goethe, died the same way, after living as a refugee in Cagnes-sur-Mer, then in the United States where he took poison in 1940 in New York. No less tragic was the case of Rudolf Olden (born 1885), a political journalist active in the defence of Carl von Ossietzky in 1929. Exiled first in Prague, then in Paris, then in London where he gave many lectures against fascism, he tried to reach the United States in 1940. His ship, the *City of Benares*, was torpedoed on the night of 17 December by a German submarine; it was carrying 247 passengers, including seventy-three children escaping from Germany. Olden refused to leave the ship and was drowned, together with his wife who remained at his side and entrusted their children to fellow passengers in order to save them.

Though it is hard to know the precise reasons that drove Tucholsky, Zweig or Toller to suicide, others such as Walter Hasenclever, Carl Einstein and Walter

Benjamin did so in the face of evident danger: the risk of falling into the hands of the German army and Gestapo.

The Social-Democratic journalist Hans Natonek told the story of a young Austrian who tried to flee France in 1940.[135] After reaching Perpignan, he studied the maps with the help of the mayor in order to cross the Spanish border illegally. He had to adjust the age on his passport from twenty to seventeen, so as to avoid military conscription. He tried three times to cross the frontier, alone and at night. Eventually he got lost and ended up at the Spanish border post. The police let him continue his journey to Lisbon, but the change of age on his passport was detected by an official, who handed him over to the German police. While being taken to prison he threw himself down a stairwell and died. The son of Alfred Döblin, Wolfgang, killed himself on 21 June 1940. He was serving in the French army, and in the course of battle he was separated from his regiment and feared falling into the hands of the Gestapo. He preferred death to being tortured. The literary critic Gerth Schreiner took his life in similar circumstances as the German troops entered the Netherlands. Rudolf Hilferding, in a letter addressed to Chancellor Brüning from Arles, on 16 September 1940, described his desperate situation and fear of being handed to the Gestapo by the Vichy government.[136] In June 1940 he took refuge together with Robert Breitscheid in the 'zone libre', equipped with an exceptional Czech visa which should have enabled him to enter the United States. After thinking of crossing the border illegally, he refrained for fear of being arrested and sent back to Germany. An attempted flight to Morocco also failed, and he was put under house arrest in his hotel. He continued to work, trying to correct his former ideas without thinking that he was in danger of death. During the night of 8 February 1941 he was arrested by the French police, together with Breitscheid, and shown the extradition demand presented by the Reich. On 10 February he either poisoned himself with veronal, or according to another account (that of Vincent Auriol) hanged himself in his cell. In a third version (Högner) he threw himself out of the window while being questioned by the Gestapo.

The expressionist playwright Walter Hasenclever (born 1890), known above all for his play *Der Sohn*, lived in exile in the south of France (1933–34), then in London (1936), Nice (1937) and Florence (1937–39). After being deprived of his German citizenship, he took refuge on the Côte d'Azur, at the home of the publisher Kurt Wolf. In 1937 he bought a farm with a vineyard in Italy, where he and his wife lived self-sufficiently until 28 April 1938, when he was arrested by the *carabinieri* and imprisoned in the fortress of Massa, in anticipation of Hitler's visit to Mussolini. This experience was so shattering for him that he decided to sell his farm and return to Cagnes-sur-Mer. When War was declared, he was twice interned,[137] ending up in May 1940 in the camp of Les Milles, at the same time as Lion Feuchtwanger and the former *Simplicissimus* editor Franz Schoenberger. After his first internment, he started writing *Die Rechtlosen* (*Those Without Rights*), a novel that described the life of exiles in the south of France. In another novel started in 1939, *Irrtum und Leidenschaft* (*Error and Passion*), his hero claims to keep on his person 'five tubes of good veronal, genuine veronal, for all occasions'. Hasenclever's internment at Les Milles filled him with utter despair, and as Feuchtwanger relates in *The Devil in France*, he thought that he would never be released, and that all the detainees would fall into the hands of the German army. He poisoned himself with veronal on 20 June 1940, after saying farewell to other internees. The following day the detainees were evacuated. Feuchtwanger insisted that Hasenclever should not be left behind. Taken to hospital at Aix-en-Provence, he died there the same day. The Nazi paper *Der Stürmer* wrote that his suicide was the only positive action in his life.

Carl Einstein (born 1885) met an equally tragic fate. An expressionist poet, passionate also about modern painting, he was famous in Germany both for his poems and for his Dadaesque novel *Bebuquin*. His play *Die schlimme Botschaft* (*Bad Tidings*), a fairly surprising version of the life of Jesus, brought him a condemnation for blasphemy and a fine of 15,000 marks. Certain revolutionary utterances that he placed in the mouth of Christ could not be pardoned. Close to George Grosz – he was involved with the magazine *Der Blutige Ernst* – he was also a fellow-traveller of the KPD. Excited in 1915 by African art, he published a remarkable history of modern art in 1926. His hatred of National Socialism soon led him to take his distance from Germany. He lived for a long time in Paris, and fought in the Spanish Civil War, his wife also serving as a nurse. After Franco's victory, he was interned with Spanish combatants at Argelès, close to Perpignan.

Political events however had broken Einstein's spirit. In May 1940 he was moved as a German to the camp at Gurs. With the advance of the German armies he was released and took refuge in a monastery. As a former soldier in the International Brigades, and long-time opponent of National Socialism, he feared being arrested and deported to Germany. On 5 July 1940 he opened his veins and threw himself into the Gave de Pau. His body was retrieved two days later. Before leaving Paris, he had confided to his friend D. H. Kahnweiler: 'I know what is going to happen. I'll be interned and the French gendarmes will be our guards. One fine day the SS will come. But I don't want that. I'll throw myself in the water.'

Franz Hessel (born 1880) was known above all for his collections of stories *Verlorene Gespielen* (*Lost Playmates*) and *Pariser Romanze*, also for his tales of wanderings through Berlin, which had a deep effect on Walter Benjamin. He settled in Paris in 1925, but returned to live in Germany and only decided to emigrate when he saw his synagogue burn and was forbidden to write. Interned in France in autumn 1939, in the Colombes stadium, he was released because his son had acquired French nationality. He then retired to Sanary, in a house put at his disposal by Aldous Huxley. Subsequently interned at Les Milles, he refused to escape and committed suicide at the camp exit on 6 January 1941. He refused to be evacuated for fear of being handed over to the Gestapo.

Walter Benjamin (born 1892) was of course an extraordinarily captivating and vulnerable person, who sometimes felt he had been catapulted into the twentieth century from the nineteenth. In a letter of 17 April 1931 he already described himself as 'a shipwrecked man on a sinking boat, clinging to the top of an already broken mast and trying to send a rescue signal'. His world was

Berlin, Baudelaire's Paris, and above all his books, for which he had an absolute passion, collecting them as much for their beauty as for their rarity and interest. They were for him almost a living extension of his work, and he could not live without them. Throughout his life Benjamin was pursued by improbable bad luck, and it was not without reason that he called himself 'the little hunchback', after the legendary character from the collection of German folk poems, *Des Knaben Wunderhorn*, who makes everything fail, turning every event into a catastrophe. Benjamin's thesis on *The Origin of German Baroque Drama*, despite being a work of genius, failed to gain him a doctoral degree. Articles he wrote were dismissed for their seeming obscurity, or else magazines refused to pay him or went bankrupt. Poor already in Berlin, trying desperately to survive as an independent writer, he was still poorer in exile. He refused to emigrate to Jerusalem, as his friend Gershom Scholem urged him, or to the United States, as advised by Adorno and Horkheimer. He had the tragicomic feeling that his place was nowhere else but in Europe, even when it was no longer safe for him to remain there.

When the threat of arrest by the German army became clearer, this 'last European' agreed however to leave for America. His friends managed to get him a US visa in Marseille. He had the transit visa that permitted him to reach Lisbon, but lacked the French exit visa which the Vichy regime would not give him. He tried to cross into Spain at the Port Bou border post, along with other refugees. Suffering a heart complaint, he found the walk very difficult. The border was closed that day, and it seemed to him that the Spanish police, who refused to look at his papers, were threatening to hand him over to the Gestapo. On the night of 27 September 1940 he took poison, though the following day he would have been able to cross the border. His death made an impression even on Franco's police, who let the rest of the group enter Spain. Benjamin requested that nothing be done to save him. His brother was interned in Germany in a concentration camp.[138]

For a third category of exiled writers, suicide was neither an act of resignation nor a final possibility of escaping Hitler. Still more tragically, it was the end of a long process leading to the steady destruction of their personality. Joseph Roth's alcoholism was as deadly in the end as Walter Hasenclever's veronal.

Exiled in Paris where he had lived before 1933 as correspondent for the *Frankfurter Zeitung*, Joseph Roth left the Hôtel de la Poste in the rue de Tournon only to die in the public ward of the Necker hospital. The author of novels, essays and short stories, his reputation as a writer was made in 1929 with *Rechts und Links* (*Right and Left*), which soon brought him international celebrity. Very rapidly, however, emigration led to a deterioration of his personality. His letters were distress signals, and even his relationship with the novelist Irmgard Keun, whom he met in 1936, could not console him. A Galician Jew and admirer of the Austro-Hungarian monarchy, Roth had left Germany without regret. He detested the country and tried to distance himself from it ever further. Long before 1933 he had written: 'My country is wherever I feel bad. Anywhere I feel good is abroad.' He left no family behind, and had no possessions. His books had been neither burned nor banned, though he had written against Hitler from Austria. If he chose exile, it was not just as an antifascist but as a Catholic and legitimist Austrian. Exile remained a creative period for him, though nothing seemed to attach him to life any more. Those émigrés who visited him depicted his unrestrained alcoholism. Klaus Mann described the devilish concoctions he ingested under the eyes of his admirers, and when Walter Mehring asked him why he was destroying himself with drink, Roth retorted that what astounded him was people who didn't drink. He attended the funeral of Ödön von Horvath, killed on 7 June 1938 by a falling branch in the Champs-Elysées, in dirty clothes and dead drunk. Roth died of alcoholism on 27 May 1939. Walter Mehring wrote in *La Bibliothèque perdue*:

> Joseph Roth collapsed like a cracked piece of wall. He died in hospital of delirium tremens three days later. At his burial outside the walls of Paris, a gentleman in a black frock-coat arrived and laid a wreath tied with a black and yellow ribbon, on behalf of His Most Catholic Majesty Otto von Habsburg. A priest without surplice said a short prayer; Jews said the Kaddish; a left-wing colleague laid a bouquet tied with a red ribbon that read '*A notre camarade*', on behalf of a circle of Muscovite writers. A crowd of grieving women sinners wept for their one beloved.[139]

Alfred Wolfenstein, seen as one of the greatest expressionist poets, spent his first years of exile in Prague, in utter poverty, then in Paris. In 1940 he tried to reach the '*zone libre*', but was arrested by the Gestapo and imprisoned in the Santé where he wrote his poems *Der Gefangene* (*The Prisoner*) and *Exodus 1940*. A Gestapo officer who appreciated his writing helped him reach southern France where he hid for some years in the homes of peasants, living in cellars, stables and haylofts. Suffering from depression, he returned to Paris and awaited the Liberation, already seriously ill. When he was discovered he was immediately taken to hospital, where he committed suicide soon after his admission.

Among the great writers that exile killed morally by accentuating the imbalance of their personality, Klaus Mann must also be mentioned. Brecht's depiction of him does him an injustice – a talented young man, a refined and bourgeois aesthete, protected from the world by the shadow of his father. In fact, this shadow began to destroy him already in his youth. Crushed by the fame of Thomas and Heinrich, he sought desperately to make his own name in the literary world. An habitué of the great capitals, at ease with Gottfried Benn in Berlin or Jean Cocteau in Paris, he wrote two autobiographies, several literary essays, plays and novels, attracting negative criticism precisely because of his name. The eldest son of Thomas Mann, he undoubtedly lived a gilded youth that separated him from other writers of his generation. At the age of eighteen he had already published his *Kaspar Hauser Legenden* and was working as a theatre critic. His first plays were quite poorly received, and the trio that he formed with his sister Erika, the person closest to him, and Pamela Wedekind (daughter of the playwright) was the talk of the town. In 1926 he stayed in Paris and made the acquaintance of René Crevel, whose inspiration he followed in his *Kindernovelle*. For all his attempts to win critical acclaim, he was constantly judged by the standard of his father or his uncle. It is true that some of his works seem a bit pallid and inadequately worked. But the best of his novels are far from negligible, in particular those of his exile years – *Mephisto* and *Der Vulkan* – as well as his admirable memoir *The Turning Point*. Throughout his exile he struggled against fascism, publishing his magazine *Die Sammlung* and giving frequent lectures both in Europe and the United States. The years he spent there, however, were not very productive. His review *Decision* only lasted for a few issues. In 1942, he asked to serve in the US Army, and was sent to North Africa where he accompanied the Fifth Army in Italy as a member of the Psychological Warfare Branch of military intelligence. On 11 July 1948 he made a first suicide attempt, and put an end to his life on 21 May the following year in Cannes, while working on a book to be called *The Last Day*, the story of a man who commits suicide at the end of the War because of the world situation.

If Klaus Mann was haunted by suicide throughout his life, as many of his texts testify,[140] it is likely that exile, the loss of confidence in his ability as a writer in the course of his stay in the United States, played as great a part in his fate as his fragile personality.[141] His death was one of the most typical of those 'delayed suicides' provoked by exile.

Finally, how can we not also remember the Austrian writer Jean Amery (born in Vienna in 1912), who escaped from concentration camp, and returned to commit suicide in 1978 at Salzburg? Or F. Hardkopf and S. Staub, who committed suicide together with their companions? Or the wife of Alfred Döblin who did not want to survive him? Macabre as such details may be, they certainly form one of the most tragic chapters in the exile story. In all these deaths whose logic it is no longer always possible today to decipher, these suicide victims whose tombs are unknown, we encounter the tragedy of a life and of an era.

The Organization of Support

A number of elements contribute to explaining the varied reception that the émigrés encountered and the difficulties they had in being accepted. The economic crisis affecting Europe and the ensuing threat of unemployment helped to fuel violently xenophobic reactions: the French example is enough to show the disproportion between the fears that the arrival of German refugees aroused and their actually very limited number.[1] They were also constantly blamed for poisoning France's relations with the Reich, whose warlike intentions these politicians and journalists failed to take into account. The different legislation and attitudes in the various European countries was a further factor in the very diverse situation facing the exiles. The greater or lesser presence of aid committees and organizations also explains why some refugees found it much harder to survive than did others. Though an analysis of the operation of these various committees would go well beyond the framework of the present study, their role and function in relation to the development of international opinion certainly needs to be sketched out.

THE ATTITUDES OF EUROPEAN COUNTRIES
TO THE ÉMIGRÉS

'How did your brother help you then?' a man was asked, dying of hunger and without hearth or home. 'Just with a sigh,' came the reply, 'but what a deep one!'

Manès Sperber

The works of H. A. Walter, M. Durzak and M. Wegner,[2] along with the correspondence, memoirs and diaries of the émigrés, underline the diversity of the conditions of asylum they encountered. Czechoslovakia and Switzerland certainly stood at opposite extremes, but as Lion Feuchtwanger emphasizes, there were some constant factors in the treatment the exiles received:

Everywhere that these troublesome guests arrived, they were undesirable [. . .]. There were no longer any countries where new and capable men would have been welcome.

Quite the contrary, these strangers who wanted bread and work were everywhere looked at askance. They were not allowed to work, scarcely even to breathe. They were asked for papers and visas which they didn't have, or not the right ones. Some had fled without managing to bring any documents, or their passports soon expired and were not renewed by the Third Reich authorities. It was also hard for these exiles to establish that they were what they claimed to be. Many countries found this an excellent pretext for sending them back. It happened that people who did not have the requisite papers were taken secretly at night by the police and expelled to neighbouring countries. The following night, the police of these other countries returned them across the border in the opposite direction.[3]

In an initial phase the situation seemed quite favourable: the German borders were still fairly permeable and those of adjacent countries not yet shut tight.[4] The barbarism that marked the Nazi seizure of power had aroused a sense of repulsion in the European conscience, and its victims enjoyed a certain sympathy. Measures to assist the refugees were taken rapidly, on the initiative of left-wing parties and religious organizations, which established a number of support committees. This wave of sympathy, however, rarely spread beyond these progressive milieus, and rapidly came up against the hostility of the right-wing press and Nazi sympathizers. Jews were seen as 'racially foreign elements', incapable of 'integration into the national community'.[5] The reasons that had driven so many men and women to flee their country were obscured by the imaginary danger they represented for the security and economy of the countries in which they sought refuge. The Europe that received these émigrés was a world in moral and economic crisis, deeply traumatized by the fear of unemployment and recession, and readily susceptible to selfish and xenophobic sentiments, anti-Semitism in particular. If these few tens of thousands of antifascist refugees could have only a marginal effect on European economies, the indigenous populations were still sensitive to all the arguments that stressed the horror of a rise in the numbers seeking work, and the risk of seeing foreigners take their work and their livelihood. These fears, irrational as they might be, did not spare any category of refugee[6] and were often sufficient to silence the upsurge of solidarity and generosity.

After a real movement of sympathy towards the victims of National Socialism, therefore, many countries sought to guard themselves against a new influx of refugees. From 1934 on, border controls were sharply reinforced and restrictions on work opportunities became still more draconian. Most of the committees set up to support the refugees collapsed one after the other for lack of resources. The European governments generally agreed that the importance of the refugee question was such that it overspilled national boundaries and had to be dealt with by the League of Nations, to arrive at an equitable distribution of these exiles. From 1935, international opinion was steadily less favourable to the refugees. Affected by the arguments of the right-wing press, it increasingly saw them as an economic threat. Apart from such rare moments as the Front Populaire in France, when a certain number of measures were taken in their favour, their situation went on deteriorating until 1939. The refugee question had by this time ceased to be debated in the context of the support committees set up in each country, and had become an 'international problem'.

Attitudes towards Germany had also shifted. The Reich was now far less isolated diplomatically. The disgust aroused by its barbarism had given way to a sense of admiration for its economic successes, especially in those right-wing milieus that were traditionally Germanophobic. The spectacular improvement of German finances, the concordat with the pope, the Berlin Olympics, were all defeats for the émigrés. Their constant appeals were in vain against the lethargy of European governments towards Germany and the general unawareness of the danger it posed for Europe. Not only were they not listened to, they were accused of 'pushing for war' to regain their lost positions. Their situation thus continued to worsen: each new wave of émigrés met more fearsome obstacles and undermined still further the sympathy enjoyed by their predecessors. After the influx of political refugees in 1933 it was the turn of 'racial émigrés' to have this sad experience, then refugees from the Saar and from Austria and Czechoslovakia.

The growing number of Jewish refugees without passports finally presented a legal problem that was submitted to the League of Nations. A similar situation had existed in the previous decade, with the massive exodus of white Russians after the October revolution, as well as Armenians after the genocide. After much difficulty, a 'Nansen passport' had been created in the 1920s for those who no longer possessed a national passport. But this agreement had been hard to negotiate, and the passport was not recognized by all countries. The situation of the antifascist exiles of 1933 was worse: they often aroused less sympathy and understanding than the white Russians (over a million) who pandered to the prevailing anti-Communism.[7] While Italian antifascists had been relatively easily absorbed, those hailing from Germany were especially unwelcome. Governments had not only to deal with an often xenophobic public opinion, but also with their right-wing parties.[8] It was often against their will that they accepted these émigrés. The massive influx of Jews from Germany or countries occupied by the Reich was to have still more tragic consequences.

THE PROBLEM OF JEWISH REFUGEES AND INTERNATIONAL OPINION

> The countries concerned could find some place in the world to put the Jews, and then tell those Anglo-Saxon states brimming over with humanity: 'Look, there they are! Either they'll die of hunger, or you'll have to put your words into practice.'
> Chvalkovsky interview with Hitler, 21 January 1939

If several thousand refugees already left Germany in 1933, these were mainly political opponents and not the great exodus that would follow the promulgation of the Nuremberg laws and the intensification of anti-Semitism. In the second half of March 1933, French consulates supplied between ten and fifteen thousand entry visas, and by September, at least 50,000 Jews had sought refuge in countries bordering on Germany, as well as in Great Britain, the United States and Palestine.[9] These refugees were a burden on countries whose economic situation was often by no means favourable. At the fifteenth session of the League of Nations, therefore, the Netherlands raised the question of the fate of these emigrants. While unable to support the burden they imposed, Holland was unwilling to forbid them entry. This conference was the first official debate on the refugee problem.

The German position was relatively simple: those who left the Reich did so 'of their own accord', and no law forbade them to return. Those who refused to do so were criminals – it was even announced that legal investigations were under way – and whilst they could if they wished forfeit German nationality by gaining naturalization in other countries, the Reich for its part refused to let other countries intervene in their favour as long as they remained German citizens. The German government, moreover, did not conceal its satisfaction that Jews were leaving its territory: 'Germany has gained a lot from the departure of political refugees. As these are especially Jews who had come from the east, it is only just that other countries besides Germany are also obliged to absorb a certain number.'[10] Since this position was evidently unacceptable, the League of Nations finally appointed a high commissioner responsible for coordinating the different measures to be taken to help refugees. This decision was taken unanimously, except for Germany, which left the League a few days later.

The designated high commissioner, James McDonald, was a specialist in international relations. He tried to open discussions with the Nazi authorities as soon as he took up the post, but was only able to coordinate various projects of financial assistance proposed by Jewish organizations.[11] Besides, the Reich did not yet exclude all Jews from German life, so as not to aggravate its economic difficulties. This relative reprieve from persecution gave many Jewish émigrés living in poverty the belief that they could return to Germany without danger. On 25 January 1934, however, Göring ordered the Gestapo to arrest all further emigrants who returned to Germany and send them to concentration camp. McDonald submitted to the British Foreign Office a plan to evacuate 100,000 German Jews over a period of five years, but this also met with defeat.

After the annexation of Austria in 1938, a new wave of refugees overwhelmed the consulates, especially the diplomatic representatives of the United States. A campaign seeking an easing of the immigration quotas established by the 1924 Immigration Act[12] was organized in America. Sumner Welles, assistant to Cordell Hunt, was charged with planning an international conference on the refugee problem, which was held at Évian a few months later. The American government made known that the quotas would not be raised. Of the thirty-three countries invited, only fascist Italy refused to take part. The situation of Jews from Germany was all the more fraught in that the Gestapo was now expelling people across the frontier at night, especially to Poland, despite the protests of neighbouring countries. They were then immediately arrested and returned to Germany, where they were interned at Dachau. The Évian conference undoubtedly raised great hopes among the refugees, but these were very soon disappointed. The French representative, Henry Béranger, suggested that the refugees should be accepted by the United States and Australia, whose economic prosperity depended on a constant influx of new immigrants. The Australian representative declared that his country would only accept British citizens. The United Kingdom claimed that it could not accept any more refugees, given the threat of unemployment, while the American government stood firm on the question of quotas. The concluding speech of the conference, given by Henry Béranger on 16 July 1938, has an ominous ring to it:

> France is happy to have shown, in this beautiful and harmonious setting of mountains and lakes, that it is able, given the trustworthiness of its institutions and the public order of its democracy, to receive all the nations of the world and afford them, in the most perfect material and moral tranquillity, a haven for the deliberations of governments aiming at the peace of all peoples, the independence of all countries, and the liberty of all citizens of the world.[13]

Behind the smokescreen of speeches and declarations of principle, the concrete results were paltry: owing to their internal problems of economic crisis and unemployment, no country was disposed to make a sacrifice to accept the refugees, and the *Völkischer Beobachter*, in its edition of 13 July, flaunted the headline: 'No one wants them'. Hitler himself, in his closing speech at the Nuremberg rally on 12 September 1938, waxed ironic on the fact that the democracies were so ready to give moral lessons on the supposedly 'cruel' treatment that Germany inflicted on the Jews, but no other country wanted to accept them.[14] The inter-governmental committee set up by the Évian conference to find a solution to the refugee problem came up against ceaseless and irresolvable difficulties. None of Germany's neighbouring countries was prepared to shelter indefinitely those refugees whom they had provisionally accepted in the name of the right of asylum. They all hoped to see them leave for other destinations, particularly Latin America. Those countries, however, which had up till then had very liberal immigration policies, took increasingly severe measures to keep out of their territory refugees without capital. The committee vainly tried to obtain from Germany a relaxation in the conditions of emigration, so that refugees would not be entirely deprived of resources on leaving Germany. Faced with this situation, a certain number of adjacent countries took increasingly severe measures to prohibit German Jews from entering their territory. As early as 31 March 1933, Switzerland had imposed more rigorous conditions for granting a residence permit. From then on it accepted only refugees in transit, and orders were given to deport any foreigner lacking a visa. On 28 March 1938, the Swiss government decided to require a visa for Austrian nationals.[15] These visas were only given parsimoniously. In May 1938, Adolf Eichmann, having stripped all Austrian Jews of their belongings, started forcing them across the Swiss border at night, leading the Swiss police chief Heinrich Rothmund to declare: 'Switzerland has no more need of these Jews than does Germany, and will be forced to take further measures so as to avoid being submerged with the complicity of the Viennese police.'[16] Though the Swiss government considered returning these refugees en masse, it refrained from this as 'acting in such a way would attract to a high degree the criticism of civilized countries'. But the Third Reich was not prepared to mitigate its emigration policy, and it was only when the Swiss threatened to require a visa for Germans visiting Switzerland that the Hitler government decided to stamp a distinctive 'J' on the passports of Jews,[17] so that they could immediately be returned if they did not have adequate financial resources or documented transit status.

The immediate result was that German nationals whose passport was stamped with a red 'J' three centimetres high on the first page were likewise refused access to Latin American countries. Even the United States government made it harder for those with this stamp to get a visa, for fear of seeing them settle in the United States illegally. The State Department warned all its diplomatic offices that bearers of such a passport still had 'the right to return to the territories of the Reich at any time'.[18] After the invasion of Czechoslovakia, the ranks of refugees were joined by a large number of Czech Jews, all facing the same difficulties as they came up against one frontier after another.[19] Britain intervened to request the Prague government to accept Jews from Sudetenland, but the Czech government held that these were 'not only an economic but a political danger'. Britain, for its part, was prepared to accept émigrés in some of its colonies, as long as they were not Jewish. It was a struggle for the League of Nations High Commissioner to get this distinction abolished.

After Eduard Benès went into exile on 5 October 1938, the Czech liberal tradition collapsed. Anti-Jewish measures were promulgated (15 November 1938), and Germany made the 'liquidation of the Jewish problem' a test of the Prague government's good will. But when Czechoslovakia tried to expel its Jews, it found the surrounding borders hermetically sealed. On 31 March 1938, a decree from the Polish president withdrew Polish nationality from any citizen who had spent five years or more continuously abroad. Jews who held Polish passports but lived in Germany were no longer permitted to return. They were expelled from the Reich by the Gestapo on 26 October 1938, and taken to the Polish border where they came up against armed sentries who pointed their guns at them. Poland responded by expelling all Germans of Jewish origin, and tried to persuade Britain and the United States to accept the immigration of these Polish Jews who had been made stateless. When Herschel Grynszpan, a boy of seventeen who had emigrated first to Belgium, then to France, learned that his family found themselves in the Zbanszy no man's land, he shot Counsellor von Rath of the German legation in Paris. In response, Germany sent between twenty and thirty thousand Jews to concentration camp. There were now some half a million persons who had left territories occupied by the Reich without the least certainty of finding asylum in a neighbouring country. The high commissioner for refugees laconically noted: 'Since the Évian conference, doors everywhere have been systematically closed to the emigrants.' On 15 November 1938, Roosevelt himself made clear once more that a modification of US quotas was out of the question. The only places refugees could find a country to accept them were in distant lands such as China, Madagascar or Tanganyika. The United States vainly appealed to Mussolini to accept some of these refugees in Italy.

In February 1939, negotiations were begun between the director of the Évian committee, the American lawyer Rublee, and Nazi minister Schacht (subsequently replaced by Wohlthat), seeking to tie the possibility of emigration of German Jews to an increase in exports from the Reich. It only remained to locate a site where this 'Jewish reservation' could be situated. Mussolini did not want it in Ethiopia, France was opposed to its being organized in Madagascar or Haiti. From summer 1938 onwards, Roosevelt was still considering Angola. The Reich authorities were quicker. On 24 January 1939, Göring set up a Central Reich Office for Emigration, entrusting its direction to Heydrich. From now on the Gestapo would be charged with the question of emigration and seeking a solution to it. Similar offices were subsequently established in Vienna, Prague and Amsterdam. Hitler demanded that the Jewish authorities organize the departure of at least a hundred people per day. Since no country was prepared to accept them, they were condemned to wander from country to country and port to port. Many reached Shanghai, despite British and American protests. Hitler agreed to release all Jews who obtained immigration papers. Yet no country was prepared to provide the least rescue plan for these Jews threatened with perishing in the camps. A German ship, the *Saint-Louis*, carried 930 emigrants to Cuba armed with disembarkation certificates purchased from the immigration service, but the Cuban president declared these null and void, and forbade disembarkation. The United States was equally opposed, and when the ship reached Florida it was intercepted by the coastguards. The refugees finally returned to Antwerp, from where they were distributed between Belgium, France and the Netherlands.

Right to the moment when war broke out, other conferences were held in London and New York to consider the problem of these refugees, but without reaching any concrete result. It soon became impossible to leave Germany. In 1942 the Reich government began the 'final solution' when it established the first extermination centre using gas at Chelmno. All Jews throughout the countries occupied by the Reich, especially those of central and eastern Europe, were now condemned to deportation and death.

RELIEF COMMITTEES AND AID ORGANIZATIONS

The relief committees had their origin in 1933, when opponents of the Nazi regime began to leave Germany. A number of organizations already in existence also joined this effort. The committees were many and varied. With the exception of Jewish organizations, financed above all by American Jews, their resources were scarce, and continued to decline while the number of people needing assistance constantly rose. They all had the same functions: to receive refugees, persuade countries to accept them, provide them with the necessary means of survival, offer legal defence and sometime aid the exiles to leave Germany or Europe when they faced immediate danger. A study of these committees is made more difficult by their number and their often ephemeral character, and a number of exiles themselves did not learn of their existence until they read the memoirs of fellow exiles. Certain particular types of these committees can be broadly distinguished.[20]

Organizations Linked to the Parties of the Left

In all countries it was these organizations that were generally the most active. They sought to fulfil as best they could the triple task of receiving refugees, preventing them from dying of hunger, and helping them with legal defence and resettlement. The aid offered by the left-wing parties was never sectarian. Even when there was scarcely any contact between the Socialist and Communist parties, and the KPD still maintained the 'social-fascist' line, it was not rare for Communist and Socialist committees in exile to aid activists of the other party. Trade unions, including the American ones, also saw it as a duty to assist German antifascist militants, as did sections of the Human Rights League. Some committees were newly established in 1933 to deal with the influx of refugees; others, whose operation has been briefly sketched above, such as International Red Aid, the Matteoti Committee, the Ligue des Droits de l'Homme (LDH), were already in existence. Several of these French organizations were non-party, including the LDH and the Ligue Internationale Contre l'Antisémitisme (LICA).

The most typical example of these committees linked to the left-wing parties was International Red Aid, founded in 1923 under the aegis of the Communist International. With national sections already established, it sought to defend all victims of capitalist repression in both moral and material respects.[21] In 1933 it began in very varied ways to collect funds for refugees, also food and clothing; in France it held popular festivals as well as making direct appeals. In the legal field, it sought to get them granted asylum and opposed expulsion measures. After an international conference of 20–21 June 1936, a Comité National de Secours was founded in France which brought together the various refugee aid agencies. This work was later taken over by the Secours Populaire Français.

The Social-Democrat equivalent of International Red Aid in France, the Matteoti Committee, likewise came to the assistance of German political refugees. In a general way, the left parties and organizations established an effective aid network from 1933 on. They sought to assist threatened activists to escape from Germany, and to provide them with papers, accommodation, work, and a minimum of money for their material survival, as well as a certain legal protection in the countries in which they operated. This solidarity effort, which assumed substantial dimensions on the French left, was echoed in several other countries. In the Netherlands, the main political organizations working to aid antifascist refugees included the Carl von Ossietzky Komitee, the Vereinigung van Vrienden van der Sowjet-Unie, the Internationale Arbeidershülp, the Comite van Künstenaars en Intellectuelen ter Destrigding van de Terreur in Duitsland, the Committe Einheid voord Democratie and Von Waakzammheid van Antinationaaalsocialistische Intellectuelen. In Sweden there were several very active Communist committees such as the Rödä Hjälpen (Red Aid), which had existed since 1930 and in 1934 established the Flüchtlingskomitee der Roten

Hilfe, with Knut Ollson as secretary. The Swedish Social-Democrats also possessed various organizations such as the Arbetarrörelsens Flyktingshjälp, which concerned itself chiefly with workers and trade-union activists, including Communists. In Prague there were also six large support committees for refugees, including Red Aid, the Vereinigung zur Unterstützung Deutscher Emigranten, and Solidarität (which replaced Red Aid after this was banned). Switzerland had the Sozialdemokratische Flüchtlingsfürsorge (directed by Wilhelm Sander), and the Fürsorge für Deutsche Emigranten beim Einheitsverband der Angestellten.

Alongside these committees devoted to the reception of émigrés, a number of others worked on the defence of activists imprisoned in Germany. The most typical example is that of the Comité Thälmann in France, the various activities of which have already been described. These committees often brought together activists and intellectuals around the figure of one or a number of prisoners, including Ernst Thälmann, the defendants in the Reichstag fire trial, Carl von Ossietzky and Edgar André. Such defence actions contributed to a rapprochement between the two main parties of the left, despite the opposition of their leaderships. Efforts were often made to unite these committees in wider bodies. In April 1937, Anna Siemsen, E. J. Gumbel and Heinrich Mann appealed in Paris, without success, for the formation of a non-party committee in support of the victims of fascism, at a meeting in the Mutualité at which the German Human Rights League, the Arbeiter Volkswohlfahrt, Red Aid, and the Internationale Hilsvereinigung der ISK were all represented.

Support from Religious Organizations

Pride of place here naturally belongs to Jewish support organizations, who were concerned above all with the material problems of Jewish refugees from Germany, even if they sought to direct them to third countries. In France, the main body was the Comité National de Secours aux Victimes de l'Antisémitisme. Founded in July 1933 after the French government had made approaches to prominent figures in the Jewish community, this functioned until the following year. Many Jewish refugees and national committees received financial assistance from international Jewish organizations such as the American Joint Distribution Committee and the movements for emigration to Palestine. In Prague there was also a Jüdisches Sozialamt directed by Chaim Hoffman, in the Netherlands the Jüdische Flüchtling-Komitee, and in Sweden the Mosaiska Församlingens Hjälpkommitte. Generally apolitical, these committees were concerned above all with gathering funds to assist the flow of refugees coming from Germany and, later, from elsewhere in central Europe. The aid of these international committees, the American ones especially, was all the more needed in that at the national level, Jewish communities often had an ambiguous attitude. While they sympathized with the sufferings of German and central European Jews, they too sometimes displayed a certain 'economic racism' and distrust, in the face of a possible rekindling of anti-Semitism occasioned by these refugees. Even while assisting them, therefore, these Jewish organizations sought to steer the refugees as fast as possible in the direction of other countries. American Jews, too, were no more desirous to see a large number of European Jews settle in the United States. If western Jews were sometimes hostile to those from the east, New York Jews, hailing mostly from Poland or Russia, had little sympathy for their German co-religionists. It is undeniable, too, that many French or Dutch Jews saw German Jews more as Germans – even '*boches*' – than as Jews. Helmut Müssener recalls the strange question that the chief rabbi of Stockholm asked the refugees: 'Why don't you return to Germany?'

This assistance from Jewish organizations was supplemented by that of the Christian churches – Secours Catholique, the Protestantische Hilfskomitee, the Römisch-katholische Komitee für Opfer der Glaubenverfolgung. Among the most effective support was that of the Quakers. Though two-thirds of their number lived in the United States and there were scarcely more than a hundred in France, they opened a Foyer d'Entraide aux Emigrés Allemands in Paris on 10 July 1933.[22]

Organizations Founded by Foreign Governments or Individuals

In a certain number of countries, governments were themselves minded to establish committees or support financially those that already existed, making available to them unused hostels, barracks and hospitals, as was the case in Paris and the Netherlands. Alongside these government organizations, there were also committees set up by prominent personalities, intellectuals or academics, which sought to support their colleagues.

In the Netherlands, three major aid committees were in existence by 1934: the Comite voor Bijzondere Joodsche Belangen, the Neutraal Vrouwencomite voor Vluchtelingen, and the Academisch Steunfonds voor Intellectuelen. In Sweden, the Insamlingen för Landsflykliga Intellektuella had been set up in 1933 by two hundred figures including the son of the former king, writers, academics and historians. Each member received a card, a duplicate of which was sent to the Comité International pour le Placement des Intellectuels Réfugiés. Founded in 1937, the Stockholm Central Committee for Aid to Refugees headed by Professor Einar Tiegen united other organizations such as the Committee for Assistance to Refugees, the Lindhagen Committee, the International Foyer, the Jewish Community Assistance Committee, the Ecumenical Aid Committee, the Quaker Aid Committee, later also the Israel Mission and Catholic Aid.

If only few such committees developed in Switzerland, the government did agree to lend money to some aid organizations. The Schweitzer Hilfswerk für Emigrantenkinder was created in this way. The Arbeiterhilfswerk paid émigrés unable to work 150 Swiss francs a day (190 francs in winter). In England, the number of committees was fairly limited. Until 1938 there was the Central British Fund, which collected funds for the émigrés. The Academic Assistance Council (under Lord Rutherford of Nelson), known later as the Society for the Protection of Science and Learning, was chiefly concerned to support intellectuals, scholars and academics. Subsequently, under pressure of public opinion, new organizations were established bringing together the Quakers, the International Christian Committee and the trade unions. The British Coordination Committee aided refugees from Germany and Czechoslovakia, and worked to evacuate them to Britain.

In France finally, among the official organizations, the Comité National de Secours aux Réfugiés Allemands should be mentioned. Directed by Raymond Raoul Lambert, who worked with Édouard Herriot at the ministry of foreign affairs, this spent 12 or 13 million francs on supporting some 25,000 refugees. After the reunion of the Saar with the Reich (13 January 1935) and the annexation of Austria, new waves of emigrants led to the formation of new committees: the Association d'Entraide pour la Sarre, the Accueil Français aux Autrichiens (comprising deputies, senators, and members of the Académie Française), and the Comité pour l'Autriche headed by François Mauriac. There was also the Assistance Médicale aux Enfants des Emigrés, financed by Swiss, American and British figures, which by May 1937 had assisted 2,400 children.

Committees Formed by the Émigrés Themselves

The fairly large number of these, whether official or clandestine, connected with the parties or independent, concerned themselves not simply with the material and legal problems of the exiles, but also with the defence of resisters arrested in Germany and the continuation of the struggle against fascism. They were often headed by famous personalities, and rarely affiliated openly to the Communist party, even if they were unofficially connected with the Comintern. A large number of these were the work of Willi Münzenberg, publisher of the *Brown Book* on the Reichstag trial. As Arthur Koestler notes in his memoir:

First, he founded the 'World Committee for the Relief of the Victims of German Fascism', with branches all over Europe and America. It was camouflaged as a philanthropic organization, and had in every country a panel of highly respectable people, from English duchesses to American columnists and French savants, who had never heard the name of Münzenberg and thought that the Comintern was a bogey invented by Dr Goebbels.[23]

These 'shop windows' made it possible to attract the maximum number of supporters. It is almost impossible today to draw up a complete list across the various countries of exile.

Specialist Aid Organizations

A certain number of émigrés received aid from bodies formed to rescue members of particular professions. Though these also existed for lawyers, musicians and psychoanalysts, we shall mention here just the most famous among those that worked to assist intellectuals and academics.

There were a good number of committees concerned with scientists. In 1933 a

Comité des Savants was formed in Paris, with the aim of supporting scientists expelled from Germany. In 1937 the Comité pour l'Organisation du Travail des Savants Étrangers was founded at the initiative of Jean Perrin and Louis Rapkine. A similar committee existed in London, under Lord Rutherford of Nelson. The greatest efforts in this field were made in the Anglo-Saxon countries. A number of aid organizations were set up here in 1933. In April of that year, too, a first group of scholar refugees in Switzerland founded the Notgemeinschaft Deutscher Wissenschaftler im Ausland, inspired by Phillipp Schwartz, a pathology professor of Hungarian origin at Frankfurt University. This body strove to facilitate the re-establishment of academics at foreign universities. In 1936 a list of 1,500 was circulated in several countries with the support of the Rockefeller Foundation. Rather similarly, the Comité International pour le Placement des Intellectuels Réfugiés was established in Geneva, including representatives of most European democracies as well as the United States. In 1940 the committee was forced to close its offices in Paris, Brussels and Amsterdam. Its assistance was now limited to refugees in Switzerland. Similar bodies existed in Belgium, Great Britain, the Netherlands, France and Denmark.

The Academic Assistance Council, established in London in 1933, was a private body that included members of British universities and scholarly societies. Founded on the initiative of Sir William Beveridge, director of the London School of Economics, its aim was to assist scholars, academics and researchers who 'for reasons of religion, political opinion or race were no longer able to pursue their work in their own country'. While Beveridge remained its honorary secretary, the famous physicist Lord Rutherford became its first official president. Until 1939 this committee was led by Walter Adams of London University, and it is estimated that from early 1933 to autumn 1938 it had found positions for at least 524 individuals in thirty-six countries (including 161 in the United States). On 22 May 1933, the Council published an appeal to alert British universities to the fate of their German colleagues, with the aim of inspiring a movement of solidarity in their support. It proposed setting up an international information centre, but held aloof from any political standpoint.[24]

Close to the Academic Assistance Council, another Hungarian played a major role in the support given to academic refugees, Leo Szilard. After leaving Berlin University, he went into exile in Vienna and contacted William Beveridge from there. Invited to join the committee, he focused on finding positions for exiled academics in foreign institutions. The Academic Assistance Council built up files on all lecturers who had been expelled from Germany, or had to flee from the Nazis when Hitler came to power. It collected funds to assist them and enable them to survive while they were waiting to find a new post. Many British academics spontaneously agreed to hand over part of their salary to support their émigré colleagues.[25] The Council soon extended its activities to other countries. Though created originally just to assist German academics, it subsequently took on those expelled by the Nazis from Austria, Hungary, Poland and Czechoslovakia, as well as Italian and Spanish antifascists.

As the economic situation in Britain hardly made it possible to accept all these academics, the Council worked in close collaboration with its American counterpart, the Emergency Committee in aid of Displaced Foreign Scholars. At the end of 1933, the university lecturers' association in the United States launched an appeal signed by 12,000 academics, protesting against 'the tyranny prevailing in German universities'. Measures were immediately envisaged to assist German academics forced into exile. In July 1933, 142 college presidents called for solidarity with the victims of Nazism, and the president of Cornell University founded a further committee to support the émigrés, appealing to foundations and non-academic milieus to finance their journey to America and their initial salaries. Several bodies were soon working actively to rescue these academic emigrants: the Emergency Committee, the Rockefeller Foundation, the Oberländer Trust and the New School for Social Research. The efforts deployed in France to assist German scholars and academics have already been mentioned.

It was harder to set up assistance for artists and writers. German literary figures, even famous ones, could not be found new positions abroad as readily as eminent scholars. Defence committees for writers were relatively few and isolated. Writers' organizations had been infiltrated by the Nazis even before their seizure of power, and those re-established in exile, like the Schutzverband (SDS), had little power either in Paris or New York. As for the exiled PEN Club, while it subsidized a few writers such as Hermann Broch, its means were very limited.

The American Guild for German Cultural Freedom, founded in New York in 1935 by Hubertus Prinz zu Löwenstein with Horace M. Kallen and Dr George N. Shuster, worked to protect artists and writers. Presided over by the governor of Connecticut, Dr Wilbur L. Cross, it included among its honorary members Senator Robert F. Wagner, Professor Carlton J. H. Hayes, Robert McIver, Alvin Johnson, Robert M. Hutchins, Frank Kingdon and Dorothy Thompson. It organized fund-raising dinners, and the money collected enabled the foundation in 1936 of the Deutsche Akademie in Exil, its literary and scientific sections subsequently presided over by Thomas Mann and Sigmund Freud. The senate of the Akademie counted twenty-one members in 1937, rising to forty-six in 1940, including Thomas and Heinrich Mann, Alfred Döblin, Lion Feuchtwanger, Bruno Frank, Leonhard Frank, O. M. Graf, Robert Musil, Alfred Neumann, Rudolf Olden, René Schickele, Ernst Toller, Fritz von Unruh, Franz Werfel, Arnold Zweig and Stefan Zweig. The Akademie tried to find positions for writers in departments of German, or work for them in the American cinema. It gave grants that enabled some exiled authors to continue their work. It awarded prizes to the best works written in exile, and made it possible to have these published. The American Guild paid $30 per month to the writers it assisted: Hermann Broch, Alfred Döblin, Robert Musil, Bertolt Brecht, E. Castonnier and Annette Kolb. It also paid the fares of a number of exiles who were still in France and trying to get to America. Its funds came from Catholic charitable organizations as well as Jewish ones.

A sister organization was born in 1937–38, led by the poet H. Richardson: the

Arden Society für Verbannte Künstler und Schriftsteller in England. Another important relief organization was the Fonds Thomas Mann (there was also an aid committee in Prague called the Thomas Mann Gesellschaft) founded in February 1937, following an appeal signed by twenty-nine writers, artists and scientists.[26] Pursuing the same ends as the American Guild, it sought to assist young writers by giving them grants and facilitating publication of their work. We should finally mention, apart from the committees, the important aid that developed among the writers themselves, the more fortunate donating part of their royalties to their poorest colleagues. Ernst Toller, Erich Maria Remarque, Thomas Mann, Lion Feuchtwanger, Stefan Zweig and Hermann Kesten played a major role in rescuing writers left in Europe in 1940 by paying their passage to America, financing the Emergency Rescue Committee or the European Film Fund.

This account of the various forms of relief organizations for the émigrés should not however foster the illusion that they had large resources at their disposal. Despite the diversity of the committees, their means were weak in relation to the mass of refugees, and could only enable these to survive the first months of exile. Even so, they often managed to lighten their moral and material suffering, to translate the wave of solidarity into active support, and to defend them with the various governments. Despite all their efforts, however, they could not prevent a large number of exiles from falling into poverty – or into the hands of the Gestapo in 1940.

First Reflections on
the Meaning of the Emigration

I was forced to leave Germany in February 1933, immediately after the Reichstag fire. This was the start of an exodus of writers and artists such as the world had never seen. I settled in Denmark and from then on devoted my entire literary work to the struggle against Nazism, writing plays and poems.

> Bertolt Brecht, testimony to the House Committee
> on Un-American Activities[1]

It matters little whether we see or not the triumph of our work or even its recognition; that has no importance, as long as it is devoted to truth and justice. As long as this is so, we shall not die, we shall always have friends and even a homeland, as we carry it within us; our country is that of the spirit.

> Ödön von Horvath, letter to Theodor Csokor of 23 March 1938

Lived initially as a colossal trauma, a source of unknown sufferings, a wrench of distressing strangeness, it would be wrong for all that to reduce the exile experience just to this negative dimension. Very soon, the majority of writers became aware that if they were still alive it was in order to struggle, to bear witness of Nazi barbarism and denounce it; that their very existence was a weapon preventing the complete victory of National Socialism. Nostalgia for their lost homeland was thus transformed into the desire to reconquer it, as Brecht asserted in his *Exile Dialogues*. The émigrés' works often took on a new and more political dimension as they sought any opportunity, even the slightest, to combat the Hitler regime.

Whether imposed or chosen, emigration became a 'task', a 'mission', a 'crusade'.[2] This moral vocabulary is typical of the earliest texts published by the exiled writers. Even if they remained nostalgic for their former existence, and dreamed of continuing their work in the same style as before 1933 despite asking themselves what the purpose of writing now was,[3] the majority of émigrés sought to define the meaning of this emigration, this battle that steadily came to be identified with their life.

EMIGRATION AS A TASK

Our function and task were clear and significant. There was a double function, to be more precise, and the task was twofold. We had to warn an unaware and drowsy world, to begin with, and also to provide the German underground movement with information and encouragement: this was the political aspect of our mission. At the same time it behoved us to preserve and develop those literary values and traditions now suppressed in the land of poets and thinkers.

Klaus Mann, *The Turning Point*

Banned, proscribed, or voluntarily exiled, these writers, who sometimes left the Reich before they were actually threatened, were aware that they embodied ideals and values deeply rooted in German culture, and now trampled on by the Nazis. Many felt themselves charged with a mission that was both political and spiritual. The destruction of the workers' parties and the enslavement of all cultural life had made them, in Heinrich Mann's fine expression, 'the voice of a people who had become mute'. As spokespeople for democracy and freedom, they affirmed the 'other Germany', the 'better Germany', certain that its genuine culture had left the Reich and was found with them in exile.[4]

The separation between the émigrés and those writers who had rejected exile does not seem to have been final. They believed that some of these would rejoin them, or that if they stayed it was to struggle against Hitler.[5] They therefore refrained from condemning them en bloc, and equating those who had remained silent with those who rallied openly to National Socialism. Often they addressed appeals to them.[6] Emigration to them meant not only the survival of German culture, but of freedom, generosity, morality and intelligence in the face of a world that seemed to be collapsing into a bloody bestiality.[7] Rejecting the assertion of Alexis Tolstoy that exile signified the death of any literature, Bruno Frei considered that emigration had saved the life of German letters.[8] In their eyes, what the Nazis had assassinated was not just their political opponents, but the entire German liberal, humanist and revolutionary cultural tradition.

Even before inquiring into the nature of the Nazi regime, and the process that had permitted its rise, the exiles were aware of the eminently moral character of their emigration. Heinrich Mann saw it less as an uprooting than as a 'duty' and 'task'. Thomas Mann viewed it as 'a battle against Evil', and it was this moral stance that united the émigrés over and above their ideological differences. The theme of a *besseres Deutschland*, found in so many of the earlier exile writings, corresponded to a reality for them: forced to leave their country, they had in some way carried its soul and truth with it. E. Saenger wrote in his diary in 1943: 'To be an emigrant means asking oneself every day and every hour when the world will be better.' He added that the role of the emigration was to embody Germany's highest spiritual demands.[9] They were certain that a future Germany would be born out of their struggle. The periodical *Gegen-Angriff*, published in Prague, had as its subtitle: 'You are the Germany of today, we are the Germany of tomorrow'.

Because they had been witness to the rise of National Socialism and had suffered from its barbarism, the émigrés also felt the duty of awakening Europe to the danger it represented. The battle against Hitler was not only that of Good against Evil, so Thomas Mann claimed, but that of life against death. And if Klaus Mann held that the exiled writer was charged with a double mission, to warn the whole world of the Hitlerite danger while remaining in touch with the opposition still in the Reich, Kurt Hiller wrote still more sharply: 'For us, the key problem of the present is as follows: How can we clean the Augean stables of Germany, what brooms do we need to brush out the filth? How can we get rid of the vermin that has established itself in our country as a result of bad management?'[10]

The majority of writers thus refused to dissociate cultural and political work. They sought on the contrary to find a thousand ways of combining these. Klaus Mann maintained that exile literature not only had to keep alive the great tradition of the German language, but produce manifestos, appeals and analyses of fascism. In all the countries still free the exiles should cry out:

> You are in danger. Hitler is dangerous. Hitler means war. Don't believe in his supposed love of peace! He's lying. Don't do a deal with him; he won't keep his promises. Don't be intimidated by him. He is not as strong as he makes believe, *not yet!* Don't let him become so. For now, a gesture, a strong word on your part would be sufficient to prevent him from this. In a few years the price will be higher, it will cost you thousands of human lives. Why wait [. . .]? Break diplomatic relations with him! Boycott him! Isolate him![11]

And Brecht, who insisted that the writer should discover 'a writing that kills', began his 'Five Difficulties in Writing the Truth' with the words:

> Whoever proposes today to engage in struggle against lies and ignorance, and to write the truth, has to come to terms with at least five difficulties. He must have the *courage* to write the truth when on all sides it is suppressed; the *intelligence* to recognize it, when it is everywhere hidden; the *art* to make a serviceable weapon of it; enough *discernment* to choose in whose hands it will become effective; and the *cunning* to distribute it among them.[12]

In all these demands, the same tasks were raised:

1. To understand how the Nazi regime had been able to establish itself;
2. To defend, preserve and enrich German culture;
3. To safeguard its values and its democratic heritage;
4. To unmask in every way possible the true face of the Third Reich;
5. To warn Europe of the danger it represented for liberty and peace;
6. To contribute to its overthrow by helping the internal resistance.

THE COMPULSION TO POLITICS

Many of our number, writers who learn the horrors of fascism and detest them, have not yet understood this doctrine, and have not revealed the roots of barbarism. They run the danger, as previously, of considering the cruelties of fascism as gratuitous.

Bertolt Brecht, speech at the First International Writers'
Congress for the Defence of Culture (June 1935)

A poet who does not fight against Hitler and the Third Reich today is certainly a weak man, and most likely without value as a poet.

Joseph Roth, 1938

Not all the writers who left Germany in 1933 were activists, even if they saw National Socialism as a monstrosity. Exile often radicalized their ideas, leading them from moral disapproval to political commitment. Their relationship to history was either suddenly or gradually transformed. This development often happened in a complex and contradictory way: liberals drew close to Communism, poets became activists, though there were also former politicians who abandoned their previous activism. It is often as hard to follow the development of the exiles' political ideas from 1933 to 1945 as to describe their connection with history in the Weimar years.

While exile served for several as a kind of historical accelerator in ideological matters, every possible combination of *Geist* and *Tat* – an opposition dear to Heinrich Mann – could be found in the émigré world. The certainty that emigration was a 'task' or a 'spiritual mission', that they had a key political role to play in the struggle against National Socialism and for the project of a future Germany, united not only the more politicized writers, but also pacifists, liberals and republicans who opposed to National Socialism their faith in humanist ideals. Doubtless some exiles maintained a distinction between their literary work and their political commitment. For many, however, these were only two facets of the same task: they issued appeals, manifestos, articles and lectures while continuing their literary creation, and saw each word, each free writing, as a political act against National Socialism and its values.[13]

This faith in the role of the emigration would however be criticized by some exiles – and not the least of their number – who for a range of different reasons kept their distance from émigré activity. Some no longer believed that exiled writers or activists were in a position to influence the course of history. Others held that such an influence could only be pernicious. Kurt Tucholsky and former Chancellor Brüning each illustrate this attitude in a different fashion.

Tucholsky, a few days before his death, sent the *Neue Weltbühne*[14] an article, 'Juden und Deutsche', in response to a book by Arnold Zweig,[15] reaffirming his distance both from Judaism and from the German emigration. He explained that he had broken with Judaism in 1911 from disgust at 'unctuous rabbis', and considered that he and his generation had experienced in Hitler's rise to power a defeat that was intellectual as well as political and moral. Instead of self-criticism, the émigrés struck him as enclosing themselves in a dangerous idealism, forgetting the mistakes committed and cradling themselves in undeserved praise: 'praise for Jews, for Socialists, for Communists'. He found it laughable that instead of asking why the Germans had chosen Hitler, the émigrés were content to maintain that they were the 'better Germany' or that 'Germany was no longer Germany'. He railed against those émigrés – 'the Paris lot' – who carried on the game when it was all lost and no victory was now possible. Tucholsky maintained that his life was too dear for him to rest content with sitting under an apple tree and praying for it to produce pears. Germany existed and it was Nazi. Those who claimed to embody Germany were trying to resurrect a ghost. He refused to associate with the émigrés or share their illusions, since 'they have not yet realized that they do not have the masses behind them, or the slightest bit of power.'[16]

Former Chancellor Brüning also kept his distance from the emigration, but in his case from a refusal to associate himself with any denunciation of Germany, even Nazi Germany. Whilst Tucholsky's position was both lucid and desperate, that of Brüning attested to his political ambivalence. Not only did he play no role in the exiles' resistance to Hitler, he often slyly attacked this.[17] He wrote anonymous pamphlets on the themes of his lectures, but refused to express himself outside of an academic context and urged Hermann Rauschning to reject any rapprochement with Willi Münzenberg. He constantly feared that émigré actions would damage Germany, and that the country would find itself in an unfavourable situation 'because a few emigrants have protested against Nazi policies'.[18] His attitude infuriated a number of British political figures, and when Brüning advised the British government to maximize its concessions to Hitler, Churchill called him a 'coward'.[19] Throughout his exile, Brüning reiterated that a future German government would not include the émigrés, whose actions had been 'detrimental to Germany'.[20]

Other émigrés kept their distance from political struggle out of an utter inability to think in political terms. They may well have been antifascists, but it was history that had forced them into exile and they swung between despair, revolt and resignation. Stefan Zweig illustrated this attitude in his own way. He remained apart from the émigré world, even though writing sometimes in their periodicals and helping them materially. He deplored the barbarism that had descended on Germany and Austria, but did not believe he had the least possibility of acting as a writer. In *The World of Yesterday*, he wrote with the naivety for which Klaus Mann criticized him:

> Foolish as I knew so superfluous an inhibition to be, I spent those years of semi-exile and exile apart from wholesome intercourse, in the delusion that it was bad form to express myself on topics of the day in a foreign land. In Austria I had not been able to combat the folly of influential circles, how then could I attempt it here? Here, where I considered myself a guest of this kindly island, knowing well that if [. . .] I were to point out the world-danger which Hitler represented, it would be considered a personal, prejudiced opinion.[21]

Besides those who refused for various reasons to join the émigré circles, there were those writers who left the Third Reich from disgust at its barbarity, and believed that their very presence outside of Germany would suffice to express their condemnation of the regime. This was Thomas Mann's position at the start of his exile. As his *Diary* shows, though his hatred for the Nazis was constant, he refrained for quite a while from taking a public position, and kept his distance from the émigré periodicals, which he treated with a certain disdain. The poet Max Hermann-Neisse described his nostalgia for Germany in poignant terms, but seemed to await the end of National Socialism as if this was just a long winter. The Alsatian expressionist writer René Schickele already lived in the south of France before 1933. Though he had published in Switzerland during the First World War the famous periodical *Die Weissen Blätter*, and was among those most bitterly hostile to the war, he held himself aloof from the émigré struggles, and only contributed to *Mass und Wert*. For Schickele as for these other writers, his condemnation of National Socialism was a mere formality. They saw in it simply an 'eruption of evil forces', and could oppose it only with an abstract morality and their own despair.[22] Even Alfred Döblin sometimes seemed to display this attitude. Though before 1933 he tried to set up a study group with a rather vague ideology, he counted nonetheless as one of the genuinely progressive writers of the Weimar Republic, and his novel *Berlin Alexanderplatz* was translated into Russian despite the protests of the BPRS. In his essay on German literature in exile, Döblin classified its various representatives on the basis of political categories,[23] even if these were somewhat arbitrary. In the exile situation, however, he contrasted literature and politics, maintaining: 'We should be left to work in peace. We are German literature abroad and we won't let any politician teach us lessons.' The writer, for Döblin, should not engage in a political movement, but rather keep his spirit pure and free. Thus, while participating in émigré meetings, he refused any militant activity. He rejected the invitation addressed him by Alexander Abusch to join the Freies Deutschland committee set up in Moscow on 28 July 1943, which included German prisoners of war along with political activists and exiled writers. His name figures on few émigré committees. He refused to have his political texts, or even literary ones, published in the exile reviews, and even opposed the publication in *Freies Deutschland* of extracts from his novel on the 1918 revolution. The magazine did however publish two years later a message of friendship to Egon Erwin Kisch on his sixtieth birthday, adding that it was uncertain whether his good wishes would be welcome, given their ideological differences. However, he specified, 'you must accept me as I am.'[24] Döblin opposed to fascism his own morality, and to Nazi literature his exile novels.

Brecht rightly criticized the dangerous illusion that this abstract conception of morality carried with it, in his speech at the International Congress for the Defence of Culture in 1935: 'The writers who experience the crimes of fascism in their flesh or that of others, and are horrified by them, are not yet, despite this lived experience and horror, in a position to combat these crimes. Many may believe that it is enough simply to describe them, especially when a great literary talent and a sincere indignation render their description striking.'[25] Whether they took refuge in morality or in literature, such opposition to fascism, Brecht held, remained purely idealistic. An attitude similar to Döblin's was displayed by Robert Musil,[26] who constantly defended culture against politics, believing in its independence, and disdained all the commitments of his contemporaries, few of whom indeed enjoyed his esteem.[27]

Throughout the 1920s, a number of writers managed to refuse any political commitment in the name of the primacy they ascribed to the aesthetic.[28] This was certainly no longer the case after 1933. Klaus Mann maintained that there was no other solution but exile, and the *Neue Deutsche Blätter* wrote in very similar terms: 'There can be no neutrality. Not for anyone, still less for a writer. Those who use the weapon of words as an ornament or a toy leave the field open to the adversary.' Exile thus led many writers to a complete reversal in their relation to history and politics.[29] They felt compelled to take part in the antifascist struggle, even if they had previously found any kind of activism repellent. The most typical example of this 'compulsion to politics' is certainly that of Thomas Mann. His *Reflections of a Non political Man*, published at the end of the First World War, affirmed both his attachment to a certain irrationalism and idealism inspired by Schopenhauer, Nietzsche and Wagner, which did not fit well with democracy, and a frank disdain for all political matters. The rise of National Socialism led him in the early 1920s to distance himself from his aristocratic vision and defend the Republic and democracy. Exile forced him to play an actual political role as spokesman for the émigré community and adversary of National Socialism. While continuing his writing, he gave numerous lectures, radio broadcasts and appeals.

In more than one way Mann found himself in a fairly unique position. His celebrity as a writer sheltered him from administrative and material worries, and gave each of his words a special weight. Though attacked in Germany, he was still the object of discreet approaches by the Nazis until he publicly declared himself an émigré. He initially believed that by saying nothing about the 'new Germany' he would impress the foreign press more than did the exiles with all their campaigns. This seeming neutrality, however, inspired by considerations of prudence, was broken in 1936 by his controversy with the critic Eduard Korrodi. Mann could now not avoid taking a clear position, and once his break with Germany was achieved, he followed this 'compulsion to politics' (*Zwang zur Politik*) that he often evoked in his correspondence. Despite the caution that was still urged on him by Schickele and Herman Hesse,[30] he waged constant public battle in support of the émigrés and against National Socialism, which he denounced from then on in all his public interventions. In a letter to K. Engelmann, he wrote on 15 December 1936:

The anger aroused in me by all this suffering, and the human misery that these despicable holders of power have caused and continue to cause, has put an obligation on me to pronounce the words and accomplish the acts which have led to my 'deprivation of nationality' [. . .]. God knows that I was not born for hatred, but these corrupters of man, these bloody madmen, I detest from the bottom of my heart, and wish them with all my soul the horrible end that they deserve.

Mann's response to the dean of the philosophy faculty of Bonn University, who had announced that he was being stripped of his doctoral title, was a genuine political manifesto, in which he reiterated the necessity of taking a position towards the events unfolding in Germany. The author who had formerly exalted 'the natural distance of the German spirit' from the political sphere now committed himself totally. Nothing expresses better this turn in his thought – and in his life – than the title of his collection of essays, *Order of the Day*, and the notes that make up 'Leiden an Deutschland' ('Germany, My Suffering') are of a rare violence. Mann recanted here his former prejudices towards politics, maintaining that: 'Politics is a function of human society, the interest that we take in it is part of the totality of the human spirit, and no more than man uniquely belongs to the realm of nature is politics uniquely included in evil.'[31]

Many texts of his, before 1936, had an activist character, even when based only on humanism. But in 'Beware Europe' (1935) and 'Humanities and Humanism' (1936), he called for a genuine political battle, and spoke of the need for humanism to 'arm itself'. Mann was no longer content to affirm his faith in democracy, as he had in the 1920s: he now emphasized the need for personal political commitment to defend it. Writings such as 'This Peace' (1938) are genuine political analyses of the international situation and the balance of forces in play. Throughout his exile in America, Mann gave numerous lectures, appeals and radio broadcasts, including his famous 'Appeals to Germans'. It is doubtless hard to imagine what Mann's political development would have been without the need to defend democracy against National Socialism. What is certain however is that, without the experience of exile, this development would not have taken the form that it did.

For other writers, exile meant less a 'compulsion to politics' than a radicalization. Lion Feuchtwanger was undoubtedly a 'progressive writer' in the 1920s. Exile however brought him close to Communism, leading him to direct, together with Willi Bredel and Bertolt Brecht, the Popular Front antifascist magazine *Das Wort*, and directly integrate the exile experience in his work, which was not the case with Thomas Mann, whose novel sequence *Joseph and His Brothers*, for example, bears no evident trace of exile. The case of Heinrich Mann is still more typical. A very progressive writer and admirer of Zola, bitter enemy of the Wilhelmine Reich and the First World War, he was constantly attacked by the Nazis, who demanded his expulsion from the Prussian Academy. He was also attacked at this time by the Communists, especially by J. R. Becher in the *Linkskurve*. As a refugee in France, Heinrich Mann developed an intense activism with his pamphlets (*Hatred*, 1933), newspaper articles (in *La Dépêche de Toulouse*) and many statements in support of the émigrés and of oppositionists imprisoned in Germany. More than any other writer, he was the soul of the German antifascist Popular Front in Paris, striving to unite around him, with his moral prestige, even writers quite hostile to Communism, and becoming himself a kind of fellow-traveller after his reconciliation with Becher. It is unlikely that without the exile experience, Heinrich Mann would have been led to such a position; it could hardly be predicted from his ideological course in the 1920s and his relations at that time with the KPD, but in the *Volksfront* era he became the party's partner of choice.

A place must also be found in this radicalization for those 'almost solitary combatants' who had never been connected with the left parties in the Weimar Republic and remained relatively isolated in exile. Armed only with their conscience, their moral and intellectual prestige, their battle was often all the more intense because of its solitary and desperate character. Such was the case with Ernst Toller, expressionist poet and pacifist, who played a major role in the Bavarian soviet republic of 1919, before becoming the most famous playwright of the Weimar years. An idealist and champion of a messianic socialism, Toller took up all the progressive causes of his time. In the 1920s he fought for freedom of expression and against all the many threats to the Republic. He struggled against intolerance, injustice, militarism and National Socialism, always trying to combine his contradictory ideals of pacifism and revolution. After 1933 he contributed to a number of émigré journals,[32] gave numerous lectures and speeches, and made appeals in Britain, the United States and Canada. Between 1933 and 1939, he made no less than 200 interventions, of which only a small number have been published.[33] For Toller, the struggle against National Socialism was a continuation of the struggle he had waged since the First World War. Remaining outside any party, he continued to believe in the power of speech and justice. His struggle to rescue Spanish children injured by bombing, following on his moral commitment to the struggle against Franco, was his last hope and his last defeat.

RESCUING THE GERMAN CULTURAL HERITAGE

Genuine literature has gone into exile. The literature of emigration *is* German literature.

Ernst Ottwalt, *Internationale Literatur* (May 1936)

At the same time as they were 'compelled to politics', the majority of exiles felt charged with a double mission: to preserve the spiritual heritage of German culture, presently confiscated by the Nazis, and keep it alive in exile while enriching it with new creations. This requirement led a certain number of writers and artists to modify substantially the conception they had had of the relationship between their own works and this heritage. For many years before 1933, discussion on this subject had frequently opposed those who remained attached to a certain literary tradition and those who claimed to combat this in the name of avant-garde currents and styles. Similar debates in the Soviet Union had opposed Lenin's conceptions to those of the futurists or Proletkult. In Germany, rereading issues of the BPRS magazine *Linkskurve*, following the polemics between Lukács and Ernst Ottwalt or Willi Bredel on the 'reportage novel' or 'proletarian novel', or the later critiques Lukács would formulate against expressionism, Brecht and Eisler, one can appreciate the complex relations that so many artists maintained with this classical 'heritage'.

The Nazi seizure of power deeply modified the antifascist writers' relationship to Germany's cultural heritage. Not only did the Nazis reject all 'avant-garde' forms, but also the entire liberal and democratic tradition, let alone the socialist and revolutionary currents, substituting this with an archaic and reactionary mythology. At the same time, they laid claim as 'ancestors' of their movement and values to such figures as Luther and Nietzsche, Goethe, Schiller and Hölderlin. The task therefore was not only to denounce this supposed kinship between classical German culture and National Socialism, and show what this supposed 'Germanity' had falsified, but also to emphasize the extent to which the classical German heritage was indissociable from those values now trampled on by the Nazis: a certain belief in freedom, justice and democracy.

Authors with quite opposing conceptions thus came to take up the defence of the classical heritage, even if they had sometimes impugned it before 1933. Lukács, in his polemics on expressionism, would oppose this classical and democratic heritage to the experimentation of the 1920s, which he deemed too formalistic. J. R. Becher, who had formerly maintained in the *Linkskurve* that the true 'proletarian classics' were Marx and Lenin, not Goethe, Gerhardt Hauptmann or Heinrich Mann, came round to praising Büchner, Lessing, Hegel, Schiller and Hölderlin as 'builders of both classic and contemporary culture'. Thomas Mann maintained in his essay of 1928:

> What would be needed, and what could finally be German, would be an alliance and pact between the idea of a conservative culture and the idea of a revolutionary society – between Greece and Moscow, to sum it up in a single formula [. . .]. I maintain that all would be well in Germany, and Germany would find its true self, the day that Karl Marx reads Friedrich Hölderlin – a meeting that, moreover, is in the process of happening. I forgot to add that a one-sided acquaintance would remain sterile.[34]

At the same time, proletarian theatre companies staged classical German plays in the USSR. Becher spoke of distributing poems of Hölderlin to sailors' clubs and having Hegel read by the Red Army. The need to unite the defence of the classics with antifascist struggle brought about a kind of abolition of frontiers between the 'avant-garde' and a certain classicism formerly viewed as 'bourgeois'. This need to defend the German heritage was all the more acute in that in Germany itself this had been either banned or systematically distorted.

The émigrés were very soon aware that Nazi rage would not only vent itself on the progressive works of the Weimar Republic, but threatened the whole of German culture. Their hatred of modern art drove the Nazis towards a kind of classicism, of which they proposed a slanted image: to the humanist Greece of Winckelmann and Goethe they opposed militarist Sparta, the 'Doric' world celebrated by Gottfried Benn. Thomas Mann described in 'Brother Hitler' the painful impression he had on seeing National Socialism lay claim to the same tradition and symbols that he had celebrated in his work, those of Luther, Nietzsche, Wagner and Romanticism. It was in vain that Ricarda Huch refused the Nazis the right to decide what was 'German'. And Thomas Mann wrote in 1937: 'It seems that I have injured the Reich and Germany by taking a position against them! They have the unbelievable audacity to identify themselves with Germany!' While the humanist ideals of German classicism were deemed subversive, the Nazis produced countless mediocre plays and propaganda films exalting a 'Nazi Schiller' (*Schiller im braunen Hemd, Schiller Waffenkamerad Hitlers*). In Goebbels's hands the Faust legend became an allegory for Hitler's Germany itself. The émigré press reported however that Schiller's *Don Carlos* was banned, as the play was judged dangerous to the state.[35]

Baldur von Schirach tried to demonstrate a harmony between the education of the Hitler Youth and the classicism of Goethe,[36] while the wearing of uniform by young people was justified by *Elective Affinities*.[37] Heinrich Mann for his part celebrated Schiller's 175th birthday with an address on 'Nation and Freedom'.[38] He exalted the poet as a 'prophet of the revolution against tyrants' and 'admirer of the French Revolution', a 'nationalist' who did not hate any people but loved them all.[39] In a further text published in the *Neue Weltbühne* (2 September 1937), he stressed that past works were written not only for the past, and it was important to 'combine the limited knowledge of today with the knowledge of the past'. The unleashed barbarism raging in the Third Reich was for Heinrich Mann the sign that the link with the German heritage had been broken. Against Hitler, therefore, he exalted not just Schiller, Goethe, Lessing and Novalis, but also Humboldt and Herder, emphasizing that the entire German heritage, from Kant to Hölderlin, was inspired by the passion for freedom. In the same fashion, Thomas Mann showed in 1939 how Goethe's ideals were inseparable from democracy, and closer indeed to those of Heine. In the 1920s, Mann had already defended democracy in the Weimar Republic by appealing to Novalis.

THE DEFENCE OF EXILED WRITERS: ACTIVITIES OF THE SDS

Among the bodies most actively engaged in protecting the émigré writers was the Schutzverband Deutscher Schrifsteller (SDS), a genuine writers' union in the Weimar era, whose politicization had attracted Nazi hatred. Banned in Germany, it was re-established in Paris in summer 1933.[40] Its official inauguration was held in September. This was a body independent of parties, even of Willi Münzenberg's committees, though it did include a number of Communist writers. Chaired first of all by the poet David Luschnat, who left Germany on account of his religious convictions, its first members reflected the diversity of German exile literature. Individuals such as Rudolf Leonhard, E. J. Gumbel, Gustav Regler, Ludwig Marcuse, Anna Seghers, H. Pol and Max Schröder were united only by their hatred of Nazism.[41] Alfred Kantorowicz, who played an important role in it, insisted on the SDS's complete independence.[42] Whereas in the Berlin days, violent opposition often followed ideological divisions, the need for a common struggle attenuated these in the exile period, even if political differences remained. Also, as Kantorowicz emphasizes, the exiled SDS was the only writers' organization that could be termed free after the Nazification of all German cultural institutions, especially the transformation of the Berlin SDS into the Reichsverband Deutscher Schriftsteller. In Paris, it managed to regroup all the exiled writers, over and above their ideological oppositions, and establish a genuine discussion platform for German literature in exile. Between September 1933 and November 1938, the SDS invited the most varied individuals, and counted among participants at its writers' evenings a large number of different writers.[43] These few examples are sufficient to show the incontestable spirit of openness that prevailed within the SDS.[44] Their names should of course be supplemented by the foreign writers who were invited to attend and speak,[45] as well as a certain number of writers who came to Paris for the 1935 Congress and received the same invitation.[46]

These meetings, monthly in 1933 then weekly from 1934 to 1938, were held in the basement of Café Mephisto, on the boulevard Saint-Germain. They included lectures followed by discussion, and readings from works in progress. Anyone could attend without a special invitation, and everyone knew what time the meetings would be held.[47] Each meeting attracted between fifty and a hundred participants, depending on its theme. A year or two after its foundation, the SDS was in a position to print a small journal on bible paper, to be smuggled into Germany clandestinely or under false cover, for those writers who, in the émigrés' opinion, might be led to take part in internal resistance.[48] The SDS strove to develop links between French and German writers by organizing a number of public meetings in the hall of the Société d'Encouragement pour l'Industrie Nationale,[49] sometimes attracting 250 people. An admission fee was charged for these meetings, and part of the takings went to assist imprisoned writers or exiles without resources. Henri Barbusse and Paul Nizan took part in these discussions, though we know almost nothing about the content of these events apart from information conveyed in émigré memoirs or in the exile press.[50] A certain number of meetings were also held around particular political events: the imprisonment of Carl von Ossietzky and Ludwig Renn, the murder of Erich Mühsam, the Saar referendum, the fiftieth birthday of Egon Erwin Kisch, the return of Gustav Regler and Arthur Koestler from the Spanish war, the anniversary of the book burnings, the commemoration of émigré writers who died in exile in camps (addresses by Ödön von Horvath and Joseph Roth).[51]

In November 1938 a special booklet was published on the activities of the SDS, with contributions from a large number of writers and other artistic and political figures.[52] The SDS also published a series of small booklets titled 'Der Deutsche Schriftsteller', devoted to political events or statements by writers on questions affecting the exiles. In July 1937 a booklet was devoted to the Spanish war. At the same time, the SDS organized exhibitions of books such as 'Das Deutsche Buch' in Paris (25 June 1937). Heinrich Mann spoke here on antifascist literature,[53] and works by Heine were exhibited alongside those by antifascist émigrés.

Finally, the SDS helped a number of writers materially. It was via the SDS that André Gide provided meals at the Cercle François Villon to a dozen or so impoverished German writers. The SDS also devoted a commemorative evening to Eugen Mewer, who died in autumn 1937 of hunger and cold. But the foremost initiative of the SDS was the Freiheitsbibliothek.

THE GERMAN LIBRARY OF BURNED BOOKS

The émigré writers have founded in Paris and other capitals a collection of burned books, known as the Freedom Library. This library is the only current shelter for the heritage of many generations. In their own country, these books are no longer so easy to find. This library undoubtedly has a practical and historical significance, but not least is its value as a symbol. It proves the indestructible essence of a spiritual culture that is too old for an explosion of barbarism to destroy it.

Heinrich Mann, *Die Neue Weltbühne*, 18 June 1936

The Freedom Library (*Freiheitsbibliothek*) or the German Library of Burned Books was set up on 10 May 1934 under the aegis of the SDS, with the assistance of Willi Münzenberg, in commemoration of the books burned in Germany a year ago that day. Its foundation committee included Romain Rolland, Heinrich Mann, Lion Feuchtwanger, H. G. Wells and Lucien Lévy-Bruhl. It set out to collect all works that had been burned, banned or silenced in Germany, to gather books and articles indispensable to the study of National Socialism, to put the émigrés' personal libraries at the disposal of all, and collect documents on the international antifascist struggle.

At its origin, there was certainly the desire to emphasize the barbarism perpetrated by the Nazi book burnings. This act, by its sadism and medieval obscurantism, struck not only every exiled author but the imagination of the entire world.[54] In the course of a conversation between Renaud de Jouvenel and Alfred Kantorowicz,[55] the establishment of an archival centre was envisaged where books, newspapers and magazines banned or burned in Germany would be collected. A committee was set up to give the project concrete form, its members including Gide, Gaston Gallimard, Charles Dullin, G. Baty and Paul Langevin. Documents on the persecution of German writers, the destruction of books, and the lists of banned works, were initially piled up in Kantorowicz's hotel room on the rue de Tournon.[56] Romain Rolland agreed to preside over the founding committee. Writers involved in its work included G. Duhamel, E. Fleg, H. R. Lenormand, Gaston Gallimard, F. Masereel, G. Baty, Paul Langevin, H. Wallon, Count Karoly, J. R. Bloch, E. J. Gumbel, Hanns Eisler, Alfred Kerr, Egon Erwin Kisch, R. Leonhard, Theodor Plievier, Kurt Rosenfeld, Joseph Roth, Anna Seghers, Lion Feuchtwanger, Bruno Frank, Rudolf Olden and Prinz Hubertus zu Löwenstein. At the same time, thanks to Ernst Toller and the Germanist Albert Malte Wagner, exiled in England, a Society of the Friends of the Burned Books was founded there, encouraged by Lady Oxford and Asquith.[57]

The German Library of Burned Books was initially established in a painter's workshop at 65 boulevard Arago. As well as volumes burned in Germany, it collected more than 10,000 press cuttings on the subject of Nazi cultural policy, the persecution of writers and proscriptions of works. Added later were works written in exile, leaflets, and letters from émigrés and prisoners. The library operated with the help of unpaid staff, and was also supported by Willi Münzenberg. It obtained the sponsorship of Lord Marley, president of the

World Committee for the Victims of Fascism, Harold Laski, Ellen Wilkinson and Professor J. B. S. Haldane, as well as Lord Rothschild and Lady Oxford. It was at the request of this last that H. G. Wells agreed to join the British support committee of the Freiheitsbibliothek.

A similar committee was established in Switzerland, on the initiative of Hans Mühlestein. Gradually a genuine library was organized, which collected not only all the banned and proscribed books, but also works by exiles and any document concerning National Socialism. This library soon held more than 200,000 newspaper articles, as well as thousands of pamphlets and leaflets. In Britain, more than a thousand people joined the Society of Friends of the Burned Books. When the Freiheitsbibliothek was opened, speeches were delivered in both Paris and London by a number of writers, and a large number of messages of support were addressed to the exiles, including one from John Dos Passos. A year after its inauguration, the Freiheitsbibliothek held more than 50,000 volumes. Its reading room became a meeting place for many émigrés and it was with good reason that Kantorowicz described it as the 'spiritual centre of German emigration in Paris'.[58] The library's collection of documents was presumably destroyed by the Gestapo in 1940, together with the SDS archives.[59]

The symbol it had embodied, however, remained alive. In autumn 1942, the New York Public Library held an exhibition of banned and burned German books. The committee of honour that sponsored the display included Eleanor Roosevelt and Albert Einstein, writers, teachers and political figures. The inauguration of this exhibition, on 1 December 1942, was accompanied by speeches given to an audience of several thousand: American politicians and writers, exiles and journalists explained the significance of this demonstration.[60] British and American writers were all the more sensitive to the phenomenon as the works of some fifty of their number were now banned in Germany.[61] Under the aegis of the Council on Books in Wartime, which comprised bookshops and libraries, other demonstrations were organized on the theme of these banned books. NBC broadcast a programme 'They Burned the Books',[62] and flags on American libraries and schools were symbolically lowered to half-mast. Evoking the events of 10 May 1933, Franklin D. Roosevelt declared:

> We all know that books burn. But we know still better that books can never be destroyed by fire. Men die, but books never die. No man and no violence can extinguish their memory. No man and no violence can lock ideas up for ever in a concentration camp. No man and no violence can chase from the world the works that express the eternal struggle of humanity against tyranny. We know that, in this War, books are weapons.

The Council on Books in Wartime made the anniversary of the 1933 book burning a 'Day of the Free Book'. Roosevelt's opponent, the Republican candidate Wendell L. Wilkie, launched the same appeal, maintaining that the flames of the burned books lit up the sky and united men today. Posters were published, the SDS organized lectures and discussions with writers and

American academics.[63] Lists of works banned or burned were circulated to bookstores and librarians, with a view to immediately reintroducing them after the destruction of fascism. Finally, summing up all these actions, Thomas Mann emphasized in his May 1943 radio broadcast to Germany that the Nazi regime would always remain in people's memory as the regime of burned books. It is indeed true that this act of barbarism more than any other struck the world imagination at this time. For the commemoration organized on 10 May 1943, hundreds of broadcasts were devoted to the burned books. Discussions were organized in schools and army barracks, as well as readings from works banned in Germany. Sinclair Lewis and Eve Curie (daughter of Pierre and Marie) wrote to American publishers to explain the meaning of these demonstrations. Works by 'degenerate' composers were also played: Mendelsohn, Gershwin, Schönberg, Shostakovitch, Kurt Weill and Hanns Eisler, and plays banned in Germany were staged in the theatre.[64] As Kantorowicz wrote, the spark struck by a few émigrés in an attic room had lit up a continent.[65]

On 10 May 1947, the 'Tag des freien Buches' was celebrated in a ruined Berlin, both exiles and anti-Nazis who had remained in Germany taking part. For this occasion, Kindler Verlag (operating under US licence) published a weekly magazine, *Sie*, with an introduction by Richard Drews and Alfred Kantorowicz, containing documents on the external and internal emigration. A *Tag des freien Buches* pamphlet was also published, written by Kantorowicz. It recalled the names of the exiled writers and the list of works banned or burned under the Third Reich. In the course of this ceremony, in which a number of Soviet representatives also took part, poems of Heine were read as well as of Mayakovsky, Heinrich Mann, Gorky and Tucholsky. Ernst Busch performed songs by Brecht and Eisler. Busch had been released in 1945 from a German prison, with his face half paralysed. For the first and last time, perhaps, in this remembrance of the burned books, exiled writers and opponents of fascism gathered together despite their ideological differences. Some of them had not met for fourteen years. A ceremony was held in the courtyard of Humboldt University, opposite the square where the book burning had been held. Peter Suhrkamp, Alfred Kantorowicz, Anna Seghers, Alfred Döblin and Erich Kästner were present along with Günther Weisenborn, and as Kantorowicz emphasizes, speeches were directed both to East and West, punctuated with extracts from *The Magic Flute* performed by a Berlin choir.

After the Second World War, Professor Hanns Wilhelm Eppelsheimer started from scratch to collect the exile publications.[66] The task was especially hard in that the exiles had been scattered across the world, had published under pseudonyms, in short-lived and poorly distributed magazines. Yet by 1950, 100 books had been collected, and by 1968 the collection held 11,000 books and periodicals, as well as 1,500 letters (largely from the Walter A. Berendsohn collection in Stockholm). These publications included not only Socialist and Communist periodicals, but also those of Otto Strasser's Schwarze Front, the Deutsche Freiheitspartei and the Jesuit Friedrich Muckermann. This library comprised three sections: the first for political literature, magazines and newspapers, pamphlets and manifestos; the second for belles-lettres, and the third for scientific publications, with works by more than 2,000 scholars including 723 professors. Thanks to the documents subsequently collected in Frankfurt, exhibitions on these banned and burned books were organized throughout the world. Similar efforts were later taken in the GDR. A plaque was also put up on the former premises of the Freiheitsbibliothek in Paris, at the initiative of the GDR and in the presence of former émigrés. Finally, when the fiftieth anniversary of the Nazi seizure of power was commemorated in 1983, many events were organized internationally celebrating the foundation of the Freiheitsbibliothek. Few émigrés would have imagined then that their enterprise would acquire such a symbolic power across the years.

WARNINGS TO EUROPE

In 1933 and during the next two or three years, the only people with an intimate understanding of what went on in the young Third Reich were a few thousand refugees.

Arthur Koestler, *The Invisible Writing*

What would the world know without us?

Heinrich Mann, *Kampf der Volksfront*, 1937

To warn the European nations and the whole world of the danger that Hitler presented to peace and the future of democracy – *their* democracies – was one of the most constant concerns of the exiles, even if they found themselves incessantly in the role of unhappy Cassandras. This denunciation of National Socialism took a number of forms.

From 1933 on, the émigrés issued copious information, including first-hand testimony, on the terror and barbarism prevailing in Germany. These documents also covered the arrest of activists and writers, the stifling of cultural life, and the sadism with which oppositionists were treated. Their denunciation of National Socialism had its first victory with the publication of the *Brown Book* on the Reichstag fire, produced by Willi Münzenberg, which contained a large number of documents on the German terror. Among these early testimonies, the descriptions of concentration camps by writers, artists and activists who had been interned there (Wolfgang Langhoff, Willi Bredel, Gerhardt Seger) were translated into several languages and played a particularly important role. *Peat-Bog Soldiers* by Langhoff, and Seger's *Oranienburg*, astounded those who knew Germany only as a civilized country. The émigrés went on to publish, especially under imprints they had themselves established such as the Éditions du Carrefour in France, a large number of books, pamphlets and collections of documents on anti-Semitism, racism, organized terror, children's education and the subjugation of the churches, comprising a mass of information on German conditions to counter Goebbels's official propaganda.

The distribution of this information required not just the establishment of magazines and publishing houses, and the production of a wealth of propaganda material – leaflets and disguised texts (*Tarnschriften*) – but also the use of public platforms. From 1933 on, the most well-known émigrés, especially writers, gave countless lectures and missed no occasion to intervene at international congresses and writers' gatherings, to mobilize world opinion against National Socialism. As the exile magazines and newspapers were printed only in relatively small editions, the exiles often tried to contribute to those periodicals published in the various countries where they had settled, when this was legally possible, so that their accounts of Nazi atrocities found a wider echo. While Heinrich Mann's contributions to *La Dépêche de Toulouse* were the most important of these, a large number of émigré writers and journalists made frequent interventions in the foreign press, despite the protests of the German embassy or Nazi sympathizers.

Every means of cultural agitation – theatre, film, cabaret, novels, poems – was used against National Socialism. It is enough to recall the depictions of everyday life in Hitler's Germany in the form of sketches by Brecht and Heinrich Mann (*Hatred*), and the antifascist cabarets of Prague, Zurich and Paris, such as Erika Mann's famous Pfeffermühle. These campaigns often acquired an international dimension, like that in support of the accused in the Reichstag trial, or for the release of Thälmann, Mühsam or Ossietzky. Undoubtedly the political analyses offered by many of the émigrés suffered from many illusions: belief in a speedy end to their exile, in the weakness of the Nazi regime and its precarious character, errors in their understanding of the real causes of Nazi victory, faith in the ability of the German resistance to overthrow the regime, etc. Mistakes of this kind were simply unavoidable. What is much more striking is the accuracy of their most pessimistic predictions, and the wealth of documents and information of all kinds that they circulated about Hitler's Germany. Few of their audience, however, took this seriously enough.

It is easy then to understand the bitterness and despair to be found in so many antifascist memoirs. They knew, but no one listened to them. They wanted to help, but their offers went unheeded. The struggle they had resolved to wage against Hitler was something with which most countries did not want to be associated. In a booklet published by Éditions du Phénix,[67] titled *Warum schweigt die Welt? (Why Is the World Silent?)*, a number of émigrés inquired as to the reasons for this failure to respond to Nazi barbarism. Georg Bernhard spoke of a kind of 'laziness of the heart' that had taken hold of the democracies. Europe wanted to sleep quietly and rejected anything that could rouse it from its lethargy. Kantorowicz underlined how, whilst France had been impassioned over the Dreyfus affair, it greeted the Nuremberg laws with indifference. So many of the Nazis' victims were faceless, and scarcely aroused indignation.[68] Paul Westheim stressed in the same pamphlet how the world seemed to have lost its conscience and become acclimatized to terror and horror: 'It's a problem for other people, those of a different nationality, a different race, a different party, a different class.' When Ernst Erich Noth declared in 1938, in *Man against Partisan*, that war could be foreseen if the democracies gave in to Hitler, he failed to arouse a reaction, any more than did the Jesuit Friedrich Muckermann, who was only permitted to speak on the French radio after 3 September 1939.

After arousing a certain curiosity, a reflex of disgust, everything the exiles revealed simply met with resignation and indifference. The atrocities that they related were minimized in the papers. After 1935, many prominent figures visited Germany and met with Hitler. Following the Concordat with the pope, the Berlin Olympiad, which the émigrés had failed in their efforts to boycott, was an indubitable diplomatic success for the Reich. Stefan Zweig sorrowfully depicted the atmosphere of jubilation that followed the Munich agreement in England:

> We, on the contrary, knew that whatever was the most monstrous was the natural thing to expect. Every one of us had the vision of a slain friend, a tortured comrade, in our mind's eye, hence had harder, sharper, more pitiless eyes. The proscribed, the hunted, the expropriated knew that no pretext was too absurd or false when robbery and power were concerned. Thus those of us who had been subjected to trial and those who as yet had been spared it, the immigrants and the English, spoke different languages. It is no exaggeration to say that besides a negligible number of Englishmen we were then the only ones in England who did not delude ourselves about the full extent of the danger.[69]

And he added: 'Here in England, too, just as in Austria, I was destined to foresee the inevitable clearly with tortured heart and tormenting clairvoyance; with the difference that I was a stranger, a tolerated guest in England and dared not utter a warning.'[70]

In fact, even those who were ready to issue appeals and warnings were not always heard, and Thomas Mann, in a speech to the American Rescue Committee in 1940, drew the tragic balance-sheet of this blindness, declaring that political development in Europe would have been different if some attention had been paid to the warnings of exiled antifascists, and that the world's 'refusal to know' (*Nicht-wissen-wollen*) was a monstrous suicide.

The Struggle against National Socialism

Those who struggle against it are brave.
Those who expose its plans are intelligent.
Only those who conquer it will save Germany.

Bertolt Brecht, 'German War Primer'

We cannot claim here to offer a comprehensive picture of the exiles' anti-Nazi activities between 1933 and 1945. It would be arbitrary, moreover, to separate political struggle from exile literature. To write novels, poems and plays, to give lectures and set up publishing houses, were political acts in as much as the object in mind was the condemnation and weakening of the Hitler regime. Each group of exiles, each country of asylum, could provide the basis for a particular study. We shall restrict ourselves here therefore to the different types of action, the forms of opposition developed by the émigrés, rather than pursue these actions in detail. The fact that they were rarely crowned with success should in no way discredit them, quite the contrary. Their failure often only makes the courage, boldness and power of invention that they required all the more admirable. The exiles hardly had any illusions about their struggle, which they readily compared with that of David against Goliath – a theme as frequently found in their writings as that of the reviled prophetess Cassandra. With the exception of the campaign for the release of the accused in the Reichstag fire trial, and the distribution of information on Nazi Germany in the first years of exile, they only rarely managed to have an influence on events. But despite this, their struggles compel admiration. The publication of the *Brown Book* was already a major exploit; without it, and the 'counter-trial' in London that accompanied it, it is likely that the Leipzig accused would all have been beheaded.

1. SUPPORT FOR THE GERMAN RESISTANCE

INTERNAL AND EXTERNAL RESISTANCE

The existence of a double front of German resistance, one represented by the political and literary émigrés that had left the country in 1933, the other by those opponents who remained in the Reich, was taken for granted by the majority of émigrés in the first years of exile. Such a combination of two fronts would enable the overthrow of the Nazi regime.[1] But this belief was already eroded somewhat by the Nazi success in the Saar plebiscite of January 1935, weakening further as the Nazi regime steadily consolidated itself and any possibility of shattering it began to seem increasingly faint. Subsequently, the victory of Hitler's armies led certain émigrés to doubt the very existence of a genuine opposition to Nazism remaining within the Reich.

From 1933 to 1935, faith in the potential force of German resistance is found among both writers and political leaders in exile, though according to Thomas Mann's diary, Robert Breitscheid and Rudolf Hilferding were far more pessimistic. A number of exiles, especially writers, were tempted to interpret the least sign of the regime's problems – the rivalry between Nazi leaders, the slightest murmur of opposition, as heralding the final collapse. On 19 February 1936, Thomas Mann wrote to René Schickele: 'Everyone from Germany whom I speak to seems to feel that the National Socialist adventure is in its final stage and that general disintegration is at hand.'[2]

Heinrich Mann particularly displayed a surprising optimism. In his speeches and articles he ceaselessly depicted the capacity of German resistance, and reading these one might well ask how the Nazis could still be in power. In 1937, he wrote in *La Dépêche de Toulouse* that the Nazi government had lost its legitimacy and no longer had majority support. He described the German workers as 'Marxists' who were resolutely opposed to fascism. Behind Hitler there were only a few industrialists, who moreover would shortly be ruined by Nazi demagogy. The army itself had only a lukewarm enthusiasm for Hitler, the bourgeoisie shunned the regime, and if the 20 million Socialist workers, the millions of disappointed petty bourgeois, the 20 million Catholics and 20 million Protestants were added up, not to mention half a million intellectuals and half a million Jews, this meant a total of 65 million opponents of Hitler. Heinrich Mann, accordingly, asked in all seriousness: 'Where are the Nazis?'[3] On 4 July 1934, he was already declaring that 'faith in the regime is steadily dwindling',[4] and shortly after that the young people 'were detaching themselves from the regime' (3 October 1934). In similar vein he announced the collapse of the reichsmark (4 July 1934), followed by strikes and hunger (2 September 1935).[5] As opposed to this optimism and an almost unavoidable misconstrual of the German situation, we should note the reticence of the young Communist activists that Gustav Regler depicts when the émigrés asked them to distribute their leaflets: they saw this as ineffective and absolutely out of touch with the German situation.

The reasons for these illusions are not hard to discern. The demagogy that marked Hitler's speeches, the fact that mythical incantations had replaced an economic programme, made it hard to believe in the German recovery, all the more so as the various Weimar governments had all failed in this. The stabilization achieved by the Nazis contributed a great deal to winning them support, and covering up the more scandalous aspects of domestic policy.[6] Few exiles imagined that the European democracies could come to terms with Hitler and maintain normal relations with the Reich. In order to govern, the Nazis had to depend first of all on other parties of the right. For many, this coalition was highly unstable, and they expected Hitler to be used and then dismissed. Other émigrés believed in an inevitable confrontation between Hitler and the army (especially after the 'night of the long knives' and the murder of General von Schleicher), or in a 'second revolution' led by proletarian elements against the 'bonzes' of the regime.[7]

It is true, however, that even if decapitated, opposition remained present and active in Germany. Depending on their ideological choices, the émigrés put their trust in various components of this potential opposition. Despite the Concordat signed with the pope, exiled Catholics and Protestants refused to believe in a possible entente between the churches and the Nazi regime. In the émigré press it was noted that as far back as 1923 the Munich archbishop, Cardinal Michael Faulhaber, had warned against the Nazis, and in 1930 Monsignor von Galen, bishop of Münster, maintained that the NSDAP programme was irreconcilable with Christian belief.[8] The stupidity of Nazi policies towards the arts, and culture in general, led many to suppose that those intellectuals who remained in Germany could be counted among the opposition, apart from the absolute sycophants of the regime. Finally, the émigrés were persuaded that even after the elimination of the parties of the left, there was still a genuine working-class opposition. Communist cells had been re-established after 1933, printing antifascist leaflets and papers in which exile writings were published. Though fifty-seven Communist deputies had died in concentration camps, and more than 20,000 activists had been arrested, Dimitrov championed a 'Trojan horse' tactic of infiltrating Nazi organizations. The Nazis similarly infiltrated the Communist cells, whose members were arrested one after another. All the same, in 1936 a total of 1,643,000 illegal leaflets were seized, and a further 927,430 in 1937,[9] while the number of Communist resisters executed or arrested remained considerable. Without being anything like as significant, Social-Democratic resistance was also very active.[10]

THE RE-ESTABLISHMENT OF PARTIES IN EXILE

Immediately after the Communist and Socialist parties were banned, they tried to reorganize in exile and establish links with underground activists who had remained in the Reich. Shortly after the arrest of Thälmann,[11] John Schehr and Hermann Remmele were sent to Moscow to explain the situation. Walter Ulbricht was put in charge of the provisional party leadership in Germany, together with Hermann Schubert. Ulbricht's task was to organize the reappearance of the party organ, *Rote Fahne*, while Schubert was responsible for liaison between districts. After Schehr's return, tensions grew between his group and that of Ulbricht and Schubert.[12] Wilhelm Pieck was given charge of the party leadership abroad (Paris), and Ulbricht that of the operational direction (*Landsleitung*) in Germany. He remained in hiding in Danzig and only joined other Communists in Paris in 1936. Schubert fled to Prague in summer 1933, and Schehr remained the only major KPD leader to remain in Germany.[13] The KPD's general staff was henceforward based first in Paris, before moving to Prague and then Moscow.

The tasks undertaken by the KPD in exile were very significant. Apart from the reappearance of *Rote Fahne* and other Communist papers, instructors were trained in Paris to direct illegal organizations in the Reich, establish contact between them, and produce propaganda material for distribution in Germany. When Ulbricht was called to work for the Comintern in Moscow, in May 1937, Franz Dahlem – whose memoirs are a significant source of information[14] – Paul Merker, Paul Bertz and Johann Koplening became the most important representatives of the exile secretariat. Alongside them were a number of figures who played a major role in the emigration:[15] Walter Hähnel was responsible for press work, Anton Ackermann for political education, Elli Schmidt for women's work, Alexander Abusch for *Rote Fahne* and relations with the SDS.[16] Gerhart Eisler edited the party's theoretical organ, *Die Internationale*, and Albert Norden was in charge of relations with various international organizations.[17] Lex Ende edited the *Deutsche Volkszeitung*, and Bruno Frei *Deutsche Informationen*; Walter Beling was responsible for the party's technical apparatus, and Willi Münzenberg for propaganda. The focus of KPD activities would now be in exile.[18]

The situation of the Social-Democrats was more complex, given the diversity of their components. While a number of their leading figures had left for exile in 1933, directly threatened by the Nazis (Otto Braun, Albert Grzesinski, Phillip Scheidemann, Robert Breitscheid, Rudolf Hilferding, W. Dittmann), followed by Otto Wels, Friedrich Stampfer, Hans Vogel, Erich Ollenhauer and Paul Hertz after the destruction of the trade unions,[19] other members who remained in Germany distanced themselves from the party's exile leadership in Prague. A new leadership was even elected, which did not however prevent the proscription and dissolution of the party.

After 1933, the Prague *Exilvorstand* saw itself as the sole representative of the SPD, and published its celebrated manifesto *Combat and Objective of Revolutionary Socialism: The Policy of the German Social-Democratic Party*. A number of Socialist groups, however, still charged it with reformism. Soon, several key members of the party left Prague for Britain and the Netherlands. New groups formed in exile, which whilst claiming allegiance to Socialism, did not accept the policy of the exiled SPD. This was the case with the SAP (which had split from the SPD in 1931), of which Willy Brandt was a prominent member, Neu Beginnen, and the Revolutionary-Socialist Work Circle (RSD). After the collapse of Czechoslovakia, the SoPaDe moved its office to Paris (where several well-known Socialist leaders and theorists were to die, including Otto Bauer and Siegfried Crummenerl), while Friedrich Stampfler emigrated to the United States, Hans Vogel and Emil Ollenhauer to Britain, and other groups formed in Denmark and Sweden. Despite the KPD's change of tactic to the Popular Front, the Socialist leadership remained hostile to any collaboration. On examining the spectrum of exiled Socialist groups, it is not always easy to establish what still united them in terms of doctrine: those of London, Sweden and New York developed political visions that were not easy to reconcile.

A certain number of right-wing oppositionists also re-established themselves in exile: National Socialist dissidents and national-revolutionaries, the best known of which was the Schwarze Front of Otto Strasser, who emigrated first to Vienna, then Prague, and finally Canada. Alliance with these *Volkssozialisten* was sometimes envisaged in America, even though Strasser's followers had never ceased to proclaim their anti-Semitism. What did virtually disappear in exile, however, was the old Centre party, of which the only symbolic remnant was a few Catholic figures.

ÉMIGRÉ LINKS WITH THE GERMAN RESISTANCE

Throughout the exile period, the émigrés – both writers and full-time political activists – sought to maintain, establish and develop links with opponents in the Reich, by associating with their struggles (exchange of information, distribution of leaflets) and supplying them with propaganda material. Writers hoped to rally to their cause those colleagues who had been unable to make the choice of exile. Socialists and Communists tried to organize clandestine resistance from abroad. Until 1938–39, all were persuaded that the real struggle would take place in Germany, and those outside could only play a supporting role.[20] Though such connections between exiles and the internal resistance were still fairly frequent until 1935, they gradually dwindled as the Hitler regime maintained itself in power, border surveillance was made more draconian, and faith in the ability to overthrow the regime evaporated. Until the end of the War, German resistance took place in desperate isolation.

The links maintained between the émigrés and anti-Nazis within the Reich crystallized around a number of specific tasks.

Exchange of Information and Contact
between Internal Opponents and Émigrés

A number of Communist activists who remained in Germany after the Nazi seizure of power immediately re-established clandestine cells. Close contact was then maintained between the party's exile leadership and the operational direction.[21] The Socialists followed the same tactic. It was practically impossible for antifascists who were actively pursued to return to Germany, even illicitly, and few of these took the risk.[22] Contact was established by way of young workers who travelled abroad to secretly meet with the exiles, in Prague, the Netherlands, the Saar and especially in Paris.[23] A number of 'border networks' were set up in countries adjacent to the Reich, not far from the frontier, which enabled brief meetings between exiles and oppositionists,[24] exchange of information and documents, and delivery of propaganda material for distribution in the Reich.

It was in this way that émigrés were kept in touch with the developing internal situation, including arrests and measures taken against the opposition. This information, concealed of course by the Reich press, was published in exile papers and magazines, and conveyed to foreign correspondents.

Material and Financial Aid

Though German workers clandestinely and symbolically organized collections in support of the Spanish Republic, it was above all the émigrés who, despite their meagre resources, supplied the underground resistance with a material aid that was far from negligible. These sums were primarily designed to help activists to survive illegally or leave the country.

Newspapers, Leaflets, Propaganda Material

The reappearance in Germany of certain banned newspapers, produced illegally in print-works set up in cellars or abroad, was envisaged right from the Nazi seizure of power. These operations required a fairly complex organization[25] and a good deal of imagination, especially as far as smuggling this material into the Reich was concerned.

At the start of its illegal activity, the KPD printed small-format leaflets for distribution in the major industrial centres. These were often newspapers for a particular factory or district. According to Wilhelm Pieck,[26] in the first months of the Nazi regime these papers were printed at more than 1,000 places, in over two million copies. The *Rote Fahne* reappeared illegally in mimeograph form in March 1933, two or three times per month, with a run of more than 300,000. Other Communist papers had a more ephemeral existence,[27] and it is impossible to know how many people they reached. Printed in haphazard workshops hidden in activists' homes, and above all in neighbouring countries, this propaganda material was then imported into Germany in highly ingenious ways, from France, the Netherlands or Czechoslovakia, thanks to the complicity of German workers or by the émigrés directly. Thus the famous Transportkolonne Otto, directed by Willi Bohn, was made up of excellent swimmers able to transport material by following the Rhine down from Lake Constance. The *Rote Fahne*, printed abroad, was smuggled into Germany in this way, and according to the Gestapo, some thirty illegal Communist papers were distributed in certain districts of Berlin. This continued until 1935, accompanied by lightning meetings. The Prague SoPaDe also published little green bulletins which were distributed in the Reich. *Neue Vorwärts* was replaced by *Sozialistische Aktion*. At least 12,000 copies were smuggled into Germany, along with other Socialist papers.[28] The émigrés took an active part in all propaganda work.[29] The number of illegal publications steadily dwindled after 1935, and their impact was above all symbolic; against the propaganda system established by Goebbels, these leaflets and papers could hardly influence public opinion, but they did show that resistance still existed, and despite the terror, opposition was not dead.

Instructions for Resistance Groups and Workers

Contact between the émigrés and opponents within the Reich also made it possible to give instructions for action to all who continued the antifascist struggle after 1933. This task was all the more difficult in that the leading organs of the workers' parties moved from one centre to another. The Communist headquarters was in Paris from 1933 to 1934, from January 1935 in Moscow, from 1935 to 1936 in Prague, from 1936 to 1940 back in Paris, then again in Moscow.[30] The Socialists were based in Prague, then in Paris, before fleeing to Britain or Sweden. The destruction of parties and unions, and the arrest of cadres, had seriously disoriented activists, and the underground resistance groups were often isolated and had no contact with each other, for fear of denunciation, arrest and Gestapo infiltration. As it became increasingly hard to maintain operational direction of the parties in Germany, instructions were conveyed by way of activists who managed to leave the Reich and meet émigrés abroad. Their aim was to try and establish resistance movements. It was the Communists who developed the broadest activity. But these acts of resistance could not do very much against the system of surveillance, informing and generalized terror that the Nazis had put in place. Those who wrote the leaflets soon realized this, and those who distributed them even sooner: the majority were eventually arrested and executed.[31]

Solidarity Campaigns Abroad

A further aspect of the support given by émigrés to resisters in Germany was participation – whether public or not – in the campaigns and committees that took on the defence of imprisoned writers or political activists. In the cases of Ernst Thälmann, the Reichstag fire defendants, Carl von Ossietzky, Erich Mühsam, Ludwig Renn and Edgar André, their names became symbols. As the exiles naturally had no means of acting directly on the Reich, they sought to support antifascists under threat of death by way of intellectual mobilization in the countries where they took refuge. It has to be acknowledged, however, that very few campaigns were able to affect the fate of detainees or the wider course of events, apart from the publication of the *Brown Book* and the release of Dimitrov. The reasons for this failure were varied. Exile propaganda could hardly match the resources of Goebbels. The content of the leaflets was often refuted by Germany's economic revival. Despite the information provided by resisters in Germany, the catastrophism of émigré analyses often contrasted with the everyday reality experienced by Germans and the hopes to which Hitler had given rise. In the same way they tended to overrate the slightest signs of political crisis or development of a resistance movement, hopes that were often soon confounded.

The failure of the mobilization against the return of the Saar was doubtless one of the most tragic illustrations of these illusions. Rich in coal, the Saar territory with its 600,000 inhabitants had been left by the Versailles treaty for later settlement. Clemenceau had claimed it for France, but the decision had been delayed for fifteen years, when a plebiscite was to be held to decide on its destiny. During this time, the Saar was administered by the League of Nations.

The plebiscite was set for 13 January 1935, and it now assumed great political importance.[32] As Koestler wrote: '[H]ere an ethnically German, but politically free population would be passing judgement on Hitler's regime after two years.'[33] The political parties combined into two fronts: the 'German front' of the pro-Nazi movements, and the Popular Front comprising Socialists, Communists and liberals. The Saarlanders were given three options: return to Germany, attachment to France, or continuation of the status quo.

From autumn 1934, as Manès Sperber recalls,[34] major campaigning activity got under way. It was unlikely that the Saar's German population would rally to the French side, so the Socialists campaigned for the status quo. Without taking this option into account, the Communists had initially launched a very strange slogan: 'For a red Saar in a Soviet Germany' (Eine rote Saar in Sowjet-Deutschland), which according to Sperber and Kantorowicz left the workers perplexed. Red Saar and Soviet Germany didn't exist, so which alternative should they vote for?[35] In June 1934, the Comintern changed its tactic and decided to campaign for the status quo: 'in order the better and more rapidly to develop the revolutionary forces. But their support of the status quo will cease the moment the proletariat of Germany takes up the victorious fight for power.'[36]

The Saar campaign was marked by a close collaboration between local and exiled antifascists. 'Almost all the Communist cadres who had found asylum in France spent their energies on the struggle. Trade unionists, journalists and artists of all kinds were dispatched to the Saar.'[37] Hubertus Friedrich Prinz zu Löwenstein, the former Reichsbanner member and editor of the weekly Das Reich, published in Saarbrücken, pronounced in favour of the status quo, as did the paper Westland.[38] Arthur Koestler was also sent to the Saar to edit a satirical weekly, Die Saar-Ente (the 'canard du Saar'), while Gustav Regler, a Saarlander himself, was charged with making a propaganda film.[39] In his memoirs, he tells of the difficulties that the presence of the Gestapo presented: his car was often burned, and on many occasions he narrowly escaped being the victim of an 'accident'. The idea was for him to be taken by ambulance to Germany, where 'overnight a Nazi doctor would have seen to our wounds and we would have ended up in a morgue'.[40] The émigrés soon became aware of the church's role in the plebiscite. It was resolutely pro-German, and the Saarland Catholics, not very political, were strongly influenced by instructions given by the ecclesiastical authorities. Even when Regler presented a worker who had been arrested and tortured by the Gestapo, this failed to arouse a sense of revolt,[41] while Socialist and Communist meetings were disrupted by unemployed thugs paid by the Nazis for starting fights.

Despite all these difficulties, the majority of exiles seemed relatively confident. If the Saarlanders would not demand attachment to France, they would keep the status quo to avoid being incorporated into Hitler's Germany. Alone perhaps among the writers, Heinrich Mann published in La Dépêche de

Toulouse an article titled 'The Supreme Danger', in which he unusually asserted a pessimistic view. He predicted that the Saar would return to Germany because of its historic traditions, and this would count as a success for the Hitler regime, though the vote would have gone the same way had Germany still been a republic. In the event, 85 per cent of Saarlanders chose attachment to Germany. Gustav Regler wrote:

> I escaped that night by way of the Forbach woods, over the Spichern mountain into Lorraine. As I passed by the German military cemetery I remembered that my grandfather had fought here in 1870 against the French. But Father had said that the soldiers lying in those graves had died for an illusion. There were no visible frontiers to be seen, but only tombstones which taught men nothing.[42]

And Manès Sperber:

> The results had a most shocking effect: they were incredible, and it took great strength of mind not to doubt their reliability. I could no longer believe the radio, and waited impatiently for the morning papers: we had not just been defeated but pulverized. [. . .] In this country of coal miners, Catholics, Socialists and Communists had not even been able to win 10 per cent of the vote against those prepared to join up with Nazi Germany. [. . .] The result of the Saarland plebiscite had shown that until a new situation emerged, no uprising against the Nazi regime could be expected of the German proletariat.[43]

Like many others, the Saar campaign, in which so many of the émigrés had placed their hopes for a rejection of National Socialism by a German-speaking population, helped to ruin their illusions. This does not mean that their anti-Nazi propaganda was in vain; on some occasions it had genuine success, an analysis has to take both sides into account. But at the end of the day, this could not have changed the fate of Europe and avoided war.

2. THE SUCCESSES OF ANTI-NAZI PROPAGANDA IN EXILE

From the first anti-Nazi leaflets distributed in the factories, to Thomas Mann's broadcasts and the foundation of the Freies Deutschland committee towards the end of the War, émigré propaganda was incessant. It targeted the German population, as well as writers, foreign powers and Wehrmacht soldiers. For all the differences of political orientation, it pursued the same goals: to weaken the regime, help encourage resistance against it leading to its overthrow, and denounce the criminal character of National Socialism by showing the threat that it represented to peace and the democratic countries. Born together with exile, this propaganda ceased only after the capitulation of Germany. While it crystallized around certain particularly crucial events – the arrests of activists and writers, the Saar plebiscite, the boycott of the Berlin Olympics – for the majority of émigrés it was a daily task. Journalists, writers and political activists devoted to it a large part of their time, resources and energy. Generally produced in the centres of exile, this propaganda could not be smuggled into Germany without the complicity of workers who agreed to distribute it. The editing, printing and distribution of even the smallest leaflet required both courage and ingenuity. One man more than any other played a key role in its production and was also responsible for the few great successes it could claim: Willi Münzenberg. A figure of exceptional capacity, who could be disconcertingly attractive, his role in the history of emigration was so great that it is hardly possible to understand this without referring to his activities for the KPD in the Weimar years.

WILLI MÜNZENBERG'S ACTIVITIES BEFORE 1933

In the Comintern hierarchy Willi occupied an exceptional position, and this for two reasons. First, he was not a 'theoretician' but an 'activist'. He took no part in the battles between factions which, every two years or so, produced a devastating earthquake in the Communist universe. He did not manoeuvre for position, and the wrangles about the dialectically correct interpretation of the line left him cold and contemptuous.

Arthur Koestler, *The Invisible Writing*

Born on 14 August 1889 in Erfurt,[44] Münzenberg was won to revolutionary ideas at an early age. He attended the Socialist Youth Congress of 1908 in Berlin, which led to the loss of his job. In 1910 he travelled to Switzerland and took part in activities there. He made contact with the Bolshevik exiles, and was in charge of the Young Socialist secretariat. Opposed to the War and the policy of the official Social-Democrats, he linked up with the Spartacists and worked on propaganda material. In 1914 he made the acquaintance of Trotsky, then of Lenin and Karl Radek. His activities led to his arrest in Switzerland, while his first published writings, on the October Revolution, appeared illegally in Germany. Released after a second arrest, he returned to Berlin, published propaganda pamphlets with the Spartacists, but was once more arrested. As secretary of the International Bureau of Socialist Youth, he travelled to Austria, Sweden and Denmark and made contact with Bolshevik delegates; with his assistance, the Young Socialist movement, with at least 80,000 members, was transformed into a Communist organization. Invited to Soviet Russia by Karl Radek, he took part in the Comintern congress of 1920, and returned to Germany disguised as a prisoner of war. The following year he travelled again to Moscow for the Third Comintern congress.

Internationale Arbeiterhilfe (IAH)
In 1921 Russia was cruelly struck by famine, affecting over twenty million people. Maxim Gorky launched an international appeal for assistance on 13 July. A committee was established linking twenty-two aid organizations, under the chairmanship of the Norwegian F. Nansen. The left parties and trade unions

lent their support, and this aid steadily took on an increasingly political character. After a voyage to Russia, Münzenberg founded the Auslandskomitee zur Organisierung der Arbeiterhilfe für die Hungernden in Russland, which included not only left organizations but also figures such as Käthe Kollwitz, Albert Einstein, George Grosz, Arthur Holitscher, Maximilian Harden, Heinrich Vogeler, Alexandre Moissi, Leonhard Frank, Anatole France and Henri Barbusse. On 21 August, the committee was able to send a shipload of supplies to Soviet Russia, and soon similar vessels departed from points across the world under the auspices of the IAH. Münzenberg's first large-scale action on an international level was followed by many others that attested to his astounding talent as organizer and propagandist. Throughout his life he excelled in setting up defence and support committees of this kind, but he understood at the same time the political advantage to be drawn from such actions. Aid to the hungry people of Soviet Russia was a springboard leading those who donated to take a more general interest in the country. Finally, what is striking in Münzenberg's actions, apart from their effectiveness, was the ingenious means he employed. Political or humanitarian argument was backed up by films, images and postcards that prefigured to a surprising degree the anti-Nazi propaganda he was subsequently to carry out.[45]

International Workers' Aid (IAH) became both a propaganda enterprise and such an effective means of action that it could set up factories in Russia, as well as over a hundred children's homes run by his organizations.[46] Thanks to his humanitarian campaigns, Münzenberg was able to rally a growing number of intellectuals and artists to Communism, by developing in them this humanitarian sympathy for Soviet Russia.[47] Käthe Kollwitz designed a poster for the famine relief that became an IAH symbol.[48] Persuaded that humanitarian aid was not enough, and that it was necessary to bring his influence to bear on the Soviet economy itself, Münzenberg bent his efforts to obtaining finance, lorries and tractors and setting up factories. The American trade unions donated $250,000 for the reconstruction of the Soviet economy, and the government officially gave concessions to the IAH, which managed factories and fishing grounds. On all sides the IAH founded enterprises, built new housing and restored old. Relations between the IAH and the Soviet government were based on mutual trust. No one checked the activities of Münzenberg's organizations, and indeed he was perhaps the only person familiar with their detailed operation. He managed large sums of money, which he distributed as he saw fit, with an exceptional business talent. His name became so popular in Soviet Russia that it was given to orphanages and to a ship, and he was made an honorary member of the Petrograd Soviet. Lenin often praised the effectiveness of the IAH, which collected funds, material, foodstuffs, clothing, tractors, and industrial equipment indispensable to the young republic – and above all, succeeded in winning it the sympathy of a large number of intellectuals and artists.

After 1922, when the famine was largely dispelled, Münzenberg continued to intensify his efforts. The charitable associations ceased their work, but he devoted himself to the reorganization of the Soviet economy. To facilitate the transactions of the IAH, he established in Berlin the Aufbau Industrie & Handels AG, the original purpose of which was to obtain licences of German films for Soviet Russia. At the same time, this company collected funds and issued shares and bonds to aid the Soviet economy. Münzenberg now had a tremendous amount of propaganda material at his disposal – newspapers, films and photographs – which he distributed internationally. In 1922 he attended the Fourth World Congress of the Comintern as a delegate from the IAH, which enjoyed working-class support across the world. The following year, the IAH came to the assistance of workers in the Ruhr, with funds sent by the Soviet government. At the Leipzig congress of the KPD, Münzenberg was elected to the central committee, and took part on 17 March in the 'International Conference for a United Front Against Fascism'. He was now in a position to intensify his political activities and make more frequent interventions on internal political questions.

The 'Münzenberg Trust' and Propaganda

Though General Seeckt imposed a ban on KPD organizations in 1923, the IAH managed to continue its activities, and organized an international congress in Berlin on 9 December. Through his various campaigns, Münzenberg had attracted the sympathy of a large number of intellectuals for the German workers. He now went on to establish feeding centres for the unemployed.[49] His position within the KPD was very strong, even if certain leaders, Ruth Fischer in particular, criticized the degree of independence his organizations enjoyed, and the lack of party control. It was true that Münzenberg did not need the party to set up IAH sections in a number of countries, including Belgium, France, Austria and Britain. He was attacked by the Social-Democrats – Friedrich Adler in particular – for organizing a headquarters of Communist propaganda under the cover of the IAH, a 'third column of KPD policy' and 'a diplomatic instrument in the service of the Soviet Union'. In 1925–26, a number of parties, even abroad, published documents on IAH activities which forced Münzenberg to defend his organizations at an international level. Questions were asked about a hidden centre of control. The IAH had received its mandate from Lenin, then from the Soviet government, the Comintern and the trade unions. Münzenberg was a master at exploiting this confused situation: attacked by the right-wing press, he insisted on the humanitarian character of his organization; criticized by fellow Communists, he appealed to the authority of the Comintern.

The Arbeiter Illustrierte Zeitung

Willi Münzenberg was one of the first in Germany to be aware of the importance of image and cinema. To oppose the ideological power of the capitalist media, he had the idea of developing this in the service of Communism, which acquired him the nickname of 'the red Hugenberg'.[50] On 1 November 1921 he launched the *Illustrierte Arbeiter Zeitung: Sowjetrussland im Wort und Bild,* subsequently transformed into the *Arbeiter Illustrierte Zeitung* (*AIZ*), the greatest picture weekly for workers in the 1920s, with a run of 420,000 copies. Münzenberg sought to enlist avant-garde artists to this project. The Dadaist Fritz Jung, who worked in the Comintern's press section, was dispatched to Russia to send back reports, while Münzenberg managed to put in place his own network of supplies for the Soviet population.   In the meantime Münzenberg had established a publishing house under the IAH umbrella which was not officially Communist: the Neue Deutsche Verlag. He now published the IAH paper *Sowjetrussland im Bild* under its aegis (later it was renamed *Sichel und Hammer*), travelled throughout Europe to spread awareness of his publications, and set up editions of *AIZ*, the proletarian picture magazine, in a number of countries.[51] The magazine offered reportages, documents and photos of outstanding quality on the lives of workers across the world. As well as photographs from the Soviet Union, it included those taken by avant-garde artists, and John Heartfield's photomontages, accompanied by reportage and literary feuilletons. *AIZ* combined positive images of the USSR with testimonies on international proletarian struggle.[52] Münzenberg's publishing house also brought out novels devoted to the German proletariat,[53] and accounts of visits to Russia by German workers' delegations.[54] Through its press and publishing activities, Münzenberg's organization continued to expand. He purchased *Welt am Abend*, and strove to make the Communist press attractive and popular.[55] To this end, he was ready to organize readers' meetings, matinées at the Scala or Wintergarten with Berlin stars such as Blandine Ebinger, Rosa Valetti and Käte Kuhl, or the Berlin comedian P. Graetz. He organized regular propaganda spectacles, derided by some orthodox elements, but very useful to the KPD when its official newspapers were banned, which did not happen to Münzenberg's.

In 1931, Münzenberg founded a new paper, *Berlin am Morgen*, directed by Bruno Frei, which soon had 60,000 subscribers. His propaganda 'trust' was still expanding, and the proletarian artist Otto Nagel offered him the publication of *Der Eulenspiegel*, the satirical paper he had founded together with Heinrich Zille. Thanks to Münzenberg, its print-run topped 50,000 copies by 1931. At the same time, he directed the Vereinigung der Arbeiterphotographen and its publication *Der Arbeiterphotograph*, which aimed to become 'the eyes of the working class', to show reality differently from how the bourgeois photographers had done. Throughout the Weimar period, Münzenberg increased his range of publications, all seeking to combine a critical and revolutionary dimension with a surprisingly modern sense of the importance of media.[56] He grasped very early the importance of cinema as a propaganda weapon. In his magazine *Film und Volk*, he repeatedly maintained that cinema could in no way be considered a neutral medium. Since the bourgeoisie used it, the working class also had to learn to master it. In 1922, accordingly, the *IAZ* established a company to distribute German films in Soviet Russia; it was also thanks to Soviet capital that he was able to produce propaganda films. He not only made films on Russia, but was the first to distribute in Germany a large number of Soviet films, from Eisenstein to Pudovkin, which played a large part in inspiring a current of sympathy for the October Revolution and the young Soviet republic among German intellectuals.[57] Finally, Münzenberg also helped to set up the Prometheus cinema company, which produced a number of important films.[58]

By deliberately keeping his distance from inner-party conflict, both in Germany and in the Soviet Union, Münzenberg was able to devote himself to his propaganda activity, and support for international workers' struggles.[59] His ideological caution did not prevent him from frequent attack. The right-wing press termed him a 'red millionaire', while Hugo Eberlein, in charge of KPD finances, distrusted the fact that he had no way at all of exercising control over the large sums at Münzenberg's disposal. The Comintern, on the other hand, was impressed by the solidity and effectiveness of his 'trust'. The Social-Democrats were understandably jealous of him for the success of his campaigns and propaganda work. To those who chided him as a 'salon Communist', he replied that in a capitalist environment it was impossible to act effectively without these methods. All the texts he wrote at this time develop the same themes: the need to defend the USSR, to unite against the Nazi threat, and to master the most modern media in the service of the working class. In 1931, the IAH congress assembled delegates from a hundred countries, and a 527–page volume was devoted to the occasion, describing in detail the operation of its various organizations. At the same time, Münzenberg intensified his publishing activity: beside Communist novelists, he also published works by Kurt Kesten, Gustav Regler, E. E. Kisch and even Kurt Tucholsky. His Universum collection with the motto 'an imprint for everyone' was a real people's library for the workers. Supported by devoted collaborators, Münzenberg expanded still further his acts of 'seduction'. Otto Nagel was charged with attracting visual artists to Communism, Otto Katz with actors, Kesten and Kisch likewise with writers and journalists. At the same time, Münzenberg continued his political campaigns: in defence of the USSR, against colonialism, against the arrest of trade unionists in China, against war, and within the Pleyel-Amsterdam movement.[60] While these efforts could not escape the collapse of the Weimar Republic, Münzenberg was always viewed by the Nazis as one of their principal enemies.

Münzenberg in Exile

On 1 September 1932, the IAH offices were occupied by the police, and on 28 February 1933 the premises of Münzenberg's various organizations and newspapers were ransacked. He was forced to emigrate to Paris, where he had already stayed when the French section of the Committee Against War and Fascism, established in Amsterdam, had organized its great meeting.[61] He managed to leave Germany by borrowing the passport of a young Communist and making use of the Carnival celebrations.

Established in Paris, Münzenberg immediately made contact with French intellectuals[62] and fellow émigrés. He rapidly set on foot a whole network of antifascist activities, established the World Committee for the Victims of German Fascism[63] and took part in the founding of the Freiheitsbibliothek. Paul Nizan agreed to work with him, as did the Swiss publisher Paul Lévy, who put at his disposal both his offices and his imprint – Éditions du Carrefour – its deficit being made up by the Comintern's financial assistance. Helped by a number of Communist émigrés, Münzenberg now began to use against fascism the propaganda techniques he had honed under the Weimar Republic, and with still greater ingenuity. Among his most famous initiatives at this time was the organization of a counter-trial on the Reichstag fire, the publication of the *Brown Book*, a compendium of information and documents on the Nazi terror that clearly established who was responsible, and the production of a large amount of propaganda material for clandestine distribution in Germany: above all else, the publication of books exposing Hitler's plans. Just as he had attracted the contribution of numerous non-Communist figures in the 1920s, Münzenberg and his fellow workers[64] now managed to rally to the antifascist cause a large number of intellectuals who were unaware of his real activities within the Comintern.

A champion of the antifascist Popular Front, and the unity of Socialists and Communists against the Nazis, Münzenberg also took an active part in building the German *Volksfront* in Paris. He played an important role in Communist propaganda during the Saar plebiscite, even if he had disapproved of the KPD's initial slogans. In July 1935, he visited the Soviet Union and noted the deterioration in the political climate. Many who had worked with him were now under suspicion.[65] The IAH itself was threatened; Stalin feared the 'foreigners' who worked for it in Russia, and it was eventually wound up. Yet Münzenberg was still active in the Popular Front movement, as well as in the World Assembly for Peace, which held its congress in Brussels on 7–8 September 1936. A major part of his activities were now devoted to support for the Spanish Republic. Just as he had founded children's homes in Soviet Russia, Münzenberg established similar ones for German refugee children in Paris, and for Spanish children. He sent Arthur Koestler to Spain as an observer on the Francoist side, and published his reports in French and German under the title *Menschenopfer unerhört*.

In October 1936, Münzenberg was invited to visit Moscow. He wanted to have a discussion with Karl Radek, but learned that Radek had just been arrested. At the same time it was suggested that Münzenberg should leave his Paris organization to work for the Comintern's agitprop department in Moscow, and he was again called before the control commission. The pretext for this was an alleged 'lack of revolutionary vigilance'.[66] Münzenberg pretended to agree, but asked to return to Paris to finish a number of projects, in particular the shipment of arms to Spain. He already had no intention of returning to the USSR. His successor took over the various organizations for which Münzenberg had been responsible,[67] while Münzenberg spent a number of weeks in a small sanatorium run by Dr Le Savouret (who had married the daughter of Plekhanov). Many of his collaborators were summoned before the control commission and arrested (for example Leo Fleg). Münzenberg then witnessed the collapse of the Front Populaire, with the sense that all the sincere hope it had kindled among the émigrés was only a manoeuvre of Stalin's.

Already when Münzenberg was in the USSR in 1936, rumours of his possible arrest were current in the 'bourgeois' press, but he refused to discuss this, and devoted himself to completing his book, *Propaganda als Waffe*, which analysed National Socialist propaganda methods.[68] The book was attacked by the KPD press, which accused Münzenberg of overestimating the impact of Nazi propaganda and underestimating that of the Communists. From 1937 on, such attacks became more frequent. Münzenberg's popularity was feared, and Stalin's suspicion of him was well-known. Finally, he was accused of making contact with 'right-wing' émigrés and expelled from the KPD on 27 October 1937.

From the very origin of the *Volksfront*, certain 'bourgeois' elements had kept their distance, such as the Deutsche Freiheitspartei centred around Otto Klepper,[69] Karl Spiecker (former press chief of Chancellor Brüning) and Father Friedrich Muckermann, who published the paper *Der Deutsche Weg* in the Netherlands.[70] Early in 1938, Klepper and Spiecker suggested that Münzenberg might like to work with them, and he now put his propaganda talent at their service. The *Freiheitsbriefe* were delivered either via the French embassy in Berlin, or by balloons released close to the German border.

Münzenberg persisted in his refusal to visit Moscow, rightly fearing that he would be arrested and executed. It was not until 10 March 1939 that he made known the reasons for his break with the party, in a text published in *Die Zukunft*. He retraced here his twenty-five years' political activity, and explained his differences on antifascist strategy and the *Volksfront*. He was not breaking with Communism, he maintained, or with the thousands of militants who believed in it, but with the leadership and apparatus of the party; he would continue the struggle against fascism. In April 1939, he was attacked by the Comintern press. He now also worked with *Die Zukunft*,[71] which saw itself as above parties, and with Freunde der Sozialistischen Einheit, which tried to establish a workers' party independent of the Second and Third Internationals. He also tried to break the narrow limits of emigration by founding a 'Franco-German union' which brought émigrés together with French or British figures. Münzenberg also established the Freunde der *Zukunft* in early 1939, as an association of writers and readers of the paper. As war approached, he gathered opposition Communists and Socialists in the 'Friends of German Socialist Unity', including Austrian Socialists and Catholics, with such varied figures as Leopold Schwarzschild and Emil Ludwig.

When the German–Soviet pact was signed, Münzenberg reacted violently in *Die Zukunft* (28 August 1939). He saw this as an utter betrayal of the antifascist struggle, and called for the defence of liberty against both Hitler and Stalin. 'You are the traitor, Stalin,' he exclaimed. From now on he attacked the USSR on many occasions, especially the Moscow trials. In spring 1940, he wrote an open letter to Stalin on the liquidation of the Bolshevik old guard.

Most of Münzenberg's contributors were interned when the War broke out, and despite the sympathy that Jean Giradoux had shown him, he was sent in 1940 to the Chambaran camp, south-east of Lyon. On 20 June, the internees were moved south as the German army advanced. It seems that Münzenberg tried to reach Marseille and from there North Africa. But the trail soon goes cold, and nothing certain about his whereabouts has been established. He was however found dead on 22 October 1940, hung from a tree near Saint-Marcellin in the Isère. The hypothesis of suicide was ruled out, and the official police version, a 'crime committed by a vagrant', is extremely dubious. Some émigrés have ascribed his death to agents of Stalin.[72] The investigations of his companion, Babette Gross, with the French police after the War failed to gather any new evidence.

Of the multifarious antifascist activities of this exceptional figure, we shall focus on one episode that gives a picture of his methods, often surprisingly bold and ingenious: the organization of the counter-trial on the Reichstag fire and the publication of the famous *Braunbuch*.

THE *BROWN BOOK* AGAINST THE LEIPZIG TRIAL

Münzenberg had hit on a new technique in mass propaganda, based on a simple observation: if a person gives money to a cause, he becomes emotionally involved in that cause. The greater the sacrifice, the stronger the bond [. . .].

Arthur Koestler, *The Invisible Writing*

The Reichstag fire, which triggered a tidal wave of political terror in Germany, struck the whole world with amazement. Willi Münzenberg understood immediately what advantage to draw from these events in the international mobilization against fascism, in particular the campaign launched by the émigrés for the release of the accused Communists. The counter-propaganda he went on to develop opposed the Nazi accusations with two exemplary initiatives: the publication of the *Brown Book*, offering a mine of information on the terror raging in Germany and the circumstances of the Reichstag fire, and the organization of a counter-trial in London, opened on 1 August 1933, at which international lawyers were led to state their position on the accusation levelled against the Communists.

The *Braunbuch über Reichtagsbrand und Hitlerterror*[73] was designed above all as a collection of information and documents showing the climate of terror in which the Reichstag fire took place, the absurdity of the Nazis' charge of a 'Communist plot' and the clear role they had themselves played in this provocation. Going one at a time through the many questions raised by the fire and its circumstances: Was the presumed incendiary Marius van der Lubbe a 'Communist agent', a provocateur or a simpleton? Would he have been able to light such a fire single-handed? Who really benefited? – Münzenberg offered answers that were plausible if not always completely convincing, on the basis of information that his contributors and other exiles had provided, and which were summarized in the *Braunbuch*. Whilst some historians have reproached Münzenberg for half-truths and hasty conclusions, the sum of documents assembled, some gathered in Germany and others in the Netherlands, was enough to persuade international opinion of the innocence of the Communists and the guilt of the Nazis. The *Braunbuch* thus pulled the Nazis up short, and they raged incessantly against the 'Münzenberg trust', in reality a simple Paris office with a handful of enthusiastic staff.

Willi Münzenberg must get the credit for carrying out a large part of the work of summarizing all this information, even if his entire staff were involved in collecting it. Otto Katz travelled to the Netherlands with a Dutch journalist to investigate the past of Van der Lubbe. It was from the material they brought back that Münzenberg developed the thesis – in fact more than questionable[74] – that the supposed homosexuality of Van der Lubbe put him in touch with the Nazis. The hypothesis that the incendiaries had entered the Reichstag through the underground passage connecting the building with the house of the Reichstag president (Göring) was advanced, it seems, by Gustav Regler. Even today it is not easy to draw the line between historical fact, deductions correctly made by Münzenberg, and what was sometime only the bluff of a genius.

The book was translated into more than twelve languages and sold by the hundred thousand.[75] Several clandestine editions circulated in Germany under false covers borrowed from Reclam: one was disguised as Goethe's *Hermann and Dorothea*, another as Schiller's *Wallenstein*.

The Reichstag fire trial was due to open in Leipzig on 21 September 1933, with the accused comprising the Dutchman Marinus Van der Lubbe, the German Communist Ernst Torgler,[76] and the Bulgarians Georgi Dimitrov, B. Popoff and W. Taneff. As the Nazis refused to allow foreign lawyers who were Communist sympathizers to act for the defendants, Münzenberg decided to convene a commission of international lawyers for a counter-trial, which would deliver its verdict *before* that of the Leipzig tribunal. With Comintern support he was able to assemble the requisite commission, its seat in London provided by the Marley committee.[77] Several very famous English lawyers agreed to take part: D. N. Pritt and Sir Stafford Cripps, who gave the opening address. Arthur Garfield – the defender of Sacco and Vanzetti – came from the United States; Georg Branting, son of the Socialist prime minister, from Sweden; V. de Moro-Giafferi[78] and Gaston Bergery from France;[79] Dr Betsy Bakker-Nort from the Netherlands, and Dr P. Vermeylen from Belgium. The president of the Swiss national council, Johannes Huber, had promised his support, but was prevented from attending by parliamentary debates. They all agreed to take part in this 'Commission of Inquiry into the Origins of the Reichstag Fire'.

The first public session of the Commission was opened by Stafford Cripps in the assembly room of the Law Society in London, on 14 September 1933. The Commission received witness statements and depositions, and in Otto Katz's fine expression, served as 'an unofficial tribunal drawing its mandate from universal conscience'. The Nazis responded violently, denouncing the Commission as a 'Marxist enterprise' of Münzenberg's, even though he had taken care that the Commission should not include any Communist members. They published a book of documents allegedly 'found' in the KPD offices,[80] revealing the 'terrorist acts' being planned by the Communists. Torgler's lawyer, the NSDAP member Dr Sack,[81] tried to gain access to the files of the London Commission, but this was naturally refused.

When the hearing began, an investigating committee travelled to the Netherlands to hear sixteen witnesses apropos the personality of Van der Lubbe. It was established that he had been a member of the Young Communists until 5 April 1931, but had been expelled for oppositional viewpoints. It was emphasized that his connections were more anarchist than Communist. During the London hearings, Stafford Cripps expressed his suspicions as to the course of the trial to be held in Leipzig. He cited a Nazi newspaper which demanded the death penalty for three of the accused even before the trial began. Refusing to take a stand on the political aspect of the affair, the Commission kept strictly to the legal ground. But beyond the Reichstag fire it was the reign of terror in Germany that was repeatedly depicted. A large number of exiles were called as witnesses.[82] These all stressed that the Communists had naturally had not the least interest in perpetrating such an outrage. Wilhelm Koenen, accused together with Torgler but who had managed to escape, also came to give evidence for the accused, as did Dimitrov's sister. As for the Nazi government, none of its démarches led the British government to forbid this counter-trial, which was strictly a private matter. On 20 September, the eve of the Leipzig trial, the London verdict was delivered. It declared the defendants innocent, and emphasized:

1. That van der Lubbe is not a member but an opponent of the Communist Party;
   That no connection whatever can be traced between the Communist Party and the burning of the Reichstag;
   That the accused Torgler, Dimitrov, Popov and Tanaev, are to be regarded [. . .] as innocent of the crime charged [. . .].
2. That the documents, the oral evidence and the other material in its possession tend to establish that van der Lubbe cannot have committed the crime alone.
3. That the examination of all the possible means of ingress and egress to and from the Reichstag make it highly probable that the incendiaries made use of the subterranean passage leading from the Reichstag to the house of the President of the Reichstag;
   That the happening of such a fire at the period in question was of great advantage to the National Socialist Party.
   That for these reasons [. . .] grave grounds exist for suspecting that the Reichstag was set on fire by or on behalf of leading personalities of the National Socialist Party.[83]

Münzenberg's genius had been to have the assertions of the *Braunbuch* confirmed by an international commission of lawyers and jurists, drawing the whole world's attention to Nazi methods. The Leipzig trial, therefore, could not but open under a bad augury. From accusers, the Nazis found themselves forced to defend themselves against international opinion and oppose the propositions of the *Braunbuch*. They had naturally not envisaged this possibility, and it was still more awkward for them that the exile propaganda continued to intensify. On 5 June 1933 a Committee Against War and Fascism met at the Salle Pleyel, while the Thälmann committee, supported by the Comintern,[84] was also to achieve a remarkable mobilization of intellectuals and workers around the defence of the accused. Under the aegis of the World Committee for the Victims of German Fascism, a 'Thälmann week' was organized in New York, as well as a counter-trial followed by a demonstration in Central Park. Münzenberg obtained permission to visit the United States, accompanied by the Socialist lawyer Kurt Rosenfeld. He spoke at several meetings, held in New York, Chicago, Cleveland, Milwaukee, Detroit, Boston and Washington. He remained in America for four weeks, despite the protests of the German embassy. The opening speech at his meeting in New York was given by Mayor La Guardia. This trip was a great propaganda success for Münzenberg: he returned not just with funds to support his committees, but with the sympathy of a large number of American public figures, who took sides with Thälmann and against Hitler.[85]

In the face of this international mobilization, the macabre character of the Leipzig trial was still more apparent: it was Nazi judges who condemned innocent men for a crime for which the Nazis were themselves to blame. The debates in the German Supreme Court, which lasted three months, were chiefly devoted to a refutation of the *Braunbuch*, which became known as the 'sixth defendant'. The Nazis wanted a long drawn-out trial, which they could use for an unprecedented anti-Communist campaign. But after the slap in the face delivered in London, they experienced a further cruel defeat: none of their judges or ministers could stand up to the principal accused, the Bulgarian Georgi Dimitrov, who with exceptional courage and intelligence refuted not just all the Nazi accusations, but steadily transformed the trial into a meeting in support of the Soviet Union and of Communism. The supreme moment of this reversal was reached when Dimitrov ridiculed Göring himself, driving him into a frenzy. Completely losing his head, Göring exclaimed in full session: 'Get out, you scum!' – a moment immortalized by a photomontage of John Heartfield.[86]

Dimitrov's dialectical genius, together with the weakness of the Nazi case, gave Münzenberg new propaganda arguments. Not only had the Nazis failed to show that the Communists were to blame, they were even unable to refute the allegations made against them. Göring was undoubtedly being ironic when he declared:

> The *Brown Book* says that I looked on while the fire was being prepared, dressed, I believe, in a blue silken Roman toga. All that is missing is an allegation that, like Nero at the fire of Rome, I was playing the fiddle . . . The *Brown Book* is a work of incitement that I have destroyed wherever I find it . . . It says that I am a senile idiot, that I have escaped from a lunatic asylum, and that my skull has collapsed in several places.[87]

Yet the coolness, precision and irony of Dimitrov's defence broke the essentials of the Nazi accusation to pieces, and Goebbels soon realized only too well how the trial had been turned around. This failure in the face of world opinion explains the relative leniency of the tribunal's verdict: Dimitrov was acquitted, together with Taneff and Popoff, all three being expelled to the Soviet Union.[88] Torgler remained interned as a 'protective measure'.[89] Only Marinus van der Lubbe was executed, on 10 January 1934. The role that he played in the Reichstag fire is still a subject of controversy.[90]

The London counter-trial and the distribution of the *Braunbuch* was perhaps the only major success of émigré propaganda in exile, apart from the release of the pacifist journalist Berthold Jacob who had been kidnapped by the Gestapo in Switzerland. All the others – the attempts to save Erich Mühsam, Carl von Ossietsky and Ernst Thälmann, the campaign on the Saar plebiscite, in support of Republican Spain and the warnings to the European democracies – all ended in defeat. This *Braunbuch*, therefore,[91] remains one of the greatest symbols of antifascist activity in exile.

Origin and Conception of the Braunbuch

When I joined the battle, the first round had already been won; the Nazis were on the defensive. They had already been forced to call Göring, Goebbels and Helldorf to the witness-stand in a desperate attempt to whitewash themselves before world public opinion. Their failure, and our final triumph – the sensational acquittal of the accused Communists – was almost entirely due to the genius of one man, Willi Münzenberg.

Arthur Koestler, *The Invisible Writing*

The book we were compiling was to be another *J'Accuse*, a full-blooded, documented attack on the Nazi regime [. . .] also refuting the tale [. . .] that the Reichstag fire was the work of a Dutch vagabond named Van der Lubbe, instigated by the Communist Dimitrov. The work of preparation was documented with as much secrecy as possible; but the book's appearance was intended to produce a major explosion.

Gustav Regler, *The Owl of Minerva*

It was an unusual kind of book, produced from information and materials gathered in haste by different authors in record time, and hurled at the Nazis like a bombshell. In a few weeks, it had been translated into seventeen languages, and according to Arthur Koestler sold over a million copies.[92] Everything was done to give it the appearance of an historic document.

The *Braunbuch* provided a mass of important evidence on the terror raging in Germany,[93] providing lists of victims, precise information on the concentration camps, documents on anti-Semitic persecution and the constriction of cultural life. The most significant part of the book was a very skilful refutation of the Nazi accusation and an accumulation of evidence which made the Nazis' own involvement in the Reichstag fire quite clear. It also included photographs of buildings and of the defendants, diagrams and plans, which together made a convincing impression, even if Koestler later acknowledged that a number of arguments remained no more than probable.[94] The only certainty that the exiles had was that the Communists were innocent and that the outrage had been perpetrated by the Nazis. Many different indications attested to this, without it being possible to establish with full certainty – but who could do this even today? – who had given the order and how the incendiaries set about their work. As Koestler again remarked: 'We had no direct proof, no access to witnesses, only underground communications to Germany. We had, in fact, not the faintest idea of the concrete circumstances. We had to rely on guesswork, on bluffing, and on the intuitive knowledge of the methods and minds of our opposite numbers in totalitarian conspiracy.'[95]

This indeed was the supreme skill demonstrated in the *Braunbuch*: to make the Reichstag fire a political mystery, not just a criminal act, and allow the reader, by inspection of the documents, to reach the conclusion that the Nazis were to blame. Rereading today the analyses of the first *Braunbuch* and its successor, one is surprised by the coherence, sometimes a bit too forced, that Münzenberg was able to establish between the various pieces of evidence brought forward – especially as the *Braunbuch* had been compiled in such haste. Its editor-in-chief was Otto Katz, a close collaborator of Münzenberg's. As well as the Comintern offices, information was provided from various exiles, from German Communists and from investigations in the Netherlands. The preparatory session of the investigating committee was held in Paris on 2 September 1933, and from the 5th to the 7th a further committee worked on the 'Van der Lubbe case' in Holland. On the 11th, the day before the plenary session in London, a meeting was held at the Salle Wagram in Paris, and the lawyer Moro-Giaferri, speaking to an audience of over ten thousand, declared: 'Göring, the incendiary is you!'

Even today, it is surprising how skilfully Münzenberg managed to give probabilities the look of established fact. Apart from the description of Van der Lubbe's personality and his relations with the Nazis, based on dubious evidence, the essentials of the *Braunbuch*'s argument rested on the terror regime in power in Germany, which provided the clear backdrop to the Reichstag fire, and especially the famous underground passage which linked the Reichstag to Göring's house. While the existence of this passage was a matter of public knowledge, it seems that Gustav Regler was the first to draw Münzenberg's attention to the use that the Nazis could have made of it.[96] The latter, on the other hand, had not foreseen the role that it would play in the *Braunbuch*'s arguments. At that time, it was impossible to prove that the Reichstag really had been set on fire by gaining entrance via this underground passage. This was a master-stroke of bluff on Münzenberg's part, but it seems that he was among the first to raise a hypothesis that is today taken as more than likely. Besides, the Nazi accusation against the Communists was so crude and botched that the *Braunbuch*'s assertions seemed in contrast a model of objective deduction. Münzenberg managed to give singular force to sometimes hazardous hypotheses. The evidence adduced by the Nazis was so clumsy and contradictory that the Leipzig judges seemed to fear throughout that it would rebound against the accusers. It was easy for the exiles to make the Nazi accusations seem absurd and propose more well-founded explanations.

Another master-stroke of Münzenberg's was to give the *Braunbuch* the aspect of a solidly structured work, whereas it was in fact a collection of chapters drafted by different authors: Otto Katz investigated in the Netherlands, Gustav Regler described torture in the concentration camps, Alexander Abusch brought the whole text together and showed that the Reichstag could not have been burned by Marinus Van der Lubbe, Rudolf Fleischmann wrote the introductory chapters and Albert Norden those dealing with the Nazi party's international connections.

The tremendous outreach of the book is of course explained by the financial means of the Comintern; according to Regler, the USSR 'considered the arrest of Dimitrov a personal provocation and did not spare its roubles'. Finally, Münzenberg's talent also succeeded in giving his crusade against fascism a moral aspect as well as a political one, which enabled him to rally to his cause – and his committees – intellectuals who would have been scared off by Communism. As Manès Sperber wrote:

> It would be as absurd to glorify Münzenberg as a diabolic seducer as to reproach him with having abused the good faith of well-intentioned philosophers and naive poets and unscrupulously misled them in his manoeuvres. The one thing, the one always effective trick that he and his collaborators used almost every time they wanted to win someone unconditionally to their cause, was to persuade them that they were just the person needed in such an important and difficult struggle.[97]

Many émigrés depict in their memoirs how astonished a number of apolitical individuals – or at least people little suspect of Communist sympathies – would have been to learn that the committee they chaired was a creation of the Comintern, something they held was a bogey invented by anti-Communist propaganda. In fact, with the exception of a few very famous intellectuals such as Henri Barbusse or J. B. S. Haldane, whose links with Communism could not be concealed, Münzenberg always sought to avoid his initiatives being publicly seen as 'Communist'.[98]

The second *Braunbuch*, titled *Dimitrov against Göring*, was published by Carrefour in 1934. It opened with a description of the execution of a Communist in Cologne, on 29 November 1934, showing what would have been the fate of the Leipzig defendants if the whole world had not mobilized in their support. Willi Münzenberg retold the story of the trial, dismantling the pillars of the 'infernal machine' and emphasizing the improbability of the accusation, thus justifying a posteriori most of the claims made in the original *Braunbuch*. Beyond the trial itself, Münzenberg offered new revelations on Nazi actions in a range of countries, denounced their attempts to take over certain newspapers, and drew broad-brush portraits of the different Nazi leaders. He went on to publish a less well-known *White Book*, following the 'night of the long knives' on 30 June 1934, depicting the terror now raging in Germany against the SA. Münzenberg went on to explain the execution of leaders such as Röhm, Heines and Schultz by the need to get rid of witnesses of the fire.

In sum, it is undeniable that the *Braunbuch* was an astounding success. Münzenberg knew exactly how to launch his theatrical coups, to pile up the pieces of evidence, and flesh out what was supposedly just a criminal matter. His descriptions of the trial – the Nazi judges, in their red robes, raising their right arm in the Hitler salute in the face of the accused, a haggard (drugged?) Van der Lubbe, unable to understand that he was to be sentenced to death, the ravings of Goebbels and Göring confronted by Dimitrov – were all presented with a dramatic sense that gave these moments such force as to give the reader the sense of having been personally present.

Antifascist Publishing and 'Disguised Writings'

> To know how to use propaganda as a weapon in the struggle for socialism is one of the
> essential condition to ensure the victory of the oppressed over their fascist oppressors.
>
> Willi Münzenberg

The establishment of antifascist publishing forms an essential chapter in the overall antifascist struggle. We shall analyse this at greater length in connection with the birth of exile literature itself, though it is often hard to separate propaganda texts from literature proper. Here we shall simply describe some of the various procedures used by Willi Münzenberg to smuggle into Germany a number of subversive texts.

Under the Weimar Republic Münzenberg had been responsible for a large part of the Communist press, and he was not prepared to stop with the *Braunbuch*. In Paris, later in Strasbourg, he established a number of publishing imprints and series (Éditions du Carrefour, Éditions Sebastian Brant), which played a large part in the development of anti-Nazi propaganda. Though the number of titles published was relatively limited, these were of great importance in terms of the information and warnings that they carried. This propaganda was organized through publishing houses set up by the émigrés, or tied to organizations of the left.[99]

Éditions Nouvelles Internationales (ENI) was established in Paris by the Internationaler Sozialistischer Kampfbund (ISK), and published some fifteen titles bearing on Germany and its politics. Other political groups also published collections of documents, including the Deutsche Anarcho-Syndikalisten (DAS) and the World Committee Against War and Fascism, which particularly published a number of appeals by Dimitrov in support of the threatened Ernst Thälmann. Éditions du Phoenix (founded around 1935) published a series of short books,[100] offering both analyses of Hitlerite racism (Anselm Ruest, Paul Westheim) and appeals to struggle against Hitler's Germany (Alfred Kantorowicz, Berthold Jacob) as well as documents. The three publishing houses which operated from 1933 to 1939 – Éditions du Carrefour, Éditions Sebastian Brant and Éditions Prométhée – were all controlled by Willi Münzenberg. Carrefour,[101] by both the number and importance of its titles – fifty-six in total between 1933 and 1938 – played a leading role in exile propaganda against the Reich. This struggle, launched with the publication of the *Braunbuch*, was continued with a number of collections of documents and statistics, describing the terror in Germany with its persecutions and Gestapo activity abroad, as well as Nazi preparations for war. Finally, alongside these documentary texts there were political or literary essays by émigré authors (E. E. Kisch, J. R. Becher, Anna Seghers, Gustav Regler, Bertolt Brecht, W. Schoenstedt, Bodo Uhse), and writings by Aragon, Barbusse and Malraux in German translation. Éditions du Carrefour disappeared in 1937, after Münzenberg's break with the Comintern. He continued his propaganda work with Éditions Sebastian Brant, though with a different perspective from that of the KPD.[102] Éditions Prométhée, for its part, was more addressed to an activist readership.[103]

To tell the truth, illegality was of the very essence of propaganda material; the texts' intrinsic value meant less than the fact that they were circulated against the law. Each leaflet was proof that the dictatorship was not all-powerful and the opposition powerless.

Manès Sperber

Just as important as the publication of these collections of documents was the development of a diverse propaganda material designed to be smuggled into Germany. This required the establishment of complex networks starting from the 'border secretariats', and presupposed the participation of opponents who remained in the Reich: workers, writers from the BPRS such as Jan Petersen, railwaymen[104] and Swedish sailors. G. Bermann Fischer dispatched for Thomas Mann's readers his letter to the dean of the Bonn philosophy faculty. Münzenberg used his astounding ingenuity as a propagandist to smuggle anti-Nazi leaflets and texts in the most anodyne disguise: prospectuses from a tourist agency, packets of photographic paper, shampoo advertisements, bags of seeds with slogans such as 'Sow new seeds in German political life and root out the Nazi weed', 'Germany smells of blood, the country must be cleaned from head to foot'.[105]

Another procedure was to have minute volumes printed on bible paper or under anodyne covers.[106] German classics were frequent victims of this surrealistic practice. Schoolchildren and students in the Reich were more than a little surprised to find under the familiar covers of the little Reclam series writings by J. R. Becher, Bertolt Brecht, O. M. Graf, Otto Katz, Alfred Kantorowicz, E. E. Kisch, Theodor Plievier, Gustav Regler, Erich Weinert, Friedrich Wolf or Heinrich Mann. In one case, the third act of Schiller's *Maid of Orleans* was replaced with the *Communist Manifesto*. An anthology of anti-fascist writings published after the 1935 congress was disguised in the Miniatur Bibliothek. Believing they had bought an essay on German mythology, then much in demand, the reader discovered after a few pages texts by Thomas Mann, Anna Seghers or O. M. Graf. A false edition of the *Niebelungen Legends* ridiculed the Nazis, while Brecht's 'Five Difficulties in Writing the Truth' (1934) was disguised as a book on first aid.

Several appeals from Heinrich Mann (*An alle Deutschen*, 1 March 1938) were disguised as travel brochures or inserted in booklets advertising winter sports in the Black Forest. His appeal *Deutsche Arbeiter* reached Germany in envelopes for stamp collectors, and *Einig gegen Hitler!* arrived in the family home in little sachets of Cola-Citron powder. The writings of Thomas Mann, for their part, were disguised in sachets of Lyon's tea. Ingenious as this propaganda doubtless was, its impact remained very limited. It caused the Gestapo a great deal of inconvenience and annoyance, but it was not of course in a position to endanger the Nazi regime, and anyone reading these underground texts was liable to be sent to concentration camp.[107]

3. FEAR AND MISERY OF THE THIRD REICH

Even today, no text conveys a stronger impression of the experience of Hitler's Germany than Brecht's short playlets published as *Fear and Misery of the Third Reich*. The climate of fear, informing, torture, suffering and moral wretchedness bursts out in every line, giving it the taste of blood. The émigrés did not stop at producing propaganda material that denounced National Socialism, in Germany as abroad, in theoretical and political terms. Having seen the dictatorship establish itself, they set out to describe its everyday experience, and show the future threat it presented to the whole of Europe. If little notice was taken of this at the time, we can still be struck today by the precision and scope of their warnings.

Terror and Massacre of Opponents

What we need is primitive cries of help, and sounds to identify our murderers.

Walter Mehring

A foreigner, returning from a trip to the Third Reich
When asked who really ruled there, answered:
Fear.

Bertolt Brecht, 'The Anxieties of the Regime'

Even if the brutalities and acts of sadism that accompanied the Nazi seizure of power aroused fairly broad reprobation across the world, the diplomatic and economic successes of the Third Reich tended to repress these from memory, and substitute for this vision of a Germany of fear and blood, the positive image of a 'strong' and 'stable' regime whose martial appearance, and above all the clever propaganda developed by Goebbels, won over a number of intellectuals.[108] The new social legislation, the gradual disappearance of unemployment, the exaltation of the mystical community formed by the people and its Führer, as much as the Concordat signed with the pope and the Berlin Olympics, wiped out the memory of the massacre of opponents, the concentration camps, the *Gleichschaltung* of all culture and the anti-Semitism that the new regime had made into a cardinal value. One of the first tasks of the émigrés, therefore, was to break these tainted images and unveil the regime in its true reality.

As early as 1933, in his pamphlet *Hatred*, Heinrich Mann denounced the sadism, bestiality and cruelty that had taken hold of Germany. The role of the exiles, he declared, was to 'open the world's eyes'. It was for the same reason that the *Braunbuch* and its successors placed the Reichstag fire in the context of the terror that explained it, publishing the names of victims and opponents murdered or sent to concentration camps. These macabre lists were soon complemented by the first accounts of the camps written by former internees themselves, especially those by Wolfgang Langhoff, Gerhart Seger, Hans Beimler and Willi Bredel.[109] The émigrés piled up first-hand evidence of the

Nazi terror, especially thanks to the publishing houses tied to Willi Münzenberg or the left parties. Under the title *The Nazis are Watching You*,[110] Münzenberg published twenty-two biographical sketches of the main Nazi leaders. In *Was geht um Deutschland vor?*,[111] Bruno Frei collated documents on murdered Socialists and Communists, emphasizing that, contrary to a reassuring image widely held abroad, the terror in 1936 was no less than in 1933, as witnessed by the number of resisters murdered or sent to camps.[112] He showed that this blind terror, far from being restricted to the most political elements, also struck pacifists and ministers of religion. Éditions du Carrefour published several volumes on the persecution of Jews in Germany,[113] giving a very detailed picture of anti-Semitic persecution. Other books dealt with religious persecution.[114]

Several texts were published in order to mobilize world opinion in a defence campaign for a particular prisoner. Most such campaigns of course proved unsuccessful. If the *Braunbuch* saved Dimitrov and his fellow defendants in the Reichstag trial, Thälmann, Erich Mühsam and Carl von Ossietzky remained in prison and succumbed to Nazi brutality. As for little-known Communist activists, they were most often beheaded by axe after a summary trial.[115] These defence actions, campaigns or publications were sustained by different groups of the German Human Rights League re-established in Strasbourg (Alfred Falk, Berthold Jacob), Paris (Hellmut von Gerlach, H. Walter, E. J. Gumbel, Kurt Gläser), London (Otto Lehmann-Russbüldt, Rudolf Olden) and Prague (K. Grossman). In January 1934 an international protest was organized on behalf of Ossietzky. Émigrés and intellectuals across the world wrote to the German authorities, calling for his release. In January 1935, a large number of organizations sent telegrams to Hitler and campaigned for Ossietzky to be given the Nobel Prize. In both Europe and the United States, the slogan 'save Carl von Ossietsky' became the common rallying cry. The Nobel Peace Prize winners for 1927 and 1931, Ludwig Quidde and Jane Addams, joined the campaign, and in association with it the International Red Cross demanded a meeting with the prisoner.[116] This international campaign disturbed the Nazis, and as a diversion they tried to propose alternative candidates such as President Masaryk and Pierre de Coubertin, using a number of writers sympathetic to fascism – such as Knut Hamsun – to orchestrate their counter-propaganda. They also tried to compromise Ossietzky by printing false interviews. Even the Nobel Prize could not save him, but the emigrants had at least won a moral victory over the Reich.

The activities of the Thälmann committee were still more large-scale, to judge from the intellectual mobilization that this committee managed to generate. Though imprisoned, Thälmann was not completely cut off from the outside world and the exiled Communist leadership.[117] After his release, Dimitrov gave the order for an international mobilization in support of the KPD leader.[118] Wilhelm Pieck also declared that 'the liberation of Thälmann is a battle to be won against fascism'.[119] In its resolution of 5 March 1933, the Comintern's political secretariat gave its directives for united action in support of Thälmann, to include Social-Democrats and trade unionists as well as Communists. A large-scale campaign was organized in the Soviet Union,[120] though it was in

France and Czechoslovakia that these actions were broadest in scope.[121] The efforts grew still more intense in 1935, on the international level and especially in the context of the Popular Front. Thälmann's name was given to the battalion of German Communists fighting to defend the Spanish Republic, and the European Conference for Right and Freedom, held in Paris on 13–14 November 1937, elected a number of German oppositionists held in prison or concentration camp as honorary members of its presidium, including Thälmann and Ossietzky.[122] This conference renewed the call for international solidarity with the prisoners, and a series of symbolic actions were undertaken, such as sending telegrams and postcards to Thälmann for his fifty-second birthday. In the USSR, his name was given to several factories. In 1938, Heinrich Mann once more sent him a message, and an association of American lawyers protested against his detention. The German Communist party, aware that the Gestapo now prevented any message from getting through to Thälmann, gave the instruction to send cards bearing his photograph to all German industrialists. Despite the scale of these actions, however, they remained ineffectual: Thälmann was eventually murdered in 1944.[123]

It was only rarely that émigrés themselves appeared at the head of these actions and committees. On the one hand, several countries restricted their political activity; on the other, it was important to give such actions the widest possible audience. Aware of the fact that Nazi terror only aroused indignation if it was possible to give the victims a face, they issued one leaflet after another, coupled with appeals and pamphlets, to make known precisely who was at risk of death. International Red Aid published a pamphlet in 1935, *Les Morts parlent aux vivants*,[124] calling not only for the rescue of Thälmann and Ossietzky but also for all Communists threatened with summary execution. Willi Bredel edited the famous booklet *L'Antifasciste Edgar André*.[125] If these texts helped to reveal the regime's atrocities, they did not save any of its victims.[126]

The Destruction of German Culture

By their participation in congresses and public meetings, as much as by their writings, the exiles sought to show what the Nazis had done to German culture. As well as Heinrich Mann's famous pamphlet *Hatred*, and various texts by Thomas Mann, most other émigrés also wrote on this question. Brecht and Toller each described the enslavement of intellectual freedom and the destruction of all genuine creation, while the exile press was packed with examples – absurd as well as distressing – showing how German culture had been injured and perverted. It was in protest against this destruction, not just of Weimar culture but of the most traditional values, that Walter Benjamin published his famous *Letters from Germans*.[127] At the same time as they described the repressive measures hitting writers and artists hostile to the new regime's 'cultural' criteria, the exiles strove to keep the classical legacy alive and develop it, by way of anthologies[128] as well as in their own work.

Germany, a Danger for Europe

On the wall was chalked:
They want war.
The man who wrote it
Has already fallen.

Bertolt Brecht

One important part of the work of exiled antifascists was to give the European democracies information that would warn them about the Hitler peril. Along with Thomas Mann's famous warning 'Europe Beware!'[129] many other volumes also appeared, leaving little room for doubt about Hitler's intentions. On the subject of Nazi propaganda, besides Münzenberg's book there was *The Brown Net* by Berthold Jacob,[130] providing a remarkable analysis of German rearmament, war preparations and Nazi activity abroad. The author gave a list, which proved correct, of the first countries to be invaded, and of the newspapers and publishing houses responsible for National Socialist propaganda abroad; also the names of anti-Semitic magazines distributed in the French colonies, a list of French figures in touch with the Nazis, and Hitlerite agents operating in France, Belgium, Switzerland, Czechoslovakia, the Netherlands and the Middle East. Albert Schreiner (sometimes together with Dorothy Woodman)[131] published a large number of documents on the operation of German industries involved in armaments. The volume that Münzenberg published under the Carrefour imprint in 1934, *Au seuil de la guerre. Documents sur le réarmament de l'Allemagne hitlérienne*, is such a mine of information that it is hard to understand how the émigrés managed to obtain it all.[132] It even included factory plans, details of the weaponry and strength of the German army, and the composition and command of particular units,[133] together with topographic references to German military installations. S. Erckner's publication *L'Allemagne, champ de manœuvre. Le fascisme et la guerre*[134] presented a very detailed analysis of the trends in German military strategy, and of the intensive militarization of both industry and population.[135] Above all, this showed clearly that Hitler's entire policy was based on the notion of revenge:

> The entire structure of Hitler's Reich has an anti-pacific and openly warlike character. It is ever more clearly apparent that a regime practising terror at home must necessarily nourish a desire for outward expansion. Everything now happening in Germany shows that its ruling caste want war and are feverishly preparing for it. The militarization of the population is proceeding at accelerated pace. In all the railway stations, maps of Europe are displayed on which data are given on the number of aeroplanes, tanks and artillery pieces possessed by German's neighbouring countries.[136]

In *Die grosse Lüge. Hitlers Verschwörung gegen den Frieden*,[137] Erckner showed how Hitler's professed desire for peace was simply a mask, while in actual fact Germany sought new territories for the output of its industries. He emphasized that war with Hitler's Germany was unavoidable, and that Germany would invade Poland. In similar vein, Carrefour published in 1936 Berthold Jacob's book *Das neue deutsche Heer und seine Führer*, a careful and well-documented study of the structures of the German army, its strength and types of armament, even very detailed diagrams of its bases and matériel, along with biographical sketches of the generals in charge of the main army divisions. Just as important in the analysis of war preparations was Helmut Klotz's work *La Nouvelle Guerre allemande*:[138] 'The march towards the new German war began on 30 January 1933. Today it is approaching its aim. In the first four years of his rule, Hitler has spent over 31 billion marks on armaments. For the year 1936–37, more than two-thirds of budgetary credits are reserved for guns, aeroplanes, submarines and gas. The machine is in motion. No one and nothing can stop it.'[139]

The Institute for the Study of Fascism

The foundation of INFA was among the most famous and symbolic of the various attempts to combat, denounce and analyse National Socialism. A text published in the magazine *Europe* (no. 34, 1934) presented it as follows:

> The Institute for the Study of Fascism has been founded to struggle ideologically against the danger that fascism presents to civilization. The Institute proposes to study all fascist movements in a systematic way, publishing regularly its analyses and the results of its activities.
>
> This will be a centre for the documentation of fascism and resistance to it, no matter under what form it manifests itself. For the first time in western Europe, all fascist literature will be collected in a single location, and archives established where all writings, manifestos, decrees etc. of fascist groups and governments will be stored, along with all the critical literature that this movement has aroused.

Founded in Paris, INFA proposed to publish a weekly bulletin in several languages, and supply information and analyses to the press. Its office, along with its archive and library, was located at 22 rue des Fossés-Saint-Bernard, then at 22 rue Buffon. It aimed to maintain specialists, correspondents and researchers, and accordingly solicited the support of all antifascist forces in France.[140] It was in operation from the end of 1933 to the first half of 1935, and its collaborators were mainly German political émigrés. Despite the project's importance, not much is known of how it functioned, developed, and then disappeared.[141] Though there are a number of émigré testimonies, they tend to contradict one another.

Arthur Koestler, for example, wrote: 'The idea was to create a centre for the study of the social structure and inner workings of Fascist regimes, more scholarly in its approach than the mass-propaganda methods of the Münzenberg Trust permitted.'[142] According to him, the idea came from Peter Maros: 'The Party was to run it, in the person of Peter, but the Institute was to finance itself, and appear to the public as one of the enterprises of the Popular Front. Various French personalities had been approached and had promised moral support and financial contributions – among them Professor Langevin and the Joliot-Curies, André Malraux, Bertrand de Jouvenel, and so on. The French Trade Unions were also interested.'[143]

'Peter Maros' in fact was Oto Bihalji-Mérin, a Yugoslav art critic. Was INFA an 'unorthodox' enterprise, as Koestler maintains? Manès Sperber for his part insists on the role played by the Comintern in its foundation, and by the International Freethinkers League – Hans Meins, who first planned the project together with Bihalji-Mérin, being a member of this. The institute operated with volunteer staff who were fed at lunchtime.[144] Its role was to analyse and describe all aspects of fascism. Koestler was in charge of the publications section and supposed to put out a bimonthly bulletin (three issues appeared), as well as pamphlets and books intended for a specialist readership, trade unions and the press.[145] Manès Sperber gives a fairly similar description of the INFA's objects: 'We were in complete agreement that it was necessary now more than ever to undertake serious study of all variants of fascism, to clarify its causes, methods and effects by objective methods. From now on, this would be precisely the task of this Institute.'[146]

It was planned to establish, in the half-dozen rooms at the INFA premises, research committees and a magazine published in several languages, also to hold public lectures. Independent of the KPD, but tied to the Comintern even if this link was not 'official', the INFA was the first project for a rigorous analysis of fascism and its mechanisms, to be conducted on the basis of abundant documentation. Until October 1934 the Institute was directed by Oto Bihalji-Mérin (aka Pierre Mérin), who had studied at the School of Fine Arts in Berlin, and worked for the cultural organizations of the KPD and BPRS. Manès Sperber was responsible for the ideological side. The INFA's staff included Austrians, Poles and Italians, whose work it was to 'gather material on fascism in order to develop an in-depth analysis'; 'publish studies on its different aspects: economic, political, ideological and military';[147] and 'provide information to political organizations who request this'.

This ambitious programme, however, was far from being realized, though INFA did publish a few books and pamphlets as well as the short-lived bulletin. Its most important initiative was in connection with the great exhibition of 1935, in one of the pavilions of the Foire de Paris at the Porte de Versailles, where for over a month public meetings and lectures on fascism were to be held. A number of organizations such as the Ligue des Droits de l'Homme, the Ligue Contre les Persécutions Raciales and the CGT agreed to finance the project. According to Koestler, this enterprise failed after the arrival of a Comintern envoy 'Jan' (Hans Meins), who allegedly transformed the INFA into a Communist propaganda office, through the offices of a mediocre cartoonist.[148] Koestler wanted to prepare an antifascist exhibition through the INFA, but the Comintern emissary supposedly withdrew this project from him and Sperber, entrusting it instead to the cartoonist. Still according to Koestler, it was the arrival of this emissary that led him to resign, followed a few weeks later by 'Peter'. The next month INFA ceased operations. 'Our Institute was an altogether too unorthodox and independent enterprise. [. . .] Such an approach must sooner or later lead to deviations from, and conflicts with, the Party line'.[149]

Manès Sperber traced the end of the INFA in fairly similar terms. The failure of the exhibition project was supposedly bound up with conflicts with functionaries from the Comintern, leading to the departure of the senior staff. A book was in preparation, its material being subsequently destroyed by the Gestapo. The exhibition planned by the INFA, however, was indeed held from 9 March to 15 May 1935, at an art gallery (83 rue de la Boétie), with a fair degree of success, including a series of lectures. This was the largest and last act of the INFA, which went under for obscure reasons, it would seem more for lack of resources than by decision of the Comintern.

Birth and Decline of the *Volksfront*

The attempt, born in Paris, at a German Popular Front (*Volksfront*), represented not just a high point of the exiles' struggle against Hitler, but the hope of a genuine reconciliation between the workers' parties, whose lack of unity had so largely contributed to the rise of the Nazis in the final years of the Weimar Republic.

The application of the Popular Front in France and Spain gave a living illustration of what the union of democratic forces could achieve. Yet for all the efforts of mobilization, and the spectacular rapprochements effected in the course of this period, the *Volksfront* was to end in defeat. It was these years of 1935 to 1937, none the less, through the Congresses in Defence of Culture and the mobilization of intellectuals in support of Republican Spain, that achieved the greatest unity of intellectuals from all countries, coming together in struggle against the fascist threat.

1. THE WRITERS' CONGRESSES FOR THE DEFENCE OF CULTURE

For a large number of writers, artists and intellectuals, the combat against National Socialism reached its apogee with the mobilization for the defence of culture held in Paris in 1935. What had been one of the fundamental demands of the exiles – to preserve German culture from its destruction or perversion by National Socialism – had gradually become the slogan of a whole generation of writers, aware of the danger that fascism imposed on culture, freedom and peace. It would be easy to wax ironic on the petty results of these mobilizations. The contrast was brutal between the idealism and emotion that marked so many interventions at these congresses and the reality of the epoch. It is also easy to reveal the political illusions that these intellectuals nourished, the gap between their dreams and aspirations, and the actual policy of the democracies that led to the victory of fascism in Spain and the Munich capitulation. Yet for all that it would be wrong to deny the symbolic value of this international mobilization.

And it was undoubtedly at this cultural level, through these meetings and writers' congresses, that the dream of a united front against fascism, extending the attempts of certain intellectual groups in the final year of the Weimar Republic, began to take concrete form. A de facto unity had already been achieved from below, outside party structures, when Socialist and Communist workers took part in common actions of anti-Nazi resistance after 1933. It began to consolidate around certain key events – the joint campaign on the Saar plebiscite, the defence of imprisoned workers. While the high point of activities leading up to the *Volksfront* was attained with the work of the Lutétia committee in 1936, it is no exaggeration to say that it was broadly prepared by the sum of actions undertaken to save imprisoned writers and activists, in which Socialists and Communists often worked together, even while the two party leaderships still abstained from any official contact; especially by the growing awareness in a large section of the intelligentsia that beyond their ideological divisions they had to combat a single enemy, and that this struggle was inseparable from their dignity as writers.

A mobilization of this kind must not be judged simply in terms of its effectiveness. Brecht, more than anyone else, underlined the impossibility of defeating naked violence with words alone. But these initiatives displayed the will to construct a new world, and a courage and generosity that were not in vain, compelling admiration still today.

THE INTERNATIONAL CONGRESS FOR THE DEFENCE OF CULTURE (PARIS, JUNE 1935)

What is the use of fixing one's eyes, with either terror or complacency, on the barbarism that comes out of barbarism? One evening, after drinking too much coffee, three pale individuals [. . .] surrounded me and begged me, with imploring gestures which I made out through the cigarette smoke, to remain a humanist and rescue culture. 'Be a man,' the big one begged. 'Be human! Despise the barbarians, detest violence in all its forms! We must rescue culture!' I promised them, I would have promised anything, I was that tired and embarrassed.

Bertolt Brecht, 'Humanism against Barbarism?'

The Congress for the Defence of Culture, held in Paris in June 1935, merits a particular study, in terms of both its origins and its development. It did not manage to restrain the process leading to war; or to use Brecht's terms here, humanism did not defeat barbarism. But it was certainly an event of key importance. From 21 to 25 June 1935, at the Mutualité, many of the greatest names in world literature were gathered together. The crowds present at this assembly could not just hear, but also see in person, Henri Barbusse, André Gide, André Malraux, Jean Cassou, Julien Benda, Paul Nizan, Louis Aragon, Jean Guéhenno, Paul Eluard, Tristan Tzara and Eugène Dabit, along with Soviet writers such as Alexis Tolstoy, V. Ivanov, Isaak Babel and Boris Pasternak, Germans and Austrians such as Robert Musil, Bertolt Brecht, Max Brod, Klaus Mann, J. R. Becher, Hans Marchwitza, Rudolf Leonhard,

Anna Seghers, Heinrich Mann, Lion Feuchtwanger, Ernst Bloch, Bodo Uhse, Gustav Regler, Erich Weinert and Ernst Toller.

Curiously enough, this congress has not been studied properly at all in France, even though it marks the culmination of a literary era of rare richness; historians in the GDR, however, subsequently wrote about it in depth.[1] The importance of the congress cannot be confined just to the history of antifascist mobilization. It requires several elements to be taken into consideration, transcending the boundaries of the present work:

- its roots in a cultural and political movement that developed steadily in France from the 1920s on, of which it appeared as the culmination;
- the development of anti-war literature after 1914, the polemics around the notion of 'proletarian culture' and in a more general sense the development of relations between writers and the PCF;[2]
- the movement of politicization of intellectuals against fascism and the revulsion that Hitler's Germany aroused among a large number of writers, including those far removed from Communism;
- the awareness that the devastating blow German culture had received could be repeated in other countries, and that denouncing Nazism was to defend freedom; in struggling for the freedom of German writers, those of other countries were also defending their own;
- the difficult construction of a Popular Front which presupposed a major evolution in the strategy of the workers' parties.

Convened at the initiative of the Association of Revolutionary Artists and Writers (AEAR) and the Vigilance Committee of Antifascist Intellectuals, writers of thirty-seven countries were invited to the congress, including some of the greatest names of German exile literature: Thomas and Heinrich Mann, Anna Seghers, Ernst Toller and Bertolt Brecht. While the central theme was the mobilization in defence of freedom of creation and cultural humanism, many other questions were also raised. In the format of round tables, groups and lectures, discussion took place on cultural heritage, humanism, relations between culture and nation, the dignity of the spirit, the role of the writer in society, literary creation and the different ways of defending civilization. The French contingent included a large number of writers who had worked around the AEAR in the last several years, and gave lectures here.[3] Several countries were strongly represented: the USSR by a sizeable delegation, Britain by E. M. Forster and Aldous Huxley, the United States by Sinclair Lewis and John Dos Passos.

The selection of subjects displayed the AEAR's desire for openness. There was scarcely a mention of 'proletarian literature' and 'bourgeois literature', but instead of 'defence of culture', 'humanism', democracy and national tradition. Fascism was perceived as a global threat that could affect the personal freedom of every writer.[4] The theme of the defence of culture was illustrated in the speeches of most of the French and foreign representatives – from Paul Vaillant-Couturier to Erich Weinert – though often in rather different senses. Some writers confined themselves to making rather vague oppositions between 'humanism and barbarism', 'culture and fascism'. Others appealed to the 'force of the spirit' (Jean Guéhenno) to conquer Nazi obscurantism, or declared their confidence in humanism (Julien Benda) and 'human comradeship' (again Guéhenno).[5] In reading these communications today, one has to admit that while they all display the same concern to defend culture against fascism, to exalt socialism and humanism, they often remain in thrall to rather abstract oppositions. Explicit political interventions were rare, apart from the speeches of Communist writers (Erich Weinert) and especially Brecht,[6] who insisted on the elementary truth that to denounce fascism and its misdeeds in the abstract is insufficient as long as its origin remains undiscovered. Brecht's speech, amid so many exalted declarations, must have seemed incongruous, since he referred not to the 'force of the spirit' but to property relations.

In the course of these debates, discussion of aesthetic matters was more frequent than political speeches. Gide criticized the theory of 'committed literature' championed in the USSR, and his lecture aroused a number of comments. It was also on the basis of literary questions that political problems were often raised. The debates on 'nation and culture', for instance, introduced new definitions of 'patriotism' and 'national culture', of the relation between the Communist movement and the democratic heritage in the light of Soviet discussion of these same themes, and of the fate of the classical tradition, perverted by the Nazis into a shoddy Teutonism.[7]

The participation of exiled writers was both substantial and symbolic. It attested to the regrouping of different factions and the possibility of forming a common front against fascism, in close association with intellectuals of other countries. While Aragon and Malraux were responsible for the choice of subjects and speakers on the French side, the German side was entrusted to J. R. Becher and Gustav Regler. The selection of themes for debate was made in the context of SDS activity in which Becher, Alexander Abusch, Albert Norden and Lorenz (Winzer) played a major part. For them, this congress was to put into practice the new strategy decided by the Comintern, and help build a united front against fascism. According to Kantorowicz, the congress was preceded by a number of discussions among émigré writers, some of whom were resident in France, while others such as Becher came from Moscow to meet their French counterparts. The relatively high number of German writers taking part shows the deep significance ascribed to it by all concerned, from the standpoint of the struggle against National Socialism. To judge by the accounts of the exiles themselves, the enthusiasm that the project aroused was as great as on the anniversary of the book burning the previous year.[8] The congress was attended by writers of a great variety of nationalities – Russian,[9] Ukrainian, Georgian, Dutch, Danish, even Chinese. Its solemn opening was held on Friday, 21 June 1935, in the great hall of the Mutualité, with Gide[10] and Malraux as joint presidents, followed by addresses from E. M. Forster, Julien Benda, Bertolt Brecht, E. E. Kisch, Louis Aragon, Luppol (USSR) and Jean Cassou, all invited to discuss the theme of 'cultural heritage'.[11]

Sessions were held from 3 to 9 p.m., attended by a large audience to judge from the accounts of the time. Loudspeakers had to be installed to transmit the speeches to the entrance hall. More than a hundred journalists were present.[12]

On the closing day, Tuesday 25 June, with Malraux in the chair, a discussion was held on the political themes dealing with fascism and exile.[13] In the afternoon the session was addressed by Henri Poulaille, R. J. Humm (Switzerland), Kirschon (USSR) and Emi Sia (China), as well as a number of German antifascist writers (Bodo Uhse, Klaus Mann, Erich Weinert, Alfred Kantorowicz). It was in this session that a solemn announcement was made of the presence of an anti-Nazi writer who had come from Germany and brought the participants greetings from resisters within the Reich. Under the pseudonym 'Klaus' – in fact the proletarian writer Jan Petersen,[14] who made his appearance in a mask – he was met with general enthusiasm, as he raised the hope of a real opposition existing within the Reich, able to link up with the work of the exiles.

The congress was a great success. Both German and French speakers explained their problems with the same enthusiasm. Political cleavages seemed to have been effaced, as well as literary ones. Writers formerly classed as 'bourgeois' converged with Communists, who for their part tolerated positions that were far from orthodox from a number of intellectuals who rallied to the antifascist cause.[15] The majority of exiled writes undoubtedly sobered up before too long: 'We believed we might be prophets in the city, but we were preaching in the desert,' wrote Gustav Regler,[16] but in those days of June 1935, many – and the émigrés above all – dreamed of seeing their cause finally understood and transformed into a broad international movement.

I gazed at the thousands of heads beneath me. This was no exile. The frontiers had been abolished and the writers' international had been called into being! I looked at Gide and the old pacifist, Barbusse, seated at the committee-table, and suddenly I forgot all my carefully composed speech. I brought two of the leaflets out of my pocket, held them in the air and challenged the Gestapo agent who was certain to be seated in the audience as a spy to come up and look at them. [. . .]

I wanted to make them all feel the sense of insecurity that, with the coming of Hitler, was spreading among mankind, and to urge them to close their ranks. [. . .]

Then something remarkable happened. With a strange, dry, rustling sound the whole assembly rose to its feet, as though I had waved a baton and called upon them to sing the choral passage of the Ninth Symphony. But what they sang was very different.

A figure beckoned to me urgently from the wings. It was the German poet, Johannes R. Becher. I went towards him behind the painted canvas fly, and he hissed at me:

'You must be mad!'

'Can't you hear what they're singing?' I asked in a voice that trembled with emotion.

'That's just it!' he said, having to shout now against the mighty chorus that arose. 'The Internationale! You've ruined everything – you've given us away! This congress can't pretend to be neutral any longer. God almighty! You'll be turned out of the Party!'

I looked at his pale face, not knowing whether to laugh or cry.[17]

They were astonishing days, in which people outbid one another in generosity and were ready to stretch out their hands to former adversaries if they were involved in the same struggle; days in which words and things were often confused, where the words 'freedom', 'humanism', 'dignity' were brandished as genuine weapons, able to destroy fascism itself.[18] The interventions of German writers were as varied as those of any other country, and marked by the same idealism. Only a handful, like Brecht, mentioned the need to recognize the social origins of fascism – property relations – in order to fight it, or tried to give a genuine theoretical analysis, as did J. R. Becher. Heinrich Mann expressed himself in terms that were moral more than political, Anna Seghers traced the significance of the lost homeland, E. E. Kisch described his work as a journalist, and Feuchtwanger the historical novel; Ernst Bloch spoke on Marxism and poetry, Alfred Kerr on the misery of exile, Rudolf Leonhard on the writer's independence, and Klaus Mann on fascism and youth. Some interventions had an autobiographical stamp: the proletarian writer Hans Marchwitza spoke of his childhood, the Great War, and his work in the Ruhr. Even if all literary and political currents were represented, this was in very varying proportions, and with demands that could not always be reconciled, despite the openness which all sought to display. Robert Musil affirmed the importance of literature against politics, drawing the fire of Bodo Uhse. Attitudes towards the Soviet Union were also a subject of polemic, and Henri Poulaille caused a scandal by taking up the defence of Victor Serge.[19] The congress audience glimpsed the possible achievement of a double aim: to rally to the struggle against fascism a large number of intellectuals of bourgeois origin who had never been politically active or perhaps even never taken a position on political events, by closely linking the defence of culture, humanist values and morals to the struggle against Nazi barbarism. It showed that it was possible to overcome the ideological and literary oppositions and cleavages among the German exiles, by transforming this movement in defence of culture into an antifascist movement on a global scale. When the congress ended, the participants envisaged the foundation of an international association of writers for the defence of culture, which would perpetuate its spirit and slogans. A committee was appointed to oversee this foundation, with 112 representatives from thirty-seven countries.[20] In his closing message, Barbusse celebrated the congress as a festival of freedom. Easy as it is today to wax ironic at such idealism, this belief in the strength of literature and the spirit,[21] it is impossible to deny the sincerity and enthusiasm of the participants, who saw the congress as a step in their own destiny. The exile press attests to the same confidence in the future: the congress laid the basis for a broad and united antifascist movement.[22]

THE SECOND INTERNATIONAL CONGRESS
OF ANTIFASCIST WRITERS (1937)

Less famous than the Congress for the Defence of Culture, this second international congress held in Spain in July 1937 was its logical sequel. Organized by the Alliance of Intellectuals for the Defence of Catalan Culture and the government of the Generalidad, with the collaboration of the propaganda commissariat, this again attracted a large number of writers from across the world, who over a two-week period defended the Republican cause in English, German, French, Catalan and Spanish. The themes for discussion echoed those of the 1935 congress,[23] displaying the same faith. The various delegations converged on Valencia from 4 July onwards: writers fighting in the International Brigades, antifascist exiles, Latin American writers (Casar Vallejo, Pablo Neruda), and literary figures from a wide range of countries, including André Malraux, Claude Aveline, André Chamson, Niccola Potenza, Octavio Paz, Carlos Pellicer, Juan Marinello, Nicolas Guillen, Alejo Carpentier, Felix Pila Rodriguez and Stephen Spender.[24] While some writers from abroad were unable to attend this congress (Romain Rolland, Thomas Mann, Louis Aragon, John Dos Passos, Ernest Hemingway, Upton Sinclair), a large number of countries were represented.[25] German exiles attending included Theodor Balk, Willi Bredel, Lion Feuchtwanger, Max Hodann, Egon Erwin Kisch, P. L. Landsberg, Hans Marchwitza, Ludwig Renn, Anna Seghers, K. Stern, Bodo Uhse, Maria von Osten, Erich Weinert and Hans Kahle.

On Sunday, 4 July, the congress was solemnly opened in the consistory of the Valencia Ayuntamiento, decked out for the occasion with an immense three-pointed red star, symbol of the Frente Popular and the International Brigades, with Juan Negrin Lopez (prime minister) and Jesus Hernandez (minister of education) in the chair.[26] Its organization responded to a proposition formulated by Ricardo Baeza and José Bergamin, Spanish delegates at the 1935 congress, and at the London congress of 1936.[27] Organized thanks to a close collaboration between the education ministry and the Alliance of Antifascist Intellectuals, its orientation was firmly to the Frente Popular. Gide's attendance was deemed undesirable, following the publication of his *Retour d'URSS*.[28] The aim of this congress was to strengthen world solidarity among antifascist writers (the addresses of Aveline and Gonzales Tunon). While more or less the same subjects were debated as in Paris two years previously, there was also a focus on questions more specifically tied to the Spanish context, especially the role of culture in the immediate struggle against fascism, and the attitude of intellectuals towards the non-intervention of the Western democracies. Several Spanish historians, however, have stressed the contrast between the abstract character of the discussions and the tragic situation of the Republic, even if this congress was a remarkable propaganda action in focusing the attention of intellectuals around the world on Republican Spain. The themes developed – the need to destroy fascism in order to defend culture (Ilya Ehrenburg), the development of a 'revolutionary humanism' (Aveline, Fernando de los Rios) – could nowhere find a wider audience than in Spain at this bloody time. It is nonetheless true, however, that the congress had no concrete solution to the questions it raised, and that were raised for the Spanish Republic in general: essentially, how to break its isolation and press the democracies to fight at its side.

The congress continued its work, however, from 2 to 13 July, with sessions also in Barcelona and Madrid, as well as cultural events (including Pablo

Casals). Reading today the different interventions at the congress, as well as the articles devoted to it by the Spanish press at the time, shows that it aroused the same illusions and hopes as its predecessor, but in far more dramatic circumstances: not just the spectre of fascism and the threat it posed to culture, but an ongoing civil war. Franco's response to the congress was not long delayed: to show writers what he thought of their discussions, he bombed Madrid.

2. BUILDING THE ANTIFASCIST POPULAR FRONT

The Left Parties in Exile

The inability of the workers' parties to form a united front to fight National Socialism was undoubtedly one of the most important factors that assisted the advance of the Nazis and Hitler's coming to power. While most historians see the lack of a united response to von Papen's coup against the Prussian government as signalling the failure of the German left, other events also show the measure of its division. One of the most symbolic events was the presidential election of 1932.[29]

At this time, from the Communist standpoint, National Socialism and Social-Democracy looked strangely similar, while only differences of degree separated Hitler, von Papen and Brüning. The KPD believed that the bourgeois government would undergo a process of gradual fascisization, while the transformation of Social-Democracy into 'social-fascism' made it impossible to distinguish this clearly from fascism proper. For the 1932 election therefore, the Communists naturally presented Ernst Thälmann as their candidate, alone able to defeat this process. Thälmann's candidacy, however, failed to attract the support of a number of organizations situated between the KPD and the SPD,[30] who launched an appeal for unity by rejecting not only the strategy of the KPD and its equation of Social-Democracy with fascism, but also the SPD's failure to put forward a candidate. Unable to find a candidate of their own, these groups finally rallied to the 'workers' candidate', with the slogan 'For Thälmann, but against the KPD's wrong policy'. Though the right-wing parties were united, the Socialists were hostile to any rapprochement with the Communists, and invited workers to vote for Marshal Hindenburg – who though violently anti-republican and honorary president of the Stahlhelme, appeared to them the lesser evil. Voting for Hindenburg, the SPD were opposing both Hitler and Thälmann.

Faced with such suicidal tactics, intellectuals – whether non-party republicans, dissident Socialists or pacifists – had no political organization of their own. Movements such as the Liga für Menschenrechte or the Deutsche Friedensgesellschaft might well call on the German left to unite around a single candidate, but they were too weak to make an impact. A certain number of intellectuals were tempted to run a symbolic candidate: the Liga für Menschenrechte proposed a vote for Carl von Ossietzky, but the majority of writers were divided, even if as Socialists or Communists they were involved in common struggle within the OSDS (Opposition im Schutzverband Deutscher Schriftsteller). Communist writers naturally supported Thälmann's candidacy, but revolutionary pacifists like Kurt Hiller – fiercely anti-Communist – rejected this. Hiller accordingly appealed in the *Weltbühne*[31] for the candidacy of a moral figure independent of party, whom both Socialists and Communists could unite behind: in particular, the president of the poetry section of the Prussian Academy of Arts, Heinrich Mann.[32] Mann himself, however, like many liberal intellectuals, supported a vote for Hindenburg,[33] seeing this as a lesser evil. And it was just this policy of the 'lesser evil' that was finally to lead to Hitler.

The KPD with its 300,000 members was the largest Communist party after that of the USSR. Yet it was destroyed by Nazi terror in a matter of weeks. Even this defeat, however, did not lead to any immediate revision of its strategy. After the Reichstag fire and the ban on its activity (9 March 1933), the party still seemed to believe in the rapid defeat of Nazism, the impossibility of Hitler holding on to power and the imminent appearance of a counter-offensive from the working class. KPD strategy towards the Social-Democrats remained unchanged. If Communist and Socialist workers undertook sporadic united action right from the beginning of resistance to Nazism, the KPD leadership still conjured up 'Social-Democratic betrayal' and the role of 'social-fascism', blaming the SPD for Hitler's coming to power. There was no theoretical analysis at this stage of the defeat suffered by the working class and the KPD, and no in-depth analysis of National Socialism, which was simply seen as the logical development of capitalism in crisis. Even worse, the KPD did not always distinguish the struggle against Nazism from the struggle against 'social-fascism'. The fact that the SPD remained legal for a while after the KPD was banned, and the division that broke out between those SPD representatives who stayed in Germany and the exiles in Prague, provided the KPD with new ideological weapons, even if the SPD refused to vote full powers to Hitler on 23 March and was subsequently itself proscribed.[34] Even when the Socialists embarked on clandestine struggle against the Nazi regime, the Communists still tended to see them as in the bourgeois camp, and thus on the side of fascism. The only concession made was that the Social-Democrat party had become anti-Nazi despite itself (*unfreiwillig*), and its position had simply become one of 'enforced opposition' (*aufgezwungene Opposition*). There was certainly no talk of defeat:[35] on the contrary, the Comintern saw Nazi victory as refutation of the Social-Democratic belief in the possibility of building socialism by way of a parliamentary majority, saving on the need for revolution. The first meetings of the exiled KPD and the Executive Committee of the Communist International minimized Hitler's victory and justified the party's tactics, throwing the responsibility for the Nazi seizure of power onto the Socialists and some Communists who had fallen into 'right-wing opportunism' (Marker, Neumann, Remmele). Communist theorists often even denied that any real change of regime had taken place in January 1933.[36]

At the same time, the KPD saw itself as the sole representative of German resistance. The optimism it displayed was no more erroneous than that of other exiled oppositionists.[37] In *Der revolutionäre Aufschwung in Deutschland*,[38] the

Communists even maintained that the SPD was no longer a serious obstacle to the rallying of the working class to revolution. The exiled Communists, for their part, and especially those in Paris, seemed to fear the influence of the Young Socialists among fellow émigrés, calling them 'demagogues' for being equally critical of both the 'Stalinist' line of the KPD and the reactionary and defeatist policy of the Social-Democrat leaders. For if, as Heckert proudly claimed,[39] the rise of Hitler had not led to any radical challenge within the KPD, it had in contrast shattered the SPD. Not only did a section of the Socialists exiled in Prague criticize the SPD leadership, but they seemed tempted to converge with 'revolutionary Marxism', even distancing themselves from the SoPaDe in their programmatic text *Revolution gegen Hitler* of summer 1933. Violent polemics broke out among intellectuals of different Socialist factions, some calling for collaboration with the Communists even while rejecting the perspective of a 'bolshevik Germany'. This was the origin of groups such as Neu Beginnen,[40] while Alexandre Schifrin viewed the efforts of Torgler (KPD) and Stampfer (SPD) to overcome the division of the German working class by the formation of a united front as perfectly correct.

These criticisms of Social-Democratic strategy, and the rapprochement to Marxism (and the KPD) of the Young Socialists, were sharply rejected by the Social-Democratic leadership. The KPD also distrusted this development, seeing it as no more than a demagogic move. Wilhelm Pieck again attacked the left Young Socialists as being 'agents of fascism' charged with preventing the workers from joining the Communist organizations.[41] The manifesto *Kämpfe und Ziele des revolutionären Sozialismus*, published in Prague on 28 January 1934, seemed to make concessions to this left-Socialist criticism, though without sparing the KPD. It was denounced by the Communists as a sectarian manoeuvre designed to attract those Socialists disheartened by their leadership's tactics, and dismissed as 'social-fascist demagogy'.[42] These criticisms aroused strong reaction from the Prague Socialists, who saw no hope of any new development on the KPD's part. The SPD's own situation was in fact very difficult at the start of the exile period: the leaders risked being rejected by those Social-Democrats remaining in Germany, who formed the right wing of the party. On their left, they feared seeing some of their more active members tempted by a rapprochement with the KPD. It was doubtless this fear that led them to undertake underground activity in Germany, so as not to leave the Communists a monopoly of antifascist struggle,[43] and to set up the Internationale Gesellschaft zur Rettung (Verteidigung) der Demokratie[44] in response to the Welthilfskomitee für die Opfer Deutschen Faschismus, more or less mirroring the latter's structures. But the project did not get anywhere,[45] and the only major Social-Democratic organization set up to assist the exiles was the Paris-based Comité de Secours aux Réfugiés Allemands.

DEVELOPMENT OF KPD STRATEGY

Whilst its hostility towards the SPD remained strong in the early exile period, and polemics and insults were exchanged, some gradual readjustments of KPD tactics were already noticeable.[46] A certain rapprochement was tentatively suggested even while the Socialists were still officially treated as 'social-fascists'. In a first phase, Communist literature still declared its faith in the imminent victory of the proletariat and the overthrow of the regime. The consolidation of Nazi power, as well as the appearance of resistance movements, showed the need to organize and develop this opposition by all means possible. The French example, moreover, gave cause for reflection: on 12 February 1934, a general strike organized in Paris by the Socialists, with associated demonstrations, had attracted 20,000 Communists. The idea gradually spread therefore of a 'united front from below' (*Einheitsfront von unten*), achieved at rank-and-file level, even while the party leaderships continued to maintain irreconcilable positions. The intensifying resistance in Germany, and the diversity of its components, who now also included Christians, had an effect on Communist strategy, which appealed to them on several occasions,[47] even foreshadowing the formation of a Popular Front (*Volksfront*) against Nazi dictatorship.[48]

The liquidation of the SA on 30 June 1934 gave rise to the hope of a weakening of the regime due to its internal contradictions.[49] It was in the weeks following the 'night of the long knives' that the Socialist attitude likewise shifted. During the meeting of the Communist International on 9–10 July, Piatnitzky proposed making a 'ninety–degree turn': the consolidation of the regime that had followed the purge of the SA seemed to have convinced the Communists of the impossibility of fighting the Nazis single-handed. But this radical change of strategy decided in Moscow, which was to galvanize all the European Communist parties, met with a number of difficulties. Fortunately it was strengthened by a whole series of events that formed the prehistory of the *Volksfront*.

In France, first of all, the development of a great anti-war movement constituted a major step in the rapprochement between Socialists and Communists. At the Seventh Congress of the Communist International (July–August 1935), Marcel Cachin declared: 'We entered thoroughly into the idea of a united front, the idea of a Popular Front as demanded by the Amsterdam congress of August 1932 [. . .] That was our beginning, our embarkation, and we reached our destination on 1 July 1935, with the first massive realization of this double tactic of the United and Popular Front!'[50]

Henri Barbusse was behind this great gathering of political, trade-union and cultural organizations.[51] The founder of the Association Républicaine des Anciens Combattants, who had been converted to Communism in the 1920s, had obtained the agreement of Romain Rolland, and on 26 June 1932 both men appealed for a struggle in defence of peace. This appeal led to the Amsterdam meeting, which brought together Communists, Socialists – who attended without their party's agreement – and many trade unionists. The 'Amsterdam committees' that were founded in many places after this congress further accentuated this rapprochement. In January 1934, the French Communists embarked on the formation of a united front with the Socialists, at more than just rank-and-file level. But the right-wing riots of February 1934 still failed to bring the two leaderships together: while the Communists accepted the idea of rank-and-file unity, this did not yet apply at the top.[52] A proposal for 'loyal agreement with a view to achieving united action by working people' was addressed by the Socialists to the PCF on 6 February, but *Humanité* continued to maintain that the Socialists 'paved the way for fascism'. On the night of 6–7 February a delegation from two Socialist districts turned up at the *Humanité* offices and were received by André Marty and Vaillant-Couturier. The Socialist proposal to organize a joint demonstration on the 8th went against the intentions of the PCF's political bureau, which had planned to organize its own demonstration and call Socialist workers to parade under Communist leadership. Socialists and Communists were preparing therefore to march separately, the former to the place de la Bastille, the latter to the place de la République. Both demonstrations were banned, and the Communist one gave rise to violent clashes around the Gare de l'Est and the République. Learning that fighting was under way in the streets, members of the Socialist Youth, responsible for guarding the district offices, joined the demonstrators and were greeted with the cry: 'Unity of action!' An article in *Humanité* the next day acknowledged this common struggle and called on Socialist and Communist workers to unite. The result was that Communist workers joined the Socialist demonstration on 12 February, and members of the permanent administrative commission of the SFIO attended the burial of workers killed during the clashes of the 9th.[53]

At the theoretical level, this united front remained questionable for a long while, each party claiming to take the lead in the antifascist movement and refusing to end its criticisms of the other. On 24 February the SFIO established an antifascist liaison centre, seeking to introduce a certain degree of coordination among the Comités de Vigilance set up by its branches. On 6 March it addressed a request to the PCF to organize a kind of central committee uniting the antifascist organizations.[54] The Communists accepted the proposal with certain conditions, but just as the Socialists feared Communist infiltration of their organizations, so the Communists refused to 'form a bloc with the Socialist party'.[55] Socialist workers were however invited by the Communists to join the Pleyel-Amsterdam movement.[56] Thanks to these various rapprochements, an antifascist demonstration was organized for 20 April, without this signalling a unity of the parties.[57] The object was still, as Thorez put it, 'to form a powerful single revolutionary front under the leadership of the Communist party'. At the end of May 1934, as requested by the Comintern Executive Committee, the PCF organized demonstrations in support of Ernst Thälmann, still threatened with a death sentence. The PCF's central committee proposed to the Socialists that they organize a joint demonstration. A meeting planned for 11 June, however, failed to materialize, as the Socialists demanded as a precondition that all polemics should cease until the demonstration was held. The Communists rejected this provision, and negotiations were broken off.[58]

On 23 June 1934 the PCF held a national conference at Ivry on 'the organization of a united front of antifascist struggle', its plan of action envisaging contact with Socialist workers with a view to thwarting the manoeuvres of Socialist leaders opposed to unity. Thorez declared: 'The bourgeoisie is trying to take the lead in the race between ourselves and fascism. And if we don't manage to do more, still more, and more again for the united front, fascism will beat the working class. We don't want fascism to triumph in France. Which is why we seek at any price to achieve unity with the Socialist workers against fascism.'[59] The conference gave the political bureau a mandate to propose to the Socialists a pact of common struggle against fascism. A plan was sent to the SFIO, but even before its own Ivry conference had pronounced on the project on 15 July, unity was already achieved when some Socialist districts united with the PCF for a major antifascist rally on the 2nd. Communists and Socialists were acclaimed on the platform, and extolled the united workers' action.[60] On the 16th, the SFIO accepted the offer of joint action, and the two parties undertook to organize a campaign throughout France to mobilize workers against fascism, for the defence of democratic freedoms, against war, against fascist terror in Germany and Austria, and for the release of Thälmann. It was also envisaged that activists of the two parties would support each other in the demonstrations, and that the Socialist and Communist leaderships would suspend all polemics, while keeping their full independence. A coordinating committee of seven delegates from each party was formed to organize action and resolve possible disputes.

On 9 October 1934, during a meeting at the Salle Bullier, Thorez launched the famous slogan of a 'Popular Front of labour, liberty and peace', and the same day the PCF proposed to the SFIO to work out a joint programme for such a front. On the 14 July demonstration the following year, the parties took a 'solemn oath to remain united, to disarm and dissolve the fascist leagues, to defend and develop democratic liberties, and assure peace for humanity'.

Moscow's attitude towards these events was fairly complex. Dimitrov had attended the Amsterdam meeting as head of the Communist delegation, as well as the first session of the World Committee Against War held in Paris in December 1932. According to Henri Barbusse, Stalin, who had been favourable to the formation of the Amsterdam committees, showed greater reserve towards a Communist–Socialist rapprochement. The united front established in France also aroused a good deal of discussion within the Comintern.[61] When its Executive Committee met on 9–10 July 1934, a number of members were hostile to the change of tactics displayed in Paris. The German Communists were themselves divided, but a number of self-criticisms were made, to the effect that the KPD had failed to recognize fascism as its real enemy. The KPD central committee then met at the end of July with the presidium of the ECCI to envisage a transition from the old strategy to the new one.[62] Whilst the KPD policy was not openly criticized, the text that emerged – 'The Enemy is Fascism' – launched new slogans of struggle, appeals to a 'people's revolution' and a 'socialist Germany'. Above all, a resolution of the central committee foresaw the formation of a 'united front of working masses against the Hitler dictatorship'.

THE STAGES OF THE *VOLKSFRONT*

Now that fascism was officially designated as the true enemy of the working class, collaboration with the Social-Democrats in this struggle became at last possible. Faced with the developing situation in France, the KPD, despite its caution, was willing to embark on negotiations with the exiled SPD leadership in Prague. In August 1934, a rapprochement had been attempted with left-wing Socialists such as the Neu Beginnen group.[63] Certain Socialists (Max Seydewitz) recognized the mistake of preferring reformism to a united strategy. Negotiations were started, but constantly threatened by the old complaints resurfacing.[64] In November 1934, the KPD addressed an 'open letter to all Social-Democrat groups and their leaders',[65] calling for the formation of a united front. The 'Platform of the Revolutionary Socialists' was discussed by Wilhelm Pieck in a widely distributed pamphlet, *Aufgaben und Zielsetzung der Einheits-front*.[66] This project of unity raised many problems, for if the KPD planned to remain the sole revolutionary party able to lead the working class, the SPD insisted that the specificities of the two parties be recognized and respected.

On 30 January 1935, the KPD central committee published a text stressing the need to unite working people against fascism, and avoid any kind of sectarianism in the interest of 'establishing an antifascist Popular Front'. On 11 February it wrote to the SoPaDe leadership to propose a joint action programme and the formation of committees equally representing both parties. The KPD efforts in this direction became increasingly urgent, and they proposed a meeting with the Prague Socialist leaders. The latter rejected most of the KPD proposals, seeing the strategy of a united front or Popular Front as a Communist 'manoeuvre' designed to increase KPD influence among the exiles. They continued to maintain that the objectives of the two parties were too different to make unity possible.

A second step in the attempt to construct a German Popular Front was made during the Saar campaign, when a Popular Front group (Volksfrontgruppe Freiheitsaktion Saar) was formed under Gustav Regler, himself a Saarlander by birth, which championed the maintenance of the status quo as the lesser evil, a thesis that was finally accepted by the Saarland Communist party. An attempt at a united front was made[67] with the support of Communist officials and intellectuals,[68] but this failed,[69] and the result was thus the defeat of this attempted unity.[70]

The most important phase in the construction of the *Volksfront* began in summer 1935, at the Seventh Congress of the Communist International, marked by Dimitrov's report on 'The Fascist Offensive and the Tasks of the Communist International in the Struggle of the Working Class against Fascism', in which he called on both workers and intellectuals to achieve unity of action against fascism. It was officially recognized for the first time that the policy of splitting the workers' movement had proved catastrophic, and that the only way leading to a genuine victory for the proletariat was through the creation of a 'broad antifascist front', a 'single anti-imperialist front'. Furthermore, Dimitrov reproached the Communist parties for a certain schematicism in their actions and their analyses of fascism. This new orientation was confirmed and reinforced by the KPD conference of October 1935, known as the 'Brussels conference'. The task now was not only, as Wilhelm Pieck had maintained in 1933–34, to construct a 'united front from below' by leading the Social-Democratic workers to reject their leaders' instructions and work with the Communists, but also a 'united front from above' with the object of uniting the two workers' parties in joint action against fascism. Pieck officially acknowledged that in the years leading up to Hitler's seizure of power, KPD strategy had been marked by serious political mistakes, especially concerning its appreciation of the balance of forces. And whilst the need to struggle against class collaboration and the government's terror methods against the workers was emphasized, the KPD recognized its poor appreciation of the Nazi danger.[71] Commenting on Hitler's speech at the Nuremberg rally, he underlined that if the Nazis were well aware of their true enemies – Marxism, parliamentary democracy, the Catholic Centre – the latter had now to unite in order to confront fascism.

It was in the wake of the Brussels conference, which clearly maintained the necessity of a Popular Front against the forces of fascism, that the German Communists made their first official approaches to the Social-Democrats, as well as to the leaders of the Centre party and the Catholics.[72] Several Communist papers[73] immediately developed this Popular Front platform and sought to expand the new strategy to its limit. The first unity proposals were unacceptable to the Socialists,[74] even if they paid great attention to the resolutions of the Comintern's seventh congress and to the Brussels conference. Not only was the 'ultra-left' line now condemned, but the term 'social-fascism' would no longer be applied to the Social-Democrats, and the difference between fascism and bourgeois democracy was clearly recognized. The KPD thus tried to distinguish between a 'reactionary wing' of the SPD and a 'revolutionary current' present within that party, susceptible of being won over to Communism or working together with it. Though Social-Democratic reformism would still be opposed, approaches were undertaken to bring the two parties together, even if in the mind of the Communists, the Popular Front was a step designed to lead towards a Soviet Germany.

Despite this theoretical development and the change of strategy, the SoPaDe leaders in Prague still distrusted the KPD's offers and published a fairly negative account of the united front concept. They maintained that unity could not be established from above, but only from below, and this by a gradual change in political practice. However, despite its mistrust and doubtless fearing attack from its left wing, the SoPaDe agreed to meet a KPD delegation at the SPD offices on 23 November 1935. Wilhelm Ulbricht and Franz Dahlem accordingly travelled to Prague, where the SPD had delegated Friedrich Stampfer and Hans Vogel to meet them. Their discussions embraced both the old polemics between Socialists and Communists in the Weimar era, and the differing conceptions of democracy that the two parties had. The SPD would only accept the idea of a united front with the Communists if the KPD abandoned its attacks on them and if they could agree on a common conception of democracy. The KPD for its part maintained that the future destiny of

Germany after the collapse of National Socialism would be the object of a consultation of all parties, and promised a loyal attitude towards the SPD. At all events, both parties showed a common desire to avoid past mistakes, and the Communists declared their faith in a Popular Front government, on condition that this was not a government of collaboration with the bourgeoisie: the two parties should on the contrary *together* oppose the counter-revolutionary forces, which had never been achieved in the Weimar Republic. No formal agreement was concluded, however, and the SPD was even opposed to a joint press communiqué, believing that making the meeting public knowledge would be a political error. Vogel would agree only to relate that the discussion had not had a negative result.

This was to be the only summit meeting between the two parties. But despite the coolness of the Socialists, it did not destroy the Communist hope of officially establishing a Popular Front. Whilst the Prague leaders rejected any unity, Robert Breitscheid in Paris agreed to meet with the Communists, and groups such as Neu Beginnen also took part in these discussions.

Whereas the project of a Popular Front aroused tremendous activity on the Communist side, it only helped to aggravate differences among the Social-Democrats. From 1935 on, the KPD made many new contacts with other left-wing groups – Socialists, Catholics, antifascist intellectuals – insisting on the major turning-point that the Seventh Congress of the Comintern had officially made. It recalled that the SoPaDe manifesto of January 1934 had acknowledged how the division of the working class had been the cause of the Nazi seizure of power. The left Socialists also sought to bring the two parties together, maintaining that the Prague SoPaDe only represented one Social-Democratic current among others. Certain groups which originally seemed set to play a major role, such as Neu Beginnen, subsequently broke up as a result of their internal contradictions. Neu Beginnen was destroyed in Germany in 1936, and survived only with difficulty in Prague and London. The left Socialists of the SAP saw the Popular Front as abandoning the authentic Leninist line, and held that a government that contained 'bourgeois elements' would be an obstacle to proletarian revolution, and break apart once the question of overthrowing the capitalist economic system was raised. The Trotskyists,[75] likewise, rejected any idea of a Popular Front, even though in 1930 Trotsky had been one of the first to defend the idea of a united front grouping Socialists and Communists.[76] The KPD's action thus had a dual perspective: to build a united front from below in Paris with left Socialists and figures from the intellectual world, so as to isolate the SoPaDe leadership in Prague, and to work for a rapprochement with the Socialists as a whole as well as with liberals, seeking to maintain contact at party level. These attempts were reinforced by the growing enthusiasm that the projected *Volksfront* aroused among intellectuals, as well as among opposi-tionists who remained in Germany.

If the party leaderships did not manage to agree, anti-Nazi workers had welcomed the news of the formation of the Frente Popular in Spain with new hope.[77] Influenced by Neu Beginnen and the 'revolutionary socialists', a number of Popular Front units were formed in Germany, with Socialist and

Communist workers. On 24 December 1936, a Berlin group, formed at Communist initiative but with the participation of Social-Democratic workers, even published a 'ten-point programme' for the formation of a *Volksfront*. This group sent a three-person delegation to Prague in January 1937, to make contact with the SoPaDe, but this refused to change its positions and remained hostile to the formation of such groups in Germany. Similar contact was made with Communists in Paris, but these were suspicious of the participation of the SAP and KPO (Communist Opposition). Besides, though the 'ten-point group' and the KPD shared the desire for a united *Volksfront*, the KPD criticized the Berlin group for not taking into account the role of the party leadership. Finding no real support from either the KPD in Paris nor the SPD in Prague, this group eventually merged with Neu Beginnen.

It was in Paris, however, that the idea of a German Popular Front really acquired concrete existence. Many reasons explain this choice: besides the example of the local Front Populaire, Paris was home to the largest number of Communist émigrés outside of the USSR, as well as a large number of prominent figures from German intellectual life. France was also a particularly important observation point to follow developments in Spain. Even if the SoPaDe still refused to support the project, the idea of a union of all antifascist forces, both exiles and oppositionists within Germany – whether Socialists, Communists, Catholics, liberals, non-party or intellectuals – constantly drew strength and won over not only left Socialists but also a large number of writers. What resulted from this was an ephemeral creation, a surge of solidarity, a dream. The *Volksfront* never formed a mass movement able to act as a united front; it was never sufficiently representative to exert a political role on the lines of the Front Populaire; it was above all an intellectual gathering, albeit the bearer of an immense hope.

The birth of the *Volksfront* in Paris was inseparable from a certain number of other movements which prepared the ground, prefiguring this gathering of antifascists from the most varied origins, and uniting, sometimes around a one-off action, all opposition to National Socialism. The Amsterdam-Pleyel movement had already brought together Socialist and Communist intellectuals, as had the World Committee Against War and Fascism. The committees formed for the release of Thälmann and Dimitrov, and other Communists and Socialists imprisoned by the Nazis, aroused a solidarity that transcended party boundaries. In Paris, Willi Münzenberg had openly favoured the idea of a *Volksfront* well before the Seventh Congress of the Comintern. Robert Breitscheid, also in Paris exile, played an important role in this gathering from the Social-Democratic side. In the cultural arena, we should also remember how the SDS, re-established in Paris, united anti-Nazi writers without sectarianism, whether they were Socialist, Communist, or liberal. Finally, the French Front Populaire, at the Montreuil meeting of June 1935, openly expressed its solidarity with the German Front for Peace (Deutsche Friedensfront). Heinrich Mann had launched an appeal[78] to German antifascists to forget old oppositions. Similar declarations could be found in Leopold Schwarzschild's *Das Neue Tage-Buch*.[79] Little by little, this idea began to attract many exiled figures, like the journalist Maximilian Scheer in the Ausschuss zur Schaffung der Deutschen Volksfront, and throughout 1935 meetings were held in Paris, attended by Communists, left Social-Democrats, liberals and antifascist intellectuals. As these were held at the Hotel Lutétia, the group became known as the *Lutétia-Kreis*. One of the first major victories of the Communists was to get the appeal protesting against the execution of the Communist activist Rudolf Claus[80] signed also by leading Social-Democrats. On 1 February, a meeting of representatives from the main workers' parties was attended by the Communists Franz Dahlem, Willi Münzenberg and H. Wehner, the Socialists Robert Breitscheid, Max Braun and Erich Kuttner, as well as SAP members Paul Fröhlich, Walter Fabian and Jacob Walcher. If the idea of a campaign in defence of German political prisoners won unanimous approval, discussion as to the future government of Germany raised many difficulties. A rather general text that envisaged the re-establishment of democratic rights was nonetheless signed.

The Lutétia committee's activities became more prominent during the year 1936. It produced its own organ, *Deutsche Informationen*,[81] and on 22 April elected an executive committee of fifteen. Soon, circles of 'Friends of the German *Volksfront*' began to spread, organizing lectures and debates. On 2 February, the day after the meeting between representatives of the main left parties, a large conference was convened by Heinrich Mann and Max Braun, following which a *Kundgebung an das deutsche Volk* (*Proclamation to the German People*) was published, signed by the 118 participants, and calling for the creation of a political platform for the *Volksfront*. The signatories included Heinrich Mann, Willi Münzenberg, Robert Breitscheid and the editor of the *Pariser Tagblatt*, Georg Bernhard. Though agreement on this platform had still not been reached by the year end, a new appeal for the formation of a *Volksfront* was published, signed by seventy-three people. On 9 March 1936, after consultation between two members from the KPD and SPD, *Deutsche Informationen* was launched, with the support of Heinrich Mann. A whole series of texts attest to a certain collaboration between Socialists and Communists by February 1936. An appeal against the remilitarization of the Rhineland was signed by Robert Breitscheid, Heinrich Mann and Walter Ulbricht, another in May 1936 was signed by members of the KPD and SPD, as well as Willy Brandt for the SAP. The *Neue Weltbühne*[82] devoted a special number to the *Volksfront*, with texts by Heinrich Mann, Siegfried Aufhäuser, Karl Böchel, Georg Bernhard, Wilhelm Sollmann, Walter Ulbricht, Lion Feuchtwanger, F. C. Weiskopf, Emil Ludwig and Ernst Toller. A KPD meeting in June 1936 established a five-point programme for a 'democratic republic'.[83] On 21 December, a new appeal was launched, *Aufruf für die deutsche Volksfront*, signed by Communists, members of the SAP, and Social-Democrats (without the agreement of the SoPaDe, which called for the preparation of a plenary conference for 10 April 1937).

Yet despite the sincerity of protagonists and participants in the Paris *Volksfront*, and for all the enthusiasm of Heinrich Mann, the political differences between the two workers' parties were far from being blurred. Distrust remained between Socialists and Communists, whilst the SAP accused the initiators of the *Volksfront* for trying to imitate too closely the Popular Fronts in France and Spain.[84] Though all agreed on the need for unity around common slogans in order to overthrow fascism, they were divided over the type of government appropriate for a future Germany.[85] The KPD's orthodoxy, moreover, its approval of the Moscow trials and the liquidation of the Trotskyists, had a disturbing effect on bourgeois and liberal intellectuals. There were difficulties too in the relationship between Walter Ulbricht and Heinrich Mann.[86] The Socialist leaders in Prague always kept their distance from the *Volksfront*, even though left Social-Democratic exiles in Paris rallied to it. The KPD's central committee too, in a resolution of 14 May 1937, maintained not unreasonably that the SoPaDe remained the main obstacle to achieving the *Volksfront*. From January 1938, Max Braun, Heinrich Mann, Robert Breitscheid and Professor Denike officially announced their intention to cease contributing to *Deutsche Informationen*.[87]

The collapse of the *Volksfront* now inevitably began to gather pace. The KPD had undoubtedly made valiant efforts to bring together all components of the exiled German left by developing a new strategy and criticizing its past theoretical and practical mistakes. In May 1938, it officially recognized the presence among resisters to Nazism of members of the former Centre party, Catholics, Socialists, and even nationalists from the Stahlhelme. In a letter to Heinrich Mann the same month, Wilhelm Pieck insisted on the need to work to bring together in Paris representatives from all German and Austrian antifascist groups, declaring that each group would have a right of veto over any appeals and manifestos. Undermined by its internal oppositions, and the refusal of the SoPaDe to join it, the *Volksfront* rapidly began to dissolve, despite the intellectual energy it had attracted, and without any single particular cause. Whilst Communist historians insist on the negative attitude of the Social-Democrat leaders and mention profound differences in the conception of the antifascist struggle, others emphasize the nefarious effect that the Moscow trials and the hunt for Trotskyists had on many left formations that had agreed to collaborate with the KPD. The USSR at that point was far indeed from offering a model of democracy, and the KPD's fidelity to its line was enough to chill the most zealous champions of the *Volksfront*. More fundamentally, we should recognize that nothing succeeded in overcoming the distrust that prevailed between the two great workers' parties: the Socialists saw only a manoeuvre by the KPD to increase its influence in exile, the SAP denounced it as an anti-Leninist deviation, while Neu Beginnen did not participate and drew closer to the SoPaDe.

The Socialist groups now tried to form a new coalition, and Heinrich Mann, the most enthusiastic artisan of the *Volksfront*, was again involved, even if Robert Breitscheid viewed him with mistrust as a fellow-traveller of the Communists. In September 1938, the remnants of the *Volksfront* coalition made a final attempt to unite, launching appeals to overthrow Hitler both to the German people and to the democratic nations, but the SAP had already refused

to take part.[88] A short time after, most of the organizations that had provided
the base of the *Volksfront* were disbanded. The dream of the *Volksfront* had
lasted a mere two years. Yet its result should not be judged as negative: if it was
unable to arouse any real mass movement, or unite all the parties of the left, it
did provide the opportunity for a rapprochement between many antifascists,
and engendered a genuinely important intellectual mobilization against Hitler.

DECLINE OF THE *VOLKSFRONT*

In seeking to analyse the main reasons for the failure of the *Volksfront* in Paris,
the first thing to bear in mind is that though it aroused immense hope, especially
among writers and intellectuals, the *Volksfront* was undermined from its
inception by various contradictions: the absence of genuine unity between
the workers' parties, a heterogeneous assemblage of personalities, and the
almost total lack of a working-class base. Despite signing joint appeals, and
the same hatred for National Socialism, the different opposition factions
remained irreconcilable as soon as the question was of a future German
government was raised. Finally, the SoPaDe in Prague remained hostile to
the project in any form, whilst the SAP condemned it for opposite reasons,
especially its extension to the liberal bourgeoisie.[89]

The reasons for the final collapse of the *Volksfront* are complex, and bear both
on the weakness of its components, the distrust among them, and the absence of
genuine links with the working class, as well as on the international context. If
opposing notions of democracy had already been an issue between Socialists and
Communists, the development of the USSR and the first Moscow trials had a
disturbing effect even on those Social-Democrats most well-disposed towards
the Popular Front. Besides, the collapse of the Popular Fronts in both France
and Spain could not but rebound on the German *Volksfront*. This unfavourable
context was then worsened by personality clashes. Above all else, Willi Münzenberg's break with the Comintern deprived the *Volksfront* of its most dynamic
personality. His replacement by Paul Merker and especially Walter Ulbricht
compromised relations with a number of non-Communist intellectuals.[90] Far
more rigid than Münzenberg, Ulbricht in no way possessed the same gift of
winning sympathy,[91] and the understanding with Heinrich Mann, a cornerstone
between the KPD and non-Communist intellectuals, was considerable shaken.
Some non-Communist émigrés accused Ulbricht of bad faith, whilst he seemed
to fear they were envisaging the possibility of a *Volksfront* without the KPD. On
1 October 1937, the non-Communist members of the committee requested the
KPD to replace Ulbricht and Merker with other representatives. Heinrich Mann
himself wrote to Wilhelm Pieck to complain about Ulbricht's actions, and an
arbitration commission was set up on 25 October, chaired by Max Braun.[92]
Ulbricht's departure for Moscow and his replacement by Franz Dahlem failed to
give the *Volksfront* a new lease of life. Collaboration between Socialists and
Communists was at an end, distrust between the two parties intensified, and
dissident Social-Democratic factions again oriented themselves towards the
SoPaDe in Prague. In September 1938, certain Socialist groups, together with

Communists close to Münzenberg who had broken with the KPD, established a group for action and deliberation, the Sozialistische Arbeitsgemeinschaft. Though certain ties with the Socialists remained (such as a joint appeal to workers of Germany and Austria after the annexation of Czechoslovakia), the various attempts by the Communists to revive contact with the SoPaDe were unsuccessful. But until 1939, for all that, the KPD remained attached to the idea of a Popular Front, and on 16 September 1938 could still publish an action programme for the German emigration as a whole.[93] The Popular Front idea was again reaffirmed at the KPD's Berne conference of 30 January to 1 February 1939. But a final attempt at antifascist regroupment – known as the 'Thomas Mann committee' and comprising Socialists (Friedrich Stampfer, Max Braun), Communists (Willi Münzenberg, Franz Dahlem) and conservative figures such as Hermann Rauschning – ended in failure.

On 25 March 1939, at Communist initiative, an action committee of German oppositionists was once again founded at the Hotel Lutétia, but this essentially attracted just Communists and intellectuals, with no other components of the German left. On 23 April 1939, Heinrich Mann launched a further appeal for the unity of the workers' parties.[94] But though certain joint actions were still undertaken by exiled Socialists and Communists, they failed to bring about any reconciliation of the two parties. The German–Soviet pact then succeeded in repelling from Communism a number of intellectuals who had already taken their distance from the KPD, and especially from the USSR, following the Moscow trials.[95]

The émigré press were similarly divided. Only the Communist press approved the pact, seeing it as Stalin's victory for peace. The Social-Democratic press, on the other hand, denounced it as a 'monstrous stroke of devilish Machiavellianism'.[96] The hostility between the two parties was brutally rekindled, the Social-Democrats maintaining that this collaboration between Nazis and Communists was not new but went back to the Weimar days. Leopold Schwarzschild, in *Das Neue Tage-Buch*, declared that socialism was the very origin of fascism, and attacked all the émigré writers whom he suspected of Communist sympathies.[97] Even setting aside such excessive reactions, it is undeniable that the pact disoriented for a while both the antifascist resistance and the exiles themselves, not excluding those who had sought refuge in the USSR. Still an adolescent in 1939, Wolfgang Leonhard evoked the consternation of German émigrés in the Soviet Union after the announcement of the pact: all antifascist films were withdrawn from distribution. Even history teaching was transformed: instead of celebrating Alexander Nevsky's victory over the Teutonic Knights as a great Russian victory, praise was heaped on Peter the Great's policy towards Prussia. Antifascist works, and even works written by émigrés, were withdrawn from public libraries, while Nazi papers could now be found there.[98] If some émigrés, for example Erich Weinert, found nothing wrong with the agreements signed between Germany and the USSR, the majority of their number saw this signature as a betrayal of their cause. Even if the pact as such might be objectively justified in various ways, it was far harder to justify texts in which France and Britain were clearly attacked,[99] and above all the assertion that the

struggle against National Socialism was not an end in itself but a means of
achieving peace. It took quite some dialectical genius on the part of certain
Communist theorists of the time to argue that the news of the pact – initially
presented by Communists as a lie of Nazi propaganda – was not a 'fascist
provocation' but a 'stroke of genius' of Stalin, who had saved peace by tying
Hitler's hands. Manès Sperber was certainly right to say: 'For the entire
antifascist movement, for the left as a whole, the Stalin–Hitler pact was the
greatest political and moral defeat that could ever have been inflicted.'[100]

Paul Friedländer, a major figure in the exiled KPD, interned at the camp of
Le Vernet, drafted a protest against the pact and was immediately expelled from
his cell.[101] We should finally recall that after the signature of the pact, the
NKVD handed over a number of German Communist refugees in the USSR to
the Gestapo. These included the physicist Hentermanns, Alex Weissbert,[102] and
Margaret Buber-Neumann, the partner of Heinz Neumann.[103]

The *Volksfront* no longer had any meaning. At the meeting of the Comintern's executive committee on 6 November 1939, Dimitrov declared the need for
a new tactic. The Socialists accused the USSR of having betrayed the cause of
antifascism, and there were those who spoke of a convergence between the two
regimes – a thesis put forward early on by Leopold Schwarzschild, and later
taken up by many right-wing Socialists – while the Communists denounced the
Socialists as 'provokers of war in the service of France and England'. In 1940
the Sozialistische Arbeitsgemeinschaft published a text, 'Die KPD und die
Solidarität der Illegalen', drawing a pessimistic balance-sheet of the perspectives
of antifascist struggle. This commented on a text by Walter Ulbricht in reply to
an article by Rudolf Hilferding on 'The Meaning of This War' which had
appeared in *Neue Vorwärts*. Hilferding saw the war as the democracies' defence
against the dictatorships, and put Hitler and Stalin on the same footing. The
article had proved controversial even among Socialists. Ulbricht's reply only
envenomed relations between the parties. He declared that the more the pact
was attacked, the more the friendship between the German and the Soviet
people would be strengthened, that the main task of the KPD now was to
support the pact and that 'the main enemy in Germany is not Hitler, but the
antifascist opponents of this pact' ('*Der Hauptfeind in Deutschland ist nicht
Hitler, sondern die antifaschisten Gegner dieses Paktes*'). It is easy to understand
how phrases like this could plunge so many émigrés into despair.[104]

3. THE INVOLVEMENT OF ÉMIGRÉS
IN THE SPANISH WAR

As long as there are fascists, we shall all be Spaniards.

Gustav Regler

The civil war transformed Spain into a battlefield, on which we thought the destiny of
freedom would be rapidly decided; at the expense of the dictatorships, of course.
There was scarcely anyone who believed that the war would last for two and a half

years, and would end with the triumph of Hitler, Mussolini and Franco, the fall of the Republic and the destruction of so many human lives. Still today, decades after that summer of 1936, the summer of our hopes, the Spanish tragedy remains, for all antifascists still living, a tormenting memory, an unforgettable insult.

Manès Sperber

THE ÉMIGRÉS AND THE SPANISH WAR

While France and Britain abstained from intervention in Spain, leaving the field clear for Franco, Germany and fascist Italy, the cause of Republican Spain attracted a broad movement of international solidarity in which many German exiles took part. The reasons for their commitment are easy to imagine: they were moral and psychological as well as directly political. To defend the Spanish Republic was to defend the Popular Front that had triumphed in Spain in January 1936. To combat Franco's rebellion was to combat fascism and thus Hitler. Any émigré compelled to beg for his bread, live off the alms of committees, and line up outside the prefecture of police to obtain a residence permit, would prefer to this long series of humiliations the glory of dying in Spain in the battle against fascism.

Spain was the first site of bloody confrontation between the democratic forces and fascism. What was at stake there was not just the fate of a republic, but the future of democracy and of Europe as a whole. The outcome of the conflict was fraught with significance. The Spanish Falange was a ready match for Nazi methods. Fascist Italy and Hitlerite Germany were ranked at its side, transforming the Spanish soil, as so many émigrés noted, into a training-ground.[105] For those who had seen themselves reduced to the impotence of exile, confrontation with Spanish fascism offered the opportunity, both symbolic and real, to oppose the barbarism that had expelled them from their own country. While the committee representing twenty-seven countries that was established in London set itself the task of supervising the non-intervention agreement – though as the Soviet ambassador remarked, it was hard to describe aid given to a legitimate government as 'intervention' – a mass of volunteers gathered in both Europe and the United States, ready to offer assistance to the Republic.[106] Despite the various legal and administrative obstacles erected for them, they managed to reach Spanish soil and form the International Brigades whose courage and exploits were immortalized by the tales of Willi Bredel, the poems of Erich Weinert and the songs of Ernst Busch.

These volunteer armies counted many Communists in their ranks, but also individuals driven to Spain by a simple idealism.[107] They often took part in the hardest battles. Of the 35,000 who joined the Brigades, over 20,000 were killed or wounded. After the defeat of the Republican army, they left Spain following a final struggle to protect the hundreds of thousands of refugees who fled across the French frontier. Even when conquered, these antifascist volunteers entered into legend, and above all into literature. Few events so marked modern literature as the story of these men of every nationality, most not even speaking Spanish, who came to die for Madrid.

When the rebellion of the fascist generals broke out on 18 July 1936, the Communist International proposed a meeting with its Socialist counterpart with the aim of holding a conference. This was rebuffed, and when the Comintern made a further attempt at joint support for the Spanish Republic towards the year end, it met with the same refusal. In 1937, faced with the threat of the fascist forces winning the war, the Comintern made further appeals for international solidarity. On 21 April 1937, representatives from twenty-one Communist parties met in Paris to discuss what action to take. Agreement with the Socialists had proved impossible, despite meetings between Franz Dahlem and Friedrich Adler. There was only the volunteer army to aid the Republic. Klaus Mann expressed very well in his novel *The Volcano* the reasons impelling so many exiles to fight in Spain. Besides their idealism,[108] the majority of antifascist exiles had no doubt that the cause for which the Spanish Republicans were fighting was their own. They served it to the end, and in many cases sacrificed their lives.[109]

What is surprising is the impressive number of poets, writers, actors, journalists and artists who transformed themselves into simple soldiers. While the case of Hans Beimler is one of the most well-known, we should recall that the poet Erich Weinert, the singer Ernst Busch, the novelist Willi Bredel, the poet Carl Einstein[110] and the writer Gustav Regler all fought in Spain, as well as Alfred Kantorowicz and Hans Kahle.[111] As Kantorowicz wrote: 'It was the émigrés' battle, their cause. They fought against barbarism, but especially the barbarism that had driven them from Germany, that had martyred them and murdered their brothers.'[112] In 1937, Ernst Busch sung: 'Our country is not lost, it's now outside Madrid.' They often arrived in Spain after facing great difficulties, sometimes as bogus reporters.[113] For many, the opportunity of armed struggle against fascism was a liberation as well as a necessity. Gustav Regler depicted this sentiment very well in his memoirs:

> My volunteers displayed an indifference to danger which I find hard to explain. [. . .] Most of them were émigrés who for three years had suffered humiliation at the hands of the Paris, Prague and Swiss police. Some had been obliged to report daily (I repeat, daily) and apply for another day's asylum. Now they had arms in their hands and a city to defend. The constant threat of death, which they laughed at or at least ignored, had restored their dignity. Many were Jews, and their bullets in the darkness were aimed at Hitler.[114]

As for Hans Beimler, who escaped from the Dachau concentration camp by strangling an SS man and taking his uniform, he declared that if he returned one day to Germany, it would be via Madrid.[115] For so many of the émigrés, death on the battlefield seemed preferable to dying of hunger and despair in exile.[116] Finally, the Spanish war was the practical application of the great antifascist Popular Front which they had dreamed of. As Arthur Koestler wrote: 'Spain was the first European country in which the new Comintern line, the People's Front, had been tried out and had led to a resounding victory for the Left-wing coalition; and also the first country in which the workers and the progressive middle class had jointly taken up arms to resist a Fascist bid for power. It was, from the beginning, a symbolic contest.'[117] In the event, the battle turned out to be cultural and political, as well as simply military.

CIVILIAN AND MILITARY ENGAGEMENT

'Red Front!' cried out the hero
and Beimler collapsed on the ground.
His cry was heard
by Spaniards, Germans,
Frenchmen and Italians.
'Red Front!' he cried and fell
onto the Spanish soil, the land of giants,
he, come from a distant land
to fall and spill his blood there.

Rafael Alberti

In the first few weeks after the rebellion, German antifascist support for the Spanish Republic was far from well-organized. A few political émigrés led by Reinhold Hoffmann went to fight in the Republican militia, and some who were already in Barcelona (Max Friedmann, Werner Hermlin, Franz Löwenstein) took part in the battles under way there. It was not until 24 July 1936 that the Thälmann detachment became part of the people's militia, and on 7 August a 'Thälmann centuria' was formed in Barcelona, at the initiative of Communists who included Hans Beimler, Albert Schreiner, Hermann Geisen and W. Wille. At the same time, the KPD's political bureau called on all German antifascists with military training to fight alongside the Spanish Popular Front. Reaching Spain in groups or individually, these fighters met up on the Aragon front and fought under the leadership of Schreiner and Geisen at Huerca, Tardienta and Alcuberria. They included many Socialist or Communist émigrés, as well as non-party people and volunteers who had come secretly from Germany.

Paris was one of the most important rallying points for these combatants.[118] If it was fairly easy to travel to Spain in the early days of the war, the French police subsequently established strict controls at the border, and many had to cross illegally.[119] A number of volunteers also reached Spain by sea, and on 9 October, the *Ciudad de Barcelona* disembarked 650 antifascist volunteers at Alicante, including a large number of German Communists[120] and Social-Democrats.[121] A large contingent of writers and artists fought alongside these workers, including Willi Bredel, Ernst Busch, Gustav Regler, Alfred Kantorowicz,[122] Erich Weinert, Walter Gorrisch, Peter Kast, Heinz Kiwitz, Hans Marchwitza, Maria von Osten, Ludwig Renn, Bodo Uhse, Eberhard Schmidt and Jeanne Stern. Antifascist women were very much involved, and several, including Gerda Taro, a photojournalist from Leipzig, were killed in Spain.[123]

At least 5,000 German volunteers fought in the XIth Brigade, but there were also German volunteers in other battalions, alongside combatants of other nationalities.[124] Franz Dahlem was involved in the political leadership of these international formations, and the Communist writer Hans Beimler was one of the coordinators of the Thälmann centuria.

On 9 November 1936, the XIth Brigade joined battle against the Francoist troops and played a major role in the defence of Madrid. Out of a strength of 1,700, only 900 survived these battles. On 1 December alone, during the defence of the university compound, Hans Beimler was killed along with Franz Vehlow (Louis Schuster), Kurt von Appen, G. Meyer, P. Baumgarten, Philipp Mayer, J. Graf, Richard Wagner and W. Wille, all members of the KPD, as well as the Social-Democrats O. Volkmann, P. Lose and H. Schwindling. Maslow and Karl Katz also fell outside Madrid. Beimler's death was made into a symbol, and hundreds of thousands attended his burial. Even today, it is impossible to be unmoved by Gustav Regler's account:

> The wood echoed with explosions; the sun broke through the clouds and lit up the birch-trees; and then the two young Germans reappeared, coming slowly and almost solemnly round the end of the earthworks. Beimler lay on the stretcher. His face was colourless; his wool-lined jacket was open, and there was a small hole in his sweater above his heart.
>
> Werner knelt beside him and quickly rose again. 'It is bad?' I asked, voicing the foolish question although I knew what had happened.[125]

In the first days of January 1937, at Villanueva-del-Pardillo northwest of Madrid, the International Brigades managed to repel two fascist battalions, but on the 7th they suffered heavy losses,[126] which grew increasingly serious despite its victory over the Italian expeditionary corps. The majority of fighters in the International Brigades left Spain during the Munich crisis, many being forced to remain in demobilization camps before obtaining permission from the Spanish government for a final battle to protect the refugees. They left Spain with iron in the soul, carrying in their pockets, as Gustav Regler relates, a handful of Spanish earth. Out of 5,000 German antifascist volunteers, some 3,000 fell in Spain. The last roll-call of the International Brigades was held on 8 and 9 February 1939, at the border crossings of Le Perthus and Port Bou. Disarmed by French *gardes mobiles*, they were subsequently interned in camps such as Le Vernet, or shipped off to North Africa. Germany demanded certain individuals after the armistice and the Vichy state handed them over to the Gestapo (Franz Dahlem, Heinrich Rau). Some managed to reach the USSR (Erich Weinert, Willi Bredel, Gottfried Grünberg, Günther Tenner), others fought in the French Resistance[127] or with the partisans in Greece or Yugoslavia.[128] Many of them took part in the Freies Deutschland movement, both in the USSR and in Mexico. Still others tried to develop antifascist activity in the Wehrmacht.[129]

These military activities were not the émigrés' only contribution to the Spanish war. Just as important was cultural and political work within the Brigades.[130] This embraced courses in political training, languages and history, agitprop events (song, theatre, music), the development of historical and political documentation, the publishing of pamphlets and leaflets,[131] even of books.[132] The work of cultural agitation and propaganda included the composition of songs (Ernst Busch, Erich Weinert), plays, and political spectacles. Each Brigade had a cultural officer, and a large number of antifascist works had their origins at the front, between battles or in demobilization camps. Finally, the exiles who fought in the International Brigades did not just bear arms; they helped to build schools, repair roads, and bring in the harvest; they cared for the wounded, and assisted the civilian population in all manner of ways.

CALLS FOR INTERNATIONAL SOLIDARITY

The struggle of German émigrés in the international arena developed with three distinct objects: to arouse in Germany a reaction against the sending of soldiers to Spain; to defeat the non-intervention policy upheld by France and Britain; and to help gather funds for military and humanitarian aid to the Spanish Republic and its victims.

On 20 December 1936 Walter Ulbricht spoke on Radio Barcelona to the German people, putting forward a programme of struggle against Hitler and explaining the work of the International Brigades. Information was broadcast on the German army's exactions on Spanish soil. Leaflets attacking German intervention were distributed in Germany,[133] and funds secretly collected in factories by Communist and Socialist workers.[134] A number of Communist writings on the Spanish war were also smuggled into the Reich. A large number of literary and political figures (Heinrich and Thomas Mann, Arnold Zweig, Ernest Hemingway, Paul Robeson, F. Masereel) were invited to speak on the German radio station outside Madrid, which broadcast daily to the Reich. Instructions conveyed by this transmitter also made it possible to organize sabotage in armaments factories and slow down the shipment of weapons to Spain.[135] Heinrich Mann wrote several appeals which were distributed in Germany, urging the population to react against Hitler's support for Franco. A number of leaflets,[136] signed by Franz Dahlem and Robert Breitscheid, called on German soldiers to refuse to serve in Spain. The exiles also distributed appeals to German women, translating calls from Spanish women that urged them not to let their sons leave their country to kill their own sons. Another appeal, *Guernica*, written after the destruction of the town, was published in March 1937 in the *Pariser Tageszeitung*. If these leaflets did not reach a wide readership in Germany, the antifascist radio in Spain was a greater problem for Goebbels.[137] The Deutsche Freiheitssender[138] invited all listeners in the Reich who manage to receive its broadcasts to send information on the situation in Germany to a Paris address. A large number of writers took part in these antifascist broadcasts, including Heinrich Mann, Lion Feuchtwanger, Gustav Regler and Rudolf Leonhard; they commented on news from Germany and the situation in Spain, and encouraged the struggle against the sending of soldiers.

At the same time, antifascists undertook several initiatives to persuade the Western democracies to abandon their policy of neutrality, taking account of the atrocities committed by Franco's troops. No less remarkable was the immense effort accomplished by the émigrés in the collection of money and medicines for victims of the civil war. In autumn 1937, Ludwig Renn made a lecture tour in the United States for the victims of Franco;[139] by spring 1938 he had made no less than ninety-five appearances, including many interviews and radio programmes. He also attended a banquet of Hollywood stars in support of Spain.[140] Gustav Regler travelled to Philadelphia and Washington to collect funds raised for Republican Spain, with Ernest Hemingway's support:

> [. . .] always to the same sort of people, attentive, ready to be won over, opposed to dictatorships and therefore in favour of the Spanish Republic. They wanted it to have its parliament, and they wanted to restore to Spain everything that literature, the cinema and painting had made famous – the pride and colourfulness, the passion and the dreaming, the bullfights and the flamenco songs, the dancers and poets. Money [. . .] was handed over to the pretty girls with collecting-boxes [. . .]. One man was so moved by my speech that he came to the rostrum saying that he had not enough money on him, but here was his winter overcoat, quite new, and would I please have it sent to my friends in the trenches.[141]

In Paris, the Freundeskreise der Deutschen Volksfront and the SDS also undertook numerous initiatives in support of the Spanish Republic. Those who had been in Spain were asked to relate their impressions[142] and read extracts from their writings. Finally, many of the exile journals, especially *AIZ* and *Weltbühne*, carried frequent reports on the war. A number of émigrés not engaged militarily developed an intensive propaganda activity through their journalism. Otto Katz (André Simone) travelled to Spain for the press agency Espagne, set up in the early days of the war by Willi Münzenberg and the minister Alvarez del Vayo. They published the book *Hitler in Spain*, based on material from the Soviet intelligence service.[143] Klaus and Erika Mann published an account of their journey to Spain in the *Pariser Tageszeitung*.[144] Münzenberg organized the Comité d'Aide aux Victimes de l'Espagne Républicaine, putting the philanthropic side to the fore as he had with German fascism. He also established a Comité d'Enquête sur l'Intervention Etrangère dans la Guerre d'Espagne, on the model of the Reichstag inquiry.[145] And it was Münzenberg who sent Koestler as a journalist[146] to report from Franco's armies. Koestler managed to win their confidence and obtain a letter of recommendation from General Franco, but he was recognized by the son of August Strindberg, a fellow-journalist working for the now-Nazi Ullstein press, and had to take flight. He returned to Madrid again to rescue documents that proved the involvement of the German military in the insurrection preparations. A large number of his articles and reports were collected in book form, and published by émigré imprints.[147] Koestler returned to Spain a third time as correspondent for the Espagne press agency, and witnessed the fall of Malaga. Recognized by a Francoist officer, he was arrested and condemned to death, but eventually exchanged for the wife of a Francoist airman.

THE SPANISH WAR AND EXILE LITERATURE

Spain caused the last twitch of Europe's dying conscience.

Arthur Koestler, *The Invisible Writing*

The very fact that the second major congress of antifascist writers for the defence of culture was held in Spain shows what the war meant for many European intellectuals. Even those who did not take an active part in its battles or propaganda work were aware of the stakes involved. And the war's dramatic development played a further part in its effect on the conscience of the world.

Though the Spanish war gave birth to countless novels, from Malraux to Hemingway, and films from Ivens to Resnais, it acquired a special significance in exile literature from the very fact that many German antifascists who fought in Spain were at the same time both actors in the events and chroniclers of them. There are few émigré autobiographies – whether those of Regler, Dahlem, Kantorowicz, Koestler, Sperber, Klaus Mann, Bredel or Uhse – that do not give the Spanish war a special place. The tragedy of the Spanish people was a tragedy for them as well, and Franco's victory a defeat for them all.

There was perhaps never a time when words and stories were so closely integrated with weapons. If a bullet could kill, a poem or a song or a leaflet could win solidarity. In 1938 Erich Weinert defined the task of the writer fighting in Spain as threefold: he fought with weapons, he encouraged his comrades with words, and as an eyewitness he focused the eyes of the whole world on bleeding Spain.

Novels, poems, songs: the Spanish civil war generated them by the thousand in the midst of battle. If many works only acquired their definitive form later on, the notes from which they were written were gathered each day, between battles, entrusted to diaries and notebooks so that none of these moments of hope and despair, of treason and solidarity, could be forgotten. The 'Spanish papers' that so many antifascist fighters brought back in their rucksacks were transformed into memoirs, novels, histories or chronicles of the International Brigades. Those who fought in their ranks were sufficiently aware of the exceptional experience of international solidarity they represented that they hung on to every little bit of their story. From fighters, Willi Bredel and Ludwig Renn made themselves into historians, tracing the actions of the regiments in which they had fought.[148] Others, such as E. E. Kisch, sent back report after report to immortalize the horror they experienced. Each episode of the war was retraced and analysed. E. Mohr described the Thälmann centuria in *Wir in fernem Vaterland geboren* (*We from a Distant Homeland*); Bodo Uhse depicted battle scenes in *Erste Schlacht* (*First Battle*, 1938), as did Gustav Regler in *Das Grosse Beispiel* (*The Great Example*) and Willi Bredel in *Begegnung am Ebro* (*Encounter on the Ebro*). Maria von Osten published her *Spanische Reportagen*, Alfred Kantorowicz immortalized the story of the Chapaev battalion, a battalion of twenty-one nationalities. It was often impossible to separate the combatant from the witness or the writer. Hans Marchwitza and Ludwig Renn wrote on

Spain as soldiers, Max Hodann and Theodor Balk as doctors in the Brigades, Franz Dahlem and Alfred Kantorowicz as political commissars.

It is not possible here to list all the books to which the Spanish war gave rise, and to which the German exiles made a major contribution. We need only recall Brecht's *Señora Carrar's Rifles*, Hermann Kesten's *The Children of Guernica*, Arthur Koestler's *Spanish Testament* and Klaus Mann's *The Volcano*, as well as the poems and songs of Ernst Busch, Hanns Eisler and Erich Weinert. It was a hope defeated, a battle lost, a wound to the world's conscience. And besides the injuries and deaths that they would carry with them, the majority of émigrés who had fought in Spain now had a growing certainty that the Western democracies would do nothing against the spread of fascism across Europe. A moral, political and psychological crisis for many émigrés, the Spanish defeat appeared as a collapse of their last hope of victory over Hitler. It was not by mere chance that before his suicide, Ernst Toller laid out on his desk in the Mayflower Hotel in New York photos of Spanish children who had been killed by fascist bombs.

Press, Publishing and Literature in Exile

Many of the émigrés have described the countless problems they came up against in trying to get their works published, to set up new publishing houses or just magazines. Isolated from one another, and lacking material resources, this was achieved only at the cost of unimaginable sacrifice and thanks to the generosity of individuals. Besides making it possible to spread information on the Third Reich in the many countries where they were refugees, this émigré press was also one of the rare links that connected them across frontiers. Writing and publishing were the only ways to break the silence to which Hitler's Germany had condemned them by destroying their books. More than just a chapter in the exile story, this production is a strange landscape in which it is hard to find one's way. While some works now forgotten were too closely tied to immediate political needs to stand the test of time, others feature among the greatest works of modern German literature. The exiles' astonishing creativity contrasted with the precariousness of their situation. Novels, poems and plays, essays or mere newspaper articles, were more than just testimonies of their struggle and their faith in culture, the power of intelligence and the word. The works of these outlaws, printed with so much difficulty, eclipse the entire literary production of the Third Reich: the worst novel in exile literature is a masterpiece of talent and intellect compared with the best '*völkisch*' novel.

1. ÉMIGRÉ PERIODICALS

Rather than a paradise for intellectuals, as is too readily maintained, the Weimar Republic was rather one for magazines and papers. From the far right to the far left, every political, artistic and literary tendency sought to assert itself by finding expression in a magazine and winning a readership however small. Certainly this was not just a German peculiarity. The same explosion of magazines could be found in most of Europe at that time. From the first expressionist publications like *Der Sturm, Die Aktion, Die Weissen Blätter* – often politicized after 1914 – to the great magazines of the Weimar Republic such as the liberal *Weltbühne* or the Communist *Linkskurve*, they played a fundamental role in German cultural life, in particular that of Berlin. Their importance should not be judged simply by the number of readers: Ossietzky's *Weltbühne* had a relatively limited circulation, but remained for all that the very symbol of the liberal intelligentsia. The role such magazines played in exile has of course no common measure with what they meant before 1933. Yet it is still symbolic that the émigrés sought to continue these in exile, often with the same title – *Weltbühne* or *Simplicissimus* – as so many symbols of freedom.

As soon as Hitler came to power, the greater part of these magazines were banned or else reappeared under Nazi control. The example of the *Neue Rundschau* is one of the most striking. Founded in 1890 by Otto Brahm and Samuel Fischer, this was not just particularly well-known, but especially hated by the Nazis for its liberal views. Its editor, Rudolf Kayser, entrusted it to Peter Suhrkamp, who from 1932 had been working at Fischer Verlag, in the hope of saving it. Suhrkamp had no hesitation in publishing in April 1933 Thomas Mann's lecture on Wagner, texts by Herman Hesse, Oskar Loerke, Hermann Kasack and Harry Kessler, or celebrating the birthday of Max Reinhardt, already condemned to exile. With the establishment of the Reichskulturkammern, however, magazines were submitted to a complete censorship. Writers who were Jewish or hostile to National Socialism were immediately eliminated, together with all the émigrés. Following the death of Samuel Fischer in 1934, his publishing house was made over to a new company directed by Peter Suhrkamp; but more than 780,000 books were now banned from sale.

Every publishing house now had a Nazi commissioner in charge. The only choices were submission to the new regime or disappearance. Ullstein became a National Socialist publishing house, while Rowohlt was eventually closed down. The *Neue Rundschau*, in order to keep publishing, now had to avoid any political subject, agree to publish texts by Nazi authors and express itself in sybilline language to avoid falling prey to censorship. Yet despite wind and weather, Peter Suhrkamp managed to keep the magazine going throughout the Hitler period, without any real concession to the regime. This was a more or less unique case.[1]

To re-establish a number of these magazines in exile under the same names, or create new ones, meant a real challenge to the Third Reich, quite apart from their cultural and political role.[2] Between 1933 and 1950, over 400 publications were established by German émigrés.[3] Some of these had already existed before 1933 and for a variety of reasons enjoyed a relative financial independence.[4] The majority were founded in exile, amid the most irksome material difficulties, and often had only an ephemeral existence. Though the relatively large number of these magazines may be surprising, it reflected both the dispersion of the émigré community[5] and its ideological diversity, which no single magazine would have been able to express. Besides, the movements of the émigrés due to the invasion of Austria and Czechoslovakia led to the disappearance of a certain number of magazines and in some cases their reappearance in other capitals (Paris, London), sometimes under other names. As the European situation steadily deteriorated, most of these magazines were banned by the countries that had accepted the émigrés and shifted to more distant lands: Argentina, Mexico, Brazil, more rarely the United States and Asia.

Little is known of the details of these magazines' finances. Those tied to the SPD received subsidies from the Socialist International, and the Communist magazines were often financed by the Comintern.[6] Some periodicals were assisted by the host countries, but these were rare cases.[7] A few others managed to exist thanks to wealthy benefactors.[8] Most commonly, however, they were dependent on subscriptions and donations from émigrés themselves, who gave more than they received from them, aware of their political as well as their literary significance.

Die Neue Weltbühne

Founded by Siegfried Jacobsohn, and directed after his death by Kurt Tucholsky and Carl von Ossietzky, *Die Weltbühne*, the political and cultural weekly, became a focal point for the entire liberal and pacifist left in the Weimar era. Often prohibited by the government for its radical attacks on the army and judiciary, and several times banned in this period, the paper was a symbol of courage, lucidity and intellectual honesty that nothing could destroy, not even the arrest of Ossietzky.[9] The magazine was proscribed immediately after the Reichstag fire, and continued publication in Vienna, but it was threatened there too by the Dolfuss regime. It was finally in Prague, therefore, that the *Neue Weltbühne* was established.

After the death of Edith Jacobsohn in 1934, the *Neue Weltbühne* appeared under the direction of Hermann Budzislawski.[10] When the Hitlerite threat grew worse and the paper risked being once again banned, it was transferred to Paris where it began publication on 23 June 1938. The paper's political stand had now come closer to that of the KPD.[11] The last issue appeared on 31 August 1939, after which it was closed down by the French government.

The evolution of the *Neue Weltbühne* in exile is fairly surprising. From being pacifist and republican, it drew near to Trotskyism under the influence of its Vienna editor Willi Schlamm,[12] before its rapprochement with the KPD. The articles it published in exile were basically political, bearing on the analysis of fascism as well as the perspectives that its collapse would open up. As a general rule, the positions it upheld were more clear-headed than those of the parties, and its analysis of the real attitude of the democracies after 1938 proved especially prophetic. At the same time, the magazine denounced the mistakes of the left parties under the Weimar Republic, continued to criticize those parties in exile, and proposed that the émigrés should separate themselves from the 'bureaucracies of the KPD and SPD'.[13] Its contributors included a certain number of 'Viennese' – Stefan Pollatschek, Peter Rodin, Wilhelm Stefan – as well as 'Berliners' such as Helmut von Gerlach, K. R. Grossman, L. Lania, H. Pol, Hans Sahl and Heinrich Mann. It is hard to know how émigré readers reacted to the magazine's various changes, especially to Willi Schlamm's criticism of the parties.

When Schlamm was dismissed from the editorship and replaced by Budzislawski, the critical tone gave way to a more constructive and optimistic perspective. In 1934 Nazism was described as 'wavering', and in 1935 the *Weltbühne* declared that Germany was in a cul-de-sac.[14] The majority of Budzislawski's political analyses proved faulty. He tended to minimize all Hitler's successes, and viewed even the annexation of Austria as less serious than if the country had been a genuine democracy. The optimistic tone continued right through the Spanish civil war.

More interesting and more exact were the analyses that the magazine published on German rearmament and war preparations. The *Neue Weltbühne* had harsh words for the appeasement policy upheld by France and Britain, and the unceasing efforts it made for the construction of a Popular Front deserve special merit. Not only did it support all the initiatives of the Paris *Volksfront*, it opened its columns to participants whether they were writers or political activists.[15] On 14 January 1938 it published an 'Appeal for a Popular Front' signed by seventy-one public figures. Even after the *Volksfront* had dissolved, the *Neue Weltbühne* persisted in its efforts to unite the émigrés, a task which alone would confirm the importance of the magazine throughout its exile years. Its articles on cultural policy, often written by Heinrich Mann or Ernst Bloch, were also of rare quality.

In the literary arena, works by exile writers published in the *Neue Weltbühne* included extracts from Brecht plays, as well as texts by J. R. Becher, Erich Weinert, Stefan Heym, Walter Mehring, Friedrich Wolf, Arthur Polgar, E. E. Kisch, Rudolf Leonhard, L. Lania, Alfred Wolfenstein, Kurt Hiller, Theodor Plievier, F. C. Weiskopf, Konrad Heiden, Hermann Rauschning, Alfred Kerr, Anna Seghers, Klaus Mann, Ludwig Marcuse, Walter Benjamin, Ernst Bloch, Alfred Kantorowicz and Golo Mann. It regularly reviewed exile publications and major cultural events such as the writers' congresses in Paris, Moscow and Madrid, activities of the SDS and the Free German Library. Notices of émigré theatrical performances were also to be found. Thanks to this wealth of information, it made a far from negligible contribution towards re-establishing links between exile groups and restoring a certain cultural unity to the emigration. Though close to the KPD at this time, it kept its independence, reacted critically to the German–Soviet pact, and did not spare its criticisms of Stalin.

Arbeiter-Illustrierte-Zeitung

Better known simply by its initials, the *AIZ* was undoubtedly one of the most exciting magazines of the Weimar years.[16] Linked to the KPD, and published by Willi Münzenberg, it reached the exceptional circulation of half a million copies between 1927 and 1933.[17] Far from being just an illustrated propaganda magazine, *AIZ* sought to practise a remarkable synthesis between modern journalism, avant-garde photography and 'proletarian reportage', offering an overview of class struggle across the world thanks to its many worker correspondents, reporters, journalists and photographers. From China to Mexico, from the remotest villages of the Soviet Union to May Day parades in Germany, from demonstrations in the United States to the life of peasants in central Europe, there were few geographical territories or political struggles that it did not reflect and echo. The *AIZ* soon managed to attract as contributors avant-garde artists such as John Heartfield, whose photomontages, often published in the magazine, remain one of its most fascinating features today. The photographs sent in by *AIZ* correspondents, moreover, made it possible to see the face of proletarian misery in many countries.

The success of the *AIZ* naturally made it one of the magazines most hated by the Nazis,[18] all the more so as Heartfield's photomontages were formidable propaganda weapons. In Berlin alone, by 1933 the magazine had some twenty-four groups of worker reporter-photographers. After the ban on the Communist publishing house Neue Deutscher Verlag, *AIZ* continued to be distributed secretly for a while, and its equipment was hidden. The editorial board was then re-established in Prague, and worked simultaneously on the anti-Nazi periodical *Gegen-Angriff*, directed by Bruno Frei.[19] Whilst continuing to report on international class struggles, *AIZ* focused its efforts on denouncing the Nazi terror in Germany and the danger that Hitler presented to the whole of Europe. This was when the most violent photomontages of Heartfield and his team were produced. We need only recall one by Karl Vanek (H. Leopold), 'The Brown Tiger of Peace', illustrating a speech of Hitler's with a tiger's head roaring under a steel helmet, Heartfield's own photomontages devoted to the Leipzig trial in which a giant Dimitrov crushes in his fist a tiny Göring, the vultures hovering over Madrid symbolizing the Francoists, or the simple Christmas tree with its branches growing in the shape of a swastika to signify that all aspects of life in Germany had been brought into line.

The paper was produced amid serious difficulties. Besides the fear that the Czech government, faced with the threat of reprisals from Hitler, would encroach ever more on its freedom, it was not easy to obtain photographic evidence from the Reich – apart from official propaganda. Yet German workers continued to photograph street scenes, SA brutality, arrests and anti-Semitic actions, often risking their lives by sending the negatives to Prague. A small-format edition of *AIZ* was published, to be smuggled into Germany.[20] The magazine was helped financially by the Czech Communist party, trade unions and individual workers.

AIZ was gradually transformed into an organ of the Popular Front. Non-Communist writers were welcomed, and out of all the exile magazines, it was almost the only one to regularly publish photographic reports showing the true face of Hitler's Germany. Heartfield's photomontages had such a success that the Nazis even had to struggle against their reproduction in Germany.[21] Associated with every struggle, *AIZ* played an active part in the campaign in support of the accused in the Leipzig trial, for the release of Thälmann and all the victims of fascism. It published lists and photographs of victims of the SA, several documents on Nazi terror, and the names of spies and Gestapo agents. Its gave active support to the *Volksfront*, devoting a special number to it (9, 1936) and establishing a '*Volksfront* column' in which political activists and writers were invited to express themselves.[22] Other special issues were devoted to anti-Semitism, the Spanish war, and Hitlerite policies.

AIZ subsequently appeared in Prague until 5 October 1938 under the name

Volks-Illustrierte. Its last number, with a mere eight pages, came off the press a few minutes before Czechoslovak mobilization was announced. An attempt to relaunch the paper in Paris came to nothing.

Das Neue Tage-Buch

Before becoming an exile publication, *Das Tage-Buch* was a well-known Berlin magazine founded in 1920 by Stefan Grossmann and subsequently directed by Leopold Schwarzschild. Independent of party, the paper saw itself more as liberal than left.

While the *Weltbühne* tackled political subjects as well as literary ones, the *Tage-Buch* was oriented more towards economic affairs. Its last number appeared on 11 March 1933, after which the editorial offices in Munich[23] were occupied by the SS, Schwarzschild escaping arrest only by fleeing to Vienna. The magazine's reappearance in Paris, in relatively good shape and without a change of style, was due to the patronage of J. C. S. Warendorf. Along with political, economic and military articles, it contained editorial comment, reportage and cultural information. *Das Neue Tage-Buch* circulated in the main centres of emigration,[24] surviving until it disappeared along with other German publications on 11 May 1940.

Das Neue Tage-Buch, known familiarly as *NTB*, continued to focus chiefly on German conditions, as its predecessor had done before 1933. The task now was to directly oppose Nazi propaganda and analyse everything from a different perspective, despite the inadequate sources of information. Its reliability, deriving from a minute reading of the German press, was never faulty throughout the exile period, in particular its analysis of the German economy and war preparations. Apart from émigrés, the magazine's readership was made up of diplomats, businessmen and bankers, and the foreign contributors to *NTB* were often quite conservative. Persuaded that Hitler was set on waging war, the magazine analysed the whole German economy from this perspective, in particular the development of the armaments industry.[25] But it was in vain that the *NTB* repeatedly warned France and Britain against their policy of appeasement. It criticized the Socialist parties for their naïve pacifism, accusing them of objectively serving Nazi policy. Far from proposing a defensive war against Germany, as has sometimes been maintained, Schwarzschild championed a system of collective defence on the part of the Western democracies.[26] As a general rule, he took a positive view of anything that might weaken Nazism. But compared with the *NTB*'s very detailed analyses of the German economy, its interpretation of Nazism remained rather vague: it was a regression to barbarism, a 'negative evolution of Homo sapiens back to Pithecanthropus', an irrational phenomenon which dragged Germany back to the Stone Age.

That was one of the basic contradictions in Schwarzschild's position: he wanted to struggle against National Socialism without seeking to recognize its economic and political origins. Behind many propositions of Schwarzschild can be detected the no less confused influence of Hermann Rauschning and his vision of Nazism as 'absolute nihilism'. It is rather hard therefore to comprehend the paper as a whole, its ideology being composite: socialist tendencies went together with conservative and reactionary elements. Though a visceral anti-Communist, Schwarzschild did admire Soviet planning.[27] He supported the *Volksfront* and defended the Spanish Republic.

When the Moscow trials began, however, *NTB* distanced itself from the USSR. After declaring that the Soviet Union was embarrassing its allies abroad, the paper started to see Stalin and Hitler as twin brothers, and after 1937 its articles acquired a virulently anti-Communist tone. Schwarzschild extolled bourgeois democracy as the only remedy against fascism and Stalinism. He increasingly viewed the USSR as the source of all European evils, and declared that Italian and German fascism had emerged from the same 'Soviet Pandora's box'. He then launched into a regular denunciation campaign of Communist exiles, especially those who had sought refuge in the United States, including both the left Socialists and any writers close to Communism. Manfred George, O. M. Graf and Klaus Mann[28] were denounced as dangerous Communists along with Lion Feuchtwanger, and even Thomas Mann was not spared.[29] Schwarzschild likewise congratulated the former Communist Boris Souvarine for his attack on certain German exiles in America. *NTB* now recruited its contributors chiefly from the anti-Communist milieu,[30] and Ludwig Marcuse later characterized Schwarzschild quite aptly as a kind of 'German McCarthy'. Almost all the tropes of the Cold War could now be found in its pages, especially in the articles of its director.

It should be stressed however that in the literary field, the *Tage-Buch* attracted such exceptional contributors as Thomas, Heinrich and Klaus Mann, Arnold Zweig, Alfred Döblin, René Schickele, E. E. Kisch, Ludwig Marcuse, Walter Mehring, Lion Feuchtwanger and Harry Kesten, who published there reviews of new books, extracts from their work in progress or essays. *NTB* was the first to publish Bruno Frank's *Der Reisepass* (*The Passport*), Lion Feucht-wanger's *Der falsche Nero* (*The False Nero*), Alfred Döblin's *November 1918*, Ödön von Horvath's *Ein Kind unserer Zeit* (*A Child of Our Time*) and Ernst Toller's *Nie wieder Friede!* (*No More Peace!*). Most of the more political émigrés, however, such as Brecht, J. R. Becher and Rudolf Leonhard, never wrote for the paper, and from 1938 on, it ceased to review works published by authors it considered to be 'Communists'. Leopold Schwarzschild, despite his intelligence and talent, was too blinded by his hatred for Communism to take an interest in the works of Brecht, Becher, Heinrich Mann or Anna Seghers.

Internationale Literatur[31]
Published in the USSR, *Internationale Literatur* escaped the vicissitudes of exile and appeared until 1945. The central organ of the International Union of Revolutionary Writers, it was published simultaneously in several languages, including German, Russian, French and (from 1935) Chinese. The editor-in-chief was initially S. Dimanov, though there was also a separate editor for each language.[32] Its committee included various international figures,[33] but apart from its editors, the most influential of these were Anissimov (director of the State Publishing House for Literature), A. Fadeyev (president of the Soviet

Writers' Union) and Bela Illès (general secretary of the IURW). In 1936 they
were joined by a large number of exiled writers, German and otherwise.[34] From
1933, the German edition *Internationale Literatur/Deutsche Blätter* became a
platform for the exiles. Questions pertaining to exile, however, were never
disassociated from the general political context.[35]

Internationale Literatur/Deutsche Blätter published political essays by German antifascists as well as extracts from their works. It reflected very precisely
Soviet preoccupations in the fields of literature and culture. Homage to the
USSR and Stalin was frequently to be found, along with extracts from works
inspired by socialist realism. Orthodox if not actually official, the magazine
often expressed the standpoint of the Soviet Communist party, and lambasted
the 'treason' of Zinoviev and Trotsky in no uncertain terms. It broadly
associated the antifascist struggle with the campaign against 'Trotskyist bandits' and 'Gestapo agents'. J. R. Becher even published several articles justifying
the Moscow trials, in the name of victory over fascism and world peace. The
magazine did not escape the psychosis of the time: that of spies, traitors and
saboteurs who had infiltrated Communist ranks. Even the editorial board was
not safe from these, Karl Schückle, Hugo Huppert, Hans Günther, Ernst
Ottwalt and Serge Tretyakov being arrested as spies, not counting authors
who had previously been published in *Internationale Literatur*, several of whom
were also arrested and deported (Isaak Babel, M. Kolzov, J. Olescha, B.
Pilniak). *Internationale Literatur* likewise reflected Soviet foreign policy. The
idea that the socialist fatherland was threatened with imminent invasion by the
Western powers recurs incessantly. Its analyses of fascism faithfully reflected
those of Stalin and the Comintern (the weakness of the fascist movement, the
rapid collapse of the Hitler regime, the gradual transformation of social-
democracy into social-fascism). The same sectarianism can often be found in
its reviews and literary essays. Alfred Kurella even accused Thomas Mann of
being close to National Socialism.[36] And yet *Internationale Literatur* published
a large range of antifascist works (Erich Weinert, Friedrich Wolf, J. R. Becher,
Willi Bredel, W. Schönstedt, G. Glaser, Balder Olden).

Dimitrov's speech on 'Revolutionary Literature in the Fight against Fascism'
heralded the new orientation that was to lead towards the *Volksfront*. *Internationale Literatur* now also ceased applying a strictly orthodox policy, and
opened its columns to writers formerly deemed 'bourgeois', such as Albert
Ehrenstein, Lion Feuchtwanger, Ernst Toller, Alfred Döblin, Max Hermann-
Neisse and Alfred Kerr. After its violent attack on him in the past, Thomas
Mann was now praised as a progressive author, and a number of writers quite
distant from Communism were also published. This opening made the review
richer in political and literary debates.[37] Extracts from a number of antifascist
novels written in exile appeared in the magazine, including Anna Seghers's fine
work *The Seventh Cross*.

The magazine naturally supported the German–Soviet pact, and published
several speeches by Molotov seeking to justify it and the new tactic towards
fascism. Fewer articles appeared on Nazi Germany, and the number of contributors declined. Information on the exile situation grew thin on the ground.

Apart from the obituaries on Ernst Weiss and Walter Hasenclever, both of whom committed suicide in France as the German armies approached, there was scarcely a mention of the tragic situation of the émigrés in the countries invaded by the Third Reich. When Hitler attacked the Soviet Union, *Internationale Literatur* stressed that the War was waged by the 'Hitler bandits' and not by the German people. After the Freies Deutschland committee was formed, the magazine opened its pages to conservative figures who were now anti-Nazi. As the Soviet army moved west, *Internationale Literatur* published a large number of documents on the concentration camps and anti-Semitism.

Even if *Internationale Literatur* never contained the major theoretical debates that appeared in *Das Wort*, it did host a number of discussions, always in close relation to the Soviet cultural context: the dissolution of the RAPP, the rise of socialist realism, the writers' congress of 1934, the inauguration of a new literary policy, and debates on realism and formalism. Lukács, Hans Günther and Alfred Kurella often took part in these discussions, which complemented *Das Wort*'s arguments over expressionism. It was symbolic that Lukács's famous essay on 'The Grandeur and Decadence of Expressionism' was published in *Internationale Literatur*, in 1934. Dogmatic the journal certainly was, but its richness is undeniable, as it formed a link between the theoretical debates of antifascist literature in exile and Soviet literature.

Das Wort

Founded under the auspices of the 1935 Writers' Congress, as the organ of the antifascist Popular Front, *Das Wort* had relatively substantial resources at its command, and of all the exile publications, this was doubtless the richest in literary and theoretical debate. Directed by Brecht, Willi Bredel and Lion Feuchtwanger, it was also the magazine most open to aesthetic discussions, and the arguments in its pages over expressionism, in 1938–39, were enough to perpetuate its memory. We have already covered the magazine's history, however, on the chapters on exile in the USSR and the formation of the antifascist Popular Front.

Die Sammlung

At the start of the exile period, Klaus Mann had the idea of establishing an antifascist literary magazine capable of rallying a large number of exiled writers. The first issue of *Die Sammlung* appeared in September 1933, published by Querido Verlag in Amsterdam with the help of Fritz Landhoff. Scheduled to appear monthly, and with Gide, Aldous Huxley and Heinrich Mann as sponsors, this was one of the most interesting exile magazines, despite only a few years of existence. Declaring itself 'an organ of intellectual regroupment' in the service of literature, and able to attract exiled writers and intellectuals of every nationality,[38] it set out to be independent of both parties and partisan passion, and to establish a place for writers with very differing political positions.[39] If it was nonpolitical in this sense, it was certainly fiercely anti-Nazi. Its first issue included texts from Thomas Mann, René Schickele, Stefan

Zweig and Alfred Döblin. On 10 October 1933, the Reichsstelle zur Förderung des deutschen Schrifttums, in publishing a list of periodicals to be banned and boycotted, singled out *Die Sammlung* for special attack, a number of its contributors not yet having had their works withdrawn from bookshops. The *Börsenblatt* very swiftly published telegrams from Thomas Mann, René Schickele and Alfred Döblin, distancing themselves from the magazine's political character and declaring that the first issue did not correspond to its initial programme. Even though these telegrams were sent at the request of Mann's publisher, G. Bermann Fischer,[40] as well as by Insel Verlag on behalf of Stefan Zweig, this reaction was also a reflex action of authors whose books were still on sale in Germany, and who feared a complete ban on their works. The Nazi censorship body had clearly announced that any writer contributing to *Die Sammlung* would immediately have their books banned in Germany. When these publishers begged their threatened authors to distance themselves from the magazine, they ceased to contribute, with the exception of Döblin.

Die Sammlung did not follow a political line, even if its hostility to Nazism was very clear. Contrary to other exile periodicals, it rarely tackled current political events, only few of which found an echo in its pages.[41] The only political subjects it broached were the struggle in the churches, the Saar issue, and the restoration of universal military service. In the domain of foreign policy, *Die Sammlung* covered the fate of Austria and the risk of annexation, the Stavisky scandal in France, the rapprochement between Socialists and Communists in the days of the *Volksfront*, Roosevelt's policies and the Jewish–Arab conflict in Palestine.

The majority of its articles were restricted to cultural questions, and the political perspectives animating these were highly diverse. It would be hard, for example, to combine the contradictory analyses of fascism put forward by Ernst Bloch, Balder Olden, Hermann Kesten and Heinrich Mann. All these viewpoints were expressed, with no attempt to either synthesize or counterpose them; liberal, conservative and Marxist perspectives were simply offered alongside each other. The magazine's philosophical and literary basis was thus rather vague. Divided between an admiration for his uncle Heinrich, and for Gottfried Benn whom the latter had sharply criticized, Klaus Mann developed a mixture of rationalism and irrationalism in his articles, rather abstractly opposing the force of the 'spirit' to National Socialism and Hitler. Distant on the whole from Marxism, most contributors to the magazine championed a militant humanism, and a glorification of freedom and culture, without any more precise political programme.

The same heterogeneity marked the choice of works published. Extracts from novels by Joseph Roth rubbed shoulders with tales by Hemingway, fragments from a diary of Kafka's, poems by Pasternak, short stories by Claire Goll, texts from Aldous Huxley, Ernst Weiss and Gide, poems by J. R. Becher, Else Lasker-Schüler and Hermann-Neisse. Its liberalism failed to give any firm basis for politics. But if this eclecticism is open to criticism, credit must be given to the exceptional quality of everything the magazine published.

Neue Deutsche Blätter

After Klaus Mann's *Die Sammlung*, this was the second major literary period-ical of the exiles. The magazine had its origin in a tour of the different centres of emigration that J. R. Becher made in July–September 1933,[42] in particular the discussions he had with two Prague émigrés, Wieland Herzfelde, who had re-established Malik Verlag in the Czech capital, and F. C. Weiskopf, who helped the magazine financially.

The first issue appeared on 20 September 1933, published by Wieland Herzfelde in Prague.[43] Its most important contributors included Anna Seghers, O. M. Graf, Herzfelde himself and Jan Petersen. It achieved a fairly sizeable print run (from 5,000 to 7,000 copies),[44] and was self-financing. Even so, the loss of its markets in the Saar and Austria, and the general development of the international situation, made its life difficult.

The object of *Neue Deutsche Blätter* was to fight fascism by way of literature. 'Whoever writes, acts!', declared the first issue. Although Communist, and hoping for a 'proletarian revolution' in Germany, *NDB* did not share the optimism of most exile magazines, and sought to bring together writers of various standpoints well before such rapprochement became the motto of the *Volksfront*. It opened its pages to several non-Marxist contributors – one of its editors, O. M. Graf, was a Social-Democrat – especially to independent Socialists such as Ernst Toller, democrats such as Lion Feuchtwanger, E. J. Gumbel, A. Holitscher, Ludwig Marcuse, Balder and Rudolf Olden, and Arnold Zweig, and liberals such as Hermann Kesten and Walter Mehring. *NDB* even avoided any attacks on non-Communist writers. On the other hand, it showed far greater severity towards writers who had made their peace with National Socialism, especially those such as Gerhart Hauptmann who had supported the left in the Weimar years.[45] It was *Neue Deutsche Blätter* that first began discussion on the existence of an 'internal emigration'.[46] Its position, ceaselessly repeated, was that there could be no neutrality towards Nazism, everyone had to choose their side. Its reviews of current works by Thomas Mann, Stefan Zweig and Max Brod were also highly critical.

NDB carried frequent and interesting reports on conditions in Germany and clerico-fascist Austria. It had precise analyses of the terror and repression, as well as of illegal resistance. Finally, the magazine publicized a large number of works by émigrés such as Anna Seghers, Bertolt Brecht, F. C. Weiskopf, Stefan Heym, J. R. Becher, Erich Weinert, Ernst Ottwalt, Balder Olden, F. Schönstedt and Friedrich Wolf. More combative than *Die Sammlung*, it was one of the most realistic exile publications in terms of the political perspectives it developed.

Mass und Wert

Mass und Wert, subtitled a 'bimonthly for free German culture', was founded in Zurich in autumn 1937. In a letter the previous February to Hermann Hesse, Thomas Mann announced that this project of establishing a literary magazine would come to fruition thanks to the generosity of a certain woman who was prepared to finance the magazine if Mann undertook its direction. Ferdinand Lion was to be its editor.[47] *Mass und Wert* did not intend to be an émigré periodical in the narrow sense. It declared itself independent of parties and groups, maintaining that it was 'not polemical but constructive'.[48] As the expression of those German writers 'forced into politics', like Thomas Mann himself, the magazine set out to be a testimony of their creations in exile. Its guidelines were laid down by Mann himself, after he had publicly broken all links with Hitler's Germany in 1936.

Mass und Wert sought to achieve a synthesis of tradition and renewal of German letters in the service of freedom, and of humanism against Nazi barbarism, a programme carried out in the book he was himself working on at the time, *Lotte in Weimar*, copious extracts of which appeared in the magazine. Keeping his distance from Marxism, even if he now termed himself a 'socialist', Mann sought to promote a 'militant humanism' and to 'work for the spiritual renewal of Europe'.

Eighteen issues of the magazine appeared between 1937 and 1940, maintaining the same intellectual rigour, and publishing extracts from antifascist works as well as essays of a high literary quality. Under the heading 'Criticism' a number of works published in exile were reviewed, while 'Comments' signalled to readers various political events that should attract their attention. Several contributors to *Mass und Wert* were liberal authors with little political footing, with a few exceptions such as Heinrich Mann. Writers whose work was extracted in the magazine included Robert Musil,[49] Georg Kaiser, Hermann Broch, Annette Kolb, Bernard von Brentano, Franz Werfel and Herman Hesse, and it also published antifascist stories by O. M. Graf and Bruno Frank. It even discussed works in other languages, such as those of Federico García Lorca, and in 1940 Sartre's *Le Mur*, in a constant effort to combine 'bourgeois' and 'socialist' literature.[50]

It would be vain to seek any precise analysis of fascism in *Mass und Wert*. The militant humanism that Thomas Mann championed was content to oppose culture to barbarism in an abstract fashion. Besides, those texts that were more sociological in character generally displayed a certain anti-Sovietism and a hostility to Marxism.[51] The magazine collapsed as a result of financial difficulties and the restriction of its readership following the annexations of Austria and Czechoslovakia.[52] On his arrival in the United States, Mann found new financial backers prepared to support him (Eugen and Agnes E. Meyer), but he decided against relaunching the publication, doubtless in the belief that it had lost any sense.

Freies Deutschland

This periodical had its origin in Mexico, among the Communist émigrés there. Many of its contributors had lived in Paris and fought in Spain, after playing a major role in antifascist struggle in Germany. If they had become refugees in Mexico, this was thanks to the sympathy of President Cardenas as well as the systematic hostility that several other European countries, and the United States, displayed towards Communist émigrés. Their number included Ludwig Renn, Bodo Uhse, E. E. Kisch, Theodor Balk and André Simone (Otto Katz). They managed to develop a significant antifascist activity in Mexico, especially around the Klub Heinrich Heine, which Anna Seghers chaired. Many maintained close connections with émigrés living in the United States, such as Gerhart Eisler, Albert Norden, Lion Feuchtwanger, Heinrich Mann, Bertolt Brecht, Fritz Lang, Erwin Piscator, O. M. Graf and Ferdinand Bruckner.

In summer 1942, André Simone, Bodo Uhse, Ludwig Renn and E. E. Kisch acquired the financial means to enable them to publish a magazine, at a time when most other exile publications had disappeared or were inaccessible.[53] The publication was to be both political and cultural, and offer a discussion platform to all antifascist émigrés. It was important to give guidelines for action in countries as distant as Mexico, where the struggle against fascism was scarcely evident. Bruno Frei was appointed its editor-in-chief, and Bodo Uhse co-editor, while Simone, Kisch and Seghers played a major role in the first issues until the arrival of Alexander Abusch and other émigrés who had fought in Spain.[54] *Freies Deutschland* initially appeared in quite unfavourable conditions.[55] Its orientation was openly Communist, and it proclaimed its solidarity with the Soviet Union. The magazine not only addressed émigrés of all tendencies, but also the German communities in Latin American countries, which included a large number of Nazi sympathizers.

Thanks to the connections that the émigrés maintained with Mexican public figures – Antonio Castro Leal, the former rector of Mexico University, was its responsible editor – many Latin American artists and writers agreed to contribute to the magazine.[56] It carried discussions on literature and the classical democratic heritage, on the universality of Hölderlin and Humboldt, while alongside writings by Communist exiles there were essays by Feuchtwanger, Thomas Mann and O. M. Graf, documents on Germany and reportage on Mexico. The magazine thus managed to attract a large number of émigrés in Latin America.

In January 1942 the Freies Deutschland movement was formed, which by 1943 had representatives throughout Latin America. This was chaired by Ludwig Renn, with Paul Merker as secretary. It held an inaugural congress on 8–9 May 1943. The magazine now became the theoretical organ of the movement, and a column regularly followed its development. In July 1943, news arrived of the foundation of the Freies Deutschland national committee in Moscow, and its publications were dispatched regularly to Mexico. *Freies Deutschland* kept going for a while after the collapse of the Hitler regime,[57] publishing information on Germany where Jürgen Kuczinski was its correspondent. At this time it carried interesting discussion on the right-wing Social-Democrats (Friedrich Stampfer) who had returned from the United States, the question of German collective responsibility, and relations between the Socialist and Communist parties. Still financed by subscriptions and collections from its readers, and never paying any fees, *Freies Deutschland* successfully brought into being a real movement in Latin America. Its survival after 1945 – in 1946 it took the name *Neues Deutschland*, proclaiming its tie with the still unformed German Democratic Republic – is explained by the problems that the exiles in Mexico had with repatriation. The United States refused Communists even a transit visa. They thus had to await repatriation on Soviet vessels, and the last issue of

Nueva Alemania: Revista Democratica bade a warm and thankful farewell to
Mexico for its hospitality.

This summary description of some of the most important émigré publications
certainly does not do justice to their number and diversity. Even a list of the titles
of all German antifascist publications in exile would require a whole volume, so it
is a deliberate choice here to retain only some particularly revealing examples of
their diversity and richness. In Prague alone, Socialists and Communists had a
dozen or so periodicals. Bruno Frei published the remarkable *Gegen-Angriff*. In
Paris there was the *Pariser Tageszeitung* and *Die Zukunft*, in Switzerland *Über die
Grenzen*, in London *Freie Deutsche Kultur*. There was no country in which the
antifascist exiles did not try and found at least one magazine, with the aim of
getting their works known, establishing links with one another, and spreading
information on Germany.[58] Now documents for study and exhibition, these
magazines attest both to the ideological diversity of the exiles and their conflicts,
and to the variety and depth of their struggles.

2. THE FOUNDATION OF NEW PUBLISHING HOUSES

As Goebbels put it, the book burnings were supposed to end once and for all these
'perversions of German art'. That eulogist of blood and soil did not believe that a free
German literature would be able to survive in exile. 'These gentlemen may continue to
dribble for a while in the émigré cafés of Prague or Paris,' he railed, 'but their lifeline
has been cut, they are corpses in waiting.' Soon, however, he had to change his tune,
and by 1935, was saying that 'the literary poison distilled by a clique of émigrés is
becoming a danger on a European scale.'

F. C. Weiskopf, *Unter fremden Himmeln*

Literature was the first sector of German culture to be completely subjected to
the 'new National Socialist values', and its policy towards books became, as
Thomas Mann declared, the very symbol of the regime: for all Europe, the
Third Reich would remain the country where books were burned. But if this
symbolic act expressed the regime's spirit very well, it was not the only coercive
measure that struck German literature. The means of pressure on publishers
were considerable,[59] including the purging of public libraries and the publication of lists of undesirable authors,[60] whose works had then to be withdrawn
from circulation.[61] Ever fuller lists of books prohibited from sale were published
by the *Börsenblatt*. By 6 December 1933, over 1,000 titles had been seized on the
orders of no less than twenty-one censorship and control bodies. When
Goebbels assumed full responsibility for this censorship, the struggle grew
more intense and widespread. Publishing houses were no longer allowed to
distribute 'undesirable works', and in theory, they were all supposed to submit
projected publications to a 'consultative agency for people's literature'. From
1935, anyone contravening these directives – a publisher or bookseller – was
likely to be arrested and immediately sent to concentration camp.[62]

The consequence of these measures was a total loss of income for a large number of German writers, and above all the bankruptcy or suppression of a number of publishing houses, while others were *gleichgestaltet*. No German publisher was permitted to publish works by authors placed on the index, and only writers who belonged to the Reichskulturkammer could be legally published. The history of publishing under the Third Reich has rarely been studied: it is a painful and fascinating example of the destruction of an entire culture which could exist only by way of books.

If these measures meant the immediate disappearance of Communist, Socialist and revolutionary publishing houses – such as Wieland Herzfelde's Malik Verlag or the Münzenberg imprints – the attitude of the major 'bourgeois' publishers was more complex. We should be aware that throughout the Weimar era, these publishers had displayed an astonishing sense of freedom and quality. A look at Ernst Rowohlt's catalogue, for example, shows how, as well as nationalist writers such as Ernst von Salomon, he had Socialist and Communist writers and various representatives of the avant-garde. Rowohlt himself agreed to join the Reichskulturkammer, but soon came into conflict with the Nazis and was finally expelled.[63] His publishing house survived only as a division of Deutsche Verlaganstalt in Stuttgart,[64] and he finally abandoned publishing altogether. Peter Suhrkamp, for his part, was eventually imprisoned in 1944. The case of publishing houses with Jewish owners raised still more complex problems. The most well-known case is that of Samuel Fischer and his son-in-law Gottfried Bermann Fischer.

Publisher in the 1920s of Thomas Mann, Gerhart Hauptmann, Hermann Hesse, George Bernard Shaw, Alfred Döblin, Jacob Wassermann, Siegfried Kracauer, Klaus and Erika Mann, and Walter Mehring, as well as of the *Neue Rundschau*, Bermann Fischer was directly threatened as both a Jew and a liberal. He decided however not to emigrate immediately, on the advice of Peter Suhrkamp. He had the idea of establishing his firm at Rapallo, but wanted to return to Germany to find out what could be rescued.[65] The Nazis' first measures was to demand that he remove from his hall all portraits of Jewish writers – a tragicomic episode, as the Nazi official simply pointed to all writers with beards, including Hermann Bahr, Ibsen and Shaw. In 1933–34, Bermann Fischer was still able to publish certain books without harassment, including those of Bahr, Joseph Conrad, Hugo von Hofmannstahl, J. Giono, B. Kellermann, Alfred Kerr, Annette Kolb, Herman Hesse, Heinrich Hauser, Carl Zuckmazer and René Schickele. Though a few authors had withdrawn their manuscripts from this 'Jewish publisher', Bermann Fischer was attacked by émigrés who accused him of having taken a fairly ambiguous position. But he was soon to come up against contradictory demands. Heinrich Hauser, author of *A Man Learns to Steal*, had decided to preface his book with a dedication to Göring. To avoid this, Bermann Fischer responded that Göring would certainly not appreciate such homage from a 'Jewish publisher'. The author then wrote directly to Göring, who declared himself delighted. Annette Kolb's novel *Die Schaukel* (*The Swing*), on the other hand, included a dedication to Jews who had done so much for German culture.

The book appeared with this notice, but a threatening letter to author and publisher then demanded its suppression in any reprint. However reluctantly, Bermann Fischer agreed to this, attracting violent attacks from the émigré press, especially Leopold Schwarzschild's *Neue Tage-Buch* (19 January 1935).[66] Bermann Fischer was defended by Annette Kolb and Herman Hesse, while Thomas Mann and other émigrés encouraged him to remain in Germany to rescue his company's heritage. René Schickele even wrote to Bermann Fischer on 4 April 1934 that the appearance of Thomas Mann's novels in Germany was more important than the entire émigré literature. But the exile press continued to describe him as a traitor. He was supported for a while by Peter Suhrkamp, who had become his adviser on political matters.

After the death of Samuel Fischer on 15 October 1934, Bermann Fischer wanted to emigrate. He asked the minister of propaganda for permission to establish himself abroad with several hundred thousand books that were considered representative of *Asphaltliteratur*. The Nazis agreed, in return for a 20 per cent levy on the stock transferred. Bermann Fischer refused to sell shares in the Fischer publishing house that remained in Germany to Bruckmann of Munich, who had become a Nazi, and it was Peter Suhrkamp who took over Fischer Verlag.[67]

Bermann Fischer wanted to found a Swiss company, by means of a share issue, in order to acquire exile copyrights that risked falling into Nazi hands. A further proposition was received from England, but it was eventually in Vienna that he decided to settle, following the chicanery he had to put up with. Swiss publishers and bookstores in fact considered that the stocks rescued from the Nazis were a threat to their own publications, and Bermann Fischer was refused permission to establish himself in Zurich. He stayed for two years in Vienna (1936–38), trying to distribute German literature that was now banned in the Reich. A number of his publications could still be sold in Germany. During this period he published many foreign authors, including Jean Giradoux and Julien Green, and above all the third volume of Thomas Mann's tetralogy *Joseph and His Brothers*. He managed to find a wide readership among the émigrés.

The invasion of Austria meant the collapse of Bermann Fischer's company in Vienna. His stocks were immediately confiscated by the Nazis. He then embarked on negotiations with the Swedish publisher Bonnier, proposing a joint venture with him, though Thomas Mann urged him to come to the United States and set up there 'the major publishing house of German emigration'.[68]

In May 1938, Bermann Fischer left for Stockholm with the intention of re-establishing there a division of Fischer Verlag, together with several of his former collaborators who had been released from concentration camp. With the aid of Dutch publishers, he managed to reissue in the Netherlands a number of titles that were banned in Germany. But as Hitler's armies advanced, the market for German books steadily shrunk. The only remaining solution for him was to leave for the United States. Alfred Harcourt agreed to continue distributing the Stockholm publications, and in March 1941, Fritz Landshoff also emigrated to the United States, after acquiring rights on the most important novels written in exile. In this way, the L. B. Fischer Publishing Corporation was founded in New

York in 1942, which as well as publishing works by German exiles, also published young American writers such as e. e. cummings, Richard Wright, Norman Mailer, Ralph Ellison, Arthur Miller and Tennessee Williams – some 141 authors from twenty-one countries. At the end of the War, Bermann Fischer published antifascist paperbacks designed for German prisoners-of-war, and planned a series of anti-Nazi educational books: this Neue Welt series expanded into the well-known Fischer Bücherei.

Bermann Fischer was of course an exceptional case: very few publishers survived the banning and confiscation of their books. Still more rare were anti-Nazi authors who managed to publish in Germany after 1933, and Thomas Mann was as exceptional as his publisher in this respect. But deprived of income, unable to write in a foreign language or get their works translated, several writers abandoned writing. A novel by Thomas Mann or Lion Feuchtwanger could become a bestseller in any language, but who would bother to translate a book that was scarcely known outside the German-speaking world? And what about poets? It was to escape this condemnation to silence that the émigré publishing houses were established.[69] Whether literary or political, they set out to break the exclusion and encirclement to which the Third Reich believed it had definitively condemned its opponents. These enterprises were quite varied, including some that were basically political and others that were basically literary, as well as more or less independent collections of 'German literature in exile' set up within foreign publishing houses. The majority only developed with great difficulty, and had a fairly precarious existence, apart from in the Soviet Union where exile publications were printed in large runs. In Europe they were often ephemeral creations, and in America it was difficult to get them going at all.

POLITICAL PUBLISHERS

These grew up soon after the Nazi seizure of power, and disappeared around 1938–39. In the first days of exile, they were mainly situated in Paris, Prague and Amsterdam. Tied to the exiled political parties, some enjoyed the support of the Socialist International or the Comintern. We have already described the operation of some of them in connection with Willi Münzenberg's activities; the most characteristic examples remain those of Éditions du Carrefour, Éditions Prométhée and Éditions Sebastian Brant. The Socialist International, for its part, set up Éditions Nouvelles Internationales in France, while in Czechoslovakia Editions Graphia was founded in Karlovy Vary in March 1933, thanks to Sudeten Social-Democrats who put the printing press of their newspaper *Volkswille* at the exiles' disposal. A number of other publishing houses were financed by the SAP, by aid and support organizations (the Thälmann committee, the Committee Against War and Fascism, Red Aid). If these published the occasional volume of a literary character, most of their publications were designed to circulate information on conditions in Germany, and be clandestinely smuggled into the country to try and counter Nazi propaganda. This kind of political publisher was to be found in most centres of emigration, and though Prague and Paris remained the largest of these, they existed also in London, Amsterdam and Stockholm.

Communist publishing houses were generally the most numerous and active, and the publication of the *Braunbuch* on the Reichstag fire by Éditions du Carrefour, with material help from the Comintern, showed what an effect these could sometimes have.[70] A number of publications were also produced by publishing houses tied to political parties in the host countries.[71]

FOREIGN PUBLISHING HOUSES
AND EXILE LITERATURE

The foundation of publishing houses by German émigrés encountered difficulties that could discourage any kind of initiative, some of these being evident enough. Not only did the exiles lack the necessary financial means, but the market for German books outside the Reich was relatively limited, with the exception of certain adjacent countries such as Czechoslovakia, Austria, Switzerland and the Netherlands, and constantly shrunk as Hitler's realm expanded, especially with the annexation of Austria and Czechoslovakia. The existence of a potential readership in these countries did not in itself constitute a market: in each of these countries censorship had to be taken into account, as they feared poisoning their relationships with Germany if they permitted the distribution of émigré works. In Switzerland, exile literature was banned at the request of writers and publishers who feared its competition.[72] Despite its quality, therefore, German literature in exile was unable to compete with production from the Reich, all the more so as the Nazis threatened reprisals against publishers or booksellers who agreed to distribute these books.[73] Often printed in atrocious conditions,[74] with only small runs and relatively expensive,[75] it was hard for such works to find even the readership formed by the émigrés themselves, and after 1939 exile literature faced almost complete asphyxiation.[76] Wielande Herzfelde summed up these problems very well in an article titled 'David against Goliath', which appeared in *Das Wort* in 1937:

Firstly, a considerable part of our potential readers live in Austria, Czechoslovakia, Switzerland or France. Austria generally does not allow our literature into the country. In Czechoslovakia as in Austria, a large section of German readers and an even larger one of German booksellers admire the Third Reich or are afraid to read or sell books that displease the Nazis. In Switzerland the first signs of a similar development are already visible. Alsace has never imported many German books: the population there speak French as well, and French books are cheaper.

Second, Goebbels tries to aggravate the difficulties that émigré publishers have in selling their books by a policy of dumping, reducing their price to the foreign buyer by 25 per cent, and at the same stroke increasing the profit margin of the bookstore.

Third, because the print runs are smaller, prices are higher; but because of their content, our literature addresses the section of the population with the least purchasing power. The high prices of these books are thus very detrimental to their distribution.

Fourth, the millions of volumes seized by the Nazis are sent abroad to be remaindered at very low prices. This poisonous literature, as they call it, is still good for [. . .] earning foreign currency, while at the same time damaging the émigré publishers. All this, of course, with no concern for copyright [. . .]

Fifth, foreign booksellers can easily obtain all books published in Germany at a good price by having them dispatched in bulk from the Leipzig warehouses. Ordering books from our publishers, which are unable to keep stocks in Leipzig, absorbs a large share of the bookseller's margin, given the high price of carriage, customs duties and currency conversion, as well as the copious correspondence required.

Sixth, the pressure of the Third Reich on the smaller states – diplomatically or through terrorist organizations in the countries in question – makes distribution that much more difficult. This is shown especially clearly in Romania, where the largest bookstore, Ignaz Hertz in Bucharest, has been placed under seal and its owner deprived of his nationality; or again in Yugoslavia where anti-Semitic bands sacked the Breyer bookstore while its owner was in prison. Such practices intimidate many booksellers and force them to be cautious, i.e. to censor themselves just as the Nazis want. In Danzig the situation is the same as in the Third Reich; the Social-Democratic bookseller Tosch has been condemned to three years in prison simply for having sold German books imported from the Netherlands.[77]

This analysis is so lucid and precise that there is scarcely anything to add. Yet the Nazis' efforts by no means managed to destroy all exile literature. In particular, they could do nothing against its quality, which contrasted so starkly with the general mediocrity of 'their' writers. The fifteen German authors most widely translated between 1933 and 1938 included eleven exiles, and at least three of the remaining four were 'internal émigrés'.[78]

It is also clear that the most well-known exile authors preferred their foreign translations to be published by major publishers rather than by the émigré presses with their limited print runs, weak distribution and poor royalties. While Thomas Mann was still able to publish his books in Germany, he did not entrust them to exile publishers, and G. Bermann Fischer was very sensible to write to him:

> I view the establishment of new publishing houses in France, Holland and so on with great scepticism. These have their justification in so far as they are genuine émigré publishers. Emil Ludwig, Feuchtwanger, Remarque, Tucholsky and Kerr can no longer appear in Germany, and if in this way they can find a way to be published for German readers abroad, that is all to the good. For authors in a different situation, however, to be published by these presses would mean abandoning the German market; they would be boycotted.[79]

One of the most rational solutions was thus to establish collections of German exile literature with existing publishing houses. The only major successes here were Emmanuel Querido and Allert de Lange in Amsterdam, and Emil Oprecht in Switzerland, who all published émigré works for political reasons.[80] The case of the two Dutch publishers was quite exceptional. It is explained both by the country's long tradition of asylum, but also by the personalities of the two publishers, firm opponents of National Socialism who were ready to put their facilities at the disposal of the émigrés and even give some of them major responsibilities.[81] Far from competing with one another, they worked closely together and managed to attract to Querido Verlag a number of exile authors formerly published by Rowohlt, Insel, Kiepenheuer or Ullstein. It was to this collaboration that some of the most famous exile works – Ernst Toller's *Ein Jugend in Deutschland* (*I Was a German*), Alfred Döblin's *Jüdische Erneuerung* (*Jewish Renewal*), Lion Feuchtwanger's *Geschwister Oppenheim* (*The Oppenheims*) and Heinrich Mann's *Der Hass* (*Hatred*) – all owed their appearance. Querido went on to publish works by Vicki Baum, Bernhard von Brentano, Albert Einstein, Oskar Maria Graf, Georg Kaiser, Alfred Kerr, Irmgard Keun, Emil Ludwig, Klaus and Thomas Mann, Roger Neumann, Erich Maria Remarque, Joseph Roth, Carl Sternheim, Anna Seghers, Jacob Wassermann and Arnold Zweig.[82] Bermann Fischer in Stockholm reissued books originated by Allert de Lange and Querido in his series Forum-Bücher, as cheap novels and anthologies.

When the Nazis invaded the Netherlands, Querido decided to relocate to the Dutch East Indies, but with the threat of Japanese invasion, only one title (by Erich Maria Remarque) could be published there, and its authors and staff were now all pursued by the Gestapo. But during its few years of operation, Querido managed to produce 110 titles, and Allert de Lange seventy.[83] Emil Oprecht, instead of establishing special series for exile works, published many of these in his existing collections.[84] Together with other investors, he established the Europa Verlag-Aktiengesellschaft, to produce books designed to reveal the ideological goals of the German and Italian regimes. He also facilitated the development of the Büchergilde Gutenberg in Switzerland,[85] and founded foreign divisions of his company as far afield as the United States, in order to distribute exile works banned by the Swiss censors.[86] After 1933, German exiles made up almost half of the titles published by Oprecht. Besides political essays he also published novels, and Thomas Mann's review *Mass und Wert*. Though the print runs were somewhat limited, Oprecht had a degree of success with books by Ignazio Silone, Hermann Rauschning, and the biography of Hitler by Konrad Heiden.[87] Among the most notable authors published by Oprecht were Ernst Bloch, Willy Brandt, Bernhard von Brentano, Ferdinand Bruckner, Louis Fürnberg, Hans Habe, Max Hermann-Neisse, Georg Kaiser, Arthur Koestler, Else Lasker-Schüler, Emil Ludwig, Heinrich and Thomas Mann, Walter Mehring, Alfred Polgar, Ludwig Renn, Friedrich Wolf and Theodor Wolff. Oprecht himself played a significant role in protecting émigrés, and was one of the few exile publishers not to suffer Gestapo reprisals.[88]

Finally, a number of European publishers, if a small minority, agreed to publish exile works in German.[89] Others opened their literature collections to a certain number of exiles.[90]

EXILE PUBLISHERS

I was formerly a German poet.

Max Hermann-Neisse

A few publishing houses banned in Germany managed to re-establish themselves in exile and survive with difficulty. Such was the case with Gottfried Bermann Fischer,[91] in Vienna and later in Stockholm, but especially with Malik Verlag and its ex-Dadaist publisher Wieland Herzfelde,[92] whose apartment the Nazis immediately sacked when they came to power, and whose stock of 40,000 volumes was seized and destroyed. Herzfelde succeeded none the less in re-establishing Malik Verlag in Prague, with support from F. C. Weiskopf, and published some forty more books, chiefly translations of Soviet authors, but also works by Willi Bredel, Oskar Maria Graf, J. R. Becher, Heinrich Mann, Bertolt Brecht and Weiskopf himself, as well as the magazine *Neue Deutsche Blätter*, whose contributors included Herzfelde, Graf, Anna Seghers and Jan Petersen. After the invasion of Czechoslovakia, and a further destruction of the company, Malik was re-established once more in Stockholm.

A number of new publishers were newly founded by the émigrés, such as Éditions du 10 Mai,[93] whose titles included Willi Bredel's account of his experience as a political commissar in the Chapaev battalion.[94] Directed by Hermann Budzislawski, editor-in-chief of *Die Weltbühne*, this imprint also published texts by Heinrich Mann, but it was unable to complete its programme and fell into the Gestapo's hands in 1940. Finally, a number of works were published on a cooperative basis, chiefly in milieus close to the KPD.

After 1939, most publishers of exile literature disappeared. The control that Germany exercised over all the occupied countries made it almost impossible for any émigré work to be published. The only remaining possibility was a kind of collective publication: émigrés financed their productions by contributing funds. The most famous example was El Libro Libre in Mexico, which managed to publish a number of titles including works by Anna Seghers, Ludwig Renn, Lion Feuchtwanger, Bodo Uhse, Heinrich Mann, Bruno Frank, Paul Merker, Alexander Abusch, Paul Mayer, E. Sommer and Theodor Balk. El Libro Libre also published works in Spanish, including *El Libro Negro del terror nazi in Europa*, under the official sponsorship of President Cardenas.[95] In 1944, Aurora Verlag was launched in New York, on the initiative of Wieland Herzfelde, with Ernst Bloch, Brecht, Ferdinand Bruckner, Alfred Döblin, Lion Feuchtwanger, Oskar Maria Graf, Heinrich Mann, E. Waldinger, Berthold Viertel and F. C. Weiskopf, but though Aurora did produce a dozen titles, such publishing opportunities were increasingly limited. Only the most famous authors from the Weimar era were translated into foreign languages, especially in the United States. Others were condemned to silence, or to very limited print runs. This was especially the case with most of the poets, who were able to publish only thanks to the generosity of fellow exiles[96] or wealthy patrons: the celebrated Phoenix-Bücher published in Paris,[97] which included texts by Mynona, Rudolf Leonhard, A. Joachim, Alfred Kantorowicz, Emil Ludwig and Berthold Jacob, were financed by Renaud de Jouvenel.[98]

Finally, we should note that in the course of the different stages of exile, a large number of authors had to abandon their manuscripts, or else these were destroyed by the Gestapo: some seized in 1933 were already burned in the auto-da-fé of 10 May. Heinrich Mann had published his collected works on three occasions: in 1909, 1917 and 1925–32. In both 1933 and 1940 he lost copies of most of his articles, and little is known of what he wrote in California. Walter Mehring lost his autobiography in the train, between Berlin, Vienna and Paris. Alfred Kantorowicz had to leave his manuscripts in France in 1940, in a cellar. Those of Walter Benjamin were preserved by Georges Bataille. Ernst Weiss's manuscript, *Der Augenzeuge* (*The Eyewitness*), was rediscovered almost by chance. Fritz von Unruh had to entrust his manuscripts to a Paris dressmaker; Johannes Wüstens managed to bury his, but he was murdered by the Nazis in Gollnow.

3. ARGUMENTS ABOUT 'EXILE LITERATURE'

> Each original German sentence, each grammatically correct expression written today, forms a bridge over the German deluge, a connection between yesterday and tomorrow.
>
> Ludwig Marcuse

All attempts to analyse exile productions in a coherent and rigorous fashion come up against difficulties which emerge both in works published by the exiles themselves, and in critical writings devoted to them. Apart from the fact that these books – political pamphlets, essays, novels, plays, poems – were written by German-language authors exiled for political, moral or racial reasons, there is no obvious common bond.[99] The diversity of exile literature is a function of at least three factors that reflect the heterogeneous nature of the emigration itself: it is the expression of writers with differing aesthetic sensibilities, and is not reducible to any definite style, even if many of these works contain common themes, and genres such as reportage, historical novel and autobiography are especially frequent. Born abroad for political and historic reasons, this literature cannot be seen as necessarily activist, and its relationship to history depends largely on the political awareness of each particular writer and their conception of literature. Bound up with the exile experience in its very origin, this is present in every work to a greater or lesser degree. But while this forms the theme or even the framework of a number of novels, and such experience is reflected in several others, there are many exile productions that bear hardly a trace of it, that show nothing of the struggle against fascism, and are scarcely distinguishable from the apolitical productions of those 'internal émigrés' who remained in the Reich.

If a number of works written in exile can indeed be termed antifascist, this adjective can be applied to exile literature as a whole only in a very crude sense, unless the term is stretched to the point of destroying any meaning.[100] For some writers, exile was a decisive experience that marked their life and determined the entire future development of their work, giving it a new meaning. For others, it was an accident on their path and did not intrinsically mark their literary production. Some again experienced exile as being 'forced into politics', while others kept their distance, as many had done under the Weimar Republic.

SPECIFIC CHARACTERISTICS OF EXILE LITERATURE

A reading of the main works devoted to exile literature, and essays written by the émigrés themselves – W. A. Berendsohn, Alfred Döblin, Golo Mann, Hermann Kesten, Alfred Kantorowicz, Wieland Herzfelde, Klaus Mann and F. C. Weiskopf – makes clear that they scarcely ever agreed on anything, and their attempts at a theory of their situation were constantly contradictory. For a start, should one refer to 'exile literature', 'literature of emigration', 'German literature in exile' or 'antifascist literature'? The very term chosen reflects the theoretical or political standpoint of its author.[101]

At many times, indeed, people have been led to leave their country for political, moral, religious or racial reasons. These included writers, whose works were deeply marked by the exile experience. And in the case of the German exiles of 1933, this is so clearly apparent that they have often been compared with their illustrious predecessors when it comes to arguing that literature does not die in exile, but the experience can even be creative, as it was for Ovid, Virgil, Dante, Heine or Victor Hugo. Reflection on exile literature goes back well before the anti-Nazi emigration. Georg Brandes was perhaps the first[102] to devote a special study to the 'literature of émigrés', in his *Hauptströmungen der Literatur des 19. Jahrhunderts*,[103] in which he debated the fate of French writers condemned to exile by the Jacobins or Napoleon.[104] In Germany, this subject first appeared with the Mainz republic of the 1790s, when the country's first true republican, Georg Forster, had to escape to France. After 1815, and especially after the July revolution, a growing number of progressive German intellectuals, journalists and writers travelled to Paris. The fifty to eighty thousand Germans living in the French capital by the 1840s, not all of them of course intellectuals, included Marx, Heine, Börne, Ruge and Weitling. In 1846, Karl Heinzen planned to publish an *Emigranten Almanach* in Paris, declaring that 'Germany has become the richest country in the world in its number of literary emigrants.'[105] The defeat of the 1848 revolution expelled a new wage of émigrés – Freiligrath, Herwegh, Weerth, Marx, Engels, Ruge, etc. – forced to flee to Zurich, London or the United States. As literary censorship was strengthened, and with the anti-socialist laws in force from 1878 to 1890, many more writers left the country, often temporarily. Karl Henkell and Oscar Panizza were forced to leave Germany, as Frank Wedekind and Albert Langen had to do later, after being accused of insulting the Kaiser. The First World War brought a further wave, with pacifists such as L. Frank, I. Goll, Stefan Zweig, R. Huelsenbeck, H. Ball, E. Hennings, Ernst Bloch, Walter Benjamin and René Schickele, just to list the major writers who took refuge in Switzerland.

It should nonetheless be noted that, however interesting it may be to examine the different waves of émigrés who left Germany before 1933, this is of little help in understanding the question of exile literature after Hitler's seizure of power. This was far too specific for analogies to be readily adduced.[106] No country was ever struck by such an intellectual haemorrhage. It was not just a few writers opposed to the regime who emigrated, but almost the entire progressive intelligentsia.[107] The composite character of Nazi ideology and the broad spread of repression forced a similar fate upon people ostensibly united only by a refusal to remain in Germany. There was never an emigration so diverse in its composition. The majority of its historians have been compelled to seek a unity for it in three different directions: its political development in relation to exile, its existence as a formal category, and the community of experience that explains its origin.

On 4 March 1933, Kurt Tucholsky wrote to Walter Hasenclever: 'In no circumstances should one participate in a literature of emigration, no matter in what guise this is established [. . .]. First of all, there will be no large emigration since, contrary to the Russian example of 1917, Europe is not able to accept these people. They will die of hunger. Secondly, like all emigrations, especially German ones, they will split into 676 little groups, each battling against the other harder than they will fight against Adolf.'

If these exiled writers never formed a genuine community, as witness the countless polemics and attacks that divided them, they remained aware for all that of their common fate. One of the first to try and illuminate the cleavages within this exile literature was undoubtedly Alfred Döblin, who preferred the expression 'German literature abroad'. In a booklet published in Paris in 1938, *Die deutsche Literatur im Ausland seit 1933. Ein Dialog zwischen Politik und Kunst*, he distinguished three currents: the first conservative and oriented to the past, the second revolutionary in spirit, and the third humanist, which had all been affected by the Nazi *Gleichschaltung*, but reacted in different ways. The conservatives were tempted to approve this, or at least accept it, the humanist group was directly threatened, while the revolutionary tendency was split into a right and a left wing. But examined more closely, we have to recognize that Döblin's classification lacks rigour, and scarcely manages to explain the basis of these respective groups. Though his indication of a conservative group may be more or less accepted, the combination of Kafka, Brecht and Jünger in the 'revolutionary in spirit' category is almost meaningless.

The second historical attempt to denote the exile community, Walter A. Berendsohn's *Einführung in die deutsche Emigranten-Literatur*[108] (in two parts eventually combined under the title *Die humanistische Front*), sought to bring all the exiles together under a 'humanist' banner, as in Döblin's third category. More precise, but over-generous in its inspiration, this classification raises several problems, the most serious of which is the very term 'humanist'. Whilst this might be unhesitatingly applied to progressive liberal writers, pacifists, republicans, Socialists and Communists, it is hard to see how it characterizes turncoats from the NSDAP such as Otto Strasser and the Schwarze Front, the SA émigrés in China, or conservatives such as Rauschning and Brüning. Would they themselves have accepted the description? And what to say of the thousands of Jews who left Germany for racial and economic reasons? Recalling the number and importance of works published in exile,[109] Berendsohn speaks of a 'literature of emigrants' (*Emigrantenliteratur*) comparable to an orchestra composed of several different instruments. Besides questioning his generosity in extending the supposed 'humanist front' to include émigrés of the far right, it must also be recognized that Berendsohn never tackles the crucial question of this literature and the role of exile in its genesis. He distinguished only two groups of writers: one continuing the neo-Romantic tradition, the other more oriented to social life.

In the same manner, F. C. Weiskopf, in his book *Unter fremden Himmeln*, seemed to view all the exiled authors as progressive, even as activists. A large number of writers find no place in his analyses, as they kept their distance from the struggles of exile, or wrote nothing of a political character.

The second type of approach, which consists in extracting a kind of formal category of 'exile literature', seems just as questionable, even if it has inspired a good deal of work. It is impossible to speak of 'exile literature' as if it was a literary 'genre' in the same sense as imaginative literature or autobiography. Besides, should we speak of 'exile literature', of 'German literature abroad', or simply of exiled authors? Hermann Kesten, in a study published in Paris in 1938,[110] declared that 'neither exile nor membership of the Reichskammer divide the two German-language literatures', that dilettantes and bad writers existed among the émigrés, and talented writers among those who had not emigrated. The divide, according to him, lay within both the Reich literature and that of the émigrés, cutting through Germany, Austria, Switzerland and Czechoslovakia. Rather than there being a 'literature of exiles' or a 'literature of emigration', there were only German authors forced into exile. Kesten maintained that neither the Nazis nor the émigrés, nor for that matter foreign critics, had succeeded in offering the slightest rigorous definition of this 'literature of emigration'. The very term struck him as a reproach, not as a concept, and he emphasized that apart from language these writers had nothing in common, not even German nationality. Long before 1933 there had been German writers living abroad, in Italy, Switzerland, France or Austria, without their works being described as 'émigré literature'.[111] Exile to him did not seem a criterion, as 'clouds drift over Ostend as well as they do over Nuremberg, and the rain the poet needs is not basically different there from that of Berlin.'

Even the fact that certain authors were no longer publishable in Germany did not strike Kesten as decisive: the works of Thomas Mann and Herman Hesse were still on sale two years after the Nazi seizure of power, even though they were opponents of the regime, whilst the writings of Otto Strasser, banned in Germany, were the product of a man strongly marked by National Socialism. Exile as such had not been able to make them into any real community, and Kesten maintained that they were still just as divided as they had been in the Weimar era by their political and religious ideas; the émigrés included Catholics, Protestants, Jews, atheists, Socialists, Communists, non-party people, pacifists, anti-Semites, Kantians, symbolists, expressionists, realists, Marxists, reactionaries and conservatives. Finally, even the exile situation was too complex to be brought under any one head. Feuchtwanger had a town in the USSR named after him, but others were dying of hunger. Erich Maria Remarque was a millionaire, while most émigrés survived on the aid of committees. Kesten thus saw the rubric 'exile literature' or 'emigrant literature' as a dangerous absurdity: it gave the illusion of a community between people and works that had never existed.

Without entering into the details of Kesten's argument, it is interesting to note that the thesis he develops is the diametric opposite of that of W. A. Berendsohn, who proudly declared: 'I hold it a fatal mistake to reject the notion of an "emigrant literature". It is a description with a good sound to it.' Hermann Kesten, however, only found the term insulting.

One of the first attempts to theorize the question of 'exile literature' – among those who believed in its existence – was that of W. M. K. Pfeiler in his study *German Literature in Exile: The Concern of Poets*.[112] Without debating its ideological unity, he viewed exile literature as a 'formal category' denoting works written by German authors forced or choosing to leave their country after the advent of National Socialism. At the same time, he held that this literature should be viewed as an integral part of German literature as a whole. To avoid the ambiguity of Berendsohn's 'humanist front', Pfeiler referred to 'German literature outside the Reich'. For him, the only link between all these authors was the German language.[113] Exile did not seem to him the decisive criterion, as a certain number of non-Nazi authors who remained in the Reich also experienced a kind of internal exile, whilst even before 1933, many works viewed as part of German literature had been written abroad. Pfeiler also refused therefore the name of 'emigrant literature', which he saw as too restrictive. And yet his definition of 'German literature in exile' as a 'formal category' remained no more than a project: the two sections of his study are respectively devoted to an analysis of works written in exile as examples of 'militant humanism', and to the poets, starting from a number of rather vague themes that he links with emigration (nostalgia for Germany, solitude, despair, hatred of fascism). What he called a 'formal category' is simply a sociological extrapolation from a small number of works selected as a function of his own premises. Like F. C. Weiskopf, he reintroduced the postulate that all German literature in exile was politically charged.[114]

The same difficulties and ambiguities can be found in more recent approaches. Werner Wordtriede, in his essay 'Vorläufige Gedanken zur einer Typologie der Exilliteratur',[115] uses as typological elements such criteria as nostalgia, suffering, loneliness, silence and uprooting, which apply to pretty well all the poets. And it would be hard to apply to Thomas Mann or Lion Feuchtwanger his claim that 'the place of all exiles is a cabin, they have no house of their own'. Stefan George certainly felt more in exile under the Weimar Republic than many antifascist émigrés did in Prague after 1933. Wordtriede's approach is too esoteric to characterize authors who emigrated for political and not just 'existential' reasons. Most of the sentiments he ascribes as specific to exile literature are also common to the German romantics. Thus Max Frisch could declare: 'We have become emigrants without leaving our homeland';[116] or Hans Magnus Enzenberger: 'Absent, I am there.'[117] Peter Weiss also felt a foreigner in Germany of the 1950s and 1960s, while Armin T. Wegner, a genuine antifascist émigré, declared at the Stockholm conference on exile literature that 'all true poets always live in exile'.[118] The notion of 'exile' then becomes so vague that it denotes the most varied attitudes: not just political emigration, but exile as existential metaphor, internal exile, rejection of a vulgar world and of modernity. It becomes confused with internal emigration, the feeling of foreignness, the aspiration to a different reality.

To avoid all these ambiguities, Jost Hermand[119] acknowledged that it was virtually impossible to offer a global definition of the 'literature of exile', noting that this expression, often rejected by the most political writers (for example Brecht), was accepted by many others. Whilst it is true that the émigrés did not have the least ideological unity – authors as varied as Thomas Mann, Brecht, Werfel, Feuchtwanger, Hermann-Neisse, Weinert and Becher – and that for an initial period Thomas Mann, Stefan Zweig and Alfred Döblin rejected any antifascist activity, it remains the case that their output is historically defined in relation to another literature, that of the Reich, which they called the 'literature of Hitler's slaves'.[120] Thus, without accepting the overly vague classification offered by Döblin, Hermand believes it is possible to distinguish within the emigration at least three attitudes: one 'resigned and sceptical', the second 'humanist', and the third 'actively antifascist'. The first group would include those authors who were sceptical as to the possibility of combining literature and politics in the Weimar era, or did not believe the émigrés could affect the course of events after 1933 by a supposed 'exile literature'. Tucholsky, for example, maintained that, in so far as the Nazi regime seemed to be desired by the majority of the German people, a minority of exiles could not change history. Others took refuge after 1933 in inwardness (Richard Beer-Hoffmann, A. Schaeffer) or in religion (Alfred Döblin, Franz Werfel), or else they wrote on the suffering of exile without taking part in antifascist struggle (Max Hermann-Neisse, Else Laske-Schüler). Among many authors in this group, the break of exile is not always apparent.

The second category of writers includes authors who were progressive but not very political, considering that their task was 'to defend humanism and culture'. Some became more political in the course of exile (Thomas Mann), others like Robert Musil continued to declare themselves apolitical. The same attitude can be found with Max Brod or Ludwig Marcuse. These often viewed Nazism as a pathological phenomenon foreign to German history, which had dragged the country back to the Stone Age. Hitler and Nazism were never analysed in political terms, but as natural or even supernatural calamities that had struck Germany like a hurricane or a bad winter. All they could oppose to fascism was their morality, their faith in culture or the cosmopolitan humanism of a Goethe.[121]

The third group comprises the genuine political exiles, who saw exile as a struggle and literature as a weapon. Many of these were Communist or Marxist writers, but they also included such lone figures as Ernst Toller and even Joseph Roth, who declared in 1934: 'A poet who doesn't struggle against Hitler and the Third Reich today is surely a weak and petty man, and most likely without value as a poet.'[122] Ferdinand Bruckner affirmed at the PEN Club congress of 1939 in New York that 'poetry is a weapon' – a thesis developed already in the 1920s by Communist writers such as Erich Weinert or Friedrich Wolf. The members of this group were often severely critical of those who throughout their exile were concerned only with the quality of literary works and completely neglected the struggle against Hitler. It was these 'activists' who dreamed of a united front of German literature in exile, able both to safeguard the German heritage and oppose Hitlerite propaganda in every country, as well as preparing for a future Germany. They were also almost the only ones to develop a genuinely political analysis of National Socialism.

Of all the classifications generally offered of exile literature, this one seems to us the most rigorous, in so far as it acknowledges the existence of a certain historical unity, but also its ideological diversity.

A third possible approach to this 'literature of exile' is to study it in close relationship with the circumstances in which it arose. It is true that some works written or published after 1933 do not bear the clear trace of exile;[123] many others however are incomprehensible outside the global phenomenon of emigration, with its train of everyday suffering and battles waged. To reread these works without taking the struggle against National Socialism into account, not to mention the psychological and material wretchedness in which many of them were written, would be to misconstrue a fundamental dimension of this exile literature. To reproach Klaus Mann for a certain weakness of style in some passages from *The Volcano*, or deplore the overly circumstantial character of this or that antifascist novel written by an émigré, would be to forget the context in which these works had their origin, and what they set out to do: bear witness, and take part in a movement of struggle, rather than attain a certain aesthetic perfection.

Several authors – Feuchtwanger, Kantorowicz, Koestler, Sperber, Zuckmayer and Klaus Mann – have described the often tragic conditions under which their works were written. They all insist on the indissoluble unity between 'exile literature' and exile itself. Feuchtwanger recalled, in 'Die Arbeitsprobleme der Schriftsteller im Exil',[124] how before 1914 he had attended a seminar on literary history at which 'inner life' and 'outward circumstances' were strictly distinguished. Discussing the case of works written in exile, the professor maintained that in no case could this circumstance have influenced a work's intimate form. In considering the works of German exiles after 1933, Feuchtwanger declared on the contrary that exile was the source, the prime matter, the very essence of the majority of these works, and it alone made them comprehensible. He maintained that not everyone has the gift of writing a novel in a hotel room, especially if they don't know how to pay the next day's bill, whether their wife and children will have anything to eat, and if the prefecture of police will agree to renew their resident's permit. These sufferings, he remarked, were rarely heroic: they were made up of everyday harassment, repeated humiliation and ridiculous bureaucratic procedures that gradually changed the very act of writing and the personality of the émigré.

If Feuchtwanger's analyses, which bring together the complaints found scattered throughout countless letters and diaries, are tragically exact, they are certainly not enough to define the essence of this 'exile literature'. But they do have the merit of insisting on the need to grasp the emigration as a whole, with its battles and defeats, its hopes and disillusions, its greatness and its failures. It is only in relation to the overall phenomenon of emigration that the majority of these writings have their meaning, whether we consider a novel or a play, the choice of the historical novel as a privileged literary genre or the importance of poetry as the language of nostalgia for a lost homeland.[125] If some works written between 1933 and 1945 may be read in complete ignorance of the lives of their authors and especially of their exile, the number of these is relatively slight in relation to all those that can only be understood in relation to this exile in its various dimensions.

POLITICS AND LITERATURE IN EXILE:
THE BIRTH OF NEW CONNECTIONS

> It is fighting to root out barbarism, to plant justice in the soil nourished by the blood of countless victims, to put into practice human reason; it is fighting for a more widespread beauty, a serener joy, for the creation of a new civilization and to safeguard an eternal flame.
>
> Kurt Hiller

Should the literature of the antifascist emigration be viewed as fundamentally political because its authors had been banned in Germany? Any simplistic response to this question would be certainly mistaken: it is possible to cite many works written in exile, in the form of novels, poems or plays that, without being propaganda or circumstantial writing, form part of the struggle of the émigrés against National Socialism. To the extent that they depict the torments of exile, Nazi barbarism, and the émigrés' struggles, these works are antifascist. A further number could be added which seem foreign to their age. If it is clear that several novels of Anna Seghers, Lion Feuchtwanger or Klaus Mann were directed against Hitler, it would be hard to see Döblin's *The Blue Tiger* as belonging to this category. Here again, the ideological choices of émigrés or historians of the emigration explain their differing analyses. For some, every work by an exile is antifascist by the very fact of the author's departure from Germany; others, however, insist on maintaining the distinction between politics and literature within the exiles' output.

The ambiguity of these standpoints bears on the very definition of 'antifascist literature'. Was this simply a progressive literature foreign to the values of National Socialism and heir to the literature of the Weimar era, or rather an openly committed literature, militant in the sense understood by the Communist writers of the 1920s?

If it is hard to speak of any genuine antifascist literature still present in the Reich – apart from illegal leaflets and writings, and a few exceptional cases – this is simply because such literature had no way of finding expression. Most often what was involved was rather a 'non-fascist' literature, which was not necessarily oppositional.[126] The mere fact that the exiles had all left the Reich because of the Nazi regime, however, meant that the Hitler government saw them all as opponents, and thus 'antifascist'. Even if an émigré took no political stand towards the regime, and kept a complete distance from émigré struggles, the mere fact of their presence outside Germany, and the banning of their works in the Reich, meant that they could be considered an opponent. Even where there was no commitment in the strict sense, a 'militant humanism' could often be recognized; not to speak the official language of Nazi ideology was equated with an act of resistance (Berendsohn, Pfeiler). This is the meaning of Heinrich Mann's assertion that all works written by the émigrés should be seen as an opposition to Hitler. Klaus Mann maintained that 'simply by its quality, this literature protested against the country that had forced it into exile'.[127] Kurt Hiller saw it as a challenge to barbarism, and Hermann Kesten as embodying 'new moral forces'.[128]

A diametrically opposing attitude can be found in a number of historians and émigrés who strictly distinguished between works written in exile and political commitment. Tucholsky refused to join the émigré circles, viewing their struggle as totally useless. Thomas Mann abstained for a while from taking a stand against the Third Reich; in his eyes, his very presence outside the country was enough to show where his sympathy lay. Alfred Döblin did not write in the émigré magazines, and rejected any political commitment, as also did René Schickele. Robert Musil was hostile to Nazism, but declared himself 'apolitical'. Each of these authors was concerned to distinguish themselves from the Communist writers with their notion of 'militant literature'; it was sufficient for them that they embodied a free German literature, unsullied by Nazism. Thus Golo Mann could write:

> It is not legitimate, however, apart from the case of political journalism, to view German literature in exile as an element in the front line of struggle against the Nazis. Its purpose was rather to maintain and conserve its traditions, and try out new forms in complete freedom. [. . .] German literature in exile, as such, did not have any striking power. What was achieved by the artists, working in isolation and each for themselves, as is their nature, did not add up in the way that the combative force of soldiers and weapons does. If isolated German writers fought with the International Brigades in Spain because they considered that the Spanish civil war was a war waged against Hitler – I will not concern myself here with whether that argument is valid – if later on they fought under the British or American flags, then for that period of time they abandoned their character of writer in favour of that of combatant. That phenomenon is not part of the history of literature, or belongs to it only in a negative fashion, in so far as their predominant feeling was that there were more important things to do than write books.[129]

But if it is true that the connection of writers to history was boundlessly complex, right through the exile period, and the works written outside Germany between 1933 and 1945 cannot all be brought under one and the same rubric, can we really imagine that an émigré writer would seek merely to pick up the threads of his literary work, unfortunately interrupted by the advent of Hitler? Was it possible to write the same works after 1933 as one might have written before 1933, and within Germany?

The most characteristic example of this kind of controversy was the polemic that followed a 1935 article by the Dutch antifascist writer Menno ter Brak, in *Das Neue Tage-Buch*.[130] This discussed a number of texts published by émigrés themselves on the tasks of German literature in exile.[131] A writer and literary critic, and a friend of Thomas Mann,[132] Brak rallied early on to the émigré cause; his criticism of exile literature set out to be constructive. What he reproached it for was not being essentially different from the literature of the Weimar era. If the exile literature had a task to accomplish, it needed not just to differentiate itself fundamentally from that of the Reich, but also to be up to the new task in hand. Brak also criticized the émigrés for their complacency in praising each other's new work without any great objectivity.

This criticism gave rise to a series of theoretical discussions that show what varied notions the émigrés had of both literature and a writer's commitment. Joseph Bornstein (writing as Erich Andermann) responded to Brak in the following issue.[133] He criticized Brak for setting an overly high ideal for émigré literature: that the émigrés wrote similar novels as they had done before 1933 was in his view to be praised, considering the situation in which they lived. It was simply the Third Reich's vicious cultural policy that had forced a number of German novels to appear abroad, and this was not enough in his view to establish a new 'intellectual category'. Far from wanting to assign it a European mission, as Brak sought to do, Bornstein maintained that the writers' only real duty was to keep alive in exile the authenticity of German literature; and one needed only to compare the production of the exiles with that of the Reich's official authors to see that the emigration had not failed in this mission.

Hans Sahl, in his own response,[134] criticized the positions of both Menno ter Brak and Bornstein, maintaining that emigration could not be simply limited to a 'common fate', nor exile literature to the task of keeping alive the Weimar legacy. If exile was a political and intellectual attitude, it could not be equated with a mere change of publisher. He also mentioned works by a certain number of writers such as J. R. Becher, Bertolt Brecht, Heinrich Mann and Ernst Toller, who seemed to him to embody the most authentic meaning of the struggle waged by the émigrés through their books. Ludwig Marcuse joined the debate to assert that there was no 'literature of emigrants', and all that this term described was the sum of German works that were written and published in exile. He rejected the idea of a literary community and could not see how the advent of Hitler obliged writers to break with the style of their former work. Taking the example of Heinrich Mann, he pointed out that the hatred he bore for Hitler was a precise continuation of the hatred he had nourished for

Wilhelm II, and that the struggle against Nazism could not be divorced from the defence of the existing progressive tradition. If there was a literature that had been totally transformed it was that of the Reich, not that of the émigrés, whose merit on the contrary was to have remained steadfast. The importance of the arguments dividing the émigrés was for Marcuse a guarantee they would not show the complacency that Menno ter Brak had denounced.

In this continuing debate, Brecht, Willi Bredel, Alfred Kurella, F. C. Weiskopf and Wieland Herzfelde stressed the need for a more militant conception of literature, and these polemics continued through to the discussions around the genesis of the *Volksfront*. For these authors, the value of exile literature could not be judged simply on its artistic quality, but rather by its ability to use means such as poetry, novel and theatre in the struggle against fascism. Throughout the emigration, however, these differences on the role of the writer in exile, and what the relationship was between literature and politics, continued to generate antagonism. It is almost impossible to settle the question, as they all contain a part of the truth. Those who made art, literature, theatre and poetry into a means of immediate political action, following the call given by Dimitrov in his 1935 speech on 'Revolutionary Literature in the Struggle against Fascism', believed in the urgency of a certain type of action, and the need to mobilize everything in achieving this. If it is completely forgotten today, for example, the political theatre of Friedrich Wolf certainly played a major role at the time. This notion of theatre certainly was not that of Brecht, and while *Mr Puntila and His Man Matti*, *The Good Person of Szechwan* and *The Caucasian Chalk Circle* are also political works, they do not all have the same relationship to history and current events. Anna Seghers wrote a magnificent novel of hope against a background of nightmare, *The Seventh Cross*, but also short stories set in Mexico and Haiti that have no direct connection with fascism. Some of Feuchtwanger's novels are inseparable from the struggle against National Socialism, others could have been written before 1933. And there is no need to investigate the political meaning of Goethe's 'militant humanism' to admire Thomas Mann's *Lotte in Weimar*. These contradictions are all part of exile literature, and indeed elements of its richness.

GERMANY, HITLER AND NATIONAL SOCIALISM THROUGH EXILE LITERATURE

> They carry the black cross
> on a bloody flag,
> poor suckers,
> they will end up nailed to it.
>
> Bertolt Brecht, 'The Horst Wessel Story'

Though many émigrés declared they were the only ones to see clearly what National Socialism meant, having been its first witnesses and victims, this does not mean that they all had a truly political understanding. They were united in the same repulsion, but divided in their analysis of the causes that made Hitler's triumph possible; this is true for writers as well as political activists. The works by exiles depicting the Third Reich are thus highly diverse in character. They reflect hopes and illusions, as well as political convictions. Despite their divergences, the majority of exiles focused on the same questions: How did the Weimar Republic collapse, and how could Nazism triumph in a civilized country? What was the foundation of National Socialism, and what did Hitler represent? Is there a secret resistance? And how can we unite with opponents within the Reich?

Even if the ideological perspectives behind them are very different, most of the novels that tackle these questions show a marked unity of style:[135] they are almost always realist, and often use information gathered from exile magazines or newspapers from the Reich,[136] sometimes inspired by immediate and well-known[137] political events, integrated with various autobiographical elements.[138] Often, actual facts have been simply transposed[139] or made into 'fables',[140] and it is far from unusual to recognize in a certain exile novel an article published in an émigré magazine or fragments from the Nazi press. Without trying to depict here all the historical landscapes found in these anti-Nazi novels, we shall offer some examples from the most well-known works which show the diversity of the literary and ideological perspectives in which the themes just mentioned are inserted.

The Collapse of the Weimar Republic and the Rise of National Socialism

The failure of a political system, the betrayals and weaknesses of certain individuals and groups, or a general crisis of European culture? Long before the exile period, a number of German writers had begun to describe their era as marked by a certain collapse of values. This theme is found in various Austrian novelists such as Stefan Zweig, who gave such sentiment its greatest expression in his autobiography *The World of Yesterday*, as well as in Robert Musil (*Young Törless, The Man Without Qualities*) and above all Hermann Broch (*The Sleepwalkers*) and Joseph Roth (*The Radetsky March*). Austria and Europe here become allegories through which a certain visage of decline can be deciphered. This was already an obsessive theme before 1914, for example in the poems of Georg Trakl or the anthology of expressionist poetry edited by Kurt Pinthus, *The Twilight of Humanity*. Karl Kraus gave a similar title, *The Last Days of Humanity*, to one of his plays. And in Germany, from naturalism to expressionism, from Heinrich Mann's novels through Carl Sternheim's plays to Gottfried Benn's essays, numerous works appeared that depicted in often similar terms this sense of a collapsing system of values.

Under the Weimar Republic images of chaos could be found on all sides – in Tucholsky's satires as well as in cabaret songs, poems and plays, in the *Threepenny Opera* and *Mahagonny*. Erich Kästner's 1931 novel *Fabian*, if not among the masterpieces of the period, nonetheless offers an astonishingly realistic depiction of a world in decomposition, of which the worst is to be expected – even if the author, some twenty-five years later, exaggerated somewhat its political significance in claiming that this satirical portrait of an amoral era was 'a warning against the abyss that Germany and Europe were marching towards'. For many authors, the collapse of the Weimar Republic was part and parcel of this maelstrom of European values: National Socialism was a product of this moral and political decomposition, a wave of mud and archaism swelling up from the depths and unleashed onto a world in crisis which had been wavering ever since the First World War. A number of writers developed these themes in their exile works, showing how Nazism was born in this decomposing world.[141]

If some saw Nazism as the end result of this crisis of Western values, the most political authors preferred to describe the political weaknesses of the Weimar Republic which Hitler had been able to exploit, especially the ambiguous attitude of the Social-Democrats: Oskar Maria Graf, *Der Abgrund* (*The Abyss*), 1936; F. C. Weiskopf, *Lissy oder die Versuchung* (*Lissy, or Temptation*);[142] Adam Scharrer, *Familie Schuhmann* (1939).[143] Gustav Regler portrayed Nazi terror in the Saarland in his novel *Im Kreuzfeuer* (*In the Crossfire*), while the concentration camps are the setting for many novels, the most famous of which is Willi Bredel's *Die Prüfung* (*The Test*).[144]

Understanding Nazism and the Role of Hitler

If literary or historical accounts of the collapse of Weimar were governed by very different ideological perspectives, according to whether their authors were Communist, Social-Democrat or liberal, these differences were still more profound when they sought to understand the essence of National Socialism. Heinrich Mann declared in 1933 that it was the émigrés who knew Nazism best, and they were certainly all privileged witnesses of it. But over and above the simple narration of events, it is clear that the antifascist exiles – writers, activists or publicists – analysed the phenomenon of National Socialism in ways that were often mutually opposed. Some of them, like Brecht, already saw it in 1933 as a social, political and economic phenomenon bound up with big capital and a bourgeoisie in crisis,[145] others described it in the most varied colours: a form of German bolshevism, a nihilism with no precise ideology, a natural calamity, a return to paganism, the eruption of the petty bourgeoisie onto the historical stage, a proletarian eschatology, a regression to the Stone Age, an incomprehensible irrational phenomenon, the coming to power of a clique of failures and imbeciles greedy to revenge, a religious movement which reminded some of Luther or Wagner, others of Muhammad and Islam, etc.

For each individual author, their conception of National Socialism generally acquired a political character. Though certain exiles had remained until their emigration prisoners of a basically unhistorical vision of Nazism, they mostly went on to change their analyses quite profoundly. Brecht's essays on fascism[146] are certainly a rare model of a direct yet quite nuanced political comprehension, but many other writers moved from an apolitical notion to a certain historical understanding of the Nazi phenomenon, whether Marxist or not.[147] In his 1933 pamphlet *Hatred*, Heinrich Mann saw the Nazis simply as a band of imbeciles, idlers and bloodthirsty failures. He did not separate fascism from Bolshevism and saw it as a typically Austrian phenomenon. By the Popular Front era, however, he had developed a basically Marxist perspective quite close to Brecht's analyses.

Finally, certain émigrés sometimes seemed tempted to develop several contradictory conceptions at the same time. Thomas Mann's conversion to democracy, being 'forced into politics', did not prevent him from depicting the Nazi phenomenon in a number of different ways that are hard to reconcile. In 'An Appeal to Reason', published in 1930, he stressed the importance of the economic crisis in the development of Nazism, but at the same time he saw this as an integral part of 'a mighty wave [. . .] of anomalous barbarism, of primitive popular vulgarity – that sweeps over the world today'.[148] As a mass phenomenon and product of the democratic age, Mann initially judged Nazism from an aristocratic standpoint: it was one of the many faces of modern mediocrity, under cover of a 'proletarian eschatology', and he wondered 'if such a phenomenon can even be qualified as German'.[149] In 'The Rebirth of Decency' of 1931, Mann stressed the Nazis' hijacking of irrationalism. And in 'Germany, My Suffering' of 1933–34, he called Hitler an 'idiot'; the Nazis were 'criminally insane', 'morbid, sadistic types', and Nazism as a whole an 'insensate orgy in a powerful and shady moral element'.[150] In the last instance, Mann deemed the Nazi phenomenon something foreign to German history and culture. Yet 'Brother Hitler' of 1938 strikes a different tone, and Mann now refuses to radically divide the tradition of philosophic irrationalism (Schopenhauer, Wagner, Nietzsche) from its 'derangement for cooks' that is Nazi irrationalism. While declaring that Hitler was a catastrophe, he also found in him: 'A brother – a rather unpleasant and mortifying brother. He makes me nervous, the relationship is painful to a degree. But I will not disclaim it. For I repeat: better, more productive, more honest, more constructive than hatred is recognition, acceptance, the readiness to make oneself one with what is deserving of our hate, even though we run the risk, morally speaking, of forgetting how to say no.'[151]

Finally, in his 1941 essay, 'Germany and the Germans', Mann seems to have abandoned the style of political analysis he had adopted in the 1930s, returning towards certain political positions of his *Reflections of a Nonpolitical Man*. Germany was now seen as an almost diabolic and irrational entity, no longer to be exalted but rather cursed, as it would for ever remain foreign to peace and democracy. This was the Germany of *Doctor Faustus*, of the pact with the Devil: 'And this devil of Luther, the devil of Faust, seems to me a very German figure; alliance with him, the pact with the demon in order to temporarily gain all the treasure and power of the world in exchange for salvation, has always been close to the German soul.'[152] Brecht subsequently criticized Mann in very harsh terms for his refusal to dissociate Germany from National Socialism, or the Germans from Hitler.

These contradictory examples taken from Thomas Mann's writings are echoed in the texts of many émigrés. At least three differing styles of approach can be distinguished:

- an apolitical or unhistorical vision that sees Nazism as a natural or supernatural catastrophe, as the eruption of diabolical forces;
- a focus on the personality of Hitler;
- the attempt to understand the mechanisms of fascism, and the reasons for its rise and triumph, in political and economic terms.

The Unhistorical Vision of National Socialism

According to this conception, fascism is an unleashing of barbarism that struck these countries with the violence of a natural element.

Bertolt Brecht, 'Five Difficulties in Writing the Truth' (1935)

This first type of depiction of National Socialism almost completely ignores social, political and economic elements. It is a vision that appears most completely in those authors who were not very political, if at all so, under the Weimar Republic, and underwent scarcely any further development in exile. They left Germany for moral reasons, disgusted by barbarism. They cursed this Nazi barbarism without really trying to fight it or discern its origin. Yet a number of themes deriving from this vision can be found even in the most political authors, if in this case associated with other analyses.

For certain émigrés, Nazism struck Germany like a natural disaster. They liked to compare it with a 'storm', a 'hurricane', an 'earthquake' or a 'tidal wave', without trying to understand it further. The only solution was to await its disappearance, as one waits for the end of winter or for a flood to ebb. Many of these themes appear in the poems of Max Hermann-Neisse, in which Nazism is described as hell or apocalypse,[153] in the expressionist poet Alfred Wolfenstein who writes of a 'wreck', 'a ship adrift', a 'madness', and equates Nazism with a kind of 'natural disturbance' which one can only wait to disappear. For others, Nazism was a 'diabolical' force[154] defying all rational comprehension, that had triggered a flood of 'primitive barbarism',[155] provoking a genuine regression to the Middle Ages[156] or even the Stone Age.[157] It was an 'absolute evil', to be exorcized rather than simply fought.[158] Such metaphors recur in several political authors, who compared Nazism with a sickness, a plague, a cancer, a gangrene,[159] and the epithet 'diabolical' is found in many writers who were political without being Marxist (Thomas Mann, Hermann Kesten). These often depicted the struggle against fascism as a moral crusade, the struggle of good against evil, a victory to be won over the realm of demons, a genuinely metaphysical battle. As in Joseph Roth's novel *The Antichrist*, the whole universe seems marked by the Apocalypse.

Brecht, in his essays on fascism, summed up the idealism of this approach in admirable terms:

It consists in saying: in this country, in the very heart of Europe, where the implantation of culture goes back a very long time, barbarism has more or less been unleashed from one day to the next, like a frightening fit of fury, equally sudden and inexplicable. The benign forces were vanquished, the malign forces have established their domination. The solution to the enigma, therefore, is that barbarism comes from barbarism. These acts come from the instincts. The instincts come from nowhere, they are simply there. The Third Reich, if we are to believe this hypothesis, would be equivalent to a natural catastrophe, such as a volcanic eruption, causing devastation in the flourishing countryside.[160]

The Focus on Hitler or the 'German Character'

In summer 1933, I had the opportunity to talk about Hitler with some relations of mine [. . .]. One of the persons present related that formerly she had often seen the house-painter in a Munich café, where for the price of a mark he let people spit at him in the face. She added that she never told this true story outside of our own circle, as in her view it was not an argument against the man. One of my friends, a Communist, then said: 'It is another argument against such a man. Against such a man, all arguments are good in my eyes.' That is also my view.

Bertolt Brecht, 'Essays on Fascism'

Just as he does in several émigré biographies, most famously in that by Konrad Heiden,[161] so Hitler frequently appears in literary works written in exile, or in historical essays, under the most varied of signs: a monster, a new Satan, a bloodthirsty imbecile, a mental case, a loser, or a mere puppet of big capital. The place ascribed to Hitler in the interpretation of National Socialism steadily decreases in the case of those authors close to Marxism. For the least political exiles, on the other hand, Hitler exercised a genuine fascination, and they sought varied and contradictory ways to grasp his personality as an explanation of the Nazi phenomenon.

The Diabolization of Hitler
While many described Nazism as a diabolical phenomenon, in several literary fictions Hitler himself appears as an archaic or devilish creature, an *Untermensch*, a prehistoric being, a false prophet. One of the most imaginative, Graf Keyserling, viewed Hitler in 1934 as a 'medium', a 'new prophet', a 'new Muhammad'[162] who had engendered in Germany a 'revolt of subterranean forces'. With the clairvoyance that marked his writings, Keyserling declared that Hitler was the leader of a movement of 'purification against a corrupt world', and Nazism 'the first non-imperialist movement in modern history'. In more realistic vein, Harry Kessler compared Hitler with a *Niebelungen* character leading Germany towards 'grandiose destruction', and embodying the supposed 'fundamental trait of the German nation, which has always been in love with death'.[163] The adjective 'diabolical' is used to refer to Hitler's sadism, his political acumen and his methods, by writers as different as Thomas Mann, Ernst Niekisch and Ernst Jünger.[164]

The image of the false prophet, the Pied Piper of Hamelin, recurs in Erich Kästner and Hermann Broch (*The Tempter*). And Joseph Roth saw Hitler in 1934 as an embodiment of the Antichrist:

[H]e has come in everyday habit, equipped even with all the signs of the lowly piety of the petit bourgeois, his innocent-seeming avarice, and the love, which he thinks sublime, for certain human ideals – as, for example, faithfulness unto death, patriotism, heroic readiness to sacrifice himself for the whole, chastity and virtue, reverence for the tradition of his fathers and of the past, reliance on the future, and respect for all the high-sounding phrases on which the average European is accustomed, and even constrained, to live.[165]

Hitler as Pathological Specimen

The explanation of Hitler as a pathological personality was common among the émigrés, even if only some of them made it an explanatory principle of Nazism. Thomas and Heinrich Mann both viewed Nazi demonstrations as 'epileptic fits'. Walter Mehring in *Die Nacht des Tyrannen* (inspired by Heiden's biography) described him as a sick victim of his frustrations. He was a mediocre barbarian, close to the caveman, scarcely able to speak an articulated human language, while his grimaces were those of an animal.[166] The Nazis also appeared as pathological criminals in Alfred Neumann's novel *Es waren ihrer sechs* (*There Were Six of Them*, Berlin 1948). Fritz von Unruh traced a grotesque portrait of Hitler in *Der nie verlor* (*Who Never Lost*, published 1948, written in 1940 and 1944): he was a perverse psychopath suspected of at least one crime in his youth, who kept in his desk drawer the ashes of the SA leaders he had killed. This vulgar creature made his generals drink champagne from his boot, and prided himself on embodying 'the spirit of evil' (*der Geist des Bösen*). In similar vein, Thomas Mann in 'Germany, My Suffering' called Hitler a 'wretch', 'impostor', 'hysterical', a 'hollow monster',[167] while the Nazis as a whole were an 'apocalyptic rabble' and 'inferior degenerates'. In Ernst Glaeser's novel *The Last Civilian*, Nazism is likewise described as an epidemic, and Hitler as a hysterical personality. More surprising, perhaps, the fine novel by Ernst Weiss, *Der Augenzeuge (The Eyewitness)*,[168] whose narrator is a doctor, describes Hitler as a morbid personality affected with hysterical blindness, a sickness contracted during the Great War – the narrator remembers treating him – which he risks communicating to the entire German people. Here the pathological dimension is elevated to something monstrous and fantastic.

Hitler as a Typical 'Loser'

The dictator's obscure and fairly wretched early years were broadly described already by his first biographers.[169] Many émigrés sought an explanation for Hitler's psychology in his defeats and frustrations. In his 1933 pamphlet *Hatred*, Heinrich Mann makes little difference between fascism and Bolshevism, and gives little sociological or political explanation of Nazism, but he does describe the movement as a gathering of 'imbeciles' and 'losers', 'greedy and criminal individuals'. He stressed that the majority of National Socialists, including Hitler himself, had never exercised any honest profession and did not know what it meant to work. They burned books that they would have been incapable of writing, and Mann reduced Nazi ideology to the expression of an almost pathological hatred against everything noble, to the sum of frustrations accumulated by shameless individuals. 'Criminals' and 'do-nothings' are words that frequently recur in Stefan Zweig, Thomas Mann and Klaus Mann, who all drew pitiable portraits of Hitler.[170] Nazism was called an 'imbeciles' vision of the world' (Niekisch), an 'unrestrained bestiality' (Bloch). In Feuchtwanger's *The Oppenheims*, the Nazis are described as failures and charlatans, and certain émigrés simply referred to Nazism as *Hitlerei*, seeing no more in it than the repugnant and pathological creation of a perverted and monstrous man.

Nazism and the 'German Character'
Finally, several authors – especially immediately after 1933, and again at the end of the War – were tempted to link National Socialism to the 'German character'. Far from representing a simple 'fall' into barbarism, a 'temporary regression to the pre-human', Nazism appeared to them as intrinsically tied up with German history, its fatal culmination. This style of interpretation was already present in Erich Kahler's book *Der deutsche Charakter in der Geschichte Europas*. He argued that a kind of 'hypertrophy of national character' in the collective psychology had led to Nazism. Fritz Jellinek, in *Die Krise der Bürger*, saw National Socialism as derived from a whole intellectual tradition, running from Luther through to Spengler. Thomas Mann also inclined towards this interpretation in his 1945 essays on Germany.[171] Here Mann, distressed like so many émigrés at there being no popular revolt against the Nazi regime, ended up lumping the German people together with Hitler. In his strange book *Doctor Faustus*, he seemed to view Germany as an irrational and maleficent entity inherently threatening European security. Far from being a perversion of German history and its intellectual tradition, National Socialism appeared as a kind of macabre apotheosis. Such propositions acquired the form of caricature in such Germanophobic journalists as William Shirer, and above all Lord Vansittart, who from 1941 onward ceaselessly expressed a hostility to Germany that refused to dissociate its people from Hitlerism. Such theses were violently attacked by Brecht, and by a number of Socialist exiles. Thomas Mann was certainly far removed from this position, but in scarcely perceptible degrees it is easy to pass from Emil Ludwig's positions to those of Vansittart. For Thomas Mann, it was a kind of conflict between irrationalism and democracy that had transformed the Germans into 'a people of romantic counter-revolution', and he saw 'original affinities between National Socialism and the German character'. Walter Mehring also approached this standpoint in his novel *Die Müller*, where he presented Nazism as the culmination of a kind of inability of the Germans to understand what freedom meant. Other writers insisted on the morbid passion of the Germans for obedience and discipline, and their 'mystique of death', to grasp how National Socialism had managed to graft itself on to the Germanic tradition.

Attempts at a Political Understanding of National Socialism

Attempts of this kind were naturally to be found in the most political authors, those who were influenced by Marxism in the Weimar era, or became politicized

in exile. Naturally, such political and economic analyses of the Nazi phenomenon broadly derived from their authors' political orientation. While Communists fairly faithfully held to the basic propositions of the Third International,
their analyses shifting with those of the Comintern, a number of other Marxists
often stressed very different factors, even if the majority of these have significant
similarities (the role of big capital, the bourgeoisie in crisis, the pauperization of
the masses, the despair of the middle classes, etc.). The major cleavage, aside
from the respective responsibility of the parties in Hitler's coming to power,
bears on the difficulty of articulating the economic and irrational factors that
many authors recognize in the rise and success of the Nazi movement.

The Significance of Irrational Factors
It was theorists as well as writers who stressed the irrational aspect of National
Socialism. Besides the risky extrapolations of those who saw Nazism as a cosmic
and 'telluric' movement (the disciples of Hermann von Keyserling), other
confused and obscure interpretations sought to explain it in terms of a mystique
of death, a nihilistic cult (Hermann Rauschning).[172] Thomas Mann saw in it the
derailment of an aspect of the German philosophic tradition of irrationalism.
Many other exiles also evoke this irrational aspect and its confused translation
into the political domain. Whilst the link that Mann established a posteriori
between hypnotism and fascism in *Mario and the Magician* is debatable, and
though his physical description of the magician is strangely reminiscent of
Hitler, Hermann Broch also depicted Hitler on several occasions in terms of
allegories such as the Pied Piper of Hamelin. *The Tempter* shows how a peaceful
Tyrolean village falls under the maleficent influence of a half-crazy vagabond,
who arouses the memory of a cult of blood and soil, and leads the inhabitants to
crime.[173] This irrational explanation of National Socialism also recurs in Ernst
Weiss's *The Eyewitness* and Feuchtwanger's *The Oppenheims*. Few Marxists, on
the other hand, were susceptible to this aspect of Nazism, apart from Ernst
Bloch and Walter Benjamin, who in their respective works *Heritage of Our
Times* and 'The Work of Art in the Age of Mechanical Reproduction',[174]
offered some remarkable analyses of this manipulation of dream, utopia and the
irrational by National Socialism: 'The position of the "Irratio" within the
inadequate capitalist "Ratio" has been all too abstractly cordoned off, instead
of its being examined from case to case [. . .]. That is why dogs and false
magicians were able to break into large, formerly socialist areas undisturbed.'[175]
Bloch stresses here the importance of the irrational factors at work in Nazi
propaganda, and the false utopias it managed to inspire, especially among the
youth. At the same time, Bloch criticized the overly mechanical interpretations
of fascism offered by the majority of Marxist theorists, deeming it essential to
understand why 'the petty bourgeois revolt only in a vague and misguided
sense'. It is notable that Bloch, along with Walter Benjamin – who wrote some
remarkable passages on the 'aestheticization of politics' by the Nazis – were
almost the only two Marxist writers to investigate this irrational dimension of
Nazism. Brecht only broached this question very reticently.[176]

The Crisis of the Middle Classes

The role of the middle classes in the development of National Socialism is emphasized by the majority of progressive writers, whether Marxist or not. Heinrich Mann depicted the fate of the impoverished masses in his booklet *Hatred*, and in *Heritage of Our Times* Ernst Bloch analysed various aspects of the ideology of the middle classes,[177] as Siegfried Kracauer also did in his study of *The Salaried Masses*.[178] Three other émigrés also investigated mass psychology: Elias Canetti, *Crowds and Power*; Hermann Broch, *Mass Psychology*, and Wilhelm Reich, *The Mass Psychology of Fascism*. The success of Hitler is ascribed to the demoralization and impoverishment of the petty bourgeoisie by Ernst Glaeser in *The Last Civilian*, and by Oskar Maria Graf in *The Abyss*. Walter Mehring, in *Die Müller*, shows through the far-flung story of a family, running from the Roman soldier Millesius press-ganged into the Roman legions, via his descendant likewise conscripted into the Prussian army, through to Dr Müller who is criticized for having a non-Aryan wife, how Nazism based itself on the tradition of passivity, spinelessness and submission to authority characteristic of *homo germanicus*, whose tragicomic saga is seen as the 'guiding thread of German history'. The Müllers served Hitler as they had served Rome and the later emperors, with the same arrivisme and stupidity, failing ever to even glimpse the meaning of freedom.[179] National Socialism thus appeared as the quintessence of the German character.

Economic Explanations of Nazism

It was not only the most political writers, Marxist or close to the KPD, who offered economic explanations of Nazism before 1933, but also journalists and essayists from very differing standpoints, such as Georg Bernhard and Leopold Schwarzschild. As a general rule, the majority of authors – of both right and left – agreed in recognizing the weakness of the Weimar Republic, and the dubious role this had played in the development of Nazism, even if they interpreted the collapse of German democracy in opposing ways. Hermann Rauschning saw it as the result of the transformation of nationalism into a 'revolutionary' movement (the NSDAP) and the replacement of Brüning by von Papen.[180] Georg Bernhard made Brüning responsible for this collapse, and argued that the entire Republic was a 'democracy *manquée*'.[181] Heinrich Mann declared: 'The Republic was doomed to succumb, having left every liberty to its enemies and taken none for itself. It had the masses behind it, and could have kept them by a mere assertion of its will.'[182]

More pessimistically, Brecht noted:

The Weimar Republic fell victim to the contradictions between the dismantling of its military potential and the development of its rationalized heavy industry, which by virtue of the conditions resulting from the world domination of capitalism, could only be rescued and used in the drive to war. It accordingly prepared for war by building up this industry. The peace policy imposed by the military victory of the other capitalist states was only considered as a lack of policy.[183]

These analyses of the mistakes of the Republic and the left forces, so well described by Tucholsky and Ossietzky,[184] recur in the majority of exile novels, with blame ascribed differently according to whether the writers are Socialist, Communist, liberal or conservative.[185] Whilst disagreement was rife as to the burden of responsibility (whether individual politicians such as Brüning or von Papen were to blame, or parties such as the SPD or KPD), the question of the link between Nazism and the German tradition was an equally complex one to face.

Was National Socialism a typically German phenomenon? Thomas Mann hesitated to say so, recalling that Hitler was 'a non-German of mean extraction'. In the same vein, the philosopher Ernst Cassirer declared in the United States: 'This Hitler is an error of history. He does not belong in German history at all.'[186] In 1933 Heinrich Mann denounced Nazism as a typically Austrian phenomenon: 'The German Republic had too many Austrians, which is one of the reasons for its fall. They entered the political parties, the press and business, dissolving everything by their innate tendencies of conformism and cleverness indifferent to all principles, if not to honesty [. . .]. The great man of Austrian origin seized hold of Germany in the same way as his compeers, even if he excelled them in his ambition.'[187]

For many left-wing émigrés, on the other hand – Walter Mehring, W. A. Berendsohn, Anna Siemsen – National Socialism was a typically Prussian phenomenon, though a certain number of right-wing authors viewed the Prussian element as a restraint on Nazi excesses. Few essays or novels by Socialist authors defend the tactics of the SPD, but writers close to the KPD frequently denounce it in rather schematic terms. In a preface to Hans Beimler's booklet, *Dachau*, F. Heckert wrote that 'Social-Democracy, cowardly, pitiful and treacherous, had weakened the German working class to the point that a band of capitalist pimps and scoundrels were able to establish their own bloody tyranny in the workers' land of Germany.'[188] The theory of social-fascism, which raged in the Communist press until the start of the *Volksfront*, was illustrated in a number of novels. If Ernst Glaeser traced the disappointment of the whole German left in *The Last Civilian*, F. C. Weiskopf made the SPD's policy directly responsible for Hitler's rise to power in his novel *Lissy, on Temptation* (1937). Oskar Maria Graf, in *The Abyss*, accused the SPD of having sabotaged the united front. In *Unsere Strasse*, however, Jan Petersen, though a proletarian writer, gave a more nuanced and objective picture of the left parties' policies.

Many authors sought to show how National Socialism was directly bound up with capitalism in crisis. They often criticized fellow émigrés for abstractly denouncing the Nazi regime without understanding what it was based upon. In an article in *Deutsche Blätter*, 'Wir wollen deutsch reden' (September 1933), Wieland Herzfelde wrote:

> It goes without saying that coherence among antifascist writers is still problematic. Many see fascism as an anachronism, an intermezzo, a return to medieval barbarism. Others talk of a sickness of the German spirit, or an anomaly contradicting the

'normal' course of historical development. They curse the Nazis as a horde of losers who have brusquely descended on the country. We, on the contrary, do not see fascism as an accident, but as the organic product of moribund capitalism.

Brecht expresses himself similarly in 'Five Difficulties in Writing the Truth', where he declares that 'fascism can only be combated as the most shameless, impudent, oppressive and lying form of capitalism'.[189] Fascism cannot be denounced without criticizing property relations, on pain of falling into hypocrisy.[190] In his 'Essays on Fascism', written between 1933 and 1939, he again maintains: 'Any proclamation against fascism which refrains from dealing with the social relations from which this arose as a natural necessity is lacking in sincerity. Those who do not want to give up the private ownership of the means of production, far from getting rid of fascism, have need of its services.'[191]

Of all the analyses of fascism offered by the émigrés, Brecht's count among the most interesting, and have lost none of their pertinence. He analyses with precision the mechanisms of Nazi ideology, how it was able to rally the petty bourgeoisie and even a section of the proletariat, and he avoids both abstract humanist protestation against Nazi barbarity and the facile schematism of Communist orthodoxy. Brecht also succeeded in his sinister and grotesque transposition of Hitler's rise to power in *The Resistible Rise of Arturo Ui*, in which all the protagonists of the time find a place (Hindenburg, Hitler, Goebbels, Göring, Röhm), along with the main events that marked Germany and Europe from 1933 to 1938. Arturo Ui is simply a megalomaniac gangster who takes over a cauliflower cartel by criminal means. It is an impressive play, even if in artistic terms somewhat abstract, and far from achieving the depth and irony of *The Threepenny Opera* with its link between the police chief Tiger Brown and the underworld boss Mackie Messer, despite the cartoons between the scenes that recall the different historical events treated symbolically on stage. Chaplin's *The Great Dictator* and Ernst Lubitsch's *To Be or Not to Be* also spring to mind. The transposition of Nazism into a gangster tale[192] enables certain connections between National Socialism and heavy industry to be represented, but certainly not the full reality of Hitler's support and the reasons for his success.

With *Arturo Ui* we reach a second kind of abstraction, which threatens certain representations of Hitler in exile literature. While the less political émigrés depicted him as a demonic character and failed to analyse the economic aspect of National Socialism, a number of Communist and Marxist writers made Hitler into such an abstract 'puppet of capitalism and heavy industry' that one might well ask how such a mediocre and insignificant figure managed to win over a large section of Germany – unless one considered, like Heinrich Mann, that the workers, Jews, intellectuals, churches, a large section of the bourgeoisie, the aristocracy and many industrialists were all in opposition. In which case, it was possible to imagine the collapse of the regime as constantly imminent, since in theory it rested only on itself.

These examples suffice to show the perplexity even of eyewitnesses in the face of Hitler's rise to power, the difficulty they experienced in grasping its mechanisms, the often contradictory analyses that they offered, and the accent that in many works was placed on certain partial aspects of National Socialism: Hitler's personality for Ernst Weiss, anti-Semitism as the essence of Nazism for Feuchtwanger.

Furthermore, the development of a theory of fascism, whether before 1933 or into the 1940s, came up against a number of obstacles. In 1945, everyone was aware that Nazism had marked the face of the world and overturned the entire global balance. An interpretation of the phenomenon was urgent and legitimate, and people were only too familiar with it. In 1933, however, there was a preliminary obstacle to overcome, even for Marxists: could one really discuss something so low? Bloch's tone in referring to Nazism attests to a mixture of horror, contempt and irony. Tucholsky sometimes seems to view the mediocrity of fascism as not worth dwelling on. Orthodox Marxists were tempted to see it simply as the aggravation of a reactionary policy, and failed to see its specific characteristics. Overall interpretations of Nazi ideology were thus fairly uncommon. The most famous in the 1930s was that of Hans Günther, a KPD member and refugee in the USSR since 1932, whose 1935 book *Der Herren eigner Geist: Die Ideologie des Nationalsozialismus* refuted the argument according to which the mediocrity of Nazism did not merit a long theoretical analysis. Far from seeing Nazism as the 'revenge of failures' or a kind of 'German atavism', Günther sought to grasp the logic of its appearance on the basis of mechanisms of capitalist ideology, whilst still recognizing its specific character. He was at any rate one of the first to investigate the function of myth and the irrational in National Socialism, and his approach – very different from that of Ernst Bloch, whom he took issue with in reviewing *Heritage of Our Times* for *Internationale Literatur* in 1936 – was certainly one of the most interesting contributions to the Marxist analysis of fascism in the 1930s, just as Franz Neumann's *Behemoth* would be ten years later.

Finally, we should note the existence of a number of 'right-wing' interpretations of National Socialism. One of the most well-known was that of Hermann Rauschning, *The Revolution of Nihilism*, which sought to disassociate Nazism from conservatism: for Rauschning, National Socialism was a revolutionary movement opposed to conservatism, 'devoid of principles and lacking a programme geared towards action'. Its 'unrestrained nihilism' had only adopted the mask of a national revolution. He thus viewed Nazism as a revolutionary movement of a socialist type, not necessarily far removed from Bolshevism, but having managed to 'shake off the Marxist scaffolding'. Rauschning's essay contained a number of sharp insights into National Socialism, especially his assertion of the immense danger it represented, able to afflict all Europe with blood and fire. At the same time, however, he was unable to make clear what the infrastructure of Nazism rested upon, and how such a destructive and nihilistic movement had managed to come legally to power.

It was only at the end of the War, and chiefly in the United States, that the first reflections on 'totalitarianism' started to develop. We should recall however that a number of émigrés were involved in these, including Leopold

Schwarzschild, whose anti-Communism had been exacerbated by the German–Soviet pact.

Everyday Life in Nazi Germany

We cannot deny the fact that the face of Germany, our homeland, has become in recent years a source of horror for the world, even the bourgeois world.

Brecht, 'Essays on Fascism'

Though it is from works published after the War, rather than those of the exiles, that everyday life under the Third Reich can be best understood, many of the émigrés already sought to represent this. It was only a rare few, however, such as Jan Petersen, Willi Bredel and Ödön von Horvath, who had first-hand knowledge of Germany after 1933. The majority of writers were forced to gather information from the papers, both those from the Reich and those of the exiles, enriched by scattered accounts from oppositionists who remained in Germany. To the degree that such contacts were broken off, and the German economy strengthened, it became increasingly hard for them to imagine the reality of Nazi Germany, and the separation between those who left for exile and those who remained sometimes became insurmountable. Apart from Petersen's *Unsere Strasse*, and Horvath's *Youth Without God*, the greater part of works depicting the reality of Hitlerite Germany were pure products of the imagination, even if the barbarism and terror were described and analysed with considerable verisimilitude by a number of authors. Thomas Mann, in 'Germany, My Suffering', evokes the enslavement of cultural life and its mediocrity.[193] Jan Petersen depicts the terror in the Berlin streets after 1933 and the sadism of the SA. Anti-Semitism and racism are the themes more commonly depicted: the anti-Semitism[194] rampant among the upper classes (Friedrich Wolf's *Professor Mamlok*), in a simple school (Horvath's *Youth Without God*), or at everyday level in Feuchtwanger's novel *The Oppenheims*,[195] the chronicle of a Jewish family in 1932–33. The macabre reality of the concentration camps is described in the essays of Wolfgang Langhoff, Gerhart Seger, and above all Willi Bredel's *The Test*.

The general climate of the years following the Nazi seizure of power lies at the heart of Irmgard Keun's 1937 novel *After Midnight*, which shows the despair of people who have contempt for Hitler but still cannot decide on exile. The very dark colours of all these novels corresponded far more to the hopes of the émigrés than to reality. It is clear for example that the economic recovery of Germany was generally underestimated in the exile novels. Unable to imagine that Hitler, with his incoherent programme, could steer Germany out of a crisis that no one before him had managed to alleviate, the émigrés generally imagined Nazi Germany as economically wretched and verging on famine. Feuchtwanger in *The Oppenheims* describes people in real economic distress, and Wolf depicted popular despair in the face of the growing deterioration of living conditions in *Zwei an der Grenze* (*Two at the Border*). Like Heinrich Mann, they anticipated that a powerful movement of internal resistance would result from this.

If we compare these exile novels with eyewitness reports given after the war, we have to recognize that it was undoubtedly Brecht's short sketches in *Fear and Misery of the Third Reich*[196] that, by the precision of the situations portrayed, the cold objectivity of their description, and the different beams of light cast on everyday life under the Nazis, with its climate of fear, hatred and generalized distrust, offered the most accurate evocation of lived experience in Hitler's Germany.

Images of Clandestine Resistance

Both in their novels and in the press, the exiles tended always to exaggerate German resistance: its scale, significance and effectiveness. We have already indicated how Heinrich Mann depicted it as ready to leap at Hitler's throat as working-class anger intensified.[197] The 'information' he cites seems so precise that the reader ends up believing it is genuine. The Germany of *The Oppenheims* is racked by general discontent, and the SA are ready to rally to working-class resistance. The famous novel by Karl Wolfskehl, *Beim Flucht erschossen* (*Shot While Trying to Escape*), shows the development of an SA man killed in rescuing a concentration-camp detainee. Klaus Mann, through the character Angel in *The Volcano*, asserts that there is a broad opposition movement to Hitler in Germany, the 'internal emigration'. And though Feuchtwanger does not directly depict this in his novel *Exile*, several of its representatives make an appearance. With a few exceptions, however, the émigrés had no knowledge of this resistance apart from what they read in the papers, and thanks to clandestine 'couriers' who informed them of the situation in the Reich. Only Willi Bredel and Jan Petersen had first-hand knowledge, and it is their novels, *The Test* and *Our Street* (*Unsere Strasse. Ein Chronik geschrieben im Herzen des faschistischen Deutchlands 1933–1936*), that alone draw on lived experience. Petersen described the struggle of Communists in the working-class district of Charlottenburg. A number of historical events recur: the arrest of militants, the Reichstag fire trial, the murder of Erich Mühsam. But he too overestimated the importance of this underground resistance, and believed like many of the émigrés in an imminent uprising against Hitler.

In the same realist style, Heinz Liepmann's novel *. . . wird mit dem Tode bestraft* (*. . . Is Condemned to Death*, 1935) depicts Communist resistance in Hamburg, the arrest of Edgar André and the bringing to heel of the trade unions. The action takes place at the time of the Reichstag fire, and focuses on the reconstruction of the underground Communist apparatus. Its originality lies in that it presents both Communist resistance and that of the Young Socialists, something fairly rare with other writers close or belonging to the KPD. Willi Bredel depicted the treatment inflicted on opponents in the concentration camps (*The Test*), and in *Dein unbekannter Bruder* (*Your Unknown Brother*, 1937) he described the fate of a young Communist, released from concentration camp, who returned to underground struggle. Bredel too still believed in the possibility of a workers' revolt that would topple Hitler.

Far more interesting among the novels describing underground resistance is Anna Seghers's *The Seventh Cross*, written in 1937–38, which deserves particular attention here. Through a tale of the escape of seven prisoners of whom six are murdered by the Gestapo or sent back to the camp, she describes admirably the terror prevailing in Germany, the difficulties of resisting it, and yet – symbolized by the successful escape of one of the seven – the certainty that night will not be eternal. While some antifascist novels fall into schematism, Anna Seghers succeeds in maintaining the steady dramatic intensity that makes this book a masterpiece. Beyond the success or failure of these men in flight from the concentration-camp hell, she raises the question whether Nazism can be conquered.[198] In her novel, the description of Germany and the balance of forces there leaves room for surges of courage and fraternity, as well as for opportunism and cowardice. Many individuals portrayed in it are neither fanatical Nazis nor oppositionists. They suffer the terror inflicted on others, but do not rise up against it. The spectacle of horror sometimes arouses heroism in them, but also fear. Even in her portraits of Nazis, nothing is overdone. The Gestapo officials themselves are more commonly mediocre bureaucrats than sadists. The resisters are not abstract figures but men prey to doubt, disoriented, aware of the limits of their actions; and Seghers displays none of the historical optimism of Petersen and Bredel: the core of the underground resistance has already been destroyed by the Gestapo. The resistance she describes is not a broad popular movement, but the act of a few isolated individuals vainly trying to remake broken connections, whose struggle is evoked without any illusion.[199]

The Communist resistance was presented with far greater realism in exile novels after 1936. Though few works matched the beauty of *The Seventh Cross*, Bruno Frank in *The Passport* (1937) depicted the opposition of an anti-Nazi prince, forced to leave Germany for his involvement in a monarchist organization. But this opposition to Nazism is not shown as anything more than individual, and does not claim to give any portrait of German conditions. It does not offer a clearly defined political perspective. Irmgard Keun's *After Midnight* is more an evocation of the impossibility of life under Nazism for a section of young people than a depiction of resistance. Their revolt against the Nazi system is desperate but leads only to suicide and death. Disgust has the upper hand over political awareness, and there is no room for any hope.

Arnold Zweig, in *Das Beil von Wandsbek* (*The Axe of Wandsbek*, 1943, set in 1937–38), depicts against a background of trials in preparation for Communist militants, the attitude of a section of the German petty bourgeoisie who had believed in the NSDAP programme and gradually discovered its absurd and bloody character. A number of resisters appear in the novel, belonging to very varied milieus, working-class or Christian (the Bekenntniskirche).[200] The execution of Munich students belonging to Die Weisse Rose gave the theme for Alfred Neumann's novel *There Were Six of Them* (1948), written in 1943–44 on the basis of articles that had appeared in the British press. Eventually the depiction of German resistance ceases to serve any political purpose and becomes simply the setting for a novel, as in Vicki Baum's *Hier stand ein Hotel*

(1947), also remotely inspired by Die Weisse Rose. Finally, some émigrés described a different kind of resistance, desertion: F. C. Weiskopf's *Himmels-fahrs Kommando* (Stockholm, 1945) is the story of a soldier who abandons the eastern front. This theme also became steadily more vague, and merged with the depictions of writers such as Alfred Andersch, who described in *Winter Coat* the demoralization of German officers at the end of the War.

The Relationship of the Émigrés to Germany and the Meaning of Antifascist Struggle

By its dynamic character, its unusual and painful experiences, exile provided very many of the émigrés with abundant literary material. Because it meant a brutal rupture in their existence, making them actors and privileged witnesses of European events, they were aware of the universal dimension that their most intimate testimonies acquired. The novels of exile are often confused with their autobiographies, as they transposed lived experience: departure from Germany in Heinz Liepmann's *Das Vaterland* (1933), Konrad Merz's *Ein Mensch fällt aus Deutschland* (1936), the Reichstag fire, the occupation of France and escape to America (Anna Seghers's *Transit*), everyday life in exile through to the war (Feuchtwanger's *Exile*, Klaus Mann's *The Volcano* of 1939). At the same time they sought to grasp the meaning of this exile and retrace its history. This constant association of the most personal and everyday experience with a historical dimension that borders on the epic, gives all these works a profile that is all more striking in that their authors wrote at such little distance from the events.

Among so many works, Klaus Mann's are among the most moving. *Flight North* (1934) depicts the fate of a young German woman of bourgeois origin who had rallied to the anti-Nazi resistance and was forced into exile in Finland. *The Pathetic Symphony* (1935) presented Tchaikovsky as an exile, not for political reasons but because he could not feel at home anywhere and died alone. *Mephisto* (1936) portrayed, in the person of an actor who was gifted but devoid of moral sense – inspired by Gustaf Gründgens[201] – those who made their peace with Hitler's Germany, refusing exile so as not to interrupt their career, and who, in Hermann Kesten's expression, had 'licked blood'.[202] *The Volcano*, in its scope and emotion, is undoubtedly the greatest antifascist novel of exile. By way of characters that are sometimes a little abstract, Klaus Mann managed to evoke the multifarious sufferings of the exiles, the hopes and disappointments of each day, in the years leading up to the Second World War.[203] The majority of its characters were inspired by real individuals. Thomas Mann is recognizable, along with Erika Mann, Martin Gumpert, and René Crevel. Through a rather surprising construction, a richness of materials and events that seem constantly on the verge of drowning the author, Klaus Mann managed to depict the life of émigrés in Paris and other capitals, and their developing struggles through to the Spanish war. And to overcome the problem of retracing the life of exiles scattered all over Europe, he uses the strange figure of the 'Angel of emigration' who protects them and records their last breath, carrying them off through the skies to show them their various destinies and revealing the meaning of these.

Lion Feuchtwanger's *Exile* (1939), better constructed perhaps than *The Volcano*, but less moving, also transposes real events – the Nazis' kidnapping of the pacifist journalist Berthold Jacob, their purchase of the Saarland newspaper *Westland*, and the Abyssinian war. Likewise using events common to the majority of exiles, he affirms a certain optimism in their 'spiritual battle', symbolized by the émigré press. The birth of the Popular Front is described here from a perspective closer to Communism than that of Klaus Mann. In *Two at the Border* (Moscow 1939), Friedrich Wolf relates the fate of a Communist worker suspected of killing an SA man, who has to flee to Czechoslovakia. Finally, many works presented as autobiographies also depict the struggle of fellow émigrés. Anna Seghers's *Transit* traces the suicide of Ernst Weiss, the desperate efforts of émigrés to leave France in 1940, without a boat or a visa, having every day to confront police harassment and avoid arrest. Hans Sahl's *The Few and the Many* (written between 1933 and 1936) evokes the emigrant milieu in Prague, Amsterdam and Paris at the moment of the outbreak of War, followed by exile in America.

Though many of the émigré novels can only be read today as documents on the exile, it is undeniable that they also include the finest works of German literature of the 1930s and 1940s. Anna Seghers's *The Seventh Cross* can be read time and again with the same emotion.

Antifascist Theatre in Exile

THE DESTRUCTION OF GERMAN THEATRE

The Weimar Republic marked the high point of German theatre. With the decline of naturalism, the development of expressionism, the experiments of Max Reinhardt and Leopold Jessner, the appearance of various forms of proletarian theatre from agitprop to the productions of the Volksbühne, and finally the birth of the epic and documentary theatre of Piscator and Brecht, Berlin became the capital of the European stage.[1] The wealth of its repertoire (consider only the works of Toller, Georg Kaiser, Carl Sternheim, Ödön von Horvath and Brecht), the beauty and novelty of its productions – from the magic of Reinhardt's lighting to the radicalism of Piscator's experiments – the importance of the plays created at this time, made Germany the country where the greatest chapter in the history of modern theatre was written. The reasons for this apogee were varied. It is partly explained by the exceptional concentration of talent that was found in Berlin, the importance of the theatre in the cultural life of the time, but also by the frequent concern to make the stage into a political platform, a means of social denunciation and criticism.[2] Following the scandal of Wedekind, few plays aroused as much argument as the early expressionist works (Toller, Hasenclever, Unruh, Kaiser, Sternheim) or the productions of Piscator, all of which appeared to present a challenge to the whole existing culture. Jews, Socialists, Communists, pacifists and progressives, the majority of figures prominent on German stage aroused the hatred and disgust of the Nazis, who begun to target this revolutionary theatre already in the 1920s.[3]

In the final years of the Weimar Republic, a large number of progressive works were either banned or violently disrupted by the SA. In 1929 the Nazis attacked Max Reinhardt, in charge of the Munich festival, as a Jew (his original name was Goldmann).[4] Jessner was attacked for his Socialist convictions and his 'absolutely un-German' productions. He was accused of having staged Schiller's *The Robbers* 'with Spartacist sauce', and Wagner's *Ring* cycle in cubist style. Piscator was regularly insulted by the Nazi press, as were Toller and

Brecht – many of whose works, such as *Mahagonny*, being interrupted by SA detachments, who had little time for his political convictions or Kurt Weill's typically 'Jewish and Negroid' music. Jewish or political actors symbolized for the Nazis the decadence of the German stage. Ernst Josef Aufricht, the producer of the *Dreigroschenoper* and director of the theatre Am Schiffbauerdam, who had staged plays by Brecht, Horvath and Mariluise Fleisser, was termed a 'red director' by the Nazis and could only stage his last productions by agreeing to pay money to the SS, who resorted to this kind of racket against Jewish directors.[5] Fritz Kortner, in his autobiography *Aller Tage Abend*, described better than anyone else the various vexations and slanders he had to put up with before deciding to go into exile.

Hitler's seizure of power immediately brought a freeze to the German stage, the rapid annihilation of its achievements and the exile of its representatives.[6] The decision to emigrate was doubtless more difficult for many actors to take than it was for writers: they generally had no chance of recommencing their careers abroad, and did not exist outside the German public and German language. This was why a number of actors, often prestigious ones, remained in the Reich, without defending the regime, as long as they did not feel directly threatened, being neither political nor Jewish. Some of these no doubt sincerely believed they would be able to maintain a certain tradition of German theatre. If Klaus Mann's *Mephisto* offers a typical portrait of such actors, and views them as objectively guilty of complicity with the Nazis, many other émigrés were less severe and refused to see them as genuine Nazi sympathizers.[7] It may be unjust to see *Mephisto* as a straightforward depiction of Gründgens,[8] but the novel remains all the same a fairly realistic depiction of German theatre after 1933, and the disarray that took hold of many of its representatives. In seeking to create a 'type', however, Klaus Mann often dispensed with nuance, and the refusal of Gründgens, Emil Jannings, H. George, W. Krauss, H. Paulsen, R. Forster or Bernhard Minetti to emigrate cannot be considered as illustrating the same attitude in each case. While George and Jannings compromised themselves severely with the Nazi regime, by agreeing to be official celebrities, Gründgens and Minetti kept their distance and tried to come to the aid of those far less favoured.[9] Bernhard Minetti, one of the most prestigious actors in contemporary German theatre, wrote: 'Why then didn't I emigrate? [. . .] I believe it was because I speak German and wanted to continue on the stage.'[10] It is true that this response could be given by many actors, who were unable to decide on exile and were led to make more or less serious compromises in order to continue their careers.[11]

Immediately after their seizure of power, the Nazis expelled from the theatres all who were known for their progressive ideas. They drove Jews off the stage and divided actors into different categories in terms of their attitudes towards Nazi ideology.[12] Progressive plays and Jewish authors were banned, and efforts were made to impose a new repertory. To fill the gap left by this destruction, the National Socialist government took over a number of Berlin theatres: the Theater des Westen became a 'people's opera', the Friedrichstrasse a 'peasant theatre', while Piscator's old theatre, Am Nollendorfplatz, served in 1934–35 as a 'National Socialist popular theatre'. The stupidity of the plays staged there,[13] the wretchedness and propaganda saturation of this 'new' theatre, condemned it to failure. As for the *'Thing Theater'*, a theatre of National Socialist agitation with aspects equally of the fairground, the *comedia del arte* and medieval mystery plays, this collapsed after 1935 despite the immense resources spent on it – its plays sometimes counting 20,000 characters. The National Socialist repertory subsequently sunk into the utmost mediocrity – as witness the plays of Hanns Johst, the falsification of the classics,[14] the exaltation of 'peasant' values – or it fell back on the operetta genre.

THE ROLE OF THEATRE
IN THE ANTIFASCIST STRUGGLE

The renaissance of German theatre in exile did not just express the desire of so many actors and directors to continue their art, but the concern to make theatre into a weapon against National Socialism. Study of the exile theatre's production techniques and repertory shows that, in its diversity, it succeeded both in continuing a number of currents and experiments of the Weimar years, and in creating new linkages between theatre and actuality.

Militant Antifascist Theatre

If the struggle against National Socialism occupied a large place in émigré theatre, for instance with the plays of Friedrich Wolf and Bertolt Brecht, it did not proceed from a single conception of the relationship between theatre and politics.[15] A first tendency seemed to prolong the agitation theatre style of the Weimar era (*Zeitstück, Aktionsdrama*). The heir of agitprop and the proletarian style of Wangenheim and Piscator, this theatre sought to produce an immediate effect on the audience on the basis of current themes. It contained a strong emotional dimension, a call to mobilization. It sought to provoke the audience to react against what it denounced. Realistic to the utmost degree, it dispensed with allegory, and was often more akin to a propaganda meeting.[16] Most commonly, it tried to bring about an awareness of the Nazi danger, and exhorted European countries to oppose Hitler. Its themes were inspired by recent political events: the year 1933, the Reichstag fire, the arrest of opponents, the crushing of the trade unions, the invasion of Austria, Czechoslovakia and Poland. Friedrich Wolf depicted the crushing of the Austrian Schutzbund in *Floridsdorf*, anti-Semitism in *Professor Mamlok*, and the infiltration of Nazi organizations by Communists in *The Trojan Horse*. Theodor Fanta portrayed youth under Nazism in *The Children of the Unknown Soldier*, Bruno Frank depicted *Kristallnacht* in *Strength Through Fire*, Brecht the Spanish war in *Señora Carrar's Rifles*, Carl Zuckmayer the opposition within Nazism in *The Devil's General*, T. T. Csokor the struggle of the Yugoslav patriots in *The Lost Son*.

Those artists who had worked in agitprop before 1933 also continued this style in exile: Gustav von Wangenheim wrote *Agents* and *Cellar Heroes*, which depicted the crimes of the SA, Ernst Toller depicted the struggle against National Socialism in the church in *Pastor Hall*, P. M. Lampel portrayed Berlin at the moment of capitulation, and F. Bruckner the resistance in *Patriots*.

Avant-Garde Theatre in Exile

The Weimar Republic had seen the development alongside this political or agitation theatre of a large number of avant-garde experiments (expressionist theatre, influence of the Bauhaus, etc.) and new techniques (Reinhardt, Jessner, Piscator, Brecht). The majority of these experiments disappeared in exile,[17] or could not be staged anywhere, not even in the USSR.[18] Most of these attempts seem 'formalist' in the light of the discredit that Meyerhold experienced, the attacks on expressionism, and the rehabilitation of Stanislavsky's theories. The classics were systematically privileged, as well as the realist style represented by Friedrich Wolf and agitprop. Exile thus saw the disappearance of a number of theatrical experiments, while others again lost their radicalism.[19] Yet some of the best works of Brecht were written in exile – *Mother Courage, The Good Person of Szechwan, The Life of Galileo, Mr Puntila and His Man Matti* – plays that cannot simply be dismissed as 'political'. A less challenging relationship to the classics can also be discerned.

A number of émigré works seemed to continue the style of the Weimar era: for instance, Bruckner's *The Races*, and Brecht's *Round Heads and Pointed Heads* with its similar theme. The same distance from everyday politics is also found in J. R. Becher's play *The Road to Füssen*, where the action takes place in front of three backdrops showing Hitler in front of the burning Reichstag, a tank factory, and a frozen soldier on the Russian steppes. In formal terms, this drama attained a certain classicism, far removed from both agitprop and socialist realism. The same procedures of transposition are to be found in Brecht's *Arturo Ui* of 1941, which achieved an astounding balance between allegory and the narration of events.

The Moral Requirement

If morality played a major role in Piscator's theatre after the Second World War ('confession theatre'), as well as in the productions of Hochhuth, Peter Weiss, and Heinard Kipphardt, it is also to be found in the exile plays of a large number of writers of bourgeois origin, who championed the 'militant humanism' dear to Thomas Mann. These works often depict fascism, but in a fairly abstract manner, as illustrating the eternal struggle between good and evil. This problematic is typical of certain plays by Georg Kaiser written after 1933 (*Napoleon in New Orleans*, 1937–41, and *The Raft of the Medusa*, 1940–43). As opposed to Brecht's allegories, those of Kaiser do not have a specific reference, but rather indicate an eternal confrontation of values or an utter despair.[20] Rudolf Leonhard wrote his play *Hostages* in the Vernet camp in France in 1941, inspired by the death of ten French hostages shot by the Gestapo. Works such as F. Hochwälder's *The Refugee* also use the historical backdrop only to raise moral problems, and if the setting of Horvath's play *Pompei* (1937) depicts the proximity of the volcano, it is hard to describe it as an antifascist work; it is simply the depiction of a world that is cold and loveless. The same escape into fiction is found in Walter Hasenclever's *Münchhausen*, the tale of the love of a man in his seventies for a young girl of seventeen. These works are not specifically antifascist, even if they were written in exile.

Comedy

The response of the satirist Karl Kraus when he was asked what he had to say about Hitler is well known: 'absolutely nothing'. The man who had lambasted the failings of Viennese society found nothing to say about Hitler as he inspired only horror and disgust. Brecht later maintained: 'When the era died of its own hand, he was that hand.'[21] As for Tucholsky, he asserted long before he was forced into exile: 'Satire has an upper limit: Buddha escapes it. It also has a lower limit: in the Germany for example the fascist forces. It's just not worth it, you can't look so low.'[22] With its bloody bestiality, Nazism made it hard to joke, and the rare satirical works it elicited were generally restricted to the person of Hitler.[23] Even Walter Benjamin reproached Ernst Bloch for speaking of the Third Reich in too sumptuous a style in his *Heritage of Our Times*.[24] Only the glacial realism of Brecht's *Fear and Misery of the Third Reich*, or the macabre humour of Ödön von Horvath, who in his *Tales of the Vienna Woods* depicted a good woman coming to the King of the Magicians to buy two boxes of soldiers for her little boy – one box of dead ones, the other of mortally wounded – seemed able to depict the reality of the time. Thus there were very few comedies on the subject of the Third Reich. The plays that Horvath wrote in exile did not have a direct bearing on Nazism:[25] in any case they could never have been staged in Vienna.[26] Only Brecht wrote in exile political comedies such as *Puntila*. Works like Hasenclever's *Ehekömedie (Marital Comedy)*, Gustav von Wangenheim's *He Still Doesn't Know*, even Bruckner's *Napoleon the First*, resemble other comedies and have no direct connection with the exile situation. This style often corresponds to a desperate effort to rediscover an audience, and the rare works that sought to analyse contemporary political errors – such as Ernst Toller's *No More Peace!* – bordered on both farce and grand guignol. One comedy written by an émigré, however, became a Broadway success: Franz Werfel's *Jacobowsky and the Colonel*, its action taking place in France in 1940.

The Social-Realist Style

A number of plays written by émigrés can be grouped under this heading, most of these writers being refugees in the USSR. Without always sharing the same style, they developed a political and aesthetic vision that was broadly similar. Almost all illustrated political themes taken from the struggle of the proletariat against fascism and the role of the Communist party. Significant in their political impact, they disappeared from theatres after the Second World War and are now found only in collections of antifascist works. The most representative authors of this style were Julius Hay,[27] Gustav von Wangen-heim,[28] J. R. Becher and Friedrich Wolf.[29]

Revival of the Classical Heritage

Since they were banned or disfigured by the Nazis, embodying as they did the old democratic ideal, the classics were often newly presented by émigré authors, as both a denunciation of National Socialism and as rescuing the German cultural heritage. This presupposed a far-reaching evolution on the part of a number of avant-garde or Communist writers in relation to their inheritance, and their recognition of the positive character of a certain 'bourgeois' tradition. This defence of the classics had two main aspects. One was to stage works banned in Germany (Lessing) or distorted into proto-Nazi manifestos (Goethe, Schiller), the other to make this classical idea of justice and humanity a means of propaganda against Hitler. There was nothing surprising, therefore, if Schiller was so often staged by the émigrés, in reaction to the Reich's *Schiller in a Brown Shirt*. Even the proletarian émigré companies of the Volga Republic offered their peasant audience classical works. New voices could be heard through old themes: in the United States, Piscator staged Shakespeare plays in his epic style; Brecht presented *Antigone* as an antifascist work after the War; even Eisler took up the theme of *Faust*. This appeal to the classics, however, did not imply agreement on theoretical positions, as shown by Lukács's famous polemic against Eisler and Ernst Bloch.[30]

The Difficult Rebirth of German Theatre in Exile

The rebirth of a German theatre in exile presented countless difficulties, despite the efforts of actors and directors expelled from Germany. Some of these certainly enjoyed an international fame: Max Reinhardt's productions had been admired across the world, Piscator's theories discussed in both the Soviet Union and the United States, but these were rare exceptions. While Ernst Toller was considered the greatest playwright of the Weimar Republic and enjoyed a real celebrity abroad, Brecht remained little known despite the success of *The Threepenny Opera*.

The first obstacle encountered was of course that of language: the most prestigious German actors had no presence outside the German-language zone, and neither Fritz Kortner nor Max Pallenberg, Alexander Granach nor Carola Neher, had the slightest chance of continuing their career in exile. Though the German repertoire did have an audience in Czechoslovakia, Switzerland and Austria, in the majority of other countries it only interested a minority of specialists, and very few foreign theatres would take the risk of staging German plays. Moreover, those countries where there was a German population feared the reactions of the Reich to such antifascist productions, as well as the no less violent reactions of Nazi sympathizers (Switzerland, Czechoslovakia, Austria and the Netherlands). Other countries such as Britain and France felt little affected by these plays.

A further factor was that most European countries were in the throes of an economic crisis that had its effects on culture as well. Often in poor circumstances, foreign theatres had little to offer the émigrés. Yet despite all these difficulties, exile theatre remains one of the most astonishing artistic experiments of the 1930s and 40s.[31] The demarcation of the term 'exile theatre' is not easy, and cannot simply be equated with that of 'antifascist theatre'. One would hesitate to include in it a certain number of plays, productions, or companies that found engagements abroad.[32] A number of stages set up by exiles, for example in Palestine and Shanghai, cannot really be described as 'antifascist'. Chronologically, too, as with literature, it is hard to define exactly when this theatre came to an end: in 1945, 1950, or even later.[33] Piscator remained in American exile well after the end of the War, and his epic theatre in the United States cannot be described as antifascist, even if it undeniably had a social and political aspect. An exhaustive study of German theatre in exile would require taking account of plays written in exile as well as those performed, together with the diversity of styles and theatrical experiments, both those in cabarets and official theatres, itinerant companies and isolated productions. A theatre of this kind, in different forms, developed in almost all countries where German exiles found refuge, and it is impossible to trace its contours in full. Besides, the authors involved were not just German: T. Csokor and F. Hochwälder were Austrian, E. E. Kisch and Franz Werfel were Czech, Julius Hay and Ödön von Horvath were Hungarian. The examples given here do not give an adequate image of the extreme richness of this exile theatre: it existed not only in Moscow, Zurich, Paris, Prague and London, but also in Argentina, Mexico, Jerusalem and Shanghai.

It is naturally hard to establish with any precision the number of 'theatre people' who left for exile. In 1932–33, German theatres employed at least 220,000 workers. The actor Curt Trepte estimated the number of those leaving for exile at around 4,000. Research made in 1972 counted more than 420 dramatic authors who went in exile, and wrote during their émigré years some 724 plays for the theatre, 108 for radio, and 398 film scripts.[34] Both the quantity and the quality of the works produced contrast strikingly with the appalling circumstances in which they were written: loss of audience and celebrity, lack of finance and publishers, precarious conditions of existence.[35] The majority of exiled authors continued to write, without knowing whether their works would be eventually performed or even published. And they did so at the cost of heavy sacrifices, making concessions to popular taste[36] or trying with difficulty to find employment in the cinema.[37] After 1933, however, exile theatres sprung up in almost every European capital.

Prague
In 1932 there were over a hundred German-language theatres in Czechoslovakia, most of them conducted by itinerant companies. Though there was a legal limit of 30 per cent on the employment of foreigners, this was considerably relaxed in favour of émigrés, who could readily find engagements or get their

works staged as long as these did not damage too seriously relations with the Reich.[38] The émigrés were assisted by Czech organizations.[39] Very rapidly, a Club of Antifascist Workers in Czech and German Theatre was established, with the object of showing the danger presented by National Socialism by way of theatre performances. Similar efforts were developed by the Communist and Socialist parties. Czech theatres produced a fairly large number of works by German exiles.

From 1935–36 a genuine émigré theatre developed. 1933 had already seen the birth in Prague of a number of émigré stages in the genres of agitprop and cabaret. These performances were most often staged in cafés, continuing the style of the Berlin political cabaret.[40] The following year, under the direction of Hedda Zinner and Fritz Erpenbeck, a large collective developed, Studio 1934, which included Germans, Austrians and Czechs.[41] Its productions used the styles of political operetta, parody, music hall and political sketch. According to contemporary reviews, they were well received. Studio 1934 went on to stage a large number of antifascist works, but the success of these disturbed the Czech government and led to the company experiencing censorship problems. It remained faithful to this cabaret style, also interpreting extracts from Brecht plays such as *St Joan of the Stockyards*.

A second attempt at antifascist theatre developed in 1935,[42] under the name of the Einheitsfront-Truppe,[43] which sought to bring together Socialists and Communists. It held readings of poems by Brecht, Becher, Bredel and Weinert, with music by Hanns Eisler. Alongside these political spectacles a number of amateur companies also sprung up, such as the Freie Deutsche Spiel-gemeinschaft in Prague, attracting especially young émigré actors who struggled for a united front of antifascist youth and interpreted revolutionary songs or extracts from plays by Becher and Brecht.

Thanks to the Association of Communist Theatre Workers (DDOC), a number of more important works were staged from 1936 on, including Clifford Odets's *Waiting for Lefty* with both Czech and exiled actors, and Johannes Wüsten's *Bessie Bosch*.[44] Finally, several antifascist works written by exiles[45] were staged in Prague, including Brecht's *Señora Carrar's Rifles* in February 1938, but these increasingly fell foul of the Czech censorship, and antifascist performances went into decline in the face of threats from the Reich.

Zurich

By virtue of its very repressive legislation, which limited political and cultural activity as well as access to its territory, Switzerland scarcely offered the exiles a favourable environment for the development of their theatre. In 1933, however, at the Zürcher Schauspielhaus, a theatrical company was established that was to count as one of the most important ensembles of the exile era.[46] The independence of this theatre, which was privately financed,[47] enabled it to escape the strict provisions of cantonal laws.[48] Opened as a boulevard theatre in 1926, the Zurich Schauspielhaus included in its repertory, after 1933, a number of modern authors such as Franz Werfel, T. Csokor, H. J. Rehfisch, F. Bruckner and F. Wolf. When the majority of Jewish actors and directors were forced to leave Germany,

Ferdinand Rieser booked them for his theatre, aware of the talent they could bring. In this way he managed to attract Kurt Horwitz, Ernst Ginsberg, Leonard Steckel, Emil Stöhr, Karl Parzla, Wolfgang Heinz, Erwin Kalser and Therese Giehse.[49] On the advice of Kurt Hirschfeld, Rieser engaged Wolfgang Langhoff (who had been interned in concentration camp) after writing directly to Goebbels.[50] The actors that Rieser engaged included a large number of highly talented left-wing figures.[51] Some antifascist productions, such as Bruckner's *The Races* and F. Wolf's *Professor Mamlok*, won real acclaim for this theatre even if they needed police protection. Rieser subsequently staged works by Horvath and Else Lasker-Schüler, making a total of nineteen émigré plays between 1933 and 1938.[52] Communist actors who had re-established a cell at this theatre took part in many propaganda actions against Hitlerite Germany.

Besides these antifascist works, the Schauspielhaus also staged classic works (Goethe, Schiller, Shakespeare), but its reputation for hostility to Nazism was so great that Rieser left Switzerland in 1938 and relocated to Paris for fear of German reprisals. The publisher Emil Oprecht now took over the financing of this theatre,[53] appointing Oskar Wälterlin to direct it,[54] who continued to develop this antifascist style but put greater emphasis on the progressive classical tradition than on current events. The success that he had up to the eve of the Second World War shows that the Swiss audience were well aware of this political dimension, and some lines from classical works were greeted with thunderous ovations.[55] Subsequently, while Europe was aflame, the Swiss audience hurried to see Goethe's *Faust* or Büchner's *Danton's Death*. Among modern authors, Brecht and Georg Kaiser were the most performed. In April 1941, the Zurich audience were still able to applaud *Mother Courage* (with Therese Giehse), and two years later *The Good Person of Szechwan* and *Galileo*.

Rather than a specific style, this Zurich ensemble managed to achieve an astonishing encounter of figures from the most varied backgrounds – from Communist to Catholic – united by the same will to struggle against fascism. In more than one way, this prepared the way for the revival of German theatre in the postwar period.

London
Though until 1938 Britain received refugees only parsimoniously, it soon became a place of asylum for a number of actors. A note from 1935 in *Das Neue Tage-Buch* signalled the presence in Britain of Elisabeth Bergner, Lucie Mannheim, Grete Mosheim, Oskar Homolka, Fritz Kortner, Conrad Veidt, Paul Grätz and Ernst Deutsch, among the greatest stars of the theatre and cinema of the 1920s. A certain number of theatrical performances were first of all given in the context of clubs established by the refugees,[56] as well as in cabarets.[57] An Austrian theatre in exile was established by Arthur Hellner, Österreichische Bühne, which performed a number of classics banned in Germany. But the English theatres generally had very little interest in émigré works, and the censorship also banned several performances in the name of 'British neutrality'.[58] Few émigré writers were performed, or managed to work with London theatres, Carl Zuckmayer being an exception here.[59] Toller's *No*

More Peace! was given a good performance on 11 June 1936, but without great success. The notices judged the play to be too naive, and the exiled actors managed to find engagements only on an individual basis. This rather surprising situation is explained particularly by the fact that there was little connection between English and German culture.

Denmark, Sweden, Norway
Because of their tolerant policy towards the émigrés, the Scandinavian countries played a relatively important role in exile theatre. Brecht and his family lived in Svendborg, Denmark from 1933 to 1939, then in Stockholm until August 1940. During the eight years he spent in Scandinavia, Brecht wrote some of his most important works.[60] His house became a meeting-place not only for other émigrés, but also for discussion on the theatre. In Denmark Brecht collaborated with amateur companies (including that of Ruth Berlau which produced *The Mother*) and managed to get some of his works successfully staged.[61] The campaign in support of Republican Spain often used *Señora Carrar's Rifles* as a propaganda piece, and the play received an enthusiastic response from the audience.[62] Curt Trepte, the former Piscator actor who was also a refugee in Sweden, also worked with the amateur companies formed by young Socialists. A number of Brecht's works were inspired by current events (*Dances, The Price of Iron*), focusing especially on the danger of supposed neutrality. Many of his plays were also performed by working-class companies under the direction of Ruth Berlau.[63] Besides these antifascist performances staged by amateur companies, there were also more official ones at other theatres. But for fear of reactions of the right-wing press, and to respect its neutrality, Sweden did not allow the performance of explicitly antifascist works, with the exception of Freidrich Wolf's *Professor Mamlok*.

Paris
Despite its wide cultural range, Paris did not offer great possibilities of development of an antifascist theatre in exile, although a large number of actors, writers and directors had emigrated there. Brecht did manage to stage *Señora Carrar's Rifles* in 1937.[64] In 1933, the show he had written to Kurt Weill's music, *The Seven Deadly Sins of the Petty Bourgeois*, was performed by Les Ballets 33 with Tilly Losch and Lotte Lenya, but without great success. *The Threepenny Opera* was also staged in Paris in 1937, by its original producer E. J. Aufricht, but its success was likewise limited.[65] The project of establishing in France a theatre company of émigrés from all countries failed for lack of resources and the necessary visas.[66] Several scenes from *Fear and Misery of the Third Reich* were also performed in May 1938, in the context of SDS activities.[67] Even if they aroused Walter Benjamin's enthusiasm,[68] they only attracted an émigré audience. The project of establishing a major antifascist theatre capable of undertaking tours was also discussed at the SDS, but without any concrete result.[69] A number of scenes from *Fear and Misery of the Third Reich* were again staged in 1938 at the Salle Iéna, with a fair degree of success as the Nazi press commented on the event.[70]

Despite these few successes, the life of exile theatre in France turned out to be very hard. Brecht lived there in relative poverty,[71] and Piscator failed to find an engagement.[72] Several émigrés described the deplorable lack of French interest in German works. Horvath's *Faith, Hope and Charity* was reviewed above all by the exile press.[73] Very few theatres were prepared to accept German works, and these were staged above all in evenings organized by the SDS or at the cabaret Die Laterne. Bruckner's plays were staged without attracting any special attention. Only Brecht's *Fear and Misery*, staged on a number of occasions, met with real success. The piece was performed again in 1939, and a final production failed only because of the mobilization.

Many émigrés, however, gave proof of a boundless imagination in seeking to re-establish themselves in the Paris theatre. E. J. Aufricht relates in his memoirs the countless approaches he made to interest the French in his projects. In despair, he leased the Théâtre Pigalle, which operated as a cinema, to stage plays at midnight after its regular shows. Together with Raymond Rouleau, he presented several productions at this 'Théâtre de Minuit', unique of its kind.[74] Hailed by the press as a surrealist undertaking, this theatre scarcely attracted any audience.

Soviet Union

We have already depicted the cultural and political context in which theatrical activity developed in the USSR. Piscator's great project of an antifascist theatre at Engels[75] remains its most amazing symbol. Without offering an exhaustive account of these activities, their great wealth and diversity must be acknowledged. These actors, writers and directors might come up against pretty rigid aesthetic principles, but they did not have to fear the Reich's censorship and threats. The multiplication of antifascist theatre was on the contrary officially encouraged.

Several circumstances explain the diversity of these theatrical experiments between 1933 and 1937. First of all, the establishment at Moscow in 1932 of an International Theatre entrusted to three companies – German, English and French.[76] Other theatres in Leningrad also presented plays in foreign languages. As political theatre, and especially the agitprop style, was rejected in most Western countries, the USSR appeared the only place where it was possible to develop these experiments. Not only were Soviet directors themselves champions of this style, but the German companies were often invited to the Soviet Union to produce or take refuge there. The productions of Piscator and von Wangenheim have already been mentioned.

For a large number of actors and directors, the USSR was the only country where they could continue their work, and with the maximum of technical and financial resources. Piscator himself was one of the first to conceive of a regrouping of 'theatre workers in exile'. The too-high cost – a million roubles – made the project fail, and the project of a 'studio for worker-actors' was substituted instead. From this time on, German exile theatre developed in a number of stages.

In 1932, a number of threatened actors and companies took refuge in the

USSR. The famous ensemble Kolonne Links, which interpreted revolutionary songs with jazz rhythms and was very popular in Berlin, had enjoyed a triumphal tour in 1929. The law that banned agitprop in 1931 led them to decide to emigrate, and it could now develop its repertoire on an international scale. The 1931 Company, which had kept going for a month after the Nazi seizure of power, emigrated first of all to Paris, but unable to do any real work there it also decided to settle in Moscow, where it merged with Kolonne Links. From this was born on 25 February 1934, at the Moskauer Klub Ausländischer Arbeiter, the Deutsches Theater Kolonne Links, which immediately included in its repertoire von Wangenheim's plays *Cellar Heroes* and *Agents*, works by Demian Bedny, as well as Brecht's *Ballad of the Reichstag Fire*. Several exiled actors joined other ensembles, such as the Deutsches Gebiettheater Dniepropetrowsk. These first achievements were soon enriched by the arrival of new figures by 1935: Ernst Busch and Erich Weinert, who gave many concerts, and Alexander Granach who guested at the famous Arts Masters Club in Moscow. Carola Neher was received with enthusiasm, just as Piscator and Brecht were on their visits to the USSR. The Klub Ausländischer Arbeiter organized performances of extracts from Brecht's works as well as those of Friedrich Wolf.

Exiled writers were able to publish their works in large editions in the Soviet Union, and often they were rapidly translated and performed in Soviet theatres. The Berlin agitprop style was thus able to develop very easily across the USSR. But the most ambitious project was the antifascist theatre at Engels in the Volga Republic, planned to receive a large number of exiles, give new life to the greatest political plans of Weimar theatre, and form a focus of revolutionary agitation against fascism. The project failed not just because of its over-ambitious scale, but above all due to Stalin's distrust, the climate of repression that fell on the USSR and struck the exiles themselves so harshly. This failure, which more or less brought about Piscator's unpublicized break with the Communist movement, sounded the knell for any similar project. Exile theatrical activity continued, but it was increasingly controlled. Though Wolf and von Wangenheim remained popular, many actors were arrested, deported and killed. From 1938 on, the disgrace of Meyerhold brought in its wake a distrust towards the whole revolutionary conception of the theatre. The disillusioned comments of Brecht on this development in his *Journals* are more than symbolic.

Shanghai

Though not a great deal is known of the life of émigrés in China, the example of the Shanghai theatre illustrates in a fairly dramatic fashion their efforts to re-establish stages on which they could preserve German culture wherever they found themselves.

With its Jewish and Communist émigrés, its special and complex legal position, Shanghai was the venue for quite unprecedented theatrical experiments. Amid very great difficulties, the actors and directors who took refuge there, as the last opportunity of leaving Europe without a visa, tried to overcome their isolation by organizing evenings of 'European culture'. Most often set up in old cinemas and disused offices, these productions – shown at the Broadway Theatre – were generally financed by the émigrés themselves[77] and operated on a subscription basis.[78] There is little information as to the standard of these performances.[79] Clearly their object was not so much to offer antifascist works, which in any case would have been banned by the Japanese censorship, as to give new life to spectacles formerly popular in Berlin. As well as works in Yiddish, therefore, plays by Klabund, Hasenclever, Lessing, Schnitzler, Lenz, Bruckner, Strindberg, Wolf, Brecht and Sophocles were staged. Few examples are as moving and surprising as these meagre Shanghai productions: a last effort to revive fragments of a world which, in proportion to its distance in space, became for them as much a myth as a spiritual homeland.

Antifascist Cabarets and Films

Far from being confined to images of a rather disturbed sexuality and decadence, as conveyed by so many modern works that take Sternberg's *Blue Angel* or Otto Dix's portraits as the symbol of the Weimar Republic, the Berlin cabarets were a focus of social criticism and freedom that the Nazis bitterly opposed. From the Cabaret of Eleven Hangmen in Munich, around Frank Wedekind and the Schwabing bohème, which ridiculed the Wilhelmine Empire and its morality, through the literary cabarets of the expressionist era and the variety spectacles of the 1920s to political satire, the Berlin cabaret attracted the greatest artists: it is enough to mention Klabund, Walter Mehring and Kurt Tucholsky. As a bastion of freedom, a symbol in Nazi eyes of the decadence of national values and 'destructive Jewish humour', the new regime persecuted its exponents as real enemies. Not content with destroying these last vestiges of freedom, Goebbels tried in every way to have its representatives murdered in exile.[80]

The last non-political cabaret, the Nachrichter of Kurt E. Heyne and Werner Kleine, was banned in October 1935. The Nazis encouraged the continuation of cabarets such as Die Entfesselten, whose humour was '*völkisch*', confined to parodies of operettas. The famous Kabarett der Komiker, founded by Kurt Robitschek, survived under the direction of Willi Schäffer until 1938, but the majority of the great figures who had created this style of cabaret had long been in exile, and often met with a tragic fate: Robitschek was murdered by the Nazis, Karl Schnog sent to concentration camp (though at least he survived), Tucholsky and Paul Nikolaus committed suicide in exile, Paul Graetz died in Hollywood in 1937, Fritz Grünbaum perished in Dachau in 1941, Max Ehrlich and Willi Rosen were gassed in Auschwitz, while Kurt Geron – Tiger Brown in *The Threepenny Opera* – and Erich Mühsam were killed in Oranienburg.

With such a prestigious past, how could the émigrés not have been tempted to try and revive cabaret in exile? The most famous example was undoubtedly Erika Mann's Pfeffermühle, founded in Munich on 1 January 1933 at the Bonbonnière. This was a literary cabaret with a strong political orientation, aimed particularly at the Nazis. The sketches, written by Erika and Klaus Mann, were performed by herself and Therese Giehse.[81] Though Erika Mann was violently attacked by the Nazis on several occasions, her cabaret managed to continue for a few weeks until Bavaria was brought into line by the new regime.[82] When she was forced to take refuge in Zurich, she immediately reopened the Pfeffermühle,[83] with a number of anti-Nazi sketches. The company went on to tour Czechoslovakia, the Netherlands, Belgium and Luxemburg with equal success, giving over 1,034 performances in seven countries. Despite the attacks of the Nazis and their Swiss sympathizers,[84] this cabaret became a symbol of antifascist struggle, dear to the entire émigré community. Erika Mann tried to revive her cabaret again in New York in 1936, but the Americans remained impervious to this type of humour, and it disappeared the following year.

Studio 34, with Hedda Zinner and Fritz Erpenbeck, was established in Prague in 1934 and mingled cabaret spectacles with agitprop scenes. The same year, other émigrés founded an antifascist cabaret in Paris, Die Laterne, with a company led by Hans Altmann, Günter Ruschin and Werner Zacharias (Florian). They were subsequently joined by Steffie Spira, Barbara Burg, Erich Berg, Alfred Buchner, the pianist Gelbtrunk, the painter Heinz Lohmar and the writer Henryk Keisch. Joseph Kosma wrote music for a number of songs. The majority of its sketches bore on émigré life, the situation in Germany and international events. Many spectacles were staged in the form of parodies. Die Laterne disappeared in 1938, though some of its participants went on to work for the cabaret Bunte Bühne.

A number of émigrés in London, who called themselves the 'black sheep', managed to establish on 21 June 1939, in the context of the Freier Deutscher Kulturbund, a cabaret in the West End[85] at which songs by Walter Mehring and Brecht were performed in English and German, with the motto: 'We play in English, jeder Deutscher versteht uns; wir spielen deutsch, but every Englishman understands.' These spectacles were chiefly devoted to the lives of émigrés and their relations with Germany. Many were inspired by John Heartfield's photomontages. To illustrate Göring's slogan vaunting the superiority of iron over butter,[86] a German family – from grandmother to new arrival – were seen learning to eat a bicycle wheel. Though these spectacles had a certain success with the public, the enterprise failed for want of money. It was also in London in 1939 that Austrian émigrés[87] launched Die Laterndl, which offered a mixture of songs and poetry, some of its sketches depicting Hitler.[88] As in Paris, a number of stage plays where also given at this cabaret. Works by Nestroy, Bruno Frank and Machiavelli were performed, as well as songs in Yiddish and from *The Threepenny Opera*.

Most surprising were the cabarets set up in concentration camps. Sometimes the SS demanded that interned cabaret artists continue their activities as an entertainment.[89] More often it was the prisoners who put on spectacles, both to escape from the pervasive fear and despair, and to show that they were still human beings. The existence of these spectacles in concentration camps is attested in several accounts. One of the most emotive is that of Walter Langhoff, who in his *The Peat-Bog-Soldiers*) describes how the prisoners in the Esterswegen camp established the Circus Konzentrationi. The celebrated 'Song of the Peat-Bog Soldiers' was sung for the first time at the end of this performance. Werner Finck, arrested in May 1933 and likewise interned at Esterswegen, created cabaret numbers for his fellow prisoners, with the motto: 'We used not dare to say anything for fear of being sent to concentration camp. Now we needn't be afraid: we're already here.'[90]

Émigrés also organized cabarets in French internment camps in 1940. Hanna Schramm relates, in her memoir of Gurs,[91] the astonishing cultural life that the detainees managed to re-establish in these camps, so as not to succumb to despair. Hannah Zweig, a relative of Stefan Zweig, led a children's theatre company. The women at Gurs managed to hire a piano, and established a cultural centre. Joined in autumn 1940 by men transferred from the Saint-Cyprien camp and Jews from Baden, including actors, painters, musicians and singers, they created a genuine cabaret with Fred Nathan, Kurt Loew and Maerker. Ernst Busch himself helped by composing texts for reviews, and sung at these performances. They performed Ibsen plays as well as Mahler's *Kindertotenlieder*. The spectacles were so astonishing that the camp staff attended together with surrounding villagers. One song by Heini Walfisch described these evenings as follows:

To those who had lost courage,
We return heart and soul,
All the sufferings of humanity
We have experienced in ourselves.
But we've made theatre . . .
Think of what that means.[92]

The making of antifascist films in exile raised still more complicated problems. Many émigré actors and directors certainly tried to find outlets in the cinema industry, especially in the United States. Several acted in antifascist films (Conrad Veidt, Peter Lorre), but apart from Fritz Lang's film *Hangmen Also Die*, the American film industry was little disposed to make antifascist films until the country entered the War. For many, cinema was simply a means of survival.[93]

In Switzerland and France, a few émigrés tried to start film companies or to work with well-known directors.[94] But these attempts rarely got beyond the state of projects, or failed to overcome all the obstacles. Apart from *Hangmen Also Die*, and *Pastor Hall* based on Ernst Toller's play about resistance to Nazism in the church, the USSR was the only country in which émigrés had a chance of making antifascist films. Starting in 1934, Piscator shot there, despite many technical problems, *The Revolt of the Fishermen of Santa Barbara*, based on a short story by Anna Seghers, and drawing the lesson of a strike that failed for lack of solidarity. As an appeal for a united front against fascism, the film appeared too late and was not widely distributed. Friedrich Wolf's play *Professor Mamlok* was also made into a film in 1938, as was von Wangenheim's *Fighters*, based around the Reichstag fire. Several émigrés worked on anti-Nazi

films shot in the Soviet Union, for instance Hans Klering and Heinrich Greif.[95]
After the disbandment of Mezhrabpom, most antifascist films were made in
other studios. Some of these used actors exiled in the USSR[96] or were inspired
by German antifascist works.[97] Many of these films are inaccessible nowadays[98]
and it is hard to get a detailed idea of them. They were never distributed outside
the Soviet Union, apart from Piscator's film and *Professor Mamlok*. The
majority were withdrawn from general release after the German–Soviet pact,
and it was impossible to see them even after the German invasion. Herbert
Rappaport, who had been G. W. Pabst's assistant, went on to work on several
antifascist films made during the War (*A Hundred for One*, 1942; *Vanmka*,
1942). A number of scenes from Brecht's *Fear and Misery of the Third Reich*
were used by Pudovkin in his film *The Murderers Are Coming*. While Conrad
Veidt and Peter Lorre played Nazi spies in Hollywood alongside Humphrey
Bogart, Heinrich Greif and Hans Klering played similar roles in more than
thirty Soviet films depicting Hitlerite Germany. If many attempts were made to
make exile films, the results were generally disappointing, for lack of financial
resources.[99]

The Émigrés and the Second World War

1. THE WAR AGAINST THE ÉMIGRÉS

We hear every day echoes of the scandalous and lying propaganda against the awakening of Germany under Hitler, inspired by world Jewry and the Third International.

Goebbels

Referred to by Goebbels as 'corpses in waiting', insulted and slandered daily in the Nazi press – which greeted their defeats, deaths and suicides as so many victories of the Third Reich over its enemies – the émigrés had to struggle against National Socialist attack throughout the exile period. If the intimidation and threats towards governments that protected them were constant, the Nazis also sought to combat their influence by unleashing their supporters against them. Almost nowhere were they safe from the Gestapo, from possible kidnapping or assassination. The fear that many exiles had of approaching a building flying the swastika flag was all too justified. Here we shall simply mention a few aspects of this underground war that Germany waged against the émigrés, the campaigns of slander, the intimidation of host countries, and the attempts to reduce to silence those whom Goebbels viewed as dangerous.

THE ÉMIGRÉS AND NAZI PROPAGANDA

The articles on the émigrés that appeared in the National Socialist press give the general tenor of these attacks. Because they had belonged to pacifist or progressive movements, had been active in or sympathized with the left parties under the Weimar Republic and declared their hatred for National Socialism, they were all branded as 'criminals'.[1] It was they who were responsible for the misery of the German people, blamed for the *Dolchstoß* of 1918, the Spartacist uprising, the Bavarian soviet republic and all subsequent disasters. Activists, intellectuals and artists were all assailed by Nazi propaganda with the same venom. After the Reichstag fire, the regime's opponents were equated with common-law criminals, and documents fabricated by the Nazis, which they claimed to have 'discovered' in KPD offices, tried to make out, both in Germany and abroad, that the Communists had been preparing a series of violent actions – assassinations, kidnappings, poisonings. Because they had left the Reich and denounced the crimes being committed there, the émigrés were 'traitors' who deserved to be expelled from collective memory, their deprivation of nationality being the most symbolic marker of this.

If the Nazi government initially did not seem to fear the influence of the émigrés abroad, it was very soon forced to recognize – especially with the success of the *Braunbuch* on the Reichstag fire trial – that the antifascist propaganda they developed could be extremely effective, and a threat to German interests in the countries where they had taken refuge. The Nazis scarcely had to fear their influence on the German population, which for all their efforts, they found very difficult to reach. But the émigrés could compromise the good relations that the Reich sought to maintain with other European countries.[2] The Gestapo therefore took very seriously the danger the émigrés represented,[3] and was led to take increasingly severe measures against their *Greuelhetze* or 'hate propaganda'.

First of all, through the intermediary of German embassies, the Nazi regime sought to prevent at all costs the distribution of the émigré press. Employing both fallacious offers and threats – towards Czechoslovakia, for example – it stressed the danger of a deterioration in relations with the Reich that this might produce. If it was unable to act against the periodicals in question directly, it sought to impede their distribution by paying sizeable sums to journalists sympathetic to National Socialism who could supposedly give the lie to this propaganda. The Nazis also tried to purchase newspapers when this was possible (as they did in the Saar). They often sought to convince conservative figures – exiled or otherwise – that any attack on the government that appeared in the foreign press damaged Germany as a whole.[4] One of the arguments most commonly used by the Nazi press was to maintain that the émigrés' 'hateful and lying propaganda' was the act of a group of 'Marxists', so as not only to limit its effect, but above all to disqualify it in the eyes of foreign governments. German writers were regularly invited to give lectures abroad in order to affirm their solidarity with the regime and refute the émigrés' accusations, and almost everywhere attempts were made to distribute propaganda films and newsreels giving a positive image of Germany and its achievements.[5] As for German publishers, they solemnly declared[6] that they would break off all contact with their foreign counterparts if these agreed to publish or distribute the 'hate-arousing works' of émigrés.

Fearing Germany's political and economic isolation, the Nazis bent their efforts to contradicting exile propaganda point by point, getting it criticized by non-Nazi personalities, and presenting the émigrés as 'international trouble-makers' who were unable to reconcile themselves to seeing the German people elect a government they did not like, and would not give up slandering it. Not only did they prevent negative information filtering out of the country in any way they could – former concentration-camp inmates were punished with death if they spoke after their release about what they had suffered and seen – but they presented certain violent displays, such as anti-Semitic persecution, as popular excesses inherent to any revolution.

There was in fact a striking contrast between the little influence that the exile press could exert and the fear it aroused in the Nazis. Far from restricting itself to slandering the exiles in the German press and abroad, the government took very severe repressive measures against the families of certain émigrés who had remained in Germany in order to force them to silence. The parents of Phillip Scheidemann were sent to concentration camp in response to an article of his that appeared in the *New York Times*.[7] After the Social-Democrat deputy Gerhard Seger escaped from Oranienburg, the Gestapo sent his wife to concentration camp together with their two-year-old daughter.[8] On some occasions the Gestapo even forced detainees to write to the directors of exile periodicals to beg them to stop publishing articles on the camps. From August 1933, German nationality was withdrawn from any émigré whose words or writings damaged the Reich.

After 1934, though the émigré propaganda had very little success – witness the failure of attempts to obtain the release of Thälmann and Ossietzky – the National Socialist press campaign steadily intensified: the *Völkischer Beobachter* and *Das Schwarze Korps* daily lambasted the 'Judeo-Marxist clique', those 'villains' and 'traitors'. But the Nazi government often used cleverer methods than crude abuse to refute information published by the émigrés. Rather than contradict accounts in the exile press case by case, it sought to discredit them globally, for example by circulating false news items that it was then easy to refute. All that was needed was to let an émigré journal know of the murder of a concentration-camp prisoner, and when this news was published, display the prisoner alive and well. Spies paid by the Gestapo had the special mission of infiltrating themselves into these magazines and giving false accounts of executions and arrests, even publishing false letters from detainees. In a number of cases this procedure had a certain success.[9] More important still was intimidation against the host countries.

INTIMIDATION AND THREATS AGAINST HOST COUNTRIES

From the start of the exile period, the Nazi government made frequent representations to foreign embassies protesting at the support or understanding that 'enemies of the Reich' enjoyed in certain countries. All antifascist activity developed by the émigrés brought official interventions that sought to obtain its banning. The counter-trial that Willi Münzenberg organized in London to show that the Nazis were responsible for the Reichstag fire was viewed as an intolerable interference in German affairs. The articles Heinrich Mann published in the *Dépêche de Toulouse* and the antifascist exhibitions organized in Paris and Prague all triggered German protests that were often very violent.

It is hard to assess the impact that these interventions and threats had on the politics of the host countries towards refugees. As a general rule, most European countries certainly did not want to poison their relations with Hitler's Germany, whether because they bore a certain sympathy for its government (Austria), because they feared its reprisals (Czechoslovakia), or because they pursued a policy of appeasement towards it (France, Great Britain). The Western democracies had to fear their own public opinion, and above all the right-wing press, which constantly railed against the 'warmongers' who sought to drag Europe into conflict so as to regain their lost positions.[10] Anti-Communism was widespread, and the ban on émigrés' practising any political activity, in the majority of host countries, was not a signal for tolerance. Certainly, the fear that France, Switzerland or Great Britain might have for Germany had no common measure with that of Czechoslovakia, which felt directly threatened, but the desire to avoid any cause of friction with Hitler helps explain the severity of the authorities and the censorship of the émigrés' political activities.

The argument according to which they constituted a disruptive factor in European politics, pushing for war, had a definite resonance in the foreign press. German diplomats issued regular warnings to this effect: the countries bordering on Germany had the choice between friendship with 68 million Germans or with a 'handful of hate-filled émigrés'. Any support given to the émigrés, any tolerance of their antifascist activities in the fields of press, publishing, exhibitions or theatrical performances, was directly equated with a demonstration of hostility towards the German people. Viewing the exiles as a 'European danger', Goebbels invited foreign countries to take defensive measures against them, in their own interest and in that of their relations with Germany. The Reich had many means at its disposal to back up its demands. It could seek the support of right-wing milieus, arouse 'spontaneous' demonstrations of its sympathizers against antifascist spectacles, directly threaten with political or economic reprisals the countries concerned, and even physically eliminate the émigrés themselves.

The Nazi arguments found zealous champions in the far-right press, which never missed an occasion to accuse the émigrés of abusing the asylum they had been granted. They were attacked for pushing for war and poisoning relations with Germany, but also for spreading Communist ideas, aggravating unemployment and economic crisis, introducing cultural elements that were foreign to the national character[11] and endangering national independence.[12] It was hoped that in this way any sympathy towards them would be silenced, and a current of opinion created that was hostile to admitting them.[13] In those countries where movements supporting National Socialism existed, Germany urged them to regular provocations against the émigrés. Violent incidents took place in Switzerland, where Nazi supporters demonstrated in theatres when émigré works were staged.[14] Similar scenarios occurred in Vienna and Prague.

Economic reprisals would affect countries that depended on Germany commercially or had substantial economic transactions with it: Czechoslovakia, Sweden and Switzerland in particular. Several countries were thus led to exert an increasing censorship on émigré activities. Despite the sympathy it might have for them, the Czech government for example had to take seriously the threats from the Reich. Thus the famous exhibition of caricatures organized in Prague in 1934, including photomontages by John Heartfield, attracted complaints from the German embassy. Seven works were withdrawn from the show at the demand of the police.[15] Austria, in its turn, protested against three other photomontages. The affair soon acquired an international resonance. Not only were solidarity demonstrations organized in Prague, but the president of the Salon des Indépendants, Paul Signac, wrote to the Comité d'Aide aux Victimes du Fascisme and offered to host the banned works in Paris.[16] John Heartfield received similar offers from a number of other countries, and subsequently exhibited '150 photo-montages politiques d'actualité' in the rue de Navarre, at the invitation of the Association des Écrivains et des Artistes Révolutionnaires. The German government threatened to break off diplomatic relations with France, but the solidarity campaign behind Heartfield made any action against it impossible. From 1933 to 1938, such protests gathered pace, with various threats against countries that supported the émigrés or tolerated their activities.[17] As a general rule, any demonstration of solidarity or even humanitarianism was considered a 'lack of courtesy' or an 'act of hostility' if it came from official circles.[18]

KIDNAPPING AND ASSASSINATION

At the same time as Germany was publicly combating émigré propaganda and threatening reprisals against governments who assisted the émigrés, the Gestapo was carrying out clandestine actions to eliminate them physically. The attempt to obtain the extradition of political refugees as 'criminals' came up against too many obstacles. Apart from Switzerland, Austria and Vichy France, few countries were prepared to deliver to Germany people who would be immediately murdered.[19] If in similar cases the police intensified the surveillance of these exiles, completely restricted their activities and sometimes agreed to collaborate with the German police, nowhere before 1940 did pressure from the Reich succeed in getting its opponents handed over.[20] Even when activists close to the KPD were involved, many countries tried to obtain their release from concentration camp if they could claim the relevant nationality.[21]

In many cases, therefore, the Nazi government resorted to illegal means to eliminate exiles it particularly hated or viewed as dangerous to the security of the Reich. Such actions were generally undertaken in various stages. The close surveillance that the Reich practised on émigrés was made possible by the cooperation of the police of certain countries of asylum (Switzerland, Austria, Denmark) and above all by the systematic infiltration of exile groups by spies, bogus 'émigrés' in the service of the Gestapo, and – still more tragically – genuine émigrés who for one reason or another had yielded to Nazi blackmail and had to pay for their rehabilitation with the betrayal of their friends. Such surveillance was easier in those countries where there were German minorities (such as the Sudeten Germans in Czechoslovakia). In his essay 'Die Aufgaben der Emigration',[22] Heinrich Mann insisted on the need for the émigrés to develop a counter-espionage of their own to prevent the Gestapo from murdering them. This was indeed the aim of most of these efforts. The general rule was to win the trust of a wanted émigré, then under some pretext lead them to return illegally to Germany or approach the border. They would then be abducted and murdered. Scenarios of this kind were fairly common, and struck a wide range of individuals.

The action of Gestapo agents abroad, however, was exposed in detail early on by the émigrés, in particular the pacifist Berthold Jacob, who subsequently fell victim to kidnapping himself.[23] On their arrival in a country, the émigrés were not just kept under surveillance by the local police, but also by Gestapo emissaries.[24] The people they had contact with were photographed, Germans in particular. The Gestapo agents not only sought to establish a detailed record of their activities, but also to divide them or make it hard for them to establish themselves in the host countries.[25] Then there were the bogus émigrés sent abroad by the Gestapo to obtain information on antifascist activities, and the most shameless attempts at corruption. Gestapo agents selected the most impoverished and least political exiles, and in exchange for a promise of return to Germany and rehabilitation, or release of relatives in concentration camps, led the émigré in question to betray others. These bogus émigrés might be Nazi sympathizers, professional policemen, or even turncoats from the left parties. The sailor Kronburg, unmasked in Paris by Red Aid when he tried to join the illegal KPD, was a former member of the SPD. Berthold Jacob described the case of the student Jürgen Warner,[26] who arrived in France in 1933, supposedly a Socialist or Communist, and offered information to the émigrés until his lifestyle demonstrated that he had been paid by the Gestapo. The former editor of the Social-Democratic paper in Spandau, Otto-Emil Fechner, was sent abroad to find out how the émigrés obtained information on the German weapons programme. Some bogus émigrés distributed false passports to antifascists which enabled their arrest when they reached the German frontier. This led to a climate of extreme distrust among the émigrés. Each new arrival was suspected and questioned. What party or political group did he belong to? Whom did he know? How had he left Germany? Even when they had escaped from concentration camp, their good luck was suspect, and the fear was that they had been aided by the Gestapo itself.

As the Reich grew increasingly aware of the danger that the émigrés represented, its provocations became more violent. A large group of Gestapo agents was expelled from Switzerland after illegal actions. If they were unable to eliminate the émigrés, these agents sought to draw suspicion on them in all kinds of ways. Berthold Jacob listed the various scenarios. Their identity papers, money or correspondence were stolen. Bogus officials from the gas or phone company would take advantage of their absence to photograph letters and leave in the émigré's home political leaflets attacking the host country. In June 1935 alone, five Gestapo agents were unmasked by the émigrés at political meetings.

On several occasions, these agents or the SS managed to murder émigrés abroad. Czechoslovakia, despite its generous asylum policy, was particularly vulnerable in this respect: Dresden was not far from the frontier, and there was a Gestapo headquarters there. Otto Strasser, leader of the Schwarze Front, was surprised to find, when his home in Prague was raided by 'Czech' police, that their vehicle was registered in Germany. The 'policemen' who had questioned him were Sudeten Nazis whose aim was to kidnap him. Their perfect knowledge of Czech enabled them to assist the Gestapo and pass themselves off as genuine policemen. In March 1934, a bogus Englishman, 'Frank', managed to corrupt two of Strasser's collaborators and almost succeeded in drawing him into a trap, by inviting him to visit the Saar where it was planned to kidnap him. Otto Strasser's radio engineer Rudolf Formis, in charge of the 'black transmitter' that broadcast to Germany, was murdered by two SS men in his Prague hotel room, with the help of a woman accomplice. In 1933, the Czech government had protested at kidnap attempts against Socialist leaders – including Otto Wels – in Karlovy Vary, by SA men operating on Czech territory. Otto Thiele, secretary of the SoPaDe, nearly fell victim to this, as did Paul Kretschmar, a former member of the Reichsbanner. Kurt Robitschek was murdered in Prague, as was the pacifist Theodor Lessing. A price of 80,000 marks had been put on his head: he was killed by the Gestapo in his villa in Marienbad on 31 August 1933.

One of the most famous actions of the Gestapo against émigrés was the kidnapping of the pacifist journalist Berthold Jacob. A contributor to the *Weltbühne,* and author of several works on Hitlerite propaganda, Nazi espionage and German war preparations, he was one of the most hated émigrés. On 9 May 1935 he was kidnapped in Switzerland and taken back to Germany. A few days later the Swiss police arrested Dr Hans Wesemann, an accomplice in the crime. This Wesemann was a former journalist, and deeply in debt.[27] He had been approached by the Gestapo to spy on the émigrés, and to try and eliminate Willi Münzenberg and Berthold Jacob. The former, too distrustful, refused to meet him. Wesemann then focused on Berthold Jacob, who ran the Service de Presse Indépendant in Strasbourg, passing on to him in 1934 various items of 'information' that had been prepared in Berlin. To attract him to the Saar, he made Jacob believe that the 'black Reichswehr' had established an arms depot there, close to the German border. It would then have been easy to drive Jacob into Germany. The plan failed, as Jacob asked the Social-Democrat leader Max Braun to accompany him, and two French policemen also joined the group.

A new ambush was set up in Basle, ten minutes from the German frontier, at a hotel where Gestapo agents were also staying, but Berthold Jacob refused to go there. In 1935, Wesemann once again proposed that he should meet a 'trustworthy' man who worked for the German defence ministry, and who, unable to compromise himself by a visit to France, had suggested meeting in Switzerland. He even offered a false passport, and Jacob accompanied him by taxi to his hotel to put the final stamps on this. The taxi was in reality a Gestapo vehicle, which crossed the Swiss border control with its lights out. The driver stopped at the German border post, pretending to be unaware that they were in Germany. Wesemann remained in Switzerland, but aroused the distrust of the Swiss police. When the kidnapping was discovered, he was accused of abduction and murder. At first he denied everything, but on seeing that he had been abandoned by Germany, he admitted having acted under orders from the Gestapo. Following protests from Switzerland, the Reich responded that Berthold Jacob had returned to Germany voluntarily to obtain information – an unsupportable claim, since no antifascist would ever have dared to present himself at the German frontier with an out-of-date passport. The Swiss Bundesrat then accused the German authorities of kidnapping on its territory. The affair was submitted to an international tribunal, and the Reich was forced to release Berthold Jacob on 18 September 1935. Wesemann was condemned to three years in prison, and subsequently emigrated to Venezuela. Berthold Jacob was interned in France in 1941, in the Vernet camp. He then tried to flee to Portugal. Recognized by the Gestapo in Lisbon, he was taken back to Germany, and died after torture in 1944.

2. THE HARDENING OF EUROPEAN POLICY IN 1938–39

REINFORCEMENT OF CONTROL AND PRIVATIONS

Though European attitudes towards refugees differed widely among the various host countries, the general hardening in 1938–39 was part of the overall international situation. While Britain opened its gates to Jewish emigration after the annexation of Austria, the French government was led to set new restrictions on refugees, putting an end to the generosity of the Popular Front.

Several of the benefits granted at that time were rapidly put in question by the Daladier government, formed on 15 April 1938, through a series of decrees that worsened the life of foreigners staying in France.[28] Departmental prefects were instructed to see that political émigrés renounced 'on our territory any action in support of the conflicts of opinion in which they were involved in their countries of origin',[29] which meant a ban on any antifascist activity. A further decree, adopted on 2 May, provided for a fine of 100 to 1,000 francs, and imprisonment from one month to a year, with subsequent expulsion, for any foreigner in an irregular situation, or any person who had facilitated their entry into the country and movement within it. Any clandestine support for refugees could now be penalized. Finally, foreigners were now forbidden, even if their papers were in order, to move house even within the same commune if this had more than 10,000 inhabitants. This last measure meant an actual assignment of residence, which contradicted the convention on the status of refugees from Germany that the French government had signed at the League of Nations on 10 February 1938, and guaranteed their freedom of movement.

After the *Anschluss*, no measures were taken to receive refugees coming from Austria, and the situation of many émigrés already settled in France became still more difficult. The fear that spies or Nazi agents would infiltrate the country with the émigrés, prefiguring the idea of a 'fifth column',[30] was not sufficient explanation for this. On 10 July 1937 France had signed an economic agreement with the Reich, and former Chancellor von Papen had visited Paris to meet French businessmen, the government's rightward turn raising hope for a better understanding with Germany, with the further aim of silencing exiled anti-fascists. Shortly after, on the eve of Ribbentrop's visit, a number of 'suspect' refugees were summoned to the prefecture of police and assigned residence away from Paris.[31] The implementation of this new regulation, despite the protests it aroused,[32] made conditions of life – and even survival[33] – increasingly hard for the émigrés, subject now to the arbitrary decision of zealous functionaries. A further decree-law aggravated these provisions still further, by establishing internment centres for those foreigners who had to be 'subjected to closer measures of surveillance'.[34]

'ENEMY ALIENS'

France, I am convinced, will want to remain in this Europe of madness, the refuge of all the persecuted. Orders will be given at all our frontiers – will they not, Monsieur le Ministre? – that those who have managed to escape Nazi rifles or the machine-guns of the Reichswehr, where these have already been installed, will find in our country that fraternal reception that has for all times been the glory and honour of France, so that there is no question of returning them, and that our police forces – sometimes, alas, too brusque – receive every instruction needed to receive these unfortunate people and steer them towards the destination, wretched but at least assured, that must be reserved for them in the name of humanity.

Jules Moch, 5 April 1933

Despite the support and assistance provided by the workers' parties, the trade unions and a number of public figures, the émigrés were poorly tolerated and regularly seen as 'foreign subjects', trouble-makers and fomenters of disorder, an economic and a political threat, who risked disturbing future relations with the Reich. This attitude, widespread on the right, was broadly developed by the reactionary press, which never stopped attacking 'Marxists and Jews'. On 20 May 1933, M. de Puymaigre, a Paris municipal councillor, demanded information on the émigrés that left no doubt at all about his wishes: 'It is not without disquiet that public opinion sees France give [. . .] such a broad welcome to expelled Germans [. . .]. Among these there are certainly several victims who deserve our interest, but also how many undesirables [. . .] besides, will these exiles not form in our country, just like the antifascist centre exposed by Mussolini, an anti-Nazi centre, and arouse in Hitler a still greater hatred for France, if this is possible?'[35]

Throughout the 1930s, *Gringoire* ceaselessly slandered the émigrés, presenting them as a constant threat to French security and well-being. The anti-Semitism of the French right was further reinforced by the fact that the refugees were Germans, whom they hated.[36] A section of public opinion in France had backed Mussolini in his war on Ethiopia, and Franco in the Spanish war, despite the warnings of some Catholic writers such as Bernanos and Mauriac. Step by step, the right-wing press developed in a direction favorable to Hitler, even though it had traditionally been hostile to Germany – Action Française in particular. In 1923, Léon Daudet had written the famous line: 'I welcome the famine in Germany', but hatred of the Third Republic's weakness was stronger than hatred of Hitler. The French right was increasingly seduced by 'strong regimes' and constantly compared 'French disorder' to 'German order'.[37] *Candide, Gringoire*, and *Je suis partout* poured a constant stream of abuse on the émigrés, as part of the vast Jewish and Masonic conspiracy that Henri Bérault permanently denounced.[38] From 1937 on, the tone became increasingly anti-Semitic, and the émigrés were simultaneously accused of 'plotting against Germany' and of being members of the 'fifth column' – an insult that by 1940 had become commonplace.[39]

After the Munich agreements, the right of asylum in France was restricted to a minimum, while public opinion saw the 'foreigners' as one of the causes of deteriorating relations with Germany.[40] The right-wing press stoked up the psychosis about infiltration of Nazi agents, and any German refugee – or tourist – was perceived as a potential spy.[41] The Munich agreements were experienced by the refugees as a total capitulation of the democracies to Hitler, who was preparing for war while declaring his will for peace. The majority of antifascist exiles were now given an assigned residence, could only move around with difficulty and were subject to strict regulation, being threatened with internment on a wide variety of pretexts. Since the interior ministry circular of 12 October 1938, all 'illegals' were classed as 'forbidden to remain'.[42] Any political refugees deemed undesirable were liable to find themselves interned in a camp.[43] At the same time as distrust towards them was increasing, refugees were required to take a more direct part in the collective effort, by helping to 'reinforce our military power and take part accordingly in our national defence burden'. Acceptance of military service became a requisite condition for naturalization, and 'refusal of military service would lead to expulsion or dispatch to a special holding centre'.[44] Recruitment commissions were established in July 1939, and a committee was also set up to 'examine the political past' of foreigners. Refugees had to present themselves at the police commissariat for their place of residence within a maximum of twenty days. At the same time, police surveillance of them was reinforced, and frontier posts were instructed that foreigners should be allowed into the country only if they had an international transit card.[45] A series of other decrees bearing on freedom of the press and publications managed to silence the majority of antifascist activities.

The situation of the émigrés continued to worsen.[46] Even those who wanted to leave France could do so now only with immense difficulty.[47] Faced with this new situation, lively discussions took place among them on the possible outcome in case of conflict. While a large number of German workers among the refugees in France wanted to enlist in the French armed forces, other émigrés were divided, especially after the German–Soviet non-aggression pact. The majority of antifascist intellectuals believed that the cause of the peoples struggling against Hitler was their own, and that a new democratic regime would only be possible in Germany with the overthrow of fascism. But the question of military engagement alongside the Allies now raised problems and divided Socialists from Communists. When war was declared, the Social-Democrats Otto Wels and Hans Vogel declared: 'The annihilation of freedom and the destruction of world peace have been the essential idea of National Socialism from the start. To defeat Hitler is therefore the goal for which we struggle, together with the democratic forces of Europe [. . .]. We shall act in the course of this war as a force allied with all the enemies of Hitler who struggle for freedom and civilization in Europe.' Franz Dahlem, on the other hand, a member of the KPD central committee, declared on 16 September 1939: 'The struggle for the overthrow of Hitler, and for the establishment of a new regime in Germany, is the proper cause of the German people. To achieve this end, it is not necessary to make a bloody war, whose victims will first and foremost be thousands of Germans and Frenchmen.'[48] This question also divided the intellectuals: some approved the attitude of the KPD, whilst others rejected it violently.[49] Seen as treason by many of the émigrés,[50] a necessity by others, the German–Soviet pact sowed confusion in many minds, not to mention doubt towards the USSR.[51] At the end of August, the right of asylum was withdrawn from all German refugees, and on 1 September they were declared 'enemy aliens'.[52] Raids were increasingly common, and many émigrés had the feeling that it was on them first of all that war had been declared.

The KPD press, which had defended the German–Soviet pact, was now treated as an ally of National Socialism and proscribed.[53] German and Austrian political activists, who had been monitored for a long while by the police, were declared 'suspect' or 'dangerous' and arrested. New official lists of 'suspects' were published. Almost everywhere in France, antifascist exiles were arrested at night by the police, and sent to prison or detention camps.[54] When war was declared, refugees were no longer seen as a potentially useful support to the French army: deprived of the right of asylum, antifascists were lumped together with all other Germans, even Nazis, and on 5 September 1939, by dispositions taken by the ministry of national defence and war, male 'citizens' of the German Reich between the ages of fifteen and fifty had immediately to travel to holding centres that were indicated on posters. Both men and women had to report to the town hall or police commissariat of their place of residence. Until new instructions were given, they were not allowed to leave the locality in which they lived without special authorization.

'THE DEVIL IN FRANCE': ACCOUNTS OF THE FRENCH CONCENTRATION CAMPS

> The Devil in France was a friendly, well-mannered Devil. His devilishness came out in his polite indifference, his *Je m'en foutisme*, his slovenliness, his bureaucratic slowness.
>
> Lion Feuchtwanger, *The Devil in France*

The Devil in France was the title that Feuchtwanger gave to his book describing the fate of émigrés after 1940, in particular his own internment at Les Milles, near Aix-en-Provence.[55] If the antifascist exiles feared for the worst after Munich, very few of them imagined that those who had ceaselessly warned of the Hitlerite danger could one day be treated as enemies. As soon as the decree was announced, thousands of them had to travel to holding centres for subsequent internment. Then a regular nightmare began for them. As Hermann

Kesten wrote: 'I had always been a friend of the French people. I left for exile in Paris as if I was going home. I was happy to live among my French friends. When I saw the poster on the walls, stating that all citizens of German, Austrian or Saarland origin had to go to a concentration camp set up in the Colombe stadium, with a knife and fork and provisions for two days, I went along.'[56]

Ernst Erich Noth did not feel the notice should apply to him: 'My first reaction was fairly close to a fit of despair. I had expected, like most of the refugees who shared or still share this fate in the camps, something quite different than to spend the first weeks of the war interned, guarded by men alongside whom I'd believed I should and would be able to fight for a common cause.'[57] While Günter Markscheffel told himself: 'In times of such disturbance as these, a foreigner should avoid making mistakes. So I went to the Colombes stadium telling myself that the sooner I presented myself there, the sooner I would be released.'[58]

Many examples could be given: the exiled antifascists all went to these internment centres willingly, persuaded that they would be released 'once the Nazis had been sifted out'. The 20,000 or so who arrived at the Colombes stadium had to stand in line for twelve hours guarded by *gardes mobiles* armed with rifles, in deplorable hygienic conditions. Water for drinking and washing was rationed, as was straw needed for bedding. The internees suffered from rain and sun, and from the insults of their guards who already viewed them as conquered enemies, and Hermann Kesten had every reason to write to René Schickele on 7 September: 'And so France is starting its war against Hitler with a war against the enemies of Hitler who took refuge in France. Such victories gained over the victims of tyrants make this kind of victor the tyrant's next victim.'[59]

The internees included Jews, political émigrés, Socialists, Communists, non-party antifascists, Saarlanders who had opted for France, members of the Foreign Legion, writers,[60] veterans of the Spanish war and escapees from Dachau. Coffee was supplied in six barrels; six others served as latrines. At night they slept on damp straw or on the bare ground, under electric lights, while the *gardes mobiles* struck them with their rifle butts if they dared to protest. When after five days they had not even been told what was to happen to them, the most pessimistic rumours spread around: they feared being handed over to Germany. 'German citizens' were soon separated out, to be taken under the protection of the Swedish Red Cross and repatriated. The others, the refugees, were referred to by their guardians as 'dogs'. In due course, 'screening commissions' began to divide the internees into categories.[61] The decree-law of 9 September, moreover, enabled the government to withdraw French nationality when this had been only recently granted.[62]

Alfred Kantorowicz describes in similar terms the holding centre at Les Milles: the detainees there included Czechs, refugees from Danzig, soldiers from the Foreign Legion, Germans who had lived in France for more than fifteen years and were married to Frenchwomen, Jews and known opponents of Nazism, some of whom had been stripped of German nationality.[63] The only choice given these refugees was between engagement in the Foreign Legion for a five-year term in Africa, or detention as 'enemies' in another camp.[64] On 17

September, the interior minister made it known that those arrested foreigners who appeared 'suspect' would not be expelled but interned. German Jews who had been placed in holding camps were authorized to leave France for America after appearing once more before the screening commission. Meanwhile – in mid September – a special section for 'undesirables' had been established in the Colombes stadium,[65] then in the Roland-Garros stadium.[66] Women were sent to the Vélodrome d'Hiver. These émigrés included men of various nationalities, but especially Communists, including members of the KPD central committee. The majority were well-known for their antifascist convictions: Friedrich Wolf, Berthold Jacob, Paul Fröhlich, Gustav Regler,[67] Willi Münzenberg. On 11 October, after a new selection, certain antifascists were piled into goods wagons and taken to the repressive camp at Le Vernet.

It was a goods train. I made the endless journey in a brake-box, consumed with bitterness and premonitions. Finally, we pulled up on a plain which I did not recognize. A camp of shabby hutments was spread out before us, and in the distance gleamed snow-clad mountain-peaks.

Gustav Regler, *The Owl of Minerva*

Located in the Ariège, close to the Pyrenees, the camp at Le Vernet had been established for fighters and refugees from Republican Spain, on the same basis as the other camps at Saint-Cyprien and Gurs.[68] Divided into three sections – A for 'common-law criminals', B for 'politicals' and C for 'suspects', it housed left-wing activists, and Communists in particular. Alongside Spaniards and stateless (Russians, Poles, Germans deprived of nationality), there were Jews of German origin. Some had already served in the French army, others in the Foreign Legion. There were also a large number of German and Italian antifascists. While the detainees in sections A and B were not required to do any particular work apart from everyday chores, those in section C were employed in the camp sawmill, where they made furniture, or had to carry bricks. Even in winter, the detainees had four daily roll-calls. The conditions of detention were appalling: they slept in filthy barracks in groups of 200, often without covers, on damp straw infested with vermin. Lacking medication or a proper infirmary, a number died soon after arriving at the camp. Prisoners were allowed to write one letter and one card each week, but not to receive any mail. Their wives could come and see them only through the barbed wire.

The majority of accounts stress the disciplinary character of the camp and the appalling conditions in which the prisoners were forced to live.[69] These included political activists,[70] scholars, writers, and specialists in every discipline. Arthur Koestler has given his account of this camp in *The Scum of the Earth*.[71] Gustav Regler described in *The Owl of Minerva* the calvary of these men, antifascist fighters who were daily insulted by the camp commander who treated them as a 'rabble of spies'. Regler found there a large number of soldiers from his own brigade:

Vernet was an eerie cemetery. The huts stood like great coffins on the plain. Every morning the dead crept out of their graves to form up in rigid squares, a pathetic soldiery, and then, under the orders of uniformed men, went about the work of clearing paths, digging drains, stopping up rat-holes, burning foul straw and cleaning their coffins. It was a busy scene, as though someone had taken the lid off a churchyard to watch the dead at their squalid employments. But sometimes one of the dead, unable to endure the cemetery, would kill himself a second time. When we cut him down from the beam from which he hung we had a feeling of picking a ripe fruit, and we felt something like envy when we laid him to rest in the real cemetery of the camp. Everything, the box and the empty grave, had a look of dignity, privacy, cleanness and even homeliness. Death restored men's private lives. A man was by himself again.[72]

'Intellectuals' were especially marked out for latrine duty by the commander, and Alfred Kantorowicz maintained that the Vernet camp bore comparison with Dachau or Buchenwald. The detainees included several well-known writers: Koestler, Kantorowicz, Regler, Friedrich Wolf[73] and Rudolf Leonhard. After having passed through various screening camps, the less 'suspect' Germans were dispatched to other internment camps in the provinces,[74] to be parked there in tents, barns or sheds, without knowing what their fate was to be. They also included Communists, Socialists, pacifists, Jews, Catholics and Protestants who had nothing in common except their opposition to Hitler.

Were they civilian detainees or military prisoners? The legal imbroglio that they posed would not be resolved until May 1940, when it was decided that these 'suspects' should not be regarded as civil detainees. When they were led to the trains taking them across France,[75] they were once more mistreated by the *gardes mobiles* and insulted by the population. They were then divided between different camps but had very similar experiences, often related in their autobiographies and their exile novels. Hermann Kesten found himself 'near the châteaux of the Loire' in an unlit stable. Many fell seriously ill, victims of lice and dysentery. A doctor treating them, himself an antifascist refugee, died after two weeks. In the majority of these camps, the superior officers embezzled some of the money allocated for food.[76] Each day the detainees were taken out on marches, and had to eat standing up. They were used for all kinds of work, often pointless, in swamps, quarries or forests, without work clothes – they had often brought with them only a city suit – and without pay. They did however obtain permission to organize literary evenings. Kesten read his poems, Walter Benjamin his Chinese epigrams: 'These were academics, businesspeople, workers, of every age, who were forced to live in shame, insecurity and mud.'[77] They had no idea what had become of their wives and children back in Paris, let alone of their means of support.[78]

The same situation was described somewhat later by Lion Feuchtwanger, at the Les Milles camp where several of the most celebrated exile figures were detained. On 8 September 1939 a large number of refugees in southern France had been imprisoned in a camp near Marseille. Kantorowicz, a former fighter in the International Brigades, described this camp guarded by soldiers with bayonets – often veterans of the First World War – who saw the refugees simply as 'Germans'. The detainees each tried to advance their particular case: some were Alsatians, whose brothers were in the French army and who hardly spoke German; others were Jewish or had been married to Frenchwomen for twenty years. Among those 'suspected' of Hitlerite sympathies there were pacifists and members of the Human Rights League: Gert Kaden, Anton Räderscheidt, and the young architect nephew of Karl Liebknecht. The Les Milles camp, ten kilometres from Aix-en-Provence, had a less harsh regime than that of Gurs or Le Vernet, as it did not house known Communist activists. The detainees included a number of other writers and artists besides Feuchtwanger: Franz Schoenenberner, Wilhelm Herzog, Walter Hasenclever, Franz Hessel, E. A. Reinhardt, Max Ernst and Max Lingner.[79] The aberrant situation had it that they were guarded by *légionnaires* including two Germans who had fled the Reich – one a Communist, the other a Social-Democrat – and had both fought in the XIth International Brigade. Alfred Kantorowicz showed the same black humour when he described these inmates carrying out different chores in the camp and always addressing each other by their titles: '*Danke schön, Herr Landsgerichtsrat, Bitte schön, Herr Professor, Herr Hofrat, Herr Doktor*,' etc., even when they were just passing bricks.

It was soon learned that all women of German origin aged between seventeen and sixty-five had been interned at Gurs in the Pyrenees. In June 1940, the Les Milles camp counted 3,000 men, including detainees from camps in the north who had also been sent there as the German army advanced. In utter despair, they were reduced to paying their guards a high price for French newspapers – banned in the camp – in order to get some news.[80] The new arrivals included some genuine Nazis who greeted each other with '*Heil Hitler!*' They were dispensed from working and allowed access to the lists of detainees. At the same time, Feuchtwanger had to wield a shovel, and send a postcard to his American publisher to tell him that he would not be able to write the article on French hospitality he had promised, as he was presently occupied in terracing work in an internment camp.

On 29 June 1940 Alfred Döblin wrote to R. Minder from a camp in Lozère: 'I am in a wretched state, unable to speak, without help, in complete disarray,' ending the letter 'I sign this as a man who was formerly called Alfred Döblin.' Walter Victor was at Montauban, Günter Markscheffel in the Mayenne. Most often they were not even allowed to inform their wives of their place of detention, which was known only by a military postcode. A number were employed as foresters or quarrymen, others sent out to farms where they worked with the peasants.

It is easy today in reading the letters, memoirs and diaries of all these antifascist writers who had sought asylum in France to divine what their feelings were: a mixture of disgust, humiliation, revolt and fear, an utter despair. Since 1933, they had ceaselessly fought Hitler and warned France of the Nazi danger. They had often enlisted as volunteers in the French army, both to struggle against National Socialism and out of solidarity with the country that had taken them in. Never did they imagine that they would spend the start of hostilities in a concentration camp.[81] They sensed a horrific injustice[82] in the victims of Nazism being treated as enemies of the democracies. 'The first (and, as the event was to prove, the only) prisoners of war of the French Republic were now safely behind barbed wire,' wrote Gustav Regler.[83] And Arthur Koestler: 'In this bewildering situation, the French bureaucracy found a welcome diversion in starting a witch-hunt among the detested anti-Nazi refugees.'[84]

The documents that describe these internments all give a striking impression of the mixture of illogic, waste and aberration[85] that marked this episode. Certainly a number of voices were raised in defence of the detainees, but their legal situation was inextricable. Arbitrarily arrested, and suspected of being 'dangerous persons', they were guilty of nothing and had not committed any crime. But the decree of 18 November 1939 had transferred to the administrative authorities a power that properly belonged to the judiciary. The parliamentary groups of the left strongly signalled the infringement of individual liberty this involved, and the danger of granting such special powers to the military. But if the minister of the interior acknowledged that 'a police operation on the scale conducted at the outbreak of hostilities may have created painful situations', he still defended its necessity and the impossibility of discriminating among those affected.

A number of French public figures took up the defence of certain individual internees, such as the son of Karl Liebknecht, the fifty-five-year-old writer Lion Feuchtwanger who before wielding a shovel in a French concentration camp had been received by Stalin, Roosevelt and the king of England,[86] Hermann Kesten, Alfred Döblin or Walter Benjamin.[87] But their protests and representations generally had little weight against the administrative machine.[88] Hostility towards the émigrés – even writers – was very prevalent in government milieus.[89] All the same, thanks to a list drawn up of 'internees to be released immediately', a number of antifascist writers and 'non-suspect political émigrés' were freed in January 1940. In February, all foreign men under forty-eight were asked to join a task force to be deployed 'by the minister of national defence and war in the execution of all works needed for national defence'. Some 9,000 refugees joined the Foreign Legion, and 5,000 this task force.[90] If some kept the memory of their internment as an unpardonable humiliation, others continued to see France as their new homeland.[91]

The situation of interned antifascists had still not been completely settled, especially those in the Gurs camp, which had received a large share of fighters from the International Brigades. Despite several representations – including from André Marty – the French government refused to consider them as civilians with the right to asylum, but treated them as soldiers in a foreign army. In April 1939 they were transferred from Saint-Cyprien and Argelès to the reception centre at Gurs, which by May 1939 housed 18,983 persons of fifty-nine nationalities. These included 5,863 former International Brigaders, of whom 605 were Germans.[92] They asked the camp commander on 9 May 1939 to release them, so that they could take part in 'the defence of culture against barbarism and the fury of war', but this was summarily rejected. Condemned to live in damp barracks on straw mattresses, sometimes without shoes, often suffering from old wounds of the Spanish war that had badly healed, they only escaped despair by organizing an orchestra, lectures, and a theatre course. Throughout the summer of 1939 their situation continued to worsen, and after war was declared they were naturally treated as enemies. The repression intensified after the official ban on the French Communist party, and these 'dangerous and undesirable foreigners' were transferred to the repressive camp of Le Vernet. Some of them enrolled in the Foreign Legion or in the task force, so that by 23 March 1940 the Gurs camp only held 2,423, and 916 by June.[93] These were soon transferred to the Le Vernet camp, and Gurs became a detention centre for women. As Hanna Schramm wrote in her fine account of this camp: 'This was how the German women and children lived at Gurs; the men were initially sent to other camps. We had lost our past, we no longer had a homeland, a black cloud hovered over our future: the menacing shadow of Hitler's final victory. The country where we had thought to find a second homeland during the years of emigration had thrown us out of its community.'[94]

A number of German artists were interned at Gurs, including the expressionist poet Alfred Mombert and his seventy-two-year-old sister. There were also the wives of a large number of well-known antifascist émigrés: Valérie Schwarzschild, Lili Jacoby, Gerda Friedmann, the wives of Carl Misch and Weichmann; Babette Gross, the companion of Willi Münzenberg, Adrienne Thomas, Toni Kesten, the wife of Kurt Wolff (the expressionist publisher who published Kafka's *Metamorphosis*) as well as Lotte H. Eisner.

3. LAST EFFORTS TO ESCAPE FROM EUROPE

I drafted in my mind, almost without stopping, a very long letter to my friends, to explain to them why I had stayed in France, where I now found myself caught in a trap. This letter was a testament full of hope: defeated, we could not return home as we no longer had a home; every place on earth where we set our feet would be for us, and us alone, the land of nowhere.

Manès Sperber

In May 1940 the French government ordered the arrest and internment of all émigrés who had been left at liberty in September 1939 or whom the screening commissions had released.[95] The men were taken to the Invalides barracks, then to the Buffalo stadium (14 May 1940) before being directed to internment camps. The women were assembled at the Vélodrome d'Hiver, then taken to Gurs.[96] After the Armistice in June, these camps resembled giant mousetraps – an expression used by several émigrés – as the German army advanced. Even when they managed to escape from the camps, it was increasingly hard to leave France, and a number of émigrés – Ernst Weiss, Walter Hasenclever and Walter Benjamin – committed suicide rather than fall into the hands of the Gestapo.

THE MOUSETRAP

All German prisoners of war and civilian prisoners, including those detained and condemned for acts in support of the German Reich, shall be handed over without delay to the German forces. The French government is bound to deliver on demand all German nationals designated by the Reich government who are located in France, as well as in French possessions, colonies, protected and mandated territories . . .

Article 19 of the Armistice convention

As the success of the German invasion became clear, the majority of detainees lived in terror of being handed over to the Gestapo. The most well-known Communists and antifascists knew very well what their fate would be: arrest, deportation to Germany, torture, concentration camp and most likely death. They therefore made constant representations to the military authorities in charge of the camps to explain their situation and the vengeance that the Nazi regime would undoubtedly wreak on them if it managed to catch them. In certain cases, officers gave their word of honour that the files of political émigrés would be destroyed before the Nazis arrived.[97] Rudolf Leonhard and Friedrich Wolf, prisoners' delegates at the Le Vernet camp, even supplied a list of those prisoners who were most at risk if the camp administration passed into German hands. The situation differed greatly from one camp to another. In some, surveillance by *gardes mobiles* was stepped up; in others, the detainees were told that if they escaped, they would not be fired on by the machine-guns posted at the gates. At the Les Milles camp, a delegation led by Feuchtwanger asked the commandant to allow threatened antifascists to reach a port as rapidly as possible.[98] While a minority of the detainees rejoiced at Hitler's success and awaited the arrival of the German army as a liberation, Hitler's enemies lived these days in fear and utter despair. The arrival of Nazi forces in Grenoble and Arles had already been announced before any order for their release was given. Though the camp guards declared that they would not fire on the detainees if there was a mass outbreak, the detainees did not know what the reaction of the *gardes mobiles* would be. Feuchtwanger believed there would be a way out, if only because he claimed to have 'fourteen books in my head'. Hasenclever no longer shared that confidence, and decided to kill himself with veronal rather than fall into the hands of the Gestapo. He was taken to the Arles hospital, where they tried in vain to save him. On 23 September, all men between fifty and sixty were released from the Les Milles camp.

By the terms of article 19 of the Armistice convention of 22 June 1940, all persons of German origin interned in France had to be returned to the Reich, whether they were prisoners of war or civilians. Though the term 'civilian prisoner' was ambiguous, since it had not been made clear in the Armistice negotiations whether this also covered émigrés who had been deprived of their nationality, this situation was cleared up by a sub-commission.[99] The German government did not seek the repatriation of émigrés or Jews who still had German nationality, but insisted on having 'information of their identity'.[100] A high official of the Berlin foreign ministry was accordingly sent on a tour of inspection to the '*zone libre*' in July, to verify that article 19 had been complied with. Not only did all prisoners condemned for a criminal act on behalf of the Reich have to be handed over to the German army, but in other cases any 'unorganized release' was ruled out. The Kundt commission charged with examining the situation proposed therefore to inspect all the camps.[101] Faced with this situation, the camp directors were divided. In several camps – particularly at Gurs – they authorized the threatened detainees and those who were actively sought by the Gestapo to hide in the surroundings of the camp for the duration of the inspection. But in the camps of Le Vernet and Rieucros, which housed so-called 'undesirables', all the political prisoners were presented.[102] The Wehrmacht declared in its report that, though the French authorities had not made any obstacles, they had enabled a number of opponents to escape the eyes of the commission.

Officially, the supposed task of the commission was to repatriate 'good Germans', i.e. Nazi sympathizers, and give opponents the opportunity to re-establish themselves in the 'national community' after re-education.[103] Between 28 July and 29 August, the commission visited thirty-one camps, sixteen prisons and ten hospitals, counting some 7,500 Germans (including 5,000 Jews) and 2,000 task-force workers of German nationality. It encouraged as many Germans as possible to return to the Reich, and promised immunity for those who had committed no crime before their departure.

The living conditions in the camps, the crushing defeat of France and their subsequent despair, undoubtedly had an effect on a number of émigrés whose political convictions were not very solid.[104] Very few, however, agreed to return to Germany.[105] In all cases, the camp directorate had to supply the commission with lists of detained Germans, which then enabled the Gestapo to actively seek them out. It was not only those who requested repatriation who were returned to Germany, but also political militants that the Vichy authorities had handed over to the Gestapo at the demand of the Reich. Two former ministers of the Weimar Republic were to perish as a result, Rudolf Hilferding and Robert Breitscheid. At the same time, the Gurs camp received thousands of Jews deported from Baden and the Palatinate.

Those detainees who had refused to return to Germany remained in the camps. A series of disturbances and revolts broke out in some of these, following the murder of a detainee trying to escape. Negotiations were held between prisoners' delegates and the camp directorate to improve living conditions, but the situation continued to deteriorate. Franz Dahlem was sent to prison. New measures taken by the Vichy government in January 1941 further aggravated the situation in the camps of Gurs and Le Vernet, and accentuated their repressive character. When new disturbances broke out at Le Vernet, this was surrounded by armoured cars on 26 February 1941, and 800 *gardes mobiles* stormed the barracks.[106] A hundred detainees managed to obtain US visas, and were transferred to the Les Milles camp with the hope of leaving for America. In 1942 a number of antifascists were handed over to the Gestapo, including Franz

Dahlem, Heinrich Rau, Sepp Wagner, Siegfried Rädel and Herbert Tschä-per.[107] Some managed to flee abroad,[108] or lived underground.[109]

ÉMIGRÉS IN OCCUPIED FRANCE

Once under the Vichy administration, the camps were far more dangerous than they had been under Daladier. Not only were opponents sought by the Gestapo at risk of being handed over to Germany and murdered,[110] but the climate of anti-Semitism struck a large number of refugees of Jewish origin.[111] The latter were systematically kept at a distance by the Kundt commission, which in no way wanted to see them return to the Reich. After the Armistice, a large number of women detainees were also released, but those without resources or who feared arrest remained in the camps.[112] The Pétain government had divided the detainees on 31 October 1940 into 'dangerous' (the Le Vernet camp), 'to be kept under surveillance' (Gurs), and 'calm elements' (Argelès). Despite reinforced surveillance, a number managed to escape.[113]

From 27 September 1940, the German military government promulgated the first decrees defining the 'Jewish race'. Jews were now forbidden to cross the demarcation line, and those remaining in the occupied zone were to be counted. At the same time as Vichy was excluding them from the civil service (13 October 1940), full powers were given to the prefects to intern foreign Jews. On 22 October 1940, 6,504 Jews were expelled from the Palatinate and Baden, and sent to Gurs with the backing of the French authorities. On 2 June 1941 the French authorities ordered a new census, and the administration made an effort to promote the emigration of detainees to other countries. For this, however, they needed one or two people to vouch for them and stand surety in the country of asylum, and make the visa application (generally for the USA) before being transferred to the transit camp at Les Milles where they would wait for a suitable ship.[114] The situation worsened in 1942, after which it became virtually impossible to leave Europe. The Vichy government now agreed to hand over Jews from Germany and other countries living in the unoccupied zone to the Nazis. Some of these managed to escape and survived illegally, while others were deported to the east.[115]

Whether they had been released by the camp authorities, thanks to the intervention of outside figures, or had simply escaped, the émigrés were forced to live a clandestine existence for a while, having to fear the Vichy police as much as the Gestapo. A certain number did manage to do so, helped by the support of French friends, *résistants*, or by the authorities themselves – not all of whom simply obeyed the occupying power, and sometimes provided false papers, feigned to believe that the escapees' papers were valid, or helped them to escape raids and searches. There were the employees at the Marseille prefecture described by Anna Seghers in *Transit*, who pretended not to notice that the certificate of release from camp was false, that the identity photo did not match the bearer, or that the 'Alsatian refugee' addressing them was a German wanted by the Gestapo.[116] Alfred Kantorowicz, whom the gendarmes at Bormes had suspected right away, nevertheless owed his life to them: they even offered to hide him if the Gestapo paid a call, and when arrest became too imminent, it was the gendarmes in Toulon who protected the former International Brigade commander, and enabled him to leave Marseille.

Those exiles remaining in Paris – who either had not been reinterned in 1940 or had been released – could reach the unoccupied zone only with great difficulty. Ernst Weiss chose to commit suicide when the Germans entered Paris.[117] Alfred Döblin gave a detailed account in his autobiography *Schicksalreise* of his flight before the German army. He left Paris after the capitulation and reached Tours, Moulins, and Le Puy, travelling in cattle-trucks and dragging his eternal suitcase, in search of his family who had been evacuated to Bordeaux.[118] A number of émigrés remained in the south of France: at Cagnes-sur-Mer with Gide and Malraux, or in Provence. Kantorowicz cut down trees for heating and burned Feuchtwanger's old library. Most émigrés, as they feared being handed to the Gestapo, tried to leave France in any way they could.

Some tried to flee via Spain. As they had neither money nor papers, they often tried to cross the Pyrenees clandestinely, at the risk of being returned by the Spanish police. Kantorowicz reached Marseille by car with French soldiers, passing himself off as Czech. Alma Mahler and Franz Werfel lived in hiding in Bordeaux in a former brothel. They then reached Biarritz and Bayonne, where they tried to obtain a Portuguese visa. When they passed Lourdes, Werfel, despairing at being able to leave France, vowed to devote a novel to Saint Bernadette if he managed to escape the Nazis.[119] He then reached Marseille and hid himself at a hotel occupied by German officers. With the aid of Varian Fry – charged by the US government with assisting intellectuals threatened with arrest by the Gestapo – he then travelled to Perpignan with Heinrich, Nelly and Golo Mann. They all crossed the Spanish frontier illegally. The Catalan police took pity on them and allowed them to continue their flight to Barcelona and Madrid. Arthur Koestler, though freed from the Le Vernet camp, had had his identity card confiscated, which forced him to report to the prefecture twice a week. He finally managed to reach Limoges, enrolled in the Foreign Legion, and was employed in Marseille as a military messenger. There he met Walter Benjamin who was waiting to embark for America, and kept a dose of morphine to hand in case he was arrested by the Gestapo. Koestler reached Casablanca, and from there Lisbon, with the help of a British official. As he was refused a visa, he travelled to Britain without papers on a Dutch vessel. Arrested on arrival in London, he asked to join the British army.

Anna Seghers has depicted the anguish and despair common to all these German antifascists seeking a visa for the US in her novel *Transit*.[120] Marseille was where the majority of them gathered, trying to escape the immense mousetrap that all Europe had become. But to emigrate, a whole series of conditions had to be met, which almost no one managed to fulfil. First of all, if he was in Paris, the refugee had to cross the demarcation line with a safe-conduct. Unable to obtain this, he had to cross clandestinely with the assistance of local peasants. If he had been released from an internment camp, he had to be in possession of a paper testifying that he had left legally. Often, however, these exiles had escaped from camp and were forced to use false certificates. To leave France, they first had to reach Marseille. The prefecture there did not allow refugees to stay if they did not have a residence permit – something that could be obtained only with a good deal of luck, recommendations, representations and support. Even so, the permit would only be for a very limited time. The émigré was often sent back to his department of origin so that he could make his application there. A residence permit could only be obtained if one's identity papers were in order, and in particular with a foreign visa showing that the émigré was preparing to leave the country.

In order to leave France, one needed not only a certificate of release from camp, and identity papers, but an exit visa from the Vichy government, which naturally would not supply this for persons wanted by the Gestapo. Applications to consulates were lengthy and desperate. A Portuguese and a Spanish transit visa were both needed, but these were only granted parsimoniously, and refused to émigrés known for their antifascist convictions, who had taken part in the Spanish war or had written against Franco. Without these two transit visas, any other visa was useless. A Mexican visa could be easily obtained,[121] but a US visa was also needed, which was only granted with difficulty. The refugee needed to provide an affidavit – a financial guarantee signed by two US citizens – as well as papers that were in order, the transit visas, and above all the attestation that this visa was granted by the US government. To obtain it, one needed powerful supporters, the intervention of people such as Thomas Mann or Hermann Kesten, which was possible only for the most well-known émigrés.[122]

Finally, sufficient funds were needed for the ticket – often bought on the black market, given the weight of demand – unless one could get it paid by a committee. By the time this confirmation and the different visas had been obtained, the boat had generally left a month ago. You then had to wait for the next one, but in wartime conditions the shipping companies did not know when this would arrive and whether it would leave. By the time the visas were obtained, the first one would be out of date or the ticket would no longer be valid. The émigré then had to begin all over again. But as he no longer had a visa testifying to his imminent departure, renewal of his residence permit was refused and he risked being sent back to his department of origin or imprisoned.

If he remained in Marseille clandestinely, he needed the complicity of a French family who would hide him, or to find a dodgy hotel that didn't look at identity papers. At all events, however, he would risk arrest as soon as he appeared in the street or visited a café, and all hotels were subject to frequent raids. If a man was arrested, his wife would often be sent to a camp, since no one was there to support her. He would often not even know where she had been interned. The majority of émigrés thus had to make innumerable applications, follow the interminable queues outside the consulates, and live in daily fear of being arrested by the police in the street, woken up in the middle of the night by a raid, denounced by a neighbour, or recognized in a café by a Gestapo agent. They did not even greet each other when they met, for fear of being spied on.

The majority of émigré letters and memoirs are filled with descriptions of this desperate quest for a visa in 1940, and the Kafkaesque procedures that were needed to obtain it. To escape the raids in Marseille, Hilde Walter hid herself away in a clinic, Alfred Kantorowicz was protected by the gendarmes in Bormes, and Franz Werfel put up at a hotel where German officers were staying. Alfred Döblin, though naturalized in France and with a son in French uniform, was at first refused authorization to leave the country. It was only on his wife's insistence that he obtained permission from a general.[123] He had to make numerous appeals to connections in the United States to obtain an American visa. But this was still dependent on possession of a ticket, which he could not buy for lack of money.[124] He had to queue outside the Spanish consulate from five in the morning to present his case. Ludwig Marcuse was at first refused a visa as he did not have a marriage certificate and could not obtain one, having lost his German nationality. Kantorowicz came up against a similar problem: he was asked to prove his place of birth. Lion Feuchtwanger, who had an emergency visa, managed to leave France thanks to the US consul, who put him up at his home so that he enjoyed extraterritorial status. Heinrich Mann and Alfred Kantorowicz had to disguise themselves as bathers to exchange information on the next departures. Rudolf Leonhard, who tried to escape in the hold of a boat, was arrested by the French police and imprisoned in Castres, from where he managed to escape. He spent the War in a monastery, where his friend, the writer and lawyer Botho Laserstein, had become a monk. He had the unusual privilege of reading various funeral orations written in his memory by his fellow émigrés.[125] In the Marseille cafés, pretending not to recognize one another, one could meet Ernst Busch, the *légionnaire* Arthur Koestler, Tristan Tzara and Walter Mehring.

Up to the last moment, they did not know if the expected ship would arrive, and if they would be able to embark, as one of their visas or authorizations might in the meantime have run out. The story Anna Seghers tells in *Transit* – of an old man who obtained an engagement as orchestral conductor in Caracas, waited several months for his ship, then died of a heart attack when he was told he could not leave because his file was short of an identity photo – was quite possibly no invention. Alfred Kantorowicz, for his part, was almost unable to leave because it was discovered, when he was already on the boat, that he figured on the list of persons wanted by the Gestapo. He owed his salvation to the generosity of a French officer who decided to let him escape regardless. Often, for want of a boat to America, the émigrés were ready to embark for any destination: South America, Martinique,[126] Cuba or Santo Domingo. The old cargo vessels that carried them resembled floating concentration camps, according to Kantorowicz. The crossing itself was not safe: sometimes the British refused to let ships pass Gibraltar. When they stopped at Dakar or Martinique they were interned once more and it often took several months to reach America. A number of them, finally, including Rudolph Olden and his wife, perished when their boat was torpedoed by the German navy, or succumbed to typhus epidemics.[127] As for those who tried to reach Spain, their fates were very varied. Though Heinrich Mann, despite his age, managed to cross the Pyrenees clandestinely, Walter Benjamin killed himself after he was threatened with being handed to the Gestapo. The pacifist Berthold Jacob was recognized in Lisbon and arrested.

Those émigrés unable to escape had to remain in France illegally or join the Resistance, if they were to avoid arrest by the Gestapo. The painter Hermann Gowa lived under a false identity, hidden by a Russian writer to the north of Nice. The brother of Ernst von Salomon, Bruno, worked as a tenant farmer at Châteauneuf-de-Grasse. Lotte Eisner became a cook, supposedly of 'Alsatian origin', and remained hidden in Figeac. Emil Alphons Reinhart was helped by an Italian who hid him in southern France, grateful that he had written a biography of Eleanore Duse, but he was finally arrested by the Gestapo. Nico Rost depicts him in his book *Goethe in Dachau*. Theodor Wolff, former editor of the *Berliner Tageblatt*, was taken back to Germany and died in Oranienburg on 23 September 1943. Siegfried Rädel, Heinrich Rau, Franz Dahlem, Robert Breitscheid and Rudolf Hilferding were handed over to the Gestapo. Though some still managed to escape from or survive in the camps, Breitscheid was murdered in Buchenwald and Hilferding took his own life.[128]

ENGAGEMENT IN THE RESISTANCE

The engagement of German antifascists in the French Resistance is still not well-known, despite a number of studies.[129] As they had fought against Hitler, and in the International Brigades, many German antifascists were ready to take part in resistance movements, alongside local partisans, in the countries occupied by the Reich. As soon as the threat of war appeared, a large number of them volunteered to fight in the French army. After the capitulation, many who remained in France joined the *maquis*, where their perfect knowledge of German was put to good effect.

The organization *Travail allemand*, formed by French and German Communists, was charged with propaganda action in the Wehrmacht and espionage missions in the occupied zone. During the summer of 1940, a number of German Communists who found themselves in the '*zone libre*' gathered in Toulouse to coordinate their activities. After making contact with the PCF, Otto Niebergall was charged in April 1941 with supervising all propaganda work carried out by this organization. The aims selected were 'demoralization of the Wehrmacht', obtaining information, infiltration of its services by anti-Nazi activists, and the establishment of resistance centres. Wives and daughters of émigrés took part in this work by forming connections with German soldiers in order to sound out their morale and their political attitudes. At the same time, the Resistance asked some German exiles to gain employment as secretaries, telephonists and translators in the German military and civilian services.

These tasks were particularly dangerous. Undermining Wehrmacht morale was punishable by death. What was most commonly attempted was to make contact with soldiers or officers, win their friendship, and bring them to express themselves freely about Hitler and the War – even, in some cases, get them to provide military information, secretly take anti-Nazi leaflets back to Germany, or set up Freies Deutschland cells. Contact with soldiers also made it possible to note from their bags the numbers of their postal sectors, so as to send them Nazi papers on which the émigrés had commented in the margins.[130]

One Communist exile, Gerhard Leo, managed to find employment as a French interpreter at the Toulouse Kommandantur. He was thus able to warn French resisters of future deportations of workers, and divert trains with military equipment. Through the military post, he managed to send many anti-Nazi leaflets to Germany, and made contact with a German soldier who saved him from arrest when the Gestapo suspected him of spying.[131] Thanks to this underground work, some anti-Nazi papers designed for soldiers attained a print run of 50,000 copies.[132] In certain cases, finally, the exiles managed to lead soldiers to desert[133] or commit acts of sabotage.[134]

An important step in this ideological work within the Wehrmacht was marked by the formation of CALPO (Comité 'Allemagne Libre' pour l'Ouest).[135] While the German army was experiencing increasingly heavy losses on the eastern front, the Nationalkomitee 'Freies Deutschland' was formed near Moscow, at the instigation of the KPD, its members including anti-Nazi figures from the widest variety of backgrounds, as well as prisoners of war, officers and rank-and-file soldiers. Besides developing an intensive ideological activity among the prisoners of war, Freies Deutschland managed to smuggle propaganda material into almost all countries occupied by the Reich, and transmit radio broadcasts to Germany informing soldiers of the real military situation. CALPO developed the aims and ideals of Freies Deutschland in France, by trying to get German soldiers to join the Resistance. This work of propaganda and espionage was carried out with great difficulty, and it is certainly hard to assess its impact. Some actions however were highly symbolic: German soldiers who joined the *maquis* after contact with the émigrés, others who warned resisters of impending dangers. But by the time that CALPO was officially recognized as a Resistance organization in June 1944, a large number of Germans who had worked for it had already been executed by the Gestapo.

Besides these acts of espionage and propaganda, a number of émigrés fought with the regular Resistance – in France, especially in the Cévennes and Lozère.[136] Some even took part in the liberation of Paris.[137] Men and women,[138] most commonly known only by their pseudonyms, rest today in French cemeteries or in common graves.

Part Two
Exile in America 1939–45: From the Second World War to McCarthyism

If I had not felt embarrassed before the others, I would have kissed the American earth.

Alma Mahler, *And the Bridge Is Love*

it is difficult for refugees to avoid either indulging in wild abuse of the 'Americans' or 'talking with their pay-checks in their mouths' as KORTNER puts it when he is having a go at those who earn well and talk well of the USA.

Bertolt Brecht, *Journals*, 14 November 1941

I leave this country in bitterness and rage. I could perfectly well understand why the Hitler bandits should put a price on my head and turn me out [. . .]. But I feel deeply wounded by the ridiculous way in which I am being expelled from this fine country [. . .]. I carry with me the image of the real American people whom I love.

Hanns Eisler, 26 March 1948

Preface to Part Two:
The Acceptance of Defeat

Until the whole European continent fell under the Nazi heel, few of the émigrés had thought of America as a place of exile. They wanted to remain close to the borders of the Reich, not to leave the orbit of German culture, and to return home as soon as possible. America, which had fed so many of the artistic myths of the Weimar era, they saw as a monster with immense landscapes and human resources linked to the power of technology and money, but more or less empty as a cultural space. Most of the émigrés did not speak English, and the images they had of the United States were disturbing and negative so they had no desire to confront the reality. If some of them had found it hard even to leave Berlin, America seemed to the majority of émigrés an almost uninhabitable world for any European intellectual. Walter Benjamin's hesitations in emigrating, the pain that Ludwig Marcuse felt when he resolved to take refuge there, and Brecht's own unease in Hollywood, were not feigned. It is hard to imagine today, when New York is just five hours away by plane and American culture is all-pervasive, how for these German exiles in 1940 it still appeared as the 'new world', how crossing the ocean was an adventure, and almost nothing was known of American reality apart from films, novels, jazz, variety shows and detective novels. American novels had certainly enjoyed great success in Germany, but they had often helped to accredit a frightful and monstrous image of the country. Many émigrés scarcely made a distinction between New York and the visions of *Metropolis*, between American society and Chaplin's *Modern Times*. Their visions of America were so many myths. Fascinated by its gigantism and its industrial might, they had only been the more deeply affected by the crisis of 1929. In his poem, 'Late Lamented Fame of the Giant City of New York', Brecht wrote:

Who is there still remembers
The fame of the giant city of New York
In the decade after the Great War?
[. . .]

What fame! What a century!
Oh we too demanded such broad-gauge overcoats of rough material
With the padded shoulders which make men so broad
That three of them fill the entire sidewalk.
[. . .]
And we too stuffed our mouths full of chewing gum (Beechnut)
Which was supposed eventually to push forward the jawbone
[. . .]

What people they were! Their boxers the strongest!
Their inventors the most practical! Their trains the fastest!
And also the most crowded!
And it all looked like lasting a thousand years.[1]
[. . .]

But one day the news was out that a catastrophe was in the process of ravaging this universe that fascinated Europe:

For one day there ran through the world the rumour of strange collapses
On a famous continent, and its banknotes, hoarded only yesterday
Were rejected in disgust like rotten stinking fish.[2]

These images of a gigantic, monstrous, fascinating America crop up again and again in Brecht's early plays. The unexpected vision of his first poems gives way to a denunciation of this false paradise in which everything can be bought if you have the money. This is the Chicago of *In the Jungle of Cities* and *St Joan of the Stockyards*, followed by the cemetery city of *Mahagonny*. It is also the America of German films of that era.

Whatever their degree of politicization, the exiles almost all found America repellent. Walter Benjamin saw scarcely a difference between the United States and Kafka's nightmare world. Franz Werfel preferred to risk his life in Europe than to cross the Atlantic. And if German film-makers of the 1920s visited Hollywood and even settled there (Sternberg, Lubitsch, Murnau), there were few artists – George Grosz being an exception – who could envisage without terror in 1933 the possibility of moving to America. Separation from Germany was already experienced as a trauma by most of the émigrés, and there were few indeed who left Europe in 1939–40 without a tear, even if this departure – often awaited for months – meant the sole chance of escaping arrest, concentration camp or death.

America, still traumatized by the crash of 1929, distrusted any new wave of immigrants. It cannot be denied, however, that following the fall of France, it displayed – especially under the personal influence of Franklin D. Roosevelt – a genuine generosity towards the refugees. We should neither embellish the picture nor blacken it. Many émigrés lived in semi-poverty in America, suffering from isolation and completely forgotten. The most political had later to confront the wave of McCarthyism that chased a number of them – including

Brecht and Eisler – back to Europe. But even those, like Eisler, who left cursing
the American government and claiming that their persecutors reminded them in
a sinister way of what they had formerly fought against in Germany, always
kept a feeling of deep and sincere gratitude towards the American people. The
diversity of émigré fates makes it almost impossible to describe this American
exile in a single image. It horrified or disconcerted them. They cursed it or
decided to remain. They carried on criticizing its values or adopted them. For
better or worse, they became Americans.

On disembarking in the new continent, they were all assailed by the same
feeling of disturbing strangeness. For a few of them, America proved a place of
gilded exile, a haven of tranquillity where they had practically nothing to fear.
For others, it brought an apprenticeship in isolation, indifference and poverty.
They regarded these cities and landscapes with amazement as well as disquie-
tude, judged the country's customs with indulgence or irony. Though the
antifascist activities conducted there – apart from the great intellectual mobilization that accompanied America's entry into the War – were extremely
limited by comparison with what they had been in Europe, America possibly
left a stronger mark on the German emigration than did any other country.
Avant-garde artists whose names were known all over Europe were often
unknown here, and their styles failed to arouse any interest. To make a living,
to work and continue to create, they had to adapt, discover mass culture and the
laws of the market. American cinema, and the way it was organized, was the
radical negation of everything that had made the grandeur of German cinema.
Fritz Lang and so many others learned this lesson painfully and had to modify
their aesthetic. Brecht tried to sell screenplays, even if he despised Hollywood.
Schoenberg, the very symbol of Europe's musical avant-garde, had to give
private lessons in order to survive. Kurt Weill certainly abandoned the radicalism that had made him so famous in the years of his collaboration with
Brecht, though it would be too easy to reproach him for his adaptation to
Broadway. In America he was able to give greater rein to the influences that had
already marked his style in the 1920s – those of jazz, blues, and Gershwin. One
may regret this change of style, but it is impossible without bad faith to remain
insensitive to the beauty of 'Lady in the Dark', 'September Song' or 'Speak
Low', all the admirable songs and music that he wrote for the American stage.
Others who were revolutionary in Europe became teachers; Piscator, for
example, found a replacement theatre in a lecture-hall, discovering that everything can be taught in America. They acquitted themselves with a dedication
and passion that nothing can belie. Piscator's young secretary was a certain
Tennessee Williams. In a photograph taken during an open-air rehearsal, the
young students in shorts include Marlon Brando and Tony Curtis. And the
young woman taking notes, Judith Malina, was later to found the Living
Theater.

Few cultural encounters were so painful, or so rich, as that between these
émigrés who embodied the high ground of European culture, physically
threatened with annihilation by the Nazis, and this America which championed
a kind of industrial culture – all too familiar today – for which the majority of

them had cultivated up till then only disgust and contempt. By giving them a visa, America saved their lives. And what would America have been without them? There is no domain of culture or science – biological research, the visual arts, cinema, theatre, art history or economics – to which these émigrés and their children did not give a sharp boost. Yet it was only in the 1970s that a new generation of Americans came to realize how for a period of ten years, everything that was deep, innovative and revolutionary in Europe of the 1920s and 30s could be found in the shadow of their cities, that Brecht, Reinhardt, Piscator, Lang, Eisler and Schoenberg had lived among them.

What should be said, then, about the political emigration? If Communists found themselves as much at home in the United States as the proverbial bear in an ants' nest, their encounter with America also toppled a number of perspectives. They learned to know it, and thus love or detest it, with greater objectivity. Without his encounter with America, the theoretical work of Herbert Marcuse would be hard to imagine. And the social sciences in America would hardly have developed as they did. For some of the émigrés, the encounter sharpened their critique of capitalism; for others, it softened it or dissolved it altogether. Eisler could remain a Communist in Hollywood, and Brecht a Marxist, but a number of radicals became reformists and a number of Socialists became conservatives. America was a strange mirage that shattered so many concealed contradictions. If it left some unchanged in their political or artistic ideas, it radically transformed others in their most intimate convictions. Former antifascists turned into theorists of anti-Communism and Cold War. Their children never learned German, and championed ideas that their fathers had fought against throughout their exile.

Finally, what remains of Weimar in America, more than just works in museums and libraries, the collapse of a body of knowledge and a number of artistic experiments, are also the tombs scattered from New York to California. Franz Werfel, Max Reinhardt, Ernst Toller, Kurt Weill and Heinrich Mann are all buried in American soil. In the immense white necropolis of the Hollywood cemetery, similar bouquets of dried flowers are piled before the urns of Rudolf Valentino and Peter Lorre, the child-killer of Fritz Lang's *M*.

The Confrontation with Nazi Germany

1. US FOREIGN POLICY AND THE THIRD REICH

ROOSEVELT'S POLICY TOWARDS NATIONAL SOCIALISM

Surprising as it may seem, America played scarcely any role in the overall foreign policy of National Socialism until the outbreak of the Second World War.[1] References to the United States were rare in Hitler's speeches, and he seems to have systematically ignored the reports of his ambassadors and military attachés on the development of American opinion towards the Third Reich. Hitler saw the tradition of American isolation as definitively established.[2] The hostility of a number of American public figures mattered as little to him as the noisy and bothersome support of pro-Nazi German-Americans.

This ignorance of America in the Nazi ideological and political edifice is explained first of all by the totally negative image of the country that the Nazis gave themselves. The United States was a great power forming a continent of its own, quite unconnected to the problems of the European states. It was an immense space devoid of culture, victim of 'Jewish jobbers and moneybags',[3] a pitiable example of political and racial decadence. It had gathered up the 'Jewish scum' of Eastern Europe, had no unity of its own, and 'National Socialism alone is destined to liberate the American people from their ruling clique and give them back the means of becoming a great nation'.[4] Nothing could be expected of this 'ethnic chaos' on the edge of the abyss, Goebbels would declare.

By historical accident, Hitler and Roosevelt took charge of their two countries' destinies at almost the same date – 30 January and 4 March 1933. The change of the governing party in America led to the appointment of a new ambassador to Berlin from a university background, William E. Dodd,[5] who was fresh to the diplomatic world and deeply disturbed on his arrival in the German capital by the style of the new regime, especially its anti-Semitism.[6] At the same time, the former Reich chancellor and president of the Reichsbank, Hans Luther, was appointed German ambassador to the US. If the American government already viewed these new diplomats sent by the Reich with mistrust, and had scarcely any sympathy for Hitler, the wave of arrests and the climate of anti-Semitism whipped up throughout Germany soon aroused the most widespread disgust. American Jews regularly protested against Nazi anti-Semitism. Several demonstrations were held from early 1933 on, both in New York and on the West Coast, with the backing of intellectuals and trade-unionists. As for the book burnings and the persecution of intellectuals, they struck the whole American intelligentsia with horror. But if Roosevelt's assessment of developments in Germany was certainly negative, he abstained from any public condemnation. His first public attacks on Nazism were made only after the outrages of *Kristallnacht*, and the Nazis held American Jews responsible for this turn in American policy. A number of remarks on racial discrimination in Germany are found in the Congressional Record from the start of the Hitler era, and on 1 April 1933 the American Jewish Congress held a meeting in Madison Square Gardens to condemn the practices of National Socialism. American opinion – even in Jewish milieus – was still cautious about the usefulness of hardening United States policy towards the Reich,[7] and the consequences of an economic boycott of Hitler Germany.[8] But for all that, the American democratic conscience clearly declared its contempt for the treatment inflicted on the Jews, and German legations were assailed with petitions, telegrams and letters of protest, to which the Nazis of course paid no attention. Roosevelt did not hide his view, in communications with Ambassador Dodd, that he found these practices a scandal, but he still saw it as an internal matter for Germany, in which the United States could do no more than protect American citizens who might be affected.[9] Hitler himself, in response to protests from Dodd, committed himself to guaranteeing the safety of American Jews in Germany. The threat of a boycott was brandished with caution, and until May 1933, the American Jewish Congress refused to envisage such a measure. Cordell Hull, the Under-Secretary of State for Foreign Affairs, disapproved of a boycott appeal published by Samuel Untermeyer in the *New York Times* and supported by the American Federation of Labor. In London as well as Washington, negotiations with Germany were undertaken with a view to stopping anti-Semitic persecutions. The Reich made promises but did nothing. The State Department, for its part, officially assured the president of the American Jewish Congress on 22 March 1933 that its ambassador was keeping it informed of the situation of Jews in Germany, and that these persecutions would soon stop.[10]

Some conservative public figures in Germany were disturbed at the possible repercussion of this hostility of American public opinion and the US government towards the Reich, but Hitler was not overly concerned by this,[11] insulting Roosevelt and the USA on frequent occasions. Between 1935 and 1937 German relations with America steadily deteriorated, reaching a new low in 1938 after *Kristallnacht*. On learning that a hundred synagogues had been fired, seventy-six of them destroyed, 7,500 Jewish shops ransacked and ninety-one Jews killed, America was struck with horror, and the former US consul-general in Berlin sent Cordell Hull a memorandum in which he wrote: 'When a country that prides itself on the superiority of its civilization commits deliberately and in cold blood acts worse than those which we have vigorously protested against in the past, I believe that the moment has come for us to take measures that go beyond mere blame. In my opinion, if we do not react to the events that have occurred in Germany, we shall be far behind the public opinion of our country.'[12]

The United States immediately recalled its ambassador, and Roosevelt declared at a press conference the next day before two hundred journalists: 'I myself could scarcely believe that such things could occur in a twentieth-century civilization. With a view to gaining a firsthand picture of the situation in Germany I have asked the Secretary of State to order our ambassador in Berlin to return at once for report and consultation.'[13]

The recall of Hugh Wilson, the US ambassador in Berlin at this time, was an important diplomatic event, as the US had not taken any such measure since the First World War. Hitler immediately recalled his ambassador in the US, fearing a break in diplomatic relations and the expulsion of German nationals. In fact, the US action was confined to replacing the ambassador with a chargé d'affaires. Nazi insults towards America now intensified, however; Roosevelt himself was treated as a 'quarrelsome Jew', and his wife as 'typically Negroid'. The Senate, however, still refused to abrogate the neutrality laws, and the Roosevelt administration found itself stymied in the face of a public opinion that was hostile to Nazism but strongly anti-interventionist, while the Nazi government increased its provocations and insults, responding to the President's message demanding an assurance that after Czechoslovakia other weak nations would not be invaded, that Germany had no intention of invading the United States.

NAZI MOVEMENTS IN THE US

All these strains are an assurance that the sound elements of the United States will one day awaken as they have awakened in Germany. [. . .] The German-Americans, rejuvenated by National Socialism, will be called to lead a new America.

Adolf Hitler

Equally disturbing for American democracy was the radicalization of a number of groups of German-Americans – with the hesitant support of the Reich – who found a role as defenders of Germany and National Socialism in the United States. American Nazi movements of this kind were found from New York to Los Angeles, Detroit to Memphis, modelling their processions, flags and demonstrations on those of the German Nazis, but they never managed to build themselves into a real political force, and aroused only moderate interest on the part of the Reich. Quite often, their noisy admiration was even judged untimely.

These pro-Nazi movements developed early on in the communities of German-Americans that were to be found in most large American cities.[14] On 12 October 1935 the Chicago National Socialists celebrated the eleventh anniversary of their organization.[15] But their situation was not an easy one: by their anti-Semitism they aroused the hostility of the majority of the American population, while the German government, aware of the negative effects of these demonstrations, generally disapproved of the activities of these groups and banned *Reichsdeutsche* from joining them.[16] The greater part of these Nazi support groups had been established haphazardly by young Germans who had emigrated to the United States in the early 1920s and found in National Socialist ideology the illusion of a certain '*völkisch*' community that attached them to Germany. The majority of their members – even the American Nazi leaders – had never been members of the NSDAP. This did not stop them from forming a number of National Socialist groupings, but even the well-known Teutonia in Chicago had little more than fifty members.

The development of these movements reflected fairly closely the electoral successes of the Nazi party in Germany. The first American Nazi newspapers, such as *Vorposten,* appeared around 1930, and for a while, the NSDAP viewed these American groups as valuable ideological allies and encouraged their development.[17] Soon, rival Nazi groups developed in Chicago and New York, each claiming to represent American National Socialism.[18] Teutonia gradually became the rallying-point for the majority of their number. But when Hitler came to power, this victory of National Socialism in Germany, far from opening the way to a new expansion of 'American Nazism', was in fact to mark its decline.

The American Nazis had no official ties to the Reich.[19] Their agitation and brutality only increased the hostility that the majority of Americans already felt towards National Socialism. Faced with the risk of a growing deterioration in relations between Berlin and Washington, therefore, Rudolph Hess ordered all American Nazi groups to stop public demonstrations, and confine their sympathy for the Reich to winning over public figures by rebutting the accusations of the 'Jewish press'. At the same time a Bund der Freunde der Hitler-Bewegung was established (in 1932), which together with Teutonia, was to become the main concentration of Nazi sympathizers.

The Bund likewise modelled its style of action on the NSDAP, calling for a boycott of Jewish shops and of newspapers opposed to Hitler.[20] These anti-Semitic and racist attacks, however, brought an increasingly lively response, especially in New York. On 27 October 1933, the leader of the Bund, Heinz Spanknäbel, was threatened with arrest as a 'foreign agent' and had to flee to Germany.[21] Facing the risk of violent confrontation with democratic movements and the hostility of a large number of political figures, the Bund was forced to undergo an 'Americanization'. The German embassy henceforth avoided being represented at its demonstrations, all the more so as the US government had ordered an inquiry into Nazi propaganda and the Bund's activities.[22] Witness hearings were held in many US cities to show that the Bund was financed by the Third Reich. Yet despite its demonstrations, its vocal admiration for Hitler and its anti-Semitism, it was impossible to prove in an irrefutable way that the Bund violated American laws. Its ideology was certainly anti-democratic, but experts were unable to establish that it presented any real danger. Disturbed however by the attitude of the US government, the Reich officials demanded that the Bund immediately cease all activities. This was only obtained with some difficulty, despite the mediation of the German embassy, and the Bund carried on attacking all non-Nazi German-American groups.

The organization of a Völkischer Tag on 6 October 1935 was a complete fiasco: the parade of Nazi activists in the New York streets came up against large police forces. Not only had the German regime ordered all members of the NSDAP to keep away from such demonstrations, but German citizens living in the United States were strongly urged to refuse any solidarity with these movements. The supreme humiliation was that the propaganda section of the NSDAP in Berlin maintained in an interview published on 7 October in the *New York Times* that it completely distanced itself from the Nazi actions in New York, which it deemed detrimental to relations between America and the Reich. Renamed the German-American Bund, the organization of Nazi sympathizers was compelled to conceal its link with the Hitler regime. In 1935 it comprised thirty-five local groups including seventeen in New York, with some 2,500 members and up to 25,000 supporters. They continued to organize large meetings in the major American cities, despite the protests of the German ambassador who sent back many negative reports on their activities. Germany reiterated the ban on Reich citizens and NSDAP members from involving themselves in the Bund's demonstrations. No warning or instruction managed to silence the zeal of the US Nazis. They did agree, however, to publish anti-Semitic articles only in the German edition of their journal *Der Weckruf*, and not in the English edition. The Deutsch-Amerikanischer Kulturverband, directed by émigré antifascists, organized demonstrations against the Bund, but apart from the Reich's public disapproval, the Bund had above all to fear the hostility of the American population and the US authorities. The procession of its paramilitaries, modelled on the SA, that was planned for New York in 1937, aroused the attention of the Deutsch-Jüdischer Club, which published the magazine *Aufbau*, and following a complaint to the mayor of New York, Fiorello La Guardia, the parade was banned.[23] Gerhart Seger, a Socialist who had escaped from concentration camp, undertook a large-scale information campaign on Nazi activities in the United States (including a lecture at the Washington Town Hall Forum on 18 December 1937), which led to a complete ban on this paramilitary formation.

For all its violence, the Bund never made a mark on US public opinion, except negatively. The extremism of its speeches and article was accompanied by a certain cowardice, and the anti-Hitler journalist Dorothy Thompson, wife of Sinclair Lewis, did not hesitate to attend meetings of the Bund in February 1939 and disrupt them with fits of laughter.[24] Other émigrés such as Joachim Remak[25] believed that, far from winning support for Hitler's Germany, the Bund succeeded in alienating from it the majority of American intellectuals and politicians, as well as the public at large. If only a few Americans felt worried by events in Europe or took the threat of fascism seriously, they were sufficiently impressed by seeing American Nazis parade in Madison Square Gardens with their uniforms and swastika flags that Thomas Mann feared a '*Kristallnacht*' against German shops, and the development of a violent anti-German sentiment as there had been during the First World War. Many Americans of

German origin also feared that the actions of the Bund would get them seen as potential Nazis. But the agitation of these groups continued to intensify. In 1940 the Bund organized violent demonstrations against the film *Pastor Hall*, based on Ernst Toller's play, which showed scenes of concentration camps. In certain cities, including Chicago, the disturbances were on such a scale that the film could not be shown, and it was withdrawn from commercial distribution. Finally, the infiltration of Nazi ideas in the German-American milieu helped to fuel the spy psychosis that many Hollywood films developed during the War, such as *Spies on the Thames* or *Defeat for the Gestapo*.

ANTI-SEMITISM AND THE WEIGHT
OF AMERICAN OPINION

If the US government showed the utmost caution in taking a public stand against Hitler's Germany, it often lagged behind public opinion in this respect. The refusal of German consuls to return to Berlin, coupled with Einstein's decision to remain in America, were the subject of lengthy comment in the US press,[26] as was the treatment inflicted on Jews in Germany. On 1 February 1933, Isaac Klimov, Berlin correspondent for the *Jewish Morning Journal* and the *Jewish Chronicle*, explained to the Reich press service that Nazi anti-Semitism was bound to have a negative effect on American public opinion. Foreign minister von Neurath hastened to declare that this was simply a matter of excesses due to 'election fever', or 'provocations' committed by Communists who had infiltrated Nazi ranks. Von Papen also declared in the *Neue Wiener Journal* on 7 March that Jewish citizens had absolutely nothing to fear. The intensification of violence against Jews, both German and foreign, put the lie to these honeyed words. The foreign press, and the English-language papers above all, were particularly indignant at the unleashing of anti-Semitism. The Reich issued both promises and warnings: any press correspondent describing anti-Semitic actions risked immediate expulsion. If on the other hand the press campaign against Germany stopped, then the Social-Democratic press would be allowed to reappear. In Britain, the German ambassador asked to meet with figures from the Jewish community in order to reassure them. Reaction from Jews in the United States was more violent. On 27 March 1933, a mass demonstration was planned at Madison Square Gardens, which the US government tried unsuccessfully to defuse by maintaining that, according to reports from its ambassador, violence against German Jews had stopped. But the boycott and ransacking of Jewish shops, the systematic expulsion of Jews from German economic and intellectual life, followed in 1938 by *Kristallnacht*, only increased the indignation of the American Jewish community, and of a large section of the non-Jewish population, those of German origin included. The US government was unable to check such spontaneous reactions. It might be impossible to declare a systematic boycott of German products, but dockers in many ports refused to unload boats flying the swastika flag. If the solidarity of trade unions and left organizations remained limited, the protests of Jewish organizations were stronger and could not be ignored by the government, all the more so as the Reich's religious policy was now also arousing the indignation of American churches.[27] Far from being restricted to trade-union, Jewish or religious circles, the repugnance that Nazism aroused did not take long to spread to the greater part of American opinion, especially thanks to the development of the mass media.

At the turn of the decade, many American journalists had written articles and essays on Germany's development, which they described as having the potential to end up in either Communism or fascism.[28] New press correspondents, resolutely hostile to Nazism, would soon exert a deep and increasing influence on American opinion. The most characteristic example was undoubtedly William J. Shirer, later known for his bestselling history of the Third Reich, who lived in Berlin from 1934 on. Virulently Germanophobic,[29] Shirer sent very many negative reports on Hitler's Germany, emphasizing the pogrom atmosphere that reigned in Berlin, despite threats to expel him from the Reich. From 1937 he worked for CBS, and relayed to America a number of extracts from Nazi speeches and demonstrations that only increased repugnance towards Nazism. Radio was still at this time a new and popular invention, and millions of Americans were stupefied to hear the voice of the new German *Führer*. If Hitler and Goebbels stressed the importance of speech in winning the masses for Nazism, the effect on US opinion was not at all favorable: most listeners to CBS were deeply shocked by the violence and hatred in Hitler's voice, and thanks to the almost daily broadcasts that the three CBS journalists in Germany relayed to the US, millions of Americans had a taste of Nazism in sound. The role of the media in the development of US policy towards the Reich can be exaggerated, but it is certain that the Roosevelt administration was forced to take account of this radicalization of American opinion; though still hostile to intervention, it expressed a feeling of disquiet and disgust towards the new German regime. And Shirer's broadcasts had a surprising impact on millions of listeners, who for a long time continued to identify Nazism with just one voice: that of Hitler.[30]

2. THE UNITED STATES AND THE REFUGEE QUESTION

THE ECONOMIC CRISIS AND THE PROBLEM OF IMMIGRATION

At the time that the problem arose of emigration from Europe to escape from Nazism, the United States had scarcely emerged from a social and economic crisis whose repercussions could still be felt.[31] Legislation on immigration was also particularly severe. Cheap labour was plentiful, with university graduates working in New York as elevator boys. More than 80 per cent of American families were not in a position to offer their children higher education. Maurice Davie, officially charged with drawing up a sociological audit of immigration from Europe from 1933 to 1943, stressed in his 'Report of the Committee for the Study of Recent Immigration from Europe', published in 1946 as *Refugees in America*, the role of this economic situation in the government's general attitude towards refugees.

The basic law on immigration of 1917 had been revised by the Immigration Act of 1924. On top of the conditions generally required for a US visa,[32] this divided the globe into three zones, each governed by a particular regime. The 'unrestricted area' comprised the dependent countries of the Western hemisphere in North, Central and South America, as well as the West Indies. 'Eligible native-born citizens' of these countries could immigrate to the US without restriction of number. The 'barred zone' comprised Asia and those Pacific islands that were not American. No further migrants were accepted from this zone apart from the Philippines (an annual quota of fifty, to start from 1934) and China (a quota of 105). The third zone comprised countries subject to strict quotas (Europe, Africa, Australia, New Zealand), for which the 1924 Act set an annual total of 150,000.

These quotas were strictly controlled by US consulates overseas. Some categories of immigrant were not subjected to the quotas,[33] or were classified as 'non-immigrant'.[34] To land in the United States, it was necessary to obtain a visa – temporary, permanent or immigrant – delivered by a consulate. The visa jurisdiction was directly under the State Department, while the Justice Department was charged with prosecuting any infraction following from an illegal stay. Obtaining a visa naturally required possession of a valid passport, certificates of civil and military status, and an affidavit of resources. A presidential order of 1930 further aggravated the conditions of immigration by demanding the strict respect of quotas, as well as forbidding access to the United States to any person unable to prove that their means of existence enabled them to avoid becoming a charge on the government for a period of several years. In legal terms, these conditions in theory prevented the majority of antifascist émigrés from reaching America.

The entry of the United States into the War in 1941 led to still more draconian measures. After the closing of American consulates in the Axis countries, control of visas was entrusted to the State Department, and to avoid infiltration of spies and saboteurs, allocation of visas became the responsibility of an Interdepartmental Visa Committee, composed of representatives of the State Department, the immigration and naturalization services, the FBI, military and naval intelligence. The majority of anti-Nazi refugees of German and Austrian origin now found themselves 'enemy aliens'. The granting of a visa was subject first to the Interdepartmental Visa Committee, then in unfavourable cases to the Interdepartmental Visa Review Committee, and finally to the Board of Appeals whose two members were appointed by the President himself. In 1942, a further text alleviated this legislation somewhat, declaring that victims of regimes against which the United States was waging war should not be considered as enemies. Maurice Davie acknowledged that while this legislation certainly prevented the infiltration of spies, it made it increasingly hard to rescue threatened persons, to the point that the rate of immigration reached its lowest figure at the very moment when requests for US visas had never been so numerous. These measures were repealed only in July 1945.

*   *   *

An examination of the official statistics confirms this fact: the regulations were in general so strictly applied between 1933 and 1944 that despite the many organizations that sought to support the émigrés, the number of European immigrants was the lowest recorded since 1820:

1891–1900	3,687,564	1921–1930	4,107,209
1901–1910	8,795,386	1931–1940	528,431
1911–1920	5,735,811	1941–1944	132,833

In fact, for the first time in American history, the number of emigrants from the United States exceeded the number of immigrants in the years 1933–44. The dry figures published in the Davie Report make a dramatic counterpoint to the stories of so many exiles who tell of the long lines waiting outside US consulates: an antifascist threatened with arrest by the Gestapo if he could not gain the support of powerful figures or committees getting the reply that he could indeed migrate to the United States by inscribing himself on the waiting list, but that 60,000 people were in front of him. The consular authorities, taking refuge behind the quota law, applied it with such extreme severity that not only were these quotas not exceeded between 1933 and 1944, but they were rarely even attained: the number of refugees admitted to the United States fell several hundred thousand short of the number legally authorized.

The United States was thus no exception to the lack of enthusiasm that the great majority of countries displayed towards the reception of refugees, an attitude shared by both conservatives and liberals. Whilst many intellectuals took a stand in support of assisting the refugees, governmental circles remained very cautious. Conservatives maintained that neutrality was part of the American tradition, liberals that war only served imperialist interests. Isolationism was upheld by supporters of Roosevelt as well as by his adversaries. Burton Wheeler, a senator for Montana and a Roosevelt supporter, subsequently became one of the leaders of the non-interventionist lobby America First,[35] in October 1941 attacking the 'royal refugees' – an allusion to the Habsburg family – who sought to drag the United States into a 'democratic' war in order to retrieve their crowns. The same position was championed by the liberal historian Charles A. Beard, which brought a violent attack in an open letter signed by progressive writers who reproached him for his egoism and cynicism. If the liberals were also hostile to the easing of legislation towards émigrés, they avoided attacking them personally.[36] Under-Secretary of State Breckinridge Long,[37] on the other hand, did not conceal the fact that he feared the refugees both economically and politically: they risked influencing US opinion in an interventionist sense.

The total number of refugees from Europe admitted to the United States between 1933 and 1945 did not exceed 300,000, according to the Committee for the Study of Recent Immigration from Europe, 53.1 per cent of whom came from Germany and Austria. It was believed that 67.5 per cent of the total left their country of origin because of fascism, though political emigrants in the strict sense made up no more than 5 per cent.[38] The largest share of refugees reaching the United States up till 1945 were either of Jewish origin, or came from other countries of asylum that had now been occupied by the Reich. The quota policy remained practically unchanged until 1938, and the maximum quota authorized for Germany and Austria was reached for the first time in 1939. These figures do not however take account of persons deemed to be non-immigrants or those benefiting from special visas, in particular the 'emergency immigrants'[39] who numbered some 30,000 in all.

If the procedure to obtain a US visa was relatively simple, very few of the antifascist émigrés were able to satisfy it. Very often they lacked any identity papers or these had long expired, as well as any financial guarantee. The Gestapo often acted more swiftly than the rescue committees, and before obtaining a visa they found themselves in concentration camp.[40] If they were well-known for their political activities or their Communist ideas, moreover, they risked being refused a US visa point blank.[41] The good will of the US consuls – even in Marseille – could not change the draconian conditions imposed on immigrants, and many of these in despair took ship for South America or the West Indies, where conditions of access were easier. Even as anti-Semitic persecution worsened, the United States refused to increase its quotas.[42] Not until 1940 were exceptional solutions envisaged, which made it possible to rescue some antifascists threatened with death.

This was the role of the Emergency Rescue Committee directed by Frank Kingdon, which sought to come to the aid of a number of figures in occupied France, facilitating an 'emergency visa' for individuals who figured on lists transmitted to the US consulates. More than 567 requests were made in August and September 1940, but the committee obtained no more than forty visas, despite several representations to President Roosevelt, explaining that the only offence of these threatened people was that they had defended democracy. Even in these circumstances, Under-Secretary of State Breckinridge Long tried to restrict the number of these visas as much as possible, on pretext that they risked making it easier for Nazi spies and 'totalitarian agents' to reach US territory. Eventually the Emergency Rescue Committee obtained some 2,000 visas, about half the number requested for antifascists remaining in France. The interventions of Eleanor Roosevelt, Thomas Mann and Albert Einstein did not succeed in bending the administration's policy. A War Refugee Board to rescue the victims of fascism was finally established in 1944 – too late!

> The American consul in Marseille is the man our fate depends on.
>
> Walter Victor, letter to Emil Oprecht, 13 July 1940

Despite the adjustments made to US immigration law *in extremis* in 1940, obtaining an American visa remained a real obstacle race for the majority of antifascist refugees. Few indeed succeeded in collecting all the papers needed: certificate of release from internment camp, exit visa from the Vichy government, Spanish and Portuguese transit visas, affidavit, and so on, that enabled them to make the application. It is easy to understand how many maintained they would sell their soul to the devil in return for a US visa. The typical situation was just as Anna Seghers depicted it: by the time all the documents had been collected, the first one would have run out and it was necessary to start all over again, with the risk of no longer being able to obtain the transit visas or the authorization to stay in Marseille, being expelled from one's department of residence or no longer finding a boat.[43] The chance of obtaining one of these emergency visas depended on having influential connections in America – Einstein, Hermann Kesten, Thomas Mann, Hubertus Prinz zu Löwenstein – and we have already mentioned how Mann, for example, refused to intervene in favour of Salomo Friedländer (Mynona), not wishing to see him among the émigrés. Those who were famous as writers or scholars could hope to obtain the backing of an institution. The same applied to the affidavit.[44] Finally, the variety of questionnaires to fill in left little prospect of Communists ever obtaining a transit or immigrant visa.

Hanns Eisler had received an official invitation from the New School for Social Research in 1937, and a visitor's visa in 1938. The Nazis had withdrawn his German nationality, but he obtained a Nansen passport from representatives of the Czechoslovak government in New York. All he now needed was to request an immigrant visa from the US government. But this could be obtained only by leaving the country, and he had to travel to Havana to request it from the US consulate there.[45] He had to wait a good while before getting a response, as in the meantime he had been referred to publicly in America as a 'Communist'. On 31 March 1938 the Havana consulate received instructions from the State Department that he was not to be granted a visa until a full inquiry had been held. In October 1938 a second memorandum stated that he would not be granted a visa, as his Communist convictions were no longer in doubt. In the meantime, however, he had obtained an extension of his visitor's visa until 21 January 1939, following a number of representations. The journalist Dorothy Thompson then launched a petition in his support, signed by a number of public figures, and got Eleanor Roosevelt to intervene for him with Secretary of State Sumner Welles, but without success. On 2 March 1939, the US authorities demanded that Eisler leave American territory immediately. This aroused new protests,[46] insisting on Eisler's antifascist convictions and his value as a musician. He was still however at risk of expulsion. President Cardenas then offered him a residence permit in Mexico, and from April to August 1939 Eisler taught at the conservatoire in Mexico City. After legal intervention on his behalf, he obtained a new tourist visa on 7 September 1939, for just two months, to allow him to return to the New School. He remained in New York after his visa ran out, and new petitions were circulated on his behalf.[47] But for all that, an order for his arrest was made on 17 July 1940, and he had to leave for Mexico to obtain a new visitor's visa. As he was still a professor at the New School, Vice-Consul Myers granted him a 'non-quota immigrant visa', which eight years later brought him a severe reprimand from the House Committee on Un-American Activities. Even armed with this visa, however, Eisler was refused re-entry to the United States and had to wait two months at the Mexican border until his fate was decided. By the time he finally obtained an immigrant visa, the whole procedure had taken two years.

THE INTERVENTION OF UNIVERSITIES

Faced with this extreme complexity of US legislation, many antifascist refugees owed their salvation to the support and intervention of American public figures and institutions. Associations of American academics took a stand against National Socialism early on, and expressed their indignation with German restrictions on academic freedom. A number of them set out to develop effective support for their threatened colleagues. Some university presidents, moreover, also saw in this German exodus an opportunity to enrich their staff at less cost, in tandem with a humanitarian operation. Universities and foundations thus worked out a rescue programme together. As teachers were not subject to the immigration quota, it was relatively easy for a German academic with an invitation or contract from an American university to enter the United States. According to the Davie Report, the number reaching America on this basis was close to 2,000.

In 1933, a number of American universities already sent invitations to German professors expelled from their posts. Columbia University took on members of the Frankfurt School and the Institut für Sozialforschung, after they had spent a period in Paris. The University of Chicago invited Leo Strauss, Paul Tillich and Arnold Bergstraesser. Yale and Harvard employed a number of academics and artists, including Paul Hindemith. Many American colleges, such as Vassar College in New York State and Black Mountain College in North Carolina, invited German scholars of Jewish origin. The Institute of Advanced Study in Princeton, where Einstein had been since 1933, took on Thomas Mann and Hermann Broch in 1938. The second wave of émigrés, in 1936–37, particularly found asylum at Californian universities (Los Angeles, San Francisco, Berkeley), which accepted artists as well as scholars. During the War the Institut für Sozialforschung was based in California, along with Arnold Schoenberg, Hanns Eisler, Ludwig Marcuse and Hans Reichenbach. Stanford University also took on a number of émigrés.

As unemployment was still rife in America, and many American academics saw the arrival of over-qualified Europeans as a threat to their career, the salaries of these professors were often paid by private foundations. Many artists – even those who had not previously taught – declared themselves teachers to avoid the quotas. Their legacy to America was immense, and the social sciences and humanities as well as the fine arts, music and drama would be unimaginable today without the contribution of these émigrés.

INDIVIDUAL INITIATIVES AND COMMITTEES

Important support in helping German exiles reach the United States was given by committees established there, well-known émigrés already settled, and individuals who for various reasons were concerned to support these émigrés. The most significant of these committees were often established by Jewish organizations, such as the German-Jewish Club of New York, the American Jewish Committee, the American Federation of German Jews and the Jewish Labor Committee, all of which were chiefly concerned with Jewish refugees expelled from Germany and Austria, and sought to establish a strong current of solidarity with them in American public opinion.

Other committees specialized in support for artists and academics, such as the Emergency Committee in Aid of Displaced Foreign Scholars, founded in 1933 by Stephen Duggan, whose object was to obtain visas for academics and settle them with American institutions. The American Guild for German Cultural Freedom played an important role and made financial awards to artists. The Guild's 'American committee' was presided over by Alvin Johnson and Governor W. L. Gross of Connecticut, its 'European committee' by Thomas Mann. The League of American Writers, at that time a very political organization, also formed a special section for the émigrés, the Exiled Writers Committee, and sought to draw the government's attention to the fate of anti-Nazi intellectuals. Finally, a number of these American committees were set up by wealthy immigrants or in film circles, especially by the director William Dieterle (of German origin), their efforts being to support actors, scriptwriters and directors forced into exile. More important still was the aid of the Emergency Rescue Committee, which granted emergency visas and was directly responsible to President Roosevelt. The directorate of this committee included representatives from various aid organizations, intellectual circles and trade unions. It played a major role in the rescue of antifascist intellectuals through 1940–42, and aided at least 2,000 immigrants. This committee, directed by Dr Frank Kingdon, president of Newark University, included both Americans and foreign advisers who monitored the endangered antifascists in various European countries.[48] The committee's financial requirements were met in a rather strange way: by banquets, raffles, and demands of the kind: 'Who will pay $500 to save Franz Werfel or Marc Chagall?' Debatable or not, some $200,000 was raised in this way.[49]

These committees and organizations were complemented by a large number of personal initiatives. If many of the émigrés complained about American bureaucracy, they often paid tribute to the generosity of the American people. A large number of prominent figures in American political and cultural life stood financial guarantee for émigrés whom they did not know, signed their affidavits and raised the money needed for their passage to the United States. Those émigrés who had succeeded in reaching America multiplied their efforts and collections to enable their less fortunate friends to join them. Piscator came to the aid of Brecht,[50] Thomas Mann helped a number of émigrés. Sometimes their aim was to act on American public opinion to show the danger of fascism in Europe and the distress of the émigrés by way of plays and films.[51] It was often actors, journalists and writers who sought to draw the attention of the administration, or of Eleanor Roosevelt,[52] to the situation of a particular threatened antifascist. Many exiles were grateful to Clifford Odets for his support, and to Ernest Hemingway, who not only paid substantial sums to help antifascists such as Alfred Kantorowicz who were still in France, but also enabled former Communist fighters in the International Brigades to reach the United States. One of the most illustrious examples of this commitment of American intellectuals to the refugees was that of Sinclair Lewis and his companion, Dorothy Thompson.

An influential journalist, Dorothy Thompson was one of the first American public figures to campaign not only in support of the émigrés, but also for United States commitment alongside the European democracies. Paradoxically, she came from a conservative background and had been a bitter adversary of Roosevelt and the New Deal. She put her hope in an 'enlightened twentieth-century imperialism'.[53] In the early 1920s she lived in Europe as correspondent for a number of American papers,[54] and it was at Gustav Stresemann's house that she met her future husband, the writer Sinclair Lewis, whose life she shared until 1942.[55] She belonged to the literary generation that throughout the 1920s, from Scott Fitzgerald to Henry Miller, fled a prosaic and materialistic America for a more or less mythical Europe, understanding nothing of its political situation. Dorothy Thompson was certainly interested in the rise of Nazism, but hardly saw it as a real danger. She could not imagine that the German people would ever accept Hitler.[56] After meeting the Führer, she drew such an unflattering portrait of him in her book *I Saw Hitler* that she was expelled from Germany on 25 August 1934.[57]

Her expulsion came as a surprise to Americans, and transformed the conversational journalist into a dedicated anti-Nazi who, while America was still very little interested in European issues, ceaselessly denounced National Socialism as a global danger.[58] Her articles in the *Saturday Evening Post* and the *Herald Tribune* made her the most famous political journalist in the United States, even if her convictions were often rather muddled and had a mixed reception.[59] At all events, she exercised a profound influence on American public opinion by her hatred of fascism and her will to support the refugees. It was thanks to her press campaigns and the affidavits that she signed that a large number of writers were able to reach America. Her house – to the great despair of her husband[60] – became a meeting-place for émigrés. Some of these she knew from her time in Berlin, being friendly with the Mann family and Ernst Toller, and she took on the actor Fritz Kortner as her secretary.

Kortner met her at the moment of her separation from Sinclair Lewis, when he was supposed to write a theatre play with her, and he remained her personal adviser until his departure from Hollywood. He seems to have had a certain influence on her political ideas, leading her to defend more forcefully Roosevelt's policy. In his autobiography, *Aller Tage Abend*, Kortner recalls the long conversations he had with her:

> In these endless debates, her liberal friends, of whom I was according to her the most pitiless and the most vehement, waged a long resistance. We believed we had gained ground, when a conversation with [Wendell] Wilkie reduced our success to nothing. After wearing out all our arguments, I begged her to think how her father would have advised her. The following day, she came with an article for the *Herald Tribune* in support of Roosevelt.[61]

After this sudden conversion, perhaps due to the influence of Kortner and other émigrés, she campaigned for Roosevelt in 1940 and played a certain role in his re-election.[62]

Dorothy Thompson could be seen at the majority of antifascist public meetings; she helped to break up a meeting of the Bund, and especially bent her efforts in support of German antifascists remaining in Europe. Her friendship with Eleanor Roosevelt, her membership of the Emergency Rescue Committee and then European PEN in America, as well as her contacts with Franz Werfel, Thomas Mann and Hermann Kesten, enabled her to help a number of émigrés, even Marxists such as Brecht or Hanns Eisler. Her famous article 'Refugee Anarchy or Organization?' seems to have played a role in Roosevelt's decision to step up assistance to the exiles.[63] After her 'betrayal' of the Republican party, she was violently attacked by conservative circles who condemned her 'Communist' connections. Indeed, her collaborators included several émigrés whose progressive ideas were well-known, who not only convinced her of the rightness of their analysis of the European situation, but even drafted some of her articles. After Fritz Kortner left for Hollywood, her closest collaborator was Hermann Budzislawski, former editor of the *Neue Weltbühne*. In the McCarthy era, however, Dorothy Thompson published in the *Saturday Evening Post* an article 'How I Was Duped by a Communist' (1949), which maintained that, despite working with him since 22 June 1941, she was actually quite unaware of his political ideas, and that he did not exert any real influence on her views.[64]

As well as the important role she played in rescuing antifascist émigrés,[65] Dorothy Thompson exercised a far from negligible influence on her husband Sinclair Lewis (the first US recipient of the Nobel Prize for Literature in 1930), who campaigned against anti-Semitism to the point of being called 'Lewisohn' by his enemies, though he was not of Jewish origin. Lewis was not especially political, and remained apart from the awakening of radical consciousness that marked so many American writers in the 1930s. His nickname 'Red' referred to his hair colour, not his politics. Though his novels made a trenchant critique of American civilization, it was particularly under his wife's influence that he took part in antifascist activity and wrote *It Can't Happen Here*, depicting a hypothetical fascist regime in the United States. Despite the opposition of Father Coughlin and the Hearst press, this work had a great success, and a play based on the novel was produced by the WPA during Roosevelt's re-election campaign in 1940. Staged in more than thirteen American cities, it made a far from negligible contribution towards raising consciousness of what was happening in Europe.[66]

It is certainly hard to assess with any certainty the impact that this sympathy for the émigrés and the common struggle against fascism had on American politics. While Fritz Kortner does not stint his praise of Dorothy Thompson, Klaus Mann depicts with irony and tenderness the 'frail girl' who accompanied Sinclair Lewis to Vienna, Munich and Berlin, and grew into a strong woman aware of her prestige, feared and admired, who sought to arouse American opinion on the meaning of the tragedy being played out in Europe. But a number of émigrés often tended to overestimate the commitment of these American supporters. Sinclair Lewis had no love for Hitler, but discussion of European politics bored him to tears. Even when émigrés met with progressive American writers at Thomas Mann's home in California, they formed two distinct groups and had little contact. Lewis's play was a courageous act of commitment, but did not remove his ambivalence towards left-wing ideas.[67] At the request of Mrs Frank Taylor, however, he took part in 1944 in radio broadcasts on the 1933 book burnings. During his time in Hollywood, he worked on a film on the European situation, *Storm in the West*, and again formed close ties with some German émigrés. Even Piscator had the idea of staging one of his plays, but collaboration proved impossible. And this astonishing writer, who could have been one of the greatest of his age, fell steadily into alcoholism and dementia.

THE ROLE OF PRESIDENT ROOSEVELT

If the émigrés formed conflicting images of America, to the point that one feels Brecht and Thomas Mann are scarcely speaking of the same country, they almost all displayed the same admiration for President Roosevelt – an admiration that bordered on veneration. The majority of them saw him as the very symbol of the struggle against fascism, of morality and democracy, calling him the 'father of the émigrés'; the whole German emigration felt a collective grief at his death. While the majority of countries closed their borders and even his own administration was hostile to the refugees, he sought to come to their aid and made this a personal concern. The genuine sorrow felt by so many of the émigrés when he died should thus be no surprise. 'Our president is dead,' Ernst Toller's wife declared to Ludwig Marcuse, who maintained that the 'antifascist émigrés' were his 'chosen people', to whom he showed more generosity than did any other country. Alfred Kantorowicz was ashamed of being German when he heard the insults that the Nazi radio heaped on the dead President. Thomas Mann opposed him as the 'archangel of Good' to the 'Hitler devil'.

In actual fact, Roosevelt's attitude towards the émigrés was fairly complex. People like to cite, as evidence of the attention he paid them, Thomas Mann's invitation to the White House during his visit of June–July 1935, when he received the title of doctor *honoris causa* from Harvard University. Through Thomas Mann, many émigrés declared, it was Weimar in exile that was being saluted. But Mann at this time was not really an émigré. And even if he subsequently maintained somewhat enigmatically that from his first meeting with Roosevelt he 'knew that Hitler was lost', no one could take seriously the idea that Roosevelt already envisaged direct intervention in Europe at that time. On the contrary, he constantly minimized the danger posed by European fascism, despite the detailed reports of his ambassadors. It was only in 1937 that he made public his hostility towards Nazism. He said nothing on the Czechoslovak crisis, and believed even after Munich that peace was still possible. His change of attitude followed that of American opinion, the growing disgust aroused by *Kristallnacht*, and the violence and sadism against Jews in

Germany. Even if Roosevelt had considerable sympathy for the Jews – and several in his own entourage – he kept his emotional reactions under wraps for a long while, trying to keep the United States out of the European conflict.

But if many of Roosevelt's positions at this time were cautious, timorous, even naïve and idealistic, if he seems to have been unwilling to understand the true meaning of Nazi triumph and the spread of fascism in Europe, and still believed America could remain uninvolved, he was sensitive early on to the question of refugees. In 1934 he addressed a note to US consulates, requesting them to show generosity in granting visas to victims of National Socialism.[68] It seems however that the consulates took scant notice. After *Kristallnacht*, he authorized the twelve to fifteen thousand refugees then staying in the United States on tourist visas to remain by renewing these every six months, and promised that they would in no case be forced to return to their country of origin.[69] At the Évian conference Roosevelt was prepared to relax the US immigration law, but he had no power to implement this. The United States simply agreed to accept a further 27,370 German refugees. The results of the conference thus fell far short of the hopes to which it had given rise. The Wagner-Rogers Bill of May 1939, which proposed to accept 20,000 refugee children, was derisory in relation to the number of victims. Certainly America was granting visas, but to scientific figures or well-known academics, not to Jewish petty traders or obscure Social-Democratic journalists. The verdict passed by a number of historians is only too true: millions of people were condemned to death by selfishness.[70] From 1940 onwards, however, Roosevelt acted more effectively. A number of American writers who had founded the Emergency Rescue Committee, directed by Frank Kingdon and William Green, president of the AFL, declared the need to support antifascist trade unionists. Despite the persistence of conservative opposition, the action of Roosevelt and his wife succeeded in rescuing a number of antifascists in danger.

We should not be surprised therefore at the gratitude so many émigrés displayed towards him, that their debt to America made some of them blind to his failings, and that Roosevelt became for the émigré community a symbol and a legend. *Der Aufbau* compared him in 1942 with a landscape, and stressed the impression of 'trust', 'goodness' and 'natural strength' that emanated from his face. Alfred Kantorowicz found him 'clear' and 'luminous', and opposed his noble spirit to the vileness of Hitler. The Socialist magazine *Die Neue Volkszeitung*, at first hostile to Roosevelt, became neutral in 1940 and supported him after Pearl Harbor. Twelve days after the Japanese attack, the director and friend of Brecht, Bertold Viertel, wrote a regular love poem addressed to him.[71] Brecht too called Roosevelt as an 'enlightened democrat'; Fritz Kortner described him as a 'powerful opponent of the devil',[72] and the New Deal as the attempt to introduce 'a certain understanding of socialism within capitalism'. He judged Roosevelt's policy to be 'moral and humane', his hostility to fascism arising from 'a sympathy with the middle classes and the proletariat'. When American forces liberated the concentration camps in 1945, *Der Aufbau* made it a personal victory for Roosevelt, titled 'FDR frees refugees and Jews'. The expression 'father of the emigration' is found in letters of most of the émigrés. Rejected only by a minority of radicals who saw him as the embodiment of capitalism, he was venerated by almost all others, and it is once again in Thomas Mann's writing that the ambiguity of this image of Roosevelt in the émigré community is most clearly expressed.

Mann had been personally invited to meet Roosevelt during his first visit to the United States.[73] He met once more with him privately, while teaching at Princeton.[74] He shared the admiration of so many émigrés for the President, and in his message to the German people of November 1940, greeted his re-election in the following words:

> He is the representative of struggling democracy, the true champion of a new, social conception of freedom, and the statesman who has distinguished most clearly between peace and appeasement. In our century of the masses, an essential part of which is the idea of the leader, it was the good fortune of America to welcome the happy appearance of a modern leader of the crowds who wants what is good and spiritual, what really does stand for the future and for liberty.[75]

Mann called Roosevelt a 'good leader', a 'spiritual leader' in the fight against Hitler, even while deploring certain of his dictatorial traits. When the regulations for 'application for a certificate of identification' were published, he immediately sent the President a telegram declaring that opponents of fascism should never be termed 'aliens of enemy nationality'. From 1943, Mann became rather more critical, and also emphasized the conservative aspects in Roosevelt's personality. The letters he wrote to his American friend Agnes E. Meyer attest to his unease at the development of the situation in Europe and his fear of seeing the United States opt for a separate peace: 'I see in FDR still a strong inclination to make peace, with the support of the church and south European fascism. This is the only objection I would have against it. At the end of the day, after all, anything is better than Hitler. This truth permeates me, and I feel personally able to accommodate myself to Communism, or to a sufficiently cultivated clerical fascism.'[76]

The tone becomes steadily harder, and yet after Roosevelt's death, in May 1945, Mann wrote to Erich von Kahler: 'Roosevelt – let me not speak of it. This is no longer the country to which we came. One feels orphaned and abandoned.'[77] When the House Committee on Un-American Activities was launched, Mann still regretted the era and spirit of Roosevelt, and contrasted this with what America was becoming. And it was this mixture of acknowledgement and admiration together with doubt for the future that best characterized the émigré community's attitude towards the man considered the very symbol of the struggle of democracy against fascism.

VARIAN FRY AND THE RESCUE
OF ÉMIGRÉ INTELLECTUALS

The various American initiatives to rescue antifascist intellectuals trapped in France in 1940 cannot be described without paying tribute to the courage and intelligence of Varian Fry, to whom many owed their escape from the Gestapo. After the fall of France, Marseille became the main centre where refugees gathered in search of a ship to cross the Atlantic. President Roosevelt's attention had been drawn to the danger that threatened the greatest represen-tatives of the European intelligentsia if they were to fall into Nazi hands. The exile committees, and a number of literary and political figures, made several representations to the President, providing lists of names of threatened in-dividuals – the Gestapo had similar lists of its own – who needed emergency help.[78] Since the majority of these refugees had neither visas and papers nor money, it was essential to intervene immediately, and the Emergency Rescue Committee accordingly sent Varian Fry to Europe.[79]

Fry was no ordinary intelligence agent. He had studied Greek and Latin, spoke several languages including French, knew Germany well and had been linked to Socialist circles in Austria before joining the American Friends of German Freedom. Though not a member of the Emergency Rescue Committee, he offered to travel to France to seek out individuals threatened by the Gestapo and help them leave the country. The director of the Museum of Modern Art in New York, Alfred Barr, provided him with funds and a list of artists to rescue, including Chagall, Max Ernst, and Lipschitz. Thomas Mann and Hermann Kesten gave him a list of writers, on which figured the names of Franz Werfel, Lion Feuchtwanger and Konrad Heiden. Karl Frank supplied a list of political figures. Final rescue operations of this kind were to be attempted in almost all countries occupied by the Reich.

When he reached Marseille, where he was to stay for thirteen months, Varian Fry set out to trace all the two hundred names on his list. Some of these were still interned, and he had to seek them out individually to enable them to leave for the United States, showing that they had visas or official invitations.[80] He obtained the transfer to Montpellier of a number of scientists (with the aid of Edouard de Rothschild), from where they travelled to America via North Africa.[81] Most of Varian Fry's actions were completely illegal. He and his assistant Frank Bohn were officially covered by the US embassy, but Fry's boldness eventually disturbed the ambassador to the point of requesting Washington to recall him immediately. Bohn did return to America, but Fry continued to seek out people in danger, constantly under the watch of the French police who inspected his offices regularly and ended up escorting him to the Spanish border in September 1941. Fry had managed by this time to contact a number of antifascists, warn them that they figured on the list of people to be arrested, provide them with money and sometimes even hide them before taking them to a ship leaving for America. He was regularly amazed by their lack of awareness: it was often a surprise to the refugees to learn that they were actively pursued, and they would have been unable to leave France without his help. In this way he succeeded in rescuing some 1,500 refugees, though a further 300 failed to leave France after Fry was expelled, and in particular, antifascists who were Communists or fellow-travellers were almost all refused entry to the United States and had to seek refuge in Latin America, especially Mexico. Hans Sahl, however, a former collaborator of Piscator's who lived later in

Hollywood, described with emotion his first meeting with Varian Fry: a young man with distinguished bearing told him in a low voice that he figured on the list of people wanted by the Gestapo, and slipped a bundle of dollars into his pocket, saying 'Sorry they're not cleaner.' It's understandable that Hans Sahl added that he burst into tears and could never forget that gesture: 'You know, since that day I have loved America.'

It was thanks to Varian Fry that Lion Feuchtwanger, Walter Mehring, Franz Werfel, Heinrich Mann, Golo Mann, Alfred Döblin, Leonhard Frank, Max Ernst and Egon Erwin Kisch managed to escape the Gestapo. Fry's courage was often helped or hindered by a series of unpredictable chances, which gave individual fates very different outcomes. It was a close-run thing that some managed to emigrate[82] while others fell into the hands of the Gestapo.[83] Fry's activities were illegal under French law as well as American. He did not conceal the fact that if his efforts were often blocked by the Gestapo and the French police, the latter sometimes helped him indirectly, as they did a number of refugees. The example of Max Ernst's escape helps to show the mixture of sadism, vileness and generosity that so many refugees encountered. After his break with surrealism, Ernst had been living since 1938 on an abandoned farm not far from Avignon. In 1939 he was interned in the disused prison of Largentière before being released on parole, then interned again in the Les Milles camp. He was released in December 1939 thanks to the intervention of Paul Eluard. Arrested again in 1940, he escaped while a petition was being circulated for his release. The Museum of Modern Art in New York did all it could to rescue him, in contact with Fry. Unable to obtain an exit visa, Ernst decided to cross the Spanish frontier with papers that were not in order. At the last station before the border he was noticed by the police, and an officer told him that he would have to send him back to an internment camp. He asked Ernst therefore to take his luggage across to the adjacent train, and make sure he did not take the one on the left, which was going to cross the frontier directly. Ernst understood the implication, but was not even able to thank the officer.

3. THE FIRST WAVES OF ÉMIGRÉS

IMAGES OF AMERICA

As the seventeen-year-old Karl Rossmann [. . .] sailed slowly into New York harbour, he suddenly saw the Statue of Liberty, which had already been in view for some time, as though in an intenser sunlight. The sword in her hand seemed only just to have been raised aloft, and the unchained winds blew about her form.

Franz Kafka, *Amerika*

I hear you say:
He's talking about America
And knows nothing about it
He's not been there.

Bertolt Brecht, 'Manual for City-Dwellers'

Though a number of film-makers, directors and writers had visited America in the Weimar era, and some had even lived there, for the majority of European authors it was an unknown and foreign land. The decade of the 1920s was certainly deeply marked by American mythologies. Musicians and composers were passionate about jazz; George Grosz dreamed of New York before settling there. Theatre and cabaret stages were invaded by a number of American myths – a certain taste for reviews, striptease, and a rather vulgar luxury – and both Fritz Lang and Brecht were inspired by American realist novels and detective stories. Without these one could hardly imagine some scenes from *Mabuse*, *In the Jungle of Cities* or *Mahagonny*. But few German writers had a more realistic idea of America. They knew it only via translations of novels – Upton Sinclair, John Dos Passos, Sinclair Lewis – or films: it was a world of dreams, myths and nightmares. For many, America meant only a backdrop of giant cities, cars, wealth and vast landscapes. In Kafka's famous novel, it is hard to recognize the Statue of Liberty holding a 'sword' and many other descriptions of New York. Brecht saw in America only an immense social chaos, both fascinating and terrifying, a paradise in which everything could be bought if you had the money. This is the image of his Chicago (*In the Jungle of Cities*, *St Joan of the Stockyards*), or *Mahagonny*, the urban trap of Standard Oil and Rockefeller, the symbol of modernity at its most dishevelled and capitalism at its most monstrous. If some saw America as the land of wealth and boundless possibilities, even if each gesture there had a disturbing strangeness (Kafka), the majority had a rather negative image. The cruelty of the American system was matched by its fragility: the crash of 1929 made an impression on all these writers, and Brecht in particular. They felt crushed by its material force, but saw it as a complete cultural desert. The decision to take refuge there went much against the grain for almost all the émigré writers. A reading of their diaries and letters shows how throughout their exile it remained a deeply foreign world in which they felt almost incapable to 'strike root' (Alfred Döblin's expression): with a few rare exceptions, Thomas Mann being for a time one of these. It is understandable, in the light of the mythologies of America current in so many German works of the Weimar era, that they initially felt the possibility of exile there as a fearsome trauma.

Stefan Zweig wrote to Hermann Kesten on 24 January 1940: 'But we have to stay here; we shall never see Europe again if we leave now. We have to stay even if our positions here are lost. Here we can fulfil our task, simply by our very presence. America would swallow us up.'[84] Klaus Mann had visited the United States in 1927, invited by his American publisher. Though he was enthusiastic about New York and the Broadway stage – which he found almost as lively as that of Berlin – American cities struck him as 'heartless and soulless', and after spending Christmas in Hollywood, at Emil Jannings's home in the German film colony, he exclaimed: 'It was not our world. We remained Europeans.'[85] Toller, who visited in 1929, drew an apocalyptic picture of the United States.[86] And even those fascinated by America in their literary work – like Brecht in his early poems[87] – never thought of living there. A number of German writers had their books published in the United States – Ernst Toller, Lion Feuchtwanger,

Thomas and Klaus Mann – and some stage directors such as Max Reinhardt were known there. But there was little connection between German and American culture outside the personal ties that Thomas Wolfe, Dorothy Thompson and Sinclair Lewis had with some writers in Munich or Berlin. Brecht made a brief trip to America in 1935, together with Eisler. Franz Werfel followed in 1937. None of them returned with a very good impression. René Schickele refused to travel to the United States, and wrote to Hermann Kesten on 11 January 1940: 'Despite everything: we have to plod on, my friend. America? Toller hanged himself there and Marcuse writes me desperate letters.' Alma Mahler wrote in her diary: 'I [. . .] wanted to leave that pest-ridden country, but Werfel, stubbornly clinging to the notion of a "last shred of Europe", refused to leave.'[88] If Walter Benjamin felt out of his element as soon as he left Berlin, for many German writers America was the very symbol of the reign of materialism, money, and lack of culture. Most of them had studied Greek and Latin, but very few could express themselves in English. Ludwig Marcuse recalled in his memoirs[89] that he would never have thought of going to the United States; the 'new world' struck him as less new than disquieting. He moved there from necessity: 'Neither Alaska nor Terra de Fuego nor Panama said to me: come here if you like!' Columbia University had sent him an affidavit, but at first he thought of refusing, since not only did he not speak English but he felt a strong repulsion towards the Anglo-Saxon world. In cultural terms, he declared that Americanism displeased him as much as Bolshevism, and he saw no difference between the cultural level of America and Africa. Carl Zuckmayer, in similar vein, maintained that the idea of ending his days in America horrified him.[90] As for Walter Benjamin, he paid for his hesitation in leaving for America with his life. It was only with great reluctance that they left Europe and embarked for America, as the only chance of rescue. As George Kaiser declared, while a refugee in Switzerland: 'I feel nostalgic for the United States, not because it is the United States but because it's no longer Europe.'

THE COMPOSITION OF THE ÉMIGRÉ COMMUNITY

Since it formed the last refuge for all those fleeing from Nazism, the waves of émigrés arriving in America were far more varied than those reaching the European countries of asylum in 1933. Hitler's seizure of power had forced into exile political opponents and a large number of intellectuals unable to live under Nazism even if they had not struggled actively against it. The promulgation of the Nuremberg laws, and the invasion of Austria and Czechoslovakia, gave rise to a Jewish emigration on an increasing scale. Those trying to reach America in 1940 belonged to all these categories and originated not only from Germany but from all countries that the Reich had now occupied.

If the majority of antifascist émigrés who left Germany in 1933 were relatively young, those seeking refuge in America towards 1940 included both old people and children. The Davie Report estimated, on the basis of data from the immigration service, that approximately 250,000 refugees reached the United

States between 1933 and 1944. At least 37,000 of these were under sixteen, often from families where the father was in concentration camp, or Jewish children sponsored by American families.[91] As well as these children, there were a large number of students from Germany, Austria, Czechoslovakia and Poland.

The composition of the émigrés in the United States was far more varied than in other European countries. Though it included political activists, artists and intellectuals, a large number of refugees were from the liberal professions and had left Germany for racial reasons. They included businessmen, industrialists and merchants, as well as academics, doctors and writers. After having been drained of their intellectuals, Germany and the countries occupied by the Reich lost a large number of scientists and members of the liberal professions, prevented from practising by the anti-Semitic laws. The refugees reaching America included more than 5,000 doctors,[92] 1,682 university professors,[93] 2,000 lawyers and jurists, about the same number of psychologists and psycho-analysts, and over 500 non-university scientific researchers. The number of artists and writers is still more astonishing. Besides such famous figures as Lipschitz, Zadkin, Masson, Mondrian, Kisling, Breton, Duchamp, Tanguy, Chagall and Léger, who all sought refuge in America, the Davie Report mentions over 717 painters and sculptors. The writers included not just the greatest names in German literature – Lion Feuchtwanger, Thomas, Heinrich and Klaus Mann, Bertolt Brecht, Alfred Döblin and Franz Werfel – but a total of more than 1,900, including journalists and publicists. As for theatre and film actors, directors and musicians, they came to over 2,000.

Up till 1938 it had been Germans above all who were forced into exile, together with a small number of Austrians and Czechs, but from that year on the United States received refugees from all countries occupied by the Reich. According to Laura Fermi,[94] 44 per cent of these immigrants were from Germany, 20 per cent from the former Austria-Hungarian lands,[95] a fairly large number of Italians[96] and French,[97] but also Russians, Belgians, Danes, Greeks, Dutch, Norwegians and Romanians.[98]

The richness of the émigré community is scarcely visible from the bare statistics. A study of its composition, in the intellectual field alone, shows that for Europe it represented, whether temporary or permanently, a genuine bloodletting. Obtaining a visa or an affidavit often depended on the connections that the émigré enjoyed in America, and it goes without saying that it was the elite in each field who found it easiest to reach the United States. No country, not even America, was in a position to offer these émigrés an adequate reintegration, and the result was very often a real waste of talent: full professors became college teachers, avant-garde composers had to work for Hollywood or teach basic composition classes, surgeons became country doctors. Though America had no problem absorbing the number of émigrés, very few were recognized at their true value. They also suffered very often from the exile situation, and both North and South America saw a large number of émigré suicides (Karl Dunker, founder of gestalt psychology, the biochemist R. Schoenheimer, writers Stefan Zweig and Ernst Toller). A fair number of émigrés who were famous in Europe lived in poverty in America. Even in old age,

Schoenberg found it hard to support his family. Bartok, who died in a New York hospital in 1945, was so poor that a collection had to be taken for his burial costs. It is hard to establish from the Davie Report, moreover, how the immigrants were divided along racial, political and economic lines.[99] Finally, if it was not until the 1960s that American historians investigated the appalling indifference that the greatest names of European culture had suffered in 1940, it should be stressed that an impressive number of émigrés went on to play a leading role in American cultural life, from the visual arts and theatre to political science and physics.[100] Though the emigration that National Socialism precipitated in 1933 was particularly one of progressive writers and artists, that of 1940 affected all sectors of intellectual life: its representatives were not necessarily antifascists, but their Jewish origin had excluded them from the cultural life of their own countries. Despite their dryness, the statistics of the Davie Report give an excellent idea of the diversity and significance of this intellectual immigration.

Doctors and Biologists

The majority of doctors, biologists and professors of medicine expelled from Germany often found themselves in the United States in the aberrant position described by Brecht in his *Exile Dialogues*. It was made very hard – if not impossible – for them to practise their profession, so as to avoid competition with the American medical establishment. From 1 July 1932 to 30 June 1944, some 6,426 doctors and biologists (classed under 'physicians') settled in the United States, or an average of 535 per year. At least 5,480 of these had left their country for political or racial reasons.[101] Despite their specialized skills and their willingness to work, the majority remained unemployed, with the exception of the few that had a world reputation. The US army refused to engage them as they were not Americans, while the navy required a minimum of twelve years' residence. In 1942 they had to appear before a commission to establish whether or not they were 'enemy aliens'. They could only obtain temporary hospital posts, or in rural communities where there had not been doctors.[102]

Psychoanalysts

Since psychoanalysis had been termed a 'degenerate Jewish science' and a large number of analysts were indeed Jewish, they were doubly forced into exile. The United States, moreover, offered a particularly favorable context for their resettlement.[103] In 1934, Ernest Jones declared at the Thirteenth International Congress of Psychoanalysis that the German movement had already lost half of its members.[104] Of the sixty-nine members of the Vienna Psychoanalytic Association, only three were left in Austria in 1945.

The analysts expelled from Hungary (Sándor Rado) or who left German early on to settle in the United States (Frank Alexander) were soon joined by a large number of members of the German Psychoanalytic Association, then of its Austrian counterpart. The American analytic movement made efforts to support them, and financed the passage of more than 150 European analysts, subsequently seeking places for them in clinics or institutes. The most well-

known names among them are those of Helene Deutch, René Spitz, Hanns
Sachs, Ernst Simmel, Karen Horney, Therese Benedek, Sigfried Bernfeld, Otto
Fenichel, Theodor Reik, Otto Rank, Ludwig Jekels, Edward Hitschmann, Paul
Federn, Hermann Nunberg and Erich Fromm. Most of these found positions at
existing institutes or established new ones: this was how the famous psychoanalytic centres in New York, Chicago, Boston and Los Angeles came into
being. Many became university professors. In their theoretical and practical
work, several of them gave rise to new and typically American developments in
psychoanalysis, especially Karen Horney and Erich Fromm, both leading
figures of Freudian revisionism in the 1950s and 60s. Some of these analysts
pioneered new research that was especially valuable: Bruno Bettelheim on
infantile autism, Geza Roheim on ethnopsychoanalysis, Heinz Hartmann,
Ernst Kris and Rudolph Loewenstein on the structure of the ego, and Erik
Erikson in sociology and history.

Physicists

If European psychoanalysts made a key contribution to the history of American
psychology and psychiatry, what about their scientific colleagues? The role of
émigré physicists in the development of the first atomic bomb is too well-known
to need repetition here. We need only note that it was in Hitler's Germany that
Otto Hahn and Fritz Strassmann discovered uranium fission, and that Leo
Szilard, who had the intuitive idea of chain reaction, emigrated to the United
States in 1937, followed two years later by Niels Bohr from Denmark. The
majority of nuclear scientists were of European origin (Fermi, Wigner, Gamow,
Bloch, Bethe, Teller, Weisskopf). The US army laboratories, and the Naval
Research Laboratory in particular, immediately recognized the military ad-
vantage to be drawn from such a discovery: Szilard, and Einstein himself, spoke
with President Roosevelt about this. The atom bomb was born in these
American university laboratories with the aid of émigrés from fascism. It
was Fermi, Szilard and Wigner who built the atomic pile at the University
of Chicago, and Emilio Segrè who isolated plutonium at Berkeley. The scientific
leadership charged with construction of the bomb at Los Alamos in New
Mexico also comprised émigrés such as Fermi, Bloch, Staub, Segrè, Bethe,
Rossi, Teller and Weisskopf. Five of the exiled physicists won Nobel Prizes.

Lawyers

According to the Davie Report, between 1,800 and 2,000 lawyers found refuge
in the United States between 1933 and 1944, including 1,000 from Germany. It
was very hard for them to find work, and one of them was quoted as saying that
it was easier for a Catholic theologian to work in a Tibetan lamasery than for a
German lawyer to continue his profession in the United States.[105] Not only did
their particular training have no validity in America, but the number of lawyers
there was already so high that it was impossible for them to find work. Several
of their number consequently had to move to quite different professions.[106] The
most fortunate managed to become teachers or businessmen, while others
applied themselves to studying US law. They were often helped by various

committees, in particular the American Committee for the Guidance of Professional Personnel and the Committee for Re-education of Refugee Lawyers, which selected the most well-known and offered them intensive training to make them employable as 'American lawyers'.[107] After the United States entered the War, a number of refugees acquired important positions in the administration, employed in the Office of Strategic Services (forerunner to the CIA), Office of Censorship, the Treasury Department or the army. David Riesmann and Robert M. W. Kemper, who both formed part of this anti-Nazi emigration, sat as judges at the Nuremberg Tribunal.

Academics

The academic exodus provoked by the Nazi seizure of power and the promulgation of the Nuremberg laws led to the emigration of a large number of teachers – republicans, progressives, pacifists, more or less Marxist or of Jewish origin. The total number of teachers who settled in the United States was far larger than the 2,000 full professors. The sympathy they received from American academic circles, and the relative ease of obtaining a visa as a teacher, explains how the United States became the principal refuge of European academic emigration in the face of the Hitler threat. Mathematicians and logicians, for example, included a large number of members of the Polish school – Witold Herewicz, Jerzy Neymann, Stan Ulam, Mark Kac, Leonid Hurwicz, Samuel Eilenberg – as well as Alfred Tarski, the pioneer of semantics. Immigrants from Hungary included Paul Erdös, C. Lanczos, G. Polya, T. Rado, O, Szazs, G. Szegö and J. von Neumann. Austrians included several members of the Vienna Circle, in particular Karl Menger and Kurt Gödel; German mathematicians included Otto Neugebauer, Emmy Noether, William Prager, Hans Lewy and Hermann Weyl.[108] American astronomy was totally transformed by the arrival of émigré scientists from a number of countries occupied by the Reich, and it is symbolic that the majority of chairs of astronomy, as well as the directorships of observatories and laboratories, were held in the 1940s by Poles, Czechs, Dutch and Germans. The same findings apply in the fields of medicine, chemistry and biology. It should be stressed that the US government was often able to find practical applications for these theoretical and highly specialized talents. The famous Research Project of Totalitarian Communication, launched at the New School for Social Research in 1941 and designed to study Nazi propaganda, was entrusted to the German émigré Hans Speier and the Austrian psychoanalyst and art historian Ernst Kris. Analysis of interrogations of prisoners of war was given to the Austrian George Rohrlich, a member of the Office of Strategic Services,[109] and Louise Holborn. Franz Neumann, Leo Löwenthal, Paul Lazarsfeld and Max Horkheimer were all associated as sociologists with government projects to combat National Socialism and analyse its methods, as were John Herz, Otto Kirchheimer, George Rohrlich, Karl Deutsch, Nathan Leites as political scientists, economists such as Walter Levy (head of the OSS petroleum division), not to mention Herbert Marcuse and Kurt Lewin. The New School for Social Research also took on a large number of economists (H. Bloch, W. Brook, G. Colm, A. Feiler, E. Heimann, J. Hirsch, G. Katona, E.

Lederer, F. Lehmann, A. Lowe, J. Marschak). Several of these were employed by the US government in various official services (Office of Strategic Services, Office of War Information, Board of Economic Warfare, etc.), in accordance with their respective specialism.

Exile sociology in America was represented by a variety of different schools. The most well-known was the Frankfurt School, with Theodor Adorno, Max Horkheimer and Herbert Marcuse, as well as Karl Wittfogel, Leo Löwenthal, Felix Weill and Otto Kirchheimer. American social psychology owes a great deal to the Austrian Paul Lazarsfeld, as also to Kurt Lewin, Kurt Koffka and Max Wertheimer. While the exiled sociologists included Marxists such as those of the Frankfurt School, the tradition of Max Weber was also represented by Hans Gerth, Kurt Wolff and Albert Salomon.[110]

It was to the United States that the entire faculty of the Berlin School of Political Sciences emigrated, and they had an immense impact on their field in America. It is sufficient to cite the names of C. J. Friedrich, Waldemar Gurian, Franz Neumann, Sigmund Neumann, Hans Morgenthau, Leo Strauss and Hannah Arendt. Historians were just as numerous, and often brought new methods with them to the United States. Sometimes they developed fields of research that were previously unexplored: Stephan Kuttner and Ernst Kantorowicz initiated a new interest in the medieval period and canon law, Karl Wittfogel developed the study of archaic Chinese society, Hajo Holborn spread the theories of Meinecke's historical school, while Hans Baron specialized in study of the Italian Renaissance. As well as these typically European sectors there was specialist historical work on Germany itself. One of the first historians of the German resistance, Hans Rothfels, was a professor of history at the University of Chicago during the war. There was also the contribution of Austro-Hungarian historians. The greatest study of the Habsburg monarchy is still that of Oscar Jaszi, of Hungarian origin and a friend of Lukács. And what should we say of the contribution of Orientalists such as Leo Oppenheim, Wolfram Eberhard, Benno Landsberger, Tibor Halasi-Kun, Kurt Weitzmann, Arno Poebel and Arnold Walther, to give only a few names – who developed in American universities, before students who often had difficulty in following them, their immense knowledge of the life of the Etruscans or Assyrians, of Indo-European or Arabic philology, archaic Chinese art and the religious customs of the indigenous people of Japan?

Philosophy was represented as well. Wittgenstein's influence in America was strengthened by the arrival of a number of representatives of logical positivism – Gustav Bergmann, Rudolf Carnap, Herbert Feigl, Philipp Frank, Carl Hempel, Hans Reichenbach, Richard von Mises. The Protestant theologian Paul Tillich, who arrived in the United States in late 1933 at the invitation of Reinhold Niebuhr, taught at the Union Theological Seminary in New York, and had a great influence on reflection on religion. The humanist tradition was represented by Ernst Cassirer, who died in New York in 1945, as well as by philologists with wide-ranging interests such as Werner Jaeger and Erich Auerbach. Finally, it was in the United States that Ernst Bloch wrote his most important philosophical work, *The Principle of Hope*.

Writers and Artists
According to the Davie Report, over 1,000 musicians emigrated to the United States between 1933 and 1944. They included orchestral conductors such as Toscanini and Bruno Walter (a friend of Thomas Mann), composers such as Arnold Schoenberg, Béla Bartok, Paul Hindemith, Hanns Eisler, Darius Milhaud, Igor Stravinsky and Ernst Toch, as well as a large number of instrumentalists including some of the great European virtuosos. The leading representatives of the Bauhaus and the European architectural avant-garde also took refuge in America – Ludwig Mies van der Rohe, Walter Gropius, Erich Mendelsohn, Marcel Breuer, L. Moholy-Nagy, Herbert Bayer. The painters who found exile in the United States included Ferdinand Léger, Marc Chagall, Marcel Duchamp, Salvador Dali, André Masson, Max Ernst, Yves Tanguy and George Grosz, as well as figures like Albers, Bazer and Feininger who were also associated with the Bauhaus. Avant-garde sculpture was represented by Lipchitz and Zadkin, art history by Erwin Panofsky, who established this teaching almost from nothing in the United States, in its systematic and scientific form.

The greatest names of German literature were also to be found in America, with Thomas, Heinrich, Klaus and Golo Mann, Franz Werfel, Alfred Döblin, Lion Feuchtwanger, Ludwig Marcuse, Hermann Kesten, Bertolt Brecht, Hans Natonek, Max Beer-Hoffmann, Siegfried Kracauer and Carl Zuckmayer, and other European languages represented by André Breton, Ferenc Molnar, André Maurois, Jules Romain, Ivan and Claire Goll. These famous names hide a large number of others: 2,000 varied writers, journalists and others who lived in their shadow.

Actors, Film-Makers and Stage Directors
Another essential component of the emigration provoked by Nazism was made up of representatives of the theatre and cinema. If the official figures only count 273, their real number was around three times that. An article by Kurt Hellmer that appeared in *Der Aufbau* in December 1944 depicted 'Berlin and Vienna on Broadway', and not without reason. And what to say of Hollywood?

The 1940s saw at least eighty émigré actors on the American stage. If Marlene Dietrich had originally left Germany for reasons unconnected with politics, her fiercely anti-Nazi convictions led her to see herself as an émigré. Other prominent actors included Helene Weigel, O. Homolka, Sig Arno, Albert and Else Bassermann, O. Karlweiss, E. Angold, H. Grade, Marianne Stewart (Schenzel), Fritz Kortner, Peter Lorre and Conrad Veidt. An article by Hans Kafka, 'What Our Immigration Did for Hollywood and Vice Versa' (22 December 1944) mentioned ninety émigré film actors, thirty-three directors, twenty-three producers, fifty-nine screenwriters and nineteen film-music composers who were working in Hollywood after being expelled from Germany. Fritz Lang, Robert Siodmack and Billy Wilder were among these émigrés, while the importance of stage directors can be gauged by the names of Max Reinhardt, Erwin Piscator, Bertolt Brecht, Salka Viertel and Leopold Jessner.

Any listing is cumbersome, and there is no space here for a full list of the antifascist emigration. Just a 'Who's Who' of Weimar in Hollywood would require a whole volume to itself. The brief indications above are designed just to break the dryness of the Davie Report, and give a few faces to mere figures. The names cited are enough to show that the intellectual haemorrhage provoked by National Socialism, both artistic and scientific, did not just bleed German culture to death, but drained the whole of Europe of its life-blood, causing a loss that was almost irreparable even if America gained a great deal from it.

IDEOLOGICAL STRUCTURES OF THE EMIGRATION

Hard as it is to describe the various ideological components of the German emigration in 1933, this task becomes almost impossible for America in the 1940s. First of all because it is no longer a question of one country and certain well-defined categories, chiefly intellectuals and political opponents, but includes political émigrés, regular immigrants, refugees from all over Europe, escapees from concentration camp, survivors of the Spanish war and from the former capitals of German emigration, people expelled from Germany, Austria, Poland, Italy, Czechoslovakia, France, the Netherlands, Belgium and Hungary. Whilst these refugees included opponents of Nazism from all origins, there were also a large number of Jews simply fleeing from Nazi anti-Semitism.

The Massive Jewish Emigration
Though a number of German Jews had thought of emigrating to America since 1933, it took the Nuremberg laws and the almost total expulsion of Jews from economic and intellectual life before a mass emigration began. The extension of anti-Semitic measures to all countries occupied by the Reich, then the deportation and extermination of the Jewish population, made emigration vital at a time when it was often no longer possible. American statistics count some 311,887 refugees of Jewish origin who found asylum in the US between 1933 and 1943. According to the fullest estimates,[111] these made up some 67.6 per cent of the total number of émigrés, divided fairly equally between refugees from Germany and from other countries occupied by the Reich. This Jewish emigration was very diverse. Whilst it included genuine opponents of Nazism, a large number were simply 'racial refugees'[112] who were forced to leave the Reich rather than leaving by political choice.

Intellectual and Artistic Emigration
The few examples mentioned above show how the emigration provoked by Nazism, and reaching America around 1940, included the elite of European culture in almost every field, to the point that it is easier to list the names of those artists and intellectuals who remained in the countries occupied by the Reich than of those who left for exile. If the emigration of 1933 was antifascist by political conviction, that of 1940 included not only opponents of the Hitler regime, but many artists and writers who fled the War and the German occupation without being active antifascists. A large number of them kept their distance from any political involvement, and the same goes for a large number of academics of Jewish origin.

The Political Emigration

This included artists, writers and intellectuals who had struggled against Hitler since 1933 or who had left the Reich for ideological reasons, as well as political activists in the strict sense. The composition of the political emigration in the United States was very different from that of the exiles who had taken refuge in European capitals from Paris to Prague. Exile in America appeared to the majority of political émigrés as the last chance of escaping the Nazis, rather than as an active choice. Besides, if France and Czechoslovakia had also accepted Communists, this was not the case with the United States. The political emigration in America was thus marked by a shift to the right in its various components.

It did indeed include both Socialists and Communists, along with conservatives and liberals, but in different proportions. The Socialists were represented by a number of quite divergent tendencies, just as in the various European capitals: there were 'left' Socialists (Gerhart Seger), conservative Socialists (Wilhelm Sollman), 'right' Socialists (Friedrich Stampfer), and members of the group Neu Beginnen (Paul Hagen). But whilst there had been a radicalization of a number of Socialists after 1933 – those who openly criticized the policy of the SPD – the Socialist emigration in America seemed on the whole to follow the opposite route and become increasingly reactionary. Reading the texts of some of the Socialists who emigrated to New York, one might wonder what, apart from a semblance of phraseology, still justified the political label: a number of them became fanatical anti-Communists and theorists of the Cold War after 1945.

It was forbidden on principle to grant US visas to members of the Communist party. The majority of exiled Communists therefore chose to emigrate to Latin America, and especially to Mexico. Yet the political refugees in New York and Hollywood did include a number of Communists – composers, journalists and writers – such as the Eisler brothers, Stefan Heym, Alfred Kantorowicz, Alfons Goldschmidt, F. C. Weiskopf and Hermann Budzislawski, who had a greater chance of obtaining a visa than did a party cadre. If American law authorized the expulsion of acknowledged Communists, the measure was not applied in the Roosevelt era, and it was often thanks to the direct intervention of American public figures that Communist exiles managed to reach the United States. Thus Dorothy Thompson came to the aid of Budzislawski, and Hemingway helped not only the former International Brigade commander Hans Kahle, but also Gustav Regler[113] and Alfred Kantorowicz. Though the latter's Communist convictions were a matter of general knowledge,[114] he was nonetheless able to work at CBS radio from 1942 on. The former collaborator of Willi Münzenberg, Otto Katz – who was hanged in Prague in 1952 after the Slansky trial – settled in Hollywood, while Erwin Piscator taught at the New School.

Above all, however, the political émigrés in America included a large number of conservatives and centrists. One of the most famous was former Chancellor Brüning,[115] whose activities were confined to lectures and open letters, and who kept his distance from other émigrés, although a certain number of conservatives would have liked to see him at the head of a German government in exile.

Hermann Rauschning was fairly close to Brüning, whilst Treviranus was still further to the right. There were also Catholics: conservatives such as Waldemar Gurian and Friedrich Muckermann, quasi-Socialists such as Hubertus Prinz zu Löwenstein, and supporters of the Habsburg monarchy.

Finally, the political emigration counted some national-bolshevik sympathizers who worked together with right-wing Socialists, and supporters of Otto Strasser's Schwarze Front – Strasser himself having been unwillingly detained in Canada.

4. LIFE IN AMERICA

ASSISTANCE TO REFUGEES

American help for antifascist refugees enabled them to leave Europe, escape Nazi persecution, reach the United States and find some kind of opening in US society. An intergovernmental committee on refugees had been established at the Évian conference of 1938. Interrupted by the War, negotiations were recommenced in 1943, and on 22 July 1944, at Roosevelt's initiative, the War Refugee Board of the United States[116] was set up, charged with rescuing the victims of Nazi persecution.[117] Between 1940 and 1944, the US government had already taken a series of measures, through the President's Advisory Committee on Political Refugees, that enabled threatened persons to come to America without being blocked by the quota system. The War Refugee Board was placed over the other émigré organizations. Its representatives had diplomatic status, and offices in a number of countries (Switzerland, Sweden, Turkey). It could not of course obtain collaboration from the Nazi government, which murdered any political refugee. If the emergency visas enabled the rescue of 4,000 persons, the WRB helped some tens of thousands of refugees to reach America.[118]

As well as these government organizations, a large number of private bodies came to the aid of the refugees.[119] If it was hard to reach America after 1940, the situation of the émigrés remained very difficult even after their arrival in New York. The number who were welcomed by American public figures, journalists or relatives was tiny in relation to all those – often unable to speak English – who were sponsored by refugee committees and charitable organizations. The Davie Report underlines how the traumas they had experienced, the humiliation, fear and despair that were the lot of the majority of émigrés, represented a psychological handicap as great as their destitution, from the standpoint of their integration into American society. The countless sufferings that they had endured formed a barrier between them and the American people, who had a very inadequate notion of what they had undergone. The US government was thus led to set up very rapidly a special programme of aid for the refugees. Jewish organizations were the most active in this, especially the Hebrew Sheltering and Immigrant Aid Society and the National Council of Jewish Women, soon backed up by specialist agencies that dealt with the émigrés by professional category. The American churches – Catholic, Protestant and, above all, Quaker – formed a number of aid committees, as did progressive and liberal circles. The National Coordinating Committee (for Aid to German Refugees), financed by Jewish organizations, assisted non-Jews as well. Faced with the influx of refugees and their requests for support, the committee soon divided in two and gave birth to the Greater New York Coordination Committee, which helped refugees to survive while they were waiting for national agencies to take responsibility for them. Finally, besides national organizations like the National Refugee Service, there was the European-Jewish Children's Aid and the Emergency Committee in Aid of Displaced Foreign Physicians, which between them had more than 900 local branches.

It should be noted that a large number of committees were set up very early on. The American Committee for Christian German Refugees had been formed in 1934, financed by Protestant churches and Jewish organizations. The Catholic Committee for Refugees was born in 1936, followed in 1938 by the American Friends Service Committee.[120] Other less well-known committees backed up these large national organizations.[121]

The most destitute refugees were taken charge of by the committees as soon as they arrived. From 1939 to 1945, the National Refugee Service assisted 35,000 people. It helped them to find housing and work, often on a temporary basis. The financial power of these American committees was so great that virtually no refugee fell to the government's charge. The committees also offered medical and psychological aid, and helped the refugees to learn English. To avoid rejection by the American population, with its high level of unemployment, the committees avoided any possibility of competition, and offered only temporary work, poorly paid and always inferior to that which the refugees had practised before their arrival in America. As employment conditions gradually became more favourable, the émigrés were able to find more stable positions.

Finally, the committees avoided too high a concentration of refugees in New York, by dividing them among the different states. A regional centre was then charged with finding them a more specific position. Some 15,000 refugees were dispersed in this way across the United States. Those who refused to leave New York risked having their financial aid withdrawn. To facilitate their integration into American society, hostels to shelter them were established by the American Friends Service Committee, and the Quakers also set up colleges and courses in English language and American history and civilization. The American Friends Service Committee, with its headquarters at Powel House in New York City, even organized friendship parties from 1943 on, designed to help émigrés meet Americans.

Intellectuals, for their part, were most often sponsored by special committees. Academics were broadly supported by the University in Exile, founded by Alvin Johnson at the New School for Social Research, and the Emergency Committee in Aid of Displaced Scholars (active from 1933 to 1945), which assisted more than 350 academics, providing 150 of these with permanent positions. The Oberlaender Trust of Philadelphia took responsibility for 330 professors from Germany and Austria. Writers were aided by the American Center of the PEN

Club. In 1943 the American Christian Committee for Refugees were founded, and in 1945 the American Committee for Émigré Scholars, Writers and Artists. The American Friends Service Committee itself assisted more than 200 refugees between 1939 and 1945.

Scientists were aided by the Emergency Committee in Aid of Displaced Foreign Physicians (founded in 1933), concerned especially with doctors and biologists, then the National Committee for Resettlement of Foreign Physicians, which operated with the help of Jewish organizations, various private funds and American doctors. The émigrés themselves set up their own professional bodies, such as the Association of Former European Jurists.

The problem of political refugees was more delicate. From 1933, the Jewish Labor Committee collected funds designed to support antifascists, more than 1,800 of whom appealed to its services. The Joint Antifascist Refugee Committee, and above all the Exiled Writers Committee, focused their efforts on those who had fought for the Spanish Republic, most of whom had settled in Mexico. Finally, the American Committee to Save Refugees sought to assist opponents of Hitler who were still in France. Just as important were the International Rescue and Relief Committee, the International Relief Association, and the Emergency Rescue Committee, which from 1940 on actively worked for writers and activists in danger of death. These various committees succeeded in rescuing at least 2,000 intellectuals, 1,000 of whom settled in the United States. Starting in 1941, the President's Advisory Committee on Political Refugees was charged by Roosevelt himself with rescuing certain individuals threatened with arrest by the Gestapo. If American aid was slow to get under way, it was in due course both generous and effective.

GEOGRAPHICAL DISTRIBUTION OF THE EXILES

The itineraries by which the émigrés reached America were often quite strange.[122] While some of them took ship in Marseille or Lisbon and disembarked in New York, others only reached the United States after long odysseys via North Africa or the West Indies. Some refugees, after spending a while in Mexico, reached Arizona via Nogales. In May 1941, Brecht had to flee the Nazi advance via Finland and the Soviet Union. He embarked at Vladivostok just as the Nazi attack on the Soviet Union was announced, crossed the Sea of Japan, and stopped over in Manila, before reaching San Pedro in California on 21 July.

The majority of the émigrés were tempted to settle where they arrived, especially as most opportunities for employment were around New York City or Hollywood. California naturally attracted actors, writers and film-makers, while by its giant scale and cosmopolitan character, New York offered the émigrés a kind of condensed version of Europe, with a number of definite advantages: the variety of its activities, its literary and theatrical life, and above all the size of its Jewish population. Both Hollywood and New York seemed able to offer the possibility of work, and escape from a sense of isolation.

US immigration policy generally sought to avoid such concentrations of émigrés, rightly believing that this would lead to the formation of ghettoes and slow down their adaptation to American society. In the case of refugees chased out of Europe by Nazism, their number was too small to pose such a danger.[123] They were consequently authorized to settle where they wished, even if the aid organizations urged them to establish themselves in the less populated states. Though the European antifascist emigration was highly mobile, the emigration to the United States had a surprisingly static character: the majority of émigrés settled around New York and Hollywood, sometimes leaving one city for the other, or remaining in states such as Pennsylvania, New Jersey, Ohio, Illinois, Massachusetts, Michigan and California. The size of America, the time and cost of travel, all explain the rareness of such moves. Whilst Kurt Weill, Erwin Piscator, George Grosz, Max Reinhardt, Hanns Eisler and Bertolt Brecht had specific reasons to settle in New York or California, Thomas Mann, with his frequent lecture tours, was almost the only exile to travel widely through the American heartland. Most émigrés, throughout their American exile, never left the regions of New York or Los Angeles. Statistically, however, all states except some in the Far West – Montana, Idaho, Nevada and Wyoming – received at least some European immigrants in 1940.

The work of the Davie Commission makes it relatively easy to understand the reasons for this distribution of the emigration. Very few exiles thought spontaneously of settling in the countryside, where they had little chance of employment (except for doctors and teachers), Carl Zuckmayer's experience as a farmer being a rare exception. New York state, accordingly, and New York City in particular, formed the greatest émigré concentration.[124] It was where the majority had disembarked, and they were reassured by the cosmopolitan character of the city and the variety of its activities. Those who spoke no English felt less at sea there. Most Jewish refugees from central Europe refused to move from there, viewing New York – or even Brooklyn – as a second homeland. New York attracted members of the liberal professions as much as it did intellectuals and actors, eager to discover Broadway. At the end of the War, 100,000 of these refugees remained there permanently.

California had the second great concentration of émigrés. Its mild climate, beauty and tranquillity were attractive,[125] so were the relatively low cost of living and the closeness of the film studios. Many film companies, particularly MGM, had helped with the rescue of émigrés by offering invitations and contracts to a number of writers, who worked there as salaried employees manufacturing 'stories'. The exiles themselves called this concentration of artists, writers and exiles in the Los Angeles, Santa Barbara and Santa Monica conurbation, 'Weimar in Hollywood'. It included the most illustrious names in German theatre, cinema and literature, forming a strange community, varied and not without conflict, but mixing relatively little with Americans.

The refugee aid committees tried to persuade a number of exiles to settle in less populated states, to avoid this massive concentration in New York and Los Angeles. But if this was viable for members of the liberal professions, it made no sense for intellectuals: already little known in these cultural metropolises, elsewhere they would simply fade into obscurity. A large number of refugees also preferred to integrate into existing communities – Jewish, Russian, Italian,

German, Polish. Settlement in other states would only increase the feeling of isolation, and many maintained either that they had never known anything of America outside of New York or California, or that they only really felt in exile after leaving New York. Only academics accepted this transplantation. German and Austrian professors taught at Winston-Salem in North Carolina, at Winthrop College, Rock Hill in South Carolina, in New Mexico and elsewhere, though the majority remained in the big universities such as Chicago and Princeton; but Darius Milhaud, Fernand Léger and André Maurois were all at Milles College, and several very well-known German and Austrian musicians at Black Mountain College, along with members of the Bauhaus, artists such as Walter Gropius, Ossip Zadkin and Lyonel Feininger.

It is quite unlikely that American students realized they had as their teachers the greatest names in the European avant-garde, and the latter often suffered cruelly from their isolation and the waste of their talents. Arnold Schoenberg complained in his letters at the feeble quality of his students, and rejoiced that the US government had at least not transformed Einstein into a physics professor at a provincial college, but what about the professors of Sanskrit or Egyptology who had to teach history to high-school students? Some of these experienced their situation as a terrible trauma, others maintained that it was through this unrewarding teaching that they started to discover and love America.

FROM ISOLATION TO ADAPTATION

I was almost twenty-nine years old and was standing on deck of the French liner *Normandie* watching the Statue of Liberty come closer and closer and beyond her – for the first time – the skyline of New York. I was so overcome with emotion that I could not control my tears. I was swept by the feeling that a new life was beginning. The Otto Preminger whose address had been Vienna was finished. The American Otto Preminger was starting.

Otto Preminger

In his autobiography, Otto Preminger comments ironically on the 'large number of European émigrés, always ready to criticize everything', who saw in every American custom only a symptom of barbarism, and sought in this way 'to protect themselves from a civilization they had discovered, but were unsure whether they would be able to adapt to'. He maintains, for his part, that he felt 'each day more in love with my new country', a feeling that never left him.[126]

Such verdicts were uncommon, and if it is hard to analyse the diversity of attitudes that the émigrés adopted towards America, this is because they were a function of several factors – knowledge of the language, ability to find work, personal connections, deeper or less deep attachment to European customs, and the émigré's age. Most of the émigrés knew nothing about the United States when they landed there. Arrival in America meant for some the certainty of having escaped death, for others the haunting feeling that they would never see Europe again. Almost all, however, arrived with a genuine hope. The finest homage to America, perhaps, is the smile of the young Greek hero in Elia Kazan's film *America, America*, when he sees from his boat the skyscrapers of New York, the city of his dreams. But they were welcomed by friends and relatives, sponsored by committees or left to their own devices, it was not long before the majority of émigrés experienced a feeling of disturbing strangeness at American life, culture and society. There is no émigré whose letters and memoirs do not betray the mixture of surprise, enchantment, fear and irony that marked their discovery of America. The replies to the questionnaire of the Davie committee, *What the Refugees Think of America*, are often surprising. Even intellectuals confessed their astonishment at discovering on their arrival neither gangsters nor Red Indians, but museums and libraries open late into the evening, and that spitting in the New York subway was subject to a fine of $500. They generally found the country either richer or poorer than they had supposed. Their image of America was born from the novels of John Dos Passos, Sinclair Lewis, Upton Sinclair, Jack London and Ernest Hemingway. Many imagined New York as a hell on earth: in fact they found the city fascinating, and declared that the first view they had of it on arrival at the port remained a unique and unforgettable impression.[127] America struck them as a liberal country. The actor Fritz Kortner, welcomed on arrival by a customs official who spoke to him in Yiddish, was struck by the absence of anti-Semitism, and enthralled that a Jew, just like any other citizen, could become a government official, a businessman, scientist, minister, writer, musician or gangster.[128] Ernst Bloch, in a lecture to the SDS in New York in 1939, recalled that if America was the land of capitalism, it had also known a bourgeois revolution, contrary to Germany, and that its 'dreams of a better life' deserved respect. He proposed accordingly to seek an original and critical relationship with America, free equally of complacency or systematic denigration. A number of refugees in California were amazed to see that roses flowered several times a year, that American cities seemed like ageless suburbs, that the New World was already so old.[129] Kurt Pinthus, fascinated by the cities of the expressionist poets, described New York as 'a crazy city, grandiose and terrible at the same time' and 'new each day'.[130] Piscator, Brecht and Grosz were all fascinated by the skyscrapers, though Fritz Kortner tried to avoid raising his eyes, so that he could feel he was still in Europe. If they were shocked by American racism,[131] they still found America more humane than they had imagined. What surprised them most was the political naivety of the Americans, their heedlessness of the European situation, the seriousness of which they still failed to recognize.[132]

After the joy of escaping Hitler, a number of émigrés became amateur analysts of American customs and tried to list everything that should not be said, so as not to shock their hosts.[133] There were those who adapted right away to the strangest customs.[134] Undoubtedly, the pace of adaptation, or rejection of it, depended a good deal on the émigré's personality and situation. There were some for whom America opened a new page in their career, while for others it ruined all their hopes. Unable to adapt to the American stage, Carl Zuckmayer became a farmer. He borrowed money from his friends and publisher to purchase agricultural equipment, and worked for two and half years unable to leave his farm. When the neighbouring farmers, distrustful of him at first, came round at the start of his third year to ask him to join their union, he was as proud as if the President had named him an honorary citizen. But in all his years of exile, his conversations with other farmers did not go beyond a discussion of different chicken sicknesses and the best varieties of maize. The Swiss author Kurt Goetz also raised chickens in California. Zuckmayer does not stint his praise on these Vermont farmers who eventually considered him one of their own, but the same situation would have reduced others to despair.

By the end of a few months or a year, certain émigrés saw America as their new homeland. Many, however, always lived in hope of an early return to Europe, even when their cities lay in ruins. If the judgements that émigrés made of France, Switzerland or Czechoslovakia did not differ all that much, the images they constructed of America were often contradictory. At the end of their exile, some of them still felt as foreign as when they first got off the boat. Others found it hard to envisage a return to Europe. Thomas Mann, at least until Roosevelt's death, gave many flattering depictions of America in his correspondence, and though at the start of his exile he had maintained that it was hard for him to imagine without fear a lengthy separation from German language and culture, by 1944 he recalled in many letters that he saw himself as an 'American citizen',[135] that his sons were serving in the US army, and that 'in the present state of affairs, [it is] in the cosmopolitan universe represented by America' that his 'type of German-ness is best integrated'. He added: 'The idea of returning to Germany is of course very foreign to me,' and even declared: 'Naturally, I have an ardent desire to tread European soil once again, but as far as I can see, though this may be a prejudgement, I shall only do so as a visitor.'[136]

George Grosz also found America more beautiful than he had imagined. He took many photographs of New York, found inspiration for his paintings and drawings, and waxed enthusiastic for American life, without really ever managing to adapt to it. For Arthur Polgar, the American landscapes were the finest in the world. Kurt Weill adapted to Broadway, and Piscator tried to come to terms with American life, whereas Alfred Döblin saw it simply as a hell with no escape route. He declared himself neither an emigrant nor an immigrant, but a temporary exile in a country where he felt he could never put down roots.[137] He described in many of his letters his impressions of Los Angeles: 'a region and not a city, the sea, and here and there ranks of buildings, a city without pedestrians, where the inhabitants are born at the wheel of a car, a desert where you scarcely meet anyone.' Like Heinrich Mann, he was almost unknown in America and spoke English only with difficulty.

Brecht's *Journals* and his poems of this period express the same negative judgements.[138] 'almost nowhere has my life ever been harder than here in this mausoleum of *easy-going*,' he wrote on 1 August 1941. He deplored the fact that 'there is no proper bread in the states' (4 October 1941) and joked about Kortner that he even complained of the Californian climate. But Brecht himself wrote on 21 January 1942: 'odd. i can't breathe in this climate. the air is totally odourless, morning and evening, in both house and garden. there are no seasons here.' The California that Polgar admired so much seemed to Brecht far too beautiful, and he felt nostalgia for the European seasons: 'i involuntarily look at each hill or lemon tree for a price tag.' He deplored above all else the mercantile relationship that governed all human relations: 'custom here requires that you try to "sell" everything [. . .] you are constantly either a buyer or a seller, you sell your piss, as it were, to the urinal. opportunism is regarded as the greatest virtue, politeness becomes cowardice.' Brecht had no pity for 'sexagenarians strolling around tarted-up and dressed like flappers, forced by the cosmetics industry and the movies to remain sexually competitive unto death' (13 February 1942). He judged America as a whole to be 'vulgar' (30 March 1942) and cursed 'the tarted-up petty bourgeois villas with their depressing prettiness' (18 June 1942). His son, on the other hand, had already visited America and collected jazz records, and eventually settled there.

To overcome their isolation, the émigrés organized a stream of receptions and dinners, often to celebrate each other's birthdays. They met at the homes of Thomas Mann or Lion Feuchtwanger, with Heinrich Mann, Hanns Eisler, Alfred Döblin, Franz Werfel, Fritz Lang and Charlie Chaplin. Some American writers attended these gatherings, but the German and Austrian emigration in Hollywood was made up of circles adjacent but not connecting, apart from a few individuals – Lang, Eisler – who were links between separate worlds.[139] With a few rare exceptions – Kurt Weill, Thomas Mann, Lion Feuchtwanger – most of the émigrés always felt poorly adapted to American life, which in some cases such as Döblin turned to hostility. Annette Kolb replied to someone who asked her how she felt in America: 'Grateful and unhappy.'[140] Fritz Landshoff wrote to Hermann Kesten on 21 November 1939: 'I'll go back to Europe. I CAN'T stay there!' Leonhard Frank used the royalties he received from MGM in 1945 for the adaptation of his novel Karl und Anna to set up home in New York: it was 4,800 kilometres nearer Europe. Faced with American culture, the émigrés had to struggle to maintain their identity, as well as battling against isolation. They were doubtless often amazed by American wealth, a certain luxury and ease of life that contrasted with what they had known in Europe, but almost all had the feeling that this was a poisoned chalice, and that if they fell prey to these siren songs, nothing of them would be left intact. They were both attracted by the opportunity of making money by working for the various culture industries – theatre, music, cinema, criticism – and tempted to reject them with contempt.

The obstacle of American culture that they felt each day was greater than the obstacle of the language. Sometimes, even when they were able to find work or a position, they refused this as it embodied for them the negation of almost every European value they had believed in.

In 1940, America was still the 'New World', and its discovery remained for every European intellectual an experience that was as intoxicating as it was traumatic. Lévi-Strauss depicts this admirably at the start of his Tristes Tropiques, when the ethnologist who had himself become a 'concentration-camp animal' found himself on the boat together with German refugees:

But the congenital lack of proportion between the two worlds permeates and distorts our judgements. Those who maintain that New York is ugly are simply the victims of an illusion of the senses. Not having yet learnt to move into a different register, they persist in judging New York as a town, and criticize the avenues, parks and monuments. And no doubt, objectively, New York is a town, but a European sensibility perceives it according to a quite different scale, the scale of European landscapes; whereas American landscapes transport us into a far vaster system for which we have no equivalent. The beauty of New York has to do not with its being a town, but with the fact, obvious as soon as we abandon our preconceptions, that it transposes the town to the level of an artificial landscape in which the principles of urbanism cease to operate, the only significant values being the rich velvety quality of the light, the sharpness of distant outlines, the awe-inspiring precipices between the skyscrapers and sombre valleys, dotted with multicoloured cars looking like flowers.[141]

FROM 'ILLUSTRIOUS IMMIGRANTS' TO PARIAHS

Here [in California] there are only two categories of author: those living in luxury and those living in the mire.

Alfred Döblin, letter to Hermann Kesten, 12 March 1943

each week [Heinrich Mann] goes to pick up his unemployment benefit of $18.50 since his contract with the film-company, like döblin's, has run out. he is over 70. his brother thomas is in the process of building a huge villa.

Bertolt Brecht, *Journals*, 3 December 1941

This great range of judgements on America was not just a function of the émigré's particular personality, his deeper or less deep roots in European culture and landscape, and his ability, in F. C. Weiskopf's happy expression, to live 'under foreign skies'. It was broadly conditioned by the difference of status that they enjoyed. If in Europe writers often enjoyed a fairly equal fame, in America there were the illustrious figures who were celebrated, and the anonymous mass of others of whom America knew nothing and did not want to know more.

In a letter to Albert Einstein of 27 November 1945, Thomas Mann questioned the timeliness of a proposal for the refugees to display their gratitude by a gift to the White House.[142] The US government certainly displayed real generosity towards the refugees after 1940, but between the treatment accorded the illustrious immigrants and the 'non-illustrious' – viewed as genuine pariahs – there was an exorbitant difference. The disproportion of lifestyles of the émigrés in the United States, and in California above all, was more marked than in any other country of exile. If some of them managed to integrate into American life with relative ease, others – even famous writers – almost died of hunger or were forced to work as elevator boys or dish-washers in restaurants. The writer Friedrich S. Grosshut and his wife worked as domestics for a rich household. Helene Weigel did cleaning work, and Fritz Kortner delivered milk. The hatred that the most disfavoured often displayed towards the richest is thus understandable. While some spent their days in splendid villas, with every kind of convenience, others knew only poverty and isolation. Those whose works had been translated into English, and had publishers and literary agents, were asked to give lectures and received a fairly high income (Thomas Mann, Lion Feuchtwanger, Erich Maria Remarque, Franz Werfel, Vicki Baum). But the unknown majority were unable to publish, and had to restrict themselves to hack work that just about enabled them to survive, or earn their living as screenwriters in Hollywood. They certainly enjoyed a real freedom of movement and action, far more than they had known in any European country, but against this they suffered from a much greater cultural isolation and from the indifference of those around them. Without being a very famous writer, Alfred Döblin had enjoyed in Paris a fairly large circle of admirers. In the United States he was completely unknown. As for Heinrich Mann, a respected and relatively well-known figure in France, in the United States he was simply the brother of 'the great novelist Thomas Mann', or worse, 'the uncle of Golo Mann'!

A number of scientists, members of the liberal professions and a few writers, had no difficulty in rebuilding their lifestyle in America.[143] The others, however, fell into one or other of the two categories that Döblin brutally defined: the poor and the well off – even if the borders were not quite so clear-cut. Thomas Mann was less rich than Feuchtwanger, Brecht less poor than Döblin or Heinrich Mann. Schoenberg was better off than Hanns Eisler, but even so had difficulty supporting his family. Old ideological or artistic oppositions were now supplemented by new rancour towards the most fortunate, even though the latter devoted a large part of their resources to assisting their poorer colleagues: saving them from a worse poverty, but not from humiliation.[144]

Thomas Mann described on several occasions Feuchtwanger's splendid house, the 'castle overlooking the sea'[145] where he continued writing his bestsellers, surrounded by his books and precious furnishings, and dictating to his secretary the next volume, which he knew in advance would sell tens if not hundreds of thousands. In friendly terms, Brecht also depicted this 'grand villa on the sea, filled with his furniture and his art objects from Berlin' (15 May 1942), with a fine garden, in Pacific Palisades. Whilst Feuchtwanger wrote a worthy text[146] on the material sufferings of the exiled writers, this was a subject he was scarcely familiar with himself. His novels remained bestsellers, in both German and English, and he enjoyed a real opulence throughout his exile.[147] Without enjoying the same luxury, Thomas Mann was also well off. As he wrote to Bruno Walter on 6 May 1943: 'We live our by now deeply habituated waiting-room days among our palms and *lemon trees*, in sociable intercourse with the Franks, Werfels, Dieterles, Neumanns [. . .].'[148] Mann had a pleasant villa, a black servant and a car, and organized brilliant soirées at which each of his friends read their latest works, and musical entertainment was given just as in the richest Munich homes. If the English editions of his works were not printed in very large runs, German editions were published in Stockholm by Bermann Fischer, and sold also in the United States. Considered a standard-bearer of the German emigration, he enjoyed immense fame and planned lecture tours with his literary agents, certain of the success he would gain:

In Montreal, the police had to be called out when the overflow crowd refused to move and was threatening to crush in the doors. In Boston something like 1,000 persons had to be turned away. I ask myself every time: What do these people expect? After all, I'm not Caruso. Won't they be completely disappointed? But they aren't. They declare that it was the greatest thing they have ever heard.[149]

Each of Mann's speeches was recorded and sold on disc. In 1944, when Germany lay in ruins, he wrote to Agnes E. Meyer: 'I am extremely fond of celebrations, birthdays, champagne, Christmas with the children and grand-children, evening readings aloud in a circle of friends.'

But what about his brother Heinrich? In 1946, the editors of *Freies Deutsch-land* wrote to Thomas Mann asking news of Heinrich, and he replied on 6 February:

His home is situated in a more urban district, further from the sea, not exactly *down town*, but in any case in Los Angeles. He lets us bring him out to the country once a week without fail, and spends with us the hours from lunch to sunset. For a change, we meet at his house and have a kind of picnic dinner, generally extraordinarily pleasant and intimate, after which he might read us the remarkable new things he has written, or ask about the work I have been doing.

Heinrich Mann, with his 'lucid joviality', divided his time between drafting 'works of genius' and discussion with his brother. He was 'very attached to his little ground floor' on South Wall Street, from where he could go out on foot to the shops. He worked in 'a well-appointed study', or in his bedroom 'equipped with an excellent radio set', and 'in the evening listens a great deal to music'. Wrapped in general esteem and consideration, Heinrich seemed therefore to enjoy a happy old age – if we believe Thomas Mann. Others however describe him as living in extreme isolation, in fairly squalid conditions, unable to go out for lack of a car, with a companion – Nelly – who though devoted to him was seriously neurotic and an alcoholic, whom Thomas Mann praised in public but not in his private letters.[150] Though he could not speak correct English, Heinrich Mann had worked first of all in the Hollywood studios for an annual salary of $6,000, as a mere employee. For eight hours a day he wrote stories that were never filmed.[151] His brother had to help him constantly by paying his rent. As he no longer received anything from his Soviet editions, he sometimes lived on two to four dollars a week. Only a few friends such as Kurt Rosenfeld and Alfred Kantorowicz prevented him from sinking into total misery, and his wife had to work as a nurse.[152] Brecht noted in his diary on 11 November 1943: 'h. m[ann] has no money to call a doctor, and his heart is worn out. his brother in that house he built, with 4–5 cars, literally lets him starve. nelly, just 45, vulgar and with a coarse prettiness, worked in a laundry, has taken to drink. the two of them sit, among cheap furniture and the few books mann managed to salvage, in a stuffy little hollywood villa with no garden.'[153] Even if this portrait is a bit overdone – out of dislike for Thomas Mann – it is certain that at the end of his life, Heinrich Mann recognized that no one in Europe was concerned about his return, and wondered where he would have less chance of dying of hunger: in America or in Europe? Apart from his few books, he literally possessed nothing, and to return to Europe he could count only on the generosity of his brother and other émigrés.

Alfred Döblin lived in a very similar situation. He worked as a screenwriter for MGM on $100 a week, and when his contract expired in October 1941, it was not renewed. He received for a while an unemployment allowance of $18 per week, and then was supported by private benefactors.[154] The letters he wrote to Hermann Kesten are full of tragicomic lamentations on the exile situation: he wrote his great novel on the 1918 revolution knowing it would not find a publisher, and constantly bewailed the fact that the author of *Berlin Alexanderplatz* had become a literal beggar. What should we say, finally, of the expressionist poet Albert Ehrenstein, who learned English at evening classes in New York and lived by writing articles for *Der Aufbau*, supported by George Grosz? While his former wife, Elisabeth Bergner, now married to the producer Paul Czinner, had a triumph on Broadway, he did not even manage to get a single collection of his poems published, and died on 8 April 1950 in a charity hospital, at the age of sixty-three. His ashes were brought back to a London cemetery, but his ex-wife, who lived a few miles away, did not even know.

Weimar in America:
The Strangers in Paradise

1. ARTISTIC CREATION IN AMERICA

THE ENCOUNTER WITH MASS CULTURE

If it is art, it is not for the masses. If it's for the masses, it's not art.
Arnold Schoenberg, letter to William Schlam, 1 July 1945

One of the most violent traumas felt by the antifascist exiles on their arrival in America was the encounter with a new type of culture, today commonly known as 'mass culture', of which the majority had previously had no experience.[1] The culture they had been familiar with in Europe – and above all in Berlin – was an elite culture, nourished by a broad classical and historical tradition, and addressed to a public that was relatively cultivated and attentive to all aesthetic innovations. If this avant-garde culture came constantly into conflict with so-called 'bourgeois' culture, as new movements were formed,[2] this conflict gave rise to a process of ongoing and critical assimilation, leading to an enrichment of classical culture. Initially marginal, these movements laid siege to the visual arts, theatre, literature and the cinema, eventually winning general recognition. It could take no more than a dozen years for a style to become the fashion, for an artist who had been hated and reviled by the critics to become a professor at the Academy of Fine Arts.

Weimar culture was an avant-garde culture, often highly political, confrontational and in breach of taboos, but it could certainly not be termed a mass culture. These artists often formed a kind of ghetto, restricted to one or two cities – Berlin or Munich – but with the necessary means for getting their creations known. They were certain of the approval of a section of the public, the progressive intelligentsia, as well as a large part of the bourgeois youth, in revolt against official ideals, eager to topple old values, who considered these artists as their allies. For all its novelty, Weimar culture was still based on a long classical tradition, even while it challenged this. It developed thanks to a weighty cultural infrastructure – cinemas, theatres, concert halls, opera houses, publishers of books and magazines – which assured its distribution to all the major cities of Germany. It also fed on foreign influences, and cannot be understood in isolation from other European cultural movements. If it was addressed to a restricted public, this public was sufficiently large to provide a livelihood. It often assumed of its audience a fairly high cultural level, developed on the basis of a succession of works, and paid scant attention to popular taste; its job was to fashion a sensibility for these new styles. Before being a style used for cinema backdrops, expressionism was the cry of revolt of a section of the youth against the values of the German Empire.

If this marginal, antagonistic and challenging culture was able to develop, it was because it had available to it certain means of distribution, without however being controlled by them. Closely linked to a certain social climate, to individual and collective forms of sensibility, and to certain personalities, public incomprehension was often a guarantee of its authenticity. Critical and politicized, and far from claiming to satisfy public taste, it set out to provoke a raising of consciousness. The paradox is that within the very system that it challenged, it enjoyed a certain autonomy. Censorship and banning only succeeded in strengthening it. The often passionate attention of the public transformed a theatrical performance, an exhibition, the publication of a novel or the release of a film into a genuine event. Constantly under threat of being stifled for lack of funds, it managed to find expression even in the most impoverished forms, and the attempt to get rid of it only made it resurge with greater strength. The government's negative attitude, which did nothing to support it, indeed actively opposed it, was offset by the impressive number of theatres in Germany and their relative independence, the audience that painters found at international exhibitions, and the large number of literary magazines that came to its defence and made it known.

Before encountering American conditions, the majority of émigrés simply saw the United States as an immense cultural desert from which a few unusual forms sometimes emerged. In reality, this 'desert' was a complex culture-industry system, operating with quite different laws, aiming at opposite results, and producing works that had scarcely any relationship to those that had made the richness of German culture of the Weimar era. The inability of the majority of émigrés to accept the laws, demands and aims of this very different system – which for them did not even deserve the name of 'culture' – explains the sense of unease, frustration and despair that many of them felt towards this 'mass culture'.

Though catering for a whole continent, American culture was often reduced to a few theatres or streets. Outside of New York, American cities had very few large theatres, opera houses or symphony orchestras, and if the film studios were the largest in the world, they would never have undertaken three-quarters of the German films of the Weimar era, which they would have found 'macabre', 'foreign to public taste', 'immoral' or 'lacking a subject'. American artists did indeed have a certain knowledge of European productions. The Hollywood studios had followed the success of actors on the other side of the Atlantic. The experiments and theories of Meyerhold, Reinhardt and Piscator were known to a certain degree in New York's avant-garde milieus, though

Brecht and his theory of epic theatre were almost unknown. Outside of Reinhardt's tours, European theatre aroused little interest. And the majority of big names in German painting and literature were to all intents ignored by the American public.

Most works created in the United States had no intention of challenging society or raising public awareness – with the exception of the Harlem theatre, and certain theatrical experiments following the crash of 1929 and the New Deal; the intention was to serve existing taste. They were addressed to the masses, aiming to satisfy the desires, needs and dreams of the greatest number, and paid no attention to an elite audience. Far from assuming a complex distribution system of theatres, galleries, press and magazines, American culture was based on means that were both technical and effective: radio, cinema and journalism. In the very conception of a work, far more importance was paid to the consumer than to the creative artist. The real cultural power, accordingly, was not in the hands of theatre critics, journalists and artists, but with those who wielded capital, the means of manufacturing these 'products', who controlled at once their conception, creation and distribution.

From the start, therefore, American culture seemed to the majority of émigrés both simplistic and crude: it corresponded to the tastes of the petty bourgeoisie and not those of an intellectual elite, and, scarcely concerned with either political awareness or formal experimentation, it sought rather to seduce, distract, arouse laughter or tears.[3] Entirely subject to money, it had no autonomy within the system. The artist – especially in the fields of music, theatre and cinema – had to accept the demands of producers and financiers of all kinds, who for their part sought to meet public tastes as faithfully as possible. Schoenberg, Eisler, Brecht and Fritz Lang all had cruel experience of this.

Lacking any avant-garde character – we are still far from the 1950s – American culture appeared astonishingly divided between a mass culture that was generally quite devoid of intellectual substance, even if it achieved amazing effects in certain areas (film, song, musical comedy, etc.), and experiments that were interesting but most often ignored and marginalized by the system and known only in some progressive milieus. In Berlin, Max Reinhardt had shown that it was possible to create an avant-garde theatre that also enjoyed commercial success. In the United States, however, quantity decidedly carried the day over quality. The value of films produced was of less interest than the size of the audience, and even music did not escape this commercial criterion.[4] Long before Herbert Marcuse offered a detailed analysis of the operation of this one-dimensional culture, the majority of antifascist émigrés discovered it with both curiosity and consternation. In almost every cultural sector, public taste played a determining role.[5] It was not for the public to learn to understand, admire and love new works that might shock its sensibility or its vision of the world, but for the creators to constantly investigate the tastes of the public in order to serve them. The value of a play was determined neither by aesthetics nor social message, but by the box-office takings. This is what would decide the run of a production, its further revival, and its possible transformation into a Hollywood film. The most common ideal was to take a successful novel, convert it into a play and then a film, so that the public was literally saturated. 'Famous plays from famous authors', declared a producer as remarkable as A. Zukor, proponent of the absurd creed: 'The public are never wrong'. It was important therefore to avoid themes that were difficult or too intellectual, not to shock the spectator's morals by overly bold ideas, and to respect a complex code of conventions that every author, producer and director had to be familiar with, under threat of seeing himself lambasted by the countless leagues in defence of morality – or still worse, confronted by a public boycott. Family and respect for American values went without saying. A dreamy kind of eroticism was permissible, as long as explicit sex was avoided. The Hollywood tradition remained surprisingly constant, seeking in the best of cases to combine a certain visual beauty, the mastery of a genre, with a fairly simple content, capable of moving or distracting the spectators, and reinforcing them in their opinions. It operated as a gigantic dream factory by manufacturing stars, even if Mae West's double entendres or Jean Harlow's low-cut dresses were seen as a threat to public morals. An astonishing mix of provocation and prudery, prosaic situations and repressed desires, this mass culture was built on taboos and did not abolish any of them. If black actors played in a film, they had to appear in unimportant scenes which could be cut without problem when these films were shown in the Southern states. Triumphant on all sides was the consumption of images, the scintillation of colour and light, the manipulation of nostalgia over authentic creation. A film was known by its main star, not by its director, and it was again public taste that engendered the star system: each artist saw their salary and roles determined by the number of letters and requests for dedicated photos that the studio received, all of which was keenly monitored by press attachés and producers, constantly informed of the number of tickets sold for each film. This gave rise to a complex hierarchy among actors, which took no account of their artistic value, but only of the commercial factor. The money-makers who prevailed at the box office were the rulers of this mini-society, this realm of socialized images, with its vamps and ingénues, its good and bad children, its sports stars and exotic comedians, its policemen and gangsters.

The success of the talkies, following Al Jolson's *The Jazz Singer*, enabled Hollywood cinema to compete directly with the theatre from the mid 1920s on, and to become the medium par excellence of this mass culture that dominated all American culture with its financial weight. Fifty million dollars was spent in six months on the modernization of the studios, and the cinema audience rose by leaps and bounds. This expansion ended by threatening the few quality theatres that remained. Despite the clouds that darkened the social and economic climate, musical comedy and operetta became the most popular genres with the American public. After the vamps and mysterious beauties of the silent films, singers and dancers were the heroes of this new culture, the great expansion of which coincided with the arrival of the exiled artists from Europe. Music – to match each image and glance – played an ever greater role in the cinema, demeaning the work of Gershwin. A painless transition led from dance film to music-hall film (*Broadway Melody*, 1940), which sought to supplant live theatre itself. A work of art that was tentacular rather than totalizing, Hollywood film with its concentration of capital drew in writers, musicians and the widest range of talent. In the gigantic shadow that it projected, all other creations could only fade into insignificance if they refused to follow its example.

Was America the 'cultural desert' that so many of the émigrés maintained? Undoubtedly it was. But a surprisingly overpopulated desert that left no room for anything but its own productions. In New York or Hollywood, the exiles were deprived of all those means of expression whose conflicting diversity had permitted the development of Weimar culture. What could become of so many artists, actors, writers, directors and musicians, in a country so poor in theatres, literary magazines and publishers, where screen writers and directors, actors and musicians, were simply employees in an immense business that could demand everything of them as they owed it everything? Not only were the émigrés unfamiliar with the tastes of the American public, most of them were unable to grasp the laws that governed the operation of such an empire. Whilst a number of exiled artists came to terms with the system by adapting their style, and several discovered themselves anew in this way, it condemned a large number to inactivity and hatred towards a world that mocked their sensitivity, their individuality and their pride as creators, not to mention their most cherished values, bearing on the meaning, function and very nature of art. The inability and refusal to accept the laws of this culture found expression in the bitter irony of Brecht's *Journals*, as he observed American society with an entomologist's curiosity; it explains the ambiguous attitude of so many émigrés towards Fritz Lang and Kurt Weill, who seemed to come to terms with the system, and also the misery and isolation of Alfred Döblin and Heinrich Mann, symbols of a culture of which they found no trace in America, aristocrats and patricians of a vanished world. How many of them would not recognize themselves in the long complaint that Schoenberg addressed to Kokoschka on 3 July 1946:

> You complain of the lack of culture in this world of entertainment. What would you say then of the world I live in, which disgusts me to death. I am not just thinking of the cinema. The following advertisement will give you an example: it shows a man who had run over a child, with the child lying dead in front of his car. He's holding his head in despair, but not to say something like 'My God, what have I done?' For underneath it the words are: 'Sorry, now it's too late to worry – take out your policy at the WW Insurance Company in time.' And I have to teach these people composition.[6]

THE ART MARKET

> No serious composer in this country is capable of living from his *art*. Only popular composers earn enough to support oneself and one's family, and then it is not *art*.
> Arnold Schoenberg, letter to Henry Allen Moe, 22 February 1945

There was another unhappy discovery that a large number of émigré writers and artists had to make: that of the art market. In selling their works in Europe and in America, the relation they had with the financial powers was completely different. European artists, of course, whether painters, directors or writers, were also concerned to win public favour. But they did not govern their creation entirely by public tastes. Brecht became famous with *The Threepenny Opera* which, despite its political dimension, was a major success in the bourgeois milieu. In the film that G. W. Pabst was to make of his play, Brecht tried to emphasize more precisely the critical dimension of his work, even though this displeased the film company. The outcome of the lawsuit that followed is well known: Brecht lost, but attracted the sympathy of all those intellectuals who admired the courage with which he had sought to have his status as author respected.

It is possible to list the names of several painters or writers who enjoyed a certain wealth under the Weimar Republic, and the profits some people received from films and plays. But the majority of those who embodied this culture of the 1920s and early 30s were fairly poor,[7] and in economic terms this avant-garde culture was highly fragile. Two failures in a row were enough to bankrupt a theatre. Piscator was imprisoned for non-payment of tax. This type of culture often depended on productions being very modest in terms of cost,[8] and on private or public patronage, i.e. state subsidies to theatres and opera houses.[9]

The majority of émigrés soon discovered that American culture operated on completely different lines. There were no subsidies to theatres, and hardly any private patronage. Those who put up the money were able to control the entire production, and the creative worker was simply their employee. American culture was entirely based on private capital, whose holders were able to exert a genuine tyranny by their demands and their tastes.[10] It operated as an industry, and the works produced were seen as commercial products whose value was calculated by the profit realized. The artistic activity of German émigrés in America is often therefore a history of their entanglements with the culture industry and the art market. Most of them were faced with a dilemma. If they rejected the laws of the market and every adaptation of their requirements to the actual operation of American culture, they would be condemned to die of hunger in this midst of this opulence; if they did adapt, they risked betraying their most fundamental aspirations and despising themselves. Writers, in order to survive, were forced to invent marketable 'stories', something they were often incapable of doing, knowing almost nothing of the laws of this genre and the tastes of the American public. Composers thus became teachers (Eisler, Schoenberg)[11] or had to write film music. Actors often agreed to play insignificant roles in 'B' movies. As for directors of film and stage, they had to come to terms with the American style. Finally, in contrast with the multiple sites of cultural creation that Europe had to offer, American culture seemed limited to two microcosms both complex and singular: Hollywood and Broadway.

In the early 1920s, a few films were still made in New York by Paramount, but the centre of gravity of the film industry had already moved to Hollywood, which had become a cultural industry of a kind almost unique in the world, and a genuine financial power. Though its population in 1920 was no more than

25,000, of whom 2,000 worked for the cinema, the advent of sound films completely transformed the situation. Hollywood now attracted thousands of new arrivals:[12] everyone who dreamed of becoming an actor, but also writers and journalists who wanted to write screenplays, musicians attracted by the lucrative composition of film music, and even a large number of established actors from New York who were fascinated by Hollywood and its enormous prestige. With its financial power, technical resources, and the personalities by which it was surrounded, the film industry was in a position to compete with any other spectacle whatsoever. It could supplant theatre, music-hall and musical comedy, or bring them into its orbit. And the greatest American writers were prepared to become salaried employees for this powerful industry.

In Europe, a number of writers had been led to collaborate with the film industry, including Arnolt Bronnen, Bertolt Brecht, Alfred Döblin, Heinrich Mann and Carl Zuckmayer. But the relationship between writer and producer here was quite different from that in America. In Berlin, a film company often tried to adapt a successful play, or use the talents of a famous writer. In America, the studio 'bought a story', reserving the right to change it as it pleased, even denature entirely its meaning and content, the better to adapt it to public taste. Émigré directors, writers and actors would soon understand that profitability was pretty well the only criterion that Hollywood recognized. Brecht and Döblin, like Ludwig Berger,[13] often expressed their surprise at the little interest producers displayed in the artistic qualities of the films they made. From being the most famous writers in Weimar Germany, they found themselves transformed in Hollywood into mere employees,[14] forced to work in unhealthy sheds, receiving less consideration than lighting technicians and make-up artists, having to manufacture 'stories' in office hours, to add to the hundreds already written, and which practically no one read. If the companies were prepared to invest gigantic sums in buying a successful title, they paid relatively little – $100 a week – to the authors they employed as screen writers. In a system of this kind, actors were forced to change their style, writers to abandon any originality, and musicians to compose hack work devoid of interest.[15]

The second American cultural metropolis, just as mythical, was Broadway. Theatres and music halls of every kind had pressed together since the start of the century between 30th and 50th Streets.[16] The most remarkable shows ran alongside the most mediocre. Broadway did not kindle the same mythology as Hollywood, but it was in a more profound sense the real heart of American theatrical and musical culture. Even if it offered far less in the way of employment possibilities for European exiles than did Hollywood, Broadway was nonetheless a kind of heritage for the émigrés, the last place where images of European culture still survived, a place at least where the attempt was made to revive them. Rather than a genuine expression of American popular culture – of which Gershwin, himself raised on this world of Broadway, was the most prestigious representative – Broadway was born from a strange encounter: with the world of German and Austrian operettas from the years just before the Great War, which had crossed the Atlantic from London. It was here that these vestiges of the old European culture mixed intimately with other musical and choreographic elements to form a style more or less unique in the world. The magic of Broadway lay less in the creation of new shows than in the transformation of existing ones, and in a style of spectacle that was almost unknown in Europe. Before creating a genuine American popular culture, Broadway managed to abolish the lines of division between genres that in Europe had remained strictly separate. While European culture distinguished between mere entertainment on the one hand and avant-garde works on the other, 'serious' and 'light' music, Broadway drew its strength, power and prestige from combining the two. Oscar Hammerstein, Irving Berlin, Cole Porter and George Gershwin were certainly rare talents, but it is undeniable that it was from this ambiguity, this rejection of distinctions, that so much of the show music and musical comedies was born, its composers being themselves European émigrés or the children of émigrés.[17] Gershwin, who declared in 1928 that 'all music is a conspiracy against silence', is himself the best example of the experience and translation of this.

With Tin Pan Alley, its phantom street and song factory, Broadway also created its own mythology, the spectacle of its rise, a world of musical dreams that steadily marked the entire American sensibility. In the years when the son of the Russian émigré Morris Gershovitz became George Gershwin, all these European influences melted together to give birth to a type of culture and spectacle, familiar today, but which had no equivalent anywhere at that time. Jazz soon came to mark all American music, and throughout the 1920s the 'review' continued to develop, a succession of song and dance numbers, as well as the music hall, a heterogeneous combination of more or less artistic attractions. The American mythologies of the post-war decade reached both Paris and Berlin, fascinating both Brecht and Paul Morand; they were seen as astonishing and almost unclassifiable. That a musician such as Gershwin could be at the same time a composer of genius and a contributor to this kind of spectacle was bound to surprise a European public. If it was aware of its superiority to the cinema, the world of Broadway rapidly understood that it could only survive by coming to terms with it. A growing number of actors, directors and composers were accordingly led to work for the film industry, and it was around the New York/Hollywood axis that American culture increasingly crystallized.

Without denying the interest of many productions that were born in this way, it is clear that they increasingly involved a certain submission to public taste, and a corresponding financial dependence, so that very few émigrés – Kurt Weill being the obvious exception – managed to find a place here or even to grasp their sense. Many had only contempt for them.

ATTITUDES TO AMERICAN CULTURE

here my profession is gold-digging, the lucky ones pan big nuggets the size of your fist out of the mud and people talk about them for a while; when i walk, i walk on clouds like a polio victim.

Bertolt Brecht, *Journals*, 1 August 1941

Confronted by this culture and its mode of operation, almost unknown in Europe, many émigrés experienced conflicting feelings. Some of them lived their exile as one long nightmare (Alfred Döblin), others managed to adapt, even to rival American creators on their own ground (Kurt Weill). Finally, the majority of émigrés were torn between a wish to profit from the system they despised, and a desire not to alienate themselves in it.

For evident reasons, it was almost impossible – apart from the few rare émigrés who were really wealthy – to reject any compromise with the system. Even if they found this culture industry repulsive, limited to the manufacture of consumer products, most of them had to try and live off it. Thomas Mann and Lion Feuchtwanger could proudly ignore the tastes of the American public. The relative incomprehension that American critics displayed towards *Doctor Faustus* did not greatly disturb its author. But this was not the case for those authors who found work as screenwriters in Hollywood. Some, like Franz Werfel or Vicki Baum, were fortunate enough to find that the film industry took an interest in their works. Directors such as Max Reinhardt and Erwin Piscator became professors, as did Hanns Eisler and Arnold Schoenberg. But they all wondered how far they could go in this collaboration without betraying themselves. If some seemed to accept the laws of the system, others constantly sought to cheat it, trying to create interesting works despite the genres imposed on them. There was certainly a gulf between *The Threepenny Opera* and the musical comedies of Broadway, and it is easy to reproach Kurt Weill for his 'adaptation' to the American style. But can his career in the United States be simply ignored? Even if situated in the 'mass culture' context, Weill's melodies are admirable, by the same standard as the music of George Gershwin, who achieved an astonishing balance between modern and popular music.

The limits of the émigrés' compromise with this 'mass culture' were often very narrow. Few European artists were able to grasp its dynamic. On the whole, the most representative artists of the Weimar era were strictly incapable of adapting to it, and their works were the very opposite of what was required of them. The majority of American musicians and critics recognized the genius of Schoenberg and the beauty of Eisler's compositions, but these remained unknown to the public at large. Until his death, Schoenberg had little opportunity to get his works performed, and he had to make a living by teaching. The presence of so many eminent German writers in Hollywood aroused only scant interest among producers. With a few exceptions, none of their screenplays was filmed, and both Brecht and Döblin were unknown to most of the studio bosses. A number of actors had to accept parts they would have refused in Germany, or were typecast as Nazi officers or spies because of their accent. Though a few émigré novels were genuine successful in film adaptation – Anna Seghers's *The Seventh Cross* and some novels by Franz Werfel, Erich Maria Remarque or Vicki Baum – these were rare exceptions. Worse, the majority of screenplays written by these Weimar writers eventually bore no trace of their original work, and it is almost impossible even to list them.

Even when collaboration with the culture industry seemed on the cards, it often collapsed because of the author's artistic convictions. The dispute that

Brecht and Fritz Lang had over a projected film on the assassination of Heydrich, *Hangmen Also Die*, is a good illustration: despite his desire to 'make money', Brecht could not accept certain sacrifices, and withdrew his name from the proposal. Schoenberg, when it was proposed that he should compose film music, made such exorbitant financial requirements, under the pretext of not prostituting his art, that he was certain to discourage producers. He had to rest content with his teaching job. Piscator gave up his theories of 'political' or 'proletarian' theatre, and taught epic theatre at the New School for Social Research. Max Reinhardt opened a drama school, and George Grosz a school of drawing, but without any great success. As for Fritz Lang, he had often to shoot scripts that had little interest, for the same commercial reasons.

This 'New Weimar', as it was called at the time, thus remained, in relation to the overall American art market, a veritable ghetto, a foreign body. It was only twenty years later that a retrospective interest in these émigrés and their work developed, and America realized what they could have brought to it. While their encounter with America was in all cases a decisive experience, it must be recognized that it scarcely modified their style. Schoenberg's music was inspired to the end of his life by the European tradition, just like Thomas Mann's *Doctor Faustus*. America did not in any way modify Brecht's theatre or Eisler's compositions. Piscator, on his return to Germany, seems to have returned to his style of the Weimar era. And if America makes an appearance in several of Feuchtwanger's novels, most works by the émigrés bear scarcely a trace of the country.

George Grosz and Kurt Weill are notable exceptions. When Grosz settled in New York in 1932, invited by the Art Students' League, he was already disgusted with Germany.[18] He opened a private school of art there together with Maurice Sterne, where he taught until 1955. Grosz's drawings soon evolved well away from the European context. They depicted street scenes and advertising billboards with warmth as well as irony. He was one of the few artists of his generation to adapt successfully to America. As he himself recognized: 'In any case, America was at that time the country where I wanted to live. Paradoxically, this desire remained with me, and it managed greatly to annoy my orthodox Marxist friends.'[19] In 1936, a New York publishing house brought out a volume of Grosz's drawings – old and new – with a preface by John Dos Passos. Some of the political themes are still there – the depiction of Nazi anti-Semitism and anti-Communism – but the radicalism of his style has already softened. He seems to have abandoned caricature for more naturalistic sketches, and he portrayed the American way of life with more tenderness than hostility. Grosz gradually became more of an illustrator than a 'committed' artist, and his ideological evolution can be read from his drawings: the former Dadaist, subsequently fellow-traveller of the KPD and friend of Piscator, now presented fascism and Communism as twins. If his drawings continued to oppose Nazism, he also did many illustrations for *Esquire* magazine that had no political content. The Spanish war still marked his work, but at the same time his political beliefs seemed to collapse. 'Many things that Germany had frozen were then reborn around me: in America I rediscovered the pleasure of painting.

I deliberately and carefully destroyed a part of my past. When I experienced a phase of deep depression, this had nothing to do with America.'[20] From 1940, he concentrated on painting landscapes and still lifes, removed from themes of actuality. Examining the drawings of American landscapes that he did at this time, it is hard indeed to detect the style of 'Ecce Homo' or 'The New Face of the Ruling Class', Grosz's chronicle of the German inflation, the crushing of the Spartacists and the hopes for revolution. He himself declared, in 1944, that he had 'finished with the satirical phase of my art', and though in the latter part of his life he returned to certain principles of Berlin Dadaism, it is clear that the encounter with America meant for him both an artistic and a political break with his past. The fact that despite distancing himself from Marxism he maintained close connections with many fellow émigrés makes it hard to see Grosz as having simply adapted to the American context. It was just that it was impossible to continue in New York an artistic style that made sense only in Berlin.

The example of Kurt Weill is equally complex, and like Grosz, he was criticized for having accepted American reality. A student of Busoni, a composer close to atonality, friend and collaborator of Georg Kaiser and Ivan Goll before meeting Brecht in 1927, Weill remains known in the history of theatre and music of the Weimar years for the music he wrote for Brecht's plays: *The Threepenny Opera* (1928), *The Rise and Fall of the City of Mahagonny* (1930), *He Who Said Yes* (1930), then in 1933 *The Seven Deadly Sins*, staged in Paris at the Théâtre des Champs-Elysées. His music was certainly far removed from the avant-garde embodied at this time by Schoenberg, who had scant regard for *The Threepenny Opera*, though it was admired by Alban Berg. Already at this time, Kurt Weill's music showed the influence of jazz, blues and Gershwin, a certain romanticism blended with social irony that gave his style its inimitable character, to the point that Ernst Bloch could see the song 'Pirate Jenny' as a national hymn.[21]

Kurt Weill found the first years of exile difficult, but in 1935 he settled in the United States,[22] where he began a new career. After collaborating with the Summer Camp and Group Theater, he composed music for the American stage. *Johnny Johnson* was staged in 1936, *The Eternal Road* in 1937 (at the Manhattan Opera House, directed by Max Reinhardt). He went on to collaborate with Ira Gershwin and Maxwell Anderson (*Knickerbocker Holiday*, 1937), and produced a whole series of compositions for musical comedies: *Railroads on Parade* (1939), *Lady in the Dark* (1941, with Ira Gershwin), *One Touch of Venus* (1943, with S. J. Perelman, directed by Elia Kazan), *The Firebrand of Florence* (with Ira Gershwin), *Street Scene* (from Elmer Rice, 1947), *Love Life* (1948, directed by Elia Kazan), *Lost in the Stars* (a 'musical tragedy' by Maxwell Anderson, 1949), *Huckleberry Finn* (with Maxwell Anderson). Were these works in fact only 'light' music, adaptations to the Broadway stage, and an artistic regression in relation to Weill's European creations? They are certainly far removed from *The Threepenny Opera* or *Mahagonny*. The social themes, if not absent, are little emphasized, and a critic like Adorno, for example, held that Weill was musically dead in his American exile. But in what way did Weill change his style? His

music in Europe had nothing 'committed' about it. He admired Brecht without
sharing his ideas. He was influenced early on by Gershwin and jazz – the Nazi
accusation that Weill's music was 'negroid' attests to this. His arrival in
America simply brought him closer to these influences on his music. Those
critics who deny Weill's American compositions their place in modern music,
seeing only an aesthetic collapse of his work, most often display their bad faith.
Like Gershwin, Kurt Weill worked for Broadway; he accepted the laws of a
genre and tried to bring it to a certain perfection. If it is easy to show what
distinguished Weill's American compositions from his works created before
1933, this is no reason to disdain them. One wonders in fact whether the critics
who have made such negative and exaggerated judgements have really listened
to his music.[23] And indeed, what would be more illusory than to imagine – as
with Grosz's drawings – that it was possible in America, in different political
circumstances and a radically different cultural context, to continue a style so
closely tied to Germany – even to Berlin – in the pre-Hitler years? It is symbolic,
moreover, that Brecht, Grosz, Weill and Piscator maintained good relations –
despite the occasional quarrel – until their deaths.[24]

Many other examples could be given to show the wide range of attitudes that
émigrés adopted towards American culture. There is certainly little comparison
between the situation of Alfred Döblin in America and that of Lion Feuchtwanger, between the relative integration Thomas Mann enjoyed and the
isolation of his brother Heinrich, the loneliness of Hindemith, Eisler and
Schoenberg and the success of Weill. But this difference in attitudes is due
less to concessions made to the system than to the ability that the émigrés had to
follow their own style without denaturing it. Kurt Weill certainly succeeded
better than anyone else. On the whole, the émigrés remained complete strangers
to American culture, made little effort to understand it, and found it hard to
abandon a real contempt towards it: a European inheritance, and an abyss that
no bridge could cross in the course of their exile. When the majority left
America, it was as foreign to them as when they took refuge there in 1940.

2. THE INTEGRATION OF ÉMIGRÉS
INTO AMERICAN CULTURAL LIFE

Again and again
As I walk through the cities
Seeking a living, I am told:
Show us what you're made of
Lay it on the table!
Deliver the goods!

Bertolt Brecht, 'Deliver the Goods'

Despite their reticence in putting their talents and their art at the service of a
world dominated by the demands of commerce and spectacle, the majority of
the émigrés had to accept a minimum degree of compromise with the system in

order to survive and continue to create. This adaptation was not made without trouble and a certain rift. While some won a new celebrity, the majority vegetated in semi-misery. To tell their story is thus also to trace the account of their disappointments. The most tragic of these was perhaps the discovery that Hollywood was a great mirage.

HOLLYWOOD, OR THE LIE MARKET

Every day, to earn my daily bread
I go to the market where lies are bought
Hopefully
I take up my place among the sellers.

Bertolt Brecht, 'Hollywood'

Even if the Hollywood story is an immense mystification, the town where so many dreams were made was also a dream town for many of the émigrés. The extreme concentration of German exiles in California in general, and Hollywood in particular, well deserved the label 'New Weimar' or 'Weimar in Hollywood'.[25] Feuchtwanger and Thomas Mann lived in Pacific Palisades, Alexander Granach and Leopold Jessner on Cherokee Avenue, Heinrich Mann in a Los Angeles suburb, and Brecht in Santa Monica. The greatest names in Weimar culture could be found within a few kilometres of each other, in some cases just a few streets, forming a strange cultural ghetto.[26]

The reasons that led them to Hollywood were varied: life there was less expensive than in New York, as well as calmer. The Californian climate seduced them and reminded them of the Mediterranean. The film industry, above all, let them hope that they might glean a few crumbs from the fabulous wealth to be found there. They were tempted therefore to settle on the periphery of this mirage city, forming a strange colony, almost completely cut off from American reality. 'I scarcely realized,' Ludwig Marcuse was to write, 'that there were also Americans living here, and I found that a poor person in Los Angeles was not as poor as they would be in New York.'[27] He did not hide the fact that after Sanary-sur-Mer, he had the impression of 'living in the Weimar Republic for the third time', and Hollywood Boulevard struck him as a real ' "Kulturdamm" of émigrés'. A constant stream of actors, writers, poets, film-makers and composers strolled down the street, and met each other even more frequently than they had done in Berlin. Marcuse ironically recalls how, coming across Leopold Jessner, who was contemplating the window of a shoe shop, he could not stop himself from exclaiming: '*Herr Intendant!*', and that many émigrés continued to imagine themselves living in Germany, the only difference being that the plays they staged and the works they played interested only an émigré public. They formed a microcosm, divided by a number of cleavages and cut off from the surrounding Americans. Many would never see Europe again, and it was not without reason that Ludwig Marcuse maintained that a fragment of Weimar in exile is buried in the Hollywood cemetery.[28]

These Hollywood exiles included a large number of writers, composers, film-makers and actors who were perpetually on the look-out for work. They came across the same obstacles and experienced the same disappointments. As Brecht put it:

> even the most experienced hollywood writers who have been fabricating one script after another for 10 years still, at a certain stage in every script, feel the hope that this time they might, by this or that subterfuge, thanks to some happy contingency, pull off something better, something not quite so low. this hope is always disappointed, but without it they could not work – and those low and dirty films could not be made.[29]

Hollywood attracted early on a large number of writers who hoped not only to get their works adapted, but to work as screen writers for one or other of the film companies. It was a hope that had already led William Faulkner, F. Scott Fitzgerald, D. Parks, S. J. Perelman, G. Oppenheimer and Henry Miller to the movie capital. Few of them had any idea exactly what this collaboration would mean. By 1930, the Hollywood style was dominated by musical comedy, and Hollywood sought to eclipse Broadway. Apart from *The Wizard of Oz* (1939), the early results were fairly mediocre, but the arrival of a certain number of prominent figures from Broadway such as Vincente Minelli was to give these productions a new dimension. Writers were invited to manufacture 'stories' with a prospect of commercial success, to be filmed with luxurious backdrops, popular stars and music. Besides this style of musical comedy, the producers also aimed to transform into films the most famous Broadway plays and the best-selling books. It was not long, however, before a number of American writers left the studios, and others agreed to work there only with iron in the soul.[30] Working conditions were disastrous in every way for these screenwriters, who were underpaid and despised. Not only did they have to abandon any personal originality, and work up the inept stories retained by tyrannical producers – Daryl Zanuck is the best-known example – on an assembly-line basis,[31] but most of their scripts were never filmed. Those fortunate enough to see their work adapted by Hollywood had the same bitter experience: however original it had been, it was immediately trans-formed into a sentimental and insipid triviality. Since in Weimar days they had known only the most successful examples of this collaboration with the cinema, most of the émigré writers were soon cruelly disillusioned.

For anti-Nazi writers exiled in America, however, work with the Hollywood studios offered less an opportunity of getting their works known – they were not that naïve – than the sole hope of making a living, given that they now received hardly any further royalties. Besides, a large number of them had only been able to emigrate to America thanks to contracts with Metro-Goldwyn-Mayer, obtaining in this way the affidavit indispensable for a US visa. On their arrival in America, therefore, Heinrich Mann, Alfred Döblin, Leonhard Frank, Alfred Polgar and Walter Mehring found themselves bound by contract to a company that knew absolutely nothing of their works.[32] A large number of them had never worked for the cinema, had difficulty expressing themselves in English (all the above except Leonhard Frank), and had nothing but contempt for this work, which they performed without the slightest enthusiasm. These exiled writers' encounter with the Hollywood studios thus often boils down to a long tale of grievances and imprecations.[33] Besides being considered as mere employees, with no one paying the slightest attention to their identity, their works and what they could contribute,[34] the stories they wrote – and according to Ludwig Marcuse, they could indeed have brought fresh blood to the mediocrity of the American cinema of the 1940s – were generally deemed 'morbid and twisted' by producers who took no further interest in them, simply waiting for their contracts to expire.

Heinrich Mann, when he arrived at the MGM studios, was almost unknown in the American literary and film world,[35] despite the triumph of Marlene Dietrich in *The Blue Angel*. He appeared to his friends 'to have aged ten years in twelve months'.[36] If Sternberg's film was well-known, no one knew the novel *Professor Unrat* that had inspired it. Thanks to his connections, Heinrich Mann had obtained contracts with both MGM and Warner Brothers. Like many writers of the Weimar era, he took a genuine interest in the meeting of cinema and literature.[37] In Hollywood, Mann had to be at his office from 10 am to 1 pm, though he did not actually do any work there. Leopold Frank, Alfred Polgar, Walter Mehring and Alfred Döblin all had the same disastrous experience. Döblin, when he arrived in New York on 9 September 1940, was met by the Emergency Rescue Committee (with Hermann Kesten, Leo Lania and Leopold Schwarzschild), settled in Beverly Hills and worked at MGM. He earned $100 a week as a 'writer' until his contract expired on 7 October 1941. He was involved in two screenplays, *Mrs Miniver* and *Random Harvest*, and subsequently received an unemployment allowance of $18 a week. Until 1945 he lived on the support of other émigrés and the Writers Fund. His attempt to obtain a grant from the Guggenheim Foundation in 1943 met with defeat,[38] and only the European Film Fund, chaired by the wife of Bruno Frank, prevented him from sinking into destitution. Döblin experienced his work for the film studios as a real humiliation: just like Heinrich Mann, all he had to do was put in a few nominal hours, which he could use for catching up on his correspondence. As he wrote to Hermann Kesten on 31 March 1941: 'I'm now engaged on a new story for the studio, but it is a hopeless attempt. The people here don't need our stories, they already have vaults full of them.'[39] On 24 July he struck an even bitterer note: 'I do not believe one can at the same time serve Louis B. Meyer and one's own work.'[40]

Alfred Neumann also wrote to Hermann Kesten on 13 August 1941 that they were indeed paid to write stories, but as no one ever read these, their salary was more like charity. Brecht, according to Fritz Kortner, lived in Hollywood in an ascetic fashion.[41] Unlike Eisler, he rarely attended evening parties given by the émigrés, had little esteem for Schoenberg – whom Eisler venerated – and could hardly stand Thomas Mann, let alone Theodor Adorno and Max Horkheimer, whose portraits he sketched with a biting irony, especially in his *Tui* novel. Brecht did invite some guests to his home, including Otto Klemperer, Heinrich Mann, Leopold Frank, Bertold and Salka Viertel, Curt Bois, Oskar Homolka, Lion Feuchtwanger, and some American and British figures such as Charlie

Chaplin, W. H. Auden, Christopher Isherwood, Aldous Huxley and Charles Laughton; he lived much the same life as he had in Europe.[42] Just as he had tried to make money in his early days by writing screenplays with Arnolt Bronnen, so Brecht tried to sell these 'roulette stories' to Hollywood, with Fritz Kortner, Charles Boyer, Thören and Vladimir Pozner.[43] He himself worked for United Artists, together with John Wexley, and was constantly in revolt against the functioning of the film industry: 'i never cease to marvel at how primitive the structure of films is. this "technique" gets by with an astonishing minimum of inventiveness, intelligence, humour and interest.'[44]

For all his efforts, however, Brecht did not succeed in selling any of his stories, and his encounter with Hollywood put paid to his image of the 'roaring twenties'; he saw it only as a shop window, a desert besides which Svendborg and the Swedish countryside seemed an 'international centre'. During his Hollywood years, Brecht worked on no less than fifty projects, the majority of which are now lost.[45] Apart from the abortive collaboration with Fritz Lang on the screenplay of *Hangmen Also Die* (1942), and his work with Feuchtwanger on *Simone* (1944) – an adaptation of his play *The Visions of Simone Machard* – it has to be recognized that this activity of Brecht's left no trace in his overall work.[46]

[The] idea that you should go to Hollywood is sheer nonsense. So far there has been absolutely no chance of anything here, otherwise I should obviously have seized it.
Arnold Schoenberg, letter to Jakob Klatzkin, 19 July 1938

Those composers for whom Hollywood was also a mirage found the same unease and disappointment. The success of *The Jazz Singer*, the development of sound film and the popularity of musical comedy, had attracted a growing number of composers wishing to offer their services to the film studios. By the 1930s, a large number of them had obtained work and been transformed into salaried employees, loaned out from one company to another to compose music on an assembly-line basis. The concern for efficiency and profitability left little room for originality or avant-garde experiment. The first composers of film music were also viewed as renegades by their fellow musicians, who saw this collaboration with Hollywood as a betrayal.[47] The composer attached to a studio worked on several films concurrently. His music had to constitute a simple 'background sound', developing in parallel with the images, matching the turns of the plot, emphasizing important moments, happy or dramatic, with appropriate musical effects. The essence of the composition had to be woven round the creation of a leitmotif, constantly repeated at a slower or more rapid tempo, as a function of the state of mind of the characters and the taste of the producer.[48] Despite this anti-artistic mode of operation, the film industry attracted several composers as notable as Miklos Rozsa and the Gershwin brothers.

As the most successful films were inspired by Broadway musical comedies, it was natural that New York composers should leave for Hollywood. George Gershwin arrived on 5 November 1930, along with his brother Ira, and worked for Fox, writing music for Fred Astaire and Ginger Rogers. He returned there after *Porgy and Bess* (1935) and made the acquaintance of Arnold Schoenberg, who expressed great esteem for his music and championed it. Many émigré composers were similarly tempted to work for the film studios. Kurt Weill, though particularly known for his compositions for Broadway, worked for Paramount in 1945 on *Lady in the Dark*.[49] Hanns Eisler, long before his American exile, had criticized the division between 'classical' and 'light' music,[50] and was interested early on in film music. A student of Schoenberg, whom he always venerated despite their political opposition, he had set to music a number of Brecht's poems, written the music for the film *Kuhle Wampe* and several films of Joris Ivens. For Eisler, film music should not be a substitute for operetta, but a new mode of expression corresponding to the technical development of the cinema. But Hollywood offered him little opportunity to put his theories into practice. He wrote music for eight films[51] as well as teaching composition, but ceaselessly lambasted the Hollywood style: 'Hollywood music was ruining his ear'.[52] Paul Dessau had the same negative experiences, and also came into conflict with Eisler over royalties.[53] As for Schoenberg, if he was tempted to work for the cinema, his pride and his awareness of what he represented led him to demand such a high price that any collaboration proved impossible.[54]

Our trade is to make beautiful images with beautiful people, and there is no room here for anyone who doesn't understand that.

Louis B. Meyer to Elia Kazan

The angels of Los Angeles
Are tired out with smiling. Desperately
Behind the fruit stalls of an evening
They buy little bottles
Containing sex odours.

Bertolt Brecht, 'Hollywood Elegies'

The émigré film-makers had their own bitter experience in trying to establish themselves in Hollywood. The 1939–45 period was one of extreme concentration in the American cinema. After the advent of the talkies, competition between the companies died down, and the majority of studios were now in the hands of a few big firms: Paramount, MGM, Fox, RKO, United Artists, Universal, Columbia and Warner Brothers. Their trade association Motion Pictures of America owned more than 4,000 cinemas and was responsible for over 90 per cent of US film production. These companies alone formed a real industrial empire, financed in turn by others – electricity companies and banks. Their gigantic resources and abundance of capital naturally made possible some exceptional productions, but it also brought considerable limitations in the artistic sense. A director might be a genius, but he was nonetheless a salaried employee, forced to follow the demands of the producer and the tastes of the public. A screenwriter had always to be aware of this. Creative freedom for the individual was thus practically absent. Only directors such as Elia Kazan and Orson Welles could grant any liberty to their actors, in accordance with the theories of the Actors' Studio. If the screenwriter simply followed public taste, the director did not choose his own scripts; they were imposed on him by the producer. He was not responsible for the selection of actors, and rarely for the setting, forced rather to follow orders in achieving a product that at all points escaped him, from the initial concept to the final editing.[55] The American audience had scant interest in formal experiments: they wanted to consume a dream and find in these films opportunities for escape, emotion and enchantment, as well as a confirmation of their values. It was not rare for one and the same script to be used for a number of films, or for a producer to demand a completely new editing, a change of actors or setting, to the detriment of the film's artistic value. The director was required to produce a profitable work, just as an actress was required to be beautiful and sensual while of course remaining moral. The slightest conflict with the producer could lead to a brusque dismissal of the director, and a ban on his working in the film industry.[56] The consequences of this system were that the film bore the style of the company that produced it, and was known for its actors rather than for its director. If these abuses were denounced early on by some American directors,[57] they had no way of putting a stop to them. They could only hope to make the least bad films possible within these constraints, marking each of them with a certain style (Vincente Minelli) or 'touch' (Ernst Lubitsch), and if they were particularly attached to a certain project, they had to seek authorization from their company to produce it themselves.[58]

The Hollywood cinema, however, had sought early on to win the collaboration of leading European actors and directors. In September 1922, Pola Negri and her director Ernst Lubitsch arrived in Hollywood,[59] engaged by Paramount, soon followed by Dimitri Buchowisetzky. Friedrich Murnau, known for *The Last of Men*, *Faust*, and *Nosferatu the Vampire*, came to shoot *Sunrise* in 1927; Paul Leni, Paul Ludwig Stein, Lothar Mendes and E. A. Dupont all followed. This exodus of German directors was followed by one of actors: Lya de Putti, Camilla Horan, Conrad Veidt and Emil Jannings also arrived in Hollywood. If none of the films these actors made in America can compare with those they made in Germany, German cinema was still temporarily decapitated by their departure. The advent of talking pictures brought a second generation of actors: Alexandre Moissi, Heinrich George, Gustav Froelich, William Dieterle, Dita Parlo, Olga Tchekowa and Marion Lessing, some of whom returned to continue their careers in Germany. Hollywood had by this time become a decisively international centre of cinema, and several films were shot simultaneously in American and German versions, often leading to a surprising casting of actors.[60] Dubbing increasingly permitted the employment of foreign actors, and if the majority of German actors returned to work in Berlin, a number of directors remained in Hollywood (Dupont, Lubitsch, Murnau).[61]

The advent of Nazism was to precipitate a new wave of émigrés in the direction of Hollywood. Fritz Lang established himself there in 1935, William

(Wilhelm) Dieterle, Max Reinhardt's main collaborator, in 1934, followed by Joe May, Walter Reisch, Alexis Thurn-Taxis, K. Neumann, Edgar G. Ulmer, Max Nosseck, Fred Zinnemann, Detlef Sierck (Douglas Sirk, who arrived in 1944) and Curt Siodmak. A further number of German actors found refuge in Hollywood after the Nazi *Gleichschaltung* of cinema and theatre: Conrad Veidt, Albert Bassermann, Peter Lorre, Fritz Kortner, Luise Rainer, Francisco Gall, Heddy Kiesler (Hedy Lamarr), Oscar Homolka, Francis Lederer, Hugo Haas, Sig Arno, Fritz von Dongen (Philipp Dorn), Willy Eichberger (Carl Esmond) and Ernö (Ernst) Verebes.

But the Hollywood system was the radical negation of most fundamental values of the German cinema. The producers feared any aesthetic complexity, which risked upsetting the audience. Whilst UFA films had been 'auteur' films, of an extreme artistic richness, the fragmentation of cinematic direction, and the absence of any control by the director over the finished product, could only lead to a deep change in their styles.

Fritz Lang had signed a contract with David O. Selznick of MGM when he was still in France. His first screenplays were not filmed, but in 1936 he began his American career with *Fury*, then *You Only Live Once*. If both of these films display a number of themes dear to Lang – the crushing of the individual by a superior force, which might be madness, the will to power, a mythological destiny, death or the crowd – they are more akin to American social films and count among his best achievements. *You and Me* (1938) was a comedy; a screenplay on anti-Nazi espionage, *Men Without a Country* (1939), was never shot. In 1940 Lang turned to Westerns, *The Return of Frank James, Western Union Pioneers*, without great originality.[62] From 1941 to 1943 he made several spy films with a bearing on Nazism – *Hunt the Man, Confirm or Deny* (1943), *Hangmen Also Die* (1942–43), *Spies on the Thames* (1943). A new version of *The Golem* was never made. In 1944–45, Lang directed *Woman in the Picture* (1944) and *The Red Street*. His next films continue the characteristic style of his American period, with a mix of thrillers and spy films: *Cloak and Dagger, The Secret Behind the Door* (1946), *House by the River* (1949), *Guerrillas* (1950), which have scant interest. He returned to Westerns in 1950–51 – *Winchester 73, The Angel of the Damned, The Demon Wakes at Night* (1951) – taking up again the theme of criminal madness. All the other films he made from 1951 to 1956 were thrillers: *Woman With the Gardenia, The Big Heat, Human Desires, While the City Sleeps, Beyond Reasonable Doubt, The Smugglers of Moonfleet*.

On his arrival in the United States, Fritz Lang spoke little English and knew scarcely anything of the operation of American cinema, though he had already visited the country in 1924. In most of the interviews with him published after the War, he declared that he had never compromised with the Hollywood film industry or made any major concessions. His uncritical champions have extolled all the films he made in this period, seeing them even as the apogee of his career. His detractors, on the other hand, speak of a real loss of genius on contact with American society, and a number of émigrés – Brecht and Fritz Kortner – deplored his too successful adaptation to the Hollywood milieu. There can certainly be no question of the interest, value and beauty of several of

the films Fritz Lang made in America, but it has to be admitted that a gulf
separates these from his German productions. *Fury* and *You Only Live Once* are
certainly remarkable, but no other film of Lang's in his American period bears
comparison with films like *Mabuse, The Three Lamps* and *M*, none of which
could have been made in America. Lang did indeed have the opportunity to
direct great actors – Sylvia Sydney, Spencer Tracy, Henry Fonda, Joan Bennett,
Marlene Dietrich and Marilyn Monroe – but none of the films of his American
period adds to his status, even if a certain atmosphere and a fantastical social
realism links them with his films made in Germany,[63] and his signature is
recognizable in certain shots and frames – of a face, or of prison bars.[64] In a
blocked situation, Lang tried not to prostitute his talent, but he was forced to
abandon his symbolism[65] and modify his style, and could practically never give
free rein to his marvellous imagination.

If Lang's is the most famous example, and perhaps the most tragic, the destinies
of other film-makers can provide further illustration. Joe May made admirable
films in Germany, such as *Asphalt* (1929), but in exile he only made films by
order, of which none has found a place in the history of the cinema. The same
went for Wilhelm Thiele, Leo Mittler, Richard Oswald and Reinhold Schünzel.
Walter Reisch, on the other hand, previously known as a scriptwriter before
being eclipsed by Willi Forst and Alexander Korda, attained a certain celebrity
with such films as *Ninotchka, Madame Curie* and *Gaslight*. Hermann Kosterlitz
was also famous under his American name of Henry Koste, as was Curtis
Bernhardt, known above all for *Death Can Wait* with Humphrey Bogart.

Hollywood sounded the knell for many an émigré film-maker's career,
leading them to oblivion or a slow decline as they were unable to adapt to
the system, or else adapted too well. But it also awakened new talents. Born in
America, but winning recognition as a film-maker first in Europe, Robert
Siodmak owed his real celebrity to Hollywood. Billy Wilder imbibed so many
Hollywood myths that he helped to revivify them, even lending them fresh
blood with Germanic legends, to the point that some of the finest American
films are to his credit. He is also the only case of a director who recommenced
his career once again, in postwar Germany, with the same talent.[66]

Actors had greater difficulty in re-establishing themselves. Compared with
Europe and especially Germany, America had very few theatres, and very
few German actors could express themselves in English without an accent.
Those who worked in Hollywood in the 1920s, such as Conrad Veidt and Emil
Jannings, were never able to find roles comparable with those they had played in
UFA films, or even – alas! – under the Third Reich, in the case of Jannings. The
majority therefore returned to Germany. A large number of actors who had
emigrated to America after 1933 did not manage to continue their career, or like
Helene Weigel, failed to find any engagements. Many had to settle for
supporting parts. If Otto Preminger[67] and Erich von Stroheim made a speciality
of the Prussian officer with monocle and shaved head, Conrad Veidt[68] and
especially Peter Lorre, with his disturbing physique,[69] excelled in the ambiguous

roles of Gestapo agents and Nazi spies (Michel Curtiz's *Casablanca*, and *Defeat for the Gestapo*, alongside Humphrey Bogart). Albert Bassermann, one of the greatest actors of the 1930s, never found any role suited to his stature, nor did Fritz Kortner, the expressionist actor, who had to be satisfied with supporting roles that he would never have agreed to play in Germany.[70] For want of finding acceptable roles, some actors who had wanted to remain in exile returned to Germany. Marlene Dietrich describes the tragic case of Rudolf Forster, 'Mack the Knife' in Pabst's film of *The Threepenny Opera*, who after humiliation in the United States went back to the Third Reich.[71]

Actresses such as Francesca Gall and Hedy Lamarr likewise failed to maintain their careers, and even Liliane Harvey's time in Hollywood failed to leave a mark on American cinema. What should we say of Oskar Homolka, Hugo Haas, Francis Lederer and Sig Arno, who had to be satisfied with insignificant roles? They were all eclipsed by a generation of American actors and actresses – exceptional, to be sure – such as Jean Harlow, Joan Crawford, Rita Hayworth, Gary Cooper, Cary Grant, Clark Gable, Humphrey Bogart and Lauren Baccall. The style of German actors, moreover, was so different from that of the Americans, so strongly marked by silent film and expressionism, that it aroused a somewhat fearful surprise on the part of the spectator, if not total incomprehension.[72]

EXILE THEATRE

remarkable how very different the situation of the drama is here after scandinavia. the obstacles there were pretty well all political, and that didn't prevent you from writing. here they are aggravated by those of a wholly commercialized theatre in addition.

Bertolt Brecht, *Journals*, 22 October 1941

kortner asks eisler about the new york theatre. eisler: i only know about that from trying to shut my ears to my wife's complaints about it.

Bertolt Brecht, *Journals*, 26 April 1942

Despite the large number of writers, actors[73] and directors who fled to the United States, no lasting 'exile theatre' was established there, even if many émigrés did contribute to the enrichment of the American stage. This somewhat paradoxical situation is explained first of all by the organization of the theatre in the United States: though there were theatres in the majority of larger American cities, and German plays had been performed since 1850, most of them operated thanks to private funds. They were guided by a concern for profitability that left little room for formal innovations. If the technical staff of these theatres received high salaries, thanks to their trade unions, this was not the case with actors, who were generally underpaid and overexploited. The émigrés were of course unable to finance a theatre, and American producers had little interest in wasting their capital on a German theatre in exile.

In the 1920s, New York had a number of German-language theatres, including the famous Schubert,[74] and a number of German directors had been invited there.[75] But around 1930 dramatic style in America underwent a profound transformation. The bourgeois comedies that had been prevailed for so long in the repertoire gave way to musical comedies,[76] often adapted from successful novels (such as Edna Faber's *Show Boat*). With their sumptuous lighting and scenery, these shows gave a new boost to Broadway, creating the taste for song that gripped America under the aegis of Ira and George Gershwin. With its 6,200 seats, Radio City Music Hall at the Rockefeller Center was the largest theatre in the world. At the centre of all these activities was a fairly well-structured group that revolved around the Gershwin brothers and included musicians, actors and writers.[77] If George Gershwin was still little known in Hollywood, he was already famous in Europe, and it was at this time that he composed his masterpiece *Porgy and Bess*. His brother Ira was considered the most talented of Broadway composers.[78] Far from being a minor and negligible genre, these shows attracted a growing number of artists. Broadway discovered surrealism through the choreography of George Balanchine, future director of the New York City Ballet. Like Berlin, New York had its Winter Garden, and throughout the 1930s it was these new shows that won public favour.

But the era of the New Deal seemed to mark a new stage in American theatrical life. In 1935 Franklin D. Roosevelt established the Federal Theater Project, which set out both to encourage progressive works and give work to unemployed actors. These initiatives seemed set to strengthen a number of theatrical efforts born in the 1920s. While the social situation deteriorated and demonstrations multiplied, a large number of artists and writers took up Friedrich Wolf's slogan 'Art is a Weapon' and moved in the direction of an activist theatre.[79] These plays were so topical that many of them were staged on Broadway. New and revolutionary theatrical experiments appeared in the early 1930s.[80] In 1935 the CPUSA published an anthology, *Proletarian Literature in the United States*, with texts by Erskine Caldwell, John Dos Passos, Maxwell Bodenheim, Muriel Rukeyser, Clifford Odets and Malcolm Cowley. From 1927, *New Masses* had published poems written by workers. Real proletarian theatre developed in the factories – Workers Laboratory Theater,[81] Workers Dramatic Council – supported by the Trade Union Unity League, International Labor Defense, Workers International Relief, etc., and inspired by the German and Soviet experiments of agitprop and Proletkult.

During the Great Depression, a number of other political theatres were established. The Group Theater (1931–35) was born on Broadway and its directors included Harold Clurman, Lee Strasberg and Cheryl Crawford. Liberal rather than radical, it sought to convey 'the moral and social pre-occupations of the time', in opposition to the lack of topical significance of American theatre. Breaking with the eclecticism of the Theater Guild and off-Broadway, these created a new style and repertoire. The Theater Guild, founded in 1918, had set out to stage plays of real artistic value. Its repertoire grew more radical in the 1920s and even included some Soviet plays. At the same time, the Independent Stage on Broadway produced a number of plays on social themes. The Popular Front slogan also marked American theatre and the League of Workers' Theater was transformed into the New Theater League. A series of progressive plays now appeared on the American stage. Between 1935 and 1937, the Theater Union sought to win a new public with foreign plays – including Brecht's *The Mother* – as well as by mixing theatre with variety shows. The same period saw the development of the Federal Theater, designed to combat unemployment among actors: it employed more than 10,000 people during its four years of existence from 1935 to 1939. Directed by Hallie Flanagan, this staged a large number of plays on political and social themes. Finally, the Group Theater (1935–41), starting from the success of Clifford Odets's works, built up a real repertoire of activist plays. All these theatres broke entirely with the style of the commercial stage. They often operated as 'collectives' and developed a style somewhat evocative of Piscator or Brecht, fuelled by contemporary problems, with Clifford Odets's *Waiting for Lefty* being the most typical example.

Yet if these experiments seemed to link up with the most revolutionary tendencies in the German theatre – for instance the epic style and certain 'living newspaper' procedures – the differences remained very significant. A number of actors who took part in these experiments (Elia Kazan, Orson Welles, Joseph Losey) were familiar with these German and Soviet experiments,[82] but only a few broke with the methods of Stanislavsky and escaped the naturalist style. Whilst productions of some works of Friedrich Wolf like *The Sailors of Cattaro* had a genuine success,[83] Brecht was very scathing about the production of *The Mother*, which was a complete flop.[84] The success of these left theatres was also closely tied to a psychological climate that depended on the Depression and the personal initiatives of F. D. Roosevelt. They were in no position to actually impose a new style or to rival Broadway. Even so, their birth was a political victory, and the mere creation of the League of Workers' Theaters made possible not just an association of several progressive groups[85] but the production of antifascist works. These experiments do not seem to have made a lasting mark on American theatre, however, and in 1938 musical comedies again had the upper hand over any other shows. This made it all the more difficult for representatives of the German theatre such as Reinhardt, Brecht and Piscator to find a place for themselves.

In the nineteenth century, emigrants had established German theatres in New York which staged classic works – from Goethe to Gerhart Hauptmann – and invited German companies.[86] But at the time that most antifascist exiles reached America, there was no possibility of founding any new theatres. European actors were thus immediately faced with the dismal situation of American actors, and only those able to express themselves without any trace of an accent could hope to find a booking. The encounter between the progressive tradition in American theatre that grew up in the 1920s and 30s, and the German theatre of the Weimar Republic, simply did not happen.[87]

Yet the dream of most émigrés was still to set up a German theatre in New York, able to play a modern repertoire. It was with this aim that Alfred Durra and Erwin Feith founded the Komödie, which staged several German authors (including Lessing) as well as cabaret shows. Ernst Lothar, former director of

the Josefstadt theatre in Vienna, established an Austrian stage together with
Raoul Auernheimer,[88] but it rapidly died for lack of funds and spectators. In a
more realist vein, the Theater of German Freemen (Freies Deutsches Theater)
of Manfred Fürst, Kurt Hellmer and Ludwig Roth sought to make contacts
with German-American trade unionists, not just to reach a mass audience but to
struggle against the influence of pro-Nazi organizations. A number of unions
supported this theatre, as did the Anti-Nazi League. Its artistic council included
a variety of figures.[89] More than seventy well-known actors worked there, as
well as a number of exiled directors. Its first production, planned for April 1941,
was cancelled for lack of funds.[90]

One fallback, however, was the radio, which produced dramatic broadcasts
by the émigrés in collaboration with the magazine *Der Aufbau*. In Los Angeles,
where there was practically no theatre at this time, the émigrés found support
from a number of figures of German origin in the film world, such as William
Dieterle, who had acted with Max Reinhardt. Leopold Jessner worked on a
production of his famous *William Tell*, but the play had to be staged in English
in order to reach an American public. The difficulty that the actors had in
mastering a foreign language, as well as adapting it to the American style, made
this production a fiasco, though it had made Jessner's reputation in the 1920s.
Premiered on 25 May 1939, the play ran for only two weeks, despite the
appearance of actors as prestigious as Ernst Deutsch and Alexander Granach.
Walter Wicclain also founded a Freie Bühne in Hollywood, to show German
plays. This was initially supported by the Jewish Club, but after 'Americanizing'
itself in 1940 the Club called for a boycott of German theatre,[91] and Wicclain
had to finance the undertaking himself.

Attempts to relaunch German cabaret in New York also proved difficult. The
American version of Erika Mann's Pfeffermühle was completely unsuccessful.
The Refugee Artists Group managed to gather two dozen Vienna cabaret
artists, including Herbert Berghof, Illa Roden, Maria Pichler, Elisabeth Neumann, Katty Mattern, Paul Lindenberg, John Banner and Fred Lorenz, who
tried to re-establish the Wiener Kleinkunstbühne on Broadway with the
assistance of Irving Berlin, Sam Harris, Al Jolson, Moss Hart and S. Kaufmann.[92] Its first season opened in March 1940 with *Reunion in New York*, but
the artistic director Herbert Berghof left to join Piscator at the New School's
Studio Theater. From 1943 New York also had a political cabaret led by Jewish
émigrés – the Ark – directed by Oscar Teller and Erich Juhn. Valeska Gert,
known for her film roles, especially in Pabst's *Dreigroschenoper* and Sternberg's
The Blue Angel, opened The Beggar's Bar in 1941, where she reinterpreted her
antifascist mimes and sketches. This cabaret in Greenwich Village attracted a
fairly large audience, beyond just intellectuals and émigrés. Tennessee Williams
worked there, and even Judy Garland declared that it was the best cabaret in
New York.[93] It continued until 1945, when Valeska Gert lost her license.
Among the more political theatrical efforts, we should mention here the Tribüne
für Freie Deutsche Literatur und Kunst in Amerika, which replaced the German-American Writers' Association as a body for German and Austrian artists.
This organized evening lectures and dramatic productions in which many exiles

took part (more than thirty productions between 1941 and 1945), as well as staging several antifascist works.[94]

A number of antifascist plays, and plays written by émigrés, were thus performed in America. Some of these were very famous, such as Friedrich Wolf's *The Sailors of Cattaro* and *Professor Mamlok*, Brecht's *The Mother* and *The Threepenny Opera* (in 1935), Ernst Toller's *No More Peace!*, and Piscator's American adaptation of Theodore Dreiser's *An American Tragedy* under the title *The Case of Clyde Griffiths*. But the greater part of these works had little success. Even Brecht's theatre aroused scant interest with the American public at this time. American actors found it hard to grasp the sense of his theories, and only marginal theatres, often linked to universities, staged his works in an experimental fashion. In the commercial theatres, they were almost always a financial catastrophe.

Émigré actors were also faced with serious difficulties. First of all because unemployment was rife among American actors, and secondly because to act in the United States they had to be free of a German accent. G. Bermann Fischer describes in his memoirs the case of Oskar Karlweis, whom Reinhardt cast for the part of Prince Orlofsky in *Die Fledermaus*, staged in New York in 1940. He played the role with great success, as his English was so comic that it immediately brought the audience into fits of laughter. The German acting style, however, was hard for the American public to understand. What was true of Fritz Kortner was generally so for actors marked by expressionism. His tour in 1938 with the American actress Katharine Cornell in Hebbel's *Herod and Marianne* was a flop. American critics were unanimous in condemning his style and faulting his 'poor command of English'. The excessive character of his acting, his way of gesticulating and rolling his eyes, stupefied and frightened the audience. In Dorothy Thompson's play *Another Sun*, which depicted the fate of émigrés in New York, he was again assassinated by the critics. A few actors managed to find successful roles on the American stage, such as Elisabeth Bergner, who played in Martin Vale's *The Two Mr Carolls* (585 performances), Oscar Karlweiss in Franz Werfel's *Jacobowsky and the Colonel* (111 performances), and Oskar Homolka in Paul Osborne's *Innocent Voyage* (265 performances), but these were rare exceptions. Ernst Deutsch, who had triumphed in Berlin in Walter Hasenclever's expressionist drama *The Son*, ended up unknown in New York. Alexander Granach was practically confined to the Yiddish theatre. Alfred Bassermann, one of the best-known German actors, who arrived in America at the age of seventy-two, managed with courage and perseverance to learn English, despite no previous familiarity at all. He played in several films, arousing the curiosity of critics, the *New York Times* even asking: 'Who is this fellow Bassermann?' The 'wonderful old man with the strange accent' was still acting on Broadway at the age of seventy-seven, and on 31 October 1944 played the role of the pope in Friedrich Wolf's play *Embezzled Heaven*, partnered by Ethel Barrymore. The only surprise for the critics was to hear the pope speak English with a Mannheim accent. He acted in Piscator's production of *Fear and Misery of the Third Reich*, and in 1946 played the role of Mephisto, aged all of eighty-two.

It would certainly have been possible with these seventy German émigrés to put together a marvellous company. But only a few of them found serious engagements. The majority had to be content with supporting roles, sometimes indeed even insignificant ones.[95] It is possible to glimpse what the encounter with American culture meant for exiled playwrights from their autobiographies, diaries and letters. Three examples will illustrate this sufficiently, those of Ernst Toller, Bertolt Brecht, and Carl Zuckmayer.

Ernst Toller, the most famous playwright of the Weimar Republic, was by no means unknown on his arrival in the United States. *The Blind Goddess* had been staged in London in 1934, as had *Miracle in America*. Toller himself had directed *Draw the Fires!* in Manchester and London in 1935.[96] *No More Peace!* was produced in 1936, and performed in the United States, as were *Masses and Man* and *The Machine Wreckers*. In 1940, a film version of *Pastor Hall* was made in England, and distributed in America with a short introduction by Eleanor Roosevelt. The majority of Toller's works – including his autobiography *I Was a German* and his *Letters from Prison*, had appeared in English translation. From autumn 1936 to spring 1937, he had given several lectures in the United States and Canada, before settling in Santa Monica. He enjoyed a great reputation as a lecturer in progressive circles. His interventions in support of the Spanish Republic had won him sympathy, and one might suppose that he was one of the most privileged exiles. On his arrival in the United States, however, he felt increasingly isolated. Soon his plays were no longer staged and he became just one exile among so many others. Like Brecht, he felt it humiliating always to have to spell his name. In New York, the greatest German dramatist of the 1920 fell steadily into oblivion, and there is no doubt that this slow decline played a major role in his decision to put an end to his life.

Brecht's case is just as exemplary. His encounters with the American stage were almost as disastrous as those with its Soviet counterpart. *The Threepenny Opera* did not attract the American public, and neither did *The Mother*, staged by the Theater Union in 1935.[97] He travelled to New York to oversee the production, but was unable to change anything. It was at the same time that Brecht made contact with Lee Strasberg, who wanted to produce *The Measures Taken*. Brecht's epic style, however, conflicted with the theories of Stanislavsky that were generally prevalent at this time. In several letters to the Dramatic Workshop, he tried to explain his concept of theatre,[98] and noted in his *Journals* on 1 November 1941: 'Nowhere is writing about theatre more difficult than here, where all they have is theatrical naturalism.'[99] All Brecht's judgements on the American theatre were negative. On 27 November 1941, he described his discussions with Homolka on European theatre and had the impression of speaking of 'a strange, sunken theatre in ancient times on a submerged continent'. American theatre struck him as an 'evening's entertainment'. Its submission to public taste, the 'whole hierarchies of experts and agents' who 'claim to know the needs and wishes of the buyer', had made theatre into just another commodity.[100] Throughout his exile, Brecht aroused scant critical interest, and no one was interested in the plays he had written during his time in Scandinavia (*Mother Courage, The Good Person of Szechwan, Arturo Ui*). He hoped that Piscator would help him, also Max Reinhardt, who had planned to produce *Fear and Misery of the Third Reich*. On 1 June 1942, Brecht again wrote in his *Journals*: ' "chances": 1) if MGM were seriously to consider filming THE THREEPENNY OPERA. 2) if jean renoir were to want to write a film with me. 3) if may wong wanted to do the GOOD PERSON OF SZECHWAN on broadway. 4) reinhardt FEAR AND MISERY.'[101]

In fact, *Fear and Misery of the Third Reich* was staged in June 1942 by Die Tribüne für Freie Deutsche Literatur und Kunst in Amerika, in a production by Berthold Viertel. *The Threepenny Opera*, staged in New York in 1933, had lasted for only twelve performances; *The Mother* was a failure in 1935, and for all the efforts of his translator and friend Eric Bentley, only extracts from the English version of *Fear and Misery of the Third Reich* were staged during his American exile. In describing the construction of his play *The Caucasian Chalk Circle*, he met with such total incomprehension – he was asked 'where is the conflict, the tension, the flesh and blood, etc.' (*Journals*, 28 May 1944) – that he had the impression 'it was like writing a play for the Tunga steppe'.[102] Brecht therefore made new approaches to the cinema. He was friendly with Charlie Chaplin and the British actor Charles Laughton, who tried to interest American theatres in his works,[103] but *Galileo* was not staged until 1947, when Brecht was already making ready to leave America. He did however write during his exile in California *The Visions of Simone Machard, Schweyk in the Second World War*, and *The Caucasian Chalk Circle*, even amid his complaints about American theatre.

Carl Zuckmayer's fate was still more surprising. After arriving in New York in 1940 as a 'guest' of Dorothy Thompson,[104] he subsequently settled in Vermont. Like the majority of other émigrés, he tried his luck with the film studios, but found the time spent in Hollywood the most painful in his life. He worked first of all on an adaptation of Arnold Zweig's novel *The Case of Sergeant Grischa*, but this was soon abandoned. He was then employed on a script on Don Juan in Italy. Zuckmayer left Hollywood in disgust and gave some lectures at the New School on Piscator's initiative, in a 'playwright class'.[105] Finding the experience unsatisfying, he decided to return to Vermont, where the countryside was reminiscent of Germany. He rented some land from an old farmer and applied himself to growing maize, while his wife reared chickens. In a few years he became a farmer like those around him, even if his neighbours still found his name 'unpronounceable'. During his years in exile, Zuckmayer almost completely abandoned literary activity for farming, raising cattle, selling milk, and taking a crafty pleasure in giving his birds the names of Nazi dignitaries. Outside of American intellectual life, he felt he had grown into a character from Karl May, and even gave his daughter the name Winnetou. During his first year as a farmer, he had no time for anything outside his work – 'the farm in the green hills' – but after the death of Stefan Zweig he wrote his celebrated appeal *Appeal to Life*. The only major work he wrote in America was

The Devil's General.[106] He maintained that in the United States he had become just a face in the crowd.

The majority of directors experienced similar problems, as shown by the fate of Max Reinhardt and Erwin Piscator, to speak only of the most famous, or even Leopold Jessner, former director of the Prussian state theatre.

After the success of *Sumurun* in 1913, Max Reinhardt was considered the most innovative director in the European theatre. The financier Otto H. Hahn, who had already brought Diaghilev and Stanislavsky to the United States, planned to establish a theatre festival, and the American Miracle Company was established to invite Reinhardt. The outbreak of war prevented the project from going forward, and after various negotiations, Reinhardt eventually came to New York in April 1923.[107] The premiere of *Mirakel* was given in January 1924 at the Century Theater, transformed for the occasion into a Gothic cathedral, and it met with great success. American critics were enthusiastic at the surprising beauty of the production, and the play was performed 298 times right across the country. Soon the project of a Reinhardt tour was envisaged, bringing to America his greatest successes in the German original. *A Midsummer Night's Dream* was staged with similar success in 1927, along with Hofmannstahl's *Jedermann* and Büchner's *Dantons Tod*. In 1928, other productions of his had further triumphs on the American stage, and he was asked to speak at several universities. His success was so great that on his departure (29 February 1928) the foundation of a Max Reinhardt Theater was immediately envisaged in New York.

Simultaneously with all this, Reinhardt was solicited by the film industry. Since the end of the First World War, A. Zukor had tried to interest him in a number of projects.[108] In 1923–24, after the production of *Mirakel* in New York, Reinhardt was again invited to make a film, on the proposition of W. R. Hearst himself, but the project again came to nothing.[109] He did however have new contacts with Hollywood in 1926, when he got to know Joseph M. Schenk, president of United Artists, and Lilian Gish. The latter came to Europe in 1928 and worked with Reinhardt and Hofmannstahl, but when the time came to start shooting, United Artists was no longer prepared to invest in a silent film.

When Reinhardt had to leave his theatre in 1933, he was invited by an American journalist, Meyer W. Weisgal, to direct a play based on the Old Testament.[110] He worked on the project with Kurt Weill and Franz Werfel, which became *The Eternal Road*. In 1934, Warner Brothers considered a film of Reinhardt's *A Midsummer Night's Dream*. *The Eternal Road* was to be staged at the Manhattan Opera House on 23 December 1935, but this was postponed until 7 January 1937, when it opened to an audience of over 3,000. Though the production had cost more than $500,000, it ran for only 153 performances and made a loss. Reinhardt had been invited in October 1933 by Norman H. Sloane, director-general of the California Chamber of Commerce, to lay the foundations for a theatre festival, and it was in his perspective that he undertook a new production of Shakespeare's *Dream* in Hollywood, San Francisco and Berkeley. Warner Brothers immediately proposed a film version, with William Dieterle as co-director, and the actors to include Olivia de Haviland and Mickey Rooney. The film marked the high-water mark of Reinhardt's American career, and he was proposed for the Nobel Prize. He sketched out other film projects – *Die Fledermaus, Tales of Hoffman* – but none of them were made. Warner Brothers also suggested that he make a film on Danton, and in 1936 he began to work on this. As he did not have the technical knowledge needed for the shooting – despite having made a number of films in Europe – Michael Curtis, his son Gottfried Reinhardt (then a scriptwriter at MGM) and Samuel Hoffenstein were charged with its direction.[111] The project was abandoned due to MGM's refusal to invest so much money on a revolutionary subject, and it was then suggested that Reinhardt should adapt Dostoyevsky's *The Gambler*. This project again ran into the sand, and put an end to his Hollywood career.[112]

Reinhardt now devoted all his efforts on the California theatre festival, at which he planned to stage *The Merchant of Venice* and *As You Like It*, but these two projects were also abandoned. Over the next few years, he still sought to establish a big theatre, and appealed to various prominent figures. He envisaged merging this project with the NewYork Center Theater, but without success. But in 1936 he did manage to stage Berlioz's *Faust*. The production was to be revived in 1940, but the outbreak of war prevented this. Reinhardt then focused his energies on launching a drama school. This was designed to revive the school he had formerly directed in Berlin, which had trained all the great German stage and screen actors of the 1920s. He obtained the financial backing for this in 1937, and the school was opened at 5959 Sunset Boulevard, in the Columbia Broadcasting System Building, under the name of the Max Reinhardt Workshop of Stage, Screen and Radio. The teachers were eminent figures, former students of Reinhardt with a radio or film background, including a number of émigrés (William Dieterle, Karl Freund, Helene Thimig-Reinhardt). For the opening he staged a Maeterlinck play – *Sister Beatrice* – and subsequently produced plays by Goldoni, Sidney Howard, Thornton Wilder, Leo Tolstoy, Hugo von Hofmannstahl, Gorky, Ibsen and Maxwell Andersen, at his school or in other theatres. But as soon as the students reached a certain level, the film studios that had given them grants recalled them, leading Reinhardt to try and establish another school in New York. In 1941 he ended all active participation in the Workshop,[113] trying instead to establish a repertory theatre. The school soon foundered for lack of resources. He then worked with Thornton Wilder on a production of *The Merchant of Yonkers*, staged by the Theater Guild on Broadway in autumn 1938. Reinhardt was not however able to select his own actors, who were imposed by the producer. The play was poorly received by the critics, and ended after thirty-nine performances. Reinhardt then tried to found another theatre in New York, in conjunction with H. E. Clurman and Stella Adler.[114] He again had to seek capital for this.[115] After an initial defeat, he founded a production company in August 1942 with Richard Myers and Eddie Dowling, and wanted to direct Eugene O'Neill, but the latter was already tied to the Theater Guild. Reinhardt then turned his attention to Maeterlinck, subsequently C. Simonov and Franz Werfel. Until 1942–43 he was unable to realize new productions, and revived *Die Fledermaus* for the New Opera Company. His business partners were very hostile to his doing any other work, and all he did was 'supervise production'. He staged I. Shaw's *Labor for the Wind*, also known as *Sons and Soldiers*. The critics were hostile, and the play ended after twenty-two performances. Reinhardt then tried to relaunch his cooperation with the New Opera Company, for a production of *La Belle Hélène*. The project foundered in 1943, after disagreement on the choice of actors. On 9 September that year Reinhardt had celebrated his seventieth birthday, surrounded by friends and admirers, who included the majority of his fellow émigrés in Hollywood and New York, and he died on 31 October. His death was mourned by the entire émigré colony, and the American press marked the disappearance of a 'working man' and 'very good fellow'. His exile in America was for Reinhardt, perhaps the greatest director of the European theatre, simply a long train of defeats, disappointments and humiliations.

Erwin Piscator's encounter with American theatre was just as problematic. After the failure of the antifascist theatre project at Engels and his return from the USSR, he lived in France where he found hardly any work. In Zurich he met Sam Spiegel, whom he told of a plan worked out with Alfred Neumann for the dramatization of Tolstoy's *War and Peace*. Spiegel put him in touch with Gilbert Miller,[116] and a contract was immediately signed for the play to be staged on Broadway in a gigantic production. But though Miller had paid a considerable sum to acquire the rights, he abandoned the project soon after Piscator's arrival in the United States, after receiving a host of contradictory opinions.

Piscator had come on a simple tourist visa, and was thus unable to request a work permit. He had the good fortune to obtain a teaching post at the New School for Social Research, thanks to Alvin Johnson, who offered him a lecture-hall in which he established the Dramatic Workshop, which opened on 1 January 1940. Piscator taught dramatic art, trained actors, and directed a team of teachers, theatre being seen here less as a site of formal experimentation than as one discipline among others. On its foundation, the Workshop counted twenty students, but by 1947–48 this had grown to a thousand. After being accustomed to realizing productions in Berlin with the most sophisticated technical means, Piscator had to work with students before a limited public, not even managing to attract critics who had little interest for this 'student theatre'. (It so happened that the students in question included Marlon Brando, Tony Curtis, Tennessee Williams and Harry Belafonte, later on also Judith Malina.) Reinhardt produced Michael Pogodin's *The Aristocrats*, and from April 1940 the Studio Theater began to stage shows at popular prices and offer a rediscovery of the classics. Piscator successively staged *King Lear*, *The Chalk Circle* (by Klabund, in March 1941), *Any Day Now* (by Philip Jordan, May 1941), *Days of Our Youth* (by F. Gabrielson, November 1941), *The Criminals* (by Ferdinand Bruckner, in 1941) and an adaptation of Lessing's *Nathan the Wise* (also by Bruckner).

After Hitler's invasion of the Soviet Union, Piscator took up his project of an epic dramatization of *War and Peace* at the New School. The work was performed in May 1942, for just a week and without attracting any notice, the New York critics being almost completely ignorant of Piscator's work in Berlin. As he could not pay his actors the union rate, this being in any case a university studio, he was threatened with a ban on employing professional actors. Continuing to use students, Piscator staged Daniel Lewis James's *Winter Soldiers* in November 1942.

Despite the very modest means at his command – no comparison with Reinhardt's projects – Piscator was reproached by the New School for making a serious dent in the college budget,[117] and his theatre was eventually closed. He then had to hunt around the New York theatres for one cheap enough to allow him to stage his productions. He discovered first of all, on 48th Street, the President Theater, which had previously been a cinema and a strip joint. Unable to hire professional actors, he continued to use students,[118] but found it hard to attract either audience or critics. But if he was unable to develop political theatre, Piscator remained faithful to his epic style, and sought to relate the plays he produced to current events: Sartre's *Les Mouches* in 1947, A. Salacrou's *Nights of Anger*, Robert Penn Warren's *The King's Fools* in January 1948, W. Borchert's *Before the Door* in March 1949, and John Matthew's *The Scapegoat* in April 1950. As these works attracted a large audience, sensitive to social themes, he decided to open a larger theatre, the Rooftop, on the Lower East Side, which offered a fairly heteroclite repertoire designed for students. He tried to reach out to a wider public with *Romeo and Juliet*, and *The Burning Bush* by Geza Herczeg and Heinz Herald. But at the same time Piscator had to end his teaching activity at the New School, which had been forced to accept Senator McCarthy carrying out investigations there. Feeling himself personally threatened, Piscator returned to West Germany in October 1951.

Certainly the work of both Reinhardt and Piscator in the United States was far from negligible; it left deep traces in the history of American theatre. Both had a posthumous fame even if during their lifetimes, and when they were in America, they found it impossible to continue their earlier experiments.[119] One might have expected that the flourish of left theatres that emerged in the 1920s and 30s would have allowed a better understanding of the émigrés' theatrical talents. By the 1940s, however, the majority of these American experiments were already dead or dying. The few attempts at exile theatre in America – the Neue Theater Gruppe 1935, Free Culture in the Land of the Free (1941), Comedie (1938), Theater of German Free Men (1941), Players from Abroad, German Jewish Club of Los Angeles, Freie Bühne – were only ephemeral creations.[120] Certainly some collaborations made their mark, like *The Eternal Road* (Weill, Reinhardt, Werfel, Norman Ben Gedder in 1937), *Another Sun* (Fritz Kortner, Dorothy Thompson in 1940), *Summer in France* (Kortner, Zuckmayer and the Guild Theater in 1941). Some émigré works were also staged, including Brecht's *The Mother* and *Fear and Misery of the Third Reich*, Ferdinand Bruckner's *The Races*, Friedrich Wolf's *Professor Mamlok* and Toller's *No More Peace!*, but these results all appear very pale in comparison with the sum of talent, attempts and energies that were available and spent.

MUSICIANS AND COMPOSERS

For it is so sad that all these people with the finest musical culture there was in Europe should be cast out and have to spend their old age in anxiety and hardship and grief

Arnold Schoenberg, letter to Alfred Hertz, 2 May 1938

Beneath the green pepper trees
The musicians play the whore, two by two
With the writers. Bach
Has written a Strumpet Voluntary. Dante wriggles
His shriveled bottom.

Bertolt Brecht, 'Hollywood Elegies'

According to the Committee for Refugee Musicians, the United States received at least sixty-nine composers of European origin, who included Arnold Schoenberg, Hanns Eisler, Igor Stravinsky, Ernst Krenek, Kurt Weill and Paul Hindemith. The diversity of their trajectories illustrates very well the difficult relationship America had with the musical avant-garde. A number of performers did indeed find employment in orchestras, though often in difficult conditions. Avant-garde composers such as Kurt Weill and Hanns Eisler worked for Hollywood or Broadway. Innovators as radical as Schoenberg became teachers.[121] A reading of their letters, memoirs and personal diaries shows that they almost all accumulated a store of bitter experience. Illustrious in Europe, whether hated or idolized, in America their works aroused only very modest interest, if not simply polite boredom. The European musical avant-garde was almost unknown, and Schoenberg did not spare the most desperate sarcasm towards the 'fossilized' aesthetics of American music, and the 'melody-crazed public' who almost never went to concerts to *hear* works, but rather to *see* singers or conductors. The majority of them often had to accept hack work – teaching, composition of film music – obsessed by the fear of poverty as well as that of demeaning themselves in the eyes of their followers. If a few such as Kurt Weill managed to adapt to this new reality, others experienced it in anguish (Schoenberg) or despised it (Eisler).

Kurt Weill had left Marseille for New York in September 1935. His European collaboration with Brecht had ended with the production of *The Seven Deadly Sins of the Petty Bourgeois* in Paris in 1933. During his exile Weill had already composed his second symphony (premiered by Bruno Walter on 11 October 1934 in Amsterdam). He was not unknown when he arrived in the United States. *The Threepenny Opera* had been staged on Broadway, and his second symphony played in New York. He rapidly linked up with progressive theatres such as the Group Theater, where he made the acquaintance of Paul Green. This gave rise to his first American composition, *Johnny Johnson* (19 November 1936). Weill seemed to have little difficulty in accepting the rules of the American market, and composed for both theatre and music hall. Less political than Brecht or Eisler, his fascination for jazz made his encounter with America more a return to sources than a rupture. Weill soon won wide popularity with the American public, thanks in particular to his work with Ira Gershwin. *Johnny Johnson*, the story of a little clerk in the First World War, somewhat reminiscent of *Schweyk*, had a great success, helped by Lee Strasberg's direction. Weill subsequently had the opportunity of working with such talented figures as Elia Kazan. Franz Werfel and Max Reinhardt's *The Eternal Road*, for which he wrote the music, including its memorable choruses, traced the history of the Jewish people and had scarcely any precedent in American theatre. After meeting Maxwell Anderson, Weill was led to work increasingly for Broadway.

A number of critics – and fellow émigrés of the time – were quick to criticize Weill for his adaptation to the American stage, accusing him of reneging on his past and his collaboration with Brecht, and bending to the demands of the American public. That shows a misunderstanding of Weill himself, and of the richness of his American compositions. It is true nonetheless that his case was almost unique in the musical field: no other émigré musician was able to recommence such a brilliant career in exile.[122] The most striking comparison is precisely with other composers who also collaborated with Brecht.

Paul Dessau had known Brecht's work since the 1920s, but did not become acquainted with him until 1943. He had begun setting some of Brecht's lyrics to music in Paris in 1936, for Slatan Dudow's production of *Fear and Misery of the Third Reich*, staged in 1938. When he emigrated the same year to the United States, he was completely unknown. He worked for a Jewish children's home in Brooklyn, and from 1941 on a chicken farm close to New York. He later found employment with the Internationale Gesellschaft für Neue Musik, and obtained a teaching job with the Jewish Men's Hebrew Association. In 1942 Brecht came to New York to discuss the production of extracts from *Fear and Misery*,[123] met Dessau and began a collaboration with him. Dessau accompanied Brecht to California in May 1943 and joined his circle there,[124] while also composing film music for Warner Brothers. Brecht's influence on Dessau was decisive in both political and artistic matters. The greatest work of his exile period was the oratorio *Deutsches Miserere* (1944–47), which incorporated a number of Brecht poems[125] and only had its first performance, in Leipzig, on 20 September 1966. Dessau also worked with Brecht on an uncompleted opera, *Travels of the God of Luck*, as well as writing music for *Mother Courage* and *The Good Person of Szechwan*.[126] He remained unknown to the American public.

The case of Hanns Eisler is just as remarkable. He arrived in the United States as a refugee in 1938, though he had already stayed there in 1935–36.[127] During these visits he gave several talks on fascism, and performed his works in most large US cities. The CPUSA and workers' organizations (in particular the Workers' Music League) gave his visit prominent coverage. It was during this tour that he obtained a contract to teach composition at the New School for Social Research. He taught there from October 1935 to January 1936, recorded a number of discs of proletarian songs and Brecht poems, and made personal contact with a number of figures in American musical life, including Aaron Copland, Marc Blitzstein and Virgil Thomson. In 1937, Eisler received a further invitation from the New School[128] and decided to return to New York to teach.

His arrival was greeted by a performance of his own works under the baton of Marc Blitzstein (27 January 1938), and Eisler explained his ideas on the political function of music in the class struggle. Throughout his exile in America, he continued to deepen the themes he had been reflecting on even before 1935: the role of music in modern society, its relationship to the proletariat, the class attitude towards the 'bourgeois tradition' of avant-gardism, the possibilities of film music, etc. In 1935 he composed his *Deutsche Sinfonie*, which was not performed until 1959 in Berlin, and set texts mainly from Brecht.

After 1938, Eisler had to break off his participation in the political discussions around music in the American workers' movement, as he had been forced to leave the country. Besides, the great progressive wave that had marked American cultural life, and especially the theatre, under the New Deal, was beginning to ebb. Eisler had met up again with Joris Ivens[129] in New York, and composed music for Ivens's feature on China, *400 Millions*. Just as important was his meeting with Joseph Losey, who had founded a 'political cabaret'[130] in 1937, with which Eisler collaborated until 1939. In 1938 Losey obtained a contract with an oil company for an advertising film shown at the world petroleum exhibition held in New York in 1939. He invited Eisler to write music for it.[131] The success of this film, on which Losey, Ivens and Eisler worked together, made his name in America as a composer of film music. He had already written music in New York for Odets's *Night Music*, and for Offmann R. Hays's *Medicine Show*.[132] In 1940, thanks to Losey and A. Johnson, he obtained a scholarship from the Rockefeller Foundation to continue his research on film music. This was the same time as Theodor Adorno was collaborating on a project on music and radio: their encounter gave rise to *Composing for the Films* in 1947.[133] Some of Eisler's most ambitious American projects had their origins around this project, including *Fourteen Ways of Describing Rain*, written for the silent film *Regen* that Joris Ivens had made in 1929, and dedicated to Arnold Schoenberg for his seventieth birthday. But despite his contacts with other New York émigrés, including Erwin Piscator and Alfred Kantorowicz, Eisler spent his exile years in a relatively marginal position, and few of the works he wrote in the United States were performed there. He left New York for California on 15 August 1942, to try and earn a living as a composer of film music,[134] and in the hope of obtaining a teaching post at the University of Los Angeles. Brecht had also settled there by this time.

Brecht and Eisler now collaborated very actively until 1947. Eisler wrote music for several Brecht plays: *The Vision of Simone Machard*, *The Life of Galileo*, *Schweyk in the Second World War*, as well as for the poems Brecht had written in Finland. By 1943 he had written eight film scores as well as seventy songs, while also continuing his teaching. Eminently sociable, Eisler shared his research on film music with several American composers. In California he was on good terms with Brecht and Helene Weigel, Lion Feuchtwanger, Fritz Kortner, Peter Lorre, Berthold and Salka Viertel, Oskar Homolka and Arnold Schoenberg. He saw only a few Americans, apart from his students and Charlie Chaplin, who asked him to help with the music for *Monsieur Verdoux* (1944–47). By his kindness, he became a link between several émigré circles who otherwise had little contact with one another. Who apart from Eisler could count among his friends Bertolt Brecht, Theodor Adorno, Thomas Mann and Arnold Schoenberg?[135] Despite his multifarious activity, and the esteem in which he was held by his students and colleagues, Eisler was one of the first victims of McCarthyism, and was expelled from the United States in 1947.[136]

Arnold Schoenberg had accepted a position with the Boston Conservatoire in 1933, when he was directing *Pelléas et Mélisande* there. On his arrival, receptions were held in his honour and he was asked to speak at a number of universities. In 1934 he moved to New York, then to Hollywood, first of all giving private lessons to film-music composers. In 1936 he wrote his Violin Concerto and his fourth string quartet, and was finally appointed professor at the University of California, being naturalized in 1941. But for all his celebrity, the early years of his exile were beset by material difficulties which aggravated his constant nostalgia for Europe. In October 1934 he wrote:

> It is perhaps expected that now that I am in a new world I should feel its amenities to be ample compensation for the loss I have sustained [. . .]. Indeed, I parted from the old world not without feeling the wrench in my very bones, for I was not prepared for the fact that it would render me not only homeless but speechless, languageless, so that to all but my old friends I could now say it only in English [. . .].[137]

Schoenberg's teaching work only aroused disappointment. His students knew nothing of the classical repertoire, and he wondered what use his teaching might be. As he was paid much less than in Berlin, he planned to teach at two universities,[138] and in order to survive, he came round to accepting the idea of composing music for a film. He did this with the same reluctance as a virtuous girl prostituting herself out of poverty, but the excessive sum he asked saved him from 'dishonour':

> Then I almost agreed to write music for a film, but fortunately asked $50,000, which, likewise fortunately, was much too much, for it would have been the end of me; and the only thing is that if I had somehow survived it we should have been able to live on it – even if modestly – for a number of years, which would have meant at last being able to finish in my lifetime at least those compositions and theoretical works that I have already begun [. . .]. And for that I should gladly have sacrificed my life and even my reputation, although I know that others, who have held their own in less strict regard than I mine, would not have failed to seize the chance of despising me for it.[139]

Even his teaching work ended up in humiliation: 'my work is as much a waste of time as if Einstein were having to teach mathematics at a secondary school'.[140] And when William Dieterle proposed he should write music for a film on Beethoven, Schoenberg set conditions that were exactly the opposite of what Hollywood expected: not to 'serve a libretto' but to 'form a poetic version of Beethoven's life'; not to 'use Beethoven's music' but compose 'variations'.[141] In 1936, Schoenberg managed to complete his fourth string quartet while giving private lessons and summer courses. Though he got his work performed thanks to a wealthy patron, he deplored the fact that his concerts had not been advertised and that his colleagues had not even taken the trouble to attend. His efforts to build up a music department at UCLA collapsed as a result of the governor's refusal to provide the funds. But Schoenberg did not despair. He wrote many letters to university presidents and American public figures, even trying to find teaching jobs for other émigré musicians. Sometimes his isolation and frustration were so great that he exclaimed: 'Composing is something I've not done for two years. I have had too much other work. And anyway: whom should one write for?'[142] If teaching prevented him from continuing his work, however, if was the only way he could support his family. For fear of poverty, he refused to accept retirement when he reached the age of seventy. He had hoped that his teaching pension would enable him to finish works he had started long ago. But after eight years' teaching at UCLA he had to continue giving private lessons,[143] and in 1945 he applied unsuccessfully to the Guggenheim Foundation for a grant. In May 1947, Schoenberg was elected to membership of the National Institute of Arts and Letters, but he continued to suffer the hostility of American composers. Bitter and often acidic, he lived the last years of his life in a psychological climate that steadily deteriorated. He also failed to appreciate how Thomas Mann, in his novel *Doctor Faustus*, had attributed the discovery of twelve-tone music to a fictitious Adrian Leverkühn. The tragicomic letters he exchanged with Mann and his friends can only be understood in the context of exile.[144] In February 1949, he declared that his music was so unknown in America – though he had ardently championed Gershwin – that he had to rejoice at any recording of his works, even if the quality was highly debatable. In 1947 Schoenberg composed *A Survivor from Warsaw*, as well as tidying up his last writings. He died in California on 13 July 1951, aged seventy-six. The composer who wrote: 'My music is not modern, it's just badly played' never hid his disdain for America and his hatred for American critics – one of the rare traits he shared with Brecht and Thomas Mann. On 29 October 1944, he wrote again to Fritz Reiner, leader of the Pittsburgh orchestra: 'The stupidity of these poor men is unsurpassed, and approached only by their arrogance and ignorance. To every man with a minimum of intelligence and knowledge I have proved to possess some knowledge and to have some ideas.'[145]

These few examples of the most celebrated German composers exiled in America certainly give only an imperfect image of their situation in the American context. As well as composers, the United States received 275 musicologists, 107 directors, 215 singers and 330 instrumentalists. Famous or not, they often had the same experiences. Music teaching was poorly developed and symphony orchestras mediocre. The majority of exiled composers could not get their works played except privately or with amateur bands. The European musical avant-garde was almost unknown in America and the only work they could find was as university teachers. Paul Hindemith taught at Yale, Ernst Krenek at Black Mountain College, Ernst Toch and Hanns Eisler at the New School for Social Research. But their talents were very largely wasted. When Adorno programmed a work of Hindemith for a radio broadcast, he immediately received a call from the mayor of New York, Fiorello La Guardia, asking him to break it off. The works that Eisler composed in America were not played until 1970. And while a few famous émigrés such as Bruno Walter and Otto Klemperer found important positions with leading orchestras, the majority had to survive in any way they could. It was thanks to the émigrés that the first chairs of musicology were established in the United States, a discipline that had not been taught before 1935.

ARCHITECTS, PAINTERS AND SCULPTORS

A large number of visual artists and architects also emigrated to the United States. According to the Davie Report, more than 717 artists settled there between 1933 and 1944,[146] as well as 380 architects.[147] These included some of the greatest representatives of the German, and indeed European, avant-garde: Lipchitz, Zadkin, Masson, Mondrian, Kisling, Breton, Duchamp, Tanguy, Chagall, Léger. But Matisse, Picasso, Brancusi, Maillol and Derain remained in France, and Schmitt-Rottluff in Germany.

A number of these painters and architects had issued from the Bauhaus, which on 19 April 1933 had to abandon its last refuge in Berlin-Steglitz and dissolve itself. As a large number of these artists had an international renown, America was able early on to offer them good opportunities to re-establish themselves. The painter and stylist Josef Albert taught at Black Mountain College in North Carolina from 1935, as did Xanti Schwinski, who had taught at the Bauhaus in Dessau. Walter Gropius, Lazlo Moholy-Nagy, Marcel Breuer and Ludwig Mise van der Rohe settled in the United States from 1937 onwards, likewise the architect Ludwig Hilbersheimer and the photographer Walter Petershans. The majority of these already had a certain celebrity across the Atlantic. The Bauhaus had received American students since 1928, and Feininger, Kandinsky, Jawlensky and Klee – the 'four blues' – had exhibited in New York.[148] It was natural that the majority of former Bauhaus members should decide to establish themselves there. Schwinski, Gropius and Breuer designed the 'Hall of Democracy' for the World's Fair of 1938, as well as the Pennsylvania pavilion. Herbert Bayer organized two exhibitions at the Museum of Modern Art in New York: 'Road to Victory' (1942) and 'Airways to Peace' (1943). The majority found a certain audience, and the magazine *More Business* paid tribute to them in 1939, speaking of a 'New Bauhaus'. The New Bauhaus had in fact already been founded by Walter Gropius in Chicago in 1937, together with Moholy-Nagy, Archipenko, Bayer, Keper and Bredendreck, joined later by the painter Johann Molzahn. But material problems forced it to close its doors in 1939, reopening as a School of Design (Institute of Design from 1944). Individually, however, the Bauhaus members continued to exert a significant influence on American architecture, as shown by the work of Gropius, Mies van der Rohe and Marcel Breuer.[149] Gropius and Breuer went on to teach at Harvard, Walter Peterhans and Ludwig Herbersheimer joined Mies van der Rohe at the Illinois Institute of Technology.[150] Gropius himself designed a large number of buildings in the United States – including the Harvard Graduate Center – as well as homes in New England and Pennsylvania. He was a consultant for the reconstruction of the old quarters of Boston and Chicago. From 1938 to 1942 he worked almost always with Marcel Breuer, then in 1945 formed The Architect Collaborature with a group of young Americans. Mies van der Rohe built skyscrapers in Chicago as well as the Seagram building in New York, the Bacardi building in Mexico City and the campus of the Illinois Institute of Technology. Historians of American architecture understandably maintain that the Bauhaus gave more to the country than any other group of émigrés. They had a still deeper effect by their teaching, popularizing the principles of modern architecture elaborated in Germany in the Weimar years. Used to collective methods, they made a large contribution to training a whole new generation of American architects.

Lazlo Moholy-Nagy, Herbert Bayer and Lionel Feininger were just as active. Bayer worked for industry, while Feininger continued his work in the same abstract expressionist style that marked his last European compositions. Albers[151] and Moholy-Nagy taught at various schools of fine art and ceaselessly attempted to re-establish the Bauhaus of the Weimar years. At the Institute of Design, Moholy-Nagy tried to combine painting, photography, collage and typography.

Relations between American and émigré painters and sculptors were more complex. The first major European painter to settle in the United States in the 1930s was Hans Hofmann, invited by the University of California, who spread an awareness of expressionism before opening his own school.[152] Abstract painting had remained little known in the 1920s,[153] but the following decade saw a number of European exhibitions in New York, where an indigenous new school of painting developed.[154] The members of this school did not hide their admiration for European painters: Pollock praised Matisse, Miro and Mondrian; Guston favoured Mondrian and Soutine; Rothko's heroes were Miro and Léger. For a long while there was no artistic milieu in the United States comparable to what Berlin, Munich or Vienna had to offer. It was only during the Great Depression that a new generation of painters gathered in Greenwich Village. The majority of them had discovered Matisse and Brancusi in the mid 1920s. Avant-garde galleries – J. B. Neumann's and Stieglitz's – soon made European discoveries more widely known. Most American painters were initially tempted by certain formal experiments. Archille Gorky was inspired by cubism, and futurism became famous thanks to David Bourliouk who settled in New York. John Graham, of Russian origin, travelled frequently to Europe where he visited André Breton, Paul Eluard, André Gide and the surrealists. Frederick Kiesler, of Austrian provenance, made expressionism known in New York and published studies on Picasso, De Chirico, Klee, Matisse, Léger, Mondrian and Brancusi, as well as on Naum Gabo, Bruno Taut, Mies van der Rohe, K. Malevitch and A. Exter.

The first émigré painters kept a fairly close connection with German artistic life, and were at the origin of this discovery of 'modernism' in America. The avant-garde of the 1920s had already aroused a real interest in New York. Marcel Duchamp and Katherine S. Dreier had founded the Société Anonyme in 1920, with Kandinsky as president and Duchamp as secretary. In 1926 a major exhibition at the Brooklyn Museum had revealed the works of Miro, Mondrian and Lissitsky. La Société gallery at 475 Fifth Avenue brought to New York the works of Archipenko, Campendouk, Bourliuok, Léger, Klee, Ernst, Kandinsky and Schwitters. New York thus offered a particularly favourable terrain for the encounter between American and European avant-garde, the latter's works being well known to members of the Art Students' League. Expressionist canvases had been hailed as a revelation by Mark Rothko, J. B. Weinmann and Max Weber, and Max Beckmann, Paul Klee and E. L. Kirchner were equally discussed.

The situation of painters on the West Coast was very different. Those who had settled there – Philip Guston, Hermann Cherry, Reuben Kadish, Jackson Pollock – were more isolated and divided between radical tendencies that were sometimes anarchical or mystic.[155] They were influenced above all by the Mexican painters: Rivera, Orozco and Siquieros. The influence of European painting was re-asserted with the foundation of the Artists' Union and the Artists' Committee of Action in November 1934. Their review *Art Front* proposed to drag American painting out of its chauvinism. It was politically committed and quick to attack European fascism. In 1936 an American Artists' Congress was held in New York. Following the Writers' Congress of 1935, in which Theodore Dreiser, Waldo Frank, Josephine Herbst, Erskine Caldwell and Malcolm Cowley had participated, the task of struggling for individual freedom and against fascism in Europe was again affirmed. After the 1929 crash, André Breton had been translated, and several exhibitions of Picasso had been successfully held at the Museum of Modern Art. Salomon Guggenheim built up his collection of 'non-objective art', and Kandinsky was one of the émigré artists most admired before 1940. The American public then discovered the works of Max Ernst, Tanguy, Masson, Selligmann, Mondrian, Léger, Lipchitz and Zadkin. Peggy Guggenheim collected both surrealist and abstract works in her gallery. This enthusiasm for European painting, and the multiplication of galleries and reviews that championed modern art, explains the relatively favourable situation that the émigré painters found on their arrival in the United States. A large number of them immediately obtained teaching posts, and they all contributed to the World Exhibition of 1938. Andreas Feininger, known in Germany for his painting, became a photographer in America. George Grosz, who had arrived in the United States in 1932 at the invitation of the New York Art Students' League, continued to paint and draw, but in a completely new style, very different from the political caricature that had made his name under the Weimar Republic.

It is in fact quite hard to isolate the effects of exiled German painters from those of other representatives of the European avant-garde, since Fernand Léger, Marc Chagall, André Masson, Marcel Duchamp, Yves Tanguy, Salvador Dali and Max Ernst also emigrated to the United States. And equally difficult to assess the impact that the encounter with America had on their styles. Lyonel Feininger, though of American origin himself, always felt in the United States a German painter in exile, though in Germany he had felt himself an American. Grosz's enthusiasm for America led him to abandon his former artistic and political convictions. He responded to American cities[156] and mythologies, which replaced those of 1920s Berlin. As a general rule, the American landscape left little trace on the exiles' painting. And while architects found it fairly easy to reconvert themselves, the majority of painters found – like Grosz[157] – that their fame dwindled and they often had to wait until the 1950s before their work aroused any real interest from the public. If some surrealists such as Yves Tanguy were inspired by American life – notably in his case by Iroquois totems and Sioux sculptures – the majority remained quite culturally isolated. The most one can find in some of their works is an obsession for scrap metal, machines and skyscrapers, as for example with Léger. In other cases, their colours became more violent on contact with America, without this development having any very definite significance.

No less important in the visual arts field was the relatively large number of art historians and writers on aesthetics who emigrated to the United States. Whereas methodologies of artistic analysis had steadily developed in Europe, these were practically unknown in America. Erwin Panofsky recalled in the epilogue to his book *Meaning in the Visual Arts*[158] the feeling he had on his arrival in the United States in 1931.[159] His discipline was represented at that time only by pioneers such as Alfred Barr and Henry Russell Hitchcock, a few students, and Panofsky himself. Translating German works into English, they were forced to invent new terms. The advent of Hitler led to the emigration from Germany and Austria of a large number of art historians who set out to develop their discipline in the universities where they taught. Julius Held, a specialist in Flemish painting,[160] and Karl Lehmann (classical archaeology),[161] both taught in New York from 1935. The Institute of Fine Arts also received Walter Friedlaender, from Freiburg, in 1936. In 1937, Martin Weinberger from Munich arrived, the following year Alfred Salmony, a specialist in Asiatic art, then Guido Schoenberger in 1939. Princeton University, which already had a department of art and archaeology, was endowed in 1935, thanks to Abraham Flexner, with a School of Humanistic Studies, within its Institute for Advanced Study. Erwin Panofsky and Kurt Weitzmann (specialist in Byzantine and Christian archaeology) joined him there to make Princeton one of the main centres of art history teaching in the United States. Hans Swarzenski arrived there in 1936, and three years later Charles de Tolnay, a specialist in the Italian Renaissance. They were followed in 1940 by Paul Frankl, a specialist in Gothic art, Richard Ettinghausen, Justus Bier and Richard Bernheimer. Almost every American university profited from this exodus. Ulrich Middledorf taught in Chicago and founded an art history department there.[162] Harvard took on the medievalist Wilhelm Koehler, Jacob Rosenberg, a specialist in Gothic and baroque art, and Otto Bench, from the national museum in Vienna. Milles College employed Alfred Salmony, Alfred Neumeyer and Otto Manechen-Felfer. It was thanks to these émigrés, and Panofsky above all, that art history became a distinct discipline in the United States, with its own rigorous methods. Panofsky's *Studies in Iconography* (1939) influenced a whole generation of students, and it is impossible to imagine the subsequent development of art history in America without the contributions of all these émigrés.

3. PRESS, LITERATURE AND PUBLISHING

EXILED WRITERS AND AMERICAN CULTURE

Some four hundred writers who were expelled from Europe by fascism took refuge in the United States. They included a large number of essayists – Arnold Brecht, Ernst Frankel, Karl Frank, Robert Kempner, Hans Leonhardt, Franz Neumann, Heinz Pol, Fritz Sternberg and Hans Weigert – as well as some of the greatest names in German and Austrian literature who have already been discussed. Their destinies were highly diverse, and if it is true that a number of remarkable works were written during their American exile – just think of Brecht's plays, Thomas Mann's *Doctor Faustus* and Döblin's *November 1918* – it is impossible to deny that the encounter of German writers with American culture was very often difficult and painful. The origins of this malaise were many. There was very little connection between German and American literature. The majority of exiled writers were condemned to live in a material and intellectual situation that was often appalling. Finally, they could no longer get their works published and had no readership there. It is not surprising therefore that Brecht should have noted in his *Journals* on 11 November 1943: 'writers are lured to hollywood after their first slim volume and squeezed dry. they write for nobody and nothing comes to anything.'[163] And Golo Mann recalled the words of his brother Klaus in winter 1947: 'The Americans will kill us all, all the intellectuals, all those who were against Hitler and for Roosevelt. This is the real fruit of the War.'[164]

The 1920s myths of America, however, had deeply marked German writers. They had often discovered the country through the novels of Theodore Dreiser, Upton Sinclair, Sinclair Lewis and John Dos Passos. Several writers had visited the United States in that decade, and their works even had some success there.[165] Cultural exchanges were established. Wieland Herzfelde had undertaken the translation of Upton Sinclair's works as early as 1921. Sinclair Lewis and Thomas Wolfe both knew Berlin and Munich well, Wolfe saying his farewell to Germany with a novel on the Olympic Games. The beginnings of exile saw new links made between German and American intellectuals on the basis of current political events. The struggle against fascism and the Spanish war brought Ernest Hemingway together with Gustav Regler, Alfred Kantorowicz and Ernst Toller. Klaus Mann and Sinclair Lewis became friends. On their arrival in the United States, these exiles had a great admiration for all the progressive writers of the 1920s, John Steinbeck and John Dos Passos arousing particular enthusiasm. But very few German writers were well-known in America apart from the famous authors of bestsellers – Lion Feuchtwanger, Thomas Mann, Franz Werfel, Erich Maria Remarque, Vicki Baum. Even Heinrich Mann and Alfred Döblin were almost unknown to American readers and publishers. Avant-garde writers were completely excluded from the literary market. Literary glory, moreover, was even more rapid and ephemeral than in Europe, as Ernst Toller learned to his cost. Having been seen as the greatest playwright of the Weimar years, he found himself suddenly quite unknown.[166] American writers who had lived in Europe chose Paris rather than Berlin.[167]

Very few had any real knowledge of German literature, with a few exceptions such as Scott Fitzgerald, a great admirer of Thomas Mann. If the majority of European intellectuals had felt concerned by the political situation of the 1930s, had taken a stand and often struggled actively against National Socialism, America was scarcely represented at the Congress for the Defence of Culture in 1935. The few writers who had immediately expressed their revulsion for Hitler's Germany included Ernest Hemingway and Henry Miller. By the early 1940s, precious little remained of the 'red decade'. Between American progressive literature and the antifascist exiles, no genuine meeting of minds seemed possible. Relations between the exiles and American writers and artists remained limited to a few individuals. Thomas Mann was friendly with Pearl S. Buck, Sinclair Lewis, Archibald McLesch, Thornton Wilder and Theodore Dreiser; Brecht with Charlie Chaplin, Charles Laughton, Joseph Losey, Orson Welles, Groucho Marx and Clifford Odets. Despite personal and political affinities, they were different in almost every way at the level of sensibility. The 'big names' of German literature fêted in America were Erich Maria Remarque, Franz Werfel and Vicki Baum, and most likely American critics would have found Döblin's novels almost incomprehensible had they read them. The majority of scripts written by German writers in Hollywood were deemed unusable by the producers. As Brecht constantly reiterated in his *Journals*: 'For the Americans, exiled writers were quite simply unable to tell stories capable of interesting a real audience; they only wrote for their colleagues.'

Contacts between exiled and American writers, therefore, even progressive ones, proved disappointing. Both Brecht and Thomas Mann, though they scarcely attended the same parties, describe in almost identical terms the two groups that émigrés and Americans formed at each gathering. They greeted each other without trying to get to know one another. Klaus Mann was friendly with Thomas Wolfe, and appreciated Southern writers such as Eudora Welty and Carson McCullers. It is unfortunate though that even Brecht did not have more contact with people such as Lillian Hellman who could have been important interlocutors. But the writers exiled in America tended to form isolated groups, to socialize among themselves, and did not make sufficient effort to meet the representatives of a culture that they did not hold in high esteem. They experienced their exile with a growing sense of unease. First of all, there was the question of language: very few were able to express themselves and write in English. They felt so deeply tied to European culture that any adaptation to America, its values and its lifestyle, seemed impossible.[168] It was not surprising therefore that they wrote so few works in America. This cannot be explained simply by the very limited number of publishers that might have been interested in their books, or the absence of an established readership; there was rather a lack of desire to write. Heinrich Mann, for example, contributed to émigré magazines, especially *Freies Deutschland*,[169] but the only major work he wrote during his American exile was his autobiography. He undertook this in the hope of extracting from it a series of broadcasts, as well as interesting the American press who, in his own words, 'knew nothing of him and did not want to know'.[170] In his last letters of 1947, he defined himself in the following words: 'Heinrich Mann, former writer first class, retired. Mind still clear, but whose serenity has turned to indifference.'[171] In Los Angeles he lived in relative isolation together with his companion Nelly – who was ill, neurotic and alcoholic – in often wretched conditions. A man who had once maintained: 'I have generally lived among foreign peoples, I'm used to Bavarians and Prussians. The room where I wrote served as my country, the room and nothing more,' a man who had felt equally at home in Munich, Berlin and Paris, scarcely managed to put down any roots in America. Only the aid of his brother and a few friends such as Alfred Kantorowicz prevented him from really sinking into utter destitution. His last work – *Lidice* – failed to interest anyone, and some of his colleagues, such as Ludwig Marcuse, deemed it incoherent and incomprehensible.

Brecht himself wrote on 21 April 1942: 'for the first time in 10 years, i am not working seriously on anything,' and declared that most of the other German writers in Hollywood had the same problem.[172] Alfred Döblin confided to Victor Zuckerkandl on 18 March 1945 that he lived in complete isolation,[173] saw no one apart from fellow émigrés, felt a stranger in America and its culture, and wondered if it actually had one. The bitterness displayed throughout his correspondence illustrates very well how he could not stand America, never ceasing to see it as a hostile and despicable world. Describing Döblin's attacks on him, Thomas Mann wrote to Walter Rilla on 22 June 1948: 'I am ashamed of the ignorant indifference he has experienced from beginning to end in this country, which has certainly contributed a great deal to his bitterness.' Psychological and cultural isolation was reinforced for the majority of writers by a disastrous economic situation. The term 'strangers in paradise' was never so apt as for them; they had been the most famous writers in Germany in the Weimar years, and living now in a country running over with wealth, they often experienced only indifference and poverty. After their contracts with MGM expired, most of the writers employed there went on to confront the most serious material difficulties, and some only survived thanks to the generosity of others.[174]

These pessimistic considerations, however, should not lead us to forget the major literary works that were born during the American exile: Bruno Frank wrote *Die Tochter* (*The Daughter*), Alfred Döblin *November 1918*, Heinrich Mann *Lidice*, *Empfang bei der Welt* (*Reception in the World*), *Der Atem* (*Breath*) and his autobiography *Ein Zeitalter wird besichtigt* (*View of an Age*). Lion Feuchtwanger was just as prolific in America as he had always been, as witness his novel *Die Füchse im Weinberg* (*Fox in the Vineyard*) and the short stories *Der Treue Peter* (*Faithful Peter*), *Die Lügentante* (*The Lying Aunt*), *Das Haus am grünen Weg* (*House on the Green Road*), *Venedig Texas* (*Venice, Texas*), *Simone*, and *Waffen für Amerika* (*Weapons for America*). He kept to his particular style of historical novel, and America played hardly any role in his stories after 1940, apart from *Der Teufel in Boston* (1946), set in the seventeenth century and depicting the witch-hunting climate which the beginnings of McCarthyism harked back to. Franz Werfel won fame in America thanks to *Jacobowksy and the Colonel* and, above all, *Song of Bernadette*, which he had vowed to write if he escaped from the Nazis.[175] His last novel, *The Star of the Unborn*,[176] displays the same mystical fervour, if with greater depth. The greatest work of German literature in American exile however was undoubtedly Thomas Mann's *Doctor Faustus*,[177] a project conceived in March 1943 following a reverie on Faust, the demonic soul, the musician Hugo Wolf, the madness of Nietzsche and the constant conviction of the author of *Buddenbrooks* that sickness, which is to the individual what decadence is to culture, can lead to the highest creations. It was when the bombing of Berlin was at its height that Mann pondered over Luther's Devil and the Faust legend.[178] This polyphonic edifice defies any summary: all the themes dear to Mann are to be found there – the link with irrationalism, music, Schopenhauer and death, and the ambiguous connection he draws between Germany and the demonic, a theme he also brings into the political essays he wrote in the United States. It was not just Faust but Germany that Mann saw as ever ready to make a pact with the Devil. Several of his analyses, like the finest pages of this novel, hark back to his early *Reflections of a Nonpolitical Man*. But the signs are now reversed: the immutable connection he makes between Germany and this irrational vision is a source not of eternal creation but of eternal danger.

EXILE PUBLISHING

The lack of a German readership interested in the exiles' works, the gigantic size of the country and the very different aesthetic criteria that prevailed, made it particularly hard for most of the exiles to find a publisher for their works, except for the few who enjoyed an international reputation. Though the United States counted at least 4,950,000 potential readers of German books in 1941, their tastes were conservative and there was little chance of interesting them in the exiles' productions. Ludwig Marcuse recalls in his autobiography[179] how the 'German-Americans' would not let the exiles contribute to their magazines, and even American Germanists kept them at a distance. Fairly conservative, these were interested at most in Thomas Mann and Franz Werfel, but more so in Gerhart Hauptmann, R. G. Binding, Hermann Stehr, Ernst Wiechert, Hans Carossa, W. Schäfer and H. G. Kolbenheyer, i.e. authors who had remained in Germany.

From 1933 to 1939, the exiles' works had managed to reach a certain number of readers, even if the German market was closed to them and their public steadily shrinking. Thanks to the readers they found in Switzerland, Austria, the Netherlands, Denmark and Czechoslovakia, even in France, the foundation of exile publishing houses, difficult as it was, was not a mere utopian dream. The same was not true in the United States. Despite their number, the émigrés formed a minuscule ghetto, lost in the immensity of the nation. Their deep ignorance of European reality meant that Americans had little sensitivity to the themes that the exiles explored. In a country of immigrants they did not seem especially original. The absence of connections with political parties, and a material situation that was often abysmal, made the founding of publishing houses almost impossible. Those established in Europe had meanwhile fallen into the hands of the Nazis. Most exile writers thus wrote knowing that they would not be published and that no one would read them before the end of the War. As for interesting American publishers in their works, it was scarcely worth the try. A number of American publishers had indeed published translations of authors who were now in exile (Ernst Toller, Thomas Mann, Lion Feuchtwanger, Vicki Baum, Erich Maria Remarque), but the number of these was small, and only the few authors of bestsellers or writers of international renown such as Thomas Mann could interest a publisher. There were indeed a few houses publishing foreign-language works, but they were too thin on the ground to absorb the exiles' production. Only political or historical essays[180] could achieve large print-runs. This was almost never the case with literary works, and few writers could hope to see their works published in German.[181] They had to hang on to their manuscripts in the hope that fascism would collapse before their death. The number of unpublished manuscripts by the exiles, or posthumous editions, shows that this was a very real fear. The most well off published their works themselves, or circulated them in typescript copies. It was in this form that Brecht presented his *Exile Poems* to Heinrich Mann on 20 December 1944.[182] Alfred Döblin could only publish a brief extract from his trilogy on the November revolution, under a pacifist imprint. More fortunate, Lion Feuchtwanger managed to get all his works published either by Viking in New York (in translation), or in Mexico (El Libro Libre) and Stockholm. Several novels by Bruno Frank were also published by Viking, while Leonhard Frank's novel *Mathilde* appeared in 1943 with the same pacifist imprint. Hans Habe published with Harcourt Brace, one of the largest US publishers, but this was an exception. The first volume of Heinrich Mann's *Henry of Navarre* had been published by Knopf in 1936, with a certain success. The second volume, which appeared in 1939, went completely unnoticed, and his 'cinematic novel' *Lidice* was published in Mexico in 1948. Franz Werfel had the rare chance of seeing his works published in German and English with equal success.

Starting in 1938, H. G. Koppells's Alliance Books (NY) imported German-language books, but in a limited number (500 to 1,000 copies per title). The War put an end to this enterprise. Only Wieland Herzfelde, with Aurora Verlag in New York, had a real antifascist publishing programme, from 1944 to 1946. It was hard therefore to envisage an émigré struggle against National Socialism in the field of literature. In 1939 Thomas Mann had suggested the publication of pamphlets written by exiles who were 'genuine representatives of the German spirit',[183] but the project came to nothing. According to Cazden's figures,[184] 353 German-language works that could be considered 'free German literature' were published in the United States between 1933 and 1954. These included 201 literary works, of which 119 were written by exiles, 89 by established writers. The others did not exist in the eyes of American publishers. There was no process of censorship, but it turned out that the only criteria recognized were commercial ones, and the antifascist exile was simply one author among others.

Publishers accepted exile works if they were likely to be successful. Viking was happy to publish *Song of Bernadette*,[185] as its success was certain. The publisher Benjamin Huebsch, despite his sympathy for the émigrés, rarely published their works as he did not see them as adequately marketable.[186]

In such a situation, the establishment of exile publishing houses in America was almost impossible, with Wieland Herzfelde's Aurora Verlag a unique achievement. Even in the best of cases, the émigrés could only find a place with existing American houses. The most remarkable case was certainly that of Kurt Wolff, former publisher of expressionist works and of Kafka, and director of the celebrated collection Der Jungste Tag, who founded Pantheon Books in New York, which in due course became one of the most famous American paperback imprints.[187] He managed to publish a number of German works, including an anthology of Stefan George (1943), *The Death of Virgil* by Hermann Broch, and *A Thousand Years of German Poetry* (1949). Gottfried Bermann Fischer, after his activities in Vienna and Stockholm, managed once again to partially re-establish his imprint in America, with the help of Harcourt Brace. Together with F. Landshoff he established the L. B. Fischer Publishing Corporation, which published a number of antifascist works, as well as American authors such as Ernest Hemingway, Sinclair Lewis, John Dos Passos, Norman Mailer and Arthur Miller.

Wieland Herzfelde had a constant struggle to try and publish exile works. After Berlin and Prague, his Malik Verlag was re-established in London. Its liquidation in 1939 enabled Herzfelde to reconstitute it in New York. With the Deutsche Schriftsteller Verband of New York, he devoted a special issue of the magazine *Direction* to 'Exiled German Writers', with texts by Oskar Maria Graf, Erich Mühsam, Ferdinand Bruckner, Bertolt Brecht, Ernest Bloch and Klaus Mann, and from 1943 he set up a new publishing house by selling ten-dollar shares to fellow émigrés. Aurora was less a conventional publishing house than a kind of cooperative, with which Ernst Bloch, Brecht, Bruckner, Döblin, Feuchtwanger, Graf, Heinrich Mann, Berthold Viertel, E. Waldinger and F. C. Weiskopf were all associated. It published scarcely a dozen titles, though these included Brecht's *Fear and Misery of the Third Reich* and Weiskopf's *Die Unsiegbaren* (*The Unvanquishable*), as well as texts by Graf, Bloch and Mann, and the anthology *Morgenröte* (*Dawn*).[188]

ANTIFASCIST MAGAZINES AND PUBLICATIONS

For lack of a readership and funds, it was also very hard to establish exile magazines. The American press displayed a genuine interest in the émigrés on their first arrival in the country, and interviewed the most famous of them. Thomas Mann's lectures in 1937 aroused commentary in most newspapers,[189] and in 1938 the *Christian Century* devoted an issue to the émigré writers under the headline: 'Welcome, Brave Exiles!' Thomas Mann was still the star of most of these articles: with his worldwide fame, fairly conservative views, an anti-fascist far from the Communists, humanist and eager to adapt to American culture, he struck them as the ideal émigré. The arrival of the *Nea Hellas* on 13

October 1940, with a cargo of immigrants on board who included Franz Werfel, Heinrich and Golo Mann, Friedrich Stampfer, Herman Budzislawski, Walther Victor, Alfred Polgar and Lion Feuchtwanger, also aroused lively interest from the New York press. Collaboration between these émigrés and American publishers, however, proved difficult from the start, as the majority could not express themselves fluently in English.[190] Those who could, such as Alfred Kantorowicz, preferred to contribute to the radio.

Those antifascist magazines that appeared in the United States were often tied to fairly small political groups. The Communists first of all had *Deutsches Volksecho*, which Stefan Heym[191] edited and which appeared from 1937 to 1939 as the organ of the *Volksfront*, financed by the CPUSA.[192] Most of its articles were written by Heym himself. The paper launched several campaigns against the Nazis (including the 'American Nazis') and disappeared after the signature of the German-Soviet pact. In 1940 *The German American* appeared,[193] edited by the former Prussian justice minister, Kurt Rosenfeld, a co-founder of the SAP whose position was now close to the Communists. Its contributors included Gerhard Eisler, Albert Norden, F. C. Weiskopf, Karl Obermann, Albert Schreiner and Alfred Kantorowicz. The paper had a circulation of 5,000 to 10,000, was financed by the trade unions, and agitated early on for an organization of anti-Nazi exiles, leading in 1944 to the creation of the Council for a Democratic Germany. Some of the contributors to *The German American* – Gerhart Eisler, Albert Norden, Albert Schreiner – published in 1945 *The Lesson of Germany*, a contribution to the discussion of Germany's future. The Social-Democrats were represented by the *Neue Volkszeitung New York*,[194] which appeared from December 1932 to August 1949. Though several émigrés had contributed to the paper, which had existed since 1877 as the *New Yorker Volkszeitung*, it was addressed above all to Americans of German origin. Gerhart Seger was its editor-in-chief from 1936 to 1949. The paper also included among its most regular contributors a number of exiled Social-Democratic figures (Friedrich Stampfer, Rudolf Katz and Karl Jacob Hirsch, less frequently William Schlamm, Emil Franzel and Wilhelm Sollmann). It was characterized on the whole by a predominance of right-wing Social-Democrats and a violent anti-Communism.

Der Aufbau played a very important role within the antifascist emigration in the United States, well beyond that of a New York Jewish magazine. Literary magazines produced by the exiles were very thin on the ground. In 1940 Klaus Mann worked to establish a magazine – *Decision* – with a project not far removed from that of *Die Sammlung*, but came up against an impressive number of obstacles, which he listed in *The Turning Point*. After many difficulties, the first issue appeared in January 1941. It tried to get contributions from both émigrés and American intellectuals, and its editorial advisors listed Stefan Zweig, Sherwood Anderson, W. H. Auden, Edward Benès, Julien Green, Vincent Sheean and Robert E. Sherwood. Thomas Mann made a substantial financial contribution to it. But right from its birth, *Decision* was seriously beset with financial problems and only managed to reach a limited readership. Despite the support of Max Ascoli, a professor at the New School for Social

Research, and Marshall Field, its situation rapidly worsened and the rate of publication slowed. *Decision* soon went under, adding to Klaus Mann's bitterness.[195]

The very limited number of exile magazines published in the United States stands in marked contrast with the editorial effervescence of the first years of exile. The situation of the émigrés in America, their intellectual and material isolation, is sufficient explanation. They also sought other means of expression, including lectures and radio broadcasts. Klaus Mann has described, not without irony, these lecture tours in which, after lunch or dinner, they had to explain the German tragedy to an audience of 'ladies'. Each objective in the struggle required the organization of such tours, whether it was collecting funds for refugees, for the Spanish Republican army or child victims of Francoist bombing. Ernst Toller spent a great part of the last years of his life on this lecture circuit. Even if the émigrés were apprehensive about the political awareness of this type of audience, they appreciated its generosity.

Thomas Mann also had to give several lecture tours: on 'the coming victory of democracy' (March–April 1938) and 'the problem of freedom' (March–April 1939). These were regular shows, planned and organized by impresarios. It goes without saying that only the star émigrés could attract such attention. Though the political tenor of these lectures, given their attendance, never went beyond the limits of liberal humanism, they were certainly far from useless, and increased American awareness of the danger of fascism. They generally had a threefold aim: to try and influence the political sphere, leading the Roosevelt administration to take a clearer position on the war in Europe and Hitler's Germany, to alert American opinion, and in particular to draw Americans of German origin away from the pro-Nazi organizations.

The émigrés recognized very well that it was hard indeed to get the American public to feel concerned. The most sinister example[196] perhaps was that of the Austrian writer Raoul Auernheimer, vice-president of Austrian PEN, who was arrested in Vienna in 1938 and sent to Dachau. After emigrating to America, and being received by Eleanor Roosevelt, he could not find a single paper in which to give an account of his imprisonment: they all replied that this would not interest their readers. If few antifascist magazines saw the light of day, a certain number of historical essays on National Socialism were published in the United States. *School for Barbarians*, the book Erika Mann published in New York in 1938 on education in Nazi Germany, was very successful,[197] and the publisher Houghton Mifflin invited Klaus and Erika to write a book on the most important exiles – *Escape to Life* – with a preface by Thomas Mann. Finally, a number of émigrés tried to develop antifascist ideas by contributing to American press and radio. Hermann Budzislawski wrote for the *New York Times*, Alfred Kantorowicz worked for CBS. Some academics and writers were able to contribute to the antifascist struggle as members of official bodies, in particular the Office for War Information or the Office of Strategic Services.[198] But all these activities together do not support the myth of a renaissance of Weimar culture in America, and more especially in Hollywood: only some ruins of it were left. The majority of émigrés experienced this encounter with American culture as a defeat.

It would be unjust, however, to make America or the Americans solely responsible for this defeat. Certainly the émigré writers' and artists' confrontation with the American culture was a *rencontre manquée*, in Hollywood above all. From their autobiographies and letters it is easy to see all the obstacles they came up against in this discovery of a world that they knew so poorly. The gulf between the operation of culture in America and in Germany was so great that the gathering of a large number of representatives of this Weimar culture in a relatively confined space on the Californian coast could not produce a visible and immediate result. The most one can say is that it prepared for the future: there was not a single sector of cultural, political and scientific life in America that did not owe something to the émigrés. It is also true that few of the exiles made any real effort to get to know America, and distinguish its negative aspects from the positive. Kurt Weill's example is fairly unique. Many of them could not get over a certain disdain for American culture, which they contemplated from the height of their European superiority. Even Brecht's notes on American culture, which give his *Journals* their rather desperate humour, seem often somewhat exaggerated.

John Russell Taylor, who wrote an interesting study on the daily life of the émigrés – *Strangers in Paradise*[199] – certainly brought a useful corrective to the rather Manichaean view of the attitude of America towards the émigrés that is found in a number of their works. David Raskin, for example, a former student of Schoenberg, recalled in an interview that they used to call the German émigrés in Hollywood 'at-homers', after their habit of starting every sentence with a comparison with Europe, invariably negative for America. Certainly, 'at home' in Berlin everything had been different. And if it is somewhat surprising that Horkheimer's Institut für Sozialforschung continued to publish its work in German, for a public either unable to read this or who no longer existed, it is still more so to see how so few émigré writers in the United States made an effort to learn English.[200] Though they could scarcely imagine that an intellectual could be unfamiliar with Latin or Greek, they saw English as a language suited only for businessmen.[201]

The gulf between the two cultures in 1940 was all the more striking given how rich the 1920s had been in encounters and promises. A number of European figures seemed able to maintain their originality while making a mark in Hollywood, for example Ernst Lubitsch and Erich von Stroheim. On his arrival in America in 1922, Lubitsch remained a symbol of European culture, with a characteristic humour and distinction, while developing a prodigious activity in the film world. Right up to his death in 1947, the 'Lubitsch touch' was a recognizable element in Hollywood. In the 1920s Hollywood had absorbed almost three-quarters of German cinematic talent. Yet even at this time a number of signals showed how hard this encounter was. A film-maker quite foreign to Hollywood values, Friedrich Murnau, managed to make a master-piece there in 1927 – *Sunrise* – which continued the magic of expressionist lighting effects.[202] Though the film won tremendous acclaim from the critics – certain American historians still see it as the finest film made in Hollywood in these years – it was only released in the larger centres and for a short while. The protection of William Fox enabled Murnau to use large sets once more for *Four Devils* in 1928. *Our Daily Bread* was re-edited without his permission, before being released under the title of *City Girl* in 1930. *Taboo* was hardly commercial, and it is hard to imagine what course Murnau's career in Hollywood would have taken if an unfortunate accident had not put an end to his life shortly after.

This generation of the 1920s would certainly have been able to serve as an essential mediation between America and the new German arrivals of the 1940s, but a series of misfortunes prevented this. Besides the sudden death of Murnau, Paul Leni, who had made some of the finest films of the silent era (*The Cabinet of Waxworks*, 1924) also died at the age of forty-four. Dupont, the creator of *Varieties*, made nothing interesting in Hollywood. The film capital, despite its resources, was unable to retain most of the foreign talent it attracted. The few figures who stayed there either made no films of value or returned eventually to Europe (V. Sjöström, M. Stiller). As for actors, the roles they were offered at that time were often devoid of artistic interest, and the advent of sound made their engagement difficult. The gap between these earlier émigrés and the new arrivals was thus almost total. Some of the most famous 'Hollywood Germans' of the 1920s were by 1940 stars of the Nazi cinema (Emil Jannings). Only a few, like the director Berthold Viertel and his wife, Salka Viertel, friends of Brecht, belonged to both generations of immigrants. Finally, if Hollywood held an immense cultural potential, this was controlled by producers whose constricted and commercial spirit can never be sufficiently stigmatized. As John Russell Taylor remarks,[203] a meeting between Samuel Goldwyn and Sergei Eisenstein must have been surrealistic.

Perhaps the very place of the encounter between the émigrés and American culture made a contribution to this defeat. The complaints of so many writers about California, Los Angeles and Hollywood, as voiced by Brecht or Döblin, may seem to us somewhat excessive. But to people used to working in the structure of a European city, America –with the exception of New York – was bound to seem something of a nightmare. If émigrés living in New York could entertain the illusion that they were still almost in Europe, Los Angeles was the radical negation of their very idea of a city. With its conurbation of 105,750 square kilometres, including Beverly Hills, Santa Monica, Pasadena and Long Beach, it was a heartless urban monster, without meeting places, with no literary café and almost no theatre of any worth.[204] The less fortunate lived in the city, the richer ones had splendid villas built in the outlying suburbs, and the poorest were generally at least fifteen kilometres from their workplace. The lack of a car – a frequent problem for the émigrés, for example Döblin and Heinrich Mann – was enough to condemn them to immobility. Cinema had pitilessly devoured most other forms of cultural expression. There were no operas, cabarets or avant-garde theatres, and by comparison with Berlin or Munich, Los Angeles really was a kind of desert.[205] This relative emptiness certainly left room – in theory – for several possibilities, but these generally required considerable financial resources. The émigrés however had nothing to offer apart from their high culture, good education and artistic sensibility. If they wanted to work, they had to bend to the existing rules and show that they were able to succeed within them. Most of the writers, actors and film-makers thought their career spoke for itself, that their European reputation had preceded them. In the eyes of American producers, though, they were worth only what they could bring in. The most prestigious European film-maker interested MGM only as a function of the profits of his last American film, as Erich Pommer and Joe May learned rapidly to their cost. As producer and director they had been leading figures in German cinema,[206] but after the failure of their first American film *Music in the Air* (1934) they risked unemployment. Besides the fact that American producers knew little or nothing of German films from the 1920s, it was unthinkable that these could be shown to an American audience. That the émigrés were political refugees worked neither in their favour nor against them, though the truth is that the majority of producers saw them as figures of fun. If they could sometimes be unexpectedly compassionate – as shown by the incontestably generous aid given by the studios to the rescue of refugees in 1940 – the émigrés, whether political or not, had to 'prove themselves', as Brecht often noted irritably in his *Journals*. A number of producers were ready to give them a chance by taking them under contract or for a test. But if the test was negative, they were dismissed without pity or confined to the production of 'B' movies.[207] The less well-known, if they were even to get this chance, had first of all to escape from poverty. Before becoming a big name in Hollywood, Billy Wilder shared a room with Peter Lorre, both practically without money or work. Even the most famous émigrés could not ignore the rules of the system and its genres.

The example of Fritz Lang illustrates very well the mechanisms at work. First of all rejected by all the producers, he was then taken under contract by David O. Selznick. His film *M* could certainly not have been made in Hollywood, even if it was offered as a model for screenwriters. For a whole year Lang was unable to interest producers in his projects, which were seen as strange and macabre.[208] He finally made *Fury* for MGM,[209] but despite the film's quality and success, he was still not accepted by the world of Hollywood. This artist full of passion, intelligence and finesse, with his imperturbable monocle, strong German accent, and voice reminiscent of a Prussian officer, left many people perplexed, and several accounts bear witness to the visceral dislike he aroused in Louis B. Meyer. Despite his genius, Lang had also to learn that he was only a salaried employee, that making a film was expensive and had to bring in money, that films were made for the audience to love and not to be inscribed in cinema history. The commercial success of *Fury* did more for Lang's American reputation than all his European films together. Just as Kurt Weill remained in the American theatre a very rare example of both commercial and artistic success, so *Fury* was the first film made by an émigré director that met the approval of the American public.

It is possible to ask why Lang succeeded despite the constraints of the system, while so many émigrés foundered. His success was possibly due less to his personal aesthetic, which he had to change considerably, than to his exceptional ability to tell stories. Whereas, after the films of Lubitsch, the first creations of William (Wilhelm) Dieterele and Michail Curtiz (Mihaly Kertesz) still represented a European dimension in American cinema, Lang, by playing down an overly obscure symbolism and attenuating his pessimistic metaphysic, managed to purge his style and make it acceptable to his new audience. Those émigré film-makers who managed to establish themselves in Hollywood had to give proof of the same facility, start their career afresh (Wilder, Siodmak),[210] or abandon it for good. It should not be surprising, therefore, if Dupont, such a big name in Germany, fell into alcoholism, or G. W. Pabst was so disconcerted by American methods of work that he refused to include in his filmography *A Modern Hero*, made in Hollywood after 1933. As for his project *War Is Declared*, with Peter Lorre, an astonishing screenplay telling the story of a man who manages, by making passengers believe that war had been declared, to spread such a climate of panic and violence on a liner that this is shipwrecked, it was the State Department itself that asked the film company to abandon it.

The study of all these failures is all the more instructive in as much as it was often the leading lights of German culture who fell victim. Their situation was all the more tragic in that what they were able to contribute interested no one, and what they were offered struck them as dishonourable. When they accepted such work, it was often out of necessity, as hack work, and while for some Hollywood meant a new departure in their career, for many film-makers it marked the beginning of a decline.[211] As for the generally negative balance of the encounter between Hollywood cinema and the exiled writers, it followed from the simple fact that most American producers believed they had no need at all for these writers; the majority of them were thus occupied in insignificant tasks or wrote scripts that were never filmed.[212] Certainly, thanks to the European Film Fund, founded by Ernst Lubitsch, Salka Viertel and Paul Kohner, the studios mobilized in support of German émigrés stranded in Europe. Louis B. Meyer was one of the first to agree to pay $100 a week to these writers and 'contracts' of this kind prevented some of them from sinking into destitution. But it would be naive to believe that this was seen by the producers as a real investment; most expected nothing in return. It was an act of charity and generosity such as Hollywood has often and paradoxically been capable. No producer there imagined that a writer like Heinrich Mann – seventy years old, knowing no English and scarcely anything of the taste of the American public – would be seriously capable of writing usable screenplays. The more clear-headed émigrés understood very soon that these salaries paid them by Hollywood were fictitious, at least when they realized that, while they earned $100 or $200 a week for completely useless work, a real screen writer earned $3,500. It was quite symbolic that once their contracts expired, neither Heinrich Mann, Alfred Döblin, Leopold Frank, Ludwig Marcuse or Walter Mehring were re-engaged.

The dream of a new Weimar, if it existed at all, had scant reality. Almost everything stood in the way of the exiles being able to re-establish a genuine community, as they had been able to do in certain European capitals or in

Mexico City. These men and women, separated by kilometres of suburb, were separated even more intellectually, and open hostility often broke out between them. Some of them lived in splendour, others struggled just to survive. All their means of expression – magazines, publishing houses, theatres, literary cafés – had disappeared. They never encountered real hostility as émigrés, even when America was at war. But in a certain sense, they no longer existed. There is certainly something fascinating in this concentration of exiled publishers, film-makers, writers, poets, actors, directors, journalists and artists, who often represented the elite of European culture. But rather than a real community, they divided into groups around one or a number of figures – Thomas Mann, Fritz Lang, Franz Werfel and Alma Mahler, Lion Feuchtwanger – who met only on symbolic and somewhat artificial occasions, unable really to conceal their differences and hostilities. What did Lion Feuchtwanger with his wealth and rare books, his 'castle' overlooking the ocean, have in common with Heinrich Mann, poor and forgotten?

It was at such gatherings, however – on 2 March 1941, for example, when the seventieth birthday of 'old Heinrich' was solemnly celebrated in Hollywood – that the illusion of a new Weimar seemed to become reality. The man who had been the life and soul of so many struggles and so many hopes now bore all the signs of age, marked by illness, who apart from his autobiography *Ein Zietalter wird besichtigt*, which his brother Thomas considered a masterpiece (but is it really?), had stopped writing anything really important. The two brothers still paid obeisance to ritual by exchanging tributes, and for an evening, the conflicts dividing the exiles seemed to be forgotten. It was perhaps only on occasions like this that Hanns Eisler, Bertolt Brecht, Arnold Schoenberg, Franz Werfel, Thomas Mann, Alfred Döblin and Theodor Adorno would all meet together. Their life in Hollywood had something schizophrenic about it. Many wrote without knowing if they would one day find a readership. Germany had turned its back on them, but they often turned their back on America. Yet even those who decided to remain there after 1945 continued to perpetuate a certain sensibility inseparable from Berlin in the 1920s.[213]

Academics in Exile

Hitler is my best friend. He shakes the tree and I collect the apples.
W. Cook, president of the Institute of Fine Arts, New York University

THE RESCUE OF ÉMIGRÉ ACADEMICS

The promulgation of the Nuremberg laws, following the earlier exodus of anti-Nazi academics, deprived Germany of a very large number of professors and researchers.[1] With the occupation of Czechoslovakia, Poland, Austria, the Netherlands and France, America became the sole refuge for a large number of threatened academics. The United States also had the most effective arrangements in place to rescue this intellectual emigration. Its deep attachment to academic freedom made Nazi discrimination appear particularly abhorrent. In May 1933, the American Association of University Professors adopted a resolution condemning the restrictions on teaching freedom applied in Germany and declared its solidarity with teachers expelled from their posts. A number of American academics immediately organized the collection of funds in order to invite them to the United States, both out of solidarity but also to enrich their departments. Several philanthropic organizations even agreed to bear the costs incurred in the reception of these foreign professors, as well as their first salary payments.

The Emergency Committee in Aid of Displaced Foreign Scholars, set up in summer 1933 under the leadership of Dr Stephen Duggan, director of the Institute of International Education (New York City), financed this first wave of the academic exodus.[2] A similar initiative was taken in 1936 by the Oberlaender Trust of the Carl Schur Memorial Foundation in Philadelphia, directed by Dr Wilbur K. Thomas, which enabled 330 academics to be brought over. Finally, between 1934 and 1940 the Carnegie Foundation paid large sums to universities accepting these exiles, and the Rockefeller Foundation took on more than 300 of them.

This resettlement of academics did not occur without a hitch. First of all, their level was often clearly superior and their knowledge more specialized than that of American academics. Several eminent scholars had to rest content with modest employment in provincial colleges. Some had to change discipline or give up teaching that was too complex and hardly interested American universities. If the resettlement of scientists was relatively easy, in the humanities the problem was much greater. Thomas Mann might well complain in his correspondence of the countless stupid questions he was asked during his lectures. But what about those German specialists who had spent their life studying Egyptian religion, Assyrian art or the Hittites, and were now required to teach a broad outline of world history? Many American academics, moreover, were hostile to the émigrés, whom they viewed as a threat to their own careers. Relations with American students also had their problems. The tragicomic laments of some stars of the German university on the vulgarity of their students, their lack of seriousness, the materialism of their colleagues and the sterility of campus life, also attest to what these American colleagues saw as their 'Teutonic background', inseparable from a certain disdain and sense of caste. Ludwig Marcuse described the encounter in his autobiography, in very moving terms. The American university was not a *Universität*: there was no central building with libraries, but a little village with streets, trees, a restaurant and pharmacy, and the agitation of life there struck him as rather like the big Wertheim department store in Berlin shortly before closing time. He was surprised by the lack of a solemn spirit or hierarchy, and even found the students to be not proper students but big children. They for their part displayed the same surprise towards these new professors who spoke English so badly, did not know the basic rules of baseball, and could not even drive a car.[3]

At least 2,000 teachers found refuge in America, and this haemorrhage from German and European universities was certainly a blessing for United States.[4] There were almost as many different types of resettlement and development as there were émigrés. Two specialists in the same discipline could often have opposite trajectories. Substantial differences could be noted even in the respective positions occupied by prominent figures such as Ernst Cassirer, Max Horkheimer, Ernst Bloch or Herbert Marcuse. We shall give a few examples.

The Institute for Advanced Study at Princeton
Famous above all for having Albert Einstein as director, and subsequently Richard Oppenheimer, this institute became one of the leading centres of German scientific emigration. The initiative for its foundation, in 1938, came from Abraham Flexner, the son of a Jewish family from Bohemia whose brother was secretary of the Refugee Economic Corporation during the Second World War. Though the Institute had not been founded by émigrés, it received some of the most celebrated academics from Germany: the mathematicians Johann von Neumann and Kurt Gödel, the art historians Erwin Panofsky and Paul Frankl, the historians and archaeologists Alfrede Vagts and Ernst Herzfeld. Thomas Mann was invited to Princeton in 1938, along with the Austrian writer Hermann Broch, who spent the years 1941–48 there. They all became members of the Institute, as did the literary historian Erich von Kahler. The conditions of work offered the émigrés there were also optimal: members were not required

either to publish or teach, and had complete freedom of research. The independence of the Institute was such that Adolf Keller termed it in 1940 a 'scientific republic'. The historian Joachim Radkau speaks of it rather as an 'island', as politics never came into play, and Flexner, then seventy years of age, seems deliberately to have chosen émigrés who were conservative or not very political. If the Institute did concern itself with the legal defence of émigrés, it never intervened in particular political questions, though very different political figures were invited there, from Hermann Rauschning to Karl Frank from the Neu Beginnen group.

Abraham Flexner had dreamed of abolishing the boundaries between disciplines, and the reception of émigrés there was all the more favourable in that Flexner himself was a specialist in European academic questions. Back in 1932 he had established a body of American and European teachers, chiefly in the fields of mathematics and economics. A passionate defender of intellectual freedom, he founded in 1933 a department of humanist studies to which Erwin Panofsky and Ernst Herzfeld were asked to contribute.

The 'University in Exile': The New School for Social Research

No less important was the work of the New School for Social Research. Located in Greenwich Village, and decorated with revolutionary frescos,[5] it had been founded at the end of the First World War, under the direction of a group of liberals around the magazine *New Republic*. For many years the School was the symbol of a progressive academic renewal in America. Thorstein Veblen taught there until 1927, as did the historian Charles A. Beard and Harry E. Barnes. Alvin Johnson became its director in 1923 and made the New School into a centre of research and training for adults. It gradually lost its avant-garde character and became an official institution. Beard and Veblen both left at that time, as its reputation as a 'centre of revolution' and nursery of socialist ideas dwindled away. The School subsequently included a Labor Research Bureau, financed by industry and directed by Croly, the *New Republic*'s publisher, who left the School however when Johnson gave up the editorship of the magazine in 1923.

During the 1920s, Johnson became more conservative. In its 'bourgeois' reorganization, the New School had lost some of its most radical representatives. From 1933 however it was to receive a large number of figures from European artistic and academic life who had been expelled from Europe by Nazism. Johnson attempted first of all to gain the support of the Rockefeller Foundation in paying the salaries of a hundred professors, though the émigré component of the School never reached this number. In 1937 it had seventeen émigrés, but by 1940 this had risen to sixty. Johnson himself called his European staff the 'University in Exile', but the name was soon abandoned in order to stress the Americanization of the émigrés. Following this influx, the New School ceased to be a school for adults and became a regular college, officially recognized as such in 1941 by New York University. Whereas the Institute for Advanced Study in Princeton had banned any political debate from its programme, and Max Horkheimer in his Institute focused on the study of fascism, the 'University in Exile' gave greater importance to sociological questions. The magazine *Social Research* became a regular discussion forum for many intellectuals, as well as taking the initiative for the English publication of *Mein Kampf*. Thanks to the émigrés, the New School rediscovered a certain political radicalism, even though émigré sociologists often had opposite opinions, for example figures close to the Frankfurt School on the one hand, and on the other the former president of the Berliner Hochschule für Politik, Albert Salomon, who openly challenged the 'revolutionary' character of other exiles' sociological theories.

In fact, Alvin Johnson was wary of teachers who were too committed. None of those he viewed as too radical could become 'members of the family'. His political sympathies lay rather with the economist Emil Lederer, opposed to Marxism, and he kept at a distance all émigrés who had a reputation as Marxists, such as the architect Werner Hegemann and the historian Hallgarten. Horkheimer and his Institute tried in vain to be accepted by the New School. When Horkheimer's Institute published in 1936 its first major work in America, *Studien über Autorität und Familie*, this received a surprisingly negative review in *Social Research*, from the pen of Hans Speier, future director of the social science section of the Rand Corporation, financed by the US air force.[6] In the scientific arena, however, Johnson showed great openness in accepting figures with the most opposing standpoints, especially in the social sciences. Max Wertheimer, founder of gestalt psychology, taught there until his death, and other members of this department were Claude Lévi-Strauss and Erwin Piscator, whose radical ideas were well known to Alvin Johnson.

Why was he so keen to support so many émigrés? In the chapter of his autobiography[7] devoted to the 'University in Exile', he emphasizes the negative impression he had formed of Germany in the 1920s, when he witnessed the violence of the extreme right in Berlin. Visiting there again in 1932, he was struck by the further deterioration of the social and political climate, and it was both the many friendships he had formed with German academics and his belief in the university as a 'bastion of freedom' that led him to make the New School into a place of work and asylum for those threatened by fascism. If the history of this 'University in Exile' occupies relatively little place in his account of the development of the New School, tribute is due to him for the very important role he played in relation to the émigrés: it was thanks to the New School that Claude Lévi-Strauss obtained a visa for the United States, and that Erwin Piscator could remain in the country as a professor. Though it did not manage to take on all the academics who applied, the New School mobilized foundations and universities in their favour and thus made a great contribution to their resettlement. It was not just Germans that Alvin Johnson helped in this way, but refugees from all countries occupied by the Reich. He personally enabled Jean Wahl, professor at the Sorbonne, to leave the camp where he had been interned. And as well as figures such as Erwin Piscator, Max Wertheimer, Arnolt Brecht, Arthur Feiler, Kurt Brandt, Hermann Kantorowicz and Claude Lévi-Strauss, the New School also welcomed Gustave Cohen, Jacques Maritain, Henri Grégoire and Boris Mirkine-Guetzévitch. It was Gustave Cohen who proposed establishing a French-language university in parallel to the New School, which took the name of the École Libre des Haute Études,[8] and at which Lévi-Strauss and Henri Focillon taught. Alvin Johnson was certainly no revolutionary, but his passion for freedom, enthusiasm and generosity compel admiration. Without him Piscator might never have been able to teach theatre in the United States, and it is to Johnson, too, that we indirectly owe the birth of the Dramatic Workshop, even if this theatre was only a lecture-hall. Though he was well aware of Piscator's radicalism in Germany, and his desire to proceed from art to politics, he simply advised him to try one day the opposite path, and go from politics to art.

Max Horkheimer's Institut für Sozialforschung
Founded in 1922,[9] out of a desire to break out of the theoretical blockage engendered by a conservative university, a dogmatic Communist party, and a reactionary Social-Democratic party with scant interest in theoretical questions, the project of constructing an institutional framework that would enable the creation of new relationships between theory and praxis, Marxism, philosophy and the social sciences led to the establishment of the Institut für Sozialforschung. This 'Frankfurt School' is still viewed today as one of the most significant and radical philosophical and sociological enterprises of the twentieth century.

The Institute was officially opened on 2 February 1923, and very soon a number of quite diverse figures with exceptional theoretical talents gathered around Pollock, Horkheimer, Wittfogel, Löwenthal and Adorno. The future of the School and its famous Institute was inevitably threatened by the rise to power of the Nazis. As a 'Marxist enterprise', largely made up of academics of Jewish origin, the Frankfurt School was forced to close on the grounds of 'tendencies hostile to the state', and the 60,000 or so volumes of its library were confiscated. The Institute's funds had fortunately been transferred abroad two years before. Max Horkheimer, Paul Tillich, Karl Mannheim and Hugo Sinzheimer were immediately expelled from their academic posts, while Karl Wittfogel was interned in a concentration camp before obtaining permission to emigrate to Britain. The Institute re-established its administrative centre in Geneva, under the name of the Société Internationale de Recherches Sociales, directed by Horkheimer and Pollock. Divisions were subsequently opened in Paris and London.[10] Since the climate for pursuing the Institute's activities in France was not very favourable, Julian Gumperz visited the United States in 1933 and concluded that it would be better to transfer the Institute there. Horkheimer went to America in May 1934 and met the president of Columbia University, Nicholas Murray Butler, who offered him premises. Though Walter Benjamin was so attached to Europe that he could not contemplate leaving without anxiety, Herbert Marcuse, Leo Löwenthal, Friedrich Pollock and Karl Wittfogel all settled in New York. The *Zeitschrift* continued being published by Félix Alcan, and the majority of its articles were still written in German, a strange fidelity to a tradition and a culture that not only cut the Frankfurt School off from the American public but also from academic grants. Throughout its exile, the School continued to deepen its research and refine its theories. Links with Europe were not entirely broken. Pollock returned several times before the War, and the Geneva office remained open, administered by A. Sternheim, then by Juliette Favez. The London office was closed in 1936, though the Paris section kept going until the War.

Though now fixed in the United States, the Institute remained isolated and rejected any Americanization. It operated with its own close milieu of researchers. Its financial independence protected it from those material worries common to most émigrés, which also explains the conflictual relations that sometimes existed between Institute members and some other exiles.[11] Max Horkheimer was deeply attached to the Institute's German past, and rejected the idea of integrating his research into the world of the American social sciences, especially at Columbia University, even though the *Zeitschrift* did publish contributions from American authors, including Margaret Mead, Charles Beard, and Harold Lasswell. In the notes for his projected *Tui* novel, Brecht commented ironically on these Frankfurt School intellectuals whom he viewed as armchair revolutionaries, jesting about the funds that the Institute possessed and claiming that Max Horkheimer was forced to establish a chair in each university where he taught in order to hide his revolutionary activities.[12] Yet the Institute certainly displayed a real generosity towards other émigrés. Walter Benjamin survived largely on the Institute's material assistance. Over 200 émigrés benefited from the material aid it dispensed from 1934 to 1944 (at least $200,000) to doctoral candidates and researchers.[13]

Members of the Institute gave lectures at the university, organized conferences and seminars, from its offices on 117th Street. Its contribution to the struggle against National Socialism was not confined to any precise campaigning actions, but lay rather in the deepening of critical theory and its application to subjects as important, from a political standpoint, as the authoritarian family, racism, and anti-Semitism. It was short-sighted of some commentators to see the School's members as 'non-activist': how else should we view studies such as *The Authoritarian Personality*, *Studien über Autorität und Familie*, and Franz Neumann's remarkable work on National Socialism, *Behemoth*? We should finally recall that Erich Fromm, who took part in the Institute's earliest work in the United States before subsequently separating from it, developed important work in America, that Karl A. Wittfogel developed there into a specialist in Chinese questions, while from 1942 Leo Löwenthal directed the research section of the Voice of America, though he was not an actual Institute member. Paul Lazarsfeld, who was a member, became an important figure in American sociology.

Yet the Frankfurt School theorists were not really discovered by American scholars until the 1960s and 70s. The Institute flourished, but in a very marginal situation. It was able to maintain its radical claims in a conservative America because its works, appearing in German, only reached a very limited readership; even the American left was unaware of it. Despite its studies of fascism and anti-Semitism, moreover, the Institute remained removed from the great debates of exile, and its contribution to exile struggles was above all of a financial order. It did achieve a remarkable balance between pure theory and empirical research, and one can believe Alice Meier, Horkheimer's secretary, when she declared: 'We were all possessed, so to speak, of the idea we must beat Hitler and fascism, and this brought us all together.'[14] In fact, the School's analysis of fascism is a very complex question that demands its own examination. The arrival of new figures shifted its theoretical perspectives. While Adorno and Horkheimer remained faithful to the approach inaugurated by *Studien über Autorität und Familie*, Franz Neumann's *Behemoth* was to have the more decisive influence, though it was far removed from Adorno and Horkheimer's dialectical Marxism, and more sensitive to the formal and legal – even anthropological – dimensions of National Socialism. Otto Kirchheimer also made an important contribution to the study of National Socialism with his study of law under the Third Reich.[15]

These few examples are naturally far from sufficient to give a satisfactory insight into the diversity of academic emigration to the United States. Academics on the whole, however, had a far more favourable fate than did writers. Many of them learned to teach in English and adopted this language for their works, even if they continued to think in German, and spoke English with a German accent to the end of their lives. How could one deny that the seduction Herbert Marcuse exerted on all those who came near him was a function of this astonishing mixture of German high culture, his roots in romanticism, and his radical critique of a world that he adopted in exile without ever feeling himself at home there? At the age of eighty, Marcuse still dreamt regularly of the street in Berlin where he lived as a child, and his accent alone summed up for him the calvary of exile. He still belonged to those who could continue a brilliant career in America and enjoy world renown. If figures as different as Panofsky, Spitzer and Auerbach became famous in America and their glory reached Europe, what should we say of those who fell into oblivion, had to interrupt their research or radically change their perspective? America was the destination of Ernst Cassirer, one of the last representatives of European humanism, and it was where Ernst Bloch wrote *The Principle of Hope*.[16] The encounter with America enriched some of the émigrés with new horizons, giving their work an added dimension (Herbert Marcuse), it considerably shifted the political itinerary of several others (Erich Fromm, Karl Wittfogel).[17] If a few of their number experienced a spiritual rebirth on their contact with American culture, many disappeared there and only a list of publications reminds us that they ever existed.

The Breakup of the Political Emigration

Despite the number of émigrés who found refuge there, the United States was not very important in the history of German emigration as a base of political activity. This was first of all because the American emigration included very few Communists, who were generally refused a visa, and so lacked its most active elements. The distance from Europe, and a feeling of impotence towards events unfolding there, also help to explain the fact that some formerly active political émigrés tended to abstain from any political activity there or even become depoliticized. The case of some Socialist émigrés who became violently anti-Communist after contact with America is particularly striking, and already foreshadows the climate of the Cold War. The most important discussions among the émigrés took place in the Jewish clubs of New York and Los Angeles, while debate among Communists was almost non-existent. A certain rapprochement was also noticeable between right-wing Socialists and conservative milieus from the Weimar Republic. It was not until the Council for a Democratic Germany was established in 1944, and the defeat of National Socialism was near, that the future of Germany was debated, opening a new chapter in the story of this political emigration.

ÉMIGRÉ POLITICAL AND CULTURAL MAGAZINES, CIRCLES AND ORGANIZATIONS

Two magazines played an important political role within the German émigré community in the United States: the *Neue Volkszeitung*, organ of the exiled Social-Democrats, and *Der Aufbau*, a Jewish magazine that oriented itself towards the émigrés as well as to American Jews and those in Palestine. Of a worldwide total of at least 400 exile magazines in existence between 1933 and 1945, very few appeared in the United States. The Austrian exiles had a dozen or so little magazines, while German exiles wrote chiefly in the two mentioned above. These cannot however be really considered as émigré periodicals. The *Volkszeitung* had already existed as a 'German-American' magazine, and the aim of *Der Aufbau* was more the integration of Jewish émigrés in American society than the struggle for a new Germany. Other magazines, such as *Das Volksecho* – of Communist inspiration – and *The German-American*, played no real political role, given the small number of Communists exiled in the United States. These tended to be more centred on *Freies Deutschland*, published in Mexico. Besides, the large number of German and Jewish magazines already published in New York[1] also helps to explain the hesitancy in establishing new ones specifically for the exiles. Finally, it should be recognized that if those exile periodicals born in Europe were generally directed by prominent figures (Leopold Schwarzschild, Georg Bernhard, Bruno Frei), this was in no way the case in America, except for Manfred George (*Der Aufbau*) and Gerhart Seger (*Volkszeitung*).

The German-Jewish Club had been founded in New York in 1924, made up of German-Jewish émigrés who had fought in the First World War. Its nationalist character gradually faded away in the 1930s. *Der Aufbau* was initially founded as the organ of this Club in 1934, and only gained wider significance with the arrival in 1939 of new émigrés who raised its intellectual level.[2] The Club was soon transformed into a genuine cultural and social organization,[3] and by the time of America's entry into the War was known as the New World Club. The magazine's title had no political significance,[4] and it never abandoned its original positions, which were close to liberalism. Published monthly until 1939, it then appeared twice weekly and enjoyed true financial independence. From this time, under the direction of Manfred George, it set out to give 'the standpoint of Jewish ethics' on world events,[5] though this desire for universality constantly came up against the particularism of *Der Aufbau*'s readers, whether they lived in New York or Palestine. The magazine was certainly read by political émigrés, but also by most Jews expelled from Germany, the majority of whom were not very political.[6]

Despite its wide readership among the émigrés, however, *Der Aufbau* did not really play a political role. The German language isolated it from American political and cultural life. The absence of theoretical debate prevented it from attracting much interest among intellectuals, even if it helped raise awareness of the refugees and thus helped to assist them. *Der Aufbau* subsequently published a supplement for readers in California, *Die Westküste*, and it set up an Advisory Board with some of the greatest names of the German emigration – Albert Einstein, Thomas Mann, Bruno Frank, Franz Werfel and Fritz von Unruh – as well as American figures such as Fred Kirchwey, Nahum Goldmann, Max Nussbaum and Friedrich Pollock.

The *Neue Volkszeitung*, established in December 1932, was not originally an émigré magazine but the continuation of the *New Yorker Volkszeitung*, founded in 1878 by Socialist émigrés at the time of Bismarck's anti-Socialist laws. The arrival of antifascist émigrés substantially shifted the magazine's profile, particularly in its attitude towards the Communists. It gradually became the official organ of the right-wing Social-Democrats, and moved away from its original positions.[7] Its peak circulation was reached in 1934, with 21,850 copies,[8] subsequently declining to between ten and fifteen thousand. Its editor-in-chief from 1936 was Gerhart Seger, who had arrived in the United States in 1934 after release from concentration camp, replaced in 1940 by Friedrich Stampfer and Wilhelm Sollmann. Far from presenting itself as an émigré magazine, the *Neue Volkszeitung* tried to reach all Americans of German origin, and contrary to *Der Aufbau*, was written entirely in German. During the War it began to criticize the ideas of the *Deutschamerikaner*, and became essentially an exile magazine, before disappearing in 1949. If the ideas it developed were relatively reactionary, the large number of eminent figures from the SPD who contributed to it contrasted with the fairly low cultural level of its readers. After the disappearance of the *Neue Vorwärts* in 1940, it became practically the only German-language Social-Democratic organ published in the United States.[9] From 1938 already, it took a reactionary turn, Rudolf Katz, Wilhelm Sollmann, William S. Schlamm, Siegfried Marck and Hans von Hentig replacing antifascism with a visceral anti-Communism.

Among the cultural organizations that played a major role in the émigré community, the Deutschamerikanischer Kulturverband (DAKV) was the most active. Asserting its desire to keep the German humanist tradition alive in the United States in opposition to Nazi barbarism, this organization set out to promote a Popular Front policy by winning Americans of German origin to the battle against National Socialism.[10] The Kulturverband aimed to be non-party, and bring together all opponents of the Nazis. Its leadership included trade unionists such as Otto Sattler, and cultural figures such as Karl Mayer and John E. Bonn. It succeeded in attracting a number of important personalities, including Thomas Mann and the anthropologist Frank Boas, dean of Columbia University. The DAKV maintained good relations with the Communist émigrés, especially Martin Hall, editor of the *Volksfront*, the KPD organ in the Midwest, who became secretary of the Kulturverband in 1938.

Right from the start, the DAKV used a wide variety of means in its anti-Nazi cultural propaganda: conferences, public meetings, exhibitions and theatrical performances, counting more than 75,000 sympathizers. In 1935 it held a Deutscher Tag to commemorate the revolution of 1848 and its refugees, arousing violent protests from the pro-Nazi Bund. More than ten thousand people – trade unionists, young people, workers, émigrés – took part in this demonstration, which was addressed by Ernst Toller, Julius Lips, Alfons Goldschmidt and Kurt Rosenfeld, as well as by Peter Lorre. At its 1937 gathering, anti-Semitism was discussed as well as Sinclair Lewis's play *It Can't Happen Here*, in the presence of Ludwig Renn, an émigré writer fighting in the International Brigades. The following year Thomas Mann was the keynote speaker, in 1939 Paul Tillich and Julius Lips, while Oskar Maria Graf presided in 1941.

The German American Writers' Association (GAWA) was also deeply affected in its structures by the massive influx of refugees, who tried to transform it into an association close to the Schutzverband. Manfred George became its secretary. Oskar Maria Graf and Ferdinand Bruckner attended its founding meeting on 7 October 1938, while Thomas Mann agreed to serve as honorary president. Without having a definite political programme, GAWA also championed the idea of a Popular Front. Though counting no more than 150 members, from 1940 onwards it organized radio broadcasts devoted to exile writers, famous or otherwise. It also intervened effectively in the rescue of a number of intellectuals stranded in Europe, obtaining affidavits for them and money for their passage to New York. The deteriorating situation in Europe helped to radicalize a number of its liberal members, but GAWA's statutes prevented it from being politically committed as an organization.

In spring 1942 the German American Emergency Committee was established, seeking to bring Americans of German extraction to a defence of American democracy and a condemnation of Hitler's Germany and the Axis powers. The founder and first president of this movement was the former left Social-Democrat Kurt Rosenfeld, an active champion of the Popular Front. Other members of this committee included Frank Boas, Walter Damrosch, Lilian Hellman, Walter Rautenstrauch, Lion Feuchtwanger, O. M. Graf and Otto Sattler. Over 50,000 German-Americans attended its founding meetings. A large number of émigrés worked on its propaganda activities, and it published a monthly directed by Gerhart Eisler and Max Schröder, *The German-American*. Jewish circles were equally active, with a good deal of debate. German émigrés including Willy Gunzburger, Joe Adler and Julius Frei had founded the Deutsch-Jüdische Club in New York in 1924, but this soon divided between conservatives and progressives. From 1933–34, with the massive influx of Jewish refugees, this club tried to widen its base by transforming itself into a mutual-aid organization. It too championed the idea of an antifascist Popular Front, but sought above all to provide immediate aid and assistance to the refugees, also supporting the actions of the Non-Sectarian Anti-Nazi League, taking part in the boycott of Germany and the Olympic Games, and backing the candidacy of Carl von Ossietzky for the Nobel Peace Prize. It held regular lectures in German and English on topical themes.

JEWISH IMMIGRATION AND THE DEBATES AROUND *DER AUFBAU*

If *Der Aufbau* and the club attached to it acquired new importance with the arrival of the émigrés of 1933, this was because they transformed a magazine of very limited interest into a liberal political organ.[11] This was far however from achieving unanimity between contributors and readers. These divisions reflected the wider situation of European and American Jewry. Read in Jerusalem as well as Brooklyn, the magazine sought to be open-minded on practical and Jewish questions. This openness however did not prevent snide comments: a group of readers living in Palestine congratulated the magazine for informing them that Mr Levy of Hamburg had opened a laundry in Brooklyn, and telling them where to find the best Polish pastries in New York. They wanted *Der Aufbau* to have a broader scope than a collection of local advertisements. Manfred George had contributed to several European Zionist magazines, but the director of the German-Jewish Club, Wilfred C. Hulse, was resolutely assimilationist. He called for the rapid Americanization of all Jewish émigrés and advised them to pay more attention to the American constitution than to news from Europe or Palestine. At the same time, *Der Aufbau* did not spare its criticism of American Jewish organizations, especially the American Jewish Committee that was resolutely anti-Zionist, and the Joint Distribution Committee, the main Jewish organization of aid to the refugees,[12] which a number of Jewish émigré figures, not just of the left,[13] termed 'pseudo-philanthropic'. The absence of any political or religious awareness among these Jews of the American establishment reminded the émigrés of those Jewish businessmen who until the last moment had dreamed of a possible compromise with Hitler's Germany and had left the country only with regret. Manfred George sought to avoid violent polemic between Jewish organizations and maintained his conception of liberalism, while mollifying the American Jewish committees and accommodating both assimilationists and Zionists. This openness was all the more necessary in that a number of contributors to *Der Aufbau*, who were better known than its editor, were equally removed both from Zionism and from the specific debates within American Jewry. This was the case with Carl Misch, for example, former political editor of the *Vossische Zeitung* and subsequently editor-in-chief of the *Pariser Tageszeitung*, or Siegfried Aufhäuser, a left Socialist who contributed to *Der Aufbau* out of contempt for the violent anti-Communism of the *Neue Volkszeitung*. *Der Aufbau* avoided any criticism of the Communists, even after the German–Soviet pact,[14] which led Manfred George to be attacked by the former editor-in-chief Rudolf Brandl, who called him a 'Communist agent'. The magazine displayed a genuine sympathy for the USSR without being close to the exiled Communists.[15]

The interest of the debates that arose round this magazine and its circle is that they symbolized the special situation of the emigration in the United States. Here the talk was less of the battle against National Socialism and more of assimilation. While this was championed in most articles by Wilfred C. Hulse, the magazine for its part declared itself 'American in spirit – German in language': the necessary 'Americanization' of the émigrés should not be reduced to a mere assimilation, of which the German Jews showed little sign; New York Jews were mostly from Eastern Europe, and the émigrés felt complete strangers among them.[16] *Der Aufbau* prudently kept its distance from such discussions. A number of American Jewish figures did indeed deplore the fact that the break with Europe in such dramatic conditions had not led to any intellectual improvement among the refugees: they had lived these events in complete passivity, and were pejoratively referred to as 'Hitler Jews', with regret that they had learned nothing from fascism. Besides, if a large section of American Jews of Russian and Polish origin were favourable to an increase in Jewish emigration to the United States, Jewish leaders in Congress feared this would fuel anti-Semitism. German Jews viewed these recently Americanized Jews from the east with a certain condescension, while the latter often refused to employ German Jews whose forefathers, a generation or so before, had used them as cheap labour. *Der Aufbau* did however manage to steer between these rocks, opening clubs in many American cities, as well as mutual-aid associations and even a Labor Council directed by Siegfried Häuser, which served as an employment agency for refugees. The magazine and its clubs took part in the war effort by collecting funds,[17] clothing and blood. Manfred George then decide to combine all these emigrant organizations in the Immigrants Victory Council, supervised by the New World Club in 1940, and planned to establish an American Federation of German Jews charged with uniting Jewish émigrés of German origin.

It should be stressed that these clubs were not simply organizations to aid the émigrés, but regular cultural centres, which held lectures, discussions, and theatrical performances. The German-Jewish Club of New York invited émigré companies to stage anti-Nazi plays, German classics, and even pieces by Clifford Odets. Lectures were given on current political topics as well as on literary works. A large number of writers and actors were invited to speak at its meetings, including Ernst Deutsch, Berthold Viertel, Albert Ehrenstein, Lion Feuchtwanger, Bruno Frank, Oskar Maria Graf, Hermann Kesten, Erika and Klaus Mann, Fritz von Unruh and Kurt Pinthus. A number of sessions were held in tribute to Thomas Mann, Franz Kafka, Stefan Zweig and Max Reinhardt. The Los Angeles club, of which Leopold Jessner became director in 1940, held similar activities. Ernst Deutsch, Fritz Kortner and Helene Thimig (the partner of Max Reinhardt) read from the works of Schiller, Heinrich Mann, Karl Kraus, Bertolt Brecht, Goethe and Rosa Luxemburg. From 1942, the German–Jewish Club collaborated with the European Film Fund (established on the initiative of William and Charlotte Dieterle, Bruno and Liesl Frank, and Ernst Lubitsch), which worked to assist the émigrés by donating a percentage of their earnings.

THE SOCIALIST EMIGRATION

In the United States as elsewhere, the Socialist emigration was deeply divided. After the transformation of the *New Yorker Volkszeitung*, now resolutely oriented to the right, certain Socialists drew nearer to the SAP (the *Kampfsignal* with Paul Hagen and Kurt Rosenfeld) or Trotskyism. Those individuals grouped around the *Volkszeitung* – Gerhart Seger, Friedrich Stampfer, Rudolf Katz – had no real link with other Socialist groups, and their growing anti-Communism had led them to break with Friedrich Adler and the Sozialistische Union in London. The émigré Socialists were also very isolated from their American counterparts. This political development had some unusual aspects. Gerhart Seger, for example, famous for his escape from the Oranienburg concentration camp and the book he wrote on his imprisonment there, did not originally belong to the right-wing tendency around Wilhelm Sollmann. But his views became increasingly conservative, even annoying Thomas Mann, who could not be accused of Communist sympathies. As for Stampfer, it is hard to pin down what still tied him to Socialism. A 'national' Social-Democrat, always keen on a certain left phraseology but without any theoretical basis, he was openly conservative. Together with Seger, the editor-in-chief of the *Volkszeitung*, Katz played a major role in the Socialist emigration in the United States. An adviser to Chiang Kai-shek, together with Max Brauner, before becoming a reader at Columbia University and editor of the *New Leader*, he became secretary of the German Labor Delegation in 1940, concerned with rescuing the émigrés.[18] Schlamm was as much a conservative as he was a Socialist. Emil Frankel belonged to those 'left people of the right' who liked to combine a Marxist and a nationalist vocabulary. These *Volkssozialisten* were ready to unite with Otto Strasser's Schwarze Front, whose programme was still openly anti-Semitic.[19] Wilhelm Sollmann was the link between the *Volkssozialisten* and the *Volkszeitung*. In the United States he became a fierce champion of the American system and violently attacked Marxism.[20]

The presence of these contradictory ideological elements, the main link between which was anti-Communism and hatred for the USSR, helps to explain their development from neo-conservatives into theorists of the American right. Sollmann stopped contributing to the *Volkszeitung* in 1940, when the paper was directed by Stampfer and still kept a certain connection with the SPD, which Sollmann completely rejected. The fact that he sought a rapprochement with a Nazi dissident such as Strasser naturally aroused the distrust of many Socialists, even anti-Communist ones. His departure from the *Volkszeitung*, however, changed nothing fundamental in the paper's political orientation, which became increasingly conservative. Siegfried Marck, in charge of book reviews, was an admirer of Hermann Rauschning, and so was Julius Epstein. Hans von Hentig came from the national-bolshevik milieu and saw only the Junkers as possible opponents of the Nazis regime. If he wrote in the Communist magazine *Freies Deutschland*, this was because he dreamt of an association between Prussianism and the Soviet Union.

It is very hard therefore to analyse in detail the political ideas of these exiled Social-Democrats in the United States, or even pin down in what way their ideas were still tied to Socialism. Most of them, apart from Emil Frankel, abandoned any reference to Marxism, but conservativism, anti-Communism and a certain admiration for right-wing ideologies (Rauschning, Strasser) were common to the majority of them. Only Seger continued to respect a certain Socialist ideal that was no longer shared by the magazine's contributors.

The relations of these exiled 'Socialists' to their American counterparts were fairly complex. The American Socialist movement had broken up in the early 1930s into a 'rearguard' and the new radicals. The rearguard was strengthened by the arrival of the German exiles: both feared Communism and groups such as Neu Beginnen. Back in June 1934, at the party congress in Detroit, the Socialists of the *Volkszeitung* encouraged a struggle against the Trotskyists, adding to the confusion created by the rivalry between the two Socialist groups of Chicago and New York. In 1936, the Socialist rearguard broke away from the party and formed the Social-Democratic Federation. The exiled Socialists were swift to attack those American Socialists who supported the Neu Beginnen group, and linked up with the most conservative elements. They did not form any distinct organization, but were simply a '*deutsche Sprachgruppe*'. In 1939, Friedrich Stampfer established a German Labor Delegation within the AFL, together with Seger and Katz, with the aim of collecting funds for Socialists trapped in Europe. According to certain accounts, however, Katz advised left Socialists against emigrating to the United States, doubtless so as to keep the existing balance within the party.

It is easy to divine from the composition of this Socialist emigration what its relationship with the Communists would be: a constant rejection and hatred. And yet Gerhart Seger, a friend of Willi Münzenberg, had been involved in the campaign in defence of the Communists accused in the Reichstag fire. Heinrich Mann had written a preface to his book *Oranienburg*, and at the beginning of exile Seger was in no way anti-Communist. His collaboration with Stampfer seems to have influenced him in this direction, as well as the German–Soviet pact, which led him to maintain the identity of the Soviet and Nazi regimes. From this time at least, Seger became a declared adversary of Communism, championing the position of Arthur Koestler.[21] The invasion of the Soviet Union by Hitler's armies did not lead him to change his tune: the *Volkszeitung* only feared this aggression would lead the democracies to sympathize with Stalinism, and it reproached Roosevelt for his understanding for the USSR.[22] It attacked as pro-Soviet the famous film *Mission to Moscow* – admired by Thomas Mann. The *Volkszeitung* even published in 1943 a serialized anti-Communist novel, *An America in Russia*, by Lili Körber, giving a systematically negative picture of the Soviet Union. At the start of the Cold War, the *Volkszeitung* stoked up American hostility to the USSR and took on the 'Hollywood Communists' in terms worthy of Senator McCarthy.[23] Apart from Siegfried Marck and Hans von Hentig, very few Social-Democrats agreed to work together with Communist exiles or write for *Freies Deutschland*. They also took their distance from American liberals and linked up more with the right, playing no role either in émigré cultural organizations. Attached to Germany, they also attacked Emil Ludwig and Lord Vansittart, and found themselves increasingly isolated. After the War, they defended Germany from a standpoint distinct from any other exiles. At a time when some people, even Thomas Mann, were tempted to see Germany as a diabolical entity, a perpetual threat to European peace, what concerned the Social-Democrats of the *Volkszeitung* was the fate of East Prussia and the conditions of German capitulation. Only Gerhart Seger focused on the political re-education of German prisoners of war interned in the United States.

THE DIFFICULT SURVIVAL OF THE COMMUNISTS

The expression used by J. Radkau to define the position of exiled Communists in the United States – like a bear in an ants' nest – is perfectly apt. American legislation, and the difficulty of obtaining a visa, discouraged a large number of Communists from even trying to emigrate there. They often preferred to go to Mexico, which was more welcoming. If KPD members exiled in Europe might expect some help from the USSR, this was not forthcoming in New York or Hollywood. The signature of the German–Soviet pact, moreover, alienated a large part of American sympathy for them until the invasion of the Soviet Union. The 'red decade' was at an end, Communism was no longer the fashion, they were under constant suspicion from the United States authorities and prey to attacks from exiled conservatives and Socialists. Socialist hostility towards the Communists had started to intensify from February 1937, when the Communists sought to put the Popular Front policy into practice and founded the *Deutsches Volksecho* under the direction of Stefan Heym,[24] with a view to winning over workers of German origin. Communist attempts to make contact with other groups often met with defeat: Stefan Heym could not connect with the Socialists of the *Volkszeitung*, and Alfons Goldschmidt, a former contributor to the *Berliner Tageblatt*, was also unsuccessful, from 1938, in winning the sympathy of a number of Jewish organizations. The Communists had more success in the cultural arena in 1937, rallying a number of intellectuals to the cause of the antifascist Popular Front, including Kurt Rosenfeld. These efforts made them still more unpopular in the eyes of the Socialists, who redoubled their attacks, worried that they might win the support of the *Deutsch-amerikaner*. They especially feared the connection between the Deutsch-amerikanischer Kulturverband and the German-American Writers' Association, which included such major figures as Thomas Mann and Ferdinand Bruckner among its members, and the secretary of which was Oskar Maria Graf.[25] The Association was vilified by the Socialists as a Stalinist body, and after the German–Soviet pact the majority of liberals left it, leading it to dissolve. The pact dealt a mortal blow to the Communists in the United States. A large section of the American population began to equate Nazis and Communists, and even fellow-travellers were seen as 'Nazi sympathizers'. Jews left the party and its cultural organizations en bloc. Even in Hollywood, it helped make the USSR suspect among the most progressive artists, and those who tried to justify it were criticized severely. The Nazi attack on the Soviet Union improved the Communists' situation considerably, the USSR and Stalin now appearing as enemies of Nazism. In 1942, accordingly, a new organization was founded to replace the DAKV and GAWA, the German-American Emergency Conference, including Otto Sattler, Oskar Maria Graf, Kurt Rosenfeld, Lion Feuchtwanger and Alfred Kantorowicz, as well as the Social-Democrats Julius Deutsch and Horst Baerensprung. Thomas Mann however refused to take part. Though the DAKV did not try to be a political organization, the German-American Emergency Conference opposed the German-American Congress for Democracy that had been founded on 14 June 1940, to which Thomas Mann belonged, together with Gerhart Seger and Max Brauer.

Among the rare successes of the Communists in the United States was the foundation of the Aurora publishing company by Wieland Herzfelde, whose role was all the more important in so far as this was the only publishing house established by the exiles in America. Its founders included a number of former members of GAWA such as O. M. Graf, Ferdinand Bruckner, Lion Feuchtwanger, Heinrich Mann, Ernst Waldinger, Berthold Viertel and F. C. Weiskopf. The cultural field, moreover, was the only place in which exiled Communists in the United States had some prospect of being active. Lacking a solid basis – the *Deutschamerikaner* being conservative or at most Socialist sympathizers – or an effective political organization, they could do little more than simply survive, and if they enjoyed a new audience during the War, the development of American politics gradually deprived them of any means of expression or action: they now risked deportation pure and simple.[26] It is even astonishing how they managed to keep going in such difficult circumstances. This was basically because they were more active than the Socialists in the émigré community, and gave it a deeper moral and political sense.

CONSERVATIVE TENDENCIES IN THE EMIGRATION

The presence among the political émigrés of a number of reactionary or conservative elements should also be mentioned; these not only formed a significant component of the emigration to the United States, but went on to play a far from negligible political role. First among them was ex-Chancellor Brüning,[27] who initially remained incognito and subsequently still refused to take part in émigré activities, which he viewed with an evident disdain. He gave no interview until 1936, and was always very cautious in his judgements on the Third Reich, refusing to criticize Germany as a whole. But even in his silence he was always heeded by the other conservative émigrés, some of whom wished him to become the head of a government in exile, as the last legitimate head of the Weimar Republic. The left, on the other hand, generally refused to see him as an émigré. He would undoubtedly have been able to play a major political role, and rally around his name conservatives, liberals, and right-wing Socialists. Emil Ludwig, at the founding meeting of the Deutsch-Amerikanischer Kulturverband, hailed him as an exceptional personality, in the same league as Rathenau or Stresemann.[28] But Brüning never abandoned his reserve. He hated the Communists and had only episodic relations with the right Social-Democrats, even if he made efforts to rescue Breitscheid and Hilferding before the French authorities handed them over to the Gestapo. The only émigré with whom Brüning, an austere and distrustful man, had a steady connection, was Treviranus, whom he knew from the First World War and who had belonged to his cabinet. He did not even keep up connections with conservative and Catholic émigrés, and turned down Otto Strasser's proposal that he should form a German National Council, despite his esteem for Strasser. He even kept his distance from the Jesuit Friedrich Muckermann, who was a member of his own party, and from Waldemar Gurian, likewise a Catholic. Nor did he collaborate with Hubertus Prinz zu Löwenstein, also a member of the Centre party, who played an important diplomatic role in the émigré world.[29] He was content to offer his opinion through intermediaries, but did not believe that the émigrés had any political influence, and knew that a large number of them – especially of the left – detested him.[30] There was in fact a striking contrast between Brüning's silence and the number of articles and rumours concerning him, some of which attacked him very violently.[31] Opinions are divided as to the influence he may have had on the US government. Though some writers deny he had any, others claim that it was he who steered the Americans to the choice of Konrad Adenauer as head of the Federal Republic.[32]

Treviranus, who was close to Brüning, often seemed to play the role of his representative in the English-speaking world, which was easier in so far as he was a Protestant. He maintained ongoing relations with the right-wing Socialists (Sollmann), as well as with Otto Strasser. He also collaborated with Karl Spiecker, a former member of the Reichsbanner. More important however was certainly the influence of Hermann Rauschning, former president of the Danzig senate, known above all for his two books *The Revolution of Nihilism* and *Hitler Speaks*. Despite the ideological confusion of his conception of Nazism, which has the most limited theoretical interest, he seduced the conservatives, and his books were reprinted time and again. Rauschning represented one of the most conservative poles of the emigration, and through his lectures he enjoyed real celebrity.[33] But despite the affinities that can be discovered between these right-wing émigrés, they never formed a structured group – though people did speak of the *Brüning-Kreis* – and their audience remained very limited.[34] At the start of the Cold War, the influence of the right-wing Socialists was far more malign than that of the old Weimar conservatives.

If the antifascist émigrés as a whole had only little influence on US policy in the 1940s, what is clear is that several conservative émigrés were at the origin of a new development of conservative ideas in America. In 1939 the celebrated *Review of Politics* was launched, under the direction of Waldemar Gurian, professor at the Catholic University of Notre Dame (South Bend, Indiana), devoted to a historical and philosophical approach to social realities. A bitter opponent of both National Socialism and Marxism, Gurian became after 1945 a specialist in Russia and the Socialist countries,[35] and remained very famous until his death in 1954. A number of conservative émigrés gathered around him, including Ferdinand A. Hermens, and the *Review of Politics* became the theoretical organ of the most conservative milieus of the emigration,[36] soon joined by American conservatives such as Mortimer Adler.[37] The University of Chicago took on many émigrés, but their ideas were generally in accord with its conservative president. It is not surprising, therefore, to find there Hans J. Morgenthau, Arnold Bertstraesser (who sympathized with Nazism in its early years), Erich von Kahler, a literary historian formerly close to the Stefan George circle, the historian Rothfels, the philosopher Leo Strauss, and David Riesmann, future author of *The Lonely Crowd*. A number of other émigrés taught there later (Paul Tillich) or were invited as guest lecturers (Hannah Arendt, Erich Voegeln, Hans Simons, Kurt Riezler, Karl Löwenstein). Morgenthau and Strauss went on to represent the 'realist' school in American political science. Despite being an émigré, Morgenthau was swift to undertake the passionate defence of US interests, and was a fierce opponent of 'political idealism'. He had a major influence on younger generations as a theorist of the 'national interest'.[38] Similar themes were developed by another émigré, John H. Herz, and by the young Henry Kissinger.

It is curious how the most conservative émigrés and those least well-known under the Weimar Republic – they were often quite young at the time – came to play a major role in the United States, helping to destroy a certain American utopianism. Even Franz Neumann, the friend of Herbert Marcuse and author of the celebrated book on National Socialism, *Behemoth*, maintained in 1958 that the political events of the last few years had destroyed his belief in the ability of social sciences to transform reality. Paul Tillich rightly spoke of the 'anti-utopian effect' of the emigration – even if it was in the United States that Ernst Bloch wrote *The Principle of Hope*.[39] Bloch himself seems to have lost his faith in any utopia with the triumph of Hitler, followed by the atom bomb on Hiroshima.[40] This entire school declared the bankruptcy of the grand proletarian utopias and its suspicion of any technological utopia. Hostility to political idealism and utopia was not simply a stock-in-trade of the right; the phenomenon is more complex. But what is certain is that it was in so far as the émigrés were part of this current that they came to influence American political thought.[41] For many of them, 'utopianism' was equivalent to 'totalitarianism', and this systematic suspicion of political utopianism that had marked the 1920s and 30s would be one of the most characteristic aspects of American conservative political thought in the 1950s and beyond. It is thus one of the most paradoxical consequences of the antifascist emigration that a number of its representatives became precursors of conservative or neo-ideological ideologies that were openly reactionary. Many of the exiles were even the most eager gravediggers of the ideas of the 'red decade' and the New Deal, even though these had helped to rescue many of them. Finally, some opponents of Nazism also became the most bitter American anti-Communists: Stefan T. Possony, Gustav Stolper, Jan Valtin, etc.

Emigration in Latin America

Though very few anti-Nazi émigrés in 1933 thought of Latin America as a place of exile,[1] the situation was quite different by 1940. Not only were antifascists who had been refused admission to most countries now ready to embark for any destination whatsoever – Shanghai, the Dominican Republic, Cuba – as long as they could find a boat, but immigration regulations in Latin America seemed less rigorous than those of the United States. Some countries did not just positively welcome this new European migration, often highly skilled, but actively sought to profit from it. Mexico made it a duty to welcome all those who had fought for the Spanish Republic. For the majority of antifascists stranded in France in 1940, these countries represented almost the sole opportunity of escaping the Gestapo, once entry to the United States proved impossible. Anna Seghers's *Transit* depicts very aptly the attempts, hopes and fears of candidates for emigration to Mexico, besieging the consulate in Marseille and never knowing whether their visa would arrive before the arrest that constantly threatened them. It was in no way surprising then that antifascist refugees could be found in at least eighteen Latin American countries – Argentina, Chile, Brazil, Uruguay, Paraguay, Bolivia, Peru, Ecuador, Colombia, Venezuela, Panama, Costa Rica, Honduras, Guatemala, Mexico, Cuba, Haiti and the Dominican Republic. Not all these countries of course were equally important in the history of German emigration. We can only mention here its most important aspects, in those countries where the émigrés were most numerous and most active.[2] The hundred thousand or so refugees who reached Latin America after 1933 included around ten thousand political exiles, including three hundred Communists who were especially active in Mexico. The choice of one country or another was often the outcome of a series of accidents. In 1938–40, most countries restricted the number of visas granted to European refugees. Failing to obtain a visa for one country, the émigrés tried all the others. Sometimes the destination of exile was simply determined by where a ship was going. But despite these limitations, the Latin American countries seemed relatively tolerant: most of them cared more about the émigrés' skills than the reasons that had led them to leave Europe. Already at the time of

Bismarck's anti-Socialist laws, and again in the 1920s, a number of German activists had found refuge there, and by the early 1930s there were over a million Germans living in Latin America, especially in Argentina, Chile, Uruguay and Brazil.[3] Whether they had adopted their new country's nationality or remained German citizens, the majority were nationalist and conservative, and formed distinct communities. The Latin American countries were always on the lookout for new capital and cheap labour. Contrary to Europe, openings for work were many and little regulated. Many European refugees accepted these conditions of exploitation, and became manual workers in industry or agriculture at derisory wages. The most disfavoured were the intellectuals, as their resettlement often proved very difficult. If many countries demanded a certificate of resources, the lack of vigilance of the immigration services made it possible to arrive with a transit visa and later obtain a residence permit. Though Brazil had a principle of not accepting Communists, Mexico was happy to receive them.

The most difficult thing was not entry to these countries but the passage there. Not only were their consulates permanently besieged by people requesting visas, but ships crossing the Atlantic from Marseille became increasingly rare due to the War. As for the cost of a ticket, this could be met only by aid committees or the help of other émigrés. Besides, it was often useless to obtain a visa for a Latin American country without an exit visa from the Vichy government and the Spanish and Portuguese transit visas. Whilst intellectuals and well-known activists could hope to receive financial support, this was certainly not the case for workers or ordinary journalists. The Atlantic crossing also became increasingly perilous due to risk of German submarines, the fate of the *City of Benares* being one of the most unfortunate examples.

The émigrés reaching Latin America between 1938 and 1940 included a large number of Jewish refugees expelled from Germany and Austria, often not very political, as well as those who had actively opposed fascism – as intellectuals or militants – since 1933. While the latter made haste to set up political and cultural organizations that could carry on the struggle against National Socialism, the former were concerned above all to assimilate, and in only few cases returned eventually to Germany. This emigration to Latin America has not been very deeply studied, apart from its most illustrious representatives. The hundred thousand German refugees who settled there were divided into some 45,000 in Argentina, 25,000 in Brazil, 2,000 in Chile, 5,000 in Bolivia, 1,500 in Mexico, 2,000 in Colombia, 7,000 in Uruguay, 800 in Paraguay, 1,000 in Ecuador, with 5,000 scattered between Peru, Venezuela, Panama, Cuba, Haiti, the Dominican Republic and the rest of Central America.[4] No exact figures are available as to how these divided between 'racial' and political refugees.

ARGENTINA AND MEXICO AS
MAJOR CENTRES OF EMIGRATION

While all the Latin American countries received German refugees, Argentina and Mexico formed the two most important exile colonies, in terms of numbers, personalities and activities.

Argentina alone received about half of the German, Austrian and Czech refugees, though it was also the country where Nazism was most implanted in the German community. Buenos Aires had long been the Latin American city that attracted the largest number of refugees. Foreigners enjoyed the same rights as native Argentinians. In 1931 a Nazi group was established in Buenos Aires. Argentina counted 278 members of the NSDAP in 1932, and some 1,500 by 1937.[5] German schools were soon dominated by Nazi ideology, while workers had to join the Arbeitsfront or risk losing their job. The process of Nazification spared neither churches nor newspapers. This strong pro-Nazi tendency in the German population was moreover welcomed with sympathy by the Argentinian military dictatorship.[6] The Communist party (founded in 1918) was illegal, and in 1935 an anti-Communist pact was signed between Argentina, Brazil and Uruguay, with their Communist parties newly banned in 1936.

On 1 August 1933, however, a parade of Germans in Nazi uniform was blocked by Argentinian workers, leading to violent confrontations, and when German buildings flew the swastika flag on 1 May 1934, popular demonstrations again took place. A further provocation by German and Austrian Nazis, celebrating the annexation of Austria, also came up against the Argentinian population, who burned the Nazi flag while singing the national anthem. Ernst Wilhelm Bohl, the head of the Nazi groups in Latin America, then ordered Hitler supporters to be more discreet in expressing themselves. The advent of a new president in 1938, Roberto M. Ortiz, also forced Argentinian Nazis to be more circumspect. Hostile to Hitler's Germany, Ortiz banned all political demonstrations by foreign organizations and let the Socialists publish a *White Book* on Nazi activities in Argentina. Some German émigrés – Heinrich Groenewald, Heinz Bier – took part in this project. But Nazi activities were once more allowed free rein in 1940, under the vice-presidency of Roman Castillo, who succeeded the sick President Ortiz. Though tens of thousands of refugees arrived in Argentina, it was now forbidden to write against Hitler in the press.

The emigration provoked by the Nazis was slow to reach Argentina. It was initially made up of Jews and political activists, to a total of 2,650 in 1935 and 2,857 in 1937. In 1936, the foreign ministers of Argentina, Uruguay and Brazil decided to coordinate their surveillance efforts on the activities of these new immigrants. Argentina asked its consulates to be less generous in granting visas, and particularly opposed from 1939 the arrival of boatloads of Jews.[7] In 1943 Buenos Aires had between eighty and a hundred thousand German-speaking inhabitants.[8] Antifascist émigrés and Nazi supporters formed two distinct communities, naturally without connection, each having its own theatres and papers, schools and cultural associations. But the power of the pro-Nazis was so strong that very few cultural bodies could resist it. One of the most famous was Vorwärts, founded by Social-Democrats in the nineteenth century, which immediately gave support to the émigrés and waged a common struggle with them against National Socialism. Though still linked to the Argentinian Socialist party, Vorwärts had abandoned its political character after 1918 to become simply a cultural organization. Yet it was never won over to nationalist ideas, despite hundreds of Nazis applying to join. The arrival of the émigrés was to radicalize the paper and its group, which soon became a genuine anti-Nazi organization. The new members included both Communists and Social-Democrats, members of the ISK and SAP. At the same time, a German-language group was formed within the illegal Argentine Communist party, led in 1937 by Erich Bunke, who remained active in Vorwärts until his return to the GDR in 1952. The organization now held regular political meetings, no longer confining itself to workers' choirs and gymnastic exercises. It even embraced antifascist theatre companies who performed extracts from Brecht plays.

Among other organs that resisted the Nazi stranglehold over the German community, the *Argentinisches Tageblatt*[9] merits a particular mention. The sole German newspaper not won over to a pro-Nazi position, it was immediately boycotted on Hitler's order by all German businesses and banks, while the German embassy regularly protested against its articles.[10] Despite court actions, the paper in no way changed its tune. Its editorial offices were burned, and two of its editors murdered by Gestapo agents. The German government however lost an action against it and the paper's courage won it an international readership. Its fiftieth anniversary was saluted by Thomas Mann, Hanns Eisler, Lion Feuchtwanger, Stefan Zweig, Robert Olden, Emil Ludwig, Sigmund Freud, Klaus Mann, Alfred Kerr, Stefan Heym and Oskar Maria Graf. The *Argentinisches Tageblatt* had several émigré contributors who provided anti-Nazi articles and cartoons. In a petty act of vengeance, the rector of Heidelberg University, Ernst Krieck, withdrew from the paper's director, Ernesto E. Aleman, the doctorate that the university had awarded him.

Those German émigrés who did not want their children to be brought up in National Socialist values established on 1 May 1934 – with the aid of Dr Alemann – the Asociacion Cultural Pestalozzi,[11] which systematically opposed Nazi propaganda. Antifascist refugees in Argentina defended this school and gave it their collaboration. Stefan Zweig visited there, along with Emil Ludwig.[12] Here again the Nazis reacted with a series of attacks, all the more so as the majority of teachers – Dr August Siemsen, H. C. Walter Damus (former teacher at the Karl-Marx-Schule in Berlin), H. Groenwald and Clément Moreau (Carl Meffert) – were all known for their progressive ideas. Chance had it that Carl Meffert, who taught design, had among his students a young Argentinian who went on to have an astonishing destiny: Ernesto Che Guevara.

Mexico played a more significant role in the history of antifascist emigration in that a large section of the Communist emigration in Latin America was concentrated there in 1940, including some of the most prominent exiled writers such as Anna Seghers. In 1938, the secretariat of the exiled KPD in Paris had considered the possibility of emigration to the United States. The arrival of former combatants from the International Brigades made this task all the more urgent. Ludwig Renn, a former Brigader, was interned at this point in a French camp (Saint-Cyprien). Franz Dahlem tried to use Renn's knowledge of English to set up this American emigration.[13] He took advantage of an invitation to the

United States to study the problem of obtaining visas (June 1939). Bodo Uhse had been invited by the League of American Writers and was staying there too. They managed to obtain affidavits for a number of imprisoned writers (Theodor Balk, Peter Katz, Hans Marchwitza). But despite all their efforts, Ludwig Renn rapidly concluded that permanent stay in the United States was almost impossible for Communists, and it was the KPD delegate in New York, Johannes Schröter, who suggested Mexico as a place of asylum and a new centre of KPD activity on the American continent.

The reasons for this choice were several. Under the presidency of Lazaro Cardenas, from 1934 to 1940, Mexico was experiencing an era of progressive reform. In 1936 the Communist party had been legalized. The far right had attempted a putsch in 1938, supported by German Nazi advisers, but this was put down by government forces. Mexico was the only country besides the USSR to actively support the Spanish Republic, supplying arms and subsidies, and welcoming its government in exile. It also refused to recognize the annexation of Austria, and made it known that it would welcome all victims of National Socialism who obtained a work contract with a Mexican company. A number of political refugees[14] and members of the Jewish bourgeoisie had already reached Mexico. In 1939 Mexico received refugees from the Spanish war, 150,000 of whom were then in France. At least 10,000 migrated there, as well as a number of former International Brigaders who were able to leave the French camps. These refugees enjoyed the same rights as Mexican nationals, though the majority of earlier German immigrants had been won over by National Socialism.

The first anti-Nazi organization to be founded in Mexico was the Liga für Deutsche Kultur (Liga pro Cultura Alemana en Mexico), established at the initiative of Ernst Toller when he visited in 1937. This aimed to unite antifascist émigrés, progressive Mexicans and anti-Nazi German-speaking Mexicans in a Popular Front movement that both Communists and Social-Democrats could join. Until 1939 this carried out a number of political and cultural activities – meetings, leaflets, pamphlets in German and Spanish – to counteract Nazi propaganda.[15] It held lectures and schools, and worked to support antifascists stranded in Europe, without distinction of party. At least thirty-nine writers and journalists were rescued by its intercession.[16] By 1940, however, it had become increasingly difficult to get to Mexico, due to both internal tension in the country[17] and the situation of the exiles under the Vichy government.

Thanks to the work of Varian Fry, a number of people interned in French camps were still able to reach Mexico,[18] but it was harder to help the Communists, and most of these had their voyage paid only as a result of an international appeal. In 1940, Mildred Rackwell went to Mexico to obtain entry visas, a task to which Bodo Uhse and Otto Katz also applied themselves. The painter Siquerios's attempted assassination of Trotsky did much to discredit the Mexican Communist party at this time. But in 1940–41 a large number of Communists – some already émigrés in the United States – did arrive in Mexico,[19] and the capital gradually became one of the last centres of political activity for the Communist exiles. In 1941, the Mexican government still supplied visas to enable women interned in the Rieucros camp (in the department of Lozère) to leave France. Paul Marker, Gerhart Eisler and Theodor Balk were rescued at the same time, even if it tremendous material problems now had to be overcome in order to reach Mexico.

ASPECTS OF ANTIFASCIST STRUGGLE
IN LATIN AMERICA

The political activities of the émigrés in the different Latin American countries depended both on their number, the personalities involved, and their political affiliation, but above all on the attitude of the government in question towards these activities. Whilst these countries had little to fear from Hitler's Germany – apart from some damage to economic relations[20] – they did have to reckon with the large German minorities who had been often won over to Nazi ideas. This exile activity also found itself in a wide variety of political environments: in Mexico it could develop on a broad scale between 1933 and 1945, but in Uruguay, Chile, Colombia, Cuba and Bolivia it was considerably restricted. In Argentina it was tolerated at first, but was violently repressed when the military again took power. Brazil was very anti-Communist and never tolerated exile activity, which was also quite impossible in Venezuela, Paraguay and Peru. The Latin American regimes were very diverse, ranging from Popular Front coalitions to overtly fascist military dictatorships. Many were directly dependent on the United States, or had strong economic ties with Germany, which flooded the German communities with propaganda material. German settlers who refused to support the Nazis were often physically threatened, and Gestapo agents did not hesitate to murder those who sympathized with the émigrés. Relatives in Germany could also become the object of reprisals. The encounter between exiled antifascists and these German colonists was often painful and violent.

The political exiles naturally aspired to continue their struggle against Hitler. But the forms of struggle were necessarily limited. Sheer geographical distance made any direct action impossible. All they could do was enlighten the country in which they had taken refuge on the meaning of European events, by way of counter-propaganda, and help as many fellow exiles as possible to leave Europe. Besides, it was difficult for these political émigrés to remain indifferent to the ideological situation of the countries in which they found themselves. Where the possibility of a Popular Front existed, they would naturally try to strengthen it, or help bring it into being. Several émigrés accordingly took part in the various attempts at a Popular Front in Argentina, Uruguay and especially Chile, where a Frente Popular was established in 1936 against President Alessandri. The Frente Popular candidate – Pedro Aguirre Cerda – was indeed elected. A Liga für Deutsche Kultur was also founded in Chile in 1939, while in Argentina a broad front of left forces was formed to resist pressure from the government and Nazi provocations. In 1937, a German group within the Argentinian Communist party tried to establish an underground Popular Front by uniting émigrés of different tendencies under the same slogans. In this way the organization Das Andere Deutschland was founded on 7 June 1937, which carried out many actions in support of victims of Nazism and constantly denounced the lies of Hitlerite propaganda. In its leaflets it attacked the Reich's policy of aggression and sought to arouse a movement of revolt against it. It also established an organization to support the émigrés, victims of fascism – Das Andere Deutschland even supported refugees from the Saar who had settled in Paraguay – and other opponents, including activists still in Europe and combatants from the International Brigades interned in French camps. The antifascist school in Buenos Aires – the Pestalozzi-Schule – organized fund-raising events to help rescue children detained in these camps. Das Andere Deutschland published a monthly magazine, designed for all its supporters in Argentina and Latin America, which spread news about Germany. First of all this was simply mimeographed, but by March 1939 had enough subscribers to be printed. It also included more general articles and book reviews.

The same Popular Front movement could be found in Uruguay,[21] where antifascist activity could develop free from restriction, thanks to a long democratic tradition.[22] To struggle against Nazi propaganda, the Uruguayan Communist party established in Montevideo in 1932 the Kulturklub Deutschsprechender Arbeiter (Club Cultural Obrero de Habla Aleman), which regularly spread news on the terror raging in Germany and made known antifascist and progressive works (J. R. Becher, Erich Weinert, Heinrich Heine). The club also organized meetings in defence of Thälmann. From 1935, under a military dictatorship, the Communist party was banned and relations with the Soviet Union broken off. The struggle of Nazi supporters against the regime's opponents, Communists and émigrés, accordingly gathered pace. The Kulturklub organized a union of antifascist schools, one of which, again called the Pestalozzi-Schule, survived until 1940. In summer 1936, its offices were closed and the *Arbeiter-Welt* banned. The government, now declaring its support for Hitler, Mussolini and Franco, restricted any democratic activity. The situation improved with the new government that came to power in 1938, and the number of émigrés in Uruguay gradually increased. A committee in defence of the Spanish Republic, founded by the émigrés, collected medicines and food. This committee subsequently assisted former combatants of the International Brigades and the Republican army, while lectures were held at the Casa de España in Montevideo in support of the Popular Front.

In March 1939 a Freier Deutscher Klub (Club Aleman Independiente) was also formed in Montevideo, in which Communists and Social-Democrats worked together until 1943. It held various activities against National Socialism, commemorated the book burnings of 1933 and sought to make contact with progressive Uruguayan intellectuals. Its bulletin reproduced a number of exile writings, in particular those of Heinrich Mann.

In 1939–40, Chile and Argentina came to play the most prominent role in the antifascist struggle in Latin America. The Popular Front policy inaugurated by Das Andere Deutschland was an example followed in several countries, including the Freie Deutscher Klub in Montevideo and the Liga pro Cultura Aleman in Mexico City. It was seriously shaken by the signing of the German–Soviet pact and the war on Finland. After the German attack on the USSR, solidarity campaigns with the Soviet Union were newly organized by most movements of émigrés and progressive intellectuals in Latin America. Despite the distance, Communist émigrés collected medicines and blankets for the Red Army (in Uruguay this was through the committee Accion Antinazi), which were sent either directly by ship to the USSR or via the Soviet consulate in Washington.

ÉMIGRÉ CULTURAL ACTIVITIES

The large number of exiles in Latin America explains the diversity and richness of the cultural activities developed there, especially in Mexico.[23] In October 1941, Anna Seghers, Egon Erwin Kisch, Bodo Uhse and Rudolf Feistman established a German-language Cultural Union, in which the Austrian musician and student of Schoenberg, Ernst Römer, was also involved. The organization was named after Heinrich Heine (Club Enrique Heine, Associacion de Intelectuales Antinazi de Habla Alemana). Its members regularly organized sessions at which antifascist works were read. During its four years' existence, this club was one of the main centres of anti-Nazi cultural agitation in Latin America. Besides lectures, concerts and dramatic performances were held,[24] sometimes attracting an audience of up to eight hundred. Among the most important plays staged was *The Threepenny Opera* – this being its first performance in Mexico – but works by J. R. Becher and Ferdinand Bruckner were also shown.

In several Latin American countries émigré theatrical activity was quite important. Argentina for example had a Freie Deutsche Bühne under the direction of Paul Walter Jacob, which staged 550 performances between 1940 and 1946. In Uruguay an exile theatre (Die Komödie) was established under the direction of Fred Heller and Albert Maurer. The Kammerspiele theatre was founded in Ecuador, which gave plays by Goethe and Schiller as well by Molière, Shaw, Wilde, Anouilh and Brecht. The Club Enrique Heine succeeded in presenting most of the musical works banned in Germany (Schoenberg, Mahler), thanks to the presence of a large number of Austrian musicians.[25] It was the émigrés who first introduced the Mexican public to Richard Strauss's *Salome*. The Club also organized a series of events around Mexican culture.[26]

One of the most well-known achievements of the émigrés in Mexico was the foundation on 30 January 1942 of the Freies Deutschland movement, presided over by Ludwig Renn. This aimed to unite all German antifascists without distinction of party, in the perspective of the construction of a new Germany. A magazine of that name had existed since November 1941, as both a political and a literary organ. Since the émigrés did not have the funds to finance this, they organized lectures for American tourists. Ludwig Renn and especially Egon Erwin Kisch, known as the most famous German reporter of the 1920s, carried out sensational exposés in order to raise Mexican currency. Further support was obtained from the first two hundred subscriptions, and *Freies Deutschland* became in fact the first exile periodical founded since the outbreak of war. It set out to unite on a global scale the opponents and adversaries of National

Socialism.[27] In its first year alone, more than 118 writers and activists contributed to it. The writers included such varied names as Heinrich and Thomas Mann, Lion Feuchtwanger, Bruno Frank, Ferdinand Bruckner, F. C. Weiskopf, Oskar Maria Graf, Berthold Viertel, Hans Marchwitza, J. R. Becher, Willi Bredel, Alfred Kurella, Theodor Plievier, Berta Lask, Anna Seghers, Bodo Uhse, Egon Erwin Kisch, Ludwig Renn, Leo Katz, K. Stern, Bruno Frei, Paul Mayer, Paul Zech, Balder Olden and Ulrich Becher. *Freies Deutschland* was distributed throughout Latin America and even in the Soviet Union. It informed its readers of the progress of the War, military operations, advances and victories of the resistance, and the most important international events, as well as publishing many reviews. Despite its scanty means, by May 1943 the magazine reached at least 20,000 readers.[28]

The antifascist emigration in Latin America comprised a large number of significant writers. Among the most important, we should mention in Argentina the expressionist poet Paul Zech as well as Balder Olden, Stefan Zweig and Ulrich Becher (Brazil), Erich Arendt (Colombia), Anna Seghers, E. E. Kisch and Ludwig Renn (Mexico). Most of these found it very hard to get their work published. Between 1909 and 1933, Paul Zech had published twenty collections of poems, nine short stories, five novels, twenty plays and eight volumes of essays. From 1933 until his death in 1948, he did not manage to publish a single work and lived in great poverty.[29] Erich Trendt wrote several poems evoking Colombia, its population and the Bogota countryside. He and his wife survived by starting a chocolate business. He did not publish his poems until he returned from exile.

On 9 May 1942 Das Freie Buch (El Libro Libre) was established in Mexico City, on the anniversary of the book burning of 1933. Its direction was collectively assumed by a group of writers including Ludwig Renn, André Simone, Bodo Uhse, E. E. Kisch and Leo Katz. Dr Paul Mayer, who was the publishing editor, had previously worked for Rowohlt. Its publications were financed by subscription: enough readers wishing to read a particular book had to order it in advance for it to be printed. Royalties went not to authors but to help finance other books. El Libro Libre was also supported by lectures. Its is remarkable that most of the books published in this way sold out in two months after their appearance. The undertaking was so unusual that a writers' delegation was received by the Mexican president. From 1942 to 1946, El Libro Libre published twenty-two works in German and four in Spanish. At least 54,000 copies were printed, including some of the most important works of exile literature.[30] The situation of this publishing enterprise steadily improved, and authors soon began to receive royalties on bookshop sales. Several other exile publishing companies were also founded in Latin America: Notbücherei Deutscher Antifaschisten in Rio de Janeiro, Estrellas, Quadriga and Cosmopolita in Argentina, which published some poetry collections (Paul Zech), but none of these attained the renown of El Libro Libre. Anna Seghers's *The Seventh Cross* went on to become a bestseller in the United States.[31]

The Émigrés in Wartime America

1. AMERICA'S ENTRY INTO WAR

THE UNITED STATES AND THE WAR IN EUROPE

We have to state that modern war, waged in the Nazi manner, is a repugnant affair. We do not like it. We do not want to join it. But this is where we are, and we shall fight with all our resources.

F. D. Roosevelt

a giant nation was rising, still half-asleep, to go to war.

Bertolt Brecht, *Journals*, 8 February 1941

Even if isolationism remained the United States' official doctrine, American opinion was profoundly shaken by the outbreak of war in September 1939. On 24 August, Roosevelt had sent a final message to Hitler calling for peace. The invasion of Poland deeply shocked American consciousness, which on the whole – with the exception of a minority of the German-American population – had been fundamentally hostile to Hitler's Germany. A poll taken in September 1939 showed that 44 per cent of Americans were prepared to accept sending troops to Europe if Britain and France risked defeat. 'No one, not even a neutral, can be asked to close his mind or his conscience,' Roosevelt again declared. On 27 October, accordingly, the neutrality law was modified and became discriminatory. Yet the United States remained in a state of expectancy, confining itself to reminding the Soviet Union of its friendly relations with Finland. Sumner Wells was sent to Europe in February 1940, with the aim of obtaining information. He met Count Ciano, President Lebrun, Daladier, Ribbentrop and Churchill. The German attack on Denmark and Norway once again brought official censure from Roosevelt, who tried to intercede with Italy to prevent it from entering the War. At the same time as the United States was multiplying its diplomatic initiatives, without the least success, it continued supplying weapons to the democracies. On 16 May, Congress voted an increase in the military budget, and on 25 May an Office for Emergency Management was established. After the fall of France, America daily grew more aware that this danger would not spare it. The many opinion polls to which Americans were regularly subjected[1] showed that in 1939 less than 0.1 per cent of the public were favourable to Germany. In March 1940, 8.7 per cent were ready to declare war on Germany, and 52 per cent wanted to aid the democracies without military commitment. By September 1941, 26 per cent of the population accepted the idea of America joining the War, and 47 per cent of sending an army to Europe to fight Hitler. If the fall of France had put an end to the myth of neutrality, from 1941, when Hitler railed against the United States, the American press denounced in increasingly violent terms the threat that Germany represented. The rejection of Japanese proposals for China made the situation in Asia ever more explosive. If an attack on Pearl Harbor had been seen as possible, it was nonetheless deemed highly improbable. On 8 December, Congress voted, unanimously but for one vote, that a state of war existed. On 11 December, Hitler declared war on the United States. The attack on Pearl Harbor and the trauma it aroused put an end to the era of diplomatic negotiations. Within a few weeks, the country's immense economic potential was put to the service of war. The population applied itself to the task just as immediately, without enthusiasm but with a sense of duty.

This new situation had its effect on the position of the émigrés. More than ever, they sought to associate themselves with the war effort against Hitler, and the certainty of an Allied victory over Germany led them to question the shape this would take, and what a future Germany would be like.

THE ÉMIGRÉ INFLUENCE ON UNITED STATES POLICY

Long before American entry into the War, a number of US public figures brandished against the émigrés the old accusation – already heard in 1939 in right-wing French papers such as *Gringoire* – that they would not stop interfering in the internal affairs of the countries that had accepted them, and were stoking up passions and hatreds, pushing for war with Germany. Though no one in America went so far as to say that Heinrich Mann wanted to declare war on Germany to regain his position in Berlin, and that there was a 'Jewish hatred' against Germany, the émigrés were reproached with campaigning against United States neutrality and seeking to influence its foreign policy.

The American right were ever ready to denounce 'Communist tendencies' at all levels of the administration, in the army, the press, the cinema and cultural life in general. Some Communist émigrés and their friends were made directly responsible. But if the facts are objectively noted, we have to acknowledge that neither in Europe nor America did the émigrés manage to have the least decisive influence on the policies of the countries in which they took refuge. In the United States, they absolutely did not have the means for this. Even when they contributed to the press and radio, they were in no position to play a significant role in forming American opinion. The administration was scarcely interested in their ideas. Hostility towards Hitler's Germany had been widespread since 1933, and is explained by other factors than the émigrés' influence. Jewish-Americans first of all were deeply sensitive to Nazi anti-Semitism, the boycott of Jewish shops, and the racial hatred that the Nazis erected into a system. It was in the large Jewish community that the first antifascist movements capable of influencing public opinion came into being.[2] The *Neue Volkszeitung*, to which Socialist émigrés contributed, certainly had regular articles on Nazi Germany, but information on the Third Reich was so common that the American population had no need of the émigrés to know what was going on in Berlin. The majority of press correspondents – such as William Shirer – were violently hostile to Germany and never refrained from distributing to America any information that could help their readers gain an exact idea of the regime's barbarity.

Besides, it is impossible to deny that American opinion was deeply pervaded by a spirit of tolerance. The Nazi regime seemed particularly abject and condemnable to it, even before the US government made any official pro-nouncement. The anti-Semitic persecutions, the burned books, the treatment inflicted on intellectuals, artists and academics, seemed hardly imaginable in a civilized country, and it was with a mixture of horror and disgust that main-stream American opinion received information on the Reich. Finally, America in the 1920s and 30s counted a certain number of left or simply progressive organizations that could only react negatively to the development of European fascism, whether it took the form of Nazi barbarity or the civil war in Spain. American opinion was always ahead of government policy in its visceral condemnation of Nazism, and it scarcely needed to wait until 1939–40 and the arrival of European refugees to display its hostility to Hitler. The accounts of the refugees could only confirm what Americans already believed. The disgust inspired by Nazism and its methods among all who felt attached to the democratic ideal was only reinforced by the stupidity of the 'American Nazis'. The parades with swastikas in the streets of New York, the gratuitous violence and the anti-Semitism proclaimed in their papers, gave a sufficient glimpse of what Nazism meant on a national scale in Germany.[3] Infinitely less dangerous to democracy than were for example Hearst and Coughlin, these American Nazis never managed to rally to their cause more than a tiny section of the German community,[4] and actually contributed to the development of antifascism. Denunciation of Nazism in the US press and within the Jewish community was so strong that it is remarkable any paper ever referred to the émigrés' analyses; these passed almost unnoticed, even if some of their political essays were made into successful books and the Deutsch-Amerikanischer Kulturverband, with many left-wing émigrés among its members, claimed to have fought with the Nazis in the streets of New York.[5]

A number of émigrés gave regular lectures against Nazism. Thomas Mann is the most famous example, though Gerhart Seger also gave many talks on Nazi propaganda in the United States.[6] But the anti-Nazi activities of the émigrés had so little weight on American opinion precisely because this was already of the same mind. Another possibility of influence was via American public figures with a certain prestige, but there again it is very hard to establish it with certainty. Though ex-Chancellor Brüning enjoyed a certain celebrity in American political circles, he never took an open stand against Germany. Thomas Mann, Ernst Toller and Klaus Mann were all received by President Roosevelt, but they were scarcely in a position to exert the slightest influence, and Klaus Mann himself acknowledged that he did not dare broach any political subject with the President.

This does not rule out that certain émigrés might have been able to exert an influence on other American public figures. One of the best-known examples is that of the journalist Dorothy Thompson, who sometimes acted as a spokesperson for émigré demands. A friend of Thomas Mann and Fritz Kortner, and associated with several of the émigrés, she violently denounced the demonstrations of the Bund, not hesitating to disrupt their meetings herself, and took part in various antifascist events alongside Thomas Mann.[7] It is certain that her close relations with German antifascists only strengthened her hatred of National Socialism. She was moved to come to the aid of all those that it threatened, and frequently intervened in favour of refugee intellectuals.[8] The influence that the émigrés might have exerted on her decision to support Roosevelt's candidacy in 1940 has often been analysed.[9] Fritz Kortner and Hans Jacob insist on the role of the émigrés in her shift of allegiance. Klaus Mann, however, who was also close to her, says nothing on the matter. It is true that after having as her secretary Fritz Kortner, who wrote articles under her name, she took on Hermann Budzislawski, the Communist émigré, who wrote political analyses for her to use. Though in the McCarthy era Thompson wrote 'How I Was Duped by a Communist', she was never unaware of Budzislawski's ideas, and as J. Radkau emphasizes,[10] the incriminating articles could have been signed by Thomas Mann. The same goes for Sinclair Lewis: the émigrés certainly provided him with information, but did not exert any real influence on his political positions. Dorothy Thompson's campaign against American neutrality, like her support for Roosevelt, was the logical conclusion of her hatred for Nazism and her desire to defend democracy. It is thus very hard to prove that the émigrés exerted the slightest influence on American policy or even on a single political figure.[11] We should also recall that the only attack on an émigré by an American politician was the famous speech by Senator Reynolds on 1 February 1939, in which he took issue with an article by Erika Mann in favour of US intervention. Fellow senators replied by asking why Erika Mann was so important that her views needed comment. Reynolds had to acknowledge in front of journalists that not only was he unaware that she was the daughter of Thomas Mann, but he did not have the slightest idea who Thomas Mann was. This simple example is enough to show the limited audience that even the most famous émigrés had in American politics.

Émigré magazines also give evidence of an extreme caution. Fearful of seeing a development of anti-Semitism in isolationist milieus, *Der Aufbau* abstained from any propaganda in favour of intervention, and even from expressing solidarity with persecuted Jews, in Poland for example. It is even surprising to note the degree to which the émigrés avoided any propaganda in favour of US entry into the War. Only the *Neue Volkszeitung* – which was not really an émigré magazine anyway – campaigned early on for intervention in Europe. When the

Nye committee[12] was established on 12 April 1934, charged with studying the influence of Wilson's decision to intervene in Europe on US policy, Nye was quite vehemently attacked by the émigré Social-Democrat Gerhart Seger, and a debate ensued between them. As a rule, however, the émigrés' caution in the positions they adopted, their refusal to get involved in American affairs, and their fear of arousing anti-Semitism, all make the assertion that they were in any way able to influence American policy highly questionable. They could only contribute to the developing hostility towards National Socialism, especially among intellectuals and in Hollywood.

ATTITUDES TOWARDS REFUGEES

being of german extraction, we are enemy aliens, and the fear is that we may have to leave the coast unless an exception is made for hitler's enemies. the japanese fishermen and farmers here are being put in camps.

Bertolt Brecht, *Journals*, 26 June 1942

How justified was this fear of Brecht's? The attitude of France and Britain at the outbreak of the War could suggest the worst: internment in camps, assignment of residence and systematic surveillance of all émigré activities. It is clear that following America's entry into the War, all nationals of the Axis powers were legally 'enemies'. Those targeted most were naturally Germans and Japanese. The sympathy for National Socialism that a fraction of the German-American community had displayed was evidently a ground for suspicion, especially with a view to possible acts of sabotage or spying. Fear of a 'fifth column', so dear to American cinema in the 1940s, was widely shared. The situation seemed all the more complicated in that the United States had not stopped accepting refugees from precisely those countries with which it was at war. Besides, the number of refugees, their dispersal, and the extent of the American continent, made surveillance almost impossible, let alone deportation or internment. The very fact that the American population was so composite in character gave the problem of loyalty a quite specific character. Aware of these difficulties, many émigrés sought immediately to display their attachment to their new homeland.

A fairly large number of refugees applied for naturalization as soon as possible after their arrival in the United States. This desire was very widespread among the 'racial émigrés', who generally did not plan to return to their countries of origin, also among a number of intellectuals and writers who had been stripped of German nationality or who did not envisage leaving America. The Davie Report's figures show a proportion of 96.5 per cent of refugees declaring that they wished to remain in the United States.[13] During the War years, the number of naturalizations overtook the number of new immigrants. Between 1935 and 1944, there were no less than 441,979 naturalizations. The procedure was more or less automatic for those who asked to join the US armed forces: not only did the army require it, but these 'enemy aliens', originating from countries at war with the United States, risked immediate execution in case of capture by the Axis powers. It was for this reason that

Congress passed in 1942 the second War Powers Act, to simplify the naturalization of members of the armed forces after three months' service. This
naturalization could be obtained even outside United States territory. In this
way 101,653 soldiers were immediately recognized as American citizens, including 10,997 in combat zones. Large as this figure was, it represented only half
the number of applications.

The conditions for naturalization were not in fact as simple as might be
supposed. The candidate had to have been in the country at least five years
(except for those in the armed forces), and naturalization was often delayed for
a further year or two in those states which had the most refugees. If the figures
show only 1 per cent of refugees having their application refused when they met
the requisite conditions, this naturalization was far from being a simple
formality. The candidate had to take a regular examination bearing on their
knowledge of English and of US political institutions. The Davie Report
certainly mentions a large number of émigrés who apologized for their poor
English, adding 'But I love America!'; yet even Thomas Mann had to pass a
rigorous exam. In a letter to Agnes E. Meyer of 7 January 1944, he described the
complex interrogation he had to undergo in order to become a US citizen.
Brecht wrote in his *Exile Dialogues*:

> Because of all this talk of freedom, I am full of enthusiasm for America and wanted to
> become an American citizen or at least move to this land of liberty. I ran from pillar to
> post. The one was busy and the other made some obstruction. The consul made me
> walk round the block four times on all fours, then insisted on a medical certificate, to
> establish that I didn't have calluses. After that, I had to declare under oath that I had
> no opinion. I swore this looking at the consul in the whites of his eyes; but he saw
> through me, and asked me also to prove that I had never had one in my life.[14]

A number of intellectuals and writers, for various reasons, never obtained
naturalization. This was the case with Lion Feuchtwanger, despite his celebrity.

When America entered the War, those refugees who were not yet naturalized were
declared 'enemy aliens' along with all citizens of Germany and its allies. A number
of them had their freedom immediately restricted. But this surveillance was fairly
limited, in no way comparable with the measures taken during the First World
War, or in Europe in 1939–40. The government understood that opinion was
broadly hostile to Hitler's Germany and that it was unnecessary to take draconian
measures towards people who had been its victims. Moreover, the FBI had
gathered a great deal of information on potential 'subversive elements' and knew
everyone who might represent some kind of danger to national security. They
were arrested on the night of 7 December 1941, or in the following weeks.

Out of five million émigrés registered in 1940, 1.1 million were classified as
'enemy aliens'. They were forbidden to live in certain areas such as military
zones, and to possess radio transmitters or cameras. German émigrés had to
register and have their fingerprints taken. Falling into the same category as the
Japanese led them to fear for the worst: but it was the Japanese who were most

heavily affected by these measures.[15] A number of protests were raised in the American press in defence of antifascist refugees. Gottfried Bermann Fischer reported a campaign in their support launched by Dorothy Thompson, and on 9 February 1941 he wrote to Thomas Mann asking him to make the same appeal to the government or send a delegation to Washington.[16] Mann then wrote directly to President Roosevelt (23 February 1941), emphasizing the injustice of classing as 'aliens of enemy nationality'[17] people who had fled their countries from being persecuted there. He asked that this discrimination be removed and that a clear line be drawn between 'potential enemies of American democracy' and 'victims of totalitarianism'. According to Bermann Fischer, this letter, signed by Thomas Mann, Albert Einstein, Bruno Frank, G. A. Borgese, Arturo Toscanini and Bruno Walter, had a successful effect. Though US nationality was only accorded to soldiers for the duration of the War, the émigrés were no longer treated en bloc as 'enemies', despite certain precautions being adopted.

The émigrés were now requested to deliver all their lectures in English.[18] An Alien Enemy Control Unit was established at the Department of Justice in order to keep check on nationals of Germany and its allies, and supervise all cases monitored by the FBI. A very small number of foreigners who gave rise to suspicion or had displayed signs of disloyalty were interned.[19] The Davie Report, moreover, points out that the immigration procedure was sufficiently rigorous that no Nazi managed to reach the United States in the guise of a refugee, nor was any suspect activity noted on the part of refugees throughout the war, as acknowledged by Thomas McColley, assistant to the director of the Alien Enemy Control Unit. The consul Paul Schwarz, in New York, was charged with gathering information on German immigrants, and Brüning provided him with information on several occasions.[20] The only effective restrictions were, from 1942, assignment of residence and the need to request a US district attorney for permission to travel a distance away. Refugees were not allowed to leave home after 7 p.m. These measures often led to absurd situations, as Ludwig Marcuse explains: Thomas Mann could go anywhere, being a Czech citizen, likewise Arthur Polgar who was Austrian, while Brecht theoretically had his residence assigned. Contrary to the situation in the First World War, there was no outbreak of violent hostility towards Americans of German origin. Ludwig Marcuse recalls just one incident: when he was talking with Alfred Döblin and Bruno Frank in a Los Angeles grocery, they were told to speak English or get out. The majority of émigrés thus accommodated themselves quite well to these measures. If Marlene Dietrich's husband moved to New York, feeling that surveillance there was less severe, very few of the exiles were distressed by these measures, with the exception of Erich Maria Remarque, who left the United States for Switzerland.

2. THE INTELLECTUAL MOBILIZATION

Like Brecht, Fritz Kortner notes in his autobiography how the majority of émigrés had the feeling after Pearl Harbor that America was like a sleeping giant. This enormous country, 'the richest on earth, found itself, when war was declared, with no army and no defence.'[21] In fact, after the initial defeats inflicted by the Japanese fleet and German submarines, mobilization of all America's energies and resources – material and moral – proved very effective.[22] No less extensive than the economic and military mobilization was the mobilization of intellectuals and émigrés in the war effort, which was surprisingly intense and rapid.

WRITERS AND THE EUROPEAN WAR

In the 1920s and 30s the United States had spawned a number of fascist or quasi-fascist movements of varying significance. As well as the Bund, there was the League for Liberty, the anti-Semitic supporters of Townsend, the Silver Shirts of William Dudley Pelley, the Hearst press, the movement for redistribution of wealth of Huey Long, the National Union for Social Justice of Charles E. Coughlin. Antifascist movements, however, developed on a more intensive scale.

In first place were the Jewish organizations that had early on developed leagues, committees and public meetings. Workers' and trade-union organizations were naturally concerned by the situation in Germany, but so were a large number of cultural movements created by film-makers, writers and actors, which went on to play an ever more important role in the politicization of intellectuals and their rallying to the War effort. This soon grew into a regular crusade for the defence of democracy. If the commitment of Hollywood film-makers and screen writers was especially effective, that of writers did not lag behind. Dorothy Thompson and Sinclair Lewis had been known for their opposition to Nazism since 1933. By their public statements and writings they made a large contribution in combating those who publicly displayed their sympathy for Hitler's Germany.[23] Many American writers denounced Nazism as a danger for global democracy. It was this awareness that led a number of them, such as Hemingway, to actively support the Spanish Republic, then enlist in the US forces. F. Scott Fitzgerald declared himself ready to fight against Germany, even though his physical debility no longer made this possible. John Steinbeck wrote his famous propaganda pamphlet for the air force, *Bombs Away*, in 1942. Hemingway asked to serve as a war correspondent for the North American Newspaper Alliance. When this was refused, he left for Cuba where he tried to organize his own counter-espionage network – the 'crook factory' – aiming to gather information on the movements of German submarines,[24] using a boat disguised as a scientific research vessel but armed with submachine-guns. Hemingway did not encounter any submarines, but he went on to take part in the Normandy landings as a correspondent for the RAF, and in the Rhineland campaign.

Military commitment in Europe or the Pacific was not the only way in which writers took part in the intellectual mobilization. One of the most astonishing documents on their activities is the thick volume *Writers' Congress. The proceedings of the conference held in October 1943 under the sponsorship of*

the Hollywood Writers' Mobilization and the University of California.[25] Twelve
hundred people took part in this congress on 1 October 1943 – a previous one
had been held in 1941 just after Pearl Harbor – which set out to study the
various ways of combining the efforts of intellectuals, writers and artists within
this mobilization. President Roosevelt sent a message to the Hollywood Writers'
Mobilization, as did other US public figures (Wendell L. Willkie, Henry A.
Wallace), to underline the importance they placed on this initiative. Messages
from British, Chinese, Latin American and Soviet delegations were also read
out.

Owen Lattimore, of the Office of War Information, explained the aims of this
body, which was charged both with information within the United States and
with counter-information abroad to combat Nazi propaganda. He called on all
American writers and intellectuals to take part in this mobilization against lies.
Almost every category of intellectual was represented, and each speaker
explained how they envisaged their involvement. Leading writers agreed to
collaborate on the production of propaganda pamphlets or make films on the
War. Others, enrolled in the Army, worked on documentaries. Scriptwriters and
animators undertook to make their characters take part in the war effort. The
question of the émigré contribution to the struggle against fascism was also
raised. A number of representatives of American writers recognized that the
émigrés had made a major contribution to making intellectuals aware of the
danger presented by Hitlerite Germany. The presence of a number of exiled
writers at this congress and the organization of seminars on a number of
questions connected with the war, the struggle against fascism and the role of
intellectuals, all contributed to giving the congress an exceptional symbolic
value. Thomas Mann and Lion Feuchtwanger took the floor and explained
their relationship to Germany and their work as writers in exile. A number of
American historians already sketched out at this stage a preliminary balance-
sheet of the contribution of the émigrés to America. This congress, with its
broad scope recalling in some ways that held in Paris in 1935, marked a
significant date in the history of the émigré community in the United States.
It showed, if only symbolically, the degree to which this mobilization, uniting
American intellectuals and émigrés, was sincere and general.

INTENSIFICATION OF ANTIFASCIST PROPAGANDA

If few writers wrote such direct propaganda texts as John Steinbeck's *Bombs
Away* (Hemingway said he would rather cut three fingers off his hand than have
written this), several were involved in propaganda activity alongside the
émigrés. The mobilization naturally reached its apogee in Hollywood, but
many writers vigorously contributed to propaganda tasks explaining the meaning of the War. Hemingway published an anthology, *Man and War*, and
contributed to a number of Hollywood films. Many animators made anti-Nazi
cartoons in which their heroes joined the Marines or infantry. Intellectuals
working on the radio organized antifascist broadcasts and a regular counter-
propaganda, to oppose Nazi broadcasts to Latin America.[26] Transmitters were

set up all around the world, designed for the US forces, and presented special programmes to which writers also contributed. Practically all sectors of American cultural life – cinema, literature, media, theatre, popular song – were affected by this unprecedented effort.

Many émigrés took part in these propaganda tasks, which were organized under the Office of War Information and the Office of Strategic Services. Aware of the impact of Nazi propaganda, the US government had this studied by sociologists, political scientists and psychoanalysts – a work to which émigrés made a notable contribution – in order to develop an effective counter-propaganda. This led to the printing of millions of leaflets in German and Italian (also in French), launched by Flying Fortresses at a rate of up to seven million a week,[27] explaining to the enemy troops that they had the choice between living for Germany and Italy or dying for Hitler and Mussolini. Thousands of safe-conducts were also dropped on the German forces, inviting them to surrender to the Allies. A small newspaper, *Amérique en Guerre*, was regularly dropped over France, explaining the US war effort and detailing the advance of the army in North Africa. The *Sterne Banner* was dropped on German cities, and the *Frontpost* in Italy, announcing the imminent defeat of the fascist regimes. Émigrés worked on most of these undertakings, drafting leaflets, writing articles, studying scientifically the mechanisms of Nazi propaganda, as well as analysing and commenting on the political situation. A large number of these refugee propagandists lost their lives in American uniform.

THE ÉMIGRÉS AND MILITARY ACTION

Concerned as they were to display their loyalty to the United States as well as fighting Hitlerite Germany, a large number of émigrés enlisted in the US Army. Following an investigation by the director of the Selective Service System, refugees originating from countries at war were enrolled in the Army and immediately naturalized. At least 33 per cent of male refugees fought with the US forces. A large number of them asked to be sent to Europe, for evident reasons: a desire to confront Hitler's armies directly, but also to know what had happened to their parents and relatives, whether they had been sent to camps or were still in Germany. Fritz Kortner's son fought in the US Army, so did Brecht's. The son of Hubertus Prinz zu Löwenstein was wounded several times during the Italian campaign, and finally killed in 1944. Not until 1949 was his father able to visit his grave. Klaus and Erika Mann both became war correspondents.[28]

A number of émigrés were assigned special missions, because of their perfect knowledge of their home country's language.[29] The Davie Report mentions young Jewish émigrés fighting in Europe and being awarded the US Bronze Star, after their fathers had been decorated with the Iron Cross in the First World War. If the role of émigré scientists in the US atom bomb project is well known, a number of scholars in the humanities were appointed to the US Army's ancillary services and even worked on counter-espionage in the OSS. Herbert Marcuse was one of its members, charged with gathering information on Hitlerite Germany. Paul Lazarsfeld studied the mechanisms of Nazi propaganda, as did the psychoanalyst Ernst Kris. Hans Simons, formerly employed in the Prussian interior ministry (1924–30), then dean and vice-president of the New School for Social Research, became an adviser to the US secret services in 1943–44. There was even a plan to organize a committee for sabotage and espionage in Germany with émigrés working for the OSS, but the State Department rejected this.

Those unable to enlist in the armed forces sought to display their loyalty towards the United States in any way possible: they helped the Red Cross, gave blood, bought and sold War Bonds, made many interventions on the radio, encouraged by the OWI, to support the war effort and explain its meaning. The CBS sent Norman Corwin to Britain. Orson Welles made a number of reports on the situation in Latin America. Larry Lesueur travelled to the Soviet Union. The magazine *Der Aufbau* had had a radio station since 1938. A Cooperating Agency for Refugee Radio Programmes was established early on, and from 1941, the *Aufbau* station also broadcast many programmes in German, including plays and information bulletins. In 1942, in the context of the German-American Loyalty Hour, the programme 'We Fight Back' was organized, with analyses of Nazism, Nazi ideology, and Nazi activities in the United States. Many broadcasts called for donations under the slogan: 'Each dollar a bullet against Goebbels'. During these broadcasts aimed at German-Americans, the music of émigré composers such as Kurt Weill or Paul Dessau was played. The German political situation was analysed by different figures, and lectures were also organized. Victor Ridder, publisher of the *New Yorker Staatszeitung*, intervened on the theme 'Why German-Americans should fight the Nazis', while Thomas Mann broadcast 'On the Meaning of This War'. A number of antifascist plays were broadcast in serial form. The 'We Fight Back' team organized a major event on the anniversary of the book burnings, in which Franz Werfel, Walter Mehring, E. J. Aufricht, Kurt Weill and Lotte Lenya took part. In the course of the evening, original manuscripts and drawings were sold to raise funds for the War Bond Drive.[30] Starting in 1942, Thomas Mann gave a monthly radio talk in both German and English, with the aid of the BBC which broadcast it to the Reich. He also wrote articles for the Office of War Information, and took part in public meetings held by Jewish organizations. These émigré activities steadily reached a prodigious diversity, especially on the East Coast, where the exiles were very numerous and the environment was most politicized.

3. HOLLYWOOD AT WAR

Though seen by many as simply a factory of dreams, an artificial world made up of fantastic and futile characters, Hollywood reacted spontaneously and with enthusiasm to the war effort, ready for the greatest sacrifices. There had perhaps never been so great a unity among actors, scriptwriters, directors and producers as during the War years, when all shared the goal of making their contribution to the common cause. The greatest Hollywood actors undertook tours across the country to sell War Bonds. Dorothy Lamour, Carole Lombard and Marlene Dietrich used their popularity to win the generosity of their admirers. While many actors and singers left for the front to distract the GI's, the goddesses of the American cinema auctioned their kisses in support of the weapons industry.

Hollywood at war was a strange world: fragile, and cut off from reality by its high salaries and myths, yet capable of a genuine generosity. Immediately after Pearl Harbor, a large number of representatives of the film industry offered their support, especially members of the Screen Actors' Guild. Producers, actors and cameramen shot films on fascism and the war, documentaries and adventure films designed to win the country to the democratic cause. The most famous Hollywood idols left the studios to become war correspondents, officers, or simple soldiers. True, the War was also a commercial theme, and in many films of the 1940s it served simply as a suitable backdrop for moving the public. In most Hollywood films one might seek in vain for the slightest political note. But the commitment of many members of the Hollywood microcosm was sincere and complete. This immense leap can only be understood on the basis of the politicization that had overtaken the cinema capital in the 1930s, and was reinforced by the presence in California of a large number of émigré writers and artists.

THE DREAM OF AN ANTIFASCIST POPULAR FRONT

A number of very different factors lay at the root of the growing politicization of Hollywood in the years 1936–39. The economic crisis had severely ravaged California, leading to poverty and unemployment.[31] This was the context in which the EPIC (End Poverty in California) movement was born, championed by Upton Sinclair, who narrowly missed being elected as governor in 1934, but was boycotted by the film producers whom he had violently attacked.[32] The disgust that a number of film workers felt towards the studio bosses, and MGM in particular, pushed them into political commitment. A certain internationalist spirit steadily grew with the rise of European fascism and the Spanish war. The Communist party enjoyed a genuine influence in Hollywood. The arrival of antifascist émigrés brought Germany that much closer. The interest that Hollywood displayed for the European situation is also explained by the fact that a large number of directors were of European origin, especially from Hungary (Wajda, Lukas, Cukor) or Germany (Lubitsch). In 1939–40, certain Californian homes became regular meeting-places for Hollywood circles and émigrés. Charlie Chaplin received them generously. At Salka Viertel's celebrated 'Sundays at Salka's', one could meet Brecht, Feuchtwanger, Vladimir Pozner, Christopher Isherwood, Charlie Chaplin, Hanns Eisler, G. Sklar and B. Taffel. Thomas Mann's house was another meeting-place, as was that of Franz Werfel and Alma Mahler. Even if these were mostly microcosms centred around one or two personalities, and separated from other microcosms formed by other émigrés, there can be no doubt that the presence of all these German exiles did not leave Hollywood indifferent. It was Nazism that had led Peter Lorre, Luise

Rainer, Max Steiner, Franz Waxman, E. W. Korngold, Hanns Eisler, Fritz Kortner, Bertolt Brecht, Billy Wilder, Max Reinhardt, Leopold Jessner, Wilhelm Dieterle, Fritz Lang, Lion Feuchtwanger and Vicki Baum to take refuge in California. The Americans were aware of this.

If the United States as a whole was not greatly affected by the German intellectual emigration, the same was not true of Hollywood, which seems to have immediately taken up the exiles' cause. The latter, moreover, were active within the antifascist organizations that had grown up in the film world. Sonja Dahl[33] became executive secretary of two antifascist groups in Hollywood. Progressive circles there did not just want to oppose fascism in Europe, but to fight in America anything that resembled it.[34] It was all these reasons that led Hollywood writers and artists to establish a kind of Popular Front, which counts as one of the greatest intellectual mobilizations that the United States has known. The image of the French Front Populaire, as well as the new tactics indicated by Dimitrov, led a number of American political and intellectual movements to establish a democratic unity against fascism. Without any rigid structures, this Popular Front combined organizations with four shared objectives: to bring the Roosevelt administration to an active commitment against National Socialism, aid the defenders of democracy and the victims of fascist regimes, combat in the United States anything that resembled the fascist movements, and promote social reforms and justice in American society.

A number of organizations and groups responded to this appeal on the basis of purely humanitarian demands (aid for the victims of the Spanish war and the Hitler regime, support for the refugees). The most important components of this Popular Front were:

• The League against War and Fascism
• The American Youth Congress
• The Joint Anti-Fascist Refugee Committee
• The League of American Writers
• Labor's Non-Partisan League
• The Workers' Alliance
• The Writers' and Artists' Committee for Medical Aid to Spain
• The Abraham Lincoln Brigade
• The National Lawyers' Guild

together with the three major antifascist organizations specific to Hollywood:

• The Hollywood Anti-Nazi League
• The Motion Picture Artists' Committee
• The Motion Picture Democratic Committee.

One of the most active figures in this movement was the writer Donald Ogden Stewart. From a bourgeois background, and successful as an author, he had the idea of introducing a 'Communist' character in one of his plays. He accordingly decided to read up on a number of Marxist works, was convinced by the ideas in them and became an activist. Settling in Hollywood in 1936, he sympathized with the Communist party, put his own wealth at the service of the committees struggling against fascism, and tirelessly collected funds for the victims of German fascism, supporting all the antifascist initiatives and operations. The Anti-Nazi League (1936–39) was one of the most active movements in the film milieu. It included such famous figures as Dorothy Parker, Donald Ogden Stewart, Fritz Lang, Fredric March, Oscar Hammerstein, as well as a large number of anonymous activists. Alongside the personalities on its letterhead, it had an executive board made up of a large number of Hollywood actors, producers such as Carl Laemmle and Jack Warner, Communist writers such as John Howard Lawson and Sam Ornitz. A number of émigrés had been involved in the League's foundation, including Hubertus Prinz zu Löwenstein, who made contact with cinematic circles by way of Willi Münzenberg and Otto Katz.[35] The latter put the prince in touch with a number of film personalities, and they immediately organized fundraising banquets to aid victims of the Nazi regime. This initiative received the support of such major producers as Thalberg, David Selznick, Sam Goldwyn and Walter Wanger.

The Hollywood League against Nazism (later called the Hollywood Anti-Nazi League) was established around the same time, holding its first public event on 23 July 1936 with 500 guests at the Wilshire Ebell Theater, followed in the autumn by a meeting at the Shrine Auditorium attended by over 10,000 people who had come to hear Eddie Cantor, Oscar Hammerstein, Dorothy Parker, Gale Sondegaard, Frank Shaw, Isaac Pacht, J. W. Buzzell (AFL) and John Lechner (American Legion), as well as a number of figures from the business world. The League soon became one of the most important organizations in the Popular Front. With its 5,000 members, it brought together a large number of figures from the cinema: actors, directors and scriptwriters. It included liberals as well as radicals and Communists, even a few conservatives. Its paper, *Hollywood Now*, published information on fascism and on Nazi activities in the United States. It had two weekly radio broadcasts, and organized a constant round of banquets and public meetings. In January 1937, for example, it held an inter-racial event against Nazism at the Philharmonic Auditorium, and another on the Spanish war at the Shrine Auditorium, with the participation of Ernst Toller and André Malraux, as well as a radio broadcast 'Four Years of Hitler'. It also held demonstrations outside German consulates against the bombardment of Almeria, called for a boycott of Japanese products when Japan invaded China, intervened against the American Nazi party congress held in Los Angeles, and made several appeals to President Roosevelt to condemn Hitler Germany. The League was also behind the Hollywood boycott of two fascist figures who came to visit: Leni Riefenstahl and Vitorio Mussolini, nephew of the *Duce*, who each played an important role in their respective country's film industries. In domestic politics, the League worked to defend Roosevelt's initiatives such as the Federal Theater Project.[36] Already at this time, it came up against a number of opponents even within Hollywood, especially the powerful Screen Playwrights, who accused it of being a Communist tool. The Anti-Nazi League sent a number of telegrams to Roosevelt, without success, to obtain the dissolution of the increasingly notorious Dies Committee.

The war in Spain was no less important than the arrival of the refugees in the mobilization of Hollywood. American antifascist organizations undertook many initiatives and demonstrations in support of the Spanish Republic, deploring the US government's neutrality.[37] Hollywood organized banquets to raise funds for the Republican side. Following André Malraux's speech at the Shrine Auditorium in January 1937, the League collected funds for ambulances and medical supplies, unable to provide weapons and matériel. Dorothy Parker and Lillian Hellman visited Spain in 1937 and returned with shattering reports. Together with left-wing writers including Dashiell Hammett, Donald Ogden Stewart, Dudley Nichols, Lester Cole, Julius and Phillip Epstein, directors such as John Ford and Lewis Milestone, and actors Melvyn Douglas, Luise Rainer, Paul Muni, Fredric March, Gale Sondergaard and John Garfield, they founded the Motion Picture Artists' Committee to Aid Republican Spain (MPAC). A large number of its members also worked with the Joint Antifascist Refugee Committee, formed by veterans of the Spanish war and directed by Dr Edward Barsky. This committee helped refugees interned in the French camps to reach the United States, as well as those who were already in Latin America.

The MPAC rapidly gained a membership of over 15,000, holding many debates, lectures and fund-raising banquets for the Spanish Republic. It formed a political cabaret, 'Sticks and Stones', to which some of the most famous Hollywood screen writers contributed. It showed John Howard Lawson's film on the Spanish civil war, *Blockade* (United Artists, 1938), and the profits enabled eighteen ambulances to be sent to Spain. A year later, the same committee also raised funds by exhibiting Picasso's *Guernica*. It was in the same context of the Popular Front that Lillian Hellman, Dorothy Parker, Hermann Shumlin, A. Macleish and Ernest Hemingway worked with historians to produce *Spanish Earth*, directed by Joris Ivens. The film was shown in Hollywood and at the White House, raising more than $35,000 for the Spanish cause. Even if these campaigns for the Spanish Republic proved unable to change the course of events, they led to a raising of consciousness and a far-reaching intellectual mobilization.

DECLINE AND COLLAPSE OF THE POPULAR FRONT

The Hollywood Popular Front was characterized by a number of mobilizations, public meetings and fund-raising activities in support of Spain and the victims of fascism, without having any very precise political structure. It brought liberals and Communists together. It is hard to know how many people were effectively involved in its actions. American historians estimate that through the various committees these campaigns mobilized at least 25 per cent of those working in the film industry, or some 15,000 people, with some fifty or seventy-five playing a leading role.[38] Very often, enthusiasm and idealism took the place of genuine political awareness. The most politicized elements were screen writers rather than actors.[39] It was these who issued all the warnings, articles and position statements against fascism. Even if being 'on the left' was fashionable in certain circles, for others it was a sincere commitment. It is certainly easy to wax ironic on the toasts made to the Red Army at these antifascist banquets attended by stars with their silk robes and Cadillacs: Hollywood however fought with the weapons at its disposal. And the $100 a plate charged for these banquets did indeed go to the Spanish Republic. One could seek in vain for the same spirit of solidarity in other sectors of American life, even cultural life. True, the Hollywood mobilization did not change the course of history, and even the support it gave to the Spanish Republic was inadequate, but these voices raised against fascism and the funds collected for the refugees were far from useless.

The reasons for the collapse of the Popular Front are several. The Nazi–Soviet pact certainly disconcerted a number of American Communists. It was difficult to understand or justify it. Many Communists saw it as a betrayal of the international antifascist struggle simply in the interest of the Soviet Union. Fellow-travellers broke ranks with the Communists, as did liberals who had seen the USSR as the sole great opponent of National Socialism. The majority of American antifascist organizations experienced irreversible splits.[40] The invasion of Finland shifted liberal opinion further against the Soviet Union. The justification for the pact given by American Communists, in maladroit terms, only managed to isolate them, while a certain number of liberals became anti-Soviet and refused any further connection with the Communists. The early enthusiasm gave way to a period of distrust that increasingly limited possible activities. One of the rare organizations to survive was the Motion Pictures Democratic Committee (MPDC), led by the actor Melvyn Douglas and the screenwriter Philip Dunne. A very popular actor, Douglas had visited Germany in 1936 and been deeply shocked. On his return he joined the Anti-Nazi League. Philip Dunne, who was very well-known in Hollywood,[41] had been active in the defence committee for Sacco and Vanzetti, and agreed to work with the Communists despite being hostile to them.[42] The Nazi–Soviet pact also broke apart the MPDC, which no longer managed to organize any real mobilizations. Torn apart by internal struggles between liberals and Communists, it steadily lost its members.

The majority of liberals left the Hollywood antifascist organizations, accusing the Communists of betrayal. They organized new committees, such as the California Citizens Council, William Allen White's Committee to Defend America by Aiding the Allies, the Union for Democratic Action and Fight for Freedom – the objectives of which were now more national than international. These 'new liberals' included a certain anti-Communism in their programmes, refusing to accept members or supporters of the CPUSA in their organizations. Melvyn Douglas himself called for a struggle against Communism.[43] Other liberals equated Communism and fascism, and expelled Communists from their ranks.[44]

THE CAMPAIGN FOR INTERVENTION

Hollywood in 1939 and 1940 also saw the most active campaign for US intervention in Europe. The isolationist cause was championed by three bodies: America First, which embodied the traditional isolationism of the right; Keep America Out of the War, of Socialist inspiration and led by pacifists; and the CPUSA, which following the Nazi–Soviet pact launched four anti-war organizations: the American League for Peace and Democracy, the Hollywood Peace Forum, the American Peace Mobilization, and the Keep America Out of the War Committee.

These organizations held frequent public meetings in support of peace, blaming Hitler's victories on the foreign policies of France and Britain, which had done so much to destabilize Europe. The various organizations linked to the Communist party bent their efforts to defend the cause of US non-intervention in the European conflict. On 6 April 1940 a 'Living Newspaper on Peace' was organized at the Olympic Auditorium in Los Angeles, written by Michael Blankfort, Gordon Kahn and Albert Maltz. Other left movements campaigned for neutrality. But the situation became increasingly confused, as some conservative figures from the film world were in favour of intervention. The entire intellectual left, which had achieved such remarkable mobilization against fascism, was now disoriented. Broken into factions, it was notable how among its former supporters, hostility towards the Soviet Union was now as widespread as that towards Germany. Doubt also started rising within the Communist movement. Irving Stone left the committee of the League of American Writers, which refused to distinguish between Hitler's war of aggression and the Allied defence. Even within the Keep America Out of the War Committee, doubts spread about the rightness of the position adopted.

On 21 June 1941, the American Peace Mobilization launched a 'National Peace Week'. But news of the invasion of the USSR reversed the entire Communist strategy: the War ceased to be a conflict between imperialist powers and became a crusade against fascism. The CPUSA immediately established the American People's Mobilization in support of the Allies. In July, the League of American Writers called for a similar mobilization, 'The Service of Our Country'.

Anti-Communism now abated within the general population in favour of a genuine sympathy towards the Soviet Union.[45] As late as autumn 1946, more than $85 million was collected for Soviet reconstruction. But the CPUSA had lost its credibility among a large number of intellectuals, and liberals distrusted its 'dialectical reversals'. It was in these difficult circumstances, however, that the mobilization effort in support of the War was to intensify among the Hollywood intellectual and cinematic milieu.

MOBILIZATION AND RADICALIZATION: CINEMA IN THE FACE OF FASCISM AND WAR

When war was declared, all men (and women) were mobilized, not just by the Army, but also for all other objects of the great 'enterprise'. We actors were no exception.

Anyone able to talk, tell stories, make jokes, sing or dance was invited to put themselves at the service of the country.

Marlene Dietrich, *My Life*

After the Pearl Harbor disaster, a large number of Hollywood figures offered their support to the government, establishing in December 1941 a Victory Committee that set out to entertain soldiers on their different bases and at the front. Some 2,327 artists took part in these unpaid tours, designed to sustain the morale of American forces. The Hollywood Writers' Mobilization was formed on the same lines, including some 3,500 members from the Screen Writers' Guild, Radio Writers' Guild, Screen Readers' Guild, Screen Cartoonists' Guild, American Newspaper Guild, Independent Publicists, etc., who immediately devoted themselves to producing propaganda material. The film industry as a whole was among the most enthusiast supporters of the war effort.

A large number of actors volunteered for the armed forces, and so even did producers. Darryl Zanuck left Twentieth Century Fox after the attack on Pearl Harbor and rejoined the army as a war photographer, leaving the studios to his assistant William Goetz. Frank Capra became a colonel and made propaganda films. John Huston found himself heading a photographic patrol in the front line at Monte Cassino and on other Italian battlefields. John Ford, Anatol Litvak and William Wyler similarly joined up. Some fought as simple soldiers, others made documentaries or other films designed to explain the purpose of the United States' involvement in the War. The greatest Hollywood actors went to sell War Bonds or took part unpaid in tours organized for the GIs,[46] if they did not themselves work on antifascist radio broadcasts.

Many authors and screenwriters also worked on propaganda tasks. Donald Ogden Stewart wrote *Keeper of the Flame* (1943) for MGM, one of the best antifascist films made in the USA. Other screenwriters fought in the army.[47] Some were employed in the cinema division of the Office of War Information (Waldo Salt, P. Dunne, R. Riskin, L. Bercovici, K. England, B. Schoenfeld). Karl Foreman and Leopold Atlas worked with Frank Capra in the Signal Corps. The years 1941–45 were a happy time for radical screenwriters: emerging from the shadow of the studios, they were called on to take part in the war effort without hiding their political ideas. Still more, the social and critical dimension of the cinema was publicly recognized. Films directly related to the events tearing Europe apart mushroomed: *Destination Tokyo* (Maltz), *Action in the North Atlantic* (Lawson), *Blood on the Sun* (Cole), *The Cross of Lorraine* (Lardner). The public taste itself seems to have evolved, and Hollywood began to investigate the possibility of making 'responsible' commercial films. Curiously enough, these films created a kind of unanimity around them: even HUAC found nothing to complain of in the radical films made during the War. Optimism seemed to have been rekindled among the Hollywood intellectuals: liberals and Communists worked together once more. The image of the Soviet Union was restored, and the CPUSA found new adherents. Throughout the War, Hollywood saw a multiplication of committees in support of victims of fascism and refugees, and the generosity shown towards them became the immediate sign of a new political awareness. The Motion Picture Democratic Committee changed its name to the Hollywood Democratic Committee, and the Hollywood Writers' Mobilization sought to attract writers from all sides. A new Popular Front was being born, cemented by the war effort.

Trade unions and writers' organizations worked together.[48] The committees reaffirmed their support for Roosevelt, bent themselves to resolving labour disputes and utilizing writers and artists in projects of national defence. These various initiatives reached a culmination in the famous Hollywood Writers' Mobilization,[49] which sought to channel the entire intellectual effort to the service of the struggle against fascism and the victory of the Allies. Contrary to the Anti-Nazi League, the Writers' Mobilization wished to be pragmatic above all. It functioned as a regular government organization. Cinema was scientifically used as a propaganda weapon, which in the 1930s had been precisely one of the criticisms most frequently addressed to the Communists. Seminars on radio, cinema, the media and literature mushroomed on all sides to obtain the greatest effectiveness in the battle against Hitler, and all the émigrés in California were associated with these. One of the most concrete results of the Hollywood intellectual mobilization, associating producers, directors, actors, American and émigré writers, was the production of a number of anti-fascist works, including several of enduring interest.

The *boys* must find it hard to explain to themselves why they have to defend Oklahoma in Africa [. . .] and as for the question 'What are we fighting for?', it is almost impossible to give them an answer.

> Thomas Mann, letter to Agnes E. Meyer, 17 February 1943

settings in russia are now all the rage here. it is possible to put a love story in a tank. Guerrillas are a substitute for wild west films.

> Bertolt Brecht, *Journals*, 28 July 1942

Though a number of Hollywood film-makers and screenwriters had been politicized, they found it impossible for a long while to put their ideas into their films: they had to take account of producers, commercial demands and public taste. Before the United States entered the War, an antifascist film would immediately have been savaged by the Hearst press. In 1939, however, a number of films made in Hollywood ostensibly declared their hostility to Nazism. The first and more famous of these, *Confessions of a Nazi Spy*, violently attacked the activities of the Bund, which it presented as a 'fifth column'. Edward G. Robinson, who was responsible for the film, and director Anatol Litvak, were immediately subjected to death threats from American Nazis. The writer was John Wexley, who would also work on the Brecht and Fritz Lang project *Hangmen Also Die*. Litvak had left Germany in 1934. This film showed for the first time the danger that pro-Nazi groups presented in the United States. It aroused a great deal of debate and remained unrivalled. Even Chaplin came up against difficulties when he wanted to make *The Great Dictator*. The government publicly made known to him that at the present time such a film would not be desirable. It was not premiered until 1940, by which time similar subjects were being tackled in a number of films: Litvak depicted the European situation in *A Rebel* and *The Gentle People*, Alfred Hitchcock in *The Fifth Column*, Ed Dmytrik in *Hitler's Children* (1943), Michael Curtiz in *Casablanca*. Fritz Lang followed *Hangmen Also Die* with *The Ministry of Fear* (1944), while Vincent Sherman directed *The Invisible Agent* in 1942 (with Conrad Veidt, Peter Lorre and Humphrey Bogart), *One Night in Lisbon*, and *International Lady*. Alongside these films that denounced Nazi espionage and infiltration there were some remarkable anti-Nazi comedies, the most famous of which remains Ernst Lubitsch's *To Be or Not to Be*. Richard Thorpe showed a worker persecuted by the Nazis in *A Pure-Blooded American*. If these films all gave a totally negative image of Hitler's Germany, it was because the producers at this time were still unconcerned by HUAC investigations. They were interventionist at a time when majority American opinion was not yet so. Several of the major producers – Darryl Zanuck, Jack and Harry Warner, Sam Goldwyn – financially supported the interventionist William Allen White Committee, and joined the Motion Picture Committee Cooperating for National Defense which distributed government propaganda films and documentaries. After Pearl Harbor this was known as the War Activities Committee. Hollywood and its émigrés thus became the favourite target of non-interventionist circles (the America First committee), which demanded that a Senate commission examine these films and rule on the propaganda they were spreading.

The opposition aroused by these first antifascist films in the conservative milieu was so great that the Dies Committee visited Hollywood from 9 to 28 September 1941 and a hearing was opened in Washington against the heads of MGM, Twentieth Century Fox, Warner Brothers and other studios. One of the films most attacked was Alexander Korda's *That Hamilton Woman*, and the Committee denounced the role played in the genesis of such films by 'non-American figures', i.e. the émigrés. The Dies Committee did not just take issue with antifascist films, but with all those that developed a certain social criticism: Fritz Lang's *Fury* (1936) and William Dieterle's two films *Blockade* (1938) and *Juarez* (1939) were particularly denounced. This situation was of course completely changed by the attack on Pearl Harbor, which not only put an end to US neutrality, but made the struggle against fascism an official political goal.

On 18 December 1941, the US government made known to the film studios that they could take part in the intellectual mobilization by making films on such themes as the nature of the enemy, his ideology, aims and methods, the Allies, the forces in struggle, the battlefront and the home front, 'what are we fighting for?' and 'the American way of life'. Hollywood set out to fulfil this task with enthusiasm, producing between 1942 and 1945 over a hundred films on the proposed themes, and 375 with a patriotic character.[50] American and émigré film-makers also worked on a wide range of films raising topical political questions.

Documentaries

Under the auspices of the War Activities Committee of the Motion Picture Industry, 16,000 cinemas showed weekly documentaries on the progress of the War. The majority of these were produced by the Office of War Information. Some of them encouraged enlistment in the armed forces (*Winning Your Wings* with Jimmy Stewart, or Frank Capra's famous film *Why We Are Fighting*). Several showed the battles waged by the US Army and its allies (*The World at War*, *Desert Victory*, *The City That Stopped Hitler*, *Our Russian Front*). Joris Ivens worked for the Special Service Division charged with producing films designed for the military and showing the moral character of their fight.[51] The films shot by Capra's unit, especially those showing combat on the Russian front, were made using Soviet footage.[52] British and Canadian documentaries were also shown in the United States.[53] The greatest American directors took part in this propaganda effort: besides the films of Colonel Frank Capra, Howard Hawks made *Air Force*, and John Huston *Report From the Aleutians*. Walt Disney, for this part, placed one of his production units at the disposal of antifascist propaganda, and his famous cartoon figures were seen at grips with the Nazis.[54]

Propaganda Films

A substantial number of films on Nazism were shot in Hollywood, showing Nazi atrocities in Europe and explaining why the United States had joined the War. These films were designed both for the American public, and especially for the military. Among the most famous were those of Capra, along with Litvak's *Why We Are Fighting*, *The Nazis Strike* (1943), *Divide and Conquer* (1943), and *The Battle for Russia* (1944), which explained to the GIs why they had to fight in Europe.[55] These films were made at the request of General Marshall, who gave Capra the idea of using extracts from Nazi films such as Leni Riefenstahl's *Triumph of the Will* to show soldiers the reality of Hitlerite Germany. Darryl Zanuck, for his part, let the US Army install its radio network at the Twentieth Century Fox studios.

Antifascist Films

Despite the War, Hollywood made few films that can really be called antifascist. The example of the conflictual collaboration between Brecht and Fritz Lang on *Hangmen Also Die*, which we shall analyse below, is enough to show how difficult it was to integrate this type of film into the American market: several owners of movie theatres feared they would lose their audience. The public were certainly ready to see films dealing with the War and Germany, but only so long as they could find their favourite actors in new adventures, even if in uniform. The majority of Hollywood films on fascism thus had a very weak political content, as the situations presented were so fanciful that it was hard to draw any lesson from them: gangsters were simply replaced by Nazi spies, mercilessly tracked down by Errol Flynn and Humphrey Bogart. The Mexican cowboy in *Valley of a Hundred Men* hunted German saboteurs like the cattle rustlers of old.

But these films cannot all be simply rejected as 'commercial'. Compromise with public taste was inevitable, in order to convey a message, and GIs were perhaps more readily persuaded that their presence in Europe was necessary if their favourite heroes were fighting alongside them. Even if they sacrificed heavily to commercial imperatives, these films made the American public more sensitive to the seriousness of events and what was at stake in the war. Films such as *Casablanca, Hangmen Also Die, The Hitler Gang, Mission to Moscow, The Seventh Cross*, and Lubitsch's *To Be or Not to Be*, cannot be viewed as insignificant. A number of émigrés also played in these films,[56] many of which raised very real issues. In 1940 George Froeschel made *The Moral Storm* for MGM, showing the breakup of a mixed Jewish–Aryan family, and in 1942 *Mrs Miniver* on the situation in Britain. It was also an émigré, Michael Curtiz,[57] who made *Casablanca*, in which Peter Lorre and Conrad Veidt – constant specialists in disturbing and sinister film roles throughout the 1940s – appeared alongside Humphrey Bogart and Ingrid Bergman.[58] Fred Zinnemann, who adapted Anna Seghers's fine novel *The Seventh Cross*, was also an émigré,[59] as were several of the actors in this film, including Helene Weigel, Alexander Granach and Felix Bressart.[60]

War Films

This was the type of film most commonly made in these years, whether depicting the War in a dramatic or a comic fashion. Even with such a subject, directors could manage to make the audience smile, if not actually laugh.[61] After Pearl Harbor, however, more realistic films were made, extolling the US armed forces[62] and the vicissitudes of combat.[63] These steadily came to embrace almost every episode of the Second World War: the Italian campaign, the Normandy landings, the war in the Pacific[64] and the liberation of France. Very few of these had any real artistic value, except for Michael Curtiz's *Mission to Moscow* and *Five Graves to Cairo*, in which Erich von Stroheim played an impressive Rommel.

'Hangmen Also Die':
A Failed Collaboration between Brecht and Fritz Lang

A particularly interesting example that illustrates the countless difficulties encountered by the émigrés when they tried to make genuinely antifascist films is provided by the experience of the collaboration between Fritz Lang and Bertolt Brecht[65] on the script for *Hangmen Also Die*.[66]

Brecht had been interested in the cinema since his youth. He had written a number of screenplays together with Arnolt Bronnen, but none of these were filmed. He had little luck with the film version of *The Threepenny Opera* directed by G. W. Pabst. Whilst Brecht wanted to accentuate the critical and political dimension of his work, the film company was only concerned to profit from the success of its songs. *Kuhle Wampe*, on the other hand, directed by S. Dudow and E. Ottwalt, seemed to match up to Brecht's initial political intentions. His entire relationship to cinema before 1933 shows that he was fascinated by its technical possibilities, even if it is not clear if he precisely understood its particular aesthetics. At the same time, Brecht distrusted the possible sidelining of his political or artistic intentions in the interest of the cinema's commercial requirements. Of the two film projects that had marked his career before 1933, he saw *The Threepenny Opera* as so far removed from his play that he launched a lawsuit against the company. He naturally lost, but drew an interesting sociological lesson from it. As for *Kuhle Wampe*, Brecht deemed the film a success and a genuine political force. The censorship authorities had the same opinion, and were quick to ban it. The film was only released, after much argument, in an amputated form.

In Hollywood, Brecht naturally sought to make new cinema contacts, even if he saw the California film industry as a 'lie market'. But these lies offered a living. In fact, despite the prodigious diversity of the scripts he came up with, none were of interest to the Hollywood producers. But if Brecht distrusted the cinema as a 'mass art', he was well aware of the propaganda possibilities it offered, especially within an apolitical population who knew so little about fascism. It was in this context that he came to collaborate with Fritz Lang in 1942. Starting from an historical fact – the assassination of Gestapo chief Reinhard Heydrich in Prague – Brecht had the idea of making an antifascist film able to reach a broad public. In the cinematic field, this was undoubtedly the biggest project envisaged by the émigrés in America. In spring 1945 Brecht also planned to make some short propaganda films with William Dieterle, designed for German prisoners of war in the United States, but the project did not get off the ground.[67]

On 27 May 1942, the Czech resistance killed 'Reichsprotektor' Reinhard Heydrich.[68] The following day, Brecht and Lang discussed (on the beach) the possibility of making a film on the hostages arrested by the Nazis after Heydrich's assassination.[69] The event was a considerable one for the exiles: not only the death of a hated figure, but a success for the antifascist resistance in Czechoslovakia. In June and July, Brecht and Lang worked on the script, which was to be called *The Hostages of Prague* or *Silent City*, and gathered as much material as they could. Very soon, however, both their artistic sensibilities and their political visions came into conflict. Brecht wanted the film to be a homage to the Czech people and resistance; Lang insisted on the need to make concessions to Hollywood taste. Brecht noted in his *Journals* on 29 June:

> i usually work with lang on the hostage story from nine in the morning till seven in the evening. there is a remarkable term that always crops up whenever the logic of events or of the continuity cries out to be discussed: 'the public will accept that'. the public accepts [. . .] commissars' corpses falling out of wardrobes and 'secret' mass meetings

during a period of nazi terror. lang 'buys' that kind of thing. interesting too that he is far more interested in surprises than in building up suspense.[70]

Brecht does not hide the fact that the financial dimension of the project is important for him,[71] but he is increasingly aware that the project is running into a blind alley, writing of the 'infinitely dismal fabrication this hostage film is that i have to occupy myself with these days' (27 July 1942).[72] From October, he worked on the script with John Wexley.[73] But soon the respective ideas of Brecht and Lang could scarcely be reconciled, each accusing the other of distancing himself from the original project. The film was now to be called *Trust the People* and was to emphasize the role of the resistance. Lang wanted a more Hollywood-type film, and Brecht noted on 16 October: 'I feel the disappointment and fear of the intellectual worker whose product is torn out and mutilated.' With Wexler's complicity, he set out to suppress some scenes, which Lang immediately restored, with the result that 'the main stupidities are now all included' (4 November). Other conflicts soon came to add themselves on the fundamental disagreement over the project. Brecht had asked for a part in the film – that of the flower seller – for Helene Weigel, but Lang was violently opposed, as Weigel had a strong German accent (24 November).[74] More than seventy pages of the script were rewritten before the work was broken off for good. Relations between Lang and Wexley deteriorated, leading Brecht to withdraw from the project, as his conception of the film was now completely opposed to Lang's. Brecht launched a complaint against Wexley,[75] with the aim of obtaining a share of the royalties, which resulted in Wexley being given sole authorship of the script. Despite the intervention of Lang and Eisler (who had written music for the film), he finally lost the case on 26 March 1943.

Hangmen Also Die appeared without Brecht's name, and the manuscript of his collaboration with Lang has been lost. If Lang viewed the film as the most political of those he made in America, Brecht described in his *Journals* with bitterness and irony the slow metamorphosis of an antifascist film into a conventional thriller. Commercial betrayal of an idea that sought to be first and foremost political? It is hard even today to know exactly what brought Brecht and Lang to this break. Brecht's version cannot be completely taken for granted, while Lang sought to minimize his differences with Brecht in the various interviews he gave. The 280 pages written by Wexley and Brecht were transformed into a script of 190 pages by a young American writer, Gunzburg, shortly before the shooting began. Chance had it that the appearance of Brecht and Lang before the Screen Writers' Guild tribunal was to be their last meeting. And eventually a secretary was paid $100 for giving the film its definitive title: *Hangmen Also Die*.

Perspectives on Germany

CONTROVERSIES OVER FASCISM AND THE GERMANS

One of the most regular and acute sources of suffering for the émigrés throughout the exile period was their relationship to Germany, which continued to steadily change. Some waited impatiently to return to the country they had been forced to leave because of Hitler, eager to contribute to its democratic renewal. Even if they had been compelled to change their nationality several times in exile, they never ceased to see themselves as Germans. Nazi Germany inspired in them a feeling of horror and disgust, but they refused to identify Hitler with the German people. As the German collapse approached, they often felt torn apart by conflicting feelings. They wished with all their heart for the end of the Hitler regime and the military destruction of the Nazis, but could not view the fate of the civilian population without despair. They listened to the Allied communiqués with a painful joy.

'My native city, however shall I find her? / Following the swarms of bombers,' Brecht wrote in a poem of this time,[1] and in his *Journals* he depicted the city of Cologne razed by the RAF: '1000 bombers were over it for one and a half hours. somebody said: if this is the start of a 2nd front then it is a good thing, for it could destroy hitler. of course, if no 2nd front follows, it is not such a good thing, for it will destroy germany.'[2] On 29 August 1943, he noted again: 'the heart stops when one reads the account of the aerial bombing of Berlin [. . .] it is impossible to see the end of the war.'[3]

J. R. Becher published a poem which ended with the invocation: 'My Germany'. Thomas Mann wrote to Agnes E. Meyer on 11 October 1944: 'My God, Aachen! Once again we have to reduce it to ashes. But the people hoisted white flags. *Poor people!*' Klaus Mann likewise asked whether it was possible to rejoice at this bombing of Germany, knowing it meant the destruction of its churches and theatres, and the death of thousands of children and civilians. He replied that if Hitler must fall, everything that led to his defeat was justified: 'The bombing weakens Hitler. I am for the bombing.'[4] In Argentina, Paul Zech wept on hearing the announcement of the bombing of Germany. But at the same time as feeling this terrible ambivalence towards the military communiqués – joy at seeing the Third Reich collapse, pain at the destruction of towns and the massacre of the civilian population – the émigrés were increasingly divided by controversies around such questions as the future of Germany, the 'responsibility of the German people', and the possible roots of National Socialism in a certain national tradition, both cultural and psychological, as some maintained. Certain questions were constantly debated among the émigrés, as well as among American intellectuals and political figures:

- Since no resistance movement managed to threaten the Nazi regime and slow down the advance of Hitler's armies, should we conclude that almost the entire German people accepted Hitler's policies?
- Was National Socialism an accident of German history or a phenomenon closely bound up with it?
- What type of future government and international control can guarantee peace in Germany and security in Europe?

The belief of many émigrés in the existence of an antifascist second front, an 'internal emigration', steadily eroded in the wake of Hitler's victories and territorial expansion. Brecht noted in his *Journals* on 15 August 1944:

but what about the question why the germans continue to fight? well, the population has the SS on its back, and besides it is without a political will in any direction, robbed of the few parliamentary institutions it had, questionable though they were, and economically under the heel of the possessing classes, as it has always been. its soldiers are fighting for their lives in the context of strategic and tactical operations [. . .]. the germans are still fighting because the ruling classes are still ruling.[5]

On 25 February 1945, Brecht again wrote:

all the while the lack of any uprisings against hitler in g[ermany] – source here of such angry comments – is perfectly comprehensible to me. for the first time i can see possibilities (from afar) when i hear that the reich is caught between a shortage of labour for the munitions industry on the one hand and unemployment on the other because raw materials are running out, the transport system is cracking up and the factories have been bombed. in st petersburg in 1917 the workers in the putilov plant rebelled when the bourgeoisie shut them out of the munitions factories.[6]

Many émigrés however were far removed from Brecht's effort of political understanding, and even hostile to it: they refused to distinguish between Germans and Nazis, and Brecht himself had to acknowledge (29 June 1942) that the 'high morale' of the German forces made a bad impression on the Americans. The majority of émigrés experienced the same doubt and fear. Thomas Mann wrote to Agnes E. Meyer on 28 January 1943: 'I would like to know how far the people themselves have fallen prey to this perversion.' He already inclined towards a certain fatalism, and confided again to Meyer on 18

June 1943: 'May the Allies triumph soon, so that the misery of Europe comes to an end; the spectacle is intolerable! What the conquerors do with their victory does not bother me so much. Everything follows its course, and history will correct the mistakes they will make. Just conquer.' When Mann heard of the execution of the White Rose students, however, he experienced a wave of sympathy towards Hitler's opponents in Germany, and wrote: 'They have gone through the fire of purgatory which we have not experienced, and in some respects they have gone beyond us.' Among many of the émigrés, however, exile had changed their deepest connection to their former homeland. Ernst Bloch already declared in 1939, in *Internationale Literatur*,[7] that impossible as it was to cast off one's roots in German culture, it was equally vain to curse one's country of asylum.

On 4 July 1942, Emil Ludwig delivered a violently anti-German lecture in Los Angeles, under the title: 'Win the War – Win the Peace'. The author of successful biographies, able to write equally well on Mussolini and Nefertiti, and detested by many of the émigrés, Ludwig kept up his denunciations of the 'German character' in a series of lectures and essays with frankly Germano-phobic titles.[8] An account of his lecture in the *New York Times*, under the heading 'Ludwig Asks Fight on German People', immediately kindled violent debate among the émigrés, who accused Ludwig of not only abjuring his German past but showing a veritable racism towards the Germans. Ludwig did not go so far as to propose enslaving the German people or wreaking vengeance on them, but he saw their sufferings as both inevitable and justified. He held it necessary to do everything to prevent a new revival of German imperialism as had happened under the Weimar Republic, maintaining that the German people had to be recognized as collectively responsible, they had to be subjected to 're-education' and all their political and cultural organizations placed under strict control.

In July 1943 the foundation of the Freies Deutschland committee was proclaimed in the Soviet Union. This set out to unite in a broad antifascist front, designed to hasten the end of the war, German soldiers and officers who were prisoners in the USSR along with Communist exiles and writers. Thomas Mann publicly hailed its manifesto.[9] On 1 August 1945 a number of émigrés met at the home of Berthold Viertel, including Brecht, Feuchtwanger, Bruno Frank, Heinrich and Thomas Mann, Hans Reichenbach and Ludwig Marcuse, and after long discussion signed an appeal[10] that hailed the establishment of the Freies Deutschland committee, advocating the creation of a 'democratic front' in Germany while maintaining the need to distinguish between the Hitler regime, those who had actively supported it, and the German people as a whole. This text however remained unpublished, as the following day Thomas Mann decided to withdraw his signature, fearing that even in this qualified form, it had the appearance of a 'patriotic declaration' with which 'the Allies could be stabbed in the back'. He held that it should not be seen as unjust if 'the Allies punished Germany for a good ten or twenty years'.

Brecht's *Journals* show the real hatred that broke out between him and Mann, at least at this time. If Thomas Mann accused Brecht and his friends of letting

Germany off the hook, Brecht responded by accusing Mann of statements (genuine or not) that he deemed were a regular incitement to murder:

> last Sunday when THOMAS MANN, with his hands in his lap, leant back and said: 'yes, they are going to have to kill half a million in germany,' it sounded absolutely bestial. it was a stuffed shirt speaking. no fighting was mentioned and none would be required for these deaths, it was a matter of punishment in cold blood, and why not revenge when even hygiene as a reason would have been bestial (for this was the resentment of an animal)?[11]

Yet Brecht was in no way tempted by any kind of German nationalism, as shown by his critical remarks on a certain nationalist sentiment displayed by J. R. Becher. On 10 November 1943 he noted in his *Journals*:

> döblin brought I[NTERNATIONALE] L[ITERATUR], 1943, iv, containing GERMAN DOCTRINE, an article by becher which stinks of nationalism. Again hitler's nationalism is quite naively accepted; Hitler just had the wrong brand, whereas becher has the right one. [. . .] i read: 'it is a new sense of community that is being formed, in order that germany's will be done, and that we should be the agents of this, and it is the highest thing of all that guards over such a common weal, the genuine of an eternal germany.' pass the sickbag, alice![12]

Both Mann's and Brecht's positions were in fact far more subtle than these few quotations suggest. One need only reread the texts that Thomas Mann devoted to the situation in Germany at this time, in particular his 'Appeals to Germans' broadcast on the radio, in which he takes care not to identify Germany with Hitler. In November 1940, Mann declared: 'No one in the world believes that the German people feel proud of the history made by despots, the wretched charlatanry made up of blood and tears', and 'I know that I only express the deepest aspiration of the German people themselves when I cry: Peace! Peace and freedom.'[13] But Mann also recognized, in December 1940, that the obedience of the German people 'becomes less pardonable every day', and his appeals became more pressing: 'Germans, save yourselves! Save your souls by refusing to believe and obey your tyrants, whose only concern is for themselves, not for you.'[14] In the same broadcast, he exclaimed: 'Your duty is to prove what the world still struggles to believe, that National Socialism and Germany are not one and the same thing. If you march with Hitler come wind and weather, right to the end, you will arouse a vengeance whose prospect horrifies all those who love Germany.'[15] And he warned the Germans that their fate would be totally different depending on whether they got rid of Hitler themselves, or this was done from without.

His message of August 1941 displays the controversies raging at this time on 'the difference between the German people and the forces reigning over them today'. Thomas Mann, for his part, held that 'National Socialism had deep roots in German life', and that Nazism was 'the degenerate and virulent form of ideas that have always born within them a germ of murderous perversion, but which have in no case been foreign to the old, the good Germany, civilized and cultivated'.[16] Nazism itself seemed to Mann to base itself on a whole tradition that included German Romanticism, nationalism and racism, to the point of forming 'today an explosive mixture that threatens civilization as a whole'. If Mann refused to simply amalgamate this tradition with Nazism, he did maintain that given 'the political immaturity of the German people', 'a long quarantine of caution and surveillance' would be inevitable after the War.

It is interesting to compare these warnings with the lecture that Thomas Mann gave on 29 May 1945 at the Library of Congress, 'Germany and the Germans', while he was working on his great novel *Doctor Faustus*. He reaffirmed there the link between National Socialism, the 'bad' Germany, and the 'good' Germany of Schopenhauer, Nietzsche and Wagner. Already in 1941, Mann had declared in 'Destiny and Duty' that 'Wagner's revolution in art was a phenomenon related to the National Socialist revolution.' In certain respects there seems to have been in his political thought a kind of regression towards the philosophical positions he had formerly defended in *Reflections of a Nonpolitical Man*, in which Germany already appeared as an irrational entity, unable to be satisfied with democracy. But while in his speeches of the 1920s Mann had invited his own class to commit itself to the defence of democracy, he seems to have believed after 1942 that an abyss would always cut the Germans off from democratic thought: 'This all seems to prove the original affinities that the German character had with National Socialism, and show that the latter is irremediably inherent to the German nature.'[17]

Thomas Mann held that it was impossible to plead for mercy for the German people without a bad conscience, and that any initiative designed to defend them could only appear as a betrayal of the Allied cause.[18] As long as Germany was not politically mature enough for democracy, it would constitute a factor of war in Europe. Without denying the importance of these questions, Brecht held that it was impossible to link National Socialism with a supposed 'German nature', and that necessary as it was to punish the Nazi criminals, it was immoral to demand punishment for the German people as a whole. Mann's position was doubtless the consequence of his philosophical options, the complex attitude he adopted towards the German irrationalist tradition, and a certain tendency to demonize Germany, for better or worse, depending on whether it was a question of denouncing its fateful character or exalting it, as he had done in the First World War. It was also the result of the increasingly bitter disappointment he felt in his American exile, noting that no popular revolt had occurred to shake the Nazi regime. Brecht believed that such a revolt was completely impossible given the effectiveness of the dictatorship and the absence of political organizations, and rightly feared that any demonization of Germany would only make the restoration of democracy more difficult. He therefore attacked Thomas Mann quite sharply, questioning the assumptions of his lecture.

Mann replied on 10 December 1943, declaring that if he had indeed spoken of the collective responsibility of the German people, he had refrained from identifying the Germans as a whole with Nazism. He reiterated all the same his disagreement with the plan to establish a Free Germany Committee in the United States, as the undertaking not only struck him as premature, but 'members of the State Department think it premature and do not want it now'. He feared such a body would be viewed as 'nothing but a patriotic effort to shield Germany from the consequences of her crimes', and concluded: 'It is too soon to pose German demands and to appeal to the world's emotions in favour of a country which still has Europe in her power and whose capability for crime has by no means been shattered.'[19] At the same time, he acknowledged the difficulty of his position: 'The questions on what should be done with Germany after victory will not go away. I shall say nothing. If clemency is advised, one may be frightfully disappointed by the Germans. If one counsels rigour, one finds oneself in a false and intolerable position towards the country whose language one writes.'[20]

On 29 April 1944 he wrote to Ernst Reuter:

> For reasons of conscience and tact, I dislike a certain patriotism of German émigrés who in the midst of the War, at a time when the enemy remains dangerously powerful and the heaviest sacrifices are still foreseeable in order to assure victory, want to open their arms wide to Germany, and demand that nothing should be done against the country on any pretext. And yet it is this Germany that has inflicted the most unheard-of treatment on other European nations.

Mann therefore refused to sign the manifesto of the Council for a Democratic Germany, judging it 'an irresponsible boldness for German émigrés to guarantee today the future good conduct of Germany, a country that has become deeply foreign to us all [. . .] Germany has begun its expiation, and is undoubtedly on its way to still harsher expiation. I have no objection to this.' He added: 'It is up to the world's responsible statesmen to take the right decisions to prevent Germany hurling the world into a new catastrophic war in ten or twenty years' time.'[21] He distrusted Germany to such a degree that he wrote on 11 October 1944: 'In no way should Klaus and Golo be sent to Germany. They would be murdered in my place.'[22] And on 20 October 1944 he repeated to Erich von Kahler that his 'disgust for everything German is at this time growing boundlessly'. He believed that the Germans had learned nothing from the War, experienced no remorse, and he railed against their bitter support for a regime from which they could no longer expect anything: 'What is happening in their brains is very strange and incomprehensible.' If Mann refrained from encouraging the destruction of Germany, he constantly railed against 'the patriotic madness of the German immigrants', their refusal to understand that National Socialism 'has not been imposed on the Germans from without, but has roots growing centuries deep in the history of German life', adding – perhaps with an eye to Brecht – 'I have to endure a good deal from imbeciles who believe themselves more German than me.'

Over and above these debates on the 'German character', the émigrés were equally divided on the real significance of National Socialism. Analysis of the

Nazi phenomenon had certainly developed a long way since 1933. The first attempts to understand it had often been superficial and rudimentary. Very few of the émigrés, even among the most political, were capable of comprehending Nazism in a genuinely theoretical and not merely schematic way. Many were happy just to denounce it in moral terms, interpreting it as a kind of regression to the Middle Ages, or seeing it as a pathological phenomenon bound up with the personality of Hitler. Ten years later, however, many émigrés had attempted a more theoretical and global approach, even if discussion among them remained very lively. Both Thomas Mann and Emil Ludwig were inclined to see Nazism as a product of German history, the monstrous fruit of a certain irrationalist tradition, an ignorance of democracy and liberty. In the majority of works written in the 1940s, the documentary aspect of lived experience – so important in 1933, when it was a question of explaining to the whole world the horror of the Nazi regime – has disappeared: they were no longer the only witnesses of Nazi barbarism, the whole of Europe had been steeped in its bloody crimes. If works on Nazism now had a less dramatic aspect, the émigré writings of this later period were nonetheless distinguished by their originality from the majority of studies of fascism written after the War, even if the latter were better documented. It should also be noted that the most well-known works on Nazism by the émigrés were not always the most important ones: Hermann Rauschning's *The Revolution of Nihilism*, for example, a runaway bestseller, is of very limited theoretical interest. In 1939 *The End of Economic Man* was published, whose author, Peter F. Drucker (of Viennese origin), sought to elucidate the phenomenon of totalitarianism. The ex-Communist Franz Borkenau published *The Totalitarian Enemy* in 1939, and Emil Lederer *The State of the Masses* in 1940. Different as these various approaches are, they all express the appearance of a theory of totalitarianism that was unknown in 1933. In 1942, Sigmund Neumann published *Permanent Revolution*, which was subsequently to have a deep influence on American political thought. It can be said that for many émigré writers in the United States, National Socialism was now placed in a broader perspective, and that the question was not so much to find a typically German origin for it as to investigate it as a symptom of the industrial age. It is also revealing that already at this time, several essays compared the Nazi and Stalinist systems in a perspective that would be further developed in the Cold War.

In contrast with the rather right-wing inspiration of these analyses, *Behemoth* by Franz Neumann, a friend of Herbert Marcuse, still remains today one of the most interesting books on National Socialism from a left-wing standpoint. In 1941, Ernst Franckel published *The Dual State*, but this new understanding of Nazism, increasingly identifying fascism and Communism, culminated only six years after the end of the War with Hannah Arendt's *The Origins of Totalitarianism*.

Among works published by Communists, one that deserves mention is Paul Merker's *Das Dritte Reich und sein Ende* (Mexico 1945), which has the merit of proposing concrete analyses of the functioning of National Socialism that are still of interest today. Less emphasis is placed on the personalities of the Nazi leaders than on the overall barbarism of its methods. These works, however, generally do not make much comparison with Italian fascism. The book by Max Ascoli and Arthur Feiler, *Fascism for Whom?*, did trace a parallel, though without drawing any real theoretical conclusion. Even with those attempting a political and economic analysis, if National Socialism is no longer identified with a fit of collective madness, a regression to the Middle Ages or the expression of a single man's hysteria, it is still considered a more or less unique phenomenon with no equivalent – even by such a progressive author as Franz Neumann.[23] But there was certainly no consensus in the works on National Socialism published by the émigrés in the 1940s. They were divided over their understanding of the class character of Nazism, the role of 'revolutionary' elements in its ideology, its relationship to socialism and to the German tradition, its significance in the capitalist system and its historical origin.

The link between fascist ideology and the middle classes is often mentioned, but this theme was already present in the sociological literature of the Weimar Republic. Hans Speier and Siegfried Kracauer had both written on the white-collar workers before 1933.[24] This identification of fascism with the middle classes was moreover criticized by some Marxists such as Richard Loewenthal, who stressed that if a large section of the middle classes did rally to fascism, the economic policy of the Third Reich was directed by quite different interests.[25] Konrad Heiden, famous for his biography of Hitler and the image of the declassed bohemian that he presented, saw Nazism rather as a phenomenon of class collapse, and emphasized the role of conservative circles in its rise, while recognizing the attraction it exercised on the middle classes. Hermann Rausch-ning refused to blame the middle classes for the rise of Nazism, and insisted on its delinquent revolutionary aspect. Gustav Stolper, on the other hand, denied any class character of Nazism and saw the only possible opposition to it in the conservative milieu.

If Marxists all emphasized the connection between Nazism, the bourgeoisie, the middle classes and heavy industry, an anti-Communist émigré such as Robert Ingrim absolutely rejected the theory of a collusion between Nazism and big capital. Friedrich Stampfer, a right-wing Social-Democrat, similarly maintained in 1939 that the bourgeoisie had opposed Nazism from the start, and it had found its main support among the workers. He thus saw future cooperation possible only with non-proletarian elements. S. Marck and Gerhart Seger maintained in 1943 that the industrialists and Junkers were responsible for Hitler's victory, while Paul Tillich and E. Heimann insisted on the role of the masses.

When it came to specifying exactly what constituted the mass character of fascism, the émigrés were similarly opposed. The Communists and some left-wing Socialists saw National Socialism as a dictatorship of big capital over the proletariat. Franz Neumann for his part maintained a close link between Nazism and capitalism. Rauschning on the other hand practically never mentioned the economic aspect of Nazism, and Eduard Hermann (who arrived in the United States in 1937) rejected any equation of National Socialism with capitalism. Franz Borkenau did not deny the ties between fascism and capitalism, but the structure of the war economy and state dirigisme seemed to him to make this relationship problematic. If big capital had supported Hitler, the Nazi state had a singular structure and was not a typical phenomenon of capitalism.[26]

Finally, in the *Aufbau* milieu, a number of analyses of National Socialism were developed that systematically compared it with Bolshevism. In 1937, Leopold Schwarzschild interpreted Nazism as a reaction to the October Revolution. Hermann Rauschning insisted on the idea of 'proletarian revolution' that he claimed to find at the basis of Nazism. W. Gurian published in 1935 an essay titled 'Bolschewismus als Weltgefahr', in which he already identified Nazism and Bolshevism. The Nazi–Soviet pact strengthened the champions of this thesis, and a 1940 issue of the *Neue Volkszeitung* bore the headline: '*Ist Hitler ein Bolschewist?*'

PERSPECTIVES FOR A FUTURE GOVERNMENT

Towards the end of the War, debate on the future of Germany steadily intensified among the exiles. It stirred up conflict among a number of prominent figures in the émigré community – Emil Ludwig, Lion Feuchtwanger, Bertolt Brecht, Thomas Mann – bringing up old oppositions and indicating future divisions. The debates were followed attentively by the American press and government, for which reason some of the émigrés were unwilling to express themselves clearly on the questions raised. April 1943 saw the publication of an article by Kingsbury Smith, close to the State Department, in the *American Mercury*, advocating a division of Germany to counteract Prussian influence.[27] Besides, the growing tension between the United States and the USSR already foreshadowed the difficulties of the postwar era.

The émigrés were naturally not invited to take part in any official discussion. All the same, the question of the future of Germany and a German government loomed increasingly large in their debates.[28] There was a simultaneous formation of several discussion groups, as the components of the political emigration in the United States were so opposed that it was impossible to bring Communists and right-wing Social-Democrats together to compare ideas. Theorists such as Friedrich Stampfer ruled out in advance any idea of reconciliation with the Communists after the War, holding them to be almost as dangerous as Hitler. In August 1941, the Social-Democrats under Albert Grzesinski[29] founded the German-American Council for the Liberation of Germany from Nazism, which gave birth to the Association of Free Germans,[30] to which Herman Kesten, Alfred Polgar and Frederick Zweig belonged, and which sent the House of Representatives a programme for a new German republic.

Thomas Mann, who kept his distance from the Social-Democrats while not having any sympathy for the Communists, placed his hopes, as expressed in his 'Appeals to Germans', in an 'abolition of national states'.[31] The Association of Free Germans only managed to rally certain Social-Democrats to its programme, and failed to make any agreement with the Socialist Neu Beginnen group. It collapsed in summer 1944, and Grzesinski then rallied to the Council for a Democratic Germany, without however obtaining the support of his party's former leaders.

The Council for a Democratic Germany was founded in March 1944, eight months after the Freies Deutschland committee. Many anti-Communist émigrés distrusted it, deeming it a pro-Soviet organization. According to Karl O. Paetel (a former 'national-bolshevik'), the foundation of the Council was in no way envisaged as a response to Freies Deutschland. If its members included a number of Communists, the majority were from bourgeois and especially clerical milieus. Paul Tillich was appointed to lead it. Brüning was invited to take part, but declined – 'unless expressly invited by the US government'. Albert H. Schreiner, a Communist, joined it, as did Brecht. In fact, the Council was less a political organization than a private club. Entry was by invitation only, and it had no means of effective action. Tillich sought to achieve a balance within the Council between the different political visions of the émigrés. It did not however claim to give a faithful image of the many tendencies within the exile community, only those it saw as susceptible of contributing to a reconstruction of democracy in Germany. The desire to maintain this balance brought the Council to complete inactivity, and Tillich itself passed severe judgement on it. Very idealistic in its aims, the Council also envisaged admitting non-Germans as members. Its very limited means[32] scarcely enabled it to move beyond the realm of intentions. It only issued a single publication, *Denkschrift über Wiederaufbau der Gewerkschaftbewegung in Deutschland* (19 July 1944), signed by Bärwald (Centre party), Aufhaüser (SPD), Hagen (Neu Beginnen), Walcher (SAP) and Schreiner (KPD). Other projects were sketched out in the fields of health and economics, without very concrete results. The Council insisted on the restoration of democracy in Germany being the work of the Germans themselves.[33] But it never managed to obtain official recognition, or even to achieve unity among its members. On many occasions *Der Aufbau* magazine distanced itself from it. Thomas Mann judged Tillich's project to be too hasty, and feared it would be badly perceived by the US government.[34] Tillich and Hagen subsequently remained in America,[35] and it is very hard to imagine a hundred or so political figures working under the leadership of a theologian.

The failure of the Council for a Democratic Germany can be ascribed above all to its absence of legitimacy – it represented only itself – and to the fact that it was no more than an assemblage of well-known figures. After 1947, moreover, under Niebuhr, the Council aligned itself with Truman's policy and accepted his anti-Communism.

Just as dangerous for the functioning of the Council – as well as for any attempted reflection on the reconstruction of democracy in Germany – were the violently anti-German positions developed by certain British and American figures, and particularly associated with Vansittart.

In 1941, Lord Vansittart (1881–1957), former under-secretary of state in the Foreign Office, published under the title *Black Record* a series of radio broadcasts on the Germans, in which he violently attacked the 'German national character', claiming that this had constantly produced wars in Europe ever since

Charlemagne. Though his argument was little more than a series of Germa-nophobic stereotypes, it rapidly aroused debate among the émigrés. Victor Gollancz, of German-Jewish origin himself, published *Shall Our Children Live or Die?*, in which like Brecht he rejected any identification of Germans with Nazis. Heinrich Fraenkel published *Vansittart's Gift for Goebbels. A German Exile's Answer to the 'Black Record'*. In 1942, the Social-Democrats Curt Geyer and Walter Loeb published a pamphlet, *Gollancz in German Wonderland*, with a preface by the Labour MP James Walker, broadly agreeing with Vansittart. There was no question for them of destroying the Germans, but a long re-education would be necessary. The SoPaDe, for its part, accused the champions of 'Vansittartism' of British nationalism. But Vansittart's supporters continued to maintain that while the émigrés might well claim it was unjust to identify the German people with National Socialism, the successes of the German army and the absence of opposition to Hitler showed that the Nazis had a broad popular base and that it was a myth to make out that a handful of Nazis were subjecting the German people to a bloody dictatorship. If the 'other Germany' existed, where was it?

The polemics aroused by Vansittart's claims soon opened new divisions among the émigrés, and considerably obstructed their discussions on the future of Germany. But contrary to the situation in Britain, the exiled Social-Demo-crats in America refrained from adopting such positions. Certain émigrés – such as Emil Ludwig – did take them up on their own account, somewhat shame-facedly, after being accused by other émigrés of being 'Vansittartists'. Friedrich Wilhelm Foerster, who was more violently anti-German, had founded a Society for the Prevention of World War III in 1943, with both American members and émigrés including Paul Winkler. Rejecting any distinction between 'German' and 'Nazi', supporters of this movement maintained that the forces who had supported Hitler were the same as had supported Bismarck and Wilhelm II. The development of this anti-German feeling led many émigrés to fear that the simplistic propositions of Vansittart and his supporters would end up influen-cing United States policy. In May 1945, Otto Nathan, an adviser to the German economics ministry before 1933, was charged with studying the problem of war reparations, and by this time several possible ways of dividing Germany were under discussion.[36]

If such violently Germanophobic movements as the Society for the Preven-tion of World War III were rejected by the majority of exiles, they were still capable of attracting support from some anti-German American patriots such as William Shirer,[37] Sigrid Schulz and E. A. Mowrer. Paradoxically enough, though these positions found a certain intellectual support, they were com-pletely rejected by the American population.[38] The American 'Vansittartists' remained isolated. Most of them had only a very summary acquaintance with German history. Emil Ludwig was rejected by a large number of émigrés; he was disliked by the most convinced antifascists, who found it hard to excuse his biography of Mussolini, and by liberal Jews. *Freies Deutschland* also attacked him in the strongest terms. But 'Vansittartism' was not a phenomenon of right or left.[39] Its supporters included émigrés who had remained faithful to the first slogans of the exile community: the destruction of Hitlerism by all means necessary, as well as others who had suffered so deeply that their relationship to their former homeland had been transformed into hatred. The 'Vansittartists' included Socialists and declared enemies of Prussia (such as F. W. Foerster), as well as Catholics and liberals. What was certain was that this current represented a dangerous ideology, at a time when the question of the fate of Germany was so forcefully in question, because of its rigidity, its refusal to distinguish between the German people and the Nazi government, its sclerosed vision of history and its taste for anathema, fixing nations into eternal stereotypes.

Other émigrés moved beyond the schematism of such visions to investigate not only the future of Germany but also that of Europe in general. If the Communists scarcely took any position on this question until 1945,[40] several Socialists of different tendencies, exiled in London or New York, worked out plans for a 'European federation' (Friedrich Stampfer) or supranational 'federal structures'.[41] Supporters of the Centre party, and liberals (Karl Spiecker, publisher of *Das Wahre Deutschland* and later a minister under Adenauer), insisted at the same time on the necessity of a European federation, as also did Arnold Brecht (a high official under the Weimar Republic, then a professor at the New School for Social Research). The same aspiration towards a federation could be found in certain theorists of the conservative right such as Hermann Rauschning. It is little probable that the division of Germany and the creation of two autonomous states, with the tensions that marked their history, corresponded to any of the programmes that so many of the émigrés worked out at the end of the War; just as it is hard to maintain that the German Democratic Republic was the realization of the utopian plans of the Communist exiles, even if many of them took part in its creation. The postwar political reality was far more complex than they had imagined in their most pessimistic forecasts. Klaus Mann wrote at the end of his autobiography: 'Let us hope that from the combat Adolf Hitler has imposed on the two great rivals and antagonists, the combat they are now waging fraternally and side by side, a collaboration will be born in the service of peace; that would be our salvation.' He added, very farsightedly:

All other problems, including the problem of Germany, would then be relatively simple to resolve [. . .]. A sincere understanding between East and West is the sine qua non: without it nothing is possible; but each step that brings it closer or consolidates it is a step in the right direction. Each step leading us away from it is a step towards disaster[42]

Who would deny the aptness of this faith in a peaceful Europe? Reading again these political programmes elaborated by the exiles – confused, contradictory, and often naïve – one is struck by the trust that they placed in European organizations, the existence of which has become so obvious for us that it takes an imaginative effort to recall a time when they did not exist. And who would deny that it is often these pages written on Europe, for example by Klaus Mann, insisting on its spiritual unity, its mission and its diversity, that prove the richest in hope and instruction?

ORIGIN AND DEVELOPMENT OF THE
FREIES DEUTSCHLAND COMMITTEE

Far more significant for this struggle among the émigrés, as it intensified towards the end of the War, was the foundation of the 'Free Germany' National Committee. The origins of the committee lay in the massive desertions from the German army, which gave the Soviet authorities the hope of rallying a number of soldiers to their cause, on the understanding that the War was lost and there was no sense in dying for Hitler. The Comintern distributed a pamphlet by General Ernst Hadermann, *Das Wort eines deutschen Hauptmanns*, which called for an armistice and the opening of negotiations to put an end to the War and the Nazi regime. The fact that Heinrich Graf von Einsiedel, a great-nephew of Bismarck, had ranged himself with the founders of Freies Deutschland, gave cause to hope that their example would be followed.

On 12 July 1943 a meeting took place at Krasnogorsk, near Moscow, of workers, peasants, representatives of the middle classes, KPD functionaries, members of the SPD, as well as delegates of soldier and officer prisoners of war in the USSR, to give an official structure to this perspective of a Popular Front: the Nationalkomitee 'Freies Deutschland'. Among the Communists who took part in the committee, the majority had been in exile in the Soviet Union since 1933 or soon after. Some soldiers had deserted to join the Red Army from ideological conviction. A large number of officers and soldiers joined the committee in the hope of putting an end to the War and overthrowing National Socialism. Freies Deutschland proposed to unite all adversaries of the Nazi regime and the War, whatever their political convictions. Conservatives as well as Communists could join, Prussian aristocrats as well as Social-Democrats or Christians.[43] There had been the idea of adopting the black, red and gold flag as the movement's symbol, but certain Soviet figures judged it inopportune to select as symbol of a new Germany the flag of the Weimar Republic with its weaknesses, division and unemployment.[44] The black, white and red banner was chosen in order to rally the army, and as a symbol of the new national government, even if some émigrés were shocked to see this reappearance of the imperial flag. According to Wolfgang Leonhard, who worked for it, the Freies Deutschland Committee was established following an appeal launched in the German POW paper *Freies Wort*. *Pravda* attached great importance to the event, and devoted a whole page to the appeal. The USSR invited officer POWs to take part in the movement. Among the first of these were Major Homann, General Hadermann, founder of the first group of antifascist officers, Major Hetz, and Lieutenant Heinrich Graf von Einsiedel. The first exiles to take part in the committee included member of the KPD leadership in exile (Wilhelm Pieck, Walter Ulbricht, Wilhelm Florin, Hermann Matern, Anton Ackermann, Edwin Hörnle, Martha Arendsee), as well as writers (J. R. Becher, Willi Bredel, Theodor Plievier, Gustav von Wangenheim, Friedrich Wolf). The committee itself was chaired by the poet Erich Weinert. The foundation ceremony of Freies Deutschland was filmed and widely distributed, and in mid October 1943, the committee met again at Ljunowo, 35 kilometres outside Moscow. According to

Wolfgang Leonhard, the committee had two kinds of bodies, official and unofficial. Though it included figures from all political horizons, the active element was made up of émigrés.[45] Freies Deutschland soon started to publish an organ whose main editors included Lothar Bolz (former editor of the German-language *Rote Zeitung* in Leningrad and the *Deutsche Zentralzeitung* in Moscow), Alfred Kurella (in charge of relations with the officers on the national committee at Ljunowo, Karl Maron (responsible for military commentary) and Ernst Held (former theatre director, responsible for culture), while Ernö Gero (Hungarian Communist who had lived in the Soviet Union since 1923) was in charge of supervising political articles. Freies Deutschland acquired new importance with the formation of the Bund Deutscher Offiziere (11–12 September 1943), which adhered to the committee's aims. On 14 September, at a session of the national committee, their activities were co-ordinated. The presidium of the national committee was expanded to include the leaders of the Bund Deutscher Offiziere, General Walther von Seydlitz and Edler von Daniels, who became vice-presidents). The following year, the orientation of the national committee again changed. Until the Teheran conference, it had addressed itself to soldiers, calling on them to return to the borders of the Reich and conclude an honourable peace with the Allies. From 1944, Freies Deutschland called for a popular uprising against Hitler and desertion across the front. It now included a large number of POWs, about 800,000 of whom were detained in the Soviet Union.

Broadcasts were soon organized in association with the Freies Deutschland Committee. Wolfgang Leonhard worked on these under the direction of Anton Ackermann (a member of the KPD central committee since 1935), who took charge of the most important commentaries. Military announcements were made by Kurt Fischer, and other broadcasts given by Fritz Erpenbeck, Lore Pieck, Hans Mahle, Max Keilson and Gustav von Wangenheim. Protestant and Catholic chaplains took part in these broadcasts, along with anti-Hitler generals and Communists. At the first meeting of the committee, its president Erich Weinert depicted the outcome of the War after the battle of Stalingrad,[46] and the desire to save Germany from the destruction to which the Nazis were condemning it. He underlined the necessity for Germans, on the front or at home, to rally to the committee, as the only way of accelerating the end of hostilities. At least twenty-one people spoke, describing the situation of Nazi Germany, declaring that the War was lost and that the greatest enemy of Germany was Hitler. The manifesto called on Germans to save their country by working together for the construction of a democratic regime.[47] The thirty-eight signatories of the committee's platform included soldiers, workers, peasants, writers, officers, Christians, Socialists and Communists, thus constituting a final attempt at a Popular Front. Throughout its existence, the committee enjoyed the material support of the Soviet Union. From 19–20 July 1943 it possessed a radio transmitter and a weekly paper, while printing presses and megaphones were brought to the front in order to distribute antifascist news, inform German soldiers on the real situation of their country and its armies, and on the existence of the committee. At the same time, members of the committee were very active among the prisoners of war, seeking to rally them to the cause of antifascism.[48]

Despite certain internal tensions and mistrust, the Freies Deutschland Committee had a genuine success, judging from the number of prisoners who rallied to the movement:[49] the figure rose from 4.5 per cent of German POWs in July 1942 to 18.1 per cent in October 1943, 34.1 per cent in January 1944, 67.1 per cent in April 1944 and 96.6 per cent in July 1944, a year after the committee was founded.

The movement soon took on a considerable scope, not just in all the camps for German POWs in the USSR, but also abroad. Committees in support of Freies Deutschland were immediately established in a number of countries.[50]

19

The Antifascist Émigrés and the Beginnings of McCarthyism

THE COLLAPSE OF LIBERALISM

If the 1920s had been the 'red decade', the New Deal represented a kind of apogee of American liberalism, an attempt to introduce a number of progressive reforms into social and political life. The admiration that so many of the émigrés, Communists as well as Socialists and liberals, had for President Roosevelt is not explained just by his attitude towards the refugees. He embodied in their eyes a certain America which, in comparison with the fascist regimes of Europe, symbolized a genuine hope for democracy and freedom. Yet from 1946 onwards, even those émigrés least suspect of Communist sympathy proclaimed their unhappiness at the development of United States policy. Thomas Mann himself declared that he could no longer recognize in America after Roosevelt's death the country he had dreamed of making his new spiritual home:

> Now we are experiencing a great lowering of morals, raw avarice, political reaction, race hatred, and all the signs of spiritual depression [. . .]. As a German I am naturally inclined toward pessimism, and occasionally I fear having to go through the whole disaster, somewhat modified, again. And then there would be no further exile – for where would I go? [. . .] But if fascism comes, I can point out that I was once Senator Taft's dinner guest. That perhaps may save me from the concentration camp.[1]

This feeling of unease towards America steadily grew. On 12 October 1947 Mann wrote: 'At one time my faith in America's humanitarian mission was very strong. In the last few years it has been exposed to slight strains. Instead of leading the world, America appears to have resolved to buy it – which is also a very grandiose thing after its fashion [. . .].'[2]

The most disturbing symptom was to be the unprecedented climate of anti-Communism, that of the 'American inquisition'.[3]

American anti-Communism was a complex phenomenon, rooted in a long tradition that was not limited to the existence of the CPUSA. Founded in 1919–

21, and led by William Z. Foster, the party had enjoyed a certain following in the crisis years that followed 1928. The Committee of National Struggle, founded in 1930 in support of the unemployed, built up millions of members until 1934–35. Though in 1932 the party had put up Foster as candidate for President, in 1936, 1940 and 1944 it supported Roosevelt. Though it never counted more than 80,000 members, Communist ideas marked a fairly wide section of the American intelligentsia, especially in the 1920s. Many writers took up the reading of Marx, happily describing themselves as 'Communists' and following the development of the Soviet Union with sympathy. The party's organ *New Masses* was moreover a cultural review of great interest. While the Hearst press ceaselessly attacked it, the CPUSA attracted a growing number of artists and intellectuals.

Despite this following, the CPUSA never had a major presence on the political stage: Communism seemed more of a moral ideal than an economic and political system. Foster's candidacy in 1932 had been supported by fifty-two writers and artists who signed the manifesto 'Culture and Crisis', published in *New Masses* in December 1931. It was also on the initiative of this magazine that the Congress of American Writers[4] was held on 1 May 1935, with Friedrich Wolf as a special guest. The attraction of Communism was felt in the theatre as well as in literature. A regular agitprop movement developed, along with a number of progressive theatres. The experience of the Group Theater remains the most famous example. To combat the unemployment that was ravaging artistic milieu, the Roosevelt administration set up the Federal Theater Project, which with authors such as Clifford Odets,[5] Elmer Rice, Maxwell Anderson and Lillian Hellman, staged progressive works that directly bore on social and economic problems. After the Seventh Congress of the Communist International, the CPUSA likewise set out to develop a Popular Front movement.

From September 1936, the Roosevelt administration seems to have been disturbed by Communist activities, which were now closely monitored by the FBI. After 1937, a noticeable anti-Communist current started to develop in the United States. In the wake of the Nazi–Soviet pact the CPUSA split into factions, and after the invasion of the Soviet Union it came under the right-wing leadership of Earl Browder, leading to the dissolution of the party in 1944, though the following year it was re-established. By this time it had lost almost all influence, on intellectuals as well as among the working class.

The anti-Communist wave that emerged in the 1940s, culminating in the McCarthy era, drew on a long tradition. As early as 1919, the American Legion had attacked Socialist demonstrations with the slogan 'Deport Bolsheviki!' The press accused Communists of inciting black Americans to revolt, and the *New York Times* eagerly described the supposed route of Communist infiltration by way of Mexico. The high point of these attacks was reached in 1920, in which year 249 Russian immigrants were expelled, followed by a further 550 in 1921.[6] Marxists had been expelled from the Socialist party, whose presidential candidate, Eugene Debs, was imprisoned for espionage. The CPUSA had to develop underground activity, and demands were made to investigate 'bolshevik' influence within the University of California. The crisis of 1929, however, led a large number of intellectuals in the direction of Communism, while right-wing critics equated the New Deal with socialism. It was in this climate that antifascist cultural organizations such as the Anti-Nazi League and the Spanish Republican Committee developed. The first commission of inquiry into 'un-American activities', formed in 1938, did not produce any conclusion. Chaired by Martin Dies, this set its sights on both Communism and fascism, which Dies seemed to have a problem in distinguishing, as he saw Hitler as a 'Marxist'. After investigating the activities of the Bund, the commission turned its attention to 'Communist' intellectuals. The Nazi-Soviet pact confirmed Dies in his idea that fascism and Communism were identical. Several Communists were arrested and sentenced to years in prison at this time, accused for example of having recruited fighters for the Spanish war. In 1940, a number of Hollywood personalities, including Fredric March, Florence Eldridge, James Cagney, Luise Rainer and Humphrey Bogart were accused of having collected funds for Spain and against Hitler. Dies soon tried to establish that Communists were preparing to sabotage American industry, and in 1941 Congress voted $150,000 for him to pursue his 'investigations'.

Though the committee's hearings were suspended after America entered the War, Dies continued to hunt out 'Soviet sympathizers' in the US administration. HUAC relaunched its activities even before the War in Europe was at an end, especially targeting the 'Hollywood tarantula'. The majority of the New Deal's cultural organizations were suspected of Communism, even individuals close to Roosevelt. In 1946, nine leaders of the Joint Anti-Fascist Committee were sentenced to prison terms. A regular spy psychosis developed: the 'reds' were not only accused of championing ideas hostile to American democracy, but of handing over strategic secrets to the USSR. Hoover requested his FBI agents to investigate all strategic projects. The revelations of the three first 'big spies' – Bentley, Budenz, Chambers – immediately led to the arrest and inquisition of several hundred people. Budenz denounced other Communists as 'spies', and in the foray, Gerhart Eisler was fingered as the 'spymaster'. Once the process had been set under way, nothing seemed able to stop it: military establishments, doctors, actors, writers, academics and generals were called to justify themselves and prove that they were not 'Communists'. The wind of madness blew in successive gusts – 1946–47, 1948–49, 1950 – and especially struck Hollywood, viewed as a regular bolshevik stronghold. The new chair of HUAC, Parnell Thomas, decided in January 1947 to pursue his investigations in this direction, and expose the 'Hollywood Communists'.

THE 'HOLLYWOOD COMMUNISTS'

Communists and people from Hollywood are the same thing.

Senator Jack Tenney

Who were these 'Hollywood Communists'? This term was used to designate a certain intellectual milieu that had radicalized in the 1920s and 30s, and developed in the shadow of the eight major film companies. The success of the talking pictures had attracted to Hollywood a growing number of writers wishing to work at the film studios, and had even created a new kind of author, the 'screenwriter', an often obscure character able to write filmscripts, stories and dialogue. In the immense Hollywood machine they were simply an 'element of production', but their number grew with the demands of the movie industry, and in 1933 the Screen Writers' Guild was established, set to remain for fifteen years the most politicized trade union in Hollywood. Actors and directors, for their part, were too tied to the production process by their high salaries to be able to criticize it. The same was not true of the screenwriters, who throughout the 1930s dreamed of seeing the cinema become a genuine art form and not just a simple commodity. Chaired by John Howard Lawson, the SWG had no specific political orientation, simply maintaining a certain faith in solidarity. By October 1934 it had 750 members, while actors established their own guild in 1933. Its first years were marked by very lively professional discussions and a series of clashes with the studios, and it broke up in 1936 after the conservatives and centrists left it. A new association, the Screen Playwrights, was founded the same year, directly competing with the SWG. But on 12 September 1938 the SWG was recognized by the government as sole representative of the cinema writers. From a professional defence organization, it had become in five years a political and cultural organization with a left-wing orientation.

This politicization of screenwriters explains why they so rapidly felt affected by European events, and the massive character of their adherence to Hollywood's antifascist movements. The CPUSA certainly played a major role within this intellectual milieu throughout the 1930s. Though weakly implanted in the working class, it attracted a large number of screenwriters – Paul Jarrico, John Howard Lawson – while the Popular Front policy created a new role of fellow-traveller. Subsequently, after the ban on the CPUSA, the Screen Writers' Guild relapsed into more conservative positions, but this left intelligentsia of the 1920s and 30s certainly contributed to the greatness of the Hollywood cinema. Its disappearance also explains how uninteresting so much of the output of the 1950s was.

Nothing predisposed Hollywood to such a rapprochement with Communism. The situation of its sympathizers, within the most capitalist of industries, was paradoxical. The CPUSA did not even possess any genuine cultural organizations, the most important being the John Reed Club and the Film and Photo League, but a large number of intellectuals agreed to take part in actions alongside the Communists, such as John Dos Passos, Sherwood Anderson, Theodore Dreiser, Waldo Frank, Edmund Wilson and Malcolm Cowley. The rise of fascism in Europe brought this movement of politicization to a head. The appeal launched in May 1935 for the organization of a Congress of American Writers was signed by many famous Hollywood figures,[7] who saw Communism and the defence of the Soviet Union as a rampart against fascism, a safeguard of American liberalism as well as a means of struggle against racism and colonialism. The fact that the Communist party did not impose any dogma or discipline on writers made this rapprochement all the more easy.

From 1935, the Hollywood screenwriters included a number of active Communists, of whom John Howard Lawson was the best known. The editor of *New Masses*, he took part in the campaigns against racism in the Southern states, the committees in support of Republican Spain and the struggle against fascism. In 1937 Hollywood counted some 145 writers, fifty to sixty actors, and fifteen to twenty directors who openly proclaimed themselves Communists. The majority took part in weekly meetings on both aesthetic and political questions. This was still of course a fairly limited number,[8] and it is hard to pin down what exactly Communism meant for them,[9] all the more so as it was more often the European situation that was responsible for their politicization than the CPUSA itself. Besides, in the McCarthy era, any left-wing sympathizer was termed 'Communist'. But the singularity of the 'Hollywood people' in relation to America in general did indeed lie in the presence of the Communist party, even it did not know very well how to behave towards them. They were motivated far more by a certain idealism than by any genuine political consciousness, and their activism often consisted in simply supporting every humanitarian cause.

The mechanisms of the film industry, its rules, taboos and laws, made it almost impossible to display any political conviction in a film. The most that was possible was a kind of social realism such as inspired *The Grapes of Wrath*. The more social films written by Communist screenwriters were eventually so toned down that it would be hard to find any critical dimension in them. These Hollywood Communists had often not read a single line of Marx or Lenin, were scarcely familiar with Eisenstein or Pudovkin, and understood nothing of economics, but they were inspired by a certain ideal of social justice, liberty, and defence of democracy which permitted a Popular Front together with mainstream liberals.

In the early 1940s, the assaults of the conservatives were directed as much against the Roosevelt administration, the cultural bodies of the New Deal – especially the Federal Theater Project – and even liberals, as against the Communists themselves. While the Dies Committee conducted its various hearings, the sensationalist press constantly spread new 'revelations' about Communist infiltration of Hollywood. Every antifascist or progressive organization was denounced as a Communist outfit, even those that were merely liberal. The situation was all the more confused in that American liberals were now highly anti-Communist, yet themselves victims of conservative attack. For this reason, and overcoming the divisions created by the Nazi–Soviet pact, a meeting was held at the Philharmonic Auditorium on 27 February 1940 to decide on a joint response. This did not prevent the Dies Committee from immediately drawing up lists of 'subversives'. A large number of progressive figures in Hollywood – Herbert Bibermann, Gale Sondergaard, Sam and Sadie Ornitz, Lionel Stander, Clifford Odets – were called to respond to a grand jury 'concerning operations of Communists in the film colony', while several actors including Humphrey Bogart, Fredric March and James Cagney were likewise accused. A committee investigating un-American activities now sat permanently in Hollywood[10] and carried out increasingly intrusive investigations. Some figures in the cinema attacked progressives with the same vehemence: Walt Disney tried to get the Hollywood Writers' Mobilization congress banned as a

Communist initiative, and Senator Tenney proceeded to two whole days of hearings on the subject.

The Tenney Committee disappeared after a while, but it had succeeded in casting suspicion on the Hollywood milieu: mere suspicion of being a 'red' would now be enough to break a career. The stand in support of intervention in Europe taken by a number of prominent figures in the film world was used to discredit them, as were the antifascist activities of the Popular Front. New investigations were launched by the Senate Subcomittee on War Propaganda. If the Dies Committee had only aroused a rather vague wave of resistance in the cinema industry, solidarity against this new subcommittee proved far stronger. The producers' association asked Wendell Willkie to represent it before the subcommittee, and underlined that out of 1,100 films made in Hollywood in the two previous years, only fifty dealt with fascism, at a time when this threatened the entire idea of democracy. A number of intellectuals – Arthur Krock, Dorothy Thompson – took up the defence of Hollywood, and the committee had to yield. Its investigations came to an end in September 1941.

This victory gave Hollywood back a certain confidence in the strength of its unity. If there were still many attacks, even during the War, liberals and radicals were reconciled in the struggle against Germany. But even before the War in Europe was ended, a new wave of hatred and slander broke on Hollywood. After the death of Roosevelt, supporters of the New Deal were dismissed from all posts and anti-Communism raised to a factor of national cohesion. The ideological machine that gave birth to McCarthyism was highly complex: it included business representatives, churchmen, political figures, intellectuals, academics, former FBI agents and former Communist activists, to which were added a Congressional committee and a general staff of conservative politicians, chiefly from the Southern states, supported by right-wing organizations such as the Knights of Columbus, Daughters of the American Revolution and the American Legion, capable between them of a formidable mobilization of public opinion. Even liberal milieus, hostile as they were to the conservative right, became transmission belts for this anti-Communism,[11] which soon developed into a regular crusade.

In January 1944, the House Committee on Un-American Activities opened an investigation into the CIO trade-union federation, then at the peak of its power. Its report concluded that the Communists had penetrated the CIO and were conducting 'subversive intrigues' in it: no less than thirty-five leading figures were accused. In April, scouts were sent to Hollywood, where in the meantime the Motion Picture Alliance for the Preservation of American Ideals (MPA) had been formed,[12] proposing to combat Communist influence on American films. Its declarations amounted to a regular invitation to HUAC. The MPA wrote a letter to the ultra-conservative Senator Robert R. Reynolds, requesting him to combat Communism in Hollywood. A coalition of liberals and radicals came together against this new threat. On 18 April 1944, two days before the arrival of the HUAC investigators, the leadership of the Screen Writers' Guild called a meeting to protest against the MPA's irresponsible actions. The meeting was held on 2 May, with representatives of seventeen organizations of cinema workers which together formed the Council of Hollywood Guilds and Unions, and whose publication *The Truth About Hollywood* denounced the witch-hunting frenzy that had struck the film industry.

It was not just the intellectual milieu that was affected by this campaign, but the United States as a whole, with the moral climate steadily deteriorating. Industrialists set out to challenge the social conquests of the New Deal, encouraging the hunt for radicals. In 1946, the Chamber of Commerce called for a systematic investigation of Communist influence on the media, and in 1948 it went on to demand laws to prohibit Communists from access to professions such as journalism, teaching, and social work. This demand was reiterated in 1952, and led to an eviction of 'Communists' from all professions that might have an influence on public opinion. In the early 1950s, Hollywood seemed to rekindle the hatred of conservative milieus. At a time when its films had nothing revolutionary about them, and were no longer innovative in any way, the cry of Communist subversion continued apace. Despite the failure of previous committees in their repeated assaults against Hollywood intellectuals, HUAC under Parnell Thomas managed to establish itself far more easily in the Cold War climate that now prevailed. The tactic employed was always the same: to intimidate by publicizing the accusations and the attitude of the accused, discrediting them if need be by a press campaign, or threatening the studio that employed them with economic sanctions. This was why a distinction was made between 'friendly witnesses', 'volunteers of information'[13] and 'unfriendly witnesses' – such as Hanns Eisler.[14] Long lists of 'Communists', real or imagined, were drawn up with the aid of 'informants',[15] while the Motion Picture Alliance also bent itself to denouncing a number of a number of progressive figures.

The launch of these investigations aroused real panic in the cinema milieu, sensitive as it was to public opinion. The producers delegated Eric Johnston to speak to the committee, as he was himself known as an anti-Communist. He assured Parnell Thomas of the producers' loyalty, seeking to deflect the HUAC investigations. But on 9 May 1947, John McDowell and Parnell Thomas arrived in Los Angeles and began the questioning of fourteen 'friendly witnesses'. The producers rightly believed that these investigations were ridiculous, and would lose them both time and money. Very few, however, followed Louis B. Meyer in openly displaying their contempt for the Committee and refusing to collaborate with it. In October 1947, forty-three members were summoned by HUAC to appear before the Committee in Washington. They included both 'friendly witnesses' and 'Communists' – nineteen left-wingers. Even today it is hard to understand the logic that impelled the Committee to choose these particular names among others: all lived in Hollywood, sixteen were writers, ten were Jewish, the majority had been members of the CPUSA and worked in antifascist organizations. In June 1947, seventeen members of the Joint Antifascist Refugee Committee were also called to give evidence. Rather than a legal battle, the accused tried to mobilize public opinion. In Hollywood they even managed to rally anti-Communist liberals who were disturbed by HUAC's actions, members of the Progressive Citizens of America, the Committee for the First Amendment[16] and the Screen Writers' Guild. Demonstrations against HUAC were held in Hollywood and New York, but many people wavered between defending their friends and the risk of damaging their career.

The hearings that opened in Washington on 20 October 1947 were a regular political show. Some witnesses treated the Committee with irony and contempt, whether they were writers, actors, or producers such as Louis B. Meyer. Others, like Jack Warner, did not hesitate to denounce 'Communists' in their studios. A parade of good Hollywood citizens appeared to display their sadness at seeing their town 'bolshevized'. Robert Taylor, Robert Montgomery, Ronald Reagan, Gary Cooper and George Murphy described the close attention they gave to reading scripts, with a view to discovering subversive tendencies or Communist ideas. At the same time, in a radio broadcast 'Hollywood Fights Back', a number of Hollywood stars including Lauren Bacall and Humphrey Bogart emphasized that the Committee represented a far greater danger than the one it claimed to combat. It was then time for the 'unfriendly witnesses', including John Howard Lawson, who attacked the Committee, constantly interrupted by Parnell Thomas.[17] Several of the accused tried to prove that the Committee's actions were a flagrant violation of the US Constitution. When the 'nineteen' returned, solidarity demonstrations were held in Hollywood and New York, showing how American opinion was divided. Progressive intellectuals were relatively optimistic at the defeats that HUAC had encountered. Many failed to foresee how they would soon figure on the blacklists which multiplied between 1947 and 1950, how they would be arrested, sentenced to prison, and have their career, broken for ever.

EFFECTS ON THE LIVES OF ÉMIGRÉS: THE CASES OF BRECHT AND EISLER

Long before the anti-Communist hysteria of McCarthyism, a number of émigrés had been denounced to the FBI as 'Communists'[18] and attacked by the Hearst press. At the end of the War, while some of them were preparing to return to Europe, the American press singled out a number of émigrés whom it accused of obeying 'Moscow's orders'. Egon Erwin Kisch, for example, on his arrival in Mexico en route for Prague, was called a 'Russian spy' in the *New York Times*. After being denounced by Louis Budenz (former editor of the *Daily Worker*) in January 1947, Gerhart Eisler, on the point of returning to Germany, was summoned to answer questions about his Communist activity in the United States. He was arrested two days before his departure and accused of being a Comintern agent. As there was no evidence to bring against him, he was prosecuted for his work in support of the Spanish Republic and for breach of the immigration laws: when he had entered the United States with a Mexican visa, he had omitted to declare his membership of the Communist party, and had used a false passport.

This accusation of 'technical perjury' was deeply absurd. Threatened with death by the Nazis, Communist émigrés were always careful not to declare their party membership. Besides, émigrés of all shades of opinion had used false papers, which were sometimes even provided by American rescue committees.[19] Parnell Thomas called to the witness stand Eisler's sister Ruth Fischer, a leader of the KPD in the 1920s, who denounced him as 'the perfect terrorist type'.[20] Though he had not undertaken any political activity in the United States, and even refrained from taking any stand on the internal situation, Eisler was accused of spreading Communism in Hollywood through his friendship with a number of progressive figures.[21] He was summoned to a HUAC hearing in Washington on 6 February 1947. Ruth Fischer immediately denounced him as a 'Comintern agent',[22] and their brother Hanns as a 'Communist in the philosophic sense'.[23]

Hanns Eisler was little known to the American public as a musician, despite his celebrity in Hollywood. It was the entire progressive culture he embodied that was denounced in his name. The 'Eisler case' thus became exemplary. The hunt was now on for the accomplices, within the New Deal programmes and the Roosevelt administration itself, who had enabled all these émigrés to establish themselves in the United States. In April 1947, Richard Nixon, then a representative for California, declared that HUAC suspected American films of carrying elements of Communist propaganda, and he did not hesitate to declare, when a subcommittee was sent to Hollywood to question Eisler, that 'the Hanns Eisler case is perhaps the most important yet to have come before the Committee'. But the questioning of Eisler in Hollywood proved disappointing, and Parnell Thomas was forced back to the weak assertion that Eisler had responded evasively when asked if he believed in capitalism. The press continued to attack Eisler in very violent terms, even though practically nothing had been found to reproach him with. It was above all his brother Gerhart who was being targeted through him. During Eisler's questioning by Parnell Thomas[24] in Washington on 24 September, the Committee sought to establish whether or not he was a Communist. Eisler remarked that he felt 'like an aboriginal trying to defend himself with arrows against an atom bomb'.[25] It was impossible to prove that he had been a member of the KPD in 1926. A large file of interviews, texts and musical scores was produced to try and show that he had regularly collaborated with American and Soviet Communist organizations. It was during this hearing that Eisler had the honour of being referred to by the chief investigator Robert Stripling as 'the Karl Marx of Communism in the field of music'. Eisler had to reject this unexpected compliment, which made him blush.

In order to convict him for having infringed the law governing visits to the United States by foreigners, a number of State Department officials in the Roosevelt administration were subpoenaed. The legislation in fact banned from entry into the United States any person who supported the overthrow of the government by force: the exiled Communists fell under the provision of this law, even if nothing specific could be charged against them. The Committee did not hesitate to use correspondence between Eleanor Roosevelt and Sumner Welles on the question of Eisler's request for a visa, to show 'attempts at Communist infiltration' within the previous administration. As it was impossible to prove anything substantial against Eisler, his file was handed over to the Justice Department, and to prevent him being simply acquitted, he was 'technically deported', i.e. expelled to a country not bordering on the United States.

A campaign of support for Hanns Eisler was rapidly formed, with a view to defending other threatened intellectuals and artists. Thomas Mann initially refused to take part, fearing possible repercussions on his family. On 10 October 1947 he wrote to Agnes E. Meyer: 'I am no longer signing any of the multi-tudinous appeals with which the desperate Left is making a nuisance of itself, for I have little desire to play the martyr once again.' He added, however:

> For personal reasons the case of Hanns Eisler touches me closely. I know the man very well; he is highly cultivated, brilliant, very amusing in conversation, and I have often had splendid talks with him [. . .]. Since the Inquisition has turned him over to the 'secular arm' for deportation, there is the danger that he will land in a German camp. I hear that Stravinsky (a White Russian!) means to start a demonstration in his favour. But I have wife and children and am not inquiring further into the matter.[26]

Mann did finally agree to join the defence committee for the Eisler brothers, together with Carey McWilliams.[27] Other American figures who joined the committee included Chaplin and Linus Pauling,[28] who were immediately attacked.[29] Thomas Mann was not alone in sensing that Eisler had to be defended.[30] Besides Chaplin and Einstein, a defence committee around Picasso was established in Paris, and in November, *Les Lettres Français* published a protest telegram signed by more than twenty French artists, including Picasso, Matisse, Eluard, Cocteau and Aragon. Eisler was one of the first victims; the blacklists now drawn up were to ruin the literary or film career of many progressive figures. After the Eisler investigation, and the campaign against the 'Hollywood Ten', the wave of systematic repression culminated in the McCarthy hysteria of the early 1950s. Those who had been spared in the first wave did not escape now. Eisler had to leave the United States. Four weeks before his departure, a number of American composers organized a farewell concert in his honour. His works were played before an audience enthusiastic at the beauty and subtlety of his music.[31]

Hanns Eisler and his family left New York for Prague on 26 March 1948. At La Guardia airport, he read a declaration to the press:

> I am not leaving this country without bitterness and anger. I could understand very well why the Hitler bandits put a price on my head and drove me out. They were the disease of the time; I was proud to be hunted by them. But I feel deeply wounded by the ridiculous manner in which I have been expelled from this fine country . . . I carry with me the image of the real American people whom I love.[32]

His brother Gerhart was arrested, and had to leave the United States illegally.[33] The investigation of Hanns Eisler inevitably led to that of Brecht, who received a summons to appear before the Committee on 19 September 1947. In July his play *The Life of Galileo* had been staged in Los Angeles, with Charles Laughton in the title role, and on the very day of his appearance before the Committee he had received a payment of $1,000 from the National Institute of Arts and Letters. Most people whom Brecht was acquainted with in Hollywood had been questioned, including Dorothy Thompson, who had helped Brecht reach the United States by financing his flight from Finland.

On 20 October, Brecht was questioned by Robert E. Stripling. The hearing was so grotesque that it scarcely seemed real.[34] The investigators spoke no German, and Brecht's English was poor. He deliberately exaggerated how badly he spoke and understood, getting on the Committee's nerves to the point that Parnell Thomas broke off the discussion and exclaimed: 'I cannot understand the interpreter any more than I can the witness.' After a hesitation about his date of birth, provoked by a mistake in English, Brecht proposed reading a very worthy declaration that he had prepared. He was prevented from doing this, and had to reply to the most ridiculous questions. Brecht was asked about his relations with Eisler, whom he had known since the 1920s, and the Committee tried in vain to establish his membership of the Communist party. Brecht tried again to read his declaration; it was submitted to the Committee chair and dismissed: 'This is a very interesting history of life in Germany, but has absolutely no bearing on the investigation. Consequently we will not allow you to read it.' Brecht was also asked about certain of his poems, and plays that were judged 'revolutionary'. He readily acknowledged that everything he had written in the context of the anti-Hitler struggle could effectively be viewed as 'revolutionary', since it worked for the overthrow of the Nazi regime. He was informed that it was not those works that were at issue. Brecht also acknowledged that a text which had appeared in a Communist magazine in East Berlin was indeed by him. The most solid element in the accusation lay in the theme of his play *The Measures Taken*, written in 1930, in which a young Communist is wrongly executed by his comrades.[35] Brecht managed to completely sidetrack the accusation by presenting the work as an adaptation of a Japanese Noh drama expressing the feeling of German workers in their struggle against Hitler, and skilfully eliminated all the controversial points.

Confronted with an interview with Tretyakov, which drew a somewhat exaggerated picture of his youthful political convictions, Brecht simply declared that he did not remember this. And when he was asked if his plays were based on the ideas of Marx, he acknowledged that he had studied these, and that he did not believe it possible in our day 'to write intelligent plays without making this kind of study'. He was also confronted with the songs he had written for *The Mother*, which had been published in a CPUSA magazine. He took issue with the translations, feigning not to recognize the original, and it was at this point that the exasperated chairman declared he could not even understand the interpreter. Brecht went on to maintain that he had never had the intention of joining the Communist party, and challenged the translation of the chorus of the 'Solidarity Song' from *Kuhle Wampe*. Having played to perfection before the Committee the role of Schweyk, he was thanked, and cited to other witnesses as an example of good will! Brecht did not wait for the first performance of *Galileo* in New

York, but left America for Switzerland. When he appeared before HUAC he already had his ticket for the passage.

The anti-Communist campaign steadily widened its scope into the early 1950s, leaving almost nothing untouched. During the Cold War, the United States rejected all proposed negotiation with the Soviet Union, and hunted out traces of 'Communist infiltration' in all the wheels of its administration and cultural life. The émigrés were always at the centre of these investigations. After the Eisler brothers and Brecht, Feuchtwanger also came under suspicion. A friend of both Eisler and Brecht, he was the author of *Moscow 1937*, and inscribed on the list of 'public Communists'. Before Arthur Miller wrote *The Crucible,* Feuchtwanger had written in 1946 *Wahn, oder der Teufel in Boston*, his own transposition of McCarthyism to the seventeenth century. Despite many requests, he had been refused US nationality and his fame did not stave off attacks in the press.[36]

The anti-Communist campaign did not even spare those émigrés who had never had anything to do with the party.[37] While the US government sought to mobilize intellectuals and public opinion behind its crusade, progressive figures whom no one could suspect of Communist sympathies, such as Thomas Mann and Albert Einstein, supported the Committee for the First Amendment, established after the 'Hollywood Ten' affair. Einstein had behind him a long past of pacifist commitment,[38] while Thomas Mann was rightly seen as one of the great representatives of European culture. His faith in liberalism led him to react vigorously to the development of American policy, and he courageously declared himself to HUAC a 'hostile witness', despite asserting his rejection of Communist ideas. His celebrity did not stop Mann being violently attacked for his contacts with the 'Soviet zone'. It was not long before the Republican George Doudero attacked 'red art', and called futurism, cubism, expressionism and surrealism 'weapons of destruction of our cultural heritage'. The prestige of Einstein and Mann helped the Arts, Sciences and Professions Committee to organize a conference for peace[39] which attracted 550 intellectuals and artists – immediately called the 'Pink Cominform'. Twenty-one figures from the socialist countries were given visas, but kept under constant surveillance by the FBI and HUAC: some progressive intellectuals such as Lillian Hellman tried to shift discussion from Cold War antagonisms to problems such as poverty and hunger which seemed to go unnoticed.

Thomas Mann followed this development with consternation. He had thought to find a new homeland in America. He declared that he hated the activities of HUAC as much as he had hated Hitler. In 1948 he saw himself labelled a 'potential Soviet agent'. His situation was morally all the more difficult in that he felt as hostile to Soviet policy as to 'the inquisition, the Cold War and the ridiculous fondness for renegade Communists'.[40] Mann avoided any display of sympathy for the new German Democratic Republic, so as not to give any excuse for American attacks, trying in this way to maintain a difficult balance.[41]

In letters written in 1949, Thomas Mann constantly deplored his humanism and liberalism being now taxed as 'Communist':

I've put all honest people's backs up because of my 'Communism', and I read every day terrible things about my moral decline. The world is raving mad. If in 1932 someone expressed the conviction that there would one day exist a world that was organized, planned, unified, thanks to a common management of the earth [. . .] he would still have been treated as more or less respectable. Today, the same words trigger against you, in unison, the fury of the entire press of the Atlantic pact.[42]

When he signed a protest against the imprisonment of lawyers defending the American Communist leaders, he was attacked once more, and noted:

Things happen, acts are being prepared, that would up till now have been unimaginable in a country where fascism had not yet broken out [. . .]. The 'Cold War' is ruining America both physically and morally, this is why I'm against it – and not against America. If the Mundt–Nixon bill is passed, I'll *run off* legs akimbo, along with my seven doctorates *honoris causa*.[43]

In 1950, Mann cancelled several lectures for fear of public reaction against him as a 'Communist'. His daughter Erika was forced to give up any work in the press or radio. He sadly noted on 3 April 1951: 'I've reached the age of seventy-five living in a foreign country which has become a homeland for me, to be now publicly accused of lying by the witch-hunters who, and this is the scandalous thing, believe in no one apart from the sayings of their own witches.'[44] And it was certainly this moral degradation of America rather than a nostalgia for Europe that led Mann to return there for the last years of his life.

'GERMANY, PALE MOTHER':
BETWEEN DREAMS AND RUINS

I know of course: it's simply luck
That I've survived so many friends. But last night in a dream
I heard those friends say of me: 'Survival of the fittest'
And I hated myself.

Bertolt Brecht, 'I, the Survivor'

There is no victory. At the end of this war there are only the vanquished.

Alfred Kantorowicz

On 30 April 1945, Hitler killed himself in his bunker. The Nazi radio announced the death of the Führer, 'fallen in his final struggle against bolshevism'. Admiral Dönitz, appointed as his successor, addressed the Wehrmacht to confirm this news. Hitler, the man who rose from nothing, had returned to nothing, leaving behind him only millions of deaths and cities in ruins. In his first speeches, calling on God as his witness, he had declared that after him Germany would no longer be recognizable. Photographs of the Reich in 1945 show in what sinister fashion his prophecy was fulfilled. Where Hanover, Nuremberg, Frankfurt, Berlin and Dresden once stood, nothing could be distinguished in many districts except heaps of charred stone and burned-out apartment blocks. The whole of Germany was plunged into misery, fear and chaos. Who then spared a thought for the émigrés? Twelve years of Hitlerism had banished their names from German memories. In an exile poem, Kurt Pinthus wrote in an astounding prophetic way that he felt buried in forgetfulness, as by a shroud of snow.

The capitulation of 8 May 1945, marking the collapse of the Third Reich, opened for all the exiles the possibility of returning to Germany. Many among them had not lived long enough to see this day, even if some seem to have survived simply in the hope of seeing Germany again, if only to die there. Others could only view such an encounter with their former homeland, which they had never ceased to dream of, with a silent anguish. What would they see there, and who would be waiting for them? Those who suffered most cruelly from their uprooting, from linguistic solitude and misery, were often the most tempted by an immediate return. The more politicized believed that their exile was now at an end, but a new mission awaited them: to help rebuild the moral and material ruins of their country, and aid the birth of a republican and democratic Germany. For others, the tie with their former homeland had become so problematic that they sometimes no longer saw themselves as 'Germans'.[45]

Encountering this vanquished Germany, they experienced contradictory feelings, made up of love, hate and pity, largely depending on their exile experiences but also on the fate of those they had left behind. When Carl Zuckmayer returned to Bavaria and found his parents again, even learning that an SS man bearing the 'mask of evil' had helped his mother to survive, he declared that he was unable to hate.[46] Fred Uhlman, for his part, visited his grandmother's tomb in the Jewish cemetery in Stuttgart, but knew he could never do the same for his parents and sister, exterminated at Auschwitz:

> I broke into tears. I wept as I had never wept in my life and as I hope never again to weep. I was now fifty years old. I wept for my murdered family, my dead friends, my poisoned memories, the countless thousands of Jews and Christians who had been massacred. I wept for Germany, for the ruins of so many old and lovely cities [. . .]. I silently shouted: 'Murder! Murder' over the Jewish tombs, no longer maintained, and my voice was full of hatred, as beyond the hedge dividing the Jewish from the Christian part, I saw Christian graves that were tidy and carefully weeded.[47]

They feared the poverty and ruins, but above all the unknown reception with which the German people would greet those who had gone into exile in 1933. Many asked themselves how far the population were contaminated by Nazism, and whether their names still meant anything after more than a decade of Hitlerism.

Heinrich Mann described in a letter to Karl Lemke on 7 November 1946 a message of sympathy he had received from a Berlin worker, who declared: 'What astonished me most is that you are still alive.' He thought that this worker had grasped his situation admirably. At the writers' congress held in Berlin in 1947, where Ricarda Huch paid homage to all the anti-Nazi writers who died in exile or in Germany, the expressionist poet and pacifist Arnim T.

Wegener was surprised to discover his name on the commemorative plaque. He was shattered, he said, to be confronted with his tomb, but he believed it was not completely wrong: as his name had been banished from German memories, and he himself condemned to exile, he had the feeling of having been dead a long while.

During these long years of exile, the youngest émigrés had become mature men and women, sometimes prematurely aged. Some of their number, including the most famous, had died or would die soon. Thomas Mann's last volume of letters contains countless messages of condolence for such deaths.[48]

The survivors of exile, in 1945, were still a most varied bunch. No more than in 1933 was there any real unity among them. If some planned to return to Germany as quickly as possible, others felt that the gulf between them and their former country could never again be bridged. And even those who sought to get back to Europe in any way possible still felt a mixture of hope, doubt and apprehension: what would they find, and whom? All had several friends dead in concentration camps, sometimes their entire family. They often returned to a desert of ruins in which they felt once again in exile.

The decision whether to return or remain in exile is complex and difficult to analyse. In many cases it was hard to foresee. How could one imagine for example that Thomas Mann, who in 1933 had maintained in his letters that he could not imagine staying out of Germany for long, would declare in 1945 that he had no desire to return there? The reasons that led the exiles to return were very varied. Some of them returned with the firm resolution to work for the political and moral reconstruction of Germany, others because in exile they had experienced only poverty and despair, and life even in a ruined Germany could not be worse than emigration. Still others were inspired by the wish to see again the country that had dreamed about ever since they left.

But the return was not so simple. Material, legal and psychological obstacles were as strong as nostalgia. The émigrés' age played a significant role. While the younger of them were ready to recommence their existence in Germany, the older ones could not envisage the perspective of return without apprehension.[49] In 1933, they had been forced to abandon everything and leave for exile, changing their language, homeland and profession. They managed only with great difficulty to rebuild the modest basis of their existence. In the course of time, some had a degree of success. In 1945, they often feared having to abandon everything once again. They were not rich in America, but in Europe they risked being even poorer. Describing the death of his brother Heinrich, Thomas Mann wrote:

> In this last period he suffered a great deal, and had aged a lot physically, but he planned in about six weeks' time to move to East Berlin where wealth and striking honours were waiting for him [. . .]. On his last evening he stayed up later than usual, listened joyfully to music for a good while, and found it hard to decide to go to bed. Then in his sleep, a brain haemorrhage, the most merciful solution.[50]

At his burial, Lion Feuchtwanger and a pastor of the Unitarian Church spoke, and Heinrich was carried to his grave accompanied by a Debussy string quartet. His death was reported at length in the German Democratic Republic, but raised scarcely a mention in West Germany.[51] Reading Heinrich Mann's correspondence one can measure his chagrin at having not received for such a long time any invitation to return. His burning desire to do so had been matched by a fear of dying there of hunger.[52] If the most famous émigrés were fairly speedily asked to return to Europe, offered academic posts and new university chairs, several had the feeling that they no longer existed in the eyes of their compatriots. Leonhard Frank sadly wrote in his diary: 'I did not become a great writer, one of the greats. I did not succeed, but I did what I could and even a bit more. Amen!' Alongside the literary and political eminences who were pressed to return to Germany, a number of émigrés felt that if they were no longer 'corpses in waiting', as Goebbels put it, they were certainly 'living dead'. Writers in particular knew they would have to wait a long while before their books were republished and they could find a new readership. Many indeed feared losing what following they still had. The majority were unable to afford the Atlantic crossing,[53] any more than they could when they reached America in 1939–40 with the aid of the refugee committees. The émigrés in Mexico had to wait for Soviet ships to be repatriated, and in the immediate postwar years those in North America had to take US military transports.[54]

The psychological obstacles were no less serious. The Nazi regime had been overthrown by the Allied armies and not by a popular uprising. The bitter resistance of the Nazis, and the absence of apparent opposition from the population, could suggest a genuine adhesion to the regime's values. The discussions at the end of the War on the connection between National Socialism and German history, and the responsibility of the German people, betrayed the fear of many that even after Hitler, Hitlerism might not be really dead. How deeply had Nazi propaganda marked the German people? If some, like Brecht, were convinced that not all Germans should be tarred with the Nazi brush, other émigrés – Thomas Mann in particular – did not hide their scepticism. They feared that Germany was still infested with National Socialism,[55] and that nothing could bridge the yawning gulf between the émigrés and those who had stayed in Germany.[56] Throughout the exile period, and especially during the War, their feelings towards Germany had steadily shifted. As Golo Mann later wrote:

> The names of French, Luxemburger, Dutch, Norwegian, Polish and Czech martyrs are engraved on monuments in all the countries surrounding Germany. There are no monuments, however, for German writers, whether they committed suicide or were discovered by the Nazis in one of the occupied countries, deported and murdered. Incontestably, their fate was less heroic, in a passive comparison. You whose countries were occupied, detested the enemy; we did too, but because we were Germans ourselves, we experienced at the same time a feeling of confusion that was unknown to you.[57]

Very few even of those who still kept a deep attachment to Germany could escape being traumatized by the ruins of their country. With a painful farsightedness, Döblin wrote that this victory over fascism was also their destruction as émigrés. What remained of the 'spiritual' Germany that they had taken with them into exile? Faced with a conquered Germany, they experienced complex feelings in which fear, pity and disgust were mingled.[58] Elias Canetti noted in 1945 that 'Hitler has transformed the Germans into Jews, in that today the word "German" has become as painful as the word "Jew".' The talk was of 'crime' and 'punishment', terms that were most often employed by authors of bourgeois origin, who often interpreted Nazism as a perversion of national character. For many of these, belief in the existence of an 'internal emigration' had eroded with the passage of time. They were therefore as fearful of returning to a devastated Germany as were their compatriots. If the most politicized of their number – activists or writers[59] – were ready to work for the reconstruction of their country, many sank into a sadness and despair that they never managed to shake off: after their return from exile, they discovered that the Germany they had fled no longer existed.[60] Their cities and their memories were no more than ruins in which they could not find an orientation.

The return of the émigrés spread from 1945 into the 1950s. The political émigrés were naturally the most eager to return, despite the difficulties of all kinds that lay in wait. Writers were often more cautious. As for those denoted as 'racial émigrés', who had left Germany because of anti-Semitism, members of the liberal professions and even a certain number of academics, many of these groups chose to remain in their countries of asylum.[61] In the first few years after the War, return to Germany was often quite difficult, as the country remained cut off from the rest of the world.[62] The logic that drove certain émigrés to return to Germany and others to remain in exile was not always clear.[63] Thomas Mann agreed to visit Europe, but it was a long while before he decided to return there to live. George Grosz never thought of returning to Berlin, Piscator awaited the official invitation that would offer him a new theatre, Eisler and Brecht were chased out of America by McCarthyism, Alfred Döblin was so unhappy in America that he had to leave.

It is hard to remain unmoved by reading the accounts of so many émigrés that depict their first contact with Germany after 1945. Before they were able to return, they tried to make contact with relatives and friends. They had remained without news since the start of the War, if not before, with only rare letters arriving via Switzerland. Sometimes it was their relations who made the first move, wanting to obtain some permission from the Russian or American military authorities, penicillin, clothing or coffee. The exiles could send them parcels via the US armed forces,[64] sympathizing with their sufferings and scarcely daring to ask why they seemed to have forgotten them when they went into exile. These attempts to renew links were all the more tragic in that some exiles discovered that their entire family had been deported and exterminated in concentration camps, others that their parents or children had become

Nazis, but now wanted their assistance to justify themselves to the de-Nazification commissions.

What were the first impressions they had on regaining their birthplace? More than anything else, a sense of disturbing foreignness. In 1939, Carl Zuckmayer had written a strange poem in which he imagined his return:

> I know I will see it all again,
> But everything will have changed;
> I will walk through extinct towns
> Where not one stone still stands upon another,
> And even where there are these old stones
> There will no longer be the familiar alleys.
> I know I will see it all again,
> And that I will find nothing more of what I left behind.[65]

Hubertus Prinz zu Löwenstein exclaimed in October 1946: 'How beautiful Germany is, despite all the ruins.' Claire Waldoff, in a letter to Elow, compared postwar Berlin to an 'illuminated cemetery'.[66] When Fred Uhlman returned to Stuttgart, he felt a complete stranger: 'The city was no more than a great cemetery under the moon, and I walked through it as one ghost among others. The windows which one day had been opened for me were empty. I waited, but no one came.'[67]

This encounter with Germany was often experienced as a violent trauma. One of the most emotive depictions of this return is undoubtedly that of Klaus Mann in *The Turning Point*. Arriving in Europe with the US Army, and working as a journalist and writer, he found Munich in such ruin that he could not find his way around. The house where he was born was still standing, though it had been altered inside. It was impossible to reach the upper floor, as the staircase had been destroyed, and a young woman had established herself acrobatically on the mezzanine. She was unaware who owned the house, but remembered that at one time it had belonged to a famous writer. Klaus Mann and another American soldier requisitioned a bed with a family. The father said how much he had hated Hitler, but in the bedroom Mann found Nazi books, which he threw on the fire with a feeling close to despair. He went to Dachau and attended the interrogation of Göring, who claimed never to have known of the existence of concentration camps, throwing all responsibility for them on Himmler. Klaus Mann asked him in German if Hitler was really dead.

Disoriented by these ruins, he tried to meet up with old friends. He called on Richard Strauss, in American uniform and without revealing his identity. The old musician complained about the Nazis: his Jewish daughter-in-law had not been allowed to go hunting, and his last operas were almost ignored. When Klaus Mann asked Strauss if he had ever thought of leaving Germany, the old man proudly replied that Germany had eighty opera houses. He did not even react when Mann corrected him: 'It used to have.' Strauss would say nothing about all that had happened under Hitler; not a word of regret. He was even vexed when Klaus Mann, this young American soldier, refused a signed photograph. Mann found old acquaintances who had survived concentration camp and looked like ghosts. Emil Jannings, ever jovial with his dogs and parrots, waxed indignant that he should be taken for a Nazi, when he considered himself almost a martyr. Winifred Wagner confided to Klaus Mann how charming she had found Hitler, so intelligent and full of good spirits. Desperate and ashamed, Mann thought of writing a play, *Are All Germans Nazis?* The unease that he felt, and that steadily grew, most likely contributed to his suicide.

Alfred Döblin returned to Germany so as to flee the disastrous situation with its solitude and poverty that he had known in Hollywood. He sincerely wanted to take part in the rebuilding of German culture, and was one of the first writers to put an end to his exile. In 1945 he visited Baden-Baden, in the French military zone, inspired by a certain faith in the future of Germany in a united Europe. At Strasbourg station he contemplated the ruins and thought they were a fitting symbol of the time. In the distance he could see the Rhine and its collapsed bridges. When he set foot on German soil, sadness gave way momentarily to fear, it was so hard for him to realize that he could walk through German streets without risking arrest by the Gestapo.[68] Carl Zuckmayer arrived in Berlin by military train in November 1946. Visiting the military government in Dahlem, he felt that Berlin had become a dead city. When he saw the Kaiser-Wilhelm-Gedächtnis-Kirche, he recalled that this bombed-out church used to be the very heart of Berlin, with its literary cafés and the cinemas of the Kurfürstendamm. He saw a child dressed in rags collecting bits of wood, and realized that he no longer knew anyone there. He met Peter Suhrkamp, released from concentration camp, and looked for his parents, with the feeling that it was impossible to hate this ruined Germany. Ludwig Marcuse described his return to Munich and Berlin in similar terms, and his inability to find his way in these devastated cities. As Klaus Mann questioned Emil Jannings, so Marcuse asked Gottfried Benn how he had been able to defend the Nazi regime. Benn blushed, stammered and found nothing to say in reply.

This confrontation with the others, those who had stayed, was often as painful as the encounter with the destroyed cities.[69] Some émigrés were fortunate enough to meet up again with their families, even in bombed-out buildings. Many others learned of their loved ones' death in concentration camp. If until 1933 they had shared a common history despite their political divisions, the distance that now separated them seemed almost unbridgeable. As Manès Sperber noted about the émigrés:

> They could not hold back a sign of indignation when people found them changed and even unrecognizable, or even when people claimed they were still the same – as if those who had remained at home all this time were trying in this way to wipe out the memory of the banishment inflicted on their victims and wash their hands of the crime they had committed towards them.[70]

The majority of émigrés asked themselves what their compatriots who had stayed in Germany had experienced, what events had taught them. If some people welcomed them effusively, many felt only hatred towards them. Since they had left Germany in 1933, they were traitors; and now they returned as conquerors.[71] They had not known the sufferings of the German people, and their accusations or questions were rejected in advance.[72] Only a rare few had the courage to appeal to the émigrés to hasten their return.

In 1946, Günter Weisenborn, spokesman 'of the Germany that did not collaborate with National Socialism', did call on the émigrés to return,[73] and a similar appeal was made to academics by Alfred Andersch on 1 January 1947. Rather later, Walter von Molo published on 13 August 1953 his celebrated *Open Letter to Thomas Mann*, calling on him to return to Germany, like a doctor to the bedside of a sick patient. Frank Thiess had made a similar appeal already on 18 August 1945. The distrust that Mann displayed towards Germany led to a scathing reply to this open letter from Thiess. He attacked Mann for his attitude towards Germany, maintaining that those who had lived for a dozen years in the Nazi hell needed no lesson from the émigrés who had spent this time in California while they were being bombed.

Often these émigré accounts of their return – which demand a whole study to themselves – were one long chronicle of the disillusion and new humiliations that they experienced. Each day they grew more aware of everything that separated them from those who had remained in Germany. Each side frequently viewed the other with distrust and hostility. Those who had left Germany were astonished to find so little regret or self-criticism, both for their political illusions and in some cases for their cowardice. After they had searched anxiously for the slightest sign of resistance and opposition on the part of all those writers who stayed in the Reich, and had been cruelly affected by their professions of faith and submission to the Nazi regime, they regarded their self-justifications, lies and complaints with a mixture of horror and disgust. Rare were the intellectuals, writers and artists belonging to the Reichskulturkammern who did not in 1945 declare themselves opponents of the regime, 'internal émigrés', making out that their public adhesion was only a ruse to conceal their real opposition to Nazism, 'to keep open the émigrés' places', as Gottfried Benn put it. To listen to them, or read them, one might suppose that it was only the sudden collapse of the Nazi regime that had prevented them from tearing off their masks and leaping on the adversary. Indeed, it is impossible to read most of the autobiographies of writers who remained in Germany during the Nazi years without a certain malaise. The degree of bad faith, lies, blindness and omissions of which they were guilty is only too often on display in their books, speeches and articles of the time. A number of émigrés, understandably, followed Ernst Busch in declaring that before shaking a German's hand, he wanted to know where he was after 1933.[74] This cleavage that divided the intellectuals often ran even within a single family. Gustav Regler's son had fought in the German army, Erwin Piscator's brother had joined the Nazi party, as had the father of Anne-Marie Hirsch, who left for exile with her Jewish husband.[75] When the slow, complex and imperfect process of de-Nazification got under way, some writers did not hesitate to ask the émigrés, in the name of

their former friendship, for certificates of good conduct – to their understandable consternation.[76] The attempt to create a real interest in 'exile
literature' did not succeed, despite the efforts of Döblin,[77] who perhaps suffered
more than any other writer from the ignorance towards émigré authors in the
early postwar years. Döblin did not manage to renew the connections, or even
establish some kind of unity among the exiles with his magazine *Das Goldene
Tor* (1951), published with French backing. Two years later, deeply shattered,
he turned his back on Germany and moved to France. Despite occasional
honours – the West Berlin senator for culture and education, Joachim Tiberius,
proposed that he should settle in Berlin, and he was given honorary membership
of the Hamburg Freie Akademie der Künste, along with Paul Hindemith and G.
Marks – he found it painful that his novels were not reissued. He was given the
literary prize of the Mainz academy, made a corresponding member of the
Akademie der Künste in East Berlin, and received a further prize from the
Bavarian academy shortly before his death. But for all this, Döblin felt that his
novels were in some way being boycotted.[78] He remained in France, living on a
modest pension, and on 6 October 1952 wrote to Arnold Zweig:

> When I came back in 1945, no one that I spoke to or read wanted to know anything of
> what had happened before. Now they have become completely open . . . They only
> speak and write about German unity, and one would have to be mad not to know
> what that means, in other words the core, the beginning [. . .] of the old song, which
> sooner or later becomes the Horst Wessel song.

Still more disillusioned, he wrote a farewell letter to the President of the Federal
Republic, Theodor Heuss, on 28 April 1953: 'This was not a return, rather a
kind of extended visit [. . .]. There is no use for me in this country where my
parents and I were born.' To the end of his life, none of Döblin's novels were
reissued, and no publisher accepted his novel *Hamlet, oder Die lange Nacht
nimmt ein Ende.*[79] He died on 26 June 1957 and was buried in France, alongside
his son Wolfgang. His wife committed suicide on 14 September.

If Döblin's case is one of the most tragic among those returning from exile,
many examples could be given of how hard they found it to reintegrate into
postwar Germany. Piscator renewed contact with Brecht after their falling-out
over a new production of *Schweyk* in America. In many letters he mooted the
idea of a joint theatre project, but Brecht believed that their styles were too
different to enable them to work together: two theatres would be needed.
Friedrich Wolf invited Piscator to settle in East Berlin, on behalf of the
Volksbühne. Piscator, however, whose relations with the Communist party
had been far from simple since his return from Engels,[80] doubted the official
character of the invitation. Faced with his hesitations, Wolf began to wonder
whether Piscator really wanted to return to Germany, or was fearful of leaving
New York for a city in ruins. Brecht invited him to come and stage a play in
Berlin and Zurich. But Piscator never received confirmation that he would be
given a theatre of his own in East Berlin.

In 1951, fearing arrest as a Communist – the FBI apparently had already taken out a warrant against him[81] – Piscator left the United States for West Germany, despite having no invitation there. He staged productions in Marburg, Tübingen and Giessen, in small theatres. At fifty-nine years old, he had to recommence his career like a beginner, despite having been one of the great directors of the Weimar period. Following his production of *War and Peace* in Berlin, on 20 March 1955, attacks on him steadily intensified. Not only was his style dismissed as 'anachronistic and outmoded' – political theatre was certainly out of fashion in the Federal Republic – but his ideological convictions were denounced in the strongest terms. Confronted with such ferocious attacks, Piscator felt once again an émigré in his own country. Several of his productions were violently criticized,[82] reaching a peak when he staged Rolf Hochhuth's *The Representative*, which raised the question of relations between Pius XII and the Third Reich. The hatred shown in this criticism was no less than he had known in the 1920s. As for the exiled playwrights, generally there was no interest in their émigré experience, which was only rarely depicted.[83]

George Grosz was offered a professorship at the Berliner Hochschule für Bildende Kunst, but he turned it down, replying that he preferred 'to be poor and a failure in the United States than a failure and poor in Germany'. Appointed a member of the West Berlin Akademie der Künste in 1958, he eventually returned to Germany on 28 May, and died there on 6 July. Even authors who were acclaimed on their return, such as Carl Zuckmayer,[84] did not always officially end their exile. Zuckmayer took Swiss nationality, and also adopted a different style from that of the 1920s. Lion Feuchtwanger was officially invited to settle in the GDR as a member of the Akademie der Künste, and awarded the Nationalpreis für Kunst und Literatur in 1953, but he was ignored in the Federal Republic, and his books not reissued there. His doctoral title from Munich University, which had been revoked by the Nazis, was restored to him on the demand of the GDR authorities; he received it in the post, without an accompanying letter. And though a proposal was made in 1957 to award him the literary prize of the city of Munich, its senate decided to keep its distance from this 'pro-Communist' writer. He preferred to put up with American anti-Communism rather than return to Germany.[85]

Thomas Mann's return was equally complex. The reasons that led him to settle in Switzerland, visiting Germany in 1949 for the Goethe celebration and in 1955 for that of Schiller, had less to do with nostalgia for Europe and Germany than with a steady deterioration in his relationship with the United States. In a letter to Einstein of 27 November 1945,[86] he already deplored 'the present moral state of the country – the growing xenophobia, anti-Semitism, etc.' In 1951, Eugene Tillinger launched a campaign against him in *The Freeman*, accusing him of sending birthday greetings to J. R. Becher, 'literary valet of the Stalinists of East Germany'. He initially reacted negatively to the suggestion by Walter von Molo that he should return to Germany.[87] Replying on 7 September 1945, he declined the historic mission that some German writers seemed to expect of him, recalling his break with Germany and the sufferings of exile, and declared that he did not see why he should now give up the advantages he had acquired in

America by returning to Germany: 'I confess that I am afraid of the German ruins – the ruins of stone and the human ones. And I fear that understanding would be difficult between someone who experienced the witches' sabbath from outside, and you who danced along with it.'

Mann acknowledged that he was touched by the testimonies of friendship he had received from Germany, but noted that these came *after* the defeat of Hitler. If he refrained from condemning en bloc the authors who had not emigrated, he declared that for him 'the books that could be published in Germany between 1933 and 1945 are worth less than nothing [. . .]. A smell of blood and shame still permeates them.'[88] Yet he admitted that throughout his exile the thought of Germany had never left him, and that he 'dreamed of feeling under his feet again the soil of the old continent'.[89] Mann still hesitated about making a trip to Europe when the *Bürgermeister* of Frankfurt invited him in January 1948, arguing his age, tiredness, and the length of the journey. His letters, however, show a gradual evolution. After his very critical position towards Germany at the end of the War, he once again declared himself its 'son'. As he steadily distanced himself from America, he was attentive to the republication of his works in the Federal Republic and increasingly interested in the development of his homeland.

Mann still feared his rediscovery of Germany. His emotional reaction would be very strong, he maintained, and he did not know what the feelings of his compatriots towards him would be: 'The émigrés are not seen in a good light,' he wrote to Hans Riesiger on 19 December 1948, 'they have not been faithful to Germany.' In spring 1949, nonetheless, Mann decided to visit Europe, though still hesitated about a return to Munich, considering this would be 'a hallucinatory adventure and a real test'. He agreed to accept the Goethe prize in Frankfurt, and went on to visit Weimar, criticizing the Soviet Union there just as he had criticized America's anti-Communist hysteria. He finally agreed to come to Munich, noting that 'To see this whole portion of an outlived past reappearing in a tattered and battered state, with the faces of people so much aged, had something ghostly about it.'[90]

Mann refused to see his old house, now half ruined, and was disturbed by the state of mind of a large number of Germans: 'Everything that after 1945 had for a moment to bend down and hide itself is now shamelessly raising its head, encouraged by the madness and short-sightedness from abroad' (1 December 1949). The growing American anti-Communism, and the attacks he had experienced himself, led him to feel increasingly a stranger there as well: 'We in this foreign land that has become so homelike are living in the wrong place, which confers a certain air of immorality upon our existence' (letter to Theodor Adorno, 9 January 1950).[91] In May 1950, Mann travelled to France and Switzerland, stopping off in Zurich, where he considered staying: 'The situation in the United States is such that I can only tell myself that in all probability I will have to give up my home there and establish in Switzerland a new and necessarily more modest existence.'

Thomas Mann, who in 1945 could not imagine any kind of return to Europe, and especially not to Germany, aspired in 1950 to 'return to the old ground': 'I would not want to repose in this soulless ground, to which I owe nothing and which knows nothing of me,' he wrote to Hans Carossa on 7 May 1951. He visited his home town of Lübeck, but settled finally in Switzerland. By the end of his life, Mann had renewed multifarious connections with Germany, and his work was again celebrated there. Unhappily, very few of the émigrés had this good fortune: the majority did not live to see their works republished, felt despised or forgotten, and a number of them left Germany again for a new exile.[92]

The situation of those émigrés who had returned to the Soviet zone of occupation had its own complications. It was naturally the Communist émigrés and their fellow-travellers who were tempted to settle in East Berlin. Their return however posed logistic problems.[93] The *Pushkin* had to make a detour of 2,000 kilometres to pick up Alexander Abusch, Paul Merker and other Communist émigrés in Mexico, and bring them to Europe. Gerhart Eisler left the United States illegally on a Polish ship. Brecht travelled cautiously to Berlin, one step at a time, passing through Switzerland, Vienna and Prague. On 30 August 1945, the group of Communist émigrés around Walter Ulbricht welcomed Willi Bredel to Berlin. J. R. Becher, Bredel, Fritz Erpenbeck and H. Willmann together launched a *Programm des Kulturbundes zur demokratischen Erneuerung Deutschlands*, which attracted a fairly large number of émigrés. Before long, these émigrés came to occupy important positions in East German cultural organizations: Erich Weinert became vice-president of the Deutsche Zentralverwaltung für Volksbildung, Gustav von Wangenheim director of the Deutsches Theater (Max Reinhardt's old theatre), while Julius Wolf reorganized the cinema.[94] New publishing houses were established, especially Aufbau Verlag, and cultural organizations rebuilt in which émigrés were called to play a major role. In 1946, an exhibition of art banned in the Hitler period was organized in Dresden, and the following year the Büchner prize was awarded to Anna Seghers. As early as 1946, the Sowjetische Militäradministration in Deutschland published a large number of Soviet novels in translation, along with a certain number of German émigré works, including J. R. Becher's poems. In so far as the young German Democratic Republic laid claim to the progressive inheritance of Weimar culture, it was only normal that the émigrés should receive special attention. Even today, it has to be recognized that it was in the GDR, not the Federal Republic, that the works of the antifascist émigrés were systematically reissued in large editions. Heinrich Mann became a popular author in the GDR at a time when his books could scarcely be found in West Germany. It was also the GDR that saw the largest number of works on the antifascist emigration. The émigrés were certainly honoured there, though it is very difficult, beyond appearances, to gauge exactly what influence they went on to exercise, even if the government was itself made up of political émigrés (Wilhelm Pieck, Walter Ulbricht) and some literary émigrés, such as Alexander Abusch, Alfred Kurella and J. R. Becher, occupied important functions.

As evidenced by documents published by the Institut für Marxismus-Leninismus beim ZK der SED and the Kulturbund der DDR,[95] the initial intentions were excellent. In February 1946, intellectuals, artists and writers, whether Communist or not, were invited to take part in a great effort to transform Germany and build a new culture.[96] In the field of literature, this effort was to involve a rediscovery of the German classics, the large-scale distribution of Soviet literature, and the development of a certain progressive culture that had its roots in that of the Weimar Republic. It was in this sense that works of a large number of writers were published and publicized.[97] If in West Berlin the main cultural initiative involved reopening the theatres, what figured most prominently in the East was the creation of new cultural structures. In May 1947 the first congress of the Kulturbund was held, and in October the first congress of German writers. The years 1947–48 were marked by the opening to Soviet culture, the multiplication of newspapers, magazines, publishing houses and libraries, in all of which the émigrés (Erich Weinert, Alexander Abusch, Arnold Zweig, Willi Bredel, J. R. Becher) were very active. On 7 October 1949, the émigré Wilhelm Pieck became the first president of the GDR. In re-reading the memoirs of these exiles who founded the 'new Germany', one realizes the weight of the hopes and dreams invested in it. It is impossible to deny however the great disillusion that was to follow; and the émigré community of 1945–46 in East Berlin was soon to break up in division. A solid core remained around Wilhelm Pieck and Walter Ulbricht, which included Paul Merker, Alexander Abusch, J. R. Becher and later Alfred Kurella, who became regular 'cultural functionaries'. For a good while, the émigrés were active in press and publishing, with such magazines as *Sonntag* (organ of the Kulturbund), *Der Aufbau*, and *Die Weltbühne*.[98] But only a few, such as Abusch and especially Becher, remained permanently in important posts. Most of the other émigrés, despite being officially fêted, were soon retired to work of minor responsibility, even if they were awarded honorific positions.[99] In the first postwar years, there was still quite close contact between émigrés in East and West. Non-Communist progressive authors were honoured in the Soviet zone. In the West, Alfred Döblin appealed in his magazine *Das Goldene Tor* for contributions from the many authors now resident in the East, as well as non-émigré authors such as Otto Flake and Hermann Kasack.

One of the last symbols of the community that still existed among the émigrés was the Tag des Freien Buches held in Berlin in 1947. On the anniversary of the book burning of 10 May 1933, a large number of émigrés from both East and West, as well as antifascists who had stayed in Germany (Peter Suhrkampf) met to celebrate cultural freedom. Manfred Hausmann, B. Kellermann, Elisabeth Langässer, Günther Weissenborn, Axel Eggelbrecht and Hermann Kasack joined émigrés from both sides of the geopolitical divide. Kindler Verlag published a special issue on the writers silenced by National Socialism. Richard Drews spoke on the 'internal emigration', Alfred Kantorowicz on the exile.[100] Kantorowicz's introduction was published with a preface by one of the cultural heads of the Soviet army, General Tulpanov, a professor at Leningrad University. A ceremony was held at the Haus der Kultur der Sowjetunion. Marshal Sokolovsky addressed a message recalling the present task of all German antifascists: to work for the birth of a humanist and socialist culture, and root out all vestiges of National Socialism. During this celebration, poems of Heine and Mayakovsky were read out, and texts by Heinrich Mann, Kurt Tucholsky and Gorky, while Ernst Busch, rescued from his bombed-out prison in 1945, sang songs by Brecht and Eisler. For the last time, representatives from all four sectors met together in the name of their common past. As Kantorowicz recalls, anti-Communists such as Birkenfeld and Nestriepke could be seen alongside party functionaries J. R. Becher and Alexander Abusch, 'East Germans' such as Anna Seghers, Friedrich Wolf and Ludwig Renn alongside 'West Germans' such as Alfred Döblin, M. Hausmann, Erich Kästner, Elisabeth Langässer and Peter Suhrkamp, whether they had chosen exile or refused to compromise with the Nazi regime.

Where the banned books had been burned on 10 May 1933, émigrés and opponents of Nazism spoke out in the name of the same demands. But the following year, a number of émigré works, such as those of Theodor Plievier, were no longer on sale in the Soviet zone.[101] The Cold War now drove a new division between those whom antifascism had scarcely managed to unite. The ideological demands of the postwar period spared neither the survivors of exile, mobilized around new causes, nor literary historians, many now rewriting their works in the light of present conditions. Former Communists who were now stalwarts of anti-Communism, such as Arthur Koestler, undertook a painful revision of their youthful illusions. The names of some émigrés disappeared altogether from collective memory. In the West, Communist writers and fellow-travellers were banned from textbooks, if they were published at all. In the East, those 'renegades' who had broken with the party – Willi Münzenberg, Gustav Regler, Arthur Koestler, Theodor Plievier – were denounced. If representatives of the 'socialist tradition' attracted much study and republication, many fell into sad oblivion: there was no republication for Tucholsky, no more than for Gustav Regler or Karl Wittfogel (that 'traitor to the working class'), Ernst Ottwalt, W. Schönstedt, Wolfgang Leonhard or Kurt Kesten. Ernst Bloch and Georg Lukács were also violently attacked. Some were eventually rehabilitated (Lukács, Ottwalt), others never.

Just as thorny a question, never publicly raised in the GDR, was that of all those émigrés, Communist or not, who fell victim to Stalinist terror, or whom the Soviet authorities handed over to the Gestapo. For many years, Ernst Ottwalt, Herwarth Walden, Karl Schmückle, Hans Günther, Heinz Neumann, Carola Neher and Zensl Mühsam[102] could not be mentioned in the GDR, a taboo that was never completely lifted. The most that could generally be said was that they 'disappeared' around 1938, but were subsequently rehabilitated.[103] For want of documents, it is often hard – apart from rare personal testimony – to depict the ideological course of former exiles in the GDR, and the degree to which they saw in the new republic the realization of their hopes or the collapse of their illusions. It is similarly difficult to know the degree to which one could take at face value the declarations of official GDR representatives (Becher, for example, who had to face the criticism of his own son living in Britain) or those who broke with the regime, such as Alfred Kantorowicz. Reality was more complex.[104] Ernst Bloch kept relatively silent after leaving the

GDR.[105] Alfred Kantorowicz used a fairly cruel Chinese legend to describe the extent of his disappointment: a peasant threatened by a frightening dragon rescues a child who pesters him to know what the dragon was like. When the peasant turns round, he finds seated in his cart not the child, but the dragon.

Study of the reintegration of the émigrés into postwar Germany, both East and West,[106] and their further development in the course of the Cold War, would require a special study. For the GDR, this is made difficult by the impossibility of distinguishing between personal rivalries, disappointments, and the political development of the country. A large number of émigrés, even former Communists or fellow-travellers, always felt a certain distrust towards the Soviet Union and Stalin, and their situation was especially uncomfortable. The examples of Brecht and Bloch, despite their differences, are sufficient to demonstrate this.

After leaving America, Brecht showed great caution in choosing his place of residence. He hesitated to return to Berlin, or even to settle in the Federal Republic. He thus chose Zurich as an 'observation post'. He very quickly felt disgusted by the 'German theatre style', its mannerism and arrogance. It seemed to him that he would have to begin his work all over again, that before seeing the ruins of Germany he had already seen those of German theatre. By order of the State Department, he was refused a visa for the US occupation zone.[107] He was however able to visit Salzburg, stating that he wanted to take Austrian nationality and attend the festival. On 22 October 1948 he arrived in East Berlin, where his verdict on the plays being staged there – among them those of Julius Hay – was as negative as that on Western productions. He put on *Mother Courage* at the Deutsches Theater on 6 January 1949, but at this point little heed was paid to his aesthetic theories.[108] He came directly up against the dogmas of socialist realism, and publication of a collection of his poems was abandoned on grounds of 'formalism'. For a long while he feared that settling in one part of a divided Germany would cause him to be considered virtually dead in the other. The project of establishing a major cultural centre around the Berliner Ensemble initially failed to arouse much enthusiasm. Its official inauguration took place on 12 November 1949, with the production of *Mr Puntila and His Man Matti*, in the presence of Otto Grotewohl, head of the new government. Brecht's relationship to the young GDR was highly complex. To the end of his life he was loyal to the regime, having a genuine sympathy for Wilhelm Pieck, if not for Walter Ulbricht. Though his productions were highly successful, he was often accused of 'formalism'. And on the question of the classical heritage and its contemporary relevance, Hanns Eisler's *Johann Faustus* (1952–53) provoked a memorable quarrel that shattered Eisler.[109]

If the GDR offered genuine advantages – even privileges – to former exiles, they were certainly not protected from criticism, and hasty judgements were often passed on their works. Brecht's attitude towards the East German regime was made up of enthusiasm, confidence and critical scepticism. He could never forgo a certain irony towards 'party jargon', and never followed the current line – as shown by his position towards the workers' uprising of 17 June 1953 – even if, like Hanns Eisler or Stefan Heym, he could not now imagine living in any other country. Moreover, the situation of former émigrés in East Berlin changed as a result of a number of political factors. Besides those who became important functionaries (J. R. Becher was appointed minister of culture in 1954), a number also fell into disgrace.[110] Erich Weinert died in East Berlin in 1953, having quarrelled with Becher. Max Schroeder, literary director of Aufbau Verlag, died in 1958. Friedrich Wolf, after serving as ambassador to Poland, lost all influence. Willi Bredel did not get any position of responsibility. Wolfgang Langhoff, director of the Deutsches Theater, was expelled from the party. True, Alexander Abusch remained responsible for culture, Albert Norden was a politburo member and head of propaganda, Otto Winzer minister of foreign affairs, Kurt Hager responsible for ideology, Klaus Gysi for the arts, and Kurt Barthel for the writers' organization. But Paul Merker, Leo Bauer and Lex Ende were accused of having connections with the American secret service, Ernst Bloch left the GDR after the Berlin Wall was built, fearing he would no longer be able to write freely, and Alfred Kantorowicz left for the West as early as August 1957.[111]

Other facts, still more tragic, should not be forgotten. Erica Wallach, who had worked as a nurse with the International Brigades at the age of fourteen, was attracted to East Berlin after her marriage to an American, and condemned to fifteen years' forced labour for spying. Egon Erwin Kisch was attacked after his death by the Czech Communist party. And Otto Katz (André Simone), collaborator of Piscator and Willi Münzenberg, was hanged in Prague as a 'traitor' on 3 December 1952, after the Slansky trial: accused of being a 'British spy' and 'Zionist agent'.[112]

The climate of Cold War was at its height. A wind of madness blew over both the United States and the Soviet Union.[113] As this paranoia set in, Oskar Maria Graf, who had written to Hitler reminding him to burn his books, made a sinister prophecy on his return to West Germany: 'Our emigration is only starting now that the war is over. Until then, we were only in the waiting-room.'

Epilogue
Cassandra

A Klee painting named 'Angelus Novus' shows an angel looking as though he is about to move away from something he is fixedly contemplating. His eyes are staring, his mouth is open, his wings are spread. This is how one pictures the angel of history. His face is turned toward the past. Where we perceive a chain of events, he sees one single catastrophe which keeps piling wreckage upon wreckage and hurls it in front of his feet. The angel would like to stay, awaken the dead, and make whole what has been smashed. But a storm is blowing from Paradise; it has got caught in his wings with such violence that the angel can no longer close them. This storm irresistibly propels him into the future to which his back is turned, while the pile of debris before him grows skyward. This storm is what we call progress.

Walter Benjamin, 'Theses on the Philosophy of History'

It begins in green and finishes in bloody red. If the author has hurled himself into the arms of his time, he will not be able to see as the historian will a hundred years later, and not even want to see with this perspective. He has been so close to events that they have flayed him and his own blows touch them. He tears his hands, he bleeds, and he washes his bloody hands – red with his own blood – shrugs his shoulders and leaves. One can still smile, after all . . .

Kurt Tucholsky

The spirit can scarcely conceive the idea of its own elimination.

Theodor Adorno

I

'The fact that exile literature had only a small effect on the struggle against National Socialism should be not the end of reflection on it, but only the beginning,' wrote Frank Trommler.[1] It is true, indeed, that there is something overwhelming about the story of these antifascist intellectuals who left Germany in 1933 – the sufferings, struggles and defeats they experienced until their return to their homeland after 1945. The abundance of material on the exile period, the rehabilitation of those who refused to come to terms with barbarism or become its accomplices, and the honour attached to their names, cannot make us forget that they were also martyrs to a lost cause, that humiliation and defeat loom larger in their story than their meagre victories. Certainly, the *Brown Book* saved Dimitrov and his fellow accused in the Reichstag fire trial. And in the early years of the Third Reich, the propaganda of the émigrés, their magazines and their eyewitness accounts were the sole source of genuine information for Europe on the scale of the Nazi terror. But reading today the tens of thousands of books, articles, appeals and leaflets written by the exiles between 1933 and 1945, now piously conserved in archives and libraries,[2] leads inevitably to examining the final defeat that closes their history. Detailed study of their autobiographies, correspondence and diaries does not refute the truth expressed in similar terms already by so many of the émigrés in 1945, when they rediscovered the ruins of Germany with both emotion and despair: at the end of the War, all that remained were the vanquished. If no movement of internal resistance had been in any real position to endanger the regime, neither had the antifascist emigration genuinely threatened it. And those who, like Brecht, sought to invent a 'writing that kills', to oppose the 'monstrous Beast' with the 'intellectual Beast', were witnesses of a further bitter yet undeniable truth: naked force was defeated only by a still stronger force. In Italy and Germany it was foreign armies that brought the death of the fascist regimes, not the regime's internal opponents. This victory was certainly theirs too, but at what price? The impact of armed resistance can be measured, but how can one measure that of intellectual resistance? Apart from sporadic successes that were often of limited duration, the émigrés never managed to restrain the fatal course of history, even if this only became fatal because their warnings went unheeded. Carl von Ossietzky, the man at death's door who mumbled through his broken teeth that he only wanted peace, Erich Mühsam, Ernst Thälmann and so many other opponents whose very names sum up the antifascist struggle, perished in Hitler's camps. The Saarlanders voted to return to Germany, the Spanish Republic was conquered despite the aid of the International Brigades, Europe refused to rouse itself from its slumber when the émigrés issued warning after warning on the danger that Nazi Germany represented. Despite Heinrich Mann's optimistic accounts of German workers and youth hurling themselves upon clandestine exile writings, it is not even certain that any one of these texts won a single person to the resistance.

Discussing Walter Benjamin's admirable *Letters to Germans*, designed for distribution in the Reich, Theodor Adorno lucidly remarked:

> This book has managed to reach Germany unscathed, and has had no political effect there: those who read this kind of literature were in any case opponents of the regime, and to increase their number is no easy task. Just like us other émigrés, Benjamin still cradled the illusion that intelligence and cunning would put an end to a power that granted the spirit no autonomy, considering it a mere means with which no confrontation need be feared.[3]

If historians differ in their analysis of the causes for the defeat of the émigrés' antifascist struggle,[4] they almost all agree in the homage they pay to its heroic character,[5] even while recognizing that it could never achieve its goal. They differ above all in the conclusions to be drawn, if indeed they draw any at all. But the study of the antifascist emigration, its vicissitudes and struggles, splendour and misery, only has any meaning for us if it can serve as material for further theoretical analysis, the present volume being only the prolegomena for this. The various works that have appeared in recent years, seeking to retrace the history of 'German literature in exile' or the 'anti-Nazi emigration', fail to resolve certain questions that arise inevitably from their passionate and erudite studies. Is the issue simply to renew the broken thread of German literature by reintegrating into it the works of these forgotten authors? If yes, then the task has already been largely accomplished. Research into exile literature no longer comes up against the kind of taboos that were so common in earlier decades. There are undoubtedly still some individuals who consider that these writers, intellectuals and activists who left Germany in 1933 and in many cases returned with the 'occupying armies' after 1945 were 'traitors', but it is impossible to deny that the efforts of the first researchers and historians – such as Hans-Albert Walter, to mention only the most celebrated of these pioneers – achieved their object: the majority of works written by the émigrés have long since been republished in Germany, and many of them translated into other languages, while each year international symposia attract historians, Germanists and sociologists to the theme of *Exilforschung*, some universities even devoting special courses to it.

The greatest German publishers have established collections that pay homage to the 'burned books'.[6] Films, theses, exhibitions and monographs are regularly devoted to them. The question today – at least in Germany – is less to 'rediscover' the exiles' works than to examine how this heritage can (or cannot) be reintegrated in a living fashion into German culture, how these works should be read, and whether it is possible to understand them outside of their historical matrix.[7] Political challenge – chiefly by German students – has now long since shattered the postwar taboos. A new readership has grown up, escaping the 'inability to mourn' that the Mitscherliches described, and claiming the right to question the past. The very fact that the first historians of exile provided the materials needed to rediscover and understand these works is sufficient to earn their writings genuine merit.

This interest has transcended the German-language zone and affected almost all European countries as well as the United States – through the very varied reflections of exiles and their children, Germanists, and historians. Its birth and development deserve theoretical investigation of their own, especially in France. Seventy years after the events that forced these authors into exile, and now that they all are dead, what is the meaning of this homage paid to their courage, their struggle and their martyrdom?

A phenomenon such as this is certainly susceptible of multiple sociological interpretations. The rediscovery of the exiles and the interest taken in their destiny is the sign that a number of taboos have disappeared – the openly xenophobic attitude of several democracies towards the refugees of 1933, of which Switzerland was the most striking example; the repressive and scarcely honourable policy of France towards exiled antifascists, whom it seemed to treat as its real enemies as soon as war was declared, handing over a number of them to the Gestapo; the ignominy of the camps in which they were interned, collaboration, etc. If it is scarcely possible to envisage an overall awareness of what these events meant, they have been reintroduced bit by bit into the collective memory. In this way, research into the antifascist emigration is also part of a certain expiation. In France and elsewhere, just as in Germany, exhibitions, symposiums and seminars have multiplied on these authors formerly rejected from German culture, seeking in this way to efface to a certain degree the shame marking the image of these countries where they sought refuge. There can be doubt that for both Switzerland and France, their attitude towards the refugees from Hitler was one of the least glorious pages of their contemporary history. The process is easier now that those responsible for this policy have died and the task of rehabilitation falls to a new generation, also as those historians of exile who experienced the epoch were often themselves émigrés or close to the Resistance. Having been a more or less censured subject in collective consciousness, tackled only by a few set on imposing this rediscovery, the history of the émigrés of 1933 has now become a focus of media attention: in the Federal Republic the 'burned poets' are the subject of documentaries, theatrical presentations, and autobiographical novels adapted for the screen.[8] What remains to be seen is what lesson will be drawn from these.

Even if this rehabilitation came very late, too late indeed for the émigrés themselves, we can only rejoice at it. Sadly, it changes nothing of what happened, and towards the exiles of 1933, the criticisms that Ivan Karamazov made of the future harmony dreamed of by Alyosha remain fully justified. The republication of burned books can in no way override the barbarism of the act, the homage paid to these poets will never wipe out the martyrdom of any of them, no more than the commercial success belatedly enjoyed by some exile works can relieve the despair that they felt throughout their exile, the feeling that they were forgotten or hated in their own country; it was in 1945, not 1985, that Alfred Döblin, Oskar Maria Graf, Leonhard Frank and so many others dreamed of seeing their works republished. The homage posthumously paid to Heinrich Mann cannot wipe out the dark shadow that fell over his last years, any more than the several biographies of Else Lasker-Schüler can lead us to forget that the author of some of the finest expressionist poems died in poverty and half-crazed in Jerusalem.

It is certainly this feeling of the immutability and horror of what was done that obscures any hope of relieving it. Funeral rites are a help only to the living. And the Dostoyevskian certainty that evil cannot be redeemed, that it is better to stay with 'unavenged sufferings', 'unappeased indignation' than to grant an illegitimate pardon, finds here again its profound truth. From religious eschatology to history, we must declare like Ivan Karamazov than compared with this sum of suffering, 'all truth is not worth such a price'. This certainty also led Theodor Adorno to some of the finest, if most pessimistic, conclusions of his *Negative Dialectics*, when he wrote:

Auschwitz demonstrated irrefutably that culture has failed. That this could happen in the midst of the traditions of philosophy, of art, and of the enlightening sciences says more than that these traditions and their spirit lacked the power to take hold of men and work a change in them. There is untruth in these fields themselves, in the autarchy that is emphatically claimed for them. All post-Auschwitz culture, including its urgent critique, is garbage.[9]

The transformation of the destiny of the anti-Nazi emigration into an object of sociological investigation, therefore, does not protect it completely from criticism and suspicion, if we accept what Adorno wrote on culture:

> In restoring itself after the things that happened without resistance in its own countryside, culture has turned entirely into the ideology it had been potentially – had been ever since it presumed, in opposition to material existence, to inspire that existence with the light denied it by the separation of the mind from manual labour. Whoever pleads for the maintenance of this radically culpable and shabby culture becomes its accomplice, while the man who says no to culture is directly furthering the barbarism which our culture showed itself to be.[10]

Anyone seeking to erect *Exilforschung* into an object of theory has in their turn to answer this question, and ask whether it is not already too late. Certainly, investigation of any historical object can be justified. But when what is involved is the fate and destruction of a culture, the fact of the impotence of intelligence and morality in the face of brute force, it is very hard to interpret it as a problem that no longer concerns us. If, as Adorno likewise maintains, '[a]ll political instruction finally should be centred upon the idea that Auschwitz should never happen again',[11] an approach to the antifascist emigration can only justify itself if it escapes the simple reconstruction of the historic past, and questions the overall meaning of this struggle, and the reasons for and lessons of its defeat. Lacking this, it threatens to lose its share of truth. It is certainly possible to trace the various conflicts among the exile groups, or analyse the exiles' lived experience. But why exactly do the experiences of Alfred Döblin, Bertolt Brecht, Heinrich and Thomas Mann, Fritz Lang and Max Reinhardt, have a special historical value, when they are so similar to those of all other exiles?

Exilforschung, therefore, must find a way between mourning and celebration. And its final meaning can only be to invite us to meditate on the tragedy of a generation, the failure of a certain faith that it had in the power of intelligence and culture. Walter Benjamin admirably proposed this critique by writing that there is no culture that is not also a document of barbarism. The questions that any investigation of the antifascist emigration raise are inseparable from those concerning its origin. They invite us to retrace the history of the Weimar Republic, understand its weaknesses and why it was incapable of establishing a genuine democracy in Germany. They also make necessary an analysis of the factors that permitted the development and triumph of National Socialism, including the responsibility of the workers' parties in this victory. In the cultural field, the questions raised by the fate of the exiles of 1933 also demands that we take into account the structure of 'Weimar culture', its relationship to the republic and politics, its richness but also its fragility. This contrast between richness and fragility was to remain in the exile period, in still more exacerbated and dramatic form. If it is hard to imagine how the Nazis managed to destroy in a few weeks a cultural world that was certainly the most remarkable in Europe, as well as the strongest Communist party in western Europe, to dismantle all the cultural and political institutions of a highly civilized nation, replacing it with a reign of violence, nonsense and barbarism that no one in their worst nightmares could have dreamed of, the weakness of effective resistance that German culture managed to oppose to National Socialism, in its institutions that were so speedily dissolved or its universities, never ceases to surprise, and this is perhaps the most bitter lesson to learn. Already in 1933, in his booklet *Hatred*, Heinrich Mann expressed this paradox remarkably well, in stressing that the Nazis burned books they were incapable of writing, or for that matter reading. It remains true, however, that a few weeks were enough to accomplish the destruction of this culture, and that the Germany that defined itself in exile as the 'other', 'better' or 'true' Germany was deprived of any cultural and political expression, and found itself in concentration camp or on the paths of exile.

The defeat of the émigrés' propaganda, struggles and actions only prolonged this initial defeat of the Weimar intelligentsia faced with the rise of National Socialism. One can certainly invoke the divisions of exile, the inability of the parties to unite, the errors of analysis and assessment of the prospects of the Hitler regime, but it remains nonetheless true that the speed with which the regime established its iron grip (as against the development of Italian fascism, for example), the *Gleichschaltung* it imposed by terror, and the annihilation of all efforts at internal opposition, immediately made problematic any action conducted from abroad, not based on any concrete force, and condemned to remain without echo in the Western democracies. All the paradoxes raised by Adorno as to the essence of culture, the various ideas of the relationship between 'spirit' and 'action' dear to Heinrich Mann, of the revolutionary force of truth when it can become a weapon, as imagined by Brecht, break down before the scandalous evidence of naked violence. It is tempting to counterpose to Hegelian mediations the Kierkegaardian category of scandal. The melancholy and despair that mark Tucholsky's *Letters of Silence* are already contained in this sinisterly prophetic fragment of 'Learning to Laugh Without Crying' that he wrote between 1925 and 1932:

A Communist had been imprisoned. The greatest European writers were asked to say what they thought of this. The Frenchman wrote an elaborate appeal, making sure to make good use of the subjunctive – 'that you would doubt' – and in this way unleashed a lively discussion in his country. G. B. Shaw composed a drama of biting irony in which he mocked his compatriots so unreservedly that for weeks the booking office had to close; moreover, the play didn't even mention the prisoner. The German would not sign the protest, as he happened to live in Munich. Two men, however, forced open the prison gates. The first to break into the cell was a Russian. But the prisoner was lying dead; the fascist had murdered him first.

On the level of fact and history, Tucholsky was sadly right, and his refusal to join the exiles' struggle after 1933 is understandable, however unjustified. He and his generation felt that they had already lost the battle. And those whom Nazism had forced into exile were unable to affect the course of events: they awaited the realization of their darkest presentiments.

But at the very moment that the defeat of this emigration is established, the impossibility of acting on history in which it found itself, a new question is raised. What defeat precisely was this? Even if some believed otherwise, it would be naive to imagine that a few tens of thousands of émigrés could by themselves modify the course of events just by dint of their intelligence, their attachment to a Germany uncontaminated by National Socialism and their faith in morality. To oppose brute force with intelligence and ethics is to bury these contradictions without resolving them. The defeat was not so much that of this exiled intelligentsia, whose truth could not change history, but of the world that refused to accept it and take it on board. Expelled from their homeland by barbarism, chased from one country to another, everywhere unwelcome, the only weapon of the émigrés was their courage and intelligence, and the astonishing moral sense that made them oppose Nazism even before it had directly threatened them. And it was undoubtedly this ethical consciousness, this certainty than any true thought contained a moment of universality that would one day be recognized, that set the stage for their strangest victory. The very fact that this emigration existed, that these writers, poets and artists left Germany, often choosing exile deliberately, facing the worst torments rather than betray themselves, was the first defeat for National Socialism. Even Carl Schmitt, the philosopher of law won over to Nazism, could declare that with the advent of Hitler, Marx and Engels had emigrated with Lenin to Moscow, but Hegel was truly dead in Germany (indeed, a fine tribute to the philosopher); the fact that the arrival of Nazism forced into exile those who embodied a certain sense of ethics, courage and intelligence was its most ignominious condemnation. As the skull appears beneath the hollow of the face, so this country that lost its poets in a matter of days had already the look of a graveyard.

By a strange reversal, therefore, it is finally the complete impotence of this emigration, which could only oppose barbarism with its ethical conscience and intelligence, that speaks most strongly to us today. There are two ways of evading this question of the relationship of intellectuals to power: the first is to imagine that they have power, the second to imagine that they have none.

II

The postwar German writer Christa Wolf quoted a significant passage from Goethe: 'This dark race is beyond help; for the most part you had to remain silent so as not to be considered mad like Cassandra, when you prophesied what already lies outside the gate.'[12]

In the not-yet-happened of history, the exiles of 1933 were condemned in their wanderings to prophesy the darkest of futures, as so many unhappy Cassandras. Long before Christa Wolf devoted this strange and remarkable novel to her, it is surprising to note that this prophetess condemned to predict what no one wanted to hear was already a common pole of comparison for the exiles. It is rare for any of the émigrés not to mention her name at least once.

The daughter of Priam and Hecuba, Cassandra was loved by Apollo, who gave her this unwelcome gift of prophecy. Being unable to withdraw it, the god discredited her predictions, and, so the myth has it, had her taken for mad. Instead of being listening to, she was shut up in a tower, where she could only continue to lament the misfortunes of her homeland. Her cries and tears soon redoubled when she learned of the departure of Paris for Greece. But her threats only aroused mockery, and it was without success that she opposed bringing the wooden horse into Troy. The night that Troy fell, she took refuge in the temple of Minerva, where Ajax violated her. She fell to Agamemnon who, touched by her beauty, took her back to Greece where she suffered the jealousy of Clytemnestra. It was in vain that she predicted to Agamemnon his own death. Clytemnestra had him murdered, along with the twins she had from her husband.

The parallelism of fate, in reading again Aeschylus's *Oresteia*, is certainly disturbing. In the 1920s, Tucholsky, Ossietzky and Toller constantly raised alarms about the Republic, denouncing the various threats to it and those who would sooner or later put an end to it. Not only did no one believe their predictions, but they were condemned to heavy fines and imprisonment. Far from being listened to, their warnings led them to be treated as 'nest soilers'. It was in vain that they urged a struggle against those working to undermine the Republic: the left parties did not heed them, indeed often attacked them, and the only platforms available to them were pacifist magazines such as the *Weltbühne* that generally reached only the converted.

After the Nazi seizure of power, and scattered across Europe, the exiles sought in vain to arouse the democracies from their lethargy, to show that Hitler was a danger to peace and a struggle against him was necessary. They were unwelcome and scarcely tolerated. They were accused of poisoning relations with Germany, and far from heeding their warnings, Europe tried to go back to sleep. They were interned in camps, rather than in a tower. As Klaus Mann declared in *The Turning Point*, it was in vain that they cried out:

> You are in danger. Hitler is dangerous. Hitler means war. Don't believe in his supposed love of peace! He's lying. Don't do a deal with him; he won't keep his promises. Don't be intimidated by him. He is not as strong as he makes believe, *not yet!* Don't let him become so. For now, a gesture, a strong word on your part would be sufficient to prevent him from this. In a few years the price will be higher, it will cost you thousands of human lives. Why wait [. . .]? Break off diplomatic relations with him! Boycott him! Isolate him![13]

This appeal failed to arouse a response. The European nations received the German émigrés' warnings with a mixture of annoyance and 'realistic scepticism'. And Klaus Mann likened the exiles to 'so many Cassandras'.[14] The reasons for not listening to them were several. As the Trojan prophetess was mad, so they were emigrants 'blinded by hate'. The terror that the Third Reich had made a principle of state was compensated for by its economic success. Hitler also represented a bulwark against Communism. And those who might have been ready to listen to their warnings often had no power to act on them. Finally, illustrating Hegel's identification of the real with rational, many could not admit that a regime as fundamentally evil as Hitler's could stay in power. The very existence of the Third Reich was enough to refute the apocalyptic propaganda of the exiles. If the idealist who rejected it in the name of morality and right was impotent against it, the realist, as Klaus Mann acknowledged, had to admit that 'the fact that the regime continued and even flourished refuted the horrors that exile propaganda spread'. Hence the permanent necessity for the émigrés to denounce the false identification of the Third Reich with Germany, and of Hitler with the German people, to constantly claim the right to represent another Germany, deprived of any official representation but gathering together opponents and victims, shadows among shadows.

Even when Nazi threats became ever more concrete, and the émigrés' predictions were realized, the refusal to listen to them persisted, and they became the butt of hatred. As Koestler wrote: 'Anti-Nazi refugees who talked about the German concentration camps and Hitler's plans for world-conquest were regarded as fanatics and fomenters of hatred',[15] and he too compared the function of the exiles in Europe at this time with 'the ever antipathetic and grating role of Cassandra';[16] in similar vein, Manès Sperber wrote: 'Even before the Nazis were in power, we had predicted that their victory over Germany would lead them within a few years to make war on the whole world. In the six years that have passed since this time, the presence of the exiles in the countries that received them was experienced as all the more importunate to the degree that their warnings were confirmed by the facts.'[17]

This is the same sense of fatality that weighed on Cassandra: by a diabolical magic, not only did people refuse to believe a prophetess whose predictions were true, but as bearer of bad news she was herself blamed for the misfortunes that she proclaimed. The strangest thing is that the political affiliation of the émigrés ultimately played little role in the credit accorded them. If Communists such as Manès Sperber, Willi Münzenberg and Arthur Koestler were not believed, no more were pacifists such as Ernst Toller, who tried in vain with his 1936 lectures in New York and San Francisco to awaken America to the danger of fascism, or Berthold Jacob, even former Nazis such as Otto Strasser. If Thomas Mann was given no credit for drawing, in 'This Peace' (1938), an astonishingly clear balance-sheet of the policy of renunciation and abdication in the face of Hitler's demands that the democracies were conducting, no more was ex-Chancellor Brüning, who declared to British politicians in 1938 that war would break out before August 1939.

From the Reichstag fire to the Munich capitulation, it is surprising to establish how accurately the antifascist exiles foresaw the course of events. They undoubtedly passed through phases of optimism in which they also predicted the coming fall of the regime. But the most far-sighted did not fail to draw the attention of western governments to the almost fatal outcome of their policy of appeasement towards Hitler. Their writings of 1933–34 already predicted what the reign of terror in Germany would mean for the future of the European democracies, warning them right away of the danger of war that Hitler's policies would mean. After the refusal to boycott the Berlin Olympics, the intensification of repressive measures and the promulgation of the Nuremberg laws, just as in the face of the Spanish war, the militarization of the Rhineland, and Hitler's aggression against Austria and Czechoslovakia, they drew each time a pessimistic forecast of the years ahead, which turned out to be only too true. As Golo Mann wrote: 'After the early illusions had evaporated, we were all led – young or old, famous or quite unknown – to play the role of Cassandra: to know and not be listened to. Not that we had any burning desire for war. But we knew that with Adolf Hitler peace was an impossibility, that each concession offered him would only inflate his boldness and reinforce his contempt for the old Europe.'[18]

Their predictions did not move anyone except their fellow exiles. Brecht thought at this time of writing a new version of Cassandra, as he had done with Antigone,[19] also declaring in his *Exile Dialogues*: 'The best school for dialectics is emigration. The most penetrating dialecticians are émigrés. It is changes that have forced them to go into exile, and changes are all they are interested in. From the tiniest signs, assuming they have the capacity for reflection, they deduce the most fantastic events.'

III

Alas! The miseries of my city, for ever disappeared! [. . .] And every remedy has been in vain! The city of Priam has met its fate; and I leave, my soul on fire, to kill myself on the ground.

Aeschylus, *Oresteia*

In April 1945, when the Allied press discovered the concentration camps, Alfred Kantorowicz raised the terrible question: If these governments had taken the émigrés' warnings seriously some twelve years before, could all this not have been avoided? He noted that it had taken a World War, with millions of deaths, for the world to discover what the émigrés had reiterated constantly since 1933, i.e. 'that the Nazis behave like Nazis'.[20]

It is undoubtedly too easy to maintain that the writings, appeals and information spread by the exiles could have prevented war if they had been taken seriously; the road of history cannot be traced in reverse. But if the democracies had taken a different stand towards Hitler, firmly resisting his initial demands, would they have been led to the capitulation of Munich? If in 1945 there were 'only the vanquished', this defeat can certainly not be laid at the door of the émigrés, who did all that they could to prevent it. As Brecht already declared, you cannot avoid a sabre blow by holding out your bare fist. It is ludicrous to imagine that with the means at their disposal, the émigrés could have acted alone on the course of history. The only weapon of the exiles was their intelligence, their sense of morality, their certainty – born from experience – that National Socialism was a perversion of history, a monstrosity, which like a cancer, threatened the entire world.

They sought to convey this truth through the thousands of leaflets, novels, essays, articles and plays that they wrote. Exile press and publishing were in no position to struggle against the immense system of propaganda that the Nazis and their supporters had established. And the few thousand readers they might expect to reach could hardly count as a political force. In Germany itself, the climate of terror made any opposition suicidal, and as Brecht declared, no one can be accused of not being cut out for martyrdom.

What was lacking was the historical mediation that might have enabled this truth to become effective. And the most typical cleavages of the literary emigration, from 1933 on, involved the belief that some had, and others did not, that such mediation between themselves and political action was possible. It was hope in the possibility of gathering all opponents of Nazism around the ideals of the left that led to the attempt at a *Volksfront*. This hope disappeared with the signing of the Nazi–Soviet pact. Others took refuge in the certainty that they embodied, despite everything, something that they called the 'other Germany', the 'better Germany', persuaded that a sense of honour and justice are never completely in vain. As Thomas Mann wrote to Lion Feuchtwanger in April 1944: 'Each in our own time, we shall leave life with the experience, a relief after all, that on this planet whose ephemeral acquaintance we have made, though not everything is literally irreproachable, what is most stupid and vile has after all been unable to maintain itself in this world for only a decade or so.'

Klaus Mann was certainly right to hold that 'the literary emigration had nothing to be ashamed of'. It remained faithful to this ideal of a more humane and less barbarous world, and was ready to sacrifice itself to this: 'Yes, we were deeply persuaded that we spoke in the name of all the *better Germans*, in the name of those martyrs and heroes that the reign of terror had reduced to silence. The protest that was stifled in the concentration camps, the whispered criticism, the repressed cry, the growing fear, questioning and anguish of the *better* German, all this was what we sought to express and make heard in an unknowing and lethargic world.'[21]

How can we not recognize that these writers, through their courage, lucidity and generosity, whether this is ascribed to them as individuals or to the ideals that they cultivated – humanism, Marxism, pacifism, republican virtue or revolutionary messianism – generally behaved very much better, not only than other professional groups, but also than writers of other nationalities in less cruel times. Although many faces of this German intellectual resistance are still unknown, it is impossible to deny that this Weimar intelligentsia inspires more admiration than the whole French intelligentsia, apart from the brief flame of idealism and generosity of the 'left bank' of the 1930s and the writers of the Resistance. While there were indeed some major authors who compromised with National Socialism, the majority adopted a more trenchant moral attitude towards it than a number of French writers did in the era of collaboration.[22]

IV

My work will return to you one day, I know, even if I will not be there for this myself.
Thomas Mann, October 1940

In this respect, German exile literature, with its richness and weakness, remained surprisingly close to the literature of the Weimar Republic; the writer represented an unhappy consciousness, often astonishingly lucid but unable to act on events. This was the tragedy of Tucholsky, Ossietzky, Toller and so many others. Far from seeing the Weimar era as a 'paradise for intellectuals',[23] we would rather be tempted to see there, as did Klaus Mann, Ludwig Marcuse and Manès Sperber, a crucial stage in an ever increasing divide between 'intelligence' and 'power'. To regret the disappearance of the plethora of literary magazines, the circles of writers and the debates on ideas in which the Weimar Republic – and Berlin above all – was so rich, would be to stick to appearances. As Fritz J. Raddatz emphasized in a famous essay,[24] the Weimar intelligentsia enjoyed an immense success but had no effect. This was certainly nothing new in Germany, where ever since the Romantic movement, the triumph of the intelligentsia has generally had as its counterpart an almost total political impotence. But this reality had never been so apparent as in the Weimar period.

Here again, it is Kurt Tucholsky who represents a kind of paradigm of the Weimar intellectual, as well as of the antifascist exile. Hated by the right, despised by the Republican state, constantly attacked by the Communists, he defined himself as an 'injured clown'. His marvellous intelligence, biting humour and stinging irony led him to revolt incessantly against everything that threatened the Republic. From his first articles in the *Schaubühne*, then the *Weltbühne*, likewise in his books, he constantly stigmatized, under the five different pseudonyms he employed in the service of his 'merry schizophrenia', the dangers that weighed on this fragile democracy. Sceptical, republican, pacifist, he did not ignore any of these. One need only read a single one of his books, or a few of his satirical commentaries, to be convinced of this. In his programmatic essay, 'We Negative Ones', published in the *Weltbühne* on 13 March 1919, he already maintained: 'We want to combat hatred with love.' Without belonging to a party or having a well-defined ideology, he declared that he felt 'confusedly that something is approaching on padded feet which threatens to destroy us.' And he was not deceived. Reading the three hundred or more articles that he wrote under the Weimar Republic is to be made aware how there was not a single danger that he failed to denounce: the reactionary and anti-Republican officers, the iniquitous judges, those who used murder as a political weapon, the Nazis. He warned, he exhorted, he cajoled, resembling, in Erich Kästner's famous expression, 'a tubby little Berliner trying to stop a catastrophe with his typewriter'. In his own words ('Learning to Laugh without Crying'): 'There are times in which, for a writer who wants to have some influence, it is not good to write. Times in which the tapping of the typewriter is not as useful as that of the machine-gun. But the latter simply obeys the former.'

Tucholsky certainly knew success. Most of his books sold from 25,000 to 50,000 copies each year. The right-wing press frothed with rage at everything he published. The Nazis tried to lynch him, but got the wrong man. The Socialists accused him of undermining the Republic's foundations, the Communists – not without truth – of being a non-party intellectual. As he wrote to Heinz Pol on 20 April 1933: 'And I won't any have any party apparatchik telling me that I'm just an intellectual! My predictions have proved right, not a single one of *Rote Fahne*'s have.' Who would seriously try and claim otherwise today? Undoubtedly, Tucholsky also made mistakes – even in his assessment of the Nazi danger – but how could one deny that his attacks, polemics and denunciations, in their bitter and often biting irony, all seem with today's hindsight surprisingly true?

What is most surprising in his work and his life is precisely this ineffective success. Like other intellectuals of the Weimar Republic, and later of the emigration, he foresaw historical development with a painful lucidity. His criticism of the Republic's weakness, his denunciation of those who would sooner or later destroy it or contribute to its fall, his exhortations calling on the German left to unite, were as well-founded as the warnings of the émigrés after 1933 on the danger that Hitler represented for world peace. As a publicist, Tucholsky was admired, feared and hated, and had genuine success. The émigrés, however, were most often only hated. They no longer had an audience. The calvary of this generation of intellectuals – leading Tucholsky, Ernst Toller and, later, Klaus Mann to suicide – was certainly to have had a clear view of historical rationality and irrationality, without being in any way able to act on it.

V

> The soothsayers who found out from time what it had in store certainly did not experience time as either homogeneous or empty. Anyone who keeps this in mind will perhaps get an idea of how past times were experienced in remembrance – namely, in just the same way. We know that the Jews were prohibited from investigating the future. The Torah and the prayers instruct them in remembrance, however. This stripped the future of its magic, to which all those succumb who turn to the soothsayers for enlightenment. This does not imply, however, that for the Jews the future turned into homogeneous, empty time. For every second of time was the strait gate through which the Messiah might enter.
>
> Walter Benjamin, 'Theses on the Philosophy of History'

This fine text of Walter Benjamin that ends his 'Theses on the Philosophy of History' can well serve as a conclusion. But to what? To this final image of revolutionary messianism Benjamin opposed his own suicide, following in the wake of Tucholsky. The Pyrenees crossing that stood in the way of a problematic salvation for Benjamin was so narrow, at least in a metaphorical sense, that he lost all hope of passing it. And the melancholy that marked Tucholsky's *Letters of Silence* also culminated in his suicide. In the light of this historical experience of the Weimar intelligentsia, of which so little account has been taken, it is strange to revisit the debates of the 1950s or, more recently, on literary 'commitment'.

If this experience still concerns us today, it is because it marked the high point of a relative autonomy of the intelligentsia, its appearance on the historical scene with the dream of playing a role there. The utopian spirit inspired this generation, before it lost almost all its dreams one by one. Expressionist poets, pacifists, revolutionary artists, political activists, anonymous representatives of 'revolutionary Yiddishland',[25] they set out to conquer a certain notion of responsibility towards history that led them into opposition to the First World War, to expressionist activism, Dadaism, the utopian Marxism of the 1920s, the defence of republican ideals, the Pleyel-Amsterdam movement, the struggle against fascism, the Congress for the Defence of Culture, engagement in the Spanish War and the European Resistance. Their generosity, today both deplored and evoked with nostalgia, and echoed in Sartre's arguments in *Situations II* and *Les Mots*, inspired the German intellectuals of the 1930s, some as early as 1914. While history continues to display the same chill of the guillotine's blade that Büchner depicted in *Danton's Death*, and when Benjamin's words that 'it is those without hope who give us hope' seem over-optimistic, the certainty that struggle for a world that is a bit less barbaric, a bit less humane, that is not in vain, seems itself to have become utopian. What divides us from the intellectuals of the 1920s and 30s is less an over-sensitive laziness, a dryness of heart, than the more or less clear remove from which we judge the chronicle of their illusions, their suspicion that over the various charnel-houses of history there still floated a little flame of meaning, and that a Messiah of some kind might come to claim his own.

VI

At the end of *Les Mots*, Sartre wrote: 'For a long time, writing was asking Death or Religion in disguise to tear my life away from chance. I was of the Church. As a militant, I wanted to save myself through works [. . .]. My retrospective illusions are in pieces. Martyrdom, salvation, immortality: all are crumbling [. . .]. I see clearly, I am free from illusions, I know my real tasks [. . .]'.[26] Here, as a distant echo, we can hear the laughter of Kurt Tucholsky, and the admirable address 'to the reader of 1985' that he wrote in 1926:

> I can't even carry on a high-level conversation with you over the heads of my contemporaries, with the theme: We two understand each another, for you are an intellectual, like me. Alas, my good friend – you are somebody's contemporary, too. Of course, when I say 'Bismarck' and you have to think hard who that was, I break out in a grin even today. You can't imagine how proud the people around me are of that man's immortality. Oh well, let's drop that. Besides, you'll want to go and have your lunch now.
>
> So long, then. This paper has turned quite yellow, yellow like the teeth of our county judges – look, the page is crumbling between your fingers: well, it is rather old. Go with God, or whatever you call that thing now. We probably don't have too much to say to one other, we little people. We are lived out, our essence has passed away with us. The appearance was everything.
>
> Oh yes. I want to shake your hand. For the sake of good manners.
>
> And now you're off.
>
> But let me tell you one more thing: You aren't any better than we were, or those before us. Not in the least, not in the very least . . .[27]

Notes

INTRODUCTION

1. Bertolt Brecht, 'Thoughts on the Duration of Exile', *Poems 1913–1956*, London 1987, p. 301.
2. 'To Those Born Later', ibid., p. 319.
3. Among these early studies we should cite: Wolf Franck, *Führer durch die deutsche Emigration*, Paris 1935; Alfred Döblin, *Die deutsche Literatur (im Ausland seit 1933). Ein Dialog zwischen Politik und Kunst*, Paris 1938; Walter A. Berendsohn, *Die humanistische Front. Einführung in die deutschen Emigration-Literatur (Erster Teil von 1933 bis Kriegenausbruch)*, Zurich 1946; F. C. Weiskopf, *Unter fremden Himmeln. Ein Abriss der deutschen Literatur im Exil 1933–1947. Mit einem Anhang von Textproben aus Werken exilierter Schriftsteller*, Berlin 1948; Richard Drews and Alfred Kantorowicz, eds, *Verboten und verbrannt. Deutsche Literatur zwölf Jahre unterdrückt*, Berlin and Munich 1947.
4. We should remember that after the Second World War a number of writers glorified under the Third Reich continued undisturbed an honoured career. This was the case with Hans Carossa, and especially with Friedrich Blunck and Hans Grimm; some of them, even among the most compromised, suddenly discovered themselves in the 1950s to have been 'internal émigrés' or even disguised anti-fascists. In the course of literary gatherings, former worthies of the Third Reich continued to read their works (Will Vesper, E. G. Kolbenheyer, Hans Grimm, R. Blunck, E. W. Möller, Heinz Schauweker, Heinrich Zillich, Gerhard Schumann). They organized magazines and cultural events, awarding prizes to works of a most reactionary stamp. Even after their death, some of them would be regularly fêted by circles of intimates and nostalgics who perpetuated their memory. An inquiry carried out in 1964 by Bavarian television indicated that in educational books, members of the Prussian Academy of Arts, as reorganized by the Nazis, were represented twenty times more than writers persecuted by the Hitler regime. The 161 works analysed included ten texts by Heinrich Böll against a hundred by Agnes Miegel, a nationalist and pro-Nazi writer. It was by way of reaction to this tendency that teachers insisted that educational manuals and programmes should contain texts by Bertolt Brecht, Alfred Döblin, Anna Seghers and Thomas Mann. (Cf. Lionel Richard, *Le Nazisme et la culture*, Paris 1978, pp. 167–171.)
5. Cf. Hans-Albert Walter, *Bedrohung und Verfolgung bis 1933. Deutsche Exilliteratur, Band I, 1933–1950*, Neuwied 1974, and the collections of articles from the Akademie der Künste of West Berlin on the theme of *Exilforschung*.
6. Especially in the East, as in the Federal Republic they were for a long while very poorly accepted, and some even left again for a new exile. In East Berlin, a large

number of former émigrés benefited from official recognition and even played an important role (A. Abusch, F. Wolf, J. R. Becher, etc.).

7. On the ideological function of the 'internal emigration' and the 'other Germany' in the Adenauer era, see Ralf Schnell, *Literarische innere Emigration, 1933–1945*, Stuttgart 1976, pp. 6ff.

8. There were some representative authors of German literature after 1945 who sought to make links with the émigrés. Günter Grass, for example, reclaimed the epic style of Alfred Döblin; Rolf Hochhuth sent Oskar Maria Graf his play *The Representative* (letter of 20 June 1963, archives of the Akademie der Künste). Heinrich Böll, in a letter to Graf of 7 May 1963, deplored the break that had set in between the two generations.

9. Thus the Gruppe 47, which came out of the magazine *Der Ruf* founded in a camp for German prisoners of war in the United States and then relaunched under the same name in Munich, inspired by Alfred Andersch and H. W. Richter, became the forum of the new West German literature with I. Bachmann, G. Eich, A. Andersch, Heinrich Böll and Günter Grass.

10. Grass remarked: 'In literature, after 1945 there was initially great astonishment: the drawers were empty. We had imagined that after the Nazi era a whole internal emigration would emerge, an opposition that had not had the right to publish, but there was nothing [. . .]. During the first few years, German literature was dominated by the émigré authors who returned, or who had not yet returned: Thomas Mann, Döblin [. . .] and whose books continued the unbroken tradition of the German novel of the nineteenth century' (*Atelier des Métamorphoses*, Paris 1978, pp. 78–9). See also the account of Brecht's return by Max Frisch in *Lettres Nouvelles*, March–April 1970, pp. 7ff. If Gottfried Benn still exercised a deep influence on the literature of the 1960s, the only writers of the 1940s who made a mark on the younger generation were the 'internal émigrés' such as Reinhold Schneider, Ernst Wiechert and Werner Bergengruen. Oskar Loerke was an influence on Elisabeth Langgässer, Hermann Kasack and H. E. Nosak. We should note that Bergengruen, the most widely read author after the war, was completely unknown to the majority of emigrants, including Brecht (ibid., p. 9).

11. Cited by H. A. Walter, *Bedrohung und Verfolgung bis 1933*, p. 14.

12. These included Ernst Bertram, Gerhard Frick, Herbert Cysarz, Franz Koch, Hans Naumann, Friedrich Neumann, K. J. Obenauer, Hermann Ponges and Gottfried Weber.

13. Frankfurt 1967.

14. Stuttgart 1962.

15. Soon after the end of the War, Hanns Wilhelm Eppelsheimer had the idea of collecting the complete published works of the émigrés. This undertaking was particularly hard as these writers had sought refuge in all parts of the world, and their publications had been printed in short runs, often with deliberately falsified publisher details so as to mislead Gestapo investigators. Author names and book titles were also disguised (*Tarnschriften*), while many publications had been lost or destroyed. Eppelsheimer thus sought first of all to compile an index. The idea was born in Zurich, with former émigrés such as Ossip Kalenter, Walter Fabian and Otto Zimmermann. A collection was also attempted by W. Sternfeld, who had emigrated to London. The number of titles assembled grew from 100 in 1950 to 12,500 by 1968 (11,000 books and journals, 1,500 letters and manuscripts). (Cited after Kurt Köster, *Zur Eröffnung der Ausstellung Exilliteratur 1933–1945*, Bad Godesberg 1968.) The Deutsche Bücherei at Leipzig also collected a large number of works proscribed under the Third Reich while their authors were in exile. This currently holds 3,294 monographs, 2,104 translations and original works in foreign languages, 78 microfilms and 14,923 issues of reviews and periodicals.

16. This library comprises three distinct domains: novels, memoirs and poems published in exile (many of which have since been republished); political publications, appeals, leaflets, manifestos (fairly rare); and scientific publications (more than two thousand

scientists left Germany), including physics, chemistry and medicine. Many of these documents have been restored, and are available in photocopy or microfilm.

17. Darmstadt 1960.
18. Hamburg 1964.
19. Munich 1964.
20. The exhibition catalogue established by Werner Berthold was twice republished. The exhibition was presented for the first time in Frankfurt from May to August 1965, then in several German cities and abroad (Switzerland, Netherlands, Belgium, Denmark, Norway, Czechoslovakia and Israel). From 17 to 19 January 1968 a conference was held in Luxemburg for writers, historians and political figures exiled between 1933 and 1945. An exhibition of exile literature was organized, accompanied by debates in which the Luxemburg foreign minister Pierre Grégoire took part, along with Golo Mann and Willy Brandt. A memorial volume comprising the main communications was published in Bad Godesberg.
21. Reissued in book form in Basle in 1977, this went through two successive editions.
22. Such as Ernst Toller, Else Lasker-Schüler, Arnim T. Wegener, Franz Jung, Ivan and Claire Goll, Albert Ehrenstein, Walter Mehring, Erich Mühsam, Alfred Döblin, Carl Einstein, Walter Benjamin, Walter Hasenclever, Max Hermann-Neisse, Paul Zech and others.
23. Neuwied 1972–74.
24. Willy Brandt, in several lectures, stressed the role played by the student movement in this rediscovery of exiled authors.
25. For example Heinz Liepmann, Alfred Kerr, Nico Rost, Theodor Balk, Egon Erwin Kisch, Robert Olden, Konrad Merz, Theodor Plievier. Similar initiatives were undertaken by publishers such as Rowohlt, Ullstein and Suhrkamp. Several films were made for television from the works of émigrés (such as Feuchtwanger's *Exile*) retracing their fate.
26. But historians in the GDR encountered other problems which could affect the objectivity of their work. Some questions were always taboo: the fate of exiles in the USSR, their liquidation by Stalin or their handover to the Gestapo, and the debates around the Nazi–Soviet pact. H. A. Walter was right to speak of a real 'schizophrenia' prevailing in research on the exile period: while the proletarian actor Hans Otto, murdered by the Nazis, was the subject of monographs and celebrations, one could seek in vain in works published in the GDR for any mention of the execution of Carola Neher, the friend of Brecht (and Polly Peachum in Pabst's movie of *The Threepenny Opera*), who was shot as a 'Trotskyist'. Authors who broke with the Communist party were sometimes omitted even if they had played an important role in the antifascist emigration (Arthur Koestler, Gustav Regler, Willi Münzenberg, Otto Katz). Alfred Kantorowicz, after himself breaking with the GDR, did not hesitate to speak of 'manipulation' in connection with the book by Klaus Jarnatz, *Literatur im Exil*, and made the same reproaches against certain works tracing the cultural life of the Weimar Republic that appeared in East Berlin. He noted for example that in the celebrated book *Aktionen-Bekenntnisse-Perspektive*, devoted to the political and literary struggles of the 1920s, 200 pages out of 675 were devoted to J. R. Becher, whereas Brecht was mentioned only on twenty occasions; the Comintern functionary Bela Illès appeared forty times, while Willi Münzenberg, who played a role in all these conflicts, was named only once. Theodor Plievier, the collaborator of Piscator and author of the play *The Emperor's Galley-Slaves*, was unmentioned, as was Kurt Tucholsky. Ernst Bloch had become a 'partisan of imperialism', Karl Wittfogel a 'traitor to the working class', while Ernst Ottwalt, Kurt Kläber and Ernst Glaeser seem never to have existed. See A. Kantorowicz, *Politik und Literatur im Exil*, Hamburg 1978, pp. 31ff.
27. In *Beiträge zur Geschichte des Buchwesens,* vol. 4, Leipzig 1969, pp. 189–294.
28. These volumes are devoted to exile in the Soviet Union, Switzerland, France, the United States, Latin America, Scandinavia, the Netherlands, Czechoslovakia and Spain.

29. The concentration of study on exile in Scandinavia is explained not just by the importance of the émigrés who found refuge there (Brecht, Tucholsky, Willy Brandt, etc.), but above all by the influence of Professor W. A. Berendsohn, specialist in Scandinavian languages and historian of exile literature who remained in Sweden after the fall of the Hitler regime.

30. One major exception was the study by William K. Pfeiler, who had lived in the United States since 1921: *German Literature in Exile. The Concern of Poets*, University of Nebraska Studies 1957. A considerable number of conferences were subsequently organized on the German exiles (University of Missouri at St Louis in 1972, University of South Carolina in 1979, University of California in 1980, etc.).

31. We need only note here James K. Lyon, *Bertolt Brecht in Amerika*, Frankfurt 1984; Edda Fuhrich-Leisler and Gisela Pronitz, *Max Reinhardt in Amerika*, Salzburg 1976, with a preface by Ronald Sanders, US ambassador to Austria; Ronald Sanders, *Kurt Weill*, New York 1980; and John Russell Taylor, *Strangers in Paradise*, London 1983.

32. Cf. Stuart Hughes, *The Sea Change. The Migration of Social Thought 1930–1965*, New York 1975.

33. As Gilbert Badia wrote: 'Publications on Hitler and the Third Reich have been innumerable, and continue to be so, even in France. But on the most consistent and sometimes more prescient opponents of Hitler there has been almost nothing. It is as if French public opinion, forty years after the event, still wanted to ignore these exiles and their warnings; as if the collective consciousness of the French sought to efface and wipe out a page of our history' (G. Badia et al., *Les Barbelés de l'exil*, Grenoble 1979, p. 7).

34. Ibid.

35. *Vivre à Gurs: Un camp de concentration français 1940–1941*, Paris 1979.

36. *Exilés en France. Souvenirs d'antifascistes allemands émigrés, 1933–1945*, Paris 1982.

37. G. Badia et al., *Les Bannis de Hitler. Accueil et luttes des exilés allemands en France, 1933–1938*, Paris 1984.

38. *Exilforschung* practically became a discipline of its own at the University of Hamburg following the creation of the Arbeitstelle für Deutsche Exilliteratur. Contending positions divide not just literary scholars and historians, critics and sociologists, but also Germanists from the Federal Republic, those of the GDR, and those from American universities. During the PEN Club conference at Bremen in 1980, Marcel Reich-Ranicki reproached historians of *Exilliteratur* for orienting their works only in relation to antifascist struggle and enclosing them in a kind of ghetto, whereas the same aesthetic criteria should be applied to them today as to any other works. This point of view was attacked by H. A. Walter and W. Emmerisch, who saw it as impossible to grasp the literature of exile outside of the dramatic context in which it was born and which formed an intrinsic dimension of it. Reich-Ranicki then asked the historians if Thomas Mann's *Lotte in Weimar* should be condemned because, whilst written in exile, it spoke only of Goethe and not of Hitler. See the account of the congress by Marcel Reich-Ranicki in the *Frankfurter Allgemeine Zeitung* for 23 September 1980. The lack of interest in exile literature in the Federal Republic in the 1950s, and the censorship exercised on the republication of certain works, was opposed on many occasions by émigré sociologists as eminent as Richard Loewenthal (Berlin) and Wolfgang Abendroth (Frankfurt).

39. In particular thanks to the works and research of Professor Walter Huder, director of the centre of archives of the Akademie der Künste in West Berlin. It is to him that we owe the preservation of a certain number of personal archives of émigrés (the AdK has gathered thirty-four of these), and making these available to historians. Exhibitions on exile theatre were organized in Berlin in 1973, the following year at Oberhausen, Munich, Saarbrücke and Offenbach, in 1975 at Regensburg, and 1976 at Bonn. Weeks on 'Burned and Banned Books' were held as part of very varied festivals in Hamburg (1981), Amsterdam (1982), Jerusalem and Osnabrück in 1983.

Some half-dozen catalogues are available on this theme. Theatre and cinema festivals have been devoted to émigré actors and directors, particularly in Berlin where as well as Marlene Dietrich and Ernst Lubitsch, the actors Elisabeth Bergner, Franz Lederer, Dolly Haas, Curt Bois, Herta Thiele and Wolfgang Zilzer were celebrated, the 33rd Berlin Festival being dedicated to them.

40. Cf. Peter Engel, 'Neue Debakel für die Exilforschung', *Berliner Allgemeine Wochenzeitung*, 7 February 1975; Peter Laemmle, 'Exilforschung in der Krise?' *Frankfurter Rundschau*, 4 September 1974.

41. The Börsenverein des Deutschen Buchhandels and the libraries of the city and University of Frankfurt published, under the title *Verbrannte Bücher, Verfremde Dichter*, an 82-page catalogue with the titles of all works prohibited or burned under the Third Reich that were again available.

42. Cf. Wendelin Zimmer, 'Lässt sich die Kultur des Exils wiedergewinnen?', in *Neue Osnabrücker Zeitung*, 17 May 1983.

43. Certain German-language writers were nationals of Austria, Czechoslovakia or Hungary.

44. According to A. Kantorowicz (*Politik und Literatur im Exil*, p. 82), more than 2,500 individuals whose profession was that of writer left Germany in 1933.

45. A part of Georg Kaiser's archive remained in Berlin, while he abandoned most of the rest in the countries where he took refuge. His last novel was discovered at Ancona where he died on 4 June 1948. The archives of Ödön von Horvath remained in Munich and Vienna; those of Alfred Kerr were found in London, in six suitcases at the back of a shed. Walter Mehring lost his autobiography in a train, Alfred Kantorowicz abandoned his manuscripts in France, in a cellar. The last novel of Ernst Weiss was found in his room, after his suicide at a Paris hotel. Walter Benjamin confided his manuscripts to Gershom Scholem in Jerusalem and Georges Bataille in Paris, but the contents of the black attaché case with which he tried in vain to cross the Pyrenees remain lost.

46. Besides the Deutsche Bibliothek at Frankfurt, we should mention the Deutsche Bücherei at Leipzig, the Archiv des DGB of the Friedrich-Ebert-Stiftung, the archival centre of the Akademie der Künste (formerly in West Berlin), and those of Marbach, Münster, Hamburg and former East Berlin. Other documents are to be found in Zurich, Amsterdam, Stockholm, New York and London. The émigré archives are divided between more than ninety-one centres and collections, and six specialized libraries containing more than 50,000 volumes. To peruse the archives on Piscator, for example, it is necessary to consult those in Berlin, in New York, and at the University of Illinois, while the fate of those in the USSR is still unknown.

47. Not to speak of the emigration in China, where Jews were to be found alongside SA men (escapees from the 'night of the long knives'). Certain of these, after serving as cadres in Chiang Kai-shek's armies, remained in Taiwan or Hong Kong.

48. R. Hirsch, for example, signed his articles 'Bichette', *Hirsch* in German meaning a roe deer.

49. Thus in Germany today the term *Exilforschung* is more current than *Erforschung der Exilliteratur*.

50. J.-M. Palmier, *L'Expressionisme comme révolte*, Paris 1975; *L'Expressionisme et les arts* (2 vols, Paris 1978, 1980); and *Piscator et le théâtre politique* (in collaboration with Maria Piscator), Paris 1983.

51. Bertolt Brecht, 'In Praise of Communism', trans. Steve Gooch, from *The Mother*, London 1978, p. 28.

CHAPTER 1   ASSASSINATION OF A CULTURE

1. On the history of these demonstrations and their consequences, see the excellent study by Hildegard Brenner, *Die Kunstpolitik des National-Sozialismus*, Frankfurt 1964, pp. 7ff.

2. Influenced by the ideas of Oswald Spengler, Spann argued that the entire culture was in crisis, and violently criticized futurism and Dadaism. The decomposition of culture, according to him, reflected that of society, and only an authoritarian state would be able to reverse this. Spann's lecture was attacked in numerous periodicals, and the rector of the university reproached for having allowed it.

3. At its origin, at least, this Kampfbund claimed to be independent of the Nazi party. In 1927 a National Socialist Society for German Culture had been founded, with its headquarters in Munich. The signatories of its founding document included Heinrich Himmler, Emil Weiss, Gregor Strasser, F. X. Schwartz, Phillip Bouler and Alfred Rosenberg. This society proposed to put into practice certain proposals already formulated in the NSDAP programme. It divided its activities by sector and *Gau*. After the lecture by Othmar Spann, this society was replaced by the Kulturbund, which brought together high officers from the military (von Epp), nationalist writers with Nazi sympathies (Kolbenheyer, Johst, Kynast, J. M. Wehner, etc.) as well as personalities such as Winifred Wagner and a considerable number of university lecturers (such as A. Bartels and Paul Schultze-Naumburg).

4. Albert Speer, a student of architecture and a Nazi sympathizer, attended one of these meetings at which the ideas of his teacher Tessenow were attacked: 'One of the speakers called for a return to old-fashioned forms and artistic principles; he attacked modernism and finally berated Der Ring, the society of architects to which Tessenow, Gropius, Mies van der Rohe, Scharoun, Mendelsohn, Taut, Behrens and Poelzig belonged.' (Albert Speer, *Inside the Third Reich*, London 1975, p. 48.) The Kampfbund was active by 1929 in more than twenty-five German cities. Lectures similar to that of Spann were given all over the country at that time, likewise that of Alfred Heuss (in Munich in March, on the crisis in music). Other speakers attacked architecture (V. Senger) and literature (E. Diderich).

5. According to Hildegard Brenner, *Kunstpolitik des National-Sozialismus*, pp. 18–19. The Kampfbund also had connections in other countries, notably Finland, Switzerland, Sweden and Austria.

6. The Kampfbund's theses were inspired by Rosenberg's monotonous historical frescoes and appeals to struggle against the corrupters of German art. The Bauhaus was violently denounced, as well as the artistic avant-garde as a whole, bearer of 'world revolution'. The Kampfbund championed three types of ideal: provincialism (around Hans Thoma, the inevitable Schultze-Naumburg, and Adolf Bühler) which proposed to break with modern art and return to Romanticism and the nineteenth century; a bourgeois variant which rejected all foreign influence and above all any social commitment in art; and finally the exaltation of racist and Nordic values.

7. At the end of 1930, the censorship authorities prohibited Pabst's film of *Die Dreigroschenoper* (Pabst was later to reconcile himself with the Nazi regime), as well as Friedrich Wolf's plays *Cyankali* and *Frauen im Not* (this latter concerning abortion). Schulze-Naumburg also had a mural by Oskar Schlemmer destroyed, banned exhibits of modern art in the Weimar Schloßmuseum, and had a number of other paintings withdrawn (those by Dix, Feininger, Kandinsky, Klee, Barlach, Heckel, Kokoschka, Marc, Nolde, Schlemmer and Schmidt-Rottluff), as well as sculptures by Lehmbruck, for being foreign to the 'Nordic-German essence'. The most tragic feature is that the German press in general scarcely took these measures seriously, seeing them as just a great joke or refusing to believe them altogether. The *Thüringscher Allgemeine Zeitung* stated: 'The only response possible is to laugh out loud.' Some journalists wondered if the Nazis would not end up by attacking roses for being red.

8. On 22 April 1930, the Thuringian minister of education announced his programme of cultural policy under the title: '*Wider die Negerkultur, für deutsches Volkstum*' ('Against Negro culture, for Germanity'). The librarian Wolfgang Hermann, future author of black lists after 1933, was already active in this government in December 1930.

9. The reactionary character of Italian futurism predated fascism. As early as 1915,

Marinetti dreamt of a futurist political movement different from the party of Corradini. The same year, after the publication of the Futurist party's manifesto, the magazine *Roma Futurista*, edited by Carli and Settimelli, established Futurist political leagues in various Italian cities. In 1919 Marinetti joined Mussolini's combat leagues. Futurists and fascists figured on a single list in the same year, and engaged in joint attacks (for example on *Avanti* in 1919). In 1924, in *Futurism and Fascism*, Marinetti still saluted Mussolini for his 'marvellous futurist temperament'. Yet this relationship of futurism to fascism should not be over-simplified. Contrary to what Benn claimed in his defence of expressionism, futurism was far from constituting a 'state art' in Italy: one need only look at the official monuments to see this. The futurists rather found themselves taken hostage. In 1934, on the occasion of the exhibition of Italian futurist 'Aeropainting' in Hamburg and Berlin, Marinetti and several other Italian futurists launched a polemic against the stupidity of Nazi censorship and its conception of 'degenerate art', condemning in particular the ideas about culture that Hitler presented at the Nuremberg congress. When Italian fascism eventually echoed the Nazi struggle against 'degenerate art' the futurists found themselves threatened. An 'anthology of degenerate art' was published in Italy in 1937, and even attacked Marinetti. Cf. G. Lista, ed., *Marinetti et le Futurisme italien*, Paris 1977.

10. In his autobiography *Double Life*, Gottfried Benn related his entanglements with the Nazi authorities and how, despite having occupied official positions, he was subsequently treated by the Nazi press and the *Völkischer Beobachter* in particular as a 'degenerate swine'. He finally had to abandon not just writing but his medical practice as well. The expressionist painter Emil Nolde, though he rallied to the NSDAP early on, encountered similar vexations. He wrote to Goebbels: 'I beg you, Herr Minister, to have a stop put to the slanderous campaign against me. I resent it all the more vigorously as I was almost alone among German artists in waging an open struggle against the invasion of German art by foreign elements, against the unhealthy art market and the intrigues around Lieberman and Cassirer, a struggle waged against enormous and superior forces and which for years on end brought me only material disadvantage. When National Socialism labelled me and my art as "degenerate" and "decadent", I had the feeling of being deeply misconstrued, as this is not the case; my art is a German art, vigorous, hard, and ardent.' (cited after Lionel Richard, *Le Nazisme et la culture*, pp. 64–5). In 1941, Nolde was forbidden to paint.

11. His sculptures were also withdrawn from public places, for example the 'Spiritual Combatants' at Kiel and the angel he had donated to Güstrow cathedral.

12. Karl Hofer was violently attacked by Rosenberg's *Deutsche Kulturwacht* (vol. 17, 1933, p. 13), which ranted: 'How much longer is the Academy going to dance to the pipes of the Jew Hofer?' He responded: 'I have never played the pipes, and unfortunately have never seen the Academy dance. Moreover, I am not Jewish.'

13. Kokoschka emigrated to Prague and then London, where he really did paint 'political canvases'. Klee returned to Berne, Max Beckmann left Germany in 1937 and settled in the United States. Kandinsky was all the more detested by the Nazis for being Russian and having belonged to the Commissariat for Fine Arts in the Soviet Union. His membership of the Bauhaus was a further mark against him. It should be emphasized, however, against the prevailing legend, that the Bauhaus was really politicized only in its Dessau period, when Walter Gropius was replaced by Hannes Meyer. The Nazis imposed on Mies van der Rohe, the new director, the elimination of its Social-Democratic members and Kandinsky. If he had little real sympathy for Communism, Kandinsky was attacked by the Nazis for having 'transformed pictorial language into a Morse code'. The majority of German museums got rid of his canvases, which were acquired by the Guggenheim collection.

14. In 1929–30, following actions by the Kampfbund, Rosenberg had obtained the dismissal of several museum directors favourable to modern art. Frick appointed

'commissars of art' charged with drawing up lists of performances to ban or monuments to destroy. In April 1933 an exhibition on 'cultural bolshevism' from 1918 to 1933 was organized at the Kunsthalle in Baden.

15. Stefan Zweig had suggested to Richard Strauss the idea of basing an opera on *The Silent Woman* by Ben Jonson. The opera was already completed when Hitler took power. A few weeks later, a decree was published that prohibited German theatres from playing works by 'non-Aryan authors'. In his memoirs, Zweig wrote: 'It went without saying that Richard Strauss would abandon further work on it and begin another with someone else. Instead, he wrote me letter after letter asking what had got into me; quite the contrary, he said, for as he was already at the orchestration he wanted me to work on the text of his next opera' (*The World of Yesterday*, London 1943, p. 281). Zweig does not conceal the fact that Strauss accepted favours from the new regime: he even composed the hymn for the Berlin Olympiad of 1936, and had numerous meetings with Göring, Goebbels and Hitler: 'Despite his art-egoism, which he always acknowledged openly and coolly, he was inwardly indifferent whatever the regime. He had served the German Kaiser as a conductor and had arranged military marches for him, later he had served the Emperor of Austria as court-conductor in Vienna, and had been *persona gratissima* likewise in the Austrian and German Republics' (p. 282). Zweig recalls that Strauss had all the more interest in attracting the regime's sympathies as his daughter-in-law was Jewish, his publisher was Jewish, and he had collaborated with Hugo von Hoffmannsthal who was similarly Jewish. Yet Strauss insisted that the name of Stefan Zweig figure alongside his own on the posters. Hitler finally authorized the opera, but it was shown only in Berlin. The correspondence between Strauss and Zweig was intercepted by the Gestapo. In these letters Strauss maintained that he 'only mimed his role as president to avoid more serious troubles'. Zweig, for his part, had never hidden the fact that he was donating his royalties to Jewish relief organizations. Goebbels demanded that Strauss should immediately resign his position as president of the Reichsmusikkammer, which he officially did on 13 July 1935, requesting a meeting with Hitler who did not respond. Strauss was never disturbed under the Nazi regime, being too distinguished, and for his eightieth birthday the performance of some of his operas was authorized, though no official figure attended. Strauss was already nearly seventy when the Nazis took power, and even if his celebrity would have enabled him to work wherever he wished, he refused to leave Germany. Though defended by many émigrés, Klaus Mann draws a fairly negative portrait of him in *The Turning Point*: the old man who gives out signed photos and praises the number of German cities with opera houses, seeming not to realize that they were now almost all in ruins.

16. The Nazis and the right-wing press frequently targeted Max Reinhardt (under his original name of Goldmann) and Leopold Jessner. In the Prussian parliament, the expressionist actor Fritz Kortner was accused of having 'Judaized' the Staatstheater by favouring the engagement of four Jewish actors (Forster, Ettlinger, Bildt and Wäsche); in fact only one of these was Jewish. The Hugenberg press denounced the 'Kortner dictatorship'. (Cf. Fritz Kortner, *Aller Tage Abend*, Munich 1969, p. 245.)

17. He had staged a play by a little-known dramatist: Benito Mussolini.

18. For instance the actor Hans Otto, thrown from a window by the Gestapo. Klaus Mann recalls that Otto's death did not leave the acting world indifferent. Several of his colleagues demanded an explanation, in response to which they were simply forbidden to attend his funeral. The following day, the actors of the Berlin Staatstheater left wreaths with red ribbons in front of the theatre. Ten of them were immediately arrested by the Gestapo.

19. Johst wrote in particular the play *Schlageter*, a homage to the nationalist student and Freikorps member who was shot by the French for sabotage during their occupation of the Ruhr. It was in response to an earlier play of his, *Der Einsame*, that Brecht wrote his *Baal*. Johst is also responsible for the phrase wrongly attributed to Göring: 'When I hear the word culture, I reach for my gun.' Whilst

he occupied various official positions under the Third Reich, Johst wrote practically nothing more and died after the War completely forgotten.

20. To give a random selection, Werner Krauss, Heinrich George, Bernhard Minetti, Gustaf Gründgens, Rudolf Forster, Paul Hörbiger, Hanns Albers and Emil Jannings.

21. Goebbels subsequently gave these two painters official responsibilities in the Strength Through Joy organization. Otto Andreas-Schreiber founded the bimonthly magazine *Kunst der Nation* in October 1933.

22. Franz Marc had been killed in the battle of Verdun. The soldiers of his battalion wrote in vain to Hitler against this insult to his memory.

23. The 'specialist' in these juxtapositions was still Schulze-Naumburg, who since 1931 had been touring Germany to present the conflicting visions of the world in art. He showed photos of deranged people and drawings by mental patients alongside expressionist portraits and works by Nolde, Kirchner, Hofer and Barlach. The Nazi press was unstinting in its praise for this racist imbecile, and asserted: 'The name of Schulze-Naumburg is a programme for us.'

24. Its title was *Dringender Appell*, launched by the Internationaler sozialistischer Kampfbund. On the significance of this appeal see the memoirs of Karola Bloch, *Aus meinem Leben*, Pfullingen 1981, p. 80.

25. The Prussian Academy of Arts had been founded by Friedrich III in 1696, with the aim of grouping talented artists who might serve as decorators for the court. A School of Fine Arts was attached to it, and a musical section was created in 1809 at the initiative of Goethe. A few rare writers were admitted in the eighteenth and nineteenth centuries, but in general the Academy still held itself aloof from literature. After the collapse of the Imperial regime in 1918, a literary section was created, and held its first meeting in 1926. Its first members included Ludwig Fulda, Gerhart Hauptmann, Arno Holz, Thomas Mann and Ricarda Huch. It was first presided over by Wilhelm von Scholz (who subsequently abdicated before the Nazis), and its object was to ensure the defence of intellectual values and oppose all attacks on liberty. Throughout the 1920s it was a site of major debates. On its history, see Inge Jens, *Dichter zwischen rechts und links. Die Geschichte der Sektion für Dichtkunst der Preussischen Akademie der Künste dargestellt nach den Dokumenten*, Munich 1971.

26. Between 1927 and 1930, ideological conflicts grew continuously sharper, setting republican writers such as Döblin and Schickele at odds with nationalists and conservatives such as W. Schäfer, Kolbenheyer, Münchhausen, Ernst, Blunck and Grimm. A large number of these debates were reported in the *Vossische Zeitung*.

27. It was Franz Werfel who on 6 December 1932 drew the section's attention to the danger of a work of P. Fechter that had reached a print run of a million copies. Heinrich Mann gave an exposé of it on 5 January 1933. Alphons Paquet, Thomas Mann and Jacob Wassermann held that the Academy should condemn the book, while Döblin, Benn and Fulda thought it dangerous to polemicize against individual works. On 16 January, the question of the 'unleashing of cultural reaction' was once more raised, but the members could not agree on an appropriate response. Von Molo, Fulda, Benn and Döblin each presented a written position.

28. The precise words were: 'This house is concerned only with art and not with politics' (*es geht um Kunst nicht um Politik*). However, neither Mann nor Kollwitz had signed this appeal in their capacity of members of the Academy.

29. On the details of this episode, see Heinrich Mann, *Ein Zeitalter wird besichtigt*, Berlin 1973, pp. 342ff.

30. This '*Treugelöbnis*' was signed by eighty-eight writers who expressed their desire to contribute to the 'reconstruction' (*Wiederaufbau*) of the Reich. The signatories included G. Benn, R. Binding, O. Loerke, W. von Molo and Ina Seidel. In fact, the SDS lost any independence with the creation of the 'chambers of culture' in November 1933.

31. This had been a very powerful organization with more than three thousand

members, constituting a genuine writers' union. It had steadily grown more political in the course of the Weimar years. In 1924, Alfred Döblin, who was then president of the SDS, wrote in the magazine *Der Schriftsteller*, the SDS organ, that politics should not be left to the professionals. In 1930, moreover, an opposition was organized within the SDS at the impulse of Communist writers. The Berlin group, being the largest section, demanded that the SDS should take up the defence of writers prosecuted for their political views. The section particularly intervened in support of Carl von Ossietzky in 1932, likewise of Ludwig Renn. It also protested against the execution of two Hungarian Communist writers by the Horthy government. The SDS reacted by declaring the Berlin section dissolved, but this remained active until the Reichstag fire. In January 1933, the Berlin section launched a magazine, *Der oppositionelle Schriftsteller*.

32. Of Jewish origin, a friend of Martin Buber, Oskar Loerke and Rudolf Pannwitz, Alfred Mombert also had links with expressionism. He did not leave the Academy, and wrote in a letter to Pannwitz on 27 March 1933: 'The Academy is an old secular institution. We cannot so easily abandon it to its fate. And one should not deal so lightly with certain people.' Oskar Loerke adopted more or less the same attitude. Mombert still published a selection of poems in 1936, which was passed over in silence, and his other books were withdrawn from libraries. Despite warnings from his friends, he refused to emigrate. In 1941, at the age of sixty-eight, the Gestapo took him together with his sister (aged seventy-two) to the internment camp of Gurs in southern France. Suffering from cancer, his friends tried to have him sent to Switzerland, but he died on 6 February 1942. He wrote a number of poetry collections during his imprisonment: *Baraken-Winter* and *In der Finsternis* (cf. A. Mombert, *Briefe 1893–1942*, Heidelberg 1961). In a letter to Hans Reinhardt, he wrote on 30 October 1940: 'It is my fate that everything I expressed prophetically in my poems I have had to live in cruel reality.' Interned in Gurs as a Jew, he still hoped to obtain permission to return to Germany.

33. The order in which they are mentioned here corresponds to that of their responses.

34. Letters of Thomas Mann that are not included in the selected English edition (*The Letters of Thomas Mann 1889–1955*, Berkeley, 1970) are cited throughout just by their dates. For further details see *Die Briefe Thomas Manns. Regesten und Register*, Frankfurt 1976–87.

35. The members that remained were Bahr, Benn, Binding, Beumelburg, Blunck, Däubler, Dörfler, Griese, Grimm, Halbe, Hauptmann, Johst, Kolbenheyer, Loerke, Mell, Miegel, von Molo, von Münchhausen, Ponten, Schäfer, Schmidtbonn, Schönherr, von Scholz, Ina Seidel, Stehr, Strauss, Stucken and Vesper.

36. Elected with fourteen votes against H. F. Blunck (six) and W. Schäfer (two).

37. The Academy maintained that it was up to it and not the police to take a position on literary questions. Certain worker-poets had been sent to concentration camp, and former Social-Democrats such as Karl Bröger and Friedrich Bischoff.

38. This slow decline of the Academy can be traced in the private diary of Oskar Loerke, one of the few genuine 'internal émigrés', and in the correspondence of Börries von Münchhausen. In a letter of February 1934 addressed to Werner Beumelburg, Münchhausen discusses in perfect seriousness whether one should attend the Academy's meeting in tails or smoking jacket.

39. Jünger declined the offer of nomination, arguing that his work had a military character and that he could not stand academic situations. He referred to the analysis of culture he had made in *Der Arbeiter*. Jünger subsequently opposed the publication of his texts in Nazi periodicals, and protested when one of his writings was reprinted without his authorization in the *Völkische Beobachter*: at no price did he want to be considered a contributor to this paper. In a private interview (January 1979), Jünger declared to me that he had never had any sympathy for the Weimar Republic or for Heinrich Mann, its defender, preferring Anatole France in matters of literature. The elimination of certain members of the Academy did not arouse in him 'an excessive chagrin' but he could not countenance membership of the new

Academy. He acknowledged that if he had had to be a member, he would rather have belonged to its predecessor. We should also note that Stefan George declined the Nazis' offer and kept his distance from the new regime, while Gerhart Hauptmann accepted membership but abstained from attending the inauguration on 7 January 1933. It is clear that, with few exceptions, those authors selected by the Nazis to figure in the 'new Academy' were scarcely representative of German literature.

40. The SDS had been created in 1908 as an organization of German writers. It was re-established in exile in Paris, in autumn 1934. Among its leading lights now were Alfred Kantorowicz, Alfred Kurella, Rudolf Leonhardt, Ludwig Marcuse, Gustav Regler, Max Schröder and Anna Seghers. Heinrich Mann was named honorary president. Communists here occupied important positions. Sections were also created in Prague, Brussels, Copenhagen and England. 1938 saw the birth of the Schutzverband Deutsch-Amerikanischer Schriftsteller. The exiled SDS defended the rights and economic interests of its members. It directed numerous appeals, conferences and texts against National Socialism and campaigned for the liberation of Ludwig Renn and Carl von Ossietzky. Its history will be recalled below.

41. A Deutsche Akademie für Dichtung succeeded the Preussische Sektion für Dichtkunst until May 1945. The literary section was re-established in East Berlin on 24 March 1950, directed by Willi Bredel. The archives of the former Academy are held at the Akademie der Künste in East Berlin.

42. Cited from the article by Claude Aveline, present at the Ragusa congress, who gave a detailed account in *Nouvelles Littéraires*, 17 June 1933.

43. Italy (Marinetti), Austria (Felix Salten), the Netherlands (Van Ammers-Küller), and German-Switzerland (E. Stickelberger).

44. Cited after the article by Claude Aveline.

45. Toller said to his German colleagues: 'I shall be accused in Germany of having spoken against my country. That is untrue. What irks me is the methods of those men in power today in Germany, who have no legitimate claim to substitute themselves for the country. Millions of people in Germany no longer have a right to speak and write freely. When I speak here, I speak for these millions who no longer have a voice. I doubt whether we will often have the opportunity, in this Europe, to meet and talk together. Anyone who rebels today is threatened. What are we to do? Overcome the fear that demeans and discourages us. We are struggling on several paths. It may be that on some of these we meet face to face. But in all of us there is the idea of a humanity freed from barbarism, from lies, from social injustice.' Toller had played an increasingly important role during previous congresses, which he attended from 1930 on. He sought to introduce a political consciousness of the moral responsibility of the writer, and prevent the PEN Club from becoming simply a literary society. He had given a fairly critical account of the 1930 Warsaw Congress in *Die Weltbühne* (8 July 1930). His proposition to invite delegates from new countries (USSR, Syria, India, Morocco) was rejected. In May 1932 he found himself violently at odds with Marinetti.

46. Toller asserted once again the following year that he was not sure that German writers were again free to speak. Marinetti replied to him by a hymn of praise for war. The PEN Club did not react to his speech, out of diplomatic considerations. After the Congress, Toller wrote a further letter to Goebbels, accusing him not only of murdering writers in Germany but wanting also to physically liquidate émigrés.

47. This 'PEN Club in exile' of German émigrés was recognized by the general secretariat of PEN. Heinrich Mann was its president and Rudolf Olden its secretary. After the occupation of Austria in March 1938 an Austrian 'PEN in exile' was also formed, presided by Franz Werfel and with Robert Neumann as secretary. The PEN Club held its next congress in Prague in 1938, the German delegates including Ernst Bloch, Wieland Herzfelde and Oskar Maria Graf. (Cf. Karola Bloch, *Aus meinem Leben*, pp. 127–8.)

48. On the details of these chambers' functioning, cf. J. Wulf, *Literatur und Dichtung im Dritten Reich. Eine Dokumentation*, Gütersloh 1963; Hildegard Brenner, *Kunstpolitik des National-Sozialismus*, Hamburg 1963; Ernest K. Bramsted, *Goebbels und die N. S. Propaganda 1925–1945*, Frankfurt 1971.

49. In which case, if they were discovered, they risked arrest by the Gestapo and being sent to concentration camp.

50. (1) insurance; (2) social, legal and professional problems of writers; (3) book trade, publishing, bookstores, literary agents; (4) contracts; (5) libraries; (6) paperbacks, reprints.

51. Hermann Kesten, commenting in 1938 on the operation of these chambers of culture in the Paris-based *Neue Tage-Buch* ('Fünf Jahre nach unsere Abreise'), maintained correctly that a regular Chinese wall now divided censored literature from free literature. The principles of the chambers of culture left the only effective options as submission or silence.

52. The weighty list of literary prizes designed to reward the most servile works of literature should be mentioned here. There were in fact also 'white lists', 'party catalogues' published by Rosenberg's *Jahresgutachteranzeiger* and the Nazi 'library' of Bouhler. The works selected in this way were distributed to school libraries, their authors invited to read their writings before gatherings of Hitler Youth and other Nazi organizations (Kraft durch Freude, National-sozialistische Kulturgemeinde, etc.). Official demonstrations designed to glorify these writers were periodically organized (e.g. the Woche der deutschen Bücher from 1934 onward).

53. Family members and close friends were often arrested as well.

54. He managed to warn Karola Bloch in good time to conceal any trace of Communist activity. The colony of progressive artists where she lived was raided by the SA.

55. He still managed to speak on 27 February at Langenselbold bei Hanau. The meeting had scarcely finished when the SA tried to apprehend him. On the details of these arrests, cf. H. A. Walter, *Bedrohung und Verfolgung bis 1933*.

56. Münzenberg had the idea, two years earlier, of getting part of the profits of his publishing programme transferred to the Soviet embassy, to avoid their confiscation.

57. On the advice of Willi Bredel, the Marx-Engels-Verlag had already shifted part of its operation to Prague. Many left-wing publishers collapsed immediately.

58. Cf. H. A. Walter, *Bedrohung und Verfolgung bis 1933*, pp. 235ff.

59. On his release from concentration camp, Wolfgang Langhoff was unable to find work and emigrated illegally. Willi Bredel, after his internment at Hamburg-Fuhlsbüttel, took refuge in Prague, Kurt Hiller, after internment at Oranienburg, returned to Berlin and was still unwilling to leave Germany. He emigrated to Prague in September 1934 and could never discover the exact reasons for his release.

60. A pacifist writer, Wegner had been arrested for writing an open letter to Hitler, demanding that in the name of defending the German people the Jews who had contributed so much to German culture should be defended. He was interned for fourteen months at Oranienburg where he was tortured daily. After his release he refused to emigrate, as he maintained that 'emigration is death'. He remained in Berlin and was re-arrested for defending a Jew he had known in concentration camp. His books were burned and he had finally to leave Germany and take refuge in Italy so as not to be sent back to a camp. His wife left for exile in Palestine. Wegner remained in exile, and it was only at the age of eighty, when he still dreamed regularly of the tortures he had experienced, that he turned to complete the book he had started when Hitler took power.

61. Ludwig Renn, a former officer, was not sent to concentration camp but to prison, as the Nazis still hoped to win him for their cause. He was promised a passport to emigrate and an amnesty if he wrote that he had never been beaten in prison. Though this was in fact true, he refused in solidarity with all those that had been tortured. He left Germany in 1936 with the help of the clandestine KPD and reached Switzerland.

62. Rudolf H. Ganz, freed from Buchenwald in 1938, was expelled from Germany in March 1939 and emigrated to England.
63. Klaus Neukrantz suffered from nervous illness after his internment, and was undoubtedly killed by the Nazis as a mental patient.
64. On Ossietzky, cf. W. Grossmann, *Ossietzky. Ein deutscher Patriot*, Frankfurt 1982; Bruno Frei, *Carl von Ossietzky*, Berlin 1966; Raimund Koplin, *C. v. Ossietzky als politiker Publizist*, Frankfurt 1964.
65. E. E. Kisch, E. J. Gumpel, K. Otten, K. Kesten, W. Mehring, R. Olden and K. Pinthus also collaborated on this.
66. In his autobiography (*Mein zwanzigstes Jahrhundert*, Munich 1960, pp. 145ff.), Ludwig Marcuse recalls having urged him in these terms: 'Don't cast yourself into hell. You won't get out. Spare yourself for the struggle. Outside your pen is a power. Don't part with it.' Ossietzky replied that an oppositionist who crosses the frontier ceases to be one, and someone who seeks to act on the minds of the people must share their fate. Thus he would go to prison as 'a living demonstration' of his ideas. The editor-in-chief of *8-Uhr Abendblattes* decided in agreement with Kurt Grossman, secretary of the League for the Rights of Man, to organize a guard of honour for Ossietzky on his way to prison. Among the figures who accompanied him were Ernst Toller, Leonhard Frank, Arnold Zweig, Erich Mühsam, Lion Feuchtwanger, Alfred Wolfenstein, Alexander Roda-Roda, Hermann Kesten, Alfons Goldschmidt, Herbert Jhering, Rudolf Olden and Hellmut von Gerlach. Ossietzky, deeply moved, saluted them and entered the prison.
67. Ossietzky benefited from the amnesty of Christmas 1932. Though the League for the Rights of Man had collected 43,600 signatures in his favour, it was impossible to obtain his release any sooner.
68. During his detention he was replaced by Hellmut von Gerlach.
69. The story of this meeting with Ossietzky was related by Kurt Grossman (*Emigration. Geschichte der Hitler-Flüchtlinge 1933–1945*, Frankfurt 1969, p. 59). The Red Cross delegate evoked 'a trembling creature with cadaverous complexion, a being who seemed not to feel anything any more'.
70. A plaque was installed after the War, with the inscription 'peace for ever' (*Frieden für immer*).
71. *Brennende Erde: Verse eines Kämpfers; Alarm: Manifeste aus zwanzig Jahren.*
72. On the death of Erich Mühsam, cf. the documents published in the magazine *Europäische Ideen*, vol. 34–36, 1977, and Kurt Hiller, 'Erich Mühsam und seine Mörder', in *Profile. Prosa aus einem Jahrzehnt*, Paris 1938. Hiller profoundly disagreed with Mühsam, though himself a libertarian. He made his acquaintance in the KZ Oranienburg.
73. Zensl Mühsam herself met a tragic end. She was arrested in the Soviet Union after being invited there by the Red Cross to give lectures on the concentration camps. Though she tried to win the support of foreign celebrities, she was condemned to twenty years in Siberia and only returned to the GDR in 1956. She died in 1962.
74. Zensl Mühsam related her last meetings with her husband. The Nazis had not only broken his teeth, but cut his beard to make 'a Jewish caricature'. He was forced to lap up dirty water and his thumbs were broken so that he could no longer write to his wife. As for his death, Zensl makes clear that the rope was tied in a fashion that Erich, with his proverbial clumsiness, could never have managed himself. Kurt Hiller also mentions the case of the Communist Dressel, whose veins the SS opened to give the appearance of suicide. In Mühsam's case, it is very likely that the camp commander who had him killed was the same as murdered Gregor Strasser, a certain Eicke.
75. We may just recall the names of Gertrud Kolmar, Arno Nadel, Camill Hoffmann, Gertrud Kantorowicz, Arthur Ernst Rutra, Moritz Seeler and Arthur Silbergleit among those who died in concentration camps, without counting those intellectuals and writers who committed suicide rather than fall prey to the tortures of the Gestapo, such as Eugen Gottlob Winkler and Jochen Klepper. Nelly Sachs owed her survival to the intervention of Selma Lagerlof.

76. For example Fritz Martini, in *Deutsche Literatur. Geschichte von der Anfängen bis zum Gegenwart* (Stuttgart 1952, p. 540), speaks of 'unplanned and improvised book burnings' (*planlos improvisierten Bücherverbrennungen*).
77. Cf. Mathias Wegner, ed., *Exil und Literatur*, p. 37. On the detail of the book burnings see also R. Drews and A. Kantorowicz, eds, *Verboten und verbrannt*; Klaus Schöffling, ed., *Dort wo man Bücher verbrennt*, Frankfurt 1983; Gerhard Sander, ed., *Die Bücherverbrennung*, Munich 1983; and the catalogue of the exhibition held at the Akademie der Künste, Berlin 1983.
78. The authors whose books were to be burned figured on the black lists with a cross against their names. They included Georg Bernhard, Lion Feuchtwanger, Friedrich Wilhelm Foerster, Sigmund Freud, Ernst Glaeser, W. Hegemann, Arthur Holitscher, Erich Kästner, Karl Kautsky, Alfred Kerr, Egon Erwin Kisch, Emil Ludwig, Heinrich Mann, Carl von Ossietzky, Ernst Ottwalt, Theodor Plievier, Erich Maria Remarque, Kurt Tucholsky, Theodor Wolff and Arnold Zweig.
79. Fire and flames played a symbolic role in several speeches of Goebbels.
80. J. Wulf, *Literatur und Dichtung im Dritten Reich*, pp. 46ff.
81. At Bonn, Frankfurt, Göttingen, Munich and Württemberg. In Berlin, the nine incantations were directed against Marx and Kautsky, Heinrich Mann, Ernst Glaeser and Erich Kästner, Freud, Remarque, Tucholsky and Ossietzky. A portrait of the sexologist Magnus Hirschfeld was burnt, and 'nine students hurled the words of fire'. Goebbels took the occasion to exhort the youth to 'have the courage to look life pitilessly in the face, and forget the fear of death'.
82. Zweig, *The World of Yesterday*, p. 277.
83. Cited by Jürgen Serke in *Die verbrannten Dichter*, Weinheim 1977.
84. The history of the Freiheitsbibliothek, established in exile in Paris, will be traced further on. Destroyed by the Nazis when they occupied France, it was re-established after the war in Frankfurt. A large number of exhibitions have since been devoted to it, in particular for the fiftieth anniversary of the book burning.
85. Bertolt Brecht, 'The Burning of the Books', *Poems 1913–1956*, p. 294. Oskar Maria Graf's article was written in the form of an open letter, 'Verbrennt mich!' published in the *Wiener Arbeiterzeitung*. Neither Jew nor Communist, he had been curiously omitted from the blacklists. Indeed, one of his works appeared on a recommended 'white list'. This shows that the Nazis had not read him and saw him simply as a 'Bavarian' writer. The work recommended, *Wir sind Gefangene . . .*, was a memoir of his youth, particularly political and virulent, which had already created a scandal. This forgetfulness was all the more curious in that his apartment had already been searched by the SA, who confiscated his manuscripts. Horrified at the idea of passing for a representative of the 'new German spirit', Graf wrote this admirable letter in which he asked what he had done to merit such dishonour. He requested that his books should be burned, purified by the flames and not left in the bloody hands of a gang of murderers. The Nazis responded to his request by organizing a special auto-da-fé for his books outside Munich University, and in June 1933 he was deprived of German nationality. On many occasions Graf showed a similar insolence. He did not hesitate to appear at the first congress of Soviet writers in Bavarian costume, to the great joy of children thrilled to see this giant in short trousers. When it was proposed that he should visit Lenin in his mausoleum, he declared himself 'enchanted to see Sleeping Beauty in her glass coffin'. Exiled in America, Oskar Maria Graf continued to express himself in the only tongue which, by its beauty, seemed worthy to him of dethroning English as a language of universal communication: the Bavarian dialect.
86. For the complete text, cf. J. Wulf, *Literatur und Dichtung im Dritten Reich*, p. 64. An article in the *Münchener Neueste Nachrichten* for 18 May 1933 stipulates that 'Russians' and 'cultural bolsheviks' should not be confused, that neither Tolstoy nor Dostoyevsky should be put on the index as without the latter there would never had been Moeller van den Bruck. It was the 'new Russians' that had to be destroyed (*alle neuen Russen vernichtet zu werden brauchen*). The proscribed authors included

Lion Feuchtwanger, Ernst Glaeser, Arthur Holitscher, Alfred Kerr, Egon Erwin Kisch, Emil Ludwig, Heinrich Mann, Ernst Ottwalt, Theodor Plievier, Erich Maria Remarque, Kurt Tucholsky and Arnold Zweig, as representatives of 'asphalt literature'. This term was subsequently adopted by certain émigrés. Thus, in a letter to Feuchtwanger of June–July 1934, Brecht wrote: 'Why shouldn't we just accept the term "asphalt literature"? [. . .] Only the swamp complains of its great black brother. Of asphalt, so patient, clean and useful' (Bertolt Brecht, *Letters 1913–1956*, London 1990, pp. 174–5). Brecht opposed 'asphalt literature' to 'blood-and-soil literature' and maintained that all real literature could be included in the former category, even 'works with a *minimum* of that rational and bourgeois wisdom that characterizes at their highest point the works of Swift, Voltaire, Lessing, Goethe, etc.' (*Ecrits sur la littérature et l'art*, vol. 3, Paris 1970, p. 49).

87. Following the *Prinzipien zur Säuberung des öffentlichen Büchereien*.
88. Stefan Zweig remarked that: 'Book dealers were warned not to display any of our books and newspapers ignored them, nevertheless the general public remained indifferent. While there was no threat of punishment in prison or concentration camp my books sold almost as well in 1933 and 1934 in spite of all difficulties and chicaneries as before.' (*The World of Yesterday*, London 1943, p. 277). Klaus Mann, however, maintains the contrary in *The Turning Point*, that after 1933 no one risked asking in a bookstore for a novel by Thomas Mann, even if he did not yet figure among the émigrés. If Mann's works continued to be distributed until his break with the Reich, a large number of bookstores already refused to sell them, according to G. Bermann Fischer, his publisher.
89. These lists were known as 'lists 2 to 4'.
90. According to H. Brenner, as many as twenty-one institutions had the power to ban books. On 6 December 1933, a thousand titles had already been proscribed, 732 new interdictions were announced in February 1934, and it is estimated that by the end of that year, at least 41,000 publications had been placed under ban by forty different instances.

CHAPTER 2   THE BEGINNINGS OF EMIGRATION

1. An overall study of the fascination that fascism exercised on a certain number of writers in the 1920s and 30s remains to be written. Alastair Hamilton laid the foundations of this in *The Appeal of Fascism*, London 1971. There is still no complete study devoted to German and French writers. For Italian intellectuals, see Michel Ostenc, *Intellectuels italiens et fascisme (1915–1920)*, Paris 1983.
2. Apart from the collaborationist French writers, the most authentic representatives of fascist literature are largely insignificant. The novels of 'Nazi writers' are read today only as documents; the like of Kolbenheyer, Bloem, Binding, Burte, Claudius, Vesper and Schumann have left little trace in German literature. (Cf. Ernst Loewy, *Literatur unterm Hakenkreuz. Das dritte Reich und seine Dichtung*, Frankfurt 1966.)
3. Italian fascism was more of a pole of attraction than Nazism. For many, anti-Semitism, absent in the beginnings of Italian fascism, seemed a mere aberration.
4. The English example is pertinent here; many 'English fascists' despised Hitler.
5. It is a vain search, therefore, to try and prove that Heidegger's philosophical theses in *Sein und Zeit* led him to believe in National Socialism, or that Gottfried Benn's irrationalism necessarily led him to support the new regime. It is equally hard to establish with certainty the intellectual logic that led Drieu la Rochelle to support a movement whose bloody brutality should have aroused his contempt; the reasons sometimes given – taste for action, fascination with death – could also be found in Malraux. Neither Stefan George nor Ernst Jünger became adepts of National Socialism. If they had been, could one establish ideological links between their works and their adherence? It is more astonishing that Gottfried Benn should have supported the Nazi regime than that Stefan George immediately distanced himself

from it, more surprising that Gerhart Hauptmann accepted its honours than that Ernst Jünger refused them with contempt.

6. For instance the 'fascism' of Yeats in England and to some extent that of Ezra Pound.

7. We thus depart here from the analysis of Walter Laqueur. Besides ascribing too much power to the intellectuals of that epoch, and unjustly reproaching the most critical of these with having worked for the Republic's destruction, it is misleading to hold that writers of left and right were totally unaware of one another: 'Just as a man of the right would not dream of attending a performance of a Krenek opera, not to mention one of the plays staged by Piscator, a left-wing intellectual would take no interest in right-wing literature about war' (*Weimar. A Cultural History*, London 1974, p. 42). Not only did the right follow with vigilance all the cultural productions of the left, but Piscator himself took part in a radio debate with Goebbels in 1930. Their respective speeches were prepared by Franz Jung and Arnolt Bronnen. If writers were divided by politics, they were nonetheless united by a certain faith in culture and ideas, which was not the case with the Nazis.

8. Cf. Jean-Pierre Fay, *Langages totalitaires*, Paris 1972, where this confusion of political language, particularly pronounced on the German right, is remarkably analysed.

9. On 20 June 1923 Karl Radek gave a curious speech at the Executive Committee of the Communist International at which he described the 'wanderer in the void' as a 'courageous soldier of the counter-revolution'. The next few weeks saw a polemic in the press of both right and left around Radek's article, as to who had the legitimate right to claim the allegiance of this 'wanderer in the void'.

10. Cf. Louis Dupeux, *National-bolchevisme. Stratégie communiste et dynamique conservatrice*, Paris 1979; also John Spalek, ' "Links Leute von recht" before and after 1933', *Jahrbuch für Internationale Germanistik*, series A, vol. 5, Berne 1979. One can easily get lost in analysing these tangled currents and their respective ideologies, at once close and distinct, which borrowed terminology and themes both from the far left and from the 'revolutionary' right. All had in common the belief in a social revolution waged from a nationalist standpoint. This is what united the Widerstand circle of Niekisch, the Schwarze Front of Otto Strasser and the social-revolutionary nationalists (Karl O. Paetel). Many were for a redistribution of wealth, the expropriation of large fortunes and sometimes even the creation of councils. The national-bolsheviks championed a rapprochement between Germany and the Soviet Union. Count Brockdorff-Rantzau, the first foreign minister of the Weimar Republic, was named the 'red count' for his admiration of Soviet Russia. A number of representatives of these currents came from old Prussian families, others had migrated from the Social-Democrats. After November 1918 a 'national-communist' movement developed in Hamburg around Heinrich Laufenberg and Fritz Wolffheim. After the arrest of Niekisch, his family were protected by Ernst Jünger, who had to burn his letters for security reasons.

11. 'Doctor Goebbels also turned up with his henchmen, whom I try in vain to recall in my memoirs, as they were still more effective than their boss [. . .]. This studio on the sixth floor, a nightmare for the other inhabitants of the building, had the look of a well-lit aquarium in which plenty of fishing was possible: cuttlefish, jellyfish, sea anemones with long tentacles, tiny sharks whose skin was still quite tender' (*La Cabane dans la vigne. Journal IV*, Paris 1980, p. 34).

12. Scheringer was condemned in the course of the trial at Ulm in 1930 in which Hitler was called as a witness, for working to set up Nazi cells in the Reichswehr. Imprisoned at Gollnow along with Communists, he then joined the KPD. His fellow-accused Ludin, detained at Rastatt, subsequently joined the SA. The third accused, Wendt, became manager of a music-hall.

13. Cf. E. von Salomon, *Le Questionnaire*, Paris 1953, pp. 344–5.

14. All the more so in that German democracy was not the culmination of a popular revolution, but an accidental solution after the collapse of the Reich and the failure

of the revolution of 1919. The Republic was implanted in a country in which anti-democratic and anti-republican ideas were paramount. Many writers, such as Thomas Mann, served a slow apprenticeship in democracy. On the various anti-democratic currents, see Kurt Sontheimer, *Anti-demokratische Denken in der Weimarer Republik*, Munich 1962, and the classic study of Armin Moehler, *Die konservative Revolution in Deutschland, 1918–1932*, Stuttgart 1950.

15. Among them, *Der Ring, Das Gewissen, Deutsche Volkstum, Die deutsche Rundschau, Die Hochschule, Archiv für Politik und Geschichte, Politik und Geschichte, Die deutscher Arbeiter*, not to speak of artistic magazines or associations of students which were just as reactionary.

16. For instance, hatred for the Republic and democracy, resort to the irrational and myth, anti-intellectualism.

17. Cf. Wilhelm Stapel, *Der christliche Staatsmann. Eine Theologie des Nationalismus*, Hamburg 1932: 'The true statesman is a master, a warrior and a priest at the same time. His opposite number is the spirit, the intellectual, the *littérateur*' (p. 195).

18. Ernst Jünger, *Der Arbeiter. Herrschaft und Gestalt*, Hamburg 1932.

19. *Der Führerfrage im neuen Deutschland*, Hamburg 1928.

20. *Der christliche Staatsmann*.

21. 'Führerschaft', in *Deutschlands Erneuerung*, 1920.

22. E. Jünger, *La Cabane dans la vigne*, pp. 36–7.

23. Moeller van den Bruck is almost the only theorist to have been the object of a thorough study. Cf. Denis Goedel, *Moeller van den Bruck (1876–1925)*, Frankfurt 1984.

24. Thomas Mann, *Three Essays*, London 1933, p. 215.

25. In his essay on Zola that appeared in Switzerland in November 1915, a veritable plea for democracy, Heinrich Mann attacked in passing 'some aestheticizing writers not engaged in politics', a direct reference to his brother.

26. T. Mann, *Reflections of a Nonpolitical Man*, New York 1983.

27. 'The German Republic', in Thomas Mann, *Order of the Day*, New York 1942, pp. 3–45.

28. *Order of the Day*, p. 47.

29. Ibid., p. 57.

30. 'Die Wiedergeburt der Anständigkeit', in Thomas Mann, *Gesammelte Werke*, ed. Peter de Mendelssohn, Frankfurt 1960–74, vol. 12, pp. 649ff.

31. Mann wrote for example to Reinhold Niebuhr on 19 February 1943: 'Had I remained at the level of *Reflections of a Nonpolitical Man*, which after all was not an anti-human book, I would have raised myself against this abomination with the same fury and *just as legitimately* as I do today as a democrat.'

32. *The Hour of Decision*, London 1934, pp. ixff.

33. French translation: *La Haine et la honte. Souvenirs d'un aristocrate allemand 1936–1944*, Paris 1969, p. 15.

34. Some of these aristocrats joined the active opposition to Nazism at this point. One of the most spectacular transformations was that of Hubertus Prinz zu Löwenstein who on 16 October 1930 became a member of the Reichsbanner, the Social-Democratic combat organization. Cf. Hubertus Prinz zu Löwenstein, *Botschafter ohne Auftrage, Lebensbericht*, Düsseldorf 1972, p. 62.

35. *La Haine et la honte*, p. 29.

36. The same scenes are described by Klaus Mann in *The Turning Point*, London 1984.

37. 'At that time he was in the process of writing *Die totale Mobilmachung*, and I understood from reading this essay that he had already arrived at a result, whereas I, like all those who were attracted to him, was still walking through the landscape of our century with my eyes open, trying to get my bearings from each passing signpost' (*Le Questionnaire*, p. 238).

38. Ibid., p. 239.

39. Ibid., p. 240.

40. Oral communication from Ernst Jünger.

41. *Le Questionnaire*, p. 241.
42. Ernst Jünger, *La Cabane dans le vigne*, p. 31.
43. *Le Questionnaire*, p. 182.
44. Ibid., p. 182.
45. Ibid., p. 188.
46. Ibid., p. 340.
47. *La Cabane dans le vigne*, p. 241.
48. 'The immense efforts of four years of war had not only led to defeat; they had led to humiliation. The disarmed country was surrounded by very dangerous neighbours armed to the teeth, corridors were cut through it and it was pillaged and bled white. It was a bad dream, a dream in grisaille. Then along comes this unknown who gets up and says what had to be said, and everyone feels that he is right. [. . .] I remember that after the meeting, men passed round with sacks which we stuffed with banknotes' (ibid., p. 243). Jünger sees his relationship to Hitler as passing through three phases: first he was fascinated, then found Hitler ridiculous, and finally frankly dangerous. He noted however in his diary (*La Cabane dans le vigne*; 31 March 1946): 'When the news of his suicide was confirmed, I felt relieved; I had sometimes feared seeing him exhibited in a cage in some foreign capital. At least this is one spectacle we were spared.'
49. The fates of the main representatives of these right-wing intellectuals, whether they were dissident National Socialists, national revolutionaries or national-bolsheviks, were both varied and unforeseen. Gregor Strasser was murdered, his brother Otto re-established the Schwarze Front in exile. The head of the Freikorps, Erhardt, 'the greatest hope of German nationalism' according to von Salomon, left Germany secretly so as to avoid arrest. The national-bolshevik Niekisch lost his sight in a concentration camp. Karl O. Paetel (a national-bolshevik friend of Jünger) went into exile, Bodo Uhse and Ludwig Renn joined the left. Fritz Wolffheim ended in concentration camp. Harro Schulze-Boysen went on to play a major role in the Rote Kapelle spy ring, and was murdered by the Nazis in December 1942.
50. Ebert had been a cooper, Severing a locksmith, Scheidemann a printer, Noske a basket-maker, Wels a decorator. Autodidacts, they formed an embourgeoisified bureaucracy that was pretty contemptuous of intellectuals.
51. Thus the victims of attacks by the Linkskurve were often the most progressive writers: Tucholsky, Heinrich Mann, Ilya Ehrenburg, Toller, Döblin, etc.
52. Despite his political clairvoyance, Carl von Ossietzky scarcely took Nazism seriously before 1932. It was with the arrival of the Nazis in the government of Thuringia that he realized the danger they represented. Between 1930 and 1932 his attacks were focused on Brüning, and he treated the Nazis with irony and contempt.
53. *Mein zwanzigstes Jahrhundert*, p. 122.
54. Alfred Döblin, *Die deutsche Literatur*, p. 13.
55. Klaus Mann, *The Turning Point*.
56. Munich 1959.
57. Kortner also recalls (*Aller Tage Abend*, p. 259) that for Kraus the great danger threatening Germany was not Hitler but Alfred Kerr. He even came to Berlin to combat him. Kraus denounced the pernicious influence of Kerr on the German theatre in a number of articles, but he wrote practically nothing against Hitler. Manès Sperber saw in Kraus's silence the failure of satire and irony in the face of sadism and vulgarity ('Grandeur et misère de la satire', in *Cahier de l'Herne* on Karl Kraus, Paris 1975, p. 122). In the final number of *Der Fackel*, Kraus could only write: 'On the subject of Hitler, nothing comes to my mind.'
58. *Aller Tage Abend*, p. 259.
59. Count Harry Kessler, *The Diaries of a Cosmopolitan 1918–1937*, London 2000.
60. Harry Graf Kessler (1868–1937) became an oppositionist under Wilhelm II and defended the Republic. Ambassador to Poland after 1919, he was also an intimate friend of Walter Rathenau.

61. Even with Nietzsche's sister Elizabeth, who confided to Kessler that she had noted Hitler's 'fascinating eyes' but saw him as more of a mystic than a political figure. She maintained that in any case, he was not a great politician (7 August 1932; *Diaries of a Cosmopolitan*, p. 426).

62. 22 Feb 1933; ibid., p. 447.

63. 1 April 1933; ibid. p. 451.

64. 24 May 1933.

65. Manès Sperber, *Au-delà de l'oubli*, Paris 1980, p. 32.

66. Gustav Regler, *The Owl of Minerva*, London 1959, p. 145, and *Le Glaive et le fourreau*, Paris 1960, pp. 161–2. [Only the first sentence appears in the English edition.]

67. *The Owl of Minerva*, p. 151.

68. Cited from H. A. Walter, *Deutsche Exilliteratur*, p. 95. Wolff, the editor-in-chief of the celebrated *Berliner Tageblatt*, was arrested by the Italians in Nice and handed to the Gestapo. This old man was murdered in a concentration camp. Goebbels celebrated his extradition to Germany in a special announcement.

69. *The World of Yesterday*, p. 271.

70. Ibid., p. 273.

71. Published in 1930 in *Zur Situation*, and reprinted in *Auf der Suche nach einem Weg*, 1931. Klaus Mann stressed that Stefan Zweig's admiration for the youth prevented him from seeing that they were heading towards an apocalypse and that their supposed radicalism 'had nothing praiseworthy about it'.

72. G. Bermann Fischer, *Bedroht-Bewahrt. Weg eines Verlegers*, Frankfurt 1967, pp. 78ff.

73. H. A. Walter, *Deutsche Exilliteratur*, pp. 101ff.

74. *Aller Tage Abend*, pp. 419ff.

75. Klaus Mann, *The Turning Point*, p. 232.

76. Vicki Baum, *Es war alles ganz anders. Erinnerungen*, Frankfurt 1962, p. 459.

77. Cited by H. A. Walter, *Deutsche Exilliteratur*, p. 106. When François-Poncet responded that in his opinion Severing would not press the button, Zweig was perplexed, and astonished at such a combination of pessimism and lack of faith in the Social-Democratic government.

78. The 'red prince', who had joined the Reichsbanner while still a student, was one of its most striking speakers. In 1932 he wrote to Hindenburg to defend the organization, which had just been dissolved, and received a hand-written reply. On 14 March 1933, when the SA burst into his apartment in the middle of the night, he asked them to get out, threatening to call the police, and requested that they take care not to damage his collection of porcelain. (Hubertus Prinz zu Löwenstein, *Botschafter ohne Aufträg*, Droste 1972, pp. 87–8.) He took part in meetings until March 1933, when members of the Reichsbanner were arrested and tortured by the SA.

79. *Diaries of a Cosmopolitan*, p. 218.

80. In his autobiography, *Leben gegen die Zeit*, Frankfurt 1969, Hiller mentions this text as lost, but a French translation was published in November 1932 by the review *Europe*.

81. Cf. André Banuls, *Heinrich Mann, le poète et la politique*, Paris 1966, pp. 341ff.

82. Gustav Regler relates that in January 1933, with the Nazis patrolling the streets, 'Only those writers who had not joined in the daily battle were alarmed and fully conscious of the danger. Kiepenheuer, the publisher, told me that he had sent the proofs of my Avignon novel to an associated publishing house in Holland. For the first time I heard the word "exile" spoken. I thought them all disgusting cowards and hurried back to my artists' colony' (*The Owl of Minerva*, p. 148).

83. Ernst Fischer, *Le Grand Rêve socialiste*, Paris 1974, pp. 231ff. This depiction is perhaps somewhat exaggerated.

84. *The Letters of Sigmund Freud and Arnold Zweig*, London 1970, p. 41.

85. This included Communists, Social-Democrats, pacifists, and individuals well-known for their republican ideas.

86. Hiller, *Leben gegen die Zeit*, pp. 222ff.

87. Three days before his release from prison, Carl von Ossietzky once against urged Communists and Socialists to unite against the Nazis and hold an urgent meeting at a round table ('Ein runder Tisch wartet').

88. For example the Human Rights League, whose secretary was Kurt Grossman, met on 30 January 1933 to decide on further action. When they learned in the course of the session that Hitler, the 'whirling dervish', had become Chancellor, they expressed their shame before this grotesque episode of German history. Ossietzky, more pessimistic, maintained that he would be chased out in either fourteen days or fourteen years. He noted quite pertinently: 'The counter-revolution has occupied the commanding heights without a fight. It dominates the valley in which we live.' On 3 February, the League held a further meeting in the Beethoven hall. The meeting was immediately banned by the prefect of police, and they had to meet in a café. (Karl Grossman, *Carl von Ossietzky*, p. 341.)

89. Regler, *The Owl of Minerva*, p. 146.

90. Ibid., p. 151.

91. A. Kantorowicz, *Deutsches Tagebuch. I. Teil*, Berlin 1959, p. 393.

92. The initiator of this group seems to have been Georg Bernhard, who from August 1932 on gathered left intellectuals regularly in his apartment in Charlottenburg, including Heinrich Mann, Count Harry Kessler, Carl Misch, Robert Olden, Otto Lehmann-Russbüldt and Kurt Grossman, who was also its secretary. Willi Münzenberg, who according to Grossmann was behind the idea of the Bernhard committee, proposed to organize a congress. Grossmann accepted on condition that it was not taken over by the Communists and that these were not officially represented in the discussion. Münzenberg partially financed the congress, which was attended by 900 people, including a hundred journalists.

93. Grossman, *Carl von Ossietzky*, p. 347.

94. In February 1933, Ossietzky launched a further appeal for antifascist unity. The text was posted up on Berlin walls. Kurt Grossmann was threatened with expulsion from the Social-Democratic party for having signed an appeal for a common struggle together with the Communists.

95. For example Hans Rothfels, *Die deutsche Opposition gegen Hitler*, Frankfurt 1958.

96. Thus Otto Strasser, former Nazi and leader of the Schwarze Front, was an opponent of Hitler just as much as Heinrich Mann, but it would be hard to consider him as an 'antifascist'.

97. Describing in his diary the banning of a concert by Bruno Walter on 21 March 1933, and the official concerts that Strauss and Furtwängler conducted, Thomas Mann simply noted: 'Lackeys.' He also expressed his indignation on 9 May 1933 when he learned that Gerhart Hauptmann had deemed it appropriate to hoist the Nazi flag on his house on 1 May. (Thomas Mann, *Diaries 1918–1939*, London 1984, pp. 134 and 157.)

98. Klaus Mann's novel *Mephisto. Roman einer Karriere* was published by Querido Verlag of Amsterdam in 1936. For many years after the War it was not republished in Germany, following a complaint by Gründgens's adopted son, Peter Gorski-Gründgens. Gründgens senior, for his part, continued his brilliant career after 1945. The novel had previously appeared in instalments in the *Pariser Tageszeitung*, with the subtitle *Ein Schlüsselroman* (a *roman à clef*). In June of that year the author protested ('Kein Schlüsselroman. Ein notwendige Erklärung von K. Mann in *Pariser Tageszeitung*'), maintaining that if the rise of an actor now celebrated in Germany was not foreign to his book, he had sought to represent 'a type and its milieu, not an individual'. Klaus Mann had known Gründgens since the 1920s, indeed Gründgens had been married to his sister Erika.

99. Gustav Regler evokes in his autobiography (*The Owl of Minerva*, pp. 103–4) the prevailing atmosphere at Heidelberg University after the Great War. Though Max Weber provoked violent attacks by calling Wilhelm II a 'crowned amateur', Alfred Weber encouraged students to travel to Berlin to combat the 'Spartacist scum'.

Students in the uniforms of their corporations hunted Ernst Toller with a view to lynching him. E. J. Gumbel had denounced in the 1920s such acts of violence committed by the far right (*Vier Jahre politischer Mord,* Berlin 1923). When he was appointed a tenured professor at Heidelberg, students demonstrated against him, calling him a 'swine', a 'traitor' and a 'Russian agent', and threatening to boycott the university's foundation anniversary if he were not dismissed. The students' association ASTA was dissolved by the minister, but still more violent attacks continued against Jewish and socialist teachers. The science faculty and the rector supported the students, and following a general referendum, Gumbel had to leave for France in 1932.

100. 'Care' (*Sorge*), for example, was identified with Odon, the aristocratic god, 'everyday banality' with Thor, and so on.

101. Cf. *Literatur und Germanistik nach der 'Machtübernahme'. Colloquium zur 50. Wiederkehr des 30. January 1933,* ed. Beda Alleman, Bonn 1983. Germanists in France, on the other hand, remained almost without exception adversaries of Nazism, and used their knowledge of German culture to denounce the falsifications introduced by National Socialism.

102. Ernst Bertram, *Nietzsche. Essai de mythologie,* Paris 1932.

103. 'I have believed for a long while that for internal reasons more than external, it is and will remain impossible to practise politics in Germany. I feel deeply that I am incapable of exerting any action on the German present, just like my brother but in a different way' (letter of 25 November 1918). Their correspondence has been published in volume form: *Thomas Mann, Ernst Bertram. Briefwechsel,* Pfullingen 1960.

104. 'Excuse me for constantly making a connection and link with my own work, the *Reflections* – I see in it not just a complement, but in some way its redemption, just as in the other sense, the truth of your legend is confirmed to a certain degree by my stammering confessions' (21 November 1918).

105. Letter of 30 July 1934; *Letters of Thomas Mann 1889–1955,* p. 191.

106. *Der Spiegel* interview.

107. This I would see as the basic mistake made in the majority of arguments around the Heidegger case. His opponents assemble very dubious documents to trace the darkest portrait possible of the philosopher (for instance the works of Paul Hühnerfeld, *In Sachen Heidegger, Versuch über ein deutsches Genie,* Munich 1962, and Guido Schneeberger, *Nachlese zu Heidegger,* Berne 1962). Heidegger's defenders, for their part, too often take refuge in a derisory apoliticism, making out that it was possible to remain in Germany under Hitler and think only of Hölderin and the pre-Socratics. Heidegger's aberration is indissociable from the entire climate of the German academy and it is hard even today to study all its implications.

108. Cf. F. K. Ringer, *The Decline of the German Mandarins. The German Academic Community 1920–1939,* Cambridge MA 1969. We should recall however that a motion of support for Hitler in spring 1933 obtained only 900 signatures out of a total of 7,000 professors.

109. Oral communication of Arno Breker.

110. We may recall that Belmondo, the neo-classical French sculptor, was like Breker a pupil of Despiau (author of a dithyrambic study on Breker published by Flammarion in 1942); Hitler admired Rodin and Maillol, the latter being indeed protected by the Nazis and receiving commissions from the Third Reich. This neo-classical style illustrated by Breker, Kolbe, Klimsch and Thorak has nothing specifically Nazi about it. The admirers of Breker's works included Stalin.

111. Speer wrote in his memoirs: 'The crucial fact appeared to me to be that I personally had to choose between a future Communist Germany or a future National Socialist Germany since the political centre between these antipodes had melted away' (*Inside the Third Reich,* p. 50).

112. Arno Breker, *Paris, Hitler et moi,* Paris 1970, p. 235.

113. G. W. Pabst, who had been awarded the French *légion d'honneur*, sent it back. He worked in France in the 1930s and completed a number of films there: *Mademoiselle Docteur* (1936), *Le Drame de Shanghai* (1938), *L'Esclave blanche* (1938) and *Jeunes filles en détresse* (1939).

114. Hans Otto (1900–1933), a well-known German actor who worked with proletarian theatre groups, was arrested and tortured by the SA, who threw him out of a window. He died on 24 November 1933. The Nazis sought to prevent the news of his death from being known. But in December of that year, Brecht addressed an open letter to the actor Heinrich George, asking what had become of Hans Otto. His death was announced in *Humanité* the same month, and a Hans Otto foundation established in Switzerland to assist émigré actors. The proletarian actor Curt Trepte, who kindly gave me much information on his late friend, wrote from Paris to Hanns Johst, responsible for the Nazi theatres, to demand an explanation. Plays in which actors won over to Nazism appeared were boycotted abroad. Émigrés then launched during performances leaflets giving the title of Brecht's open letter to Heinrich George, 'Heinrich George, where is your colleague Hans Otto?' A ceremony in his memory was organized in the United States in 1943. Cf. Curt Trepte and Jutta Wandetsky, *Hans Otto, Schauspieler und Revolutionär*, Berlin 1970.

115. This was despite the fact that in the 1920 he used to joke about his 'little Jewish head'. According to Lotte H. Eisner (oral communication), Jannings was in fact half-Jewish.

116. Reck-Malleczwesen, *La Haine et la honte*, p. 89.

117. In his memoirs, *Paris, Hitler et moi*, Arno Breker recounts that at Nuremberg, when the judges asked Jannings why he continued to work for the Nazis, he exclaimed: 'Your lordships, I happen to have a contract with me here of the kind drawn up before the making of a film. It can serve as an example of all the films that I made between 1933 and 1945. Consider, if you please, the amount of money that this contract brought me . . . Then please allow me to ask you this question: would you yourself have refused such a sum?' (p. 204). The same negative impressions are recorded by Gottfried Bermann Fischer (*Bedroht-Bewahrt*, pp. 77–8). On his return from Hollywood in 1932, Jannings, despite having acted for Jewish directors, displayed such public cynicism towards current events that Bermann Fischer and Curt Goetz left the room. Jannings refused from then on to acknowledge Bermann Fischer. He died in 1950 at the age of sixty-five, embittered by the criticisms that had been made of him. When Klaus Mann met him in 1945, Jannings professed astonishment that anyone could criticize his attitude under the Third Reich.

118. Unable to find appropriate roles in Hollywood, he left a note to his actor friends in exile that he was 'going back to Adolf's'.

119. For instance Herta Thiele, who starred in *Kuhle Wampe*, remained in Germany for a while but went into exile later, giving up her career rather than playing the part of a young Nazi girl.

120. Klaus Mann, *Mephisto*, Harmondsworth 1995, p. 263.

121. Heinrich George was not de-Nazified and died in a Soviet army camp. F. Marian (*Jew Süss*) died in an accident and his wife was drowned. The son of Werner Krauss committed suicide. Veit Harlan was accused in 1945 of crimes against humanity. Actresses such as Zarah Leander, who could not be reproached with anything very precise in political terms, were the object of violent press campaigns.

122. It is not correct therefore to maintain, as did Walter Laqueur, that 'relatively few non-Jewish intellectuals emigrated, however much they disapproved of the regime, and [. . .] of these a few later returned to Germany' (*Weimar: A Cultural History*, p. 268). Those who left Germany in 1933 were opponents of the regime, and in their majority it was not as Jews that they chose exile. The massive Jewish emigration of 1938 included a large number of petty-bourgeois and businesspeople who emigrated for 'racial' reasons without being oppositionists. Writers who emigrated without being Jewish include: Fritz von Unruh, Max Hermann-Neisse, Leonhard

Frank, Erwin Piscator, Thomas Mann, Heinrich Mann, Klaus Mann, Georg Kaiser, René Schickele, Annette Kolbe, Oskar Maria Graf, Erich Maria Remarque, J. R. Becher, Irmgard Keun, Gustav Regler, H. H. Jahn and Bodo Uhse.

123. Stefan George's work contained the appeal for racial regeneration, exaltation of blood and expectation of a 'mystic leader', but his 'new realm' should not be confused with the Third Reich. Nowhere did George champion any form of racism or glorify the Nordic race. Even in the Great War George was not a confined nationalist; he also celebrated Mediterranean civilization, 'the kingdom of wheat and wine'. His cult of art for art's sake and his disdainful aristocratism were hard to reconcile with the Third Reich and its folklore of the masses. George expressly insisted in his last wishes that his body should be cremated in Locarno and not returned to Germany.

124. Jünger's attitude towards National Socialism was complex. It would be wrong to present him as a declared opponent of the regime, which he served as an army officer, but he was not just the mere 'herald of barbarism' that Thomas Mann called him. His nationalism and his cult of war won the appreciation of Hitler, to whom he dedicated his first writings (*Feuer und Blut*). Hitler sent him an inscribed copy of *Mein Kampf*, and in 1927 offered him a seat as Reichstag deputy, which he refused. Goebbels sought in vain to rally him to the Nazi regime, but later described him as a 'dangerous man'; his book *Der Arbeiter* was greeted in the *Völkische Beobachter* with the words: 'Jünger is getting close to the zone of bullets in the head.' When that newspaper published an extract from *Adventurous Heart* (6–7 March 1934), Jünger protested: 'This must give the impression that I am a contributor to your paper, which is in no way the case.' He likewise refused to join the new literature section of the Prussian Academy after its reconstruction by the Nazis. In 1943 Goebbels insisted on the suppression of a passage from his *Gärten und Strassen*. Jünger did not agree and the book was banned.

125. The only description of the Hitler epoch given in *Le Questionnaire* is ironic and disenchanted. Insolent and provocative, von Salomon had only contempt for the Nazis. He accommodated himself to the regime by keeping a low profile.

126. Representing the worse verbal excesses of expressionism, Arnolt Bronnen had already been reproached by the critic Alfred Kerr for 'a language devoid of sense', and his love of 'chaos for its own sake'. In his memoir, *Arnolt Bronnen gibt zu Protokoll* (Hamburg 1954), he wrote: 'This man [Jünger], brown-haired, slim, sinewy and small, awakened in me the same fascination as Bert Brecht had experienced towards me five years earlier.' He noted on Goebbels: 'He did not have at that time the anti-Semitic attitude of Otto Strasser, not the petty-bourgeois drugstore atmosphere of Gregor Strasser, nor Adolf Hitler's guttural mix of dialects, nor the hot-headed fanaticism of Streicher and Rosenberg. There was an intelligence there, at least I thought so at the time; later I discovered it was just the residue of a former intelligence.'

127. Ernst von Salomon wrote in *Le Questionnaire*: 'The novel was titled *O. S.*, and it was excellent. But suddenly all hell broke loose. Arnolt Bronnen, in a state of shock, could wipe his monocle as much as he liked, but everyone wrote that he was a traitor, a fascist. Bronnen carefully examined all that he had written up till then and had to admit: "If that is fascism, then I am a fascist." And as he continuously heard and read that he belonged to some obscure group around Jünger, he gravitated towards this Jünger' (p. 247).

128. 'In personal terms, there was no call for me to leave Berlin, I lived off my medical practice and had nothing to do with politics' (*Double vie*, p. 72).

129. Ibid., p. 73.

130. Benn cites this letter in its entirety in *Double vie*, where he seeks to justify his attitude. Klaus Mann wrote: 'What motive could have led you to lend your name, which for us is a symbol of the highest intellectual class and a fanatical purity, to a group of people whose nullity is unparalleled in European history and whose moral ignominy has provoked the disgust of the whole world? How many friends will you

not lose if you make common cause with people who deserve only spiritual hatred! And what friends will you gain in the end on the wrong side of this divide? Who can understand you?' (*Double vie*, p. 78).

131. In *The New State and the Intellectuals* (1933), Benn wrote: 'Those who hailed enthusiastically any revolutionary impulse on the part of Marxism, recognized this as a revelatory value and were ready to lend it unlimited credence, held that it was a matter of their intellectual honour for them to consider the revolution carried out in a national' spirit as immoral, sterile, and running against the direction of history' (*Un poète et le monde*, Paris 1965, p. 165).

132. Ibid., p. 81.

133. Ibid., p. 82.

134. Ibid., p. 84.

135. Though Benn still occupied an official position in the Academy's literature section, by 22 April 1933 he had already ceased to believe in Hitler. Oskar Loerke noted in his diary: 'Benn thought that we would not just be cast out but also physically eliminated' (O. Loerke, *Tagebücher 1903–1939*, Heidelberg 1955). His correspondence with Ina Seidel also shows that he had by then taken his distance from the new regime. He was not allowed to publish anything under the Third Reich, he was forbidden to practise medicine, dismissed by the Nazis as a 'degenerate' and attacked in scatological language in the *Völkische Beobachter*. In 1938 all his writings were banned and he had to enrol in the army as a doctor. After the War, Benn was denounced and arrested a number of times by the Soviet army. He died in poverty in Berlin on 7 July 1956, just as his work was beginning to be rediscovered.

136. Cited by Peter Gay, *Weimar Culture: The Outsider as Insider*, London 1968, p. 3.

137. R. Binding, *Briefe*, Hamburg 1957, p. 182 (letter of 6 April 1933).

138. Romain Rolland wrote on this subject: 'Gerhart Hauptmann is a great artist, but for many years now it has been impossible to pardon his moral abdication in favour of the masters of the day, who dispense honours, money, luxury and success. And this abdication has become unpardonable by his silence at this time. [. . .] What! He was not even capable like Furtwängler to protest against the expulsion of artists who were the honour of Germany! No, this is not the time to write *literary* panegyrics for men who renege, like Hauptmann, on the holy audacity of their youth! There's been enough *literature* for a while; now is the time to sort *characters*' (letter from Romain Rolland to Serge Radine, 18 October 1933; *Cahiers Romain Rolland* 17, 1967).

139. In an interview with the Hungarian writer Ferenc Körmendy, Hauptmann supposedly said: 'This filthy Austrian painter's assistant has ruined Germany, but tomorrow it'll be the world! This bastard has robbed the Germans of all we had of value – he's made us a nation of slaves! But that's not enough for him. This scum will bring war to the whole world, this miserable brown comedian, this Nazi hangman is rushing us into a world war, into destruction!' (Cited by A. Hamilton, *The Appeal of Fascism*, p. 165.)

140. G. Bermann Fischer recalls in his memoirs (*Bedroht-Bewahrt*, p. 125) that when Hauptmann's *The Rats* was being performed at the Burgtheater in Vienna in 1937, the playwright had asked him to invite artists and writers to a reception at his (Hauptmann's) house. Three days before the reception, Hauptmann cancelled the invitation, on the pretext that he did not want to be seen together with émigrés.

141. Hitler had the courtesy on this occasion to present Hauptmann with a swastika-decorated vase.

142. 'Warum ich nicht Deutschland verliesse', *Die Welt*, 10 November 1962; interview with Ferenc Körmendy as note 139. Thomas Mann, on the other hand, wrote: 'I can't blame old Hauptmann for keeping silent. Why talk himself out of all his possessions and his country as well?' (letter to Alexander M. Frey, 12 June 1933; *Letters of Thomas Mann 1889–1955*, p. 171). Arno Breker (*Paris, Hitler et moi*, p. 64) and Veit Harlan (*Le Cinéma selon Goebbels*, p. 78) both testify as to the distrust of the Nazis towards Harlan.

143. In his clandestine diary, Oskar Loerke, a friend of Benn, noted on 22 April 1933 that he and other writers wept on hearing Benn's speech 'The New State and the Intellectuals' (*Tagebücher*, p. 272).
144. Anti-Nazi writers, being politically committed, certainly were forced to emigrate. But this was not the case for writers not known for any political stance, who instead of going into exile, could have continued to live in Germany. Exile for them was a moral choice.
145. Cf. Ernst Loewy, *Literatur unterm Hakenkreuz*, Frankfurt 1966.
146. Epigones, since the great representatives of this neo-Romanticism did not stray into the Nazi ranks. This applies to Stefan George, and above all to Ricarda Huch, who left the Academy in 1933.
147. And even after. Geneviève Bianquis, for example, in her *Histoire de la littérature allemande* (Paris 1936), mentioned a number of writers who rallied to the Nazi regime (H. F. Blunck, H. Grimm, H. Carossa, E. G. Kolbenheyer, R. G. Binding) in far from praising terms, and concluded: 'In the meantime, German literature is not dead, but it is thinner and constrained, fearful and over-disciplined. We cannot permit ourselves any further prognosis' (p. 206). It was notable, moreover, that despite their limited print runs and the whole Nazi propaganda against them, books by émigrés still sold better than those of the Reich's official authors. That is why Thomas Mann could not unreasonably maintain apropos Jünger: 'He is too good for the Nazis.'
148. The publisher Bermann Fischer related how on the evening of 30 June 1934, he was enjoying himself with friends when someone announced the murder of Röhm. Erich Kleiber, a friend of Fischer's, got up and intoned a hymn to Hitler; the publisher had never expected that he might have been a Nazi. Hauser and Rehberg, two young dramatic actors, appeared one day at the publishing house in SA uniforms. Others, less opportunist, could simply be classed as lacking awareness, such as Samuel Fischer's friend Leo von König, who voted for Hitler because 'the Weimar Republic conducted itself in a wretched fashion' (*Bedroht-Bewahrt*, p. 80).
149. 'According to the paper's director, [Sieburg's] influence could be useful to me' (E. E. Noth, *Mémoires d'un allemand*, p. 249).
150. The *Braunbuch* mentions a rather obscure role that Sieburg allegedly played in the service of the German government in the Stavisky affair. According to Münzenberg, he paid money to a number of French newspapers to win their sympathy for the Nazi government.
151. *Vor Deutschland wird gewarnt*, p. 15. A similar expression was used about Sieburg by F. C. Wieskopf in the *Neue Deutsche Blätter* for 10 September 1933.
152. In 1935 Kurt Tucholsky wrote to W. Hasenclever about an article of Sieburg's that he 'no longer paints with oil but with mayonnaise'. In the *Braunbuch* he was described as follows: 'Sieburg is a former poet. He is one of those chameleons who always enthuses for whoever is in power at the moment. He was an admirer of Karl Liebknecht at the time that he thought he saw in this martyr of the workers' movement the victor of the morrow. He discovered the "high qualities" of Friedrich Ebert at the very moment that the government was hunting down Liebknecht. He hymned Noske just as he had hymned Liebknecht before. He threw himself into the arms of Stresemann when this politician's star was riding high. He then swore by Brüning, by von Papen, and by Schleicher. And today he swears by Hitler.' [This passage does not appear in the English edition of the *Brown Book*.]
153. Figures given by Hans Helmuth Knütter, *Die deutsche Exil-Literatur*, p. 35. According to Helmut Müssener (*Exil in Schweden*, Munich 1974, pp. 44–5), 60,000 people had left Germany by 1934, of whom 50,000 were Jews. The number of exiles rose to 80,500 in 1935, 100,000 in 1936 (4,000 left the Saarland when it was reattached to Germany that year), and 150,000 in 1937, reaching 400,000 by the end of 1939. In 1935, the émigrés included five to six thousand Social-Democrats, 8,000 Communists, 2,000 pacifists, 1,000 Catholics and 2,000 other oppositionists of various kinds. The total number of political exiles is hard to assess, but seems to be

more than 35,000. According to the Sternfeld/Tiedemann index, more than two thousand writers and journalists left Germany after 1933, as well as 1,684 academics (figure from Helga Pross, *Die deutsche akademische Emigration nach den Vereinigten Staaten 1933–1941*, Berlin 1955). All these are just approximate estimates, given the diversity of countries in which the exiles took refuge. Many political or illegal émigrés, moreover, did not declare themselves to the police. After the stabilization phase of 1934–38, their number rose considerably with the addition of refugees from Austria and Czechoslovakia, and the massive exodus of German Jews.

154. As one of Klaus Mann's characters in *The Volcano* put it, 'I was just fed up with Germany' (*Le Volcan*, Paris 1982, p. 34).

155. The most acerbic critics were Alfred Döblin and above all Kurt Tucholsky, who wrote to Arnold Zweig on 15 December 1935: 'How could they! How not to understand in March 1933 that the moment had come to emigrate in inverse proportions. Not, as today, one in ten, but already at that time one who remained for nine who had or would have to go. Was there *a single* rabbi who guided his people? A single man? None. [. . .] If you had said to the average Jew in 1933 that he would have to leave Germany in the conditions as they were in 1935 and after, he would have laughed in your face. [. . .] Heroism meant choosing the best deal. So why did they not choose this route?' (*Chroniques allemandes*, Paris 1982, p. 321.)

156. In his memoir *Ein Zeitalter wird besichtigt* (p. 344), Heinrich Mann maintained that the hatred towards him after his expulsion from the Academy had at least made him as popular as *Der blaue Engel*. Kurt Hiller and Willi Bredel had been meanwhile arrested.

157. The principal laws that affected writers were the *Gesetz zum Schutz der Nation* (28 February 1933), and the *Gesetz zum Schutz des deutschen Blutes und der deutschen Ehre*, which excluded from literary activity all authors who were Jewish or hostile to National Socialism. The purge was carried out by Goebbels's Ministerium für Volksaufklärung und Propaganda, by the Reichskulturkammern, and by Rosenberg's Reichsstelle zur Förderung des deutschen Schrifttums. The works of undesirable authors were divided into four categories: (1) non-Aryan; (2) Communist and Marxist; (3) writers not belonging to any group but who had expressed their hostility to the regime in previous works; (4) writers whose works did not contain oppositional elements but who refused to join the Reichskulturkammer for literature.

158. A friend of George Grosz, he emigrated to Switzerland then to England. Though a 'pure Aryan', he refused to remain in Germany, as 'no civilized man can live among a band of assassins.' He maintained that he remained a German poet in exile, even if his country no longer existed for him except as a dream.

159. To take some random examples, ex-Chancellor Brüning, Arnolt Brecht, and former interior and justice minister Erich Kochweser, who emigrated to Brazil and went into the export–import business.

160. Benn acknowledged later in his autobiography (*Double vie*, p. 77) that Klaus Mann had been more far-sighted than him. 'A boy of twenty-seven judged the situation better than I did, and precisely predicted the development of things; he thought more clearly.' Gustav Regler noted in his memoirs (*The Owl of Minerva*, p. 167) on the subject of Benn's speech: '[In a newspaper] I found a passage from the poet Gottfried Benn, answered by Klaus Mann. [. . .] Benn assured us exiles that if we had stayed the German people would not have treated us "too badly". I said bitterly, "Not too badly! Not too many broken bones. Only one eye gouged out, not both. Only one kidney smashed. They would have burnt our flesh only with cigarettes – not cigars!"' The same reproach of having left Germany, forgetting what would have happened to them had they stayed, recurred again after 1945 in the arguments of the 'internal emigration'.

161. No less than seventeen bodies were charged with surveying literature.

162. Kessler, *Diaries of a Cosmopolitan*, p. 449 (28 February 1933).

163. *Deutsche Exilliteratur*, p. 28.
164. On each occasion, the SA ransacked apartments, destroyed manuscripts, burned libraries or threw books out of the window, as well as lynching whomever they found, whether friends, relations, or simply other tenants. Hermann Kantorowicz, a pacifist, escaped the SA, but his brother, a dentist in Bonn, was sent to the camp at Börgermoor. Alfred Kantorowicz's father and brothers were later exterminated in the gas chambers. The brother of Alfred Döblin, an actor, was murdered by the Nazis. Gertrud Kolmar, who was unwilling to abandon her aged father, remained in Germany. He was murdered in 1941, and she herself in 1943.
165. Ludwig Marcuse, *Mein zwanzigstes Jahrhundert*, p. 156.
166. Leonhard Franck, *Links wo das Herz ist*, Munich 1952, p. 95.
167. 'In any case, I was not going to run away! I would not let Berlin be taken from me! Half an hour later I went to the station [. . .]' (*The Owl of Minerva*, p. 158).
168. 'I said that this must be an exaggeration. He glared at me and then apologized for doing so. Leading me down the Tauentzienstrasse, he told me in a toneless, monotonous voice that the block of flats in the Fehrbelliner Platz, where my apartment was, had that morning been methodically surrounded and besieged by the new police in a textbook military manoeuvre. [. . .] My own apartment had been looted, with others' (ibid., p. 157).
169. 'As you're what they call "Aryan" and your old parents are well connected, your errors would surely be forgiven, especially if you explained that this was all due to ignorance, the folly of youth.' So Klaus Mann has one of his characters say in *The Volcano*, thinking no doubt of his own case. (*Le Volcan*, p. 10).
170. Hermann Kesten, *Der Geist der Unruhe*, Cologne 1959, pp. 222–37.
171. Alfred Döblin, *Die deutsche Literatur im Ausland seit 1933*, p. 4.
172. *Verbannung*, p. 35.
173. Ibid.
174. The majority of writers left alone, so as to put police surveillance off the scent, intending that their wives should rejoin them later. Most frequently they took nothing with them – Döblin a single suitcase, Heinrich Mann an umbrella. They often thought of returning in a few days. In the meantime they learned that their homes had been ransacked by the SA and return was impossible. Their emigration often signified a family breakup, the abandoning of parents when these preferred to die in Germany (or later Austria) rather than confront the misery of exile. Stefan Zweig abandoned his mother, Gustav Regler his son (who went on to fight in Hitler's army). Sometimes their wives hesitated to emigrate. Albert Ehrenstein complained bitterly in a letter to Hermann Kesten (12 July 1933) of having to leave his Siamese cat in Berlin, wondering if 'this little fellow will also get a National Socialist education. I could not survive it' (*Deutsche Literatur im Exil*, p. 51).
175. Count Harry Kessler noted in his diary on 20 June 1935 (*Diaries of a Cosmopolitan*. p. 468): 'Today my poor domestic furnishings in Weimar are being auctioned. That closes the main chapter of my life and is the end of a home built up with great love.' Thomas Mann's diary shows how large material considerations loomed in his hesitation to opt for emigration (his house in Munich, his royalties and bank deposits). Most often, leaving their library was a genuine drama. Well before the advent of Hitler, Walter Benjamin, learning that the library of one of his friends had been destroyed by a fire in his apartment, wondered how one could survive such a disaster. His letters to Gershom Scholem and Brecht (16 October 1933; 5 March 1934) perfectly symbolize the agony felt by so many exiles at abandoning their manuscripts, their archives and their books. The most fortunate managed to transfer these abroad. Benjamin sent his books to Brecht in Denmark, and copies of his texts to Scholem in Jerusalem. (Both Benjamin and Scholem were to lose their brothers in concentration camp.) E. E. Kisch wrote to his mother (*Briefe*, Berlin 1978, p. 244) to announce the arrival in Prague of some forty boxes of books. Walter Mehring had to abandon his immense library (and that of his father; cf. *La Bibliothèque perdue*, p. 193). Kurt Pinthus complains in a letter to Walter Hasen-

clever (3 September and 4 October 1937; *Verbannung*, pp. 140–1) of having left all his books in Berlin. Stefan Zweig had to sell his collection of association copies and manuscripts, or donate them to the national library in Vienna; Walter Benjamin had to sell in exile his celebrated lithograph by Paul Klee, the 'Angelus Novus'.

176. The publisher Bermann Fischer wrote in *Bedroht-Bewahrt* (p. 122): 'How can I describe the farewell to Germany? How can I speak of what I felt when I met my fellow-workers at the publishing house for the last time? An end. It was like a living death for me.'

177. *Letters of Thomas Mann 1889–1955*, p. 168.

178. Döblin, *Briefe*, p. 179.

179. Kortner, *Aller Tage Abend*, p. 251.

180. Ibid., p. 249.

181. K. Mann, *The Turning Point*, p. 261.

182. W. Herzog, *Menschen, die ich begegnete*, pp. 259ff.

183. Kurt Grossmann, secretary of the Human Rights League, watched the Reichstag burn and thought of organizing a protest meeting for the next day. His friends urged him to flee. He destroyed his archives and files, and threw the addresses of his organization's members into the Spree, before catching the train for Prague.

184. The results were dubious. Goebbels wrote in *The Battle for Berlin*, apropos the city's police chief Dr Bernhard Weiss: 'Dr Weiss! This was almost an incendiary slogan. Every National Socialist knew him. Every activist was imprinted with his physiognomy in the most living and precise fashion, thanks to thousands of satirical papers, photographs and caricatures.' [This passage does not appear in the English edition.] But H. A. Walter reports that Dr Weiss left Germany by train, travelling in the same compartment as SA leader Röhm who failed to recognize him.

185. Armand Bérard recounts in his memoir, *Au temps du danger allemand*, Paris 1976, that General von Bredow, who had been given a French visa on 11 March 1933, was arrested despite this at Aachen and had his passport confiscated.

186. Bérard mentions (ibid., pp. 185–92) a measure taken by ambassador François-Poncet who authorized him to 'visa and stamp at home any piece of identity of individuals who had to flee'. He thus indicates the active support of the French embassy in Berlin to antifascists who wanted to quit Germany illegally. Bérard makes clear however that the means at their disposal were very limited: 'We were shattered by this cyclone of madness. We simplified the formalities to the minimum for the now massive departures to France' (ibid., p. 193).

187. Dolfuss's Austria for example required a minimum of 1000 marks.

188. Though he had Hungarian nationality, von Horvath was under threat from the Nazis, who had already tried to have him arrested in Austria. He did however return to Germany before establishing himself in Vienna.

189. This pacifist writer had served as a nurse in the same regiment as Hitler.

190. Not to mention the emigration of scientists, which was also considerable. The above examples are drawn only from the literary world.

191. 1934 saw the definitive emigration of E. Castonnier, G. Fischer, W. Gurian, K. J. Hirsch, K. von Kauffungen, W. Jablonski, K. Kesten; 1935 that of Schalom ben Chorin, A. Berend, L. Derleth, W. Victor, Irmgard Keun (who returned to Germany later and lived underground), K. O. Paetel, E. Brehm, W. Fabian, Ossip K. Flechtheim, R. Löwenthal and P. Merker. In 1936, G. Bermann Fischer, R. Frank, E. Franzen, G. Fröschel, M. Gumpert and M. Kuczinski. In 1937, E. Ezck, K. Pinthus. In 1938 J. Bab, P. Gan, F. Hessel, M. Osborn, R. Friedenthal, S. Haffner, Monty Jacobs, E. Maria Lanfau, H. Hauser, G. Kaiser, M. Kaléko, H. J. Schoeps, H. Sinsheimer, M. Tau. In 1939, M. Beheim-Schwarzbach, M. Beradt, W. Bock, J. Gebser, J. Mass, A. Schaeffer, H. Ullstein, P. Mayer and U. Rukser.

192. Stefan Zweig's mother remained in Austria, as did the widow of the publisher Samuel Fischer. Gertrud Kolmar refused to abandon her aged father, and they were both gassed. Sigmund Freud wrote to Ernst Freud on 12 May 1938: 'Anna will certainly find it easy to manage, and this is the main thing, because for us old people

between 73 and 82 the whole undertaking would have made no sense' (*The Letters of Sigmund Freud*, London 1961, p. 438).

193. Lithuania, Poland, Czechoslovakia, Austria, Switzerland, France, the Netherlands, Belgium, Luxemburg and Denmark.

194. On 5 March 1933, all trains to Switzerland were surveyed and searched. Recognized antifascists were immediately arrested. The Nazis very rapidly took account of the ideological danger that émigrés represented in view of their testimony and propaganda. On 1 November 1933 Hitler invited other European countries to worry about their own problems and not about German émigrés who, he maintained, 'would poison their wells', and whose departure from Germany was a blessing. When the sixth international conference on the unification of criminal law was held in Copenhagen in September 1935, Nazi jurists tried to have it accepted that German political refugees whose return was demanded for reasons of public safety should be returned to the Reich. The conference evidently decided against this demand.

195. G. Badia, *Les Barbelés de l'exil*, pp. 15ff.

196. Badia mentions that close to 90 per cent of German émigrés reaching France were male, and of the 11 per cent female, only 3 per cent were married. 'Three-quarters of the refugees fell into the age category of 25 to 40, with about a quarter each in the ranges 20–25, 25–30 and 30–40' (ibid.).

197. The KPD had planned for a number of illegally functioning networks before 1933, but these were rapidly dismantled. Even so, the Communists were already used to underground activity in the 1920s (false names and secret meeting-places, etc.). The same went for the Schwarze Front of Otto Strasser, whose activists arranged meetings in mountain huts, disguising their rendezvous as tourist excursions. (Cf. Otto Strasser, *Hitler and I*, London 1940.) Strasser himself changed his appearance to escape from the Nazis, something that writers were generally incapable of doing.

198. Manès Sperber, *Au-delà de l'oubli*, Paris 1979, p. 9.

199. This train journey was also not without risk. Ernst Niekisch mentions the case of the schoolteacher Toni Pfühl who committed suicide in 1933 in an express train (*Gewagtes Leben*, p. 110). The writer Alfons Paquet, a colleague of Piscator's whose works had been burned, was arrested at the border and sentenced to a long prison term. He died on 8 February 1944 during an Allied air raid on Frankfurt.

200. Cf. *Im Kampf bewährt*, Berlin 1977, pp. 470ff.

201. Otto Strasser left Germany with a chauffeur disguised as an SA man. The police, who suspected something, let him continue on his way, as they knew how skilfully he could use his machine pistol. Ruth Fischer and Arkadi Maslow crossed Czechoslovakia, Austria and Switzerland by motorbike before reaching France. Willi Münzenberg's secretary, Hans Schulz, was warned by the police of his imminent arrest. His wife was the daughter of the former Berlin chief of police, the Social-Democrat Karl Zörgrebel.

202. Karl O. Paetel, the national-bolshevik, was accompanied on skis to the Czech frontier by the Dresden SA leader. Klaus Mann was warned of the danger he ran by his Nazi chauffeur. Gustav Regler escaped arrest thanks to a former member of the Communist Red Front who has gone over to the SA and simply told him: 'Don't have it in for me, we've lost.' For a long while the émigrés continued to believe in the possibility of winning over the SA, as unemployed or proletarian elements who had been duped by the Nazis; a tactic envisaged for a moment by Heinz Neumann. W. Langhoff, in *The Peat-Bog Soldiers*, evokes the discussions that prisoners had with SA men. More symbolically, the interesting novel by Walter Schoenstedt published in France in 1934, *Auf der Flucht erschossen. Ein SA Roman 1933*, was dedicated to the Sturmführer SA from Düsseldorf Heinz Bässler, killed by the Nazis in 1933. It sought to show how a former worker who had gone over to the SA becomes aware of his mistake and tries to redeem himself by helping a Communist prisoner who was his friend to escape from concentration camp.

203. G. Regler, 'Briefe an meinen Sohn'; *Deutsche Blätter*, vol. 26, 1945, pp. 3–9.

204. The illusion of the imminent collapse of the Nazi regime was widely shared by the émigrés at the start of their exile. Though Thomas Mann seems fairly clear-headed in his *Diaries*, his publisher Bermann Fischer wrote him on 17 July 1933 that one should not trust the atmosphere surrounding the emigrants, and 'there is no risk in returning to Germany'. As for Kurt Tucholsky, he wrote to Walter Hasenclever in the wake of the Reichstag fire that there was no need to worry about the fate of Carl von Ossietzky, he would be released in two or three weeks, and anyway he was safer in prison than outside, as the Nazis wouldn't dare try anything against him. (*Politische Briefe*, ed. F. Raddatz, Reinbek 1969, p. 13.)
205. *Die deutsche akademische Emigration nach den Vereinigten Staaten*, Berlin 1955, p. 18.
206. 'Vorläufige Gedanken zu einer Typologie der Exilliteratur', in *Akzente* 15, 1968, pp. 556–75.
207. Cf. the critique made by Jost Hermand in 'Schreiben in der Fremde. Gedanken zur deutschen Exilliteratur seit 1789', in *Exil und innere Emigration*, Third Wisconsin Workshop, Frankfurt 1972, p. 9.
208. Peter Stahlberger, *Der zürcher Verleger Emil Oprecht und die deutsche politische Emigration*, Zurich 1970.
209. The criteria proposed by Herbert E. Tutas, *N-S Propaganda und deutsches Exil* (Worms 1973, p. 10) also lead to confusion. He makes an opposition between political émigrés (*politische Emigrante*), who fought fascism in exile, and those who sought to assimilate into their new milieu, whom he terms *Auswanderer*. The first point to make against this is that a writer who left Germany in 1933 without being persecuted for racial reasons was viewed by the Nazis as a political opponent, whatever his stance in exile. The notion of *Auswanderer* is itself unclear. Hanns Eisler and Kurt Weill left Germany in 1933 because they were opposed to Nazism and their music was considered 'bolshevik' or 'negroid'. Eisler, in the United States, was completely uninvolved in politics, though he never reneged on his Communist convictions. Kurt Weill, for his part, started a successful new career on Broadway. Should we conclude that he was not a 'political emigrant' but a mere '*Auswanderer*'?
210. L. Marcuse, *Mein zwanzigstes Jahrhundert*, p. 244.
211. Bad Godesberg conference, p. 37.
212. A. Kantorowicz, *Politik und Literatur im Exil*, pp. 7 and 20.
213. The polemics that marked the last years of cultural and political life under the Weimar Republic were further exacerbated by exile. Ideological and literary differences, not to speak of personal rivalry, were intensified by bitterness, despair and a psychosis of treason. Polemics over the respective responsibility of the two great workers' parties towards the Nazi victory continued to oppose Socialists and Communists after Hitler's seizure of power, and even in the concentration camps. Left-wing Socialists and Social-Democrats were divided on the question of the correctness of the 'policy of tolerance' adopted towards Hitler, and over the slogans of struggle against the Nazi regime. New groupings – Neu Beginnen, Revolutionäre Sozialisten Deutschlands (K. Böchel, S. Aufhäuser) marked the rupture of Social-Democratic unity. The Popular Front policy adopted by the Communists rekindled these tensions and the climate of distrust between the two parties. Often, as with the quarrel over expressionism and the avant-garde in the review *Das Wort* (1938–39), the issues were both cultural and political. Cleavages of this kind continued to multiply throughout the exile years, with different themes and objects. This is also shown by the discussions that divided émigrés in the United States on the issue of the responsibility of the German people. Exile memoirs, for their part, often revolve round a settling of accounts, with their political past or their former colleagues.
214. Hans Mayer, 'Konfrontation der inneren und äusseren Emigration. Erinnerungen und Deutung', Third Wisconsin Workshop, p. 79.
215. Ibid.
216. *Politik und Literatur im Exil*, p. 25.
217. Figures cited after Léon Poliakov, *Le Bréviaire de la haine*, Paris 1951.
218. Gershom Scholem relates in his autobiography, *From Berlin to Jerusalem* (New

York 1980) how Berlin Jews celebrated Christmas with a fir tree, not 'as Jews' but from attachment to German tradition.

219. Oral communication. In France, likewise, Durkheim and Bergson were no less chauvinistic than Maurras and Barrès.

220. Cf. the fine study by Michael Löwy, 'Messianisme juif et utopies libertaires en Europe Centrale (1905–1923)', *Archives de sciences sociales des religions* 51, 1981.

221. In 1912, Moritz Goldstein published in *Der Kunstwart* the celebrated essay in which he maintained: 'We Jews, let us manage the intellectual heritage of a people that denies us the right and capacity to do so.' Jewish youth, attracted by Zionism or Communism, found itself profoundly divided. The Zionists treated the Communists as 'red assimilationists', while the latter did not hesitate to describe Zionists as 'Jewish fascists'. Relations on this score between Walter Benjamin and Gershom Scholem are exemplary (cf. Gershom Scholem, *Walter Benjamin, Histoire d'une amitié*, Paris 1980). Whereas Scholem emigrated to Palestine in the early 1920s, Benjamin hesitated for two decades about making the journey. He could only see in the Zionist project an 'act of violence' (*Briefe*, vol. 1, p. 208). Moreover, Jews from central Europe had made a large contribution to the rise of the workers' movement, being often in the vanguard of a whole range or organizations – from the Bund and Poale Zion to the Communist and Socialist parties. Often issuing from traditionalist and religious families, this generation was to take part in all struggles of the era – from the October Revolution to the French Resistance, by way of Spartakus and the Spanish War – dreaming of a red Palestine or a working-class messianism. (Cf. Alain Brossat and Sylvia Klingberg, *Le Yiddishland révolutionnaire*, Paris 1983.)

222. Telegram from the Berlin Jewish community in April 1933 to the chief rabbi in London, and protest by Leo Baeck, the Berlin chief rabbi, against the 'parties of the left'. (Cf. L. Poliakov, *Le Bréviaire de la Haine*, p. 12.)

223. Gershom Scholem analysed in detail in many of his essays the ambiguous cultural assimilation of German Jews. He claimed that there had never been a 'Judeo-German dialogue', that intellectuals and writers had been accepted only to the extent that they renounced their identity or even struggled against it' (*Fidélité et utopie. Essais sur le judaisme contemporain*, Paris 1978, pp. 79ff.). Theodor Lessing, in his book *Deutschland und seine Juden*, Prague 1933, maintained that he was at the same time 'Zionist and socialist', but above all he was German: 'And when I say German, this is not a merely verbal profession of faith inspired by fear, in tune with the nationalist madness of the present time. It is the relationship of a drop of water to its source, of a tree to its roots. A profession of faith in the language that is mine, in the bread that feeds my son, in the earth where those who loved me rest, where they grew up, the land that I love.' In exile, Lessing did not cease to maintain that Germany was and remained his homeland. A doctor in both philosophy and medicine, and a pacifist, a price of 80,000 marks was put on his head, and he was murdered in Marienbad on 30 August 1933.

224. In his letter to Arnold Zweig of 15 December 1935, Kurt Tucholsky claimed to have 'left Judaism' in 1911, as since from an early age he'd had 'a holy terror of unctuous rabbis' and 'felt more than I realized the cowardice of that society' (*Chroniques allemandes*, p. 317).

225. In his autobiography, *Schicksalreise* (Frankfurt 1949), Döblin wrote: 'And what about Judaism? I heard already at home in Stettin that my parents were of Jewish origin and that we were a Jewish family. Apart from that I noticed nothing particularly different about us' (pp. 156–7). Further he notes that he had no desire to go to Palestine, but he wanted at some point to 'know more about the Jews', since he knew so little. Where then were there Jews? 'In Poland, I was told. So I went to Poland' (p. 164). Döblin claims that this was the first time in his life that he saw Jews, that he was surprised by their appearance and their language, and described them with an ethnic curiosity. They saw him as a foreigner, and he equally saw them as foreign. Palestine, moreover, meant nothing to German Jews who were not Zionist. Arnold Zweig returned from there with strongly negative impressions, as

witness the letters he wrote to Sigmund Freud, and Else Lasker-Schüler hesitated a long while before deciding to emigrate there. When people wanted to translate her poems into Hebrew, she replied: 'They're Jewish enough as they are.' Armin T. Wegner separated from his wife rather than move to Palestine.

226. 'All that I knew was that Germany was my country, my homeland, with no start or finish, while being Jewish was basically no more important than being born with brown hair and not red. We were Swabian before anything else, then German, and then Jewish' (Fred Uhlmann, *L'Ami retrouvé*, p. 64). [In *The Making of an Englishman* and other writings, this author wrote under the Anglicized name of Uhlman.]

227. Cited after L. Poliakov, *Le Bréviaire de la haine*, p. 14.

228. In March 1937, out of 150,000 Jews still in Berlin, 60,000 were assisted by such organizations. In June 1939 Walter Benjamin wrote to Margarete Steffin: 'Karl Kraus died too soon after all. Listen to this: the Vienna gas board has stopped supplying gas to Jews. A consequence of the gas consumption of the Jewish population was that the gas company lost money, since it was precisely the biggest users who did not pay their bills. The Jews preferred to use the gas to commit suicide' (*Letters of Walter Benjamin*, p. 609).

229. It was Tucholsky, of course, who judged most severely this attitude of Jews who refused to go into exile ('Herr Wendriner steht unter Diktatur'). He endlessly stigmatized their cowardice and lack of clear-headedness. Yet few Jews could imagine in 1933 what anti-Semitism would be like in 1938 or 1940, and Tucholsky takes little account of the fact that no European country was prepared to accept Jewish refugees from Germany. In his *Mémoires d'un Allemand*, E. E. Noth recalls the joke that Erich Maria Remarque made when he was asked in the United States if he was homesick for Germany: 'What makes you think that I'm Jewish?' Rudolf H. Ganz, released from Buchenwald in 1938, wrote: 'At the moment when we had to leave our home town of Frankfurt, we felt in our hearts the injustice done to us: we were forced to leave Germany because we were Jews' (*Verbannung*, p. 32).

230. The poet Ernst Lissauer, during the First World War, had written a 'Hassgesang gegen England', which brought him a decoration from the Kaiser. Forced into exile as a Jew in 1936, he died in Vienna the same year in utter isolation, the political émigrés refusing to pardon his xenophobic patriotism.

231. Theodor Csokor, *Zeugen einer Zeit. Briefe aus dem Exil 1933–1950*, Munich 1964, p. 73.

232. Cf. also Thomas Mann, 'Leiden an Deutschland', *Werke,* vol. 12, pp. 684ff.

233. Hans Jacob, *Kind meiner Zeit. Lebenserinnerungen*, Cologne 1962, p. 186.

234. Cf. *Verbannung*, p. 193.

235. Ibid., pp. 192–3.

236. Heinrich Mann, *Verteidigung der Kultur*, Hildesheim 1960, p. 12.

237. H. Mann, *Ein Zeitalter wird besichtigt*.

238. Letter to H. Kesten, July 1933, in *Deutsche Literatur im Exil*.

239. Letter to H. Kesten, 12 July 1933, ibid.

240. Letter to H. Kesten, 6 September 1933, ibid.

241. Letter to H. Kesten, 6 September, ibid., p. 69. Golo Mann wrote in the same fashion: 'It would be quite wrong to equate the literary emigration from Germany with a Jewish emigration, treating it as if it were something enforced [. . .]. Besides, those Jewish writers who left Germany in the months after Hitler's seizure of power did so not because they were Jews but because they were writers. The majority of Jews in other professions remained in Germany for too long, which was damaging for them, since they could not believe the fate that lay in store for them anymore than Europe wanted to do so' (Bad Godesberg conference, p. 36).

242. Son of the last emperor Charles, Otto was brought up in exile after 1918. He protested against the suppression of the Austrian state and hoped to symbolize the rejection of the *Anschluss* and serve as a rallying point for the Austrian émigrés.

Moving to the United States, he sometimes attracted anti-émigré attacks, from the likes of the isolationist Senator Burton Wheeler who in 1940 railed against the 'royal refugees' who 'left their country with the gold' and now urged the USA to go to war against Germany to defend a democracy that they had been incapable of giving their people. (Cf. Joachim Radkau, *Die deutsche Emigration in den USA*, p. 86.)

243. Author of *Between Hitler and Mussolini*, London 1942, Starhemberg settled in South America.

244. Executed in France on 12 December 1942.

245. Founder in 1936 of the American Guild for German Cultural Freedom.

246. A fanatical anti-Communist, he emigrated to Switzerland then the USA.

247. Cf. the study by Joseph Rovan, 'L'émigration monarchiste autrichienne en France', in *Les Barbelés de l'exil*, pp. 138ff.

248. Otto Strasser, *Hitler and I*, p. 133. The movement's symbol was a tiepin composed of a hammer and a sword. The Black Front was organized into lodges inspired by the Freemasons. Otto Strasser, who unlike his brother Gregor (killed by the Nazis in 1934) had never held Hitler in much esteem, criticized the Nazi movement for its 'embourgeoisification' (*Verbonzung*) and for sacrificing the socialist part of its programme to the interests of heavy industry. His group never managed to form a mass movement and was banned on 4 February 1933.

249. Ulrich von Hutten (the Reformation warrior immortalized by Schiller) had been Strasser's pseudonym when he wrote for the *Völkische Beobachter* while Hitler was in prison. Besides the *Huttenbriefe* and the *Deutsche Revolution*, he also published *Dritte Front. Grüne Hefte zur europäische Politik*.

250. Thyssen's book *I Paid Hitler* was published in London in 1941.

251. The expression was coined in 1932 by Kurt Hiller to describe the 'national-revolutionary' Karl Otto Paetel, then applied also to the national-bolsheviks. Vague enough, it was generally used to designate people influenced as much by Otto Strasser as by Ernst Niekisch. Their ideologies sometimes borrowed both from theorists of the conservative revolution and from Communism.

252. Cf. Erich Matthias, ed., *Mit dem Gesicht nach Deutschland. Dokumentation über die sozialdemokratische Emigration*, Düsseldorf 1968.

253. Cf. the issues of *Probleme des Sozialismus*, published in Karlovy Vary by Graphia, and *Revolution gegen Hitler*, 1933.

254. Works on German exile literature often displayed fluctuations and hesitations in the case of these writers. For the Nazis, any opponent, even an anti-Marxist, was most likely a 'Communist of Jewish origin': Kurt Hiller was described in this way when he was arrested. Besides cadres, functionaries and activists there were writers who were KPD members (J. R. Becher), others who were close to the party without being members (Brecht), some who were more or less orthodox Marxists and others with a generally Marxist orientation. This classification used by Matthias Wegener was rejected by Alfred Kantorowicz, who deemed it insufficiently rigorous. Besides, there was relatively little contact between party functionaries and writers themselves, and relationships among these were complex enough: Friedrich Wolf, a doctor at Stuttgart, only rarely met Willi Bredel, a journalist in Hamburg, or Wieland Herfzfelde, a publisher in Berlin.

255. Klaus Mann for example judged negatively Gide's publication of his *Retour d'URSS*. As the Soviet Union was the only hope for defeating Hitler, nothing should be done or said that might weaken its prestige. The majority of Communists followed the same reasoning. Their attacks were all the more violent after they broke with the party.

256. Gustav Regler had little time for the refugee writers in Moscow. Brecht was wary of them and described them as a 'clique'. Some of them attacked others for acting as spies and slanderers. Julius Hay, the Hungarian Communist writer, reproached Walter Ulbricht and Georg Lukács for turning any literary discussion into a tribunal. Regler recalls that K. Schückle (brother-in-law of the Germanist Friedrich

Gundolf), who was accused of 'deviating from the party line', was interrogated by his friends and collaborators on *Internationale Literatur*, including J. R. Becher and Willi Bredel.

257. *Deutsche Literatur im Exil*, p. 16.
258. Walter A. Berendsohn, *Die humanistische Front*, pp. 136–8. The same reproaches could be made of his *Reallexicon*, Berlin 1958.
259. 'Deutsche Literatur im Exil', in *Handbuch der deutschen Gegenwartsliteratur*, Munich 1977, pp. 677–94.
260. W. K. Pfeiler, *German Literature in Exile*, Lincoln 1957.
261. Baden-Baden 1947.
262. These included Ernst Morwitz, Ernst Kantorowicz, Karl Wolfskehl, Edith Landmann, Robert Böhringer and S. Valentin.
263. Ernst Toller took the opportunity of writers' congresses to address German authors who had not gone into exile. His autobiography, *I Was a German*, asks the painful question: 'And where are my friends in Germany?' (London 1934, p. 13.) In May 1939, Klaus Mann addressed an appeal 'An die Schriftsteller im Dritten Reich', which he managed to convey to a number of figures in the world of literature and art: W. E. Süskind, E. Ebermayer, J. Ponten, E. Penzoldt, E. Kästner, G. Kiepenheuer, F. Sieburg, Hans Riesiger, Ricarda Huch, H. Carossa, G. Gründgens, E. Engel, G. Benn, E. Jünger and H. Johst. In ironic and emotional terms, he reminded them that even if ties seemed broken between them and the exiles, they had in common their love for Germany, a language and a vocation. He urged them to struggle against barbarism: 'Don't you hear the cries from the concentration camps when you compose your sonnets?'
264. This was the case with a number of actors and directors (G. W. Pabst, G. Gründgens, R. Forster).
265. *Cahiers Romain Rolland* 21, Paris 1972, p. 157.
266. Ibid., p. 161.
267. In a letter to René Schickele, Thomas Mann wrote: 'I often envy Hesse, who has been out of Germany so many years, but for whom Germany is not closed' (2 April 1934; *Letters of Thomas Mann 1889–1955*, p. 185).
268. Hermann Hesse had been a Swiss citizen since 1924, but his books were published in Germany. In 1936 he was attacked by the Nazi critic Will Vesper. Despite expressing himself on Hitler in very negative terms in 1932, Hesse never took a public stance on the Nazi regime and was attacked in both the Nazi and émigré press. His books were gradually withdrawn from bookshops in Germany, and *The Glass Bead Game* appeared only in 1943. He continued to dissociate poetry and politics, even if he was visited by émigrés such as Brentano, Kläber, Brecht and Peter Weiss.
269. Between 1933 and 1945, twenty books by Herman Hesse were available in Germany, selling a total of 481,000 copies. In Switzerland in the same period, he sold only 35,000 copies of two titles. (Cf. Bernhard Zeller, *Hermann Hesse*, Frankfurt 1963.)
270. Letter to Karl Kerényi, 20 February 1934; *Letters of Thomas Mann 1889–1955*, p. 184.
271. A reading of Thomas Mann's diaries in 1933 and 1934, as well as his correspondence with his publisher G. Bermann Fischer, shows the extent to which material considerations were important in the prudent political attitude Mann adopted, and how distant he was from the émigrés at this time. While a portion of his assets had already been confiscated by the Nazis, Mann feared being stripped completely of his belongings and his royalties. The same considerations led Bermann Fischer to adopt an attitude that was not always unambiguous.
272. His lecture of 10 February 1933 on 'The Sufferings and Greatness of Richard Wagner', held in the auditorium maximum of Munich University, was disrupted by the SA. Mann was to repeat this in Amsterdam, Brussels and Paris. While he had a real admiration for Wagner, this was tempered by a criticism of his nationalism and

a reprise of a number of Nietzsche's criticisms. In response to this lecture, the Nazis circulated a 'Protest from Wagner's city of Munich', signed by academics, theatre directors, musicians and journalists.

273. K. Mann, *The Turning Point*, p. 264.

274. All these passages are quoted from the same letter; *Letters of Thomas Mann 1889–1955*, pp. 168–9.

275. *Letters of Thomas Mann 1889–1955*, pp. 170–1. He again comments in a letter to A. M. Frey: 'That I, at the age of fifty-eight, should never again see Germany, this is what truly appears to me more and more impossible' (27 August 1933).

276. As well as his brother Heinrich, Mann kept up a regular correspondence with René Schickele, Leonhard Frank and Bruno Walter. He met Feuchtwanger and noted in his diary the revolt and indignation he felt at the fate of Ossietzky and Mühsam, 'whom I had little to do with, but that does not stop it hurting me when I hear his fate mentioned' (*Diaries*, 28 May 1933).

277. This was in particular *The Tales of Jacob*, the first part of *Joseph and His Brothers*. While bookstores were wary of displaying his books, they still sold very well. *Tales of Jacob* was a great success, selling 10,000 copies in its first week, and 25,000 by the end of 1933.

278. G. Bermann Fischer played at this point a fairly ambiguous role in Thomas Mann's relation to the Reich. In a letter of 25 June 1947 addressed to the editor of the *Neue Zeitung*, Mann mentions the offers he was made to return to Germany: 'Bermann Fischer, who hoped at this time to keep his publishing house in Berlin, promised to come and pick me up by car at the border and drive me back to the capital. He sent the editor of *Neue Rundschau* to Sanary-sur-Mer [. . .] to persuade me to return to the cradle. I turned him down.'

279. G. Bermann Fischer, *Bedroht-Bewahrt*, p. 203.

280. They did not yet dare to ban his works. Mann however had already paid to the Munich authorities the tax required to 'flee the Reich'.

281. He withdrew at the same time from PEN Club, the Rotary Club, and the Völkerbunds-Komitee.

282. Letter to Julius Meier-Gräfe, 23 December 1933. *Tales of Jacob* was however severely criticized by the Nazi press.

283. 28 March 1933; *Diaries*, p. 138. Mann evokes 'the misery of refugee journalists in Prague, Zurich, etc.'

284. As requested for example by the Social-Democrat Franco Ender. Mann also refused to meet Brecht. (*Tagebücher*, 27 April 1933.)

285. *Letters of Thomas Mann 1889–1955*, p. 177.

286. Letter to René Schickele, 10 August 1934.

287. Letter to René Schickele, 12 October 1934.

288. Letter to René Schickele, 10 August 1934.

289. Letter to A. Neumann, 14 October 1934.

290. Letter to A. M. Frey, 16 November 1934.

291. Letter to A. Kubin of 9 November 1935.

292. Schwarzschild's article was provoked by the decision of G. Bermann Fischer, the responsible head of Fischer Verlag, to leave a part of his publishing house in Berlin and establish another in Vienna for the émigrés. In Schwarzschild's eyes, this was a difficult compromise to accept, and meant a break with Fischer's progressive tradition. This attack – unjust, since the German section of the publishing house was directed in Berlin by Peter Suhrkamp, who was far from being a Nazi – elicited responses from Thomas Mann, Herman Hesse and Annette Kolb. Schwarzschild replied to this defence of Bermann Fischer in an open letter to Thomas Mann (*Das Neue Tage-Buch*, vol. 4, 1936, pp. 82ff). It was this reply that gave a pretext for Korrodi's attack.

293. 'But he who baseness in his heart despises/From hearth and home by baseness will be banned/Whenever a servile nation baseness prizes/Far wiser to renounce the Fatherland/Than to endure in all its childish guises/Blind hatred and the rabble's

heavy hand' (*The Letters of Thomas Mann 1889–1955*, pp. 205–10 [translation modified]).

294. In a letter to René Schickele of 19 November 1936, Mann noted: 'My correspondence swelled a good deal in the wake of my impromptu in the NZZ'.

295. Heinrich Mann recalls in *Ein Zeitalter wird besichtigt* that on his arrival in the United States, Thomas declared: 'Wherever I am, there is German culture.' This phrase, which could be interpreted as attesting to an immense bigheadedness, was not wrong. Throughout his exile, Mann appeared as the symbol of anti-Nazi Germany, and was often able to play the role of spokesperson for the emigration.

296. *The Letters of Thomas Mann 1889–1955*, p. 210.

297. Ibid.

298. H. A. Walter (*Bedrohung und Verfolgung*, pp. 231–2) recalls that Paul Roubiczek gave a fairly unfavourable portrait of Glaeser already at that time. Before leaving Germany, Glaeser had signed a contract with Roubiczek for the publication of his book *The Last Civilian*. When Roubiczek had to emigrate and established a publishing house in exile together with Peter de Mendelssohn, Glaeser, still in Germany, wanted to take back his book. Roubiczek made public the fact that Glaeser had signed a contract with him, which seems to have decided Glaeser to leave Germany. He subsequently put pressure on his publisher for money, failing which he claimed he would return to Germany. (Cf. also E. E. Noth, *Mémoirs d'un Allemand*, p. 467.)

299. Ibid., p. 470.

300. Ibid.

301. The case of Ernst Glaeser is often juxtaposed with that of Bernard von Brentano, a Communist writer, member of the BPRS and friend of Brecht, who emigrated to Switzerland and broken by exile became a reactionary. Kantorowicz maintains that Brentano was never a renegade to the emigration. F. C. Weiskopf (*Unter fremden Himmeln*, p. 22) reports a suit for defamation that Brentano launched in Switerland in 1947 against a Zurich journalist who had referred to him as a sympathizer with the Reich. According to some witnesses, he had called the invasion of Poland 'as fine as a short story by Kleist'. Joseph Breitbach also distanced himself from the émigrés, reproaching them with not seeing what there was positive in National Socialism. Grete von Urbanitsky, an Austrian exile, also linked up with the Nazis in France after 1940 and returned to Austria.

302. 1 March 1948; Brecht, *Journals*, trans. H. Rorrison, ed. J. Willett, London 1993, p. 386. Ernst Glaeser sought in vain to recommence a literary career after 1945, but no longer wrote any major works.

303. Gustav Regler wrote in his memoirs: 'The VOKS – a kind of Soviet cultural office – had sent invitations across the world. There was talk of Ernst Glaeser, the pacifist who, to general astonishment, proclaimed his fidelity to Germany at the moment when its government was preparing a new war' (*Le Glaive et le fourreau*, p. 223). [Not in the English edition of *The Owl of Minverva*.]

304. E. E. Noth, *Mémoirs d'un Allemand*, p. 467.

305. Arthur Koestler,*The Invisible Writing*, London 1969, pp. 292–3.

306. Walter von Molo asked him to come 'like a good doctor' to the bedside of the German people. The affected tone of the letter displeased Mann, who noted: 'these words had a very false ring, and in my Diary I sought to remove this untimely derangement' (*The Genesis of a Novel*, London 1961, p. 108).

307. Born in Latvia in 1890, and well-known as a novelist and essayist, Thiess had published a certain number of works under the Nazi regime.

308. T. Mann, *Genesis of a Novel*, p. 114.

309. Cf. *Thomas Mann, Frank Thiess, Walter von Molo. Ein Streitgespräch über die äusseren und die inneren Emigration*, Dortmund 1964; and F. G. Grossner, ed., *Die grosse Kontroverse – ein Briefwechsel in Deutschland*, Hamburg 1963.

310. G. Benn, *Double vie*, pp. 94ff.

311. Ralf Schnell, in *Literarische innere Emigration 1933–1945*, Stuttgart 1976, refers to the 'emigrant-defaming Adenauer era'.
312. Reinhold Grimm, 'Innere Emigration als Lebensform', Third Wisconsin Workshop, vol. 1, *Exil und innere Emigration*, 1972, pp. 39ff.
313. Joseph Klepper, *Under dem Schatten deiner Flügel. Aus den Tagebüchern der Jahre 1932–42*, Stuttgart 1955, p. 100; 28 August 1938.
314. Ernst Barlach, *Briefe II (1925–1938)*, ed. F. Dross, Munich 1969, p. 30.
315. *Ausgewählte Briefe*, Wiesbaden 1957, p. 62. In *Double Vie* (pp. 100–1), Gottfried Benn claims paternity for this expression.
316. Ernst Niekisch, *Erinnerungen eines deutschen Revolutionärs. Gewagtes Leben*, vol. 1, Cologne 1974, p. 239. This attitude was a continuation of that which Niekisch had chosen after the collapse of the Bavarian soviet republic. Following the arrest of Mühsam and Toller, he refused to take refuge abroad and was imprisoned together with Toller.
317. In Amsterdam he met the exiled Social-Democratic leaders, in Paris Bodo Uhse and Bruno von Salomon. In Basle, Niekisch had discussions with political editors and talked with Emil Oprecht about the possibility of publishing his book *Das Reich der niederen Dämonen*. He also met in Zurich the lawyer who had defended him in 1919, Philipp Löwenfeld. Niekisch mentions too the suspicion with which certain émigrés viewed him, given that he had left Germany with his passport in order.
318. 'You up there, I hate you when I wake and when I sleep, and I will still hate and curse you from my tomb; may your children and grandchildren bear the weight of my curse. I have no other weapon against you than this curse, which I know will dry up my heart, and I don't know if I will survive your ruin . . . But I know perfectly well that if one truly loves Germany, one must hate with all one's heart this Germany. [. . .] I weep, but it is from rage and shame rather than from sadness' (F. P. Reck-Malleczwesen, *La Haine et la honte*, p. 68).
319. Ibid.
320. Ibid.
321. We may also mention the diary of Jochen Klepper, *Unter dem Schatten deiner Flügel*, which resembles the notes written by this religious author, the son of a minister and contributor to the religious press and radio under the Third Reich. A Social-Democrat and married to a Jewish woman, he was denounced, sacked from his job, and expelled from the Reichsschrifttumskammer. His diary is a recital of the everyday suffering and humiliation experienced during the Hitler years. On 11 December 1942, after his young sister-in-law had been deported, he committed suicide together with his wife.
322. T. Mann, 'Leiden an Deutschland'.
323. T. Mann, *Order of the Day*, p. 170.
324. K. Mann, *Der Vulkan*, Frankfurt 1961, pp. 411ff.
325. Thomas Mann wrote in a letter to Konrad Engelmann on 15 December 1936: 'I am keeping well, I live and work as before, and truly have nothing to envy those who remained in Germany.'
326. Cited after Alfred Kantorowicz in *Politik und Literatur im Exil*, p. 17.
327. Cf. Brecht's poem 'To Those Brought into Line' (1935).
328. Freiburg 1961, p. 148.
329. Munich 1957, pp. 13ff.
330. Münster 1964.
331. 24 March 1933.
332. The Nazis sought in certain works to show that the Third Reich was the culmination of the tradition of romanticism and Germanity that Huch had exalted. This involved a complete falsification of her work, as Ricarda Huch was hostile to any '*völkisch*' dimension. She did not miss an opportunity to show her hostility to the regime, and condemn its methods and values. Her entire correspondence displays her hatred of the Nazi regime. (Cf. M. Baum, *Leuchtende Spur. Das Leben Ricarda Huchs*, Tübingen 1950.)

333. A. Kantorowicz, *Politik und Literatur im Exil*, p. 18.
334. Bad Godesberg conference, p. 40.
335. Cited in *Verbannung*, p. 275.
336. He claims to have used it in a letter sent in 1933 or 1934 to Hinkel, the official responsible for culture. Berendsohn also mentions the expression as having been coined by Thiess.
337. *Der lautlose Aufstand. Bericht über die Wiederstandsbewegung des deutschen Volkes 1933–1945*, ed. G. Weisenborn, Hamburg 1953, p. 218.
338. 'Innere Emigration als Lebensform', p. 43.
339. Cf. his novel *Stürmische Frühling*.
340. Frank Thiess, who joined the Reichsschriftumskammer, had proved his Aryan ancestry (letter from the Reichsschriftumskammer to the anti-Semitic journal *Der Stürmer*, July 1944, cited by J. Wulf, *Literatur und Dichtung im Dritten Reich*, p. 493). His work was never subject to official proscription, but was translated in ten countries. Some literary historians have stressed that his novel *Das Reich der Dämonen* was in fact banned. In fact, a notification of 18 July 1941 simply demanded a reworking of the manuscript because it gave a bad representation of the past of the Germanic tribes.
341. Among this type of work we may cite at random the essays and anthologies of F. Krause, *Dokumente des anderen Deutschlands*; Karl O. Paetel, *Deutsche innere Emigration. Anti-national-sozialistische Zeugnisse aus Deutschland*, New York 1946; and G. Weisenborn, *Der lautlose Aufstand*.
342. *Deutsche Literatur in der Entscheidung*, Karlsruhe 1948, p. 2.
343. Third Wisconsin Workshop, 1972.
344. *Die deutsche Opposition gegen Hitler. Eine Würdigung*, Krefeld 1949.
345. Adam Kuckhoff took part in the Harry Schutze-Boyssen resistance group. Arrested by the Gestapo in 1942, he was beheaded on 6 August 1943, leaving his five-year-old son a poem in which he wrote that humanity as a whole would now be his father. We should also recall the case of Gottlob Winkler, accused in 1933 of having torn up Nazi posters, who wrote numerous poems in prison and committed suicide at the age of twenty-four.
346. Thomas Mann, *Germany and the Germans*, Washington, 1963, pp. 51–2.
347. *Literarische innere Emigration*, p. 49.
348. *Weimarer Beiträge*, 2nd year, 1970, vol. 6.
349. Ibid., p. 71.
350. The political attitudes of writers and artists who remained in Germany were very complex. While certain were fanatical partisans of the regime, the majority displayed an astonishing mix of opportunism, cowardice and indeed courage. Some, even though members of the Reich's cultural organizations, found ways of helping the émigrés. The attitudes of these towards them were also very diverse. After the War Alfred Döblin attacked Hans Carossa, whereas J. R. Becher and Thomas Mann renewed links with him. Though servile to the Nazi regime, Carossa came to the aid of the expressionist poet A. Mombert when he was interned at Gurs.
351. In his study of *Ernst Jünger* (New York 1946), Karl O. Paetel, himself an exile, maintained that no émigré had the right to reproach a writer for having remained in Germany, and refused to give a special value to emigration. He claimed that he himself left Germany so as not to be arrested again by the Gestapo, and that someone who was not concerned with the 'either/or' should have remained, 'as he was more important there than in some vestibule of a refugee organization'.
352. Between 1933 and 1944, 427 titles by 104 authors were classified as 'undesirable', without their authors being oppositionists.
353. The majority of these tracts have disappeared. No issue of *Stich und Hieb* has survived. A facsimile of its second issue was published in *AIZ* 48 (Prague 1933): the magazine measured nine centimetres by six. (Cf. Wolfgang Emmerich, 'Die Literatur des antifaschistischen Widerstands in Deutschland', in *Die deutsche*

Literatur im Dritten Reich, ed. Horst Denkler and Karl Prüm, Stuttgart 1976, pp. 427ff.)

354. According to W. Emmerich, 80 per cent of this literature was produced by the Communists. The material was often smuggled in the form of clichés and photocopies in double-bottomed suitcases, else under an insignificant label, or it crossed the border on skis, by balloon, or with the help of dockers.

355. Brecht's text 'Five Difficulties in Writing the Truth' circulated disguised as a first-aid manual. A fragment of Ludwig Renn's novel *Krieg* was renamed *Der Frontsoldat*. Thomas Mann's exchange of letters with Bonn University (1937) was transformed into a false popular edition of the *Niebelungenlied*. A collection of socialist songs of struggle became Johann Strauss's opus 314, 'The Blue Danube'. Certain anti-Nazi publications imitated famous Nazi titles or appeared in the form of little Insel Verlag classics (the Reclam collection). It was not unusual to find Communist poems in a treatise on homoeopathy or texts of Marx inserted into novels by Wiechert.

356. Heinz Gittig has catalogued about 585 for the whole Nazi period. (Cf. Heinz Gittig, *Illegale anti-fascistische Tarnschfriften 1933 bis 1945*, Leipzig 1972.)

CHAPTER 3   THE STAGES OF EXILE IN EUROPE

1. Among the most important: Czechoslovakia, France, Austria, Poland, Luxemburg, the Netherlands, Belgium, Switzerland, Britain, Denmark, Norway, Sweden, Finland, the Soviet Union, Bulgaria, Turkey, Romania, Yugoslavia, Japan, Australia, the United States, Canada, Mexico, Cuba, Brazil, Chile, Bolivia, Argentina, Paraguay, Uruguay, Venezuela and Equador.

2. *Die deutsche Exilliteratur 1933–1945*, pp. 40–1. The distinction is not always sharp. Certain émigrés for example refused to see Austria as a 'country of exile'; few exiles took refuge there and the government was violently opposed to anti-Nazi activity on its soil.

3. Stefan Zweig recalls in *The World of Yesterday* (p. 320) how in England he met refugees ready to leave for Haiti, the Dominican Republic or Shanghai if only they could obtain a visa: '[A]n old worn-out man with children and grandchildren, atremble with the hope of going to a country which hitherto he would not have been able to find on the map, there only to beg his way through and again be a stranger and purposeless! Someone next to him asked in eager desperation how one could get to Shanghai. [. . .] There they crowded, erstwhile university professors, bankers, merchants, landed proprietors, musicians; each ready to drag the miserable ruins of his existence over earth and oceans anywhere, to do and suffer anything, only away, away from Europe, only away!'

4. It goes without saying that no monograph can claim to give a full picture of the various stations of exile. Helmut Müssener has devoted several hundred pages just to the study of Socialist emigration in Sweden (*Exil in Schweden*, Munich 1974). The series of volumes published by Editions Röderberg, Leipzig, remains an indispensable work of reference, likewise the works of H. A. Walter.

5. Czechoslovakia granted the right of asylum to all 'illegal' refugees that reached its territory. Clandestine crossing of the border from Germany was relatively easy.

6. Cf. H. A. Walter, *Deutsche Exilliteratur*, vol. 2, p. 142; Kurt Grossman, 'Die Exilsituation in der Tschechoslowakei', in M. Durzak, ed., *Die deutsche Exilliteratur*, p. 64; Gertruda Albrechtova 'Zur Frage des deutschen antifaschistischen Exil' in *Historica* VIII, Prague 1964, p. 181; Hansjörg Schneider, *Exiltheater in der Tschechoslowakei 1933–1938*, Berlin 1969.

7. After the Reichstag fire, the Czechoslovak minister of the interior reinforced border controls in order to avoid a massive influx of Communist refugees. It was recommended to forbid them access to Czech territory unless they had valid passports, or return them to Germany if they had entered illegally. In fact, these

measures were soon revoked. The policy on admission of Communist writers was not always clear. While Julius Hay was refused, A. Durus, F. Erpenbeck, B. Frei, John Heartfield and Wieland Herzfelde were admitted. Ruth Fischer and Arkadi Maslow were placed under police surveillance. Certain émigrés such as Herbert Wehner were arrested and expelled to the USSR.

8. Many witnesses (H. Riegl, W. Sternfeld) confirm that police measures were rarely carried out. Certain émigrés were expelled to the Prague suburbs. Whatever their politics, the government protected them from attempts at kidnapping and assassination by the Gestapo.

9. Many anti-Nazi leaflets and journals distributed in Germany were printed in Czechoslovakia, in particular the bulletins of the SoPaDe.

10. A bank employee and gymnastics teacher, Heinlein rapidly transformed sporting practice into military exercises. He was used by the Nazis to provoke tension among the Sudeten Germans, calling them to unite in the Heimatsfront. His supporters saluted him with the cry: 'Heil Heinlein!'

11. Cited from Berthold Jacob, *Le Filet brun*, Paris 1936.

12. The Prague émigrés were all the more menaced in that a Gestapo headquarters was situated in Dresden and no visa was needed for travel between the two countries.

13. This measure struck Wilhelm Pieck, F. Hecker, Robert Breitscheid, Lion Feuchtwanger, Ernst Toller and Kurt Tucholsky on 14 July 1933.

14. When Heinrich Mann sought to obtain Czech citizenship in the district of Reichenberg, Heinlein organized a demonstration against him. He was nonetheless accepted in the district of Litomysl in August 1935, and his brother a year later.

15. The law on foreigners of 28 March 1935 stipulated that if émigrés carried out political activity or interfered in Czech political life they would be expelled, though not to their country of origin.

16. In the wake of this intervention, seven photomontages had to be withdrawn from the exhibition for 'insulting the president of the Reich and other leaders of the German state'. The greater part of these had been already published in *AIZ*.

17. Eight hundred and one refugees had reached Czechoslovakia by June 1933, followed by a further 201 by November 1934, 144 more by December 1935, 1,594 by December 1936 and 1,399 by December 1937. Many subsequently emigrated to other countries, particularly France and the USSR.

18. H. Mann, *Ein Zeitalter wird besichtigt*, p. 472.

19. Most subsequently left for further exile. Paul Reimann and Rudolf Popper published a collection of their writings in London in 1944. A certain number such as Paul Kornfeld, the expressionist playwright, perished in concentration camp. F. C. Weiskopf attacked Josef Roth who wanted to restore the Austro-Hungarian monarchy. Weiskopf tried to establish an American-Czech journal in the United States, and planned in future to write only in Czech.

20. The editorial board of the *NDB* included writers such as Wieland Herzfelde, Anna Seghers, Oskar Maria Graf and Jan Petersen (who remained underground in Germany until 1935), as well as writers for Malik Verlag and Czechs such as R. Fuchs, E. E. Kisch, Theodor Balk and Louis Fürnberg.

21. Cf. E. Goldstücker, *Weltfreunde. Konferenz über die Prager-deutsche Literatur*, Neuwied 1967; and Erich Matthias, *Sozialdemokratie und Nation. Ein Beitrag zur Ideengeschichte des sozialdemokratischen Emigration in der Prager Zeit des Parteivorstandes 1933–1938*, Stuttgart 1952.

22. Cf. J. Rovan, *Histoire de la social-démocratie allemande*, Paris 1978, pp. 206ff.

23. Cf. the memoir of Wilhelm Eidelmann, 'Deutschland, Tschechoslowakei, Frankreich, Algerien, Sowjetunion. Stationen eines langen Weges', in *Im Kampf bewährt*, Berlin 1977.

24. They were based in a disused factory.

25. The Czech edition included a local page devoted to the Sudeten Germans, with the collaboration of Professor F. X. Salda, in charge of the Refugee Aid Committee.

26. In particular E. E. Kisch, F. C. Weiskopf, W. Herzfelde, H. Pol, T. Balk, M. Zimmering, E. Ottwalt, Peter Nickl and Stefan Heym, as well as Ernst Toller, Hans Eisler, F. Leschnitzer, G. Lukács, J. R. Becher, J. Roth, E. Weinert and Klaus Mann.

27. The Bertolt-Brecht-Klub had been founded in 1934 with the production of *Die Dreigroschenoper*. Directed by F. C. Wieskopf and Wieland Herzfelde, its declared object was to promote sporting education among young people. It held cultural functions and organized public meetings (the campaigns against the Berlin Olympics, for the liberation of Carl von Ossietzky, etc.). The majority of émigrés, Communists in particular, took part, often under pseudonyms. There was also a Hans-Otto-Klub for actors, and an Oskar-Kokoschka-Bund for plastic artists.

28. *Weltfreunde. Konferenz über die Prager-deutsche Literatur*. Other publishing houses were set up by émigrés or published their texts: Orbis, Rohrer, Grunow, Graphia. Malik Verlag published among others works by Adam Scharrer, Willi Bredel, and Oskar Maria Graf.

29. *Simplicissimus* was one of the most famous German satirical journals. It reappeared in Prague in both German and Czech, directed by Heinz Pol, seeking to give new life to Thomas T. Heine's original publication under the title *Die Wahre Simplicissimus*. Heine disavowed the journal for fear of Nazi reaction, and threatened the Prague editorial team with legal action. They acknowledged in an article that Heine had no connection with their journal. The first number of *Simplicus* appeared on 25 January 1934, railing at Heine's *Simplicissimus* for making peace with the Nazis. It ceased publication on 26 June 1935 for lack of financial means. Its contributors include Alfred Kerr, Heinrich Mann, Balder Olden and Theodor Plievier.

30. After having tried to kidnap Otto Strasser on Czech territory, Himmler managed to assassinate the engineer Rudolf Formis who was in charge of the 'black transmitter', luring him into an ambush with a woman (16 January 1935). The Czech government protested at this murder, but Goebbels denied any responsibility, simply asking if Strasser would be prosecuted for establishing an illegal transmitter. Strasser was in fact condemned to four months in prison on 6 January 1936, but pardoned by President Benes. The clandestine transmitter was placed by the Czechs in the Prague museum. German radio officially acknowledged on 22 November 1939 that Formis had been murdered by the SS.

31. Max Brod, *Une vie combative*, Paris 1964, pp. 343–4.

32. 'We never felt threatened in our persons or in our lives, but certainly we were disagreeably obstructed every way we turned. There were some ridiculous anomalies! [. . .] Though I had been critic of the *Prager Tagblatt* for both German and Czech theatre, I was no longer authorized, by instruction of my government, to write articles on the German-language theatre, but only the Czech' (ibid.).

33. Karl Kraus had defended Else Lasker-Schüler, and taken Brecht's side against the critic Alfred Kerr who had accused *Die Dreigroschenoper* of plagiarism. Kraus was moreover better esteemed in Germany than in Austria. Robert Musil lived in Berlin.

34. Theodor Coskor wrote from Switzerland to Ö. von Horvath on 30 November 1933: 'We are already completely in exile, whether we live in Bavaria or Vienna.'

35. P. M. Lützeler (*Die deutsche Exilliteratur 1933–1945*, p. 57) emphasizes that the political climate in Austria was as unfavorable to the émigrés as the restrictions that affected them. Following the Dolfuss–Mussolini meeting of 18–19 August 1933, Austrian politics was increasingly oriented towards internal repression, aiming at the complete elimination of the left.

36. This Steinhäusl was ultimately imprisoned for having taken part in the coup that cost Dolfuss's life. Freed by the Nazis after the *Anschluss*, he was reappointed chief of police but died in November 1939, in the course of a brawl between the SA and members of the Austrian secret police.

37. Essentially that of the Social-Democratic party, since the Austrian Communist party played only a very minor role.

38. Such mediation was attempted by the French Socialists in the name of the International Federation of Trade Unions. Mediation from the Catholic side (Hubertus Prinz zu Löwenstein, Georg Baron Franckenstein) was equally ineffective.

39. Berthold Jacob wrote (*Le Filet brun*, p. 138): 'Throughout this period of affected loyalism, the Munich transmitter kept silent, the Austrian Legion was removed from the Bavarian frontier and Habitch kept out of the spotlight. Hardly had the regrouping of Nazi forces been completed than the underhand agitation recommenced, just as it had been before July 1934. The National Socialist offensive took off again, the day that Mussolini finished his preparations for the war in Abyssinia. National Socialism was preparing its second major offensive against Austria.'

40. Karl Münichreiter, head of the Schutzbund, was executed under martial law, while already mortally wounded.

41. Fischer hid for a while at the home of the writer Elias Canetti.

42. According to Manès Sperber (*Au-delà de l'oubli*, p. 39), there were 1,200 dead, 5,000 wounded and 10,000 arrested in the wake of the February 1934 fighting.

43. Stefan Zweig's blindness was very typical of a certain number of liberal intellectuals. In *The World of Yesterday* he wrote: 'Singular as it might seem I was in Vienna during these historic February days without seing anything of the historic events which were then occurring and without the slightest inkling that they were happening. Cannon were thundering, buildings were being occupied, hundreds of corpses were being carried off – I saw not a single one' (pp. 290–1). Even when the government intervened against the workers with machine-guns, Zweig was unaware: 'If all Austria had been seized then, were it by Socialists, National Socialists, or Communists, I would have known it as little as did the citizens of Munich who woke up one morning only to learn from the *Münchener Neueste Nachrichten* that their city was in Hitler's hands' (ibid., p. 291).

44. *Rote Sturmfahne über Floridsdorf*. Though nothing could be proved against him, Hay spent several months in prison and was nearly expelled to his home country, Hungary, at the risk of being sent to his death. He owed his release to the intervention of a number of Austrian writers, and was able to emigrate to Switzerland.

45. While a few writers such as Franz Werfel seem to have sought a compromise with the Austrian clerico-fascist regime, perhaps under the influence of Alma Mahler whose ideas were particularly reactionary, the majority of Austrian authors kept their distance, for example Hermann Broch, Elias Canetti and Robert Musil. Politicized to very different degrees, they all tackled the question of fascism in their works. Broch and Canetti both examined in particular the relationship between fascism and mass psychology.

46. Cf. H. A. Walter, *Asylpraxis*, pp. 98–9.

47. On 2 May 1935, Freud wrote: 'The times are gloomy; fortunately it is not my job to brighten them' (*Letters of Sigmund Freud*, p. 421). Apropos his essay on Moses, Freud wrote on 30 September 1934: 'Concern for these uninitiated compels me to keep the completed essay secret. For we live here in an atmosphere of Catholic orthodoxy' (ibid., p. 418). The Austrian government was also very discreet when Freud's eightieth birthday was celebrated in 1936. Freud wrote to Arnold Zweig on 22 June of that year: 'Austria seems bent on becoming National Socialist. Fate seems to be conspiring with that gang. With even less regret do I wait for the curtain to fall for me' (*Letters of Sigmund Freud and Arnold Zweig*, p. 133). And again on 20 December 1937: 'In your interest I can scarcely regret that you have not chosen Vienna as your new home. The government here is different but the people in their worship of anti-Semitism are entirely at one with their brothers in the Reich. The noose around our necks is being tightened all the time even if we are not actually being throttled' (ibid., p. 154). Freud's four sisters, unable to leave Austria in time, were deported and gassed.

48. *Letters of Sigmund Freud*, p. 415.

49. To quote a few passages from Alma Mahler's memoirs, written between 1933 and 1938: 'Both of us felt that there must be something to a face that had enthralled thirty millions. [. . .] Then I saw the face I had been waiting for: clutching eyes – young, frightened features – no Duce! An adolescent [sic!], rather, who would never mature, would never achieve wisdom' (*And the Bridge Is Love*, London 1959, p. 197). 'In February 1934 the Austrian Social-Democrats paid the price of their stupendous blunders. [. . .] The crowning folly of this power-mad crew was to undermine the influence of the village clergy, and thus to pave the way for the "ersatz religion" of Nazism.' (p. 202). 'It is God who sent Hitler and who one day will make him fall with His merciful hand' (February 1934 [not in the English edition]).

50. Thus Manès Sperber wrote: 'I am not an émigré. Vienna, for me, was not a land of asylum but the homeland to which I returned' (*Au-delà de l'oubli*, p. 10). All the same, Sperber settled in Yugoslavia.

51. Cf. 'Erinnerungen an Ödön von Horvath' in Jenö Krammer, ed., *Ödön von Horvath*, Vienna 1969.

52. In T. Krischke, ed., *Materialen zum Ödön von Horvath*, Frankfurt 1970, p. 94.

53. Cf. H. A. Walter, *Asylpraxis*, pp. 98–9.

54. Cited by Paul Lützeler, *Hermann Broch. Eine Biographie*, Frankfurt 1985, p. 61.

55. Robert Musil left Berlin in 1933 when the support committee that had enabled him to live was dissolved. It had comprised principally Jews and left-wing figures. Though he commented on National Socialism in a satirical fashion, he was not directly threatened. The second (unfinished) volume of *The Man Without Qualities* had been published by Rowohlt. From 1933 to 1938 Musil lived in Vienna without resources. Bruno Fürst tried, as Kurt Gläser had done in Berlin, to establish a 'Musil society' that would enable him to finish his book. But few Austrian critics had heard of him, or else they confused him with the orientalist Alois Musil. Six people each agreed to pay Musil 100 schillings a month. He refused the donation, preferring poverty to begging. Rowohlt ceded the rights to the first volume of *The Man Without Qualities* to G. Bermann Fischer, and his situation improved a bit. He left Vienna in August 1938 and settled in Zurich.

56. Cf. H. A. Walter, *Asylpraxis*, p. 82 for the details of these measures. The ban on foreigners working was explained by the fact that in 1935 the Netherlands had more than 425,000 unemployed. In July 1934 the country had known severe social conflict.

57. The latter relates that the Dutch police explained to him how to cross the Belgian frontier illegally.

58. On the history of antifascist emigration in Holland, cf. H. A. Walter, *Asylpraxis*, the volume edited by M. Durzak, and above all the compendium edited by Hans Würzner, *Zur deutschen Exilliteratur in den Niederlanden 1933–1940*, Amsterdam 1977. The most recent study is that by K. Hermsdorf and H. Fetting, *Exil in den Niederlanden*, Stuttgart 1981.

59. These committees are not well known. After the German invasion they were often clandestine, for fear of the Gestapo.

60. Ex-Chancellor Brüning himself travelled regularly to meet former political figures from the Catholic and Centre milieu. These meetings became increasingly difficult due to Gestapo surveillance, its agents not hesitating to intervene on Dutch territory.

61. Heinz Liepmann for example was accused in 1934 of insult to the head of state of a friendly nation. In his novel *Vaterland* he had accused Hindenburg of corruption. After 1935 he emigrated to France, to England the next year and in 1937 to New York.

62. Following the intervention of the Dutch government, they were sentenced to prison rather than executed. Some of them, however, such as Franz Bobzien, perished in concentration camp. The expulsions had been decided on by the mayor of Laren, a National Socialist sympathizer, in contradiction to Dutch law.

63. The author of novels describing the Cologne petty bourgeoisie, she emigrated to Holland, invited by the publisher Allert de Lange, who wanted to bring out her books which were now banned in Germany. Her novel *Nach Mitternacht*, depicting Nazi Germany, was published by Querido Verlag. In *Bilder und Gedichte der Emigration*, Cologne 1947, she described her stay in Ostend and her relations with Stefan Zweig, Ernst Toller, Hermann Kesten, Egon Erwin Kisch and above all her partner Joseph Roth.

64. Nico Rost (1896–1967), the translator of Anna Seghers, had lived in Berlin since 1923 as a correspondent. He knew Else Lasker-Schüler, Gottfried Benn and Franz Kafka. His links with progressive writers led him to be interned for a while at the Oranienburg concentration camp. He published many articles on the German émigrés, especially on Gustav Regler, Willi Bredel, Bertolt Brecht and Heinrich Mann. Another intermediary between Dutch literature and that of the German émigrés was the critic Menno ter Brak. An article of his, published by *Das Neue Tage-Buch* in 1934, was the starting-point for one of the most important discussions of exile literature. A member of the Dutch Vigilance Committee of Antifascist Intellectuals, he committed suicide when German troops entered Holland.

65. Fritz Helmut Landshoff emigrated in 1940 to London, then to New York, where he established the G. B. Fischer Corporation together with G. Bermann Fischer. After 1941 he was director of a division of Querido in the United States, and remained in Holland after the War.

66. Arrested by Gestapo in 1940, Gerard de Lange was thrown from a window. He managed to escape and hide himself in Amsterdam. Arrested at the Belgian frontier while trying to escape to Switzerland, he was deported to Bergen-Belsen where he died in 1945.

67. This measure threatened in particular René Schickele, Alfred Döblin, Thomas Mann, Stefan Zweig and more particularly all writers published by S. Fischer Verlag.

68. Account should also be taken of the sympathy for Germany displayed by certain milieus in Holland. It was out of fear of an official ban that Querido abandoned publishing certain texts by Heinrich Mann.

69. He lived there until 1944. Just before the War, Sternheim, more and more disturbed by nervous crises, was trying to correct a copy of *Mein Kampf* in terms of his aesthetic principles of stylistic concision. He reduced the compendious work to a single slim volume. This copy was subsequently burned solemnly by the Nazis. Even so, Sternheim was able to remain in Belgium under German occupation thanks to the protection of the German governor of Brussels, General von Falkenhausen. He died on 3 November 1942, his burial followed by a handful of people. His son Carl Eduard, a Wehrmacht officer, was beheaded in 1944 for having refused to retract remarks directed against Hitler. His other son, Klaus, committed suicide in Mexico, his daughter was interned in Ravensbrück and survived. Sternheim's autobiography, *Vorkriegseuropa im Gleichnis meines Leben* was published in 1936 by Querido.

70. Among the famous names in the dramatic world in Antwerp at that time were Ernst Busch (who sung Brecht in Dutch), Alexandre Moissi, Henny Porten, Leopold Jessner, Albert Bassermann, Tilla Durieux, Ernst Deutsch, Max Reinhardt, Erika Mann and Hermann Thimig.

71. Gerd Roloff, *Exil und Exilliteratur in der deutschen Presse 1945–1949*, Worms 1976, p. 117, emphasizes that in Flanders, even after the War, lists of books publicly banned by the Catholic church were broadly inspired by the Nazi lists. Writers such as Döblin and Becher were kept on the index, while 'blood and soil' literature was praised. Cf. Joris Baers, *Lectuur Repertorium*, 1952 and 1954.

72. If Britain was not a major country of asylum in 1933, the situation changed radically in 1938 with the intensification of anti-Semitic persecution. The rescue of Jews from Austria and Czechoslovakia became a moral issue for the British government and public opinion. By October 1941, 32,000 refugees of German origin and 27,000 Austrian Jews had been given asylum there.

73. Ernst Niekisch, who travelled to England in 1934, was almost rejected, the authorities fearing that he would settle there. He could only stay by showing his return ticket to Germany. His case is all the more significant in that Niekisch possessed a valid German passport.
74. In principle, no work permit was granted to German exiles. The only people who could settle permanently in Britain were academics or scientists invited by institutions or foundations, actors and directors, and industrialists.
75. Fred Uhlman, *The Making of an Englishman*, London 1960.
76. Sebastian Haffner, *Anmerkungen zu Hitler*, Munich 1978.
77. His trilogy *The Sleepwalkers* was published in London in 1932. Broch had thought at that time of moving to England, but the lukewarm reception of his book dissuaded him, despite the praise he received from T. S. Eliot. After being imprisoned for a while in Austria, he obtained a British visa thanks to the support of his translators, Mr and Mrs Muir. Broch finally emigrated to the United States, as his financial position in Britain was dangerously precarious. On 23 August 1938 he wrote to the critic Carl Seelig: 'My finances can be summed up as follows: I receive a pension of £7 per month from the PEN Club, provisionally for three months though with the prospect of an extension. And I am supposed to receive from the American Guild a one-off assistance of 90 dollars. Apart from this I have nothing. Out of the £7 pension, moreover, I have to repay my friends Muir for their expenses, as they are not rolling in money. [. . .] Looking this horror in its so-called face has been far too strong confirmation of my old thesis that artistic activity is superfluous at this time' (Hermann Broch, *Lettres 1939–1951*, Paris 1961, p. 188).
78. Author of *Men Crucified*, 1941, on Dachau and other Nazi camps.
79. G. Tergit mentions the works of Ruth Feiner and Hilde Spiel, published both as serials in the press and as volumes; *Die deutsche Walpurgisnacht* by Dusio Koffler; and R. Friedenthal's collection *Brot und Salz*.
80. Alfred Kerr however noted a certain hostility towards refugees even in liberal milieus. They were reproached for being badly dressed and unhappy. Cf. *Verbannung*, p. 136.
81. Christopher Isherwood, *Prater Violet*, Harmondsworth 1961.
82. Ibid., pp. 104–5. The story takes place at the time of the crushing of the Schutzbund. When the Austrian director prophesies war, he is met with a mixture of sarcasm and pity. In *Christopher and His Kind* (London 1977), Isherwood explained how the director 'Friedrich Bergmann' was in actual fact Berthold Viertel, who had been invited to London to make a film inspired by the novel of the Austrian writer Ernst Lothar, *Petite amie*.
83. Club 1943 counted among its active members H. Fischer, H. Flesch, H. Friedmann, Monty Jacobs, F. Koffka, W. Sternfeld, and K. Wolff. It organized lectures every Sunday, and published the symposium *In Tyrannos. Four Centuries of Struggle against Tyranny*. Members of Der Freie Deutsche Kulturbund in Great Britain included Bruno Viertel, Oskar Kokoschka, Stefan Zweig, Alfred Kerr and W. Unger. The antagonism between Communists and non-Communists in it was very strong. In general, Socialists boycotted all cultural activities organized by the Communists. Alfred Kerr, president of the League, resigned in 1939, and Club 1943 was set up as a counter to it.
84. *Verbannung*, pp. 136ff.
85. *The World of Yesterday*, p. 326. Stefan Zweig's example is all the more tragic in that his hostility to Nazism was universally known, and he enjoyed an international reputation. The same was the case with Feuchtwanger in France, received by Stalin and Roosevelt but interned in a camp as a German citizen.
86. Cf. 'Internierungslager und Lageruniversität', in *Verbannung*, p. 115.
87. F. Uhlman, *The Making of an Englishman*, p. 233.
88. Werner Mittenzwei, author of the volume *Exil in der Schweiz*, Stuttgart 1978, speaks of the 'destruction of the illusion of a classical country of exile' (p. 15). Cf.

also H. A. Walter, *Asylpraxis und Lebensbedingungen in Europa* (vol. 2, pp. 132ff.), and *Die deutsche Exilliteratur*, pp. 101ff.

89. A visa was only required if the refugee sought work. He could remain for two years without being disturbed by the authorities, simply having to present himself to the police. The proclaimed tolerance and neutrality, however, prohibited any political activity.

90. In 1936, Switzerland had 124,000 unemployed. (Cf. H. A. Walter, *Asylpraxis*, p. 108.)

91. The very negative image that the majority of émigrés give of Switzerland bears only on its administrative and police procedures. The Swiss population, for its part, often came to the aid of refugees. Since the Second World War, many Swiss historians have worked to clarify this inglorious page in their country's history, with remarkable objectivity. Cf. Edgar Bonjour, *Geschichte der schweizerischen Neutralität*, Basle 1965; *Geistige Landesverteidigung während des zweiten Weltkrieges*, Zurich 1971; Alfred A. Häsler, *Das Boot ist voll. Die Schweiz und die Flüchtlinge 1933–45*, Zurich 1962; C. Ludwig, *Die Flüchtlingpolitik der Schweiz seit 1933 bis zum Gegenwart*, Berne 1957.

92. Eduart von Steiger made famous the image of Switzerland as a lifeboat (*Rettungsboot*) 'filled to the brim' and unable to accept anyone else.

93. Arthur Koestler wrote in his memoirs: 'In Switzerland, every alien who does not belong to the privileged category of tourists is subject to periodical police check-ups. His means of subsistence, his morals and politics are legitimate objects of scrutiny, and the smallness of the country enables the police to supervise the alien's life fairly thoroughly' (*The Invisible Writing*, p. 342). A week after his arrival in Switzerland in March 1934, Koestler was accused by the police of unmarried cohabiting. Following his marriage, the spited police chief exclaimed: 'I suppose this marriage was arranged to cover up the fact that you are working as his housekeeper without a labour permit.' (p. 348). Else Lasker-Schüler was arrested for vagabondage. Albert Ehrenstein was almost returned to Germany. Ernst and Karola Bloch were arrested and imprisoned, she being described as a 'Comintern agent'. Their residence permit was not renewed, and they had to leave Switzerland on 15 September 1934.

94. Chief of police for foreigners until 1945, Rothmund struggled with all the legal weapons at his disposal against the arrival of refugees, and Jews above all. Though hostile to the Nazis, he was yet more hostile to their victims. Concerned to keep Switzerland 'clean and healthy', he viewed this protection of his country against the influx of refugees as a genuine mission, and did not hesitate to collaborate with Dr Hans Globke, the Nazi 'specialist' in racial laws, even agreeing in 1938 to visit the Sachsenhausen concentration camp. Though himself an avowed anti-Semite, Rothmund believed that Nazi measures were too strict: he saw a large number of Jews as a danger to his country, but a small number as an advantage. It was he who discussed with the Reich authorities the best means to make the character of Jewish refugee clear on their passport (compulsory Jewish name or red ink). He finally agreed that a 'J' should be stamped on the passport. Switzerland was the only country to use such official discrimination. In 1958 Rothmund had to answer for his actions before the Bundesrat.

95. Karola Bloch (then Piotrkowski) took refuge in Switzerland after the Reichstag fire, with a letter of recommendation from her professor of architecture to the dean of Zurich University, Professor Weis. This man had been won to the Nazi cause. At the Technische Hochschule, students demonstrated against their Jewish comrades with the slogan '*Raus mit den Juden*' (*Aus meinem Leben*, pp. 84–5).

96. The case of the psychiatrist C. G. Jung is all too well known. His articles on 'Jewish psychoanalysis' as opposed to the 'Aryan unconscious of the young Germanic peoples' were utterly in the '*völkisch*' style.

97. The law on foreigners prohibited all work, even voluntary. The psychological consequences of this ban on the refugees were naturally catastrophic. If the émigrés broke this law they could be condemned to a prison sentence.

98. *Asylpraxis*, pp. 119ff.
99. Someone who was threatened with expulsion could obtain a stay of execution only by paying a very large bail, quite impossible for any émigré, especially a political refugee. Moreover, the expulsion was noted on their passport as a warning to other countries. The Swiss authorities did not hesitate to turn antifascists back at the frontier – a very rare case in Europe – at the risk of condemning them to death.
100. Anyone contravening the ban on writing could be taken to the frontier in forty-eight hours. This happened to Karl Schnog who published a poem, and Werner Helwig who wrote a few sheets published in Liechtenstein. Robert Baum Jungk and Jakob Haringer were imprisoned for the same reason. Cf. F. C. Weiskopf, *Unter fremden Himmeln*, pp. 32–3.
101. Writing under a pseudonym was both dangerous and impossible; because of the particularity of the Swiss-German language, German writers were immediately recognizable as such. Though after the invasion of Austria and Czechoslovakia Switzerland remained one of the few countries where a German-language readership still existed, restrictions on the distribution of émigré works were maintained.
102. Manès Sperber recalls how the Association of Swiss Writers constantly reminded the police that they should ensure that the ban on émigrés writing and publishing was not infringed (*Au-delà de l'oubli*, p. 221).
103. Max Frisch noted in his diary, many years later: 'A memory of 1936, when I intended to marry a Jewish student from Berlin and went to the Zurich town hall to obtain the necessary papers, I was given without asking for it a certificate of Aryan origin with the city stamp. Unfortunately, I immediately tore up this document.' (*Journal 1966–1971*, p. 170.) It should be borne in mind that Switzerland at this time sported a number of overtly pro-Nazi organizations: Gruppe Nationalsozialistischer Eidgenossen, Volksbund, Nationalsozialistische Schweizerische Arbeiterpartei, Fédération fasciste, etc.
104. In 1942, 1,056 people were returned, 3,344 in 1943, 3,986 in 1944 and 1,365 in 1945. This return to the border (*Ausschaffung*) often meant death.
105. Known for his lecture tours in Switzerland, he obtained in 1933 a permit to stay for fifteen days. Following intervention from Swiss writers this was extended for a further two weeks.
106. Around Hans Teunberg, Walter Fisch (arrested by the police), Paul Betz and Conrad Blenke.
107. They had to carry antifascist literature in waterproof bags by swimming the Rhine. This was the work of the famous Transportkolonne Otto.
108. Some German contributors to these papers were expelled to France.
109. W. Mittenzwei, *Exil in der Schweitz*, p. 62.
110. Cf. Peter Stahlberger, *Der zürcher Verleger Emil Oprecht und die deutsche politische Emigration 1933–45*, Zurich 1970.
111. Oprecht published in particular the famous three-volume biography of Hitler written by Konrad Heiden, as well as Walter Rode's *Deutschland ist Caliban*, and *Der deutsche Charakter in der Geschichte Europas* by Erich Kahler. He also published essays by Hermann Rauschning and Alexander Emmerich, Ernst Bloch's *Heritage of Our Times* and essays by Heinrich Mann.
112. After 1940, many works published by Oprecht were banned or confiscated by the Swiss authorities. These included *Lied am Grenzpfahl*, a volume of poems by Hans Reinow, and the new edition of Hermann Rauschning's *Gespräche mit Hitler*.
113. In a letter to R. J. Humm, Hesse wrote in March 1933: 'I have at my house beds ready prepared, and I expect tomorrow the first guest who has escaped from Germany' (*Lettres*, Paris 1981, p. 71).
114. Erika Mann obtained British nationality by marriage to W. H. Auden.
115. These included ones at Leysin, Cossonay, Gordola, Murimoos, Oberglatt, Raron, Sugiez, Sumiswald and Vermes. A certain number of émigrés were also imprisoned under military guard. Manès Sperber, who had reached Switzerland illegally, gave himself up to the police in Zurich. He was interned in a holding camp under military

discipline, then in a labour camp: 'We slept on straw mattresses that became so damp and dirty that we regularly had to take then out into the courtyard to air, even in rain or snow; they had then to be carried back to the dormitory, where sleepers had only a narrow space between them [. . .]. The worst thing was the disdainful and brutally contemptuous tone in which the soldiers, NCOs and most of the officers spoke to the refugees. Doubtless they had received orders to treat us as leper.' (*Au-delà de l'oubli*, p. 210).

116. The German Social-Democrat Otto Krille, for example, former member of the Reichsbanner, and in charge of helping the children of émigrés, was arrested by the police in the dead of night. Though a sick man of sixty-two, he was given the choice of being sent to internment camp or deported back to Germany. He had in fact sent the daughter of a Swiss historian an *anti*-Communist manuscript on Hans Beimler, killed during the Spanish Civil War, but was accused of spreading KPD propaganda and influencing the children in his charge in favour of Communism. His case was discussed at a national level.

117. The role of German antifascists in the Spanish Civil War, and its significance for the exiles, will be examined below.

118. Cf. Silvia Schlenstedt, *Exil und antifaschistischer Kampf im Spanien*, Stuttgart 1981, pp. 191ff., and Alfred Kantorowicz, 'Die Exilsituation in Spanien', in *Die deutsche Exilliteratur*, pp. 90ff.

119. This was done by F. Arnau and R. Hausmann.

120. *Exil und antifaschistischer Kampf im Spanien*, pp. 197–8.

121. There were fifty or sixty of them, according to S. Schlenstedt; ibid., p. 200.

122. Karl Otten managed to leave Spain and reach Marseille on an English ship. He related his escape in his novel *Torquemadas Schatten*, Antwerp 1937–38.

123. Among them Günter Bodek, Ursula Amman, Werner Heilbrunn and Alexander Maas (cf. *Exil und antifaschistischer Kampf im Spanien*, p. 203).

124. The engineer Max Friedmann built schools, writers such as Ludwig Renn and Gustav Regler fought as soldiers or political commissars. Ludwig Renn became an officer. Hans Kahler trained Spanish cadres for the army.

125. This episode is traced from documents of the time in J.-M. Palmier and Maria Piscator, *Piscator et le théâtre politique*, Paris 1982.

126. Cited after S. Schlenstedt, *Exil und antifaschistischer Kampf im Spanien*, p. 236.

127. The history of the antifascist *Volksfront* is traced in Chapter 8.

128. Those in charge of the broadcasts were Communist exiles: Gerhart Eisler, Hans Teubner and Kurt Hager.

129. A certain number of these diaries and testimonies were subsequently published, for example those of Willi Bredel and Alfred Kantorowicz which count among the most well-known. Maria Osten published her *Reports from Spain* in Moscow in 1937. At the end of that year there appeared in Madrid *The History of the Thälmann Battalion*, reprinted in Oslo by Lise Linbeack in 1938. A large number of testimonies were also published by Max Hodann, Theodor Balk and Bodo Uhse. Kantorowicz published a history of the Chapaev battalion in Madrid in 1938, Willi Bredel one of the 11th Brigade in 1937. Important accounts of the Spanish war by antifascists include Arthur Koestler, *Spanish Testament*; Gustav Regler, *The Owl of Minerva*; and Hermann Kesten, *The Children of Guernica*.

130. Cf. *La Solidarité des peuples avec la république espagnole 1936–1939*, collective volume, Moscow 1974.

131. German emigration to the Scandinavian countries has been studied in comprehensive detail. See for example Helmut Müssener, *Exil in Schweden*, and 'Die Exilsituation in Skandinavien', in *Die deutsche Exilliteratur 1933–1945*, pp. 110ff. Also H. A. Walter, *Deutsche Exilliteratur*, second edition, pp. 57ff.

132. He was arrested and executed in 1941.

133. A strange writer, who made his living from building and repairing organs, Jahn settled on the island of Bornholm after having been driven out of Hamburg for his

stand against the Nazis in February 1932, when he gave a celebrated lecture: 'Vote for Hitler, vote for war'.

134. It was near Stockholm that Brecht wrote *Mother Courage and Her Children*, conceiving the leading role for the Swedish actress Naima Wilfstrand. In 1940 he moved to Finland where he wrote *Mr Puntila and His Man Matti*, then in 1941 he reached the United States, travelling via the USSR.

135. Walter A. Berendsohn relates in *Verbannung* (pp. 100ff.) the dramatic circumstances in which he had to flee Denmark. He first had to leave town without attracting the attention of German soldiers. The German exiles, in small groups, were taken charge of by sailors who ferried them in small boats to the Swedish coast. Besides the danger of encountering German patrols, there was also the problem of heavy waves that sometimes submerged their embarkation. The émigrés, for the most part unable to row, had to bale out water with their hats. The crossing took a good nine hours. On arrival in Sweden, they were met by the police who took them to a hotel and gave them dry clothes. Mathias Wegner (*Exil und Literatur. Deutsche Schriftsteller im Ausland 1933–1945*, Frankfurt 1968, p. 52) writes that German émigrés were often able to remain hidden in Denmark even after the German occupation, an agreement between the Danish government and the Reich providing for the protection of émigrés who had sought refuge there. This measure was only abolished in 1943 following acts of sabotage carried out by the Danish resistance. The Nazis then insisted on the death penalty for antifascists. Starting in November-December 1943, the Danish resistance movement helped a number of individuals threatened with arrest to leave for Sweden.

136. Willy Brandt first settled in Copenhagen with the Danish poet Oscar Hansen, then in Oslo. He was involved in support for the refugees and wrote articles for *Arbeiderbladet*, the Norwegian Socialist party's newspaper. Brandt learned Norwegian in three months. He had known the country since 1931, and found affinities between the SAP and the NAP, which had broken with the Comintern in 1923. He subsequently worked with a group of Norwegian intellectuals (Mot Dag). After studying history at the University of Oslo, he devoted himself to politics and journalism. Many witnesses attest that he had a considerable influence on Norwegian Socialist circles at this time.

137. In 1934 Sweden had 114,800 unemployed, the number falling to 18,200 in 1937, 16,200 in 1938, and 13,400 in 1940. Cf. H. Müssener, *Exil in Schweden*, p. 52.

138. In the 1936 elections they won 17,483 and 3,025 votes respectively.

139. *Exil in Schweden*, pp. 62–3 and 77–9.

140. Similar warnings about immigrant competition were launched by Swedish doctors. Foreign doctors would want to practise medicine, despite their failure to understand the 'Swedish psyche' and language.

141. Sweden's interest to Germany was in terms of armaments. The powerful Bofors factories belonged to Krupp, and the Junkers works had a Swedish division. Though these industries had been brought under state control in 1935, the Nazis maintained close relations with Sweden. Rudolf Hess and Hermann Göring (married to a Swede) visited the country often and spoke to the German community there. Sweden also had its own pro-Nazi movements, one of them led by Göring's brother-in-law. Assault sections were established on the German model, as well as a Nazi newspaper financed by German capital. After its bankruptcy, however, the director Dr Wellin had to take refuge in Germany.

142. Peter Weiss remained in Stockholm until his death on 10 May 1982. Born outside Berlin in 1916, the son of a Jewish industrialist, he stayed in England, Switzerland and Czechoslovakia before reaching Sweden. Known first of all as a painter, he directed films and documentaries, writing in German and Swedish, before devoting himself to the theatre.

143. Naima Wifstrand had translated *Señora Carrar's Rifles* into Swedish, and in March 1938 played the leading role under Hermann Greid's direction. Helene Weigel taught at the drama school run by this actress, who played the role of Mother

Courage, with Weigel as her mute daughter. Brecht's idea was that his wife could act in the Swedish production without having to speak.

144. Cf. Klaus Völker, *Bertolt Brecht. Eine Biographie*, Munich 1976, pp. 284ff.

145. Her brother and mother perished in concentration camp.

146. His younger brother, Alexander Weiss, also wrote in Swedish after 1945, without enjoying his brother's success. Peter Weiss only became famous as a German writer in 1964, with his *Marat-Sade*. A number of his texts were marked by the suffering and solitude of exile, for instance his *Aesthetik des Widerstandes*.

147. The manuscript of her book *In der Wohnungen des Todes* was taken to Germany by the actor Curt Trepte, and published in Berlin by Aufbau Verlag in 1947. *Sternverdunklung* appeared with Bermann Fischer in Amsterdam in 1949.

148. Many German writers who took refuge in Sweden were of course totally unknown. Publishers clearly preferred historical and political essays to novels or poetry. The cases of Hildegard Kaeser, who published ten novels in exile, or Herbert Connor, who managed to write in Swedish, were obviously exceptional.

149. *Asylpraxis und Lebensbedingungen*, vol. 2, p. 32.

150. Among the most damning testimonies: Margaret Buber-Neumann, *Under Two Dictators*, London 1949; Susanne Leonhard, *Gestohlne Leben. Schicksal einer politischen Emigranten in der Sowjetunion*, Frankfurt 1956; Waltraut Nicolas, *Die Kraft, das Ärgste zu ertragen. Frauenschicksale in Sowjetgefängnisse*, Bonn 1958.

151. In M. Durzak, ed., *Die deutsche Exilliteratur 1933–45*. It is true that the author of this study was a Polish Germanist, which perhaps explains the somewhat forced celebration of the USSR as the 'homeland of antifascist exiles' with a complete lack of reservations.

152. Besides the autobiographies cited above, cf. Ruth von Mayenburg, *Hotel Lux*, Munich 1981; Andreas W. Mytze, *Ernst Ottwalt*, Berlin 1981; Peter Diezel, *Exiltheater in der Sowjetunion 1932–1937*, Berlin 1978; and two issues of the magazine *Europäische Ideen* (14–16 and 34–36).

153. *Literatur im Exil*, Berlin 1966.

154. H. Willmann worked for the Foreign Workers' Publishing Cooperative; J. R. Becher edited *Internationale Literatur*; Alfred Kurella was in charge of a section of a large library.

155. On 29 September 1933, Litvinov declared before the Central Committee: 'We naturally sympathize with the sufferings of the German comrades, but we Communists are the last to let our policy be determined by sentiment.'

156. H. A. Walter cited as an example of this an anonymous article published in early summer 1933 in the *Neue Weltbühne*, expressing astonishment at the paucity of effort displayed by the USSR in coming to the aid of endangered émigrés. The author asked how a country of 180 million inhabitants, with 141 nationalities, could not find room for a thousand antifascists in danger of death.

157. A. Lacis mentions in his memoirs the desire of Walter Benjamin to emigrate to the Soviet Union. She dissuaded him and notes that 'to prepare a position for Benjamin in the USSR would not have been easy – a period of general distrust towards foreigners had begun'. Benjamin thanked her in a letter of 1935 for 'not giving him false illusions'.

158. 'Des machines allemandes pour construire le socialisme', cited by H. A. Walter, *Asylpraxis*, p. 135.

159. An echo of this disappointment with the conditions of asylum in the USSR can also be found in several émigré journals. For example *Das Neue Tagebuch* 6, of 9 February 1935, commenting on the explanation of this attitude in terms of the difficulty of finding decent housing for German Communist workers in the large industrial centres, as these would supposedly not have accepted the same conditions as Soviet citizens. The journal deemed this a plausible explanation, though it seems less so today, taking into account the situation of German workers in 1933 and the terror from which they fled.

160. Well before 1933, many German writers and artists had visited the Soviet Union, invited by Soviet cultural organizations or by Lunacharsky himself. The impressions they brought back were generally very favourable. A few examples would be A. Holitscher, H. Kesten, B. Lask, E. E. Kisch, F. C. Weiskopf, B. Frei, H. Lorbeer, L. Renn, O. Heller, F. Rubiner, F. Jung and L. von Koerber. In the Weimar period a number of technicians and scientists, not necessarily all won to Communist ideas, went to work in the USSR. According to K. Jarmatz, at least 20,000 workers and specialists were already there in 1932.

161. The story of this strange Comintern hotel has been told by Ernst Fischer's companion Ruth von Mayenburg in her book *Hotel Lux*. She traces a fairly sinister and Kafkaesque portrait of it. Manès Sperber reports in a similar vein: 'Anna Seghers and I had heard J. R. Becher, forced to leave his Paris exile for Moscow, but who returned often to France, describe in a fit of cynicism that he pleasantly combined with black humour, how certain comrades lived, especially the functionaries of the German Communist party installed at the Hotel Lux. Each was careful not to compromise himself with a friend whom the police might possibly come and arrest during the night' (*Au-delà de l'oubli*, p. 109). W. Leonhard asserted that the Hotel Lux was 'a world unto itself'. It housed the majority of Comintern members and a certain number of émigrés. Every kind of business could be carried out at the hotel, which had its shops and polyclinic as well as housing representatives of the police and army. After the dissolution of the Comintern, special buses continued to ferry Communist cadres from the Hotel Lux to the different organizations that employed them. Famous occupants of the Hotel Lux included Wilhelm Pieck, Walter Ulbricht, Anton Ackermann, Anna Pauker, Heinz Neumann, J. Berman, Ernö Gerö, Louis Fürnberg, Ernst Fischer and F. Honner as well as writers, children of émigrés and even Spanish refugees.

162. Cf. M. Buber-Neumann, *Under Two Dictators*, p. 10.

163. The conditions of life of the majority of Soviet citizens were scarcely favorable for the reception of German émigrés. Many Moscow families nonetheless shared an apartment of 25 square metres with one or two exiles.

164. The majority of exile accounts confirm the negative descriptions of Margaret Buber-Neumann. Once their passport was taken away they felt that they were prisoners. Klaus Jarmatz, in his presentation of the exile experience in the Soviet Union (*Literatur im Exil*) does give a very complete account of émigré activity, but omits to mention that the majority perished in labour camps after 1938. Jarmatz mentions the arrest of Ernst Ottwalt, but gives not the slightest explanation for his disappearance.

165. Among the most well-known of these, *Hundert Tage illegaler Kampf*; *Die illegale Presse der KPD im Bild und Wort im Kampf gegen die faschistische Diktatur*; *Kampf deutscher revolutionärer Dichter gegen den Faschismus*; *Zeit der Entscheidung*. Several works by German exiles which had been burned on 10 May 1933 were accessible only in Soviet editions, for example the novels of Willi Bredel.

166. Besides the German national minorities (the Volga Germans in particular) there were the German workers employed in the USSR in the context of the first Five-Year Plan. The 1930s also saw the publication of the *Deutsche Zentralzeitung*, a particular rich forum for émigré debates between 1933 and 1939. This was read by many émigrés outside the USSR.

167. For its first year after its foundation in June 1931, the magazine was published under the title *Literatur der Weltrevolution*, then twice a month from 1933 and monthly from 1935. Established after the famous Congress of Proletarian Writers at Kharkov, it was initially designed to inform Russian readers about foreign literature. The subtitle *Deutsche Blätter* was added to the German edition in 1937. Articles on fascism included A. Gabor, 'Das Kulturprogramm des Faschismus' (3/1933), F. Wolf, 'Die Dramatik des deutschen Faschismus' (8/1936) and J. R. Becher, 'Deutsche Lehre' (4/1943).

168. *Manifeste des Nationalkomitees 'Freies Deutschland' an die Wehrmacht und das deutsche Volk.*

169. Cf. H. Haarmann, I. Schirmer, D. Walach, *Das 'Engels' Projekt. Ein antifaschistisches Theater*, Worms 1975. On the specific role of Piscator, cf. Maria Piscator and J.-M. Palmier, *Erwin Piscator et le théâtre politique*.

170. Brecht's attitude towards the USSR was always fairly critical and ambiguous. He visited there in 1932 but did not share the enthusiasm that gripped so many German writers. In 1935 he was received by Piscator in Moscow at the Foreign Workers' Club where a number of Berlin agitprop actors were staying. He met his friend Carola Neher, as well as Bernhard Reich and S. Tretyakov. Some of his plays were already known to the Soviet public, and at Lunacharsky's request, Tairov had staged *Die Dreigroschenoper*, though very badly and to Brecht's diapproval. In general, his work seemed too bold for a Soviet audience. Brecht returned to the USSR in 1936, while Tretyakov was translating other plays of his and Nikolai Okhlopov considered staging *St Joan of the Stockyards*. His relations with the Moscow exiles were fairly bad; he quarrelled with the Hungarian playwright Julius Hay, and had scant appreciation for the German émigrés there, as shown by his reactions to the great argument on expressionism and his remarks to Walter Benjamin. It should be noted that Brecht did not publish his response to Lukács's articles on realism and formalism until much later, after his return from exile – for fear that he might end up having to live in Moscow. At this time he rejected the idea, emphasizing that he was not sure of finding work, either for himself or for Helene Weigel. His real reticence, however, was clearly political. He wrote in his *Journals* in January 1939: 'koltsov too arrested in moscow. my last connection there. nobody knows anything about tretiakov, who is supposed to have been a "japanese spy". nobody knows anything about neher who is supposed to have done some business for the trotskyists in prague on her husband's instructions. reich and asya lacis don't write to me any more, and grete gets no answer from her acquaintances in the caucasus or leningrad. béla kun too is arrested, the only one of the politicians i saw. meyerhold has lost his theatre, but is supposed to be allowed to direct opera. literature and art are up the creek, political theory has gone to the dogs' (p. 20).

171. According to Horst Dühnke, *Die KPD von 1933 bis 1945*, Cologne 1972, four members of the KPD's exiled political bureau fell victim to Stalin's terror, together with ten members of its central committee, fifteen high functionaries, and several hundred militants. Up to 70 per cent of German Communist émigrés in the USSR suffered arrest or deportation.

172. On the details of these arrests, cf. M. Buber-Neumann, *Under Two Dictators*.

173. The majority of Polish antifascists in the USSR were executed, along with almost all the Comintern's Polish cadres. The same went for writers. Bruno Jasienski, author of *Ich verbrenne Paris. Der Mensch verändert die Haut*, died in a camp as a 'Trotskyist' in 1942, together with Domski. Boris Lewytsky recalls in *Vom rotem Terror zur sozialistischen Gesetzlichkeit*, Munich 1961, pp. 94–5, how in 1942 a conference of Communist cadres was called in Moscow, to include almost all members of the Polish central committee. On arrival at the frontier, they were immediately arrested and shot. Vera Kostrewa, a party veteran, perished under interrogation in a Moscow prison. A large number of Polish Socialists who had been imprisoned in Poland managed to reach the USSR following an exchange, but were executed in 1937. The Yugoslavs were also cruelly affected. Karlo Steiner, who relates how Tito asked Khrushchev to release the survivors, wrote an astonishing book that traces his own fate, *7000 jours en Sibérie*, Paris 1983.

174. It is not easy to establish a complete list of German Communist victims of Stalin's terror. The most well-known include Hugo Eberlein, the German delegate to the founding congress of the Comintern, Hermann Remmele and Heinz Neumann, members of the political bureau, Leo Flieg, the organization secretary, Hans Klippenberger, head of the KPD's military section, Willi Leow, head of the Red Front combatants, August Kreuzburg and Hermann Schubert, members of the central committee, and Willy Koska, head of the German Rote Hilfe. Besides cadres, a significant number of journalists and editors were also arrested: the editor-

in-chief of *Rote Fahne*, Heinrich Susskind, and Werner Hirsch, the journalists Alfred Rebe and Beutling, H. Kurella (brother of Alfred Kurella), former editor of the *Ruhr-Echo* and then head of the defence committee for Ernst Thälmann in Paris, Nikolaus Birkenhauer, former editor of *Rotes Aufbauen*, and Kurt Sauerland. Others who perished included Fritz Schulte, Paul Dietrich, Felix Halle, Johannes Ludwig and Gerhard Gluck.

175. Cf. David Pike, *Deutsche Schriftsteller im sowjetischen Exil*, pp. 417ff.
176. Arthur Koestler and Julius Hay relate the improbable fate of Elga Schweiger, who lost her job and was arrested because an informer had told the police that in the way she arranged the ashtrays on which she was designing decorative motifs for a Leningrad factory, a swastika could be discerned.
177. A number of Ottwalt's writings were republished in the GDR after 1968. Cf. A. W. Mytze, *E. Ottwalt*, Berlin 1977. Ottwalt's wife, Waltraut Nicolas, described her investigation into the fate of her husband in *Viele Tausende Tage*, Stuttgart 1960. It was ironic that the Soviet prosecutor at Nuremberg, R. Rudenko, should cite antifascist texts of Ottwalt's in support of his accusations. When Ottwalt's wife wrote to the general to ask why Ottwalt had been detained in a camp, she did not receive a reply. The Red Cross established that Ottwalt had died on 24 April 1943 at Archangelsk on the Arctic Sea. In his novel *Ruhe und Ordnung*, Ottwalt had written: 'If I have to die, I at least want to know why.'
178. His daughter, Sina Walden, investigated her father's fate in Moscow in 1966, and was told for the first time of her father's decease. Cf. 'Nachricht über meinem Vater', *E.I.*, vol. 14/15, 1976, p. 14.
179. Cf. Rudolf Rocker, 'Der Leidensweg von Zenzl Mühsam', *E.I.*, vol. 34/36, pp. 10ff.
180. *Under Two Dictators*, p. 153.
181. Cited from *E.I.*, vol. 14/15, p. 61.
182. For a long while ignored and even repressed, this history of German antifascist emigration in France has been the subject of a good number of detailed works in recent years. The most important of these were published under the direction of Gilbert Badia, who was the first to form interdisciplinary research teams on the subject. In the context of this collective work, the following books were successively published: *Les Barbelés de l'exil*, Grenoble 1970; *Exilés en France. Souvenirs d'antifascistes allemands émigrés 1933–1945*, Paris 1982; *Les Bannis d'Hitler. Acceuil et lutte des éxilés allemands en France 1933–1939*, Paris 1984. From an earlier period we should mention the monograph by Ruth Fabian and Corinna Coulmas, *Die deutsche Emigration in Frankreich nach 1933*, Munich 1978. The volume by Hanna Schramm and Barbara Vormeier, *Vivre à Gurs. Un camp de concentration français 1940–1941*, is an exemplary study on the repressive legislation affecting the émigrés. More political, finally, is the study by Ursula Lankau-Alex, *Volksfront für Deutschland?*, Frankfurt 1977, which takes a particularly interesting approach to the attempt in France to form a German Popular Front. Recent years have also seen the publication in several languages of autobiographies or novels by émigrés, such as Klaus Mann's *The Turning Point* and Lion Feuchtwanger's *The Devil in France*, enabling readers without a knowledge of German to retrace their story. Undoubtedly the often infamous treatment to which these antifascists were subjected was responsible for the strange amnesia that prevailed towards them for a long time. For a detailed study of the vicissitudes of this emigration, I would recommend all these works. My debt to the research of Gilbert Badia, Hélène Roussel, Jacques Omnès, Jean-Baptiste Joly and Jean-Philippe Mathieu is immense.
183. The number of German refugees did not vary greatly up to the War. The arrival in 1935 of 5,000 to 6,000 refugees from the Saar, then in 1938 of Austrians after the *Anschluss*, was offset by the departure of many refugees for the United States, South America and Palestine. It should be noted that the total is quite modest when one considers that at this time France counted 580,000 Poles, 490,000 Spaniards, 800,000 Italians and 30,000 Germans who were not refugees.

184. Fred Uhlman wrote in *The Making of an Englishman* (pp. 137–8): 'Paris was the obvious choice for me. Most of the expatriated German intellectuals and artists went there. The politicians mainly went to Prague, and the businessmen to London. Since 1830 France had always been regarded by liberal-minded Germans as the home of political and religious liberty [. . .]. And as the frontiers of France stood wide open I was in no doubt as to where I should go.'

185. Cf. G. Badia, 'L'émigration en France, ses conditions et ses problèmes', in *Les Barbelés de l'exil*, p. 15. Badia notes that three-quarters of the émigrés fell into the age range of twenty-five to forty, while 60 per cent were under thirty. Only 0.6 per cent were over sixty years old.

186. G. Badia reports a statistic from the ministry of the interior that mentions 6,320 refugees in the Paris region in August 1933, and 7,304 by November.

187. As well as Socialists, these included monarchist supporters of Otto von Habsburg.

188. *Volksfront für Deutschland?*, pp. 40–2.

189. The German émigrés included a number of French-speakers: Walter Benjamin, Heinrich Mann, E. E. Noth, Alfred Kerr, Alfred Döblin and Carl Einstein.

190. *Les Nouvelles Littéraires*, for example, regularly published accounts of the book burnings and repression against writers. This weekly had a permanent correspondent in Berlin, and gave voice to several opponents of the Nazis such as E. E. Noth, Ricarda Huch and Egon Erwin Kisch.

191. Even if persecuted, German Jews for many French people were still *boches*.

192. This committee included two Germans, Willi Münzenberg and B. Schulz, and campaigned first of all in support of those accused in the Reichstag fire trial.

193. In particular that of Gabriel Péri, 28 March 1933. Cf. G. Badia, *Les Barbelés de l'exil*, pp. 24–5.

194. *Journal officiel*, 1933, p. 1893, cited by G. Badia, ibid.

195. All the same, as Gilbert Badia emphasizes, the visa was valid only for two months and the safe-conduct for twenty days. Besides, any political activity was forbidden 'on pain of immediate expulsion'.

196. It was precisely these articles that were the pride of *Gringoire* and its disturbing success. Cf. Jean Butin, *Henri Béraud. Sa longue marche de la Gerbe d'or au pain noir*, Paris 1979.

197. *Les Barbelés de l'exil*, pp. 27ff.

198. G. Badia has established that one refugee in ten was refused residence from autumn 1933 on.

199. *Les Barbelés de l'exil*, pp. 27ff.

200. All that was promised these refugees was a permit to work if they managed to find a job. If their passports were not valid or no longer recognized by certain countries, they were given a Nansen passport.

201. *Les Barbelés de l'exil*, p. 55.

202. In 1937, Münzenberg was replaced by Siegfried Rädel. The German members of the commission were appointed by the Fédération des Émigrés d'Allemagne en France, an association of twenty-one émigré organizations.

203. Cited by G. Badia, *Les Barbelés de l'exil*, p. 59. This circular may be interpreted as a concession to the right-wing press and its campaign against 'German spies' and 'undesirable elements' pressing against the French borders.

204. The total for 1937; cf. *Les Barbelés de l'exil*, ibid.

205. This hardening of attitude towards the émigrés will be analysed below.

206. On the operation of this committee, see the study by J. B. Joly in *Les Bannis de Hitler*, pp. 37ff. I have drawn on this work for much historical data.

207. One of its directors, the senator Henry Bérenger, represented France at the League of Nations on all questions concerning German refugees.

208. Robert de Rothschild especially disapproved of the orientation taken by Pierre Dreyfus's Comité de Défense and Bernard Lecache's Ligue Internationale Contre l'Antisémitisme, many of whose members were Jews from Eastern Europe.

209. Cited by J. B. Joly in *Les Bannis de Hitler*, p. 44.

210. Neither Victor Basch, president of the Ligue des Droits de l'Homme, nor Pierre Dreyfus, was a member.

211. J. B. Joly sums up the situation very well: 'If French Jews ultimately did concern themselves with the German émigrés [. . .] this was no more than verbally, and above all to maintain a situation of monopolistic influence within the different Jewish communities in France and to avoid political demonstrations of which they feared they would ultimately be the victims.' (*Les Bannis de Hitler*, p. 45).

212. J. B. Joly makes the point that though 51 per cent of German émigrés were considered political victims, only 19 per cent of Polish Jews were given this classification.

213. Between October 1933 and February 1934, only 293 émigrés out of 1,397 new arrivals were taken up by the committee (cf. *Les Bannis de Hitler*, p. 47). The financing of the refugee aid was effected in large part by American Jewish committees and the Universal Israelite Allliance.

214. Described by Feuchtwanger in his novel *Exile*.

215. Cf. Jacques Omnès, 'L'accueil des émigrés politiques (1933–1938). L'exemple du Secours Rouge, de la Ligue des droits de l'homme et du parti socialiste', in *Les Bannis de Hitler*, pp. 65ff.

216. These included for instance members of the German Human Rights League, as well republicans, Socialists and pacifists.

217. All information here unless otherwise noted is taken from the study by J. Omnès.

218. On the details of this commission, cf. Marcel Livian, *Le Parti socialiste et l'immigration. Le gouvernement Léon Blum, la main-d'œuvre immigrée et les réfugiés politiques (1920–1940)*, Paris 1982.

219. Its existence was very precarious and it was closed down in March 1934, doubtless owing to political differences between its members. The help of the SFIO was generally less effective than that of Secours Rouge, which managed to achieve significant mobilizations in support of the refugees,

220. J. Omnès, 'L'accueil des émigrés politiques', p. 72. One example is when German refugees housed in a Strasbourg barracks were sent back to the Saarland frontier in June 1935.

221. Set up in 1923 and controlled by the Communist International, the aim of International Red Aid was to defend 'victims of class struggle' in material, legal and moral terms. The French section had 35,000 members in 1933.

222. In 1935 the Paris prefect of police, Chiappe, maintained: 'It goes without saying that I will not tolerate any intrusion of these Germans into our political life, any more than their participation in any form whatsoever in the atrocious campaign of conscientious objectors. No more will I accept that they should demonstrate or plot in our country against the present government of Germany. Any of them who is tempted to do so will be expelled from our borders within twenty-four hours' (cited from *Les Bannis de Hitler*, p. 70).

223. J. Omnès, 'L'accueil des émigrés politiques', p. 73.

224. Ibid., p. 82.

225. On the detailed development of these aid groups, cf. *Les Bannis de Hitler*, in particular J. Omnès's analyses, which are notable for their documentation and precision.

226. On the academic emigration in France, see J. P. Mathieu in *Les Bannis de Hitler*, pp. 133ff.

227. H. R. Lottmann, *Rive Gauche*, Paris 1981.

228. Gide, for example, wrote in his *Journal* on 27 July 1931: 'I should like to cry aloud my affection for Russia' (vol. 3, p. 179). And on 23 April 1932: 'And if my life were necessary to ensure the success of the USSR, I should give it at once . . .' (p. 232).

229. E. E. Noth, *Mémoires d'un Allemand*, p. 25.

230. Marcel supported the émigrés without sharing their ideas. At this time he was closely linked linked to Thierry Maulnier and J. Benoit-Mechin.

231. E. Dabit, who took part in many meetings with German émigrés, published in *Europe* a review of Noth's novel *L'Enfant écartelé*.

232. G. Regler, *Le Glaive et le fourreau*, p. 229. [This passage does not appear in the English edition of *The Owl of Minerva*.]
233. Clara Malraux, *Voici que vient l'été*, Paris 1973, p. 207.
234. M. Sperber, *Au-delà de l'oubli*, p. 58.
235. A. Koestler, *The Invisible Writing*, p. 302.
236. M. Sperber, *Au-delà de l'oubli*, p. 144.
237. André Gide, *Littérature engagée*, Paris 1950.
238. Ideological oppositions only became unbridgeable a few years later. At this time, Drieu la Rochelle and Malraux still saw one another. Lucien Combelle, Gide's secretary, also kept on terms with Drieu. Robert Brasillach was an admirer of André Chamson.
239. Kurella and Thirion met for the first time in spring 1931. Cf. A. Thirion, *Révolutionnaires sans révolution*, Paris 1972, pp. 308ff.
240. Along with Franz Werfel's novel *Barbara oder die Frommigkeit*, and E. von Salomon's *Die Geachteten*.
241. The interviewer was Vladimir Pozner.
242. 'Far more than used to be the case in Berlin, you sense in Paris the rhythm of a metropolis where lines of force emanating from all points of the globe meet up and cross' (M. Sperber, *Au-delà de l'oubli*, p. 82). E. E. Noth wrote in similar vein: 'The French capital was naturally also the capital of world literature' (*Mémoirs d'un Allemand*, p. 122).
243. Cited by Babette Gross, *Willi Münzenberg. Eine politische Biographie*, Stuttgart 1967, p. 254.
244. M. Sperber, *Au-dela de l'oubli*, p. 77.
245. A. Koestler, *The Invisible Writing*, p. 302.
246. E. E. Noth, *Mémoires d'un Allemand*, p. 252.
247. L. Marcuse, *Autobiographie*, p. 181.
248. Cf. the article by Gert Korinthenberg in the *Hannoverscher Allgemeine*, 25 May 1983.
249. Close links had been formed before 1933 between the KPD and PCF. Meetings had been held in both Paris and Berlin in which Ernst Thälmann and Maurice Thorez took part.
250. Noske and Severing accommodated themselves to the Nazi regime, while Breitscheid and Hilferding were arrested by the Gestapo. Otto Wels died in France.
251. These included the ISK (Internationaler Sozialistischer Kampfbund), the SAP (Sozialistische Arbeiterpartei), the Links Opposition, the KPD-Opposition and the Trotskyists.
252. German and French Communists worked together on the Thälmann committee, even though no émigré took part officially, on the World Committee against War and Fascism, International Red Aid and International Workers' Aid.
253. Cf. Gilbert Badia, *Les Barbelés de l'exil*, p. 47.
254. This was in fact first set up in Paris, then moved to Prague, subsequently back to Paris and finally Moscow. In May 1933, the KPD delegated to Paris Wilhelm Pieck, W. Florin and Franz Dahlem, members of its political bureau.
255. The Comintern seems to have encouraged this aid to the Socialists, doubtless hoping to win them over the KPD influence. Cf. *Volksfront für Deutschland?*, p. 52.
256. This was located at 1 rue Mondétour, then at 83 boulevard du Montparnasse, the headquarters of International Workers' Aid.
257. Jacques Omnès has carried out a deeper study of this question.
258. Cf. A. Thirion, *Révolutionnaires sans révolution*, on the role of Alfred Kurella and for discussion of the differences between Thorez and Doriot.
259. The most far-reaching studies at the present time are those of J. Omnès.
260. G. Badia suggests (*Les Barbelés de l'exil*, pp. 40–41) that it was the strength of the PCF and the tightening of links between the French and German Communist parties that explains this decision. Indeed, on 2 December 1932 a joint public meeting had been held at the Salle Bullier in Paris, at which Thorez and Thälmann

called for the abrogation of the Versailles treaty, the complete liberation of the German people, the self-determination of the peoples of Alsace-Lorraine, and unity with the German proletariat. On 15 January 1933, Thorez developed the same themes in Berlin.

261. They did however meet in 1937 and 1938, and more frequently up to the War. Dahlem attended the PCF's Arles congress (25–29 December 1937).
262. Cf. Michel Bilis, *Socialistes et pacifistes 1933–1939*, Paris 1979, pp. 20ff.
263. Both were Jewish and from Alsace. Grumbach had been a *Vorwärts* reporter before 1914. Weill had been an SPD member for fifteen years and had worked together with Kurt Eisner. For three years he had been a Reichstag deputy.
264. This functioned under the responsibility of the party secretariat, and was presided over by Jules Moch. It had no legal existence, but a certain number of deputies and lawyers joined it.
265. The Matteoti Committee had been formed in 1926. Salomon Grumbach was the Socialist party's official representative on this committee.
266. On all these questions, cf. Marcel Livian, *Le Parti socialiste et l'immigration*, Paris 1981, pp. 24ff.
267. Early in 1934, jurists on the Immigration Commission submitted to the Socialist party the project of creating a *Revue pratique de droit* devoted to legislation bearing on foreigners (ibid., p. 51).
268. Ibid., p. 59.
269. Above all, arbitrary expulsion practically ceased under the Blum government.
270. M. Livian, *Le Parti socialiste et l'immigration*, p. 154 (internment of R. Liebknecht, Lion Feuchtwanger, etc.).
271. Some forty or so political publicists were exiled in Paris, including Georg Bernhard, R. Breitscheid, H. Budzislawski, W. Eildermann, G. Eisler, B. Frei, E. E. Kisch, H. Buckhardt, G. Markscheffel, A. Maslow, A. Norden, M. Scheer, M. Schroeder, H. Stenitz, A. Weingarten and P. Westheim.
272. Cf. *Exil in Frankreich*, p. 78. Its editorial team included Bernhard Kurt Caro, Hans Jacob and Fritz Woll. Among its contributors were Henri Barbusse, Romain Rolland, E. Benes, L. Renn, O. M. Graf, Heinrich Mann, K. Heiden and H. von Gerlach. Its orientation was 'bourgeois liberal'.
273. Cf. *Exil in Frankreich*, p. 81.
274. Noth also contributed to the *Cahiers de Sud*, and was close to its director Jean Ballard. He wrote in *Nouvelles Littéraires* as well as in *Vendredi, Europe, Europe Nouvelle* and *Temps Présents*. Noth found it more useful to discuss Nazism, Germany and Hitler in the French press than in that of the exiles.
275. Besides the proceedings of the Congress for the Defence of Culture in 1935, *Commune* also included beween 1935 and 1937 contributions and texts by a number of German émigrés, including Alfred Kantorowicz, Gustav Regler, Ludwig Renn, Theodor Plievier, Anna Seghers, Bertolt Brecht, E. E. Kisch, Alfred Kurella, Erwin Piscator and Wieland Herzfelde.
276. Issued in book form under the title *Propos d'exil. La Dépêche de Toulouse*, 1983.
277. In *Les Barbelés de l'exil*, pp. 357ff.
278. On the history and operation of these publishing houses, see Hélène Roussel's excellent study already cited.
279. We shall return to the history of the INFA further on. Cf. the study by Jacques Omnès in *Les Bannis de Hitler*, pp. 185ff.
280. Ibid., pp. 193.
281. On the different hypotheses as to its disappearance, see the study by Jacques Omnès cited above, pp. 197–8.
282. On its history, cf. Gilbert Badia, 'Le Comité Thaelmann', in *Les Bannis de Hitler*, pp. 199ff.
283. Ibid., p. 211. All the historical details here are taken from this study.
284. Workers' delegates from the Saar were able to talk to him under surveillance; cf. 'Le Comité Thaelmann', p. 222.

285. Ibid., p. 236.
286. *Rundschau* 27, p. 1360; 20 June 1935. Cited after G. Badia, 'Le Comité Thaelmann', p. 245.
287. G. Badia explains (ibid., p. 247) how in September 1935 the Communist activist Alfred Benjamin was arrested on the place de la République, then imprisoned and expelled from France, for having 'appealed in the neighbourhood of the Bourse for solidarity towards the leader of a Berlin transport union who had been arrested by the Gestapo and was under threat of death'.
288. Ibid., p. 249.
289. The intellectual cover was all the more useful in that the French government was far from approving all these demonstrations. G. Badia cites for example the story of an exhibition on the Third Reich organized by the Thälmann committee in 1938, at 10 rue de Lancry, showing photographs, caricatures and documentary placards. An album titled *Cinq ans de dictature hitlérienne* was also on sale, devoted to the Nazi persecution of artists and intellectuals. The prefecture of police had a permanent observer at the exhibition. The German ambassador tried to have it banned at the start, protesting against certain documents and photographs as well as the album mentioned above. The prefect of police demanded the withdrawal of these incriminating documents and banned the sale of the album. It was indicated in the exhibition that these documents had been suppressed on the intervention of the German embassy. The police then had the word 'German embassy' erased. G. Badia depicts the perplexity that the police commissioner in charge of the affair experienced when it transpired that one of the banned photographs was of Hitler in a top hat shaking the hand of Hindenburg. This photo had been published in 1934, in an official Nazi album, which was then sold at a neighbouring café. When the embassy made further protests, the quai d'Orsay again complied. Cf. G. Badia, 'Heurs et malheurs d'une exposition sur le IIIe Reich', in *Les Bannis de Hitler*, pp. 261ff.
290. Ibid., p. 256; also G. Badia, 'Une tentative de Front populaire allemand à Paris (1935–1938)', *Cahiers d'Histoire de l'Institut de recherches marxistes* 2, Oct.–Dec. 1981, p. 99.
291. The committee had its office at the home of the émigré writer Rudolf Leonhard; cf. G. Badia, 'Une tentative . . .', p. 104.
292. The vicissitudes of the *Volksfront* and the reasons for its failure are analysed in Chapter 8.
293. Musil took part in some debates, but rejected the prominent role that the organizers wished to confer on him as a spokesman of exile literature. André Breton had been excluded, though his communication was read by Paul Eluard. Breton had apparently struck Ilya Ehrenburg in a café, accusing him of having slandered the surrealists in his book *Vu par un écrivain d'URSS*. Ehrenburg denounced this as a 'fascist' action, and the Soviet delegation threatened to leave.
294. Cf. *Les Bannis de Hitler*, p. 365; 'Exil in Frankreich', pp. 139ff.
295. Its history will be analysed in Chapter 7.
296. Already in 1933 the IAA held more than 200,000 press cuttings.
297. See the study by Jean-Philippe Mathieu in *Les Bannis de Hitler*, pp. 133ff.
298. The total number of émigré scientists in France varied between one and two hundred. Prominent figures in the French teaching world who came to their assistance included André Honorat, J. Bédier, A. Mayer, P. Langevin, S. Lévi, C. Bouglé, P. Rivet, P. Boyer, E. Tonnelat, J. Perrin, A. Colville, P. Renouvin, A. Lichtenberger, E. Vermeil, L. Lévy-Bruhl and M. Halbwachs.
299. Cf. J. P. Mathieu, in *Les Bannis de Hitler*, pp. 163ff.
300. Cf. the study by Hélène Roussel in *Les Bannis de Hitler*, pp. 327ff.
301. Contacts had been established with French Trotskyist activists, including Maurice Nadaud, P. Voglein and Daniel Guérin, as well as such figures as Elie Faure and Jean Langevin.
302. Cf. Hélène Roussel in *Les Bannis de Hitler*, pp. 334ff.

303. Radvanyi had been one of the directors of MASCH in Berlin.
304. Participation was two francs per session for the People's University, and three francs for the Free German University (H. Roussel, *Les Bannis de Hitler*, p. 337).
305. A large number of German academics exiled in France, from a range of different disciplines, contributed to it. It even planned an article by Walter Benjamin on 'Hegel's Concept of Matter'.
306. Cf. Martin Jay, *The Dialectical Imagination*, London 1973, p. 29.
307. Not that Bouglé shared the Institute's convictions. He belonged to the Radical-Socialists and was marked by the ideas of Proudhon. But having studied in Germany, he was very concerned by National Socialism.
308. In the Camille Demouslins cellar at the Palais Royal, then in 1936 at Raymond Duncan's, rue de Seine, and in 1937 again at the Palais Royal.
309. Among those French actors most remembered today: F. Lemarque, Léon Noel, and Y. Deniau. Cf. *Les Bannis de Hitler*, p. 376; 'Exil in Frankreich', pp. 283–4.
310. Helene Weigel came to Paris from Copenhagen to interpret the role of Señora Carrar. Despite the precarious conditions of work and existence, the actors managed to achieve a genuine production under the direction of Slatan Dudow, even if the chairs had been bought at the flea market. The play was staged on 16 and 17 October 1937 at the Salle Adyar, accompanied by René Clair's film *Le Dernier Milliardaire* and a recital of Brecht songs by Helene Weigel. The eight scenes of *Fear and Misery of the Third Reich* had been produced at the initiative of the SDS in the Salle d'Iéna, also under Dudow's direction. These all seem to have enjoyed a genuine success.
311. *Les Criminels* was produced in Paris in 1929 by the Pitoëff company, followed by *Le Mal de la jeunesse* in 1932, *Les Races* was staged in 1934 at the Théâtre de l'Œuvre.
312. See E. J. Aufricht, *Erzähle, damit du dein Recht erweist*, Munich 1969, pp. 109–18.
313. Geron was subsequently arrested and murdered by the Gestapo while trying to reach the Netherlands.
314. Luck had it that he won enough in the National Lottery to buy six cows (*Erzähle, damit du dein Recht erweist*, p. 126).
315. Even though he was a member of the Croix de Feu.
316. With the slogan: 'Madame wants to go to the theatre, Monsieur to the cinema; they both go to the Théâtre Pigalle.'
317. Cf. *Les Bannis de Hitler*, p. 373.
318. See Laszlo Glozes, *Wolf photographe*, Centre Georges Pompidou, 1980.
319. For instance the closure of the Bauhaus, and the impossibility of exhibiting paintings influenced by Dadaism, expressionism, futurism, Neue Sachlichkeit or abstract art, led to the departure of many artists. Some were directly threatened by virtue of their political commitment, especially if they had contributed to antifascist propaganda. Others saw their status of artists rejected, and were termed 'judeo-bolshevik'.
320. A certain number of artists also departed for Prague (especially satirists or Dadaists such as Wieland Herzfelde), moving later to England or the United States.
321. A number of German painters and critics had stayed in Paris from the early 1920s. The critic and poet Carl Einstein had settled in France and was a friend of Braque and Picasso. Many of these exiles have been unjustly forgotten. A large part of the work of Max Raphael was written in France. Though his aesthetic writings have been republished and commented on in Germany, these works of his Paris period have not been collected for publication. Paul Westheim, a famous art critic who emigrated to Paris, has been likewise forgotten.
322. The Third Reich's policy on art was implemented far less rapidly than that in literature. While books were burned in May 1933, exhibitions of 'degenerate art' only started in 1937, even if academies and museums had been 'purified' much sooner.

323. Cf. Hélène Roussel, *Les Bannis de Hitler*, p. 291; also *Widerstand statt Anpassung. Deutsche Kunst im Widerstand gegen den Faschismus 1933–1945*, Berlin 1980.
324. The Heartfield exhibition in Prague was violently attacked by the Nazis, who demanded the withdrawal of a number of works. Heartfield was then invited to exhibit in Paris by the Association of Revolutionary Artists and Writers, and *150 photomontages d'actualité* were presented in the rue de Navarin. Tristan Tzara, L. Moussinac and Louis Aragon attended the inauguration.
325. Fred Uhlmann, a lawyer, started his career as a painter in Paris before becoming a writer in England.
326. It should be noted that the artistic direction of the International Exhibition Against Fascism organized by the INFA from 9 to 15 March 1935 was entrusted to Frans Masereel, who also worked with young German artists. During the exhibition, émigré German painters also took part in the finishing of the Peace Pavilion.
327. Cf. Hélène Roussel, *Les Bannis de Hitler*, p. 292. Among the painters exhibited there were Wollheim, Isenburger, Schülein, Lipmann-Wulf, Edith Auerbach, Eugénie Fuchs and Käthe Münzer. Some of these were quite well known, others less so. The following year, the committee presented work by seventeen artists.
328. The painters participating included H. Lohmar, A. Hermann, K. Hagen, H. Kiwitz, H. Kralik and E. Öhl. *Les Bannis de Hitler*, p. 295.
329. Ibid., p. 297; Dieter Schiller, *Exil in Frankreich*, pp. 317ff.
330. H. Roussel, *Les Bannis de Hitler*, p. 298.
331. Ibid., pp. 298–9.
332. On the debates over this exhibition, see ibid., pp. 300–1.
333. Among the French artists, or artists living in France, who signed Westheim's protest, were Masereel, Zadkine, Matisse, Dufy and Lipchitz.
334. The very name of the exhibition, 'Banned Art', was changed to 'Twentieth-Century German Art'. H. Roussel notes that 'the most lively reaction [. . .] came from Oskar Kokoschka, Max Ernst and Gert Wollheim, who as a sign of protest forbade their canvases from being shown unless the British committee agreed to exhibit Kokoschka's "Portrait of a Man" which the Gestapo had just slashed in Vienna after the *Anschluss*' (*Les Bannis de Hitler*, p. 307).
335. The elected bureau also included Heinz Lohmar, Paul Westheim, Gert Wollheim, Victor Tischler, Max Ernst and Sabin Spiro.
336. *Les Bannis de Hitler*, p. 308.
337. As Hélène Roussel writes: 'It was a time when dissension between the component parts of the German *Volksfront* was worsening (while the French Popular Front was withering away), when mutual accusations were hurled as the French government's policy towards the émigrés grew harsher' (ibid., p. 311).
338. Thus Max Ernst represented surrealism, Wollheim the Neue Sachlichkeit, Spiro the heritage of impressionism, Otto Freundlich abstraction. Realism was also present in the person of Erwin Öhl.
339. Particular homage was paid to E. L. Kirschner, who had just committed suicide. Barlach, many works of whose had been damaged by the Nazis, was also exhibited.
340. This regrouping was undertaken at the SDS's initiative.
341. Though a few émigrés stayed for a while in Martinique (including Alfred Kantorowicz), this was generally because the ship taking them to the US made a stop there and they were interned, or that departure to the French West Indies was the only way for them to leave Europe from Marseille. The case of the Dominican Republic, which received a large number of antifascist refugees and Spanish Communists, is more complex. In order to differentiate the Dominican population, mainly of mixed race, more sharply from that of neighbouring Haiti which was almost completely black, the government strove to 'whiten' it by accepting all European immigrants.
342. 'Sammlung Theater in Exil', manuscript held at the Akademie der Künste, Berlin.
343. The city had 4,000 German refugees at the start of 1939, and 17,000 by August, according to certain sources. The United States consul-general requested the State Department to intervene with the Reich authorities. The British government also

advised shipping companies not to accept Jewish refugees for Shanghai. Because of these measures, many people interned in concentration camp could not be saved.

344. Cf. 'Shanghai – Eine Emigration am Rande. Bericht von Alfred Dreifuss', in *Exil in den USA*, Leipzig 1980; Manfred Durzak, *Die deutsche Exilliteratur 1933–1945*, p. 51; and *Aufbau. Reconstruction. Dokumente einer Kultur in Exil*, Cologne 1972, pp. 157–65.

345. Over a period of seven years, thirty-seven premieres of thirty plays by exiles were held. (*Die deutsche Exilliteratur 1933–1945*, p. 51.)

346. Cf. Alfred Dreifuss, in *Exil in den USA*, p. 455.

347. The journey was often undertaken in a number of stages: Trieste, Venice, Brindisi, Suez, Bombay, Colombo, Singapore, Hong Kong and Shanghai in three weeks.

348. *Die Zeit* devoted two reports to this curious individual, on 30 November and 7 December 1979.

349. The main contributor to this paper was Richard Paulick.

350. Turkey at this time was still cut off from European culture. Its Greek citizens had been exchanged against Turks from Greece, and a large number of Armenians exterminated. Old tradition seemed to be perpetuated in a medieval environment, and the Turkish literary heritage was completely forgotten. The revolution undertaken by Mustafa Kemal was quite enormous. Cf. Liselotte Dieckmann, 'Akademische Emigranten in der Türkei', in *Verbannung*, p. 122; Laura Fermi, *Illustrious Immigrants*, Chicago 1968, pp. 66–9.

351. At least a hundred German academics (professors or researchers) settled in Turkey. Beside mathematicians such as von Miser, these included specialists in Romance languages with a world reputation today such as Leo Spitzer and Erich Auerbach. The composer Paul Hindemith worked on the reorganization of musical education in Turkey until his departure for the United States in 1939. On his arrival in 1933, he directed a national Turkish school of drama and opera, then the national theatre.

352. According to testimonies by the émigrés, the majority of academics were subject to police surveillance and worked in deplorable conditions.

353. Hans Güterbock was the most well-known specialist on this subject.

354. Güterbock was the only German academic to master Turkish, after eight years of effort, and to teach in this language. He was a professional linguist.

355. Though the émigrés could teach the most sophisticated surgical techniques, the prevailing conditions of hygiene in Turkish hospitals were so catastrophic that any sick person could die from them.

356. 'Akademische Emigranten in der Türkei', pp. 122ff.

357. The poet Georg Mannheim, for example, claimed that it was not in Palestine but in Germany that he was in exile.

358. Gershom Scholem, *Von Berlin bis Jerusalem*, Frankfurt 1977, p. 190.

359. An allocation of £1,000 sterling was even granted to German Jews wishing to emigrate to Palestine. On the relations between Hitler and the Zionists, see Eliahu ben Elissar, *La Diplomatie du IIIe Reich et les juifs 1933–1939*, Paris 1969.

360. Curt D. Wormann recalls that the language spoken by German Jews was for Palestinian Jews the language of Hitler, and some émigrés even spoke of a kind of anti-Semitism towards European Jews on the part of their Palestinian co-religionists (Curt D. Wortmann, 'German Jews in Israel', *Leo Baeck Yearbook* XV, 1970, pp. 73–103).

361. *Letters of Sigmund Freud and Arnold Zweig*, p. 57.

362. Letter of 21 November 1935; ibid., p. 113.

363. Freud replied to him on 21 February 1936: 'In Palestine at any rate you have your personal safety and your human rights. And where would you think of going? You would find America, I would say from all my impressions, far more unbearable. Everywhere else you would be a scarcely tolerated alien.' (Ibid., p. 122).

364. Arnold Zweig did in fact write some of his most important works in Palestine (*Erziehung vor Verdun, Einsetzung eines Königs, Versunkene Tage, Bonaparte in Jaffa*), but no translation of any his works into Hebrew appeared until 1943.

365. Max Brod was more Zionist and more religious than the majority of Jewish writers of his generation (for instance Kafka or Franz Werfel). Even he, however, hesitated to emigrate to Palestine. In his autobiography, *Une vie combative*, p. 358, he wrote: 'It was precisely the best friends I had in Palestine who warned me against emigrating there. People in the intellectual professions, and especially those above a certain age [. . .] were not particularly wanted, they told me. The real need was for young and vigorous people: pioneers, men of action, engineers, tractor drivers, chicken farmers, loggers and herdsmen.'

366. *Die deutsche Exilliteratur*, p. 50.

367. Willy Haas, *Die literarische Welt*, Frankfurt 1983, p. 205.

368. Happily there were enough Indians who spoke German fluently, and could translate his work into Hindi. Haas, for his part, scarcely spoke any English.

CHAPTER 4   EXILE AS EVERYDAY TRAGEDY

1. The exiles of 1933 were themselves struck by the similarity of experience that they found in the writings of Ovid, Dante, Victor Hugo, Panait Istrati, Gorky and Heine. They took an interest in the calvaries of their illustrious predecessors, seeking analogies with their own fate and struggles. Heinrich Mann, at a lecture delivered during the exhibition 'Das Deutsche Buch' in Paris on 25 June 1937, recalled what exile meant for Victor Hugo, Heine and Marx. He stressed that they each wrote some of their greatest works in exile, that the Huguenots also left deep traces in Germany, and that Theodor Fontane was a French novelist who found his way into German letters as an exile. Books by Heine were displayed at this exhibition as well as antifascist works. In 1935, Alfred Kantorowicz declared in *In unserem Lager ist Deutschland* that Victor Hugo, who spend twenty years of his life in exile, also wrote 'illegal texts', and that his book *Le Crime du 2 décembre* was 'the *Braunbuch* of its time' (p. 15). He compared Hugo with the émigrés of 1933, maintaining that he too was an 'investigating magistrate of history'. Referring to the *Tarnschriften*, he explained that in Hugo's day even fishing boats were searched for illegal leaflets. Whole passages of Hugo's *Chastisements*, according to Kantor-owicz, could be applied directly to Hitler. The émigrés published several Heine collections, and Heinrich Mann published a homage to the poet, 'Sein Denkmal', in the *DZZ* for 17 February 1936, on the eightieth anniversary of Heine's death. Hermann Kesten compiled a Heine anthology for Querido Verlag in 1939, and Max Brod for Allert de Lange in 1934. In his poem 'A Visit to Poets in Exile', Brecht has them all meet up in the same prison.

2. There is a certain injustice even in this, for if the German emigration has aroused so much research, this is in part due to the literary quality of its representatives. It is also by virtue of its writers that the more recent Latin American emigration has imposed itself on world consciousness. The lecture by Julio Cortazar, 'Exil et littérature', in *Littérature latino-américaine d'aujourd'hui* (10–18, 1980), describes experiences that scarcely differ from those of the German emigrants of 1933.

3. In his novel *The Desert* (Paris 1939), E. E. Noth has one of his characters say: 'It was one of the hardest costs of exile, this distrust towards your compatriots; not only those unknown to you, but even those you've known before, but can't tell which way they've moved.'

4. See the volumes of letters and documents edited by Hermann Kesten, *Deutsche Literatur in Exil. Briefe europäischer Autoren 1933–1949*; and *Verbannung. Auf-zeichnungen deutscher Schriftsteller im Exil*, edited by Egon Schwarz and Matthias Wegner, Hamburg 1964. The impression of sadness that these volumes convey cannot be sufficiently stressed. As Kesten wrote in his preface: 'To publish these letters of exile is to leave for exile a second time [. . .]. You float between sky and land. You sit at a table with so many dead' (p. 15). Kesten estimates that German

writers in exile exchanged more than a million letters; he himself wrote and received more than ten thousand between 1933 and 1949.

5. In the United States, Brecht felt a real humiliation in having to spell his name. Ernst Toller, the greatest dramatist of the Weimar Republic, had to indicate his profession. His plays were no longer staged, and he was completely unfamiliar to the American public. Max Reinhardt lived in the same solitude. When an American journalist described him as 'an unimportant theatre director', Erwin Piscator, who was present at the time, hastened to slap him round the face. Heinrich Mann and Alfred Döblin suffered a similar lack of recognition.

6. Leonhard Frank wrote that the French police considered German émigrés as dirt (*Unrat*). Franz Blei, Golo Mann and Manès Sperber all recall that France first waged war against the émigrés.

7. In Sweden, Tucholsky no longer wished to speak of Germany and saw himself as a writer who had ceased to write. Ödön von Horvath similarly questioned himself on his reasons for writing, and this was also the theme of the great novel by Hermann Broch, *The Death of Virgil*.

8. Arthur Koestler wrote in *The Invisible Writing*: 'For a long while, I was not aware of having lost my privileged status as a free traveller and joined the grey horde of European political exiles. The transformation took place, so to speak, under anaesthesia. For a while, nothing seemed to change in my way of life.'

9. 'In exile, years pass like motionless shadows', Hermann Kesten confided to Klaus Mann on 2 December 1938. Alfred Döblin wrote to Oskar Loerke after his first year of exile: 'This year has lasted half a century' (26 February 1934). Manès Sperber remarked: 'Like a man who has lost his shadow, I had lost the future, and only the past remained for me. On the temporal level, I lived on credit; on the spatial level I was removed from all the fields of battle. I listened assiduously to the news on the radio, hoping that the enemy would finally cease to be victorious everywhere that he attacked' (*Au-delà de l'oubli*, p. 199).

10. Golo Mann remarked that 'seen as a whole, the life of the émigrés was a combination of tremendous freedom and slavery. You were free from all commitments, you were only too free. But the human being cannot do without certain commitments, and you were also outside all your rights.' (Bad Godesberg conference 1968, p. 38). Manès Sperber also noted that 'in exile, the beds were not the same as at home', that 'emigration was more like a state of war, or those sunless holidays that extend in desolation, as the only school building has burned down or a dangerous epidemic has cut short the habits of everyday life. Many émigrés queued up outside cinemas in broad daylight, as the matinée prices were especially low, or went to warm themselves in the sun of deserted parks [. . .]. On the one hand, time was always short for the émigrés [. . .] On the other, they had far more time than they needed, as it was rigorously forbidden to work' (*Au-delà de l'oubli*, p. 104). At the start of his exile, Arthur Koestler could still compare himself with 'a schoolboy who has escaped from an austere college to a matinée in a circus' (*The Invisible Writing*, p. 199).

11. M. Sperber, *Au-delà de l'oubli*, p. 75.

12. Regler wrote to his son on each birthday, but never received a reply, even when he was wounded during the Spanish war. He subsequently published these letters. The open letter that John Becher wrote in January 1951 to his father, J. R. Becher, by then minister of culture in the GDR, elicits the same emotion. He accused his father of becoming a bureaucrat and asked if this was the ideal he had struggled for over so many years. (J. R. Becher's wife had remained in England and refused to return to East Berlin.) Cf. Hans Daiber, *Vor Deutschland wird gewarnt*, pp. 208ff.

13. G. Regler, *The Owl of Minerva*, p. 186.

14. Ibid., p. 168.

15. A. Mahler, *Mémoires*, p. 315.

16. Lion Feuchtwanger, 'Grösse und Erbärmlichkeit des Exils', *Verbannung*, p. 195.

17. M. Sperber, *Au-delà de l'oubli*, p. 76.

18. As early as 1937, Erich Stern wrote *Die Emigration als psychologische Problem*.
19. K. Mann, *The Turning Point*, p. 266.
20. H. Mann, *Ein Zeitalter wird besichtigt*, p. 49.
21. K. Mann, *The Turning Point*, p. 266.
22. Arthur Koestler wrote in *The Invisible Writing*: 'Next to his passport, the refugee's main preoccupation is his identity card or *permit de séjour*. The passport proves his right to exist; the permit his right to reside where he does. The third essential document is the working permit which would grant him the right to earn a living. But this he is in most cases unable to obtain.' (p. 342). Many émigrés gained the impression that exile meant a loss of identity. Stefan Zweig maintained that from the moment he had to live with the papers of a refugee, he was no longer himself. Alfred Döblin also remarked that the émigré could no longer say 'I', since he no longer acted. He was driven by events and by the authorities.
23. Bruno Frank even published with Querido Verlag in 1937 a novel titled *Der Reisepass*.
24. *Die Kriegs- und Nachkriegsgeneration*, 1938.
25. Cf. his letter to Herman Hesse of 23 April 1933 and his *Diaries*.
26. Though the German consulate in Berne agreed to renew Thomas Mann's passport, other émigrés naturally did not meet with the same favour. Most, moreover, would not even have dared to enter a building flying the swastika flag, for fear of being arrested and murdered. Alexander Moritz Frey, Walter Meckauer and Carl Zuckmayer were among those who did succeed in getting their exile papers renewed.
27. For instance the former minister Trevinarius, a friend of Ex-Chancellor Brüning, waited six months to obtain a British passport, and Brüning himself complained of the difficulties he encountered in travelling to England with a Netherlands *Ausweis*.
28. Bruno von Salomon, the brother of Ernst von Salomon, had moved from right to left. He fought in Spain in the International Brigades, then returned to France where he was considered an 'undesirable foreigner' and expelled to Belgium. In Belgium, he was arrested for unauthorized crossing of the frontier and given a prison sentence. The Belgian gendarmes then returned him to the border, where the French police immediately arrested him for illegal entry to France; as he had already been expelled, he was now sentenced to prison. On release from prison he was expelled once again to Belgium, where he was once more imprisoned before being returned to France. Kantorowicz was quite right to speak of a literal ping-pong game played with refugees who lacked valid papers. It should be added that Bruno von Salomon joined the French Resistance, after first being interned in a camp in the north of France as a 'German', His wife was interned in a camp in the south, and succumbed to madness as a result of these traumas.
29. Alfred Kantorowicz ('Exil in Frankreich', in M. Durzak, ed., *Die deutsche Exil-literatur*, pp. 58ff.) related the odyssey of his marriage in France. His companion was only allowed to follow him if they were officially married. Hitler had delayed his matrimonial plans, but he now decided to marry her. Since he had no valid papers, the marriage was refused. To obtain permission, he would have to apply to the German consulate, which would have advised him to return to Germany in order to get new papers. There he would immediately have been interned and executed. When the passport of Arthur Koestler's companion expired, he had to do violence to his convictions and marry her in order for her to obtain a Hungarian passport: 'so, with a joint sigh of resignation, we decided to go through with that archaic ceremony' (*The Invisible Writing*, p. 342).
30. Principally in case of war and treason.
31. *Pflicht zur Treue gegen Reich und Volk*. Anyone could be accused of infringing this if they made negative statements about the Reich and its institutions.
32. The first of these lists was published in the *Reichsanzeiger* 198, 25 August 1933.
33. These were individuals long hated by the Nazis.
34. For example, Social-Democrats such as Robert Breitscheid, Albert Grzesinski and

Philipp Scheidemann figured on the first list, but Rudolf Hilferding was not deprived of nationality until 1935. The Communists F. Heckert, P. Maslowski, Willi Münzenberg, Hans Neumann and Wilhelm Pieck figured on the first list, but others such as Walter Ulbricht and Wilhelm Florin had to wait until *Liste 8* (February 1937). The same went for writers. Pacifists such as Hellmut von Gerlach and Berthold Jacob, as well as the critic Alfred Kerr, figured on the first list, while Brecht, Walter Mehring and Friedrich Wolf, well-known enemies of fascism, were included only on *Liste 4* (June 1935). Ludwig Marcuse did not lose his nationality until 1937. As German residents whose assets were confiscated by the Gestapo in the wake of their exile, these included Joseph Roth (Austrian), Max Brod (Czech), Anna Seghers (Hungarian), Erich Kästner (not in fact an exile) and Emil Ludwig (Swiss).

35. K. Mann, *Der Wendepunkt*, p. 294. [Not in the English edition of *The Turning Point*.]
36. Alfred Kantorowicz points out that after two and a half years of vacillation, the League of Nations had still not provided German refugees with identity papers. The League's High Commissioner James MacDonald had not been able to persuade the member states to issue special passports to refugees whose legal situation had been made desperate by their *Ausbürgerung*.
37. What this meant in concrete terms was that an exile could only obtain legal authorization to work if he had been granted nationality, and this nationality was only granted if he had work. A German deprived of nationality in 1933 could hope to acquire French nationality in 1936, Austrian in 1937, British, Italian or Netherlands in 1938, Swiss in 1939 and Belgian in 1943. It was ruled of course that he could be allowed to stay in these countries without papers or nationality.
38. In France, for instance, German émigrés deprived of their nationality received an identity card that had to be regularly renewed. Some 'stateless' people of German origin were refused a residence permit but were allowed to stay in the country until their fate was determined. French citizenship was more readily granted if the émigré did military service or had a son of military age.
39. Christopher Isherwood relates in his autobiography *Christopher and His Kind* (London 1976, pp. 192ff.) the procedures he went through to 'purchase' Mexican nationality (at a cost of about £1,000) for his German friend Heinz. These nationalizations were negotiated by the states concerned in an official fashion, by certain senior officials or by a consul.
40. With the assistance of Paul Reynaud, as H. A. Walter indicates (*Asylpraxis*, p. 24).
41. After first asking Christopher Isherwood to marry her, she married W. H. Auden. Isherwood had refused for fear of compromising Heinz, and from a horror of marriage. We should recall that Erika Mann's first husband, Gustaf Gründgens, now held a senior position in the Reich's theatre.
42. He had first of all tried to obtain Swiss nationality (letter to Heinrich Mann of 20 August 1936). Heinrich was also given Czech nationality, despite the protest of pro-Nazi elements.
43. Such passports were often signed only by a consul and not by the interior minister. Moreover, if in many cases they made it possible to travel, their bearer did not automatically acquire nationality. Many émigrés learned this at their cost.
44. L. Marcuse, *Mein zwanzigstes Jahrhundert*, p. 249.
45. S. Zweig, *The World of Yesterday*, p. 308.
46. Ibid., p. 309.
47. Ibid., p. 310.
48. In *Verbannung*, pp. 85–6.
49. Letter from Tony Kesten, 3 April 1940.
50. 'Innere und äussere Emigration', in *Verbannung*, p. 274.
51. They often did not even have a fixed address, especially in 1939–40, so as to avoid arrest by the French police or Gestapo.
52. Thomas Mann wrote to René Schickele on 23 April 1932 that he was looking for a

house with at least six bedrooms, 'For the winter, we have been offered a fine house close to Nice', he confided to A. M. Frey on 27 August 1933. Franz Werfel and Alma Mahler also suggested to him their house in Venice. Though he had to pay 'tax for fleeing the Reich', the blocking of his royalties was lifted in 1933. He wrote again to Schickele on 2 April 1934: 'I less and less see why I should be excluded from Germany for the sake of these idiots, or should leave them my belongings, house and property. [. . .]. To have our own furniture would mean a great saving in rent for us, and it would also be a psychic reassurance to be surrounded by objects of our previous life' (*Letters of Thomas Mann 1889–1955*, p. 185).

53. Thomas Mann, *Mélanges à Feuchtwanger*, Berlin 1954, p. 9.
54. 'Alltag in der Emigration', in *Verbannung*, p. 64.
55. A. Koestler, *The Invisible Writing*, p. 235.
56. Among them Kurt Tucholsky (who already lived in France), Walter Hasenclever, Count Harry Kessler, E. J. Aufricht, Hermann Rauschning (in Danzig) and Max Horkheimer, who was able to rescue part of the Frankfurt Institute's funds.
57. This was generally from 20 to 40 per cent. When G. Bermann Fischer obtained permission to transfer a division of his publishing house to Vienna, he had to pay 40 per cent of the profit realized or realizable by the sale of works deemed 'undesirable' in Germany but tolerated if they were sold in Austria.
58. Heinrich Mann transferred some of his assets in Czechoslovakia for protection, his first wife being Czech. Thomas Mann had his books sent to a false address in Switzerland. Erika, despite the danger, returned to Munich to retrieve her father's manuscripts. Most writers had to abandon a large part of their books. Walter Mehring wrote a moving story on this theme, 'The Lost Library'.
59. Heinrich Mann's goods in Berlin were immediately confiscated. Brecht left Germany carrying his soldier's canteen, his manuscripts, his smoking equipment including ashtrays, a few masks, and a small radio to hear the news.
60. A German lawyer clearly could not continue his career in France, any more than a doctor could practise his profession there, even an important specialist.
61. *The Correspondence of Walter Benjamin*, p. 509.
62. Publishers naturally ceased paying royalties on books that were confiscated or banned. They often allowed the émigrés to republish abroad, protesting for form's sake that these works had appeared without their knowledge. Other publishers sold stock off as remainders abroad, which deprived the émigrés of income and threatened their new editions.
63. Cf. H. A. Walter, *Asylpraxis*, p. 183.
64. Querido Verlag paid its authors stipends of 100 to 200 marks per month. One of its most favoured authors, Heinrich Mann, received 400 marks. The majority of poetry collections were published only on subscription and without royalties. Émigré works published in the Soviet Union did achieve print runs of two to fifty thousand, but the earnings could be spent only in the USSR.
65. Cited by H. A. Walter, *Asylpraxis*, p. 199.
66. *The Correspondence of Walter Benjamin*, p. 402.
67. Letter of 19 April 1933, ibid., p. 410.
68. Ibid., p. 416.
69. Letter to Gretel Adorno of June 1933, ibid., p. 421. The 15th was Benjamin's birthday.
70. Horkheimer tried to get Benjamin an American scholarship. See Benjamin's letter to Adorno of 7 January 1935; ibid., p. 472.
71. Ibid., p. 484.
72. These were 50 to 75 per cent lower than those paid in the Weimar era, which were already low by all accounts.
73. Joseph Roth wrote to Hermann Kesten on 29 June 1933: 'I await the cheque impatiently [. . .] I write very poorly and very sadly in the absence of money.' Ernst Weiss wrote on 19 November 1933: 'The fees would do me good, it's a hungry and aimless time.' Kesten in turn wrote to Walter Landauer on 3 June 1938: 'I am in a

new hotel without a cent. Have I been forgotten at the publishing house? [. . .] Here no one lends to anyone. Four times a day when I go out, I'm told with contempt: "The money's not here yet." '

74. In 1932, Kurt Gläser, director of the Staatliche Kunstbibliothek, had founded a 'Musil society' to enable him to complete *The Man Without Qualities*.

75. Musil was in fact not at all well-known in his native Austria.

76. Some émigré writers besides Thomas Mann and Lion Feuchtwanger did get their works translated, but their number was no more than thirty at the most (according to H. A. Walter), with no more than ten works for the most favoured authors. These were all writers whose work was already well known before 1933: Thomas Mann, Erich Maria Remarque, Heinrich Mann, Joseph Roth, Anna Segers, Franz Werfel, Arnold and Stefan Zweig, Arthur Koestler, Bruno Frank, E. Glaeser, Vicki Baum and Lion Feuchtwanger. Such authors as Georg Kaiser, Rudolf Leonhard and Fritz von Unruh only managed four translations; Hermann Broch, Irmgard Keun, and Gustav Regler three; Walter Hasenclever and René Schickele two. The number of translations was not of course proportional to the value of the work: Vicky Baum was abundantly translated, whilst Musil and Broch remained un-known to the wider public.

77. For instance the books by Hermann Rauschning, *The Revolution of Nihilism* and *Hitler Speaks*, had an international success. The biography of Hitler by Rudolf Olden sold more than 15,000 copies, as did the French translation of Maximilian Scheer's essay *Das deutsche Volk klagt an* (34,000 copies). The same went for the first accounts of concentration camps. Wolfgang Langhoff's *Les Soldats du marais* sold more than 50,000, Willi Bredel's *Die Prüfung* over 100,000. Heinrich Mann's essay *La Haine*, published by Galllimard in 1933, also topped the 100,000 mark.

78. This applied for example to translations into Swedish, Serbian, Czech and Yiddish.

79. Except in the USSR, where print runs were very large (including translation into national languages such as Ukrainian). The Swedish translation of Döblin's novel *Giganten* brought him 600 marks, with a similar amount for the Italian translation, whereas he earned only $500 for a selection of texts of Confucius (cited by H. A. Walter, *Asylpraxis*, p. 208).

80. Several émigrés such as Lotte H. Eisner worked as 'slaves' for other translators. Arthur Koestler, in order to survive, had not only to write articles for *Das Neue Tage-Buch*, but a chapter of an English guide to Paris and 630 pages on 'sexual anomalies and perversions'; he had to translate novels, rewrite one of his plays as a short story for a literary award, draft film screenplays that he never managed to sell, and draw up the synopsis for an encyclopaedia of psychology. As he himself remarked: 'The hectic pace deprived me of any professional satisfaction, and made me feel a cheap hack' (*The Invisible Writing*, p. 346).

81. There was a regular star system among the émigrés. Thomas Mann and Emil Ludwig gave lecture tours in the United States, organized by actual impresarios. In 1930 alone, Mann spoke in fifteen American cities. Ludwig also toured the United States in 1935–36, and Ernst Toller toured Britain and Canada. Hubertus Prinz zu Löwenstein likewise travelled to the United States in 1938, and Stefan Zweig, the same year, gave a number of lectures in Latin America.

82. Joseph Roth lectured in Poland in 1937. In his letters, he complained bitterly of playing the performing animal in a dinner jacket, and having to give the same lecture each night in insignificant places. Thomas Mann also complained of the mediocrity of his audience. But Roth acknowledged that without these lectures he would already have died of hunger.

83. Gerhard Seger, who escaped from the Oranienburg concentration camp, gave lectures in almost every European country as well as in the United States, over a period of seven months, as well as ninety-four interviews (cited after H. A. Walter, *Asylpraxis*, p. 217).

84. When Arnold Zweig gave lectures in Palestine, a collection was taken to pay him.

Whilst Thomas Mann earned $500 dollars a lecture, Robert Musil was only paid 100 Swiss francs.

85. A few émigrés did contribute to the *Times Literary Supplement*, as well as to the British liberal or left-wing press. The Swedish press generally refused articles by German refugees, for fear of the Reich's reactions or in the name of a supposed political objectivity. Thomas Mann warmly recommended Julius Meier-Graefe to the *Neue Zürcher Zeitung*. Heinrich Mann published an article each month in the *Dépêche de Toulouse*. E. E. Noth and Alfred Kerr contributed to *Les Nouvelles Littéraires*. But journalists or former contributors to the major German papers, the *Vossische Zeitung*, *Neue Weltbühne* or *Frankfurter Zeitung*, had most often to rest content with provincial or regional papers. If it had not been for his exile, it is hard to conceive that Heinrich Mann would have become a regular contributor to the *Dépêche de Toulouse*.

86. Max Brod, as editor of the *Prager Tagblatt*, maintained (cf. H. A. Walter, *Asylpraxis*, p. 221) that he would have needed a special number each day to publish all the articles sent in by émigrés. According to the Sternfeld/Tiedemann index (ibid.), 200 exiles contributed to thirty Swiss papers and twenty-three German-language papers in Prague, forty-eight exiles wrote for twenty-four British periodicals, thirty-nine for twenty-eight French periodicals, twenty-one for ten in the Netherlands, and twenty for thirteen Austrian papers.

87. He had to use the pseudonym Axel Kjellström.

88. Piscator wrote a screenplay based on *Schweyk*, and planned to set up a production company in Mexico.

89. For example Carl Zuckmayer in London and Brecht in Hollywood, as well as Bruno Frank, Stefan Zweig, Joseph Roth, F. Bruckner, W. Herzog, L. Frank, F. T. Coskor, H. Liepmann, Leo Lania, A. Neumann and W. Haas.

90. Elisabeth Castonnier managed to rent a hotel room by selling her bracelet. Wolfgang Hallgarten sold his violin, and Walter Benjamin had to part with his Paul Klee engraving 'Angelus Novus', which held such a major place in his work. Many others sacrificed their libraries and manuscript collections.

91. Manès Sperber recalls of his INFA contributors: 'After the Marseille outrage that killed King Alexander of Yugoslavia and Foreign Minister Louis Barthou, on 9 October 1934, the Paris police hunted down foreigners with a vigour that was both untiring and pointless. When a foreigner visibly without resources was arrested, he had not only to present his identity papers, but also prove that he possessed the sum of 20 francs. If not, he could be imprisoned for vagabondage and expelled. Many of our contributors did not generally have this sum in their possession, and were sometimes completely without money for days on end. We gave each of them 20 francs, therefore, before they left our office, which they had to refund on return so that someone else could use this vademecum.' (*Au-delà de l'oubli*, p. 60).

92. In his *Exile Dialogues*, Brecht has one of his characters relate the Kafkaesque adventure of an émigré physicist in a Scandinavian country who can only live off the support of his colleagues though he wants to help them. When he falls sick, he cannot even ask a fellow émigré to help him, as this man is not allowed to practise medicine. He is reduced to requesting a consultation in the hotel toilets.

93. For instance the Social-Democratic journalist Günter Markscheffel, who emigrated to France in 1933, was successively a farmhand, an assembly-line worker in a lock factory, and a lift repairman in the mines. He went on to learn soldering and boiler-making.

94. Alfred Kantorowicz, for example, during his final months in France received £10 from an English friend of his father, £2 from the PEN Club, £5 from the editor of *Penguin New Writing*, 500 francs from the Fonds Thomas Mann, 400 francs sent from the United States by Ernst and Karola Bloch, 400 francs from Lion Feuchtwanger and $500 sent by Ernest Hemingway.

95. In Switzerland, the publisher Emil Oprecht invited twenty or so émigrés for a daily meal. Sylain Guggenheim protected Else Lasker-Schüler, Eduard Korrodi helped

Alfred Kerr. Carl Seelig and Herman Hesse acted similarly. In France, Paul Vaillant-Couturier, Marcel Cachin, André and Clara Malraux and André Gide showed genuine solidarity. In London Gilbert Murray took in Rudolf Olden. The Polish writer Sliwinski sheltered Csokor. Brecht enjoyed the assistance of Karin Michaelis in Denmark, as did Kantorowicz. In the United States, besides President Roosevelt and his wife Eleanor, many writers (Dos Passos and Hemingway in particular, as well as Sinclair Lewis) came to their support.

96. A. Mahler, *Mémoires*, p. 260.

97. G. Bermann Fischer had the idea in 1938 (letter of 17 November to Thomas Mann) of a collection of letters by exiled writers describing their situation. He was aware of their exemplary character. Mann encouraged the project and offered to write a preface. Similar anthologies were envisaged by many émigrés; that of Hermann Kesten became the most well-known.

98. A random list would include such factors as celebrity, material resources, age, knowledge of language and culture, family situation, party membership, previous connections, first experiences of exile and the attitude of the country of arrival.

99. *Verbannung*, p. 54. Walter Mehring noted in similar vein his departure from Vienna: 'I understood the angels' advice to Lot, which holds for all other exiles as well: don't turn round, even once, to look on Sodom and Gomorrah' (*La Bibliothèque perdue*, p. 21).

100. 'Schreiben in der Fremde', in *Exil und innere Emgiration*, Frankfurt 1972, p. 15.

101. *Führer durch die deutsche Emigration*, Paris 1935, p. 7.

102. Stefan Zweig wrote in his last letters: 'People speak of the bombing so lightly, but when I read that houses collapse, I collapse with them.' And again: 'I cannot be in the room when someone triumphantly proclaims that "Berlin has been well and truly bombed".'

103. K. Mann, *The Turning Point*, p. 288.

104. *Exil in Frankreich*, p. 100.

105. A. Kantorowicz, *Deutsches Tagebuch*, p. 77.

106. Cited by Ludwig Marcuse, *Mein zwanzigstes Jahrhundert*, p. 350.

107. *Letters of Sigmund Freud*, pp. 441–2.

108. Heinrich Brüning, *Journal*, pp. 194–5.

109. M. Sperber, *Au-delà de l'oubli*, p. 208.

110. Brüning, *Journal*, p. 323.

111. B. Brecht, *Dialogues d'exilés*, p. 80.

112. Thomas Mann managed to rescue some of his books and a part of his furniture, by agreeing to pay the tax on leaving the Reich, and he entered into negotiations with the Nazis through the intermediary of a lawyer in order to avoid the confiscation of his house by the SA. This was in vain, and he had to leave more than 150,000 marks in Germany.

113. Thomas Mann, *Tagebücher*, ed. Peter de Mendelssohn and Inge Jens, Frankfurt 1979–95.

114. Brecht commented ironically on Kurt Weill writing to him in English from the United States. E. E. Noth also tried not to speak German but only French. Tucholsky also avoided speaking German.

115. Brecht, *Dialogues d'exilés*, p. 125.

116. *Verbannung*, p. 175.

117. Sometimes a writer lost the sense of nuance in his mother tongue, adopting foreign words and constructions. Ernst Weiss complained in a letter written a short while before his suicide that he 'couldn't keep his mother tongue on ice'. While Brecht, like George Grosz, ironically used English words in his diary and letters, Rudolf Fuchs mixed English and German without being aware of this. Brecht also coined new German words from an English base – *sich hineinmusklen* for *to muscle in*. Ernst Weiss and Lion Feuchtwanger used expressions in their novels that are not always clear in German. And when in Thomas Mann's *Joseph in Egypt* the pharaoh

Amenhopet exclaims '*So lange!*' by way of farewell, F. C. Weiskopf might well ask (*Unter fremden Himmeln*, p. 50) whether the irony was deliberate.

118. G. Bermann Fischer, *Bewahrt-Bedroht*, p. 252.

119. Letter of 23 Dec 1933 to Gretl Adorno; *The Correspondence of Walter Benjamin*, p. 432.

120. However, René Schickele, Ivan and Claire Goll, Anette Kolbe, E. J. Gumbel, Rudolf Leonhard, Max Beer, Alfred Kerr and Heinrich Mann wrote in French, Werner Bock in Spanish; Stefan Heym, F. Höllering, Leo Lania, Klaus Mann and Franz Schoenberger wrote in English.

121. The conflicting situation of belonging to more than one language was often encountered by the younger émigrés. Erich Fried (born 1921) left for England at the age of seventeen. He wrote for publication in German only after spending more than thirty years in England. Peter Weiss left Germany with his father in 1934. He lived successively in England, Czechoslovakia, Switzerland and Sweden. His first published works were in Swedish, and he only started publishing in German in 1947. His brother, eight years younger, continued to write in Swedish. Michael Hamburger, born in Berlin in 1924, forgot German in exile and started writing in his native tongue seven years after returning to Berlin. He became one of the best English translators of Hölderlin.

122. Brecht noted in his diary for 17 November 1944: 'now and again i forget a German word, i, who only now and again recall an english one. when i try to find it what comes to mind is not high german words, but dialect expressions.' (*Journals*, p. 334).

123. When the singer and actress Blandine Ebinger asked Max Reinhardt, about to leave for America, whether he was sad, he simply responded: 'I'll miss hearing German' (communication from Blandine Ebinger, 1983).

124. Just as Bruno Bettelheim undertook a psychological study of concentration-camp internees, whom he described as suffering a kind of autism, so it would be possible to analyse the destruction of the exile personality in such cases as Joseph Roth or Ernst Weiss. Klaus Mann, who committed suicide soon after the War, had admirably depicted this destruction in the case of two characters in his novel *The Volcano*, Kikjou and Martin, who used cocaine to escape the pain of exile. Stephan Hermlin also described in his story 'Voyage du peintre à Paris' (*Dans un monde de ténèbres*, Paris 1982), the slow collapse into madness of the painter Hans Reichel in the course of his Paris exile. Arnold Zweig, in his correspondence with Freud, mentioned a possible conference on 'emigration and neurosis' (*Letters of Sigmund Freud and Arnold Zweig*, p. 137).

125. Manès Sperber wrote: 'Why am I writing, then, and for whom? I came to the conclusion that my activity is pointless and that I would be the only reader of my texts. I spent my time covering pages of my notebook with words – a message in a bottle that would never reach the shore.' (*Au-delà de l'oubli*, p. 200). Arthur Koestler remarked: 'But to abandon his native language and traditions means in most cases death to the writer, and his transformation into a nondescript, cosmopolitan journalist or literary hack' (*The Invisible Writing*, p. 211).

126. *Verbannung*, pp. 120ff.

127. According to Walter Mehring (*La Bibliothèque perdue*, pp. 260–1), Weiss discovered his vocation as a writer by editing the account of an autopsy of a prostitute murderess who was knocked down in the place de Prague, and died while he was operating on her. She became the heroine of *La Bête déchainée*. Many of Weiss's characters are doctors or murderers, some even in combination.

128. In his autobiography, Ludwig Marcuse wrote: 'Ernst Toller was in a bad way. His charming wife [. . .] had left him. His lucky star had abandoned him. He was no longer able to work. His stock was at its lowest. When an American journalist greeted him in a slovenly fashion, he became ill with pain. Reflection on his fall pained him enormously.' (*Mein zwanzigstes Jahrhundert*, p. 253).

129. On several occasions Maria Piscator stopped him from throwing himself out of the window (oral communication, December 1981).

130. Klaus Mann relates that on his last meeting with Toller, a few days before his suicide, he repeatedly said: 'I can't sleep any more.' [Not in the English edition of *The Turning Point*.] Klaus Mann spoke at Toller's funeral, ashamed of his tears.

131. We should also recall that Toller's autobiography, *I Was a German*, was originally dedicated to 'my nephew Harry, who blew his brains out in 1928, at the age of eighteen'.

132. In an interview published in the *New York Times* book pages, he confided on 28 July 1940: 'I no longer possessed the courage to deal with private psychological facts, every "story" appeared to me totally irrelevant when seen in contrast to history' (cited after M. Wegner, *Exil und Literatur*, p. 94).

133. *Deutsche Literatur im Exil*, p. 130.

134. G. Bermann Fischer met Zweig on a New York street before his departure for Brazil: the world-famous writer seemed like a wreck, lamenting over 'the victory of evil powers'.

135. *Verbannung*, p. 323.

136. Brüning, *Lettres*, p. 323.

137. Hasenclever was interned at Fort Carré, close to Antibes. He owed his first release to his state of health, the second to Jean Giradoux, then commissioner-general of information.

138. Benjamin had written to Gershom Scholem on 16 June 1933: 'My brother is in a concentration camp. God only knows what he has to endure there. But the rumours about his wounds are exaggerated in at least one respect. He did not lose an eye' (*The Correspondence of Walter Benjamin*, p. 417). Gershom Scholem's brother Werner was also arrested in 1933 and died in Buchenwald.

139. *La Bibliothèque perdue*, p. 276.

140. We should recall that he describes on several occasions, especially in his autobiography, the suicide of members of his family (two aunts), that of the daughter of Arthur Schnitzler, the son of Hugo von Hofmannstahl, and of his friend René Crevel. In 1930 he devoted an essay, 'Selbstmord', to all those friends of his who had taken their own life.

141. It seems that Klaus Mann was curiously condemned to live in reality the conflicts that his father had described in his work. Relations between the two were always strained, as Thomas Mann acknowledged in a letter of 6 July 1949 to Herman Hesse after his son's death: 'My relationship to him was difficult, and not without feelings of guilt, for my very existence cast a shadow on him from the start [. . .]. He worked with such facility and speed that there is a scattering of flaws and oversights in his books' (*Letters of Thomas Mann 1889–1955*, p. 415). On relations between Klaus Mann and his father, see also my preface to the French translation of his autobiography: *Le Tournant*, Paris 1985.

CHAPTER 5   THE ORGANIZATION OF SUPPORT

1. Despite the xenophobic campaigns orchestrated by the right-wing press, Germans never represented more than 2 to 3 per cent of the foreigners living in France at that time.

2. Cf. H. A. Walter, *Asylpraxis und Lebensbedingungen in Europa*, vol. 2; M. Durzak, ed., *Die deutsche Exilliteratur 1933–1945*; M. Wegner, *Exil und Literatur*.

3. *Verbannung*, p. 194.

4. The first countries to react were Austria and Switzerland.

5. In Switzerland, Sweden and Norway, for instance.

6. Academics feared for their careers, writers feared German competitors (in Switzerland), and the Jewish population was not always well-disposed to the influx of these German Jews, for fear of unemployment but especially of a renewal of an anti-Semitism that would strike them as well.

7. In 1933 there were 200,000 white Russians in Paris, as against 7,200 antifascists.

8. In particular, fascist groups sympathetic to the Third Reich. Some countries also feared economic reprisals, or felt directly threatened by Germany. A large section of the bourgeoisie often saw Hitlerism as a bulwark against Communism.
9. Cited after Eliahu ben Elissar, *La Diplomatie du IIIe Reich et les Juifs*, p. 96.
10. Ibid., p. 198.
11. The figures for Jewish emigration were approximately: 63,400 in 1933, 45,000 in 1934, and 35,500 in 1939. These fairly low figures are explained by the decree of 18 May 1934 on the sale of émigré goods, and the tax to be paid on 'fleeing the Reich', which by 1940 had brought in over a billion marks.
12. Out of 153,774 visas granted, 83,575 were for applicants from Great Britain and France. Those from Germany and Austria received only 27,000.
13. Cited after *La Diplomatie du IIIe Reich et les Juifs*, pp. 250–1.
14. The German secretary of state Weizäcker summarized the results of the conference with the words: 'Though many countries produce Jews, it seems that none of them are prepared to consume them.' (ibid., p. 251). The Gestapo didn't miss the opportunity to note that the Australian representative had spoken of 'the danger that Jewish emigration would constitute for his race'.
15. Ibid., p. 268.
16. Ibid., p. 270.
17. After the *Anschluss*, Austrian Jews had German passports. The Nazi government also wanted passports of Swiss Jews visiting Germany to be similarly stamped, but Switzerland refused.
18. An evident lie, as the émigrés often had to sign a commitment not to return to Germany in order to go into exile.
19. Göring ironically remarked on 12 November 1938: 'In the morning the Czechs snatched them up and directed them to Hungary. From Hungary, return to Germany, then return to Czechoslovakia. So they had a round trip, ending up on an old barge in the Danube. They camped out there, and as soon as they set foot on land they were sent back again.' (cited from *La Diplomatie du IIIe Reich et les Juifs*, p. 286).
20. The committees operating in France have been subject to notable studies in the various volumes published under the direction of Gilbert Badia, to which I can only refer the reader.
21. Cf. the study by Jacques Omnès, 'L'aide du Secours rouge puis du Secours populaire aux émigrés politiques allemands en France (1933–1939)', in *Cahiers d'Histoire de l'Institute de Recherches Marxistes* 7, pp. 123ff.
22. This *foyer* took in 60 to 80 German émigrés each day, organizing cultural activities for them and a daily meal. It offered sewing and shoe-repair workshops, a children's nursery and social assistance. It gave loans for travel and rent. The Quakers were active on this until 1937, when they also occupied themselves with Spanish refugees. In the 1920s they had assisted children of German families suffering from unemployment and inflation, and were also active in the Nordic countries.
23. A. Koestler, *The Invisible Writing*, p. 242.
24. 'Our action should not appear as arising from a hostile sentiment towards the people of a neighbouring country, it does not represent a judgement on forms of government or other political considerations between countries. Our sole aim is to relieve suffering, and defend culture and science.'
25. After the foundation of the Council, the LSE faculty donated 3 per cent for the higher salaries and 2 per cent on the lower ones. The Princeton staff gave 5 per cent of their salaries.
26. Among the signatures were Martin Andersen-Nexö, W. H. Auden, Menno ter Braak, Lion Feuchtwanger, Bruno and Leonhard Frank, Sigmund Freud, André Gide, Julien Green, Aldous Huxley, Oskar Kokoschka, Heinrich and Thomas Mann, André Maurois, Jules Romains, Ignazio Silone, Upton Sinclair, H. G. Wells, Franz Werfel and Stefan Zweig.

CHAPTER 6 FIRST REFLECTIONS ON
THE MEANING OF THE EMIGRATION

1. [Cf. 'Appendix' to F. Ewen, *Brecht*, London 1970, p. 498, where a slightly different version of this text is given.
2. Cf. Willi Bredel, 'Lehre und Aufgabe', *Das Wort* 4, 1936; Heinrich Mann, 'Der Sinn dieser Emigration', reprinted in *Verteidigung der Kultur*. Arthur Koestler spoke of a genuine crusade, Hermann Kesten called emigration 'the finest and most difficult of missions'.
3. This is the theme of Hermann Broch's fine novel *The Death of Virgil*, in which the poets is tempted to destroy his *Aeneid*. In his poem 'To Those Born Later', Brecht asks himself: 'What kind of times are they, when / A talk about trees is almost a crime / Because it implies silence about so many horrors?' (*Poems 1913–1956*, p. 318.) Horvath likewise maintained: 'To write plays has become ridiculous. We no longer have a single theatre where they could be staged.'
4. In the pamphlet *In unserem Lager ist Deutschland*, Alfred Kantorowicz quoted a letter from Romain Rolland which declared: 'Everything that we have loved and honoured in Germany is in your camp. With you are Goethe and Beethoven, Lessing and Marx. They are with you in the battle you are waging. I have no doubt of your victory.' Walter Benjamin published his celebrated *Letters from Germans* to show that genuine Germanity had no connection with the bloody glorification of the Germanic element perpetrated by the Nazis. Leopold Schwarzschild constantly reaffirmed that 'all German literature is in exile'. Thomas Mann declared on his arrival in the United States that wherever he was, German culture was to be found.
5. Belief in the existence of an 'internal emigration', an 'opposition *intra muros*', was common among most authors in the early exile period. Ernst Toller declared in his autobiography *I Was a German*: 'And where are my friends in Germany?' It was also for those still in the Reich that Brecht wrote his 'Five Difficulties in Writing the Truth' ('Fünf Schwierigkeiten beim Schreiben der Wahrheit', in Bertolt Brecht, *Versuche*, Frankfurt 1957–59, vol. 15, pp. 137–41).
6. For instance Klaus Mann and Ernst Toller, at the PEN Club congress in Ragusa (now Dubrovnik).
7. Cf. Ernst Bloch, *Heritage of Our Times*; Heinrich Mann, *Hatred*.
8. In *Weltfreund*, p. 369.
9. In *Verbannung*, p. 173.
10. Kurt Hiller, *Profile. Prosa aus einem Jahrzehnt*, Paris 1938, p. 236.
11. Klaus Mann, *Der Wendepunkt*, Frankfurt 1952, p. 292. [This passage does not appear in the English edition of *The Turning Point*.]
12. 'Fünf Schwierigkeiten . . .'; Bertolt Brecht, *Écrits sur l'art et la littérature*, vol. 2, Paris 1970, p. 12.
13. The distinction between 'political' and 'non-political' émigrés is thus hard to apply to writers. Some of these were already aware before 1933 that they were engaged in a political struggle, and saw themselves as activists. This was the case with Communist writers, or proletarian writers close to the KPD's organizations. Thomas Mann's appeals for a union of democrats and liberals to defend the Republic against the Nazis were a specific form of political struggle, even if he never really viewed himself as a 'writer-activist'. On the other hand, some writers who were highly politicized before 1933, such as Kurt Kläber or Ernst Glaeser, ceased to play a political role in emigration. The distinction between 'bourgeois' and 'revolutionary' writers also has little sense after 1933, in so far as Heinrich Mann, Klaus Mann and Ernst Toller became 'activists' in their own way, as indeed did Thomas Mann. Finally, because they had left the Reich in 1933, all writers who refused to return to Germany were considered by the Nazis as opponents.
14. No. 36, 1936.
15. This was *Bilanz der deutschen Judenheit*, published by Querido Verlag in 1934.

16. This text was reproduced in the SS organ *Schwarze Korps* (27 February 1936). In his clear-headed fashion, Tucholsky went on to write: 'A country is not just what it *does*, it is also what it accepts and supports. What ghosts that lot in Paris are, playing with something that no longer exists! Their way of squinting from the bank of the Rhine and still feeling themselves Germans – Good God! The Germans don't want you! They hardly notice you' (letter to Arnold Zweig, 15 December 1935; *Chroniques allemandes*, Paris 1982, p. 322).

17. Count Harry Kessler noted in his diary for 20 July 1935 that on his first night in Paris, Brüning 'is hiding himself because on no account does he want to have anything to do with any émigré clique. [. . .] Their exaggerated fuss at the outset, and their dissemination of stories which turned out to be untrue, did great harm' (*Diaries of a Cosmopolitan*, p. 469).

18. Letter to H. Rauschning of 8 April 1939. (Cf. H. Brüning, *Journals and Letters*, Harvard, p. 243.) In a letter to E. Rosenstock of 3 February 1940, Brüning still maintained that 'those who want to combat Nazism from within Germany must keep silent until a propitious moment', and that exile discussions 'do more harm than good'. He believed that he had not been able to prevent Hitler coming to power, and the emigration could only make Germany detested.

19. Letter to Ian Andersen, 9 August 1939.

20. Letter to J. Fisahn, 16 June 1941.

21. S. Zweig, *The World of Yesterday*, p. 295.

22. René Schickele wrote in 1933 *Die Witwe Bosca* (*Widow Bosca*), which according to him 'sought to represent by way of a chance individual in the street the ill fate impregnated with death and the need for vengeance on an impious age that worships idols.' In his last work in German, *Die Flaschenpost* (*Letter in a Bottle*, 1937), his hero takes refuge in an asylum in order to feel free and escape the mad world outside. Schickele has him say these prophetic words: 'Everything today drives towards destruction, instinctively, unconsciously, under a thousand pretexts. The world is ready to die.' Schickele himself died in Vence on 31 January 1940. Hermann Hesse wrote in similar terms to R. J. Humm on 8 July 1938: 'I see the world of today as a madhouse, and real life as a poor sensationalist play' (*Lettres*, p. 99).

23. *Die deutsche Literatur im Ausland seit 1933*.

24. *Freies Deutschland* 6, May 1945, p. 20.

25. Brecht, 'Sur le réalisme', *Écrits sur l'Art et la Littérature*, vol. 2, p. 31.

26. Musil too spent the exile years in extreme solitude. In a letter to G. Bermann Fischer of 12 January 1934, he claimed not to see any other Germans, especially no émigrés. In France, however, he did have contact with Robert Minder, Jules Romains and Jean Giradoux. Musil had practically no connection with exile circles, and did not even belong to the 'Friends of the *Volksfront*'. He only attended the Congress for the Defence of Culture as a guest.

27. Musil depicts on several occasions in his *Journal* (vol. 2, Paris 1981, especially pp. 404–5, 419, 423, 431, 459) his relationship to politics. 'Thomas Mann and his ilk write for people who exist; I wrote for people who do not exist,' he noted. He maintained that the writer who believes in a political mission 'succumbs to an illusion', and that 'the first duty of a writer is to serve not his country but his country's literature'. There is an 'intellectual extraterritoriality', and if some people confuse the pen and the sword, he for his part felt that he was 'fencing with a candle'. He accordingly rejected any idea of committed literature. In his *Notebook 13* he wrote: 'I do not struggle against fascism, but within democracy for its future, thus equally against democracy' (ibid., p. 508). If literature did have a task to fulfil, it was to fight 'for a higher moral nature'. As for the émigrés, he wrote: 'The "front of antifascist intellectuals" assumes that the true, the good and the beautiful exist. Only the Catholic Church has this right.' The same attitude can be found in Herman Hesse, who in a letter to Eduard Korrodi of 15 February 1936 described the attacks he was subjected to by both Nazis and émigrés. Hesse continued to

claim 'the position of outside and above party from which I have to apply the little bit of humanity and Christianity that I possess' (*Lettres*, p. 91). What he wrote about his novel *The Glass Bead Game*: 'to create an intellectual space in which I can breathe and live despite the poison spread over the world, and where I can have my refuge, my fortress' (ibid., p. 188) is reminiscent of the attitude of Ernst Jünger (*On the Marble Cliffs*) or Ernst Wiechert.

28. Such was the attitude displayed by Gottfried Benn in all his theoretical essays up to 1933. He railed against the democratic enthusiasm of other writers as an 'illusion of rationalists in short pants'.

29. The radicalization of some writers who became activists after 1933 is as surprising as the silence of certain others. The proletarian writer Kurt Kläber, member of the BPRS and author of *Barrikaden an der Ruhr*, went into exile in Switzerland and tended his garden without taking any further part in political struggle. He published children's books under a pseudonym. B. von Brentano, a friend of Brecht, also took no part in émigré struggles, nor did Erich Maria Remarque, despite being detested by the Nazis for his pacifist novel *All Quiet on the Western Front*. It was only in 1939 that Remarque took a fairly clear political stand.

30. Letters of 9 November and 19 November 1936; *Lettres*, pp. 490–1.

31. 'Leiden an Deutschland'.

32. These included *Das Wort, Pariser Tagblatt, Pariser Tageszeitung, Die Neue Weltbühne, Das Neue Tage-Buch, Die Sammlung, Neue Deutsche Blätter* and *Internationale Literatur*.

33. Toller attacked the Nazi government at the PEN Club's congress in Ragusa (Dubrovnik) of 1933. He defended imprisoned writers at the following year's congress in Edinburgh, and the same year attended the Congress of Soviet Writers. From May to September 1935 he campaigned in France and England to obtain work permits for émigrés. From October 1936 to February 1937 he toured the United States speaking on Hitler's Germany. He travelled through Spain during the civil war to gather evidence on the crimes of Franco, with a view to persuading the democracies to revise their attitude of 'neutrality'. He spoke on the radio in Madrid, sent messages to Roosevelt, and collected funds and food for the Spanish Republic. Until his death, Toller always believed in a certain power of speech.

34. Thomas Mann, 'Die Förderung des Tages', *Preussische Jahrbücher*, April 1928; *Gesammelte Werke*, vol. 11, p. 649.

35. Reported by Friedrich Wolf to the First Congress of American Writers, and by Alfred Kantorowicz ('In unserem Lager ist Deutschland', p. 24). The banned production had been shown in Bremen in April 1935. This Nazi recuperation of the classics was not without its problems. Schiller was appointed a 'national hero', and in 1938, a few weeks after the annexation of Austria, *Wilhelm Tell* was shown at the Vienna Burgtheater to celebrate Hitler's birthday. By 1941, however, the play was considered an encouragement to separatism and banned. It was not even studied now in schools. The actor Bernhard Minetti related in an interview (*Revue*, Jan.–Mar. 1983) the interesting reaction of Goebbels when he was told that the audience applauded Don Carlos's response: 'Sire, grant us the liberty to think.' He was content to ask what the following line was: 'A strange fantasy,' the reporter replied. Goebbels added that this was his opinion too.

36. *Frankfurter Zeitung*, 16 June 1937.

37. Cf. H. Gerstner and K. Schworm, *Deutsche Dichter unserer Zeit*, Munich 1939.

38. This text was published in *La Dépêche de Toulouse*, 3 October 1934.

39. H. Mann, *Verteidigung der Kultur*, p. 96.

40. The initiative for this seems to have come from Leonhard and Kantorowicz. Among other founders mentioned by Kantorowicz in his article in *Das Wort* (12, 1938, pp. 60–76) were Anna Seghers, Alfred Kurella, Theodor Balk, E. Leonhard, Gustav Regler, Ludwig Marcuse, F. Schiff, H. A. Joachim, Max Schröder and Bruno Frei.

41. The first SDS meetings in Paris were held at the Quaker meeting house, rue Guy de la Brosse, then at the home of Raymond Duncan, rue de Seine.
42. Alfred Kantorowicz, *Politik und Literatur in Exil*, p. 150. He maintained, counter to some historians of the emigration (Matthias Wegner in particular) that the SDS was not 'a charitable organization dominated by the Communists'. Though its members did indeed include Communist writers, others such as David Luschnat were Christian or pacifist. L. Schwarzschild and K. Heiden, who founded the Bund Freier Presse und Literatur, did not do so in opposition to the SDS, but following differences over the Popular Front. Kantorowicz emphasized that SDS sessions were attended by writers as far from Marxism as K. O. Paetel, H. A. Joachim, Manfred George, Paul Westheim, Alfred Döblin, Joseph Roth, Alfred Wolfenstein, Ludwig Marcuse and Hermann Kesten. Klaus Mann also stresses in *The Turning Point* the freedom of spirit that prevailed.
43. A. Kantorowicz, *Politik und Literatur in Exil*, p. 156, cites the following names in chronological order of their interventions. The political characterizations are also Kantorowicz's, and follow from the vocabulary of the time. E. G. Gumbel (pacifist), A. Kurella (Communist), L. Marcuse (liberal), E. E. Kisch, A. Seghers, G. Regler (Communist), D. Luschnat (Christian), A. Kerr (liberal), A. Kantorowicz (Communist), E. Leonhardt (liberal), Kurt Stern (Communist), M. Scheer (non-party, close to the KPD), Bodo Uhse (Communist), Hellmut von Gerlach (pacifist), A. Rüst (anarchist), A. Souchy (anarcho-syndicalist), Theodor Balk (Communist), Paul Westheim, G. Bernhard, G. Stern (essayists), W. Herzfelde (Communist), J. R. Becher (Communist), A. Koestler (Communist), R. Musil (non-political, liberal), Max Brod (liberal), E. Bloch (Marxist), H. Mann (republican), L. Schwarzschild (liberal conservative), H. Marchwitza (Communist), B. Frei (Communist), C. Misch (democrat), F. Lieb (Protestant theologian), A. Döblin (liberal), Piscator (Communist), E. E. Noth (liberal conservative), K. O. Paetel (national-revolutionary), Brecht (Marxist), J. Schmidt (Communist), W. Berendsohn (liberal), H. Siemsen (non-party), J. Roth (monarchist), W. Bredel (Communist), F. Wolf (Communist), A. Zweig (liberal), L. Feuchtwanger (liberal).
44. The BPRS, in contrast, which was re-established in Prague, Vienna and Paris, maintained a narrow (and somewhat sectarian) distinction between 'antifascist writers' and 'non-fascist writers'. According to J. R. Becher, its Paris section counted some thirty members in 1933.
45. For example Henri Barbusse, Paul Nizan, A. Viollis, André Malraux, E. Fleg, H. R. Lenormand, A. Charpentier, Louis Aragon, Ilya Ehrenburg, J. R. Bloch, R. Lalo, A. Hamon, H. Jeanson, Paul Vailliant-Couturier, E. Faure, J. Guéhenno, J. Cassou, E. Dabit, H. Lichtenberger, E. Vermeil, M. Aub, Pablo Neruda, Tristan Tzara, A. del Vayo, L. Araquistain, L. Durtain, J. Benjamin, Zang Hei King and B. Crémieux.
46. For instance Karin Michaelis and Martin Anderse-Nexö.
47. Kantorowicz explains that the proprietor was paid for the tea and coffee ordered by a collection, to which those present gave between 1 and 5 francs.
48. This included texts by Romain Rolland, Bertolt Brecht, Heinrich Mann, Stefan Zweig, Franz Werfel and Thomas Mann. It is hard to measure its impact.
49. Located on the place Saint-Germain-des-Prés, where the Deux Magots café now stands. The object of this was to provide the exiled writers with a certain protection, as well as putting them in touch with publishers and newspaper editors, and defending them with the French authorities. The SDS was legally incorporated in France in 1934, and also helped some little known authors to publish their works. It also financed the publication of several works by Brecht.
50. Many of these events were devoted to imprisoned writers. Exiled authors often came to read their own works. Some meetings were held around a theoretical subject, such as: 'How do we situate ourselves in relation to Germany?', 'The theoretical and practical question of reportage', 'The Third Reich in the mirror of exile literature', 'The social novel', 'Dostoyevsky and political literature'. Carl

Einstein spoke on art, Gustav Regler on the historical novel, Paul Westheim and J. Schmidt on Nazi culture, E. Schlesinger on antifascist literature for children, and Döblin on the literature of emigration.

51. Besides the demonstrations in support of Ossietzky and Renn, the SDS set up in autumn 1934 an Erich Mühsam Fund designed to rescue writers imprisoned in Germany, to protect their wives and children, as well as the widows and orphans of those who had been murdered.

52. These included Thomas Mann, Romain Rolland, Stefan Zweig, Franz Werfel, Alfred Kerr, A. Ehrenstein, R. Breuer, Gustav Regler, H. Marchwitza, E. Lasker-Schüler, E. Kuttner, B. Viertel, M. Hermann-Neisse, R. Leonhard, K. A. Wittfogel, Wilhelm Pieck and Klaus Mann.

53. Reproduced in *Neue Weltbühne*, 15 August 1937.

54. On 14 May 1933 Romain Rolland wrote a letter to the *Kölnische Zeitung*, in which as a mediator between German and French culture, he expressed his disgust as a demonstration of this kind. Following the 'official' response of R. Binding and other writers who declared their support for the 'Hitler revolution', Rolland expressed his support for the émigrés and the SDS, maintaining that the genuine Germany was in their camp.

55. Kantorowicz had made the French diplomat's acquaintance in 1928–29, when he was correspondent for the *Vossische Zeitung*.

56. Joseph Roth, Walter Hasenclever, Gustav Regler, J. R. Becher, H. Sahl, Ernst and Karola Bloch, E. Weinter, Hermann Kesten and Egon Erwin Kisch all lived here, among others.

57. Widow of the former British prime minister.

58. The British committee comprised H. G. Wells (president), Margot Oxford, L. Golding, Wickham Steed, J. B. S. Haldane, Hubertus Prinz zu Löwenstein and J. C. Haldane. In France, Max Schröder was responsible for its operation from 1934 to 1936. Kantorowicz was its secretary (information from Kantorowicz's memoirs).

59. A. Kantorowicz, *Deutsches Tagebuch*, p. 70.

60. More than 10,000 took part in this action. Those present included Newbold Morris, Clifton Fadiman, O. M. Graf, Professor A. Domin (representing Italian exiles), Karin Michaelis (Denmark) and Geneviève Tabouis (France). Oskar Maria Graf was also co-founder of the Schutzverband Deutsch-Amerikanischer Schriftsteller.

61. These were books by Sinclair Lewis, Upton Sinclair, Ernest Hemingway, John Steinbeck, Pearl S. Buck, L. Bromfield, Langston Hughes, Theodore Dreiser, John Dos Passos, Richard Wright, Carl Sandburg, Stephen Vincent Benet, Sherwood Anderson, George Bernhard Shaw, H. G. Wells, Aldous Huxley, Bertrand Russell, D. H. Lawrence, Christopher Caudwell, Stephen Spender and Winston Churchill.

62. Written by Stephen Vincent Benet. A book for schools was derived from this, and widely distributed in the United States: *Ten Years Ago the Nazis Lighted the Way of Their Own Destruction*. Records were also made with extracts from Nazi speeches and texts by Schiller and Goethe.

63. Associated with this action were the Metropolitan Library Council, the Book and Magazine Union, the Poetry Society, the associations of booksellers and librarians, trade unionists, the Joint Committee for the Restoration of Burned and Banished Books in Europe, whose members included F. D. Roosevelt, Franz Werfel and Albert Einstein.

64. Plays by Shaw, Gorky, Friedrich Wolf, Walter Hasenclever, Ernst Toller, Ödön von Horvath, Carl Zuckmayer, Werner Herzog, Julius Hay and Hugo von Hofmannsthal. Many American magazines (*Saturday Review of Literature, Free World Magazine*, etc.) devoted special issues to this event.

65. In 1944 once again, the Women's Council for Postwar Europe declared its wish to see the burned books rapidly republished in Europe, and asked for the anniversary of 10 May 1933 to be kept as a symbol of the union of peoples in the struggle for liberty. On 10 May 1944, an event was held at the Town Hall Club in New York on

the theme 'The Restoration of Books in War-Devastated Countries'. The *New York Times* of 7 May 1944 also celebrated the anniversary.

66. This project was initiated in Zurich in 1948 with Ossip Kalenter, Walter Fabian and Otto Zimmermann.

67. Located at 2 rue Charles Matrat, Issy-les-Moulineaux, in 1936.

68. 'It is not lists of names of thousands of victims that move people. Just one name, one fate, one man, whether called Müller or Cohn, acts more effectively than thousands of others.' (A. Kantorowicz, *Deutsches Tagebuch*, p. 18).

69. S. Zweig, *The World of Yesterday*, pp. 314–5.

70. Ibid., p. 315.

CHAPTER 7   THE STRUGGLE AGAINST NATIONAL SOCIALISM

1. In *Das wahre Deutschland* (edited by K. Spiecker and H. A. Kluthe), the latter still maintained in October 1939 'that we should not overestimate the political importance of the emigration, and believe that a counter-government in exile could transform Germany. The revolution can only come from within.' The role of the émigrés was to support the German resistance. The same faith in an opposition from both within and without was reaffirmed by Thomas Mann in 'The Artist and Society'.

2. *Letters of Thomas Mann 1889–1955*, p. 211.

3. *Neue Weltbühne*, 26 September 1935.

4. *La Dépêche de Toulouse*.

5. As A. Banuls writes in *Heinrich Mann, le poète et le politique* (p. 374), 'Hope latches on here to the slightest tales, rumours and anecdotes, related unchecked and without precision, complacently exaggerated and transformed into pious images; even these quotations have an invented air, the polemicist having a way of making everything seem improbable.'

6. A former émigré, Sebastian Haffner, who subsequently became a political commentator in Britain, wrote in his book on Hitler: 'During the first six years of a reign that would last twelve years, Hitler surprised both friends and enemies by a series of achievements of which scarcely anyone, at the start, would have believed him capable [. . .]. In January 1933, when Hitler became Chancellor of the Reich, there had been six million unemployed in Germany. Just three years later, in 1936, the return to full employment was a reality. A state of crying distress and poverty of the masses had given way to a modest but tranquil well-being.'

7. Various scenarios were imagined by the émigrés. Brüning believed in a coup by the army, perhaps led by Göring. In January 1936, he maintained that Göring might restore the monarchy, which would lead to a parliamentary regime. In 1939 he still believed that Göring would eliminate Himmler. The Communists believed in the possibility of influencing the SA and showing them that the proletarian character of the regime was a myth. Ernst Niekisch, talking with Karl Mannheim in London in 1934, spoke of the need to ally with the SA against Hitler. The Sozialistische Arbeiterpartei (SAP) put its faith in a confrontation between the army and the Nazi leaders. Wels and the SoPaDe held that the army's Prussian ethic could not be reconciled with the situation of the working class.

8. Gustav Regler even wrote a short story, 'Death in St Michael's Church', about a wounded Communist prisoner who took refuge in the church where Mgr Faulhaber was in the middle of preaching. Pursued by the Nazis, he came to die in a confessional. The story won the Heinrich Mann Prize for the best antifascist short story.

9. Cited after P. Hoffman, *Widerstand, Staatsrecht, Attentat*.

10. After 1933 the *Roter Stosstrup* reappeared, organ of a group with that name, whose earlier activists had been arrested. *Neu Beginnen* continued until 1938, though its

activists were also arrested (Fritz Erler was condemned to ten years' imprisonment in 1938, but survived to play a role in the SPD after the War, as did Kurt Schumacher, who was interned in concentration camp.) Kernels of resistance were also organized by the Communist Opposition (KPO) around August Thalheimer and Heinrich Brandler. Otto Engert was executed in January 1945. The SAP also managed to keep going for a while despite arrests, as did the ISK (Internationaler Sozialistischer Kampfbund), directed in Germany by Helmut von Rauschenplatt, who was arrested in 1935. The networks of *Unser Wort* were dismantled in 1938, along with those of the 'councilists' (Rote Kämpfer), disciples of Gorter and Pannekoek, arrested in 1937. A certain number of activists from the Socialist Youth (B. Wager, H. Frieb, A. Brunner) tried to obtain weapons and were executed in 1942.

11. The evening of the Reichstag fire, Thälmann was attending a clandestine meeting of the KPD's political bureau and it was impossible to warn him. He escaped immediate arrest and was only apprehended on 3 March.
12. Factional struggles had been significant in the KPD during the Weimar years, and continued to be so in exile, according to some historians. Remmele, who had questioned the KPD line after its 'bolshevization', was called to appear before the Comintern's control commission (cf. H. Dühnke, *Die KPD von 1933 bis 1945*, Cologne 1972, p. 110). The rivalry between Ulbricht and Schehr also continued. Many historians ascribe the failure of an escape attempt for Thälmann involving a Communist prison guard to his rivalry with Ulbricht. Communist historians generally rebut this claim, maintaining that the attempt failed because Thälmann was moved to another prison. Cf. the differences between the accounts of H. Dühnke and Klaus Mammach.
13. Schubert was denounced to the Gestapo by Alfred Kattener, who had likewise denounced Thälmann. Kattener was executed for this by the Communists, and the Nazis immediately murdered a thousand Communists in reprisal.
14. In particular, *Am Vorabend des zweiten Weltkrieges*, vol. 2, Berlin 1977.
15. Cf. *Exil in Frankreich*, pp. 60ff.
16. He worked particularly with Rudolf Leonhard and Anna Seghers.
17. The Comintern's office in Basle, and the World Front Against Imperialist War and Fascism.
18. After the confiscation of the KPD's assets (24 May 1933) and the law against the re-establishment of parties (14 July), illegal work became increasingly difficult for the Communists, and their leaders were finally ordered to retreat abroad. The question of the KPD's preparedness for illegality was long disputed between Communist and non-Communist historians. According to some, especially in the GDR, this had been envisaged since 1932. Its effectiveness, in that case, is far from clear, given the large number of arrests. Many excellent works on the activities of the KPD in exile were published in the GDR, and a good summary is given by Klaus Mammach, *Widerstand 1933–39*, Berlin 1984.
19. For a detailed account of the Social-Democratic emigration, cf. J. Rovan, *Histoire de la social-démocratie allemande*.
20. The importance of this German resistance was systematically exaggerated by the exiles, whether wilfully or not. Here again, it was Heinrich Mann who gave the most optimistic descriptions. As A. Banuls wrote (*Heinrich Mann, le poète et la politique*, p. 375): 'He also knew what the Ruhr miners were whispering, and the dockers of Hamburg; he explained what workers who had "left work to discuss together" had "agreed" about the occupation of Prague; he reconstituted their emotional dialogue.' Heinrich Mann went as far as to give details that defy all probability: in their workshop, workers had hung up for several days a portrait of Léon Blum . . . Fine examples of what Manès Sperber rightly called 'intoxication of the mind'.
21. One of the most remarkable examples is that of the proletarian writer Jan Petersen (Hans Schwalm), a former member of the BPRS, who continued illegal political work after 1933, and with the help of other young writers, maintained contact with

the exiles and provided them with information. The *Neue Deutsche Blätter* carried a column, 'Stimmen aus Deutschland', which published testimonies smuggled out in this way. Texts by émigrés were also published in the underground paper *Stich und Hieb*. Most member of Petersen's group were arrested in 1935 or soon after. Author of the remarkable novel *Unsere Strasse*, Petersen brought the greetings of underground Germany to the 1935 Congress for the Defence of Culture, appearing on the platform in a mask.

22. It is hardly necessary to spell out that these illegal returns took place in very risky conditions. The Gestapo was often informed of them by spies who infiltrated the émigré milieu. It regularly organized bogus rendezvous near the border or within Germany in order to murder them.

23. See Gustav Regler, *The Owl of Minerva*, pp. 174–5, where these meetings in Paris between oppositionists from Germany and Communist exiles are described. Robert Uhrig, a KPD cadre who remained in the Reich, was still able to meet émigrés in Prague in 1938. He was subsequently arrested, and executed in 1944. 'Couriers' were sent into Germany from Czechoslovakia, but this type of operation was often suicidal. Even if they were armed, the majority were killed by police bullets or arrested (cf. K. Mammach, *Widerstand 1933–1939*, p. 45). Out of five activists sent on 4 July 1935, four were killed at the frontier. When cadres tried to travel to Prague in May 1935, they had a gun battle with the SS. One of them was killed, but Kurt Hager, though wounded, was narrowly saved by the Czech Communists.

24. The Social-Democrat activist Günter Markscheffel relates (*Exilés en France*, p. 73) how he participated in underground Socialist activity directed at Germany. Working with a team that assembled and repaired elevators in the Lorraine mines, close to the border, he made contact with miners from the Saar (one section of the mines crossed from French to German territory) and with their assistance, met underground Social-Democrats from Coblenz, Mainz, Ludwigshafen, etc. He was sent into Germany several times to gather information on the political situation. Arrested by the French police and taken to the prefecture in Metz, he was ordered to leave the frontier departments, as he represented 'a danger to good relations between France and Germany'.

25. On the details of the underground press, cf. Jürgen Stroech, *Die illegale Presse*, Leipzig 1979.

26. *Wir kämpfen für ein Rätedeutschland*, p. 61.

27. To mention only the main ones: *Hamburger Volkszeitung, Süddeutsche Arbeiterzeitung, Thüringer Volksblatt, Ruhr-Echo, Lenins Weg, Neue Arbeiterzeitung, Der Funke, Die Rote Einheitsfront*.

28. Including the *Zeitschrift für Sozialismus, Sozialistische Warte*, and *Neue Front*. The SAP also printed clandestine literature, and Willy Brandt visited Germany as late as 1936, living there for six months as a 'student' with Norwegian identity papers. The Communist Opposition distributed an illegal paper *Gegen den Strom*.

29. As well as leaflets and papers, a number of radio transmitters operated in Czechoslovakia, the USSR, and later the United States. Otto Strasser's 'black transmitter' operated in Prague from 1933 to 1935, until the assassination of engineer Rudolf Formis by the Gestapo.

30. Cf. Horst Dühnke, *Die KPD von 1933 bis 1945*, p. 183.

31. Some historians even speak of a waste of human lives, comparing the number of Communists arrested and executed for distributing leaflets with the very weak impact that they had. In Leipzig alone, between September 1934 and April 1935, 2,000 Communists were arrested for distributing illegal literature.

32. On the Saar campaign, see the exhibition catalogue *Zur 50–jährigen Wiederkehr der Saarabstimmung von 13. January 1935*, Saarbrücken 1985.

33. A. Koestler, *The Invisible Writing*, p. 327.

34. M. Sperber, *Au-delà de l'oubli*, p. 66.

35. Koestler wrote: 'The Comintern's attitude to the Saar reflected the struggle between the old, radical line and the "People's-Front" line. The idiotic slogan of the "Red

Saar" had obviously been designed by the German Central Committee for the purpose of evading the issue until that struggle was settled' (*The Invisible Writing*, p. 330).

36. Cited by Koestler, ibid., , p. 331.
37. Manès Sperber, *Au-delà de l'oubli*, p. 66.
38. When this was urgently bought up by Goebbels, the editorial staff produced another paper, *Grenzland*, supporting the same objectives. Cf. *Das Neue Tage-Buch*, 4 December 1934.
39. This film, shot by Soviet technicians and directed by Joris Ivens, was deemed inadequate by Béla Kun, though its distribution was nonetheless authorized. According to Regler, however, the film was still not shown, the Saarland Communists criticizing him for not celebrating Stalin. Regler claimed that the real reason was fear of the Nazis' subsequent reaction (*The Owl of Minverva*, p. 224). Regler also wrote an interesting novel on the Saar, *La Sarre en feu* (Paris 1934), dedicated to Herbert Becker, who was murdered in the Saar by the Nazis in October 1934. The novel's optimism was cruelly rebutted by the plebiscite.
40. *The Owl of Minverva*, p. 225.
41. Ibid., p. 226.
42. Ibid., p. 229.
43. M. Sperber, *Au-delà de l'oubli*, p. 69.
44. Apart from the remarkable political biography by his companion, Babette Gross, *Willi Münzenberg. Eine politische Biographie*, his varied work and activity have not been greatly studied. Babette Gross met Münzenberg in 1922; her sister Margaret Buber married Heinz Neumann, a KPD leader, and died in a Siberian camp. Cf. also M. Buber-Neumann, *La Révolution mondiale*; Arthur Koestler, *The Invisible Writing*; and Manès Sperber, *Le Pont inachevé*.
45. In Britain and the Scandinavian countries Münzenberg organized *Blumentage*: children sold bouquets of flowers for the IAH. In Germany, they collected money by singing revolutionary songs in working-class districts.
46. Between June 1922 and May 1923, the IAH sent four thousand tons of foodstuffs to Russia.
47. He got artists and writers such as Arthur Holitscher, Franz Jung and M. Andersen-Nexö invited to Russia, all of whom brought back enthusiastic accounts that Münzenberg then published.
48. Münzenberg even enlisted Gabriel d'Annunzio in the IAH campaign, persuading him to publish an appeal in support of Russian peasants.
49. In Berlin alone, fifty-eight IAH kitchens dispensed more than 7,000 meals each day.
50. Hugenberg, leader of the Nationalist party and boss of the UFA film company, was backed by the Krupp corporation.
51. Editorship of the *AIZ* was initially entrusted to Franz Höllerling, an Austrian journalist and friend of Brecht and John Heartfield, then to Lilly Corpus, secretary to Ruth Fischer and the companion of J. R. Becher.
52. *AIZ* had such great success that the PCF planned to publish a similar illustrated weekly in conjunction with the IAH. Münzenberg sent Babette Gross and Lilly Corpus to Paris to discuss this, and contacts were made with Hachette and with the Banque Ouvrière et Paysanne. The first issue appeared on 1 May 1928: *Nos Regards. Illustré Mondial du Travail.*
53. For example, Larissa Reissner's novel *Hamburg auf den Barrikaden*, which was immediately banned for incitement to civil war.
54. *Was sahen die deutschen Arbeiter in Russland.*
55. Münzenberg always refused to attack the Social-Democrats, and championed the unity of the workers' parties.
56. Münzenberg did not hesitate to resort to stock-exchange speculation to support his enterprises. He was even involved in a cigarette-manufacturing company based in Dresden: KPD leaders appeared on its boxes. The Nazis, for their part, had already launched their own cigarette brand, adorned with a swastika.

57. Between 1924 and 1931, Mezhrabpom distributed 241 Soviet films. Many writers contributed to its work, as well as actors and directors (Erwin Piscator, Karl Junghanns, Hans Richter, Joris Ivens, Lotte Lenya, Paul Wegener, Alexander Granach and Fritz Gershow). Münzenberg distributed Soviet films in the United States, Mexico, Argentina and Canada, and organized a campaign for the screening of *Battleship Potemkin*, which had been banned in Germany.
58. In particular *1 x 1 = 3*; *Hunger in Waldenburg*; and *Mutter Krausens fährt ins Glück*.
59. In 1924, the IAH assisted workers in China.
60. See Chapter 8, note 55.
61. This was presided over by Henri Barbusse. Romain Rolland and Maxim Gorky sent personal representatives. Münzenberg's address was greeted with an ovation.
62. He lived in the home of Marie-Claude Vogel, daughter of the publisher of *Vu* and *Jardin des Modes*, a friend of the Soviet Union, who later married the daughter of Paul Vaillant-Couturier. Barbusse and Vogel introduced Münzenberg to Gaston Bergery, a Radical-Socialist who had established his own anti-fascist movement Front Commun. Bergery welcomed Münzenberg's initiatives whilst keeping his independence from the Communists. He approached interior minister Camille Chautemps to obtain political asylum for Münzenberg as well as a French identity card as a political refugee.
63. The French section of this was directed by Count Karoly, exiled in Paris. Lord Marley offered his services to the committee, as did a number of British intellectuals.
64. Münzenberg's close collaborators including Otto Katz, Hans Schulz and Else Lange, as well as Communist functionaries and workers from his Berlin publishing operation such as Karl Sauerland, editor of *Der Rote Aufbau*, Bruno Frei, Alexander Abusch, and Communist writers such as Gustav Regler, Arthur Koestler and H. Siemsens.
65. These included L. Magyar, the friend of Eugen Varga, and Otto Unger, co-founder of the youth international.
66. He was criticized for having taken on as a collaborator a certain Liliane Klein, whose father was supposedly a spy for Franco. She was only a typist and had no access to any important document. On three occasions Münzenberg was called before the Comintern's control commission.
67. It was thanks to Togliatti that Münzenberg managed to leave the Soviet Union. Before his departure he met the former German Communist leader Heinz Neumann, who had been questioned for months by the Comintern control commission and was arrested and deported not long after. Münzenberg left copies of his archives in the safe of a Catholic press agency in Paris; they were later burned by the Gestapo. The originals, entrusted to German Communists, were left by Friedrich Wolf in his hotel room when he left Paris, and subsequently used by the Gestapo as evidence against various collaborators of Münzenberg's (such as Josef Füllenbach). These also disappeared.
68. No criticism of the USSR is to be found in this book. The name of Dimitrov is mentioned three times, that of Stalin once (with praise).
69. The Prussian finance minister before von Papen's 'constitutional coup', he later became financial adviser to Chiang Kai-shek.
70. Founded in 1937, the DFP published the *Freiheitsbriefe* which were illegally distributed in Germany until the start of the War (a total of 75 issues).
71. Arthur Koestler was editor-in-chief of this paper. Its contributors included Catholics (Werner Thormann), German writers such as Thomas and Heinrich Mann, Stefan Zweig, Joseph Roth, René Schickele, Arnold Zweig, Alfred Döblin, Alfred Kerr, Rudolf Olden, E. J. Gumbel, Manès Sperber and Max Hodann, as well as French (G. Bidault, Y. Delbos). Sperber wrote: 'The paper's political line was of course antifascist, and especially hostile to Nazism and all aspects of the Third Reich. The paper took a resolute position for the Spanish Republic and the united front, for unity of action in the struggle against all forms of fascism. As we were all

persuaded that Russia was our surest ally, we decided unanimously that *Die Zukunft* should not attack the USSR or its rulers, and to publish nothing negative on this subject' (*Au-delà de l'oubli*, p. 148). Koestler obtained a contribution from Freud, then left the editorship to write *Zero and Infinity*. Ludwig Marcuse was responsible for the cultural section.

72. A number of Münzenberg's collaborators were killed by the Gestapo; others fell victim to Stalin's terror. Margaret Buber-Neumann, sister of Babette Gross, noted about Münzenberg's death: 'The theory of a common crime has been put forward. But he had too little money to tempt a murderer. Others suspected the Gestapo, but this had every interest in taking him alive. For Moscow, on the contrary, alive he was dangerous. He knew too much about the Comintern's secret activities, and could have been the most fearsome opponent' (*La Révolution mondiale*, p. 387). The same theory of Stalinist assassination was developed by Koestler (*The Invisible Writing*, p. 497) and Kurt Kesten (*Deutsche Rundschau*, 1957, pp. 484ff.), though it has never been in any way proved. Münzenberg's successor, Otto Katz, a friend of Piscator, better known under the name of André Simone, was accused during the Slansky trial of being a 'British agent' and 'Zionist conspirator'; he was hanged in Prague in 1952.

73. The English edition is *The Brown Book of the Hitler Terror and the Burning of the Reichstag. Prepared by the World Committee for the Victims of German Fascism (president: Einstein), with an Introduction by Lord Marley*, London 1933. This was followed by *The Reichstag Fire Trial. The Second Brown Book of the Hitler Terror, Based on Material Collected by the World Committee for the Relief of the Victims of German Fascism, with an Introductory Chapter Specially Written for the Book by Georgi Dimitrov, a Foreword by D. N. Pritt, K.C., an Appendix on Murder in Hitler-Germany by Lion Feuchtwanger and 21 Illustrations from Original Sources*, London 1934.

74. See note 94 below. Dutch friends of Van der Lubbe published in response to the *Braunbuch* the *Roedboeck van der Lubbe en de Rijksdag Brand*, Amsterdam 1933.

75. According to Babette Gross, the original edition sold more than 70,000 copies. Translations were published right away in the Netherlands, Sweden, France, Czechoslovakia, Finland, the United States, Romania, Denmark, Spain, the USSR, and even Greece and Palestine.

76. Leader of the Communist fraction in the Reichstag. Torgler had left the building around 8.15 p.m. on 27 February, together with Wilhelm Koenen. Accused of involvement in the fire, he immediately went with his lawyer Kurt Rosenfeld to the police to prove his innocence, and was straight away arrested. Dimitrov was of course well-known, but Taneff and Popoff who had been arrested with him in a Berlin restaurant were unknown functionaries.

77. The Marley Committee (World Assistance Committee for the Victims of German Fascism), chaired by Lord Marley, included among its members Albert Einstein and Paul Langevin. Its secretary was Dorothy Woodman, member of the Labour party and the Fabian Society. The Marley committee included both Communists and Social-Democrats, who agreed to work with the campaign to refute the thesis of a leftist conspiracy.

78. After the War, Moro-Giafferi became procurator-general at the Haute Cour de Justice.

79. A former Radical deputy (1928), Bergery was one of the initiators of the Front Commun Contre le Fascisme (1933), though he went on to vote full powers for Marshal Pétain in 1940. After serving as the Vichy government's ambassador to the Soviet Union, he was brought before the French supreme court after the War, but acquitted in 1949.

80. *Bewaffeneter Aufstand*. Of course this volume had little credibility.

81. He had previously defended Walter Rathenau's murderers, as well as the defendants in the Reichswehr trial at Ulm.

82. These included R. Breitscheid, A. Grzesinski, P. Hertz and G. Bernhard.

83. *The Brown Book of the Hitler Terror*, p. 37.
84. Mirow Abraham, head of its department for international relations, was in charge of liaison between the Thälmann committee and the Comintern.
85. These included Sinclair Lewis, Malcolm Cowley and Granville Hicks, as well as many scientists, academics and journalists.
86. This showed a giant Dimitrov questioning a minuscule Göring with the words: 'Are you afraid of my questions, Mr President?'
87. Cited from Arthur Koestler, *The Invisible Writing*, p. 243.
88. Dimitrov took over the leadership of the Communist International. No one knows what became of Taneff. On Dimitrov, see Arthur Koestler, *The Invisible Writing*, pp. 238ff.; Jean Mérot, *Dimitrov, un révolutionnaire de notre temps*, Paris 1962; Georgi Dimitrov, *Selected Works*; and *Georgi Dimitrov, Leipzig 1933*, Sofia 1968.
89. Torgler's case was very strange. Contrary to what is stated in the second *Brown Book*, he was not sent to the Oranienburg concentration camp but remained in Berlin under Göring's protection, subsequently transferred to the police prison at Plötzensee. Released in 1936, he earned his living as a commercial traveller. He was expelled from the KPD in 1935, and joined the SPD after the War. (Cf. G. Badia, *Feu au Reichstag*, Paris 1983, pp. 247–8.)
90. On this controversy, see Gilbert Badia, *Feu au Reichstag*, and *Der Reichstagbrand-prozess und Georgi Dimitroff*, Berlin 1982.
91. The *Braunbuch* was reissued in both West and East Germany, particularly by Röderberg Verlag, Leipzig 1983.
92. 'It became the bible of the anti-Fascist crusade,' wrote Koestler (*The Invisible Writing*, p. 243). The precise sales figures are hard to estimate in any detail. Koestler's figure is substantially higher than that given by Babette Gross, which is rather more likely.
93. In the preface to the second *Braunbuch*, Münzenberg wrote: 'The allegations of the book, marshalling as they did the proofs of National Socialist complicity in the burning of the Reichstag were a crushing blow for the German government' (*The Reichstag Fire Trial*, p. 31). He maintained that the book had been read by millions, and that many articles had been devoted to it in the international press. In Britain it was called by the *Manchester Guardian* 'the most important work that has yet been produced on the Hitlerite dictatorship' (ibid.). Though Göring had threatened with death anyone found with the book in their possession, thousands of copies were secretly distributed in the Reich.
94. These documents were collated by the Comintern's information section. Koestler and Regler both stress the hypothetical character of some of the information presented. When it was republished in the GDR, Alexander Abusch rejected this thesis and saw almost the whole of its information as well-founded. For a detailed examination of the historical truth of the *Braunbuch*'s claims, see Gilbert Badia, *Feu au Reichstag*, pp. 87ff. While the descriptions of Nazi terror are certainly irrefutable, the portrait given of Van der Lubbe is certainly historically false. He was certainly blackened in order to show him as an unsavoury individual manipulated by the Nazis. The idea of Van der Lubbe having connections with the Nazis that derived from his supposed homosexuality (affirmed in the *Braunbuch* on very shaky grounds, and denied by his Dutch friends) is highly unlikely.
95. A. Koestler, *The Invisible Writing*, pp. 241–2.
96. As a former member of the Freikorps troops who defended the Reichstag against the Spartacists in 1919, Regler had been aware of the underground passage from that time. According to his memoirs (*The Owl of Minerva*, pp 160–1), he had the building's plans photographed for Münzenberg at the Strasbourg library.
97. M. Sperber, *Au-delà de l'oubli*, p. 95.
98. Manès Sperber again remarks: 'It was well known to many writers, musicians, painters, professors, priests of all kinds, people of the theatre or cinema and a great many other representatives of the intellectual professions that Münzenberg was a leading figure in the international movement financed and led by Moscow. They

knew who he was and this in no way lessened their admiration for Willi: was he not a great example of tolerance and independence from any party, in a struggle for culture, peace and freedom?' (*Au-delà de l'oubli*, p. 94.)

99. The most complete account of these publications and their operation is that by Hélène Roussel (in *Les Barbelés de l'Exil*, pp. 357ff.). This excellent essay contains a full list of titles published by these imprints, and their history.

100. Fourteen in all; cf. *Les Barbelés de l'Exil*, pp. 380–2.

101. This was put at the disposal of Willi Münzenberg by Paul Lévy, and the imprint was financed with funds provided by the Comintern. From 1934, it was located at 169 boulevard Saint-Germain, then at 83 boulevard du Montparnasse.

102. Münzenberg now sought to unite all adversaries of the Nazis, along lines similar to those developed by *Die Zukunft*, also published by Éditions Sebastian Brant.

103. Directed by the Comintern, its books were published successively in Basle, Strasbourg and Paris.

104. Gustav Regler recalls in his memoirs that in October 1934, the management of the Reichsbahn reported the discovery of some 699 subversive texts in trains arriving from Belgium and the Netherlands. More than 1,860 forbidden booklets and other printed matter were seized from travellers (*Le Glaive et le fourreau*, pp. 195ff. [Not in the English edition of *The Owl of Minerva*)].

105. 'The Gestapo overlooked a pamphlet which, ostensibly giving instructions for the development of photographic film, was accompanied by a free sample of printing-paper. The paper came in an authentic Kodak packet, and no amateur photographer would expose it to daylight' (Gustav Regler, *The Owl of Minerva*, p. 174).

106. On the story of these disguised writings, see Heinz Gittig, *Illegale antifaschistische Tarnschriften 1933–45*, and F. C. Weiskopf, *Unter fremden Himmeln*, pp. 82ff.

107. Even if Heinrich Mann, with the utopianism that marked nearly all his articles, maintained in the *Dépêche de Toulouse* on 31 July 1937: 'We know that those writings of ours that have reached Germany have been devoured by workers there, and a section of the youth fight to get them.'

108. This development was particularly clear in France among intellectuals close to Action Française, who shifted from the Germanophobia that had marked the right in the 1920s to a Germanolatry that heralded the collaboration of the occupation. Robert Brasillach was the most typical case of this.

109. W. Langhoff, *Les Soldats du marais*, Paris 1934; G. Seger, *Oranienburg. Erster authentischer Bericht eines aus dem Konzentrationslager Geflüchteten. Mit einem Geleitword von H. Mann*, Karlsbad 1934; H. Beimler, *Au camp d'assassins de Dachau: Quatre semaines aux mains des bandits à chemises brunes*, Paris 1934.

110. This was inspired by a famous book on wild animals. The Nazis had already used it for a book *The Jews Are Watching You*, devoted to the supposed 'Jewification' of German life.

111. Paris 1936.

112. In Wuppertal, 11,000 workers were arrested in 1935 and accused of being hostile to the regime. The previous year over a hundred people had been condemned in Hamburg, In 1933, 116 had been condemned to a total of 491 years in prison, and several beheaded.

113. In 1936, Carrefour published *Was soll mit den Juden geschehen*, and *Der gelbe Fleck. Die Ausrottung von 50,000 deutschen Juden. Mit einem Vorwort von Lion Feuchtwanger*.

114. For instance Fritz Lieb's *Christ und Antichrist im dritten Reich* (1936).

115. Mobilization was unable to save Edgar André, former leader of the Red Front Fighters.

116. Hellmut von Gerlach built up the campaign for Ossietzky in Paris, Rudolf Olden and Otto Lehmann-Russbüldt in London, Willy Brandt in Oslo, Kurt Singer in Stockholm, K. Grossmann in Prague. After von Gerlach's death in August 1935, Hilde Walter took over. Many actions were held in the United States (with Otto Nathan, Kurt Rosenfeld, W. Hegemann and G. Hartung). The Swiss Social-

Democrat Hans Oprecht, brother of Emil Oprecht, director of Europa Verlag, gathered the signatures of 124 Swiss parliamentarians and that of the theologian Karl Barth. Willy Brandt, Hilde Walter and Kurt Grossmann collected the signatures of 69 members of the Norwegian parliament. Petitions were circulated in almost all countries, even Turkey, and a large number of American newspapers joined the campaign.

117. Thanks to the visits of his wife, Thälmann was able to receive messages and send information out. Cf. the collective biography *Thälmann*, Berlin 1982, pp. 685ff.

118. Cf. *Ausgewählte Schriften in drei Bänden*, vol. 3, Berlin 1958, pp. 58–9.

119. Preface to *Die Welt im Kampf für Thälmann*, Paris 1936.

120. The name of Thälmann was given to IAH brigades, and many Soviet towns made him an honorary citizen.

121. In France, more than fifty public meetings were organized in his support. By 1934, 20,000 pamphlets on Thälmann had appeared, along with 30,000 badges with his picture and 32,000 postcards. 15,600 posters were produced, and 260,000 leaflets, while over 100,000 signatures were collected in his defence (*Thälmann*, pp. 692–3).

122. The leading body of the International Centre for Right and Freedom in Germany included Marcel Cachin, Léon Jouhaux, André Malraux, Romain Rolland and Thomas Mann.

123. Thälmann was imprisoned in Berlin, Hanover, Bautzen and finally Buchenwald, where he was murdered on 18 August 1944. The Nazis made out that he had been killed by an Allied air raid on 28 August. As a final homage, detainees organized a funeral rite – illegally, of course. A Soviet painter drew his portrait in charcoal on a piece of cardboard. The Communist writer Bruno Apitz played the violin, and prisoners recited poems. Thälmann's wife and daughter were also arrested and imprisoned by the Gestapo, finally being liberated by the Red Army. The trial of Wolfgang Otto, a former SS man accused of having taken part in the murder, opened in Krefeld on 6 November 1985.

124. Published under the pseudonym Pierre, with a preface by Francis Jourdain.

125. Bureau d'éditions de Paris, 4 rue Saint-Germain-l'Auxerrois. This publisher also brought out in the same series: H. Beimler, *Au camp d'assassins de Dachau*, O. Piatnisky, *Les horreurs fascistes en Allemagne*, 1935; *Où en est l'Allemagne*, 1935; and *Cent jours de lutte* (on the KPD's illegal press), 1933.

126. Edgar (Etkar) André was beheaded by axe in Hamburg on 4 November 1936. He had been arrested on 5 March 1933 for fighting against the SA.

127. Some of these letters had been published in 1931–32 in the *Frankfurter Zeitung*. The volume appeared in Switzerland in 1936 under the pseudonym Detlev, designed to be smuggled into Germany.

128. For instance the volumes published in London in the Living Thoughts Library series. Thomas Mann introduced works by Schopenhauer, Stefan Zweig and Tolstoy, Heinrich Mann introduced Nietzsche, and Arnold Zweig Spinoza. Alfred Wolfenstein's anthology *Stimmen der Völker. Die schönsten Gedichte aller Zeiten und Länder* was published in Amsterdam in 1938. He declared: 'The meaning of these poems is "humanity" through the magic of art.' Emigrés were often keen to publish texts by the classical authors to whom they laid claim. Innumerable anthologies of Heine were compiled by the émigrés between 1933 and 1939.

129. T. Mann, 'Achtung Europa!', *Aufsätze der Zeit*, Stockholm 1938.

130. Éditions de la Nouvelle Critique, 1936. Berthold Jacob, a pacifist journalist subsequently kidnapped by the Gestapo, gave a figure of 25,000 Nazi agents working abroad.

131. Albert Schreiner, a Communist journalist and future head of the general staff of the XIIIth International Brigade, wrote a number of books of astonishing precision on the Nazis' war preparations.

132. A number of these volumes were specifically commissioned by Münzenberg, who was persuaded of the imminence of war. According to Gustav Regler, documents were sometimes stolen from German embassies abroad.

133. Cf. also A. Müller (A. Schreiner), *Hitlers motorisierte Stossarmee, Heeres- und Wirtschaftsmotorisierung im III. Reich*, Strasbourg 1936.

134. Erckner was a former officer. This volume was introduced by Professor Paul Langevin, Lucien Lévy-Bruhl and M. Prenant, and published by INFA.

135. 'In Hitler's Germany, everything – absolutely everything, people and things – exist only for the purpose of war, in other words uniquely under their military form'. (*L'Allemagne, champ de manuvre*, p. 19).

136. Ibid., p. 215.

137. Éditions du Carrefour, 1936.

138. Publications de l'Office Central d'Information, Paris 1937.

139. *La Nouvelle Guerre allemande*, p. 17.

140. Its sponsoring committee included P. Langevin, L. Lévy-Bruhl, M. Willard and P. Soupault; its executive was made up Prenant, Wallon, Masereel, Jourdain and Cogniot.

141. Cf. the excellent study by Jaques Omnès in *Les Bannis de Hitler*, pp. 185–198.

142. A. Koestler, *The Invisible Writing*, p. 296.

143. Ibid., p. 297.

144. Ernst Heidelberger, who worked there in 1934 along with other young German émigrés, recalls that their task was to clip articles for archiving from the Nazi press. About twenty people worked there, in quite a family atmosphere, even though they knew each other only under pseudonyms (oral communication, 27 February 1983).

145. One of the first initiatives of INFA was the publication of six articles by Koestler in *l'Intransigeant*, on 'underground Germany'. Koestler met with a number of French figures who agreed to donate funds for the INFA, as well as giving advice or letters of introduction.

146. M. Sperber, *Au-delà de l'oubli*, p. 50.

147. The astonishing detail of the documentation gathered by the German émigrés around Willi Münzenberg and the INFA needs to be stressed. What is surprising rather is that so little trace of this is to be found in the press, or in studies and articles on Germany published in France at this time. A number of French figures do however seem to have followed Münzenberg's publications fairly closely. Several such texts for example were bequeathed to the Bibliothèque Saint-Geneviève, in various collections belonging to relatively well-known personalities. These books and pamphlets constitute a more or less unique mass of information on the Third Reich. It is curious to note, on the other hand, the success of Hermann Rauschning's book *Hitler Speaks*, which some still see today as a 'historical source', though it is most likely that three-quarters of what Rauschning says was either the fruit of laborious compilation or of highly dubious authenticity.

148. Unfortunately Koestler's memoirs must be used with caution, as they were written after his break with Communism and he depicts his past from a resolutely hostile standpoint. Since INFA had been tied to the Comintern from its beginnings, its 'taking in hand' seems questionable, and Koestler says nothing to suggest that the institute was even anything other than 'orthodox'.

149. A. Koestler, *The Invisible Writing*, p. 317.

CHAPTER 8   BIRTH AND DECLINE OF THE *VOLKSFRONT*

1. See the excellent presentation by Wolfgang Klein, *Paris 1935. Erster Internationaler Schriftstellerkongress zur Verteidigung der Kultur. Reden und Dokumente*, Berlin 1982.

2. This has to be examined, if only on account of the role that Henri Barbusse played both in the proletarian literature movement and in the preparation of the 1935 congress.

3. Among their number: P. Abraham, Alain, Louis Aragon, J. R. Bloch, Jean Cassou, René Crevel, E. Dabit, André Gide, J. Giono, Jean Guéhenno, L. Guilloux, André

0

Malraux, V. Marguerite, L. Mouissgnac, Paul Nizan, Romain Rolland, C. Vildrac and Paul Vaillant-Couturier.
4. This theme was notable in Gide's lecture and in the message from Gorky, too sick to travel to the congress.
5. 'What is needed for the defence of culture is human comradeship. [. . .] If this congress has been witness to one thing, it is precisely the great new desire of all writers for communion. [. . .]. I even envisage here such a literary school [. . .]. For my part, I look to the future without pessimism' (reprinted in Jean Guéhenno, *Entre le passé et l'avenir*, Paris 1979, pp. 260ff).
6. 'An Indispensable Precision for Any Struggle Against Barbarism', 'Rede auf dem 1. Internationalen Schriftstellerkongress, *Versuche*, vol. 15, pp. 137–41.
7. These subjects were debated by André Chamson and Henri Barbusse; cf. *Europe*, July 1935. In France, the question of heritage arose from the subject of relations between classical and proletarian literature. Aragon, Gide, Benda, G. Friedmann, Malraux and P. Gérôme all brought up this theme.
8. Herbert R. Lottman has well evoked the fevered atmosphere of the 1935 congress in his study *La Rive Gauche* (Paris 1981), with both passion and nostalgia. Writers who rallied in support of the German antifascists at this time included Gide, Romain Rolland, Theodore Dreiser, John Steinbeck, H. G. Wells, Bertrand Russell, Steven Spender, W. H. Auden, Ernest Hemingway, Pablo Neruda and Garcia Lorca.
9. Though Gorky was unable to attend, Boris Pasternak, Ilya Ehrenburg, Isaak Babel, Mikhail Koltsov and V. Ivanov all took part.
10. Clara Malraux noted in her memoirs (*La Fin et la commencement*, Paris 1976, p. 105): 'A writers' congress in Paris is fully justified to defend what others destroy [. . .]. Gide, for his part, took part in the ceremony with the fervour of a first communion.'
11. Cf. A. Kantorowicz, *Politik und Literatur im Exil*, p. 209. The full proceedings are reissued in *Paris 1935. Erster Internationaler Schriftstellerkongress*.
12. The successive sessions were as follows. 'The Role of the Writer in Society', chaired by Waldo Franck (USA), with contributions from Aldous Huxley, John Strachey, Martin Andersen-Nexö, Karin Michaelis, V. Ivanov, J. R. Bloch, M. Kolzov, Alfred Kerr, Ernst Toller and P. Abraham; 'The Individual', chaired by Heinrich Mann and J. R. Bloch, contributors Gide, Musil, Max Brod, René Crevel (Klaus Mann's friend, who sadly committed suicide while the congress was still in progress), Ilya Ehrenburg, Menno ter Braak and Malraux. Heinrich Mann's concluding remarks were apparently drowned by thunderous applause. On 23 June, 'Humanism' chaired by Henri Barbusse and Paul Nizan, in which Waldo Franck, Luc Durtain, J. R. Becher, Jakub Kadri (Turkey) and Valle-Inclan (Spain) successively spoke, followed the same evening by 'Nation and Culture' chaired by Jean Guéhenno and E. M. Forster, with the participation of Henri Barbusse, Anna Seghers, A. Williams-Ellis, André Chamson, Mikitenko, Tobidsé (Georgia), Michael Gold (USA) and even Tristan Tzara. Monday's discussion, with Martin Andersen-Nexö in the chair, was again devoted to 'Nation and Culture' as well as to 'The Problem of Creation and the Dignity of Thought' (chair Carlo Sforza, or Valle-Inclan in Kantorowicz's account; the printed programme does not always agree with the account given in *Das Neue Tage-Buch*). Heinrich Mann, Lion Feuchtwanger, Ernrst Bloch, Gustav Regler, Tichonov, Lahuti (USSR), Nezval (Czechoslovakia), Léon Moussignac and H. R. Lenormand also took part.
13. In particular, the foundation of an international union of exiled writers, ways of assisting them, and the organization of an antifascist magazine (*Das Wort*).
14. Hans Schwalm, who wrote as Jan Petersen, was a member of the BPRS and had remained in Berlin to continue clandestine agitation in the working-class districts. He signed various articles in the *Neue Deutsche Blätter* with three asterisks. After the congress, he was unable to return to Germany as he had planned.

15. 'At this congress Gide proclaimed his allegiance to Communism. The Party had the sense not to attempt to subject him to any form of discipline; he spoke his own language. With him were Malraux and some of his personal friends, partly sceptical, partly fired with enthusiasm by his speech. Louis Aragon, flattered and filled with pride at the success of this sensational conversion, for which he took the credit, was among the admirers. Gide's declaration was everywhere regarded as an event of world-importance, so hopeful was everyone in those days, and so profoundly did we still believe in the influence of writers' (Gustav Regler, *The Owl of Minerva*, p. 230).

16. G. Regler, *Le Glaive et le fourreau*, p. 261. [Not in the English edition of *The Owl of Minerva*.]

17. G. Regler, *The Owl of Minerva*, p. 232.

18. Brecht for example wrote to George Grosz in July 1935: '[. . .] I can give you a piece of vital information. We have just rescued culture. It took 4 (four) days [. . .]. If necessary, we'll sacrifice ten to twenty million people.' (*Letters 1913–1956*, p. 208).

19. Professor Salvemini (Italy) mentioned the Siberian labour camps and the deportation of Victor Serge. Magdalena Pa, a French Trotskyist, demanded that the congress take a stand on Serge's fate, as an example of an attack on freedom of thought. Anna Seghers, countered that it was not the right moment to discuss such things: 'When a house is burning,' she declared, 'you can't stop to help someone with a splinter in their finger.' Victor Serge was released, nonetheless, thanks to his friends' intervention. Chance had it that he left France, where he had lived as a refugee, in March 1941, on the same ship as Anna Seghers and Claude Lévi-Strauss.

20. The Germans included were J. R. Becher, Alfred Kantorowicz, Anna Seghers and Ernst Toller. Its twelve-member presidium was made up of E. M. Forster, Aldous Huxley, G. B. Shaw, Sinclair Lewis, S. Lagerlot, Valle-Inclan, Heinrich and Thomas Mann, Maxim Gorky, André Gide, Romain Rolland and Henri Barbusse.

21. This was of course mocked both then and later by various right-wing writers. Robert Brasillach wrote in *Notre avant-garde*, Paris 1941: 'The false revolution of 1936 was indeed a revolution of intellectuals. Hurling themselves after emoluments, all they came out with were reports and theses' (p. 161). As for Céline, he wrote in 1938: 'Never would I have taken the stage to howl . . . No! No! No! I've never microphoned or macrophoned at meetings! . . . I love you Stalin! My beloved Litvinov! My Comintern! . . . I've never voted in my life! I've never signed manifestos . . . for those martyred here, those tortured there . . . You can rest assured . . . it's always a Jew involved . . . a kike or mason committee' (Cited from H. R. Lottman, *La Rive Gauche*, p. 7).

22. The congress received widespread praise in the exile press, and its texts were often reproduced, especially those of Heinrich Mann. The pacifist Leonard Frank declared during a discussion: 'Whoever lives at a time of war and fascism has the duty to struggle against war and fascism. We must form a united front.'

23. The work of the writer in society, the dignity of thought, the individual, humanism, nation and culture, the problem of Spanish culture, cultural heritage, literary creation, relations between writers and the Republic, etc.

24. For details of the Congress sessions and interventions, see the Spanish re-issue *Il Congreso internacional de escritores antifascistes*, 3 vols, Barcelona 1978.

25. The Spanish anarchists, for their part, boycotted the congress.

26. Writers attending included A. Malraux, L. Renn, J. Benda, M. Kolzov, A. Tolstoy, M. Andersen-Nexö, W. H. Auden, M. Cowley, A. Machado, José Bergamin and P. Neruda.

27. This was held from 19 to 23 June 1936, with Ernst Toller in the chair. Its participants included Malraux, Julien Benda, Jean Cassou, Paul Nizan, Gustav Regler, H. G. Wells and Ralph Bates. A total of seventeen nations were represented.

28. Maria Teresa Leon and Rafael Alberti had met Stalin in 1937, and according to the former, Stalin made the absence of Gide a condition for sending a Soviet delega-

tion. A number of Spanish historians see this as not very credible. Cf. Manuel Aznar Sold, *Pensamiento Literario y compromiso antifascista de la Inteligensia espanola républicana*, p. 139.

29. In her study *Volksfront für Deutschland?*, Ursula Langkau-Alex rightly maintains that all the forces were already in play here that later formed the basis of the Popular Front in exile, as well as its internal divisions.

30. In particular, the Internationaler Sozialistischer Kampfbund (ISK), the Sozialistische Arbeiterpartei (SAP), Linke Opposition (LO) and KPD-Oppposition (KPO).

31. Vol. 28, no. 6, 1932, pp. 194–8.

32. Detested by the bourgeoisie for several of his works, especially *Der Untertan* and *Professor Unrat* (filmed as *The Blue Angel*), Heinrich Mann was viewed by the Communists as a 'progressive bourgeois writer', though his written protest against the execution of 'traitors and saboteurs' in the USSR had aroused the KPD's hostility. His desire to remain above party had also provoked a fairly violent attack by J. R. Becher, and Mann had become a favourite target of the *Linkskurve*. Becher of course found Hiller's proposal quite ridiculous.

33. Cf. Langkau-Alex, *Volksfront für Deutschland?*, p. 34.

34. We should note here that Otto Wels had temporarily withdrawn the SPD from the Socialist International, while Theodor Leipart, the trade-union leader, wrote a letter to Hitler on 21 March. This only reinforced Communist suspicions, and Fritz Heckert wrote in 'Was geht in Deutschland vor? Bericht an das EKKI' (*Communist Internationale* 7, pp. 114ff.), that Hitler had got rid of a faithful dog that had outlived its usefulness. When Leipart was arrested, Heckert concluded that it was to punish him for not having managed to attract the workers to the Nazi camp.

35. Several documents even assert that anyone talking of a defeat in this connection had no place in the Communist movement, this being a sign of political blindness. (Cf. Horst Dühnke, *Die KPD von 1933 bis 1945*, pp. 70ff.)

36. Through to 1935, Communists continued to describe fascism as a desperate attempt by the bourgeoisie to stem proletarian revolution. Even after the Brussels conference, scarcely any attention was paid to the underlying basis of Nazi ideology. Wilhelm Pieck declared that Jews who remained in Germany were 'more or less safe', and that the Nazis' racist ideology simply signalled a hatred for the USSR which had successfully resolved the racial question (ibid., p. 73).

37. Thus on the plebiscite to confirm Hitler's decision to leave the League of Nations, which received 95.1 per cent support, the KPD maintained that the 4.9 per cent against were votes for Thälmann.

38. *Rundschau* 24, 1935, p. 893.

39. *Inprecorr* 10, 1933, p. 341.

40. From the name of the programmatic text published in summer 1933 under the pseudonym of Milles. The ancestry of this group lay in the 'Leninist Organization' founded in 1929.

41. Wilhelm Pieck, *Wir kämpfen für ein Rätedeutschland*, 1936, pp. 47ff. Cited after *Die KPD von 1933 bis 1945*, p. 83.

42. *Rundschau*, 14, 1934, pp. 508ff.

43. Cf. *Volksfront für Deutschland?*, pp. 68ff.

44. Though avowedly non-party, this organization was directed by Social-Democrats. It was also involved in distributing antifascist papers and leaflets. Robert Breitscheid and Friedrich Adler both played an active role in it.

45. It aroused little enthusiasm in Prague. In Paris, it duplicated the work of the Welthilfskomitee and the Ligue des Droits de l'Homme, whose counterpart was also very active in England.

46. We should recall that from 1933 on, common actions against the Nazis had been undertaken by Communist and Socialist workers, while the KPD had made certain approaches towards forming a united front, but met with the refusal of the Socialists. The expression 'social-fascism' was still used in June 1933 in Willi Münzenberg's magazine *Unsere Zeit*, published in Paris. Fritz Heckert, a member

of the KPD's central committee from 1919 to 1936, published in Basle in 1933 *Ist die Sozialdemokratie noch die soziale Hauptstütze der Bourgeoisie?* in which he argued how social-reformism evolved towards social-chauvinism and then social-fascism. The Nazi seizure of power was still blamed on the Social-Democrats. The same thesis was upheld by Wilhelm Pieck in *Wir kämpfen für eine Rätedeutschland*, which denounced the left Socialists as 'support troops of fascism' allied to the 'Trotskyist gang'.

47. 'An die christlichen Werktätiger Deutschlands', *Rundschau* 58 (1934), p. 2588, and 60, p. 2673.

48. Some historians (e.g. Dühnke, *Die KPD von 1933 bis 1945*, p. 88) see this as the first use of this term as a slogan.

49. Forty to fifty per cent of SA men were of proletarian origin. In 1934, Walter Ulbricht launched an appeal, 'Comrades in the SA', seeking to rally these errant workers to Communism. (*Rundschau* 41, p. 1648.)

50. 'In Paris, the apotheosis was reached in a scene on Bastille Day 1935 in the Salle Bullier where, acclaimed by a delirious crowd of many thousands, the veteran Communist leader, Marcel Cachin, embraced the Social-Fascist reptile Léon Blum, and kissed him on both cheeks, while half of the audience wept and the other half sang first the Marseillaise, then the Internationale' (Arthur Koestler, *The Invisible Writing*, p. 395).

51. With the support of Maurice Thorez.

52. On 6 February, André Marty wrote in *Humanité*: 'It is impossible to struggle against fascism without struggling also against social-democracy'; he even proposed a demonstration against both enemies.

53. Vaillant-Couturier, however, still published in *Humanité* his notorious article: 'Who paid for the bullets?', while Jacques Duclos declared in an article in *Cahiers du bolchévisme* (1 February) that the united front did not mean keeping silent about social-democratic responsibilities.

54. It was envisaged that this would watch over the defence of working-class rights, and form self-defence groups against threatened fascist aggression.

55. Resolution of the PCF central committee, 21 March 1934.

56. This movement, comprising 3,200 delegates from fifteen European countries who had met at the Salle Pleyel in 1933, included 2,590 French representatives of whom 1,153 were Communists or non-party fellow-travellers, 190 Socialists, 26 anarchists, 11 Radical-Socialist republicans, 4 Christians and 15 from miscellaneous groups.

57. Maurice Thorez could still write in *Humanité* for 13 April 1934: 'All this loose talk about a marriage between Communists and Socialists is fundamentally foreign to the spirit of bolshevism. We do not plan to unite with the social-democrats. You don't mix fire and water.'

58. *Le Populaire*, 6 and 13 June 1934.

59. *Par l'unité d'action, nous vaincrons le fascisme*, July 1934.

60. 'This slogan of united action has entered hearts and minds. Nothing will now uproot it,' Jacques Duclos declared.

61. *Die KPD von 1933 bis 1945*, p. 97.

62. This was within the group that gathered around Pieck and Ulbricht.

63. Neu Beginnen was seen as 'Communist' by right-wing Socialists, and 'elite Leninist' or 'Trotskyist' by the Communists, who attacked it for criticizing the KPD leadership as well as the SPD. Ursula Langkau-Alex (*Volksfront für Deutschland?*, p. 71) mentions that one of the first steps in the rapprochement of the two parties was the Deutschsprachige Sozialistische Gruppe which in spring 1933 brought together mainly young exiles belonging to different left parties – KPD, SPD, SAP, LO – and sought to overcome antagonism between them by way of discussion. According to this author, in summer 1933 young Communists were called to order by KPD functionaries. She also mentions an article in the *Pariser Tagblatt*, 'Junge Sozialisten in der Emigration' (17 January 1934) which described the Communist

tactic as 'Stalinist' and attacked it for always seeking the main enemy in other workers' parties. We should also recall here that Socialists and Communists gave evidence together at the Reichstag counter-trial in 1933, and that joint solidarity actions were undertaken even though the SoPaDe was hostile to such collaboration.

64. For example the polemic of November–December 1934 between Aufhäuser and Ulbricht.
65. *Die Rundschau* 60, 1934, pp. 2739ff.
66. Ibid., 63, 1934, p. 2869.
67. The slogan of a 'red Saarland' proposed by Walter Ulbricht was criticized by the Comintern in July 1934.
68. These included E. Gentsch, M. Reimann, P. Daub, A. Abusch, P. Dietrich, Gustav Regler and Arthur Koestler.
69. The Saarland Catholics, in particular, supported reattachment to the Reich.
70. Though Wilhelm Pieck still maintained the result was a defeat for Hitler, as the Nazis won only 85 per cent of the vote in place of the 98 per cent they claimed.
71. 'We were still directing our main attack against Social-Democracy at a time when we should have directed it against the fascist movement' (*Wir kämpfen für eine Rätedeutschland*, p. 25).
72. Several appeals for the formation of this united front of German antifascists had been made after the Montreuil rally of 21 June 1935. The idea of a conference for the creation of a united front was mooted by Pieck in his 'Notizen zur Lage der KPD' (1 July 1935), and on 11 July, the KPD's political bureau projected a meeting with the Social-Democrats. In the *Pariser Tagblatt* 561 for 26 June 1935, the writer Konrad Heiden launched the slogan: 'Put an end to our fragmentation' ('Heraus aus der Zersplitterung'). This same article contained the first sketch of a political platform for the *Volksfront*.
73. Among the most important: *Gegen-Angriff* edited first by Alexander Abusch, then Bruno Frei, subsequently replaced by the *Deutsche Volkszeitung* (edited by Frei in Prague), which contained a regular *Volksfront* column. Münzenberg's *AIZ* published a number of articles by writers, Communist and other, who supported the *Volksfront*: Heinrich and Thomas Mann, Robert Breitscheid, Willi Bredel, E. E. Kisch, Theodor Plievier, Wedding, Anna Seghers, Arnold Zweig and Münzenberg himself. Just as important was another paper that Münzenberg edited, *Unsere Zeit* (December 1933 to 1935), which continued the IAH paper *Der Rote Aufbau*. Its contributors included Theodor Balk, Henri Barbusse, A. Abusch, K. Billinger, Brecht, Bruno Frei, A. Kantorowicz, K. Kesten, J. Petersen, G. Regler, B. Uhse and E. Weinert.
74. The SPD was supposed to break with the bourgeoisie, accept united action being organized in advance, recognize the need for revolutionary struggle and the dictatorship of the proletariat, and give no support to imperialist war. Unity of action had to be established on the basis of democratic centralism, as per the Bolshevik example.
75. The exiled KPD multiplied its attacks against the Trotskyists, seeing them as 'fascist agents'. The Comintern *Rundschau* was to hail the Moscow trials as a victory against fascism and its Trotskyist ally. Pieck intervened himself with an article of 11 February 1937, 'Hitler-Faschismus und Trotskysmus'. Many Communist articles from this time maintained that the Trotsykists were agents of Göring, seeking to unleash a war against the USSR with the help of German and Japanese fascism. The elimination of Stalin's opponents in the Moscow trials, the Trotskyists in particular, was even presented as a victory of the Popular Front.
76. Cf. Leon Trotsky, *The Struggle Against Fascism in Germany*, New York 1971.
77. Despite Gestapo surveillance, a number of workers left Germany to fight in the International Brigades, and funds for the Spanish Republic were secretly collected in German factories.
78. 'Die grosse Neuheit', *Die Neue Weltbühne*, 36, 1935.
79. 'Eine Aufgabe wird sichtbar', *Das Neue Tage-Buch*, 31, 1935.

80. On 17 December 1935. According to Heinrich Mann, this was the first action of the German *Volksfront*. Alongside the Communists Willi Münzenberg, W. Koenen and Hans Beimler were the names of the Social-Democrats V. Schiff, Robert Breitscheid, Max Braun and E. Kirschmann. The appeal was then countersigned at Heinrich Mann's proposal by twenty-four exiled writers and journalists, including ten Communists.
81. Edited jointly by the Communist Bruno Frei and the Socialist Max Braun, *Deutsche Information* appeared three times a week. Articles signed by Communists and Socialists could also be found in the *Mitteilungen der deutschen Freiheitsbibliothek*, even though the SoPaDe, in a circular of 24 January 1936, once again forbade its activists from collaborating with the Communists. As a general rule, Social-Democrat émigrés in France did not respect this ban.
82. The *Neue Weltbühne*, organ of the liberal and pacifist intellectual left under the Weimar Republic (Ossietzky, Tucholsky), in exile championed positions close to the KPD, after a brief Trotskyist interlude under the editorship of Willi Schlamm.
83. Cf. *Die KPD von 1933 bis 1945*, p. 239. The emphasis was placed on civil liberty, culture and democracy.
84. The SAP acknowledged the usefulness of a tactical alliance with liberals and anti-bourgeois intellectuals, but saw in this a danger for a future government. Moreover, the SAP never hid its distrust towards the Soviet Union and its sympathy for the Spanish POUM.
85. In particular, in the areas of economics, civil liberty, democracy and the role of parties.
86. Several accounts testify that Heinrich Mann declared on the subject of his discussions with Walter Ulbricht that he could not have a relationship with a man who 'suddenly makes out that the table you're sitting at is not a table but a duck-pond, and tries to force you to accept this' (Alfred Kantorowicz, *Politik und Literatur im Exil*, p. 63).
87. From November 1937 the Socialists published *Deutsche Mitteilungen*.
88. These appeals were signed by several Communists and fellow-travellers such as Heinrich Mann, Franz Dahlem, Paul Merker, Leonhard Frank, E. E. Kisch, Anna Seghers, Willi Bredel, Rudolf Leonhard, A. Kantorowicz, Albert Schreiner and even Alfred Kerr.
89. In 1937 the SAP broke into a number of factions, and its relations with the KPD became increasingly antagonistic. The Communists accused certain SAP leaders of 'Trotskyism' and being hand in glove with the Gestapo.
90. Cf. G. Badia, *Une tentative de Front Populaire allemand à Paris (1935–1939)*, p. 118.
91. Otto Katz, it seems, made many approaches to intellectuals at this time, but without great success.
92. Heinrich Mann feared that Ulbricht was only making 'a popular front for himself' (letter to Max Braun of 25 October 1937, cited by Alfred Kantorowicz, *Deutsches Tagebuch*, p. 48). The bad relationship between the two is attested by a number of witnesses, including Kantorowicz and Babette Gross, Willi Münzenberg's companion. (Cf. also *Une tentative de Front Populaire allemand*, p. 113.)
93. *Une tentative . . .*, pp. 114–15.
94. 'A disinterested man, outside of parties, but ready to serve his people, addresses this prayer to the workers' parties: achieve the unity of the working class, achieve it without further delay.' (*Deutsche Volkszeitung*, 23 April 1939, cited by G. Badia, *Une tentative de Front Populaire allemand*, p. 116.)
95. The majority of émigrés kept their doubts about the Soviet Union under wraps until the time of the German–Soviet pact, as it seemed the sole power able to oppose fascism. Even after his break with the KPD, Arthur Koestler declared that the Soviet Union represented 'our last and only hope on a planet in rapid decay'. He added: 'I clung tenaciously to this belief for another year and a half, until the Hitler-

Stalin pact destroyed this last shred of illusion' (*The Invisible Writing*, pp. 473–4). Manès Sperber followed a similar course.

96. Cf. Ingrid Lederer, 'Munich et le pacte germano–soviétique dans la presse des émigrés', in *Les Barbelés de l'exil*, p. 115.

97. This included the unfortunate Klaus Mann, likewise attacked as a Soviet agent.

98. Works withdrawn included Heinrich Mann's *Professor Unrat* and Lion Feuchtwanger's *The Oppenheims*. A number of Communist plays criticizing Germany were likewise banned.

99. There were – alas! – countless such attacks, which can only be understood as an unconditional desire to justify Stalin's policy. For even if it was possible to view the German–Soviet pact as an attempt by the USSR to gain time, it is hard to comprehend how Molotov could declare in 1939 that 'the wish to destroy Hitlerism is both absurd and criminal', how the Communist parties of France, Germany and Britain could term the preparations for war against Hitler as 'imperialist', how Poland could be simply termed 'fascist and reactionary', or how the Third Reich's concentration camps could be equated with prison camps in India and workers be given the task of 'unmasking anti-Hitlerite phrase-mongering'. Walter Ulbricht, for his part, showed no hesitation in speaking of an imperialist war prepared by France and Britain, which aimed to dismember Germany as a step towards attacking the Soviet Union.

100. M. Sperber, *Au-delà de l'oubli*, p. 164. The situation was all the more absurd in that, after encouraging the émigrés to join the French army to combat Hitler, the Communist party now encouraged them to avoid any military obligation. In the meantime, as Sperber puts it, the French army had again become 'imperialist'.

101. According to Babette Gross, the party apparatus opposed his being granted a US visa, and he was deported to Auschwitz and later murdered. Gustav Regler, after his break with the party, states that he was also denounced to the American police in a letter claiming that he was a Gestapo spy (cf. *The Owl of Minerva*, p. 363). Such statements should be treated with caution, as their authors were now anti-Communist; Koestler's memoirs in particular are not always exact.

102. His wife Eva was accused of having decorated pottery with motifs which, viewed from a certain angle, could look like swastikas, while Alex Weissbert supposedly intended to kill Stalin during a hunting party.

103. Between late 1939 and June 1940, some 500 German and Austrian Communists were handed over to Germany. Recalled to Moscow from Siberian prison camps, they were then taken west to the Polish border. Margaret Buber-Neumann was on the convoy that reached Brest–Litovsk on 3 February 1940: 'An NKVD officer accompanied by a group of soldiers led us to the railway bridge spanning the Bud. Officers came towards us from the other side; we recognized the SS uniform. The SS officer and his NKVD colleague saluted each other with the utmost cordiality' (*La Révolution mondiale*, p. 397).

104. In France, this was the start of the famous crisis that would lead Paul Nizan to break with Communism.

105. We should recall that Italy supplied the rebels with some 1,000 planes, 950 tanks and automatic machine-guns, 1,426 mortars, 250,000 rifles, 7.5 million shells and 14 billion lire's worth of matériel. Germany, by June 1938, had provided 650 planes, 200 tanks, and 700 artillery pieces. More than 200,000 Italian soldiers fought in Spain, while the German Condor Legion counted some 50,000. (Cf. *La Solidarité des peuples et la république espagnole*, Moscow 1974, pp. 11–12.)

106. As early as August 1936, many Americans already asked to join the Spanish armed forces.

107. The example of Malraux is the most famous in France. In England the volunteers included Winston Churchill's nephew Esmond Romilly.

108. It is hard to gauge the exact motivations, both political and personal, that drove so many volunteers to Spain. The case of antifascist workers and émigrés who joined the International Brigades is relatively clear, while for intellectuals it was more

usually a wave of idealism and revolt. Malraux, for his part, was driven by his cult of heroism and death as well as by his political convictions. (Cf. Clara Malraux's account, *Voici que vient l'été*, Paris 1973, in which she describes her companion as impatient to 'erect his own statue'.)

109. Apart from the number of German antifascists who died in Spain, Arthur Koestler narrowly avoided execution. Some members of the International Brigades captured by the Francoists had their eyes put out before being sent back.

110. Carl Einstein fought with the anarcho-syndicalists. His wife became a nurse and was subsequently interned in France along with the remainder of the Republican army. He committed suicide in 1940.

111. The scion of a Prussian officer family, Hans Kahle became a Socialist in 1914 and headed the XIth Brigade under the nom de guerre of 'Hans'. He led the offensive at Guadalajara and on the Ebro. A friend of Hemingway's, he was subsequently a refugee in Britain and the United States, becoming a journalist on the New York *Daily Worker*.

112. A. Kantorowicz, *Deutsches Tagebuch*, pp. 51ff.

113. Gustav Regler travelled to Spain with the pretext of delivering a van with a printing press, a projector and some rolls of film, in his capacity as German secretary of the International Writers' Association.

114. G. Regler, *The Owl of Minerva*, p. 284.

115. Ibid., p. 285.

116. 'We had no feeling that he must be revenged. Each of us reckoned with a similar end, and it was very much more agreeable to contemplate than, for example, the prospect of lying sick in a Paris hospital, begging alms from some charitable organization' (ibid., p. 286).

117. A. Koestler, *The Invisible Writing*, p. 381.

118. The group led by Gustav Szinda, head of the general staff of the XIth International Brigade, left from Paris.

119. They had to go first to Perpignan, then by bus to the Pyrenees, which they crossed illegally to reach Figueras.

120. Hans Kahle, Fritz Rettmann, Heinrich Wieland, Alfred Neumann, Heinrich Rau, Max Roscher, Otto Kühne, Franz Klamm, Fritz Dickel, Arthur Dorf.

121. Paul Bergman, Ernst Braun, Kurt Braun, Kurt Brödinger, Herbert Seifert, Hans Martens.

122. Kantorowicz fought as an officer. His wife was an announcer on the German-language broadcasts of Radio Madrid. He also worked on the Brigade archives.

123. Women volunteers included doctors (Ursula Aman, Rosa Coutelle), nurses (E. Bier, A. Dörfel, A. Schmidt), and wives of male volunteers (K. Wohlrath, K. Dahlem, L. Möller, G. Friedmann, S. Hager).

124. Thus the Edgar André battalion included Germans, Poles, Hungarians, French, Yugoslavs, British, Czechs, Slovaks and Irish. There were also Germans in the XIIth and XIIIth Brigades.

125. G. Regler, *The Owl of Minerva*, p. 286.

126. The Thälmann battalion lost 220 men in the battles of Brihuega, Trijueque and Torija, and a further 600 in those of Brunete, Quijorna and Villanueva-del-Pardillo. In the year 1938 alone, it lost over 1,000 men.

127. Former members of the Brigades who joined the *maquis* included Otto Kuhle, Max Friedmann, Kungler, W. Schwarze, H. Priess, H. Kokowitsch, K. Weber, F. Fugmann, M. Brings, A. Mahnke, H. Schürmann, W. Vesper and F. Blume.

128. Kurt Lohberger was an exemplary case. Interned in a French camp and then handed to the Gestapo, he was sent to Greece in a disciplinary unit, but managed to escape and join the partisans, later heading a German antifascist centuria in a regiment of the Greek Popular Army (ELA).

129. Hermann Geisen and Kurt B. Garbarini, former International Brigaders, started antifascist propaganda in the German army in Belgium in 1941. They were arrested,

and beheaded in a Berlin prison. A number of generals in the GDR, such as Heinz Hoffmann, had been members of the International Brigades.

130. Cf. Silvia Schlenstedt, *Exil und antifaschistisches Kampf in Spanien*, p. 287.
131. These included wall newspapers, leaflets, and Brigade newspapers. Each Brigade had one or more of these; the XIth: *Ataquemos, Hans Beimler, Todos Unidos, Der 12 Februar*; the XIIth: *A l'Assaut*; the XIIIth: *Adelante*. These papers were often produced in several languages.
132. A number of volumes were described as 'Copyright XI Brigada Internacional' or 'Ediciones del Comisariado de las Brigadas Internacionales'.
133. In Saxony, the Ruhr, and Silesia. At Aachen, seventy workers were arrested for collecting money for Spain. According to Gestapo figures, some 3,000 young people were arrested for expressing support for the Spanish Republic.
134. In particular by workers in Düsseldorf and Duisburg. A women's demonstration was organized outside the NSDAP offices in Munich.
135. In particular in Hamburg and Bremen. A number of German vessels refused to transport containers of weapons to Spain.
136. These included Heinrich Mann's *Es ist Zeit, Deutsche Soldaten! Euch schickt ein Schurke nach Spanien!*
137. German-language broadcasts were also transmitted from Barcelona starting in January 1937.
138. This transmitted antifascist broadcasts in Germany on 29.8 metres short-wave, as well as in Portuguese, Italian and Bulgarian. Gerhard Eisler and Erich Glückauf were in charge of the programming.
139. Ludwig Renn had fought in the International Brigades as an officer in July 1937. He made many appearances in the United States, Canada and Cuba, speaking to the League of American Writers as well as in many universities, to the League Against War and Fascism (in Pittsburgh) and at the protest meeting against five years of Nazi terror held at Carnegie Hall. Some of these meetings attracted more than 5,000 people. Unaccustomed to civilian manners, Renn recalled in his memoirs how he had to acquire an evening suit to address the American public.
140. This was chaired by Vicki Baum, with an introduction by Ernst Toller.
141. G. Regler, *The Owl of Minerva*, p. 315 [translation modified].
142. In particular, R. Leonhard, Bodo Uhse, E. E. Kisch, H. Marchwitza, W. Bredel and E. Brent. On 7 February 1938 Arthur Koestler told of his imprisonment by the Francoists, the episode he was to draw on for his *Spanish Testament*. Hubertus Prinz zu Löwenstein also went to Spain as a reporter. He gave lectures in America to win the sympathy of American Catholics – no easy task – for the Republican cause.
143. Babette Gross, *Willi Münzenberg*, p. 321.
144. Klaus Mann published a total of ten articles on the Spanish conflict.
145. A. Koestler, *The Invisible Writing*, p. 382.
146. Koestler had a press card in the name of Peter Lloyd of Budapest. To deflect suspicion, he also represented the London *News Chronicle*.
147. Koestler's *Menschenopfer unerhört* and Otto Katz's *Spione und Verschwörer in Spanien* were both published by Carrefour.
148. Cf. in particular Willi Bredel, *Spanienkrieg* (2 vols), Berlin 1977, and Patrick v. zur Mühlen, *Spanien war ihre Hoffnung*, Berne 1985.

CHAPTER 9   PRESS, PUBLISHING AND LITERATURE IN EXILE

1. *Das Innere Reich* managed to keep going until 1944 (cf. the study by Horst Denkler, 'Janusköpfig. Zur ideologischer Physiognomie der Zeitschrift *Das Innere Reich*', in *Die deutsche Literatur im dritten Reich*, pp. 382ff.). Fairly conservative, this magazine often fell into exaltation of the 'Nordic' and 'heroic'. It belonged to

the publisher Langen Müller. *Die Literatur* had to make concessions to the regime. *Die Deutsche Rundschau* kept going until 1942, as did *Hochland*, a Catholic journal. Peter Suhrkamp was eventually arrested on 13 April 1944 and sent to concentration camp; *Neue Rundschau* was then taken over by a Nazi commissioner.

2. H. A. Walter thus refers to them as 'documents of a powerless opposition'; *Die deutsche Exilliteratur*, vol. 7, p. 7.
3. The figure given by H. A. Walter, ibid., p. 8.
4. *Das Neue Tage-Buch, Die Neue Weltbühne, Der Zeitschrift für Sozialforschung, Internationale Literatur.*
5. Tucholsky regretted in his correspondence this fragmentation of émigré magazines, and held it would have been preferable to establish a single one of quality. (*Ausgewählte Briefe 1931–1936*, Hamburg 1962, p. 320.)
6. Thus *Das Wort, Internationale Literatur* and *Deutsche Zentralzeitung*, the organ of Freies Deutschland, were subsidized by the Soviet Union.
7. Willy Haas's *Welt im Wort* received support from the Czech government, and *Das Neue Tagebuch* from the British.
8. *Das Neue Tage-Buch* was assisted by the Dutch lawyer Warendorf, Thomas Mann's *Mass und Wert* by Agnes Meyer in the USA and Emil Oprecht in Switzerland. A. M. Schwarzenbach financed Klaus Mann's *Die Sammlung*.
9. In 1932, Ossietzky had already considered founding a new *Weltbühne* in Vienna in case it was banned in Germany.
10. The financial transactions concerning the purchase of the paper are obscure and contradictory.
11. In Prague the authorities mistakenly viewed it as Social-Democratic.
12. Trotsky himself contributed to it at this time.
13. On the detailed political development of the *Neue Weltbühne*, cf. H. A. Walter, *Die deutsche Exilliteratur,* pp. 49ff.
14. The same optimism was notably expressed by Ernst Bloch and Heinrich Mann until 1938.
15. Articles appeared at this time by Communists such as Walter Ulbricht and Franz Dahlem, and left Social-Democrats who supported the *Volksfront* (Aufhäuser, Sedewitz, Döchel, Schifrin). Among writers, there were frequent contributions from Heinrich Mann, Ernst Bloch, Kurt Hiller, H. von Gerlach, E. J. Gumbel, R. Olden, Lion Feuchtwanger and E. Ludwig. Later on they were joined by Bodo Uhse, Arnold Zweig, Klaus Mann, O. M. Graf, E. E. Kisch and J. R. Becher.
16. It appeared from 1921 to 1938.
17. On the magazine's history in these years, see Babette Gross, *Willi Münzenberg*, and Heinz Willmann, *Geschichte der Arbeiter-Illustrierte-Zeitung, 1921–1938*, Berlin 1975.
18. Several *AIZ* contributors, such as Herbert Wiedemann, were sent to concentration camp and died there. Erich Rinka and Heinz Willmann were also arrested by the Gestapo.
19. The editorial board now comprised F. C. Weiskopf, Louis Fürnberg, Fritz Erpenbeck and Heinz Willman.
20. Copies of *AIZ* circulated in Germany in the guise of booklets designed for the Berlin Olympics of 1936, also in the form of recipes for puddings and packets of washing powder. Copies were often left in trains, or launched over the border from balloons.
21. When the SS paper *Das Schwarze Korps* published an odious attack on John Heartfield which reproduced a number of his 'infamous photomontages', it rapidly sold out. Himmler was forced to destroy any remaining copies.
22. These included Robert Breitscheid, Heinrich Mann, Salomon Grunbach and Arnold Zweig.
23. It was from fear of repression by von Papen's government that Leopold Schwarzschild moved the editorial office to Munich in 1932.
24. Its offices were now on Faubourg Saint-Honoré, and its contributors somewhat

reduced in number. Schwarzschild was joined by Joseph Bornstein and Rudi Aron, and the editors contributed about half of the paper. While the *Tage-Buch* had a print run of at least 15,000 copies before 1933, in exile it never rose above 9,000.

25. L. Schwarzschild, J. Bornstein and B. Jacob published a number of articles on the German arms industry under the pseudonym Milles. The *Neue Tage-Buch* also contained very exact information on German aviation and weapons factories, and in 1936 described the role that tanks would play in the next German offensive.

26. This project was not without its contradictions, since among the 'democracies' it included fascist Italy and clerico-fascist Austria. (Cf. H. A. Walter, *Die deutsche Exilliteratur*, pp. 134ff.) The *Neue Tage-Buch* even published an article by Dolfuss, and when some readers protested, Schwarzschild retorted that even if Dolfuss was a fascist, his struggle against Hitler would be that of a fascist against a gorilla.

27. The *Neue Tage-Buch* published an article by Leo Lania in praise of Stalin.

28. Klaus Mann had formerly contributed to the paper. He noted in his autobiography: 'Schwarzschild's magazine certainly played a very vital role at this time. No other émigré journal was taken so seriously in the international arena. No other did so much to explain the true character and the sinister potential of National Socialism' (*Le Tournant*, p. 315). [This passage does not appear in the English edition of *The Turning Point*.] But this did not stop *NTB* from calling him a 'Soviet agent'.

29. Curiously enough, Schwarzschild never attacked Heinrich Mann. H. A. Walter suggests that this was out of prudence, as Mann was on very good terms with the brother of Albert Sarraut, interior minister in the Daladier government. (Cf. *Die deutsche Exilliteratur*, p. 153.)

30. H. Rauschning began to contribute regularly in autumn 1939.

31. The subtitle of its early issues, '*Literatur der Weltrevolution*', was subsequently replaced by '*Zentralorgan der IVRS*', and from January 1937, by '*Deutsche Blätter*'.

32. Paul Vaillant-Couturier was responsible for the French edition, Serge Tretyakov for the Russian, Emi Sia for the Chinese. Directed until 1933 by Hans Günther, the German edition was then taken over by J. R. Becher. Günther and Karl Schmücke remained as associate editors, subsequently replaced by Hugo Hupper and Franz Leschnitzer.

33. Martin Andersen-Nexö, Henri Barbusse, J. R. Becher, M. Gold, Maxim Gorki, John Dos Passos, Upton Sinclair, A. Serafimovitch, Erich Weinert, etc.

34. Willi Bredel, Hans Günther, E. Ottwalt, Theodor Plievier, Erich Weinert, Friedrich Wolf, A. Barta, A. Gabor, Georg Lukács, S. Tretyakov and G. Sawatsky. The names of Günther, Ottwalt and Tretyakov subsequently disappeared.

35. The role of the USSR as the socialist fatherland, construction of a classless society, bastion of resistance and antifascist struggle, etc.

36. Kurella wrote in all seriousness on Mann's *Tales of Jacob* that its subject was 'simply the return of the German people to barbarism. One is almost ashamed to have emerged from the same culture as this poet who represents Germany . . . The fate of such a man is deeply disturbing – a German, to a not negligible degree connected to our culture and heritage, who finds himself on such a sad aberration . . . Where does Herr Thomas Mann's journey lead: From Berlin to Bandol – or from Bandol to Berlin?' (Cited by H. A. Walter in *Die deutsche Exilliteratur*, p. 199.)

37. Some of these texts related to debates in *Das Wort*, for instance the famous exchange of letters between Anna Seghers and Georg Lukács on realism, published in *Internationale Literatur* in May 1939.

38. Romain Rolland, J. R. Bloch, Carlo Sforza, Bernadetto Croce, Ignazio Stilone, Wickham Steed, Stephen Spender, Christopher Isherwood, Ernest Hemingway, S. Asch, Ilya Ehrenburg, Boris Pasternak, P. Lagerkvist, Menno ter Brak.

39. Its contributors included Marxists (J. R. Becher, Bertolt Brecht, A. Kurella, A. Kantorowicz, A. Scharrer), Socialists (Ernst Toller, O. M. Graf, Harry Kesten), independent democrats (Heinrich Mann, Alfred Döblin, Arnold Zweig), Zionists

(Max Brod, H. Infeld), liberals (Alfred Kerr, W. Mehring, R. Olden), monarchists (Josef Roth) and apolitical (J. Wassermann, Else Lasker-Schüler).

40. Attacked by the émigrés, Mann made this clear in a text published in *Neue Deutsche Blätter* 3, 1933, p. 130, declaring that he had been forced to send his telegram. Bermann Fischer acknowledged this in his memoirs (*Bedroht-Bewahrt*, p. 96), stating that he had acted reluctantly, but had his hands tied; he admired *Die Sammlung* himself.

41. As H. A. Walter stresses (*Die deutsche Exilliteratur*, p. 247), *Die Sammlung* had nothing to say on the most important German political events of these years, such as the withdrawal from the League of Nations, the establishment of a 'people's court' to judge political crimes, the massacre of the SA, the assassination of Dolfuss, the plenary powers given to Hitler after the death of Hindenburg, and the debates over the *Volksfront*. Even the Reichstag fire trial attracted only a brief editorial comment.

42. Wieland Herzfelde was its editor for Czechoslovakia and Germany, O. M. Graf for Switzerland, Austria and Hungary, Anna Seghers for Western Europe.

43. In accordance with Czechoslovak legislation, Guido Lagus, a friend of Weiskopf and an engineer, took formal responsibility for the periodical.

44. The circulation of *Die Sammlung* never rose above 3,000.

45. Hermann Kesten particularly attacked Beumelburg, Dwinger, Ernst Jünger, Ernst von Salomon and F. Schauwecker. Ernst Fischer echoed these attacks against 'non-political' writers who had stayed in Germany.

46. In the same sense, *NDB* supported Klaus Mann when a number of writers not yet banned in the Reich took their distance from *Die Sammlung*.

47. The woman in question was Aline Mayrisch de St Hubert, widow of the Luxemburg steel magnate Émile Mayrisch. Its founders also included Jean Schlumberger, J. Breitbach and René Schickele. The magazine was published by Emil Oprecht, with the writer Konrad Falke as Swiss co-publisher.

48. See *Mass und Wert. Zürich 1937–1940, Bibilographie einer Zeitschrift*, Berlin 1973.

49. *The Man Without Qualities.*

50. Though it was in *Mass und Wert* that Walter Benjamin published his essay on Brecht, 'What is Epic Theatre?', many hostile reference to Brecht could also be found in the magazine.

51. For instance Golo Mann's articles in 1940.

52. Its subscriptions fell from 6,000 to 1,500.

53. See *Freies Deutschland. Mexico 1941–46. Bibliographie einer Zeitschrift*, Berlin 1975, p. 7.

54. Abusch took over as editor-in-chief with the third issue.

55. The émigrés lacked financial resources, and had to organize collections to finance their magazine. They did not have a printing press at their disposal, the German community in Mexico being sympathetic to Nazism. Besides, none of the typographers knew German.

56. In particular Pablo Neruda. Xavier Guerrero designed the woodcut for its cover.

57. In 1946, it still printed 3,300 copies.

58. Among other names would be *Zeitspiegel* (London), *Demokratische Post* (Mexico), *Aufbau* (New York), *Der Kampf* (Switzerland), *Das Blaue Heft* (England), *Die Freie Tribüne* (Argentina), *Das Andere Deutschland* (Mexico) and *Deutsche Blätter* (Chile).

59. Besides the celebrated documents published by J. Wulf (*Literatur und Dichtung im Drittten Reich*, Gütersloh 1963), cf. Hildegard Brenner, *La Politique artistique du National Socialisme*, Paris 1980.

60. Stigmatized as 'cultural bolsheviks' or representatives of 'asphalt literature'.

61. According to three criteria, these had to be destroyed by fire, or locked away pending investigation of whether they should be ranked in the first or second categories. The black lists were drawn up by a librarian, Dr Hermann.

62. The art publisher Reinhardt Piper, who published Kandinsky's and Franz Marc's

Blaue Reiter Almanach, recalls in his memoirs (*Bücherwelt. Erinnerungen eines Verlegers*, Munich 1979) his Kafkaesque entanglements with the authorities when he wanted to publish a book illustrated by A. Kubin. Publishers were not all obliged to submit manuscripts in advance, but they risked confiscation on appearance. Having experienced this already with an Ernst Barlach book, Piper decided to find out if he would be able to publish Kubin. But neither the Reichskulturkammer for literature nor that for fine arts knew which of them was responsible. Sent from one functionary to another, he was eventually told that Kubin was considered 'suspect' even though his works were exhibited in German galleries. The book projected in 1937 eventually appeared in 1942.

63. Ernst von Salomon recalled in *Le Questionnaire*, where he draws an admirable portrait of Ernst Rowohlt, that he refused to dismiss his staff as Goebbels had demanded. He was also attacked for publishing authors who were not members of the Reichskulturkammern. Harassed ceaselessly by the censorship commissions, Rowohlt eventually left Germany for Brazil, where he worked for his brother-in-law's firm from 1939 to 1940 without officially becoming an émigré. He returned to Germany, and as a former officer from the First World War, was immediately sent to Greece, then to the Russian front. In 1943 he was expelled from the army, his past being considered politically suspect: in 1921 he had signed a petition in support of Max Hölz.

64. Cf. E. von Salomon, *Le Questionnaire*, p. 275.

65. Cf. Gottfried Bermann Fischer, *Bedroht-Bewahrt*.

66. Even Thomas Mann described this concession as 'ignominious' (*Tagebücher*, 4 October 1933).

67. Suhrkamp was subsequently watched by a Nazi spy who had slipped his way into the company. He was denounced and sent to concentration camp, being released only in 1945.

68. Letter from Thomas Mann to Bermann Fischer, 8 April 1938.

69. The number of publishing houses founded by exiles, or publishers who had a special section for 'exile literature', was quite significant. Some of the most famous were Éditions du Carrefour (Paris), Querido and Allert de Lange (Amsterdam), Oprecht, Helbling and Europa (Zurich), Ring Verlag (Basle), Malik Verlag (Prague, London), Spiegel Verlag (Switzerland), Julius Kittl's Nachfolger (Czechoslovakia), Bermann Fischer (Vienna, Stockholm), Neue Verlag (Stockholm), Villi Verkauf Verlag (Jerusalem), Éditorial Cosmopolitan (Buenos Aires), Aurora, Friedrich Krause, Frederic Ungar (USA), Vita Nova Verlag (Lucerne) and Vegaar (Moscow). According to F. C. Weiskopf (*Unter fremden Himmeln*, p. 78), at least 2,000 titles were published in exile.

70. The PCF's publishing office produced in 1938 the magazine *Internationale Bücherschau*, along with antifascist booklets and works from Éditions du Carrefour. Hélène Roussel, in *Les Barbélés de l'exil*, p. 394, signals the role of the Coopérative Étoile printing works, which employed German typographers and facilitated the printing of German-language books, often in the form of 'disguised writings'.

71. Especially in France and Czechoslovakia.

72. For a long while Bermann Fischer refused any contact with the Swiss publisher E. Oprecht, wrongly believing that he was responsible for this ban. Only Thomas Mann managed to reconcile them (Bermann Fischer, *Bedroht-Bewahrt*, p. 194).

73. They risked being deprived of other German books, and were no longer invited to the Leipzig book fair.

74. For instance, Willi Bredel's collection *Der Spitzel* was published by Malik Verlag, registered in London, but actually located in Prague, with its books being printed in Oslo. Erich Maria Remarque's *Drei Kameraden* was published by Querido in the Dutch East Indies and printed in Stockholm, though the publishing house was by then in New York. René Schickele's *Das Vermächtnis* was known to critics but not readers, as the bombing of Amsterdam destroyed the entire edition.

75. Books from the Reich were very cheap by comparison.

76. After the reunification of the Saar to Germany, the annexation of Czechoslovakia and Austria, and the occupation of the Netherlands, the only countries where there were significant markets for these émigré books were Latin America, the United States and the USSR. In Switzerland, their distribution was always clandestine.
77. *Das Wort*, 4, pp. 55–58. Cited after Hélène Roussel, *Les Barbelés de l'exil*, p. 361.
78. According to W. A. Berendsohn, *Die humanistische Front* (p. 155), there were in this period 115 translations of Stefan Zweig, 87 of Vicky Baum, 80 of Lion Feuchtwanger, 74 of Thomas Mann, 60 of Emil Ludwig, 57 of Jacob Wasssermann, 40 of Franz Werfel, 34 of B. Traven, 30 of Gina Klaus, 28 of Joseph Roth and 28 of Arnold Zweig. Of the four authors still living in Germany, there were 59 translations of Erich Kästner, 49 of Hans Fallada and 20 of Ernst Wiechert, none of whom could be seen as a Nazi writer, and 134 of H. Courths-Mahler, a writer of popular fiction. The Verein für das Deutschtum im Ausland was right to complain in January 1938 that exile works were ten times more widely translated than novels from the Reich.
79. *Briefwechsel, Thomas Mann – G. Bermann Fischer*, Frankfurt 1973.
80. A number of authors owed their release from internment camps in France to the intervention of their publisher, especially Oprecht. Querido, for his part, made significant payments to several exile writers, to prevent them from dying of hunger.
81. Fritz Landshoff, who previously worked for Kiepenheuer, directed Querido's series of exile literature, Walter Landauer did likewise at Allert de Lange, who also employed both Hermann Kesten and Klaus Mann on their editorial team.
82. Many of these authors contributed to Klaus Mann's *Die Sammlung*.
83. Allert de Lange concentrated more on essays, including works by Freud, Kracauer, F. Blei, Brecht, Max Brod, F. Bruckner, Ödön von Horvath, Hermann Kesten, Irmgard Keun, E. E. Kisch, T. Plievier, René Schickele and Stefan Zweig.
84. Emil Oprecht Verlag had been founded in Zurich in 1925.
85. This was a popular library.
86. A member of the Swiss Socialist Party, Oprecht chiefly distributed Socialist writings in this way, especially those from Verlaganstalt Graphia of Czechoslovakia. He did also publish other authors, especially in the areas of history and sociology.
87. Cf. W. Mittenzwei, 'Exil in der Schweiz', and Hugo Kunoff, 'Literaturbetrieb in der Vertreibung', in *Die deutsche Exilliteratur*, p. 188.
88. He protected writers from Nazi sympathizers, hid them and defended them against the authorities, as well as publishing anti-Nazi leaflets. His books were boycotted by the Reich and he was not allowed to exhibit at the Leipzig book fair. Walter Landauer, head of the Fischer company in Vienna, remained in the city in hiding. A man offered to help him cross to Switzerland, but instead handed him over to the Gestapo. Emmanuel Querido was arrested in Amsterdam and murdered. Fritz Landshoff took refuge in London, and in 1949 Querido Verlag merged with Bermann Fischer Verlag.
89. This was more common in the USSR. In Paris, Félix Alcan published the journal of the Institut für Sozialforschung, and other works from the Frankfurt School.
90. An example of this was the Feux Croisés collection published by Plon, then under the direction of Gabriel Marcel, which published Wolfgang Langhoff's *Peat-Bog Soldiers* and Ödön von Horvath's *Youth without God*.
91. Forum Bücher was published jointly by Bermann Fischer in Stockholm, and Allert de Lange and Querido in Amsterdam. Its directing committee included Thomas Mann, René Schickele, Franz Werfel and Stefan Zweig.
92. Malik was hated both for its avant-garde publications and its Communist sympathies. Throughout the 1920s Herzfelde had published Soviet authors (Gorky, Ehrenburg, Mayakovsky), German Communist poets such as J. R. Becher, the famous albums of George Grosz, and the magazines *Neue Jugend*, *Die Pleite*, *Der Gegner* and *Jedermann sein eignes Fussball*.
93. Founded with the support of French writers, including Aragon.
94. The fate of Bredel's manuscript was typical of many exile works. According to F. C.

Wieskopf: 'The manuscript had been buried in the ruins of a Barcelona house, following aerial bombardment, and turned up only by a lucky chance. It was due to be published by Malik Verlag. It had already been typeset when the Wehrmacht occupied Sudetenland and northern Bohemia where the printer was located. The SS confiscated the type and melted it down. But an antifascist typographer had apparently taken a set of proofs and brought them to Prague, from where they travelled to Paris through Germany in the suitcase of an American journalist' (Cited in *Les Barbelés de l'exil*, pp. 392–3).

95. Cf. *Freies Deutschland. Mexico*, p. 10.

96. Hanna Fuchs, who emigrated to France in 1933 at the age of twenty-six, self-published her collection *Chimären* in 1938. Peter Grund did the same with *Der zärtliche Vorstoss in 66 Gedichten*, thanks to a subscription headed by Gide, Heinrich Mann and Arnold Zweig (cf. *Les Barbelés de l'exil*, p. 390). After the suppression of Social-Democratic publishers in Austria and Czechoslovakia, a number of political works were also published at the author's expense, including the essays of Helmut Klotz, an officer and former Nazi party member who went on to produce several works of a military nature (ibid., p. 391). Paul Zech, scarcely able to publish anything in Argentina, decided against committing suicide in the hope of being able to publish his poems on return to Germany.

97. Les Éditions du Phoenix were directed from 1935 to 1937 by Anselm Ruest (Ernst Samuel).

98. *Les Barbelés de l'exil*, p. 386.

99. Historians, moreover, do not agree on the time-frame of this exile literature. For Wilhelm Sternfeld and Eva Tiedmann (*Deutsche Exilliteratur 1933–1945*, Heidelberg 1970, p. 2), it comes to an end in 1948, or 1950 for those who did not return to Germany. Walter A. Berendsohn, on the other hand, maintains that 'exile literature' ended only with the death of the last antifascist exile.

100. Gertrude Albrecht, for example, in *Die Tschechoslowakei als Asylland der deutschen antifaschistischen Literatur von 1933–1938*, Prague 1964, rejects using the term 'antifascist' as a synonym for exile. For her it only designates those 'who decided to fight fascism as soldiers, political activists or artists, on the basis of their ideological positions'. She thus refuses to view the members of Strasser's Schwarze Front as antifascists, as well as right-wing Socialists, those who remained politically inactive in exile, businessmen, a large fraction of the Jewish petty bourgeoisie and certain academics. In this perspective, only those writers could be called antifascist who effectively struggled against National Socialism in their writings, or took part in the struggles of emigration. But this overly restrictive definition raises as many questions as the over-generous one of W. A. Berendsohn and his 'humanist front', since the articulation between exile literature and politics was a complex one. In the eyes of the Nazis, those who left the Reich and refused to return were opponents, and in that sense antifascist. Besides, should only those works that spoke directly of National Socialism and the struggles of exile be viewed as antifascist? In that case, it would be hard to include the works written in exile by Thomas Mann or Alfred Döblin. And what about the poems of Max Hermann-Neisse? Was not any work that escaped Nazi values, any free work, already in itself the negation of National Socialism, which sought to bring all culture into its embrace?

101. This notion of *Exilliteratur* is actively ambiguous. What exactly does it denote? If restricted to belles-lettres, i.e. literature in the traditional sense, then it ignores appeals, speeches, lectures, political articles – all so important in exile – and includes only novels, poetry, reportage and plays written in exile. Russian and German prefer more precise terms to designate this *Publizistik*. But if *Exilliteratur* means simply everything written by German émigrés in the years 1933 to 1945, it would also have to embrace scientific and technical writing by exiles, from physics to psychoanalysis. As for trying to restrict the concept by tying it to writings that reflect the experience of exile, this again comes up against countless problems that still flare up today in connection with reintegrating these works into German

literature as a whole. Some novels written in exile are closely linked to its lived experience, others far less so, or not at all. Does the fact that a novel was written in exile give it a particular significance? Yes, according to a number of historians; no, some literary critics respond, criticizing the former for making *Exilliteratur* into an almost mystical category. If works written in exile are to be re-integrated into the history of German literature, it is important not to restrict these to their political significance; else what would become of Thomas Mann's *Joseph* novels, or his *Lotte in Weimar*? Some historians retort, not without reason, that to separate such works from their context is an unacceptable amputation. Literary critics tend to maintain that works written in exile should be judged according to the same criteria as others, and that a bad novel written in exile is no better for that, even if it may be an interesting sociological document. This type of debate is almost a constant in most conferences devoted to *Exilliteratur* or *Exilforschung* in the Federal Republic.

102. According to Johst Hermand, in 'Schreiben in der Fremde. Gedanken zur deutschen Exilliteratur seit 1789. Exil und Innere Emigration', *Third Wisconsin Workshop*, Frankfurt 1973.

103. Berlin 1924.

104. Sénancourt, Nodier, Contant, Madame de Stael, Chateaubriand.

105. Cf. F. C. Wieskopf, *Unter fremden Himmeln*, pp. 13–14.

106. Even a comparison with the exile of certain Russian writers after 1917 would remain superficial.

107. F. C. Weiskopf (ibid., p. 15), who has analysed these waves of émigrés in detail, notes quite correctly that it was less 'a mass of literary émigrés' than an entire literature in exile; practically the whole of German letters abandoned the Reich.

108. *Privatdozent* in German literature at Hamburg, and a specialist in Scandinavian literature, Berendsohn left Germany in July 1933 for Denmark before settling permanently in Stockholm. In 1938 he was asked by an English publisher to write an essay on German literature in exile. His first volume, *Von 1933 bis zum Kriegesausbruch*, was completed in 1939 and published in Zurich in 1945. The second part was finally published in book form by Georg Heintz Verlag in 1976.

109. Berendsohn mentions 800 titles published in exile between 1939 and 1946, including 92 in Britain, 144 in Switzerland, 64 in the Soviet Union, 168 in the United States, 75 in Palestine, 40 in Argentina, 24 in Mexico and 72 in Sweden.

110. 'Fünf Jahre nach unsere Abreise', *Das Neue Tage-Buch*, 1938.

111. Herman Hesse lived in Switzerland, Carl Sternhein in Belgium, Carl Einstein and Kurt Tucholsky in France. In Prague there was a significant German literature. Finally, a number of exiled writers (Manès Sperber, E. E. Kisch, Arthur Koestler, Joseph Roth, Ernst Weiss, Ödön von Horvath) were not German nationals.

112. *University of Nebraska Studies* 16, 1957.

113. Pfeiler maintained that it was no more aberrant to group such different writers under the same heading of 'German literature in exile' than to see Kafka and Schnitzler as belonging to German literature. Language was the sole criterion.

114. Cf. in particular his chapter on 'The Writer in Exile and His Function'.

115. *Akzente* 15, 1968, pp. 556–75.

116. Cited after Jost Hermand, *Schreiben in der Fremde*, p. 9.

117. *Gedichte*, Frankfurt 1962, p. 47.

118. Cited after Jost Hermand, *Schreiben in der Fremde*, p. 10.

119. Ibid., p. 10.

120. Though this term is also too vague, and fails to take into account the different degrees of collaboration among authors remaining in Germany: Hauptmann, Jünger, Benn and Wiechert could hardly be considered Hitler's slaves.

121. As in Thomas Mann's *Lotte in Weimar* (1939).

122. Cited by F. C. Weiskopf, *Unter fremden Himmeln*, p. 44.

123. Thomas Mann's *Joseph* novels, and those of Franz Werfel or Vicki Baum, even Erich Maria Remarque.

124. *Sinn und Form*, vol. 3, 1954, pp. 348ff.

125. The poems written by émigrés are worth being studied as a whole from a purely formal standpoint: it would emerge that poetry was often the very language of exile. The exile never stops dreaming of the receding landscapes that he keeps only in his memory and will never see again, and on the strangeness of the new ones he discovers. We may cite at random here Brecht's *Svendborg Poems*, Thomas Kramer's *Neue Gedichte* (1944), Helmut Hirsch's *Amerika, du Morgenröte, Verse eines Flüchtlings* (1939–42), Berthold Viertel's *Der Lebenslauf. Gedichte* (1946), Max Hermann-Neisse, *Um uns die Fremde*, and Paul Zech, *Neue Welt. Verse der Emigration*.

126. Walter A. Berendsohn correctly analyses the ambiguity of this 'non-fascist' literature in the case of the work of Erich Wiechert (*Die humanistische Front*, vol. 2, p. 20), pointing out that some novels deemed representative of the 'internal emigration' display unmistakable affinities with 'blood and soil' literature, for instance Wiechert's *Hinternovelle* of 1935. Besides, the effectiveness of Nazi censorship and the coercion of the ministry of propaganda and the Reichskulturkammer made any literary opposition virtually impossible.

127. K. Mann, *Das Wendepunkt*, p. 292. [This passage does not appear in the English edition of *The Turning Point*.]

128. *Das Wort* 4/5, 1937.

129. Golo Mann, *Exil et Présent*, Bad Godesberg colloquium, 1968, p. 39.

130. Menno ter Brak, 'Emigranten-Literatur', *Das Neue Tage-Buch*, 52, 1934, pp. 1244–5.

131. Especially Heinrich Mann, *Der Sinn dieser Emigration*, Paris 1934.

132. A contributor to *Het Vaderland* and editor of the magazine *Forum*, Brak committed suicide in 1940 as the German army invaded the Netherlands.

133. 'Grössere Strenge gegen die Dichter?', *Das Neue Tage-Buch*, 1, 1935, pp. 1276–68.

134. Cf. *Verbannung*, p. 238.

135. Realism is a constant in the greater part of exile literature, even in the case of allegorical tales. And this literature shows scarcely any of the formal experiment that was widespread in the Weimar era. The majority of exile writers sought to be understood by the maximum number of readers, and this no doubt explains this constant preoccupation with realism, the frequency of a narrative style or fictional reportage. This is true for the novels of Anna Seghers, Ernst Weiss and Jan Petersen, as much as for Klaus Mann or Gustav Regler.

136. Certain novels by Gustav Regler (*Im Kreuzfeuer*) or Heinz Liepmann (*Das Vaterland*) even contain the names of actual SS men and accounts directly drawn from the exile press.

137. Precisely to prevent their informants inside the Reich from being discovered.

138. Cf. Klaus Mann, *The Volcano*; Lion Feuchtwanger, *Exile*; Anna Seghers, *Transit*.

139. As in Jan Petersen's *Unsere Strasse*, Hans Sahl's *Die Wenigen und die Vielen*, and Willi Bredel's *Die Prüfung*, as well as Anna Seghers's *The Seventh Cross*.

140. Anna Seghers, *The Seventh Cross* (1942); Arnold Zweig, *Das Beil von Wandsbeck* (1943), Friedrich Wolf, *Zwei an der Grenze*, and Willi Bredel, *Dein unbekannter Bruder* (1937).

141. This was already depicted by Joseph Roth in *Das Spinnennetz* (1923) and Lion Feuchtwanger in *Erfolg* (written between 1927 and 1929). The attraction of fascism for the petty bourgeoisie is a recurrent theme in many works of the late 1920s and early 1930s, for instance the plays of Ödön von Horvath, Ernst Glaeser's *Der letzte Zivilist* (1935), Ernst Weiss's *Der arme Verschwender* (1936), or Bodo Uhse's *Söldner und Soldat* (1935). Particular episodes in the rise of Nazism are the theme of many novels: Feuchtwanger depicted it against the backdrop of the Munich bohème (*Erfolg*), Hans Marchwitza in the Ruhr (*Die Kumiaks*, 1934). The Nazi seizure of power and the terror accompanying this were revisited in Ernst Ottwalt, *Erwachen und Gleichstaltung der Stadt Billiger*, 1934, and Jan Petersen, *Unsere Strasse*. Popular reactions to Nazism were conveyed by Anna Seghers, *Der Kopflohn*, 1933 and Adam Scharrer, *Maulwürfe*; anti-Semitism by Lion Feuchtwanger in *Die Geschwister Oppenheim*, 1933, which depicts the elections of March

1933, the Reichstag fire and the boycott of Jewish shops, as well as by Martin Haller (*Ein Mann sucht sein Heimat*, 1936) and Friedrich Wolf (*Professor Mamlok*).

142. These two novels especially depicted the problem of the lack of working-class unity.

143. Cf. Gisela Berglund, *Deutsche Opposition gegen Hitler im Presse und Roman des Exils*, Stockholm 1972; Heinz D. Osterle, *Die Deutschen im Spiegel des sozial-kritischen Romans der Emigranten 1933–1950* (dissertation, Brown University, USA, 1964); and H. A. Walter, 'Das Bild Deutschlands im Exilroman', *Neue Rundschau*, 1966, pp. 438–52.

144. A number of these early antifascist novels have since been republished in the Federal Republic by Fischer Verlag, in its *Bibliothek der verbrannten Bücher*.

145. These were basically Marxist writers close to the KPD. The development of their notions of fascism often reflected that of the Communist International, especially following the change of tactic announced by Dimitrov.

146. B. Brecht, *Écrits sur la politique et la société*, Paris 1970. These essays were written between 1933 and 1939.

147. At the start of the exile period, the number of political analyses of National Socialism was fairly limited, but this situation had changed radically by the 1940s. Theoretical discussion of the nature of fascism was richest in the United States. Besides the traditional Marxist conception, a fairly large number of political analyses were put forward, as to its class origin, connection with the economy and the bourgeoisie, and above all the common features it might or might not have with Stalinism.

148. T. Mann, *Order of the Day*, p. 55.

149. Ibid.

150. T. Mann, 'Leiden an Deutschland', *Gesammelte Werke* vol. 12.

151. T. Mann, *Order of the Day*, p. 157.

152. *Germany and the Germans*.

153. One of his poems is simply titled 'Apokalypse 1933'; *Die Sammlung*, 4, 1933–34, p. 208.

154. Brüning wrote in 1936 of 'devilish forces at work', as did Thomas Mann and Hermann Kesten.

155. Thomas Mann spoke of a 'return to primitive savagery' in 'Leiden an Deutschland'.

156. Denunciation of the supposedly mediaeval character of Nazism is found in Thomas Mann, who equates Nazi demonstrations with Saint Vitus's dance, and in Ernst Bloch, who likewise wrote in the *Heritage of Our Times*: 'Here are medieval lanes again, Saint Vitus's dance, Jews beaten to death, the poisoning of wells and the plague, faces and gestures as if on the Mocking of Christ and other Gothic panels' (p. 56).

157. Walter Berendsohn used the terms *dämonisch*, *krankhaft*, *teuflisch*, *wahnsinnig*, *bestialisch*, and *rohertes Untermenschentum*. The idea of a regression to an uncivilized age is found again in Leopold Schwarzschild, who compared Hitler to a gorilla. In Walter Mehring's 1937 novel *Die Nacht des Tyrannen*, Hitler is seen as a beast comparable with cavemen, Attila or the creatures of the *Nibelungenlied*.

158. Whereas Wieland Herzfelde stressed in September 1933 the necessity of 'discovering the economic roots of evil', a number of émigrés stuck with the moral condemnation of National Socialism. René Schickele, in 1934, described it as the 'catastrophe of a man without conscience', and Franz Werfel saw it as a phenomenon of 'spiritual numbness'.

159. In *The Volcano*, Klaus Mann wrote of a 'return to night and death'; the image of plague is used by Brecht, Thomas Mann, Alfred Kurella and Heinrich Mann. In Horvath's novel *Youth Without God*, young people in the Third Reich have 'the faces of fish'. Koestler evoked 'the malign tumour that Germany had become, devouring Europe's living tissue'. Walter Mehring also described Nazism as a sickness transmitted to Germany by a monster.

160. B. Brecht, *Écrits sur la politique et la société*, p. 190.

161. This two-volume work was published by Emil Oprecht in 1936, and the same year in English as *Hitler: A Biography*. Its success is explained by the concrete questions that Heiden raised: e.g. Does Hitler want war? How long can the Nazi regime last? The core of Heiden's interpretation of National Socialism rested on the personality of Hitler, whom he systematically demonized. The Nazis were 'losers', able only to appear as representatives of 'non-values'.

162. *La Révolution allemande et la responsabilité de l'esprit*, Paris 1934. These surprising divagations came with a preface by Paul Valéry. The identification of Hitler with Muhammad was also found in the French pacifist J. R. Bloch (*Offrandes à la politique*, Paris 1933, pp. 79–80).

163. H. Kessler, *Diaries of a Cosmopolitan 1918–1937*, p. 461.

164. Cf. Ernst Niekisch, *Gewagtes Leben*, p. 253. Both Niekisch and Thomas Mann referred to Hitler as a 'hypnotist'. According to Niekisch, he unleashed 'primitive and barbaric elements' in the Germans. Jünger appealed to astrology to understand Hitler's personality. The faces of both Goebbels and Hitler were those of 'evil demons'. While Niekisch depicted a realm of 'underground demons', Jünger often used the image of 'lemurs' in his *Wartime Diaries* and his allegorical tale *On the Marble Cliffs*. For Rudolf Olden, Hitler was a puppet of the army and Junkers, his intention to re-establish a Prussian military state. For Ernst Bloch, he was a false messiah, akin to Sabbatai Zewi, with heavy industry behind him. Leo Schwarzschild occasionally described Hitler as an imitation of Bolshevism, and for Franz Schoenberner he was 'the best-paid employee of big capital'.

165. Joseph Roth, *Antichrist*, London 1935, p. 6.

166. We should recall that in Chaplin's *Great Dictator*, begun in 1937 though only shown for the first time on 15 October 1940, Hitler's speeches are composed of unintelligible onomatopoeias, yet for all that they give the illusion of the genuine article. Niekisch held that the Nazis' voices were 'scarcely human', and the same image recurs in Brecht with the speeches of Arturo Ui. John Heartfield's photomontages also represented Hitler as a monkey wearing a military cap.

167. Thomas Mann, 'Leiden an Deutschland'.

168. Ernst Weiss committed suicide as the German army entered Paris. His novel was discovered by chance in 1945, and published twenty-three years later.

169. The argument, however, cuts both ways. If a number of émigrés stressed Hitler's obscure origin in order to deny him any ability to play a political role, the myth of the 'man who rose from nothing' was copiously exploited in Nazi propaganda, to emphasize both the extraordinary character of his destiny and his belonging to the masses. Hitler's elimination of various indications of his past threw the ineluctable nature of his mission into still sharper relief. The poverty and wretchedness he had supposedly known in Vienna has been largely put in question by more recent biographies.

170. 'He started out with his uneducated voice marked by suburban inflections, drawling though menacing. But soon his rhetoric expanded to a vulgar drama of scurrilous force, crying and shaking with rage [. . .]. Now he was the complete rowdy, Venus rising from the sewer, showing his warts with no shame' (Heinrich Mann, *La Haine*, p. 34). Thomas Mann, in 'Brother Hitler' (*Order of the Day*, p. 154), termed Hitler a 'failure', 'extremely lazy', 'a man who has spent long periods in institutions', 'a total good-for-nothing'. Stefan Zweig explained that Germans like himself could not conceive 'that a man who had not even finished high school, to say nothing of college, who had lodged in doss-houses and whose mode of life for years is a mystery to this day', could rise to the highest position in the state (*The World of Yesterday*, p. 274). Even Brecht in his poems refers to Hitler as a 'house-painter'.

171. We shall analyse these below.

172. Even if Golo Mann, in his preface to the reissue of *La Révolution du nihilisme*, saw in it 'something new, experienced, and true', compared with the political propositions of a large number of German émigrés, it is hard to understand how the philosophico-political bric-a-brac of Rauschning's analyses could find the audience

that it did. In his analysis of the 'Führer's charisma', he does indeed denounce the staging and trickery involved, but he still ties National Socialism closely to Hitler, whose influence was founded in 'an irrational element, in the medium-like gift of the revolutionary' (*Germany's Revolution of Nihilism*, London 1939, pp. 36–7).

173. Broch wrote three successive versions of the novel, but left it unfinished. The first version was written in 1934–35. It has a certain affinity with Hanns Heinz Ewers's novel *The Sorcerer's Apprentice*, whose hero, Frank Braun, likewise rekindles this archaic and bloody cult via a contagious madness.

174. Reprinted in *Illuminations*, London 1970.

175. E. Bloch, *Heritage of Our Times*, p. 2.

176. Brecht may perhaps be reproached for an excess of rationalism in his 'Essays on Fascism', where as a convinced Marxist, he seeks to explain everything in terms of economics and the class struggle. Whilst he admirably dismantles the illusion that 'barbarism comes from barbarism', it is not clear in his analyses exactly what made Nazi propaganda so successful (precisely what Bloch tried to explain). His investigation of the reasons why 'certain petty-bourgeois and even proletarian layers threaten to pass over to fascism' seems today too marked by the formulae of the time, e.g. 'the imminence of world war that raises the national question', the 'inability of social-democracy to imagine the future', and so on. If Bloch managed to explain how German youth could be attracted to Nazism by the distorted idealism of Hitlerite propaganda, Brecht merely maintains that 'youth is exposed to the influence of Hitler because of its place in the production process' (*Essais sur le fascisme*, pp. 172–3). Everything Brecht says is certainly true, but it is impossible to avoid the impression that the reality was more complex. The theme of the seduction of youth by National Socialism was tackled by a number of authors. In 1934, Ernst Erich Noth published *The Tragedy of German Youth*, and Heinrich Mann an essay on 'The Betrayal of Youth'. In 1935 Bodo Uhse retraced his own itinerary as a young Nazi (*Söldner und Soldat*, Paris 1935), and Anna Seghers, in *Die Toten bleiben jung* (completed after 1945), also depicts the reasons that drove various categories of Germans, including young people, to believe in Hitler.

177. 'He feels considerably better behind his desk and shop counter since he is Nordic or fully recognized in his blondness at least as regards his blood' (*Heritage of Our Times*, p. 44).

178. Siegfried Kracauer, *The Salaried Masses*, London 1998.

179. 'And once again, this unconcern for freedom, nothing less than Prussian, gave rise in the German people to a saviour who chastised with scorpions. A new dawn seemed to revivify the pallid tint of the Müller family' (*Les Müller*, Paris 1982, p. 226).

180. *German's Revolution of Nihilism*, p. 8ff.

181. George Bernhard, *Le Suicide de la République allemande*, Paris 1933.

182. H. Mann, *La Haine*, p. 53.

183. B. Brecht, *Écrits sur la politique et la société*, p. 141.

184. See for example, Carl von Ossietzky, *Rechenschaft, Publizistik aus den Jahren 1913–1933*, Berlin 1985.

185. Alfred Kantorowicz, in *Politik und Literatur im Exil*, p. 22, declared that the question of which parties were to blame for Hitler's rise to power was one of the most burning issues in émigré debates. This can be seen from reading various exile analyses of the Weimar Republic: Otto Braun, *Von Weimar zu Hitler*, New York 1940; Albert Grzesinski, *La Tragicomédie de la République allemande*, Paris 1934; A. Rosenberg, *Geschichte der deutschen Republik*, Karlovy Vary 1935; Hubertus Prinz zu Löwenstein, *Die Tragödie eines Volkes. Deutschland 1918–1934*, Amsterdam 1934.

186. Cited by Jost Hermand, *Exil und innere Emigration*, p. 18.

187. H. Mann, *La Haine*, pp. 27–9.

188. H. Beimler, *The Nazi Murder Camp of Dachau*, London 1934. It is often hard to understand in Communist novels or essays how 'a band of pimps' could grow into

one of the largest German parties. Heinrich Mann wrote in similar vein: 'Some malcontents were sulking in the Munich bars in the guise of customers. There were seven of them, including the tall man spying on the rest. [. . .] These seven scoundrels, the tall one still included, told themselves in their little corner that they needed only knock the wound made to national vanity rather sharply, to re-open it again' (*La Haine*, p. 31). But how could a band of pimps, or a handful of losers and scoundrels, win political power?

189. B. Brecht, 'Cinq difficultés pour écrire la verité', p. 17.
190. 'They are not against the property relations that give rise to barbarism, they are simply against barbarism. They raise their voices against the barbarism in which the same property relations prevail, but where the butchers wash their hands before serving the meat' (ibid.).
191. B. Brecht, *Écrits sur la politique et la société*, p. 146.
192. Arturo Ui, a mediocre and blood-stained character, owes his rise simply to Hindsborough (Hindenburg), an honorable and honest old man, compromised by greedy business deals. Ui forces shopkeepers to pay for his men to protect them from attacks which they themselves commit, and to only buy their cauliflowers from his cartel. This gangster of low intelligence is detested by all, even by his acolytes who fear him.
193. The evocation of the mediocrity of cultural life under the Third Reich recurs in the letters of Kurt Tucholsky (for instance his letter to Walter Hasenclever of 17 May 1933; *Politische Briefe*, Frankfurt 1974, p. 24), in Heinrich Mann's essays (*Vertei-digung der Kultur*), in Klaus Mann's novel *Mephisto*, and in Brecht's essays on fascism.
194. It should be noted that the depiction of anti-Semitism played very different ideological roles for different authors. For Marxist or Communist writers, this was simply one aspect of National Socialism. For Bruckner (*Die Rassen*), it was a genuine pathological delirium, and almost inexplicable. For Friedrich Wolf, it was an economic problem, whereas for Feuchtwanger it was the very essence of the Nazi phenomenon. Brecht depicts it as a symptom of the regime's barbarity, the irrationality of its ideology, and unmasks its political and economic purpose.
195. The title was subsequently changed to *Die Geschwister Oppermann*. Though the novel does not portray any real individuals, it does present a genuine sociological depiction of the German bourgeoisie and petty bourgeoisie (though not the workers). Like Wolf's *Professor Mamlok*, it turns on a break provoked by events. The action of Feuchtwanger's novel takes place between significant dates (30 January to 28 February 1933). Wolf's play is set between May 1932 (the re-election of Hindenburg) and April 1933 (the dismissal of Jews from public service). In both the Oppermann and Mamlok households, there is the same attachment to tradition, the same faith in institutions, humanism and intelligence.
196. The play was finished in 1938, and extracts staged successfully in Paris, London, New York and Stockholm. Eight of these were presented in Paris that year, in a production by Slatan Dudow. Brecht used almost exclusively information taken from newspapers or the radio, which he transformed into sketches of an astonishing dramatic intensity.
197. Heinrich Mann's articles in *La Dépêche de Toulouse* often show a surprising optimism. He describes workers laughing at a speech by the Labour Front leader Ley, and preparing a violent uprising. The big industrialists gather in Paris to discuss their complaints; the conservative leaders are in prison. On 26 September 1935, Mann claimed that by adding together Protestants, Jews, Socialist workers, petty bourgeois and intellectuals, there were a total of some 65 million opposi-tionists. On 28 January 1938, he maintained that 'five years after the establishment of the regime, nothing remains of the fascination it had previously exercised on the masses'. The same year he proclaimed the advance of an immense anti-Nazi 'internal front', that 'faith in the regime is constantly dwindling', and that young people 'are taking their distance from a worn-out regime'. The latter, 'on the edge of

bankruptcy', is 'frightened by the illegal opposition' (31 March 1936). In 1937, Mann described the proliferation of acts of sabotage: 'strikes are unleashed, barns and armaments factories are set on fire'. On 1 December 1938, he revealed that 'the regime does not have an army'. As A. Banuls points out (*Heinrich Mann*, pp. 375–6), Mann seemed to have the confidence of all oppositionists in the Reich. He knew what the workers are saying, likewise the staff in the film industry; he managed to reconstitute their dialogues and complaints. His was one of the most tragic cases of that 'intoxication by hope' to which so many exiles fell prey. With his talent and generosity, Heinrich Mann managed to amplify the slightest rumour. Reading his articles, one has the impression he is describing reality, yet the facts he relates are all highly unlikely.

198. When the prisoners see seven trees being cut down to make so many crosses, they exclaim: 'All of us felt how ruthlessly and fearfully outward powers could strike to the very core of man, but at the same time we felt that at the very core there was something that was unassailable and inviolable.' (Anna Seghers, *The Seventh Cross*, London 1943, p. 322.)

199. It is also Anna Seghers who best described the solitude of former Communists who remained in the Reich and were forced to hide their past, as well as the omnipresent climate of terror, the all-powerful police apparatus and the constant fear of denunciation. Not everyone that her hero Georg encounters has been won over to Nazism, but they fear for their safety and their lives. He for his part is unable to find his old comrades to ask for their help. He can only count on unknown strangers to help him cross the border. And the hunted and wounded man staying in his home town can only hope for the silence of some and the solidarity of others, those who without being resisters maintained an ideal of humanity.

200. The Christian resistance was depicted also by Hubertus Prinz zu Löwenstein, Ludwig Marcuse and Gustav Regler.

201. 'So intense was the fascination of his shameful glory that I decided to portray Mephisto–Gründgens in a satirical novel. [. . .] Gründgens was just one among others [. . .]. He served me as a focus around which I could make gyrate the pathetic and nauseous crowd of petty climbers and crooks' (Klaus Mann, *The Turning Point*, p. 282).

202. In a review of Klaus Mann's novel in *Das Neue Tage-Buch*.

203. The action proceeds from 15 April 1933 to 14 September 1938.

CHAPTER 10 ANTIFASCIST THEATRE IN EXILE

1. A large number of authors, actors and directors enjoyed world renown in the Weimar era. To take only Max Reinhardt, we can recall that between 1900 and 1933 he was invited to undertake productions in Prague, Vienna, Budapest, Riga, St Petersburg, New York, Paris, Warsaw, Hollywood, Rome, Florence, Oxford and Venice. Ernst Toller's plays were shown in all major German cities, and between 1923 and 1932 his *Hinkemann* was performed in more than thirteen countries, in thirty-eight different productions. Lunacharsky, the Soviet commissar for art and education, wrote reviews of Walter Hasenclever's plays.

2. The majority of plays written under the Weimar Republic had a political dimension, even for example Jessner's productions of the classics. Though the term *Zeitstücke* was coined above all for Piscator's repertoire, a large number of works of the time were 'current' or 'historical', for example those of Ferdinand Bruckner, Friedrich Wolf, Peter Martin Lampel, Berta Lask and Hans Josef Rehfisch, who all sought to intervene more or less directly on political events. The Nazis later tried made an effort to imitate this theatre of agitation by creating a 'National Socialist popular theatre', unmatched in its pitiful heaviness. Despite his political hatred for Piscator, Goebbels maintained a certain admiration for his work.

3. Max Reinhardt was Jewish, L. Jessner Jewish and Socialist, Erwin Piscator a

Communist, Brecht a Marxist. The majority of other leading playwrights were pacifist and anti-Nazi, like von Horvath and Ernst Toller, who had played a major role in the Bavarian soviet republic and symbolized in person the theatre of this era.

4. He was charged with being the agent of an invasion that threatened Germany 'with the aid of Black Americanism, of imperialist France which arms its Blacks, and the Mongol waves of Bolshevism attacking from the east' (cited after Hildegard Brenner, *Deutsche Literatur in Exil 1933–1947*, p. 29).

5. Cf. E. J. Aufricht, *Erzähle, damit du dein Reicht erweist*, p. 119.

6. Piscator had been in the USSR since 1931, Max Reinhardt left Germany in March 1933, Friedrich Wolf, Gustav von Wangenheim, Ferdinand Bruckner and Bertolt Brecht took the road of exile in the first months of the Nazi regime, Horvath left the country in 1934, P. M. Lampel when he came out of prison in 1936. Georg Kaiser, even though his works had been burned, did not leave Germany until 1938.

7. Fritz Kortner, for example, maintains that Rudolph Forster, who played Mackie Messer in Pabst's film of the *Dreigroschenoper*, was a genuine 'internal émigré'.

8. Whether or not Klaus Mann's book was indeed a *roman à clef*, the actual Gründgens can clearly be recognized in the character of Höfgens. Otto Ullrich, the proletarian actor in the novel, was inspired by Hans Otto who was murdered by the Nazis. Counsellor Brückner was a portrait of Thomas Mann, Hans Jostfinkel was clearly Hanns Johst, and Max Reinhardt, Erika Mann and others can also be recognized.

9. After the Second World War, Gründgens played again with Brecht, who seems to have maintained his friendship with him. (Cf. Curt Reiss, *Gustaf Gründgens. Eine Biographie*, Munich 1978.) Without wishing to echo the hagiography that surrounds Gründgens in the Federal Republic, it has to be recognized that he never hid his sympathy for the Jews, he employed artists who were anti-Nazi or banned under the Nuremberg laws, defended directors who had been attacked (Jürgen Fehling after his production of Schiller's *Don Carlos*), and even protected and gave work to Jewish actors (Theo Lingen, Otto Wernicke, Paul Bildt, Paul Henckels, Erich Ziegel and others). When Ernst Busch, the proletarian singer and actor, and friend of Brecht, was arrested by the Gestapo in 1941 and imprisoned in Berlin, it was Gründgens whom he asked to come to his aid; Gründgens found him a lawyer who managed to save him from the death penalty. Busch was sent to concentration camp, but freed by the Red Army in 1945. Bernhard Minetti who worked with him maintains that Gründgens was 'a screen against Goebbels and Nazi ideology'.

10. *Revue*, January–March 1983, p. 2.

11. Bernhard Minetti had to act in mediocre plays, including one by Johst on Schlageter. In 1932, he had played Karl Moor in Schiller's *The Robbers*.

12. According to Minetti (*Revue*, pp. 12–13), the Nazis divided actors into five categories: those won over to Nazism, sympathizers, neutrals, anti-Nazis and 'Communists'. Those in the last category were arrested or murdered (Hans Otto, Wolfgang Hinz) if they failed to escape. Minetti himself was 'suspected of sympathy for the left'.

13. All of these have long been forgotten. To mention some random titles: W. Matthiessen's *Sacred Earth*, W. G. Klincke's *The Hermit*, and H. C. Kaerpel's *Hockewanzel*.

14. Such as the Nazi buffooneries that made Schiller into an SA man or a companion of Hitler. *Hamlet* became a 'Nordic tragedy', and *Faust* a representation of the 'Germanic soul'. Even Gründgens was criticized for failing to give the character Spiegelberg in Schiller's *The Robbers* anti-Semitic characteristics. According to the Nazis, he should have found a double of Tucholsky to act the part.

15. This is evidenced for example by the arguments that often broke out between Brecht and Julius Hay, who had attacked him in *Das Wort* and considered epic theatre to be 'idealist and bourgeois'. Brecht complained to J. R. Becher (11 March 1937) and Piscator (March 1937; cf. *Letters, and Journals* for 27 July 1938). If unlike Hay, Wolf and Wangenheim, Brecht never wrote propaganda plays in exile, he

acknowledged that 'LIFE OF GALILEI is technically a serious step backwards, like SENORA CARRAR all too opportunistic' (*Journals*, 25 February 1939; p. 23).

16. This was a constant aspect of Piscator's productions, also to be found in Friederich Wolf, *The Sailors of Cattaro* (1930), which depicted the revolt of the German navy in 1918.

17. With the exception of some works by Brecht or Bruckner, exile theatre saw a general lowering of standards. Horvath no longer wrote major plays in exile, and the political works of Friedrich Wolf were not as good as he had written under the Weimar Republic. The same goes for Ernst Toller. The causes for this decline were many: form was often sacrificed to the desire to act on the present, political plays had little chance of being staged, many authors experienced poverty and stopped writing.

18. We should recall that even Brecht was not well known in the Soviet Union at this time, despite his close ties to Tretyakov. Tairov had produced *The Threepenny Opera* with a very limited success. The companies most appreciated in the Soviet Union were the agitprop ones (Truppe 1931, Kolonne Links). In 1935 an article by Lukács appeared in a Soviet magazine (*Literaturnyi Kritik* 11, reprinted in *Alternative* 16/1972, pp. 124–30), in which he maintained the superiority of Wangenheim's plays over those of Brecht, in the wake of the famous polemics in the *Linkskurve* in which he took issue with Willi Bredel and Ernst Ottwalt.

19. For example, Piscator in American exile spoke only of 'epic theatre' rather than political theatre, and he had to abandon the radicalism of his previous productions in this very different context.

20. Kaiser's *Raft of the Medusa* was inspired by a real incident: the torpedoing of a British ship carrying child victims of bombing to Canada. Thirteen children were rescued, but a young girl threw one of them overboard so that there would not be this unlucky number. When her friend discovered the murder, he refused to be rescued by an Allied plane, but drew down on himself the machine-guns of the German plane that was following them.

21. B. Brecht, *Schriften II*, p. 174.

22. K. Tucholsky, *Apprendre à rire sans pleurer*, p. 291.

23. For instance the Lubitsch film *To Be or Not to Be*, a masterpiece of Jewish humour, which shows how a mediocre actor playing the part of Hitler in Warsaw at the moment when the Nazis invade Poland is mistaken for the Führer in the most ridiculous situations.

24. *The Correspondence of Walter Benjamin*, p. 478.

25. If *Youth Without God* is a macabre depiction of young people under the Third Reich, *The Last Judgment*, *Don Juan's Return from the War* and *The Divorce of Figaro* were far removed from the political context of 1936. Theodor Csokor wrote to him on 12 August 1933 that 'only comedy is able to show such bestiality in its raw state'. Horvath tried to express the backdrop of Hitler's Germany in sketches for other plays (*Spring Is Here*, *Towards Heaven*), but failed to rediscover the macabre irony of *Tales of the Vienna Woods*.

26. Austrian theatres had stopped staging Horvath's plays even before 1933.

27. *Tanjka Opens Her Eyes* (1937), *Credit* (1936).

28. *Disturbers of the Peace* (1938).

29. Sometimes with a more revolutionary-romantic than realist dimension, as in *Peter's Homecoming*.

30. Cf. E. Bloch and H. Eisler, 'Die Kunst zu erben', in *Die Neue Weltbühne*, 6 January 1938; and G. Lukács, 'Es geht um Realismus', *Das Wort* 6, 1938.

31. Among the several works devoted to German exile theatre, see in particular: H. C. Wächter, *Theater im Exil. Sozialgeschichte des deutschen Exiltheaters 1933–45*, Munich 1973; Peter Dietzel, *Exiltheater in der Sowjetunion 1932–1937*, Berlin 1978, F. N. Mennemier and Frithjof Trapp, *Deutsche Exildramatik 1933–1950*, Munich 1980; *Theater im Exil 1933–45* (exhibition catalogue), Akademie der Künste,

Berlin; Hans Jörg Schneider, *Exiltheater in der Tschechoslowakei 1933–38*, Berlin 1979.

32. A distinction should be made between theatres and companies established by exiles, foreign theatres that received exiled German companies, actors or directors, and those that performed antifascist works.

33. Kurt Weill, for example, remained in America and adapted to the Broadway style. Moreover, many émigré works were still banned after the War, or performed only with difficulty. A large number of German theatres had been destroyed by bombing. Their managers had often collaborated with the Nazis, and the anti-Communist climate in West Germany after 1945 inevitably had its effect on the émigré works. F. Bruckner's *Die Befreiten* (*The Liberated*) was banned in Vienna in 1945 for its criticism of the occupying powers, as also was F. Hochwälder's *Der Flüchtling* (*The Refugee*). A press campaign against Friedrich Wolf's plays in Bonn led to the interruption of performances. Piscator was hated just as much after his return to Germany as he had been in the Weimar period. Many authors, such as Ödön von Horvath, fell into oblivion and were only rediscovered thirty years later. Postwar German theatre much preferred to perform foreign plays, and showed scant interest in émigré works. It was only in 1962 that Piscator was appointed manager of the Freie Volksbühne – rightly so, and with the support of Willy Brandt. Brecht was the only one of these writers to enjoy real fame after 1945. Though Friedrich Wolf had been one of the most celebrated Communist authors of the 1920s, he was no longer performed even in the GDR. In West Germany, Bruckner was hardly known. Attempts to replay the works of exiles came up against a lack of interest on the part of the public. It was not until 1970 that Toller's plays again met with a certain success. The exile works of Peter Martin Lampel, for example, have never been published as far as I am aware.

34. Cited by F. Mennemier and F. Trapp, *Deutsche Exildramatik 1933–1950*, p. 19.

35. We should recall that this was one of the reasons for Toller's suicide, that Piscator found no engagement in Paris and had great trouble in finding a theatre in New York. Both Brecht and Reinhardt vegetated in the US. Horvath and Hasenclever were scarcely performed at all after 1933. The greatest Berlin theatre critic, Alfred Kerr, lived in utmost oblivion in exile.

36. Hasenclever, Horvath, Bruckner and Hay all wrote comedies to try and obtain commercial success.

37. Brecht never managed to sell his screenplays in Hollywood, and this was also the case with most other émigrés. As for Horvath, he wrote (*Gesammelte Werke*, vol. 4, p. 669): 'I wrote for the cinema in order to buy a new suit. This was my lowest point in moral terms. All I had left was a tie.'

38. Some productions of works by E. Kästner or F. Bruckner (*The Races*) were all the same banned or suspended.

39. Verband der Freunde der Sowjetunion, Linksfront, Liga für Menschenrechte, *Die Tat* Club and Bertolt Brecht Club, and especially the Czechoslovak Revolutionary Association of Theatre Workers.

40. The proletarian company Das Rote Sprachrohr continued its productions in Prague with Maxim Vallentin.

41. H. Schneider, *Exiltheater in der Tschechoslowakei 1933–38*, pp. 176ff.

42. With Gerhard Hinze, Nina and Erich Freund, Charlotte Küter, Paul Lewitt and former members of Das Rote Sprachrohr.

43. There also existed a Neue Deutsche Theater, but though this took on quite a number of exiled authors, it produced rather classic plays.

44. This play had been published in 1936 in *Das Wort*, and depicted the underground resistance in Germany.

45. Horvath, L. Frank, E. E. Kisch, L. Lania, F. Bruckner.

46. Cf. W. Mittenzwei, *Exil in der Schweiz*, pp. 350ff.

47. It belonged to a businessman, Ferdinand Rieser.

48. A few famous actors such as Hertha Thiele (who played in *Kuhle Wampe*), worked in Berne and Basle, but they often had to give way to Swiss actors.
49. Therese Giehse played an important part in Erika Mann's antifascist cabaret Die Pfeffermühle.
50. Langhoff was 'amnestied' in 1934. It is doubtful whether his release was due just to Rieser's letter.
51. Some of these, such as L. Steckel and Lindtberg, had worked with Piscator.
52. Cf. *Exil in der Schweiz*, p. 360.
53. Through the company Neue Schauspiel AG.
54. Oskar Wälterlin, who came from Basle, had worked as a stage manager at the Frankfurt opera until the advent of Hitler.
55. Many of these plays extolled resistance – *William Tell*, *Nathan the Wise*, *The Maid of Orleans*. Some lines from *Götz von Berlichingen*, such as 'Long live liberty. If it survives us, we can die happily,' were especially acclaimed.
56. The Freie Deutscher Kulturbund, for example, gave performance of Brecht's *Fear and Misery of the Third Reich* and *Señora Carrar's Rifles*.
57. Das Laterndl was established by Martin Miller in 1940–41.
58. Bruckner's *The Races*, produced by Robert Klein in 1934, was banned, as was *Professor Mamlok* in 1939.
59. Kurt Weill managed to collaborate on certain spectacles such as *My Kingdom for a Cow*, after the libretto of Robert Vambery, on 1 July 1935.
60. It was the Danish novelist Karin Michaelis who offered to find Brecht a home. He lived on the island of Thurö near Fünen. In Denmark, he wrote *Round Heads and Pointed Heads*, *The Horatii and the Curiatii*, *German Satires*, *Señora Carrar's Rifles*, and *Fear and Misery of the Third Reich*. In Sweden, then in Finland, he wrote *Mr Puntila and His Man Matti*, *The Life of Galileo*, *The Resistible Rise of Arturo Ui*, and *The Good Person of Szechwan*.
61. *The Mother*, *The Seven Deadly Sins*, *Round Heads and Pointed Heads*, *The Threepenny Opera* (by Per Knutzen in 1937) and *Señora Carrar's Rifles*.
62. The performance was preceded by a film on the Spanish war. A large number of roles were played by amateurs.
63. *The Trial of Lucullus* was also staged by a company of Jewish actors at the Haus der Jüdischen Gemeinde, under the direction of Hermann Greid.
64. This was staged by émigré actors under the direction of Slatan Dudow.
65. In a production by Raymond Rouleau with Helene Weigel and Yvette Guilbert (in the role of Mrs Peachum). The play had already been staged in 1930 without much success (twenty-eight performances). There was also a French version of G. W. Pabst's film, with Albert Préjean and even Antonin Artaud.
66. René Dufour, 'Zeittheater der Emigration', in *Pariser Tageszeitung* 489, 15 October 1937.
67. In a production by Slatan Dudow, with Helene Weigel.
68. Walter Benjamin, 'Brechts Einakter', *Die Neue Weltbühne*, 30 June 1938, p. 827.
69. 'Ein deutsches Theater in Paris. Diskussion im SDS', *Pariser Tageszeitung*, 25 May 1938, p. 3.
70. *Das Schwarze Korps* for 7 July 1938 devoted a very violent article to it, depicting the 'boat of Jewish culture moored in Paris', and stressing that the play that claimed to show the horror of Nazi Germany only made the audience laugh: 'At all events it is very sad if the Jews who emigrated with Brecht no longer know whether they should laugh or cry.' Cited by H. C. Wächter, *Theater im Exil*, p. 57.
71. Several witnesses relate that he scarcely dared to appear in society because of his worn-out clothes. At the same time, Peter Lorre, equally poor, walked through London in a procession accompanied by a giant photograph of him as an advertisement for the film *M*.
72. A number of letters describe his approaches to the Théâtre des Champs-Elysées (documents communicated by Maria Piscator).
73. Production by Alwin Kronacher.

74. See p. 214 above.
75. See pp. 179–81 above, as well as the study I wrote with Maria Piscator, *Piscator et le théâtre politique*.
76. Cf. Peter Dietzel, *Exilliteratur in der Sowjetunion 1932–1937*, Berlin 1970.
77. In particular by the European Jewish Artists Society.
78. At least three performances per week were given in cinemas.
79. Cf. A. Dreifuss, 'Shanghai. Eine Emigration am Rande', in *Exil in der USA*, Leipzig 1979.
80. Cf. Werner Finck, *Alte Narr, was nun? Geschichte meiner Zeit*, Munich 1972; Rainer Otto and Walter Rösler, *Kabaretgeschichte*, Berlin 1972. The last two cabarets remaining in Berlin – the Katacombe and Tingel-Tangel – were closed by Goebbels in May 1935, as he had scant appreciation for Werner Finck's pleasantries at the regime's expense. Neither Jewish nor of the left, in fact a fairly conservative Protestant, Finck's case posed a thorny problem to the Nazis. Goebbels sent him to concentration camp, but he was released by Göring.
81. A celebrated actor with the Munich Kammerspiel, Therese Giehse continued her career in Zurich with Brecht. In France she is particularly known for one of her last roles: as the Jewish grandmother in Louis Malle's *Lacombe Lucien* (1974).
82. Cf. K. Mann, *The Turning Point*, pp. 261–2.
83. The company included Therese Giehse, Sybille Schloss, Magnus Henning, Igor Pahlem, Robert Trösch, Lotte Goslar, Gilly Wang and Paul Lindenberg (K. Mann, *The Turning Point*, p. 262).
84. Erika Mann was the object of venomous attacks in the Nazi press, and deprived of German nationality on the third list, but she became a British citizen by a *marriage blanc* with W. H. Auden, after first approaching Christopher Isherwood. The Nazis tried to have her performances banned, both by diplomatic approaches and by mobilizing their supporters (in Switzerland and the Sudetenland). A bomb was once discovered under the stage in Zurich, and performances had to be protected by the police. Subsequently, Erika Mann's authorization as an actor was withdrawn by the Swiss authorities.
85. With Annemarie Hase, Charlotte Küter, Bettz Loewen, Mowgli Sussmann, Paul Demel, Erich Freund, Felix Knüpfer, Paul Lewitt, Eddie Regon and Friedrich Richter. Several of its sets were designed by Erich E. Stern and John Heartfield.
86. 'Iron has always made an empire strong, butter and dripping only make a people fat.'
87. Fritz Schrecker and Johann Müller.
88. Die Laterndl gave a rendition of National Socialism as Wagnerian opera, with Hitler in the role of Wotan, Göring as Donner, Goebbels as Loge, and finance minister Schacht hoarding the Rheingold. In another sketch, Hitler demanded America as a German protectorate. Its most popular sketches were titled: *Von Adam bis Adolf* and *No Orchids for Mr Hitler*.
89. For instance Max Ehrlich, Willi Rosen and Otto Walburg, arrested by the Gestapo in the Netherlands.
90. *Alte Narr, was nun?*, pp. 70ff.
91. Hanna Schramm and Barbara Vormeier, *Vivre à Gurs*.
92. Ibid., p. 139.
93. Hanns Eisler taught film music in Hollywood, and tried to interest Brecht in a film on Richard Tauber. Brecht, Döblin, Franz Werfel, Carl Zuckmayer, Hand Sahl, Leopold Frank, Stefan Zweig and Alfred Wolfenstein all tried to sell scripts to the Hollywood film studios, but with little success.
94. For example E. J. Aufricht and Max Ophuls in France, or Piscator in Mexico.
95. Greif worked with Michael Romm (particularly known today for his 1965 film *Everyday Fascism*) on the shooting of *Mensch no. 217* (1944).
96. In 1936, Karl Brunner shot for Sojusdetfilmstudio a film depicting the involvement of children in German resistance, after a script by Béla Balazs. Alexander Granach acted in *The Gypsy Camp*, Herbert Rappoport (Austrian) in *Professor Mamlok*.

97. S. Roschal made a film based on Feuchtwanger's novel *Die Geschwister Opper-mann*, and another film was made from Langhoff's *Peat-Bog Soldiers*.
98. Piscator's finest film, *The Revolt of the Fishermen of Santa Barbara*, has been to all intents unavailable since the War. Those copies still in existence are in bad condition and made up of reels taken from different versions (Swedish, Dutch, Russian). The film based on Wangenheim's *Fighters* was reconstituted by the GDR Staatliche Filmarchiv and re-released on 27 February 1963 for the thirtieth anniversary of the Reichstag fire.
99. Cf. Maria Hilchenbach, *Kino im Exil*, Munich 1982.

CHAPTER 11   THE EMIGRÉS AND THE SECOND WORLD WAR

1. Nazi terminology divided the refugees into 'criminal elements', 'non-German refugees', 'Marxist criminals and agitators' and 'frightened or intimidated citizens' – the latter being those who had allegedly left Germany under the effect of the irresponsible propaganda of the old parties. Only these last were encouraged to return to Germany. Cf. Hanna Schramm and Barbara Vormeier, *Vivre à Gurs*, p. 191.
2. If the Nazis had nothing to fear from the majority of émigré magazines published in Prague or Paris, this was not the case with Willi Münzenberg's publications, which, thanks to both Comintern support and his international contacts, could launch campaigns hostile to the Reich that might well influence foreign governments. Moreover, the émigré press attacked two basic principles of Nazism: the centralization of all German information under Goebbels's ministry of propaganda, and the identification of the Nazi government with the German people. The articles published on anti-Semitic persecution had a particular resonance in Britain and the United States, arousing a reaction of disgust among the population. The Nazi government feared a boycott of Germany, or measures of economic sanctions against the Reich.
3. Cf. H. E. Tutas, *N. S. Propaganda und deutscher Exil 1933–1939*, Worms 1973, and *Nationalsozialismus und Exil*, Munich 1975.
4. They needed only show that any accusation against the regime tarnished the image of Germany. Thus ex-Chancellor Brüning, though an émigré himself, hated those émigrés who criticized the Nazi regime, as they damaged 'Germany's stature'. Neurath and Schwerin, both conservatives, published rejoinders in the British press to the allegations of anti-Semitic persecution.
5. The greatest diplomatic success of Germany in this field was the organization of the Olympic Games in Berlin.
6. On the occasion of the German Book Week of 1936, in Weimar.
7. This appeared on 27 June 1933. The article had in fact been written for a Swiss newspaper, and a series of translation errors made it into an incendiary text. Scheidemann protested, and applied to the Gestapo to get his parents released. The Nazis exploited this affair as a victory, and gave it great publicity.
8. This operation failed, as Gerhart Seger published in any case his account of Oranienburg, and the arrest of his wife and daughter aroused the indignation of women's movements in Britain. The staunch Conservative Lady Astor campaigned for their release, and the British government made an official representation. The Nazis were forced to free them, and allow them to leave for Britain.
9. The UFA cinema news, for example, showed a man who supposedly figured in the *Braunbuch* on the list of victims of the Hitler terror. In fact this man did not appear on the list, but no one bothered to check this, and the Nazi version was believed.
10. The French *Gringoire* is a good example. Its columnist Henri Béraud ceaselessly attacked the émigrés and accused them of wanting to kindle a 'Jewish war'; he blamed Heinrich Mann in particular for preparing this.

11. They were accused of seeking to influence political figures won to their cause, and thus steering the politics of their host countries.

12. In Switzerland, the right-wing press maintained that the Jews were unassimilable elements. In France, refugees were accused of being Communists and carriers of disease. In Sweden, they were blamed for theft or for disloyal competition. The *Völkische Beobachter*, for its part, described the economic damage supposedly due to the acceptance of émigrés.

13. The arguments deployed varied from one country to another: in Switzerland, the racial danger was emphasized, in France the economic burden the émigrés represented and the risk that they included 'revolutionaries' or 'spies'; in Austria, the claim was that they would strengthen the left, in Britain that they would introduce Communism.

14. Productions of works by Friedrich Wolf, Ödön von Horvath and Ferdinand Bruckner were attacked on many occasions, as were Erika Mann's cabaret performances. Works by émigrés were often refused performance for fear of attacks. (For example in Vienna; letter from F. Bruckner to Otto Preminger of 19 July 1934.)

15. Cf. Wieland Herzfelde, *John Heartfield*, Dresden 1962, pp. 70ff.

16. Henri Barbusse, Louis Aragon and L. Moussinac all declared their solidarity with Heartfield.

17. The German embassy in Prague protested not only against Heartfield's photomontages, but also against the reappearance of *Simplicus* (formerly *Simplicissimus*), the anti-Nazi weekly; the Berne embassy protested against the distribution of Heinrich Mann's works in Switzerland and the authorization given to Erika Mann to stage her antifascist cabaret. In Budapest, the German embassy demanded the seizure of the book *Adolf Hitler, Your Victims Accuse You*. During the War, Switzerland forbade the distribution of Hermann Rauschning's book *The Revolution of Nihilism* and Otto Braun's *From Weimar to Hitler*. We have already traced the fate of the famous antifascist exhibition mounted in Paris and the interventions of the German embassy towards it.

18. In March 1937, the Danish fascist journal *National Socialisten* published a series of 'revelations' emanating from German sources on the presence of 20,000 German refugees in the country who were 'eating our children's bread'. In fact there were only 2,000. The Reich protested violently when the Danish government allocated 25,000 crowns for the shelter of German refugees, on the pretext that this was helping to create a base of anti-German propaganda. The *Volkswille* applauded, on the other hand, when political émigrés were imprisoned in the Netherlands, under the headline: 'A concentration camp for German émigrés in Holland'.

19. The right of asylum had been generally recognized by all European countries since the French Revolution, and only a handful were ready to risk infringing it: Switzerland hesitated to allow the extradition of the Communist leader Heinz Neumann, accused by the Reich of murder, as this demand had too much of a political character. Neumann was eventually allowed to leave for Russia. Austria, on the other hand, expelled to Germany refugees who had illegally reached its territory. The Netherlands refused to hand over refugees accused of murdering Nazi activists during the 1932 elections. The few countries that extradited refugees to the Reich did so under duress. Paragraph 19 of the Franco-German armistice required German antifascists to be delivered to Germany, which the Vichy government carried out. In 1938 Czechoslovakia was forced to hand over Peter Forster, accused of murdering an SS guard while escaping from concentration camp, and he was hanged in Buchenwald. The Nazis almost always tried to get refugees arrested on false pretences (theft, murder, fraud, corruption). The former mayor of Altona, Max Brauer, was arrested by the French police in Paris, but the extradition demand was rejected. This did not rule out cowardice and stupidity. The Belgian Sûreté Publique handed the Communist Heinrich Bell and a number of Jewish refugees to the Gestapo at the German border, claiming that they had

flouted the conditions of 'political émigrés'. This extradition gave rise to such a strong press campaign that the Belgian government was forced to make representations to Heydrich in Berlin to get Bell's return.

20. Thus the Nazi government tried in vain to get the Danish government to hand over refugees, including Brecht.

21. This was the case with E. E. Kisch. Public opinion was generally more generous than governments towards the émigrés. Even if they were not much loved, the Nazis were still less so.

22. Heinrich Mann, *Verteidigung der Kultur*, Hildesheim 1960, p. 10.

23. B. Jacob, *Le Filet brun*, pp. 60ff.

24. Even Brüning complained of the constant surveillance he was subjected to in the Netherlands, which made any contact with Germans impossible (letter to G. Messerschmitt, 22 May 1939). Willi Münzenberg also maintained in the *Brown Book*: 'Some of these spies merely watched hotels and photographed the exiles as they came out. Others tried to penetrate antifascist organizations.'

25. For example by introducing weapons or forged currency into their homes, then denouncing them to the police. (B. Jacob, *Le Filet brun*, p. 64).

26. Ibid., pp. 66–7.

27. In the course of his trial, he admitted: 'I lived in poverty as an émigré. No country allowed me to earn a living. In October 1934 I returned to Germany. The visit made a great impression on me. I understood that I had betrayed the cause of a Great Germany and agreed to make amends' (*Le Filet brun*, p. 207).

28. On the details of these repressive measures, cf. Gilbert Badia, 'L'émigration en France, ses conditions, ses problèmes', in *Les Barbelés de l'exil*, pp. 80ff.

29. Circular of interior minister Albert Sarraut to all prefects (1 April 1938). All these quotations are cited from G. Badia's text. A 'methodical, energetic and prompt action' was encouraged, 'with a view of disembarrassing our country of the too numerous undesirable elements circulating here or intervening in an unacceptable fashion in political or social quarrels and conflicts that are only our affair' (ibid., p. 81).

30. This expression was first used by the Republican General Miaja in the Spanish civil war to refer to the Francoists who had launched four columns against Madrid, with a fifth made up of their supporters within the city. Many antifascists were treated by the French public as 'fifth columnists' or 'Nazi agents' when they were arrested in 1940. (Cf. also Max Gallo, *Cinquième colonne 1930–1940*, Paris 1970.)

31. Günter Markscheffel, a Social-Democrat activist exiled in France, wrote: 'Several political émigrés were sent to small provincial towns for the duration of Ribbentrop's visit to Paris. I was thus able for the first time to confirm the efficiency of the French administration, which, as I was to perceive later, was very well informed on any German involved in political activity who did not want to lose contact with his homeland' ('Exilés en France', p. 74). When Markscheffel tried to renew his *permit de séjour*, the prefect of police sent him to the Sûreté Générale, and he was only given authorization for a further week.

32. From a number of French public figures, and the Ligue des Droits de l'Homme. (Cf. G. Badia, 'L'émigration en France', pp. 86–7.)

33. 'Non-resident' foreigners were also not allowed to marry in France.

34. These camps were controlled by the interior ministry and the ministry for colonies, which suggests that the deportation of some anti-Nazis was already envisaged. Anyone escaping was liable to a penalty of six months' to three years' imprisonment.

35. B. Vormeier, *Vivre à Gurs*, p. 196.

36. On the different components of the fascisant right wing, cf. 'Visages de fascistes français', *Revue d'histoire de la Deuxième Guerre mondiale* 97, January 1975.

37. This development can be traced in writers such as Robert Brassilach.

38. *Gringoire*, from 1937 on, ceaselessly denounced the misdeeds of the Front Populaire and extolled Franco. From a print run of 155,000 copies that year, it reached

650,000 by the start of the War; it regularly referred to Heinrich Mann as a 'German Jew'. Henri Béraud called for the émigrés to be sent to Russia, as well as for the disbanding of the PCF and Secours Rouge.

39. Leonhard Frank and Lotte Eisner both recall, while interned in French camps, being called 'fifth columnists' and 'Nazi spies' by people who threw stones at them. Ludwig Marcuse declared that 'the classic country of hospitality stopped behaving very hospitably a while ago'. The Provence papers *Le Petit Marseillais* and *L'Eclaireur de Nice* echoed the right-wing press and attacked foreigners for preparing war and poisoning relations with Germany (*Verbannung*, p. 69).

40. On 8 November 1938, the day after the assassination of the German ambassador von Rath, *Action Française* declared: 'It was precisely one of these undesirables who committed yesterday a crime which, in revenging the Jews, seriously compromises the interests of France' (cited after B. Vormeier, *Vivre à Gurs*, p. 235).

41. *Le Jour* (10 September 1938) waxed indignant that no measures had been envisaged, in case of conflict, to check agents of the German secret services who had slipped in among the refugees. It was assumed that this would all be left to improvization and the arbitrary decision of the police: 'Would it not have been better to set up well-guarded concentration camps?' (ibid., p. 234).

42. Cf. G. Badia, *Les Barbelès de l'exil*, pp. 80ff.

43. Those antifascists who, to avoid imprisonment, requested an assignment of residence, were often condemned to six months in prison, if not actually expelled. On the details of this legislation, cf. *Les Barbelès de l'exil*, and *Vivre à Gurs*, pp. 236ff.

44. The first 'special holding centre' was established in the town of Mende (Lozère).

45. It was now necessary to have a visa from the host country in order to cross France.

46. 'Then it was Munich. I found myself by chance in Paris when Daladier returned, and witnessed the explosion of joy of the French people. I felt then for the first time the fearsome loneliness to which a political émigré can fall prey. I was disoriented and depressed in the midst of this rejoicing crowd [. . .]. Most people accused us of sowing panic, seeing things in the worst colours, and they remained deaf to our warnings' (Günter Markscheffel, 'Exilés en France', p. 75).

47. Ludwig Marcuse decided after Munich to leave France for America. According to Manès Sperber, very few émigrés made this decision, still believing in the possibility of a fight. (*Au-delà de l'oubli*, p. 153).

48. Cited by B. Vormeier, *Vivre à Gurs*, p. 244.

49. Manès Sperber wrote: 'Following the party's new line, the French army had now become an imperialist force and did not compel obedience. This was a difficult, even a dangerous decision, for volunteers who had already joined up. The new situation reduced more than one of these to despair. It paralysed their courage and such enthusiasm as they still retained' (*Au-delà de l'oubli*, p. 165).

50. Kurt Tucholsky had written already to Arnold Zweig on 15 December 1935: 'We must begin everything again from the beginning [. . .]. Don't listen to this ridiculous Stalin, who betrays his own people.' The same day he wrote to his brother Fritz: '[. . .] and when they invite you again to a congress, you have to reply: there's been a misunderstanding; I'm an antifascist, I'm afraid of meeting at your congress your business colleagues.'

51. Franz Dahlem declared: 'Whilst the Moscow negotiations between Britain and France on the one hand and the Soviet Union on the other did not lead to success, which was not the fault of the Soviet Union, this non-aggression pact opens a new path and prevents a general conflagration in Europe' (F. Dahlem, *Am Vorabend des zweiten Weltkrieges*, vol. 2, pp. 446–7). Many émigrés initially believed that the announcement of the pact was a lie from Goebbels's propaganda ministry. Manès Sperber, who describes this incredulity (*Au-delà de l'oubli*, p. 162), maintained: 'For the antifascist movement in its entirety, for the whole of the left, the Stalin-Hitler pact was the greatest political and moral defeat it had ever experienced' (p. 164). E. Heidelberger states that he saw it as a catastrophe: 'In as much as we were

antifascists, we were completely bewildered: it was unthinkable for us that Stalin could shake Hitler's hand' ('Exilés en France', p. 201).

52. The decree of 1 September 1939 made clear in its article 2 b): 'All foreigners located in metropolitan France, in Africa or in the French colonies [. . .] are assumed to be enemies.'

53. The *Deutsche Volkszeitung* had already been banned in August 1939, the police claiming that the subtitle 'anti-Hitler newspaper' disguised a Nazi propaganda cell (cf. Florimond Bonte, *Les Antifascistes allemands dans la résistance française*, Paris 1964, pp. 267–8). R. Leonhard, a radio broadcaster, was asked to read scripts attacking the USSR; when he refused, and read texts he had written himself, he was arrested the next day by the police.

54. Arthur Koestler described the attitude of the French government towards the émigrés in *The Scum of the Earth* (London 1968), as did Feuchtwanger in *The Devil in France*. Learning that the police had visited his home to arrest him, Koestler tried to find out the reason; but the division and separation of the police services prevented him from discovering the origin and motive.

55. On the camps in Provence, besides the research conducted by Gilbert Badia's team, see the special number of the magazine *Ex*: '*Les camps en provinces. Exil, internement, déportation 1933–1942*'.

56. *Verbannung*, pp. 73–4.

57. E. E. Noth, *L'Allemagne exilée en France*, Paris 1939, p. 7.

58. 'Exilés en France', p. 75.

59. *Verbannung*, p. 109.

60. Including Leonhard Frank, Alfred Kerr, Konrad Heiden, Joseph Bornstein, and several editors of anti-Nazi papers.

61. Foreigners unable to leave, foreigners who were suspect from a national point of view or dangerous to public order, and undesirables.

62. The Vichy government subsequently ordered a systematic check on all naturalizations, which started in July 1940.

63. *Exil in Frankreich*, p. 35.

64. Few refugees generally agreed to join the Foreign Legion, after being banned from fighting in regular French units. A certain number did do so, under threat of otherwise being treated as enemies, with confiscation of their belongings, or being left in camps. In the crisis days of September 1938, a large number of antifascists had volunteered for the French army, 'in the firm belief that in case of war we would fight with the regular forces' (E. Heidelberger, *Exilés en France*, p. 201). Heidelberger joined the Legion, considering that it was at all events part of the French army and would fight against Hitler. The families of men who joined the Legion also received the same allowances as those of conscripts. After being stationed near Lyon, many were sent to Algeria, some of these guarding the border with Libya. In accordance with international conventions, they were not sent into combat against German troops. Kantorowicz relates the fate of other *légionnaires* who were sent to Syria.

65. On the details of these different measures, cf. Barbara Vormeier, *Vivre à Gurs*, pp. 248ff.

66. 'The Roland-Garros stadium, a "sorting camp", was made up of three barracks resembling vast barns, with roofs that came down very low and allowed an abundant flow of rain [. . .]. For one hour a day we were allowed out of these barracks, which stank of smoke, damp straw and infection, to walk on the tennis court and the tiers of the amphitheatre' (from the account by F. Bondy, in *Vivre à Gurs*, p. 303). The internees there included the antifascist writer Balder Olden, whose wife was interned in the Vélodrome d'Hiver.

67. Gustav Regler presented himself to the authorities of his *arrondissement* to enrol in the French army. He was thanked and requested to return fourteen hours later. At six o'clock the next morning his door was broken down by five policemen, revolvers in hand, and he was taken to the coal cellar of the Palais de Justice. His wounds

from the Spanish war had still not healed, and a young policemen almost vomited on seeing them. (*The Owl of Minerva*, p. 331).

68. F. Bondy recalled: 'Among the Spaniards and International Brigaders at Le Vernet, I saw several who had lost both arms, blind men, old people and children. In section B, I saw a boy of about twelve who had lost an arm' (*Vivre à Gurs*, p. 305). A deaf mute had scribbled to me on a scrap of paper: 'Am I accused of proselytising?'

69. Cf. in particular the account by F. Bondy in *Vivre à Gurs*, pp. 309ff.

70. The Communists Dahlem, Merker, Rau and Eisler found themselves at Le Vernet, which led Regler to write with a mischievous irony (he had broken with the party after the Spanish war): 'There were possibly a few dozen profiteers among the prisoners, as well as the full strength of the Central Committee of the German Communist Party; but the majority was composed of opponents of the Third Reich' (*The Owl of Minerva*, p. 333).

71. Koestler was arrested on 2 October 1939. He was prosecuted as a 'Communist agent' even though his break with the party the previous year and his opposition to the German–Soviet pact was a matter of general knowledge.

72. G. Regler, *The Owl of Minerva*, p. 334.

73. In a letter to a woman friend (18 January 1940; *Verbannung*, p. 78), Friedrich Wolf described life at the camp, and washing in the icy water of the Ariège. To sustain his morale, he reread *Madame Bovary* and Hemingway's *A Farewell to Arms*.

74. The largest of these were: Mesaly du Maine (Orne), Montargis (Loiret), Danigny (Orne), Montbard (Côte d'Or), Saint-Julien (Oise), Villerbon (Loir-et-Cher), Villemalar (Loir-et-Cher), Marolles (Loir-et-Cher) and Saint-Jean-de-la-Ruelle (Loir-et).

75. They were unaware of their destinations. 'Trucks under heavy escort drove us to a goods station, where we were loaded into wagons for an unknown destination' (G. Markscheffel, *Exilés en France*, p. 303).

76. The same facts are reported by Lotte H. Eisner and Hermann Kesten, for different camps. Eisner, interned in the Pyrenees, relates that every evening the commander of her block came armed with a dog-whip to seek out the best-looking woman of the group with a view to buying her favours in return for food (ibid., p. 303).

77. *Verbannung*, p. 77.

78. Cf. letter of H. Kesten to his wife, 12 October 1939, in *Verbannung*.

79. Lion Feuchtwanger, *The Devil in France*.

80. Newspaper reading was strictly forbidden by the camp authorities.

81. These really were concentration camps, and the treatment inflicted on the detainees in some of them, like Le Vernet, is reminiscent of the first German concentration camps for political opponents, minus their sadism. Erich Weinert recalls that when refugees from the Spanish Republican army arrived at the French border, under the watchful eye of the *gardes mobiles*, they were directed to a village where a freshly painted sign read: 'To the concentration camp' (*Vivre à Gurs*, p. 258). See also the analysis of the repressive camp conditions in *Les Barbelés de l'exil*, p. 290. The description of the Vernet camp is particularly illuminating. The expression 'concentration camp' also appears in official documents from the interior ministry. Three camps were established in 1939, and the expression was taken over by the Vichy government.

82. At the time that these anti-Nazis were imprisoned in camps, Kantorowicz recalls that *Paris-Match* showed the luxurious apartment of the Thyssens, now exiled in France though they had given Hitler the support of heavy industry (*Exil in Frankreich*, p. 101).

83. G. Regler, *The Owl of Minerva*, p. 333.

84. A. Koestler, *The Invisible Writing*, p. 510.

85. As G. Badia remarks: 'The foreigners – in particular the German and Austrian émigrés, who included a notable proportion of skilled workers – could have been involved in the French war effort' (*Les Barbelés de l'exil*, p. 89). A large number were ready to serve in the French army. As for those who enrolled in the Foreign

Legion, they found themselves under the command of officers who did not hide their pro-Hitler sympathies and made them sing Nazi songs (Claude Vernier, *Tendre exil*, Paris 1983, p. 123). Others were made to carry stones to a hilltop only to throw them into the sea in a pretence of training – as described by Anna Seghers in *Transit*.

86. Somerset Maugham and Jean Giradoux both intervened on his behalf.
87. Walter Benjamin had been interned in 1939 close to Nevers (letter to Adrienne Monnier, 21 September 1939; *The Correspondence of Walter Benjamin*, pp. 613–14). He was defended by Valéry and J. Romains, and requested B. Crémieux to attest to his 'loyalty' (letter to Gisèle Freund, 2 November 1939; ibid., pp. 616–17). He escaped a second internment in 1940 thanks to the intervention of the diplomat Alexis Saint-Léger (Saint-John Perse), whose poems he had translated.
88. Walter Benjamin wrote to Max Horkheimer on 30 November 1939: 'It was not at all easy to obtain my release. Even though it is not rare to leave the camp for reasons of illness, among others, it is not often that a person may walk out through the front door, namely because of a decision made by the interministerial committee' (*Correspondence*, p. 618). His case was taken up by a number of committees, by French writers, the PEN Club, Maurice Halbwachs and the World Jewish Congress. Franz Blei was defended by Gide, Duhamel and Giradoux; Döblin by R. Minder, A. Rivaux, E. Vermeil and J. Giradoux; Hermann Kesten by J. Romains.
89. Alfred Kantorowicz (*Exil in Frankreich*, pp. 98–9) records Albert Sarraut's deep hostility towards the German antifascists, and his opposition to any humanitarian aid. Interior minister from 1937 to 1940, Sarraut was deported to Germany on 6 June 1944, and his wife was murdered.
90. B. Vormeier, *Vivre à Gurs*, p. 256.
91. It is surprising to read, therefore, E. E. Noth's *L'Allemagne exilée en France* (Paris 1939), in which he describes his internment in dithyrambic terms: 'For those emerging from the Nazi camps, it was a real revelation to find oneself in France, in a camp which had no more in common than the name with the hideous reality that this denoted in Germany, where you did not have to suspect each guard as your murderer of tomorrow, nor recognize him as your torturer of today [. . .] It will be a particularly moving claim to the glory of France that none of those who came out of this holding camp, or will come out of it, will be able to say, without an unworthy bad faith, that they had been unhappy there' (p. 22). Unawareness, naivety or prudence? Many émigrés would have to grit their teeth on reading these lines.
92. B. Voermeier, *Vivre à Gurs*, p. 260.
93. Ibid., p. 8.
94. Ibid.
95. All men between seventeen and fifty-five were arrested, including task-force members, and all women who were unmarried or without children.
96. Two thousand three hundred and sixty-four women had arrived in Gurs by 23 May 1940. They were subsequently joined by women and children from other departments, making a total of 6,356.
97. It seems that such promises were not kept. Cf. *Les Barbelés de l'exil*, p. 325.
98. Lion Feuchtwanger gave a detailed account of the discussions between the detainees' delegation and the camp commander in *The Devil in France*. We should remember that the antifascists had been deprived of their identity papers, so that if they escaped, they risked being immediately arrested in the wake of a police raid. Feuchtwanger, who escaped from the Les Milles camp – after the German invasion, surveillance there was not very strict – was told by the camp commander that it would be best to return, as the prisoners were to be evacuated. The situation was all the more tragic as the official order did not arrive, the German army was advancing, and the railway cars needed for the evacuation were hardly available, or arrived several days late. The émigrés were often transported in goods trucks.
99. Cf. B. Vormeier, *Vivre à Gurs*, p. 264; G. Badia, *Les Barbelés de l'exil*, p. 325.
100. B. Vormeier, *Vivre à Gurs*, p. 261.

101. Besides Kundt, this included a scientific assistant, two representatives of the Wehr-macht, two Red Cross doctors, four representatives of the NSDAP, an interpreter, and it clearly seems, three members of the Gestapo (*Vivre à Gurs*, p. 266).
102. Apart from four, Barbara Vormeier maintains, though she does not give their names.
103. A re-education camp had already been established in Strasbourg in June 1940.
104. Life in the camps had become so insupportable that some detainees were tempted by a 're-education' period of a few weeks. Candidates were given a certain sum of money, taken to Paris by train, and put up at a hotel before leaving for Strasbourg.
105. Some 800 in all. The commission counted 2,500 Aryans and 2,000 task-force members. Those repatriated included some antifascists who had fought in the International Brigades, and even Jews. The commission's report spoke of detainees who cried 'Heil Hitler!' and were 'radiant with joy'. The writer added: 'Soon I was struck by the fact that there were among them a few Jews and individuals with a very Oriental physique' (*Vivre à Gurs*, p. 268).
106. *Les Barbelés de l'exil*, p. 331.
107. They were sent to camps, where some of them perished. Tschäper, former commander of the IInd Brigade, escaped from Sachsenhausen, but was recaptured and executed in November 1944.
108. Gerhard Eisler, Paul Merker and Gustav Regler emigrated to Mexico, Paul Bertz to Switzerland.
109. Franz Dahlem was taken from the Le Vernet camp and handed over to the Gestapo. Imprisoned at Clastres, an attempt to spring him failed. He was trans-ferred to the prison of Cherche-Midi, then to the Mauthausen concentration camp. In summer 1943, Rudolf Leonhard managed to escape together with seventeen fellow detainees – German, Spanish, Austrian and Yugoslav. Thanks to a prison guard who was in touch with the Resistance, they obtained civilian clothes, a map of the town, and the address of a safe house where they were given false papers. They then joined the *maquis*.
110. A number of those who had been repatriated 'under the protection of the Reich' were immediately sent to concentration camp.
111. In October 1940, there was a plan to round up all German Jews located in France in concentration camps. Kantorowicz described the situation of apolitical German Jews interned in the '*zone libre*', who crossed the demarcation line and asked to be repatriated, not being political opponents. The Gestapo sent them back to the '*zone libre*' and they were imprisoned near Marseille.
112. By the end of summer 1940, the number of detainees at Gurs had fallen from 6,356 to 2,523 (*Vivre à Gurs*, p. 273).
113. If they were caught trying to escape from Gurs, they were sent to Le Vernet, and from there they were sent to prison. Several were killed or wounded in the course of escape attempts. From summer 1942 on, escape and assisting escape were punished with a prison term of three to five years.
114. Persons over sixty-five, sick, infirm and women with children were interned in other camps in southern France.
115. Other German and Austrian Jews, arrested by the French police on 26 April 1942, were taken to Drancy and sent to Auschwitz. After June 1942, Jews who were not born in France were arrested and deported. As Manès Sperber writes: 'They went to hunt out Jews in the darkest cellars and the furthest corners of barns, especially children who had been hidden there. Laval insisted that children should be deported together with their parents' (*Au-delà de l'oubli*, p. 211).
116. 'I presented myself at the Nice prefecture to request a residence permit, which was refused. I was given to understand that I should not insist on this, and the best would be not to make any further representation. It was only later, when Malraux requested an explanation from the prefect, that I learned the reasons for this refusal: I figured on the list of persons to extradite. If I avoided presenting myself to the police, and acted as non-existent, they also could ignore my presence' (ibid., p. 196).

117. Anna Seghers depicted his suicide, under the name of Weidel, in her novel *Transit*.
118. They were actually in Toulon (*Schicksalreise*, p. 173).
119. Alma Mahler wrote in her memoirs: 'Werfel was unnerved by the confusing rumours he brought home daily from the Czech consulate. The armistice signed by the French obliged them to "surrender on demand" all Germans (which then meant also all former Austrians and Czechs) named by the German Government. Werfel would hear from someone that he was "first on the list", and would collapse in tears' (*And the Bridge Is Love*, p. 242).
120. Anna Seghers depicted the anguish and despair common to all these German antifascists seeking a US visa in her novel *Transit*.
121. The Mexican consulate offered visas to all former fighters in the International Brigades. The consul Gilberto Bosquez tried to get a number of detainees released by declaring that they were under his government's protection.
122. Feuchtwanger needed an 'emergency visa', as provided for on Bullitt's initiative, to leave France.
123. 'She was crying. She protested violently and questioned the officers who would not reply. I kept quiet. She was of course completely right, but what did it mean to be "right" in such circumstances. She was thinking in human terms, but this was an administrative situation, not a human one' (Alfred Döblin, *Schicksalreise*, p. 274).
124. Money for the voyage was then lent him by an official at the prefecture.
125. Leonhard committed suicide following his return to Germany in 1952.
126. A number of émigrés stayed in Martinique, unable to go any further. Anna Seghers and Alfred Kantorowicz were interned there temporarily. Robert Breuer, former press chief of the Prussian government, remained there, as did the historian Kurt Kesten who died in Martinique.
127. A number of ships were blocked at Casablanca. Max Schroeder was there for two weeks before being interned in a military barracks 200 kilometres inland, where with other antifascists he suffered from the climate as well as from rats and scorpions. A number of them perished from dysentery or malaria. Claude Lévi-Strauss, who left France for America with these refugees, described in his memoires what the departure was like: 'Far from being a solitary adventure, it was more like the deportation of convicts. What amazed me even more than the way we were treated was the number of passengers. [. . .] The rest of my companions, men, women and children, were herded into the hold, with neither air nor light, and where the ship's carpenters had hastily run up bunk beds with straw mattresses' (*Tristes Tropiques*, London 1972, p. 24).
128. Both men had obtained exit visas by applying to Vincent Auriol and Léon Blum. Despite warnings from the sub-prefect J. Des Vallières, they remained in Arles working at the library, while waiting for a boat. They were arrested by the French police on 8 February 1941, who claimed they wanted to protect them from the Gestapo, but they were taken to Vichy and handed to the German police the same day. The exact circumstances of Hilferding's death are not known. According to different accounts he hung himself, took veronal, or was thrown from a window by the Gestapo. His trace is lost on 11 February 1941 in the infirmary of the Fresnes prison.
129. Cf. *Exilés en France. Souvenirs d'antifascistes allemands émigrés*, and especially F. Bonte, *Les Antifascistes allemands dans la résistance française*.
130. Ernst Melis, who actively worked on editing antifascist papers designed for soldiers (*Soldat am Mittelmeer, Unser Vaterland, Deutsches Volksecho*), drew his information from discussions with soldiers in trains. He passed himself off as director of a commercial business. Melis had escaped from a camp near Clermont-Ferrand. Having collected French uniforms abandoned by soldiers who feared being taken prisoner by the German army, he obtained official demobilization with false papers, making out that he was Czech.
131. After Toulouse, Melis carried out his propaganda activity in Castres, but he was discovered and arrested by the Gestapo following denunciation by a police

informer whom he had taken for an anti-Nazi. To gain time, he maintained that the man was his accomplice, and he was sent to Paris to be judged by the Wehrmacht's high tribunal. The train was attacked by the Resistance. As he made his escape, his guards tried to shoot him in the head, but missed. He was freed by the partisans and ended up as a lieutenant in the France-Tireurs Partisans. After the war he was in charge of foreign news for *Neues Deutschland* in the GDR.

132. The main organ in the occupied zone was *Soldat im Westen*, the first issue of which appeared on 23 June 1941; in 1942, *Soldat am Mittelmeer* was launched for the '*zone libre*'. They were subsequently replaced by *Volk und Vaterland* and *Unser Vaterland*.

133. The call to desert was given to German soldiers if they were deployed in actions against French patriots or were sent to the Russian front. This appeal intensified in 1944, when they were invited to join Freies Deutschland.

134. Sabotage of war materials was organized in this way, as was the systematic waste of the German army's resources (petrol, and spare parts for weapons).

135. Established in Paris in September 1942, with Otto Niebergall as its president. When the general secretary was sent to concentration camp, H. Hauser took over, and was also responsible for editing *Volk und Vaterland*. (F. Bonte, *Les Antifascistes allemands dans la résistance française*, p. 312).

136. They included Otto Kühne, Martin Kalb, Richard Hilgert, Max Dankner, Paul Hartmann, Hermann Meyer and Max Frank, all of whom had previously fought in the International Brigades.

137. For example the Gingold brothers, members of the Free German Youth established after the Front Populaire, which carried out agitation within the German army in Paris. Denounced and arrested by the Gestapo, Peter Gingold managed an incredible escape thanks to his knowledge of Paris geography. Leading the Gestapo to believe that he had agreed to denounce his comrades, he was taken to a building at 8 boulevard Saint-Martin where they were supposed to hide out. While the Gestapo were waiting, he came out on the rue des Boulangers. Cf. F. Bonte, *Les Antifascistes allemands dans la résistance française*, p. 300, and his account in *Exilés en France*, pp. 262ff.

138. The wives and daughters of émigrés played a fundamental part in these activities. We need only recall how Käthe Dahlem spied on Wehrmacht soldiers by passing herself off as an Alsatian. Else Fugger, a liaison agent, was arrested and died in concentration camp. Erna Stahlmann produced leaflets and antifascist papers. Arrested and interned in Germany, she managed to escape and lived underground in Berlin. Dora Schaul formed such good links with German soldiers whom she managed to rally to antifascism that at the Liberation she narrowly avoided having her head shaved as a 'collaborator'.

PREFACE TO PART TWO

1. 'B. Brecht, 'Late Lamented Fame of the Giant City of New York', *Poems 1913–1956*, p. 167.
2. Ibid., p. 171.

CHAPTER 12   THE CONFRONTATION WITH NAZI GERMANY

1. Cf. *Mein Kampf*; but also the accounts of German ambassadors in the United States: Hans Luther, *Politiker ohne Partei*, Stuttgart 1969, and H. H. Dieckhoff, *Zur Vorgeschichte des Roosevelt-Kriege*, Berlin 1943.
2. 'Hitler had [a] firm, preconceived opinion which no argument could shake [. . .] that North America would never take part in a European war again, and that, with her millions of unemployed, the United States was on the brink of a revolution from the outbreak of which only Hitler could save her.' (*Hitler Speaks*, London 1937, p. 75.)

3. Ibid., p. 76.
4. Ibid., p. 77.
5. Aged sixty-three at that time, Dodd, who had studied in Leipzig, was known for his works on the history of the American South. He was chosen for his declared liberal ideas.
6. The German ambassador in Washington, Prittwitz, had given up his position when the Nazis came to power. The German consul in New York at the time, Paul Schwarz, was of Jewish origin, as was his counterpart in Chicago, H. F. Simons.
7. Both the American Jewish Committee and B'nai B'rith were cautious in their condemnations of Germany. The Jewish Labor Committee, more to the left, demanded immediate action.
8. The Non-Sectarian Anti-Nazi League called for an active boycott of Germany. This measure was approved by German émigrés, who believed at the time that the Nazi government could be defeated by an economic crisis. If the League still maintained in 1935 that 'boycott is a substitute for war', it soon became apparent that such measures were ineffectual. The effects of the boycott could even be contradictory: it risked leading the Nazis to take still severer measures against the Jews, or trigger anti-Semitic reactions among people doing business with Germany. Conservative circles, moreover, were hostile to any boycott.
9. *Ambassador Dodd's Diary*, New York 1941, p. 5.
10. In his *Souvenirs d'une ambassade à Berlin*, Paris 1946, the French ambassador at this time, A. François-Poncet, stressed Dodd's hatred for the Nazis (p. 271). An intransigent liberal, he always refused to attend the Nazi party congress in Nuremberg, and sent regular reports to Washington on the possibility of war.
11. A sum of $6,000 was allocated to the German consul in New York for a pro-Nazi counter-offensive in the US press, to be headed by the American journalist Viereck, and for establishing a *Deutsch-Amerikanischer Handelsbulletin*. Further support was provided by Colonel Edwin Emerson, founder of the Friends of Germany.
12. Cf. E. Ben Elissar, *La Diplomatie du IIIe Reich et les juifs*, p. 352 [retranslated from the French].
13. Arthur D. Morse, *While Six Million Died. A Chronicle of American Apathy*, New York 1968, p. 231.
14. As early as 1923, Kurt George Wilhelm Ludecke had organized the collection of funds for the NSDAP in the United States. In 1924, the Teutonia group was founded in Chicago, publishing *Amerika's Deutsche Post*. These early 'American Nazis' included Fritz Gissibl, founder of Teutonia and subsequently director of Friends of the New Germany. He returned to Germany in 1930 and worked for the Deutsches Ausland-Institut. Walter Kappe, a member of Teutonia, published the papers of Friends of the New Germany and the German-American Bund. Sepp Schuster, former member of the NSDAP in Germany, was active in the Friends of the New Germany, as was Heinz Spanknäbel who established a Teutonia group in Detroit. Other Nazi groups were set up wherever there were German émigrés: the Swastika League, Friends of the Hitler Movement, and Friends of Germany.
15. The opening address was given by Walter Kappe.
16. The official ban on German citizens living in the United States from belonging to these groups was published by Rudolf Hess on 11 October 1935. These Nazi groups immediately lost two-thirds of their members.
17. They were supposed to collect funds for the NSDAP and win American public figures to Nazi ideas.
18. The New York group had at its disposal a large quantity of propaganda material brought to America on German ships; its Chicago rival had more connection with the German press in the United States.
19. Apart from organizations such as the Volksbund für das Deutschtum im Ausland, which published racist manuals and periodicals, the Deutsches Ausland-Institut and the Auslandorganisation der NSDAP. These distributed a large amount of

propaganda material abroad, and established files on all German public figures living abroad.

20. In particular the *New Yorker Staatszeitung* directed by V. F. Ridder, an anti-Nazi Catholic.

21. He was replaced by Fritz Gissibl, then Reinhold Walter and Hubert Schnuch.

22. The commission of inquiry was set up at the request of Samuel Dickstein, a spokesman of the Jewish community in the House of Representatives. The McCormick-Dickstein committee stressed the overtly racist character of the Bund's supporters and their ties with American fascist organizations. It was also pointed out that German consulates were used as propaganda centres.

23. La Guardia's mother, who came from Austria, was Jewish.

24. Cf. Sheean Vincent, *Dorothy und Red. Die Geschichte von Dorothy Thompson und Sinclair Lewis*, Munich 1964.

25. Cited by Joachim Radkau, *Die deutsche Emigration*, p. 68.

26. The new German consul, Kiep, tried to persuade Einstein to return to Germany. But when the latter twice asked the consulate in Los Angeles to guarantee his safety, he received an evasive reply.

27. The Greater New York Federation of Churches protested on 21 March 1933 in an appeal signed by thirty-five public figures.

28. H. R. Knickerbocker, for example, correspondent for the *New York Evening Post*, published *The German Crisis* (New York 1932) in which he described Berlin as the reddest town outside Russia, but predicted Hitler's victory and a civil war. Attending both Nazi and Communist meetings, he gave readers of his articles a mass of information, though he was worried less for the future of democracy than for US investments in what he described as a regular battlefield. He concluded that it was America's good fortune to be divided from Europe by the Atlantic Ocean.

29. In his *Berlin Diary*, Shirer did not hid his antipathy to the German people, whom he judged to be in their totality 'sadistic and perverse', and completely infested by the 'Nazi tarantula'.

30. Radio played a significant role as an accelerator of history, to the point that the translator of Hitler's speeches, a Harvard graduate of German origin, Hans von Kaltenborn, immediately changed his name to H. V. Kaltenborn so as to play down its German connotation. We should recall that this was the time of the panic provoked by Orson Welles's radio broadcast *The War of the Worlds*, based on H. G. Wells's novel, which depicted the Martians landing in New Jersey. The reportage style and Welles's narration gave such an illusion of authenticity that more than 1.7 million people believed the country had been invaded by the Martians, and the police and state governor had to intervene to put an end to the panic.

31. In 1932, for example, there were 21,794 unemployed university graduates. Apart from the cinema, all US industries were affected. Thousands of unemployed lined up in the Manhattan streets. In Washington state the unemployed started fires, hoping to be taken on to extinguish them. New York had more than a million unemployed, out of 15 to 17 million for the nation as a whole. In September 1932, *Fortune* magazine estimated that America had at least 34 million people (unemployed, women, children) with no income, or 28 per cent of the population.

32. 'No alien is admissible if he fails to meet certain physical, mental, moral and financial requirements.'

33. Wives and unmarried children under twenty-one, husbands and wives of US citizens, ministers of religion, teachers, their wives and unmarried children under eighteen, students desirous of carrying out study or research in the US.

34. Members of foreign governments, with their families, domestic staff, employees, temporary visitors, foreigners in transit, and 'treaty aliens' entering the United States under the terms of commercial and shipping agreements.

35. He violently attacked Dorothy Thompson for defending the cause of antifascist émigrés and campaigning for American commitment alongside the democracies, claiming that she was prepared to sacrifice a million Americans for a European war.

He ironically thanked her for wanting to sacrifice her son, already of military age, whilst his own son was still only twelve.

36. The liberal Senator Reynold, however, attacked Erika Mann for an interview published in the *World Telegram* on 27 January 1939: he did not know who she was and admitted he had never heard of Thomas Mann.

37. He became directly responsible for visas in 1940.

38. Cited in *Exil in den USA*, p. 41.

39. Walter Benjamin wrote to Gretel Adorno on 17 January 1940 (*The Correspondence of Walter Benjamin*, pp. 626–7): 'In the meantime, I went to the American consulate, where I was given the usual questionnaire. Question number 14 is as follows: "Are you the minister of any sect or a professor at a school, seminary, academy or university?" If I am correct, this question will have important consequences for me since, on the one hand, a "yes" would make it possible to get in regardless of the quota (a nonquota visa) and since, on the other hand, the consulate claims that it would take at least five or six years to be admitted under the quota.' Max Born wrote to Einstein on 31 May 1939: 'What to do with a fifty-five-year-old dentist? The Gestapo will send him to concentration camp if he doesn't emigrate in a hurry. But his number on the list is 60,000!' (*Correspondance*, Paris 1972, p. 155). It was because of these quota requirements that Erwin Piscator emigrated to the United States not as a stage director but as a 'professor'.

40. The American historian Arthur D. Morse, in *While Six Million Died*, describes the slowness of the US bureaucracy.

41. In his autobiography *In Search of Myself* (New York 1944), Hans Natonek described his meeting with the former Dadaist Walter Mehring in Marseille. Mehring was on his way to the US consulate with his books, but had cut out their titles. He wanted to prove by his books that he was a writer, but feared that their titles alone would get him counted as a subversive (p. 127).

42. The question was put to Roosevelt at a press conference after *Kristallnacht*, and he replied that the quotas would remain unchanged. Roosevelt received a petition in support of the refugees, launched under the aegis of the Jewish Peoples Committee, with 120,000 signatures. At the Évian conference he had proposed the establishment of a centre of Jewish emigration in Angola.

43. Leonhard Frank, for example, obtained a US visa but was unable to use it, for want of a valid passport. Cf. his letter to Emil Oprecht of 12 August 1940, in *Verbannung*.

44. The affidavit, a financial guarantee, had to be signed by two US citizens. Anna Seghers, in *Transit*, tells the story of a woman refugee who obtained an affidavit from an American couple she met by accident, on condition that she brought their two pet hares with her to the United States.

45. Cf. *Exil in den USA*, pp. 47ff. Eisler did however have a letter of recommendation from the director of the New School, Alvin Johnson, stating that he was a professor, which enabled him to receive a non-quota visa.

46. The film director George Cukor wrote to President Roosevelt on Eisler's behalf on 25 March 1939, and Clifford Odets also campaigned for him.

47. Signed by William Dieterle, Oscar Wagner, Rudolph Kolisch, the German Writers' Association and Joseph Losey. They all emphasized Eisler's immense value as a composer of film music, and the interest of American critics in his work.

48. Sigrid Undset did so for Scandinavia, Maurice Maeterlinck for Belgium, Jules Romains for France, Thomas Mann and Hermann Kesten for the German-speaking countries.

49. On the details of these 'lunch meetings' organized by the Emergency Rescue Committee, cf. letter from Mildred Adams to Hermann Kesten of 10 July 1940: *Deutsche Literatur im Exil*, pp. 140–1.

50. Brecht was in Sweden at this time, and travelled via the USSR. Piscator first asked Elemer Rice for support, then wrote to Erika and Klaus Mann, Hanns Eisler, Kurt Weill, Fritz Kortner, Charlie Chaplin, Paul Gree and Robert Sherwood. Letter published in J.-M. Palmier and M. Piscator, *Piscator et la théatre politique*.

51. In New York, Otto Preminger staged several works between 1938 and 1941, including *Margin for Error* (1939), an anti-Nazi comedy by Claire Booth Luce. The previous year he had played the role of a Nazi in Irving Pichel's Twentieth Century Fox film *The Pied Piper*. Warner Brothers made *Confessions of a Nazi Spy* with Anatole Litwak in spring 1939, which helped demonstrate the danger of the Bund's activities and strengthened the vigilance of the antifascist leagues, especially the Anti-Nazi Federation which was close to the CPUSA.

52. According to some historians, Eleanor Roosevelt played a decisive role in establishing the emergency visa quota.

53. Roosevelt himself referred to her as the 'Wall Street oracle', and Klaus Mann thought she initially despised Roosevelt as much as Hitler.

54. The *Philadelphia Public Ledger* and the *New York Evening Post*.

55. Klaus Mann wrote in *The Turning Point*: 'I recall a rather sumptuous reception [. . .] at the home of Mrs Sinclair Lewis, Dorothy Thompson. The brisk and attractive American correspondent whom we had known years before in Munich, Berlin, and Vienna, was now at the point of becoming a national figure' (p. 296).

56. Even Thomas Mann wrote to René Schickele on 19 February 1936: 'Everyone from Germany whom I speak to seems to feel that the National Socialist adventure is in its final stage and that general disintegration is at hand' (*Letters of Thomas Mann 1889–1955*, p. 211).

57. Hitler had made a most unpleasant impression on her, and she wrote that a man like that could never become a dictator; he therefore decided to expel her as soon as he had seized power. Klaus Mann ironically noted: 'For Dorothy, however, this mistake paid off well: her interview was the beginning of a brilliant career. By expelling her, that idiot Adolf [. . .] immediately laid the basis of her glory' (*Der Wendepunkt*, p. 350). [This passage and that in note 58 do not appear in the English edition of *The Turning Point*.]

58. 'Her regular commentaries on political, cultural and humanitarian questions appearead in hundreds of American papers. Her words had weight, her advice was listened to' (ibid.).

59. Winston Churchill maintained that she played a decisive role in support of the Allies. The American historian Mary R. Beard held that by focusing on Communism and fascism, she played particularly on her readers' emotions, 'speculating on the fear and attraction that acts of violence exerted' (*American in Midpassage* 1949), cited by J. Radkau, *Die deutsche Emigration*, pp. 70–1.

60. Sinclair Lewis was the author of a remarkable novel on fascism and American isolationism, *It Can't Happen Here*, but he did not share his wife's activism and maintained that if he were ever involved in divorce proceedings, he would cite Hitler as co-respondent.

61. Fritz Kortner, *Aller Tage Abend*, pp. 318.

62. Brecht wrote in his *Journals*: 'KORTNER [. . .] thought fit in 1940 to join roosevelt's election campaign. he persuaded the columnist dorothy thompson (formerly mrs sinclair lewis) to drop wilkie and back roosevelt, a highly significant turn of events. he wrote speeches and articles for her etc. even the "stürmer" had a picture of him as a semitic devil, dictating thompson speeches. but he didn't have the fare to go to the white house for tea after the election' (18 November 1941; *Journals*, p. 171).

63. She declared: 'Practically everybody who in world opinion stood for what was called German culture prior to 1933 is now a refugee.' This phrase was quoted on the cover of the book *Escape to Life*, one of the first published on the émigrés in the United States.

64. When this article appeared, Budzislawski was a professor in the GDR. He did not deny her claim that he had not advised her on political matters. Max Jordan attacked Dorothy Thompson in the *Review of Politics* (5, 1943) for speaking of a 'dictatorship of the people' as democracy, and of a 'world revolution for civilization based on reason, realism and morality'. J. Radkau correctly remarked that similar

expressions could be found in Thomas Mann, who was scarcely known for Communist sympathies.

65. Dorothy Thompson also signed the affidavit that enabled Carl Zuckmayer and his family to immigrate.

66. Klaus Mann depicted the atmosphere the play created: 'Most Americans thanked God for the ocean that divided the New World from the Old. Behind a barrier of such dimension they felt safe despite the earthquakes elsewhere. [. . .] It was sad for the Europeans, but a *cordon sanitaire* and five thousand miles gave perfect immunity even from a bacillus such as fascism. A fascist danger in the United States, the land of Washington and Lincoln? Impossible, it can't happen here' (*Der Wendepunkt*, pp. 347ff.) [This passage does not appear in the English edition of *The Turning Point*.]

67. 320,000 copies of the book were sold, and radical groups in several cities invited Lewis to speak of his work. He violently disclaimed any sympathy for Marxism, and sometimes insulted his audience when they found him 'radical'. (Cf. Mark Shirer, *Sinclair Lewis. An American Biography*, New York 1961, pp. 630ff.)

68. Maldwyn Alken Jones, *American Immigration*, Chicago 1966, p. 280.

69. *Der Aufbau* reported in 1939 on a group of Austrian immigrants in Chicago who decided to commit collective suicide if they were expelled from America.

70. Cf. Arthur Morse, *While Six Million Died*; Alfred Häsler, *Das Boot ist voll*, Zurich 1967.

71. 'He who watches over us like a father, if he could see how we listened to his speeches' (cited by J. Radkau, *Die deutsche Emigration*, p. 74). *Der Aufbau* published several poems in memory of the President written by refugees.

72. F. Kortner, *Aller Tage Abend*, p. 279. He wrote: 'For the first time as a mature man, I lived in complete agreement with a government and the majority of the country' (p. 291).

73. Roosevelt had been a student in Munich. Cf. Thomas Mann's letter to G. Bermann Fischer, 10 July 1935: *Letters of Thomas Mann 1889–1955*, p. 197.

74. Cf. Katia Mann's account in *Unwritten Memories*, London 1975, p. 105.

75. T. Mann, *Gesammelte Werke*, vol. 11, p. 989.

76. Letter of 5 January 1943.

77. *Letters of Thomas Mann*, p. 351 (1 May 1945).

78. The Unitarian Committee sent representatives to Europe to assist the refugees, particularly to Lisbon. The French ambassador there, G. Henri Haye, gave the US government the names of fifty threatened émigrés. Ex-Chancellor Brüning tried to assist Breitscheid and Hilferding. Hermann Kesten and Thomas Mann also worked to rescue these émigrés. Finally, Roosevelt gave the president of the AFL, William Green, 'ten emergency visas' designed to rescue Socialist and trade-union leaders whose names had been telegraphed to the US consulate in Marseille. These visas could only be granted if the émigré in question had never been a member of the Nazi or Communist party, and if they were 'prominent opponents' of Hitler. The Rescue Committee had about a thousand emergency visas but no financial means, hence the need to organize banquets and raffles.

79. Varian Fry died in 1967. He left an interesting autobiography, *Surrender on Demand*, New York 1945. On his activities, see also: H. J. Greenwald, *When France Fell*, London 1958; Hans Sahl, *The Few and the Many*, New York 1962; and the memoirs of Fry's French collaborator Daniel Bénédite, *La Filière marseillaise*, Paris 1984.

80. Fry also rescued Jean Wahl in this way.

81. These included the chemist Alexandre Gero, the physicist Hans Ekstein, and Leo Oppenheim. Curiously, the French government only agreed to transfer these after dressing them in military uniform as mountain infantry.

82. Arrested by the police in a Perpignan café, Walter Mehring was sent to the Saint-Cyprien camp. Arriving there, he claimed that he had come to see his brother. As he had no authorization for this, the gendarmes expelled him immediately.

83. Varian Fry was unable to save Ernst Weiss, Carl Einstein or Walter Hasenclever.
84. *Deutsche Literatur im Exil*, p. 130.
85. K. Mann, *Der Wendepunkt*, p. 197. [Not in the English edition of *The Turning Point*.]
86. E. Toller, *Quer Durch*, 1929.
87. For example 'Come With Me to Georgia', 'Song of a Man in San Francisco', 'Flight Above the Ocean' and 'Hosannah Rockefeller'.
88. A. Mahler, *And the Bridge Is Love*, p. 231.
89. *Mein zwanzigstes Jahrhundert*.
90. 'Als Emigrant in Amerika', in *Verbannung*, p. 148. Zuckmayer reports a conversation he had with Franz Werfel in 1938: 'We knew exactly what there was there and what there was not, from bad food to intellectual and erotic frigidity [. . .]. A country of unimaginative standardization, flat materialism, a mechanism devoid of spirit. A country without tradition or culture, with no aspiration to beauty, without metaphysics, the country of chemical fertilizer and the can-opener, without grace and without dunghills, without classics or dirt, Apollo or Dionysus.'
91. In particular, by European Jewish Children's Aid, which brought over a thousand Jewish children to American between 1934 and 1944 (*Refugees in America*, p. 211).
92. Or a third the number of doctors there were at this time in the United States.
93. Three hundred and thirteen of these were '*ordentliche Professoren*', one hundred and nine '*ausserordentliche Professoren*', two hundred and eighty-four regular professors, seventy-five honorary professors and thirty-two '*Privatdozenten*'.
94. L. Fermi, *Illustrious Immigrants*, pp. 99ff.
95. A large number of Hungarian intellectuals had studied in Germany. Others became refugees after the collapse of the Béla Kun government in 1919. The most famous of them include the physicists E. Wigner, L. Sziland, E. Teller, and T. von Karman, the mathematicians J. von Neumann, P. Erdös, C. Lamezos, G. Poly, T. Rado, O. Szazs and G. Syejö, the psychoanalysts F. Alexander, T. Benedek, S. Rado, G. Roheim, musicians B. Bartok, A. Dorati, J. Szigeti, the artists L. Moholy-Nagy, G. Kepes, M. Breuer, the writer F. Molnar, the economists W. Fellner, K. Polanyi and T. Scitovsky, and the art historian C. von Tolnay.
96. These included G. A. Borgese, R. Poggioli and Toscanini in the field of arts, and politicians opposed to fascism including Don Luigi Sturzo, Carlo Sforza, A. Natoli, R. Raccialdi and A. Tarchiani. In 1940 they formed in America an antifascist movement, the Mazzini Society, designed to combat Mussolini's propaganda among Americans of Italian extraction, then in 1942 the Free Italian Movement, which held a congress in Montevideo in 1942, under the leadership of Count Sforza.
97. Among the French: Fernand Léger, André Masson, Marc Chagall, André Breton, André Maurois, Yvan and Claire Goll, Claude Lévi-Strauss, Marcel Duchamp and Yves Tanguy.
98. Maurice Maeterlinck was Belgian, Sigrid Undset was Norwegian, Peter Debye was Dutch, Niels Bohr and Hendrik Dam were Danish, Felix Bloch was Swiss and Severo Ochoa was Spanish.
99. Toscanini for example, an antifascist, had lived in the United States in the 1920s. He returned to Italy, clashed with the regime (he refused to play the fascist hymn at his concerts) and left again for the United States where he worked as conductor for a radio orchestra. Some scientists, such as John von Neumann, Eugen Wigner and F. Alexander, had left Germany by 1930.
100. Bloch, Dam and Ochoa all won the Nobel Prize for their work on DNA and nuclear physics. The presence of European painters – Duchamp, Léger, Mondrian – deeply marked the development of American painting, and Kurt Weill's style lived on in the American theatre.
101. Fifty-seven point six per cent were Germans, 19 per cent Austrians, 6.9 per cent Poles, 4.6 per cent Hungarians, 4.2 per cent Czechs, 2.3 per cent Russians, 1.3 per cent Italians, 0.7 per cent French and 0.4 per cent Swiss. 83 per cent of the total were Jewish.

102. The Davie Report noted the surprise and joy of villagers in isolated Appalachian communities at the arrival of doctors who had been professors in Germany and Austria.

103. Freud and Jung had visited the United States in 1909, and both the American Psychoanalytic Association and the New York Psychoanalytic Society were formed in 1911. A large number of American doctors travelled to Europe to undertake analysis; often with Freud himself, and several European analysts came to America to teach (Sándor Ferenczi in 1928, Otto Rank in 1924, Paul Schilder in 1928).

104. Wilhelm Reich had left for Sweden, Otto Fenichel was in Oslo, then California, Theodor Reik in The Hague, then California, Beata Rank in Vienna, then Paris, Annie Reich in Prague and Edith Weigert in Turkey.

105. *Refugees in America*, p. 287.

106. Law professors, jurists and advocates became window-cleaners, factory workers, mechanics or firemen in New York.

107. They had to be at least thirty-five years of age. Some 135 of them succeeded in this way, and twenty-five became law professors at universities.

108. It is of course impossible here to trace the destiny of all these scholars in America. A number of indications are provided by *Refugees in America* and by Laura Fermi, *Illustrious Immigrants*.

109. It is notable that the US government never hesitated to entrust very high responsibilities – in atomic research and other military fields, economics, law and elsewhere – to 'enemy aliens'. This phenomenon, quite astounding in its scope, has no equivalent in other countries. If the exiles' talents were often squandered in the cultural and artistic domains, this was by no means the case with science, where immediate practical applications were sought from this unimaginable sum of techniques, knowledge, theories, analyses and possibilities that the European emigration represented.

110. One American specialist, Morris Janowitz, estimated that the contribution of American-born scholars in the social science fields was no greater than 15 per cent (cited from L. Fermi, *Illustrious Immigrants*, p. 337).

111. *Refugees in America*, p. 74.

112. An ambiguous term, but preferable to 'economic immigrant': it was not in the hope of a better life that so many Jews tried to get to America at this time, but simply to save their lives. The notion of a 'Jewish race', of course, has no meaning outside anti-Semitic discourse.

113. On his arrival in the United States, Regler was even welcomed by a phone call from Eleanor Roosevelt: 'I'm so glad you have reached our shores safely' (cited in *The Owl of Minerva*, pp. 355–6.)

114. When Brecht was summoned before the House Committee on Un-American Activities following the prosecution of the Eisler brothers, he was questioned by Parnell Thomas on his connections with Kantorowicz.

115. After reaching the United States in 1934, Brüning lived incognito at first under the name Henry Anderson, and spent several months at the Immaculate Conception Seminary on Long Island before he started teaching at Harvard.

116. This included the Secretary of State, the Treasury Secretary and the Secretary for War.

117. Its task was to enable victims to find temporary asylum abroad, especially in Switzerland where there were 8,000 Jewish orphans.

118. These individuals had a special legal status: they were neither regularly admitted emigrants, not visitors, but 'guests' for the duration of the War. Their rights were so limited that they were interned in camps such as Fort Ontario, run by the army. They could not go out of the camps or work outside, and they were subsequently assigned a residence. Some students worked in schools. Their conduct was exemplary and at the end of the War, President Truman offered them the possibility of remaining in the United States.

119. Among them, the American Jewish Joint Distribution Committee, the Unitarian

Service Committee, the War Relief Services of the National Catholic Welfare Conference, the Emergency Rescue Committee, the Hebrew Sheltering and Immigrant Aid Society, Hadassah, the Jewish Labor Committee, the National Refugee Service and various Zionist organizations.

120. Between 1939 and 1942, the National Refugee Service spent $2 million per year on the refugees, peaking at $3.5 million in 1940; the Christian organizations spent between $300,000 and $400,000.

121. The Episcopal Committee for European Refugees, the National Lutheran Council, the Congregational Christian Committee for War Victims and Services, the Federal Council of Churches of Christ in America, the Greater New York Federation of Churches, the Board of Missions of the Presbyterian Church, etc.

122. Thomas Mann's publisher, G. Bermann Fischer, fled from Denmark to Finland, then by plane from Finland to Moscow. He crossed Mongolia on the Trans-Siberian, and took a ship from Vladivostok to Tsurugo, a small port on the Japanese coast. He then travelled by train via Yokohama to Tokyo. In the meantime his visas had expired and he had to get them renewed. The US consul could not handle this without the agreement of the State Department, and advised him to try and get to Canada. The British consul could also do nothing without approval from London, and it was finally the Danish consul who obtained a visa for him. From Tokyo he travelled to Honolulu, then San Francisco and Los Angeles.

123. Even if all the refugees had settled in New York, they would scarcely have increased the city's population by 3 per cent (*Refugees in America*, p. 77).

124. According to the Davie Report, 3 per cent of refugees settled in towns of less than 2,500 inhabitants, 13.8 per cent in towns with between 2,500 and 100,000, and 82.9 per cent in towns with over 100,000. New York alone received 18.6 per cent of the refugees.

125. 'One of the motives for my transplantation to California was precisely the immediate desire to be freed by distance from the obligations that New York constantly imposes,' Thomas Mann wrote in a letter of 29 August 1943.

126. *Otto Preminger: An Autbiography*, Garden City, NY, 1977, p. 3.

127. Amazement at the first images of the American continent or New York recurs in almost all exile letters and memoirs. Otto Preminger cried on seeing the Statue of Liberty and the skyline of New York. Piscator and his wife were struck dumb with emotion, as was Claude Lévi-Strauss when he first saw the American continent.

128. F. Kortner, *Aller Tage Abend*, p. 292.

129. Claude Lévi-Strauss noted in *Tristes Tropiques*: 'What struck me when I visited New York or Chicago in 1941 [. . .] was not the newness of these places but their premature ageing. It did not surprise me to find that these towns lacked ten centuries of history, but I was staggered to discover that so many of their districts were already fifty years old and that they should display the signs of decrepitude with such a lack of shame, when the one adornment to which they could lay claim was that of youth, a quality as transitory for them as for living creatures' (p. 96).

130. Letter from Kurt Pinthus to Walter Hasenclever, 3 September 1937; *Verbannung*, p. 140.

131. Piscator had to give his first interview in the lobby of his hotel, as the reception refused to let the black journalist take the elevator.

132. 'It can't happen here,' people often said to Klaus Mann, and Piscator was told: 'It's not your war, you're not Jewish.' Henry Miller wrote to Anaïs Nin on 7 August 1941: 'It must seem very strange now to those escaping from Europe – to arrive here in the land of ease and luxury and indifference' (Henry Miller, *Letters to Anaïs Nin*, p. 302).

133. Arnold Schoenberg wrote to Felix Greissle on 7 June 1938: 'Only I do beg you: be very careful. Here they go in for much more politeness than we do. Above all, one never makes a scene; one never contradicts; one never says: "to be quite honest", but if one does, one takes good care not really to be so' (*Correspondence*, p. 204).

134. Cf. the letter from Franz Schoenberger to Hermann Kesten in which he described his marriage in Reno after seeing a billboard: 'Come to Reno – Get Married – Wedding Chapel Reno', in which couples stood as witnesses for each other.

135. Letter from Thomas Mann to President Benes, 29 July 1944.

136. Ibid.

137. Alfred Döblin, *Briefe*, p. 296.

138. The quotes in this paragraph are from pp. 157, 161, 193, 197 and 240 in the English edition of Brecht's *Journals*.

139. Even if they lived only a few kilometres away, there were great enmities among the refugees. Fritz Kortner was hostile to Fritz Lang, who in turn got on badly with Brecht. Brecht was friendly with Eisler, but Eisler was close to Adorno, Thomas Mann and Schoenberg, whom Brecht could hardly stand. Brecht had scarcely any contact with Thomas Mann, though he was on friendly terms with Heinrich Mann. Döblin was friendly with Brecht but not with Thomas Mann, though he was with Lion Feuchtwanger, who managed the prodigious feat of counting both Mann and Brecht among his best friends – and so on.

140. Quoted by Alma Mahler, *And the Bridge Is Love*.

141. C. Lévi-Strauss, *Tristes Tropiques*, p. 79.

142. *Letters of Thomas Mann 1889–1955*, p. 356. The idea was to purchase the portrait of George Washington by Gilbert Stuart, which was on sale for $75,000. Thomas Mann asked, not without reason, whether it would not be preferable to use this sum on 'starving children in Europe'.

143. Brecht for example wrote: 'at a garden party i met the twin clowns horkheimer and pollock, two tuis from the frankfurt sociological institute. horkheimer is a millionaire, pollock merely from a well-off background, which means horkheimer can buy himself a university chair "as a front for the institute's revolutionary activities" wherever he happens to be staying' (*Journals*, August 1941; p. 160).

144. Thomas Mann wrote on 23 September 1946 to Otto Basler: 'Döblin [. . .] supposedly wanted to kill me [. . .], he is bitter at having lived in this country a life unworthy of his talent, obscure and poor, while he undoubtedly spitefully overestimates the fame and glory of my life [. . .]. I've never heaped up gold like Feuchtwanger or Werfel. I have of course learned English, which Döblin is too proud to do.'

145. The phrase is no exaggeration: it was an old and immense residence in the Spanish style, reminiscent of a mosque. (Cf. the photographs reproduced in Joseph Pischer, *Lion Feuchtwanger*, Leipzig 1976, p. 183.)

146. *Der Schriftsteller in Exil* (Writers' Congress in Hollywood, 1943); the only tragic period in Feuchtwanger's life was his internment in a French camp.

147. Feuchtwanger used his wealth to help the poorest exiles. He contributed substantially to Brecht's passage to the United States, and financed both *Freies Deutschland*, and the publishing of émigré magazines and books (Aurora). He invited to his home the majority of German writers living in California.

148. *Letters of Thomas Mann*, p. 315.

149. Letter to Agnes Meyer, 27 October 1943; *Letters of Thomas Mann*, p. 326.

150. Thus he wrote to Wihelm Herzog on 18 January 1944: 'This great original, already 72 years old, deliberately pushes away the past and has scarcely any memory. On the other hand, he is still more sensitive than I am. Unfortunately, however, he has a wife who is a real handful.' On 7 January 1945, he wrote again to Agnes E. Meyer: 'My brother, who (fortunately) has lost his wife, will spend a few weeks with us. It was high time that death untied that bond. It was ruinous, and we have a great deal to do to set him back on his feet.'

151. There was a project, however, to adapt his last work, the cinema-novel *Lidice*.

152. 'My good woman is working as a *nurse* in the hospital. It is beyond her strength and I am ashamed. But what can be done?' he wrote to Eva Lips on 14 December 1944. Nelly Mann committed suicide two days later, her fifth attempt.

153. B. Brecht, *Journals*, p. 307.
154. Liels Frank and the wife of William Dieterle regularly sent him money, as he had no other resources.

CHAPTER 13 WEIMAR IN AMERICA: THE STRANGERS IN PARADISE

1. Walter Benjamin had already discussed this problem in his famous essay 'The Work of Art in the Age of Mechanical Reproduction'. It was no accident that the theorists who most discussed this 'cultural industry' were precisely Theodor Adorno and Herbert Marcuse, who both emigrated to America.
2. For instance the wave of 'secessions' in painting and the new schools of literature, from naturalism through expressionism to Dadaism.
3. Klaus Mann noted in *Der Wendepunkt* (p. 343) that America in the 1920s had not yet found its genuine voice: music-hall stars, boxers and actors in silent films were more famous than writers. He often expressed his unease at the lecture tours he gave: the public came to see a 'personality', and it mattered little whether it was a novelist, a politician or a tennis champion. [Not in the English edition of *The Turning Point*.]
4. Schoenberg for example noted sadly in a letter to G. F. Stegmann on 26 January 1949: 'The mentality of the Americans goes always for mass-production and they try now to do the same in music – to produce music on the "running-band". One is astonished if one sees lists of American composers, and one is astonished by the production. There are many composers who have already written many symphonies and sometimes one is doubtful if a composer who announces his 5th Symphony has already written the first, second, third and fourth' (*Correspondence*, pp. 266–7). On 12 April the same year he wrote to Rudolf Kolisch on the same subject: 'This is what they now mean to flood Europe with, treating it as a colony' (p. 270).
5. Opinion polls, for instance, were widely used to gauge public reaction. Each film was preceded by previews, with a view to measuring the spectators' laughter, tears and applause. On the basis of the first reactions of this audience sample, the producer – who personally attended each projection – decided on the kind of release the film would have, the number of theatres, which scenes to cut, and what changes to make to the editing. Brecht noted in his *Journals*: 'the so-called gallup poll test plays a particular role here, using a certain system to assemble a representative selection of different social groups, they sample the views of the population [. . .]. in actual fact it is a test of the efficacy of publicity and propaganda' (12 July 1942; *Journals*, p. 247).
6. Letter to Henry Allen Moe, 22 February 1945; *Correspondence*, p. 233.
7. Several writers of the Weimar era had to practise another profession in order to earn a living: Alfred Döblin, Gottfried Benn, R. Goering and Friedrich Wolf were doctors, and a large number of painters were teachers. Those like Thomas Mann and Lion Feuchtwanger who could live on their royalties alone were rare exceptions. Gottfried Benn maintained in *Double vie* (p. 61), that he could not take more than three weeks off work, and that his literary activity brought him only 4.50 marks per month. Döblin was relatively poor, as was Brecht before *The Threepenny Opera*. Even the success of *The Blue Angel* hardly enriched Heinrich Mann. Walter Benjamin lived in semi-poverty in Berlin, as did many other 'independent writers', who were at the mercy of publishers' advances (always low) and the fees paid (rather rarely) by magazines.
8. Apart from a few films such as *Metropolis*, whose production budget was very high for the time, actors' salaries were often quite low, and the earnings of films made by UFA stood no comparison with those of American films. If Max Reinhardt managed to cover the costs of most of his theatres, this was not the case with Piscator or Aufricht, who were always on the verge of bankruptcy.

9. Piscator, for example, staged revolutionary plays thanks to a wealthy patron who was partnered to an actress. Many German theatres were dependent on subsidies from the Reich or provincial governments. German publishers took on a large number of books that they knew would never turn a profit.

10. Hollywood producers, for example, could select a script and have it rewritten as they wanted, and they had sole responsibility for the choice of director, actors, scenery and budget. They had all the personnel required for a film available as simple employees, as well as the capital, the studios, and the screening rooms. Even scripts were often written to please the personal tastes of the producers: Daryl Zanuck and Louis B. Mayer had complete freedom to impose their slightest caprices on actors, writer and director. If these refused to obey, they were deemed to have broken their contract and were dismissed. The solidarity between producers then made it impossible for them to get any further work in the film industry: the actor or director would have to 'end his days on Broadway', as the expression went.

11. Schoenberg's *Correspondence* and Brecht's *Journals* are two extraordinary documents in this regard, illustrating what the discovery of this 'art market' meant for many of the émigrés. But what Brecht described with a caustic irony, Schoenberg experienced in an utter despair that blighted his last years. On 12 November 1945 he wrote again to Hermann Schercher: 'It's a pity, there is plenty of talent, but the teaching is superficial, and the outlook is focused on money-making' (*Correspondence*, p. 237).

12. *Film Daily* noted in 1942 that the Hollywood studios employed more than 30,000 individuals, with an annual payroll of $157,300,000. There were at that time seventy-four producers of feature films, thirty-eight producers of shorts, nine cartoon and six newsreel companies, with 550 actors, 345 writers and 115 directors under contract. Cinema made use of 276 different industries at this time for the manufacture of films. A total of 8,000 extras earned $3,368,823, and the studios paid $4,975,000 for screenplays. In total, film production represented an annual investment of $3,061,000,000, and over 200,000 people depended on it.

13. Ludwig Berger, *Wir sind vom gleichen Stoff, aus dem die Träume sind*, Tübingen 1953, p. 247.

14. Cf. Vicki Baum, *Es war alles ganz anders*, Frankfurt 1962, p. 247.

15. The majority of works by Schoenberg, Hindemith, Krenek, Eisler and Dessau were practically never played in the United States, for lack of adequate interpreters and above all lack of public interest. These composers all had to get their works performed before an audience of specialists, or fellow émigrés.

16. Cf. Alain Lacombe, *George Gershwin. Une chronique de Broadway*, Fondettes 1990.

17. Ibid., p. 19.

18. This exile indeed saved his life. In his autobiography, he noted: 'On 12 January 1933 we embarked at Bremerhaven [. . .]. By 23 March we were in New York . . . Hitler had been appointed Reich Chancellor on 30 January . . . I soon received letters informing me that they had come to look for me at my empty apartment in Berlin, then at my studio. I wonder if I would have got out alive' (cited from *George Grosz*, p. 169).

19. Ibid., p. 172.

20. Ibid., p. 181.

21. Ernst Bloch, *Heritage of Our Times*, pp. 212–3.

22. His Second Symphony was premiered in Amsterdam in 1934 by Bruno Walter.

23. Cf. *Über Kurt Weill*, Suhrkamp 1975; Kurt Weill, *Ausgewählte Schriften*, Frankfurt 1975; *Kurt Weill für Sie porträtiert*, Leipzig 1980.

24. In 1935 Brecht and Grosz envisaged the possibility of collaboration in America (cf. Brecht, *Letters 1913–1956*, p. 208). Grosz's relations with Piscator and Heartfield remained cordial, even if he was no longer interested in Marxism. Relations between Brecht and Weill seemed at first to deteriorate in the United States. Weill was opposed to an American production of *The Threepenny Opera*, a supposedly 'Negro version' by Clarence Muse. Brecht asked Adorno to intercede, but Weill

796 WEIMAR IN EXILE

'responded with a nasty letter full of attacks on me and praise of broadway, which will put on anything if it is good, and has been developing the experiments europe pioneered.' Brecht ironically noted that Weill replied in English, starting with the words: 'It's easier for me and I like it better' (*Journals*, 15 April 1942; p. 222). In 1943, however, Weill thought of producing *The Good Person of Szechwan*, and collaborating on a staging of *Schweyk*, while Lotte Lenya recorded some of Brecht's songs for the Office of War Information (in particular, the 'Ballad of the Nazi Soldier's Wife'). They met up in New York in May 1943, then in California. Weill also acted as intermediary between Brecht and Piscator when they quarrelled over *Schweyk*. Their relationship continued until Weill's death in 1950.

25. The expression was used early on by François Bondy. It is also found in letters of Thomas Mann. Vladimir Pozner, in an interview (*Cinéma* 65, p. 70), spoke of Hollywood as 'a kind of twentieth-century Weimar'. Henry Miller wrote in a letter to Anaïs Nin: 'Hollywood was an oasis – I find Europe here again – through all the émigrés' (8 June 1941).

26. A list of names would include Max Reinhardt, Bertolt Brecht, Salka and Bertold Viertel, Franz Werfel and Alma Mahler, Hanns Eisler, Paul Dessau, Walter Mehring, Elisabeth Bergner, Max Horkheimer, Theodor Adorno, Herbert Marcuse, Friedrich Pollock, Heinrich Mann, Ludwig Marcuse, Karl Wittfogel, Peter Lorre, Fritzi Massary, Blandine Ebinger, Hans Reichenbach, Alfred Döblin, Fritz Lang, Fritz Kortner and Bruno Frank.

27. L. Marcuse, *Mein zwanzigstes Jahrhundert*, p. 266.

28. The cemetery holds the remains of Leopold Jessner, Else Heims, Gisela Werbezirk, Heinrich Mann, Franz Werfel, Bruno Frank and Lion Feuchtwanger. Jessner requested burial in the Jewish sector of the cemetery, for none of his friends to be present and for his coffin to be carried by ten Polish Jews who did not know who he was.

29. B. Brecht, *Journals*, p. 262 (25 October 1942).

30. Henry Miller wrote to Anais Nin on 19 May 1941: 'Had an offer of a job doing script work here, but promptly refused. Terrible world here – the movies, I mean. Hollow as sawdust. The real men are the technicians – they are really geniuses. It's all technique. The human element is just nil' (*Letters to Anaïs Nin*, p. 290). He ended up agreeing, and tried to adapt J. Wassermann's novel *The Maurizius Case*. Faulkner worked in Hollywood for $300 a week.

31. Vincente Minelli wrote in his memoirs: 'Writers would prepare scripts; other writers were working right behind them on the same project. A fine writer would delivery a perfectly workable script. Three or four other writers would then have a crack at it. The process could completely demoralize a man' (*I Remember It Well*, New York 1974, p. 115).

32. According to Marlene Dietrich (*My Life*, p. 213), Hollywood circles, led by Ernst Lubitsch and Billy Wilder, had already organized collections to rescue concentration-camp detainees and enable a number of antifascist actors, directors and writers to reach Hollywood. Dietrich herself took part in this rescue of émigrés. Ludwig Marcuse recounts (*Mein zwanzigstes Jahrhundert*, p. 272) that Louis B. Mayer did not even know that his studio employed exiled German writers. Even if he had done, it is quite impossible that he had the faintest idea who Alfred Döblin, Heinrich Mann or Bertolt Brecht were.

33. Cf. Brecht's *Journals* and Döblin's correspondence. Indeed, one can hardly imagine either of them working for the MGM studios. Döblin's novels or stories would have met with complete incomprehension from an American public.

34. Their works were of course completely unknown to American critics.

35. He was simply the brother of 'the great novelist Thomas Mann'. The *New York Times* even announced the arrival in the United States of Thomas Mann's son Golo, accompanied by his uncle Heinrich. Thomas Mann was sufficiently aware of this situation that he asked his other brother, Victor, not to publish his recollections

of the family under the title *Thomas and His Brothers*, so as not to wound Heinrich. On 1 May 1955 he wrote again to Guido Devescovi: 'I can assure you that a chariness concerning the obscuring "grande ombra" has marked my whole life since *Buddenbrooks*. [. . .] [M]y basic attitude toward him and his somewhat formidably intellectual work was always that of the little brother looking up at the elder. [. . .] [I]t was an indescribable shock to me, and seemed like a dream, when shortly before his death Heinrich dedicated one of his books to me with the words: "To my great brother, who wrote *Doctor Faustus*"' (*Letters of Thomas Mann*, p. 475).

36. L. Marcuse, *Mein zwanzigstes Jahrhundert*, p. 230.
37. Besides *The Blue Angel*, the screenplay for which was written by Carl Zuckmayer, Heinrich Mann at the start of his exile tried to interest MGM in a film adaptation of *Die kleine Stadt, ein ernstes Leben*, likewise Twentieth Century Fox in spring 1940. The only project of his that came to fruition was the mediocre remake of *Professor Unrat* by Dymtryk.
38. It was Siegfried Kracauer who received this.
39. *Deutsche Literatur im Exil*, p. 185.
40. Ibid., p. 193.
41. F. Kortner, *Autobiographie*, p. 319.
42. As his biographer F. Ewen writes: 'His cigars no longer came from the same country, but their smoke was just as thick. Press cuttings and photographs were still heaped everywhere. Brecht had lost nothing of his curiosity and liveliness of mind, nor indeed of his quarrelsome humour (which rarely extended to discourtesy)' (*Bertolt Brecht*, London 1970, p. 382). Helene Weigel also made the same Viennese strudel.
43. I would like to thank Vladimir Pozner here for all the helpful information he provided.
44. B. Brecht, *Journals*, p. 254 (20 August 1942).
45. A fairly complete list was published by Wolfgang Gersch in *Film bei Brecht*, Berlin 1975, p. 355.
46. It is not at all clear, anyway, that Brecht's conceptions could be brought into line with the rules of film. On this point see my introduction to Béla Balazs, *L'Esprit du cinéma*, Paris 1977, and the interview with Vladimir Pozner in *Cinéma* 62, no. 65, in which he depicts the difficulties he had in working with Brecht.
47. Igor Stravinsky declared: 'There are no musical problems in the cinema, and the only interest of film music is to feed its composer.' According to Goffredo Petrassi: 'Film music is a purely practical background music and is reason for existence lies entirely in its precise functionality in relation to images' (quoted by A. Lacombe and C. Roche, *La Musique du film*, Fondettes 1979, p. 32).
48. The tyrannical tastes of David O. Selznick in music also came to the fore when he had Max Steiner write the music for *Gone With the Wind*.
49. Vincente Minelli wrote in his memoirs: 'I did meet another émigré from New York, and points east. Kurt Weill. I don't know what he was doing at Paramount . . . as he probably didn't know about me. He thought my fascination with surrealism and his intense interest in psychiatry would work well together. *Lady in the Dark*, which he wrote with Ira Gershwin in 1941, was the culmination of his interest' (*I Remember it Well*, p. 94).
50. Cf. A. Betz, *Musique et Politique. Hanns Eisler*, 1982; Jürgen Schebera, *Hanns Eisler im USA Exil*, Berlin 1978.
51. *Hangmen Also Die* (Fritz Lang, 1943), *None But the Lonely Heart* (Clifford Odets, 1944), *Spanish Main* (Borzage, 1945), *Jealousy* (Machate, 1945), *Deadline at Dawn* (Cluma, 1946), *A Scandal in Paris* (Sirk 1946), *Women on the Beach* (Renoir, 1947), and *So Well Remembered* (Dymtryk 1947).
52. B. Brecht, 20 July 1945; *Journals*, p. 349.
53. From 1943 he worked for Warner Brothers.
54. When Schoenberg was asked to write music for a film, he explained to Alma Mahler: 'If I do commit suicide, I want at least to live well on it' (Alma Mahler-Werfel, *And the Bridge Is Love*, p. 257).

55. It should be remembered that the Hollywood director was responsible neither for the script nor the choice of actors, often imposed on him by the producer as a function of those who were available or were loaned by other studios, also that he could not control the editing. At previews, opinions were sought from the costumer and the lighting technician, reactions of a sample audience were studied, and it was common at this point for some scenes to be cut or others added without the director being consulted.

56. Otto Preminger, for example, who came from Austria to work for Fox, was unable to make any film after he quarrelled with Daryl Zanuck in 1938 over the making of *Kidnapped*. He was removed from the film, and after his contract expired he found no further work in Hollywood until Zanuck took part in the artistic mobilization that followed the United States's entry into the War. Preminger had to leave Hollywood and work on Broadway until Zanuck pardoned him and allowed him to direct new films.

57. In 1939, Frank Capra wrote in the *New York Times*, in the name of the association of film directors of which he was president: 'There are now only half a dozen directors who can shoot a film as they please and direct all the works that they sign. We have worked for three years to set up a union, and the only demand we have made to the producers is for the director to have two weeks' preparation for a class A movie and one week for a B movie, as well as the right to supervise the uncut version of the film, to read the script they are going to work on and to rough-cut the film for presentation to the studio management. [. . .] I can promise you that at the present time, 80 per cent of directors shoot exactly as they are told to shoot, without daring to make the slightest change, and 90 per cent are not even consulted on the subject or on the form that is given after cutting. This is the true situation of what is supposed to be the work of a director' (cited after M. Bardèche and R. Brasillach, *Histoire du cinéma* [retranslated from the French]).

58. Some directors thus became producers of their own films when they had a passionate interest in a certain subject (Cecil B. de Mille, John Ford, Howard Hawks, Leo MacCarey, Frank Lloyd, Frank Capra, Mervyn LeRoy, King Vidor, Billy Wilder). A large number of films made in Hollywood and seen today as the greatest of American cinema had no success at all at the time and were viewed as inept by the producers. Elia Kazan's films are a good example, as are those of Otto Preminger. In the 1940s, the big studios generally produced around fifteen major films each year, ten run-of-the-mill, and thirty-five 'B' movies.

59. Lubitsch swiftly changed his style, moving from historical films to the ironical style that culminated in *To Be or Not to Be*.

60. Thus *Hollywood Revue of 1929* (in German, *Wir schalten um auf Hollywood*), by Charles F. Reisner, included Heinrich George, Dita Parlo and Sergei Eisenstein among its cast.

61. Erich von Stroheim had emigrated in 1911, and began his career playing German officers in patriotic films. He only became a director in the 1920s. Joseph (von) Sternberg, born in Vienna in 1894, had been brought up in New York.

62. F. Courtade wrote in his essay on Lang (*Le Terrain vague*, 1963, p. 61): 'If we remove the name of the director of this generic product, what remains? A run-of-the-mill little Western, a bread-and-butter work carried out conscientiously, that does not even deserve a mention in a history of the cinema.'

63. Lang's American films display a social transposition of many themes that in his German films had an almost metaphysical form. In *I Want to Live* and *Fury*, fate is embodied by the crowd, *Man Chase* raises the problem of individualism, *Woman in the Painting* and *The Red Street* criticize Anglo-Saxon puritanism.

64. It was only with Jean-Luc Godard's *Le Mépris*, in which Lang appears as himself, reciting verses of Hölderlin and playing the director of genius at loggerheads with an imbecile producer, that his martyrdom in Hollywood could be understood.

65. He acknowledged for example (interview in *Positif* 94, April 1968, p. 10), that he had to give up this symbolism in *Fury*.

66. Among his most remarkable films are early works such as *Menschen am Sonntag* (1929) and *Emil and the Detectives*, though these were eclipsed by American works such as *A Foreign Affair* (with Marlene Dietrich, 1948), *Sunset Boulevard* (with Eric von Stroheim and Gloria Swanson, 1950), *Witness for the Prosecution* (with Marlene Dietrich, 1957), *Some Like It Hot* (with Marilyn Monroe, 1959) and *Fedora*, made in Germany in 1978.

67. Otto Preminger, son of an Austro-Hungarian judge of Jewish origin, came to Hollywood in 1935, invited by MGM. He had been an actor with Max Reinhardt, and succeeded him in 1933 at the head of the Josefstadttheater. He became famous with his interpretation of the Nazi consul with scar and monocle in *Margin for Error*. He was later replaced by Kurt Katsch, also an émigré, who managed to play the role by learning the text by heart without understanding its meaning, as he knew no English. Alex(ander) Granach also played the role of Gestapo agent, as did Ludwig Donath, who went on to take the part of Hitler.

68. Conrad Veidt had interpreted such famous roles as the murderous sleepwalker in *The Cabinet of Dr Caligari*, and the eponymous *Student of Prague*. He died in Hollywood in 1943.

69. Born in 1904 (in the Carpathians!), Peter Lorre undoubtedly reached the summit of his art in the role of the murderer in *M* (1931). He acted under Pabst in France in 1934 (*Du haut en bas*) and in England under Hitchcock (*The Man Who Knew Too Much*). In the United States, he played in Sternberg's *Crime and Punishment* and Karl Freund's *The Hands of Orlac*, above all in *The Enigmatic Mr Moto* of 1939. His disturbing physique got him roles in John Huston's *The Maltese Falcon*, *Defeat for the Gestapo*, *The Invisible Agent* and *Casablanca* (1942). He never managed to revive his career in Germany, despite his remarkable film *Der Verlorene* (1951), called in Germany a 'film of ruins'. He died in Hollywood in 1964.

70. Kortner had played in particular Dr Schön in Pabst's *Lulu*, and *The Monster of the Shadows* by Robison. Those actors who stayed in Germany met a similar fate: apart from the exceptional successes of Emil Jannings, Heinrich George and Werner Krauss, not to mention Gustaf Gründgens, a large number of major stars from the 1920s had to take supporting parts.

71. Cf. Rudolf Forster's autobiography, *Das Spiel, mein Leben*, Frankfurt 1967. Otto Preminger also describes in his memoirs Forster's departure from Hollywood. He left only a brief note at the theatre: 'Dear Otto, I'm leaving for Germany to rejoin Adolf. Regards, Rudolf.' Fritz Kortner considered him the very embodiment of the 'internal émigré'.

72. Brecht noted in his *Journals* on 11 July 1942: 'kortner cannot get any part. eisler recounts that the people at RKO laughed out loud when the screen test was shown: he rolled his eyes. real acting is frowned upon here and only accepted from negroes. stars don't act parts, they step into "situations" ' (p. 247). After the War, Kortner, who had been so humiliated in America, refused to admit that he had been a famous actor in the 1920s, or to remember the roles he had played (communication from Lotte H. Eisner). He particularly detested Fritz Lang, whom he reproached – unjustly, to be sure – for 'speaking with a check in his mug'. To survive in Hollywood, Kortner had to deliver milk.

73. More than seventy German or Austrian actors played on the Broadway stage between 1933 and 1945, and there was an equally large number of directors and playwrights in New York.

74. Tilla Durieux had even played there in *Ein Tür steht offen*.

75. An offer had been made to Max Reinhardt in 1933 to produce *A Midsummer Night's Dream* at the Hollywood Bowl. Warner Brothers was going to make a film of it with Wilhelm Dieterle. Even Louis B. Meyer himself visited Reinhardt in Salzburg.

76. Among the most famous: *Band Wagon*, *Ziegfeld Follies of 1931*, *Earl Carroll's Vanities*, *George White's Scandals*.

77. For examples Yip Harburg, Harpo Marx, Dashiell Hammett, Lillian Hellman, Heywood Brown, John O'Hara and Dorothy Parker.
78. All America whistled 'Embraceable You', 'They Can't Take That Away From Me', 'A Foggy Day', 'Who Cares?' 'Lady Be Good', 'Long Ago and Far Away', 'I Can't Get Started', 'The Man That Got Away', etc.
79. Friedrich Wolf hailed this creation in 1935, when he took part in the Congress of American Writers. He described on this occasion the fate of writers, actors and directors detained in the Nazi concentration camps.
80. Cf. Malcolm Goldstein, *The Political Stage. American Drama and Theater of the Great Depression*, New York 1974.
81. Founded in 1926 by Albert Prentis, Louis De Santes and Florence Rauh. It was supported by John Dos Passos, Nathan Fine and John Howard Lawson.
82. Losey visited the Soviet Union and attended Meyerhold's rehearsals. He met Brecht, Eisenstein and Joris Ivens as well as Hanns Eisler and Erwin Piscator.
83. More than 100,000 spectators in 1934.
84. Staged in 1935, it lasted for only thirty-eight performances.
85. There were over 300 of these.
86. Such as the Irving Place Theater, which functioned from 1880 to 1913.
87. It was only after his death that Piscator was celebrated as a theatrical genius by a number of American directors. Brecht became known in the United States only a good while after his return to Germany.
88. This staged Bruno Frank's *Sturm in Wasserglas* and Arthur Schnitzler's *Liebelei*, with excellent actors such as Ernst Deutsch, Dolly Haas and Oscar Karlweiss.
89. F. Bruckner, F. Czernin, B. Frank, M. George, F. Kortner, E. Ludwig, E. Mann, H. H. Seger, D. Thomson, F. von Unruh, F. Werfel, C. Zuckmayer.
90. Only $1,000 was raised, out of a target of $25,000 to $30,000. Cf. *Exil in den USA*, p. 357.
91. Ibid., p. 360.
92. These American artists all came to the aid of the émigrés. They offered money and advice, and obtained the Music Box theatre for them on Broadway, as well as free English lessons (ibid., p. 361).
93. Ibid., p. 364.
94. The Tribüne staged both Goethe and Brecht, as well as plays by E. E. Kisch, Stefan Heym, Bruno Viertel, Anna Seghers, Bertolt Brecht, F. C. Weiskopf, Wieland Herzfelde and Carl Zuckmayer. It also organized ceremonies to remember writers held in concentration camp or murdered by the Nazis, as well as an exhibition 'Deutsche Kunst im Exil'. During these sessions, poems and extracts from plays were also read.
95. It is worth noting that the New York stage saw the appearance between 1933 and 1945 of Edith Angold, Tara Birell, Else Bassermann, Lili Darvas, Francisca Gal, Adrienne Gessner, Dolly Haas, Lotte Lenya, Eleonora Mendelsohn, Lydia St. Clair, Elleen Schwanecke, Marianne Stewart, Lily Valenti, Sigfried Arno, Curt Bois, Rudolf Forster, Hugo Haas, Paul Henried, Hans Jaray, Franz Lederer and John Wengraf, among others. Cf. *Theater im Exil 1933–1945*, p. 229.
96. Cf. R. Eichenlaub, *Ernst Toller et l'Expressionisme politique*, thesis, Strasbourg 1976, pp. 587 ff.
97. On 9 November 1935 Brecht even sent an insulting letter describing the director as a dilettante. Cf. his letter to Piscator of 8 December 1935, *Letters 1913–1956*, pp. 221 ff.
98. Cf. Brecht's letters to Piscator in 1935–36.
99. B. Brecht, *Journals*, p. 170.
100. B. Brecht, *Journals*, p. 185. Fritz Kortner made similar negative judgements in his autobiography (*Aller Tage Abend*, p. 298), where he described American theatre as 'flat, banal, lacking the religious or metaphysical background that made the greatness of European theatre'. He also deplored its commercial aspect: 'Everything that makes money seems angelic to the Americans.'

101. B. Brecht, *Journals*, 1 June 1942; p. 237.
102. Ibid., p. 385.
103. In 1943, Orson Welles and Mike Todd had thought of adapting *Galileo* for the cinema, but the project failed. Joseph Losey had been earmarked to co-direct the film.
104. She intervened with Roosevelt himself to enable Zuckmayer to remain in the United States, after he had been deprived of his nationality. (Cf. C. Zuckmayer, *Als wär's ein Stück von mir*, Frankfurt 1980, p. 459.)
105. Zuckmayer was put out by the questions of his students, such as 'How long should a love scene last?', and recalled a pharmacist who loved the theatre offering him five dollars an hour to give him private lessons in humour.
106. The play was inspired by the life of the Luftwaffe General Udet who died in an accident. Zuckmayer had known him since the First World War and was aware of his hostility to the Nazi regime.
107. Cf. Edda Fuhrich-Leisler and Gisela Prossmith, *Max Reinhardt in Amerika*, Salzburg 1976, p. 39.
108. *Paradise Lost*, after Milton, and *Ben Hur*, neither of which came to fruition.
109. Hearst had offered $100,000, Reinhardt wanted $150,000.
110. In November 1933, Reinhardt had produced a French version of *Die Fledermaus* at the Théâtre Pigalle in Paris.
111. Charles Laughton was to have played the role of Danton, Spencer Tracy that of Robespierre, with Vladimir Sokoloff as Marat.
112. MGM seems to have confused Danton with Dante.
113. Direction of the school was then taken over by his wife Helene Thimig.
114. Stella Adler also worked with Piscator. Like her brother, the actor Harry Adler, she fell victim to McCarthyism.
115. Fritz Kortner described in his memoirs (*Aller Tage Abend*, p. 321) how Reinhardt and his wife lived in splendid isolation in America. Despite a precarious material situation, they could not give up a couple of Austrian servants. Reinhardt's two sons, Gottfried and Wolfgang, both worked in the film industry. According to Kortner, Reinhardt was haunted by the memory of his past glory, and died unhappy. In Hollywood he felt he was living 'in a charcoal-burner's hut'. People who had formerly crossed the Atlantic to attend the Salzburg Festival no longer remembered him in exile. Reinhardt was deeply isolated when he died, his hands and lungs paralysed. Only his immense blue eyes still gave evidence of his eternal youth.
116. On the details of Piscator's exile in the United States, cf. J.-M. Palmier and M. Piscator, *Piscator et le théâtre politique*, pp. 120ff.
117. Oral communication from the administration of the New School.
118. Maria Piscator well remembered the disciplinary trouble her husband had with Tony Curtis and Marlon Brando; they just wouldn't turn up for lectures on time. Piscator with his Protestant-Germanic seriousness found it hard to tolerate these unusual students.
119. Alma Mahler wrote in her diary: 'Max Reinhardt, the indestructible genius [. . .] had been one of the first people we saw after our arrival on the Coast. I had found him aged but beautiful to look at, side-tracked and sad, but not embittered' (*And the Bridge Is Love*, p. 253).
120. Adolphe Weiss, a former student of Schoenberg, played in a Federal orchestra for the unemployed; his case was not unique.
121. In conditions that were often humiliating or derisory. Certain avant-garde composers found themselves teaching elementary music in high schools. Ernst Krenek taught at Vassar College in New York State. Schoenberg only earned from teaching in the United States about two-fifths of his European salary, and complained constantly at the mediocrity of his students.
122. Kurt Weill's posthumous celebrity was admirably served by the talent of his wife Lotte Lenya, who carried on rendering his classic songs in her raucous voice, both in Europe and America.

123. This production was staged on 6 March 1943 at the New School's Studio Theater, with Elisabeth Bergner and Peter Lorre.
124. Brecht worked regularly in Hollywood at this time with Eisler and Dessau; the latter married his collaborator Elisabeth Hauptmann.
125. Including 'Germany, Pale Mother', which Eisler also set in his *Deutsche Sinfonie*.
126. In 1954 he went on to compose music for *The Caucasian Chalk Circle*.
127. Eisler actually made two visits to the United States, the first on the occasion of a lecture tour on behalf of the Committee of Aid to the Victims of German Fascism.
128. He had meanwhile lived in Prague, since returning from the International Brigades in Spain.
129. He had collaborated with Ivens in the Soviet Union in 1932, on the film *Heldenlied*, and on *Neue Erde* in the Netherlands in 1934.
130. This political cabaret was held in the crypt of a disused church on East 54th Street. Performances took place on Sunday afternoons, being partly financed by the Theater Art Committee, and showing anti-Nazi plays written and performed by Howard da Silva, Martin Gable and Kate Smith.
131. The characters in this documentary, *Petre Roleum and His Cousins*, had the shape of drops of oil, and in this way Losey unwittingly created the logo of the Esso company. (Cf. Michel Ciment, *Le Livre de Losey*, Paris 1979, p. 79.)
132. Eisler also wrote in 1938, for the CPUSA's commemoration of the October Revolution, music for Hays's play *A Song About America*, under the pseudonym of John Garden.
133. Hanns Eisler, *Composing for the Films*, New York 1947.
134. In 1941 he had written the music for *Forgotten Village*, based on a story by John Steinbeck.
135. This did not prevent a dispute later opposing Eisler and Adorno on the subject of the film music book. According to Louise Eisler-Fischer, Eisler and Adorno dictated the manuscript directly and it was typed up by Gretl Adorno. When it appeared in 1947, the book bore only Eisler's name, Adorno being unwilling now to figure alongside a Communist. He went on to attack Eisler in 1969 when the book was republished in West Germany. [Adorno's name was reinstated on the book's reissue in 1994.]
136. Eisler's fate in the McCarthy era is discussed Chapter 19 below.
137. A. Schoenberg, *Correspondence*, pp. 191–2.
138. The University of Southern California as well as UCLA.
139. Letter to K. Kulka, 23 January 1936; *Correspondence*, p. 197.
140. Letter to Hermann Scherchen, 16 March 1936; ibid., p. 198.
141. Letter to Charlotte Dieterle, 30 July 1936; ibid., p. 199.
142. Letter to Alma Mahler-Werfel; ibid., p. 205.
143. Schoenberg was forced to retire under university regulations. As he had only taught for eight years, he received a pension of $38 per month and had to support a wife and three children, aged thirteen, eight and four.
144. 'I didn't read "Dr. Faustus" myself, owing to my nervous eye-affliction. But from my wife and also from other quarters I heard that he had attributed my 12–note method to his hero, without mentioning my name. I drew his attention to the fact that historians might make use of this in order to do me an injustice. After prolonged reluctance he declared himself prepared to insert, in all subsequent copies in all languages, a statement concerning my being the originator of this method' (letter of 25 May 1948 to Josef Rufer; *Correspondence*, p. 255). The quarrel between Mann and Schoenberg continued until 1950. They were then reconciled, but Schoenberg died before they could see one another again.
145. *Correspondence*, p. 222.
146. *Refugees in America*, pp. 324–5.
147. L. Fermi, *Illustrious Emigrants*, p. 233.
148. A Bauhaus exhibition had also been organized in New York in 1931, at the Museum of Modern Art.

149. Cf. *Exil in den USA*, p. 295; L. Fermi, *Illustrious Emigrants*, p. 234; William J. Jordy, 'The Aftermath of the Bauhaus in America', in *The Intellectual Migration. Europe and America 1930–1960*, Harvard 1969, pp. 485ff.

150. Other émigré architects who were not members of the Bauhaus also exerted a large influence in the United States, such as Erich Mendelsohn, F. Kiesler and Hans Hofmann.

151. Albers taught at Black Mountain College until 1949, then at Yale until 1960. Gropius directed the architecture section of the Harvard Graduate School of Design.

152. Hofmann had taught in New York in 1915.

153. There were a few Dadaist groups in New York, around Arensberg and Stieglitz, who established relations early on with Marcel Duchamp. Duchamp became a focus of interest for New York artists in the years around the First World War. Arensberg hosted visits by Albert Gleizes, Francis Picabia and Man Ray. A. Cravan gave lectures in New York in a completely drunken state, narrowly escaping arrest thanks to Ray's intercession. A number of poets were also marked by this avant-garde: William Carlos Williams and e. e. cummings. But movements such as Dada in New York were more 'radical chic' than genuinely challenging, as opposed to its Berlin counterpart that declared its revolutionary convictions.

154. Cf. Dore Ashton, *The New York School*, New York 1972; Abraham A. Davidson, *The Story of American Painting*, New York 1981.

155. Thus Philippe Guston's cult of the 'blue triangle', and Jackson Pollock's passion for theosophy and the teaching of Krishnamurti.

156. Cf. the volume *George Grosz: New York*, edited by Walter Huder and Karl Riha, New York 1985, which reproduces a number of his American drawings, especially those of New York street scenes. We should recall that in Berlin Grosz had already imagined himself in New York. He had painted skyscrapers on his walls and hung up a signed photograph of Henry Ford which bore the dedication: 'To George Grosz the artist from his admirer Henry Ford'. Grosz had discovered America through the novels of Karl May. As an exile in the United States, he drew passers-by on Fifth Avenue, billboards and shop windows, attentive to all the emotions that the city aroused in him.

157. Grosz however made an effort to adapt to American conditions. He taught drawing in New York, latterly at Columbia University, without having great success. An avant-garde artist in Europe, and close to the Dadaists, Grosz was seen in America as just another illustrator. His last works, however, in which he returned to the style of Dadaist montage, were an astonishing anticipation of American Pop Art. He played no part in American artistic life, despite exhibiting in 1938 at the Art Institute of Chicago and in 1946 at the Associated American Artists Gallery in New York. The 1950s were dominated by the cult of abstraction, and it was only after Grosz's death that his drawings were feverishly collected. He sold practically nothing throughout his exile in America, and even his splendid still lifes did not interest the American public. As for Wieland Herzfelde, another leading figure in the Dada movement, he kept a tiny stamp shop in NewYork, designed letterheads and survived thanks to the support of his son, a figure skater. The former Berlin Dadaist Richard Huelsenbeck set up in New York as a psychologist.

158. Erwin Panofsky, 'Three Decades of Art History in the United States. Impressions of a Transplanted European', epilogue to *Meaning in the Visual Arts*, Harmondsworth 1970.

159. Panofsky taught in New York in 1931, then returned as an exile to teach at Princeton in 1934.

160. He became a professor at Columbia University.

161. Former director of the German archeological institute in Rome, then of the archeological museum at Münster, he had been in charge of the Samothrace excavations.

162. Teachers already there included Ludwig Bachofen, Otto von Simson and John Rewald, specialists in cubism.

163. B. Brecht, *Journals*, p. 307.

164. Cited by Peter T. Hoffer, *Klaus Mann*, p. 21.

165. Klaus Mann visited the United States with his sister Erika in 1927, for a lecture tour. People came to meet 'the literary Mann twins', with a curiosity unusual in Europe. His reputation as a Bohemian and somewhat eccentric writer had already preceded him. In 1929 they published their account of their journey as *Rund herum. Das Abenteuer einer Weltreise* (reissued Munich 1965). If Klaus Mann was fascinated by American cities, which often struck him as inhuman (he commented ironically on the vision of America in Brecht's poems, advising him to spend a while there), he also stressed the prevailing atmosphere of conflict and racism. He loved New York but found Los Angeles horrific.

166. No one felt more keenly the ephemeral character of literary fame in the United States than F. Scott Fitzgerald. When he worked in Hollywood in 1940, he could not find a single one of his titles in a bookstore, though he had been the very symbol of a generation ten years earlier.

167. Gertrude Stein declared that the twentieth century was to be found 'where Paris was'.

168. It should be borne in mind that the majority of exiled writers in America were over forty. Klaus and Erika Mann were exceptional in being young enough to adapt to a new country, a new culture and a new language. Brecht was forty-three on his arrival in the United States, Toller forty, Werfel fifty, Ehrenstein fifty-five, Leonhard Frank fifty-eight, Fritz von Unruh fifty-five, Yvan Goll fifty-one, Franz Pfemfert sixty-one, Alfred Döblin sixty-two, Thomas Mann sixty-three and Heinrich Mann sixty-nine.

169. He was so poor that he was the only paid contributor. Cf. A. Abusch, *Freies Deutschland*, p. 18.

170. Cited by A. Banuls, *Heinrich Mann*, p. 399.

171. Ibid., p. 409.

172. B. Brecht, *Journals*, p. 223.

173. It is possible that it was this isolation and its results that led Döblin to convert to Catholicism, along with his wife and son, in November 1941.

174. Thomas Mann himself wrote to MGM in support of Alfred Döblin, Arthur Polgar, H. Lustig and Walter Mehring.

175. Walter Mehring ironically wrote in *La Bibliothèque perdue* (p. 264): 'With the Antichrist's Wehrmacht close on his heels, he begged pardon for the errors of his youth and his admiration for Zola, the detractor of the little shepherdess. She transported him with dry feet across the sea to America, raised his novel *Song of Bernadette* to a bestseller and poured over him the fabulous Californian golden rain of "Lanterne Magica Motion Pictures" of Hollywood, finally to summon him up to heaven after a convulsing embolism when he had written the last line of his masterpiece *The Star of the Unborn*.'

176. Hailed by Thomas Mann as a great novel, it did not dissolve the bad feeling that existed between Werfel and other émigrés, who reproached him for his wealth. Even Adorno and Horkheimer had little sympathy for him, citing his novels in their *Dialectic of Enlightenment* as an example of the *Kulturindustrie*. Translated in 1942, *The Star of the Unborn* was chosen as a 'book of the month' and sold 300,000 copies. Werfel earned $100,000 for the film rights.

177. Mann also wrote in the United States *Lotte in Weimar* and *Joseph the Provider*.

178. T. Mann, *The Genesis of a Novel*, pp. 84ff.

179. L. Marcuse, *Mein zwanzigstes Jahrhundert*, p. 289.

180. For example Hans Leonhardt, *The Nazi Conquest of Danzig*; K. Heiden, *Der Führer, Hitler's Rise to Power*; Hans Natonek, *In Search of Myself*; Erna Barscha, *My American Adventure*; Klaus and Erika Mann, *Escape to Life*; and Leo Lania, *The Darkest Hour*.

181. Even Thomas Mann could only get his books published in German in very small runs. The American public's awareness of him was entirely through translation. The same went for Hermann Broch, whose book *The Death of Virgil* was translated at the same time as he finished the original German. Thomas Mann wrote to Marianne Lindel on 8 October 1944 regarding *Joseph the Provider*: 'One has to imagine a music in need of translation, to understand the melancholy of my situation, also that the 1,800 German copies in America are a greater joy for me than the 200,000 English ones.' The German edition of Mann's book had in fact been originally printed in Stockholm, bound in Switzerland, and photostatically reprinted in the United States.

182. Brecht's *Dreigroschenroman* had been published in 1934 by Allert de Lange in Amsterdam, and his *Svendborger Gedichte* in 1938 by Malik Verlag in London.

183. He had in mind Wilhelm Dieterle, Bruno Frank, Leopold Frank, Lotte Lehmann, Max Reinhardt, Ludwig Renn, René Schickele, Paul Tillich, Stefan Zweig and Fritz von Unruh.

184. *Exil in den USA*, p. 225.

185. Werfel received $12,500 for his book. Over 327,000 copies were sold between July and October 1942.

186. He was quoted as saying: 'There is great temptation to help authors by publishing their books, but it is ruinous, and much wiser to make them a gift of the amount that one expects to lose' (*Exil in den USA*, p. 227).

187. On the activities of Kurt Wolff in America, cf. Kurt Wolff, *Briefwechsel eines Verlegers 1911–1963*, Frankfurt 1980.

188. *Morgenröte*, published by Aurora in 1944, contained texts by Bloch, Brecht, Bruckner, Döblin, Feuchtwanger, Herzfelde, Heinrich Mann and Weiskopf, with a preface by Heinrich Mann in which he declared: 'German literature has always been oriented towards justice and peace [. . .] It is doubtful whether any country has as many poems and tales able to fill a whole volume with prayers for peace. German literature does have these.' The book had a total of 144 texts on war and peace, by 103 authors. Schiller, Lessing, Grillparzer, Büchner, Hölderlin and Nietzsche were represented alongside J. R. Becher, E. E. Kisch, Arnold Zweig, Bodo Uhse and Ernst Bloch.

189. *New York Herald Tribune, New York Times, Brooklyn Daily Eagle, Life*, etc.

190. Brecht noted on 21 April 1942: 'i sent a piece about hitler to READER'S DIGEST (sales 3.5 million) for their series "my most unforgettable character". it came back very promptly. feuchtwanger tells me thomas mann and werfel, who has been very successful here, had their contributions sent back too. the magazine submits readers' contributions to half a dozen experts. one checks whether the thing is brown, a second whether it stinks, a third that there are no solid lumps in it etc. that is how strictly it is checked to see that it is real shit before they accept it' (*Journals*, p. 223).

191. Later a well-known writer in the GDR, Heym emigrated to the USA in 1935, aged twenty-two, after winning a scholarship to the University of Chicago. He lived there in poverty before working for the *Volksfront* movement in Chicago, directed by Martin Hall.

192. It was founded on 20 February 1937 as a weekly, and achieved a print run of 30,000.

193. This was published in New York from 1942 to 1949. Cf. *Exil in den USA*, p. 145.

194. Its political role will be discussed in the following chapter.

195. On Klaus Mann's negative experiences in American exile, cf. Ilsedore B. Jonas, 'Klaus Mann im amerikanische Exile', in Rudolf Wolff, ed., *Klaus Mann Werk und Wirkung*, Bonn 1984, pp. 119ff.

196. *Exil in den USA*, pp. 152–3.

197. It sold 40,000 copies right away, and was translated into German as *Zehn Millionen Kinder* (Querido Verlag).

198. Herbert Marcuse worked for the OSS, which led him to be attacked in the late 1960s for having worked for the CIA, on the pretext that some members of the OSS went on to work for this successor.

199. John Russell Taylor, *Strangers in Paradise*, London 1983.

200. The younger ones were an exception here. Exiled authors who switched to writing in English were generally essayists or academics (Ernst Cassirer, Herbert Marcuse). Among the most famous, only Kurt Weill was really able to write and compose using all the resources of the English language. Some exiles, such as Kurt Kesten, enrolled at university to study and obtain an American diploma, after already having their doctorate in Germany. But even among the youngest exiles this unease with the language persisted. It is symbolic that Bertolt Brecht's son Stephan, who settled permanently in NewYork, titled one of his poems 'Die Muttersprache, die schönste verloren' (*Gedichte*, Berlin 1985).

201. Paul Tillich gave lectures in English at the Union Theological Seminary in New York. But according to Karola Bloch (*Aus meinem Leben*, p. 136), he had to seriously improve his knowledge of the language as his students were unable to understand him. Eisler, who wanted to work in Hollywood, made the same efforts with his lectures, without really succeeding: when he spoke to his colleagues in English, most of them thought he was speaking German. He strongly advised Ernst Bloch to start studying English, but Bloch declared that he had enough of a problem battling with German, and saw such an effort as worthless. To convince Eisler of this, he addressed a black American in German, and got a reply in Bavarian dialect, the man having worked as a cigarette seller in Munich (ibid.). By the end of his exile, Bloch could manage to read the *New York Times*, and thought such a level was amply sufficient. Oskar Maria Graf did have a good knowledge of English, but deliberately spoke only Bavarian. As for Brecht, by exaggerating a bit he threw the House Committee on Un-American Activities into confusion, with Parnell Thomas unable to grasp anything of his responses to their questions.

202. The scene of the hunt for the body in the lake, by torchlight, was plagiarized by Veit Harlan in his anti-Semitic film of *Jew Süss*.

203. J. R. Taylor, *Strangers in Paradise*, p. 30.

204. See *Strangers in Paradise* for a description of Los Angeles in 1940.

205. Theatre there, like cinema, was only a popular commercial distraction. Those forms of cultural expression that had existed in the 1920s and early 30s were mostly well on the decline, and public taste hardly permitted any innovations. It was equally difficult both to find orchestras capable of playing Schoenberg's atonal music and an audience to listen to it.

206. Pommer had been one of the production heads at UFA, Joe May directed *Das indische Grabmal* (1921) and *Asphalt* (1929).

207. As well as the case of Joe May, we could mention that of William Thiele, director of *Die drei von der Tankstelle* and *Liebewalzer*.

208. He took advantage of this forced – but paid – vacation to perfect his English and study the sand paintings of the Navajo Indians in Arizona.

209. MGM suppressed a scene in which black people appeared, and another one with a kiss that was deemed too passionate.

210. On his career in the United States, cf. R. Siodmak, *Zwischen Berlin und Hollywood*, Munich 1980.

211. Some of them made no more films, others produced only commercial or insignificant ones. For instance the Czech film-makers Gustav Machaty (director of a film deemed at the time pornographic, *Ekstase*, with Hedy Kiesler, later known as Heddy Lamarr) and Hugo Haas, the Dane Kay Nielsen, who worked for Walt Disney, and the Dutchman Oskar Fischiner, formerly close to the Bauhaus, a technical assistant on Fritz Lang's *Frau im Mond* (1928), and a pioneer of abstract cinema, whom MGM had no idea what to do with, and who also ended up for Disney. While John Cage and Edgar Varèse considered him a genius, he was completely ignored by Hollywood. Kenneth Anger was a student of his.

212. One exception is Alfred Döblin's work on *Mrs Miniver* and *Random Harvest*.

213. They still met up until the 1980s: in California around Martha Feuchtwanger, in New York with Lotte Lenya or Maria Piscator. Anyone who has had the

opportunity to spend a short while with them – even a simple Christmas party in New York in the company of these survivors of Weimar – cannot forget the mixture of emotion and strangeness felt in hearing them speak of a time and a culture that they kept alive, as if for them time had stood still. Until her death, Lotte Lenya attended the Broadway theatres with the same enthusiasm that she had displayed in Berlin. And in Maria Piscator's apartment close to Central Park, in the company of Mozart's harp and a fascinating collection of old bibles translated by her husband's ancestor Johannes Piscator, it was not incongruous to evoke the memory of Alfred Kerr or Max Reinhardt's last productions in Salzburg, forgetting that half a century had passed in between.

CHAPTER 14 ACADEMICS IN EXILE

1. It should be recalled here that the application of the laws of 7 April 1933 already led to the dismissal of all government employees who did not meet the principles of the 'new Germany' for either racial or political reasons (membership of the KPD or left organizations, Marxist activities, hostility to the state, non-Aryan origin). Further laws of 4 November 1935 subsequently expelled from public function those teachers of Jewish extraction who were still at their posts. Finally, those of 26 January 1937 made absolute fidelity to Hitler the first condition of any government position. It is estimated that between 1933 and 1938 about one-third of teachers were eliminated.
2. According to the Davie Report, *Refugees in America*, the Committee sponsored 355 professors and spent over a million dollars.
3. From what the director of the New School for Social Research said, this was also the feeling that many students there had towards Piscator (oral communication).
4. The contribution of émigré academics to American culture was one of the first themes of research on the refugees. M. R. Davie drew a first balance-sheet of it in his report of 1947. In February 1945, the New York Jewish Club 1933 examined their influence in Hollywood. Subsequently, the works of Franz Neumann and Helga Pross on academic emigration studied the contribution in more detail, as did Laura Fermi in *Illustrious Immigrants*. More recently, the 1977 study by H. Stuart Hughes, *The Sea Change. The Migration of Social Thought 1930–1965*, showed the influence exercised by Mannheim, Fromm, Neumann, Arendt, Horkheimer, Adorno, Marcuse, Haltmann, Erikson and Tilllich on American social science. In 1952, the University of Pennsylvania organized a conference on the theme 'The Cultural Migration' which was attended by a number of the émigré professors. Its conclusions were as diverse as the judgements of these émigrés themselves. Erwin Panofsky rightly stressed that the teaching of art history in the United States owed everything to the émigrés, and the same was true of a large number of other disciplines. But though these influences are clear enough in psychology, psychoanalysis and art, it is harder to gauge the political aspect of this impact. Theodor Adorno was fairly pessimistic, and Herbert Marcuse still more so, emphasizing not without reason that the émigrés had given birth to a new conservatism. Ernst Bloch was unable to convince an American publisher to take on any of his books. *Die Prinzip Hoffnung* was rejected by Oxford University Press, and *Subjekt–Objekt* first appeared in 1949 in Spanish translation in Mexico.
5. 'Revolutionary scenes' in the style of Mexican realist painting can be seen there, with portraits of Marx, Engels, Lenin and Stalin; they remained in place despite protests by the students in the McCarthy era.
6. The work was judged to be 'somewhat thin'. The reason for this animosity was both the radicalism of the Frankfurt School, and its use of Freudian concepts to which Max Wertheimer was fiercely opposed.
7. Alvin Johnson, *Pioneer's Progress*, New York 1952, pp. 332ff.
8. Gustave Cohen obtained General de Gaulle's approval for the project.

9. On the history of the Frankfurt School, see Martin Jay, *The Dialectical Imagination*, London 1973. The idea for its foundation went back to Felix J. Weill, and its birth was prepared by the formation of the Erste Marxistische Arbeitswoche in Thuringia in 1922, attended by Georg Lukács, Karl Korsch, Richard Sorge, Friedrich Pollock, Karl A. Wittfogel, B. Forgarasi, Karl Schmückl, Klara Zetkin and Hede Gumperz.

10. We should recall here that Céléstin Bouglé, Durkheim's former publisher, and director of the centre of documentation of the École Normale Supérieure since 1920, proposed that Max Horkheimer should set up offices for the Institute in the ENS buildings on the rue d'Ulm. The proposal was backed by Maurice Halbwachs, George Scelle and Bergson. In London, Alexander Fargharson, director of the *Sociological Review*, also put its offices at Horkheimer's disposal. The Institute's *Zeitschrift* was published in Paris by the Librairie Félix Alcan.

11. The sources of conflict were varied. The Institute's relative wealth and financial independence were enviable. Its relationship to the most political exiles, however, was complex. Karola Bloch recalls in her memoirs (*Aus meinem Leben*, p. 136) the problems that her husband had in emigrating to the United States. When he applied for a teaching post, he wrote to Max Horkheimer who refused point blank, deeming Bloch too close to Communism. Brecht met with the same political reticence from Institute members.

12. Brecht noted on 10 October 1943: 'this frankfurter institute is a goldmine for the TUI NOVEL' (*Journals*, p. 302).

13. Cf. Martin Jay, *The Dialectical Imagination*, pp. 114–15.

14. Ibid., p. 143.

15. His study *Punishment and Social Structure* (1939) was the first important work of the Institute to be published in English.

16. On the exile of Cassirer in the United States, cf. *Mein Leben mit Ernst Cassirer. Erinnerungen von Toni Cassirer*, Hildesheim 1981. Cassirer was first of all invited to Yale University. He remained in America from 4 June 1941 to 13 April 1945. Ernst Bloch, for his part, failed to find any teaching post whatsoever.

17. Formerly radical in his political ideas, Wittfogel was accused by several colleagues of taking an active part in the McCarthy witch-hunts. The American historian Moses L. Finley had to emigrate to Britain as a result of one of his denunciations (personal communication).

CHAPTER 15 THE BREAKUP OF THE POLITICAL EMIGRATION

1. There were 102 Jewish newspapers and magazines in New York in 1941, including six dailies. More than half of these were already in existence before 1933.

2. Einstein himself was involved with it.

3. In April 1937, *Der Aufbau* was directed by a professional journalist, Rudolf Brandl. The Club already had a social section, and even a cemetery in New Jersey.

4. The title *Der Aufbau* did not literally mean a 'reconstruction': it originally signalled the opening of new Jewish stores in New York. The English subtitle *Reconstruction* was added later. Rabbi Mordenchai M. Kaplan founded a 'Reconstructionist' movement in 1935, as the left wing of religious conservatism, which had no connection with the magazine. (Cf. J. Radkau, *Die deutsche Emigration in den USA*, p. 128.)

5. George was attacked by R. Brandt in 1939 as a 'Communist agent'. In Germany, he had contributed mostly to Zionist magazines, and worked for the Ullstein publishing house.

6. The print runs of émigré magazines, in the meantime, steadily dwindled. *Neue Vorwärts* in Paris had a circulation of 5,000, *Mass und Wert* shrank from 6,000 in 1937 to 1,500 in 1940. *Der Aufbau* however rose from 3,000 copies in 1939 to 30,000

in 1944. It played a major role through to the 1960s, and was sold at newsstands in both New York and London.

7. The *Volkszeitung* had opposed United States entry into the First World War. An influential member of its editorial board, Ludwig Lores, a former student of Sombart, invited Trotsky to the United States in 1917, and while still editor-in-chief of the magazine, participated in the founding of the CPUSA, being expelled for Trotskyism in 1925. When the magazine became violently anti-Communist, a section of its editorial board founded the *Kampfsignal*, the title of the SAP organ established in Germany in 1931.

8. Cf. J. Radkau, *Die deutsche Emigration in den USA*, p. 145.

9. The *Sozialistische Mitteilungen* appeared in England.

10. In 1940 *Der Aufbau* deplored the fact that Chinese and blacks seemed more aware of the need to struggle against National Socialism than did *Deutschamerikaner*, who were often apolitical or conservative.

11. Cf. the reissue of major articles from the magazine in *Aufbau. Reconstruction. Dokumente einer Kultur in Exil*, ed. Will Schaber, Cologne 1972.

12. The Joint Distribution Committee provided considerable aid to European Jews, which continued to expand: $340,000 in 1938, $15 million in 1944, $69 million in 1947.

13. Hannah Arendt for example deplored in 1941 that American Jews saw Rothschild as a more representative figure than Heine, and were more proud of a Jewish minister than of Kafka or Chaplin.

14. It held that the pact should be judged only in terms of the balance of forces and not from a moral standpoint, pointing out that it had kept half of Poland from destruction. These judgements on the USSR were fairly naive: *Der Aufbau* saw the USSR as the ideal country for Jews.

15. *Der Aufbau* opposed in due course both the Nationalkomitee 'Freies Deutschland' in Moscow and Paul Tillich's Council for a Democratic Germany.

16. Besides the fact that complete assimilation would also have meant the disappearance of this German-language magazine, antagonism between German and eastern Jews had several aspects. Fritz Kortner recalled in his autobiography the disappointment of the immigration official who welcomed him to New York that he did not speak Yiddish. J. Radkau (*Die deutsche Emigration in den USA*) mentions a reader's letter sent to *Der Aufbau* which complained of the arrogance of German Jews, just arrived in America, towards Jewish-Americans of Russian or Polish origin.

17. One of its most spectacular actions was to donate to the US air force a plane named *Loyalty*.

18. Rudolf Katz was not a convinced antifascist; he had written several articles praising Mussolini during the Ethiopian war, which puzzled Italian émigrés. (Cf. J. Radkau, *Die deutsche Emigration in den USA*, p. 150.)

19. Richard Loewenthal of Neu Beginnen saw them more as left National Socialists than right-wing Socialists.

20. Under the name of William F. Sollmann, this former Social-Democrat later became a right-wing political scientist, opposing Tocqueville to Marx.

21. Thomas Mann wrote to Siegfried Marck on 15 April 1944: 'G. Seger came to visit me the other day. I told him in no uncertain terms that it raised my hackles to see the *Volkszeitung* attach Russia. He distanced himself from this and declared that Katz and Stampfer also went a bit far for his taste.'

22. In 1942 the Socialist Federation protested against Roosevelt's pardon of the CPUSA leader Earl Browder, which was particularly disingenuous given that he had been condemned for infringement of passport legislation; a large number of émigrés were in a quite irregular situation in this respect.

23. It even suspected the Vatican of Communist sympathies.

24. According to its editor, the *Volksecho* had 35,000 readers, though its circulation was not much more than 8,000. (Cf. J. Radkau, *Die deutsche Emigration in den USA*, p. 170.)

25. Though not a writer of top rank, O. M. Graf enjoyed great popularity among the émigrés. They admired his courage in 1933 when he insisted that his books be burned along with those of his friends. Converted to socialism by his admiration for Tolstoy, he had been arrested after the fall of the Bavarian soviet republic, and his rather erotic Bavarian stories had won him the popular nickname of 'Porno-Graf'. In the United States he was a link between Marxists such as Brecht and a large number of other writers with whom Brecht hardly sympathized.

26. This provision was already in force during the exile period, but was never applied. A number of Communists managed to reach the United States under Roosevelt, as long as they were not known political leaders. Stefan Heym was an army sergeant and decorated, Hermann Budzislawski became a major journalist and succeeded Fritz Kortner as Dorothy Thompson's secretary. Hans Kahle, former International Brigade commander, came to America thanks to Hemingway's protection and contributed to both the *Daily Worker* and *Time*. Alfred Kantorowicz, within a year of his arrival, worked for CBS and was in charge of foreign news.

27. He lived in the United States from 1934 under the name of Henry Anderson.

28. In 1944, the *St Louis Globe-Democrat* still maintained that the émigrés saw Brüning as their natural leader.

29. On Hubertus Prinz zu Löwenstein, see above, Chapter 2, note 78 Attached to the tradition of the German Reich, his ideas were somewhat confused, as shown by his book *Als Katholik im republikanischen Spanien*. In the United States he founded in 1936 the American Guild for German Cultural Freedom, to which Thomas Mann belonged. They quarrelled when the Guild published an article criticizing the Allies' policy towards Germany.

30. Not only had the Weimar Republic's economic crisis worsened under Brüning, but he had contributed to creating an increasingly authoritarian and presidential regime.

31. Some émigrés feared that he would return to power in 1945.

32. J. Radkau, *Die deutsche Emigration in den USA*, p. 191. It should be stressed, moreover, that one of the difficulties in appreciating Brüning's actual influence was that this was never expressed in a direct way. In his correspondence, he would advise such and such a person to enter this or that group, in order to influence it or shift its orientation. He thus recommended Fritz Ezmath to join the group of left Socialists in New York, to prevent them from writing a programme (letter of 27 January 1941). A professor of political science at the University of Chicago, Ezmath was charged by Brüning with all kinds of missions; in 1941 he was placed under surveillance by the FBI. Brüning acted similarly with W. Sollmann (letter of 4 February 1941).

33. In the preface to a new German edition of *The Revolution of Nihilism* in 1964, Golo Mann claimed that Rauschning had exercised an influence on American politics via Dorothy Thompson and Walter Lippmann; I do not see this as adequately established.

34. A projected meeting in New York in 1939, to be addressed by Rudolf Katz, secretary of the German Labor Delegation, Rauschning, Brüning, Stampfer and Thomas Mann, failed due to the reticence of each towards the others.

35. Gurian was born in St Petersburg.

36. Its contributors included Fritz Morstein Marc, Sigmund Neumann, Hans Barth, Albert Salomon, Stefan T. Possony, Peter F. Drucker, Hannah Arendt, Fritz Redlich, Fritz Karl Mann and Hans Kohn.

37. Thomas Mann denounced Adler's ideas as 'intellectual fascism'. A professor at the University of Chicago, he was a fierce champion of isolationism.

38. Hans J. Morgenthau, *In Defense of the National Interest*, London 1952.

39. Bloch however never had any influence in America.

40. Cf. J. Radkau, *Die deutsche Emigration in den USA*, p. 247. A parallel suspicion of technological utopias can be traced in Morgenthau, who stressed in 1946 that

Nazism was not just a return to irrationalism; the gas chambers were also a model of technological rationality.

41. As well as the émigrés' ideological contribution to conservatism, we should also mention the role they played in the development of the theory of 'totalitarianism', for instance Hannah Arendt. The major theorists of neoliberalism in the 1950s – Ludwig von Mises, Friedrich von Hayek, Wilhelm Röpke, were all German émigrés.

CHAPTER 16   EMIGRATION IN LATIN AMERICA

1. Paul Zech, who had a brother in Argentina, was an exception. Balder Olden, though he obtained a visa for the United States, chose instead to go to South America, deeming it 'more human'.
2. Cf. Wolfgang Kiessling, *Exil in Lateinamerika*, Leipzig 1981.
3. Brazil had 700,000 Germans, Argentina 220,000, Paraguay 35,000, Uruguay 6,000, and the Central American countries 5,000. At least 120 German papers were published in Latin America, of which nine had circulations ranging from 10,000 to 45,000. (Cf. W. Kiessling, *Exil in Lateinamerika*, p. 53.)
4. Figures from W. Kiessling, *Exil in Lateinamerika*, p. 51.
5. There were 2,903 in Brazil, and 985 in Chile (ibid., p. 64).
6. From 1933 to 1938, power was in the hands of General Augustin B. Justo, a violent anti-Communist.
7. Many settled in Paraguay and in Bolivia, but conditions of life were very hard in these less developed countries.
8. The finest description of the city is still that of Paul Zech, published in *Die Sammlung* in 1935.
9. Founded in 1889 by a Swiss immigrant, Johann Jakob Alemann.
10. The *Argentinisches Tageblatt* regularly called the Nazis murderers and thieves, exposed Göring's morphine addiction and gangsterism and compared Hitler to Attila.
11. It should be borne in mind that the Union of Overseas Germans subsidized thousands of schools abroad. After the Nazi seizure of power, those that refused the new values had their subsidies withdrawn. The writer Maria Kahle, who made a propaganda tour in South America, mentioned on her return to Berlin that the Union was supporting over 1,400 schools. In Buenos Aires, schools that rejected Nazi ideology were attacked by armed bands. Nazi branches were also numerous in Brazil. On 11 July 1935 some 15,000 Nazi supporters from fifty-two groups demonstrated in the São Paulo region.
12. A specialist in 'racist pedagogy' and publisher of *Volk im Werden*, he was known above all for his attacks on Heidegger.
13. Ludwig Renn had already visited the United States in 1935, as well as Cuba, to obtain aid for Spain.
14. For instance the educationalist Otto Rühle, co-founder of *Die Internationale*, who rallied to Trotsky for a while. He died on 24 June 1943 and his wife committed suicide shortly after.
15. The individual most active in it was Alfons Goldschmidt. Ludwig Renn, who reached Mexico by bus from New York on 6 November 1939, also played an important role.
16. These included Friedrich Wolf, Hermann Budzislawski, Alfred Kantorowicz, Leonhard Frank and Franz Werfel.
17. The 1940 elections were accompanied by violent confrontations.
18. Bodo Uhse was forced to leave the United States in December 1939. Despite his friends' efforts, it was not until March 1940 that he obtained a visa for Mexico.
19. For example Franz Pfemfert, the friend of Karl Liebknecht and Rosa Luxemburg and publisher of the well-known magazine *Die Aktion*, who died in Mexico on 25 May 1954. His manuscript autobiography is believed to be lost.

20. From 1933, Germany tried to compete with Britain in Mexico, Ecuador, Paraguay and Colombia.
21. In 1930, Uruguay, with two million inhabitants including several thousand German speakers who had come from Germany and Switzerland in the mid nineteenth century, already had Communists who had arrived after the First World War.
22. The 1919 constitution guaranteed freedom of assembly and the right to strike. Uruguay established diplomatic relations with the Soviet Union in 1926.
23. In other countries these were often more symbolic, given the hostile political milieu in which they developed.
24. Between 1941 and 1946 the Club held sixty-eight events: twenty-three literary, six musical, eleven political, nine scientific, five on foreign cultures, three on cinema and one on visual arts. It also staged seven dramatic performances.
25. Ernst Römer was conductor of the Mexico Philharmonic Orchestra at this time.
26. On the painting of Siquieros and Rivera, as well as on Maya legends.
27. The first issues were edited by Bruno Frei, Bodo Uhse and André Simone. First of all directed by Bruno Frei, *Freies Deutschland* subsequently had Alexander Abusch as its editor-in-chief.
28. According to Alexander Abusch. Other less important magazines also existed in Latin America, for example *Volksblatt*, published first in Buenos Aires (1941–43), then in Uruguay.
29. Paul Zech, one of the great expressionist poets, was arrested in 1933 when he was dining with a Jewish family. He was finally released after being locked in a cellar for three days, but his library and manuscripts were ransacked. In summer 1933 had joined his brother who already lived in Argentina, but they quarrelled over politics and he went to live in a Buenos Aires suburb, stopping mail delivery for reasons of security. Throughout his exile he experienced great poverty. He saw himself as a prisoner in Argentina, and refused to read Spanish books so as not to change his sense of the German language. His books interested so few readers (sometimes only ten) that he ended up copying out his last volumes by hand and binding them himself. He contributed to *Deutsche Blätter* as its Argentine correspondent. Zech died on 7 September 1946, leaving some fifty manuscripts: novels, tales and Indian legends. His companion, Hilde Herb, whom he had not managed to bring to Argentina, committed suicide in Berlin.
30. E. E. Kisch, *Marktplatz der Sensationen* (1942), Lion Feuchtwanger, *Unholdes Frankreich* (1942), Theodor Balk, *Führer durch Sowjetkrieg und Frieden* (1942) and *Das verlorene Manuscript* (1943), Anna Seghers, *Das siebte Kreuz* (1943), Paul Merker, *Was wird aus Deutschland?* (1943) and *El Libro negro del terror nazi en Europa* (1943), Bruno Frank, *Die Tochter* (1943), and Heinrich Mann, *Lidice* (1943). 1944 saw the appearance of Bodo Uhse, *Leutnant Bertram*, Leo Katz, *Die Totenjäger*, F. C. Weiskopf, *Von einem neuen Tag*, Paul Mayer, *Gedichte*, Ludwig Renn, *Adel im Untergang*, E. E. Kisch, *Entdeckungen in Mexico* and Theodor Plievier, *Stalingrad*.
31. If few of the works written in Mexican exile are known today, this is not the case with Anna Seghers, who wrote some of her most moving books there. She began *The Seventh Cross* in France in 1938 – the first chapter appeared in *Internationale Literatur*, published in Moscow, in 1939 – and completed it at the time of the invasion of France. Several copies were lost, but one reached the United States thanks to F. C. Weiskopf. Seghers had reached Mexico via Gibraltar, Martinique and the Dominican Republic. Several of her stories bear the mark of her unusual encounters. From 1948 to 1961 she wrote a whole cycle of novels on the Caribbean, after starting her novel *Transit* in the Dominican Republic in 1941. She was unable to reach Mexico from Cuba and had to go via New York. She settled in Vera Cruz, then in Mexico City, where the original German version of *The Seventh Cross* was published by El Libro Libre. Her entrancing short story 'Das wirkliche Blau' is perhaps the most perfect example of this encounter between the émigrés' sensibility and a world that was exotic and unknown, and bound to move them deeply.

CHAPTER 17   THE ÉMIGRÉS IN WARTIME AMERICA

1. Cf. J. B. Duroselle, *De Wilson à Roosevelt*, p. 293.
2. For example the Non-Sectarian Anti-Nazi League, the Jewish Labor Committee, the American Jewish Committee.
3. In 1939, there were some 2,500 members of American Nazi groups, and around 25,000 supporters.
4. The Bund called the refugees 'refu-Jews'. The German ambassador mentioned in his reports the effects of the 'Jewish counter-offensive', but never those of the émigrés.
5. The émigrés grouped around *Der Aufbau* protested on many occasions when the Bund was given permission to parade in the streets.
6. For instance at the Washington Town Hall Forum, in 1937.
7. On 25 September 1938, for example, at Madison Square Gardens, in support of Czechoslovakia.
8. Dorothy Thompson attracted the attention of President Roosevelt in 1938 to the fate of German antifascists remaining in Europe.
9. Cf. in particular J. Radkau, *Die deutsche Emigration in den USA*, p. 71 and Fritz Kortner, *Aller Tage Abend*, pp. 316ff., where he presents her political shift as a victory for the émigrés.
10. J. Radkau, *Die deutsche Emigration in den USA*, p. 71.
11. Even if Hubertus Prinz zu Löwenstein enjoyed a certain audience in Catholic circles through his lectures, and knew some important figures such as Winston Churchill and John Foster Dulles, it is very hard to show that he exerted any influence.
12. Gerald Nye was senator for North Dakota.
13. The Davie Report states (*Refugees in America*, p. 189) that the majority of refugees made their demand for naturalization as soon as they arrived in the United States.
14. B. Brecht, *Dialogues d'exilés*, p. 71.
15. It should be noted that the majority of Japanese (numerous in Hawaii and California) were arrested and had their belongings confiscated. They were interned in camps in Arizona and Colorado. More than five hundred discriminatory measures were voted against them after Pearl Harbor. From 1943, the government sent recruiting agents to the internment camps, and a number of detainees agreed to serve in the US Army. They fought in special units, were sent to the front lines and often on suicide missions. Three-quarters of the Japanese in the 442nd combat unit, for example, fell in the Vosges, where a monument at Biffontaine perpetuates their memory.
16. G. Bermann Fischer, *Bedroht-Bewahrt*, p. 269.
17. According to the Davie Report, the term 'alien of enemy nationality' was finally preferred to that of 'enemy alien', as being more 'friendly'. The 600,000 Italians in the United States were exempted as a group at the end of 1942.
18. Brüning planned to give a course on the history of the constitution, but was dissuaded from doing so.
19. One of the few émigrés suspected was Hasso von Seebach. In fact, only 23,000 émigrés out of 5 million were questioned, and 10,000 interned.
20. Letter to Paul Schwarz of 3 June 1942 in Brüning, *Correspondence*.
21. F. Kortner, *Aller Tage Abend*, p. 322.
22. We should note that by 1944 the United States produced some two-fifths of all the world's munitions, and between 1941 and 1945 some 299,600 military aircraft, 86,400 tanks, 2,725,000 machine-guns, 70,000 warships and 6,000 merchant ships. This effectiveness contrasted with the chaotic period of the War Resource Board of 1939, replaced in 1941 by the War Production Board, then the Office of War Mobilization in 1943.
23. These included Charles Lindbergh.
24. Cf. Carlos Baker, *Hemingway*, New York 1963, pp. 444ff.

25. University of California Press, 1944. I would like to thank Vladimir Pozner, in exile with Brecht in Los Angeles at this time, for lending me this book.
26. Under the direction of the Coordinator of Inter-American Affairs.
27. James Monroe even invented a leaflet bomb, which enabled 80,000 leaflets to be dropped at a time.
28. Erika Mann served as a war correspondent in Portugal, Great Britain, Sweden, Iran and Palestine. Klaus Mann became a sergeant at the age of 36 and took part in the Italian campaign. He worked on the editorial team of *Stars and Stripes*. Golo Mann joined the US Navy, writing leaflets designed for the German population and serving in the Psychological Warfare Branch.
29. They often served as interpreters.
30. For the sum of $8,900. A manuscript of a Brecht poem reached $500. Klaus Mann sold his collection of manuscripts and association copies for $1,000.
31. In June 1934, California had 700,000 unemployed.
32. In particular by writing *Upton Sinclair Presents William Fox*, in 1933. Californian business circles called him a 'bolshevik', their propaganda against him being worked out in the MGM studios.
33. She later married the American painter Edward Bibermann.
34. Apart from movements such as the Ku Klux Klan, the American Nazi party, the followers of Father Coughlin, Gerald L. K. Smith, Dudley Pelley and Huey Long, and the American Liberty League, California also had a number of pro-fascist paramilitary formations: the Light Horse Cavalry, the Hollywood Hussars and the California Esquadrille, who aimed to 'save America' and found a number of sympathizers in Hollywood, including actors such as Gary Cooper, Victor McLaglen and George Brent.
35. Otto Katz worked with the Soviet film company Mezhrabpom, and had been sent to the United States as early as 1933 by Willi Münzenberg in order to raise funds.
36. The Federal Theater Project was criticized by opponents of the New Deal for employing too many left-wingers and focusing on racial conflict, poverty and the depression. A coalition of Southern Democrats and Republicans managed to cut off its funding. The same alliance in Congress brought into being the House of Representatives Committee on Un-American Activities, known initially as the Dies Committee, from the name of its chair, Martin Dies, a representative for Texas. Dies maintained that the Anti-Nazi League was simply a façade for the Communist party, and proposed to visit Hollywood in September 1937 in order to question a number of film personalities on supposed anti-American activities. These accusations encouraged the opponents of the Popular Front. Moreover, the big film bosses feared that the antifascist campaign would result in a boycott of American films in Germany and Italy. Jack Warner himself only once attacked Nazism publicly, when the Nazis murdered a Warner Brothers representative who was Jewish.
37. The Roosevelt administration had declared itself neutral out of fear of offending the Catholic hierarchy, who supported Franco, as well as not wanting to find itself on the same side as the Soviet Union. Congress had voted for an arms embargo on the belligerent countries.
38. They included Communists and liberals. No one at this time thought of hiding their political ideas. It is remarkable that not one of the leaders of the Hollywood Popular Front escaped questioning in the McCarthy era.
39. Some 57 per cent of individuals blacklisted in the McCarthy era were screenwriters, and between 20 and 25 per cent actors.
40. The American Labor Party, for example, broke into an anti-pact group (led by David Dubinsky) and a pro-pact group (led by Vito Marcantonio).
41. Melvyn Douglas's career was broken off in 1950, when Richard Nixon accused him of being a Communist. Philip Dunne had written the script for the film *How Green Was My Valley*.

42. It is hard to tell, however, who at this time really was a Communist rather than just a fellow-traveller.

43. Actors wishing to defend their careers were now increasingly forced to separate themselves from any 'red' or 'pink' organization linked to the CPUSA. Melvyn Douglas became a target for the right, and was constantly accused of being a Communist. When he was nominated by Eleanor Roosevelt to head the Arts Council of the Office of Civilian Defense's Voluntary Participation Branch, the press pointed out that his real name was Hesselburg. He was forced to resign, and enlisted in the Army.

44. On 7 May 1940, the American Civil Liberties Union expelled its director Elizabeth Gurley Flynn, accused of being a Communist.

45. A Gallup poll in July 1944 indicated that 72 per cent of Americans were favorable to the USSR as against only 4 per cent to Germany. A similar reversal was also notable among the émigrés. The majority of these, however, had very complex feelings towards the Soviet Union. Feuchtwanger expressed himself quite critically about Stalin, and Heinrich Mann likewise distrusted him. Brecht never believed in the Moscow trials. Ernest Bloch, however, though not really close to the KPD, justified them in a perspective that was similar to Merleau-Ponty's in his *Humanism and Terror*. Klaus Mann never had any great sympathy for the USSR, but he noted in *The Turning Point* (p. 355): 'The fact that Russia seems free, at this point, of the pernicious Fifth Column bacillus is perhaps mainly due to the relentless purges of 1937.' Even Thomas Mann, who had termed the German–Soviet pact as 'one of the greatest perversions of history', now went to see films praising the Soviet Union.

46. The majority of Hollywood singers performed for the benefit of the California Shipbuilding Corporation. Marlene Dietrich tells in her memoirs how she got up at three in the morning to sing for the night shift, and performed several sets each hour. She took part in all the welfare galas for the government service, and raised $1,025 for the Red Cross by selling kisses. In 1944 she toured several US bases, singing for the GIs in Algeria, Italy and France, often using the headlights of a Jeep. By way of reprisal, the Nazis sent her sister, who remained in Germany, to concentration camp. Dietrich herself, during one of her tours to the front, was almost captured by her close namesake, the SS general Sepp Dietriche, and the 88th Airborne division had to intervene to prevent this.

47. Michael Wilson and Michael Blankfort fought in the US Navy, Edward Muebsch and Ben Maddow in the Army in Europe. Budd Schubert was also in the Navy, Arthur Strawn and Stanley Rubin in the Air Force.

48. In Hollywood and Los Angeles, the Unity for Victory Committee, the Screen Actors' Guild and the Californian Federation of Labor.

49. This had its equivalent in New York and Washington DC in the Writers' War Board.

50. *Hollywood Quarterly*, cited in *Exil in den USA*, p. 430.

51. These included *Know Your Allies Know Your Enemies*, *Secret Magazine* and *The Negro Soldier*.

52. Among the most famous were *The Battle for Russia*, *The City That Stopped Hitler*, *Heroic Stalingrad*. The commentary was written by John Wexley, author of *Confessions of a Nazi Spy* and a friend of Brecht.

53. Made by the Crown Film Unit, whose cameramen were authorized to shoot in combat zones.

54. A number of anti-Nazi cartoons were made. MGM produced a parody of *Three Little Pigs*, with Hitler in the role of the Big Bad Wolf. In Walt Disney's *Der Fuehrer's Face*, Donald Duck imitated Hitler and assiduously read *Mein Kampf*.

55. Cf. Frank Capra, *The Name Above the Title*, London 1972, pp. 335–6.

56. Fritz Kortner, Helene Thimig, Alexander Granach and Reinhold Schnüzel all acted in *The Hitler Gang*.

57. Born in Hungary, Curtiz had made films in Austria and Germany.

816 WEIMAR IN EXILE

58. Other less well-known émigrés acting in this film included Paul von Heinreid, Curt Bois, Ilka Grüning, Ludwig Stössel and Szöke Szakall.
59. He had directed *Menschen am Sonntag* together with Robert Siodmak in 1929.
60. The leading role was played by Spencer Tracy.
61. To cite some examples: R. Wallace's *The Wife Takes a Flyer*, Franz Borzage's *Stage Door Canteen*, D. Daves's *Hollywood Canteen* and Billy Wilder's *Uniforms and Short Skirts*.
62. For example: *Thirty Seconds over Tokyo* by M. Le Roy, *Memphis Belle* by William Wyler, *Air Force* by Howard Hawks, *A Yank in the RAF* by H. King, *Dive Bomber* by Michael Curtiz, *I Wanted Wings* by Mitchell Leisen, and *The Purple Heart* by Lewis Milestone.
63. *Story of GI Joe* by W. Wellman depicted the Italian campaign. H. Shumlin's films *I Love a Soldier*, *A Guy Named Joe* and *Watch on the Rhine* should also be mentioned.
64. John Farrone's *Wake Island*, T. Garnett's *Bataan Patrol*, R. Walsh's *Adventures in Burma*.
65. Brecht and Fritz Lang were acquainted long before 1933. They had met in Munich, introduced by Peter Lorre. Lang subsequently helped to pay Brecht's passage to the United States.
66. Produced by Arnold Pressburger for Twentieth Century Fox. Lang had already directed *Man Hunt* for Fox, which tackled the subject of fascism.
67. Brecht and Dieterle worked first of all on a film based on his 'Ballad of the Nazi Soldier's Wife', then on *Schweyk in the Second World War*, designed to contribute to the Council for a Democratic Germany, but the project seems to have been abandoned by the US authorities.
68. SS-Gruppenführer in 1934, head of Reich security in 1938, Reinhard Heydrich (1904–42) organized the massive deportation of Jews from Poland (*Aktion Reinhard*). He died of wounds received in Prague on 27 May 1942 from a bomb thrown by Czech resisters who had been dropped by parachute. The authors of the attack were immediately executed by the SS. By way of reprisal, the village of Lidice was destroyed by an SS unit, and its inhabitants deported to Ravensbrück. In Prague, 1,331 Czechs were hung, including 201 women. Goebbels also had 500 Jews arrested in Berlin, 152 of whom were executed.
69. B. Brecht, *Journals*, p. 236. The idea seems to have come from Lang. He obtained a contract of $7,500 for Brecht, who had only asked for $3,000.
70. Ibid., p. 243.
71. 'All this recent time, hack work on the hostages story with Lang. I am supposed to receive $5,000 and then $3,000 for the further collaboration' (18 July 1942; ibid., p. 248).
72. Ibid., p. 249.
73. This collaboration became necessary because Brecht spoke English poorly and could not write it, while Wexley, a member of the CPUSA, spoke perfect German.
74. Lang wanted the Czech characters, even the least important, to be played by actors who spoke correct English. He accordingly rejected Helene Weigel and Oskar Homolka. He justified this decision by saying that if the Czechs spoke English with a German accent, the audience would lose the thread of the story and take them for Germans.
75. Cf. *Filmkritik* 223, July 1975. The political and artistic differences between Brecht and Lang were compounded by a financial conflict between Brecht and Wexler, who was favoured over Brecht in the contract. The two appeared before the Screen Writers' Guild tribunal. Despite the evidence of Lang and Eisler, the tribunal declared that Wexley was entitled to declare himself sole author of the script, even though Lang himself agreed that some scenes were typically Brechtian. The tribunal's argument was specious: according to Lang, it believed that Brecht would return to Germany in due course while Wexley would remain in the United States. It was thus more useful for Wexley than for Brecht to be seen as the script's sole author. In fact, in the McCarthy era Wexley's name disappeared from films altogether.

CHAPTER 18   PERSPECTIVES ON GERMANY

1. Bertolt Brecht, 'Homecoming', *Poems 1913–1956*, p. 392.
2. Brecht, *Journals*, p. 237 (1 June 1942).
3. Ibid.
4. *Der Wendepunkt*, p. 434. [This passage does not appear in the English edition of *The Turning Point*.]
5. Brecht, *Journals*, p. 324.
6. Ibid., p. 344.
7. 'Zerstörte Sprache – Zerstörte Kultur'.
8. 'Barbarians and Musicians' (1939), 'The Germans, Double History of a Nation' (1941), 'How to Treat the Germans' (1943), 'The Moral Conquest of Germany'. Close to the Social-Democrats, Emil Ludwig was not a real émigré, having lived in Switzerland since 1906. The Nazis never missed the occasion to point out that his real name was Ludwig Cohn.
9. His message was published in *Freies Deutschland* on 6 August 1943.
10. Cf. Brecht, *Journals*, p. 288, where the manifesto is reproduced in its entirety along with Brecht's comments on the attitude of Thomas Mann.
11. Brecht, *Journals*, p. 291 (9 August 1943).
12. Ibid., p. 306.
13. Thomas Mann, *Gesammelte Werke*, vol. 11, p. 989.
14. Ibid., p. 991.
15. Ibid., p. 994.
16. Ibid., p. 1010.
17. Ibid., p. 1018.
18. This was in his lecture 'The War and the Peace', delivered at Columbia University in mid November 1943. The same ambivalence towards Germany can be found among several of the émigrés. Theodor Adorno wrote in 1944: 'To the question what is to be done with defeated Germany, I could say only two things in reply. Firstly: at no price, on no conditions, would I wish to be an executioner or to supply legitimations for executioners. Secondly: I should not wish, least of all with legal machinery, to stay the hand of anyone who was avenging past misdeeds' (*Minima Moralia*, London 1973, p. 56).
19. Letter to Bertolt Brecht, 10 December 1943; *Letters of Thomas Mann 1889–1955*, pp. 327–8.
20. Letter to Erich von Kahler, 16 January 1944.
21. Letter to Clifton Fadiman, 29 May 1944.
22. Letter to Agnes E. Meyer, 29 March 1945.
23. *Behemoth* was certainly inspired by Hobbes, but also by Jewish eschatology, in which Behemoth and Leviathan were the monsters that respectively dominated the earth and the sea. *Behemoth* depicted the Nazi regime as a 'chaos', a 'non-state', the situation of radical evil and absolute injustice.
24. As well as analysing the role of the middle classes in the rise of Nazism his book *The Salaried Masses*, Kracauer also described the psychological mechanisms of German cinema in *From Caligari to Hitler*, London 1947.
25. Loewenthal particularly distinguished the mass base, the party and the state.
26. Similar discussions had already begun in the political articles by Leopold Schwarzschild and his friends during their Paris exile. For more details of their respective positions, cf. J. Radkau, *Die deutsche Emigration in den USA*, pp. 236ff. Here we can do no more than just sketch them.
27. The role of Prussia in the genesis of National Socialism was far from being unanimously agreed among the émigrés. Some of them, such as Sebastian Haffner, became nostalgic historians and eulogists of Prussia in the 1980s.
28. Such debate had indeed begun early on in the émigré ranks. On 15 July 1939, Leopold Schwarzschild published in *Das Neue Tage-Buch* an article, 'Am Tag danach', in which he proposed the occupation of Germany after the fall of Nazism

and the dismantling of its institutions. Hermann Budzislawski replied to him in the *Neue Weltbühne* (no. 31, 2 August 1939), and so did Hubertus Prinz zu Löwenstein (*Nach Hitlers Fall*). The latter accused Schwarzschild of wanting to liberate Germany by replacing one dictatorship by another. Schwarzschild's thesis was defended in France at this time by Henri de Kerillis, and attacked by Léon Blum (cf. Hubertus Prinz zu Löwenstein, *Botschafter ohne Auftrag*, p. 173).

29. Former Prussian minister of the interior and head of the Berlin police.
30. Its leadership included B. Katz and Max Brauer. Hermann Rauschning and Otto Strasser were both members of the Association.
31. *Gesammelte Werke*, vol. 11, p. 1013.
32. The American Association for a Democratic Germany functioned from June to October 1944, with funds of $4,228. (Cf. J. Radkau, *Die deutsche Emigration in den USA*, p. 198.)
33. This demand was attacked in the *New York Herald Tribune* by William Shirer, who accused them of having not a word of regret for the past; Shirer somehow forgot that the émigrés themselves had been victims of Nazism.
34. He also feared that his name would be used to gain publicity, without managing to interest anyone in his ideas. Alfred Kantorowicz did not join the Council, 'for lack of time' as he declared in his *Deutsches Tagebuch* (p. 164). But he did sign its manifesto, which led to a violent attack on him by the Social-Democrat Rheinhardt on the New York radio station WINS, as a 'Stalinist agent' hiding behind a pseudonym. The Council, for its part, was accused of being pan-Germanist.
35. Tillich was offered professorships by a number of German universities, but declined. He made many visits to Germany, taught for two years in Hamburg, and received an impressive number of distinctions in the Federal Republic, but he remained in the United States until his death in Chicago in 1965.
36. Hubertus Prinz zu Löwenstein had campaigned since 1940 against a territorial amputation of Germany. He worked with J. F. Dulles on a memorandum, *Foundation of an Equitable Peace* (1943), then on the Post-War World Council. His defence of Germany led him to quarrel with Thomas Mann. He broke with the Freies Deutschland committee in Mexico on learning that the USSR planned to give Poland a piece of East Prussia, an act that he attacked as 'neo-Nazism'. For him, the only way of establishing a democratic Germany in a federal Europe was to restore the former republican government, based on the Weimar constitution, along with the black, red and gold flag. In 1945 the new mayor of Weimar, recently freed from concentration camp, hoisted the republican flag, but this was banned by the Allies.
37. Shirer had even attacked articles by the Social-Democrat Friedrich Stampfer published in the *Neue Volkszeitung* at the end of 1943, which argued for a continental federation in opposition to Soviet hegemony.
38. A Gallup poll in July 1942 found that 79 per cent of Americans viewed the German government as their enemy, but only 6 per cent saw the German people in this light.
39. Lord Vansittart detested Germany in general, as did H. G. Wells. Curt Geyer had been active in the USDP, then the KPD, before rallying to the right-wing Social-Democrats. Leopold Schwarzschild was anti-Communist, and his distrust of Germany drew roots from his old-established pacifist convictions.
40. The KPD press followed the Allies' discussions and international conferences without taking a position in favour of any particular settlement. The Freies Deutschland Committee called for the restoration of the sovereignty of oppressed peoples, the perspective of a policy of peace in cooperation with the USSR, but refrained from responding to the various Social-Democrat proposals. It should be noted that the French Communist party had rejected the idea of a global federation in the Socialist party's proposal for joint Resistance activity, on the grounds that it would restrict national sovereignty. It was also the idea of national sovereignty that Kurt Hager maintained in his article of 1945 in the *Freie Tribüne*.

41. On the diversity of Socialist plans at this time, cf. Johannes Klotz, *Das kommende Deutschland* (Pahl-Rugenstein, Hochschulschriften 132).
42. Klaus Mann, *Der Wendepunkt*. [Not in the English edition of *The Turning Point*.]
43. *Christen im Nationalkomitee 'Freies Deutschland'*, ed. Klaus Drobisch, Berlin 1972.
44. Cf. Wolfgang Leonhard, op. cit., pp. 285–6.
45. The son of Wilhelm Pieck played an important role on it.
46. The battle of Stalingrad, which saw the capitulation of the German Sixth Army under the command of Field-Marshal Paulus, led to a complete massacre of the German forces. Out of an effective strength of 330,000 men, only 6,000 returned. It was after this battle, at which the encircled army was completely abandoned by the Nazis, while Göring celebrated the glorious death of men who were still alive beneath the rubble, that a number of German officers realized the madness of Hitler's orders. Cf. Joachim Wieder, *Stalingrad ou la responsabilité du soldat*, Paris 1983. I would like to thank the author, an officer of the general staff at Stalingrad and an antifascist, for the account he gave me of his adhesion to Freies Deutschland.
47. The slogans launched in the appeal were: 'For people and fatherland! Against Hitler and his war! For an immediate peace! For the salvation of the German people! For a free and independent Germany!'
48. Delegates from the five main POW camps had taken part in the founding meeting of the Committee.
49. It is still hard to establish whether soldiers recruited in the POW camps were genuinely won over to the antifascist cause, or were simply aware that the War was lost and that this would give them a chance of being better treated by the Soviets. Joachim Wieder, a member of the Freies Deutschland Committee, confirmed to me that many soldiers joined for very understandable practical reasons rather than for ideological ones.
50. Cf. among others: H. K. Bergman, *Die Bewegung 'Freies Deutschland' in der Schweiz 1943–47*, Munich 1974.

CHAPTER 19   THE ANTIFASCIST ÉMIGRÉS AND THE BEGINNINGS OF MCCARTHYISM

1. Letter to Agnes E. Meyer, 1 December 1946; *Letters of Thomas Mann 1889–1955*, p. 373.
2. Letter to Mr Gray (draft), 12 October 1947; ibid., p. 383.
3. Cf. C. Belfrage, *The American Inquisition 1945–1960*, New York 1973. Also Larry Ceplair and Steven Englund, *The Inquisition in Hollywood. Politics in the Film Community 1930–1960*, Berkeley 1979.
4. The figures most active in this included Erskine Caldwell, Jack Conroy, Theodore Dreiser, Langston Hughes, Nathanael West and Richard Wright. (Cf. *1935. New York 1937. Reden und Dokumente der Schriftstellerkongresse*, ed. von Brüning, Berlin 1984.)
5. Cf. Margaret Brenman-Gibson, *Clifford Odets*, New York 1982.
6. C. Belfrage, *The American Inquisition*, p. 12. The spectre of bolshevism led to a regular psychosis. One of the most famous examples was the campaign launched in the early 1920s against the American dancer Isadora Duncan, who had married the Russian poet Sergei Yessenin. She was accused of bolshevik propaganda after dancing with a red veil.
7. Guy Endore, John Howard Lawson, Melvin Levy, Samuel Ornitz, Georg Sklar, Phillip Stevenson, Nathanael West, Erskine Caldwell, Theodore Dreiser and Richard Wright.
8. Senator McCarthy's committee listed two hundred, which would represent some 15 per cent of the number of screenwriters.
9. 'We were not only Communists, we were American again. We were readily convinced that [Marxism and Americanism] were not only compatible but insepar-

able' (George Charney, *A Long Journey*, Chicago 1968, p. 59). Cited after L. Ceplair and S. Englund, *The Inquisition in Hollywood*, p. 55.

10. Cf. L. Ceplair and S. Englund, *The Inquisition in Hollywood*.
11. These included J. B. Matthews, John Rankin, Parnell Thomas, F. Spellmann, Robert Taft, E. Johnston, William F. Buckley, James Burnham and Arthur Schlesinger Jr.
12. Led by Sam Wood, a fanatical anti-Communist, and supported by Walt Disney, John Wayne and Gary Cooper. Wood died of a heart attack in September 1949, brought on by a fit of rage against a screenwriter whose dismissal for Communist activities he was demanding. He had specified in his will that only people who could prove they had no connection with Communism would be allowed to attended his funeral.
13. See the interesting study by Victor Navalsky, *Les Délateurs. Le cinéma américain et la chasse au sorcières*, Paris 1982, which studied the motivations of the 'friendly witnesses'.
14. Nineteen writers were summoned to appear before HUAC in October 1947. Of the eleven who were actually questioned, ten were condemned to prison terms – the 'Hollywood Ten'; the eleventh, Bertolt Brecht, immediately left the United States.
15. These were FBI agents who infiltrated progressive organizations, and sometimes even Hollywood figures such as Edward Dmytryk and Elia Kazan.
16. The Committee for the First Amendment was founded by William Wyler, Phillip Dune, John Huston and Alexander Knox. It won the support of Humphrey Bogart, Danny Kaye, Myrna Loy, Katherine Hepburn, Fredric March and Richard Rodgers.
17. Brecht declared that Hitler would not have come to power if there had been more people like John Howard Lawson in Germany.
18. Hermann Kesten was denounced to the FBI as a 'Communist' and 'former Nazi' by a fellow émigré, Eva Landshoff (letter from A. Neumann to H. Kesten, 13 August 1941; *Deutsche Literatur in Exil*).
19. Heinrich Mann, Franz Werfel and Lion Feuchtwanger had all used false papers.
20. In the United States, Ruth Fischer had financed an information bulletin on Stalinism in Europe, *The Network*, in which she denounced émigré figures as 'Stalinist spies'; she did the same in the *American Mercury*. Under this rubric she attacked Elisabeth Bergner, Paul Tillich, Fritz Kortner, Ludwig Marcuse, Albert Grzesinski and Thomas Mann. Her denunciations were no less dangerous for coming from a pathological and indeed paranoid personality. Chaplin said to Eisler on hearing that he had been denounced by his sister: 'It's like Shakespeare in your family.' (Cited in A. Betz, *Hanns Eisler*, p. 165).
21. In particular Clifford Odets, Chaplin, and Stella Adler.
22. The former editor of the *Daily Worker*, Louis Budenz, had called Gerhart Eisler the real leader of the CPUSA. In autumn 1946, Fischer published a series of articles on her brother, to back up her denunciation.
23. Cf. A. Betz, *Hanns Eisler*, pp. 167ff; Jürgen Schebera, *Hanns Eisler in den USA-Exil*, pp. 139ff.
24. Parnell Thomas, the chair of HUAC, was subsequently imprisoned for misappropriation of public funds.
25. A. Betz, *Hanns Eisler*, p. 169.
26. *Letters of Thomas Mann 1889–1955*, pp. 390–1.
27. 'Thomas Mann joined with a retired bishop and California's former Immigration and Housing Commissioner Carey McWilliams in a committee to defend Gerhart Eisler' (C. Belfrage, *The American Inquisition*, p. 64).
28. The scientist Linus Pauling was working on nuclear research. He was later accused of being a 'Jap-lover' for having employed a Japanese caretaker at his Pasadena home.
29. Harry Cain, a senator for Washington state, demanded the immediate expulsion of Chaplin for having tried to mobilize 'the Communist Picasso' in favour of Eisler.

Chaplin was accused of having used the word 'comrades' in speaking to actors. He was boycotted throughout the United States, and cinemas were covered with inscriptions such as 'Send Chaplin to Russia'.

30. Eisler and Thomas Mann were on close terms, as is clear from Mann's letter quoted above. Eisler accused Brecht – who could never stand Thomas Mann – of failing to see 'what was deeply human' in him.

31. Eisler's musical works won praise in the American press. Premiered at this concert were his violin sonata, quintet 'La Pluie', and his second septet.

32. Quoted by A. Betz, *Hanns Eisler*, p. 173.

33. Gerhart Eisler managed to board the *Batory* with a box of chocolates and a large bouquet of flowers. He settled down on a deckchair until he was discovered to be a 'clandestine passenger'. In Southampton he was handed to the British police, who allowed him to continue to Berlin.

34. A recording on disc was made of this, presented by Brecht's English translator Eric Bentley, and issued by Folkways in 1961.

35. Even at the time it was written, this play aroused controversy within the KPD, as its moral is very debatable and hard to justify.

36. On the situation of Lion Feuchtwanger in the United States after 1945, cf. his correspondence with Arnold Zweig, especially the letters of March 1947. He was attacked by the press in 1949 for having signed, along with Heinrich Mann, a telegram of congratulation to Wilhelm Pieck on the foundation of the German Democratic Republic. Feuchtwanger never wrote his projected novel on exile life in California in the McCarthy era (*Die sieben Weisen*).

37. Those émigrés who had never been involved in any political activity in the United States, devoting themselves entirely to their work, were also disturbed. Ernst Bloch was summoned to hearings in Boston several times as a 'premature antifascist'. He was only known from articles of his that had appeared in émigré publications, especially *Freies Deutschland* in Mexico. On several occasions attempts were made to make him confess that he was a Communist, by questions of the kind: 'Did you never frequent company in which Communism was spoken of?' Bloch asked this official of the Immigration Service if he had ever frequented company in which Communism was not spoken of. After several hearings, Bloch declared that if he was not to be given US nationality, he preferred to carry on with his work rather than waste time traveling from Cambridge to Boston. He was summoned for one last time and questioned on American history. He knew this so well that the officials were impressed. (Karola Bloch, *Aus Meinem Leben*, pp. 175–6).

38. In exile in the United States since 1933, Einstein had been referred to by Dean Rusk as 'a baby in politics'. When he took US citizenship in 1946, the right-wing press called Einstein a 'Jewish Communist refugee'.

39. Held in March 1949, at the Waldorf-Astoria hotel in New York. A similar conference was held in Paris, with the participation of James Farrell, Richard Wright, Jean-Paul Sartre, Albert Camus and Carlo Levi.

40. C. Belfrage, *The American Inquisition*, p. 94.

41. Thomas Mann refused to the end of his life the three great prizes of Communist provenance that were offered him: the National Prize of the GDR, the Stalin Prize, and the World Peace Prize, though without giving any publicity to his refusal. He declined the proposal to give his name to a foundation at Leipzig University. After accepting the Goethe Prize in Weimar, however, he agreed to become honorary president of the Academy of Fine Arts in Munich.

42. Letter to S. Marck, 1 January 1950. In a letter to Adorno of 9 January 1950, Mann recalled that 'Recently, the Beverly Wilshire Hotel refused its hall for a *dinner* of the Arts, Sciences and Professions Council because a *communist* like Doctor Mann was to speak at it' (*Letters of Thomas Mann*, p. 423).

43. Letter to Walter H. Perl, 25 March 1950.

44. Letter to the editors of *Der Aufbau*.

45. Although the majority of exile groups imagined in the War years the possibility of a

'European federation' that would triumph over nationalism, they had no very clear idea what this would consist of. Thomas Mann wrote in 1945 on 'Germany and the Germans': 'It is in this hospitable *cosmopolis*, the racial and national universe that goes by the name of America, that my kind of German-ness is best preserved.' Before obtaining US citizenship, Mann had already acquired Czech nationality. Klaus Mann wrote in *Der Wendepunkt*: 'I am no longer a German. Am I still an émigré? My ambition would be to become a world citizen with American nationality' (p. 396). [This passage does not appear in the English edition of *The Turning Point*.]

46. C. Zuckmayer, *Als wär's ein Stück von mir. Erinnerungen*, pp. 540ff.

47. Fred Uhlmann, *Il fait beau à Paris aujourd'hui*, pp. 137–8.

48. Franz Werfel, Bruno Frank, R. Beer-Hoffmann, Else Lasker-Schüler, Georg Kaiser and Alfred Wolfenstein died in 1945, Salomo Friedländer in 1946, Egon Erwin Kisch, Karl Wolfskehl, Alfred Kerr, Emil Ludwig and Adam Scharrer in 1948, Klaus Mann and Balder Olden in 1949, Albert Ehrenstein, Heinrich Mann, Yvan Goll and Leopold Schwarzschild in 1950, Hermann Broch in 1951, Alfred Neumann in 1952, Rudolf Leonhard, Bruno Viertel, Erich Weinert and Friedrich Wolf in 1953, Julius Bab, Martin Gumpert, Thomas Mann, Theodor Plievier, Alfred Polgar and F. C. Wieskopf in 1955, Bertolt Brecht in 1956, Alfred Döblin and Louis Fürnberg in 1957, Lion Feuchtwanger and J. R. Becher in 1958.

49. The list of émigrés who died before 1945 includes the following names: Max Reinhardt, Sigmund Freud, Stefan Zweig, Hellmut von Gerlach, Arno Goldschmidt, F. Hessel, W. Hegemann, A. Holitscher, Ödön von Horvath, Georg Kaiser, H. G. Kessler, Monty Jacobs, Robert Musil, Max Hermann-Neisse, Rudolf Olden, Joseph Roth, René Schickele, Jakob Wassermann, Paul Zech, Kurt Tucholsky, Walter Benjamin, W. Hasenclever, Ernst Weiss and Carl Einstein. Brecht was only forty-seven in 1945, while Carl Zuckmayer was forty-nine, George Grosz fifty-two, Hermann Broch fifty-nine, Ernst Bloch sixty, Lion Feuchtwanger sixty-one, Alfred Döblin sixty-seven, Thomas Mann seventy, Heinrich Mann seventy-four, and Else Lasker-Schüler seventy-seven when she died at the beginning of the year.

50. *Aufbau*, 1963, p. 65.

51. Thomas Mann wrote to Emil Belzner on 21 March 1950: 'That *not a word* came from Bonn, Frankfurt, Munich or Lübeck, his birthplace – it's wretched.'

52. Heinrich Mann, who suffered cruelly from poverty and oblivion in America, had received in 1949 an invitation from the GDR authorities to settle in East Berlin: a house had been put at his disposal by the new Akademie der Künste. As his Czech passport was no longer valid, he had to wait to get it renewed, and had booked a place on a Polish ship due to leave New York on 28 April 1950. He died on 12 March. A fragment of his ashes was taken to East Berlin in 1961.

53. Some, like Ernst and Karola Bloch, had to sell their libraries once more. In the case of academics, their families were generally only able to join them a year later.

54. A place on a military vessel was available only if travelling on official business, which presupposed important connections.

55. Thomas Mann mentioned in a letter to Viktor Mann (27 March 1947) the declaration by Ernst Wiechert, who had moved to Switzerland unable to endure the situation in postwar Germany, that 'if Hitler came back tomorrow, sixty to eighty per cent of the people would receive him with hurrahs' (*Letters of Thomas Mann*, p. 385).

56. On 11 March 1947, Mann wrote to Manfred George: 'From Furtwängler's memorandum, as from so many other documents, I see once again what an abysmal gulf lies between our experience and that of the people who remained behind in Germany. Communication across this gulf is completely impossible [. . .]' (ibid., p. 383).

57. Golo Mann, *Colloque sur la littérature de l'exil*, p. 40.

58. Letter of 2 December 1945 to Carl Seelig.

59. This was generally the case with Communist writers, but also for Piscator, who, after returning to Germany, tried to achieve a moral catharsis through his 'theatre of confession' and productions such as Rolf Hochhuth's play *The Representative.*
60. Lotte Eisner decided against revisiting Berlin, where she had spent her youth.
61. Paul Tillich, for example, turned down a university chair in Hamburg and remained in the United States. Walter A. Berendsohn, one of the first historians of exile literature, stayed in Sweden. Many academics who had settled in the United States abandoned the idea of returning to Europe. Their children often became Germanists, translators – even historians of exile literature.
62. Carl Zuckmayer recalled in his memoirs (*Als wär's ein Stück von mir,* p. 528) that in the first postwar years it was almost impossible to visit Germany except through the occupation forces. Even post and parcels were prohibited. There were no regular shipping lines between America and Europe, only military vessels. Even those German émigrés who had kept their nationality were not authorized to visit Germany. Those who had become US citizens were expressly forbidden to visit Germany without special permission, or unless they were in the military. When Zuckmayer tried to visit Germany, he had to fill in almost as many forms as if he had been a former leader of the Hitler Youth. He had to wait a long while until was commissioned by the State Department to investigate the state of German cultural institutions.
63. Many émigrés returned to their native country simply to die there. Egon Erwin Kisch returned to Prague in 1946, and died in 1948. And what can be said of those like Jean Amery who returned to Germany or Austria before taking their own life?
64. The complicity of American soldiers was needed, who then forwarded the parcels to the émigrés' families. Sometimes the émigrés sent photos of their children or grandchildren. Among the most moving correspondence in this period is that of Piscator. After having had practically no news of his many relatives still in Germany since his arrival in America, he now found himself asked for assistance (family correspondence, archives of the Akademie der Künste, West Berlin).
65. C. Zuckmayer, *Als wär's ein Stück von mir,* p. 527.
66. Letter of 11 December 1953, Akademie der Künste. Anne-Marie Hirsch described 'a field of ruins and snow, an image of the end of the world' (*Retour à Weimar,* p. 54).
67. F. Uhlmann, *Il fait beau à Paris aujourd'hui,* p. 137.
68. Alfred Döblin, *Vaterland, Muttersprache. Deutsche Schriftsteller und ihr Staat von 1945 bis heute,* Berlin 1979, pp. 26–7.
69. Already in a poem of 1939, 'An einem Freund in Deutschland', Max Hermann-Neisse had written: 'If we meet again one day, neither of us will be able to understand the other.'
70. M. Sperber, *Au-delà de l'oubli,* pp. 74–5.
71. Klaus Mann wore American uniform on his return to Germany. Alfred Döblin gave lectures in Baden-Baden, Mainz and Wiesbaden in French uniform; he was officially given charge of the direction of public education. Stefan Heym was also in the US forces. Carl Zuckmayer was carrying out a mission for the State Department and Hans Habe, who established a press company in 1945 that immediately published a dozen newspapers with a combined circulation of 4.5 million, was a counter-espionage officer in the US Army. Willy Brandt began his postwar career in Berlin as Norwegian press attaché. Many émigrés had sons fighting in French or US uniform (Brecht, Döblin, Thomas Mann). Heinrich Fraenkel wore British uniform, as did Peter de Mendelssohn and W. Hildesheimer. J. R. Becher, Friedrich Wolf. Ludwig Renn and Willi Bredel returned to Germany with the Red Army.
72. See for example the debate between Frank Thiess and Thomas Mann, or Ernst von Salomon's *The Questionnaire.*
73. 'Here, in the ocean of ruins that is Berlin, living in cold and misery, we solemnly call on the writers of our nation!' The appeal was addressed among others to Ernst Bloch, Bertolt Brecht, Hermann Broch, Ferdinand Bruckner, Albert Ehrenstein,

Lion Feuchtwanger, Leonhard Frank, Oskar Maria Graf, Wieland Herzfelde, Hermann Hesse, E. Huelsenbeck, Alfred Kerr, K. Kläber, Rudolf Leonhard, Ludwig Marcuse, Thomas Mann, Heinrich Mann, Walter Mehring, P. Meyer, Alfred Neumann, Roger Neumann, Balder Olden, Heinrich Pol, H. J. Rehfisch, Erich Maria Remarque, Anna Seghers, A. Schaeffer, M. Scheer, Fritz von Unruh, Bodo Uhse, Bruno Viertel, Ernst Waldinger and Arnold Zweig.

74. Oral testimony of Lotte Eisner.
75. Cf. *Retour à Weimar*.
76. Several German writers asked Thomas Mann to intervene in the de-Nazification process, but in many cases he refused to testify in their favour. He renewed his connection with Hans Carossa, but rejected a request from Rudolf W. Blunck, interned by the British army in 1945 (letter to Blunck of 19 November 1945). Mann did however defend Furtwängler (letter to Manfred George, 11 March 1947; *Letters of Thomas Mann*, pp. 383–4). His position towards his old friend Ernst Bertram, dismissed from his university post, was more complex: 'I am against Bertram's being recalled to an academic teaching position. [. . .] But I am decidedly for his being granted a decent retirement salary and the right to determine his own rules for his creative work' (letter to Werner Schmitz, 30 July 1948; *Letters of Thomas Mann*, p. 404). He remained hostile to Ernst Jünger, even if he considered him a great stylist. In a letter to Agnes E. Meyer of 15 December 1945, Mann described Jünger as a 'pioneer and glacial sybarite of barbarism'.
77. In a short work published by P. Keppler Verlag in Baden-Baden in 1947, *Die literarische Situation*, Döblin already raised the question of the relationship of new German literature to that of the émigrés.
78. Letter to Leopold Marcuse, 16 August 1952. Similar complaints can be found in letters from Walter Mehring and Albert Ehrenstein. The fact that émigré works found so little place in the German book market in the postwar years is also explained by the attitude of the US Army, which saturated its occupation zone with American works, and also had control over publications. It should be noted that Ernest Hemingway's *A Farewell to Arms* was published by Rowohlt in 1946 in an edition of 600,000 copies, while *Life*, *Harper's* and *Reader's Digest* became the foundations of a new culture. But the novels of Erskine Caldwell and William Faulkner were not authorized by the occupying authorities, as they gave a negative image of America. Any publication had to be passed by the Book Translation Unit.
79. This was published in the GDR in 1956 by Rütter und Loenig, and in the Federal Republic the following year by Albert Langen Müller.
80. See Chapter 3, section 8.
81. Oral communication from Stella Adler.
82. His production of Leopold Frank's *Karl und Anna* was suspended following demonstrations by ex-soldiers.
83. H. Müssener cites the case of Ferdinand Bruckner, an exile in the United States. Out of 543 reviews of his plays between 1946 and 1958, only fifty-five mentioned his emigration. More than 390 either failed completely to mention his absence from Germany between 1933 and 1945, or referred to this without giving any explanation (*Rückkehr aus dem Exil im Spiegel zeitgenössischer Kritik*. Akademie der Künste. Sammlung Theater im Exil).
84. His play *The Devil's General* had 3,238 performances between 1947 and 1950.
85. Feuchtwanger died in California on 21 December 1958, aged seventy-four.
86. *Letters of Thomas Mann*, p. 356.
87. Letter to Agnes E. Meyer, 25 August 1945; *Letters of Thomas Mann*, p. 354.
88. Letter to Walter von Molo, 7 September 1945.
89. Ibid.
90. Letter to Emil Preetorius, 20 October 1949; *Letters of Thomas Mann*, p. 420.
91. *Letters of Thomas Mann*, p. 423.
92. The case of Heinrich Mann and his reception in West Germany deserves a study of its own. Not only was he completely ignored in the postwar years, his books not

reissued and his name forgotten, but in 1975, when the town of Lübeck celebrated with acclaim the centenary of his brother, the bust of Heinrich in the Behnhaus was not to be seen. Thomas Mann had been made an 'honorary citizen' of Lübeck in his lifetime, and after his death was called its 'greatest son'. But the town was still not reconciled with Heinrich. It was not until 1971 that the first symposium on his work was held in the Federal Republic, and an Arbeitkreis Heinrich Mann was established. In 1981 Lübeck finally voted funds to commemorate him. Many other émigrés had an equally strange fate. Ernst Weiss's novel *Der Augenzeuge* was published posthumously by Suhrkamp in 1963, and his work was only rediscovered in 1982. Leonhard Frank still awaits rediscovery. The city council of Würzburg, his home town, refused to name a street after him, though he was one of the great pacifist writers of the expressionist generation. He was not excused for having been praised in the GDR.

The expressionist poet Albert Ehrenstein returned to Germany in 1949. But after being unable to get his work published in exile, he could not find a publisher in Germany either. He decided therefore to return to America, where he wrote practically nothing more. He died in a charity hospital in Manhattan on 8 April 1950. He had lived throughout his exile in furnished rooms, writing reviews for *Aufbau* or the *Austro-American Tribune*. It was often not until the 1970s that émigré works were properly republished, and enjoyed a certain popularity with the new generation. (On the reception of the exiles in the Federal Republic, cf. Gerhard Worms, *Exil und Exilliteratur in der deutschen Presse, 1945–1949*, Worms 1976.)

93. As a general rule, the British and American occupation authorities made no effort to facilitate the return of 'progressive' émigrés to Germany. While the Soviet zone welcomed all the Communists, it was very difficult for these to reach there. SPD members were immobilized for a long while in London, while the US embassy refused visas to those in Sweden. Fritz von Unruh had a long wait before obtaining authorization to return to Germany. Paradoxically enough, the Allies preferred to appoint newly 'de-Nazified' German figures as professors or officials, rather than use the skills of the émigrés. Hubertus Prinz zu Löwenstein asked to return to Germany in 1945, but the US State Department replied to him that the Soviet authorities were against this (*Botschafter ohne Auftrag*, p. 219).

94. His son Konrad Wolf became one of the best film-makers in the GDR.

95. . . . *einer neuen Zeit Beginn. Erinnerungen an die Anfänge unserer Kultur-revolution 1945–1949*, Berlin 1980.

96. *Die geistige Erneuerung unseres Volkes.*

97. Alexander Abusch, J. R. Becher, Bertolt Brecht, Willi Bredel, E. Claudius, Paul Dessau, Hanns Eisler, Lion Feuchtwanger, Heinrich and Thomas Mann, Hans Marchwitza, O. Nagel, Ludwig Renn, Anna Seghers, Adam Scharrer, Bodo Uhse, Günther Weissenborn, Friedrich Wolf, Erich Weinert and Arnold Zweig.

98. Unfortunately this never achieved the interest of its illustrious predecessor.

99. J. R. Becher was a government minister, Friedrich Wolf ambassador to Poland, F. C. Weiskopf ambassador to Sweden and later China. Arnold Zweig served as president of the Akademie der Künste, Anna Seghers as vice-president of the Kulturbund zur Demokratischer Erneuerung Deutschlands. Hans Mayer, Alfred Kantorowicz, Ernst Bloch, Wieland Herzfelde and John Heartfield were variously university professors or directors of magazines.

100. Cf. *Politik und Literatur im Exil*, p. 303.

101. Pliever was never a Communist, though he had spent eleven years in the Soviet Union. In 1947 he moved to West Germany. Up to this point he had been attacked by the anti-Communist press as a 'Communist' and 'un-German nest soiler'. Now he was called a 'traitor' and 'renegade' in the GDR, and his name disappeared from works on the exile period published there. Pliever had been seen in the Weimar period as a 'proletarian writer'. His novel *Stalingrad* was published in Moscow in

1945, and the following year by El Libre Libro in Mexico. He died in Switzerland on 12 March 1955, with acerbic obituaries in the East German press.

102. Detained in the Soviet Union for many years.

103. But the circumstances of their disappearance have never been explained. Cf. in particular Klaus Jarmatz, Simone Barck and Peter Diesel, *Exil in der URSS*, Leipzig 1979. Though most exiles who sought refuge in the Soviet Union are mentioned, nothing is said of their 'disappearance'. If one was grateful for the homage paid in the GDR to the actor Hans Otto, murdered by the Gestapo, there was no recognition of Carola Neher, shot as a 'Trotskyist agent'.

104. Cf. for example Stephan Hermlin, *Meine Friede. Rückkehr*, Berlin 1985, and the dialogue between Stephan Heym and Günter Grass in Brussels on 21 November 1984; Goethe Institut (Impression Berlin 1984).

105. Cf. Karola Bloch's memoir *Aus meinem Leben*.

106. Wilhelm Hoegner, for example, became minister-president of Bavaria, and Rudolf Katz in north Germany. Erich Ollenhauer was leader of the SPD, Ernst Reuter mayor of Berlin, Max Brauer mayor of Hamburg, Ludwig Rosenberg a trade-union leader, Fritz Baader head of the Institut für Weltwirtschaft at Kiel, Karol Gerold editor of the *Frankfurter Rundschau*. Some émigrés found work in publishing (R. Hirsch at Insel Verlag, G. Bermann Fischer with his former company). Willi Haas took up his work as theatre critic (*Die Welt* in Hamburg), Piscator was appointed director of the Berlin Volksbühne, Fritz Kortner opened a theatre school in Munich.

107. Brecht wanted to visit Munich to see Erich Engel, who had produced *The Threepenny Opera* there in 1928.

108. Cf. K. Völker, *Brecht*, p. 352.

109. Hanns Eisler's work was not staged until the early 1970s, in Tübingen.

110. For example Alfred Kantorowicz, who never had much sympathy for Walter Ulbricht – indeed, few of the émigrés painted a very pleasant picture of him – and also had difficult relations with J. R. Becher. His magazine *Ost und West* was eventually suppressed.

111. The case of Ernst Bloch is one of the saddest. He had never been able to teach or publish in the United States (some of his works would not appear until 1972), but Werner Krauss offered him a professorship at Leipzig University. On his arrival, he was appointed a member of the Academy of Sciences and honoured by several party bodies. But before long he was attacked by Kurt Hager. Following the arrest of one of his friends, W. Harich, on 9 December 1956, he was increasingly under suspicion (among other things, for defending Georg Lukács, a friend of his youth). A lecture on 'questions of Blochian philosophy' was held on 5 April 1957, and he was termed a 'revisionist'. His attachment to reflection on religion and its messianic sense was declared incompatible with Marxism, and he was downgraded from a 'Marxist thinker' to a 'mystical left Hegelian'. He soon lost the right to teach, his books were no longer published, and his pupils and disciples subjected to scandalous harassment. After the building of the Wall, he decided to move to the Federal Republic, where he taught at Tübingen.

112. Otto Katz's 'confessions' need no comment: a 'Zionist and Trotskyist traitor' sold to the 'American-British imperialists', he declared: 'I have helped to prepare war against the country where my parents were born, against the people who offered me every possibility of a happy and honest life. This is why I beg the State Tribunal to inflict on me the most rigorous punishment' (Eugen Löbl, *Procès à Prague*, Paris 1969). He was rehabilitated in 1963.

113. Anna Louise Strong was arrested in the USSR as a 'Washington agent', Cardinal Mindszenty condemned to life imprisonment in Hungary for 'plotting with the Americans'. Fifteen Protestant ministers were condemned for treason in Bulgaria, while General MacArthur denounced Agnes Smedley and Gunther Stein (of German-Jewish origin) as 'pro-Japanese traitors'.

EPILOGUE: CASSANDRA

1. 'Emigration und Nachkriegliteratur', in *Exil und innere Emigration*, Frankfurt 1972.
2. Piscator's former secretary, Hans Sahl, wrote sadly in a poem ('Wir sind die letzten'): 'Research institutes ask us for dead people's laundry lists / Museums keep the bywords of our agony / Under glass, like relics.'
3. Preface to Walter Benjamin, *Letters from Germans*. (French translation: *Une série de lettres*, Paris 1979, p. 12.)
4. Cf. Jacques Droz, *Histoire de l'antifascisme en Europe 1923–1939*, Paris 1985.
5. 'It is in full awareness, therefore, of both its positive and negative aspects, that the historian has to tackle the history of antifascism: yet its human face, which bears a heroic will for freely chosen sacrifice, cannot be dissociated from a political battle beset with enormous errors of judgement and often with a very narrow perspective' (ibid., p. 11).
6. If these works have had only a limited success in recent years, this is no longer due to any particular ideological context, but more often to an inevitably ageing of literary styles. What above all has survived of these works of the 1920s and 30s is a certain boldness of form. In this respect, G. Trakl and Gottfried Benn, Carl Einstein and Ödön von Horvath, undoubtedly surpass Franz Werfel, Heinrich Mann and Friedrich Wolf. Their works would certainly have been able to play a great role after 1945, but this is no longer the case today. Even with writers as prestigious as Lion Feuchtwanger and Arnold Döblin, it is impossible to deny that while some of their novels can still exert an attraction today, others fail to speak to a contemporary readership. This is the case with Heinrich Mann, even though his writing can be admirable and moving, and his style often reminiscent of Anatole France. And while Döblin's *Berlin Alexanderplatz* remains a masterpiece, likewise his early short stories written in the *Sturm* period, this is hardly the case with *The Three Jumps of Wang Lun* or *The Blue Tiger*. As for the proletarian plays and realist novels of the Weimar period, their interest today is essentially as historical documents.
7. Once again, if *all* exile writings are important for an understanding of the exile experience, this does not mean that all the émigrés' works have literary value. The historian and critic are constantly faced with this contradiction: the works written in exile can be genuinely understood only on the basis of this exile, even though to confine them to a genre of 'exile literature' is to condemn them to a ghetto existence.
8. In 1968, the life of Ernst Toller and his participation in the Bavarian soviet republic formed the basis for Tankred Dorst's play *Toller*. Klaus Mann's *Mephisto* gave birth to one of the most interesting works by Ariane Mnouchkine in 1979, and later to Miklos Forman's film. Lion Feuchtwanger's *Exil* was filmed for German television.
9. Theodor Adorno, *Negative Dialectics*, London 1973, pp. 366–7. Adorno wrote in similar terms in *Critical Models*, New York 1998: 'The concept of a cultural resurrection after Auschwitz is illusory and absurd, and every work created since then has to pay the bitter price for this' (p. 48).
10. T. Adorno, *Negative Dialectics*, p. 367. Adorno's pessimistic position, to be sure, has its own ambiguities.
11. T. Adorno, *Critical Models*, p. 203.
12. Cited by Christa Wolf, *Cassandra*, Harmondsworth 1984.
13. Klaus Mann, *Der Wendepunkt*, Frankfurt 1952, p. 292. [This passage does not appear in the English edition of *The Turning Point*.]
14. Ibid.
15. A. Koestler, *The Invisible Writing*, p. 231.
16. Ibid., p. 232.
17. M. Sperber, *Au-delà de l'oubli*, p. 152: 'our Cassandra cries'.
18. Bad Godesberg colloquium on *Exilliteratur*, p. 40.

19. B. Brecht, *Journals*, 18 April 1941.
20. Alfred Kantorowicz, *Deutsches Tagebuch*, p. 79.
21. K. Mann, *Der Wendepunkt*, p. 293. [Not in the English edition of *The Turning Point*.]
22. Cf. for example the texts and documents cited by Pierre Assouline in *L'Épuration des intellectuels*, Brussels 1985. Few major German writers compromised themselves with the Nazi regime, which was not the case with French writers.
23. Régis Debray, *Le Scribe*, Paris 1980, p. 112: 'In Germany for instance, the Weimar Republic is recognized on all sides as the lost paradise of the intellectuals.'
24. Fritz J. Raddatz, *Erfolg oder Wirkung*, Munich 1972.
25. Cf. Alain Brossat and Sylvia Klingberg, *Le Yiddishland révolutionnaire*, Paris 1983.
26. Jean-Paul Sartre, *Words*, Harmondsworth 1967, p. 156.
27. 'Gruss nach vorn', in K. Tucholsky,*Germany, Germany*, Manchester 1990, p. 24.

Index

Heymann, F. 94
Heyne, Kurt E. 422
Hilbersheimer, Ludwig 535
Hilferding, Rudolf 6, 10, 91, 94, 100, 107,
111, 184, 202, 218, 262, 300, 302, 352,
443, 449, 568
Hiller, Kurt 16, 38–9, 40, 52, 67, 72, 108,
113, 150, 283, 339, 364, 390
Hindemith, Paul 25–7, 35, 468, 484, 510,
530, 534, 639
Hinkel, Hans 26
Hinze, G. 179
Hirsch, Anne-Marie 638
Hirsch, J. 482
Hirsch, Karl Jacob 545
Hirsch, Paul 150
Hirsch, Werner 39, 91, 182
Hirschfeld, H. M. 94
Hirschfeld, Kurt 94, 418
Hirschfeld, Magnus 197
Hitchcock, Alfred 599
Hitchcock, Henry Russell 538
Hitler, Adolf 3, 4, 24, 27, 36, 42, 53, 58,
60, 63, 65, 97, 271, 273, 300–1, 339,
362, 384, 397–9, 400, 402–4, 457–9, 463,
470, 581, 607, 631, 654–6
Hitschmann, Edward 481
Hochwälder, F. 413–14, 417
Hodann, Max 38, 39, 337, 360
Hoegner, Wilhelm 156–7
Hoernler, Erwin 174
Hofer, Karl 26, 216
Hoffenstein, Samuel 527
Hoffman, Heinrich 28
Hoffman, Ludwig 9
Hoffmann, Hans 536
Hoffmann, Reinhold 355
Hoffmannsthal, Hugo von 101, 375, 527
Hofmann, Martha 144
Hohenlohe-Langenburg, Max Karl Prinz
zu 106, 235
Hokheimer, Max 242
Holborn, Hajo 483
Holborn, Louise 482
Holitscher, Arthur 44, 94, 173, 309, 371
Höllering, F. 93
Hollos, J. 93
Holz, Arno 55
Holz, Karl 45
Holz, Max 181
Homann, Major 616
Homann, W. 169
Homolka, Oskar 418, 484, 513, 517, 519,
523, 532
Hönig, Eugen 28

Honigsheim, Paul 212
Honorat, André 188, 211
Hoover, J. Edgar 621
Horan, Camilla 516
Horch, F. 143
Horkheimer, Max 212, 240, 264, 482–3,
513, 553–8
Horney, Karen 481
Hörnle, Edwin 616
Hornung, Walter 146
Horvath, Ödön von 53, 94, 99, 114, 214,
239, 245, 254, 257, 265, 292, 367, 405,
410–11, 414, 416, 418, 420
Horwitz, Kurt 418
Hose, Heinz 145
Hotopp, Albert 174, 182
Howard, Sidney 527
Huber, Johannes 316
Huch, Ricarda 31, 101, 119, 290, 632
Huder, Professor Walter 8
Huebsch, Benjamin 544
Hull, Cordell 458, 458–9
Hulse, Wilfred C. 562, 563
Humm, R. J. 157, 335
Huppert, Hugo 368
Hurwicz, Leonid 482
Huston, John 597, 600
Hutchins, Robert M. 279
Huxley, Aldous 146, 196, 209, 263, 333,
369–70, 514

Ibsen, Henrik 527
Ilberg, W. 137
Illès, Bela 368
Ingrim, Robert 611
Isherwood, Christopher 152, 514, 591
Istrati, Panait 50
Ivanov, V. 332
Ivens, Joris 165, 515, 532

Jacob, Berthold 10, 40, 70, 319, 322, 325,
327–8, 382, 431–3, 438, 449, 655
Jacob, Hans 94, 104, 583
Jacob, Paul Walter 578
Jacobs, Monty 150, 151
Jacobsohn, Edith 93, 363
Jacobsohn, Siegfried 40, 258, 363
Jacoby, Lili 442
Jaeger, Werner 483
Jahn, Hans Henry 47, 89, 94, 127, 167,
246
Jameson, Storm 144
Jannings, Emil 66, 79, 220, 411, 516, 518,
548, 637
Jarmatz, Klaus 9, 172

Thomas, Dr Wilbur K. 552
Thompson, Dorothy 279, 461, 467, 470–2, 478, 486, 523, 525, 529, 583, 586–7, 624, 629
Thomson, Virgil 531
Thoor, J. 93
Thorez, Maurice 200, 342–3
Thurn-Taxis, Alexis 517
Thyssen, Fritz 109
Tiberius, Joachim 639
Tichauer, T. 187
Tiegen, Einar 276
Tietjen, Hans 27
Tillich, Paul 107, 126, 468, 483, 556, 561, 569–70, 611, 613
Tillinger, Eugene 640
Tischler, Victor 216
Toch, Ernst 484, 534
Toller, Christine 252
Toller, Ernst 2, 3, 6, 16, 30, 32–3, 38–40, 43, 45, 47, 52, 53, 62, 71, 101, 108, 146, 147, 150, 161, 165, 177, 184, 196, 207, 230, 246, 249, 253, 258–60, 279–80, 289, 293, 333, 348, 360, 367, 368, 371, 380, 388, 391, 410, 413, 414, 415, 418–19, 424, 456, 462, 470, 472, 477, 479, 523–4, 529, 539, 543, 546, 561, 583, 593, 654–5, 658–9
Tolnay, Charles de 538
Tolstoy, Alexis 282, 332
Tolstoy, Leo 527
Tombrock, Hans 170
Tonnelat, E. 194
Torberg, Freidrich 144
Torgler, Ernst 316–18, 340
Toscanini, Arturo 484, 586
Trakl, Georg 393
Trebitsch, Siegfried 236
Trendt, Erich 579
Trepte, Curt 170–71, 174, 178, 416, 419
Tretyakov, Serge 174, 177, 368, 629
Treviranus, Gottfried 487, 568–9
Trommler, Frank 647
Trösch, Robert 178
Tschäper, Herbert 445
Tucholsky, Kurt 2, 15–17, 24, 43, 45, 53, 61, 62, 69–72, 86, 103, 157–8, 170, 194, 223, 230, 235, 250, 256–9, 284–5, 312, 363, 384, 387, 390, 393, 402, 404, 414, 422, 644, 652–4, 658–9, 660
Tunon, Aveline 337
Tunon, Gonzales 337
Turek, L. 137
Türk, W. 93
Tzara, Tristan 332, 448

Uhde, Wilhelm von 70
Uhlmann, Fred 104, 149, 151, 153, 216, 632, 636
Uhse, Bodo 52, 89, 94, 109, 165, 211, 235, 254, 322, 333, 335–7, 355, 359, 372–3, 381, 575, 578–9
Ulam, Stan 482
Ulbricht, Walter 10, 111–12, 175–6, 184, 200, 232, 301–2, 348–50, 352, 357, 616, 642–3, 645
Ulbricht, Wilhelm 345
Ulmer, Edgar G. 517
Ulrich, Ludwig 27
Unruh, Fritz von 2, 3, 6, 31, 53, 67, 72, 89, 101, 108, 113, 279, 382, 398, 410, 560, 564
Untermeyer, Samuel 458

Vagts, Alfrede 553
Valentin, Veit 150
Valéry, Paul 193–4
Valetti, ROsa 311
Valle-Inclan, Del 209
Vallejo, Casar 337
Vallentin, Maxim 174, 178–9, 182
Valliant-Couturier, Paul 191, 333
Valter, Klara 181
Valtin, Jan 570
Vanek, Karl 365
Vansittart, Lord 399, 566, 613–15
Vary, Karlovy 377
Vayo, Alvarez del 358
Veblen, Thorstein 554
Vehlow, Franz 165, 356
Veidt, Conrad 418, 424–5, 484, 516–18, 601
Verebes, Ernö 517
Verder, Hans 171
Verlag, Querido 133, 145, 171, 224, 369
Vermeil, Edmond 194
Vermeylen, Dr P. 316
Verner, Waldemar 166
Vesper, Will 84, 115
Victor, Walter 157, 238, 440, 545
Viénot, Paul 201
Viertel, Berthold 93, 151, 381, 525, 532, 544, 548, 564, 567, 579, 606
Viertel, Bertold 473, 513
Viertel, Salka 484, 513, 532, 548, 550, 591
Voegeln, Erich 569
Vogel, Hans 110, 302, 345–6, 435–6
Vogeler, Heinrich 174, 217, 232, 309
Volkmann, Otto 165, 356
Vordtriede, Werner 98
Vormeier, Barbara 11